ecial Edition

Using

Using Windows® 95

Second Edition

QUE®

Special Edition

Using

Using Windows® 95

Second Edition

Ron Person, Robert Voss, et al.

Special Edition Using Windows® 95, Second Edition

Copyright© 1997 by Que® Corporation.

All rights reserved. Printed in the United States of America. No part of this book may be used or reproduced in any form or by any means, or stored in a database or retrieval system, without prior written permission of the publisher except in the case of brief quotations embodied in critical articles and reviews. Making copies of any part of this book for any purpose other than your own personal use is a violation of United States copyright laws. For information, address Que Corporation, 201 W. 103rd Street, Indianapolis, IN 46290. You may reach Que's direct sales line by calling 1-800-428-5331.

Library of Congress Catalog No.: 97-68670

ISBN: 0-7897-1381-0
ISBN: 0-7897-1528-7 (International)

This book is sold *as is*, without warranty of any kind, either express or implied, respecting the contents of this book, including but not limited to implied warranties for the book's quality, performance, merchantability, or fitness for any particular purpose. Neither Que Corporation nor its dealers or distributors shall be liable to the purchaser or any other person or entity with respect to any liability, loss, or damage caused or alleged to have been caused directly or indirectly by this book.

99 98 97 6 5 4 3 2 1

Interpretation of the printing code: the rightmost double-digit number is the year of the book's printing; the rightmost single-digit number, the number of the book's printing. For example, a printing code of 97-1 shows that the first printing of the book occurred in 1997.

All terms mentioned in this book that are known to be trademarks or service marks have been appropriately capitalized. Que cannot attest to the accuracy of this information. Use of a term in this book should not be regarded as affecting the validity of any trademark or service mark.

Screen reproductions in this book were created using Collage Plus from Inner Media, Inc., Hollis, NH.

Contents at a Glance

Table of Contents

V Working with Applications

VII Sharing Data Between Applications

VIII Networking with Windows

Credits

PRESIDENT
Roland Elgey

SENIOR VICE PRESIDENT/PUBLISHING
Don Fowley

PUBLISHER
Joseph B. Wikert

PUBLISHING DIRECTOR
Brad R. Koch

MANAGER OF PUBLISHING OPERATIONS
Linda H. Buehler

GENERAL MANAGER
Joe Muldoon

DIRECTOR OF EDITORIAL SERVICES
Carla Hall

MANAGING EDITOR
Thomas F. Hayes

DIRECTOR OF ACQUISITIONS
Cheryl D. Willoughby

ACQUISITIONS EDITOR
Angie Wethington

PRODUCT DIRECTOR
Stephen Miller

PRODUCTION EDITOR
Audra Gable

EDITORS
Judy Ohm
SanDee Phillips

PRODUCT MARKETING MANAGER
Kourtnaye Sturgeon

ASSISTANT PRODUCT MARKETING MANAGER
Gretchen Schlesinger

TECHNICAL EDITORS
Brad Lindaas
Nadeem Muhammed

MEDIA DEVELOPMENT SPECIALIST
David Garratt

ACQUISITIONS COORDINATOR
Tracy M. Williams

SOFTWARE RELATIONS COORDINATOR
Susan D. Gallagher

EDITORIAL ASSISTANTS
Virginia Stoller
Jeff Chandler

BOOK DESIGNERS
Ruth Harvey
Kim Scott

COVER DESIGNER
Sandra Schroeder

PRODUCTION TEAM
Marcia Deboy
Maribeth Echard
Kay Hoskin
Tim Neville

INDEXERS
Ginny Bess
Chris Wilcox
Tim Wright

Composed in *Century Old Style* and *ITC Franklin Gothic* by Que Corporation.

I dedicate this work to my father and mother, Norman and Marjorie Person, who have shown me the world and its opportunities.

-Ron Person

I dedicate the work in this book to Andrew Cohen, my spiritual teacher, for his unwavering love and guidance, and to my mother for all that she has given me.

-Bob Voss

About the Authors

Ron Person has written more than 22 books for Que Corporation, including four international bestsellers. His books include *Platinum Edition Using Windows 95, Special Edition Using Windows 95, Special Edition Using Excel for Windows 95*, and *Special Edition Using Word for Windows 95*. He has an M.S. in physics from The Ohio State University and an M.B.A from Hardin-Simmons University. Ron was one of Microsoft's original Consulting Partners.

Robert L. Bogue owns Thor Projects, a consulting company located in Indianapolis. Thor Projects specializes in solving the networking and integration needs of medium-sized organizations. Rob has been involved with more than 50 book projects on topics ranging from Visual Basic to Windows NT to NetWare to Microsoft Office. He can be reached at **Rob.Bogue@Cyber-Wizard.com** or 317-844-5310.

Jim Boyce, the lead author for *Windows NT Installation and Configuration Handbook*, is a Contributing Editor and columnist for *WINDOWS Magazine* and a regular contributor to other computer publications. He has been involved with computers since the late seventies, and has worked with computers as a user, programmer, and systems manager in a variety of capacities. He has a wide range of experience in the DOS, Windows, and UNIX environments. Jim has authored and coauthored over two dozen books on computers and software.

Jerry Cox has been involved in computers since 1982. He has worked the last 10 years as a computer sales consultant for MicroAge Computer Center of Fort Wayne. He has received certifications from Apple, IBM, Hewlett-Packard, and Compaq. He has tech edited *Upgrading and Troubleshooting PCs* 2nd, 3rd, and 4th editions, *Upgrading and Troubleshooting PCs Workbook, Winn Rosch's Hardware Bible, Peter Norton's Inside the PC Premiere Edition, Easy Troubleshooting and Upgrading PCs, Using the PS/1,* and several other Prentice Hall/ Macmillan titles.

Dick Cravens lives and works in Columbia, MO, where he is a product manager designing the Next Big Thing from DATASTORM TECHNOLOGIES, Inc., a publisher of fax, data and TCP/IP communications software for Windows PCs. In previous lives, he designed training programs for support technicians, has answered a gazillion questions about modems, worked as production manager for an advertising agency, sold television programming to evil cable TV empires, managed a chain of one-hour photo shops, ran a commercial photographic studio, and chased Angus cows, kind of in that order. Since he just bought the classic fixer-upper bungalow and has an addiction to way-cool-wicked-fast computer stuff, he writes the occasional computer book, too. His son Jesse, budding MUD freak, abuses the hand-me-down computers, slops the cats, and orders the pizzas.

Michael Desmond is Senior Editor of News at *PC World* magazine, the world's largest computer publication with a circulation rate base of over 1.1 million readers. He is also vice-president of the Computer Press Association, an organization dedicated to promoting the computer press, its writers, and editors. In 1996, Michael earned a Jesse H. Neal award from the American Business Press for runnerup in the best investigative article category. Previously executive editor at *Multimedia World* magazine, Michael has an M.S. in Journalism from Northwestern University's Medill School of Journalism, and a B.A. in Soviet Studies from Middlebury College in Vermont. Michael has also written for other publications, including *Working Woman* and *Video* magazines, and is a contributing author to *Platinum Edition Using Windows 95* from Que Publishing. A native of Cleveland, Ohio, Michael is an inveterate Cleveland Indians fan, and will never ever forgive Art Modell for moving the Cleveland Browns football team to Baltimore.

Glenn Fincher has worked in the computer industry for the last 12 years. Working in the fast-moving electronic manufacturing industry, the early years were spent in Test Engineering at SCI Systems, Inc., the world's largest computer contract manufacturer. Spending the bulk of the SCI years in component, board, and unit test, he became intimately familiar with the building blocks of today's computer technology. Joining Intergraph Corporation in 1991 as a Customer Support Analyst, he has applied his wealth of computer knowledge to providing Intergraph's customers with quality, timely, and accurate support for the MicroStation CAD product. Leading the software certification efforts for the successful release of MicroStation 5.0, he continues to be involved in the day-to-day world of Intergraph's partner Bentley Systems' MicroStation product. Sharing the knowledge gained in the experience of these years in the industry has always been a priority, so it is no surprise that he is in demand as a speaker, writer, and presenter throughout Intergraph. With his present involvement in Intergraph's WWW effort as Webmaster for Intergraph's Software Solutions, Glenn continues to remain at the leading edge of this industry. Continually seeking to stay on this edge has required both the support and understanding of wife Jan and their three children—Ashely, Will, and Aimee—without whom this and all his other endeavors would have been a lonely journey indeed. Glenn can be reached by electronic mail at **gtfinche@ingr.com**.

William S. Holderby is a computer engineering graduate from the University of Central Florida. He has 20 years of experience in systems design and applications development for the federal government and commercial markets. Mr. Holderby frequently contributes magazine articles covering computer systems technology. He is a network systems developer and integrator and is currently working with the Naval Computer Telecommunications Station based in New Orleans, Louisiana.

Gerald "Jerry" Paul Honeycutt, Jr. provides business-oriented technical leadership to the Internet community and software development industry. He has served companies such as The Travelers, IBM, Nielsen North America, IRM, Howard Systems International, and NCR. Jerry has participated in the industry since before the days of Microsoft Windows 1.0, and is completely hooked on Windows 95 and the Internet.

Jerry is the author of *Using Microsoft Plus!, Using the Internet with Windows 95, Windows 95 Registry & Customization Handbook, Special Edition Using the Windows 95 Registry, VBScript by Example, Special Edition Using the Internet 3E, Using the Internet 2E, and Windows NT;* and *Windows 95 Registry and Customization Handbook* published by Que. He is also a contributing author on *Special Edition Using Netscape 2, Platinum Edition Using Windows 95, Visual Basic for Applications Database Solutions, Special Edition Using Netscape 3, Windows 95 Exam Guide, Netscape Navigator 3 Starter Kit, Using Java Workshop, Using JScript*, and *Internet Explorer ActiveX and Plug-Ins Companion* published by Que. He has been printed in *Computer Language* magazine and is a regular speaker at the Windows World and Comdex trade shows on topics related to software development, Windows 95, and the Internet.

Jerry graduated from the University of Texas at Dallas in 1992 with a B.S. degree in Computer Science. He currently lives in the Dallas suburb of Frisco, Texas with Becky, two Westies, Corky and Turbo, and a cat called Scratches. Jerry is an avid golfer with a passion for fine photography. Feel free to contact Jerry on the Internet at **jerry@honeycutt.com** or visit his Web site at **http://rampages.onramp.net/~jerry**.

Peter Kent lives in Lakewood, Colorado. He's spent the last 14 years training users, documenting software, and designing user interfaces. Working as an independent consultant for the last nine years, Peter has worked for companies such as MasterCard, Amgen, Data General, and Dvorak Development and Publishing. Much of his consulting work has been in the telecommunications business.

Peter is the author of the best-selling Internet book *The Complete Idiot's Guide to the Internet* published by Que. He has also written another six Internet-related books—including *The Complete Idiot's Guide to the World Wide Web*—and a variety of other works, such as *The Technical Writer's Freelancing Guide* and books on Windows NT and Windows 3.1. His articles have appeared in many periodicals, including *Internet World*, *Windows Magazine*, *Windows User*, *The Dallas Times Herald*, and *Computerworld*. Peter can be reached electronically at Microsoft Network/PeterKent, CompuServe/**71601,1266**, Internet/**pkent@lab-press.com**.

Doug Kilarski is a freelance writer and an accomplished computer industry analyst. Doug is a former technical editor for *Computer Shopper* magazine and former editor-in-chief for *Computer Monthly* and *Resale World* magazines. He is currently developing global marketing and distribution strategies for the internetworking and telephony industries. Doug can be reached on the Internet at **dkilarski@mcimail.com**.

Bradley Lindaas is a project consultant for Follett Software Company, a library automation solutions provider based outside of Chicago. Brad started his career working in a computer lab while attending the University of Wisconsin, Madison, where he received his B.A. in English Literature. After graduating, he took a job with Softmart, an outsourcer of software technical support and Microsoft Windows 95 Launch Partner, working with MS-DOS, Windows 3.1, and then Windows 95.

After Softmart, Brad worked for Wingra Technologies of Madison, Wisconsin, supporting their UNIX- and VAX-based e-mail integration product called Missive. Currently, he consults K-12 schools on the implementation of district-wide technology plans involving Follett's library automation products running on Windows NT Server and Novell. Brad is a Microsoft Certified Professional and can be reached at **lindaas@fsc.follett.com**.

Gordon Meltzer has been teaching himself about computers since they were made with vacuum tubes. Recently, Gordon had designed and built workgroup networks for a music marketing division of Time-Warner and several New York City law firms. He is a consultant on computing issues to NBC Post Production, also in Manhattan.

Gordon has produced a number of jazz records for people like Miles Davis, Michel LeGrand, Al Di Meola, and Wallace Roney, and has a special interest in using computers in the business side of the music business.

Brady P. Merkel is a Senior Software Consultant and Technical Webmaster for Intergraph Corporation in Huntsville, Alabama. He has coauthored popular Internet books such as *Web Publishing with Word for Windows* and *Building Integrated Office Applications.* One of his ongoing projects includes the development of Intergraph Online, Intergraph Corporation's World Wide Web server at **http://www.intergraph.com**. Brady can be reached by e-mail at **bpmerkel@ingr.com**.

Francis Moss has been involved with computers for 12 years, a Microsoft beta tester for five years, and a writer—primarily in television but more recently, books—for 15 years. With his writing partner, he is coauthor of *Internet for Kids* from Price Stern Sloan. He likes computers because he enjoys cursing at unarmed inanimate objects. With his wife and two children, he lives in North Hollywood, California. He can be reached at **fcmoss@directnet.com**.

Michael O'Mara is a freelance author and technical writer. Previously, he was a staff author with The Cobb Group where he wrote innumerable articles about leading computer software programs and served as Editor-in-Chief of several monthly software journals. He has co-authored or contributed to other Que books including *Using DOS*; *Using Windows 3.11*; *Special Edition Using CompuServe*; *Special Edition Using Windows 95*; *Special Edition Using Windows NT Workstation 3.51*; *10 Minute Guide to Freelance Graphics 96 for Windows 95*; and *Using Your PC*. He can be reached at **76376.3441@compuserve.com**.

Sue Plumley has owned and operated her own business for eight years; Humble Opinions provides training, consulting, and network installation, management, and maintenance to banking, education, medical, and industrial facilities. In addition, Sue has authored and coauthored over 50 books for Que Corporation and its sister imprints, including *10 Minute Guide to Lotus Notes 4*, *Special Edition Using Windows NT Workstation*, and *Easy Windows 95*. You can reach Sue via the Internet at **splumley@citynet.net** or on CompuServe at **76470,2526**.

Kenneth W. Poore is a marketing consultant for the Technical Information Management and Delivery division of Intergraph Corporation in Huntsville, Alabama. He currently develops strategic product plans, but has written technology white papers, conducted customer training, and worked in presales and marketing roles over the past 10 years. Ken lives with his wife Molly in Harvest, Alabama and can be reached at **kwpoore@ingr.com**.

Paul Robichaux, who has been an Internet user since 1986 and a software developer since 1983, is currently a software developer for LJL Enterprises (**http://www.ljl.com**), where he writes data security and cryptography software for Win32 and MacOS platforms. In his spare time, he writes computer books and develops Macintosh applications; he still manages to spend plenty of time with his wife and young son. He can be reached via e-mail at **paulr@hiwaay.net**.

Rob Tidrow has been using computers for the past six years and has used Windows for the past four years. Mr. Tidrow is a technical writer and recently was the Manager of Product Development for New Riders Publishing, a division of Macmillan Computer Publishing. Rob is coauthor of the best-selling *Windows for Non-Nerds*, and has coauthored several other books including *Inside the World Wide Web*, *New Riders' Official CompuServe Yellow Pages*, *Inside Microsoft Office Professional*, *Inside WordPerfect 6 for Windows*, *Riding the Internet Highway, Deluxe Edition*, and the *AutoCAD Student Workbook*. In the past, Mr. Tidrow created technical documentation and instructional programs for use in a variety of industrial settings. He has a degree in English from Indiana University. He resides in Indianapolis with his wife, Tammy, and two boys, Adam and Wesley. You can reach him on the Internet at **rtidrow@iquest.net**.

Robert Voss, is an independent software trainer with extensive experience training in Windows 95, Microsoft Word, and Microsoft Excel. Bob has worked with Ron Person on several of Que's bestselling books, including *Special Edition Using Word 6 for Windows*, *Special Edition Using Microsoft Excel 97*, and the Using Windows 95 books.

Craig Zacker has been employed as a network administrator, a technical writer and editor, a Webmaster, a technical support engineer and supervisor, a courseware developer, and a freelance network consultant. He now spends most of his time tinkering with computers and writing about them. His previous credits for Que include *Special Edition Using NetWare 4.1*, *Platinum Edition Using Windows 95*, *Windows NT 4.0 Workstation Advanced Technical Reference*, and *Upgrading and Repairing Networks*, among others. He can be reached at **craigz@tiac.net**.

We'd Like to Hear from You!

Que Corporation has a long-standing reputation for high-quality books and products. To ensure your continued satisfaction, we also understand the importance of customer service and support.

Tech Support

If you need assistance with the information in this book or with a CD/disk accompanying the book, please access Macmillan Computer Publishing's online Knowledge Base at **http://www.superlibrary.com/general/support**. If you do not find the answer to your questions on our Web site, you may contact Macmillan Technical Support by phone at **317/581-3833** or via e-mail at **support@mcp.com**.

Also be sure to visit Que's Web resource center for all the latest information, enhancements, errata, downloads, and more. It's located at **http://www.quecorp.com/**.

Orders, Catalogs, and Customer Service

To order other Que or Macmillan Computer Publishing books, catalogs, or products, please contact our Customer Service Department at **800/428-5331**, fax us at **800/882-8583** (International Fax: 317/228-4400), or visit our online bookstore at **http://www.mcp.com/**.

Comments and Suggestions

We want you to let us know what you like or dislike most about this book or other Que products. Your comments will help us to continue publishing the best books available on computer topics in today's market.

Lisa Wagner
Senior Product Director
Que Corporation
201 West 103rd Street, 4B
Indianapolis, Indiana 46290 USA
Fax: 317/581-4663 E-mail: **lwagner@que.mcp.com**

Please be sure to include the book's title and author as well as your name and phone or fax number. We will carefully review your comments and share them with the author. Please note that due to the high volume of mail we receive, we may not be able to reply to every message.

Thank you for choosing Que!

Introduction

In this latest *Special Edition Using Windows 95*, we have created a book that conveniently separates the standard Windows 95 procedures from the new procedures available through Internet Explorer 4 and integrated shell components. Whether you use the original release of Windows 95 or the more recent Windows 95b (OSR2), you will find standard Windows procedures in chapters by themselves. Then when you are ready to make the free upgrade to Internet Explorer 4 and integrated shell components, you can turn to the chapter dedicated to the Internet Explorer 4 suite and integrated shell components.

These new chapters will help you understand how Windows 95 is integrating the World Wide Web with desktop computing. If you work in a small office, you can now use Office 97 and FrontPage 97 to create your own small intranet as easily as giant multinational companies create extranets. In both intranets and extranets, you can create webs of linked Word, Excel, and Web page documents. Company manuals can be available online for instant access and quick updating. You can even research business and personal opportunities from your desktop via the Web instead of making long trips to the library. Many corporations are installing NetMeeting so employees can do collaborative work on shared documents.

How to Use This Book

This book was designed and written from the ground up with three important purposes in mind:

- First, *Special Edition Using Windows 95, Second Edition* makes it easy for you to find any task you need to accomplish and see how to do it most effectively.
- Second, you can depend on *Special Edition Using Windows 95, Second Edition* to keep up with the most current changes and updates to Windows technology. This edition contains the information intermediate and advanced users need to take advantage of the OSR2 release of Windows 95, as well as the free add-ins that make use of Internet capabilities, Internet Explorer 4, and the integrated shell components.
- Third, this book is an update to the international bestseller *Special Edition Using Windows 95.*

With those goals in mind, how do you use this book?

OSR 2

If you have used the original release of Windows 95, you may just want to skim through this book and watch for the OSR2 icon (it appears to the left of this paragraph). You should especially note the information in Chapter 15, "Working with Disks and Disk Drives," and its discussion on whether you should upgrade to the new OSR2 hard disk format. Throughout the book, improvements to Windows 95 that are attributed to OSR2 are noted with an OSR2 icon.

Changes to the user interface to make Windows 95 operate in a more "Web-like" manner are collected in Chapter 11, "Navigating with the Shell Integration Components," and Chapter 14, "File Management Using the Shell Integration Components." The new Internet Explorer 4 and additional Internet tools are described in detail in Chapter 17, "Getting Connected to the Internet," Chapter 18, "Browsing the Internet with Explorer," Chapter 19, "Working with the Active Desktop," Chapter 20, "Subscribing to Web Sites and Offline Browsing," and Chapter 21, "Using Outlook Express Mail and News."

Special Edition Using Windows 95, Second Edition was written for the intermediate and advanced Windows computer user. You may be experienced with Windows 3.x or Windows 95. Either way, you will find comprehensive coverage on Windows 95 features and the new Internet components. Throughout the book are techniques for customizing Windows 95 to work the way you need Windows to work.

How This Book Is Organized

Special Edition Using Windows 95, Second Edition is a comprehensive book on Windows 95 and its new Internet Explorer 4.0 Suite. The book is divided into eight parts, 43 chapters, and two appendixes to help you quickly find the coverage you need. The parts begin with the most common and basic topics and move forward into more specialized or advanced subjects. The rest of this section describes the content more specifically, chapter by chapter.

Part I: Installing and Configuring Windows 95

Chapter 1, "What's New in Windows 95 and the Internet Explorer 4.0 Suite," shows you an overview of the features in Windows 95 that have been added with OSR2, Internet Explorer 4, and integrated shell components. After reading this chapter, you will see how Windows 95 is becoming more Web-centric.

Chapter 2, "Installing Windows," shows you the preparation and procedures for installing Windows 95. You will also learn the advantages and disadvantages of using Windows 95b, also known as OSR2. If you decide to use OSR2 and you don't yet have it, this chapter will tell you how to get it and install it safely.

Chapter 3 is "Configuring Windows 95." You will need this chapter if you are installing or reinstalling Windows or if you want to change or optimize your computer's basic hardware. You'll learn about installing a printer, a modem, and PC Cards.

Chapter 4, "Configuring Multimedia Windows 95," teaches you about all those spiffy multimedia devices your computer came with. Here you'll learn about sound, video, and CD-ROMs, including how to configure them with Windows and how to optimize their use.

Chapter 5, "Controlling Printers," teaches how much more there is to printing than File, Print. It shows you how to optimize your print queues, install or remove printer drivers, and diagnose common printing problems.

Chapter 6, "Working with Fonts," explains fonts and how Windows 95 uses them. It also shows you how to install and manage fonts in Windows 95.

Chapter 7 is "Plug and Play and Legacy Device Installation." The objective of Plug and Play is to make new device installation a "hands-off" process. Thus, much of this chapter is devoted to explaining what happens "behind-the-scenes" to make Plug and Play work. This chapter also describes how to install the many older "legacy" devices that do not take advantage of Plug and Play. And for those times when hardware doesn't install correctly, we've included descriptions on how to use the Device Manager to troubleshoot and resolve the problem.

Chapter 8, "Special Features for Notebook Users," describes how to take advantage of Windows 95 support for laptops. It includes advanced power management, docking stations, file synchronization with My Briefcase, and all of the other new features that are of particular use to laptop users. We've included in-depth installation and use instructions for using Windows 95's new infrared communication. This software upgrade is available free in Service Pack 1 and is incorporated into the OEM Service Release 2 (OSR2) release of Windows 95 that is sold with new computers.

Part II: Navigation Skills

Chapter 9, "Understanding Windows 95," will help you get started with Windows 95 if you're new to Windows 95. It describes the new operating methods such as the Start button, right-mouse button menus, properties sheets, and how to create shortcuts to documents and applications.

Chapter 10, "Navigating and Controlling Windows," shows you how to start Windows and the myriad ways of starting applications and documents. You will also learn about the extensive Help system built into Windows 95.

Chapter 11, "Navigating with the Shell Integration Components," explains the new operating procedures available when integrated shell components are installed. When integrated shell components are installed, Windows 95 takes on much more of the look and feel of a Web page and Web operating procedures. From within Windows, you can now single-click to start applications or documents, view folders in a Web view using HTML pages as a background, and more.

Part III: Working with Files and Folders

Chapter 12, "Managing Files and Folders with My Computer," explains one way of looking at files and folders. Each folder's contents appears within its own window. If you are used to a Macintosh or some other graphical environment, you may want to use this method of managing files.

Chapter 13, "Managing Files and Folders with Windows Explorer," is devoted to showing you how to use Windows Explorer and folder windows to work with and manage the files on your computer. The chapter includes many tips that enhance Windows Explorer.

Chapter 14, "File Management Using the Shell Integration Components," shows you how file management changes when you have integrated shell components installed. You'll learn about new features such as single-clicking to activate documents and applications, selecting multiple files with single-click activation enabled, using the new Web view of folders so that files and folders appear over an HTML page, and much more.

Chapter 15, "Working with Disks and Disk Drives," shows you how to work with and maintain your floppy and hard disks. Windows 95 comes with a tool to help you check for and repair some kinds of damage. You can monitor the performance of your system using the System Monitor. You can improve the performance of your hard disks by using Disk Defragmenter, and you can enable your system to act as if it has more memory (RAM) than is actually installed by using *virtual memory.* This chapter covers all these topics and more. To increase the effective size of your hard disk you can use DriveSpace 3, available with Plus! or the OEM Service Release 2 (OSR2) version of Windows to compress your hard disk, giving it two to three times more storage. The new FAT32 file system that comes with the OEM Service Release 2 (OSR2) version of Windows is also covered.

Chapter 16, "Backing Up and Protecting Your Data," explains how to copy one or more files from your hard disk to another location (usually a floppy disk, a tape drive, or another computer on your network), restore your backed up files to any location you choose (including their original locations), and compare files on your backup disks with the original files to ensure their validity.

Part IV: Working with the Internet

Chapter 17, "Getting Connected to the Internet," introduces you to the Internet and World Wide Web, two of the fastest growing and most talked about topics in computing. You learn what TCP/IP is, how to choose an Internet service provider, and how to connect to the Internet with the Internet Connection Wizard.

Chapter 18, "Browsing the Internet with Explorer," covers what to do once you get connected to the Internet. You see how to use Microsoft's new Internet Explorer 4.0, an impressive Web browser with more capability than Netscape Navigator. You can use IE 4.0 to browse through the World Wide Web, download files via FTP, and subscribe to Web sites you can later browse offline.

Chapter 19, "Working with the Active Desktop," is a real centerpiece for the concept of Webtop computing. With the Active Desktop, you can put live Web pages and other objects directly on your desk and schedule them for updating. As another option, you can create a Web (HTML) page that becomes your desktop. This enables you to create kiosk-like interfaces displaying links to your most frequently used applications, documents, and Web links.

Chapter 20, "Subscribing to Web Sites and Browsing Offline," will soon become an invaluable source of news and research. But then the problem arises that you must stay online to browse. Microsoft has solved this problem with the newly proposed open standards for Webcasting and the offline browsing capabilities in Internet Explorer 4. You can download any Web site on a schedule you dictate, and then later browse the Web site offline.

Chapter 21 is "Using Outlook Express Mail and News." If you don't have a newsgroup reader or e-mail program, you'll definitely want to use Outlook Express. Many people with Office 97 who feel that Outlook is overkill are using Outlook Express to quickly and efficiently read their e-mail and get information from online newsgroups.

Chapter 22, "Using FrontPage Express and IE 4 Components," describes the programs that come with the Internet Explorer 4.0 suite. FrontPage Express is a scaled-down FrontPage, intended for creating and editing Web pages. The Task Scheduler is the new robust agent that schedules and automatically runs tasks you specify, from copying files to running the disk defragmenter. NetMeeting enables workgroups to do collaborative editing on documents, share chat sessions and whiteboard, and more. It works well even with 28.8K modems.

Part V: Working with Applications

Chapter 23 is "Application Management Fundamentals." If you are coming from a Windows 3.1 or DOS background, you'll definitely want to read this chapter before working with Windows 95 applications. Here is where you will learn how to create *shortcuts* (a great time-saving feature), as well as how to perform such ordinary tasks as resizing windows, opening and saving documents, and using the all-important right mouse button.

Chapter 24, "Installing, Running, and Uninstalling Windows Applications," shows you how to install Windows applications (both Windows 95 and earlier applications are covered), how to run applications, and how to remove applications. It also includes coverage of uninstalling software with Windows 95's new Remove feature. Tips and techniques show you how to uninstall earlier applications and how to improve your productivity with application tips such as Shortcuts and Scraps on the desktop.

Chapter 25, “Installing, Running, and Uninstalling MS-DOS Applications,” shows you how to use DOS programs in Windows. This version of Windows makes more memory available to DOS applications and runs DOS games faster and better than previous versions.

Chapter 26, “Using Microsoft Exchange and Messaging,” shows how to use Microsoft Exchange and Messaging to organize “received” electronic mail and faxes in one convenient location. You learn how to use the universal inbox and how to compose, store, organize, and send messages via e-mail and fax.

Chapter 27 is “Using Fax, Address Book, and Phone Dialer.” Windows 95 includes fax services that integrate with the Universal Inbox to give you an easy way to send faxes from within documents. You can use the built-in address book to make it easy to send e-mail and fax messages through the Universal Inbox. This chapter also includes the new Windows Address Book.

Chapter 28, “Using WordPad and Paint,” teaches you about two of the most frequently used accessory programs that come with Windows 95. This chapter gives you some bare-bones instructions on using WordPad and Paint, as well as tips on how they can be used with your larger applications.

Chapter 29 is “Using Calculator, Calendar, and Other Accessories.” This chapter covers a collection of small accessories that are like a grab bag of small tools. They are helpful, but not always necessary. Keep them around, though, for that occasional odd job.

Chapter 30, “Communicating with HyperTerminal,” shows you how to use HyperTerminal, a basic communications tool. It’s an excellent tool for testing modems or for downloading drivers and utilities from bulletin board services.

Part VI: Customizing Windows

Chapter 31, “Customizing the Taskbar and Start Menu,” describes some of the highly productive ways you can modify Windows 95 to more closely fit the way you work. You will learn how to move, reshape, and hide the taskbar. You will also learn how to add frequently used programs and documents to the Start menu and even create submenus.

Chapter 32 is “Customizing the Desktop Settings.” Windows 95 is a visually attractive environment. If you don’t think so, modify it so you think it is. By changing the desktop settings, you can change screen resolution, use larger fonts for menus, change background colors and window element colors, and much more.

Chapter 33, “Customizing Your System Settings,” describes how to change the myriad little features that you usually set only once—such as which sound plays for which Windows event, the language displayed by Windows, the date and time, and so forth.

Part VII: Sharing Data Between Applications

Chapter 34 is “Simple Ways of Sharing Data Between Applications.” Generally, all Windows applications provide some means for sharing data with another application. This chapter shows how to use the most basic and commonly used of these means, including cutting, copying, and pasting within and between documents in Windows and DOS applications, as well as how to link data from one document to another.

Chapter 35, "Advanced Ways of Sharing Data Between Applications with OLE," shows how to create and modify documents based on the concept of *compound documents*—documents you create by using multiple types of data. You see how to build documents that incorporate different types of data, such as text from a word processor or spreadsheet and graphics. You also learn how to use this data within a single application without having to switch between applications to edit the different data types.

Part VIII: Networking with Windows

Chapter 36, "Setting Up a Windows 95 Peer-to-Peer Network," shows you how to set up your own workgroup network. You will learn how to install the network cards and install and configure the network client and protocol. It also covers how to share resources in a workgroup.

Chapter 37 is "Sharing Windows 95 Peer-to-Peer Resources." In this chapter, you will learn much more about setting up peer-to-peer security, and sharing resources such as drives, printers, and modems.

Chapter 38, "Connecting Windows 95 to a Novell Network," takes a more in-depth look at effectively using Windows 95 as a Network Client to the popular corporate network, Novell's NetWare. The chapter includes coverage on installing Microsoft's Client for NetWare.

Chapter 39, "Using Novell Network Resources in Windows 95," gives you an overview for using NetWare utilities, connecting to other servers, and creating network backups.

Chapter 40, "Connecting Windows 95 to Windows NT Server 4.0," familiarizes you with the various options you have available in Windows 95 to quickly get connected in a Windows NT networked environment. Then the chapter walks you through the process of getting connected.

Chapter 41, "Using Windows NT Server Resources in Windows 95," gives you an overview of server utilities and sharing resources.

Chapter 42, "Working with Network Printers," describes how to manage network printers, print via drag and drop, and install and optimize network printers.

Chapter 43, "Network Management and Security," gives you a good briefing on what to be aware of for network security. You learn how to manage user profiles, set up security, and troubleshoot problems.

Appendixes

Appendix A, "What's on the CD?," describes the software and utilities you find on the CD that accompanies this book.

Appendix B is "Additional Help and Resources." This book can't cover it all. But we can tell you where to find what wouldn't fit between our covers. This appendix lists the telephone and fax support numbers for Microsoft and third-party suppliers. You'll also learn how to use the Internet, The Microsoft Network, CompuServe, and TechNet CDs to get the same databases of support information available to Microsoft's telephone support staff and consultants.

Special Features in the Book

Que has over a decade of experience writing and developing the most successful computer books available. With that experience, we've learned what special features help readers the most. Look for these special features throughout the book to enhance your learning experience.

Chapter Road Maps A sidebar on the first page of each chapter contains a list of topics to be covered in the chapter. This list serves as a road map to the chapter so you can tell at a glance what is covered. It also provides a useful outline of the key topics you'll be reading about.

Notes Notes present interesting or useful information that isn't necessarily essential to the discussion. This secondary track of information enhances your understanding of Windows, but you can safely skip notes and not be in danger of missing crucial information. Notes look like this:

NOTE Ctrl+Esc is a shortcut key combination used to access the Start menu. Throughout this book, when you see a key+key combination, that signifies a shortcut to accessing an application or opening a menu.

Tips Tips present short advice on quick or often overlooked procedures. These include shortcuts that save you time. A tip looks like this:

Nearly every item in Windows 95 contains a properties sheet you can customize. Right-click an item and choose Properties to see its properties sheet.

Cautions Cautions serve to warn you about potential problems that a procedure may cause, unexpected results, and mistakes to avoid.

CAUTION

If you have a similar printer that could use the same drivers, do not remove the software. Deleting the associated software might remove that driver from use by other printers.

Troubleshooting No matter how carefully you follow the steps in the book, you eventually come across something that just doesn't work the way you think it should. Troubleshooting sections anticipate these common errors or hidden pitfalls and present solutions. A troubleshooting section looks like this:

TROUBLESHOOTING

I've always been able to set the number of copies I print from the control panel of my printer. When I print in Windows 95, however, I always get one copy no matter how I set the printer. In Windows 95, the settings in your programs for the number of copies to be printed overrides the setting on your printer. To print multiple copies, change the setting in the program you are printing from.

Internet References Throughout this book, you will find Internet references that point you to World Wide Web addresses or online addresses where you can find out additional information about topics. Internet references look like this:

ON THE WEB

You can learn about the Registry's organization on the Internet, too. *PC Magazine* has a three-part description of the Registry on the Web that you can read by pointing your Web browser at:

www.zdnet.com/~pcmag/issues/1418/pcm00083.htm

www.zdnet.com/~pcmag/issues/1419/pcm00116.htm

www.zdnet.com/~pcmag/issues/1422/pcm00140.htm

Cross References Throughout the book, you see references to other sections and pages in the book (like the one that follows this paragraph). These cross references point you to related topics and discussions in other parts of the book.

See "Improved Performance and Reliability," **p. xxx**

Conventions

In addition to these special features, several conventions are used in this book to make it easier to read and understand. These conventions include the following.

Underlined Hot Keys, or Mnemonics In this book, hot keys appear underlined like they appear on-screen. In Windows, many menus, commands, buttons, and other options have these hot keys. To use a hot key shortcut, press Alt and the key for the underlined character. For instance, to choose the Properties button, press Alt and then R.

Shortcut Key Combinations In this book, shortcut key combinations are joined with plus signs (+). For example, Ctrl+V means hold down the Ctrl key and then press the V key.

Menu Commands

Instructions for choosing menu commands have this form:

> Choose File, New.

This example means open the File menu and select New, which is one way to open a new file.

Instructions involving the new Windows 95 Start menu are an exception. When you are to choose something through the Start menu, the form is as follows:

> Open the Start menu and choose Programs, Accessories, WordPad.

In this case, you open the WordPad word processing accessory. Notice that in the Start menu you simply drag the mouse pointer and point at the option or command you want to choose (even through a whole series of submenus); you don't need to click anything.

This book also has certain typeface enhancements to indicate special text, as described in the following table.

Typeface	Description
Italic	Italic is used to indicate terms and variables in commands or addresses.
Boldface	Bold is used to indicate text you type, as well as Internet addresses and other locators in the online world.
MYFILE.DOC	File names and directories are set in all caps to distinguish them from regular text, as in MYFILE.DOC.

PART I

Installing and Configuring Windows 95

CHAPTER 1

What's New in Windows 95 and the Internet Explorer 4.0 Suite

by Ron Person

Learn how Windows 95 has received three updates since its release

Microsoft promised continuous free updates and we've had three of them. Learn what each update does.

How the updates affect your use of Windows 95

Service Pack 1 and OSR2 fixed or improved the internal workings of Windows 95, but the IE 4 Suite could really change the way you work.

Which of the updates are important to how you use Windows 95

OSR2 helps hard disk efficiency, multimedia, and adds new devices, but Internet Explorer 4 Suite will change your work habits.

See the future of Windows 95

Install Windows 95 and then update with OSR2, Internet Explorer 4 Suite, and the integrated shell components and you are looking at the next release of Windows.

Waves of technology change have swept through business in the last twenty-five years: personal computers, Windows 3.1/95, the Internet. It appears that another wave is rising: Web-centric desktop computing. Microsoft even calls it Webtop computing in contrast to the previous desktop computing.

Windows 95 combined with Internet Explorer 4 and the integrated shell components creates a personal computing environment that integrates work with the Internet and World Wide Web. This chapter gives you an overview of how Windows 95 is changing with its new updates. ■

NOTE If you are an experienced Windows 95 user who is familiar with Web browsing, you will want to read Chapter 11, "Navigating with the Shell Integration Components," Chapter 19, "Working with the Active Desktop," and Chapter 20, "Subscribing to Web Sites and Offline Browsing," for the major impact of the switch to Webtop computing.

If you are an experienced Windows 3.x user, you should start with Chapter 10, "Navigating and Controlling Windows," to see a few of the main user interface changes.

Keeping Your Copy of Windows 95 Up-to-Date

Windows 95 was released August 24, 1995. After its release, Microsoft stated that they would not release a new version for a couple of years, but they would release updates to Windows 95. There have been three significant updates since the first release.

The first update was in the first quarter of 1996 with the release of Service Pack 1. Service Pack 1 primarily contained patches to software problems, additional multimedia software, and additional hardware drivers.

To order a copy of the Microsoft Windows 95 Service Pack 1, call 800-360-7561 and request the Windows 95 Service Pack. There is a shipping and handling charge of $14.95. Service Pack 1 also can be downloaded from the Internet, The Microsoft Network, and CompuServe.

ON THE WEB

You can get a free upgrade by downloading portions or all of the Service Pack from Microsoft's site on the World Wide Web. To find the Service Pack on the World Wide Web use the URL:

http://www.microsoft.com/windows/software/updates.htm

The second major update was in October of 1996 when Microsoft released Windows 95b, also known as OEM System Release 2 (OSR2). This was only released to hardware manufacturers. OSR2 included all the changes from Service Pack 1, as well as a new FAT32 disk format that improved large disk performance and efficiency, additional drivers, and multimedia improvements. There was no significant change to the user interface. Personal computer owners had to purchase a new computer or hard drive to get a full copy. However, Appendix A describes how you can download large portions of OSR2 from the Microsoft Web site for free. Throughout this book, OSR2 enhancements are indicated by the icon shown at left.

The third major update is significant. It foretells a major change in Windows 95. This update includes the Internet Explorer 4 Suite (IE4) and integrated shell components. The Internet Explorer 4 Suite brings a collection of software to Windows 95 that centers work around the World Wide Web. The software in the suite includes arguably the best browser, an intermediate level personal Web page editor, a very useful mail and news reader, collaborative software that enables you to simultaneously do team editing over the Internet, and a multicast animated audio player for online education and information. Throughout this book, IE4 enhancements are indicated by the icon shown at left.

Chapter 18, "Browsing the Internet with Explorer," explains how to get a free copy of Internet Explorer 4 and the integrated shell components.

Installing Windows 95 OSR2 and Internet Explorer 4

You don't have to be a hardware guru to install Windows 95. In previous versions of Windows, you were often forced into making choices about hardware configurations. It was up to you to select the appropriate options and settings so that hardware and software were compatible. Windows 95 takes care of many of those decisions and options for you.

Most new computers come with Windows 95b (OSR2) installed. Installing OSR2 over an existing Windows 95 or Windows 3.1 is not difficult but it does require some extra work. If you want to convert your FAT16 formatted hard disk to the more efficient FAT32, then you will need to back up all your data, repartition and reformat your hard disk, install OSR2, and reinstall your applications and data. It takes a lot of time, but it's not particularly difficult, especially if you follow the instructions in Chapter 2, "Installing Windows."

Upgrading your existing Windows 95 to include the Internet Explorer 4 Suite and the integrated shell components is almost completely automatic. Use an existing Internet browser to access the Microsoft Web site and download the updates. If you want, they install automatically. Chapter 18, "Browsing the Internet with Explorer" describes how to install the Internet Explorer 4 Suite.

▶ **See** "Installing the Windows 95b (OSR2) Service Release," **p. 47**

▶ **See** "Installing Internet Explorer 4," **p. 477**

Improving Windows with OSR2

OEM Service Release 2 incorporates the changes from Service Pack 1, but it also includes a number of additional enhancements. One of its most significant enhancements is the new 32-bit file allocation system (FAT32) that enables Windows to support hard drives up to 2 terabytes in size. FAT32 uses a more efficient cluster size, so it is up to 40% more efficient with large hard disks (over 512M).

▶ **See** "Installing FAT32," **p. 52**

If you are currently using Windows 95 with a FAT16 hard drive, you can change to the more efficient FAT32, but it requires more work than a simple upgrade. You may want to use third-party software to improve disk efficiency or wait for the next release of Windows. Read the section "The FAT32 File System" in Chapter 15 to learn more about the tradeoffs and alternatives.

OSR2 includes a wide range of enhancements. Some of the enhancements are:

DriveSpace Supports compressed volumes up to 2G

New storage devices Support for floptical drives, Zip drives, CD changes, removable IDE media, and IDE Bus Mastering

PC Card	Support for newer PC Card 32, 3.3 volt PC Cards, network/modem PC Cards and GPS
Internet	Includes Internet Explorer 3, Internet Connection Wizard, Internet Mail and News, NetMeeting, and Personal Web Server
Improved multimedia	Includes DirectX 2.0, Active Movie, OpenGL, and support for Intel's MMX processor
IrDA 2.0	Improved infrared communication
Netware	Full support for NetWare 4.x including NetWare Directory Services
Automatic ScanDisk	ScanDisk runs automatically when you restart Windows after an abnormal shutdown
Online Services	Installable client software for America Online 3.0, CompuServe 3.0, and AT&T WorldNet

Some OSR2 enhancements are available individually for free from the Internet. For information on downloading and installing components from OSR2, refer to Table 2.1, "Summary of Features in Windows 95 OSR2 Update," in Chapter 2.

See "Installing the Windows 95b (OSR2) Service Release," **p. 47**

CAUTION

Be aware that there is some risk of hardware and software incompatibilities with OSR2, and any disk utilities you have that are designed to work with the FAT16 file system will not work. You will need to obtain updated versions or patches for your disk utilities. The versions of ScanDisk and Disk Defragmenter that come with OSR2 are compatible with FAT32.

ON THE WEB

Check out the following WWW site for in-depth coverage of OSR2 and the FAT32 file system:

http://www.users.cts.com/king/s/serwin/osr2.html

A Web-Oriented Interface

To most personal computer users, the interface they see on-screen is the computer. Because of that, the world of DOS computers was too difficult for many people. There was a lot of learning involved just to start with simple tasks. And there was no way to learn as you worked. The advent of Windows, with its mouse and drop-down menus, improved computer usability quite a bit. With a few hours of instruction on Windows, you could learn on your own by exploring. The work-to-learning ratio improved significantly.

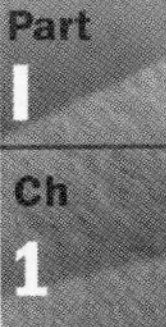

Now the explosive growth of the Internet and World Wide Web is causing another change in how people expect to work with computers. Microsoft is moving the Windows 95 interface closer toward a Web-like user environment. Combined with something called the Active Desktop, we can expect to see work on our desktop and work involving the Internet become seamless. One procedure and one learning methodology works for all tasks.

One simple, but immediately apparent way that Windows 95 is changing is by giving you the choice of double-clicking or single-clicking to activate applications or documents. The standard Windows 95 method is to double-click, but the new Web-like method uses a single-click.

A less apparent but more profound change is the integrated shell. When you install Internet Explorer 4 and the integrated shell components, the Windows Explorer, My Computer, and Internet Explorer are one. Just type a different address in the Address bar and you can watch them change. For example, start the Windows Explorer; then type My Computer in its Address bar and press Enter. It changes into a My Computer window. Type an URL in that Address bar and press Enter; the My Computer window transforms into the Internet Explorer. As you make these changes, note that the toolbars and menus change accordingly.

See "Switching Between Single- and Double-Click Activation," **p. 284**

See "Consistent Navigation Between Explorer and My Computer," **p. 297**

Perhaps the most significant change to the user interface is the Active Desktop. The Active Desktop is really the piece that transforms desktop computing into Webtop computing. The Active Desktop can display live information being Webcast over the Internet.

The Active Desktop is a new graphical layer to the desktop that is underneath the shortcut icons. You can switch the Active Desktop between three different environments. It can be a standard Windows 95 desktop. Or it can be an Active Desktop and display objects such as graphics, Web pages, ActiveX components, or Java applets. The Web pages, ActiveX components, and Java applets can be online with the Internet to display updated information. Or it can display a local HTML page. This last sounds rather dry until you read through the examples shown in Chapter 19, "Working with the Active Desktop."

See "What Is Active Desktop?," **p. 514**

The metaphor of viewing Windows as an extension of the Web continues with Web views of folders. Most Windows users are familiar with the Large Icon, Small Icon, Detail and List views of file, and folder information. The Web view of files and folders is yet another view, except this view displays a folder's contents on an HTML page. You can use any HTML editor to modify a folder's HTML page and thus modify how the files or folders appear. For example, you can display help information next to each file telling the user which files or folders to use. Or you can completely hide the files and folders and create an HTML page that contains text links to the applications or documents. Users can then read a link to see if it is what they want, and click the link of the file they want opened. The Internet Explorer 4 Suite comes with FrontPage Express, a simple HTML editor, so intermediate level users can make personal Web pages for their own Web views.

See "Viewing Files and Folders with Web Views," **p. 365**

In addition to these major changes that move Windows 95 in a new direction, there are minor changes implemented with the integrated shell components that go a long way in making Windows 95 a little easier to use. For example, you no longer have to use arcane tricks to reorganize menu items on the Start menu. Now you can just drag and drop menu items to a new position.

Most users have enjoyed the power of the Windows taskbar and the customizable toolbars in Office applications. With integrated shell components, you get a lot of Windows toolbars you can use on the desktop. The Address toolbar is good for quickly entering a pathname or URL and opening an Explorer. The Links toolbar stores your most frequently used links. The Desktop toolbar serves the same purpose as shortcut icons on the desktop—a handy feature because you can now hide desktop icons to make the desktop look cleaner. Quick Launch is a toolbar that gives you quick access to the Internet Explorer Suite. Of course, you can always create your own toolbar.

See "Displaying Built-In Desktop Toolbars," **p. 289**

See "Creating Toolbars to Open Folders, Applications, Documents, and Web Sites," **p. 291**

Internet Explorer 4 Suite

Microsoft has developed not just Internet Explorer 4 to upgrade Windows 95, they have created a suite of products designed to create an integrated work environment on the Web. Internet Explorer 4 Suite includes the following free products:

Internet Explorer 4	Microsoft's Internet browser that schedules downloads and includes offline browsing
Outlook Express Mail and News	Integrated e-mail and news reader
FrontPage Express	An HTML editor useful for creating personal Web pages
Task Manager	A task scheduler that uses the Explorer metaphor to schedule tasks such as backing up files or defragmenting disks
NetMeeting	Collaborative software that enables teams to work over the Internet using shared applications, chat space, whiteboard, audio, and video
NetShow	Animated audio that can be multicast over the Internet or intranet to improve corporate training

Internet Explorer 4: Offline Browsing and Webcasting

The new Internet Explorer 4 is not just faster, it is easier to navigate with and includes a subscription feature that enables you to schedule automatic updates to Web sites you want copied to your local drive. Once the Web sites are updated on your hard drive, you can browse them offline by using Internet Explorer 4's new offline browsing feature.

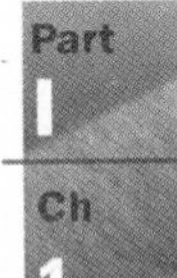

Internet Explorer 4 also introduces *Webcasting*. Webcasting gives you three different alternatives for downloading Web sites to your local drive. You can use a Webcrawler to download any Web site to a depth you specify on the schedule you specify. The Webcrawler approach works with any Web site—it even enters your password automatically in protected Web sites.

The second method of Webcasting displays in Internet Explorer 4 a table of contents listing information contained in the Web site. You can subscribe to the category of information you want regardless of how the information is physically linked in the site. The third method of Webcasting involves push technology that enables content providers such as the *Wall Street Journal* to tailor information for you or your corporation and then feed it to your desktop.

See "Navigating the World Wide Web," **p. 482**

See "Subscribing to Any Web Site," **p. 526**

See "Subscribing to Sites that Use the Channel Definition Format," **p. 536**

Stay in Touch with Outlook Express Mail and News

A very nice addition in the Internet Explorer 4 Suite is Outlook Express Mail and News. It is a complete mail and news reader that works stand-alone or from menus and buttons in Internet Explorer 4.

Outlook Express enables you to filter and store messages by category. Your messages can be plain text, include multiple attached files, or be robust Web pages. In fact, you can even send a Web page from within Internet Explorer 4 to another Outlook Express user.

See "Using Outlook Express Mail," **p. 543**

See "Using Outlook Express News," **p. 584**

FrontPage Express, Everyone's Web Page Editor

If you have seen FrontPage 97, the award-winning Web site development software, then you've seen FrontPage Express. FrontPage Express is very much the page editing portion of FrontPage 97, except it's free with Internet Explorer 4 Suite. FrontPage Express is included in the suite because the Web-centric approach to the new Windows 95 enhancements demands that you have a Web page editor if you want to customize your system.

A new view in My Computer or Windows Explorer displays files and folders within a Web (HTML) page you can modify. Using FrontPage Express, you can make major changes to how files and folders display. In fact, you can hide the files and folders and just display instructions and hyperlinks to the documents or applications you want opened.

See "Using FrontPage Express," **p. 612**

NetMeeting and the Future of Collaboration

There is a major marketing and development push within Microsoft to help corporations realize the benefits of collaborative work over the Internet. At TechEd, Microsoft's annual technical training conference, many major corporations attended a presentation on NetMeeting to see how it can be used to reduce support and training costs.

NetMeeting enables multiple Windows 95 users to connect over the Internet and share an application and document, whiteboard, chat session, telephone, and even video. When using a shared document, whiteboard, and chat session, NetMeeting runs with sufficient zip so that it's very useful. Many companies expect to use it to reduce training and support costs. Studies have found that the length of time to resolve a user's problem via remote training over the Internet is about the same time as it would take using normal telephone support. But unlike telephone support, NetMeeting produces few callbacks because the support person can see the screen of the person having difficulty, and the person with the problem can watch the resolution.

NetMeeting also has a lot of potential as a group editing and collaboration tool. It supports international telephone standards and will support group conference standards so that telecommuters can work with their compatriots at home, on the road, in the office, or in a group meeting.

▶ **See** "Group Collaboration with NetMeeting 2.0," **p. 647**

CHAPTER 2

Installing Windows

by Dick Cravens and Robert Voss

Everyone knows the old saying about first impressions. Setup may be the first exposure you'll have to Windows 95, and it will positively affect your opinion of the newest addition to the Windows product family. Microsoft has completely rewritten Setup for Windows 95, adding significant capabilities and stability to the program. You'll be amazed at the depth of Setup's capabilities as it automatically detects and configures hardware and software that literally brought earlier versions of the program to their knees. This chapter explains the basics of both installing Windows 95 for the first time and updating Windows 95 to the newer Windows 95b, also known as OSR2.

Windows 95 system requirements

Find out the minimum requirements for installing Windows 95.

Improvements in Windows 95 Setup

Find the improvements in the Windows 95 Setup.

How Windows 95 Setup works

Learn about the four basic phases involved in Setup.

Using Windows 95 Setup for a typical installation

Learn the steps involved in a standard Windows installation.

Advanced installation techniques

Find out about the different Windows installations.

Installing Windows 95b (OSR2)

Learn the advantages and disadvantages of the newest release of Windows 95.

Removing Windows 95

Learn how to reverse Windows Setup.

Understanding Windows 95 Setup Requirements

Before you begin to install Windows 95, be sure that your system meets the minimum system requirements. To run Windows 95, you need a system that includes the following:

- An 80386 or later processor (25 MHz or faster)—at least a Pentium/100 is recommended for working effectively with Windows 95 applications.
- A Microsoft- or Logitech-compatible mouse. (If you have another type of mouse, be sure to have the drivers for it handy when you begin installation.)
- A high-density (1.44M) 3.5-inch floppy drive or CD-ROM drive
- Although you can run Windows 95 with 8M of RAM, 16M is recommended as a minimum, and 32M or more is recommended if you want to run multiple or large graphic and photo-editing applications.
- VGA graphics video display (Super VGA recommended)
- Microsoft Windows 3.0 or later (including Windows for Workgroups) if you're installing the upgrade version of Windows 95. (The full, non-upgrade version of Windows 95 doesn't require a previous installation of Windows.)
- 417K free conventional memory
- 25M to 40M of free hard drive storage space (depending upon your upgrade path and installation options) partitioned with the FAT file system. Most consultants recommend at least a 1G hard drive for computers running Windows 95 and Office 95/97. The price is not significantly more than that of a 500M hard drive.
- Up to 14M of additional free hard drive storage space for the Windows 95 swap file (depending upon the amount of RAM installed on your system)

Microsoft designed the retail version of Windows 95 as an upgrade-only product, which means you must have a previous version of MS-DOS or Windows to install Windows 95. Because Windows 3.x requires MS-DOS, most users will have both.

Although Windows 95 will certainly install on a 386 computer with 4M of RAM, you won't be able to do much with it. To experience the full performance potential of the new Windows, you really need at least 16M of memory. You will see a real performance increase when running multiple applications if you have 32M or more of RAM. Processor speed is certainly important, and with the drop in price for Pentium systems, it is hard to justify spending the money to upgrade an older 386 or 486 system to run Windows 95. The response of Windows 95 on a Pentium system with 16M or more of RAM is dramatically better than that of a 486 system.

On the other hand, if you're looking at adding significant amounts of memory, plus replacing *both* your drive and video subsystems, it may pay to check out a completely new computer with the faster CPU. Check with your hardware vendor and review your options.

NOTE Windows 95 works with the major drive compression utilities on the market:

- Microsoft DriveSpace and DoubleSpace
- Stacker versions 3.x and 4.x
- Addstor SuperStor

Other compression software may work fine, but it's best to check with the vendor to confirm this prior to installation.

Also, be aware that disk compression may affect the estimate of free drive space available for installation. If you're using compression, be cautious about trusting space estimates. Compression yield depends upon many factors, including data types, so allow extra space if you're installing on a compressed drive.

If you are using the OSR2 service release of Windows 95 and you have the new FAT32 file system installed, you should definitely check with the vendor of any third-party disk compression utilities to make sure you have a version of the utility that supports FAT32. (See "Installing the Windows 95b (OSR2) Service Release," later in this chapter.) Although OSR2 comes with DriveSpace 3, you will not be able to compress your hard drive if you have installed the FAT32 file system. FAT32 volumes cannot be compressed using DriveSpace 3.

Preparing to Install Windows 95 Setup

Although Windows 95 Setup does an amazing job of configuring most systems, you can save time and trouble with some useful tips and tricks for preparing your machine for installation. Before you begin your installation, you need to take some steps to get your system ready for the upgrade and to prepare for the setup process. You also need to determine if you are going to be upgrading from Windows 3.1x, installing Windows from MS-DOS (or another operating system), or reformatting your hard disk and doing a clean install. The following sections help you get ready for installing Windows 95.

Getting Your System Ready for Windows 95 Setup

There are several steps you need to take before you are ready to run Windows 95 Setup. Before you install Windows 95, make sure you do each of the following things:

- Confirm that your system meets the minimum Windows 95 hardware and software requirements.
- Confirm the boot drive sequence for your system.
- Confirm that you have a working boot floppy disk for your current operating system configuration.
- Back up your critical data and system configuration files (a complete system backup is preferred).
- Confirm that your current Windows installation is in the best possible working order.
- Defragment your hard drive(s).

- Know the location of all required drivers for any peripherals, including network interface cards.
- Know all the user names and passwords you'll need to log in to your network.
- Disable all memory-resident programs (loaded in AUTOEXEC.BAT and CONFIG.SYS files).
- Disable antivirus programs, screen savers, disk scan utilities, and any similar programs.
- Disable third-party memory managers, replacing them with HIMEM.SYS and EMM386.EXE.
- Remove any substitute shells or shell extensions, such as Norton Desktop for Windows.
- Prune your program groups in Program Manager to remove programs you don't use.

Although this list may seem like a lot to do before you can upgrade to Windows 95, bear in mind that changing the operating system on your computer is no small matter. In fact, you should follow most of these procedures for any major change in your computing system. Anything less is simply flirting with the computing demons well known to the experienced PC user.

NOTE Although it's usually wise to make backup copies of the installation disks for a new program before you begin, it is not possible with Windows 95. Microsoft uses a proprietary disk format for Windows 95 floppies that neither MS-DOS nor Windows 3.x can duplicate. Microsoft includes an offer to purchase a second set of disks in the retail Windows 95 package. Take care of your original disks or take advantage of this offer!

The first item in the list is obvious. Less clear is the need to have a confirmed boot backup plan for your system. This comes in two parts: having a boot floppy disk and configuring your system to use it. A good boot disk is not just a bootable floppy but one that configures your system as closely as possible to the current boot session configurations you normally use via your hard drive. It's worth the time it takes to create this "boot backup." The few minutes it takes to do it may save you hours of hair-pulling later.

A great boot disk is worthless if your system can't read it. Most systems are configured to search the drives during startup to find a bootable disk, but some are configured to look only at a specific drive, to save time at startup, or for security reasons. If in doubt about your system, *test it.* If you create a boot disk and the system won't read it from a cold start, check the system CMOS settings and correct the boot sequence (see your computer's manual regarding access to the CMOS setup). The ideal is for the system to search Drive A and then continue to the next floppy (if present) before looking for startup information on Drive C. Although you can configure a system for a reverse of this order (C and then A), some systems will fail by looking at C and then staring off into digital space. Check yours to make sure it's set to search A first, before you learn the hard way.

A complete system backup is part of the most ideal preparation for any system change. If you don't have the facility for a full backup, then consider backing up your critical operating system data as a minimum preparation. These are the recommended files:

- CONFIG.SYS and AUTOEXEC.BAT (located in the root directory of your boot drive, usually C)
- Any files listed in CONFIG.SYS and AUTOEXEC.BAT
- Any network configuration files (include any login scripts) such as CFG, INI, or DAT files in your network driver or root directory
- Your complete DOS directory
- Any initialization (INI) files for Windows applications
- Any Program Information Files (PIF) for MS-DOS applications
- Registry data files (DAT) in your Windows directory
- Password files (PWL) in your Windows directory

You can search painlessly by using the recursion function of the MS-DOS dir command. (The command **dir c:*.ini /s** will search your entire C drive for initialization files.)

Whereas most INI and PIF files reside in the Windows directory, some applications store them in their own directory. Be sure to search all the directories and subdirectories on your hard disk for these files.

You can also skip the search step and copy all the desired files using the recursion switch for the **xcopy** command. For example, the **xcopy c:*.pif /s a:** command copies all PIF files on Drive C to your A drive in one fell swoop, complete with a directory structure if you need to re-create it later.

If you routinely use a backup utility, you may want to simply rely on your last backup prior to installation, or make a new one for just the file types mentioned here. Consult your backup software documentation for more information on how to accomplish this. If your Windows 3.1x system is working, Windows 95 can use those previous settings to confirm your peripheral configurations. If those settings are incorrect, Windows 95 has no real choice but to try them and fail. Even if your current installation and peripherals are working perfectly, be sure to have your device driver floppy disks handy in case Windows 95 Setup needs to refer to them during installation (especially if you're setting up a dual-boot system).

Defragmenting your hard drive prior to installation ensures that Windows 95 will find enough contiguous drive space to create the swap files it needs for virtual memory support. Defragmentation also makes your system run faster (especially during file copy sessions) because the drive system doesn't have to search frantically for free drive clusters.

Another worthwhile precaution is to disable all memory-resident programs (TSRs), antivirus programs, screen savers, utilities that scan your disk automatically for errors, and any other programs of this nature that might interfere with the setup procedure. Also, if you have a laptop that is set to automatically go into suspend mode after a period of inactivity, disable this feature. Also disable any third-party memory managers and replace them with HIMEM.SYS and EMM386.EXE. You may run into problems after you install Windows 95 if you don't do this.

If you have installed a substitute shell for Program Manager, such as Norton Desktop for Windows, you should remove it. Edit the SHELL= line in the [boot] section of SYSTEM.INI to read SHELL=PROGMAN.EXE.

There is no harm in leaving the program groups you have set up in Program Manager as they are, because they are all placed in the Programs submenu of the Start Menu. However, your Programs menu will be much easier to read and use if you consolidate your program groups into about 10 groups. Put all your file and disk management programs into a group called System Maintenance, for example. After you have installed Windows 95, you can easily reorganize the Start Menu submenus to suit your needs.

Upgrading from Windows 3.1

Most users upgrade to Windows 95 from Windows 3.1. Microsoft has designed the Setup program to make this upgrade as simple as possible and is even able to use the existing configuration in Windows 3.1 to help configure your system in Windows 95. The Program Groups you have created in Windows 3.1, for example, will carry over to Windows 95 as items in the Start menu.

Doing a Clean Install

A disadvantage to installing Windows 95 on a system with Windows 3.x is that you inevitably end up with bits and pieces of Windows 3.1x left on your hard disk. It is very difficult—if not impossible—to remove all the traces of Windows 3.x. A solution to this problem is to do a clean install by repartitioning and reformatting your hard disk and then installing Windows 95 from scratch. Although this process takes you much longer than installing from Windows 3.x, you have the satisfaction of starting with a very clean system. In some cases, users have reported that the performance of Windows 95 improved significantly when they did a clean install.

To clean install Windows 95, follow these steps:

1. Create a boot disk for your system and copy FDISK.EXE and FORMAT.COM from the \DOS subdirectory onto the disk.

   If you have a CD-ROM on your system and you will be installing Windows 95 from a CD-ROM, be sure to copy the drivers for the CD-ROM on the disk, as well as AUTOEXEC.BAT and CONFIG.SYS files for loading the drivers at startup.
2. Carefully back up all of your data files, configuration (INI) and DAT files for your applications, and so on.
3. Reboot your computer using the boot disk.
4. Repartition your hard disk using FDISK.

CAUTION

Repartitioning your hard drive destroys all the information on it. Make sure you have a reliable backup of all your important data.

5. Reformat the drive using FORMAT.COM.
6. Reinstall MS-DOS.

   You must use MS-DOS version 3.2 or higher (or an equivalent OEM version). If you use version 3.2, make sure it supports partitions greater than 32M.
7. Reboot your computer and run Setup from the DOS prompt, as described in "Installing Windows 95 from MS-DOS," later in this chapter.
8. Reinstall all of your applications and restore your data files from your backups.

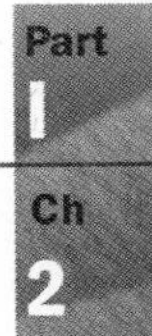

NOTE If you are installing the final version of Windows 95 on a system that had beta versions of Windows 95, Microsoft recommends that you perform a clean install to remove any traces of the earlier versions.

CAUTION

If your computer system is completely new and has no operating system installed, or if you are doing a clean install, be sure you have the non-upgrade version of Windows 95 or your Windows 3.1x disks. Otherwise, you'll get in trouble, because the standard upgrade version requires a previous version of Windows (or at least earlier Windows disks) to operate. If Windows 3.1x is not installed on your system, the Windows 95 Setup program will ask you for the first Windows 3.1 install disk during the installation.

How Windows 95 Setup Works

Before you begin to install Windows 95, it's probably a good idea to know what to expect and when to expect it. Windows 95 Setup has four basic phases:

- Detection
- Question and answer
- File copy
- Startup

Phase One: Setup Detection—Software, then Hardware

Windows 95 Setup starts by detecting what environment it was started from. If you opt to install from within a running Windows 3.1x installation, Setup skips a few steps and gets straight down to the business of analyzing your hardware. If you don't have Windows installed, or choose to start from the MS-DOS prompt, Setup first copies and executes a "mini-window" that runs the remainder of the Setup program and then moves on to hardware detection.

Setup checks your system for the following:

- An extended memory manager and cache program. If neither is found, HIMEM.SYS or SMARTDRV.EXE is loaded.
- Installed hardware devices.

- Connected peripherals.
- IRQs, I/O, and DMA addresses available.
- IRQs, I/O, and DMA addresses in use.

Don't be surprised if the hardware detection phase takes a few minutes. Windows 95 Setup uses a variety of techniques to perform this hardware query. Most PCs respond well to this procedure, which results in the creation of a hardware tree in the Registry. Older PCs may represent a problem if the devices are not industry-standard for IRQs or I/O addresses; newer machines with Plug and Play technology report their configurations more quickly, fully, and accurately.

When the hardware detection phase finishes, Setup displays a dialog box offering you an opportunity to review the detected equipment and settings for accuracy. If they are correct, you can proceed to the next phase. You can deal with any problem directly or tell Windows to ignore it for the time being.

Phase Two: Providing Additional Information

Once Setup has the basic information regarding your hardware, it knows most of what it needs to install Windows on your system. However, a few details still need to be completed, and you also can exercise options regarding exactly which Windows components you want to install. Setup guides you through this process with a few clear dialog boxes. We'll look at these options in more detail when we install Windows later in this chapter.

Phase Three: Copy Chores

Unlike Windows 3.1, Windows 95 Setup asks most questions up front and lets you relax during the actual installation process. Once you tell it what you want, it completes the dreary chores by itself, asking only for disk changes. If you are installing from a CD-ROM drive, you don't even have to worry about that!

When all Windows 95 files are copied, Setup upgrades the existing version of MS-DOS on your boot drive with the Windows 95 operating system.

Phase Four: System Startup

When it has replaced the MS-DOS operating system, Setup then restarts your system and finishes the final cleanup chores required for installation. When this is finished, you're ready to roll with Windows 95.

Starting the Windows 95 Setup Wizard

Now that you have an overview of the basic logic and operation of Windows 95 Setup and some tips for how to prepare your system, you are ready to begin installation.

This section begins by showing you two primary ways to install Windows 95:

- Installing from a working Windows 3.1x system
- Installing from an MS-DOS-only system (or Windows 3.0, Windows NT, and OS/2).

Setup installs a "mini-window" to run from if Windows is not on your computer. If you're running Windows NT, you need to return your system to MS-DOS (via NT's dual-boot option) before starting Windows 95 Setup. The same is true if you're running OS/2 or Windows 3.0.

Installing Windows 95 from Windows 3.x

You can run Windows 95 Setup from any installation of Windows 3.1 or later. If you don't have at least version 3.1, then skip to the section covering MS-DOS installations, later in this chapter.

See "Installing Windows 95 from MS-DOS," **p. 39**

Starting Windows 95 Setup is just like running any other Windows Setup program. If you haven't already done so, start your current version of Windows. Once it's running, you have a couple of choices how to start Setup: from the Program Manager or File Manager.

Before you go further, make sure you have the installation disk set or CD-ROM in the appropriate drive. These examples assume you are using floppies in Drive A. If you have a CD-ROM drive, simply substitute the appropriate drive letter for A.

Starting Setup from Program Manager To start Setup from Program Manager, choose File, Run from the main Program Manager menu. Windows displays the Run dialog box (see Figure 2.1). Type **a:setup** and click OK to begin the installation process.

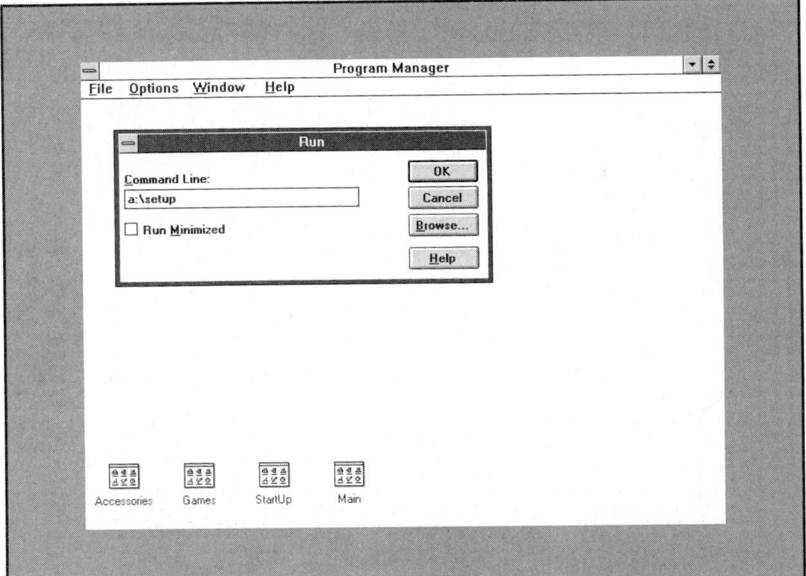

FIG. 2.1
Specify the appropriate drive letter, followed by **setup**.

If you're not sure what drive your Windows 95 Setup disk is in, you can choose Browse to find it. Windows displays the Browse dialog box to help you (see Figure 2.2).

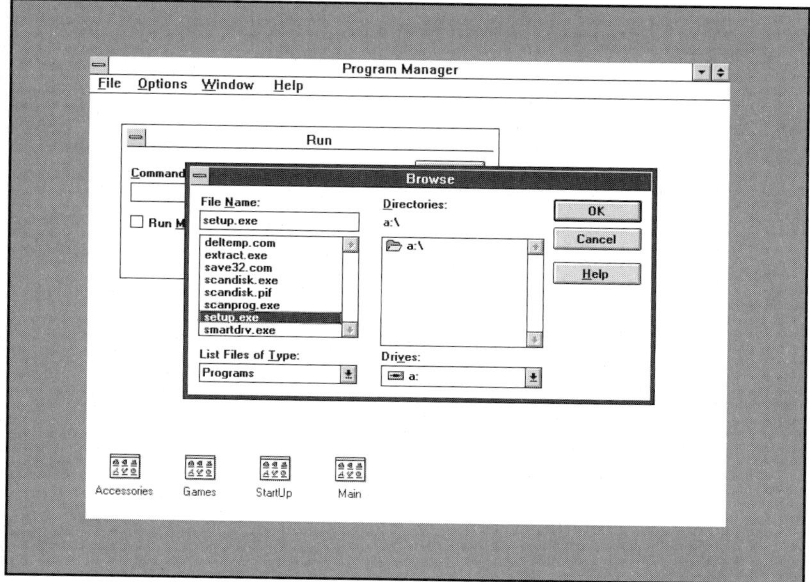

FIG. 2.2
You can search for the Setup disk using the Browse dialog box tools.

When you select SETUP.EXE, Windows loads and runs the Windows 95 Setup program. After a few seconds, Setup displays the welcome screen shown in Figure 2.3.

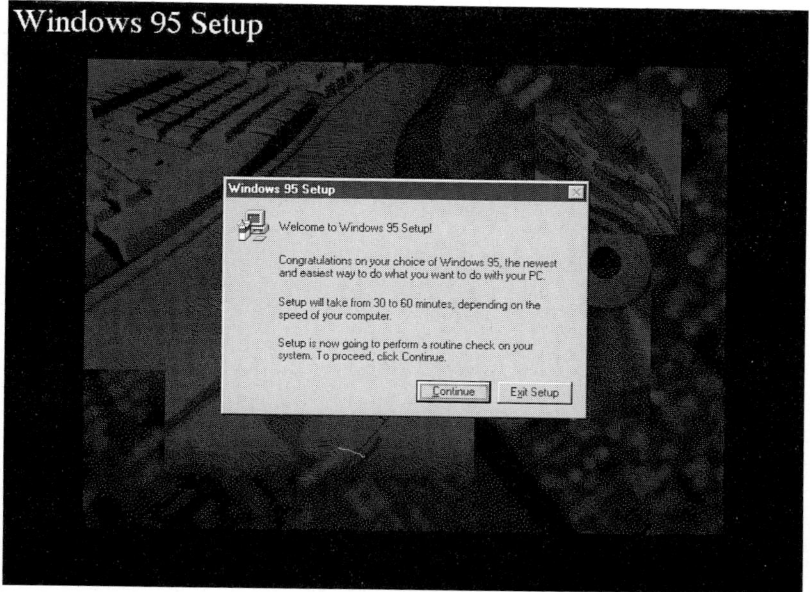

FIG. 2.3
The opening screen for the Windows 95 Setup program.

Starting Setup from File Manager Some users may be more familiar with File Manager. Start File Manager from the Program Manager Main program group by double-clicking the File Manager icon. When the File Manager window appears, click the icon for the appropriate drive where you've loaded your Windows 95 installation disk or CD-ROM. File Manager then displays the contents of the drive as shown in Figure 2.4.

To start Setup, double-click SETUP.EXE. Windows loads the program and Setup displays the welcome screen.

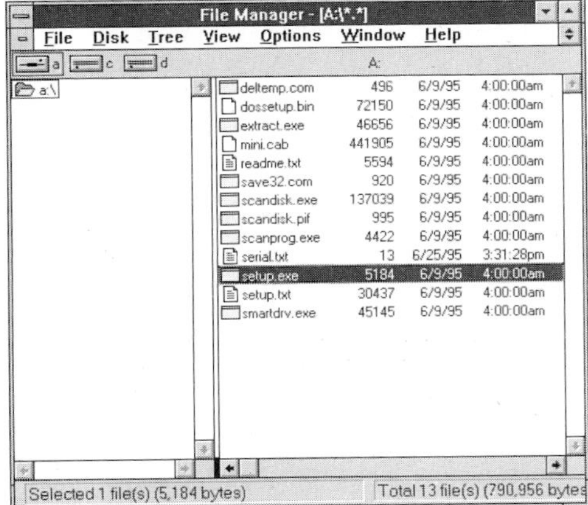

FIG. 2.4
You can start Windows 95 Setup from File Manager.

Getting Down to Business with Setup To continue Windows 95 Setup, click Continue. Setup displays the message box shown in Figure 2.5.

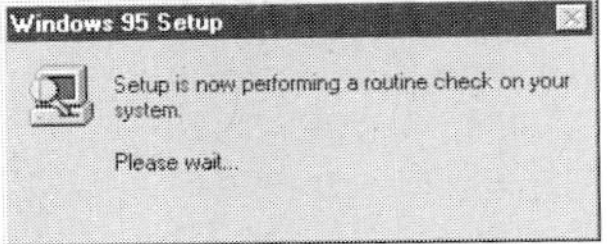

FIG. 2.5
Setup keeps you informed during its investigations.

Setup performs a brief check of your hardware, current operating system, and current running programs before proceeding. It then displays the End-User License Agreement. Read it and click Yes to continue. Windows copies files to your hard drive to prepare for the rest of the installation.

If you're installing from floppy disks, Setup frequently asks you for new disks via the Insert Disk dialog box. You can speed the process by having the disk ready and pressing the Enter key after you switch disks.

Windows may display the dialog box seen in Figure 2.6. If you have any open programs, you should close them before proceeding. This is especially wise if you have any unsaved documents in other applications.

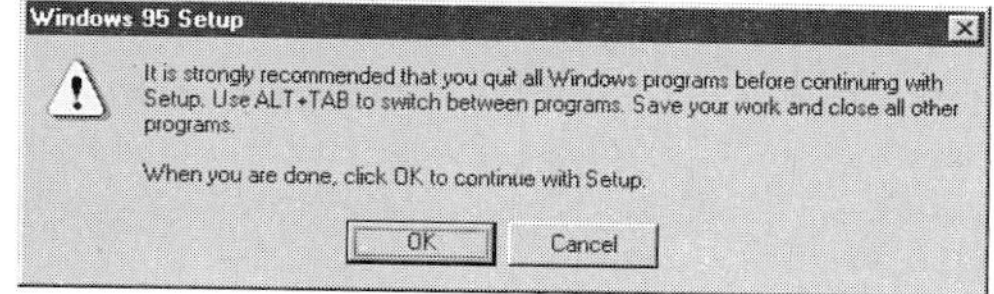

FIG. 2.6
Although Windows 95 Setup is well-behaved, it's always best to close any open applications installing Windows 95.

Take the time to use Alt+Tab to close any other open applications or documents. (You won't be able to close Program Manager without exiting Windows.) When you finish, use Alt+Tab to return to Windows 95 Setup, and click OK to proceed. Setup then displays the main Windows 95 Setup Wizard dialog box (see Figure 2.7).

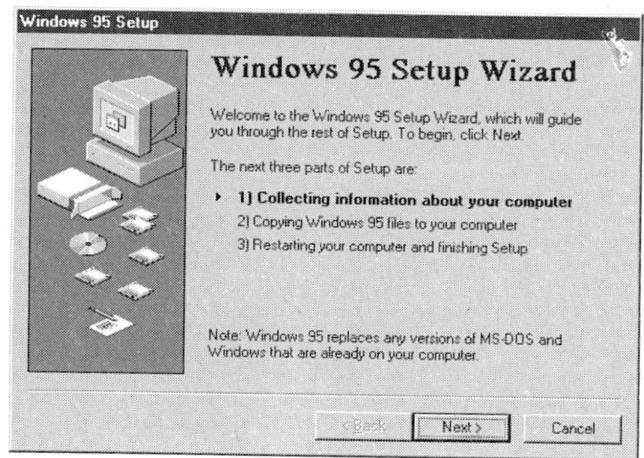

FIG. 2.7
The opening screen of the Setup Wizard. It tells you Setup is about to collect information about your computer.

Setup begins the first major phase requiring user interaction by collecting information about your system and how you'll use it. Click Next > to proceed. Windows displays the Choose Directory dialog box (see Figure 2.8).

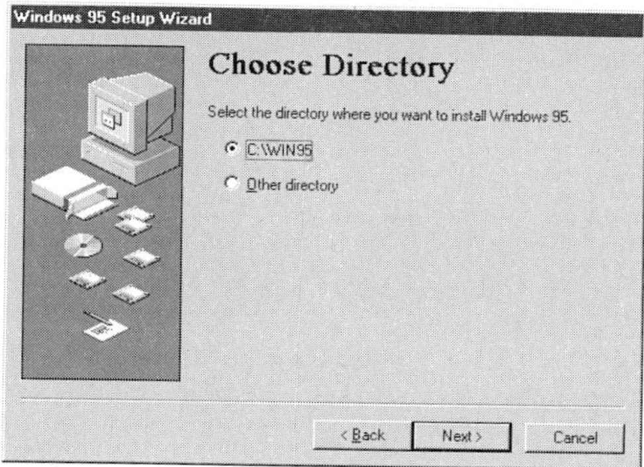

FIG. 2.8
Most users will choose to install Windows 95 as an upgrade to their existing Windows 3.x installation (usually in C:\WINDOWS). Choose Next > to confirm this option.

By default, Setup will install Windows 95 in your existing Windows directory. Accepting this option will upgrade your existing Windows 3.x installation to Windows 95. You will no longer be able to run Windows 3.x on your computer. By installing Windows 95 in another directory, you can create what is called a dual-boot system, which gives you the option of running either Windows 3.x or Windows 95. Creating a dual-boot system is beyond the scope of this book and is not something most users would want or need to do now that Windows 95 has proven to be very stable and easy-to-use.

The next option is a great idea. Windows 95 Setup presents the dialog box shown in Figure 2.9 and asks you if you want to save your Windows 3.1 and DOS system files. Saving these files takes only about 6–9M of disk space and it's highly recommended that you do this. Saving these files allows you to uninstall Windows 95 (as described later in this chapter) if you ever need to revert to your Windows 3.1 setup. Notice this is *not* a full backup of your system or applications. This just saves the system files needed to uninstall Windows 95 and revert to your original setup. Choose to save these files and then click Next to continue.

Setup next checks your system for available installed components and disk space. You don't need to take any action for Setup to move to the next stage, Setup Options. As soon as Setup determines your available drive space, it asks you to confirm what type of installation you want (see Figure 2.9).

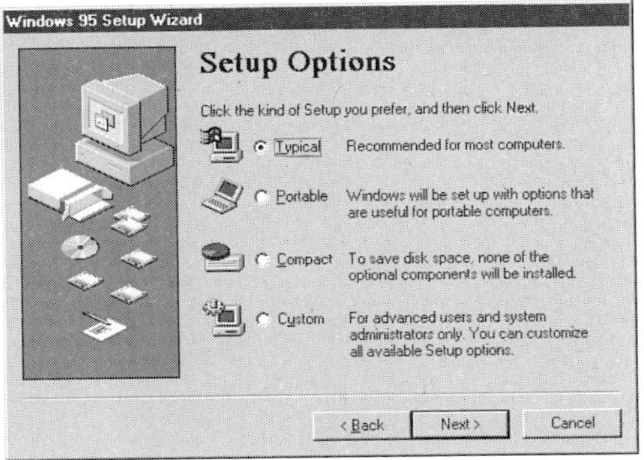

FIG. 2.9 You can choose from Typical, Portable, Compact, or Custom installation profiles.

Your choice here depends upon how you use your computer and how you use Windows. With the Typical installation option, you need only provide some user and computer information and tell Setup if you want an emergency startup disk (highly recommended).

NOTE The "Typical" selection won't install all Windows accessories or games that you may expect. To confirm all components, use the "Custom" option next described.

The Portable setup option is best for laptop or mobile computer users. Setup installs the Windows Briefcase tools for file synchronization and transfer.

The Compact setup option is for systems where you must absolutely minimize the Windows "footprint." This option is for those with truly frugal drive budgets. Windows itself is completely installed, but all extraneous accessories are not—disk compression and maintenance tools are the only accessories installed.

See "Using Custom Setup Mode," **p. 41**

The Custom option allows you to select exactly which components will be installed. You can, for example, choose not to install Windows accessories that you won't be using, and select components, that are not installed when you choose the Typical installation. If you want to install Microsoft Exchange (the MAPI mail service), Microsoft Fax, the Microsoft Network, the Network Administration Tools or the Online User's Guide, you must use the Custom installation.

The Typical Windows 95 Setup Process

For now, let's look at a typical setup, as that is what most Windows 95 users will need. To continue the installation, confirm the default selection (Typical) by clicking Next > or pressing Enter. Windows displays the User Information dialog box (see Figure 2.10).

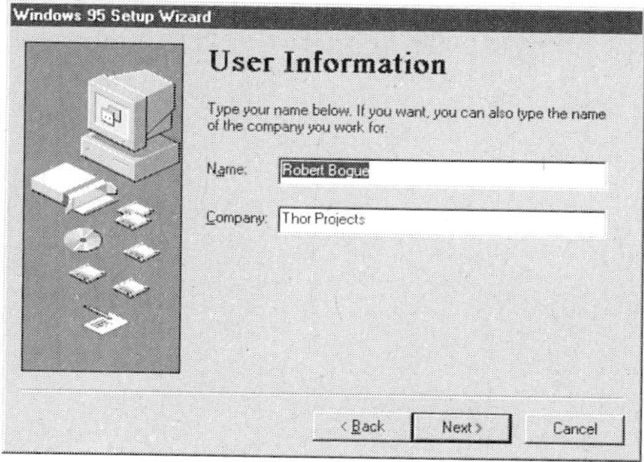

FIG. 2.10 Providing your name helps Windows properly identify you in later application installations and helps Windows identify your system on the Windows Network.

Fill in the appropriate information for your installation, and click Next > or press Enter. The next stage in Setup is further analysis of your peripheral hardware. Setup displays the Analyzing Your Computer dialog box as shown in Figure 2.11.

FIG. 2.11 Depending upon what hardware is installed on your system, Windows will display several options in this dialog box. Confirm or deny your peripheral stance, and Setup does the rest.

Click Next > or press Enter, and Setup then checks your entire system to profile your peripherals (display adapter, sound cards, CD-ROM drives, and so on). When Setup finishes this investigation, the Windows Components dialog box appears (see Figure 2.12). Be sure to check any items you want Windows to sense, or it will skip them!

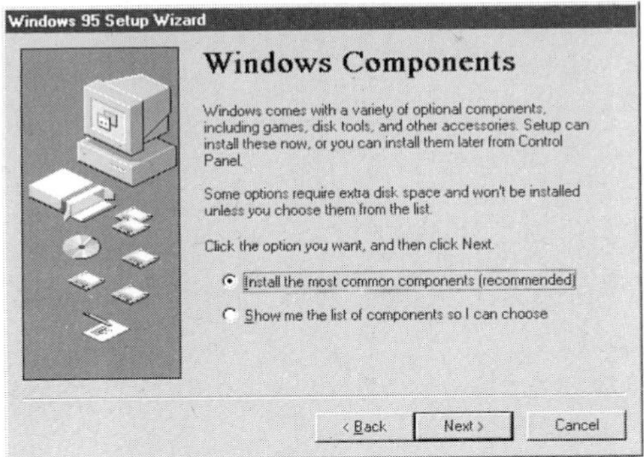

FIG. 2.12
In the Typical setup mode, Setup allows you to alter the Windows component defaults.

If you're setting Windows up on a single-user, non-networked machine, odds are that the default settings are just fine for you. Click Next > or press Enter, and Setup displays the Startup Disk dialog box (see Figure 2.13).

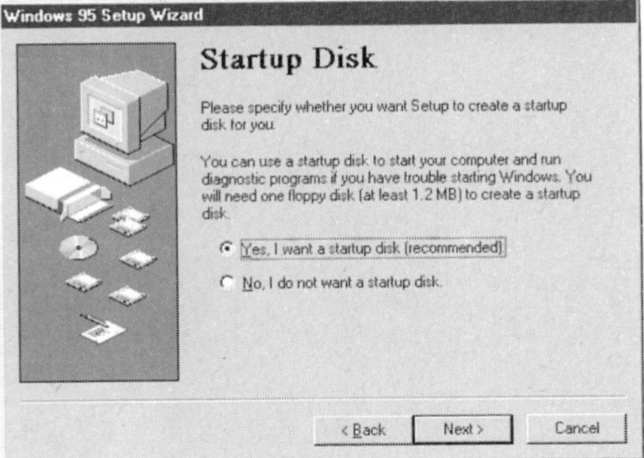

FIG. 2.13
Create a Startup Disk now and avoid regrets later.

Be smart and click Next > or press Enter to tell Setup to create a startup disk. Setup won't prompt you to do it immediately, so you have a few minutes to find a blank floppy disk. The Startup Disk contains all the files your computer needs to run in case the system files on your hard drive should become corrupt.

Click Next > or press Enter, and Setup proceeds to the next major section of Windows 95 installation.

If you installed Windows 95 from a CD-ROM, you should add some additional files to your Startup disk when you finish installing Windows 95 to enable you to access the CD-ROM should you ever have to reinstall Windows. You will need HIMEM.SYS, MSCDEX.EXE (needed to access your CD-ROM drive) and the driver file(s) for your CD-ROM. You should then create AUTOEXEC.BAT and CONFIG.SYS files that load HIMEM.SYS, run MSCDEX.EXE and the driver(s) for your CD-ROM. If you have other devices that are necessary to run in MS-DOS mode, copy the appropriate driver files and their lines from the CONFIG.SYS or AUTOEXEC.BAT files from Drive C.

The AUTOEXEC.BAT should be similar to:

```
MSCDEX.EXE  /D:OEMCD001 /L:D
```

Make sure you have copied the MSCDEX.EXE and CD-ROM driver files to the startup disk.

The CONFIG.SYS file on the startup disk should be similar to:

```
DEVICE=HIMEM.SYS
BUFFERS=20
FILES=60
DEVICE=SAMPLE.SYS /D:OEMCD001
LASTDRIVE=Z
```

The SAMPLE.SYS file is the real-mode driver file used by your CD-ROM. The OEMCD001 statement must match in the AUTOEXEC.BAT and CONFIG.SYS. Look in previous startup disks for examples of these lines.

The following are examples of AUTOEXEC.BAT and CONFIG.SYS files used on a startup disk:

AUTOEXEC.BAT:

```
MSCDEX.EXE /D:MSCD000
```

CONFIG.SYS:

```
DEVICE=A:\HIMEM.SYS
DEVICE=TAISATAP.SYS /D:MSCD000 /N:1
```

The previous startup disk included the files HIMEM.SYS, MSCDEX.EXE, and TAISATAP.SYS, the driver for a specific vendor's CD-ROM.

Here are two examples of a startup disk for a Toshiba laptop.

AUTOEXEC.BAT:

```
LH A:MSCDEX /L:D /D:TOSCD001 /M:10
```

CONFIG.SYS:

```
DEVICE=A:\HIMEM.SYS
DEVICEHIGH=A:\TOSCDROM.SYS /D:TOSCD001
DOS=HIGH,UMB
```

The files on this startup disk included HIMEM.SYS, MSCDEX.EXE, and TOSCDROM.SYS, the driver for Toshiba laptop CD-ROM drives.

The Big Copy Job Having completed its inquiries, Setup can now begin moving the Windows 95 files to your hard drive. Setup displays the Start Copying Files dialog box.

Simply click Next > or press Enter, and Setup continues. The next displayed screen is the Windows 95 Setup background with a "gas gauge" at the bottom that indicates copy progress. If you are installing from CD-ROM, you won't have to do much at this point. If you are installing from floppy disks and you chose to create a Startup Disk, Windows Setup prompts you to insert a disk (see Figure 2.14).

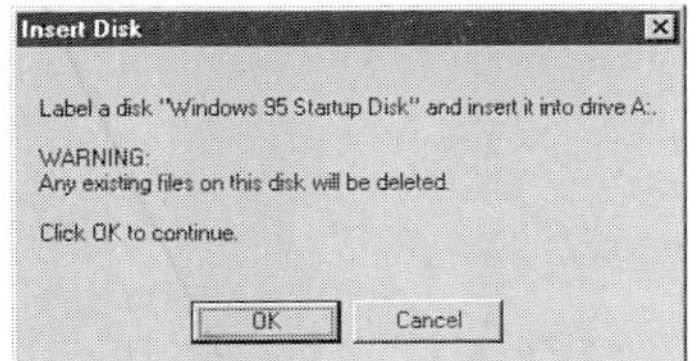

FIG. 2.14
Now is the time to invest in some computing insurance by creating your Windows 95 Startup Disk. Be sure you don't need any of the data on the disk, because Windows will overwrite it.

Right in the middle of installation may seem like a strange time to create a boot disk, but this also is a good way to get you to do it. When the gas gauge shows full, your Startup Disk is done, and Setup returns you to the installation.

TROUBLESHOOTING

My system froze up while the Startup disk was being made. Run Setup again and bypass making a Startup disk during setup. After Windows 95 is installed, create a startup disk using the Startup Disk tab in the Add/Remove Programs Properties dialog box.

Completing the Setup Process

After Setup has copied all Windows 95 files to your hard drive, the Finishing Setup dialog box appears, as shown in Figure 2.15.

Up to this point, Setup has operated as a 16-bit Windows 3.1 application. When you choose Finish and your system reboots, you'll actually be entering the world of Windows 95 computing for the first time.

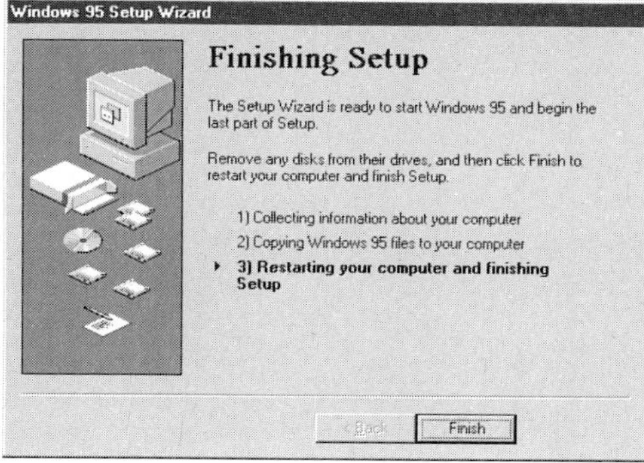

FIG. 2.15
Setup needs to restart your system to complete the installation process.

Restarting Setup, Starting Windows 95

During the Copy phase of Setup, all primary Windows 95 files were created on your hard drive, and many other components of the operating system were initialized as well. When you restarted Windows 95 Setup, MS-DOS was replaced with the new Windows 95 Real Mode kernel, and your hard drive's boot sector was updated to run only the new operating system.

When Setup resumes, it continues the Windows 95 installation by updating remaining configuration files and asks you for a few more questions regarding your system peripherals. Most of these tasks are done by a system called the Run-Once Module, which basically fires up the appropriate system wizards to help you complete your installation.

The process begins with a quick scan of the system hardware. After this quick scan, Setup runs several short routines that can be performed only from within Windows 95 (setting up Control Panels for all appropriate devices, setting up program icons in the Start menu, initializing Windows Help, and confirming the local time zone) as shown in Figure 2.16.

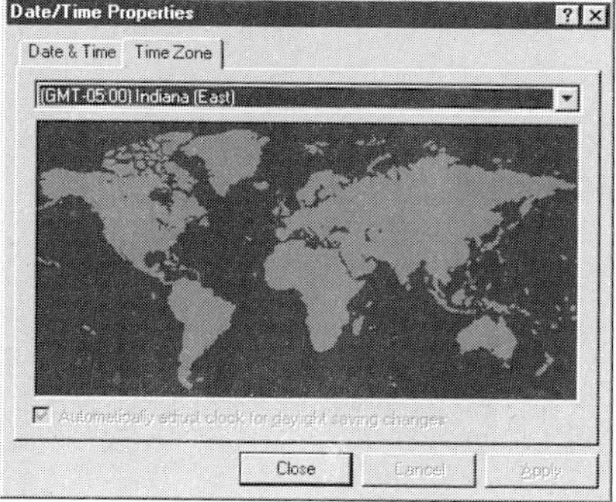

FIG. 2.16
Once Windows 95 is running, it can complete Windows 95-specific setup tasks.

A really nice touch is the Time Zone dialog box. Simply click the map near your part of the planet and Windows 95 adjusts the system clock accordingly, even down to daylight savings time. If you've already adjusted your system clock, you may want to uncheck the DST option.

When the Run-Once tasks finish, Setup is complete, and you're in the world of Windows 95 at last (see Figure 2.17).

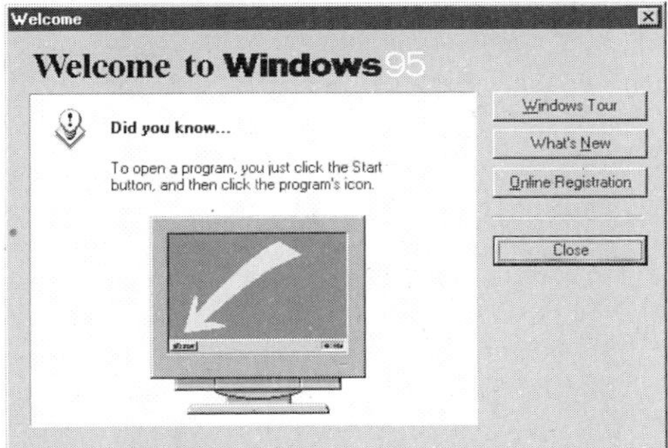

FIG. 2.17
The Welcome to Windows 95 dialog box gives you the basic tips for navigation and registration.

Our demonstration of a "typical" Windows 95 Setup run is complete. Next, you can learn how to install Windows 95 from MS-DOS, and then you can visit some issues regarding Custom Setup and other advanced setup options.

TROUBLESHOOTING

When I run Setup, it hangs during the system check. The first thing to do is to check your hard disk for viruses. Viruses are a common cause for Setup hanging up during the routine check performed by ScanDisk. After you check for viruses, run ScanDisk from the DOS prompt and then run Setup again. If Setup still hangs, run ScanDisk again with the /IS switch to bypass the routine check.

Installing Windows 95 from MS-DOS

If you don't have an installation of Windows version 3.1 or later, or are using Windows NT or OS/2, you need to start Windows 95 Setup from the MS-DOS prompt.

Starting Windows 95 Setup from MS-DOS is just like running any other MS-DOS program. If you're using a plain MS-DOS machine, you need version MS-DOS 3.2 or later. To begin, simply boot the machine just as for any other computing session. If you're using another operating system, you need to use the dual-boot feature or boot from a floppy disk to attain MS-DOS operation.

We'll again assume you are using floppy disks in Drive A. If you have a CD-ROM drive, substitute the appropriate drive letter for A in the following examples.

The first step in starting Windows 95 Setup from the MS-DOS prompt is to enter the command at the prompt. At the prompt, type **a:setup** and press Enter.

MS-DOS then runs the Windows 95 Setup program, which starts by running the Windows 95 version of ScanDisk. The first thing you see on screen is a message saying "Please wait while

Setup initializes. Setup is now going to perform a routine check on your system. To continue, press ENTER. To quit Setup, press ESC." Press Enter to continue. Setup then starts ScanDisk (as shown in Figure 2.18), which runs automatically to check out your drives to make sure they're sound before beginning the Windows 95 installation. Follow the prompts to deal with any drive anomalies.

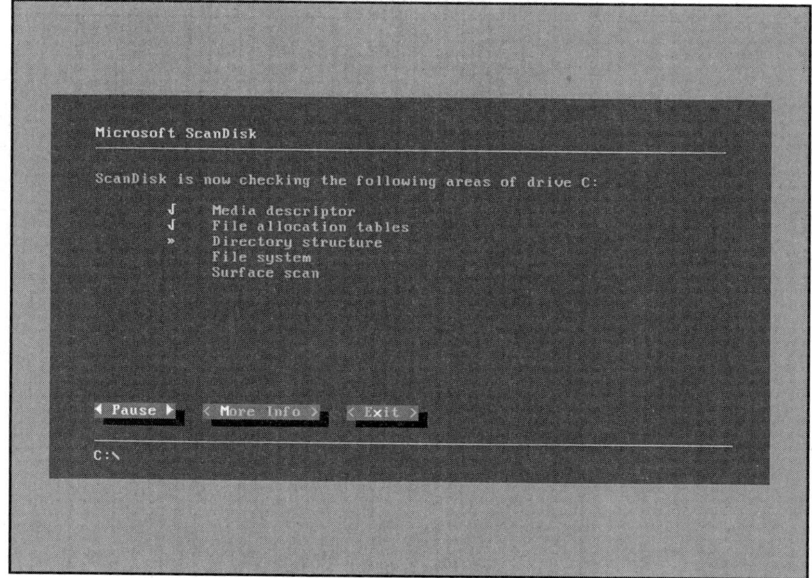

FIG. 2.18
Setup needs to check out your disk before it begins.

When ScanDisk finishes, exit back to MS-DOS, and Setup continues. Setup copies a small version of Windows 3.1 to your system so the graphical portions of Setup can run. Once that is complete, Setup displays the Welcome screen shown in Figure 2.19.

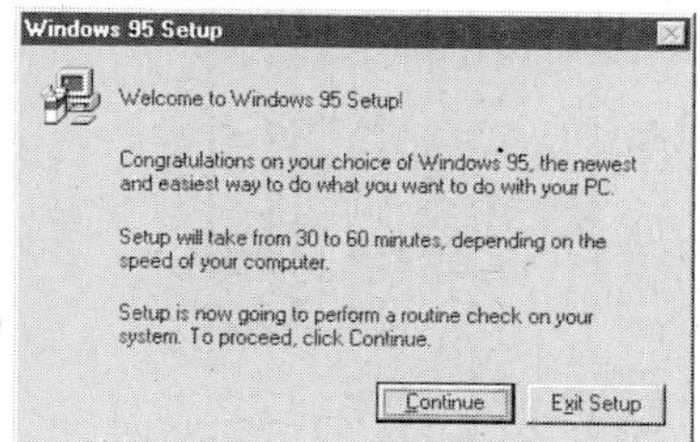

FIG. 2.19
From this point on, Setup is the same whether you started from MS-DOS or the latest version of Windows.

See "Installing Windows 95 from Windows 3.x," **p. 29**

The remaining Setup procedures are nearly identical to those listed earlier in this chapter for installing from Windows 3.1. If you're installing Windows 95 as your first version of Windows, you have to install all of your Windows applications after Windows 95 Setup is complete.

Advanced Installation Techniques

As simple as Windows 95 Setup can be, some situations still demand special considerations to meet special needs. There are as many different Windows installations as there are Windows users, and Windows 95 Setup is flexible enough to meet most needs.

In this section, you learn about

- Installing with custom options
- Using safe recovery and safe detection

Using Custom Setup Mode

Microsoft's Windows 95 development team has done an admirable job of establishing compatibility with a wide variety of peripheral components, but no one can perfectly predict all of the equipment variables in the churning world of the PC hardware market.

Installing Windows 95 for special setups is straightforward if you have the appropriate information ready before you begin. The Custom setup option allows you to specify application settings, network configuration options, device configurations, and gives you more control over the installation of Windows 95 components.

CAUTION

The Custom installation mode puts a lot of power in your hands. If you don't have the specific experience in network or device configuration, you're better off leaving this to Windows 95 Setup auto-detection, or your MIS department.

Before you begin, know the exact name and model number of the card or device you're installing. Have any special device driver files handy (the original floppy disk is fine, if you don't know where the drivers are on your hard drive). Find out the logical memory address defaults for the component, if applicable (see the peripheral documentation).

To use Windows 95 Setup in Custom mode, simply proceed with installation as described earlier in this chapter up to the point of selecting the Setup Options dialog box (shown in Figure 2.20).

At this point, select the Custom option and click Next > to proceed. Don't expect Setup to change drastically from this point on. You will see a few more dialog boxes, in which Setup asks you the appropriate questions regarding additional options. The next screen you see is the User Information dialog box. When you complete this dialog box, Setup displays the Analyzing Your Computer dialog box shown in Figure 2.21.

Customizing Hardware Support If you know you have nonstandard or unsupported devices in your installation, select the No, I Want to Modify the Hardware List option button. Then click Next > to proceed. Setup displays the screen shown in Figure 2.22.

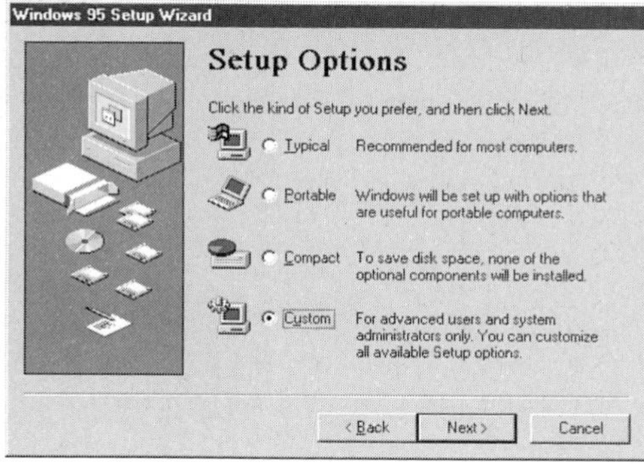

FIG. 2.20
Select the Custom option to gain more control over your system configuration.

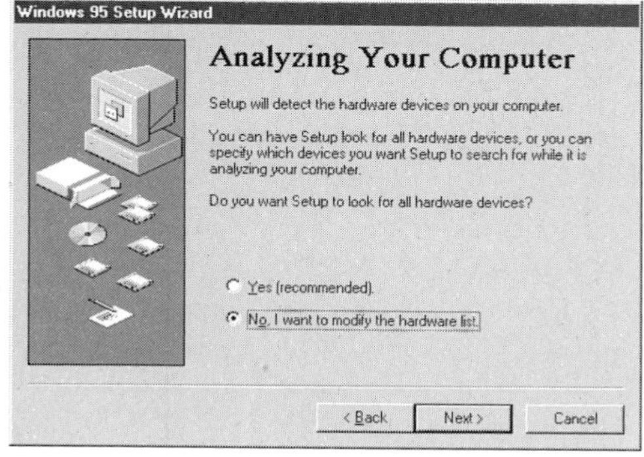

FIG. 2.21
If you know you're going to need to alter your device configurations, you can select the option easily in this dialog box.

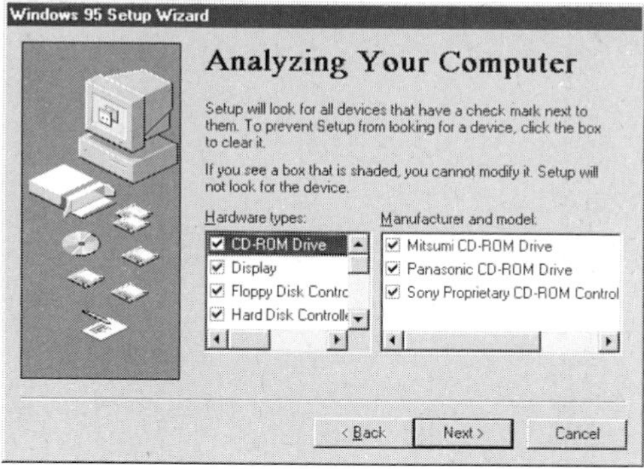

FIG. 2.22
Select the device type in the left window and the specific device name in the right. Changing the item on the left changes the list on the right.

Here's where you need the information about your system mentioned earlier. If you *know* that you have an unusual peripheral, look for it here. Setup guides you through installing any special drivers for the device at the appropriate time.

If your device doesn't appear in the lists here, it means one of two things: Either Windows 95 has native 32-bit support for the device or no support for it. If Setup didn't detect your device

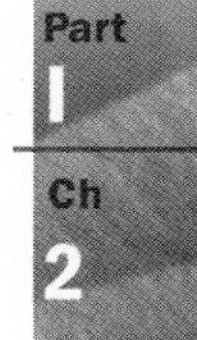

earlier in the installation, you need to tell it to install it now. If it was detected, and the Windows installation didn't work, you can tell Windows to skip it this round. You can manually install the device later using the Add New Hardware control panel.

When you've selected all the device types you want configured, click Next > to proceed. After completing its analysis of your selected equipment, Setup displays the Select Components dialog box, as shown in Figure 2.23.

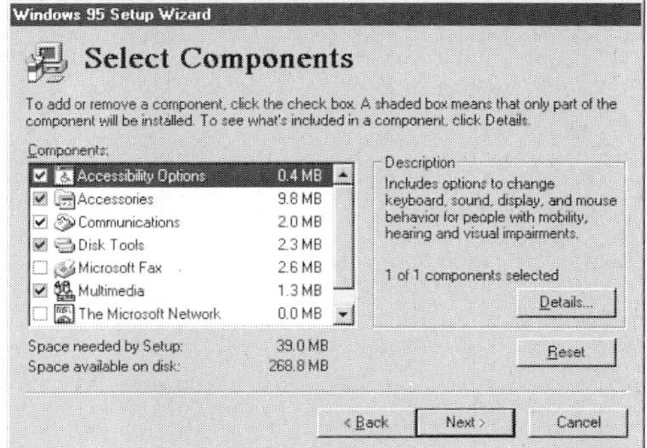

FIG. 2.23 Select the Windows 95 components you want Setup to install. Setup can provide additional information about each option when you click Details.

When you've selected all of the Windows 95 components you want installed, click Next > to proceed. The remainder of the installation depends on what hardware and software component options you've selected. Setup attempts to locate your devices and prompts you when it needs additional information such as device driver files. In the next section, we look at an example of this (specifically, the basic steps to install network support under Windows 95).

Installing Windows 95 Network Features If you've selected network support, Setup next displays the Network Configuration dialog box shown in Figure 2.24.

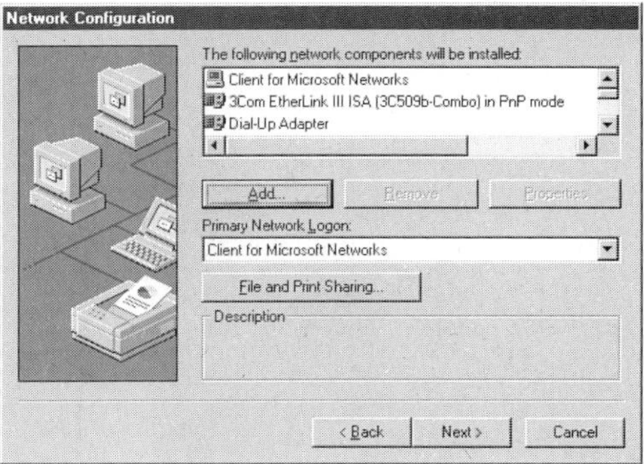

FIG. 2.24 You can install network support for multiple adapters and protocols from this one Setup screen.

To begin configuring your network options, click Add. Setup displays the Select Network Component Type dialog box (see Figure 2.25).

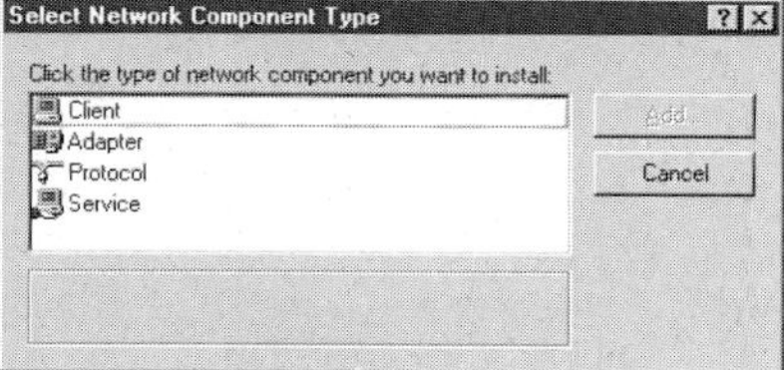

FIG. 2.25
Click the network component type you want to install.

When you select the component type you want to install, Setup displays another selection dialog box for that component classification. For example, if you select Protocol and then click Add, Setup displays the Select Network Protocol dialog box shown in Figure 2.26.

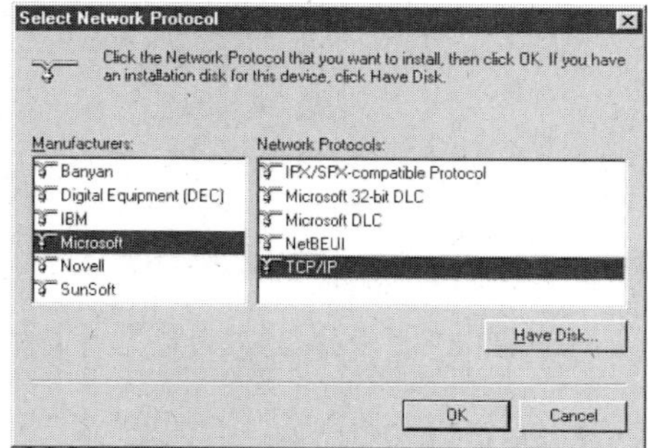

FIG. 2.26
Select the protocol publisher in the left list, and then select the specific protocol type in the right list.

When you've selected the appropriate protocols network adapter, you can either click OK (to let Setup determine if Windows 95 has native drivers for these types) or click Have Disk to install your own drivers.

Setup may make assumptions about other network support components based upon the adapter type you select. For example, selecting the Intel EtherExpress 16 or 16TP results in Setup selecting clients and protocols for both Netware and Microsoft network types.

Using Safe Recovery

If Setup fails during your installation, it has the capability to recover gracefully. Setup Safe Recovery automatically skips problem configuration items to allow the installation to finish, and then allows you to go back to the problem and correct it.

Save Recovery also can be used in repairing damaged installations. If you run Setup after a complete Windows 95 installation, it first asks whether you want to confirm or repair your installation, or whether you want to completely reinstall Windows 95 (see Figure 2.27).

FIG. 2.27
You also can use Safe Recovery after a complete installation to repair later damage.

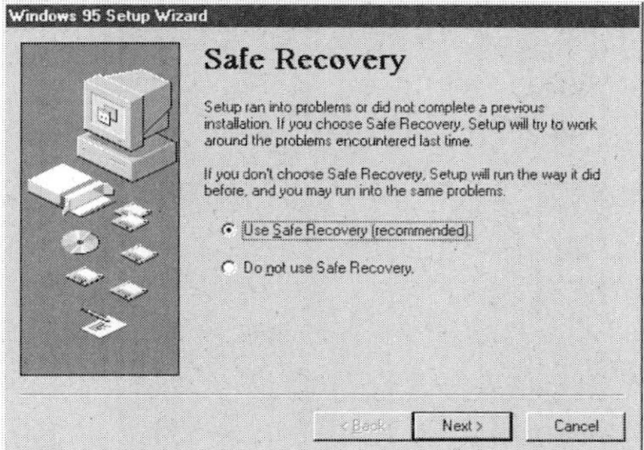

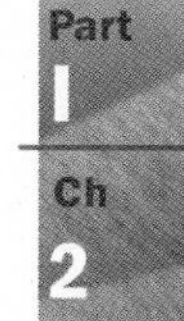

Using Safe Detection

Windows 95 Setup looks for system components in a variety of ways. Setup can detect communication ports, display adapters, processor type, drive controllers, sound cards, and network adapters. Setup also looks for system hardware resources such as IRQs, DMA channels, and I/O addresses to avoid conflicts between devices. Setup can detect both the newer Plug and Play devices and older "legacy" peripherals.

Safe Detection works on four classes of devices:

- Sound cards
- Network adapters
- SCSI controllers
- CD-ROM controllers

One problem with such auto-detection routines is failure during the detection process itself. Plug and Play devices basically identify or announce themselves to the system, but older adapters require interactive tests to locate them and confirm operation. Whereas most devices respond well to this, some don't. In addition, if there's any duplication of IRQ, DMA, or I/O addresses between devices, your system can lock up tighter than a drum during installation.

Windows 95 Setup can recover from such failures. Setup keeps track of the process of testing devices during installation and knows at what point a device failed. When you restart it, Setup knows not to touch that subsystem again until corrections have been applied, such as loading 16-bit device drivers if the 32-bit native Windows 95 drivers have failed.

Removing Windows 95

If you decide you want to return to your previous Windows 3.x installation, want to clean up your system before you trade or sell it, or you simply don't want to use Windows 95, you can remove all traces of Windows 95. To use the uninstall feature to uninstall Windows 95, you had to use the (highly recommended) option to save your old Windows 3.1x and DOS system files during Windows setup.

If you were using drive compression with Windows 95, you need to uncompress your hard drive before uninstalling Windows 95. If you have more files than will fit on your uncompressed drive, you will need to delete files before proceeding.

If you have installed any programs since installing Windows 95, they probably will have to be reconfigured to work with Windows 3.1, or you may have to uninstall them from Windows 95 and reinstall them in Windows 3.1. Of course, any applications written to work with Windows 95 (like Office 97) will not run in Windows 3.1.

Once you are ready to uninstall, open the Start menu and choose Settings, Control Panel. Double-click the Add/Remove Programs icon. Click the Install/Uninstall tab. This shows the properties sheet shown in Figure 2.28.

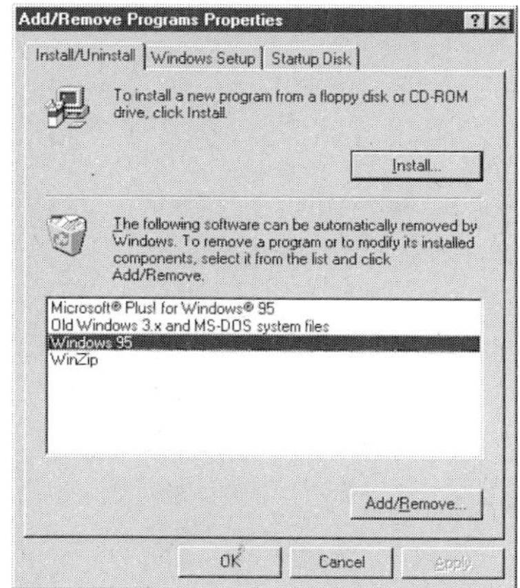

FIG. 2.28
The Install/Uninstall page of the Add/Remove Programs properties sheet includes an option to uninstall Windows 95.

Select Windows 95 and then click Add/Remove. This opens the warning dialog box shown in Figure 2.29.

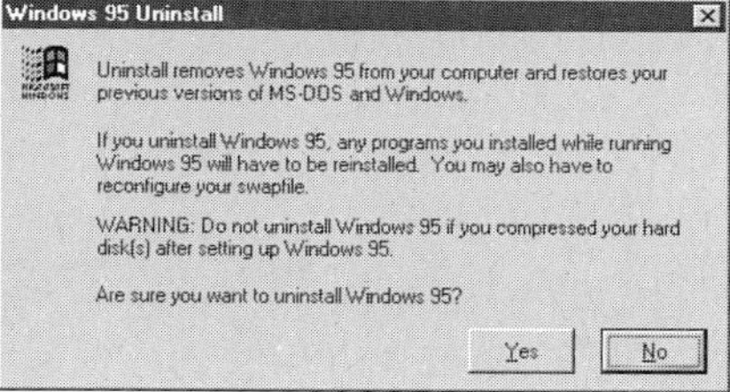

FIG. 2.29
If you are sure you want to uninstall Windows 95, click Yes. The uninstaller removes Windows 95 and restores your old DOS and Windows system files.

Your system should now boot straight to your previous version of MS-DOS. You may need to set up a new Windows 3.1 swap file because your old swap file (if you were using a permanent swap file) no longer exists.

TROUBLESHOOTING

When I start my system after uninstalling Windows 95, I get an error message saying I have a corrupt swap file. What should I do? This is normal after uninstalling Windows 95. Choose OK in the Delete dialog box that appears. Next, open Control Panel, open the Enhanced application, and choose the Virtual Memory button. Set the swap file size to none. Reboot the computer and use the Enhanced application to set up a new permanent swap file.

Installing the Windows 95b (OSR2) Service Release

The Microsoft OEM (Original Equipment Manufacturer) Service Release 2 update (OSR2), incorporates all of the enhancements included in the Service Pak 1, patches and fixes that have been released since Service Pack 1, and many new components. OSR2 is not being sold at the retail level, but has been released to OEMs to install on new systems. You can, however, download some of the new components from Microsoft's Web site and install them on your computer without having to obtain the OSR2 update. Other components are available only when you install Windows 95 from the Windows 95 OSR2 installation disks or CD-ROM. The new FAT32 file system, which is discussed in this chapter, is one of these components.

Table 2.1 summarizes the features found in OSR2. We have included the URL on the Web for those components that can be downloaded individually.

Table 2.1 Summary of Features in Windows 95 OSR2 Update

Feature	Description	Is It Available as a Separate Component?	URL Address to Download Component
Hardware			
FAT32	New 32-bit file allocation system (FAT) that supports single-volume hard disks up to 2 terabytes in size and uses more efficient cluster sizes (4K for drives up to 8G). Includes new versions of disk utilities (e.g., ScanDisk) that work with FAT32 partitions, are included. See section in this chapter for details.	No	
DriveSpace	New version that was available on Microsoft Plus pack as DriveSpace 3, supports compressed volumes up to 2G in size.	No	

continues

Table 2.1 Continued

Feature	Description	Is It Available as a Separate Component?	URL Address to Download Component
Hardware			
Advance Power	Support for APM v.1.2 BIOS Management features.	No	
Storage enhancements	Support for new storage hardware, including 120M Floptical disk drives, Zip drives, CD changers, removable IDE media, and IDE Bus Mastering.	No	
PCMCIA enhancements	Support for PC Card 32, 3.3 volt PCMCIA cards, network/modem PCMCIA cards, and Global Positioning Satellite (GPS) PCMCIA cards.	No	
CDFS enhancements	Support for CD-I format CD-ROMs and ISO 9660 disks (up to 4G in size).	No	
PCI Bridging/ Docking	Support for PCI devices used in PCI docking stations.	No	
Internet			
Internet Explorer 3.0	Version 3.0 of the Explorer. Many enhancements over previous release, but now superseded by Internet Explorer 4.0.	Yes	**http://www.microsoft.com/ie/download/**
Internet Connection Wizard	A Wizard to help you find an Internet service provider and set up your computer to use the Internet.	Yes	**http://ie/download/www.microsoft.com/**
Internet Mail and News	Applications that allow you to send and receive e-mail and read and send messages to Internet newsgroups.	Yes	**http://ie/download/www.microsoft.com/**
NetMeeting	Collaboration software for exchanging data, communicating by voice and using a whiteboard, chatting, and remotely viewing and working with programs.	Yes	**http://www.microsoft.com/ie/download/**

Feature	Description	Is It Available as a Separate Component?	URL Address to Download Component
Personal Web Server	A server application that allows you to publish HTML Web pages on the Internet (or intranets) and to transfer files using the FTP protocol.	Yes	**http://www.microsoft.com/ie/download/**
DirectX 2.0	Microsoft's state-of-the art technologies for high-performance 2-D and 3-D graphics, sound, video, and game input.	Yes	**http://www.microsoft.com/ie/download/**
Intel MMX support	Support for software developers who want to take advantage of Intel's MMX processor to provide higher performance video and audio.	No	
Other Features			
Dial-Up Networking enhancements	Scripting to automate dial-up and other enhancements to the user interface.	Yes	**http://www.microsoft.com/windows-support/default-sl.htm**
Voice Modem support	Support for modems using the VoiceView and AT+V protocols, allowing voice and data communication on a single line, and other telephone functions (such as voice messaging).	Yes	**http://www.microsoft.com/windows-support/default-sl.htm**
Service for Novell NetWare 4.x	Full support for NetWare 4.x, including NetWare Directory Services.	Yes	**http://www.microsoft.com/windows/software/msnds.htm**
32-bit DLC support	Support for 32-bit Data Link Control protocol.	Yes	**http://www.microsoft.com/windows/software/dlc.htm**
IrDA 2.0 support	Support for the latest version of the IrDA, which includes infrared connectivity to LANs.	Yes	**http://www.microsoft.com/windows/software/irda.htm**

continues

Table 2.1 Continued

Feature	Description	Is It Available as a Separate Component?	URL Address to Download Component
NDIS 4.0	Support for NDIS 4.0 network interface cards.	No	
Wang Imaging application	An application for scanning and annotating images and viewing a variety of file formats, including JPG, XIF, TIFF, BMP, and FAX.	Yes	**http://www.microsoft.com/windows/software/img_us.htm**
MSN 1.3	A new version of The Microsoft Network client.	Yes	**http://www.msn.com**
Fixes/updates	All the fixes and updates because of the original release of Windows 95.	Yes	**http://www.microsoft.com/windows95/info/system-updates.htm**
Automatic ScanDisk	ScanDisk now runs automatically when you turn on your computer if Windows 95 was not shut down normally.	No	
Online Services Folder	Client software for America Online 3.0, CompuServe 3.0, CompuServe WOW!, and AT&T WorldNet.	No	

Do You Want to Upgrade to OSR2?

So why bother upgrading an existing system to OSR2? The most compelling reason for upgrading to OSR2 is the new FAT32 file system that comes with OSR2. The original version of Windows 95, as well as DOS, uses a file system called FAT16, a 16-bit file system. There are two major drawbacks to the FAT16 file system in this age of larger and larger hard disks. First, FAT16 can only support single disk volumes (partitions) of up to 2G. With larger hard disks, you are forced to partition your drive into 2G or smaller volumes. Second, the cluster size increases dramatically as you increase partition size. A 2G partition, for example, uses 32K clusters, which means a small file, such as a shortcut on your desktop that is typically around 1K in size, will use 32K of disk space. This results in very inefficient use of hard disk space, especially if there are many small files on your hard disk. This storage waste is called *slack*. The smaller the cluster size, the less *slack* there is.

With the OSR2 release, Microsoft has introduced a new file system called FAT32. The FAT32 file system supports single disk volumes (partitions) up to 2 terabytes in size and uses much smaller clusters. For partitions up to 8G, FAT32 uses 4K clusters, resulting in much more efficient file storage.

Other reasons for upgrading to OSR2 are the enhancements for supporting the CDFS (CD-ROM File System), IrDA 2.0 devices, the 32-bit CardBus and improved-power management features for portables. There is also support for some of the newer storage media, as listed in the previous table.

What are the main disadvantages of using OSR2? First of all, it is not that easy to get a copy of the upgrade. Because of Microsoft's policy on the distribution of OSR2, you either have to purchase a new system or buy a new hard drive or motherboard from a vendor who will sell you a copy of OSR2 with the item you purchase. You can't run down to your local software dealer to buy a copy of OSR2.

In addition, the installation process for upgrading to OSR2 is time-consuming and can be daunting to the unprepared. This is especially true if you want to format your hard drive with the new FAT32 file system (you can install OSR2 without converting to FAT32). You need to back up your hard disk, repartition and reformat your hard disk with new versions of FDISK and Format (that come on the OSR2 CD-ROM), install OSR2 and then reinstall your software applications. Or, you can use one of the methods for installing OSR2 over your existing Windows 95 and then using third-party utilities for converting from FAT16 to FAT32.

Also be aware that you may encounter hardware and software incompatibilities with OSR2, and any disk utilities you have that are designed to work with the FAT16 file system will not work. You will need to obtain updated versions or patches for your disk utilities. The versions of ScanDisk and Disk Defragmenter that come with OSR2 are compatible with FAT32.

If you are currently dual-booting your system with Windows 95 and either Windows 3.1 or Windows NT, you will lose this capability if you install OSR2. OSR2 is the only operating system that can access FAT32 partitions. There are third-party utilities and patches on the Internet that will apparently restore dual-boot capability, but Microsoft is not currently supporting dual-booting.

Another serious consideration is that you may lose the support of your PC company if you install OSR2 on a system that did not come with OSR2. In fact, some computer companies are installing OSR2 on new computers without FAT32 installed and state that you will invalidate your technical support and warranty if you install it. So, be careful and know what you are getting into.

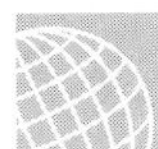

ON THE WEB

Check out the following WWW site for in-depth coverage of OSR2 and the FAT32 file system:

http://www.users.cts.com/king/s/serwin/osr2.html

Alternatives to OSR2

If you are not interested in FAT32 but would like to take advantage of some of the other components in OSR2, check Table 2.1 to see if those components can be downloaded individually. If this is the case, you don't need to upgrade to OSR2 to take advantage of the OSR2 enhancements that interest you.

If increasing the storage efficiency of your hard disk is your main concern, converting to the FAT32 file system in OSR2 is not your only option for cutting down on disk storage waste resulting from large cluster size. With PowerQuest's Partition Magic utility, you can repartition your hard disk into smaller logical drives that use smaller cluster sizes. Partition Magic enables you to do this dynamically, so you don't have to back up and then restore your data and applications (as you do with FDISK). For more information on Partition Magic, call PowerQuest at 801-226-8977 or visit their Web site.

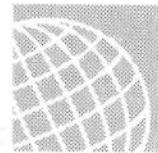

ON THE WEB

PowerQuest: **http://www.powerquest.com**.

If you decide you don't want to risk upgrading to OSR2 and the FAT32 file system, don't despair. The next major release of Windows (due in early 1998) will incorporate all of the features in OSR2, including FAT32, and by then Microsoft will have enough confidence in the compatibility of the new software to back it up with technical support. Also, by then the upgrade procedure should be much simpler.

Installing FAT32

If you do decide you want to upgrade to OSR2, you need to get a copy of the OSR2 CD-ROM or floppy disks. The OSR2 update is not available through retail channels. Microsoft has stipulated three legitimate means for purchasing the upgrade: with a new system, with a new hard drive, or with a new motherboard. So, if you are not purchasing a new system with Windows 95 installed, you will need to purchase either a motherboard or hard drive from a company that is willing to sell you a copy of OSR2 with your purchase.

Microsoft's official explanation for this policy is that because most of the enhancements apply to new hardware devices, there is no reason to upgrade existing systems. The common wisdom is that Microsoft doesn't want to support people attempting to upgrade to the new version because of the complications involved. In fact, if you can get a hold of a copy of the OSR2 CD-ROM and attempt to upgrade from the original Windows 95, you will get an error message. To install OSR2 on an existing system, you either need to repartition and reformat your hard disk and install from scratch or use the workaround described in this chapter.

Once you have obtained a copy of the OSR2 upgrade, there are several steps you need to go through to successfully upgrade your system. We will show you two methods for installing OSR2 on your system. The first approach involves repartitioning and reformatting your hard disk with the new versions of FDISK and FORMAT that Microsoft has released with OSR2. You need the updated versions of these utilities to format your hard disk with the new FAT32 file system. Once you have reformatted your hard disk, you then install OSR2 from scratch.

The second method for upgrading eliminates the need for repartitioning and reformatting the hard disk when you install OSR2. Using this method does not enable you to use FAT32.

Installing OSR2 from Scratch If you decide you want to install OSR2 on your system starting from scratch, there are several steps you will need to complete. The first step is to create a startup disk using the OSR2 CD-ROM or disks. The startup disk will include the updated versions of FDISK and FORMAT and will be used to repartition and reformat your hard disk with the FAT32 file system.

To create an OSR2 startup disk, follow these steps.

1. Insert the Windows 95 OSR2 CD-ROM in your CD-ROM drive and a blank, high-density disk in your floppy disk drive.
2. Open the Start menu and choose Setting, Control Panel.
3. Double-click the Add/Remove Programs icon.
4. Click the Startup Disk tab and choose Create Disk. Follow the instructions that appear on screen.

   Windows copies files from the Windows 95 CD-ROM to create the startup disk. Because you inserted the OSR2 version of Windows 95 in step 1, the newer versions of FDISK.EXE and FORMAT.COM will be copied to the startup disk.

Once you have created the OSR2 startup disk, copy the files needed to access your CD-ROM drive from the DOS prompt onto the startup disk. This will enable you to access the Windows 95 OSR2 CD-ROM from the DOS prompt after you have partitioned and formatted your hard drive using the OSR2 startup disk. See the tip in the section "The Typical Windows 95 Setup Process" (earlier in this chapter) that shows you what files you need to add to your startup disk to access your CD-ROM.

CAUTION

Be sure you back up all critical files on your hard disk before you repartition and reformat your hard disk. You will lose all the data on your hard disk when you repartition it.

Once you have created an OSR2 startup disk, you are ready to repartition your hard disk. To partition your hard disk using the FAT32 file system, follow these steps:

1. Insert the startup disk you just created into the floppy disk drive and reboot your computer.
2. Run FDISK from the A:> prompt.

   If your hard disk is larger than 512M, a message will appear informing you that your hard disk is larger than 512M and that you have the option of enabling large disk support. You are warned that if you do so, you will not be able to access the drive using other operating systems and that some disk utilities not designed for the FAT32 file system will not work.
3. Assuming that you accept these caveats, type **Y** and press Enter.

4. Use FDISK to delete the existing DOS partitions on your hard disk.

   Do not proceed with this step unless you have backed up your files on the hard disk.

5. Once you have deleted all existing DOS partitions, use FDISK to create a new Primary DOS partition. Make this partition the active partition.

   At this point, you can use FDISK to partition your drive into smaller, logical drives. Keep in mind, however, that one of the benefits of the FAT32 file system is that you can create a single partition of up to 2 terabytes and that partitions up to 8G in size will use 4K clusters.

6. When you have finished partitioning your hard disk, exit FDISK and reboot your computer using the startup disk.

7. Use the Format command on the startup disk to reformat your hard disk.

Once you have repartitioned and reformatted your hard drive using the OSR2 startup disk, you can install OSR2 from the OSR2 CD-ROM (or disks). Reboot your computer and run Setup from the DOS prompt. If your CD-ROM is designated as drive D:, for example, type **d:setup**. The procedure from this point onwards is identical to the procedure described in the earlier sections of this chapter, so please refer to these sections for details on the Window setup. Congratulations, you now have a system with a state-of-the-art, 32-bit file system!

Upgrading to OSR2 Without Reformatting The OSR2 release of Windows 95 is not designed to be an upgrade. If you try to upgrade a system that has the original release of Windows 95 installed, you will get a message box informing you that you cannot upgrade your system. However, there is an alternative to the laborious process described in the previous section for installing OSR2 from scratch. The following workaround will enable you to trick the OSR2 setup program into thinking you are installing Windows 95 on a system that does not have the original version of Windows installed. Be aware of the fact that this procedure is not supported by Microsoft so you can't call them for help if you get into trouble.

NOTE If you use the workaround to upgrade to OSR2 without reformatting, you cannot use the OSR2 system to convert from FAT16 to FAT32. Conversion utilities are available from sources other than Microsoft that can do this.

To upgrade your system to OSR2, follow these steps:

1. Create a temporary folder on your hard disk and name it FLAT.

2. Copy all of the setup files from the WIN95 folder on the OSR2 CD-ROM to the FLAT folder.

3. Extract the file named SETUPPP.INF from the PRECOPY2.CAB file.

   To extract the file, open an MS-DOS window and switch to the FLAT directory. Type the following at the DOS prompt:

   extract precopy2.cab setuppp.inf

4. Close the DOS window to return to Windows.

5. Using Notepad, make the following change in the file LAYOUT.INF (which is located in the FLAT folder):

   Change SETUPPP.INF=2,,4550 to SETUPPP.INF=0,,4550

6. Save the changes in LAYOUT.INF.
7. Using Notepad again, make the following change in SETUPPP.INF:

   Change ProductType=9 to ProductType=1

8. Save the changes in SETUPPP.INF.
9. Run SETUP from the FLAT folder by double-clicking SETUP in Windows Explorer. OSR2 will now run as an upgrade.

TIP Before you start the upgrade procedure, create a temporary folder and move all the items in your Windows\Start Menu\Programs\StartUp folder. When you have finished the upgrade, move these items back to the StartUp folder. This step will save you the trouble of having to restore these items to the StartUp folder.

You may wonder how you can tell if a system is using the OSR2 version of Windows 95. To find out, right-click My Computer and choose Properties. On the System heading in the General tab, the version number for Windows 95 will appear as 4.00.950 B, as shown in Figure 2.30.

From the DOS prompt, type **ver**. If you are running OSR2, the version number will be listed as Version 4.00.1111.

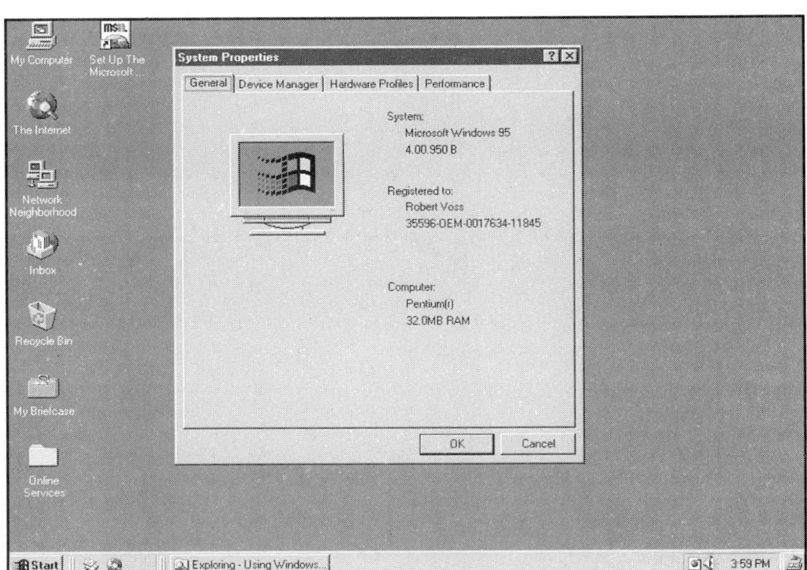

FIG. 2.30
View the System properties sheet to find out if a system is using the OSR2 release of Windows 95 (designated as 4.00.950 B).

To verify that you have installed the FAT32 file system, double-click My Computer, right-click the icon for your hard drive and choose Properties. If your hard disk is using FAT32, you will see the FAT32 file system designation in the General tab (see Figure 2.31).

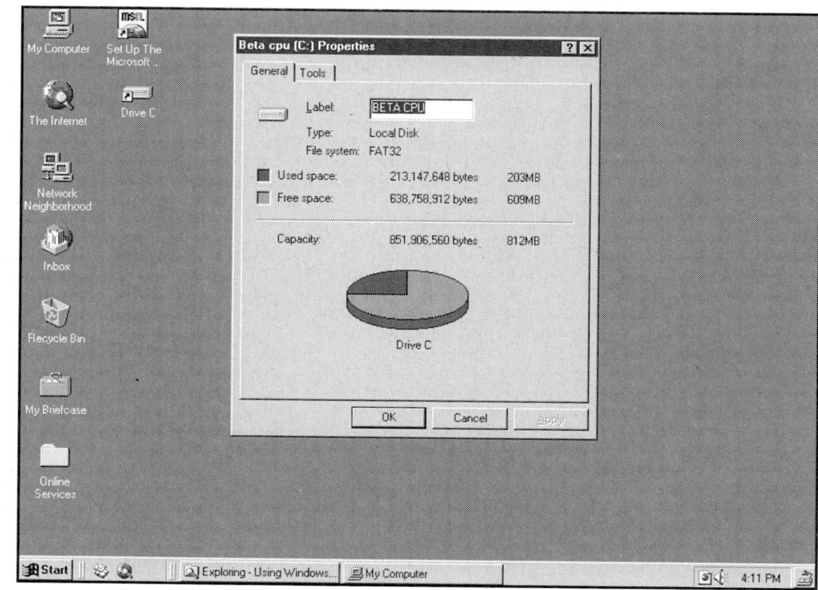

FIG. 2.31
If your hard disk is using FAT32, you will see the FAT32 designation in the properties sheet for the hard disk.

CHAPTER 3

Configuring Windows 95

One of the most important features Windows 95 brought to personal computers was an improved way to install and configure hardware. Windows 95's simple wizards and the Control Panel make setting up new equipment (and tweaking old configurations) much more intuitive and efficient. This chapter covers the installation and configuration of three of the most common hardware devices: printers, modems, and PC cards for notebook computers.

Installing and configuring printers

Learn how to install a new printer using the Add Printer Wizard or Plug and Play and how to configure your printer for optimal performance.

Installing PC card devices

Find out how to set up your computer to support PC Cards and to install the specific drivers for a device.

Installing and configuring modems

Look here to find out how to install Plug and Play and legacy modems and how to configure your modem to optimize data communications.

Installing and Configuring Printers

Windows 95 has greatly simplified the installation of printers. If you have a Plug and Play printer and computer, it can be as simple as connecting the printer to the computer, starting Windows 95, and following the directions in a few Wizard boxes. Even if you don't have Plug and Play components, the Add Printer Wizard takes you through the installation process step by step. After you've installed your printer, turn to Chapter 5, "Controlling Printers," to learn how to work with printers in Windows 95.

The printer installation process depends largely on the make and model of your printer. The following sections describe how to fully install a printer—with an emphasis on printer differences.

Installing a New Printer

Before you install a printer, you should follow these preliminary steps:

- Determine your printer's make and model (for example, Hewlett-Packard 4).
- Refer to the printer manual, or print a test page using the printer's test feature, to find the amount of RAM contained in your printer (for example, 2M).
- Identify the type of communications interface required to connect your printer to the computer (for example, serial, parallel, or a special interface).
- Identify any special features or functions supported by your printer, such as PostScript compatibility. Some printers are multimode and may require installation as two separate printers (such as the HP LaserJet IV with PostScript option).
- Find the location of a suitable port on your computer to connect your printer. The selected port must correspond to the same port type as required by your printer (that is, serial to serial, parallel to parallel).

This information is required by the Windows Add Printer Wizard later in the installation process.

Installing a Printer with the Add Printer Wizard The Windows 95 print architecture incorporates a printer installation wizard to step you through the labor-intensive chore of installing a printer.

To use the Add Printer Wizard, follow these steps:

1. Open the Start menu and choose Settings, Printers. If the control panel is open, double-click the Printer folder. The Printers window appears and shows each installed printer as an icon (see Figure 3.1). Don't worry if you have no installed printers yet: The window also includes the Add New Printer icon. The program associated with the Add New Printer icon is the Add Printer Wizard.

   If there are no printers installed, the Add New Printer Wizard will automatically be loaded.

2. Double-click the Add New Printer icon to start the Add Printer Wizard. Windows displays the initial Wizard screen.
3. Choose Next. Windows displays the Add Printer Wizard screen shown in Figure 3.2.

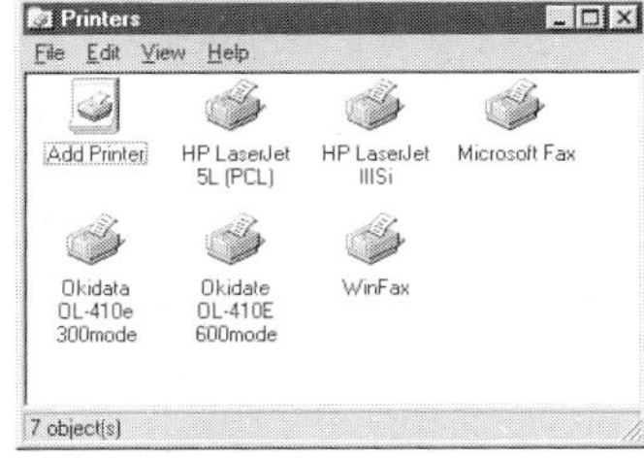

FIG. 3.1
Start a printer installation by opening the Printer folder.

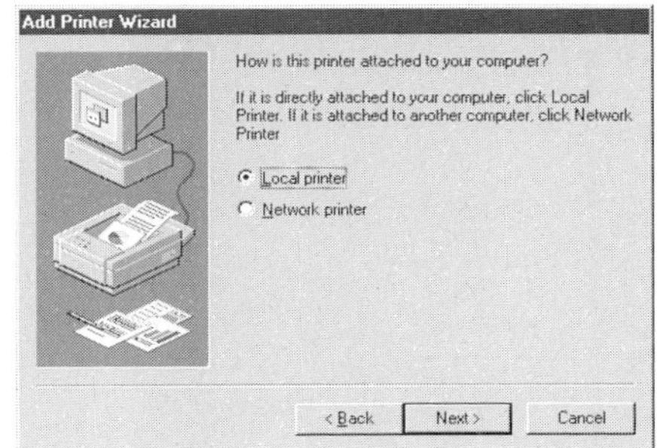

FIG. 3.2
The Add Printer Wizard steps you through the printer installation procedure by first asking whether you are installing a local or network printer.

4. Choose the Local Printer option to install a printer attached directly to your computer. Choose Next. The screen shown in Figure 3.3 appears.

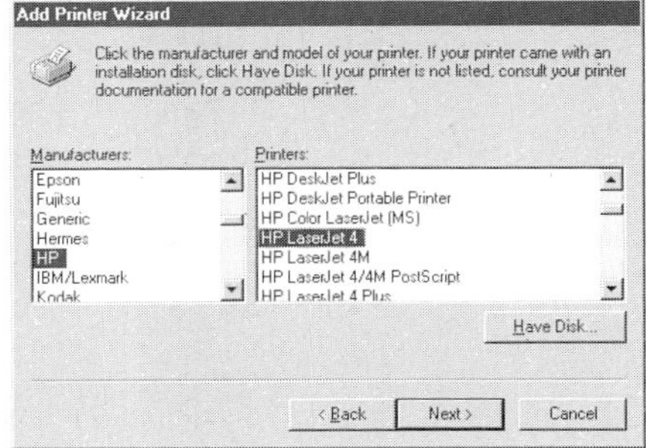

FIG. 3.3
Select the make and model of the printer you are installing from the lists provided.

5. Locate the make and model of your printer by scrolling through the wizard's screen lists (Windows 95 has drivers that support over 300 printers). Select the appropriate options, then choose Next to display the screen shown in Figure 3.4.

   If you're adding a printer after initial installation, you need the Windows 95 installation disks or CD. Windows will ask for these if it does not have an existing driver available. You also can use a manufacturer's disk to install custom printer drivers.

   If you are installing a new driver for an existing printer, click the Have Disk button and locate the new driver in the Install From Disk dialog box. Choose OK.

Scroll the screen on the far left to select your printer's manufacturer, and then select the appropriate printer model. If your printer isn't on the list, you can install your printer by choosing either the generic printer or the Have Disk button. If your printer came with its own software driver, insert the disk from your printer manufacturer and choose the Have Disk button to complete the requirements of this screen.

Many laser printers are Hewlett Packard compatible and many dot-matrix printers are Epson compatible. If you can't get a driver or the generic driver doesn't work well, try one of the commonly emulated printers.

NOTE If your printer is not listed, you should contact your printer manufacturer for an updated driver. Choose a generic printer until you get an updated driver version.

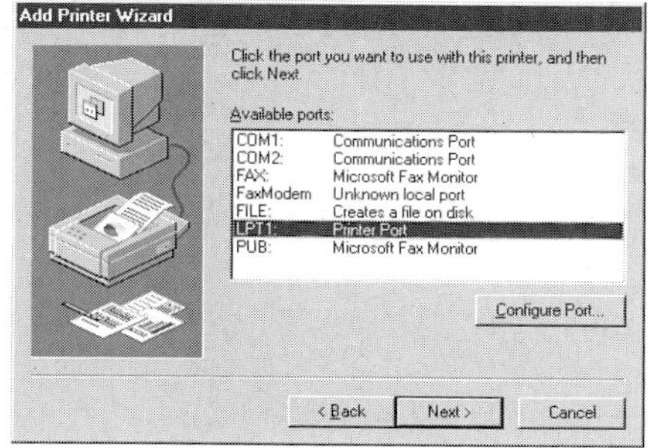

FIG. 3.4 Select the printer port to which you want to attach the printer.

6. Provide the printer port information. The wizard screen shown in Figure 3.4 displays ports based on the survey Windows did of your computer hardware. You may have several COM and LPT ports. Refer to the list of information you compiled before you started the installation and choose the port to which you want to attach the printer. The port selected in Figure 3.4 is LPT1, a very typical selection.
7. Click the Configure Port button. The wizard displays the Configure Port window (see Figure 3.5). The window contains a check box that enables Windows 95 to spool your MS-DOS print jobs. This is the only configuration in the Add Printer Wizard for the LPT1 port. This check box should always be selected to enable MS-DOS printing, unless your MS-DOS applications prove to be incompatible with Windows 95 printing. Put a check in the Check Port State Before Printing check box if you want Windows 95 to determine whether the printer port is available prior to starting the print job.

FIG. 3.5 Configure your parallel printer port to enable MS-DOS applications to use the same driver.

8. After you configure the port, choose OK and Next to open the dialog box shown in Figure 3.6. Use this dialog box to name the new printer and define it as your default printer, if desired. In the Printer Name field, type the name of the printer. The name can be up to 128 characters long and can contain spaces and nonalphanumeric symbols. The printer's name should include location or ownership.

NOTE If you have access to two printers of the same type, add unique identifiers to their names, such as "HP LaserJet 4 Room 5, Building 10" and "HP LaserJet 4 Room 25, Building 15."

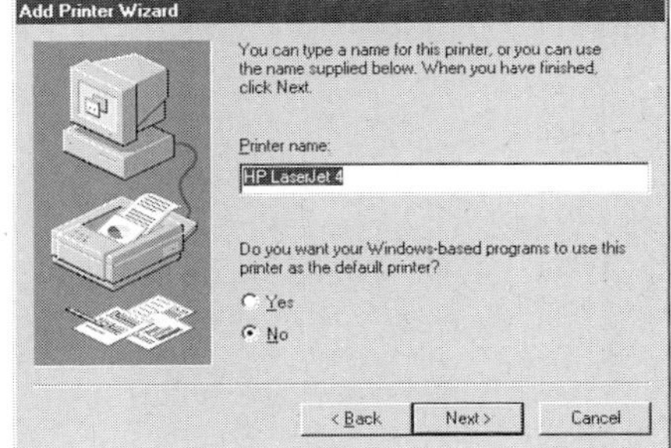

FIG. 3.6 The printer name and default status are specified using this wizard screen.

9. Choose Yes to set this printer as the system default. By setting this printer as your default, you instruct all applications to use this printer, unless you tell the application to use a different printer. (You can set the default to any other installed printer at any time.) Click Next to continue. The final wizard screen appears (see Figure 3.7).

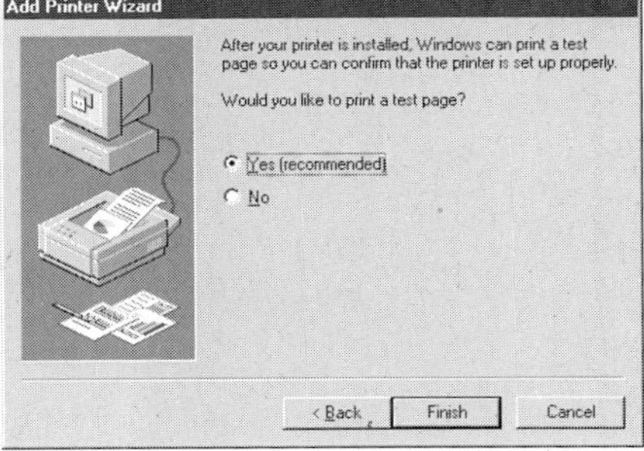

FIG. 3.7 Printing a test page is the final step in configuring and testing your printer installation.

10. Specify whether you want to print a test page. Printing one will test the overall operation of the printer based on the settings you just entered. Choose Yes and click Finish to print the test page.

NOTE The test page contains information specific to your printer, its configuration, and the drivers that Windows will use to interface with it. After this page is printed, save it for future reference. If others use your computer, you might have to return to a known installation configuration someday.

You also can get information on your printer using the MSINFO32.EXE utility located in the \Program Files\Common Files\Microsoft Shared\MSInfo folder. Run this utility and click Printing in the left pane of the Microsoft System Information window to view information on all installed printers.

Installing a Plug and Play Printer Plug and Play printers interact with Windows to automatically configure printers by using a dialog box transparent to the user. Many printer manufacturers have cooperated with Microsoft to make configuration easier and to automatically update the software when you make changes to the printer hardware configuration.

If your printer is Plug and Play compatible, see Chapter 7, "Plug and Play and Legacy Device Installation," for an explanation of how Plug and Play devices are installed.

Renaming an Existing Printer Use the Printers folder to rename printers named during installation. The Printers folder displays all installed printers; their individual names are located immediately below the printer's icon (refer to Figure 3.1).

To rename a printer after it is installed, follow these steps:

1. Open the Start menu, choose Settings, Printers, and the Printers folder appears. If the Control Panel is open, double-click the Printers folder.
2. Select the desired printer and choose File, Rename or right-click the printer name and choose Rename. You can also click the printer name, wait a second, and click a second time. Windows creates a text box around the printer name and highlights it.
3. Change the name by typing a new name or editing portions of the existing name.
4. When you finish, press Enter. The new printer name is used throughout the Windows operating system.

See "Changing Settings and Properties with the Right Mouse Button," **p. 673**

Deleting an Existing Printer You can delete an installed printer from the Printers folder that displays all installed printers as icons. To delete a printer from the Printers folder, follow these steps:

1. Select the printer you want to delete and press the Delete key or right-click the printer and choose Delete. Windows opens a dialog box and asks if you're sure you want to delete the printer.
2. Choose OK; the printer is now deleted. Windows then asks whether it can remove the associated software from your hard disk.

CAUTION

If you have a similar printer that could use the same drivers, do not remove the software. Deleting the associated software might remove that driver from use by other printers.

3. Choose OK to remove the deleted printer's software driver.

The printer and its driver are now removed. Windows signifies this event by removing that printer icon from the Printers folder.

NOTE If you plan to reattach this printer in the future, do not remove the software drivers. This can save you time when reattaching the printer.

NOTE If a new driver becomes available for your printer, you can update your existing driver by using the Add Printer Wizard. A new driver can add new capabilities, correct bugs, or increase the performance of your printer. In step 5 of the steps in the section "Installing a Printer with the Add Printer Wizard," choose the Have Disk button to specify the location of the new driver, and then continue as if adding a new printer.

One source for new drivers is the printer manufacturer. Most manufacturers have a private BBS or a site on CompuServe or the Internet where you can download updated drivers. Check your printer manual for online addresses. You also can find updated drivers in the Windows 95 Driver Library (W95DL), which is available at several online locations:

CompuServe: **GO MSL**

Microsoft Download Service (MSDL): (206) 936-6735

Internet (anonymous FTP): **ftp.microsoft.com** (SOFTLIB/MSLFILES directory)

World Wide Web: **http://www.microsoft.com/windows/software**

Configuring Your Printer

If you change printer settings frequently, you can install duplicate printers and configure each printer with its own set of properties. This eliminates repeated property changes.

By now, you have installed one or more printers for use by Windows 95 applications. Both Windows and MS-DOS applications can use these resources without further effort. The initial installation of the printer created a default configuration. You might want to make changes to that configuration. Because few default configurations satisfy all printing requirements, you might want to change the printer's configuration frequently.

NOTE Windows 3.1 provided a setting to change the priority of background printing. This feature does not appear in Windows 95. However, the print spooler in Windows 95, which uses 32-bit device drivers and DLLs, handles background printing much more smoothly than does the spooler in Windows 3.1, eliminating the need to optimize the background printing settings.

Options for Your Printer Printer properties are preset during installation of the printer. The preset values for the many variables might not meet your current printing needs. You might also have to make changes to meet special printing needs or to solve any performance problems that arise.

Like many other printing issues discussed in this chapter, the exact options available depend on the capabilities of your printer. The following discussion focuses on the basic procedures so you must adapt these to fit your specific printer.

To change printer options, open the Printer properties sheet (see Figure 3.8). Use one of these two methods:

- If the Print Manager is open for the printer whose options you want to change, choose Printer, Properties.
- Open the Printer control panel and select the printer whose options you want to change. Choose File, Properties or right-click the printer icon and choose Properties from the shortcut menu.

This sheet has several tabbed pages. The settings on each page depend on the manufacturer, printer model, and printer options.

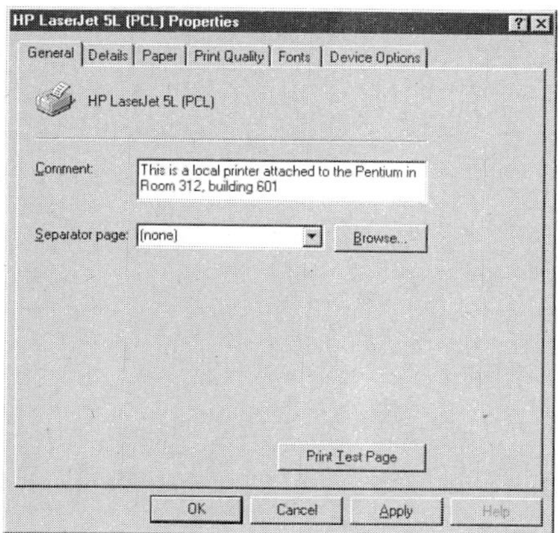

FIG. 3.8
Use the General tab page of the Printer properties sheet to get and specify basic information about the printer.

The Printer properties sheet typically contains the following information. (The details of these tabs will change with different printers.)

- **General page**. Enables you to identify your printer, print a test page, and choose a separator page to separate print jobs of different users. Each page includes a user name and job-specific information such as date, time, and file name.
- **Details page**. Contains controls to attach or change ports, add or delete ports, change time-out periods, and specify how Windows will process print files. Use the Details page to configure enhanced metafile printing and the spooler.
- **Sharing page**. Enables a printer to be shared with other workstations attached to your computer over a network.
- **Paper page**. Provides several controls that set the printer's default paper handling, orientation, and number of pages to be printed.

- **Graphics page**. Sets the resolution, halftone capabilities, scaling, and other options that define how the printer treats graphic files.
- **Fonts page**. Enables you to adjust how fonts are treated by Windows for this printer. Configurable fonts include printer, cartridge, and software fonts.

TIP Be certain to accurately configure the available printer memory. An incorrect value in this variable can change the speed of your printouts or cause your printer to time-out or fail during printing sessions.

- **Device Options page**. Configures the options associated with the printer's hardware, such as the printer memory capacity settings, page protection, and other device-specific options. The number and type of controls are specific to the printer's make, model, and hardware.

TROUBLESHOOTING

I've always been able to set the number of copies I print from the control panel of my printer. When I print in Windows 95, however, I always get one copy no matter how I set the printer. In Windows 95, the settings in your programs for the number of copies to be printed overrides the setting on your printer. To print multiple copies, change the setting in the program you are printing from.

I'd like to be able to print multiple copies from WordPad, but this option is not available. WordPad and Paint do not support printing multiple copies, so if your printer does not support printing multiple copies, this option will not be available.

When I try to print a page, I receive the message, "Not enough memory to render page." If your printer has bidirectional communication with your computer, there may be a problem with the amount of memory the printer driver detected. To have Windows 95 recheck the printer for memory, follow these steps:

1. With the printer online, open the Start menu and choose Settings, Printers.
2. Right-click the icon for the printer you want to check and choose Properties.
3. Select the Device Options tab and choose the Restore Defaults button.
4. Click OK.

Printing with Color Microsoft uses licensed Image Color Matching (ICM) technology from Kodak to create an image environment that treats color consistently from the screen to the printed page. The Windows ICM goal is to be able to repeatedly and consistently reproduce color-matched images from source to destination.

ICM provides more consistent, repeatable quality among various brands of printers and scanners and provides a higher quality color rendering (the term *color* includes grayscale rendering). To fully benefit from ICM technology, choose a color printer that is compliant with Kodak's ICM specifications.

Setting Color Printing Properties Figure 3.9 shows the Graphics page of the Printer properties sheet for a color printer. The controls on this page allow you to configure your printer to produce the best color possible.

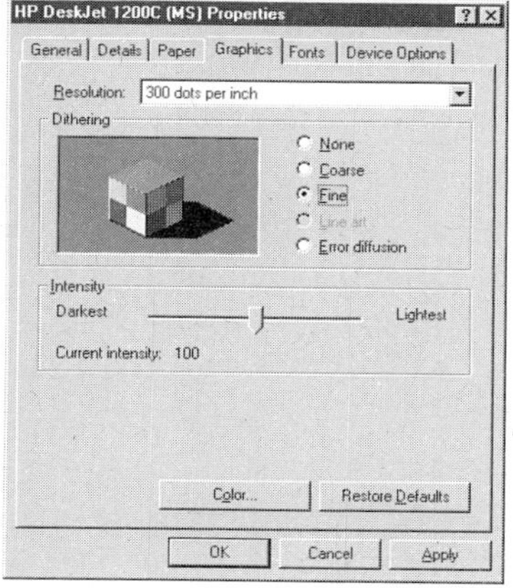

FIG. 3.9
The Graphics page of the Printer properties sheet for a color printer lets you adjust color and output quality.

- **Resolution**. This drop-down list box specifies the number of dots per inch (dpi) that the printer can produce. The higher the dpi, the clearer the graphics.
- **Dithering**. This error-correcting tool, used by Windows 95, more accurately represents an object's color and grayscale.
- **Intensity**. This brightness control lightens or darkens a printout to more accurately reflect its screen appearance and to compensate for deficiencies in toner or paper quality.

To access the color settings for a color printer, click the Color button. Use the Graphics—Color dialog box to set ICM compliance alternatives (see Figure 3.10).

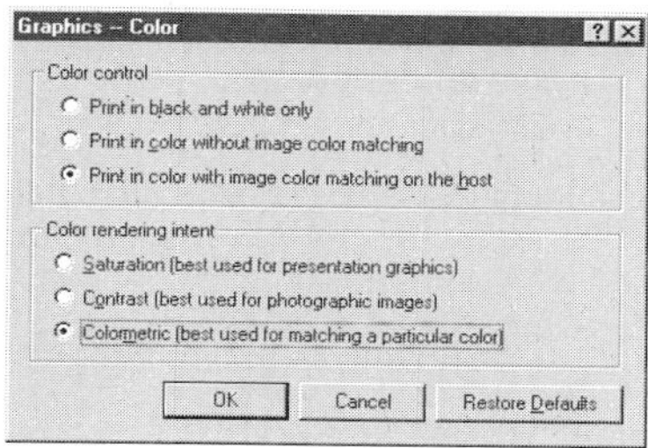

FIG. 3.10
Display this box by choosing the Color button on the Graphics page.

Use the color settings to adjust the level of compliance of your printer with the ICM standards. The dialog box is also useful for trial-and-error adjustment of color printer output quality. Following is a list of the settings:

- **Color Control**. A macro command that enables you to direct the printer to print only black and white or to specify whether you want ICM technology.

- **Color Rendering Intent.** Provides the best ICM settings for three of the major uses of color printing: presentations, photographs, and true color screen display printing. Select the choice that works best for your purpose.

Configuring the Printer Port In addition to configuring settings that affect the printer itself, you can make a few configuration changes to the port to which the printer is attached. These options vary depending on which port you use to print. The most common printing port is an LPT port, usually LPT1 (or LPT2, if you have a second LPT port). You might have to change the printer port if you attach a printer to a serial port or add a printer switch.

Follow these steps to change the configuration options for port LPT1:

1. Open the Start menu and choose Settings, Control Panel.
2. Double-click the System icon.
3. Windows displays the System Properties dialog box. Choose the Device Manager tab to configure printer ports (see Figure 3.11).

FIG. 3.11
The Device Manager tab of the System properties sheet identifies the port, its present state of operation, and the hardware configuration being used.

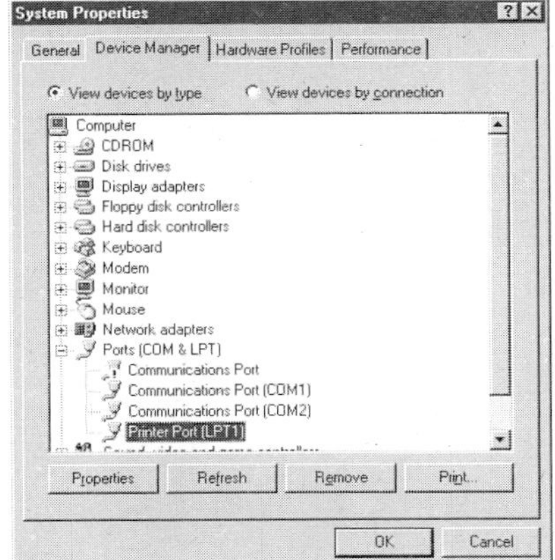

4. Double-click the Printer Ports icon to show the attached ports. Choose the printer port whose configuration you want to change, such as LPT1 or COM1. For this example, choose LPT1. If your printer is attached to another parallel port or a COM (serial) port, choose that port instead.
5. Click Properties. The Printer Port properties sheet shown in Figure 3.12 appears. Note that Printer Port Properties are divided among three tabs: General, Driver, and Resources.

OSR 2 **NOTE** If you have the OEM Service Release 2 (OSR2) version of Windows 95 installed, the General tab shown in Figure 3.12 will look slightly different. The Device Usage box will consist of a simple check box that allows you to disable the device, in this case, the printer port, for the current hardware configuration.

FIG. 3.12
The General page of the Printer Port properties sheet provides current status and information about the port's hardware.

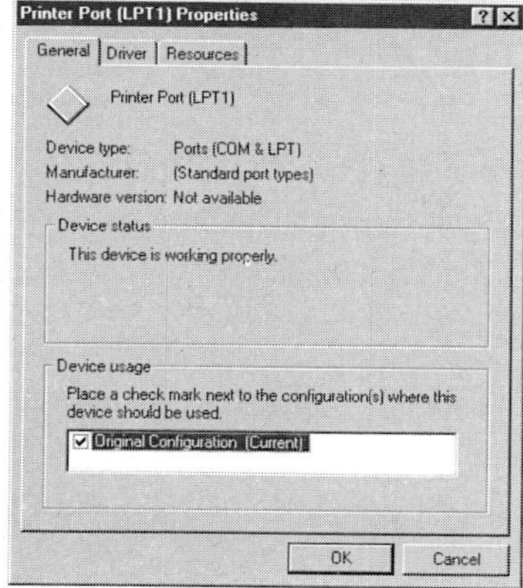

6. Choose the Driver tab.
7. Verify that the driver file selected on the Driver page is the most current printer driver available (see Figure 3.13). Note that the VXD extension signifies a 32-bit virtual driver that can be expected to provide the best performance. If you have a driver with a DRV extension, you are not using a 32-bit driver. Check with your printer manufacturer for the latest version.

FIG. 3.13
The Driver page of the Printer Port properties sheet provides the name and version of the currently installed port driver.

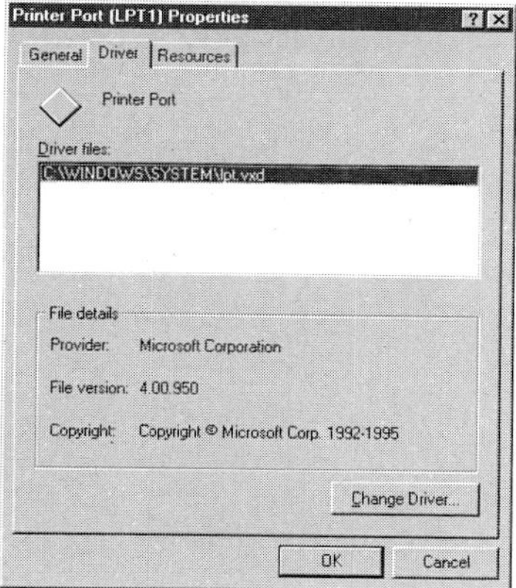

8. To install a different driver, click Change Driver. Windows displays the Select Device dialog box shown in Figure 3.14. Use this dialog box to load a new driver from either a vendor-supplied disk or to choose a previously installed driver. If you have a vendor-supplied disk that contains the new port driver, choose Have Disk.
9. Windows displays an instruction window that directs you to insert the manufacturer's disk in Drive A. The window also allows you to browse and select a driver from another location. Windows requests a vendor disk so insert the appropriate vendor disk and click

OK. Otherwise, click Cancel to stop the installation process. Windows installs the vendor software and links it to the selected printer port.

FIG. 3.14
Select a new or existing printer port driver.

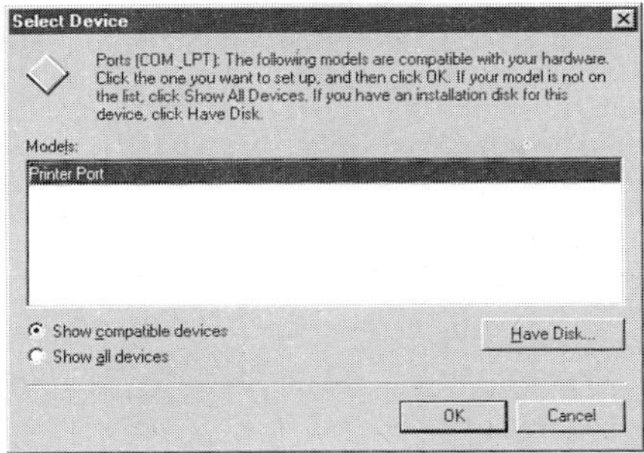

If you have the OSR2 version of Windows, the Driver tab appears as shown in Figure 3.15, and the procedure for installing a different driver differs from the steps just outlined. To install a new driver in OSR2, follow these steps:

1. Click the Update Driver tab to display the Update Device Driver Wizard dialog box shown in Figure 3.16.
2. Leave the Yes option selected to have Windows search for an updated driver. Click Next.

   or

   Select the No option and click Next to select the driver from a list.
3. If you selected the Yes option in step 2, click Finish when Windows 95 finds the driver.

   If an updated driver is not found, click Other Locations in the Update Device Driver Wizard and change to the location where the updated driver is located.

   If you selected the No option in step 2, select the correct items from the Manufacturer and Models lists and click Finish.

You will be prompted to insert the disk or CD-ROM on which the updated driver is located, if you haven't done this already. The wizard will search for the driver and install it on your computer. Select Yes when you are prompted to restart the computer to complete the setup.

The Resources page contains detailed information about the printer port's addresses and any configuration conflicts. Review this information to verify that Windows has properly installed the driver. In the background, Windows cross-checked the port's configuration with the system startup settings. Windows can and does spot configuration problems, but doesn't necessarily notify the user. The resources contain the Input/Output Range of addresses. The addresses of the LPT1 port are shown under the Setting column. If a device uses an interrupt, that interrupt is also shown. If Windows spots a problem, it will designate that a conflict exists and list the information in this window. You can then choose alternative configurations to test other configurations.

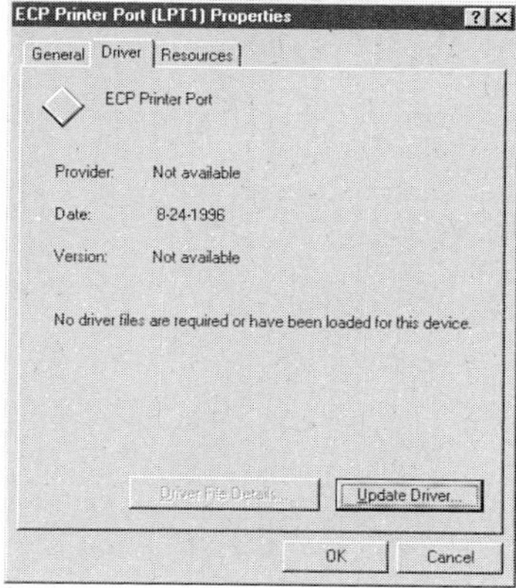

FIG. 3.15
The Driver page as it appears in the OSR2 version of Windows 95.

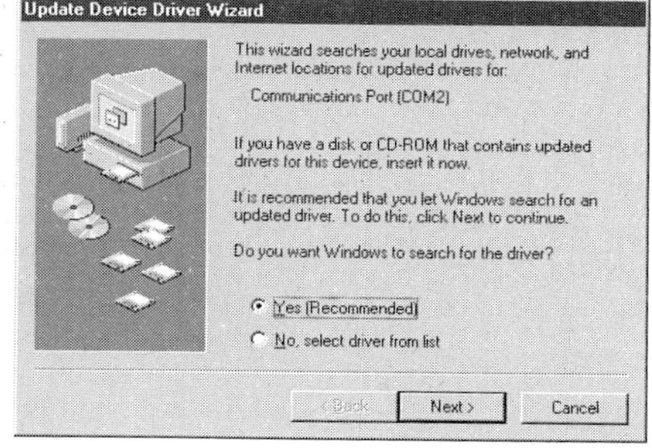

FIG. 3.16
Use the Update Device Driver Wizard to search for and install updated drivers.

To configure the printer port, click the Resources tab. The critical information is the Conflicting Device List (see Figure 3.17). This list contains all items that conflict with your printer port. When installing new hardware, always verify that its address and interrupts do not conflict with existing hardware properties.

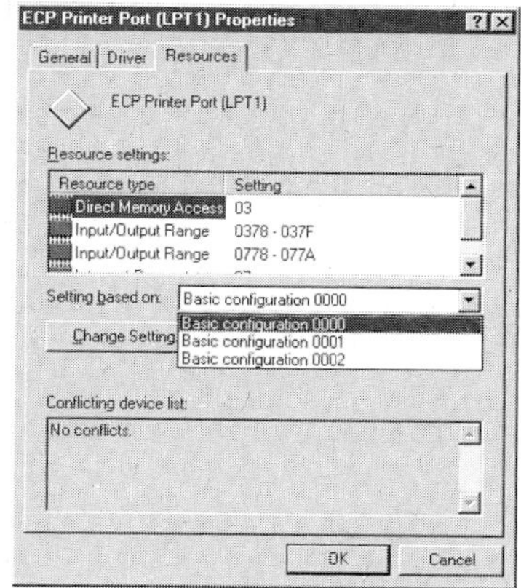

FIG. 3.17
The Resources page of the Printer Port properties sheet displays detailed hardware information vital to port operation and the diagnosis of communications problems.

You should normally choose Use Automatic Settings. If you have any conflict problems, the Settings Based On list box provides several optional configurations that Windows can use to configure the printer port.

To use this control, first clear the Use Automatic Settings check box and then use the Settings Based On option to select from a list of Windows configurations (see Figure 3.17). Each configuration shows the port configured to different devices and interrupts. As each configuration is considered, problems associated with the new configuration are shown in the Conflicting Device List information box at the bottom of the page.

NOTE Carefully review the hardware properties for all devices to identify potential conflicts. Windows cannot discover and display all problems in normal operation. Use the Device Manager to check for conflicting devices because it can prevent problems later.

Most printer installations do not require changes to the printer port settings. However, unusual address conflicts from older equipment or Enhanced Capability Ports (ECP) technology provide more configuration options. The number of possible decisions and potential conflicts between pieces of hardware increase as the number of options increase. Select OK to complete the port configuration.

Using PC Card Devices

Many notebook computers contain one or two special bus slots called *PC Card slots* (formerly PCMCIA slots) that accommodate adapters (the size of a credit card) for various functions. Although initially only flash memory cards were available in PCMCIA format, today many types of devices—including modems, hard disks, network cards, sound cards, and other devices—are available in PC Card/PCMCIA format. In addition, PC Card docking stations enable you to use PC Card devices in desktop computers, making it possible, for example, to use the same PC Card modem in a notebook and a desktop computer.

NOTE There are three official types of PC Card slots, referred to as Type I, Type II, and Type III. The specification for a fourth type of slot—Type IV—is being finalized by the PCMCIA organization (Personal Computer Memory Card International Association). One of the primary differences between the types of PC Card slots is that each higher-numbered slot accommodates a thicker PC Card than the previous slot. PC Card hard disks, for example, generally require a Type III slot, but modems can be installed in a Type I or Type II slot. Most of today's newer notebook computers can accommodate one Type III device, or two Type II devices (or any combination of two Type I and Type II devices).

The primary advantage of PC Card devices for portable computer users is that these devices make it possible to expand the capabilities of portable computers in the same way you can expand desktop systems, enabling you to add optional hardware to the portable computer. Windows 95 improves on the PCMCIA support in DOS and Windows 3.x by providing 32-bit device drivers to support the PC Card controllers in most computers. This makes it possible for Windows 95 to support a wide variety of PC Card devices without requiring 16-bit, real-mode drivers that slow down the system and use conventional memory.

Another improvement for PC Card devices in Windows 95 is expanded support for *hot swapping,* which is the ability to remove and insert PC Card devices in the computer without turning off the computer. If you need to temporarily remove your hard disk card to use a modem, for example, you first use the PC Card object in the Control Panel to turn off the hard disk card. Then, you remove the hard disk card from its slot and insert the modem. Windows 95 disables the hard disk driver(s) temporarily and enables the modem drivers.

▶ **See** "Installing Plug and Play Hardware," **p. 181**

The Windows 95 OEM Service Release 2 (OSR2) has several PC Card enhancements. OSR2 supports the newer PC Card 32 (Cardbus) cards, which provide 32-bit I/O using a 33MHz bus, similar to the PCI bus architecture found on desktops. These cards enable much higher data transfer than the original 16-bit cards, up to 132M/second versus a maximum of 20M/second with 16-bit cards. For applications that demand high data throughput, such as video conferencing over a Fast Ethernet network, the need for this technology becomes apparent. Another benefit is that CardBus cards use less power (3.3 volts), extending battery life.

OSR2 also supports multifunction network/modem and Global Positioning Satellite (GPS) PC Cards. To learn how to obtain and install OSR2 see Chapter 2, "Installing Windows."

Installing PC Card Support

Each computer with PC Card slots or a PC Card docking station includes a PC Card controller that enables the CPU to communicate with the PC Card bus. This controller requires a set of drivers that enable the operating system (in this case, Windows 95) to communicate using the PC Card bus. In addition, each PC Card device requires a device-specific driver that enables the device to function and communicate with the operating system. If you are using a PC Card network card, for example, Windows 95 requires a set of drivers for the PC Card slot itself and a separate driver for the network card.

When you install Windows 95, Setup automatically detects your computer's PC Card controller and installs support for it. Setup does not, however, enable the 32-bit PC Card controller drivers. Setup takes this approach because some portable computers require that you continue to use 16-bit drivers (which come with the portable computer) to control the PC Card slots.

NOTE Windows 95 supports 32-bit drivers for systems based on either an Intel PCIC-compatible PC Card controller or Databook PC Card controller.

In addition to enabling 32-bit PC Card support (if your computer supports it), you must install the drivers for the PC Card devices you'll be using. In many cases, Windows 95 can install these devices automatically using Plug and Play, even on systems without a Plug and Play BIOS. To install a PC Card modem, for example, simply insert the modem in its slot. Windows 95 detects the new device and starts the Add New Modem Wizard to install the modem driver.

Enabling 32-Bit PC Card Support After you install Windows 95, you must use the PC Card object in the Control Panel to enable 32-bit support for your PC Card controller. Enabling 32-bit support provides better overall system performance and more effective memory use. In addition, enabling 32-bit PC Card support is required to support Plug and Play installation of PC Card devices and hot swapping.

NOTE When Windows 95 enables 32-bit PC Card support, your existing 16-bit real-mode PC Card drivers are disabled. If you are installing Windows 95 from a network server, you must have local access to the Windows 95 source (cabinet) files. Therefore, you must have a set of Windows 95 floppy disks or have a CD-ROM connected to your portable PC to enable Windows 95 to read the 32-bit driver files for the PC Card controller. Optionally, you can copy the Windows 95 cabinet files from the network server to your portable computer's hard disk prior to enabling 32-bit support.

To enable 32-bit PC Card support for your computer, follow these steps:

1. Verify that you have local access to the Windows 95 cabinet files, as explained in the previous note.
2. Open the Start menu and choose Settings, Control Panel.
3. Double-click the PC Card (PCMCIA) program icon. The first time you open this object, the PC Card (PCMCIA) Wizard appears (see Figure 3.18).

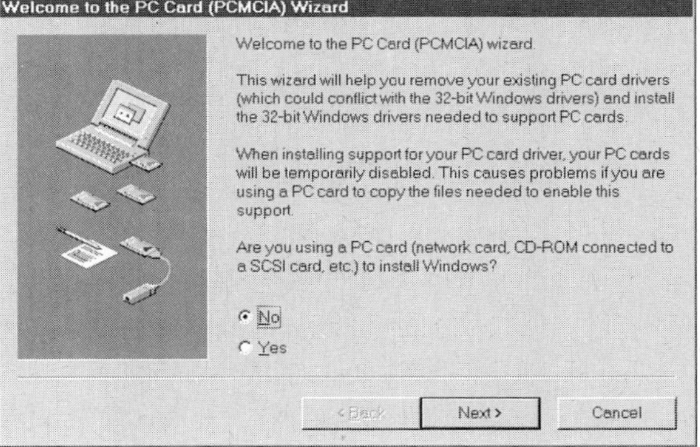

FIG. 3.18 The opening dialog box of the PC Card (PCMCIA) Wizard checks to see whether you are using a PC Card to install the new PC Card drivers.

4. Choose No and then Next to inform the Wizard that you are not setting up Windows 95 from a network server.
5. If the PC Card Wizard detects existing real-mode PC Card drivers, it displays a dialog box that enables you to view the drivers and control the way the wizard handles the existing drivers. If you want the wizard to automatically remove the drivers, choose the No option button and then choose Next. If you want to view and verify the deletion of the existing real-mode PC Card drivers, choose Yes and then choose Next.
6. If you select Yes, the wizard displays a set of dialog boxes that show the device entries it will delete in CONFIG.SYS, AUTOEXEC.BAT, and SYSTEM.INI. (Figure 3.19 shows the dialog box for the CONFIG.SYS file.) If you do not want the wizard to delete a specific driver from one of these files, clear the line in the appropriate dialog box by clicking it, and then choose Next.

FIG. 3.19
To verify your drivers, choose Yes.

7. After the PC Card Wizard removes the real-mode drivers (if any) as directed by you, it displays a final dialog box that prompts you to choose Finish to complete the PC Card setup process and enable 32-bit PC Card support. Choose the Finish button to complete the process. Windows 95 shuts down your computer so the change can take effect.

Installing PC Card Devices After you enable 32-bit PC Card support, Windows 95 can typically install PC Card devices automatically. If you insert a network card in the computer, for example, Windows 95 detects the new card and automatically installs the necessary drivers for the card. If, for some reason, Windows 95 does not automatically recognize your PC Card device, you must manually install support for it.

To manually install a PC Card device other than a modem or network adapter, use the following procedure:

1. Insert the new PC Card device in the appropriate slot. (Check the PC Card device's manual to determine if the device must be installed in a specific slot.)

NOTE If you are installing a PC Card network adapter, use the Network object in the Control Panel to install it. If you are installing a PC Card modem, use the Modems object in the Control Panel.

2. Open the Control Panel and double-click the Add New Hardware program icon to start the Add New Hardware Wizard. Then choose Next.
3. Choose Yes and then Next to enable the wizard to automatically detect your new PC Card device.
4. If the wizard is unable to detect the new device, the wizard displays a hardware selection dialog box similar to the one shown in Figure 3.20. Choose the type of device you are installing and choose Next.
5. From the Manufacturers list, choose the manufacturer of the device you are installing. Then, from the Models list, choose the device model. If your manufacturer or model is not listed and you have a driver disk for the device, choose Have Disk and then follow the prompts to direct the wizard to the directory on the floppy disk where the necessary files are located.

FIG. 3.20
Choose the type of device you are installing and then choose Next.

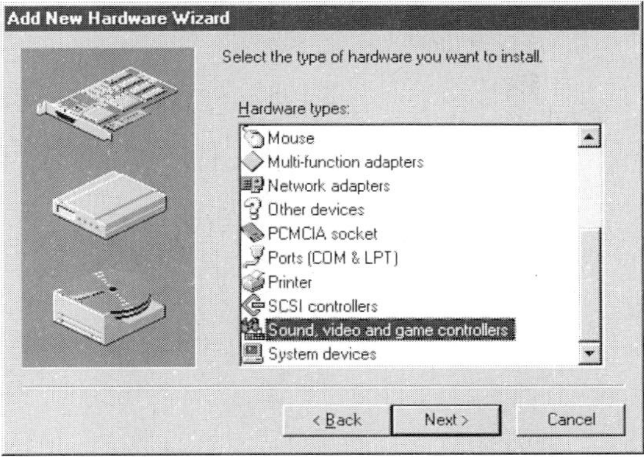

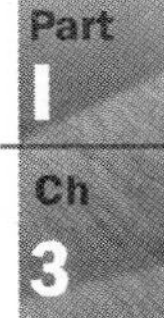

6. After you have selected the correct manufacturer and model, choose OK to complete the setup process.

See "Installing a Plug and Play Modem," **p. 77**

Hot Swapping PC Cards

Windows 95 enables you to remove a PC Card device and replace it with another without turning off the system. This capability enables you to quickly swap PC Card devices. Before you remove a device, however, you should first shut it down. To do so, choose the PC Card object in the Control Panel. Windows 95 displays a PC Card (PCMCIA) properties sheet, which displays information about the computer's PC Card slots and any currently inserted devices.

To remove a PC Card device from the system, first select the device from the list on the Socket Status tab and then choose Stop. Windows 95 shuts down the device and temporarily disables its drivers (the socket is listed as empty). You then can remove the PC Card device.

Insert the new device in the proper slot. If you have previously installed support for the device, Windows 95 detects the device and automatically enables its drivers. If you have not used the device in the computer previously, Windows 95 detects the new hardware and automatically installs support for the device.

TROUBLESHOOTING

The System Agent reports the ScanDisk error message, "Check was stopped because of an error," but the ScanDisk log file does not show an error. This occurs if you created a ScanDisk with a PC Card or docking station disk drive and later removed that drive. To resolve that problem, delete the existing ScanDisk task and schedule separate new ScanDisk tasks for permanent and removable drives.

Installing and Configuring Your Modem

Modems and the technology that they use—serial communications—have been a problem for Windows since Version 1.0. In Windows 95, however, Microsoft finally got it right—and then some. The operating system now incorporates a rich, reliable, full-featured communications subsystem that is capable of operating today's fastest modems. Windows 95 is an extensible system that works well with tomorrow's communications devices, such as ISDN adapters, parallel-port modems, and cable modems. These forthcoming devices work at speeds beyond even the fastest of today's modems. Windows 95 can handle all these devices at the same time.

Understanding the Windows 95 Communications System

In the past, getting good performance from modems running with Windows often meant changing the part of Windows that controlled all the serial ports and, therefore, controlled the modems. Various companies supplied these *enhanced communications drivers*, which were sold with high-speed modems, by themselves, or with communications programs. (Often, you couldn't get the modem working without a special driver.) Although literally thousands of enhanced communications drivers were available, all of them worked by taking over control of the modem and serial ports in Windows.

Windows 95 doesn't need these third-party drivers to make communications fly. The sophisticated Plug and Play communications subsystem in Windows 95 is designed to automatically recognize, install, and configure modems when they are installed. Even if you have a standard modem that does not support Plug and Play, Windows provides a Wizard to help you install and configure the modem.

Whichever type of modem you choose to install, Windows can use it to communicate more reliably and with better data throughput than ever before. The three reasons for this are:

- New 32-bit TAPI communications system for 32-bit applications
- Improved 16-bit communications driver for older 16-bit programs
- Support for the new 16550-compatible UART (Universal Asynchronous Receiver Transmitter) chips found in new modems and modern serial ports

Windows uses these features to give you more control over your communications with your modem and to make your modem do a better job for you. Windows also has special capabilities for 32-bit communications programs far beyond the capabilities of its predecessor. You learn more about TAPI (Telephony Applications Programming Interface) capabilities in the section "Working Smarter with TAPI and 32-Bit Windows Programs," later in this chapter.

▶ **See** "How Plug and Play Works," **p. 79**

OSR 2 NOTE Microsoft has updated the Unimodem driver that was released with the original Windows 95. The new Unimodem V driver supports voice modems, including VoiceView and AT+V modems. Voice modems enable you to switch back and forth between voice and data communication and can perform telephony functions such as answering and forwarding calls and recording messages.

For more information on the Unimodem V driver and instructions on how to download it, visit the following Web site:

http://www.microsoft.com/kb/articles/q139/3/83.htm

If you have the OEM Service Release 2 (OSR2) version of Windows 95, the new Unimodem V driver is already installed on your system. For more information on OSR2, see "Installing the Windows 95b (OSR2) Service Release," in Chapter 2.

Installing a Plug and Play Modem

Like other devices that support this new technology, Plug and Play modems communicate with Windows to cooperate in setting themselves up. These modems always contain the serial communications port and modulator/demodulator/dialer on the same card, so that Windows can configure them to work together at the same time.

See "Understanding Plug and Play Hardware," **p. 178**

See "Understanding Windows 95 Setup Requirements," **p. 22**

Many Plug and Play modems are located on PC Cards (formerly known as PCMCIA cards). These cards can support full Plug and Play functionality, including hot swapping.

NOTE ISA stands for Industry Standard Architecture. ISA cards are the familiar add-in peripheral cards that have been used in PCs since IBM set the standard.

Some Plug and Play modems may be on ISA cards. These cannot benefit from hot swapping because they are designed to be fixed inside the computer and not removed during operation.

Make sure any internal ISA card modem you buy includes the modern 16550 type of UART chip. All PC Card modems already do. If you're buying a serial port card to put in an ISA slot, check to make sure you're buying one with the 16550 chip or a compatible.

NOTE Internal modems consist of three main functional sections. The Serial Communications Port handles communications with your computer. The Modulator/Demodulator handles communications over the phone lines with another modem. The Dialer handles communications with the telephone network and gets your call connected.

External modems don't contain the Serial Communications Port—they attach to one that is built into your computer.

Plug and Play modems add another section that identifies the modem's capabilities and resource needs to Windows 95 setup.

See "How Windows 95 Setup Works," **p. 27**

During Windows setup, information is exchanged between your modem and the system. This is what happens, automatically, when Windows comes to the part of setup in which your modem will be configured.

1. Windows searches through all the system's input-output (I/O) ports and finds the Plug and Play circuits on the modem.
2. The system assigns the card an identification number, which Windows stores in its information files.
3. Windows asks the modem about its speeds and specifications. The modem gives the information to Windows Setup.
4. Setup then assigns a communications port number (COM1, COM2, and so on) and resources to be used by the port. These resources are an interrupt and an I/O address. If the Plug and Play modem is on a PC Card, Windows also assigns a memory address to the modem.

Plug and Play in Action If a Plug and Play modem is installed in your computer before you install Windows, the modem setup occurs automatically. This section examines what happens if you have a PC Card modem installed in PC Card slot 1 when you install Windows 95.

First, Windows configures the PC Card slots. The PC Card Wizard appears during installation (see Figure 3.21).

CAUTION

Notice in Figure 3.21 that the wizard warns you that it is about to disable all PC Cards while it works. If you're installing Windows from a CD-ROM connected through a PC Card, Setup will fail. For a workaround, use floppy disks for this portion of Setup, or copy all the Windows 95 CAB files to your hard disk from the CD-ROM before you disable the PC card.

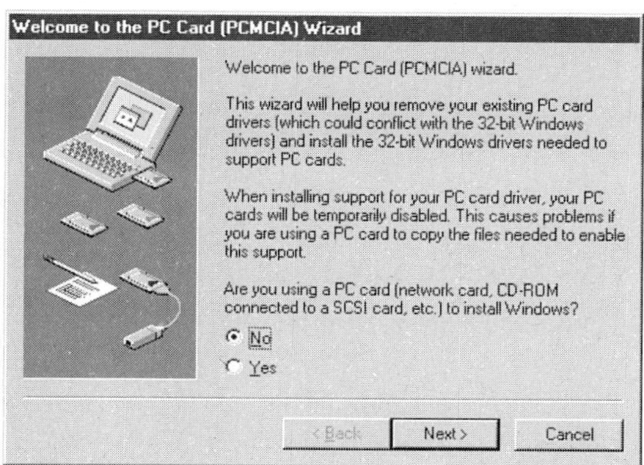

FIG. 3.21
The PC Card Wizard begins installing your PC Card modem.

Next, Windows proposes removing the old DOS-based 16-bit Card and Socket Services drivers from the CONFIG.SYS, AUTOEXEC.BAT, and SYSTEM.INI files. To review the changes before proceeding, choose Yes and then click the Next button. Figure 3.22 shows the real-mode 16-bit drivers in CONFIG.SYS. They are the last five lines in the file. For best results, you should permit the wizard to remove the old drivers. Click Next to accept the changes. After the wizard processes CONFIG.SYS, it processes the next two files in the same way.

FIG. 3.22 Real-mode drivers in CONFIG.SYS that will be removed by Windows 95.

NOTE Technically speaking, the statements are not actually removed from the file. Instead, the wizard *comments out* (switches off) the statements by inserting a "REM-Removed By PC Card Wizard" statement at the beginning of each line in which the drivers are referenced.

When the wizard finishes setting up the PC Card slots, it installs the 32-bit protected-mode Card and Socket Services driver software for them. These drivers control all the Plug and Play features.

After the drivers are installed, you need to restart Windows to activate the new drivers. Click Finish in the wizard dialog box, close any other applications that you may have running, and click Yes when you're ready to shut down.

Windows loads with the 32-bit drivers enabled for the first time. Now it can "see" (and therefore configure) the modem in your PC Card slot. Using the new, protected-mode 32-bit Card and Socket Services, Windows can install any modem in your PC Card slot. In Figure 3.23, Windows detected a new modem and installed the software drivers for it automatically.

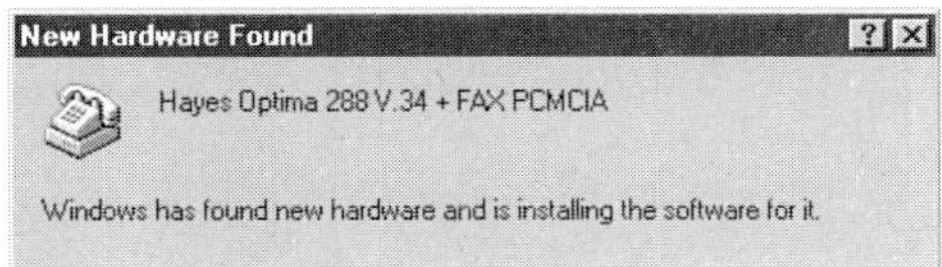

FIG. 3.23 Windows Setup finds your modem.

Your Plug and Play modem is now installed. Next, the modem must be configured to allow all advanced features in Windows to operate, which is discussed in the "Advanced Settings" section later in this chapter. The following section explains what Windows really did, via the wizard.

How Plug and Play Works The Windows user interface for the installation of the Plug and Play modem is the Setup Wizard. The wizard does all the setup work, and a lot happens behind the scenes.

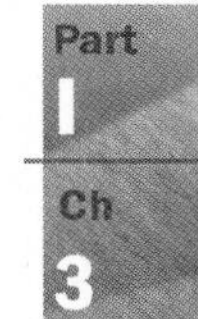

What has actually happened during the Plug and Play modem installation is this:

1. Windows asks the modem to identify itself and the modem responds. Windows installs the software to run the modem and then the wizard tells you its job is complete and your modem is installed.
2. Windows installs the Unimodem driver for any modems that support AT (Attention) commands. Most modems do. Windows then looks in its database of INF files. If information is found on the specific modem, it installs the modem mini-driver.

NOTE Windows assigns the IBM-compatible standard communications port names to ports and modems. The names will be assigned in order, using the standard resources:

Port Name	I/O Port Resource
Com1	3F8
Com2	2F8
Com3	3E8
Com4	2E8

CAUTION

If Windows finds a modem configured to a base address that is not listed in the previous table, it will assign COM5 to that modem. Programs designed for Windows 3.1 or DOS may not be able to work with a modem on this port. The workaround is to change the nonstandard address in Device Manager control panel.

▶ **See** "Understanding the Device Manager," **p. 191**

TROUBLESHOOTING

I can't get the modem to install. First, check Device Manager to see whether the hardware communications port exists and is working properly. If the Port doesn't exist in Device Manager's list of ports, follow the steps in the section "Installing a Legacy Modem" later in this chapter to install the communications port. A legacy modem is a modem that does not incorporate the Plug and Play standards. Turn your external modem off and then on again. If you are using an internal modem, shut down Windows, turn off the computer, and try again.

Installing a Legacy Modem

Legacy modems don't have the hardware in them to identify themselves to Windows 95 setup. They can't tell Windows about their capabilities or their resource requirements. Legacy modems are not Plug and Play devices. They can, however, be either internal or external modems.

▶ **See** "Installing Legacy (Non-PnP) Hardware," **p. 182**

An *internal modem* is one that fits into a slot in the computer bus and contains the serial port on the modem.

An *external modem* does not contain the serial port. The external modem connects via cable to the serial port inside the computer.

Windows considers the serial port to be a separate device from the modem, even if you have an internal modem, in which both the modem and the serial port are on the same add-in card. Windows configures these devices separately. You should be aware of the process that Windows uses to perform the configurations.

If you're trying to install an internal modem, Windows may act differently with different modems. You may be able to install the serial port at the same time you install the modem. If Windows cannot detect and initialize the port, however, you may have to use the Add New Hardware option in the Control Panel to set up the port.

See "Advanced Installation Techniques," **p. 41**

In Windows 95, you can install a legacy modem in any of the following ways:

- Use the Add New Hardware Wizard.
- Click the Modem icon in Control Panel.
- Start a 32-bit program that uses a modem. If no modem is installed, Windows suggests you install one.

The following procedure uses the Add New Hardware Wizard to install the modem. Follow these steps:

1. Open the Start menu and choose Settings, Control Panel.
2. Double-click the Add New Hardware icon. The Add New Hardware Wizard window appears.
3. Click Next.
4. You should allow Windows to try to find your modem by itself, so choose Yes when the wizard asks if you want Windows to detect it automatically. You'll see a progress report during the detection process.

   If Windows can, it sets up the serial port and the modem at the same time. Windows may not find the modem when it finds the port. In that case, run Add New Hardware Wizard again.

   The report from the Add New Hardware Wizard, shown in Figure 3.24, indicates that Windows has found a new Communications Port. View this report by clicking the Details button.
5. Click Finish.
6. When you are prompted, restart the computer.

After Windows restarts, look in Control Panel's Device Manager. On the Resources page, you'll see that a new Communications Port, COM3, has been added (see Figure 3.25).

NOTE Many times Windows will not find the port and the modem on the same pass through the installation process. Don't be concerned—follow the next steps.

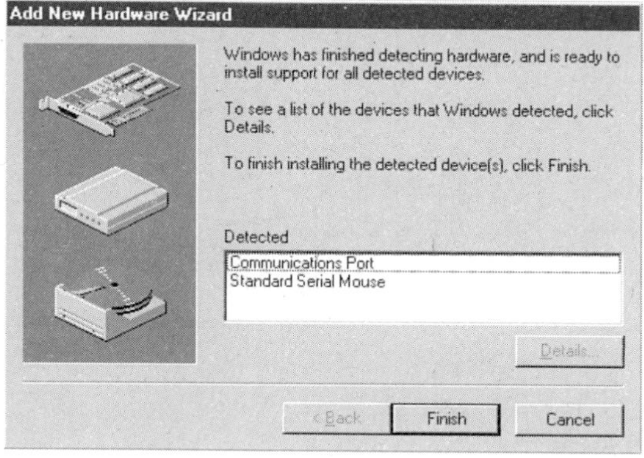

FIG. 3.24
This report from the Add New Hardware Wizard shows two new devices detected.

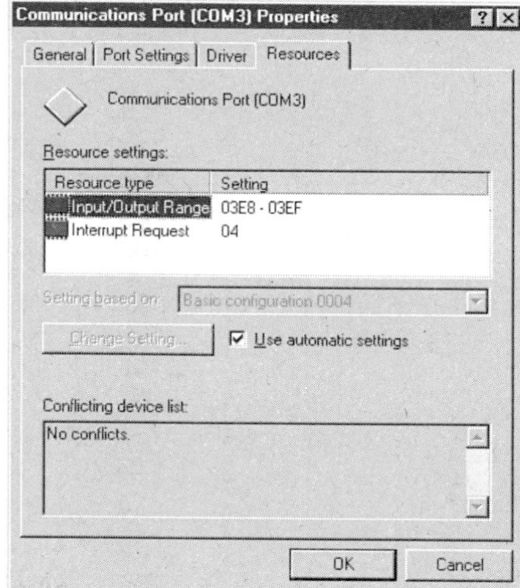

FIG. 3.25
The new communications port and its resources.

In this common example, Windows could not detect and install the port and modem in one step. Therefore, you need to visit the Control Panel again. Now that COM3 is working properly, Windows should be able to detect and install the modem connected to that port.

Double-click the Modems icon in the Control Panel. When the Install New Modem Wizard starts, choose Other.

In the next dialog box, the wizard asks for another chance to detect the modem. Click Next but don't tell the wizard what modem you have because you want to see whether Windows can find out if the port is working. Figure 3.26 shows the window that appears just before automatic modem detection.

At the end of the modem installation process, Windows reports that it found the modem attached to COM3 (see Figure 3.27). Because the reported type matches the type that is installed, you have finished the installation of the standard legacy modem. To close the dialog box, click Next.

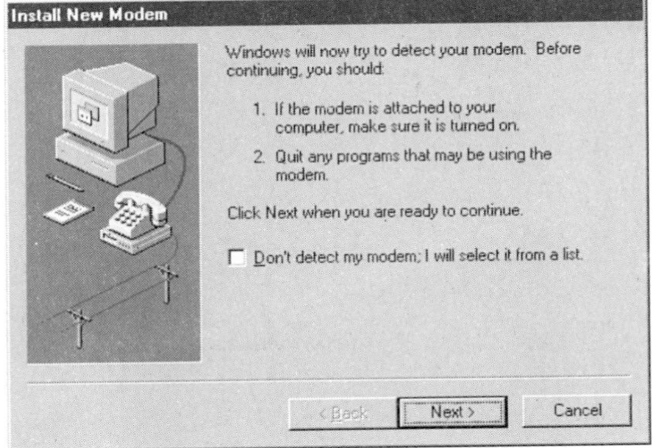

FIG. 3.26
The Modem Installation Wizard set to auto-detect your modem.

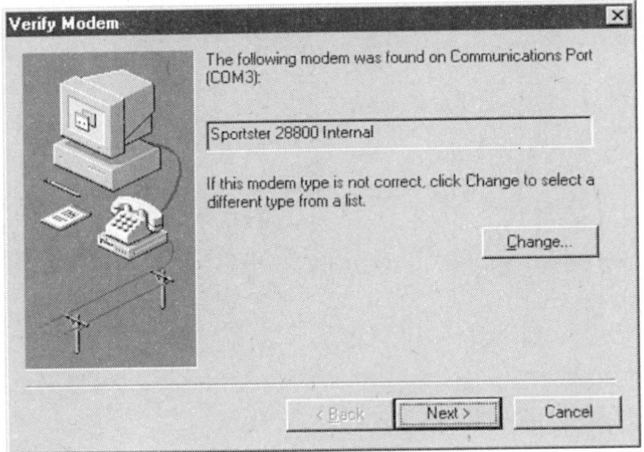

FIG. 3.27
The Modem Wizard has detected the new modem.

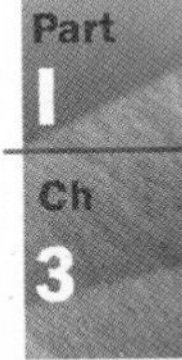

NOTE Windows chooses slow port speeds by default. If you have a fast computer, change the port speeds in the Modems Properties Control Panel to the modem's maximum speed. See "Configuring Your Modem," later in this chapter.

TROUBLESHOOTING

When I use the modem, another program—or the entire system—locks up or crashes. How do I fix it? This problem usually results from an interrupt conflict. Two devices may be trying to use the same interrupt. If you have a serial mouse on COM1, which uses Interrupt 4, and you set up a modem on COM3, which by default also uses Interrupt 4, a conflict will exist.

Use Device Manager to look for a modem or mouse icon that has a yellow exclamation point. Double-click the icon and choose Resources. If a conflict is listed, Windows offers to start the Hardware Conflict Troubleshooter. This program can help you resolve interrupt conflicts by reassigning resources such as interrupts.

Understanding the Unimodem Driver

Most of the modems on the market use a variation of the AT command set, which Dennis Hayes developed for the original Smartmodem in 1980. The command set has evolved over the years, and each manufacturer has its own set of proprietary extensions for advanced features. Still, the most basic commands are the same for all modems that use AT commands. The fact that this lowest common denominator of commands exists for the vast majority of modems allowed Microsoft to write a universal modem driver—the Unimodem driver.

Table 3.1 shows the basic AT commands used by the Unimodem driver.

Table 3.1 Modem Commands for Unimodem Driver

AT Command	Function
AT	Attention
ATZ	Reset modem
ATD	Dial modem
ATI	Identify modem
ATH	Hang up modem
ATO	Go off hook in originate mode

Once the Unimodem driver is talking to the modem, these commands provide enough functionality for the driver to interrogate the modem, find its manufacturer and model number, and try to find a match in its modem database. If a match is found, the driver tells Windows to install the mini-driver that matches the modem. This mini-driver works with the modem to enable advanced features such as data compression and error correction. These features are likely to be implemented differently by each manufacturer.

Even without a mini-driver, the Unimodem driver can make a partially Hayes-compatible modem dial, connect, and disconnect. Modems that are running with only the Unidriver will be shown in Control Panel as a Standard modem.

Using Drivers Provided by Modem Manufacturers

You may encounter a modem that comes with a Windows 95 driver disk. This disk indicates that Windows 95 has no appropriate mini-driver, or the modem has features that are not supported by the Unimodem driver.

To install the modem with its own driver software, follow these steps:

1. Double-click the Modem icon in Control Panel.
2. Choose Add.
3. Choose PC Card or Other, as appropriate.

4. Choose Don't Detect My Modem, I Will Select It.
5. Now choose Have Disk.
6. Insert the manufacturer's driver disk into the proper disk drive when you are prompted, and then choose OK.

Your modem's drivers are installed in Windows and the modem's special features are enabled.

Configuring Your Modem

Now that your hardware is installed, you can configure Windows to work cooperatively with it. Windows can take some information from you and supply that information to communications programs to allow them to function more effectively.

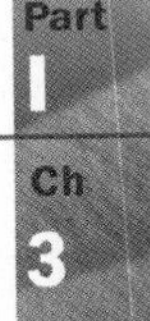

Windows automatically collects the following information from you:

- Your location
- Your area code
- Access number(s) needed to get an outside line
- Type of dialing used at this location (tone or pulse)

This information, however, is not enough to make your modem operate at peak efficiency and at maximum data-transfer rates. You should tell Windows other things about your modem, including the following:

- Maximum port speed (computer to modem)
- Default data-formatting properties
- How to handle situations involving no dial tone
- How long the modem should try to connect before stopping
- Whether to use error control and compression for robust and fast communication
- Your modem's error control and compression features
- What kind of flow control to use with your modem
- How to handle low-speed connections
- How to record a log file of the modem's interaction with the system to be used in troubleshooting
- How to manually send extra AT commands to the modem during initialization

The following sections explain these items.

General Properties Use the Modems Control Panel to select the modem that you are working with, and then choose Properties. The Modem properties sheet, which has two sheets, appears. The General properties, as shown in Figure 3.28, contains settings that can make your modem work better when the proper values are selected.

FIG. 3.28
The General page of a modem's properties sheet displays basic information about your modem.

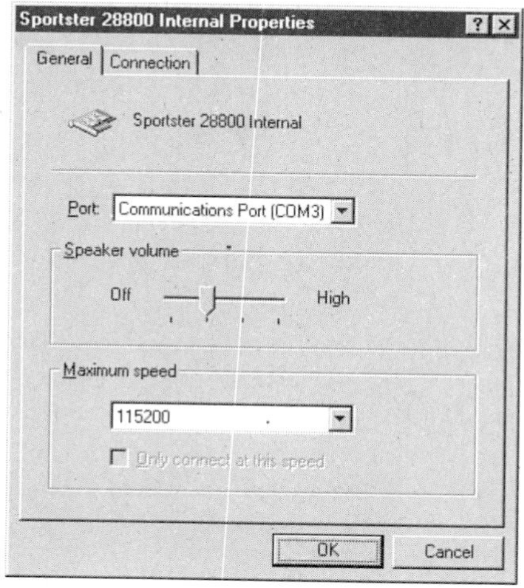

Port The Port option shows the communications port to which Windows assigned the modem. If the modem is an internal Plug and Play type, in which Windows can configure the serial port, you may have a choice in setting which communications port to use with the modem. If other communications ports are used, or if the modem cannot be configured by Windows (you must use jumpers to set its port and address), you will not be able to change the communications port assigned to this modem.

Speaker Volume The Speaker Volume control is a handy way to tell 32-bit Windows 95 communications programs how loud to set the volume of the modem's speaker.

The volume control slider works with modems that have physical speakers and with modems (such as PC Cards) that rely on the computer's speaker for their sound. If the volume control is grayed out, the modem has no speaker and no way of using the speaker in the computer. (Many ISDN Terminal Adapters will have the Speaker Volume grayed out.)

NOTE DOS and 16-bit Windows communications programs ignore the Speaker Volume setting; instead, they set modem volume themselves. These older programs set the volume themselves because when they were written, the operating system had no way to keep track of your preferences.

Maximum Speed The Maximum Speed parameter is extremely important. This setting has nothing to do with the speed at which your modem connects to another modem—it represents the speed at which your *computer* connects to your modem.

Why is this important? Any modem that operates at 9600 bps (formerly referred to as the baud) or faster typically supports data compression. The International Telecommunications Union (ITU), the professional society that sets worldwide communications standards, has established four data compression standards. Your modem may support one or all of these standards.

Table 3.2 shows the standards, the modem speed associated with each standard, and the port speed that you should use with your modem. These general guidelines work for almost all modems.

Table 3.2 Modem Port Speed Settings

Modem Speed	ITU Standard	Port Speed
9600	v.32	19,200
14400	v.32bis	57,600
19200	v.32ter	57,600
28800	v.34	115,200

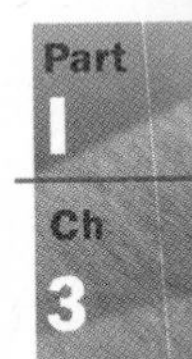

NOTE You may not be able to set the port speed as high as 115,200 on older, slower computers. These computers may not have the right type of serial port hardware, which is based on the type 16550A chip. In such a case, use 57,600.

When two modems that are using one of the ITU standards (or one of the older, but still widely used Microcom MNP compression standards) connect, the modems examine the data that they are sending to see whether it can be compressed. If so, the modems compress the data. Sending compressed data raises the effective speed of the modem. Modem speed can approach the speed of the port if the data can be greatly compressed.

See "Advanced Settings," **p. 89**

Compression works only if the port speed is fast enough to feed the data to the modem as quickly as the modem needs it. If a 14,400 v.32bis modem compresses data into half the space that the data takes up on disk, the port must feed data to the modem at least twice as fast as the 14,400 connect speed. Setting the port to 57,600 allows for the high-speed data feed to the modem and also takes care of some overhead for processing.

Only Connect at This Speed Check this box if you don't want your modem to adjust its speed to match the speed of the modem on the other end. Checking this box allows only high-speed connections between two high-speed modems.

Sometimes bad conditions on the telephone line can make two high-speed modems connect at low speeds. Checking this box prevents the low-speed connection from taking place. In that case, you will have to keep trying the call until the modems can connect at the highest speed.

Connection Properties To define the default modem settings used for new connections, open the Connection page of the Modems Control Panel, as shown in Figure 3.29.

FIG. 3.29
Use the Connection page to set your default modem connection settings.

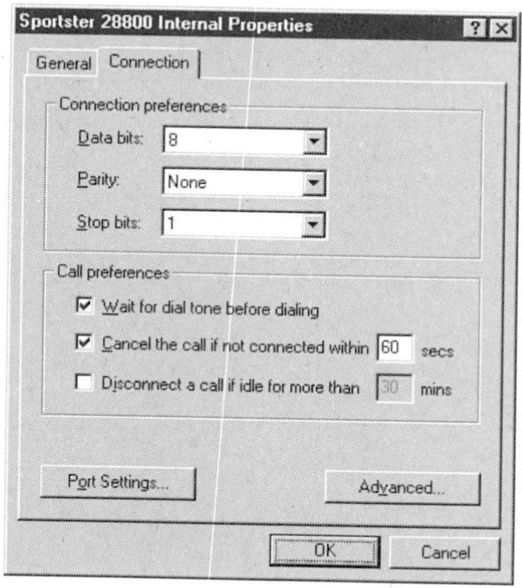

Connection Preferences The default settings—8 bits, no parity, and 1 stop bit—work for most online services, BBSs, remote access and remote control programs, data transfer services, dial-up networking, and so on. Change these settings only if the resource you are dialing requires different values.

Wait for Dial Tone Before Calling When this option is enabled, Windows cancels the connection if no dial tone is present when the modem tries to dial. Under normal circumstances, this option should be checked; however, uncheck it if you have any of the following situations:

- You have to dial the phone manually for your modem.
- You are using a phone system with a dial tone that your modem fails to detect.
- You want to speed up the dialing process by a few milliseconds so that the modem does not wait for a dial tone before dialing.

Cancel the Call If Not Connected Within X Seconds If the modem you are calling does not answer within 60 seconds, a problem may exist. When you choose this option, you are notified if your call did not connect so that you can check to see whether you have the right phone number. If 60 seconds is not long enough, type a longer duration in the text box.

Disconnect a Call If Idle for More than X Minutes This option can save you money if you use commercial online services regularly. If you get interrupted or called away from your computer, Windows disconnects from the service so you won't continue to accumulate expensive online charges.

Advanced Settings At the bottom of the Connection page is the Advanced button. When you click this button, you see the dialog box shown in Figure 3.30.

FIG. 3.30
Use the Advanced Connection Settings dialog box to configure modem error control, flow control, modulation, log files, and additional settings.

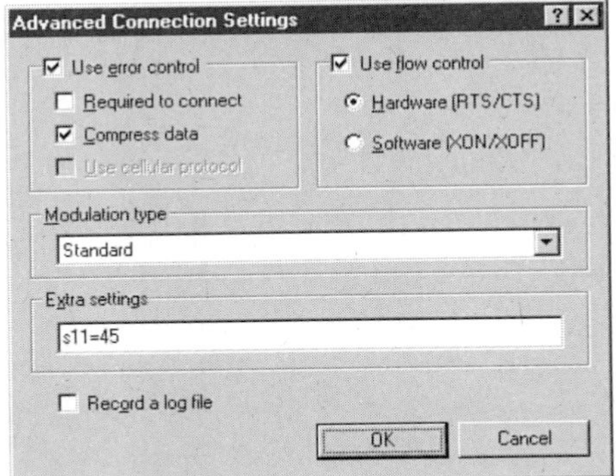

The Use Error Control, Compress Data, and Use Flow Control options in the Advanced Connection Settings dialog box work with one another and with the port speed setting in the General page of the Modem properties sheet.

Your choices in Advanced Connection Settings will determine if your modem will work as fast, and as reliably, as intended by its manufacturer.

Error Control For modems with data speeds of 9,600bps or faster, Windows turns on the Use Error Control option automatically. When using error control, such as V.42 or MNP 4, the receiving modem verifies data when it arrives. If a bad data transmission is detected, the receiving modem requests the data again.

When modems connect, they negotiate the highest level of error control and compression. If you don't want error control or compression, simply uncheck the Use Error Control check box. To insist that connections use error control, check the Required to Connect check box.

Check the Use Cellular Protocol check box if you use a cellular modem. The cellular error control protocol offers more robust connections for mobile communications moving between cells.

If your modem supports compression, such as the V.42bis or MNP 5 compression standards, choose the Compress Data option. MNP 5 offers 2X compression. MNP 5 doesn't sense when it is sending previously compressed data, such as a ZIP or GIF file, and results in slower effective throughput. Better, V.42bis offers 4× compression and senses when data has already been compressed. Refer to your modem manual to see what level of compression your modem supports.

Flow Control Use flow control to throttle data between your computer and the modem. If data buffers on either side become full, the receiving side will notify the sender to hold off for a moment. If you do not use flow control, data collisions occur resulting in garbled or illegible information.

In the Use Flow Control section of the dialog box, check the Use Flow Control check box and choose Hardware if you are using an internal or PC Card modem. You also should choose Hardware when using an external modem rated at 9,600bps or faster, but be sure you are using a hardware-handshaking cable that includes the necessary lines for the Request To Send/Clear To Send (RTS/CTS) handshake. If you don't choose Hardware, high port speeds can cause data overrun errors, and result in excessively slow throughput.

Choose Software if you cannot use Hardware flow control. Software flow control (also referred to as XON/XOFF flow control) uses byte sequences in the data of the connection, and can cause problems when transmitting binary files.

Modulation Type The Modulation Type setting controls how Windows handles connections at 300 and 1200bps. If you connect with an old modem at 300 or 1200bps, you have to decide whether to use U.S. or European standards. Bell works with American modems and CCITT V.21 works with modems in the rest of the world. If you want to connect to a CCITT V.21 or V.22 modem, make sure that your modem can use these standards.

NOTE American and European modems used different standards until 9600bps modems became popular. At that time, American manufacturers adopted the standards set by the CCITT (in English, the International Telegraph & Telephone Consultative Committee) and its successor, the ITU (International Telecommunications Union). Now modems all over the world can communicate at 9600bps and faster.

Extra Settings If you need to send the modem an AT command that Windows does not include automatically in its initialization procedure, type the command in the Extra Settings box.

Windows hides extra settings away in this obscure location because Windows architects believe the operating system should handle all details of communicating with the modem. The user should be isolated from sending raw AT commands. Because each brand of modem implements the AT command set differently, an AT command that works on one 28.8 Kbps modem may not work the same on any other brand of modem.

However, if you are certain about your modem's implementation of the AT command set, Extra Settings is the place to send additional commands at modem initialization time, just before the modem dials out.

For example, if you want to turn off the speaker completely on a Hayes modem, enter ATM0 (that's a zero after the M) in the Extra Settings dialog box.

Using Log Files If you repeatedly have trouble making a connection, tell Windows to keep a record of the commands that it sends to the modem and the replies from the modem. This record can be useful in troubleshooting the problem. You can look for responses from the modem that contain the word "ERROR" and see what commands caused the errors. To activate this feature, choose the Record a Log File option.

NOTE The log file is stored in the Windows directory as MODEMLOG.TXT. You can use Notepad to examine the log file.

When you are done making your choices in the Advanced Connection Settings dialog box, click OK. This returns you to the Modem properties sheet.

Understanding Your Modem and Your Telephone System

Dialing Properties is a new concept for Windows 95. Dialing Properties gives you a way to control how your calls are dialed. You can create and choose from a list of dialing locations, each of which can be in a different area code or country. Windows will still dial the modem properly. Finally, the system knows how to do these things!

Dialing Properties also works with your modem to tell it whether you need to dial an access code to get an outside line. It allows you to make a calling card call with your modem. Dialing Properties can disable call waiting so that your modem calls won't be interrupted by an incoming call. With Dialing Properties, you can also tell your modem whether it can use touch tones on your phone line or if the modem must use rotary pulse dialing.

To control Dialing Properties, choose Dialing Properties from the Modem properties sheet.

The preceding sections explain how some of the properties settings for your modem control the way that the modem call is made. So far, the only actual dialing parameter that you've given the modem is whether to use tone or pulse dialing.

Many of the things that a modem needs to do to complete a call depend on where you and your computer are. A modem that's being used at home, for example, usually dials differently from a modem that's being used in a hotel room or at the office. Knowing the phone number of the computer that you want to dial with the modem isn't enough—you also have area codes and outside line codes to deal with. In addition, you may want to make a credit card call.

These issues used to be problems. Windows 95, however, collects information from you so that communications programs handle these issues in a seamless, elegant fashion.

Figure 3.31 shows the Dialing properties sheet where you specify location information. This information tells your modem how to work wherever you go with your computer. If you are using your modem at home, where you don't need to dial a code for an outside line but do have the call-waiting feature, your settings may look like the ones shown in Figure 3.31.

FIG. 3.31
You can set location information in the Dialing properties sheet.

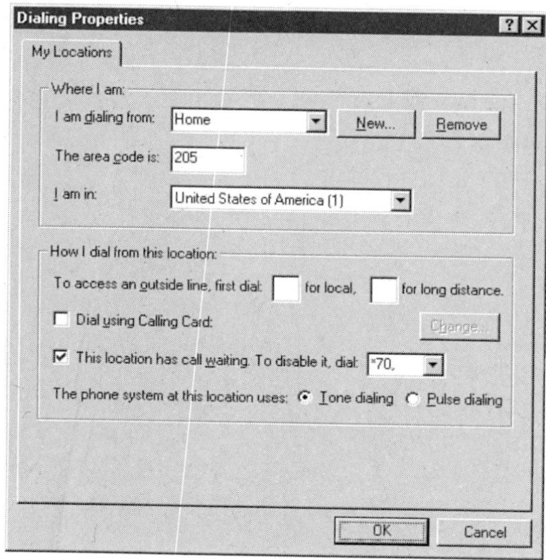

Suppose, however, that you're working in a hotel room in Washington, D.C.; that you need to dial 9 to get an outside line (or 91 to get a long distance outside line); and that you want to charge the call to a credit card.

To make a credit card call, you need to check the Dial Using Credit Card box. Your Dialing Properties settings would look like the ones shown in Figure 3.32.

FIG. 3.32
Making a calling card call with your modem is easy.

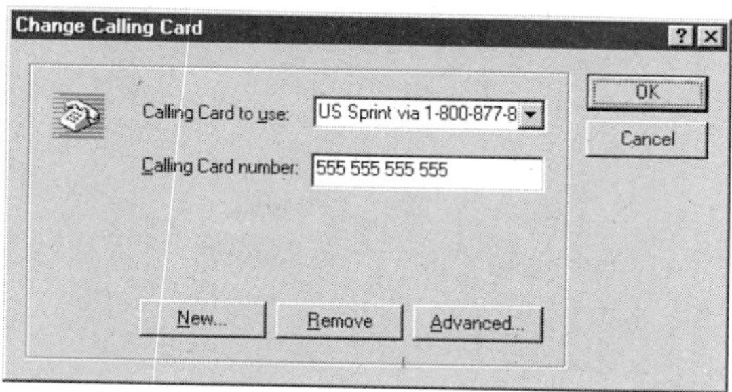

In the Dialing properties sheet, Windows has created your first Location for you, based on information you gave Setup during Windows installation. Windows has named this the Default Location.

Create additional locations by choosing New on the Dialing properties sheet. Name the Location and fill out the country and area code for the Location. You also can remove a location by choosing Remove.

▶ **See** "Working Smarter with TAPI and 32-Bit Windows Programs," **p. 96**

When you use a communications program that is TAPI-aware and Windows 95-aware, you can specify your location before dialing. Examples of programs that take advantage of Locations are Windows HyperTerminal; Windows Phone Dialer; the Microsoft Network online service; Microsoft Exchange; and any of Exchange's MAPI modules, such as CompuServe Mail and Dial-Up Networking.

To learn more about Microsoft Exchange and MAPI modules that use modems, see Chapter 26, "Using Microsoft Exchange and Messaging."

Getting Your Modem to Dial After you define your modem settings, you need to test the modem to verify that it dials properly. Phone Dialer, an accessory that comes with Windows 95, is a good program to perform the test. Run Phone Dialer by opening the Start menu, and choosing Programs, Accessories, Phone Dialer. Figure 3.33 shows the main Phone Dialer dialog box.

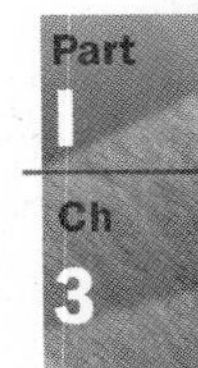

FIG. 3.33
Use Phone Dialer to test dial your modem.

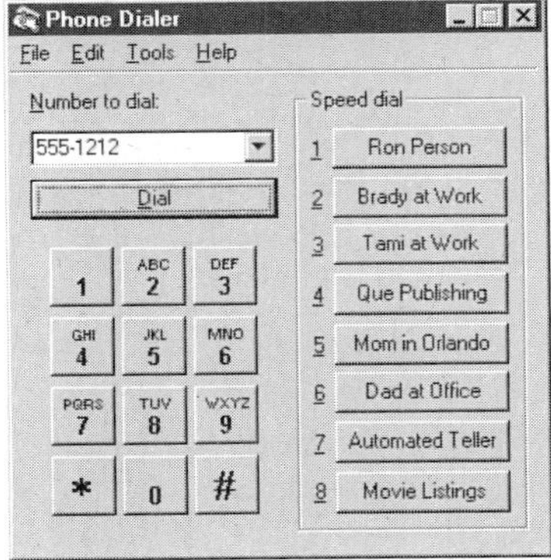

When you tell Phone Dialer to dial the number shown in the Number to Dial box, it knows how to handle the area code. Because you defined your location in Dialing Properties, Phone Dialer knows if you are dialing a number in the same area code as your computer; in that case, it leaves off the area code and dials the call as a local call, as shown in Figure 3.34. Phone Dialer also knows whether to dial 1 before the number, based on what you define as your dialing properties. When you must dial 1 and the area code for long distance calls in your same area code, select the Dial as a Long Distance Call check box in the Dialing properties sheet.

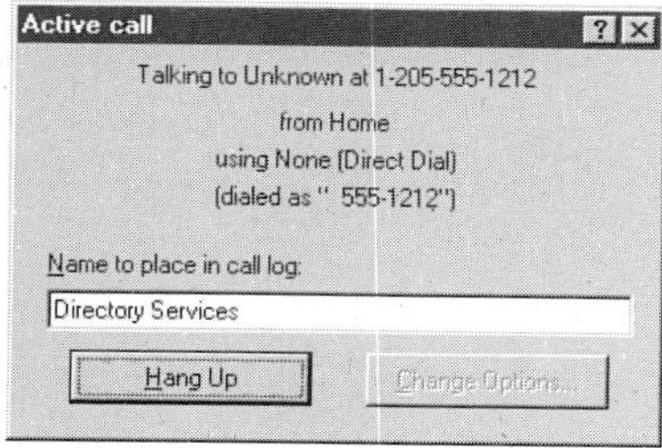

FIG. 3.34
When calling in the same area code, Windows dials only seven digits.

TROUBLESHOOTING

The modem won't dial. In the Modems Control Panel, check to see whether the modem displayed matches your model. If not, choose Add New Modem to install your modem. If any modems that are not in your system appear in the Control Panel, delete their entries.

In the System Control Panel, choose Device Manager. Choose Modems, select your modem, double-click to display the properties sheet, and click the General tab. The page shown in Figure 3.35 indicates that the device is used in the current configuration and that it is working properly.

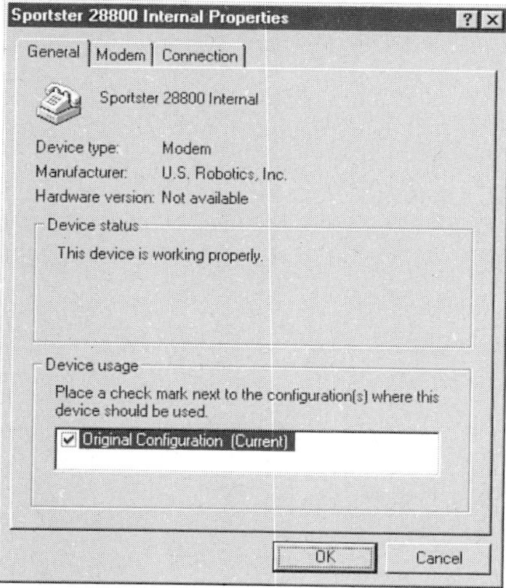

FIG. 3.35
Use Device Manager to see if your modem is working properly.

Make sure that the communications port is set correctly. Click the Modem tab, shown in Figure 3.36, and check the port name and port speed.

FIG. 3.36
Check the communications Port and Maximum Speed if your modem is not working properly.

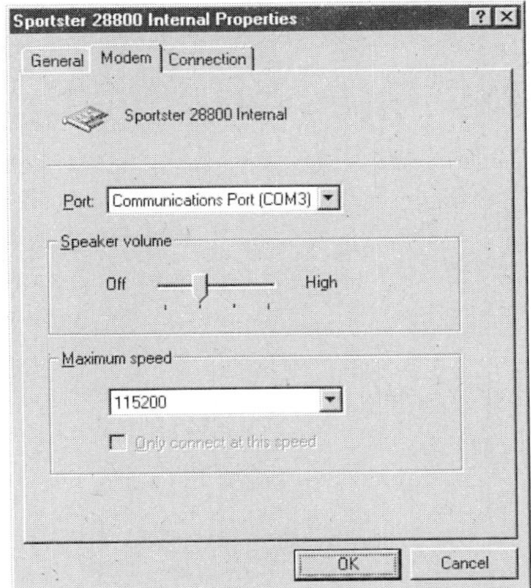

Make sure the port name matches the port that your application wants to use. If the port is set to COM2, for example, make sure your application is trying to use the modem on COM2.

You also can try lowering the port speed. Perhaps your serial port hardware does not support the selected speed. Try a range of speeds between the data speed of your modem and the maximum speed. Use the highest setting that works reliably.

If these suggestions do not work, use Windows built-in diagnostic tool that tests the communication from your computer to the modem. To use the modem diagnostic tool, start the Modems Control Panel. When the Modem properties sheet appears, click the Diagnostics tab.

Select your modem and choose More Info. Windows issues a series of interrogatory commands to the modem and notes the responses. Figure 3.37 shows sample results. Use the results to verify that the modem is responding to Windows commands. Also, some modems respond with their model number. Cross-check this with your modem settings. Refer to your modem reference manual for the meaning of the responses.

TROUBLESHOOTING

My modem connects, but it doesn't stay connected. If your phone line has call waiting, incoming calls may be throwing you offline. Use Dialing Properties to disable call waiting. You reach the Dialing properties sheet by choosing Dialing Properties from the Modem properties sheet.

If that doesn't work, flow control may be set incorrectly. For 9600bps and faster modems, make sure that flow control is set to Hardware.

To get to the flow control setting, use Control Panel, double-click the Modem icon, and then choose Properties. Click the Connection tab and then choose Advanced.

continues

continued

Also check all cables for quality by swapping them with cables that you know to be good; swap serial cables for external modems as well as your regular phone cables.

My Windows 95 application keeps dialing the wrong number. Check to see whether the Dialing Location properties are set correctly. To do this, open the Control Panel and double-click the Modem icon. Then click Dialing Properties. Make sure the entry in I Am Dialing From matches your location, and that the area code and country shown match where you are as well. If they don't, Windows 95 programs will be dialing phone numbers incorrectly.

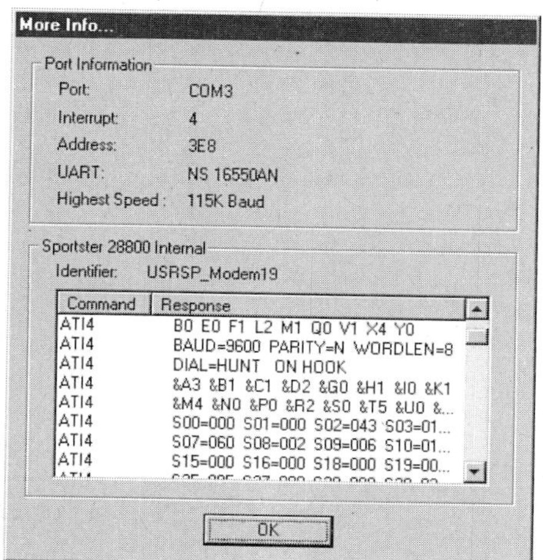

FIG. 3.37
Use Modem Diagnostics to show modem responses to basic information commands.

Working Smarter with TAPI and 32-Bit Windows Programs

Telephony Applications Programming Interface, or TAPI, lets your modem do more for you in Windows 95.

TAPI uses all the information that you gave Windows during the modem configuration process to set up not only your modem, but also all the 32-bit Windows 95 communications programs. Phone dialer, HyperTerminal, Microsoft Exchange, and Dial-Up Networking all share one modem because of TAPI. Communications programs that are written specifically for Windows 95 talk to TAPI, which issues appropriate commands to the modem. *Device independence* is the way Windows uses TAPI for all communications, instead of making each communications program learn to talk to every other modem. Device independence frees the program developer from having to know everything about your modem.

TAPI provides the following major benefits, which were covered earlier in the section "Understanding Your Modem and Your Telephone System."

- The capability to define locations to make dialing effortless
- Support for 16550A UART chips for better throughput

In addition, TAPI provides the following benefits, which are the subject of the following sections:

- Sharing of modems by applications
- Sharing fax modems over a network

Sharing a Modem Under TAPI You know the problem from Windows 3.1: Your system has one modem, which is used for data and for faxes, and you want to leave the modem under the control of the fax program so that the modem is ready for incoming faxes. When you try to make a data call with the modem, however, an error message appears, telling you that the port is already in use. You have to disable the fax program, use the data program, and re-enable the fax program.

Now suppose that you are using Windows 95. At 3 P.M., Microsoft Fax is waiting for an incoming fax to arrive. At the same time, the CompuServe Mail driver in Microsoft Exchange is scheduled to check CompuServe to see whether any new mail has arrived. Without missing a beat, TAPI allows the mail driver to use the modem; then TAPI hands modem control back to Microsoft Fax. The importance and convenience of this cooperation cannot be overstated.

TROUBLESHOOTING

My Windows 95 communications programs work fine, but I can't access the modem with a DOS or old Windows communications program. How can I make my legacy communications programs work? You ran into the TAPI gotcha. TAPI works only if all the communications programs you will be using are TAPI-aware, 32-bit, Windows 95 programs. If Microsoft Fax is waiting for an incoming fax or Dial-Up Networking is waiting for an incoming call, DOS and old Windows programs cannot access the modem; this capability is reserved for TAPI-enabled Windows 95 applications.

Sharing a Fax Modem over a Network TAPI allows any user on a Windows 95 network to send faxes via another network user's fax modem. The user who has the fax modem enables the modem as a shared device; TAPI does the rest.

NOTE Data modems cannot be shared over a network.

Understanding File Transfer Errors

Errors occur in file transfers with DOS and old Windows programs. Fortunately, you can track them down and fix them.

If you're using DOS and Windows 3.1 communications programs, you've probably upgraded from Windows 3.1 to Windows 95. There are settings in the old Windows 3.1 SYSTEM.INI file that can cause problems in your new installation of Windows 95.

To correct these problems, some manual editing of SYSTEM.INI may be necessary. You can use NOTEPAD.EXE to perform these tasks.

In the [boot] section of your SYSTEM.INI file, make sure there is a line that states COMM.DRV=COMM.DRV. If it doesn't, edit it so it does.

This will make sure Windows 95 is using its own communications driver for older, 16-bit programs.

In the [386Enh] section, make sure a line exists that says DEVICE=*VCD. If you don't see DEVICE=*VCD, type it on a line by itself anywhere in the [386Enh] section. Use NOTEPAD.EXE to do this.

Next, set the FIFO buffer to 512 bytes. Determine the communications port that you're using with these DOS and old Windows programs. If the port is COM2, for example, add the line COM2BUFFER=512 in the [386Enh] section of your SYSTEM.INI file. Use the same syntax for other ports. You can add COM2BUFFER=512 on a line by itself, anywhere in the [386Enh] section of SYSTEM.INI. You can use NOTEPAD.EXE to do this.

CHAPTER 4

Configuring Multimedia Windows 95

Working with the video tools in Windows 95

A discussion of video compression/ decompression drivers in Windows, including MPEG video.

Understanding video file formats

DirectVideo technology: what it is and how to take advantage of it.

Learning how to install and configure sound boards

Look here for the procedures and pitfalls for installing sound hardware.

Windows 95 sound capabilities

A guide to WAVs, CODECs, and MIDI files.

Using Windows 95 sound accessories

Make the most of your sound card with the software built into Windows 95.

Installing a CD-ROM Drive

Windows 95 makes the task easier than it used to be.

Using your CD-ROM drive with Windows and other applications

Details on using AutoPlay, installing from the CD, and sharing a CD-ROM across a network.

Microsoft has touted Windows 95 as a true multimedia operating system, and for good reason. Today, most PCs sold come equipped with a CD-ROM drive and sound board. Not surprisingly, the number of CD-ROM titles sold for these systems has skyrocketed, and much of the hardware and CD-ROM titles have been designed to deliver compelling graphics, video, and sound. With Windows 95, Microsoft has ensured that it will be a dominant player in multimedia computing.

With this move towards multimedia, it is vital that you know how to work with the multimedia features in Windows 95. You may have purchased a computer system that came with all the multimedia components preinstalled. In this case, you are ready to go and won't need to bother learning how to install these components. However, if you are upgrading your system to make it multimedia-capable or need to modify multimedia components, this chapter has instructions on how to install these components.

Once your multimedia system is up and running, you will want to learn how to work with multimedia in Windows 95. This chapter shows you how to use the multimedia applications that come with Windows 95 and get the most out of your multimedia experience.

Optimizing Video and Animation

Windows 95 has certainly given a boost to digital video. The 32-bit architecture of Windows 95 helps streamline video playback and eliminate pesky resource problems. Better yet, Windows 95 puts video capability directly into the operating system, which means that virtually anyone who has Windows 95 is able to work with AVI files.

At the core of Windows-based video is the Media Control Interface, or MCI. MCI is an architecture that gives programs a standard, script-based interface to Windows multimedia resources, such as the Media Player, video playback windows, and audio controls. In addition, MCI enables programmatic control of video and audio so that development tools like Visual Basic, or even application macro scripts, can invoke and control video playback and editing. MCI is also at the core of object linking and embedding (OLE) video clips, where video clips are played within OLE-aware documents such as spreadsheets.

Beyond MCI and the familiar Media Player interface, users will notice that the device and video compression drivers needed to work with video are all preinstalled in Windows 95. As a result, you can distribute AVI video files to virtually any Windows 95 user and be assured that the file can be played back.

Working with the Video Tools in Windows 95

Windows 95 puts a wealth of video-centric tools into the hands of PC users. To help you get up to speed, here is a rundown of their operation.

The Video Properties Box The properties sheet for AVI files displays valuable data that can help you optimize video playback. Right-click any AVI file in an Explorer or Browser window, and select Properties from the context menu. You'll see a tabbed sheet that opens to the General page. Here, you're able to browse all the usual file information, like file name, size, and creation date.

Click the Details tab. Here you'll see the length of the video clip, the audio compression and fidelity, as well as the compression scheme, resolution, color depth, and frame rates of the clip (see Figure 4.1). It even provides the data rate, in KB/Sec (kilobytes per second), so you can tell if your CD-ROM drive is up to the task of playing the clip.

You also can preview the AVI file from the properties sheet. Click the Preview tab and you'll see the opening frame of the video (see Figure 4.2). To view the video, click the play button or drag the slider control to move through the clip.

Using the Windows 95 Media Player The Media Player is the multimedia headquarters for Windows 95 and closely resembles the application found in Windows 3.1. One key exception: This Media Player is a 32-bit application with all the advantages and benefits that implies.

Media Player supports a wide variety of formats such as Video for Windows video (AVI), sound (WAV), MIDI (MID), animation (FLC and FLI), and CD audio. It also accepts driver updates that let it support a variety of other formats including QuickTime for Windows MOV files, MPEG video files, and other media types.

To play videos with Media Player, double-click an AVI file in an Explorer or Browser window. Media Player loads the AVI file and immediately starts playing it.

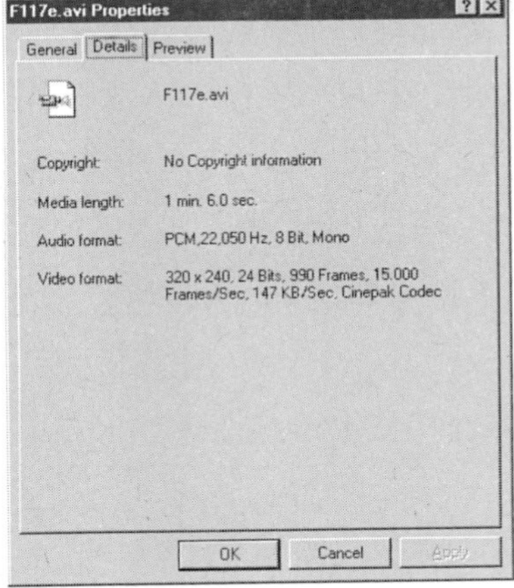

FIG. 4.1
The Details page reveals information such as data rates, color depth, and resolution.

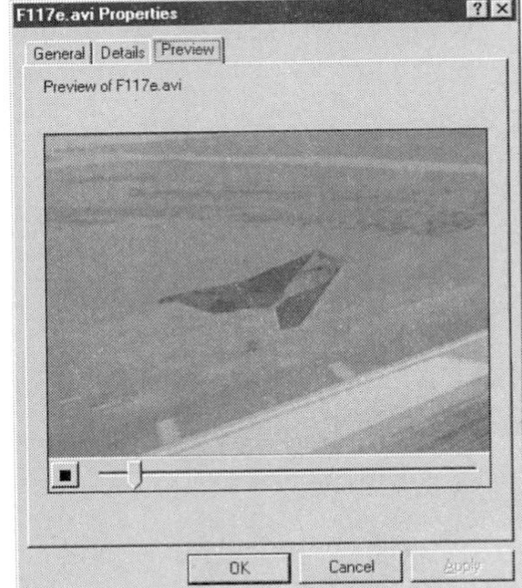

FIG. 4.2
The Preview page lets you sample AVI files.

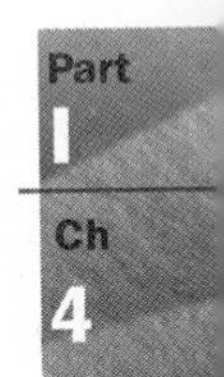

NOTE The numbered hot key for selections beneath the Device menu vary depending on what multimedia drivers are loaded onto your system.

You can open an AVI file from Media Player by following these steps:

1. Choose Device, then click the Video for Windows option.
2. Select an AVI file in the Open dialog box, then click Open.
3. Click the play button in Media Player (see Figure 4.3).

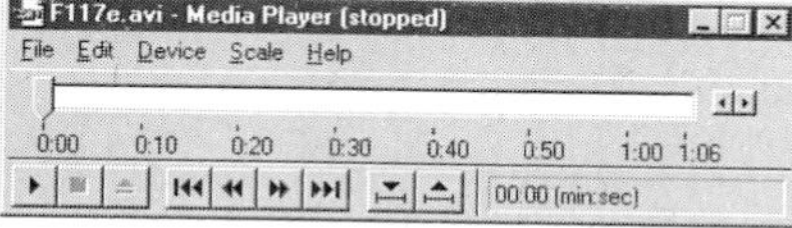

FIG. 4.3
The Windows 95 Media Player uses simple, VCR-like controls.

When a video is playing, the play button changes to a pause button. You can stop the video by clicking the stop button or pause the video by clicking the pause button. To fast forward or rewind the video, click the double-arrow buttons. You also can advance to the beginning and end of a clip or section of video by clicking the Previous Mark and Next Mark controls. Finally, the Scroll Forward and Scroll Backward buttons just to the right of the slider bar allow you to do single-frame playback, which is great for finding a specific frame.

When you double-click a video file to play it with Media Player, the video appears in a window without the Media Player controls. You can call up the Media Player controls while watching a video by double-clicking the movie's title bar.

Sizing Video Windows Media Player gives you the option of playing back a video clip at various sizes. Although you can stretch a video window by grabbing it by the edge, doing so may distort the original image.

Most AVI clips measure either 320×240 or 160×120 pixels, an aspect ratio of 4:3. To change the video window size while preserving the aspect ratio, go to Media Player's properties sheet by choosing Device, Properties.

Click the Windows drop-down list box to see the available selection of window sizes for video playback (see Figure 4.4). You can select from Double original size, 1/16 of screen size, 1/4 of screen size, 1/2 of screen size, and Maximized. The monitor image in the Video properties sheet shows an approximation of what the resized video will look like, complete with blocky pixelation.

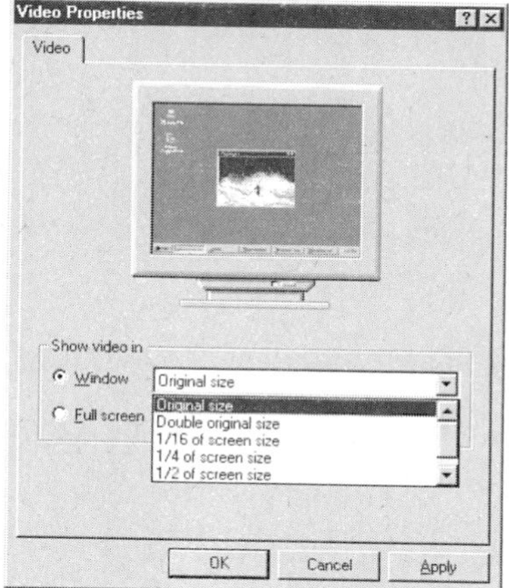

FIG. 4.4
Expand and shrink video windows from the Video properties sheet.

You can vary the size of a video in four increments by selecting Ctrl+1 (normal) through Ctrl+4 (full-screen), while the movie's window is selected.

Unless you have video-enhancing hardware and drivers for Windows 95, you usually get the best results by playing videos at Original size. Stretching or shrinking video forces the CPU to do additional processing, causing lost frames.

If you want the best full screen video, click the Full screen option button and not the Maximized setting on the drop-down list. Windows 95 can streamline video playback when it does not have to manage graphical user interface (GUI).

Working Scale Settings When Media Player plays a video clip, it uses a frame- or time-based scale to measure progress. This scheme lets you find specific points in the video so you can easily edit, play, or copy selected parts of video files. For example, a frame-based scale lets you perform frame-accurate video editing and tracking. To have Media Player display the scale by frames, choose Scale, Frames. To have the scale expressed in minutes and seconds, choose Scale, Time. The display beneath the video progress slider bar changes to reflect the new setting. You can even do this while a clip is playing.

Setting Playback Options You can customize the look and function of a video window during playback with Media Player. For instance, you can set a video to play back continually so that it starts again at the beginning once it finishes playing. Choose Edit, Options (or press Ctrl+O) to see the Options dialog box (see Figure 4.5).

FIG. 4.5 You can control the look and behavior of video clips in the Media Player's Options dialog box.

When checked, the controls in this dialog box allow you to do the following:

- **Auto Rewind** queues the video clip back to the beginning after the clip finishes playing.
- **Auto Repeat** forces the clip to play in a loop until the user stops playback.
- **Control Bar On Playback** puts start/stop and slider bar controls on video files embedded into other applications using the OLE object linking and embedding technology of Windows.

- **Caption** lets you change the text that appears in the control bar on OLE-embedded video clips.
- **Border around object** draws a border around an embedded video while it plays.
- **Play in client document** lets the embedded video run inside the OLE application document without invoking a separate video window.
- **Dither picture to VGA colors** if the color in a video clip looks distorted.

Controlling the Volume If a clip is too loud for your tastes, you can adjust the volume by choosing Device, Volume Control. The Windows 95 Volume Control dialog box appears with slider controls to handle the volume, balance, and mute settings for all the various audio inputs and outputs.

You also can adjust volume by clicking the speaker icon located in the taskbar, invoking a slider control that adjusts volume.

Inserting Video Objects in a Document You can use Media Player to cut and paste a portion of a video into a document. You can then play the video by double-clicking it. To copy a portion of a video to your document, do the following:

1. Position the trackbar thumb on the starting frame of the portion of the video you want to copy.
2. Click the Start Selection button.
3. Position the trackbar thumb on the last frame of the portion you want to copy.
4. Click the End Selection button.
5. Select Edit, Copy Object to copy that portion of the video to the Clipboard.
6. Open the document and paste the video clip by choosing Edit, Paste.

When you double-click the object in the document, the video clip plays.

If you want to deselect the clip, select Edit, Selection from Media Player's menu. Then select None and click OK.

Media Player Secrets There are many features in Media Player that you won't find in the interface or the Help file. Some of these features can help you understand and take advantage of video on your multimedia PC.

For example, pressing Ctrl+F5 when the Media Player application is open invokes the Send MCI String Command dialog box. From here, you can enter a variety of powerful text commands to play, adjust, or get information on video files. Here's a quick list of Media Player secrets:

- **Count frames**: Media Player tracks how many frames drop during playback. To see how many frames dropped after a clip has played, press Ctrl+F5 to invoke the MCI String Command dialog box (see Figure 4.6). Type **status frames skipped** in the Command box and click Send. You'll see how many frames were dropped during video playback.

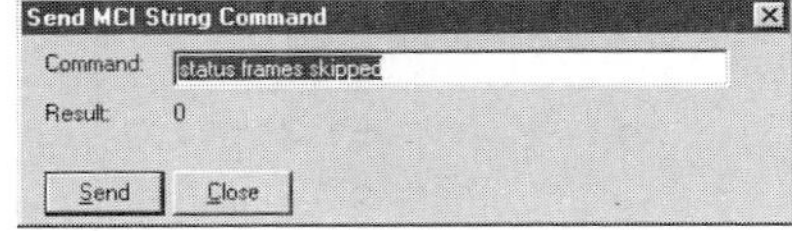

FIG. 4.6
Use the status frames skipped MCI call to see how many frames were dropped during playback.

- **More MCI command tricks**: You can type other commands in the Command dialog box that appears after pressing Ctrl+F5. For example, to pause a video, press Ctrl+F5 and type **pause**. You also can type **stop**, **play**, and **close** in the MCI String Command dialog box.
- **Drag-and-drop video**: Media Player won't look at your CD-ROM drive for video by default, thus forcing you to do lots of pointing and clicking. Take a shortcut by dragging the icon of an AVI file in a Browser or Explorer window onto the Media Player application. You'll now see the mouse cursor with a plus sign. Release the button and the file opens and begins playing right away in the background.
- **Compact video playback**: With a video window open, double-click the Media Player application title bar. You'll get a consolidated video window (without a separate Media Player window) that includes pause buttons, a start/stop button, and a slider bar (see Figure 4.7).

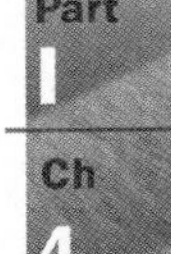

FIG. 4.7
The consolidated video window saves screen space.

- **Change video size**: This tip is particularly useful when using the compact playback window. Expand a video window to full screen by pressing Ctrl+4 and return to original size by pressing Ctrl+1. Ctrl+2 doubles the window size and Ctrl+3 quadruples it.

TROUBLESHOOTING

When I attempt to play an .AVI file, I see a message like, "Video not available, cannot find 'vids:cvid' decompressor." This is an indication that the codec needed to play this movie is not installed. Open the Control Panel and double-click the Add/Remove Programs icon. In the Windows Setup page, click Multimedia and then click Details. Select the Video Compression check box and choose OK. Close the Add/Remove Programs page to install the codecs.

continues

continued

If you want to play a movie compressed with specialized hardware or a third party codec, you'll have to install the appropriate hardware or contact the manufacturer for a specialized decompressor.

When I attempt to play an .AVI file, I see a message like, "MMSYSTEM266: The device could not be loaded. Verify the driver is installed correctly." You need to reinstall several Multimedia files that have been lost or corrupted. Unfortunately, the Add/Remove Programs tool won't capture them if you simply reinstall the Multimedia components. Instead, you need to run the Windows 95 Setup from within Windows 95 by selecting Run from the Start menu and typing **Setup**. When prompted, choose to copy all the Windows files again.

OSR 2

Using ActiveMovie With the release of Internet Browser 3.0, Microsoft introduced ActiveMovie technology to Windows multimedia. ActiveMovie gives Windows the capability to play back all standard video and audio formats, including MPEG and QuickTime. (See "Understanding Video File Formats and Compression," in the next section for more on video file formats.) ActiveMovie also supports ActiveMovie Streaming Format (ASF). This enables audio and video files to begin playing immediately instead of waiting until the entire multimedia has downloaded. Another benefit of ActiveMovie is that the DirectX technology, discussed later in this chapter, is integrated into ActiveMovie, allowing enhanced video playback on systems that have the hardware to take advantage of this technology.

ActiveMovie is available in two ways, depending upon your version of Windows and Internet Explorer. If you want to use Internet Explorer 3, download Internet Explorer 3 from the Microsoft Web site. As you do, you are given the option of also installing ActiveMovie. If your computer has the OEM Service Release 2 version of Windows 95 (OSR2) installed, ActiveMovie is incorporated into Windows.

ActiveMovie is the default player in the OSR2 release of Windows 95 and is the player used to play back videos when you double-click a video file. Even if your computer uses OSR2 you can still open Media Player from the Accessories, Multimedia submenu in the Start menu and use it to play your video files. Note that Media Player will not play back MPEG files.

The advantage to Media Player is that it gives you much more control over your playback, as described in the previous sections. The ActiveMovie component that comes with OSR2 and Internet Explorer 3.0 only has Play, Pause, and Stop controls.

To use ActiveMovie, double-click the video file you want to view in My Computer or Explorer or click Start, Programs, Accessories, Multimedia, ActiveMovie Control. The ActiveMovie control appears on screen with the Open dialog box overlaying it. Select the file you want to view and choose Open. You can pause and stop the video as it plays and view the elapsed time in the box at the bottom of the viewer.

NOTE If you have a newer computer, purchased after the fall of 1996, it probably came with the OSR2 version of Windows installed. If not, there are ways to upgrade to OSR2. To find out more about the OSR2 release of Windows 95 and how to install it on your computer, see "Installing the Windows 95b (OSR2) Service Release," in Chapter 2.

ON THE WEB

To download ActiveMovie from the Web, visit the following URL:

http://www.microsoft.com/IE/download

Understanding Video File Formats and Compression

Digital video puts excessive strain on the most powerful PCs. Video files consist of a long string of color images, which are played one after the other in rapid succession to create the illusion of fluid motion. For digital video, 30 frames per second is considered full motion, although many video clips are recorded at 15 or 24 frames per second to ease playback. Also, don't forget the work that goes into synchronizing the audio that goes with each video image.

Some standard file formats and compression technologies were needed to enable digital video. Standards, however, could not overcome the challenge of managing so much data. For that, technologies had to be created that took the pressure off the PC's CPU. In 1992, Video for Windows 1.0 helped establish some key standards. More recently, the PC platform has embraced the elements needed to enhance video.

Understanding Video File Formats To handle this flood of data, video file formats were needed that gave the PC a place to start. Today, there are a variety of video formats. Among those you are most likely to encounter are: Video for Windows (AVI), QuickTime for Windows (MOV), MPEG (MPG), and Motion JPEG (MJG). These video formats are described next.

Audio Visual Interleave—AVI The standard video file format for Windows is called *AVI*, which stands for Audio Visual Interleaved. AVI is the most common Windows video file format and can be played back on virtually any PC running Windows 3.11 or later.

As the name suggests, the audio data and video data are meshed together in the file, allowing systems to synchronize sound and images. Ironically, video playback is slaved to the audio track, ensuring that you always hear all of the audio, even if your system drops video frames. Although you can still make sense of a video that drops even a majority of its frames, the loss of audio data makes it impossible to understand what's being presented. For this reason, even when frames are lost, the soundtrack goes on uninterrupted—except in extreme cases.

AVI video files can be compressed using a variety of schemes, including Intel's Indeo, Radius' Cinepak, and Microsoft's Video 1. Whereas each of these produces a video with distinctive characteristics, the AVI format itself is unchanged. You can play the video, provided that you have the proper decompression driver (Windows 95 ships with all of these).

Apple's QuickTime Video for Windows—MOV Apple made a splash in the video world with its QuickTime technology, which multimedia developers snatched up for use in their titles. When Apple developed QuickTime for Windows, it immediately became a force on the PC because so many multimedia titles used QuickTime as their video format. QuickTime for Windows files generally carry the MOV extension. Although Windows 95 does not ship with QuickTime drivers, a large percentage of multimedia titles use QuickTime video so they will install the drivers during setup.

Like AVI files, QuickTime MOV files can be compressed using a variety of compression schemes, although Radius' Cinepak is generally the most popular. The QuickTime drivers include tools for handling decompression, so as long as you have QuickTime installed, you should be able to play back MOV files (see Figure 4.8).

FIG. 4.8
Select the Advanced tab of the Multimedia properties sheet to see if QuickTime for Windows is installed.

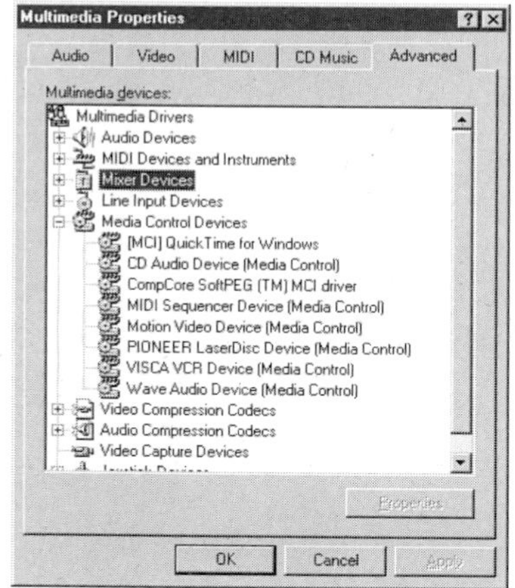

NOTE To see if your system is QuickTime-ready, click the Multimedia icon in the Control Panel; then click the Advanced tab, and click the plus sign next to Media Control Devices. You should see an entry called (MCI) QuickTime for Windows. If you don't, you need to install QuickTime before MOV files can be played.

The Next Big Thing in Video—MPEG MPEG video is being hyped as the next big thing in multimedia. Unlike Video for Windows and QuickTime for Windows, MPEG is both a file format and a codec scheme. MPEG videos are crunched down to a very small size using the MPEG compression scheme, which does all sorts of mathematics and interframe comparisons. The result is video of much higher visual quality than other schemes, yet uses a tiny 150 kilobits per second (kb/sec) of data—low enough to run off a single-speed CD-ROM drive. But MPEG is very complex, and high-end PCs have only recently reached the level where they can play back MPEG video without expensive add-in cards.

NOTE As with QuickTime, you can check the Advanced page of the Multimedia properties sheet for MPEG drivers. Click the plus sign next to Media Control Devices and look for an entry that refers to MPEG.

To get MPEG playback capability, you need one of several MPEG software players. Xing, Mediamatics, and CompCore all sell MPEG player software that you can purchase. In addition, many graphics boards come with MPEG player software as part of their bundle. Those with Pentium-75 or slower machines should buy a dedicated MPEG add-in board to get acceptable MPEG performance.

NOTE If you have the OEM Service Release 2 (OSR2) version of Windows installed on your system, you now have MPEG playback capability with the new ActiveMovie application. OSR2 comes with several MPEG codecs.

Understanding Video Compression Schemes (codecs) The only way digital video can be played on a PC is to reduce the amount of data required to store and move it. Video compression/decompression algorithms, referred to as *codecs*, do just that, reducing streams of full color images into compact code. Your system's CPU must decode the compressed video before it can be displayed to screen, a time-consuming task that often results in dropped frames.

NOTE Don't confuse video codecs with video file formats. A file format like AVI or MOV can often be compressed using a number of codecs. For example, AVI files can be compressed using Indeo, Cinepak, Video1, and TrueMotion codecs, just to name a few.

Unlike file compression utilities like PKZip or Stacker, video compression schemes actually throw out a good deal of image data to achieve compact file sizes. For this reason, video codecs are referred to as "lossy," whereas file compressors are referred to as "lossless."

NOTE Whereas lossless compression schemes like PKZip achieve compression ratios of about 2:1, lossy video compression schemes can shrink files sizes by 100 times or more, for ratios of 100:1.

Video codecs save a great deal of space by discarding redundant data. For example, MPEG only saves changes that occur between video frames instead of storing all the data in every single frame. In addition, codecs can discard color, brightness, and other visual data because much of the detail is not actually visible to the human eye. However, most software codecs, such as Indeo and Cinepak, must throw out a great deal of visual information to achieve data rates of about 300 Kbps. The result is grainy video and visual artifacts such as banding and color distortion.

Before your system can decompress a video file, you need to have a driver installed that lets the system know how to do it. To see if you have drivers installed to handle, for example, Cinepak video, go back to the Multimedia properties sheet in Control Panel's Multimedia icon. Click the Advanced tab and then click the plus (+) sign next to Video Compression Codecs. You'll see a list of installed codecs (see Figure 4.9).

Among the most common video codecs are:

- Indeo
- Cinepak
- Video 1
- RLE
- TrueMotion
- MPEG
- Motion JPEG

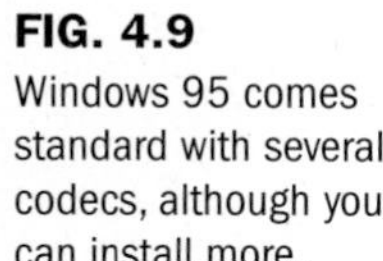

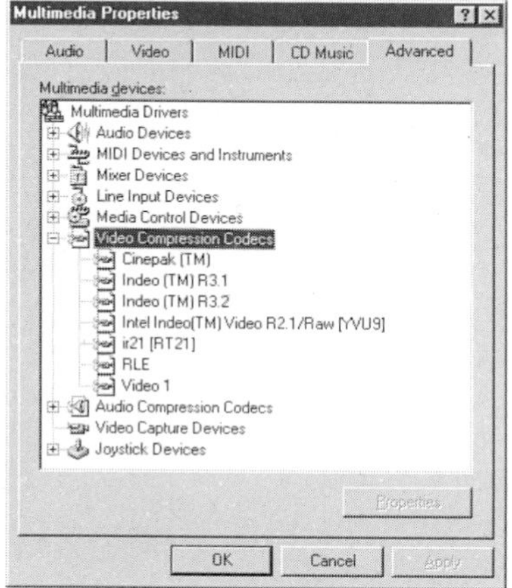

FIG. 4.9
Windows 95 comes standard with several codecs, although you can install more.

Intel Indeo 3.2 Intel's Indeo codec was among the first on the PC and is among the most prevalent. Indeo 3.2 is included with Windows 95, making it a universal playback compression scheme. To play an Indeo-compressed AVI file, you need to open the file from Media Player. Media Player automatically detects the codec used to compress the file and invokes the Indeo driver to decode it. Indeo is generally favored for video clips that contain less motion and activity that are used for clips such as interviews and speeches.

Radius Cinepak 8.02 Cinepak was developed by Radius and is also bundled with Windows 95. The Cinepak codec is popular with title vendors because it is able to compress high action sequences without too much loss of visual quality and CPU effort. However, the latest release of Indeo (3.2) has largely closed the performance gap. Cinepak-compressed files can be found in both Video for Windows and QuickTime for Windows files.

Microsoft Video 1 Microsoft Video 1 was included in the first Video for Windows release in 1992, but it lacks the sophistication to handle rich, full-color video. Although the Video 1 codec works well for animation and other simple video compression tasks, it is limited to 8-bit color and lacks interframe compression.

MPEG The original release of Windows 95 did not include support for MPEG. However, the OSR2 release of Windows does include MPEG codecs and ActiveMovie, a video player that is capable of playing back MPEG files. Users of the original version of Windows 95 can get MPEG playback by purchasing a separate playback utility from companies like Xing, CompCore, and Mediamatics, or they can download ActiveMovie from Microsoft's Web site.

Many graphics boards come bundled with MPEG playback software. Check your board's software for MPEG video drivers.

NOTE If your system has the Windows 95 OEM Service Release 2 (OSR2) version of Windows installed, the new ActiveMovie technology, which was released with Internet Browser 3.0, is now incorporated into Windows. You can use ActiveMovie to play back all the standard video and audio formats, including MPEG. ActiveMovie is the default multimedia in OSR2 instead of Media Player. You can also download ActiveMovie as a separate component. See "Using ActiveMovie," earlier in this chapter, for more information on ActiveMovie.

The secret to MPEG is its complex interframe compression, where only changes between frames are stored in the MPEG video file. The problem is that this scheme requires a lot of processing horsepower, which is why it takes a Pentium-90 PC (or better) to handle MPEG adequately in software. Older systems can play back MPEG video using an add-in card, such as the RealMagic Rave or Number Nine MPEG-Plus, to handle the decompression.

The Editor's Choice—Motion JPEG Motion JPEG, like MPEG, is both a file format and a codec. Actually, Motion JPEG is an outgrowth of the JPEG (Joint Photographic Experts Group) file format, which is a popular still-image compression scheme for files posted on the Internet. Motion JPEG's main appeal is to video artists and editors because every frame is compressed individually. By contrast, MPEG compression stores only the changes that occur between frames of video—so if you want to go back and edit a frame, it's likely that some visual data is missing.

Video capture boards such as the Reveal VideoStudio Pro and miroVideo DC-20 capture to Motion JPEG format. Files compressed to Motion JPEG format often look better than QuickTime or Video for Windows clips but require more CPU and greater data bandwidth. The files, however, can be recompressed to AVI or MOV, although video quality will likely degrade.

The Future of Codecs: MPEG-2 New codecs are constantly being developed and updated to meet the needs of digital video. MPEG-1, for example, has a big brother by the name of MPEG-2, which is a broadcast-quality compression scheme used with DSS services such as DirecTV. MPEG-2 excels where MPEG-1 breaks down—for instance, in the display of high action sequences where the efficiencies of interframe compression are lost. But MPEG-2 requires 10 times the bandwidth of MPEG-1—as much as 1.5Mbps—meaning that current CD-ROM drives are unable to keep up. In addition, MPEG-2's large file sizes mean that CD-ROM discs could only hold scant minutes of MPEG-2 video. For this reason, MPEG-2 is likely to remain a consumer video codec until PC users adopt super-density compact discs with several gigabytes of storage capacity.

The Future of Codecs: Indeo Video Interactive Perhaps more relevant is Intel's Indeo Video Interactive, also known as Indeo 4.0. This intriguing codec breaks with the past by adopting a wavelet-based compression scheme that reduces access times and visual artifacts. Intel has claimed—and some independent CD-ROM title developers have confirmed—that Indeo 4.0 can challenge MPEG video for visual quality. However, like MPEG, Indeo 4.0 needs a Pentium CPU to handle the complex decompression. It's also unclear if Indeo 4.0 can actually match MPEG quality at the low 150 Kbps data rate that MPEG maintains.

Indeo 4.0 provides powerful streaming and branching technologies that enable video to be used in interactive games. For example, multiple video streams can be played on a single display—providing, say, a simultaneous rear view video while the player looks forward. The format also enables much faster access so video can be employed in fast action games without annoying delays. These features could turn Indeo 4.0 into *the* codec for Windows 95.

Finally, Indeo 4.0 includes powerful chromakey and overlay support. For example, Indeo 4.0 videos do not have to be constrained to a video window. Instead, video images can float on the Windows desktop and interact with other Windows elements. These features provide exciting new opportunities for hobbyists and publishers alike.

Windows Video Primer: DirectVideo and Other Nifty Things in Windows 95

To lessen the load, video files are compressed down to smaller sizes to conserve disc space, ease bus traffic, and enable higher frame rates. In fact, without compression, video playback would be impossible on even the most powerful PCs. Compression has its own costs because the CPU must take time to decode the encoded video stream.

There's more to playing digital video than simply decompression. The CPU also must handle a variety of other tasks to turn an encoded pile of bits into a smooth train of images that make video:

- **Decompression**: The encoded video file is reassembled by the CPU using the appropriate driver, such as an Indeo, Cinepak, or MPEG decoder. Some compression/decompression schemes require a great deal of computing power but yield better looking images at lower data rates.
- **Color space conversion**: To save disc space, the color data in video files is usually saved using a compact format called YUV, which is optimized to the sensitivities of the human eye. This YUV color data must be converted to the standard RGB (Red, Green, Blue) format recognized by graphics cards and monitors. Color space conversion can take up to 30 percent of the CPU processing time during video playback.

NOTE YUV represents luminance, hue, and saturation and is a method for composing color video signals that was originally applied to television broadcasting. The main advantage of YUV color is that it is much more compact than the RGB format used by computers.

- **Image scaling**: This step occurs when the user changes the size of the video window from its original size. Often, 320×240 pixel videos are displayed at full screen to ease viewing. However, the CPU must calculate and create all the new pixels that appear in the image, which further strains the system. In addition, the image that results appears blocky and pixelated because the CPU simply replicates pixels to fill in the larger window.

Improved Video Performance The big problem with video is that it's, well, *big*. Really big. Consider: A modest video saved at 320×240 pixels and 15 frames per second would push 3M of data per second through your system if played uncompressed. Even with compression, video floods your system with data, taxing your CD-ROM drive, clogging the system bus, and pushing your processor to the limit. When these demands outstrip your PC, Windows has no choice but to drop frames to keep up.

A number of recent performance enhancements make it possible for Windows 95 to play back 320×240 video files at 30 frames per second. Even better, these videos can be stretched up to 640×480 pixels and beyond, and still enjoy smooth motion, provided you have the right drivers and multimedia hardware installed. Among the enhancements are:

- **DirectDraw**. DirectDraw allows accelerated access to the memory on your graphics card, key for pushing 30 frames of video each second. In essence, DirectDraw is a graphics shortcut that lets video software talk directly to your graphics hardware, eliminating Windows' slow graphics engine. DirectDraw also provides pixel scaling and color-space conversion features.
- **DirectVideo**. The second half of Microsoft's video-improvement plan, DirectVideo opens the door to hardware-accelerated video under Windows 95. DirectVideo lets inexpensive graphics hardware take over key video playback tasks from the CPU by providing an interface into DirectDraw.

NOTE Like other DirectX components, DirectDraw and DirectVideo both ship separately from the Windows 95 operating system. Most users will get DirectDraw and DirectVideo when they install software that uses DirectX technology, such as games or titles.

With the OEM Service Release 2 version of Windows 95 (OSR2), the DirectX technology is incorporated directly into Windows 95.

- **CDFS**. The CD File System improves throughput from the CD-ROM by providing an optimized, 32-bit, protected-mode file system. The result is improved performance of CD-ROM drives in Windows 95, which reduces dropped frames. CDFS also takes some of the burden off the system CPU, allowing it more time to decompress video files (see Figure 4.10).
- **Multitasking**. Windows 95's preemptive multitasking minimizes pauses and delays during video playback. These breaks in the continuity can ruin the viewing experience. Video can continue to play even while other processes, such as display of separate graphics, run in the background.

Enhanced CD-ROM and file management benefit all aspects of your computer's performance, but DirectDraw and DirectVideo are aimed squarely at improving multimedia and video. The good news is that you don't need to throw out your existing graphics hardware to play games and software using Direct X technologies. However, you will enjoy much better video playback if your graphics card includes the proper drivers and video-intelligent hardware.

DirectVideo works by first checking the graphics card and finding out what video-accelerating features, if any, are supported in the hardware. Windows then knows to send key tasks, like color space conversion and pixel scaling, straight to the graphics card, if it is properly configured. If the card lacks enhanced video support, all the video-handling tasks are sent straight to the system CPU.

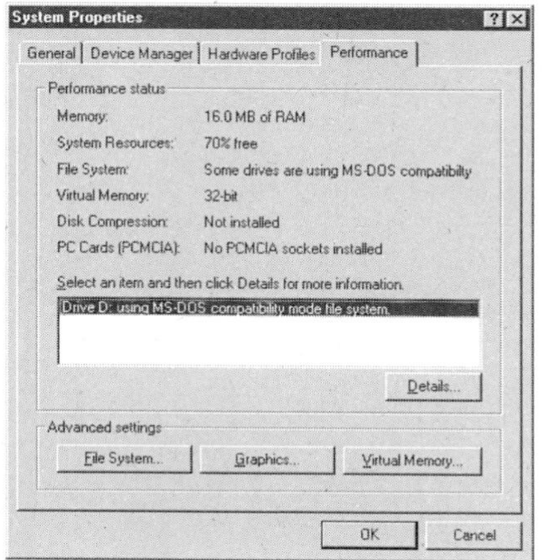

FIG. 4.10
Windows 95 may not recognize your CD-ROM drive and use slower compatibility-mode drivers. Check the Performance page of the System properties sheet to see if your CD-ROM drive is not fully optimized.

NOTE The newest graphics hardware does little good without the proper drivers. Otherwise, Windows 95 sends all the video tasks straight to the system CPU, even if you have a video-accelerating card. In fact, Windows 95 can fail to install the specific driver you need. Check the installed driver from the Display properties sheet by clicking the Change Display Type button.

Older graphic boards lack video enhancing hardware; you won't see much improvement in video performance even with DirectVideo installed. However, most mid-range graphic boards sold since the release of Windows 95 are video-savvy. Of course, you'll need DirectDraw and DirectVideo drivers to let Windows 95 know that the multimedia features are there. Contact your graphics card vendor and make sure you have the latest DirectVideo-enabled drivers.

CAUTION

If you only have 16-bit drivers for multimedia graphics boards, such as the Jazz Jakarta or miroVideo 20TD, Windows 95 will probably be unable to provide the full functionality that these boards had under Windows 3.1. Contact the board's vendor to get 32-bit drivers.

New Developments in Windows 95 Video Windows 95 delivers many improvements to desktop video playback, but Microsoft has announced a limited road map of features, functions, and new video types that should enhance the quality of CD-ROM games and titles. This section gives you a sneak peek at what to expect next.

Among the key technologies promised by Microsoft are:

- Surround Video
- WinToon

Surround Video Microsoft's Surround Video, a scheme similar to Apple's QuickTime VR, lets developers build 360-degree, photo-realistic scenes. Users will be able to interact with on-screen objects, images, and videos as they traverse immersive scenes.

Surround Video scenes consist of a series of photographs stitched together into a 360-degree panorama, allowing users to turn and view an entire scene. Games can use Surround Video to put photo-realistic backgrounds behind interactive elements. Surround Video is actually even better suited for creating virtual tours built from actual photos.

For users, Surround Video is something that comes as part of the games and other software they purchase.

Installing and Configuring Sound Options

Just as digital video has improved over the last three years, PC audio has come a long way. The original Sound Blaster board delivered audio quality about on par with that of a dashboard AM option. Today, sound boards have evolved to handle CD-quality sound, reproduce realistic MIDI scores, and even create compelling 3-D audio for games and titles. Most importantly, the majority of PCs sold now include installed sound boards.

In the past, intractable audio conflicts and difficult installations made PC-based audio difficult to manage. Windows 95 has improved the situation, providing a set of standard interfaces and applications that make working with audio easier than before. In addition, Windows 95 reduces the amount of CPU processing needed to play back audio, which enhances game play.

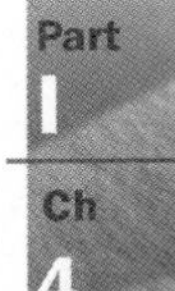

In this section, you will be introduced to some basic concepts about audio files. You will also learn how to install and configure a sound board and how to use the sound tools that come with Windows 95.

MIDI and WAV Sound Files

Your system has the capability to utilize two types of audio files:

- Digital audio (WAV files)
- MIDI (musical instrument digital interface)

Windows 95 includes built-in support for both MIDI and WAV waveform audio. However, you need to install an additional sound device, such as an add-on board, before you can realize these capabilities.

WAV, or sound wave, files take up a great deal of disk storage space compared to MIDI files because WAV files record the entire sound to your hard disk. Although WAV files take up more disk space than MIDI files, the sound is generally better. MIDI doesn't save the entire sound but keeps a record of how the sound is played. The MIDI file then consults the "instructions" when you want to play the sound back and attempts to reproduce that original sound as best it can—sometimes not very successfully if you are using a less expensive 8-bit sound card.

You can use MIDI files to great effect when integrated into a computer-based presentation, for example. On the other hand, you can attach simple WAV files to electronic-mail for distribution to a third party on a network.

MIDI uses either FM synthesis or wave table synthesis to reproduce the required sound. FM synthesis uses artificial sounds that are similar to the required sound, and wave table synthesis uses actual stored samples of sounds from real instruments.

With sampled sound, a small example of the instrument's sound is stored. When sound from that type of instrument needs to be reproduced, the sample is retrieved and it undergoes various changes, such as pitch variation, in order to reproduce a relatively accurate rendition.

Because a MIDI file essentially contains just the instructions on how to play a specific sound, the method of reproducing that sound depends on the quality of the sound board that will be playing it. When it comes to sound boards, what you pay for is what you get. A low-cost, 8-bit board is going to give you a low-quality sound reproduction. On the other hand, if you invest in a high-end, 16-bit board with extensive wave table synthesis capabilities and a good set of speakers, you are probably going to get great sound reproduction.

NOTE Many new PCs are billed as "multimedia-ready" with built-in CD-ROM and sound board capabilities, but these PCs rarely contain high-end sound cards. What you often get is average-quality sound, which is adequate for the average user. If you want a new PC capable of playing back recording-quality sound, buy a PC with a built-in CD-ROM drive and then add a high-end sound board of your choice.

Recording sound to your hard drive takes a great deal of disk space. Therefore, Windows 95 offers two groups of sound-compression technologies, or codecs (coders/decoders). The first technique enables the compression of voice data, such as TrueSpeech. The second method enables you to compress a type of high-quality musical sound. These capabilities, for example, allow for the use of voice compression during recording, which lets the resulting sound file be compressed in real-time, that is, as it is recorded.

Another sound capability, called *polymessage MIDI support*, enables Windows 95 to handle multiple MIDI instructions at the same time. The result is that less processor resources are required, which frees up the CPU for other operations.

Sound Blaster and Windows

Creative Labs' Sound Blaster family of add-on audio boards has become something of an industry standard among multimedia PCs. If you don't have a Sound Blaster board installed, you probably have one that is Sound Blaster-compatible.

CAUTION

Boards that are advertised as Sound Blaster-compatible are not always true to their claim. The result can be distorted or inadequate sound reproduction. However, most games or CDs that fall under the multimedia label probably support Sound Blaster. Check the packaging thoroughly and if the retail outlet is unable to verify compatibility, don't be afraid to contact the manufacturer directly.

Because of Sound Blaster's popularity, even Windows 95 comes with a compatible driver for supporting Sound Blaster programs. But if you don't want Sound Blaster, Windows 95 includes a less popular alternative in the form of the Microsoft Windows Sound System. Windows 95's built-in audio supports capabilities required for Microsoft's own sound specifications.

Even if you use MS Windows Sound System, you are still going to need an audio board, or at least a "multimedia-ready" PC with enhanced sound capabilities and speakers, for listening to and recording CD-quality sound. The average built-in PC speakers are totally inadequate for the task.

Configuration of Sound Options

Any number of things can lead to sound features not working properly. Many elements need to be configured properly in relation to one another. Any time one element doesn't function properly (especially with respect to the next step in the sound playing or recording process), audio problems are likely to result. This section describes how proper configuration can help you avoid sound problems.

Many times the problems are the result of hardware conflicts or wrong settings for specific components, such as IRQs or DMA channels. Hardware conflicts occur when two hardware devices want to use the same system resources. Fortunately, Windows 95 includes a very useful feature called the *Device Manager*, which keeps a centralized graphical registry of all system resources as they relate to the different PC components. As a result, you can more easily locate hardware problems in Windows 95 than you could in the previous DOS/Windows combination.

Sound problems are often the result of an error in installing a new sound device and are likely caused by wrongly assigned resources. The next section discusses the installation of a sound board using Windows 95's extremely useful Add New Hardware Wizard, which reduces the possibility of conflicts.

TROUBLESHOOTING

I get no sound at all, and when I do it is distorted. Common settings problems, such as an IRQ conflict or a wrong DMA channel selected, can result in no sound coming out at all. A wrong DMA driver setting may also result in distorted WAV file playback.

Distorted sound can also result from using sound files stored on a compressed disk. If the files with distorted sounds are located on a compressed disk, try playing them from a disk that is not compressed, if possible, and see if that makes a difference. If it does, you may want to decompress your disk if you are working a lot with sound files.

To define the hardware settings, you need to configure groups of pins, called *jumpers*, on the audio board. Jumpers are essential to the smooth running of the audio board and you must configure them according to available settings as defined by Windows 95 before installing the board. Jumper configuration can vary depending on the board being installed. As a result, a thorough reading of the documentation accompanying your new board is a must.

Adding a Sound Board

The first step in configuring sound is to install a suitable audio board. Thankfully, Windows 95 simplifies the installation of sound cards by recommending a hardware configuration for you via the Add New Hardware Wizard.

Windows 95 has made installation easier by implementing the Plug and Play standard and by providing an Add New Hardware Wizard. Microsoft designed its new Plug and Play standard to make it easier to add hardware components to existing PCs. If you are installing a sound card that conforms to the Plug and Play standard, it may be as simple as installing the card and turning on your computer. Windows should recognize the device and install its device drivers.

If you are installing a legacy sound card that is not Plug and Play, the Add New Hardware Wizard will still simplify the process by recommending a hardware configuration that does not conflict with devices already installed in your computer. The wizard takes you through the installation of a hardware device step by step.

CAUTION

You might want to use the sound board's own installation program instead, because the wizard can run into problems identifying the correct interrupts for some components.

As an example of the process as it relates to sound devices, this section reviews the installation of a Sound Blaster board. In this case, the Sound Blaster 16 AWE-32, using the Add New Hardware Wizard.

You can access the Add New Hardware Wizard through the Control Panel feature or by choosing "sound cards, setting up" from the Help Topics Index page. This example takes you through the Control Panel option.

CAUTION

With virtually all sound boards, installation problems may occur when you try to install enhanced utilities that come with the board, *after* you have installed the component using Windows 95's Add New Hardware Wizard. This is because hardly any option allows you to install the utilities separately from the drivers. However, this may be necessary because Windows 95 will have already installed the board without including the separate software utilities.

See "Installing Legacy CD-ROM Drives," **p. 133**

CAUTION

Some cards come with CD controllers already built in. When this happens, you need to install it in Windows 95 and then configure the CD portion at the same time you install the sound card.

1. Don't install the card itself until the Add New Hardware Wizard has recommended specific resource settings.
2. Open the Start menu; then choose Settings, Control Panel.
3. Double-click the Add New Hardware icon. The Add New Hardware Wizard appears (see Figure 4.11).

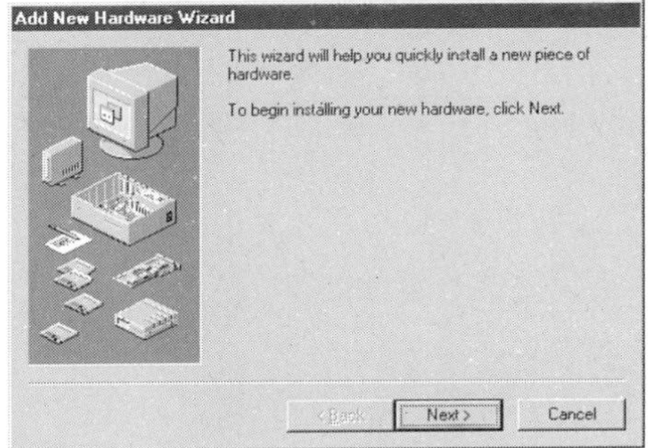

FIG. 4.11
The Add New Hardware Wizard eases the pain of adding hardware components by taking you through the installation step by step.

4. Click Next. The wizard then asks you whether you want Windows 95 to search for new hardware (see Figure 4.12).

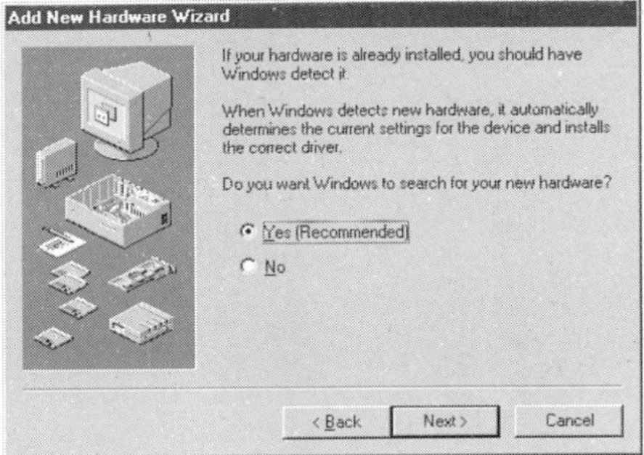

FIG. 4.12
You can choose to have Windows 95 automatically search for new hardware.

5. At this point, select the No option button as, in this case, we are only going through the steps to install sound devices.
6. Click Next. The Hardware Types list appears (see Figure 4.13).
7. Select the type of hardware device you want to add from the wizard's Hardware Type list box. In this case, select Sound, Video and Game Controllers, and then click Next. The hardware Manufacturers and Models lists appear for the device you selected (see Figure 4.14).
8. Click the sound board manufacturer's name in the left window. A list of products that Windows 95 is familiar with appears in the right window.
9. Select the board you want to add. In this case, Creative Labs Sound Blaster 16 or AWE-32.

You may need to install a driver from a floppy disk. If that is the case, you need to take a couple of extra steps. Don't click Next yet, but continue with step 10. If you don't need to install a driver from a floppy disk, go to step 13.

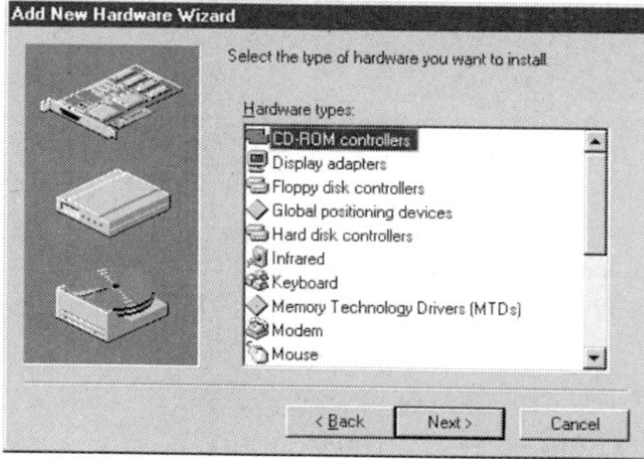

FIG. 4.13 Select the type of hardware you want to install from the wizard's Hardware Type list.

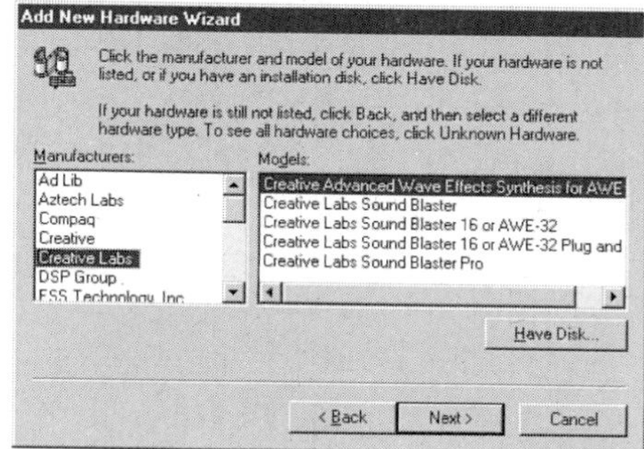

FIG. 4.14 Select the manufacturer and hardware model you want to add from these lists.

10. From the Add New Hardware Wizard dialog box, click Have Disk. The Install From Disk dialog box appears (see Figure 4.15).

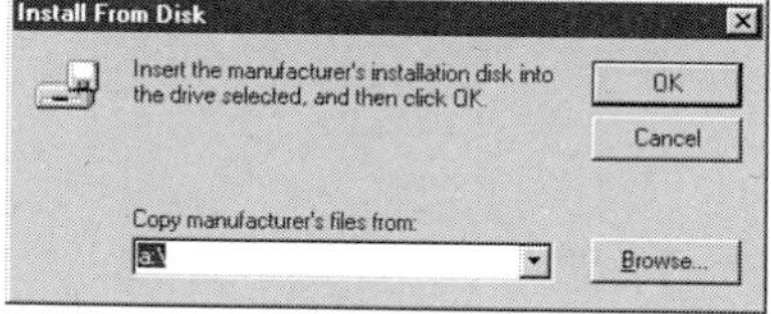

FIG. 4.15 You need to insert the installation disk into the selected drive to install a new device driver from a floppy disk.

11. Specify the directory and disk where the manufacturer's files should be copied from.
12. Click OK. The Install From Disk dialog box disappears and you are back to the Add New Hardware Wizard.
13. Now you can click Next. The wizard window changes to display the settings it wants you to use for the new board (see Figure 4.16). This list of settings is important; it is based on available settings as defined in the Windows 95 Device Manager Registry.

FIG. 4.16
The Add New Hardware Wizard gives you the settings to use for your new board based on what settings are available.

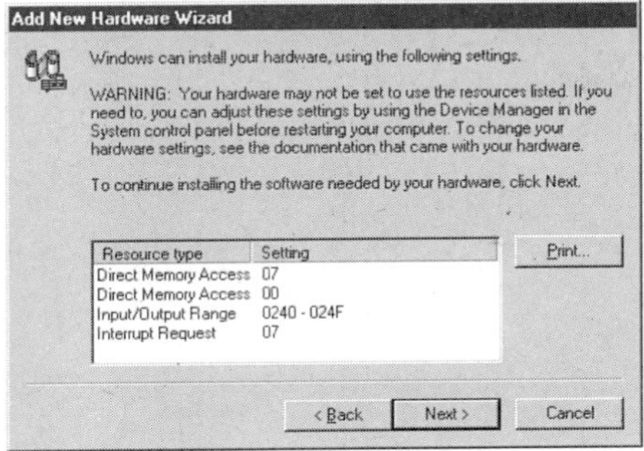

14. Write down these settings or print them out. The new board should have these settings before you install it.
15. Insert the floppy disks containing the drivers that the wizard requests.
16. Shut down your PC.
17. Configure the new sound card according to the settings given during the wizard process. See the documentation that comes with your sound board on how to make changes to I/O configuration settings, as well as IRQ and DMA changes.
18. Install the sound card, using instructions that came with the card.

NOTE You also can install the sound card prior to running the Add New Hardware Wizard and then choose Yes to the question, "Do you want Windows to search for your new hardware?" However, this method is less reliable when installing legacy devices.

Adding or Changing Hardware Drivers Anytime you add a component or peripheral to your PC, you need to make sure a software driver is also installed. The driver acts as a liaison between the computer operating system and the device so that they can communicate. You may need to change drivers if an updated one becomes available. With Windows 95, you can add or change hardware device drivers using Device Manager, which is the centralized registry of system properties and configurations. Follow these steps to update a sound card driver:

1. Open the Start menu; then choose Settings, Control Panel.
2. Open the System control item in the list box.
3. When the System properties sheet appears, click the Device Manager tab (see Figure 4.17).
4. Click the plus sign next to Sound, Video and Game Controllers.
5. Double-click the specific hardware device you are interested in, in this case, your sound card.

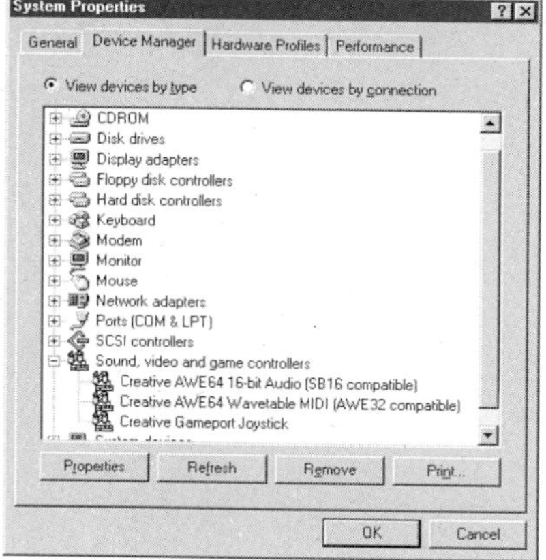

FIG. 4.17
Device Manager enables you to change driver settings.

6. In the properties sheet that appears, click the Driver tab (see Figure 4.18).

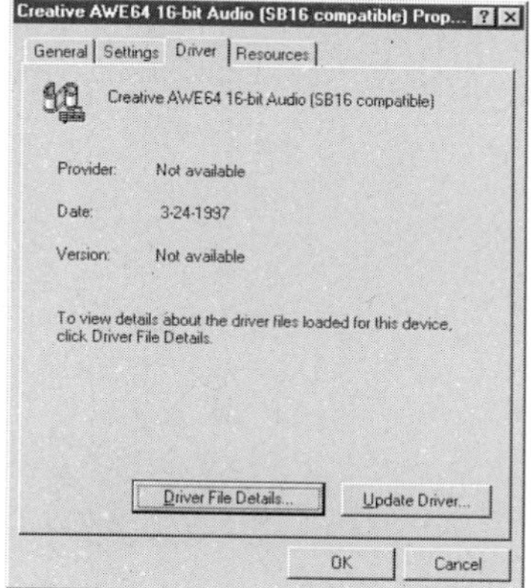

FIG. 4.18
The Driver page for your sound card (in this case, Sound Blaster AWE32) enables you to change drivers.

7. Click Change Driver, and the Select Device dialog box appears. A list details the models compatible with your hardware. Make sure the Show Compatible Devices option is selected. If the hardware model you want to set up is not on the list, you should select the Show All Devices option (use this category with caution, as it includes drivers that are, by definition, incompatible with your hardware). The list changes to show all such devices.
8. Click the device you want to set up, and then click OK.

   The Select Device dialog box disappears, leaving the Driver page showing the driver files and their correct directory path.
9. Click OK to return to the Device Manager device type list.
10. Click OK to exit System Properties.

If you have the OSR2 version of Windows, the Driver tab appears as shown in Figure 4.19, and the procedure for installing a different driver differs from the steps just outlined.

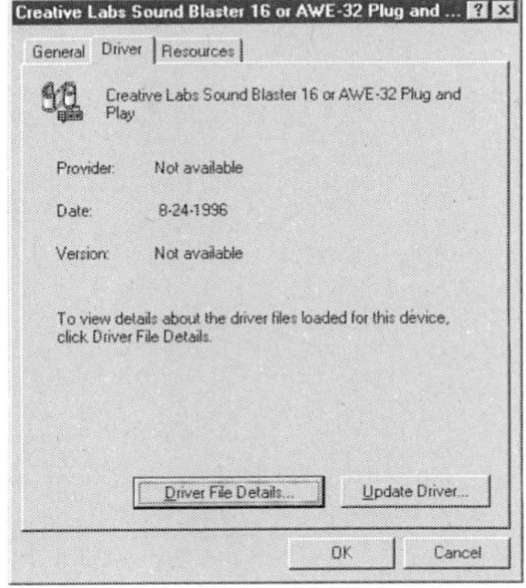

FIG. 4.19
The Driver page as it appears in the OSR2 version of Windows 95.

To install a new driver in OSR2, follow these steps:

1. Click the Update Driver tab to display the Update Device Driver Wizard dialog box shown in Figure 4.20.

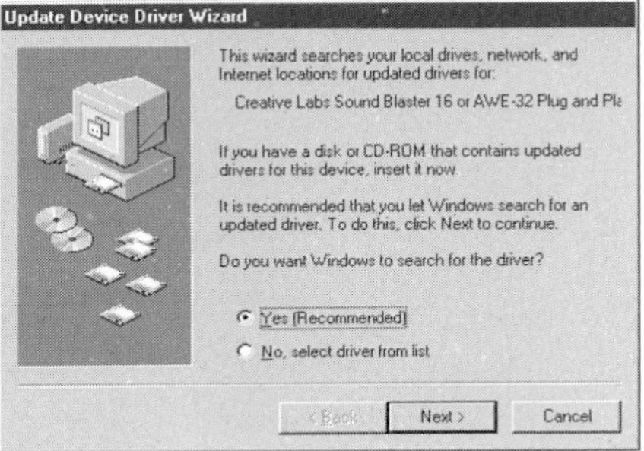

FIG. 4.20
Use the Update Device Driver Wizard to search for and install updated drivers.

2. Leave the Yes option selected to have Windows search for an updated driver. Click Next. Click Finish when Windows 95 finds the driver. If an updated driver is not found, click Other Locations in the Update Device Driver Wizard and change to the location where the updated driver is located.

   or

   Select the No option and click Next to select the driver from a list. Select the correct items from the Manufacturer and Models lists and click Finish.

You will be prompted to insert the disk or CD-ROM on which the updated driver is located, if you haven't done this already. The wizard will search for the driver and install it on your computer. Select Yes when you are prompted to restart the computer to complete the setup.

TROUBLESHOOTING

I get a hissing during playback of sound files. If you hear a hissing during the playback of a sound file, the file may be recording in 8 bits and playing back in 16 bits. The 16-bit board doesn't realize that the 8-bit file isn't the same high quality as a 16-bit file, so playing the file with expectations of higher sound quality emphasizes the lower detail.

Setting Up a MIDI Instrument One of the added features of a relatively high-quality sound board is the capability to plug a MIDI instrument into a MIDI port and play sampled sound. Here is a quick overview of setting up a MIDI instrument:

1. Plug the instrument into the sound card's MIDI port.
2. Open the Start menu; then choose Settings, Control Panel.
3. Double-click the Multimedia icon.
4. In the Multimedia properties sheet that appears, click the MIDI tab (see Figure 4.21).

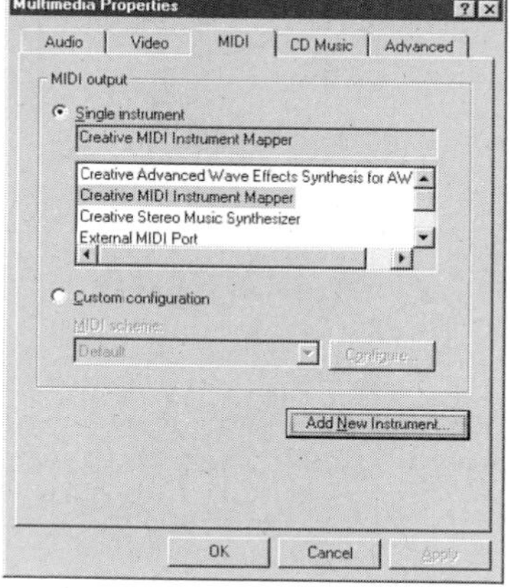

FIG. 4.21
Configure your new MIDI instrument using the Multimedia properties sheet.

5. Click Add New Instrument.
6. Follow the on-screen instructions to install the instrument.
7. Choose Single Instrument on the MIDI page.
8. Select the instrument you just installed and click OK. Your new MIDI instrument is now installed.

Moving a MIDI Instrument to Another Sound Board You can move MIDI instruments between sound boards using these steps:

1. Open the Start menu; choose Settings, Control Panel.
2. Double-click the Multimedia icon.
3. On the Multimedia properties sheet, click the Advanced tab (see Figure 4.22).

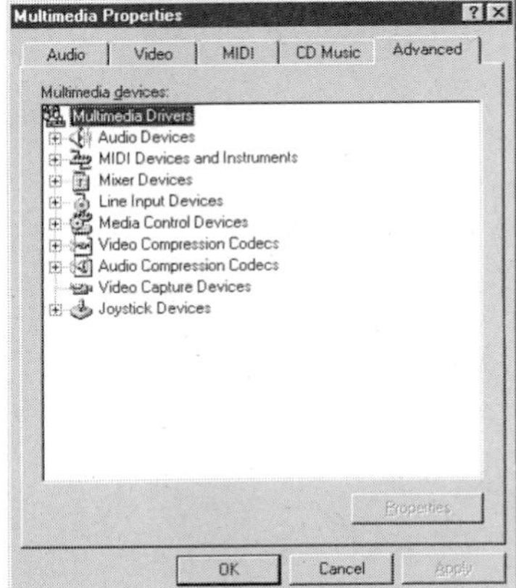

FIG. 4.22 The Advanced page in the Multimedia properties sheet is where you specify the MIDI instrument you want to move.

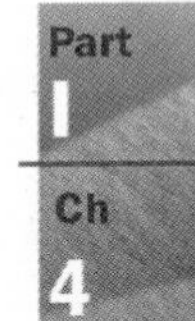

4. Click the plus sign next to MIDI Devices and Instruments. A sublist of devices appears under MIDI Devices and Instruments.
5. From the resulting list (see Figure 4.23), click the plus sign next to the sound board your MIDI instrument was connected to.

FIG. 4.23 Clicking the plus sign next to MIDI Devices and Instruments brings up a list of devices.

6. Click the instrument you want to move, and then click Properties.
7. Click the Detail tab.

8. From the MIDI Port list, select the name of the sound board to which you want to connect the instrument.
9. Connect your MIDI instrument into the new sound board you just specified, using the appropriate port, according to the instructions that come with your sound board.

Windows 95 Sound Accessories

Windows 95 has some useful sound accessories related to the recording and playing of sound, either from audio CDs or specially recorded files.

CD Player enables you to play audio CDs from your CD drive while you are working in another application. CD Player offers many of the controls found in stand-alone audio CD players and looks and operates much the same way. In addition, CD Player enables you to edit your play list for each CD, and the program remembers that list each time the disc is inserted.

Sound Recorder is a very rudimentary digital recording system. This feature enables you to make small, recorded files that you can edit and mix into other sound files (although these capabilities are somewhat limited).

Using CD Player CD Player enables you to play audio CDs in the background while you are working in another application. To access CD Player follow these steps:

1. Open the Start menu; then choose Programs, Accessories.
2. Choose Multimedia and then choose CD Player.

If you have used a stand-alone audio CD player, the controls on CD Player should be quite familiar (see Figure 4.24).

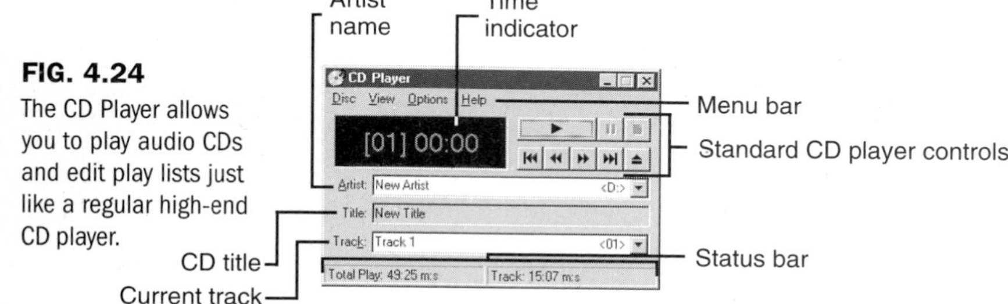

FIG. 4.24
The CD Player allows you to play audio CDs and edit play lists just like a regular high-end CD player.

CD Player includes a number of advanced functions that you access from the menu bar, such as Random Order, Continuous Play, and the ability to edit your play list.

The main CD Player screen offers four menus: Disc, View, Options, and Help. The Disc menu offers two options:

- Edit Play List enables you to edit your personal play list (see Figure 4.25).
- Exit closes the CD Player window and turns off the audio CD at the same time.

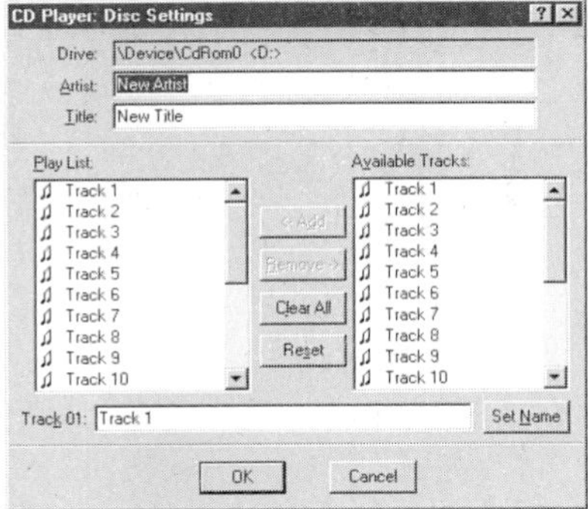

FIG. 4.25
You can customize each CD's play list by choosing the Edit Play List option from the Disc menu.

The View menu offers three sets of options. The first enables you to customize the general CD Player screen:

- Toolbar enables you to display or remove the toolbar. There are seven icons on the toolbar:
  - Edit Play List enables you to edit your play list.
  - Track Time Elapsed tracks the time elapsed since the start of the track.
  - Track Time Remaining lets you know how much time is remaining on the track.
  - Disc Time Remaining shows you how much time is left on the audio CD currently playing.
  - Random Track Order plays the track in random order.
  - Continuous Play starts the CD over again after the last track has played.
  - Intro Play plays the beginning 10 seconds of each track before moving to the next one.
- Disc/Track Info enables you to display or remove the CD disc and track information at the bottom of the general CD Player screen.
- Status Bar enables you to display or remove the status bar at the bottom of the window.

The second set of options on the View menu enable you to change the time displayed in the time indicator window:

- Track Time Elapsed shows how much time has elapsed on the current track.
- Track Time Remaining shows how much time is left on the current track.
- Disc Time Remaining shows how much time is left on the current CD.

The third set on the View menu has a single option:

- Volume Control enables you to set the control levels for volume, wave, and MIDI (see Figure 4.26).

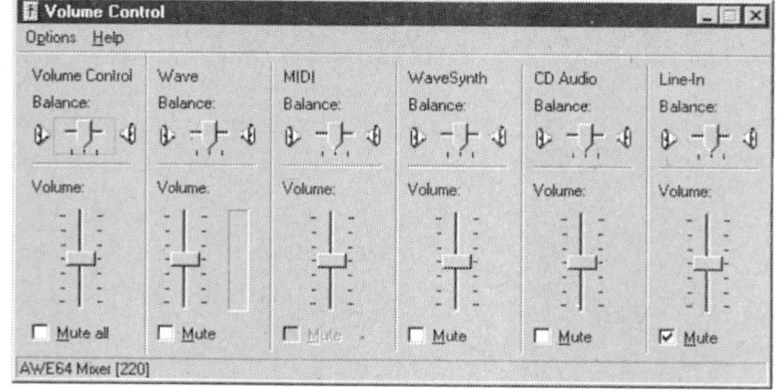

FIG. 4.26 In addition to controlling volume, you can also set WAV and MIDI file balance via the Volume Control option in the View menu.

The Options menu offers four options:

- Random Order enables you to play tracks from different CDs in random order, which can be especially useful if you have more than one CD drive.
- Continuous Play enables you to repeat the track.
- Intro Play plays the first ten seconds of each track.
- Preferences enables you to set preferences for the CD Player (see Figure 4.27).

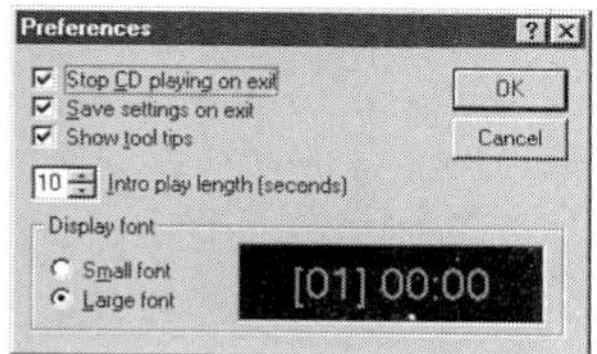

FIG. 4.27 Preferences enables you to set general preferences for CD Player, such as the length of the introduction for each track in seconds, when you choose Intro Play from the Options menu.

The Help menu offers two options:

- Help Topics offers help concerning CD Player (see Figure 4.28).
- About CD Player lets you know how much memory is being used.

Editing a Play List A play list is a list of tracks from an audio CD that you want to play. With CD Player, you can specify the tracks you want played from a CD and the order in which they should run.

You can change the play list by first choosing the Edit Play List from the Disc menu in CD Player. The CD Player: Disc Settings dialog box appears (refer to Figure 4.25).

The left window shows the desired Play List and the right window lists all Available Tracks on the audio CD. To remove a track from the Play List, highlight it and choose Remove. To add a track to the Play List from the Available Tracks list, highlight it and click Add.

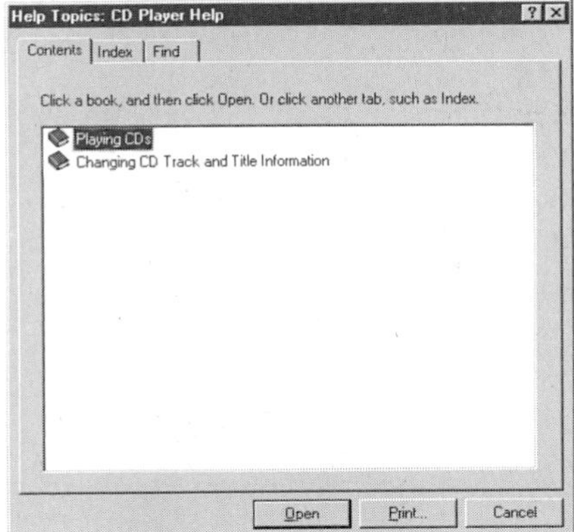

FIG. 4.28
Find help by topic with the Help Topics index option.

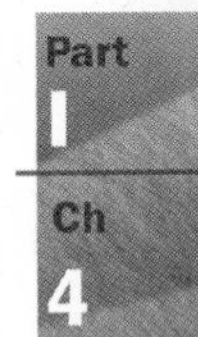

Using Sound Recorder The Sound Recorder feature in Windows 95 provides an introduction to the world of digital recording. Using Sound Recorder you can record small sound files to your hard drive to include in multimedia presentations or attach to documents for distribution among colleagues. You can even e-mail the file across your in-house local area network or the Internet. Sound Recorder does not have the advanced features of high-end digital recorders, but it does provide features suitable for most users' needs.

This section provides an overview of the basic features of Sound Recorder. To access Sound Recorder, you do much the same as you do to access CD Player:

1. Open the Start menu; then choose Programs, Accessories.
2. Choose Multimedia.
3. Choose Sound Recorder to open the Sound Recorder dialog box (see Figure 4.29).

CAUTION

Most sound cards have both line and microphone inputs, and attaching a powered microphone—like the one that comes with the Windows Sound System—to the wrong input can damage your speakers. Microphone inputs are amplified because they expect a much lower signal than line inputs, so test your connection at a low volume to be sure you won't overdrive the system.

FIG. 4.29
Sound Recorder enables you to record sounds for future playback.

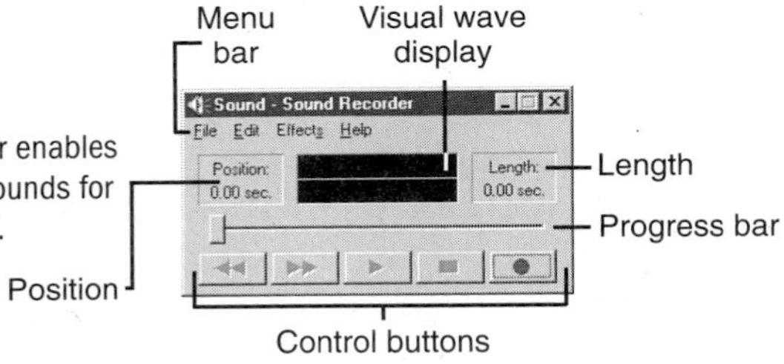

Menu bar
Visual wave display
Length
Progress bar
Position
Control buttons

The Sound Recorder display shows several important bits of information:

- **Position.** Your current location in a sound file, akin to a cursor in a Word document.
- **Length.** Total size of the file, in seconds.
- **Visual Wave display.** A graphic representation of the sound sample. More sophisticated sound editors allow you to edit start and end points in this display and show "clipping limits," where the sound will distort from over-amplification.

The *control buttons* control such operations as fast forward and rewind, like a regular tape recorder.

TROUBLESHOOTING

When I play video and sound files together, they appear out of step with each other. If you are trying to play video with sound and it isn't synchronized, you again may have a computer that isn't fast enough. You can try improving performance and adding RAM, but if you have an older, slower processor and a relatively slow hard drive, you may need to think about upgrading to a new PC with faster video capabilities built in.

The File menu contains a number of familiar and self-explanatory options, as well as two not-so-common ones. Revert enables you to undo a deleted section of a sound file, and Properties enables you to change the properties of the file and change the quality of the recording (see Figure 4.30).

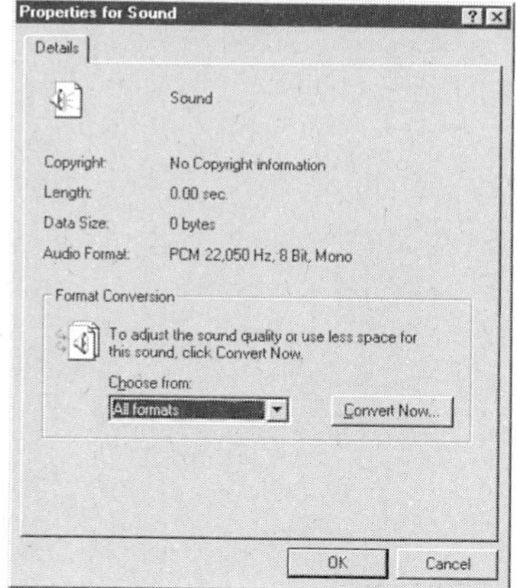

FIG. 4.30
The Properties option from the File menu enables you to change the quality of the recording by changing the format.

NOTE The Revert command works only if you have *not* saved the sound file you partially deleted.

The Edit menu offers a variety of options, some of which may sound familiar but actually accomplish tasks not normally associated with those commands:

- Copy copies a sound (used in conjunction with paste).
- Paste Insert inserts a sound into a document.
- Paste Mix inserts a mixed sound file.
- Insert File enables you to insert a file into another file at the point where you position the slider.
- Mix with File enables you to mix another file with the file playing at the point where you position the slider.
- Delete Before Current Position deletes everything before a specified point, once you have moved the slider to the point in the sound file where you want to cut.
- Delete After Current Position deletes everything after a specified point, once you have moved the slider to the point in the sound file where you want to cut.
- Audio Properties opens the Audio properties sheet, from where you can change various properties, such as volume, for both recording and playback (see Figure 4.31).

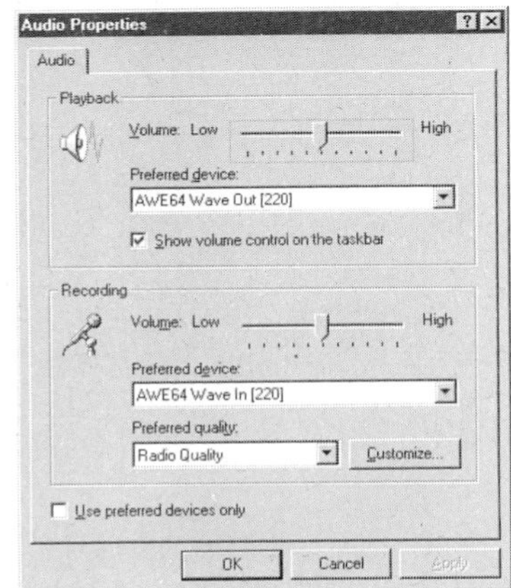

FIG. 4.31 Change recording and playback specifications, such as volume level and designated reproduction device, using the Audio Properties option.

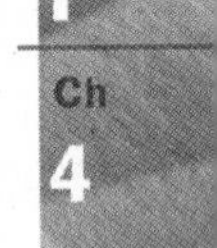

The Effects menu offers options that allow for effects to be added to the sound file:

- Increase Volume [by 25%] increases the volume of a sound file.
- Decrease Volume decreases the volume of a sound file.
- Increase Speed [by 100%] increases the speed of a sound file.
- Decrease Speed decreases the speed of a sound file.
- Add Echo adds an echo to a sound file.
- Reverse plays a sound file in reverse.

TIP You cannot change the speed of a sound file, or add an echo to a sound file, if it is compressed.

See "Compressing a Disk," **p. 397**

The Help menu offers two options:

- Help Topics accesses the Sound Recorder Help section of the general Windows 95 Help Topics feature.
- About Sound Recorder lets you know who the product is licensed to, how much memory the PC contains, and how much is currently being used.

Common Problems with Sound

Many problems can occur when you are trying to get sound capabilities working on a PC because of the complexity of the operation between the system and the components. Windows 95's Plug and Play and easy-to-use Device Manager Registry help keep track of available IRQs and I/O addresses, but things can still go wrong.

One of the most problematic and intimidating steps required in installing sound devices, or any hardware for that matter, is figuring out available IRQ, DMA, and I/O settings that you can use. If you get the setting wrong and use one that is already assigned to another device, the sound component you are adding will not work properly.

Fortunately, the Device Manager Registry keeps track of which device is using what resources. This feature is useful because when you want to add a new hardware component, you can just start the Add New Hardware Wizard, which takes you step by step through installing the device. During the installation process, the wizard gives you suggested free I/O, IRQ, and DMA settings that you should use for the new device, such as a sound board. You take those settings and configure your board or hardware component to match the settings before you install it. The new device should now work because Windows 95 figured out what free settings to give you in the first place. For more information, refer to the "Adding a Sound Board" section earlier in this chapter.

Should hardware conflicts occur, Windows 95 includes the Help option from the Start menu plus an especially useful feature: the Hardware Conflict Troubleshooter. You access the step-by-step Troubleshooter by choosing "hardware, troubleshooting conflicts" from the Help Topics Index. If you have a hardware conflict, start the troubleshooting wizard and it will take you through an investigative process that should resolve most hardware conflicts, or at least identify the conflict.

Installing and Using a CD-ROM Drive

The CD-ROM has become nearly as essential to computing as the floppy drive; more so, in fact, when you consider that e-mail has effectively replaced floppies around the office and software is increasingly shipped on CD rather than disk, making the CD-ROM a more common sight than the floppy disk for many people. Most new computers, in fact, ship with a CD-ROM drive already installed. Demand for CD-ROM software titles has mushroomed and vendors are rushing to satisfy the demand.

Most multimedia applications rely on such a quantity of sounds, videos, and images that they would not be possible without this ubiquitous little silver disc. A multimedia encyclopedia like Encarta, for instance, consumes about 600M—the equivalent of 500 floppy disks! Also, software vendors ship software on CD for economic reasons: A single CD-ROM is significantly less expensive to press—less than a dollar—than a handful of floppy disks.

Increasingly, popular software packages, such as Microsoft Office, ship on CD as well. Installing an application as large as Office is much quicker from CD-ROM: Swapping disks can take more than 90 minutes, whereas a CD-ROM installation is done in about 15 minutes.

In this section, you learn how to install and configure a CD-ROM drive and how to use your CD-ROM.

Installing Plug and Play CD-ROM Drives

In Chapter 7, "Plug and Play and Legacy Device Installation," you learned what Plug and Play is and how to install Plug and Play devices. Installing a Plug and Play CD-ROM adapter is similar to installing other Plug and Play devices. They are simpler to install than legacy CD-ROM adapters because you don't have to worry about IRQ, DMA, and I/O port settings. Driver configuration is automatic, too.

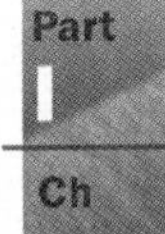

Windows will take care of the details: It identifies the hardware, identifies the resource requirements, creates the configuration, programs the device, loads the 32-bit device drivers, and notifies the system of the change. It will appear in My Computer the next time you boot Windows.

Installing Legacy CD-ROM Drives

Installing legacy CD-ROM drives is not as easy as installing Plug and Play drives. However, Windows Add New Hardware Wizard greatly simplifies the task. This wizard looks for clues in your computer that tell it what hardware is installed. Some clues include the following:

- Signatures or strings in ROM
- I/O ports at specific addresses that would indicate a specifically known hardware class
- Plug and Play devices that will report their own ID
- Drivers loaded in memory before you run Setup
- DEVICE=lines in the CONFIG.SYS that indicate specific device drivers to the wizard

▶ **See** "Installing Legacy (Non-PnP) Hardware," **p. 182**

CD-ROM Types Supported Windows supports three types of CD-ROM drives: SCSI, IDE, and proprietary CD-ROM drives.

- **SCSI**. Often pronounced *skuzzy*, a Small Computer System Interface adapter allows you to connect multiple pieces of hardware to a single adapter: scanners, hard drives, CD-ROM drives, and others. SCSI devices are known for their speed.
- **IDE**. An Interface Device Electronics adapter, commonly integrated into the motherboard, provides an interface for your floppy and hard disks. CD-ROM drives made for IDE adapters are less expensive than drives made for SCSI adapters.

- **Proprietary**. Some CD-ROM manufacturers, such as Sony and Mitsumi, sell drives that require a proprietary adapter. These drives require you to use an open slot for the adapter.

CAUTION

When buying a Plug and Play adapter, be wary of packaging that says "Plug and Play Ready" on the box. You may be up for an expensive upgrade when you are ready to use this adapter in a Plug and Play computer. Verify that it is truly a Plug and Play device before you purchase it.

Installing the CD-ROM on an Existing Adapter If you install your CD-ROM drive to an existing adapter that Windows already recognizes, you do not need to do anything else. All you have to do is complete the physical installation and connect the drive and cables as described in your manufacturer's documentation. Your CD-ROM drive will appear in your device list the next time you boot Windows.

Installing a CD-ROM and Adapter By installing the driver for your new CD-ROM adapter before actually installing the hardware, you can let Windows suggest a configuration that does not conflict with existing devices in your computer. Therefore, make sure that you have not installed your adapter in your computer before following these steps.

See "Adding or Changing Hardware Drivers," **p. 121**

NOTE If you are installing one of the popular combination sound/CD-ROM adapters, install the sound card device drivers as described in "Adding a Sound Board," earlier in this chapter before continuing installation as described in this section.

If you are absolutely sure that your CD-ROM adapter will not conflict with existing devices in your computer, go ahead and install the adapter and allow Windows to automatically detect it.

To install a legacy CD-ROM adapter and drive in your computer, follow these steps:

1. Open the Control Panel and double-click the Add New Hardware icon. The Add New Hardware Wizard opens.
2. Click Next. The wizard allows you to choose between automatically detecting new hardware and manually installing new hardware. Select No and click Next.
3. Choose your adapter from the dialog box shown in Figure 4.32.
4. Select a manufacturer from the Manufacturers list and a specific model from the Models list (see Figure 4.33). Make sure that your selection matches your adapter exactly. Click Next. The wizard displays information about the recommended settings for this device.
5. Click Print to output the recommended settings to the printer or write them down on paper. You'll use these settings to configure your hardware before installing it in your computer.

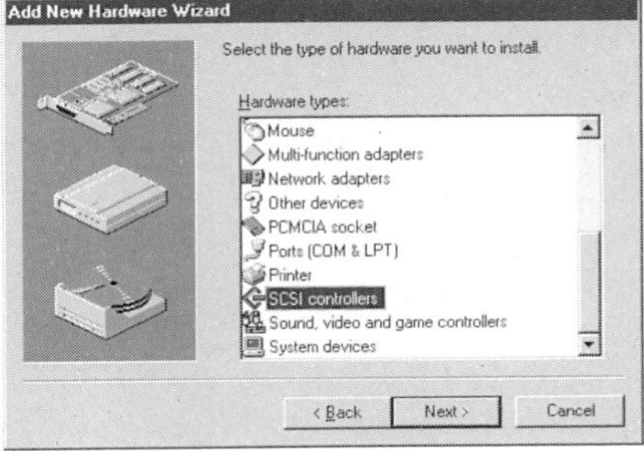

FIG. 4.32
Select either CD-ROM Controllers or SCSI Controllers from the list, depending on which type of adapter you are installing.

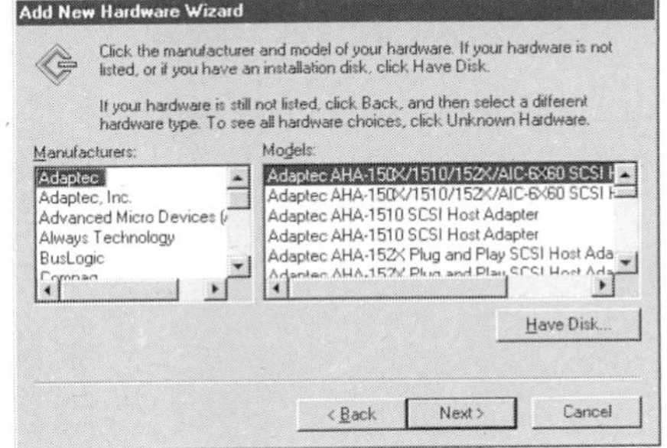

FIG. 4.33
Select a manufacturer and model. If your exact adapter doesn't appear in these lists, you'll need a disk from the manufacturer.

6. Click Next; then click Finish, and Windows installs the necessary drivers on your computer.
7. After Windows has installed the drivers, shut down Windows and turn off your computer.

See "Installing Legacy Cards After Setting Up Drivers," **p. 188**

8. Configure and install the CD-ROM adapter and drive using the instructions provided by the manufacturer and the settings recommended by Windows. For additional information on setting an adapter's I/O address, IRQ line, and DMA address, see Chapter 7, "Plug and Play and Legacy Device Installation."

NOTE If you are installing a separate sound card, don't forget to connect the audio output of the CD-ROM drive to the audio input of the sound card. See your manufacturer's instructions for more information.

Congratulations! You have successfully installed your CD-ROM adapter and can start enjoying the benefits right away.

See "Using CD Player," **p. 126**

TROUBLESHOOTING

I successfully installed my CD-ROM (I can see the files on the CD-ROM using the Explorer), but it won't play audio CDs. First, check the volume by clicking the Volume icon in the system tray. Then, run Media Player, select Device, and make sure that there is a menu entry that says CD Audio. If not, install the MCI CD Audio driver. Otherwise, if your CD-ROM plays but you can't hear the music, plug your speakers or headphones into the external audio jack of the CD-ROM. If you hear music using the external audio jack but not through your sound card, your CD-ROM is not properly connected to your sound card. Connect your CD-ROM to your sound card by following the manufacturer's instructions.

I tried to connect my CD-ROM to the sound card but the cable doesn't fit both cards. You'll need a new cable that is capable of connecting your CD-ROM drive to your sound card. If you are using commonly available hardware, contact the manufacturer and they can provide you with a cable.

My computer dies during setup after installing my new CD-ROM adapter. Restart your computer. Run Setup again and it will ask you if you want to use Safe Recovery to continue the installation. Choose Safe Recovery and click Next. Continue using the steps described in this section. Setup will skip the portions of the hardware detection that caused the failure.

Optimizing CD-ROM Drives in Windows 95

Windows 95 incorporates a new file system specifically designed and optimized for CD-ROM drives. CDFS (CD File System) is a 32-bit, protected-mode file system that provides the following benefits:

- Replaces MSCDEX, which loads in conventional memory, with a driver that occupies no conventional memory.
- Improves performance of your applications by providing 32-bit, protected-mode caching. Your multimedia applications run more smoothly.
- Requires no configuration. CDFS is a dynamic cache.

The CD-ROM cache is separate from your disk cache because it is specifically optimized for use with a CD-ROM drive. Windows normally caches the CD-ROM to memory. However, when Windows needs more memory for your applications, it swaps the cache to the hard drive instead of discarding it altogether. The next time Windows needs that particular data, it reads it from the hard drive instead of the CD-ROM. This significantly improves performance as reading data from the hard drive is about ten times faster than reading data from the CD-ROM.

To optimize your CD-ROM, use the following steps:

1. Right-click My Computer and select Properties.
2. Click the Performance page of the System Properties property sheet, click File System, and select the CD-ROM tab. A CD-ROM tab appears.

3. Drag the Supplemental cache size slider to the setting indicated here.

Installed RAM	Cache Size
Up to 8M	114K
8M to 12M	626K
12M and over	1138K

4. Select the type of CD-ROM in the Optimize Access Pattern For list, and then click OK.

Using Your CD-ROM Drive

With a few exceptions, using your CD-ROM drive in Windows is no different than using any other drive. Figure 4.34 shows the D drive icon in My Computer as a CD-ROM. You access it in My Computer or Explorer just like the other drives in your computer: Double-click the icon to open its folder, or right-click to display its context menu.

FIG. 4.34
Double-click the CD-ROM icon to open it in a folder. Right-click it and select Properties to see its size or share it.

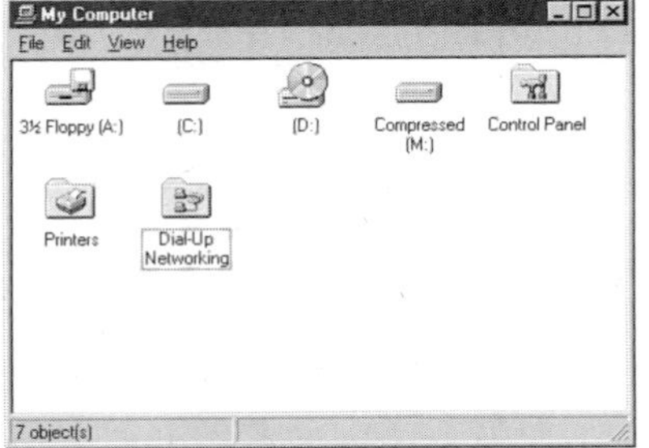

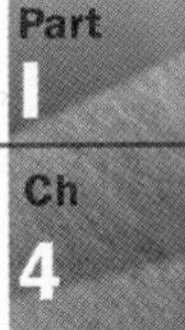

TROUBLESHOOTING

I have a CD-ROM installed in my machine but it doesn't show up in My Computer or the Explorer.

If you are using an external CD-ROM drive, make sure that it is turned on. At times, Windows may skip detecting your CD-ROM drive when you install Windows for the first time. In this case, use the Add New Hardware Wizard to allow Windows to automatically detect your CD-ROM as described in "Installing Legacy CD-ROM Drives" earlier in this chapter. If your CD-ROM drive still does not show up in My Computer, right-click My Computer and select Properties. Click the Device Manager page, select your CD-ROM, and click Properties. A description of the problem and a possible solution is displayed in the Device Status area. If your CD-ROM does not appear in the Device Manager at all, consult the manual that came with your CD-ROM for more troubleshooting information or call the vendor's support line.

▶ **See** "Troubleshooting Hardware Installation," **p. 191**

Playing a CD-ROM Automatically Windows automatically detects when you insert a CD-ROM into the drive. As a result, it displays the label of the CD-ROM next to the drive letter in My Computer. When you remove the CD-ROM, it clears the label.

▶ **See** "Adding and Removing Windows Components," **p. 695**

Some CD-ROMs for Windows 95 are set up to automatically run when they are inserted into the CD-ROM drive. If Windows detects an AutoPlay CD-ROM, it runs the appropriate program on the disk. The Windows 95 CD-ROM is a good example. After you have installed Windows 95, reinsert the CD-ROM in the drive. Almost immediately, a window opens, which gives you the opportunity to add or remove Windows components by clicking Add/Remove Software.

In the future, software vendors will use AutoPlay as a significant marketing tool (or "Spin and Grin," as Microsoft calls it). However, AutoPlay is more than a marketing tool. AutoPlay simplifies installation for countless first-time users who would otherwise spend hours figuring out how to install these products. In the future, installation instructions for many programs using Spin and Grin will simply say, "Insert this CD in your drive and follow the on-screen instructions."

To disable AutoPlay, hold down the Shift key while inserting a CD-ROM in the drive.

TROUBLESHOOTING

Windows doesn't automatically recognize a CD-ROM when I insert it. I have to refresh My Computer or Explorer to see the CD-ROM's contents. Right-click My Computer, select Properties, select the CD-ROM in the device list, click the Properties button, and select the Settings page of the properties sheet. Make sure the Auto Insert Notification option is checked.

Sharing Your CD-ROM Drive on a Peer-to-Peer Network If other users on your peer-to-peer network don't have a CD-ROM drive, you may want to share yours. Sharing your CD-ROM drive is similar to sharing any other drive on your computer.

With Windows 95 file-sharing for Novell Networks, you can share a CD-ROM drive with other Novell clients, even though Novell is a client/server network.

However, there are two considerations when sharing a CD-ROM drive

- If a user *maps* to your shared CD-ROM drive and no disc is in it, a message appears that says "X:\ is not available."
- You are sharing a drive, not a particular CD-ROM title. Therefore, if you share the drive with the Windows 95 CD-ROM in it, and then change the disc, you will be sharing the new disc.

Installing a Software Application from a CD-ROM Drive Installing software from a CD-ROM drive is similar to installing from floppy disk, but it's a lot easier. You can double-click the Add/Remove Programs icon in the Control Panel or run the Setup program on the CD-ROM directly. For Windows 95 applications, you should install using the Control Panel. For legacy software (software written for older versions of Windows), either method is appropriate.

In addition to installing an application using the preceding methods, some software is AutoPlay-enabled as described earlier in this chapter. In this case, insert the CD-ROM in the drive and follow the instructions. For information on partial installations, see the section "Partial Installation," later in this chapter.

▶ **See** "Installing Applications in Windows 95," **p. 688**

TROUBLESHOOTING

When I try to install a program from a CD-ROM using the Control Panel, it complains that Windows was unable to locate the installation program. Your CD-ROM did not have a SETUP.EXE or INSTALL.EXE file in its root directory. Click Browse to search the CD-ROM for another setup program such as WINSTALL.EXE or try to run the program directly if there is no setup program.

I successfully installed a program from a CD-ROM on my hard drive. When I run the program now, I get an error that says File not found. Or, if I try to use Help, the Help window pops up and displays an error that says Help file not found. First, make sure that you have inserted the CD-ROM you used to install the program in the drive because the program is probably looking for program or data files on the CD. If you still get the error message, make sure that the CD-ROM is still assigned to the same drive letter it was when you installed the program. If it is not, you will need to reassign the drive or reinstall the program. You can change the drive letter to which the CD-ROM is assigned by selecting the CD-ROM drive in the Device Manager, clicking the Properties button, and clicking the Settings page of the property sheet. Select a new drive letter in the Start Drive Letter list box.

Complete Installation Some applications automatically do a complete installation. All of the files required to run the program are copied to the hard drive. This is typical of applications that don't require a large amount of space, but are distributed on CD-ROM for convenience. Also, some applications, that by default install only partially, will give you the opportunity to do a complete install when performance is important.

Partial Installation Other applications enable you to do a partial installation. In this case, only core components are copied to the hard drive, whereas other files such as data or help files are left on the CD-ROM. The advantage to this method is that you don't lose a significant amount of hard drive space to store the application. However, the disadvantage is that you must place the CD-ROM in the drive to run the application, and the application will run slower than if you installed it to your hard drive.

Running Applications from the CD-ROM Drive

A very limited number of applications can be run directly from the CD-ROM drive. Many multimedia preview discs exist that contain programs you can run directly on the CD-ROM. However, the performance of applications that are run directly from the CD-ROM is poorer than if you copy the files to your hard drive because a quad-speed CD-ROM transfers data at about 600K per second, whereas a hard drive can transfer data up to 5M per second. See the HoverHavoc game on your Windows 95 CD-ROM in \Funstuff\Hover for an example of an application you can run directly from the CD-ROM.

▶ **See** "Moving and Copying Files and Folders," **p. 319**

If the CD-ROM contains a SETUP.EXE file in the root directory, you probably can't run the application from the CD-ROM.

Although programs generally can't be run directly from the CD-ROM, many other types of files can be used directly:

- **Data Files**. Data files include clip art, bitmaps, documents, and other files that you don't use often and would normally occupy a lot of space on your hard drive. You can use these files directly from the CD-ROM or copy them individually to your hard drive.
- **Font**. A collection of fonts that you install via the Control Panel. Once the font is installed, you don't need the CD-ROM in the drive to use the font.
- **Multimedia**. Some CD-ROMs are packed with sounds and videos you can preview directly from the CD-ROM. For example, see the Funstuff directory on your Windows 95 CD-ROM.

  ▶ **See** "Understanding Fonts," **p. 160**

  ▶ **See** "Using CD Player," **p. 126**
- **Audio CD**. Your favorite audio CD. You can play audio CDs on your computer as you work in other applications.

Double-click \Funstuff\Video\Goodtime.avi on your Windows 95 CD-ROM to see a great example video!

CHAPTER 5

Controlling Printers

by William S. Holderby

Microsoft has packed a great deal of experience into the features of the Windows 95 printing system. To appreciate this system, take a look at the changes Microsoft has made to enable faster printing while producing a higher quality output. Although some changes, at first glance, appear to be ho-hum, don't be fooled. Windows 95's new print model is both faster than its predecessors and designed with the user in mind.

This chapter discusses each of the new printing features and how they work together to produce a quality print job.

Rapid return from printing is enabled by the 32-bit printer drivers, preemptive spooler, and enhanced meta file spooling.

Deferred printing enables you to configure your PC to conveniently print to a file when you are on the road or away from your printer. Once the printer has been reattached, simply release the print files to the appropriate printer.

Bidirectional printer communications sends print files to your printer and listens for a response. Windows can quickly identify a printer that cannot accept a print file.

Extended capability port support enables Windows 95 to use the latest in high-speed parallel port technology to connect your printer.

How to print from Windows applications and to manage print jobs

Find out how to start a print job from a Windows application and to manage print jobs using the Print Manager.

How to print from MS-DOS applications

Learn about the changes in how Windows 95 handles printing from MS-DOS applications.

How to use the special printing features for laptop and docking station users

Set up a hardware profile that allows you to manage print jobs when you are not connected to your printer.

How to solve common printing problems

Look here to learn about the tools that come with Windows 95 for diagnosing printing problems and for a list of common printing problems you can use to troubleshoot your printer.

Before you can print from Windows, you need to install your printer. If you haven't done this already, see "Installing and Configuring Printers," in Chapter 3.

Printing from Applications

When you print from an application under Windows 95, you use the same commands and techniques available under previous versions of Windows; however, there have been changes. You find that application printing now takes less time, the operating system releases your resources quicker, and the color/gray scale found in the printer output is substantially more consistent and accurate. However, many details of the printing architecture are transparent to application users.

Basic Windows 95 Printing Procedure

Depending on the application from which you are printing, you may have some slightly different printing options. In this section, we look at the printing options available to all applications written for the Windows 95 operating system. The two most common Windows 95 applications are WordPad and Paint, included with Windows 95. The options you see in these applications are the same as the options in many Windows 95 applications.

To print from an application, perform the following steps:

1. Open the file you want to print.
2. Choose the printing command. In most Windows applications, do this by choosing File, Print. Figure 5.1 shows a typical Print dialog box. The controls in this dialog box let you specify the portion of the file you want to print and the printer designated to complete the job.

NOTE Most Windows applications that have toolbars also have a button for printing (similar to the one shown here). In some applications (such as Word, Excel, and other MS Office applications), clicking the Print button immediately prints the document using the current print settings—there are no dialog boxes to go through. Other applications open the Print dialog box shown in Figure 5.1 after you click the Print button.

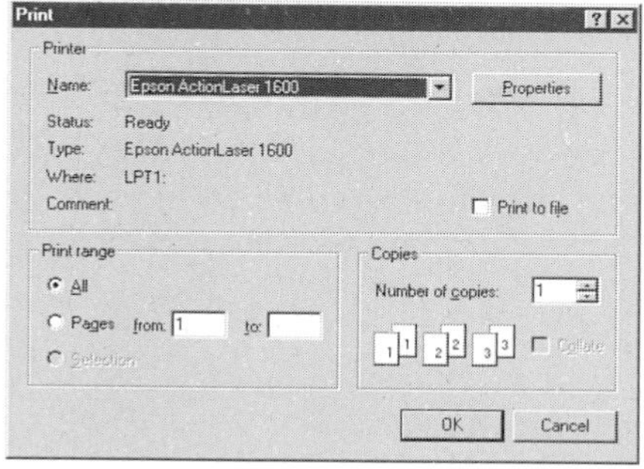

FIG. 5.1 A typical application's Print dialog box lets you send a print job to a specific printer.

3. Determine whether the printer shown in the Name box is the printer you want to use for this document. If it is not the desired printer, click the drop-down arrow for this box and select the desired printer.
4. Specify the number of copies you want to print by clicking the up and down arrows on the Number of Copies control. You may also select the default setting and type a number to replace the default number 1.
5. By default, most applications choose All as the print range. If you want to print something other than the entire document, you must define the print range. To do this, choose one of the three option buttons in the Print Range box:
   - **All.** Prints all pages contained within the document.
   - **Selection.** Prints only those portions of the document you selected using the selection features of the application.
   - **Pages.** Prints the page range you specify in the boxes located to the right of the option button. Specify a beginning page in the From box and an ending page in the To box.

NOTE The Selection option is not available in all applications. In applications that do have this option, it is available only when you select part of the document.

Some applications allow you to specify more complicated ranges. See "Applications with Special Print Options," later in this chapter.

The sheets-of-paper icons next to the collate option show whether or not the printer collates the print job.

6. If you print more than one copy of the document, you can have the copies collated (each copy of the multipage document prints completely before the next copy of the document). To collate copies, select the Collate check box. If you don't select this option, all the copies of each page are printed together (for example, four copies of page 1 print and then four copies of page 2). The Collate option is not available in all applications.

   See "The Print Manager," **p. 145**

7. To output the printer information to a print file, select the Print to File check box. Print files were used in earlier versions of Windows to store print jobs, but Windows 95 uses Deferred Printing to create its own spooled print file, eliminating the need to check this box. Print files also are used for transferring printouts between computers with dissimilar applications.
8. To begin printing, choose OK. If you change your mind and don't want to print, click Cancel to return to the document without making any changes or starting the print job.

This basic printing procedure applies to most applications, even if their Print dialog boxes are slightly different than the one shown in Figure 5.1. Some applications have additional options, as discussed in the next two sections.

NOTE If you plan to print to a file frequently, set up a bogus printer. For example, set up a second PostScript printer to create EPS files. Use the Options, Printer Setup command (or the Printers application in Control Panel) to install a new printer; accept the current driver if you already have a PostScript printer installed or add the PostScript driver if you don't have one installed. Follow the preceding procedures to direct this printer's output to an EPS file. When you're ready to print from the application, choose File, Print Setup to select the bogus printer and print.

Applications with Special Print Options

Some applications take the basic printing features in Windows 95 and add a few features of their own. This section looks at some of the additional features you may find in other programs, with Word 97 as an example. Although these features vary from application to application, this section should give you an idea of what to look for.

Figure 5.2 shows the Word 97 Print dialog box.

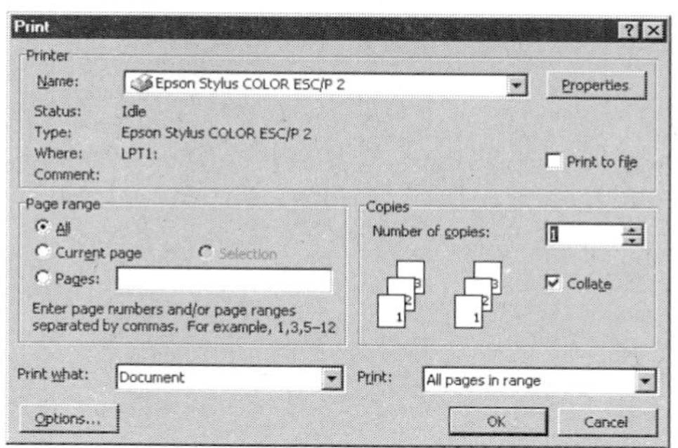

FIG. 5.2
The Print dialog box in Word 97 includes several enhancements not found in the standard Windows 95 Print dialog box.

Here is a quick summary of some of the additional (and different) options provided by this application compared to the standard Windows 95 printing options:

- The Current Page option in the Page Range section. When you select this option, Word prints the page in which the insertion point is currently located.
- An enhanced Pages option. This enhanced option allows you to specify a page range in the variable box located to the right of the Pages label. The range can be individual pages separated by a comma, a page range separated by a hyphen, or both: for example, 1,2,4–8,10. In this example, pages 1, 2, 4, 5, 6, 7, 8, and 10 are printed.
- The Print What drop-down list. In Word, you can select to print the document itself or other information such as summary information, annotations, and styles.
- The Print option. From this drop-down list, you select to print odd, even, or all pages in the range.
- The Options button. When you click this button, Word displays the Options dialog box, opened to the Print tab. Use this dialog box to set printing options specific to Word.

NOTE For a more complete discussion of Word's printing features, see Que's *Special Edition Using Word 97, Bestseller Edition*.

Keep in mind that the options described here are not the same in all applications.

Windows 3.1 Applications with Special Print Options

The other common type of Print dialog box you may encounter is from a Windows 3.1 application that has a customized dialog box, such as the one for Word 6 shown in Figure 5.3.

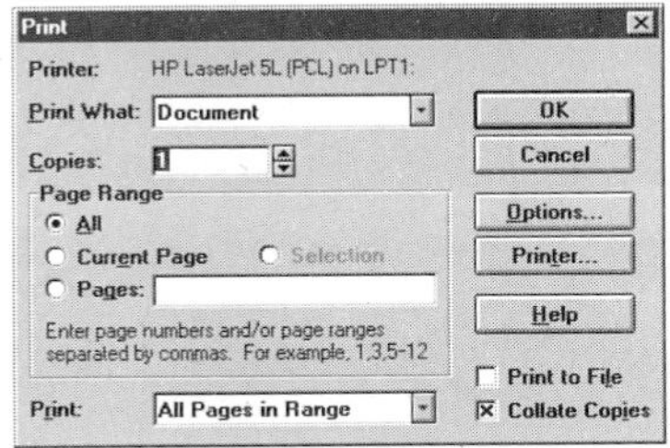

FIG. 5.3 The Word 6 dialog box is still styled like a Windows 3.1 dialog box.

Most options in this dialog box are the same as those shown in Figures 5.1 and 5.2. However, there are some differences:

- There is no status entry or comment field that describes the printer's current activity.
- You select a different printer by clicking the Printer button and selecting from a dialog box instead of choosing a printer from a drop-down list.
- There is no Properties button.

As with the other printing options discussed in this chapter, the options displayed in the Print dialog box vary from application to application.

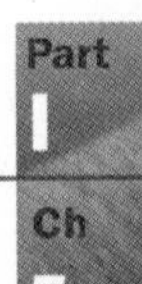

Managing Print Jobs

Like Windows 3.1, Windows 95 offers the option of printing directly to the configured port or using its Print Manager. For most applications, the Print Manager provides facilities to better manage the printing of documents.

The Print Manager

To start the Print Manager, open the Start menu and choose Settings; then choose Printers and double-click the icon for the printer you want to manage in the Printer control panel (see Figure 5.4). Depending on the printers you have installed, your control panel will differ from the one shown in the figure.

If you have a shortcut to your printer on your desktop, you can open its control panel by double-clicking the shortcut icon. To create a shortcut for your printer, see "Create a Desktop Printer Icon," later in this chapter.

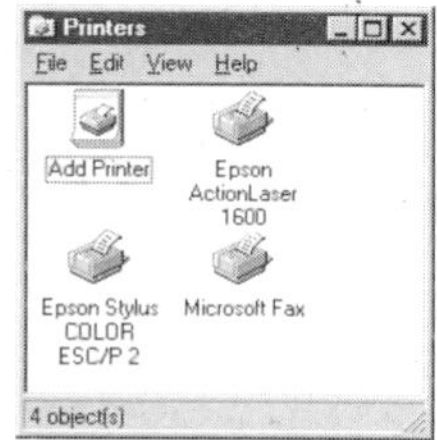

FIG. 5.4
The Printer control panel has icons for each of your installed printers as well as the icon to add a new printer.

Unlike Windows 3.1, Windows 95 uses a separate Print Manager for each printer. Therefore, make certain that you choose the correct Print Manager to view the status of your print jobs.

The Print Manager shown in Figure 5.5 displays the current printer status for each print job.

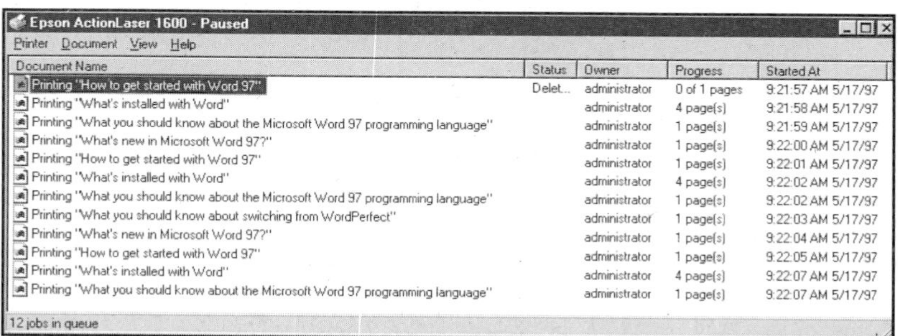

FIG. 5.5
Each printer has its own Print Manager; make sure that you select the correct printer from the Printer control panel for the print jobs you want to check.

The printer status includes the following information:

- The Document Name section shows the name of each application that has submitted a print job as well as the name of each document job in the print queue.
- The Status column describes the current condition of each print job, such as paused or spooling.

▶ **See** "Managing Print Files and Sharing," **p. 1059**

- The Owner column gives the user's name associated with each document. A print job on your printer may belong to someone else when you share your printer.
- The Progress column shows the relative progress of each job in the print queue. The progress of each job monitors the printing of each document and provides information concerning the number of pages printed and the number of pages left to print.

By default, print jobs are listed in the order they entered the queue. You can sort them according to name, status, owner, progress, or start time by clicking the appropriate column heading.

- The Started At column provides the time and date when each job entered the queue. This is important for those users with deferred print jobs.

Controlling Printing

The Print Manager coordinates and schedules the printing of files received from your applications. These applications may be Windows-based or MS-DOS-based.

The Print Manager pull-down menus provide you with the following capabilities, all of which the next several sections describe:

- Pause Printing
- Purge Printing
- Work Offline
- Set Printer as Default
- Change a Printer's Properties
- Pause a Selected Document's Printing
- Cancel a Selected Document's Printing
- View the Status Bar
- Access Windows Help

▶ **See** "Managing Print Files and Sharing," **p. 1059**

NOTE If you are using a network printer, you can cancel only your own print jobs. You cannot pause printing, even of your own documents. Canceling someone else's print jobs or pausing printing requires network supervisor rights.

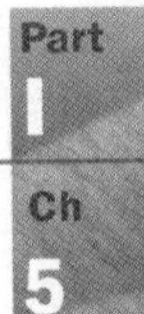

Pausing Printing Pausing a printer temporarily stops print jobs from being sent to a printer. Once you restart a paused printer, all pending print jobs start and sequentially enter the printer queue. This feature is useful when changing toner or performing printer maintenance.

To pause printing, choose Printer, Pause Printing. The Print jobs pause and the Print Manager's title bar displays `Paused`.

To restart printing, choose Printer, Pause Printing again, which is now prefaced by a check mark. The Pause Printing check mark disappears and printing resumes.

Purging Print Jobs The Purge Print Jobs command permanently removes all queued print jobs. Choose Printer, Purge Print Jobs. The documents listed by the Print Manager disappear.

TROUBLESHOOTING

The printer started my print job and the Purge Print Jobs command won't stop it. Purging print jobs stops Windows 95 from sending print jobs to the printer. However, it does not purge the print jobs currently being processed by the printer. You may have to reset the printer to terminate unwanted printing.

Working Offline Windows 95 enables you to initiate a print job without being physically attached to a printer. This feature is known as Deferred Printing, or Working Offline. Deferred Printing is available for network printers and laptop users with docking stations. Deferred Printing tracks deferred print jobs and releases them under configuration control when the computer is connected to the printer locally or networked, or attached through a docking station.

The Work Offline command is only available for laptop computers and network printers. Use the Pause Printing command to delay printing on a computer that uses a local printer. See the section "Pausing Printing" earlier in this chapter for more information on that option.

See "Using Your Laptop with a Docking System," **p. 198**

See "Printing on a NetWare Network," **p. 1054**

See "Printing on a Microsoft Network," **p. 1056**

NOTE The spooler must be turned on for you to use Deferred Printing.

To configure a printer to work offline, choose Printer, Work Off-Line. A check mark appears in front of the Work Off-Line command. The Printer is now configured to work offline and defer printouts. The Print Manager changes its title to read "User Intervention Required." This information is then placed in the status line of each print job being sent to this printer. The Print manager defers printouts until you change the status of the Work Off-Line flag.

To change the status of the Work Off-Line flag, choose Work Off-Line for a second time. The check mark disappears and the deferred printouts are sent to the printer.

The taskbar normally displays a clock at the lower right of the screen. This box also displays a printer when a document is being printed. If deferred documents are pending, the icon changes to include a question mark circled in red.

See "Printing on a NetWare Network," **p. 1054**

See "Printing on a Microsoft Network," **p. 1056**

To print documents that have been deferred, follow these steps:

1. Physically connect the target printer to the system by putting the laptop in the docking station or connecting to the network printer.
2. From the Print Manager window, choose Printer. Then choose the Work Off-Line option to remove its check mark.
3. Verify that printing begins immediately to the target printer and that the deferred print jobs are no longer displayed by the Print Manager.

Setting a Default Printer If you have more than one printer available (either locally or on a network), you can choose the printer to be used as the default. The default printer is used by all applications unless you choose another printer from within the application.

To set a printer as the default, start that printer's Print Manager and then choose Printer, Set as Default. A check mark appears next to the Set as Default command on the pull-down menu, signifying that this printer is now the Windows default printer.

To remove the printer as the system default, select the Set as Default option again to reset the flag. Alternatively, from the Print Manager of another printer, select the Printer, Set as Default command. Windows allows only one default printer.

Pausing a Document You may pause a document to stop the Print Manager from sending it to the printer. Pausing suspends processing of the print job, but it does not stop the document from being spooled. The Print Manager displays a list of documents being printed; any paused print jobs are labeled "Paused."

To pause a document, choose one or more documents from the list of documents in the print queue. (Choosing a document highlights the document's entry in the Print Manager.) Choose Document, Pause. The selected documents now display a `Paused` status.

To release a paused document, choose the paused documents from the list of documents in the print queue. Choose Document, Pause. The selected documents no longer display a "Paused" status.

Canceling a Document from Printing You also can permanently remove selected documents from the list of documents being printed. To cancel documents, choose one or more documents from the documents in the print queue; then choose Document, Cancel.

CAUTION

Once you cancel a document, Windows immediately removes that document from the print queue. You do not receive a confirmation prompt. You might try Pause first and make certain that you want this document's printout terminated.

Turning the Status Bar Off and On The status bar lists the status of the print queue and contains the number of print jobs remaining to be printed. To turn off the display of the status bar, choose View, Status Bar. Repeat this action to turn the status bar display back on. The Status Bar option is a standard Windows toggle control: if the option is not preceded by a check mark, the status bar is not visible.

Closing Print Manager

To close the Print Manager, choose Printer, Close; or click the Close button.

TIP Closing the Print Manager in Windows 95 does not purge the associated print jobs (unlike Windows 3.1). Printing continues based on the Print Manager's settings.

To rearrange the print queue, select a document, drag it to the correct queue position, and drop it. Dragging and dropping a document in the print queue works only with documents that are not currently being printed.

Drag-and-Drop Printing from the Desktop

A new feature of the Windows 95 operating system is the capability to print a document without first opening the associated application or the File Manager. Using desktop icons, you can quickly run print jobs from the desktop.

In earlier versions of Windows, printing used a four-step operation: open an application, load a file, initiate printing, and finally shut down the application after printing. Windows 95 uses a two-step printing procedure that is quick and convenient. However, before you can print from the desktop, you must take certain steps to set up your system.

Create a Desktop Printer Icon

Before you can drag-and-drop documents to desktop icons, you must first create the icons. Although some icons are automatically created during Windows setup, printer icons are not.

▶ **See** "Starting from Shortcuts," **p. 237**

To create a shortcut icon for a printer, follow these steps:

1. Open the Start menu, choose Settings, and then choose Printers. You also can open the Printers folder by double-clicking the Printers icon in the Control Panel window. The Printer's folder is now open.
2. Select the desired printer, drag it onto the desktop, and release it.
3. Windows displays a question window that asks permission to create a shortcut (see Figure 5.6). Answer Yes and Windows creates the shortcut icon. If you answer No, the icon disappears from the desktop.

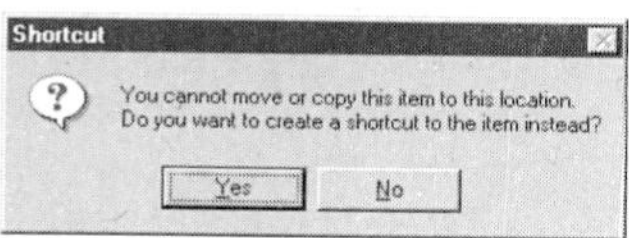

FIG. 5.6
A Windows question window asks your permission to create a shortcut.

▶ **See** "Modifying and Deleting Shortcuts," **p. 265**

After you create the shortcut to the printer, you can modify it by creating a shortcut key or changing the icon. Chapter 10, "Navigating and Controlling Windows," discusses modifying shortcuts.

Print from the Desktop

Once you create a shortcut icon on the desktop for your printer, you can print any document from the desktop.

▶ **See** "Managing Files and Folders with My Computer," **p. 301**

▶ **See** "Managing Your Files and Folders," **p. 316**

To print from the desktop, follow these steps:

1. Open any folder (either in My Computer or Windows Explorer) that contains a printable document.
2. Select that document using the left mouse button.
3. While holding down the left mouse button, drag the document's icon from its folder to a printer desktop icon. Don't worry: This action makes no changes to the file.
4. When the document icon is on top of the printer desktop icon, release the mouse button.

Make sure that the document is associated with an application and that the application is available to Windows, or your printing will be terminated.

Windows starts the associated application configured to handle that file type. Windows executes that application's print command. Once the printing has been committed to the background print spooler, Windows releases the associated application, closes it, and background prints the spooled files.

Why all the fuss about such a simple control function? Consider the time it saves you: If you have to print documents quickly, simply point, click, and drag the document to the printer; then you can go back to your other applications. Windows delivers hard copy with minimum effort. Also, if you use more than one printer, you can create a shortcut for each of the printers you use. Then, instead of having to open the application and select the printer you are connected to, you can simply drag and drop the document on to the correct printer icon.

Another way to quickly print a file is to add a shortcut for your printer to the Send To folder (which is in the Windows folder). You can then right-click a file in the Explorer or a folder window, choose Send To, and choose the printer from the Send To list. If you have multiple printers or multiple configurations for the same printer, add shortcuts for each one to the Send To folder.

Desktop Printing of Multiple Documents

Using Windows, you can print several files at once by dragging them to the shortcut icon on the desktop. Follow these steps to print several files at once:

1. Select several documents to print by dragging around them, or by holding down the Ctrl key and clicking the documents.
2. Drag the selected documents to the desktop printer icon.
3. Drop the documents on the icon.
4. The message window shown in Figure 5.7 displays. Select Yes to print. Select No only if you want to stop all documents from printing.

Windows starts each of the applications associated with the selected documents and begins printing.

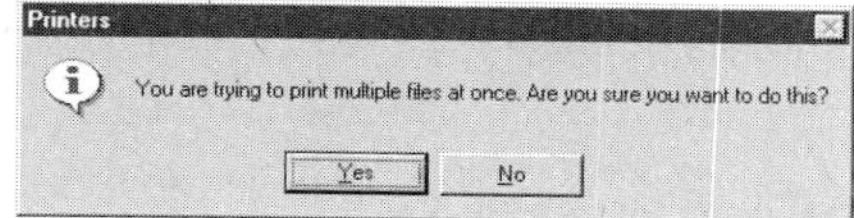

FIG. 5.7
A message window asks permission to print the multiple documents.

You can select and print multiple documents created using different applications.

NOTE Before trying to print multiple documents, check whether your system has the resources (enough memory) to support the number of applications Windows has to open to print the files. A quick check would be to start the applications prior to printing and look for an out-of-memory or other diagnostic message that indicates Windows cannot support the application load.

Printing from MS-DOS Applications

Windows provides support for printing from MS-DOS applications in much the same way it does for printing from Windows applications. The print stream is spooled using the RAW setting for the print spooler. The result is a faster return to MS-DOS applications and the ability to mix Windows and MS-DOS print streams (avoiding contention problems that occurred under Windows 3.1).

Under Windows 3.1, MS-DOS applications could not access the Windows printing facilities. In the past, printing from a DOS application was neither robust nor fail-safe. When printing simultaneously from both Windows and MS-DOS applications, you often received notice of a printer conflict. In most cases, this caused either the MS-DOS application or the Windows application to stall, and you had to reboot.

The major change Windows 95 brings to MS-DOS applications is direct access to the Windows print spooler. MS-DOS applications no longer compete for a share of the printer; you can actually use the Print Manager to queue your MS-DOS printouts with those of Windows applications.

When you print from an MS-DOS application in the Windows environment, the DOS application spools print jobs to the 32-bit print spooler, which takes the output destined for the printer port and spools it before printing. Windows automatically installs the print spooler for MS-DOS applications; the spooler is transparent to users. Although your MS-DOS printouts automatically use the 32-bit spooler, they cannot be processed into Enhanced Meta Files.

Printing from a Docking Station

Every time you start Windows, it performs an inventory check of all attached hardware. Windows also provides a choice of configurations during startup, if there is more than one configuration. You must choose one of the selections from this list.

You can configure Windows to work offline when the PC is undocked and online when the PC is docked. You can set the system configurations for the printer port to be configured only when the laptop is attached to the docking station. You also can configure the port to be automatically unavailable when the system is being used as a laptop.

Configuring a Hardware Profile

A hardware profile specifies whether Windows will use or not use a specific peripheral. Hardware profiles provide a tool that you can use to specify the hardware configurations to operate your system. You change and create the hardware configurations through the Control Panel's System icon.

Because the printer is not a system resource, it is not part of the hardware configuration. However, the printer is attached to the system through the LPT1 port. This port *is* a system resource and can be configured to be available when the computer is in a docking station. You can configure the port as unavailable when you use the system as a laptop.

Use the following steps to create the hardware profile:

1. Open the Start menu; choose Settings and then choose Control Panel.
2. Double-click the System icon. The System Properties dialog box appears.
3. Choose the Hardware Profiles tab. The tab contains a text window with a single item: Dock 1. When Windows is first installed at a docking station, it creates the Dock 1 setting in the text window.
4. Select the Dock 1 setting and click Copy.

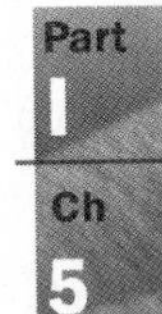

NOTE Windows will automatically detect most docking stations and create a Dock 1 profile. Even if you initially install Windows on a laptop, Windows checks the system components each time it starts and creates profiles automatically when it finds changes.

5. Change the name of the newly created configuration from *Dock 1* to *Lap Top* or some other name that indicates that the laptop is not in its docking station. Click OK.
6. Choose the Device Manager tab from the System Properties dialog box.
7. Select the port (COM or LPT) from the Device Manager tab.
8. Choose the printer's port (LPT1). The Printer Port (LPT1) Properties dialog box that appears contains a Device Usage block with a hardware configuration window (see Figure 5.8). The Device Usage block now contains two hardware configurations: the initial Dock 1 and the new Lap Top. The two items are check box controls. A check in the Dock 1 box directs Windows to include port LPT1 in its hardware configuration whenever a docking station has been detected.
9. Check the Dock 1 box. Don't check the Lap Top box.
10. Reboot your Windows system. During initial bootup, Windows asks for a configuration. Choose Lap Top.

FIG. 5.8
The Printer Port Properties dialog box showing the currently configured hardware profile.

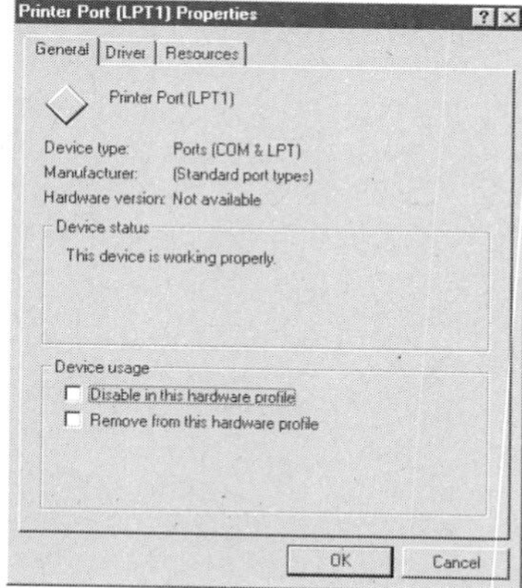

To verify that you have configured the hardware profile correctly, do not change the hardware and follow these steps:

1. After Windows starts, open the Start menu; choose Settings and then choose Control Panel.
2. Double-click Device Manager.
3. Select the port (COM or LPT) from the Device Manager tab.
4. Note that the printer port is now offline, signified by a red X through the port's icon. Printing now results in a diagnostic message that the printer is not attached. The Print Manager deletes all print files. Therefore, you must set the printer to Work Off-Line so that the system will save all print files.

Repeat the process first by rebooting Windows, this time selecting the Dock 1 configuration setting. The printer port returns. The saved print files can then be released for printing.

Common Printer Problems

You install a printer only on occasion. But you troubleshoot printer problems frequently. The most useful tool in identifying and correcting printer problems is a thorough knowledge of your printer's installation and properties. During installation, test your printer and the wide range of properties available to better identify a starting point for dissecting most problems.

Windows provides fundamental troubleshooting aid with Bi-Directional Printer Communication. If a printer can talk to its drivers, many potential causes for problems can be routinely identified.

Advance preparation is always an excellent safeguard against any PC problem. The following checklists can be useful when you are diagnosing a local printer problem.

Before the Problem: Initial Preparation

Following initial installation of the printer, perform these steps:

1. Make a test-page printout and save the resulting printout for future use. The test page can contain important configuration information including the current printer driver, memory size, and port information. On PostScript printers, it will contain version level and settings.
2. If your printer can perform a self test, make a printer self-test printout. For most printers, this test page contains the printer's internal configuration. This information may contain the number of pages printed, memory size, a list of configured options, and internal software revision level. Save the printout for future use. This information may be useful in describing your printer to its manufacturer at a later date, for upgrading or troubleshooting.
3. Note the proper configuration of your printer's indicators: the Ready or Online light and the display status.
4. Make a record of your printer's internal menu settings for paper size, orientation, interface, and so on.
5. Record the installation results and the information from the Printer Properties screens.

Diagnosing the Problem: Basic Troubleshooting

For a local printer, perform the following steps to start diagnosing a problem:

1. Verify that all cabling is free of nicks, tears, or separations.
2. Verify that all cabling is fully inserted and locked at both the PC and the printer ends.
3. Verify that the printer is online and that all proper indicators are lit (for example, that the Online or Ready indicators are lit).
4. Verify that the printer is properly loaded with paper and that there are no existing paper jams.
5. Verify that the printer has toner (laser), ink (inkjet), or a good ribbon (dot-matrix).
6. Verify that cabinet doors and interlocks are closed and locked.
7. Verify that the printer's display, if available, shows a normal status.
8. Verify that the Windows printer driver can communicate with the printer using the Printer Properties screens. You should be able to print a test page to verify communication. If you cannot print a test page, Windows generates a diagnostic message providing you with a starting point to diagnose the problem.
9. Verify that the Windows Printer Properties screens display the same information that was contained in the Properties screens when you installed the printer.
10. Attempt to print to the errant printer using another application and a different type of print file (for example, print a text file or a graphics file).

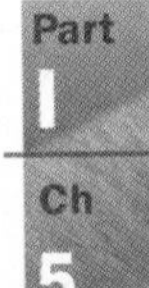

Troubleshooting Tools

If the basic troubleshooting steps listed in the preceding section fail, Windows comes with three important tools you can use to further investigate printer problems. The first tool is Windows 95's new Help file. Initiate the Help file from the Print Manager's Help menu. Then select the Troubleshooting icon.

The Troubleshooter steps you through several of the most probable causes of printing problems (see Figure 5.9). Primarily, this tool verifies that the printer can communicate with the PC. If basic communication is lost, none of the software tools can provide any real assistance. You must resort to hardware exchange until you resolve which component or components are defective. However, with the exception of toner and paper problems, most printing problems are not hardware failures; the problems are primarily software settings or corrupted printer drivers.

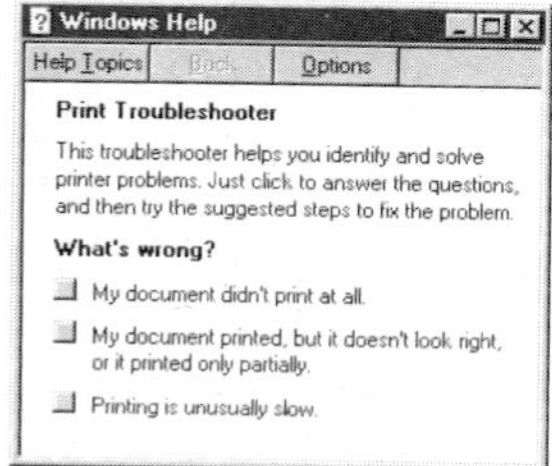

FIG. 5.9
The Windows Print Troubleshooter assists you in isolating problems using logical fault-isolation techniques.

The Windows 95 Print Manager provides a diagnostic tool that can aid you during the process of equipment interchange. The diagnostic screen shown in Figure 5.10 is usually the first indication you receive that a printer fault has occurred. The information on this screen varies (Windows provides as much detail as possible about the problem). The increased amount of information is a result of the Bidirectional Communications between the PC and the printer. For those printers without bidirectional capability, you will receive a standard "Unable to print" diagnostic.

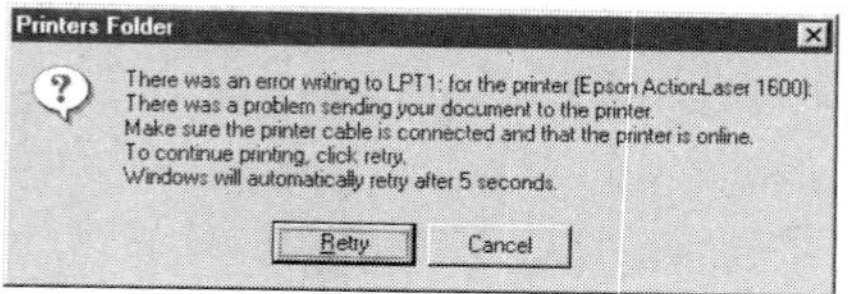

FIG. 5.10
The Print Manager diagnostic reports problems as they are found and continues until either the problem is fixed or the print job is canceled.

If you click the diagnostic's Retry button, Windows continues to monitor the printer's status at approximately five-second intervals. If you click the Cancel button, the diagnostic discontinues and the Print Manager pauses the print file.

The third troubleshooting tool is the Enhanced Print Troubleshooter, shown in Figure 5.11. This software application steps you through your problem by asking you questions concerning the problem. As you answer each question, Windows provides you with a range of possible alternatives to help you narrow in on the potential source of the problem. Clicking the hot buttons next to the most accurate answer brings up another screen with additional insight and questions. This tool is a Windows 95 executable file named EPTS.EXE.

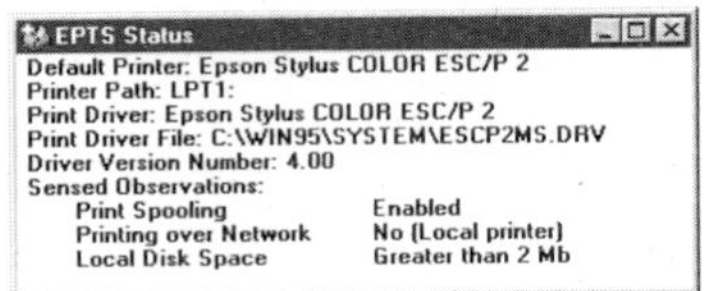

FIG. 5.11
The Enhanced Print Troubleshooter steps you through a printer problem using plain English-language prompts.

Most Common Printer Problems

The most common printing problems are printing supplies running out or a change that has recently taken place in either the printer or the operating system. In any event, a checklist is an excellent place to start because it lets you consider each possible problem. The most common problems, in order of probability, are listed here:

- **The printer is either not selected or is not the default.**

  Make the printer the system default using the Print Manager's Printer menu.

- **The printer doesn't appear to be turned on.**

  Verify that the printer has been plugged in and that the power is in the on position.

- **The printer does not begin printing even though my PC says that I am printing a document.**

  If your system is attached to more than one printer, make sure the appropriate printer is being printed to by checking the Print Manager of each attached printer to find the current print job.

- **The printer is offline.**

  Set the printer online.

- **The printer is out of paper.**

  Reload the printer's paper supply.

- **The printer is out of toner.**

  Reload the printer's supply of toner.

- **The printer is out of ink.**

  Reload the printer's ink cartridge.

- **The printer's ribbon is no longer functional.**

  Remove and replace the printer's ribbon with a new one.

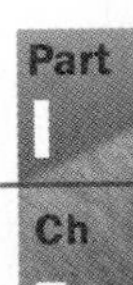

- **The printer's door is open or has a failed interlock.**

  Check for open doors or covers.

- **The printer cable is not properly connected to either the printer or PC.**

  Replace or reseat the cable.

- **The Printer is not connected to the correct port.**

  Remove the cable and connect it to the appropriate port.

- **The printer's software configuration has changed or the drivers have been corrupted.**

  Delete and reinstall the printer.

- **New hardware has been added to either the printer or the PC and a conflict has resulted in addressing or interrupts.**

  Review the installation records of the printer and reconfigure it if required.

- **Additional software has been added to Windows that changed the printer's configuration files.**

  Check the printer's configuration for driver files that have changed using the printed test page created during installation.

- **An application has indicated that it can no longer print to a corrupted print driver and to the selected printer.**

  Delete and reinstall the printer.

- **The operating system has been stalled during a print operation.**

  Reboot Windows 95 and verify printer operation, by printing a test document.

- **A printout stops halfway through printing a large detailed graphic.**

  Using your application, set the print quality to draft. If the graphic printout completes, check your printer's documentation to possibly increase the amount of memory in your printer. If it doesn't complete, run a printer self-test to print a test page.

- **A printer with a cartridge option does not report that the cartridge is installed.**

  Turn the printer off and then check to verify that the cartridge is properly seated. Turn the printer on and test it again.

- **A hardware problem may have occurred in either the PC or printer that stops during the printing of a document.**

  Reinitiate printing the document. If it fails again, review the installation records of the printer and note any changes. ●

CHAPTER 6

Working with Fonts

by William S. Holderby

- **Using fonts in Windows 95**

  Learn how to choose fonts for your screen display and your printed documents. Get to know the terminology for font technology.

- **Working with TrueType and other fonts**

  Understand the font files and the way Windows 95 uses them. Learn about TrueType and other font technologies.

- **Installing and deleting fonts**

  Learn how to install new fonts you purchase. Recognize font files and what's safe to move around or delete.

- **Installing printer fonts**

  Learn how to install proprietary fonts from your printer manufacturer. Understand the choices you can make when you use printer fonts instead of Windows 95 fonts.

The term *font* refers to one complete set of characters in a given typeface design, size, weight, and style, such as Arial 12-point bold. A *typeface* is a family of fonts of different sizes, weights, and styles that share a design. The terms font and typeface are frequently used interchangeably in Windows 95. Each font has a distinctive look, and there is sometimes an obvious personality trait for the font that makes it unsuitable for body text, or for small print.

Fonts have specifications, which include font size (such as 12-point and 14-point) and font style (such as **bold,** *italic,* and SMALL CAPS). Font styles are sometimes referred to as *attributes.*

Font technology is the term for the way fonts are created, stored, and used. The technology has improved a great deal over the years. More font types are available than ever before, and working with fonts has never been easier.

Changing fonts in Windows 95 is straightforward and almost effortless, whether you want to resize, change the spacing, or change the orientation (rotation).

This chapter deals with the standard font offerings that Windows 95 uses to print text. Although Windows 95 comes equipped with several font technologies, the Windows preference is the TrueType font technology. Microsoft developed TrueType technology to provide standard fonts, capable of being both displayed and printed with minimal changes in appearance. Microsoft included TrueType fonts with previous versions of Windows, however, Windows 95 offers new architectural features that improve their display speed for both the operating system and applications, for example, the 32-bit Rasterizer.

See "TrueType Fonts," p. 165

Understanding Fonts

Individual fonts belong to a family of similar fonts that share various characteristics such as style, size, and special effects. For example, a Times Roman font is really more than a single entity because a character set is associated with the font. To review fonts, you should first understand a few terms:

- *Font size* is the definition of how large or small a font character is displayed or printed. Sizes are normally described in points; there are approximately 72 points in an inch.
- *Font style* consists of bold, normal, italic, or bold italic. The style determines how the characters belonging to a font are displayed.
- *Font effects* defines color, special instructions (such as an underline or strikethrough), and in some cases, gradient grayscale fill for outlined fonts.

The presence of serifs is important to you as a design issue because the serifs add a decorative "complication" to characters. This means that if you create a document with sections of very small characters (for instance, less than 7 or 8 points), you'll want to use a sans serif font to make it easier to read. Also, many designers feel that sans serif is the appropriate font type for headlines.

- *Serif fonts* have projections (serifs) that extend the upper and lower strokes of the set's characters beyond their normal boundaries. The Courier font is an example of a serif font. Sans serif fonts, such as Arial, do not have these projections.
- *Font spacing* refers to the space between characters on the screen or printed page. Fixed-spaced fonts have the same space between each character. Courier is a fixed-spaced font. Proportional-spaced fonts, such as Arial, adjust the inter-character space based on the shape of the individual characters.
- *Font width* describes the width of individual characters. These widths can be fixed, normal, condensed, or expanded. In Windows, certain fonts are fixed, such as the OEM font. Other fonts use variable width to display characters that are out of proportion.

Font technology can seem complex and confusing because of the large number of fonts in use and the advantages touted by various vendors. The introduction of TrueType fonts, which provide standard font choices in all your Windows applications, has eliminated much of the confusion. Windows 95 supports numerous other font technologies from many vendors, including Adobe, Bitstream, and other software suppliers.

See "Reviewing Types of Fonts," p. 163

32-Bit TrueType Font Rasterizer

Microsoft has included a new *rasterizer* that improves the time it takes to create TrueType fonts. A rasterizer prepares a TrueType font for either display or printing from a file that contains a mathematical model of the fonts characters. The Microsoft 32-bit TrueType Font Rasterizer was developed as part of the new Windows 32-bit printing architecture. A scalable font such as TrueType can be made larger or smaller without losing its distinctive shape and appearance, that is, the appearance of a character shown in size 6 is identical to the same font character at size 18. The Rasterizer creates new sizes and parameters to use in displaying font characters of different sizes, orientations, and effects (for example, Arial 12 Bold, Italic). With Microsoft Plus! installed, you can smooth display mode curves and reduce the jagged effects of font enlargement by selecting the Smooth Edges of Screen Fonts option in the Plus! tab of the Display Properties dialog box. With this option selected, the rasterizer uses a technique called *anti-aliasing* to render a smoother font.

In Windows 95, a single file—the TTF file—replaces the FOT and TTF TrueType font families. The TTF file contains all the information needed to create fonts of different sizes and complexity.

If you upgraded to Windows 95 from Windows 3.x, you can remove all the files with an extension of FOT. This will give you a little bit of additional disk space (the files aren't very large but if you have a lot of fonts, there can be quite a few of them). The .FOT files are in the Windows\System subdirectory.

Registry-Based Font Support

In Windows 3.1, fonts were identified and loaded using INI files. Windows 3.1 dutifully loaded each font during startup. The time Windows 3.1 took to start increased as more and more fonts were loaded into the system. In addition, the number of fonts available was restricted under Windows 3.1.

Windows 95 attaches fonts through the Registry. Because Windows has immediate access to these fonts, as needed, it no longer has to load all of them, thereby reducing time and overhead. The Registry also provides better management and enables access to many more fonts. Windows uses the Registry instead of the INI files to configure software options for Windows access. The Registry provides a systematic structure and interface that is available to all software regardless of manufacturer.

Changing to Registry-based fonts provides the following benefits:

- The number of fonts that Windows can configure is limited only by available disk space. The number of fonts you can simultaneously use and print in the same document is approximately 1,000.
- Registry-based fonts create an environment where more than one person can use your PC hardware. Each user can individually configure a unique environment, which can include individual font selection.
- Improved font handling through the universal Registry enables an efficient standard access for both Windows and applications.

Windows 3.1 used initialization files to identify which font files were available for use. Most 16-bit Windows applications use the WIN.INI file to identify which fonts are installed. Under Windows 95, 32-bit applications use the system Registry to access installed fonts. Windows still maintains the WIN.INI file to stay compatible with the 16-bit applications.

Required Fonts for Windows

The number of fonts that Windows 95 requires is defined by the applications that you plan to run under the operating system. If you are primarily interested in word processing, then 10 to 12 scalable fonts are more than adequate. A page of text may require only one or two fonts for emphasis. If you plan to use CAD (computer-aided design), desktop publishing, or imaging applications, consult these packages for their special requirements. Because fonts provide an additional dimension you can use to create special effects or to distinguish a particular area of a document, CAD or desktop publishing documents may require a large number of fonts.

The following list describes the standard Windows fonts that are shipped with the operating system:

- *System fonts* are used by Windows to draw menus and controls and to create specialized control text. System fonts are proportional fonts that Windows can size and manipulate quickly. Therefore, Windows uses these fonts to save time when it creates your screen environment.
- *Fixed-width fonts* are included with Windows 95 to maintain compatibility with earlier versions of Windows 2.0 and 3.0.
- *OEM fonts* are provided to support older installed products. The term *OEM* refers to Original Equipment Manufacturers. This font family includes a character set designed to be compatible with older equipment and software applications.

Fonts You Should Keep

Unlike Windows 3.1, Windows 95 does not slow down when loaded with additional fonts. However, these extra fonts do take up valuable disk real estate. You should carefully weigh the value of these fonts before you load them on your system. Microsoft has optimized the font-handling drivers for the TrueType font family, but you still may use other fonts. The decision about which fonts to keep depends on which applications you use.

The only way to make this determination is to experiment by adding, changing, displaying, printing, and eventually deleting unneeded fonts. Experiment with all the fonts on both the display and printed page before you make this decision.

NOTE Experimenting with other font families from various manufacturers provides you with a wide range of optional selections. You can add other font families to Windows, such as fonts from Adobe. However, Adobe fonts require more Windows resources because they require the Adobe Type Manager (ATM) to be running. You may want to look for TrueType fonts that will serve your needs if your applications don't specifically require ATM.

Reviewing Types of Fonts

Some fonts are designed to be compatible with special printing devices. These fonts use mathematical outline descriptions to create their character set. The resulting characters can be scaled and rotated. However, fonts designed for special printers are often difficult to display. To solve this problem, Adobe has created the Adobe Type Manager (ATM), a Windows application that converts Adobe PostScript printer fonts into displayable characters for use by Windows 95 applications.

NOTE Many printer vendors have designed custom software drivers to support their printers. Your printer manufacturer may have special Windows 95 handler software.

These output devices involve different font handling technology and drivers:

- PostScript printers use PostScript meta file printing that is similar to, but not compatible with, Windows Enhanced Meta Files (EMF).
- Dot-matrix printers range from older, very simple models to newer Near Letter Quality (NLQ) printers. Many of the older dot-matrix printers did not support downloading of soft fonts, and some of the newer printers may provide better results using proprietary drivers.
- Hewlett-Packard PCL printers use various levels of HP's Printer Control Language (PCL). For example, the Laserjet II supported level 4, and Laserjet III supports level 5 PCL. Both Windows and HP provide up-to-date drivers that provide the best font settings.
- Plotters primarily use vector fonts as plotter software converts plotter outputs into a series of straight lines.
- Specialized OEM printers may use proprietary fonts to create unique symbols or increase the speed of graphic character creation. Most of the specialized printers provide optimum performance when they are interfaced with their manufacturer's proprietary drivers.

NOTE If your printer came with special drivers, check with the manufacturer for the latest updated Windows 95 driver.

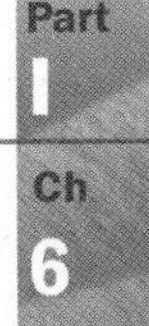

Windows supports three font *technologies* by default. A technology determines how a font is created, stored, and what device limitations it has. The three font technologies supported by Windows are:

- **Raster fonts.** Fonts that are bitmapped for fast display. These fonts are created in specific sizes and rotation angles.
- **Vector fonts.** Fonts that are created from mathematical line models, each character consisting of a series of lines (vectors). Vector fonts are an outgrowth of plotter technology. Pen Plotters are used extensively in Computer Aided Design (CAD) to create line drawings.

- **TrueType fonts.** Scalable, rotatable fonts created from mathematical models. These fonts are a compromise between displayable and printable fonts.

The following sections discuss these and some other font technologies.

Raster Fonts

The name *raster fonts* describes a font set that was designed primarily for the raster display. You cannot scale raster fonts in odd multiples or rotate them effectively. Raster fonts consist of arrays of dots and are stored in bitmap files with the extension FON. Raster fonts need separate files for each point size, resolution, and display device. Therefore, each raster font file has a letter designating its targeted device:

D = printer

E = VGA display

F = 8514 display

The Courier raster font has three files associated with it: COURD.FON for the printer font, COURE.FON for the VGA font, and COURF.FON for the fonts optimized for the 8514 display. Each raster file is optimized for its intended display device and contains attribute-specific information:

- Font type
- Font character set
- Font sizes
- Font optimized resolution

You can scale raster fonts in even multiples up to the point where they no longer appear smooth. By their nature, bitmaps that are expanded too far lose their orderly appearance and smoothness. However, these fonts are quickly displayed and reduce the Windows screen refresh time.

Raster fonts are printable only if the chosen font set is compatible with your printer's horizontal and vertical resolution.

NOTE Not all printers can print raster fonts acceptably. Before you combine any font type with your printer, you should first test the compatibility. You can test the appearance of printed fonts by creating a page of text using that font type and then printing that page. Another way to test printed fonts is print the font family from the Control Panel's Font folder shown later in this chapter.

Five raster fonts are supplied with Windows 95, and several other vendors supply additional font sizes. The supplied raster fonts are MS Serif, MS Sans Serif, Courier, System, and Terminal.

Vector Fonts

Vector fonts are derived from lines or vectors that describe each character's shape. You can scale vector fonts to any size or aspect ratio. The characters are stored as a set of points and interconnecting lines that Windows 95 can use to scale the font to any required size. These fonts are very applicable for plotting and CAD. As with the raster fonts, vector fonts are stored in FON files.

The way Windows 95 treats this font type is to rasterize the various characters by using function calls to the Graphics Device Interface (GDI). The number of calls required for each font increases the display time required to create the characters and to refresh the display. The fonts are useful for CAD and desktop publishing because they are readily extensible. Large vector font sizes maintain the same aspect ratio as smaller sizes. Windows 95 supplies three vector fonts: ROMAN, SCRIPT, and MODERN. Additional fonts are available from several sources, including CAD and desktop publishing software vendors.

TrueType Fonts

TrueType fonts use *scalable* font technology. Scalable fonts have many advantages over raster fonts and have greatly simplified the use and management of fonts. Scalable fonts are stored in files that contain both the outline information and the ratios necessary to scale the font. Windows uses this information to render the fonts, that is, to produce the dots needed to display and print the font.

Windows 95 supplies many TrueType fonts, including Arial (ARIAL.TTF), New Courier (COUR.TTF), Times New Roman (TIMES.TTF), and Swiss (TT0007M_.TTF). Because TrueType fonts are included with Windows, scalable fonts are available to all users at no extra cost. A market still exists for Adobe PostScript Type 1 fonts, because these fonts are the standard in the typesetting world. For most users, however, TrueType fonts are more than sufficient.

Other Fonts

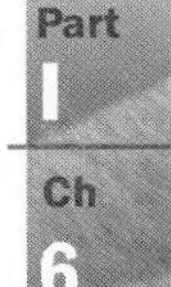

In addition to raster, vector, and TrueType fonts, other fonts exist that perform specialized services. Your printer may have an entire set of fonts or may be configured with font sets through the use of font cartridges or additional cards. The following list describes additional Windows 95 fonts:

- **System fonts.** 8514SYS.FON and VGASYS.FON.
- **OEM fonts.** 8514OEM.FON and VGAOEM.FON.
- **Fixed fonts.** 8514FIX.FON and VGAFIX.FON.
- **MS-DOS legacy fonts.** Several MS-DOS-compatible font files for DOS applications to use while running in the Windows 95 environment. These files provide backward compatibility to the real-mode DOS environment. Files included are CGA40WOA.FON, CGA80WOA.FON, DOSAPP.FON, EGA40WOA.FON, and EGA80WOA.FON. Although these fonts are primarily used for application display, the DOSAPP.FON is a good choice for printing.

- **Printer soft fonts.** Depending on your printing hardware, you may download soft fonts to your printer. Downloading fonts reduces the time taken by the printer to process printouts. You download soft fonts once to speed up subsequent print jobs.

Installing and Deleting Fonts

During the Windows installation process, Windows loads its standard suite of font files onto the system disk. Windows and your applications use these files as default fonts. You have the option of installing and deleting fonts from your system to change the look of your desktop environment, word-processing, spreadsheet applications, or for use by special application needs, such as CAD.

CAUTION

Be careful when deleting seemingly useless font sets. Deleting certain sets such as fixed, OEM, or system fonts may drastically alter the look and proportion of your Windows desktop and applications. When you delete fonts, you may see applications and even Windows dialog boxes change appearance. Even though Windows substitutes existing fonts to replace deleted ones, you may not like the substitution. Make sure you have a backup copy of all fonts you delete, as you may want to replace them for aesthetic reasons.

Installing New Fonts

Windows enables you to quickly install new fonts using the Control Panel; you can install fonts from the Windows disks or from vendor supplied disks. This procedure installs new Fonts into Windows Registry for use by both Windows and applications.

1. Open the Start menu and choose Settings; then choose Control Panel. Double-click the Fonts folder in the Control Panel. Windows displays the Fonts window that contains a list of all the fonts currently registered by the system (see Figure 6.1).
2. You can display the list as individual icons with the name of each font below the icons. Or you can display a detailed list that contains the name of the font, the name and extension of the font file, the size of the file, and the date of its creation. To change the look of this list, choose View and then choose Large Icons, List, or Details. See Figure 6.1 for an example of Details view.

NOTE On occasion, you may want to look at the list of font types displayed without their many variations, such as Bold. You may choose this option in conjunction with other View menu selections by choosing View, Hide Variations (Bold, Italic, and so on).

3. Choose Files, Install. Windows displays the Add Fonts dialog box, shown in Figure 6.2.
4. Using the Drives and Folders controls, choose the location of the font you want to install. This location may be a directory on the hard drive or a manufacturer's floppy disk.
5. Windows displays a roster in the List of Fonts window. Select the font or fonts to add. If these fonts are in a location other than the Windows font directory, you may have the

files automatically copied to this directory by checking the Copy Fonts to Windows Folder box at the bottom of the Add Fonts dialog box.

6. Click OK to add the selected font(s). Windows installs the new fonts and enters them in its Registry.

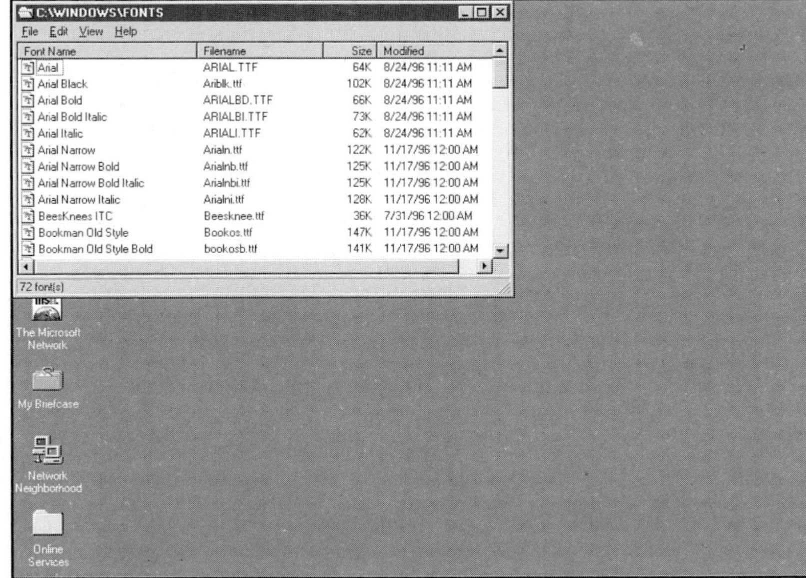

FIG. 6.1
The Fonts window shows which fonts are loaded along with their file name, size, and configuration date.

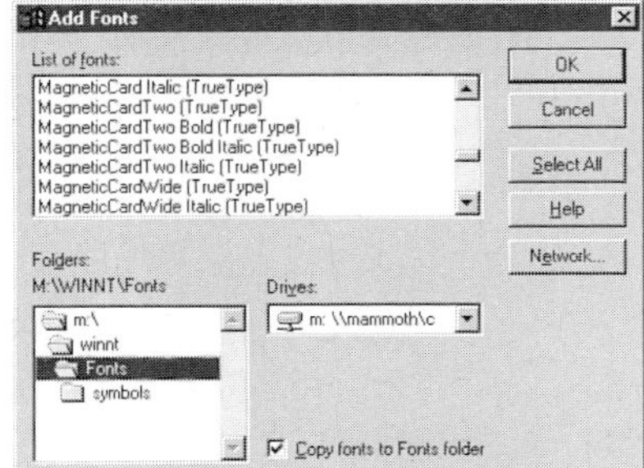

FIG. 6.2
The Add Fonts dialog box provides the controls needed to add a new font to Windows 95.

Deleting Fonts from the Hard Disk

Windows also enables you to quickly delete installed fonts from the Control Panel. The following procedure deletes unwanted fonts and removes them from the Windows Registry.

1. Open the Start menu and choose Settings; then choose Control Panel. Double-click the Fonts folder in the Control Panel. In the Fonts window, Windows displays the fonts currently registered by the system (refer to Figure 6.1).

2. Highlight the font or fonts to delete.
3. Choose File, Delete.

If you mistakenly delete fonts, you may recover them from the Recycle Bin.

See "Restoring Deleted Files," p. 323

4. Windows displays a warning asking if you want to delete these fonts. Choose Yes. Windows shows the font being sent to the Recycle bin as it removes the deleted fonts from the Registry.

NOTE For faster deletion, you can also delete fonts by dragging and dropping them from the Fonts Folder into the Recycle bin, using the Windows Explorer.

Using TrueType Fonts

TrueType fonts are an integral part of Windows 95 and many font styles come bundled with the operating system, as described earlier. TrueType scalable fonts offer several advantages over previous font technologies:

- A single font file can print and display the font over a wide range of point sizes. Raster files require many font files to cover the same range of sizes.
- The same font file can render both screen display and printer output. Raster fonts require a screen font and printer font file for each font set.
- The technology for scalable fonts has standardized the production of fonts, bringing the cost of font production way down.
- You can use the same font with any printer that has a Windows printer driver. Individual printer manufacturers don't need to worry about creating fonts for their printers.
- By using the same font file to render both the screen and printer fonts, the match between what you see on your screen and the printer output is very close.

TrueType fonts have certain limitations, however. The anti-aliasing technology described earlier in this chapter needs a 256-color mode or higher, requiring more complex and higher-priced hardware. For specific printing applications and CAD applications, PostScript fonts repeatedly provide better printing results. In addition, not every printer is compatible with TrueType fonts, causing some printers to treat TrueType fonts as graphics and thus reducing printer speed.

Windows enables you to easily identify your TrueType fonts. Open the Fonts windows in the Control Panel. Choose View, Large Icon to display your fonts as icons. TrueType fonts are designated with an icon containing the letters T_T. In the List and Details view, TrueType fonts are shown prefaced by a smaller icon showing T_T. In the Details view, TrueType fonts also are denoted by their file type TTF. Other font types are shown as file type FON.

If you work with many MS-DOS applications, note that TrueType and other fonts are also distinguishable by their file extensions. TrueType fonts have the TTF extension; other font types have the FON extension.

Adding or Removing TrueType Fonts

You add or delete TrueType fonts the same way you add or delete other font types. To add or remove TrueType fonts, use the previously described Add a Font or Delete a Font procedures, selecting only fonts with TTF file extensions.

Using Windows 3.1 TrueType Fonts

In Windows 3.1, each TrueType font was maintained by two files, TTF and FOT. Windows 95 eliminates the need for an FOT by implementing faster font creation. You can add your existing TrueType fonts to Windows 95 by specifying the TTF file when adding a font. Windows will not ask for a separate FOT file and accepts Windows 3.1 TrueType fonts as well as fonts created from most existing applications.

Using Only TrueType Fonts

To select only TrueType fonts in your applications, you can set the appropriate font option. Microsoft has integrated TrueType fonts into the Windows operating system. If you want to only use TrueType fonts in your applications, follow this procedure:

1. Choose the Fonts folder from the Control Panel. Windows displays the Fonts folder containing a list of the registered fonts.
2. Choose View, Options.
3. Choose the TrueType tab in the Options dialog box (see Figure 6.3).

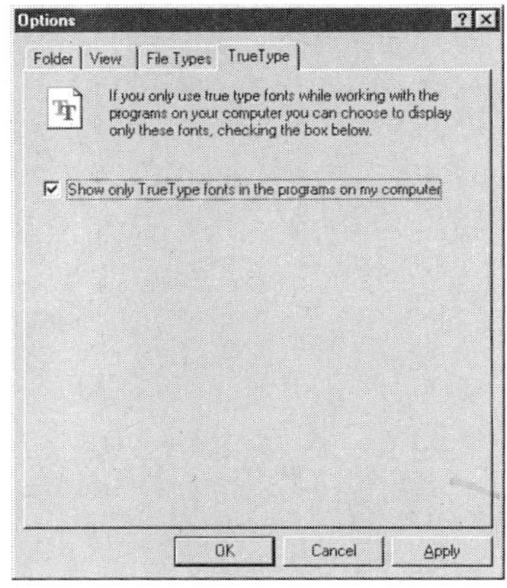

FIG. 6.3 To configure only TrueType fonts for applications, check the box in the Options dialog box that reads Show Only TrueType Fonts in the Programs on My Computer.

4. Check the box that reads Show Only TrueType Fonts in the Programs on my Computer. Now, only TrueType fonts are shown as available to applications.

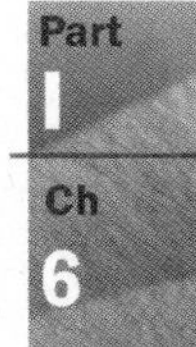

Using Other Font Configurations

See "Viewing and Changing the Properties of a File or Folder," **p. 327**

Each printer in your Windows 95 system is configurable through its Printer Properties pages. The printer property options vary from printer to printer. Many printers support downloaded soft fonts. And many of these printers support TrueType fonts as downloaded soft fonts or support printing them as graphics. You can set these options on the appropriate Printer Properties Fonts page, but you should understand the ramifications of any changes you make.

Downloading TrueType fonts as soft fonts stores the fonts in your printer. If your printer has adequate memory to store fonts, downloading speeds up the printing operation. If the printer is unable to store these fonts, you usually receive a "memory overflow" error on the printer following the download. Printing TrueType fonts as graphics increases your printing time, but on some printers, it substantially improves the look and quality of the printed font.

PostScript printers provide an option to substitute PostScript fonts for TrueType fonts by use of a Font Substitution Table. The Printer Properties Fonts page for those printers enables you to change which fonts are substituted by changing the table.

Managing Fonts in Windows 95

In Windows 95, fonts are a managed resource. Applications can quickly access fonts through standardized registration, making your fonts quickly available for viewing, printing, comparing, sorting, adding, and deleting.

Previewing and Printing Font Samples

Before you use a font, you may want to preview it or print a sample before committing it to a document. Windows provides quick access to this information by performing the following steps:

1. In the Control Panel, double-click the Fonts folder. Windows displays the Fonts window containing the list of registered fonts.
2. Select the font you want to view and choose File, Open; or double-click the font to view it. Windows displays the font in various sizes (see Figure 6.4).

You also can print a sample from the Fonts folder by selecting the font and choosing File, Print.

3. To print the sample page, choose Print.
4. When you are done previewing and printing the font, choose Done.

FIG. 6.4
A sample of a font type showing sizes and font detail information.

Showing Font Properties

Fonts, like most other Windows objects, have properties. The properties include version information that may contain important information for purposes of upgrading your fonts. Although at present there is no way to change these font properties, you can view the information contained in these screens in the following procedure.

1. Double-click the Fonts icon in the Control Panel. Windows displays the Fonts window containing the list of registered fonts.
2. Select the font you want to view.
3. Choose File, Properties. Windows displays a properties sheet like the one shown in Figure 6.5. The properties sheet contains version and management information for each font type registered by Windows.

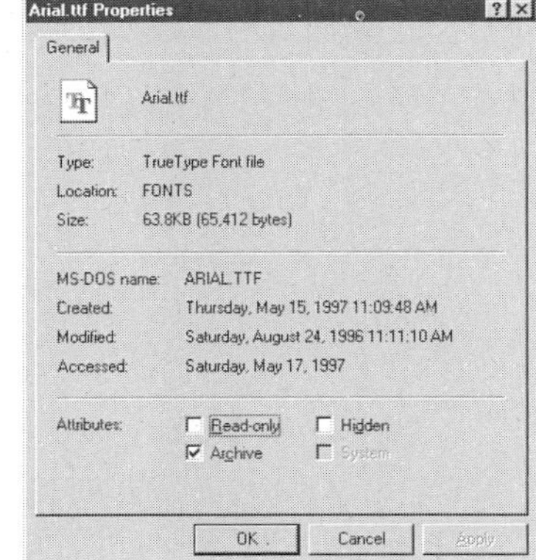

FIG. 6.5
A properties sheet for the Arial TrueType font provides file and configuration information.

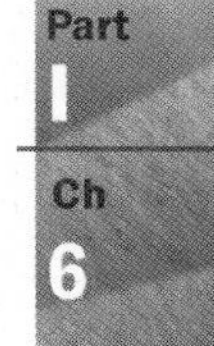

Viewing Fonts by Similarity

Fonts are distinguished by their differences, but they also can be grouped by similar features. Grouping fonts by similarity may be important to you when you find subtle differences in the text in a document or when your printed document doesn't match the display. Substituting a similar font may correct this problem. You will find fonts listed by similarity, except where Windows has insufficient Panose information to make a comparison. *Panose* refers to a Windows internal description that assigns each font a Panose ID number. Windows uses several internal descriptions to categorize fonts. The Panose information is used to register a font class and a means to compare similar font features. You can group similar fonts by following this procedure.

1. Double-click the Fonts icon in the Control Panel to open the Fonts folder with a list of registered fonts.
2. To change the way the fonts are displayed, choose View, Details, List, or Large Icons.
3. To see which fonts are similar to a specific font, choose View, List Files by Similarity. Windows redisplays the Font list as shown in Figure 6.6.
4. Open the List Fonts by Similarity To drop-down list, and select a font from the list to use as a master against which you test other fonts for similarity. The list now shows all fonts with an assessment of their similarity to the master font. Fonts are shown as being very similar, fairly similar, not similar, or no Panose information available.

You can test the similarity of other fonts by selecting the "List Fonts by Similarity to" control and choosing another font type.

FIG. 6.6
This list shows how closely other font types match the Arial font.

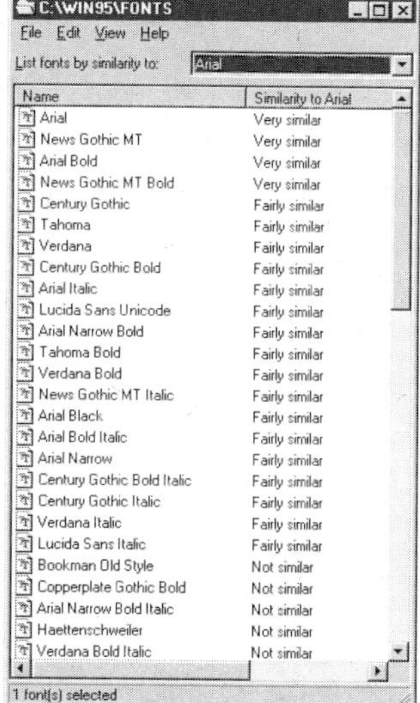

Installing Printer Fonts

Printer fonts reside in the printer as a cartridge or within the printer's memory. You can install printer fonts through Windows or through installation applications that usually accompany your printer. Follow these steps to install printer fonts using Windows:

1. Open the Print Manager for the selected printer.

   See "The Print Manager," **p. 145**

2. Choose Printer, Properties.
3. Choose the Fonts tab on the properties sheet. See the Printer Properties Fonts page shown in Figure 6.7. Note that each printer type is supported by a different set of Properties pages, which depend on the make, model, and hardware configuration of the printer.

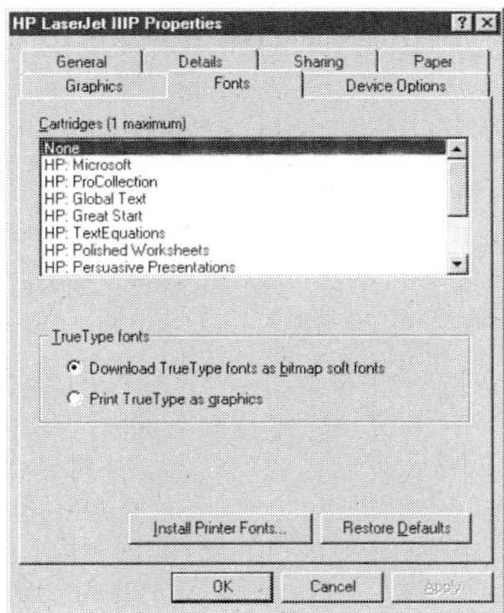

FIG. 6.7
The Printer Properties Fonts page displays the available font options for the selected printer and allows you to install new printer fonts.

4. Choose Install Printer Fonts. A dialog box similar to the one in Figure 6.8 appears. The printer fonts installer for your printer may look different from the one shown in the figure, but all installers perform similar functions.

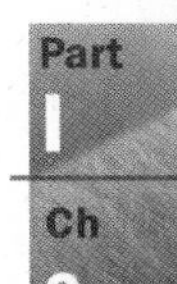

FIG. 6.8
The HP Font Installer dialog box.

NOTE The HP Fonts Installer shown in Figure 6.8 cannot be used to download TrueType fonts to HP Printers. PCL printers can download only PCL-compatible fonts. Be certain that your printer and the fonts being specified for download are compatible. Refer to the installer's help file for more information on compatible fonts.

5. Select the fonts to be installed in the list on the right side of the Font Installer dialog box.
6. Choose Copy to move the selected fonts to the left window.
7. Choose Add Fonts to register the printer's fonts. A dialog box appears, asking for the location of the fonts. This box provides a Browse button to enable you to find the disk location of the fonts to be installed.
8. Identify where the font files are located and click OK to enable Windows to install the selected fonts.

Downloading Fonts as Permanent or Temporary

Most Printer Properties Fonts pages include a set of option button controls that enable you to select whether a font is to be temporarily or permanently downloaded.

Download frequently used fonts as permanent. This allows you to print faster. However, permanent downloaded fonts limit the amount of printer memory available for printing. Therefore, to stay within normal printer memory limits, keep the number of fonts you specify as permanent to three of four.

Downloading fonts as temporary does not store the font in the printer's memory until it is needed. The font is loaded only temporarily in the printer before a document is printed and removed after the printing is completed. This increases printing time, but it also increases the amount of available printer memory and reduces print overrun errors. Downloading fonts as temporary is the default setting and works well with most applications.

CHAPTER 7

Plug and Play and Legacy Device Installation

by Michael Desmond

Installing Plug and Play hardware

Learn how to take full advantage of Windows 95's revolutionary Plug and Play technology.

Installing legacy (non-PnP) hardware

This guide to working with older hardware helps you avoid trouble-some conflicts during installation.

Troubleshooting hardware installation

When things go wrong, this section helps you get out of trouble and back to work.

Windows 95 brings a host of important capabilities to the desktop PC, including the Plug and Play (PnP) technology. Anyone who has stayed up all night or stayed in all weekend trying to get a new sound card to work will tell you that. PCs are built specifically for flexibility and upgrades, yet installing an adapter card can be a grueling and sometimes futile exercise.

Microsoft recruited the participation of companies such as Intel, Compaq, Phoenix Technologies, and others to develop an industry standard for managing PC hardware and peripherals. Windows 95 Plug and Play enables PCs, peripherals, and the Windows 95 operating system to communicate with each other, allowing for automatic configuration of hardware.

Plug and Play can take the complexity out of hardware installations, but there is a catch; for Plug in Play to work to its full potential, the PC's motherboard, add-in cards, and operating system must all be Plug and Play-compliant. But even if your hardware is not PnP-compliant, Windows 95 can make educated guesses about your PC's configuration to ease installations.

TROUBLESHOOTING

When I use the Add New Hardware Wizard, it fails to detect a device upgrade for an unsupported device. What am I doing wrong? If you have upgraded a sound card or other device that uses Windows 3.1 drivers, the new sound card may not be detected by the Add New Hardware Wizard. This occurs because Windows 95 is still seeing the reference to the older card's 16-bit drivers in the SYSTEM.INI file. To resolve the problem, you must go into SYSTEM.INI with a text editor, such as NOTEPAD.EXE, and remove the lines referring to the 16-bit drivers. Run the Add New Hardware Wizard, and the new sound card or other device should be set up correctly.

This chapter helps you understand how Plug and Play works—and more importantly, what to do when it doesn't. You learn how to use the Add New Hardware Wizard and other tools to work with peripherals that are not Plug and Play-compliant. You also learn how to handle conflicts.

Installing Plug and Play Hardware

Plug and Play can make adding peripherals easy for users of all levels of expertise. With the proper hardware, installing peripherals can be as simple as plugging in an add-in card and starting up the PC. This section guides you through the steps involved in setting up a Plug and Play device. You also learn how Plug and Play technology works.

How Windows 95 Plug and Play Works

Because it addresses so many components in the PC, Plug and Play is a complex technology. Plug and Play enables all parts of the PC to communicate to each other, from the low level BIOS to the various add-in cards. When Windows 95 starts, the operating system and PC go through a series of steps to establish configurations, arbitrate conflicts, and record changes.

The Components of Plug and Play To understand how Plug and Play works, you have to know what elements are involved. Four major technologies work together under Plug and Play:

- **System BIOS (basic input/output system).** The system BIOS is the low-level code that boots your system, detects the hard disk, and manages basic operations. Plug and Play systems employ a specially tuned BIOS that has the intelligence to detect hardware and manage configuration changes.

NOTE Under the Plug and Play specification, PnP BIOSes are identified as Plug and Play BIOS version 1.0a or later. To find out what BIOS version you have, look for the BIOS information on your monitor at the beginning of the bootup process.

- **Operating system.** The operating system interacts with the BIOS and hardware, playing a critical role in Plug and Play. Windows 95 is the first Plug and Play operating system, but Microsoft intends to bring the technology to Windows NT in the future.

- **Hardware peripherals.** To be Plug and Play-compliant, adapter cards and other hardware must include circuitry that stores configuration data and allows interaction with other PnP components. PCI add-in cards, by definition, are PnP-compliant, while ISA and EISA cards must be specifically designed for PnP. External peripherals such as modems or printers can be PnP as well.
- **Device drivers.** Drivers let your peripherals talk to Windows 95. Under Windows 95's Plug and Play, hardware must employ 32-bit *virtual device drivers* (called VxDs), as opposed to the 16-bit, real-mode drivers used under DOS/Windows 3.x.

NOTE The 32-bit VxDs for most devices are supplied by the hardware vendors. If the appropriate driver is not available on the Windows 95 CD-ROM or disks, contact your peripheral manufacturer to get the latest PnP-compliant drivers.

Walking Through the PnP Process Each time you boot up the system, a series of steps occurs that launches the Plug and Play process. All the hardware on the system is checked at boot time, so if new hardware has been installed, it will be detected and the appropriate steps taken by the PnP system.

The list below details the steps that Windows 95 goes through during system startup:

1. The system BIOS identifies the devices on the motherboard (including the type of bus), as well as external devices such as disk drives, keyboard, video display, and other adapter cards that are required for the boot process.
2. The system BIOS determines the resource (IRQ, DMA, I/O, and memory address) requirements of each boot device. The BIOS also determines which devices are legacy devices with fixed resource requirements and which are PnP devices with flexible resource requirements. Note that some devices don't require all four resource types.

NOTE Microsoft uses the term *legacy device* to refer to older hardware peripherals that do not comply with the Plug and Play specification. As a general rule, any ISA card bought before 1995 is probably a legacy device.

3. Windows 95 allocates resources to each PnP device, after allowing for legacy devices with fixed resource assignments. If many legacy and PnP devices are in use, Windows 95 may require many iterations of the allocation process to eliminate all resource conflicts by changing the resource assignments of the PnP devices.
4. Windows 95 creates a final system configuration and stores the resource allocation data for this configuration in the registration database (the Registry).
5. Windows 95 searches the \WINDOWS\SYSTEM directory to find the required driver for the device. If the device driver is missing, a dialog box appears asking you to insert into drive A the manufacturer's floppy disk containing the driver software. Windows 95 loads the driver into memory and then completes its startup operations.

Note that Windows 95 makes educated guesses about the identity and resource requirements of legacy devices. Windows 95 includes a large database of resource settings for legacy devices, allowing it to detect and configure itself to a variety of existing hardware. However, this detection is not perfect, and it forces dynamic PnP peripherals to be configured around the static settings of legacy hardware.

Understanding Plug and Play Hardware

Of course, Windows 95 Plug and Play works best on systems properly equipped to support it. This section helps you to determine if your existing PC is Plug and Play-ready; and if not, what you can do to upgrade it. This section also can help you to determine whether a new system you plan to buy is PnP-compliant.

Determining Whether Your PC Supports Plug and Play So is your PC Plug and Play? To make that claim, a system must have a BIOS that conforms to Plug and Play version 1.0a or later. Vendors generally began building Plug and Play into motherboards at the beginning of 1995, so older PCs probably won't support direct PnP features.

NOTE Even if your BIOS is PnP-compliant, you won't have a true Plug and Play system until all the peripherals in your system are PnP, too. Remember, legacy devices force Windows 95 to make educated guesses about their requirements and their resources can't be dynamically allocated.

How can you find out if your Windows 95 system is PnP-ready? Go to Windows 95's System Properties sheet and do the following:

1. Click the Device Manager tab of the System Properties sheet to display Devices by Type. (Click the View Devices by Type option button if necessary.)
2. Double-click the System Devices icon in the device list to expand the System Devices list.
3. If your PC supports Plug and Play, you see a Plug and Play BIOS entry (see Figure 7.1). The I/O Read Data Port for ISA Plug and Play Enumerator item appears regardless of whether your PC is Plug and Play.

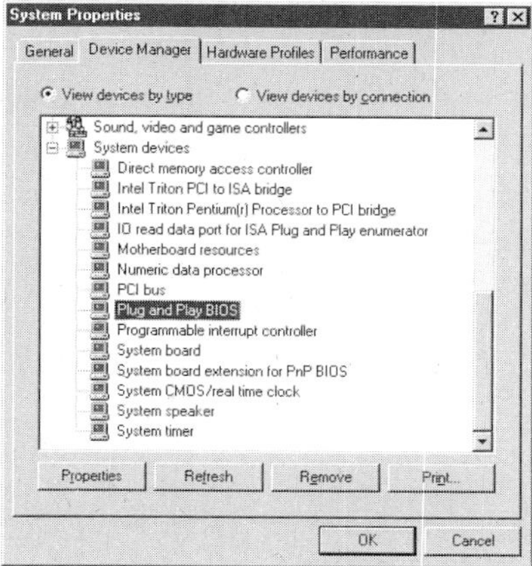

FIG. 7.1 Check the System Devices list to determine whether your PC has Plug and Play BIOS.

4. Double-click the Plug and Play BIOS icon to open the properties sheet for the Plug and Play BIOS.
5. Click the Driver tab to display the device driver (BIOS.VXD) that Windows 95 uses to connect to the PnP feature of your system BIOS (see Figure 7.2).
6. To leave the sheet, click OK, and then click OK on the System properties sheet.

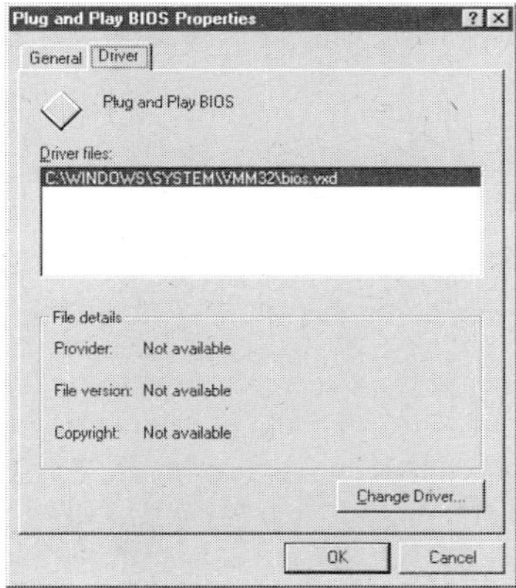

FIG. 7.2 Click the Driver tab to check the properties of Windows 95's Plug and Play BIOS device driver.

What does a Plug and Play BIOS do exactly? As the cornerstone of PnP functionality, the BIOS adds three major enhancements to conventional PC BIOSes:

- *Resource management* handles the basic system resources: direct memory access (DMA), interrupt requests (IRQs), input/output (I/0), and shared memory address ranges. Resource management allows various devices to access limited system resources without causing conflicts. The Plug and Play BIOS resource manager configures boot devices on the motherboard and any PnP devices in the system.
- *Runtime management* of configuration is available with PnP. PnP BIOS includes the capability to reconfigure devices after the operating system loads. This feature is particularly important for notebook PCs that have PCMCIA (also known as PC Card) devices that you can change at will. Previously, the operating system considered all devices detected by the BIOS to be static, which required restarting the system anytime a PC Card or other device was swapped out.
- *Event management* detects when devices have been removed or added to the system while the computer is running. PnP BIOS 1.0a provides event management, such as detecting when your notebook PC is connected to a docking adapter. (Note that installing or removing desktop add-in cards while the PC is running is not a safe practice.) Event management relies on runtime management to reconfigure the system.

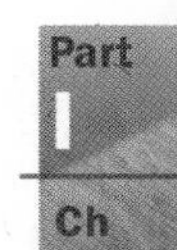

CAUTION

Some brands of computers whose motherboards were produced in 1994 display messages during the boot process, indicating that the motherboard supports Plug and Play. Many of these motherboards, however, have early versions of the PnP BIOS, which do not conform to the 1.0a specification. Even if your computer displays a PnP message during the boot process, check Device Manager for the Plug and Play BIOS entry to verify that you have PnP BIOS 1.0a.

Upgrading to Plug and Play If you have an older 486 or Pentium PC, you may not be able to take advantage of Plug and Play. The problem is that the BIOS in these systems was written before there was a PnP standard to support. Still, you may be able to upgrade your PC to support PnP, so that future installations of PnP-compliant hardware go more smoothly.

Generally, there are three options for upgrading an older PC to a Plug and Play BIOS:

- **Flash the BIOS.** This is an option for those systems with a Flash BIOS, a nonvolatile memory chip (NVRAM) that retains BIOS instructions when the power is turned off. Updating a Flash BIOS is as easy as running an upgrade utility from a floppy disk. The utility writes a newer BIOS to the NVRAM chip, effectively turning your PC into a PnP system. Contact your system vendor for an updated Flash BIOS.
- **Replace the BIOS chip.** If your system is two years old or more, you probably don't have a Flash BIOS. But you may be able to replace the BIOS chip, which is often seated into a socket on the motherboard. You'll need to call your PC or motherboard vendor about a PnP BIOS upgrade kit, which lets you pull the existing BIOS chip(s) and plug in the replacement(s).
- **Replace the motherboard.** This is the most radical (and expensive) approach, but it's the only solution if the BIOS chip is soldered directly onto the motherboard and is not Flash-upgradable. You need to make sure the new motherboard fits in your system's chassis and accepts your existing add-in cards, memory, and processor.

NOTE While a motherboard upgrade can update older BIOSes to Plug and Play, it may make more sense to wait to purchase a new system. A new PC comes with updated peripherals, such as a larger hard drive and faster graphics board, which improve overall system performance.

Purchasing a Plug and Play System Owners of older PCs may have to do a little investigating to determine if their systems support Plug and Play, but newer systems should be PnP-compliant right out of the box. Now that Microsoft has committed to bringing PnP to its other Windows operating system—Windows NT—the presence of PnP on Intel-compatible PCs becomes even more important.

Making sure you have a PnP-ready PC is not difficult. Generally, any machine that displays the "Designed for Windows 95" logo is PnP-compliant. Lacking that logo, look for the following:

- **Plug and Play BIOS 1.0a or later.** Also make sure that the system uses a Flash BIOS, because future updates to the PnP specification or other system architectures may require a BIOS upgrade.
- **PCI bus expansion slots.** Unlike ISA peripherals, all PCI cards are PnP-compliant. Even in non-PnP systems, PCI cards arbitrate configuration among themselves and offer the further convenience of being software-configurable. Also, the VESA Local Bus (VLB) standard is on the wane as Pentium systems replace 486s, which makes VLB peripherals harder to find.

You should also check if the ISA peripherals installed in the PC, such as sound boards or modems, are PnP-compliant. Remember, the presence of non-PnP or legacy hardware in your system makes the task of hardware configuration more difficult and prone to failure. You should also check on the CD-ROM and fixed disks to ensure that they are designed for the specification.

TROUBLESHOOTING

Why does my PCI graphics card show an IRQ conflict in the System properties sheet? Under Plug and Play, PCI cards can share IRQs; however, Windows 95 does not support PCI cards that try to share IRQs with non-PCI devices. While Windows 95 display drivers do not require IRQ resources, PCI graphics cards request an IRQ in order to maintain full compatibility. As a result, all PCI graphics cards attempt to assign an IRQ. You must use Device Manager to assign a new IRQ setting to the device that is conflicting with the PCI graphics card.

Why does Device Manager show a resource conflict with a PCI-to-ISA bridge? There is no conflict here. If your Plug and Play BIOS reports both a PCI and an ISA bus, the Device Manager may report a conflict with that component. Users see an exclamation point in a yellow circle next to the PCI-to-ISA bridge entry in Device Manager. However, the PCI and ISA buses both work normally; there is no actual conflict. If you want, you can contact your hardware vendor to see if an updated Plug and Play BIOS is available that will only report a PCI bus.

Installing Plug and Play Hardware

If you've been through a few nightmarish upgrades, you'll find installing a PnP adapter card into a PnP-compliant PC to be a refreshing experience. To install both a new card and its 32-bit VxD driver, do the following:

1. Turn off power to the PC.
2. Open the case and install the adapter card, following the instructions provided with the card.
3. Close the case and turn on your PC.
4. Insert the driver software floppy disk in your A or B drive, if requested, and follow the steps for installing the driver software.
5. Restart Windows 95, if requested.

It's that easy. If the driver for your card is included with Windows 95, you may not need the card's floppy disk; Windows 95 automatically sets up the driver for your device. (Note that in this case, you may need to put the Windows 95 CD-ROM or requested floppy disk into the appropriate drive so the bundled VxD can be loaded.)

Windows 95 and your hardware may both provide a 32-bit VxD for your device. Compare the dates of the driver files using Explorer, and install the more recent file.

The same basic procedure applies for PnP-compatible external devices, such as printers, scanners, or external modems. If your PC has PnP-compliant serial and parallel ports, you will follow a procedure similar to the one in the preceding list. When you add or change a peripheral device, you don't need to open the PC, and in some cases (modems, for example), a new driver is not required.

See "Using Your Laptop with a Docking System," **p. 198**

Installing Legacy (non-PnP) Hardware

As a Plug and Play operating system, Windows 95 may eventually make even complex upgrades a simple matter of plugging in a card and booting to a new configuration. But the existence of millions of add-in cards and external peripherals with no PnP support means that day is still sometime in the future. Understanding this, Microsoft has gone to great effort to ensure that non-PnP peripherals are adequately supported under the new regime.

The effort seems to have paid off. While installing legacy devices can still be tricky, the experience is simpler and less hazardous than under 16-bit Windows 3.x. This section shows you how to install legacy devices.

How Windows 95 Operates with Legacy Hardware

Windows 95 cannot fully automate the configuration of legacy devices; however, it does interact with non-PnP devices to ease the process. Detection routines, for example, allow Windows 95 to recognize popular add-in cards such as Creative Labs Soundblaster boards, even though they lack PnP capability. The System Properties sheet, meanwhile, provides a one-stop shop for determining hardware conflicts, editing resource setting values, and optimizing performance. Finally, Windows 95's automated handling of PnP devices makes managing the remaining legacy hardware that much easier.

Almost all PC adapter cards require at least one interrupt request (IRQ) level and a set of I/O base memory addresses for communication with your PC's processor. Some cards require one or more DMA (Direct Memory Access) channels for high-speed communication with your PC's RAM. IRQs, I/O memory, and DMA channels collectively are called *device resources*.

Legacy adapter cards use the following two methods for setting device resource values:

- *Mechanical jumpers* that create a short circuit between two pins of a multipin header. Jumpers are commonly used to designate resource values for sound cards, and they must be set to match the resource settings of Windows 95. If jumper settings do not match those set in Windows 95, the device will not operate.

- *Nonvolatile memory (NVM)* for storing resource assignments. Nonvolatile memory—such as electrically erasable, programmable read-only memory (EEPROM)—retains data when you turn off your PC's power. Network adapter cards and sound cards commonly use NVM. Usually, you must run a setup program for the card to match the board settings to those of the operating system.

NOTE PCI adapter cards do not have jumpers or nonvolatile memory to designate resource values. Instead, the system BIOS and Windows 95 automatically allocate resources needed by PCI adapter cards during the boot process.

The following sections describe how Windows 95 deals with a variety of legacy adapter cards. Later chapters of this book describe in detail the installation process for specific device types, such as modems, CD-ROM drives, and sound cards.

See "Installing and Configuring Your Modem," **p. 76**

See "Installing and Configuring Sound Options," **p. 115**

See "Installing and Using a CD-ROM Drive," **p. 132**

Legacy Device Detection During Windows 95 Setup

When you run Windows 95's setup program, Windows 95 attempts to detect all the hardware devices in your PC, including legacy devices, such as ISA sound cards and network adapters. It then installs 32-bit protected mode drivers for peripherals for which updated drivers are available. However, Windows 95 often keeps references to real-mode (16-bit) device drivers in the CONFIG.SYS and AUTOEXEC.BAT files, which are used when the system runs DOS software in DOS-only mode.

If Windows can't identify the legacy device, you need to install the device manually. This procedure is described in the section "Installing Legacy Cards After Setting Up Drivers," later in this chapter.

Setting Resource Values for Legacy Adapter Cards

You must set the IRQ, I/O base address, and DMA channel parameters of a new adapter card to values that do not conflict with the resource values that are already assigned to system devices, PCI slots, or other legacy adapter cards. One of the problems with the basic design of IBM-compatible PCs is that only 16 interrupts are available, and the majority of these interrupts are likely to be in use. Therefore, your choice of IRQs is limited.

NOTE The word "base" in *I/O base address* refers to the location at which the block of I/O addresses for the adapter card begins. The actual number of address bytes occupied by the I/O system of the adapter card varies with the type of card. I/O addresses are separated by 16 bytes, and most adapter cards require fewer than 16 bytes of I/O address space.

Table 7.1 lists the PC's IRQs and most common use of each interrupt level.

Table 7.1 Interrupt Assignments and Options for ISA Cards Installed in 80×86-Based PCs

IRQ	Function	Most Common Use
0	Internal timer	Dedicated; not accessible
1	Keyboard	Dedicated; not accessible
2	Tied to IRQ9	Dedicated; see IRQ9
3	Second serial port	COM2 and COM4; usually assigned to a modem
4	First serial port	COM1 and COM3; usually for a serial mouse
5	Second parallel printer	Often used for bus mouse, network, and scanner cards
6	Floppy disk drives	Dedicated; do not use
7	First parallel printer	Used by some scanner cards; otherwise available
8	Time-of-day clock	Dedicated; not accessible
9	IRQ2 on 80×86 computers	IRQ2 is rerouted to IRQ9; often shown as IRQ2/9
10	Unassigned	Good choice for sound card, if offered
11	Unassigned	Not a common option; use if 12 is assigned
12	Usually unassigned	Sometimes dedicated to an IBM-style mouse port
13	80×87 coprocessor	Dedicated; do not use even if an 80×87 is not installed
14	Fixed-disk drive	Dedicated; do not use
15	Usually unassigned	Used for secondary disk controller, if installed

Assigning IRQs is a real shell game, with many legacy devices being limited to just two or three specific IRQ numbers. In addition, many ISA boards won't support high IRQ numbers (any setting above IRQ9), which further limits your options.

When you install a new legacy device, you should assign it the highest IRQ number that it will support, leaving the lower IRQs for cards that don't support interrupts above IRQ9 or IRQ10. The Soundblaster 16 audio adapter card, for example, supports only IRQ2/9, IRQ5 (default), IRQ7, and IRQ10.

Virtually all PCs come with two serial port devices (COM1 and COM2) and one parallel port (LPT1) device. COM1 is usually occupied by the serial mouse, unless your PC has a separate IBM PS/2-compatible mouse port that requires an assignable interrupt. The default interrupt for the Soundblaster and most MPC-compatible audio adapter cards is IRQ5, the same setting preferred by many network adapters. Although IRQ5 is assigned to the second parallel printer

(LPT2), few users have two printers, and printers seldom require an interrupt—so IRQ5 is a good candidate when space gets tight.

TIP If you can't get sound on a networked PC, it may be that the network and sound cards are conflicting. IRQ5 is the preferred setting for both network adapters and sound cards, which makes this problem very common.

NOTE Most legacy PC adapter cards use jumpers to set resource values. Cards that store resource settings in nonvolatile RAM require that you run their setup applications to set IRQ, I/O base address, and DMA channel (if applicable). If the setup program unavoidably installs real-mode drivers for the device, don't forget to disable the real-mode drivers by adding temporary REM prefixes before restarting Windows 95. See the section "Changing Resource Settings," later in this chapter.

Installing Adapter Cards with Automatic Detection

The easiest way to install a new legacy card in a Windows 95 system is to use the Add New Hardware Wizard's automatic detection feature to identify your added card. The wizard also can determine if you have removed a card. Auto-detection is best suited for PCs that have few or no specialty adapter cards, such as sound and video capture cards.

The following steps describe the automatic-detection process in installing a Creative Labs Sound Blaster AWE 32 card:

1. Set non-conflicting resource values for your new adapter card, using jumpers or the card's setup program.
2. Shut down Windows 95, and turn off the power on your PC.
3. Install the new adapter card in an empty ISA slot, and make any required external connections, such as audio inputs and speaker outputs for sound cards.
4. Turn the PC power on, and restart Windows 95.
5. Launch Control Panel, and double-click the Add New Hardware icon to start the Add New Hardware Wizard (see Figure 7.3).

FIG. 7.3
The Add New Hardware Wizard provides a step-by-step guide to installing new devices into your PC.

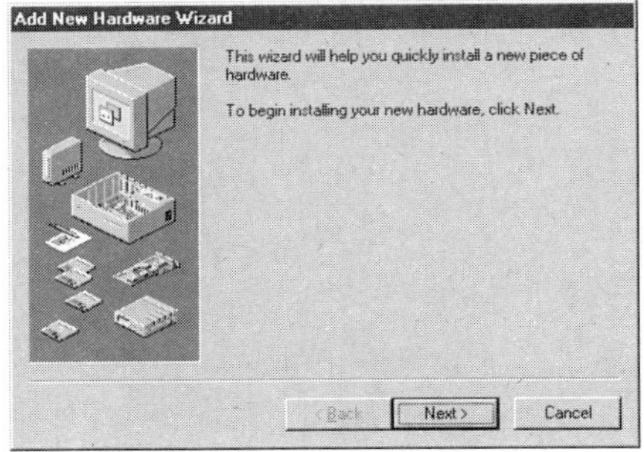

Part I
Ch 7

6. Click the Next button. The next wizard dialog box appears. You can choose manual or automatic hardware detection and installation. Accept the default Yes (Recommended) option (see Figure 7.4).

FIG. 7.4
The Add New Hardware routine lets you choose between automatic or manual hardware detection. Be warned that automatic selection can take a while, particularly on slower machines.

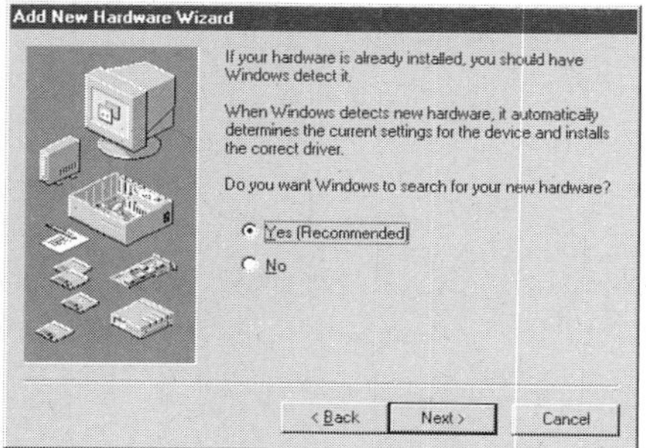

7. Click the Next button to display the wizard's warning that the detection process may take several minutes.
8. Click the Next button to start the detection process. After a few minutes of intense disk activity, often interspersed with periods of seeming inactivity, the wizard advises you that detection is complete (see Figure 7.5).

FIG. 7.5
The Wizard has finally finished the detection process.

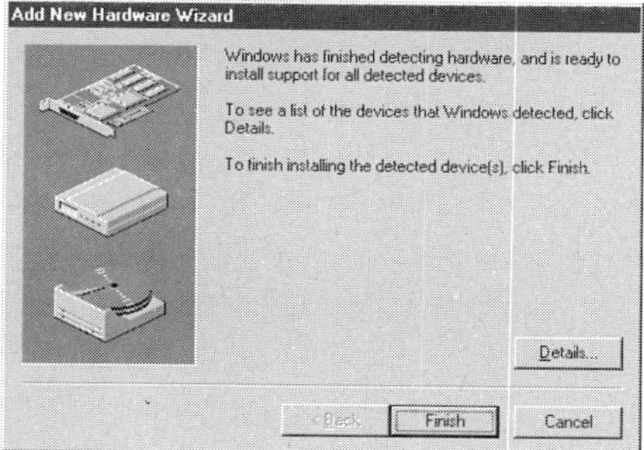

9. Click the Details button to display what the wizard detected. Figure 7.6 shows that the Sound Blaster AWE-32 was detected.

   If the wizard does not detect your newly installed card, you must install the card manually. Click Cancel to terminate the automatic detection process.

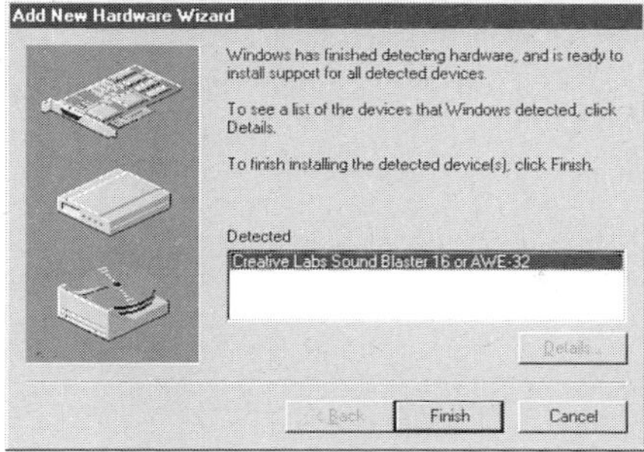

FIG. 7.6
The wizard detected the Sound Blaster AWE-32 sound card.

10. Click the Finish button to install the required drivers from the Windows 95 CD-ROM or floppy disks. The message box shown in Figure 7.7 indicates the expected medium, in this case, the Windows 95 CD-ROM.

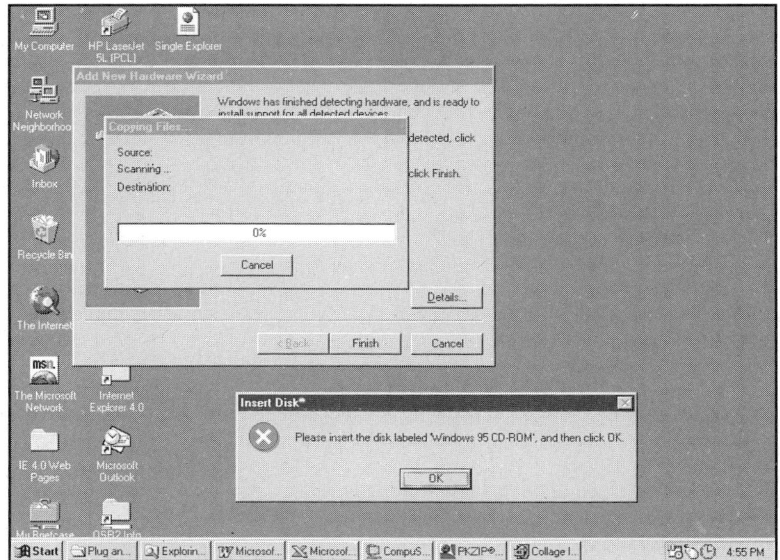

FIG. 7.7
If the driver software isn't available on your hard drive, Windows 95 prompts you to install the media that contains the drivers.

11. Insert the Windows 95 CD-ROM into the drive, and click OK to install the drivers.
12. If Windows 95 can't find the required device driver file in the expected location, you will be prompted to browse for the necessary files.
13. When driver installation is complete, a message box advises you that system settings have changed and asks whether you want to restart Windows 95. Click Restart Now so that your driver change takes effect.

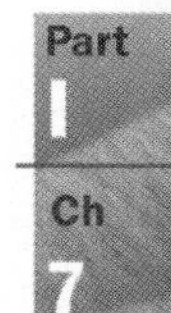

Installing Legacy Cards After Setting Up Drivers

The alternative to automatic device detection is to install the new adapter card *after* you install its driver software. The advantage to this method is that you can determine in advance resource settings that don't conflict with existing devices.

The following steps describe the process of reinstalling the drivers for the Sound Blaster AWE-32 card:

1. Launch the Add New Hardware Wizard from Control Panel, and click the Next button in the opening dialog box to display the wizard dialog box. Here you choose between manual and automatic hardware detection and installation (refer to Figure 7.4).
2. Choose the No option to select manual installation; then click the Next button to display the wizard's Hardware Types dialog box (see Figure 7.8).

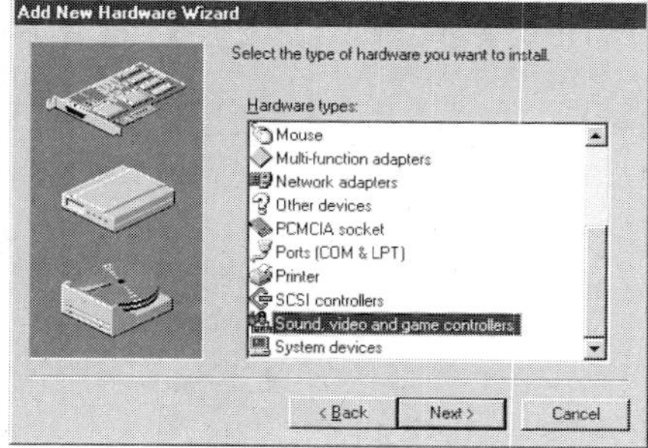

FIG. 7.8 The Add New Hardware Wizard's Hardware Types dialog box lists a variety of adapter card categories.

3. Select the card type in the Hardware Types list; then click the Next button to display the Manufacturers and Models dialog box (see Figure 7.9).

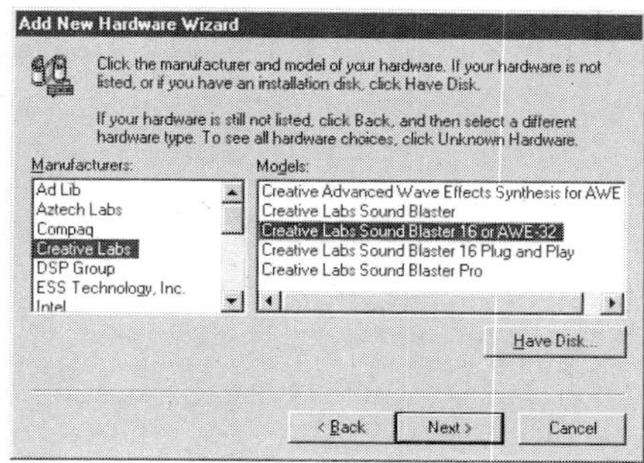

FIG. 7.9 The Wizard dialog box lists manufacturers and models of devices for whose drivers are included with Windows 95.

4. Make the appropriate selections in the Manufacturers and Models list boxes; then click the Next button to display the default settings for the new device.

NOTE If you don't see the manufacturer or model in the list boxes, you need a floppy disk or CD-ROM that contains Windows 95 drivers for your device (Windows 3.1 or later drivers won't work). If you have the required Windows 95 drivers, click the Have Disk button to install the drivers from floppy disk or CD-ROM. If you don't have Windows 95 drivers, click the Cancel button to terminate the installation.

5. Windows 95 can't determine what resource value settings you made for your new or replacement adapter card, so the default settings for the device appear in the wizard's Resource Settings dialog box (see Figure 7.10). You should write down or print these default settings.

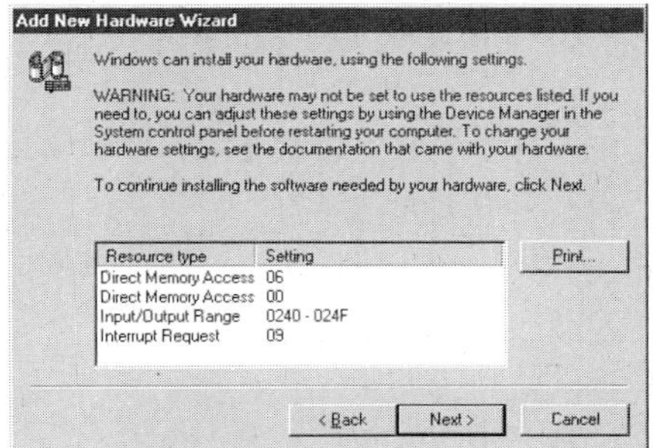

FIG. 7.10 Default values for the Sound Blaster AWE-32 card appear when you open the Resource Setting dialog box.

6. Click the Next button to display the System Settings Change message box (see Figure 7.11).

   If the default settings in the preceding step correspond to the resource settings of your card, click the Yes button to shut down Windows 95. If you haven't installed the card (which is the normal situation for manual device detection), turn off the power to your PC, install the card, turn the power back on, and restart Windows 95 with the new card activated.

   If any of the resource values in the preceding step are incorrect, or you receive a "resource conflict" message, click the No button in the System Settings Change message box so that you can alter the resource values as necessary.

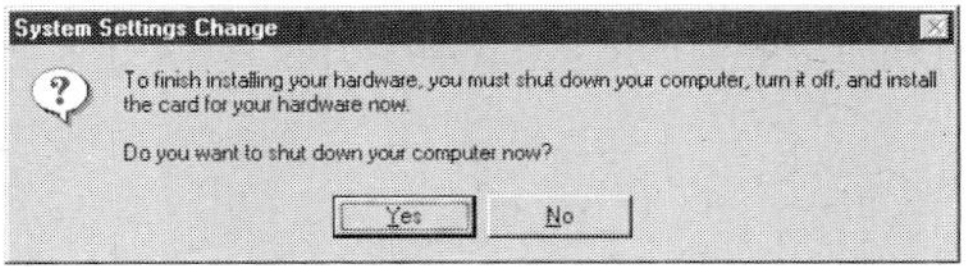

FIG. 7.11 The System Settings Change message box gives you the option to restart Windows 95.

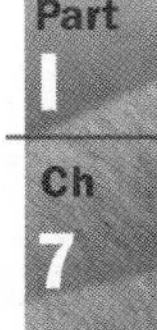

7. Open Control Panel's System Properties sheet, click the Device Manager tab, and expand the entries for the type of device that you're installing. Exclamation points superimposed on the device's icon(s) indicate that the device is not yet fully installed or has been removed from your PC.

8. If you're replacing a card, entries for both cards appear in the Device Manager list. To remove the old entry, select the entry and click the Remove button. A message box requests that you confirm the removal process (see Figure 7.12).

FIG. 7.12
Windows 95 asks for confirmation before you remove a device from the Device Manager.

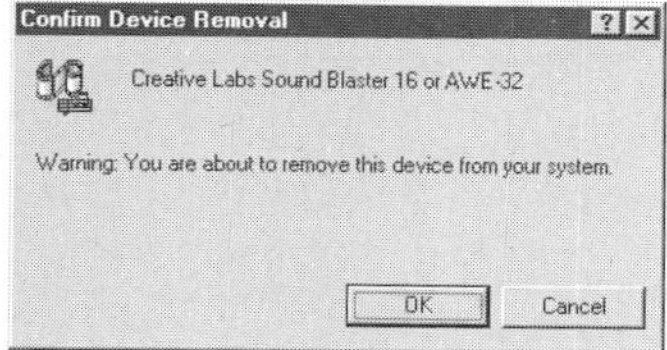

9. Double-click the entry for the new adapter card to display the Properties sheet for the device.
10. In the Resource Settings list box, select the resource whose value you want to change; then click the Change Settings button to display the Edit Interrupt Request dialog box for the resource.
11. Use the spin buttons of the Value text box to select the value that corresponds to the preset value for your adapter card. If a conflict with the existing card occurs, the card that has the conflicting value is identified in the Conflict Information text box (see Figure 7.13).
12. Change the Value setting to a value that displays No devices are conflicting in the Conflict Information box; then make the corresponding change in the card, using the jumpers or nonvolatile RAM. (Turn off power to your PC before making jumper changes.)

FIG. 7.13
Change the IRQ setting for the new adapter card to avoid a conflict.

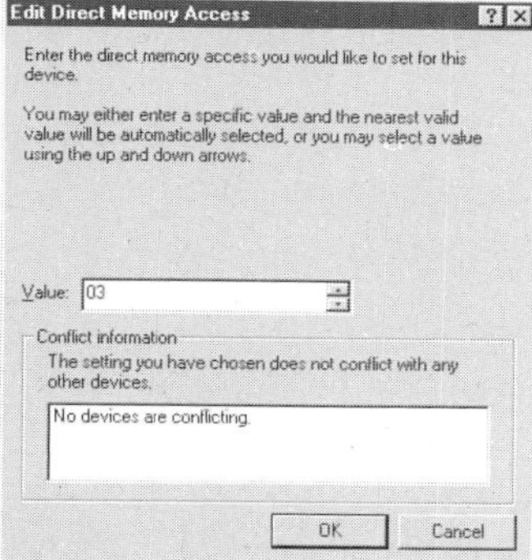

13. After making all the changes necessary to remove resource conflicts, click OK to close the resource's Edit Input/Output Range dialog box, and then click OK to close the Properties page for the specific device.
14. Click OK to close the System Properties sheet.
15. Shut down and restart Windows 95 so that your new settings take effect.

The process of manually installing a legacy device described in the preceding steps appears to be complex, but it is a much more foolproof method than the one used by Windows 3.x. For example, the capability to detect potential resource conflicts before the new setting is locked in helps eliminate many problems associated with installing new devices under Windows 3.x.

NOTE Windows 95 includes drivers for an extraordinary number of popular devices but not for low-volume products, such as digital videocapture and MPEG-1 playback cards. Most manufacturers of specialty legacy devices should provide 32-bit protected-mode drivers for Windows 95. You can find updated Windows 95 drivers on manufacturer's forums on CompuServe, America Online, and Microsoft Network, as well as on World Wide Web sites.

Removing Unneeded Drivers for Legacy Devices

If you remove a legacy device from your PC and don't intend to reinstall it, it's good Windows 95 housekeeping to remove the driver for the device from the Device Manager list. Follow these steps to remove the Device Manager entry for permanently removed adapter cards:

1. Double-click Control Panel's System icon to open the System Properties sheet.
2. Click the Device Manager tab, and double-click the icon for the hardware type of the device removed to display the list of installed devices. An exclamation point superimposed on a device icon indicates a removed or inoperable device.
3. Click the list item to select the device you want to remove, and then click the Remove button.
4. Confirm that you want to remove the device by clicking OK in the Confirm Device Removal message box.

If you have more than one hardware configuration, a modified version of the Confirm Device Removal message box appears. Make sure the Remove from All Configurations option button is selected; then click OK to remove the device and close the message box.

Troubleshooting Hardware Installation

Windows 95 is clearly superior to Windows 3.x when it comes to installing and managing hardware, but it is not perfect. The peaceful coexistence that Windows 95 tries to foster between PnP and legacy devices can break down into bitter conflict, particularly when new legacy hardware is being installed. But Windows 95 does provide a wealth of tools for managing these conflicts when they occur. This section helps you troubleshoot hardware installation problems under Windows 95, with tips for using the Device Manager and other tools.

Understanding the Device Manager

The Device Manager displays all the system components in hierarchical format, allowing you to dig down to individual devices and subsystems. In essence, the Device Manager is the user interface for the Windows 95 Registry. But unlike working in the Registry, the Device Manager is designed to avoid the kind of catastrophic crashes that making changes in the Registry can cause.

The Device Manager gives you quick access to hardware configurations for virtually all the devices in your PC. To open the Device Manager, double-click the System icon in Control Panel and click the Device Manager tab. You will see a list of items, some with a plus (+) sign to the left. This plus sign indicates that more detailed device information is available. Selecting the plus sign expands the display to show any listings below that item.

The Device Manager displays hardware information from two separate perspectives, by device type and by device connection. By default, Device Manager opens with the View Devices by Type option button selected (see Figure 7.14). In this mode, similar devices are grouped under a single item, such as the entry under Ports (COM & LPT). Clicking the View Devices by Connection option button shows the same information, but now most of the devices appear under the Plug and Play BIOS item (see Figure 7.15).

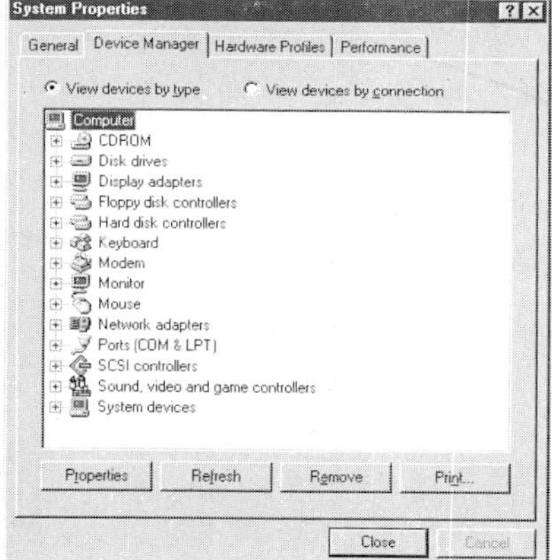

FIG. 7.14
The Device Manager showing devices listed by type.

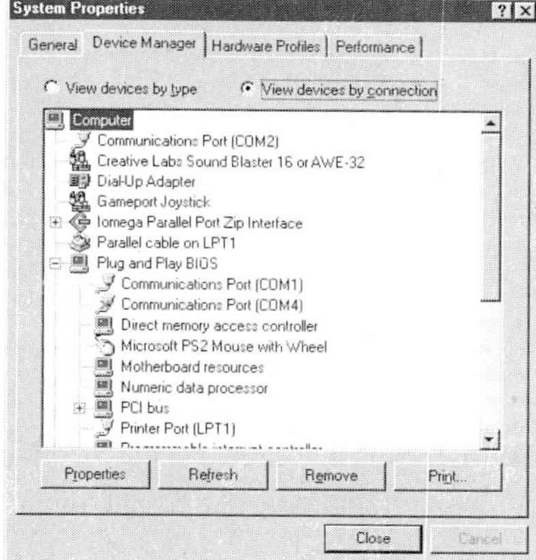

FIG. 7.15
The second option button lets you view components by their physical connections in the system.

To access the configuration for a sound card, do the following:

1. Go to the Device Manager page of the System Properties sheet.
2. Click the plus (+) sign found next to the Sound, video, and game controllers item.
3. Click the specific sound hardware item that appears on the sheet.
4. Click the Properties button to display the tabbed properties sheet for the sound hardware device.

Changing Resource Settings

After you are at the General page of a device's properties sheet, you can access the IRQ, I/O address, and DMA resource settings by clicking the Resources tab. Here you see the resources that are currently assigned to that device. Any conflicts are indicated with an asterisk next to the resource having a problem.

To change the resource settings for a device, do the following:

1. In the Resource Settings box, click the resource item you want to view or edit.
2. Click to clear the Use Automatic Settings check box (see Figure 7.16).

FIG. 7.16
Before you can make changes to device settings, you must disable the Use automatic settings item.

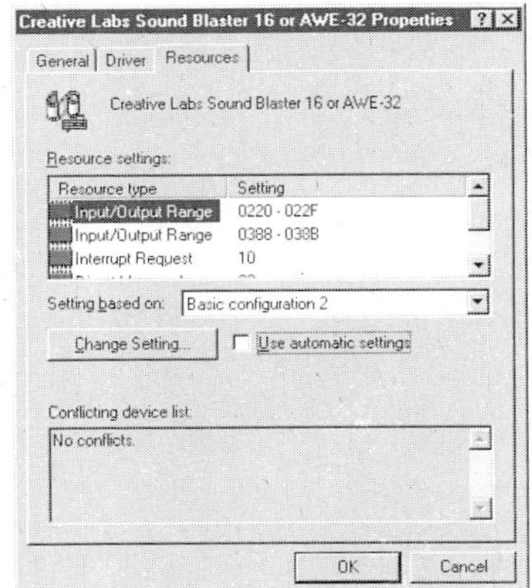

3. Click the enabled Change Setting button.
4. In the Resource Edit dialog box, click the spinner buttons to switch among system resources.

NOTE Device Manager shows all the resources, indicating those that are already in use by another peripheral. Be sure you don't create a conflict by assigning a resource to a device that is already being used by another device.

TROUBLESHOOTING

Why do I get a Resource Conflict message when I install a Plug and Play adapter card? Most PC adapter cards require at least one I/O base address and one or more interrupts. (The section "Setting Resource Values for Legacy Adapter Cards" describes I/O base addresses and interrupts.) Most adapter cards support only a few of the available I/O base addresses and interrupts. If you already have several legacy adapter cards in your PC, you may have a situation where the I/O base addresses or, more likely, the interrupts supported by the new card are occupied by existing legacy cards. In this case, you need to change the settings of one or more of your legacy cards to free the required resource(s) for use by your new card.

The worst-case condition occurs in PCI-bus PCs where all of the available interrupts are assigned before you install the new card. (In many PCI-bus PCs, PCI slots consume one interrupt each, whether or not the slot is in use.) The only solution in this instance is to free an interrupt by reconfiguring your PC's system BIOS to reassign an interrupt from an unused PCI slot. Obviously, this action will disable that slot, rendering it useless. If your system BIOS does not permit reconfiguration, you must remove an existing adapter card to free an interrupt.

You can get an effective roster of system settings by double-clicking the Computer icon at the top of the Device Manager tree. Doing so brings up the Computer Properties sheet, which features two tabs: View Resources and Reserve Resources (see Figure 7.17).

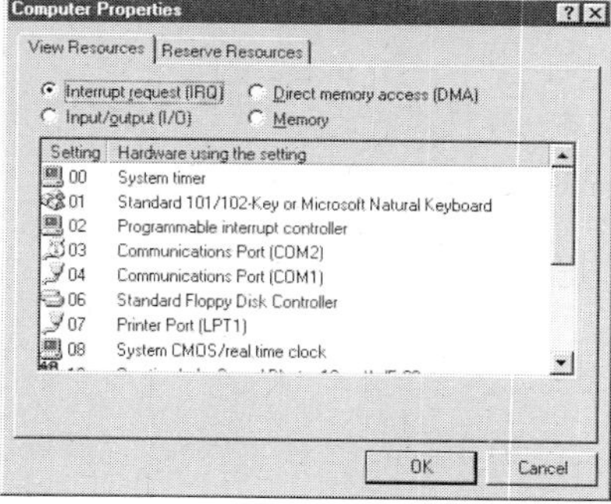

FIG. 7.17
The Computer Properties sheet provides a bird's-eye view of your system resource status.

The View Resources tab displays these four option buttons that cause the page to display the status of key system resources:

- Interrupt Request (IRQs)
- Input/Output (I/O)
- Direct Memory Address (DMA)
- Memory

Clicking the option button brings up a list of occupied settings and the devices that are using them.

NOTE The View Resources page of the Computer Properties sheet is an excellent place to get an overview of your system's resource status.

The Reserve Resources page lets you view any resources that have been excluded from use by hardware devices (see Figure 7.18). You also can use this page to reserve resources.

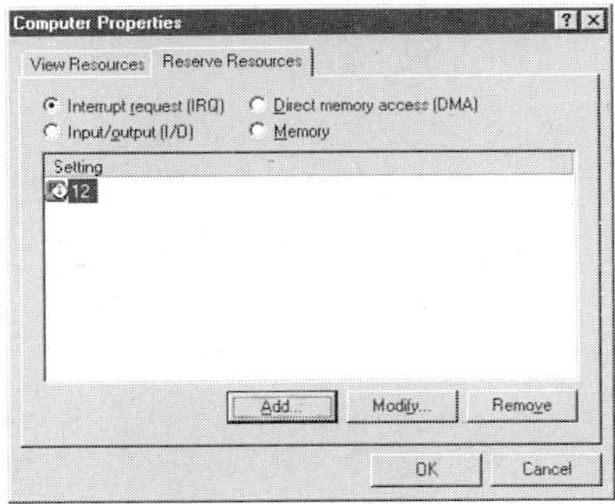

FIG. 7.18 The Reserve Resources page lets you set aside key resource settings to avoid conflicts.

TROUBLESHOOTING

Why does my system hang during shutdown? This problem can occur when a system BIOS expects a PS/2-style mouse port to occupy IRQ12, but a software-configured PnP adapter occupies it instead. You need to change the software-configurable device in Device Manager to another IRQ number. You might also consider reserving IRQ12 in Device Manager, so Plug and Play does not later assign a device to that resource. Also consider getting a BIOS upgrade that allows you to make full use of IRQ12.

Follow these steps to reserve IRQ12 (some older BIOSes won't recognize an IRQ12 device unless it is a PS/2 mouse):

1. Click the Reserve Resources tab.
2. Click the Interrupt Request (IRQ) option button.
3. Click the Add button to bring up the Edit Resource Setting sheet (see Figure 7.19).
4. Use the spinner controls to select the IRQ you want to change.

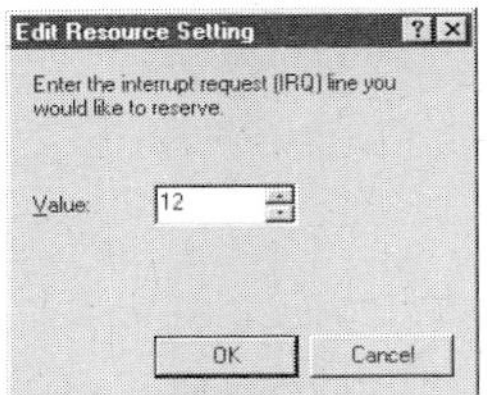

FIG. 7.19 Set the resource to reserve in the Edit Resource sheet.

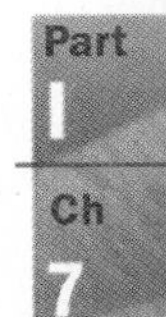

5. Click OK to change the settings.
6. If a device is currently logged into the IRQ being reserved, the Resource Conflict Warning sheet will apprise you of the possible problem and ask for confirmation (see Figure 7.20).

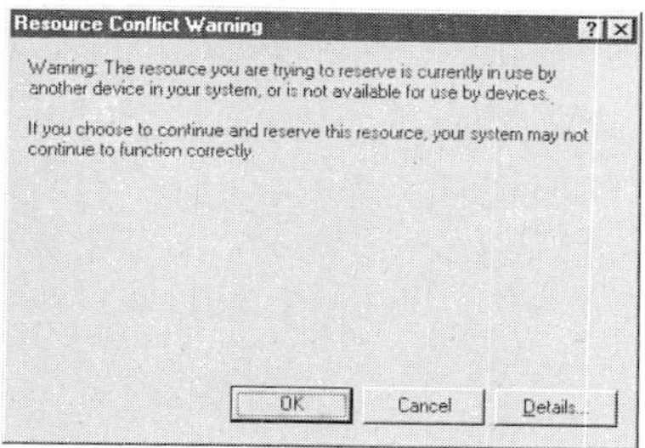

FIG. 7.20
If Windows 95 detects a device already using the resource being reserved, it will warn you and ask for confirmation.

Checking for Resource Conflicts with the Device Manager

The Device Manager is an excellent tool for resolving hardware resource conflicts, allowing you to see if any devices are experiencing a conflict. Device Manager displays an exclamation point or a strikethrough symbol through the icon of any item with a conflict, allowing you to quickly zero in on problems. The symbols indicate different situations:

- **Exclamation point inside a yellow circle.** Indicates a device that is experiencing a direct conflict with another device.
- **Red X symbol.** Indicates a device that is disabled, either due to a conflict or by user selection.

Unfortunately, it is not possible to cover all the various things that can go wrong during hardware installation under Windows 95. Many problems are the result of interactions between specific types of hardware. If you discover a problem with hardware you are installing, you should seek guidance from the vendor, since they should know about potential driver updates and other fixes that can help resolve the problem.

TROUBLESHOOTING

I can't get my second IDE drive to appear in My Computer or Explorer. Most PCs with recent system BIOSes automatically detect an additional drive connected to the primary IDE controller as a primary slave drive. If you have an older BIOS, you need to use the PC's BIOS setup application to specify the type of drive installed (number of cylinders, number of heads, landing zone, and other drive parameters). If you connect a third drive to a PC with a recent BIOS, you need to enable the secondary IDE controller in the BIOS setup program so BIOS can recognize the drive. IDE CD-ROM drives connected to sound cards usually can be installed as secondary, tertiary, or quaternary IDE drives. Use the default (secondary) setting for an IDE CD-ROM if you don't have a secondary IDE controller in your PC; if your PC has a secondary IDE controller, use the tertiary I/O base address and interrupt for the CD-ROM.

CHAPTER 8

Special Features for Notebook Users

by Jim Boyce and Doug Kilarski

Many business professionals want to take their office with them. Portable technology and Windows 95 make a hard-to-beat combination. Portable PCs enable you to work nearly anywhere, and Windows 95's features for portable computing—which include 32-bit support for PC Card (PCMCIA) devices, file synchronization, Dial-Up Networking, remote mail, and more—make Windows 95 a perfect operating system for your portable PC. Not only does Windows 95 make it easy for you to take your work with you, but features such as Dial-Up Networking and remote mail enable you to keep in touch with coworkers and access disk and printer resources in your main office from anywhere in the world.

Laptop computers must deal with changing hardware configurations

Learn how laptops can now automatically reconfigure themselves when inserted into docking stations.

Direct Cable Connection and infrared communication

Look here to find out how to move files between notebook computers and other computers using cables or IrDA ports. It's now easier.

Use Dial-Up Networking to connect your laptop to a network

Find out how your laptop can become even more flexible by accessing corporate data while in the field or at home.

Synchronize files between laptop and desktop with the Briefcase

Taking files off your desktop or network presents a problem when you return files that have been changed. This brief section outlines the advantages to using the Briefcase.

NOTE What were formerly called "PCMCIA" devices are now referred to as "PC Card" devices.

Simply put, Windows 95 enables users to better utilize their portable PCs. Mobile users have universally asked for three areas of portable-specific features:

- Get the most out of their portable PC hardware
- Maintain access to office LAN resources
- Keep organized

Windows 95 delivers on all three points. PC Card, Plug and Play, disk compression, power management, and support for port replicators and docking stations all complement portable PC hardware. Windows 95 architectural enhancements conserve battery power and manage configuration changes, which helps extend the life of older portables. Dial-Up Networking enables you to access your office file server(s) using your modem and to send e-mail to and receive e-mail from coworkers. Windows 95 keeps users organized as well. Using an advanced file synchronization system called Briefcase and a deferred printing option, roaming users remain "in sync" with their desktop environments (and vice versa).

To help you understand how to get the most from Windows 95's features for portable computing, this chapter explores the following topics:

- Using a docking system
- Using a direct cable connection to share resources
- Using power management
- Using Dial-Up Networking
- Synchronizing files with Briefcase
- Using mouse trails

Using Your Laptop with a Docking System

With Windows 95, *hot-docking support* integrates hardware and software for quick and easy docking. Docking and undocking can occur when the power is on or off. Windows 95 automatically detects any configuration changes and manages any conflicts or file disruptions. Windows 95 also loads and unloads hardware drivers as required. To undock your PC when Windows 95 is running, open the Start menu and choose Eject PC. Windows 95 reconfigures the system automatically for the undocked configuration and then prompts you to remove the PC from the docking station.

Creating and Modifying Hardware Profiles

Windows 95 enables you to create multiple hardware profiles to accommodate different hardware configurations, such as when your PC is docked and when it is undocked. Windows 95 automatically creates two hardware profiles for you: one for the docked configuration and a second for the undocked configuration. Windows 95 detects which profile is required at startup and automatically uses the correct one.

NOTE If your portable PC contains a Plug and Play BIOS, Windows 95 does not have to use multiple hardware profiles to accommodate hot docking. Instead, the Plug and Play BIOS can detect which devices are available, and Windows 95 can configure the system accordingly.

If you want to change an existing profile or create a new one, you can do so through the Control Panel. Use the following procedure to create a new hardware profile:

1. Open the Start menu and choose Settings, Control Panel.
2. Choose the System object to display the System properties sheet.
3. Click the Hardware Profiles tab to display the Hardware Profiles page (see Figure 8.1).

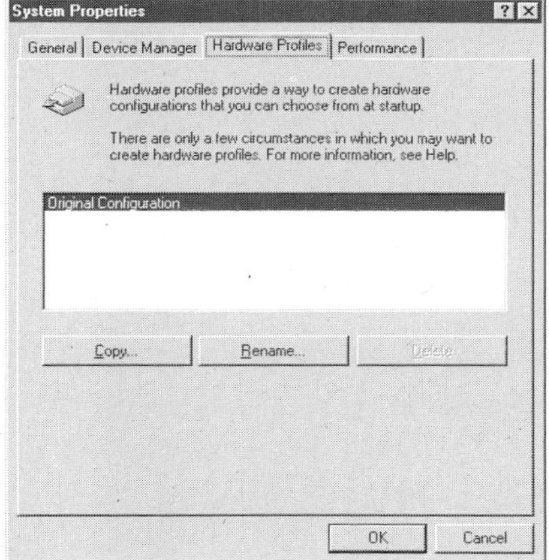

FIG. 8.1
The Hardware Profiles page enables you to modify and create hardware profiles.

4. Select the hardware profile you want to use as a basis for the new profile, and then choose Copy. Windows 95 displays a Copy Profile dialog box in which you specify the name for the new hardware profile (see Figure 8.2).

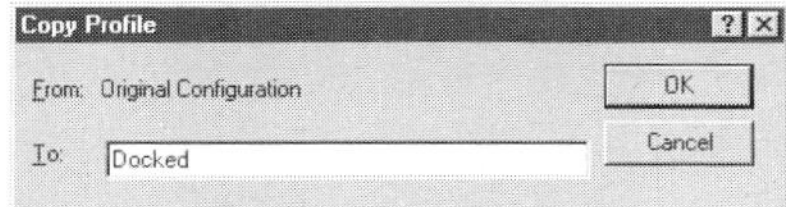

FIG. 8.2
Specify a name for the hardware profile.

5. Enter a name for the new profile and choose OK. The new hardware profile appears in the Hardware Profiles list.

In some cases, you might want to modify a hardware profile. If Windows 95 is unable to properly detect the hardware in a particular configuration, for example, you can modify the profile to add and remove hardware from the profile.

To modify a hardware profile, use the following procedure:

1. Open the Control Panel and double-click the System icon. Then click the Device Manager tab to display the Device Manager properties sheet (see Figure 8.3).

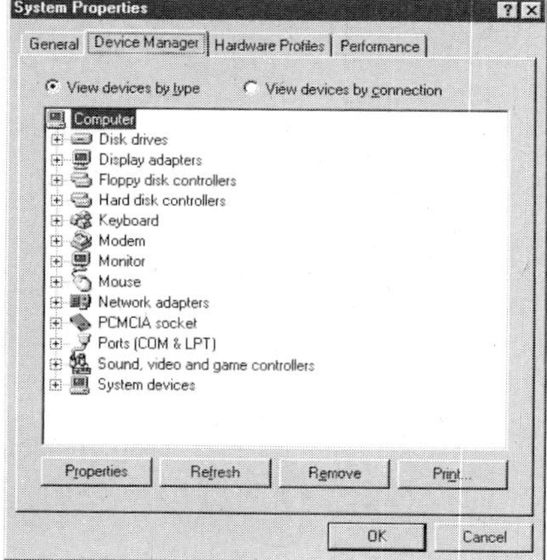

FIG. 8.3
Use the Device Manager page to modify a hardware profile.

2. Select the hardware device that you want to add or remove from a particular profile, and then choose Properties to display the General page of its properties sheet (see Figure 8.4).

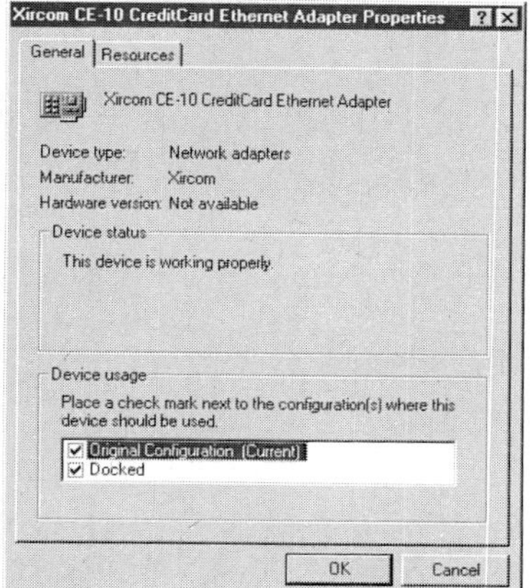

FIG. 8.4
Use the Device Usage list to add and remove hardware from a profile.

3. At the bottom of the device's General page is a Device Usage list that defines which profiles use a device. Place a check in the check box beside a hardware profile to enable the device for that profile. Clear the check box to disable the device for that profile.
4. Choose OK to apply the changes.

When you start the system, Windows 95 detects the hardware configuration you are using and automatically applies the appropriate hardware profile. If the hardware profiles are so similar that Windows 95 cannot determine which profile to use, Windows 95 displays a menu containing a list of the available profiles and prompts you to select the profile to be used.

Working with Different Configurations Most hardware settings in Windows 95 are stored relative to the current hardware profile. Changes that you make to a device's settings are applied to the current profile, but not to other hardware profiles. Therefore, it's possible to maintain different settings for the same device in two or more different hardware profiles. For example, you might use a display resolution of 640×480 in one profile, but use 800×600 in a different profile. Such is probably the case when you are using an external monitor with your PC. You probably use 640×480 with the portable's LCD display and a higher resolution with the external monitor.

To configure unique settings for a device, first start Windows 95 using the hardware profile in which you want the changes to be made. If you want to use a high-resolution mode with an external monitor, for example, select the hardware profile you normally use with the external monitor (or create a profile for use with the external monitor as explained in the previous section). After you start Windows 95 with the appropriate hardware profile, change the settings for the device. The changes are applied to the current hardware profile and do not affect other profiles you have created.

TROUBLESHOOTING

My LCD monitor is not working properly. Windows 95 might not automatically select the LCD monitor type when you are using your portable PC's internal LCD display. Therefore, you should check the monitor type in the hardware profile that is used when you are working with the internal display. To set the monitor type, right-click the desktop and choose Properties. Click the Settings tab to display the Settings page. Choose Change Display Type to display the Change Display Type dialog box. Choose the Change button to display the Select Device dialog box. Choose the Show All Devices option button, choose Standard Monitor Types from the Manufacturers list, and then choose the appropriate Laptop Display Panel selection from the Models list.

Using Deferred Printing

When your portable PC is docked, you probably have access to a printer connected to the docking station or that is available across the network. When your PC is not docked, however, it is unlikely that you'll have access to a printer. Windows 95 addresses that problem through *deferred printing*. When you print a document, Windows 95 places the document in the printer's queue, where it remains even when you turn off your computer.

See "Controlling Printers," **p. 141**

When you dock your computer, Windows 95 senses that the printer is available and begins spooling the document to the printer. Windows 95 automatically handles deferred printing. You simply print the document, and when the printer becomes available, Windows 95 begins sending the document to the printer.

Sharing Local Resources via Parallel or Serial Connection

A growing number of portable users also have a desktop system. They regularly transfer files between systems by using either a floppy disk or a direct parallel or serial cable, and a third-party application to handle the transfer. Windows 95 includes a feature called Direct Cable Connection that integrates the same capability within Windows 95; essentially, you can use a serial or parallel cable to network together your portable and desktop PCs, creating a small peer-to-peer network. The two computers then can access each other's files and other resources (such as a fax modem) as if they were joined by a traditional network interface.

In a direct cable connection, one computer acts as the host (server) and the other computer acts as a guest (client). The host PC also can act as a gateway, enabling the client to access the network to which the host is connected. The host can serve as a gateway for NetBEUI or IPX/SPX protocols but cannot serve as a gateway for TCP/IP.

Setting Up Direct Cable Connection

If you select the Portable option when you install Windows 95, Setup installs Direct Cable Connection on your PC. If you use a different option or deselected the Direct Cable Connection option during Setup, you must install it. To add Direct Cable Connection, use the following procedure:

1. Open the Start menu and choose Settings, Control Panel.
2. Choose the Add/Remove Programs object.
3. Click the Windows Setup tab to display the Windows Setup page.
4. Select Communications from the Components list, and then choose Details.
5. Place a check beside Direct Cable Connection, and then choose OK.
6. Choose OK again to cause Windows 95 to add Direct Cable Connection to your PC.

NOTE If Direct Cable Connection is already checked in the Components list, the software is already installed on your PC.

After installing the Direct Cable Connection software, you must connect the two computers with an appropriate cable. You can use either a parallel or null-modem serial cable to connect your two PCs. The types of cables you can use for the connection include the following:

- Standard 4-bit null-modem cable, and LapLink and InterLink cables made prior to 1992.
- Extended Capabilities Port (ECP) cable. To use this type of cable, your parallel port must be configured as an ECP port in your system BIOS.
- Universal Cable Module (UCM) cable, which supports connecting together different types of parallel ports. You can use a UCM cable to connect together two ECP ports for fastest performance.

As previously indicated, configuring your parallel ports as ECP ports provides the best performance. To use ECP, however, your PC's ports must be ECP-capable, and the ports must be configured as ECP ports in the system BIOS. Older PCs do not contain ECP-capable parallel ports.

The final step in setting up the Direct Cable Connection is to ensure that both the guest and host computers use the same network protocol. You can use the NetBEUI, IPX/SPX, or TCP/IP protocols. In addition, you must use an appropriate network client, such as Client for NetWare Networks or Client for Microsoft Networks. The host computer must run either the File and Printer Sharing for Microsoft Networks service or the File and Printer Sharing for NetWare Networks service.

Setting Up the Host

In a Direct Cable Connection between two PCs, one PC acts as the host and the other PC acts as the guest. The first step in enabling the connection is to configure the host. To do so, use the following procedure:

1. Open the Start menu and choose Programs, Accessories, Direct Cable Connection. Windows 95 displays the dialog box shown in Figure 8.5.

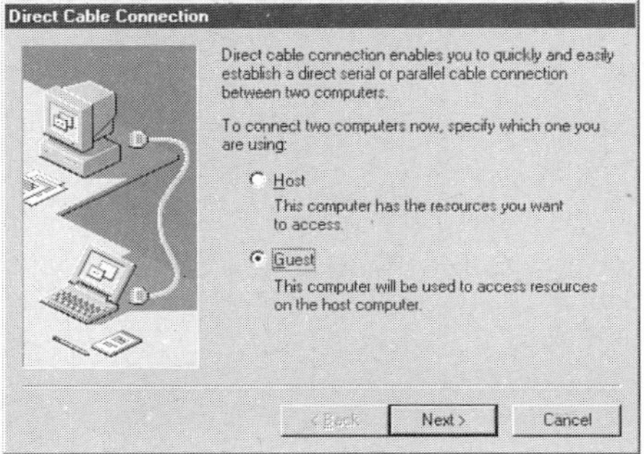

FIG. 8.5 Choose whether the PC will act as host or guest.

2. Select the Host option button and then choose Next >. Windows 95 displays the dialog box shown in Figure 8.6.

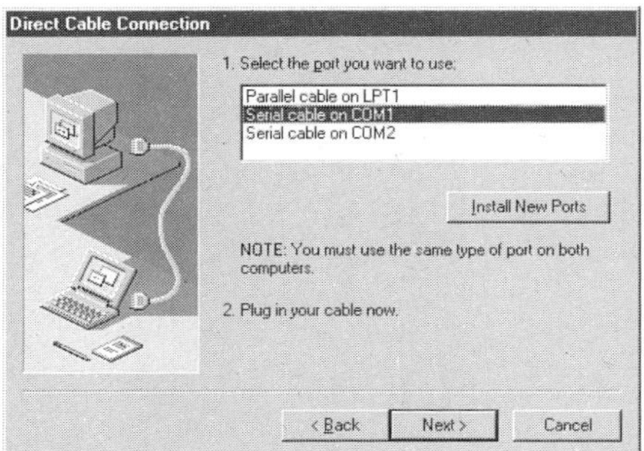

FIG. 8.6 Select the port to be used by the connection.

3. Choose the port you want to use on the host for the connection. You can choose one of the host's parallel or serial ports. After selecting the port, choose Next >.
4. Specify whether you want to use password protection to prevent unauthorized access to the host. To use password protection, enable the Use Password Protection check box. Then choose Set Password, which displays a simple dialog box in which you enter the password that must be provided by the guest computer to access the host. When you've specified the desired password settings, choose Finish to complete host setup.

Setting Up the Guest

After configuring the host, you're ready to configure the guest computer. To do so, use the following procedure:

1. On the guest computer, open the Start menu and choose Programs, Accessories, Direct Computer Connection.
2. From the Direct Cable Connection dialog box, choose Guest and then Next >.
3. Choose the port on the guest PC through which the connection will be made, and then choose Next.
4. Choose Finish to complete the setup.

Before you begin sharing files using the Direct Cable Connection, you must share a directory in which the files will be transferred. To set up sharing, refer to Chapter 37.

Using the Direct Cable Connection

When you want to begin using your mini-network connection, you need to start the Direct Cable Connection software on both the host and the guest computers. On the host, open the Start menu and choose Programs, Accessories, Direct Cable Connection. Windows 95 displays a dialog box similar to the one shown in Figure 8.7.

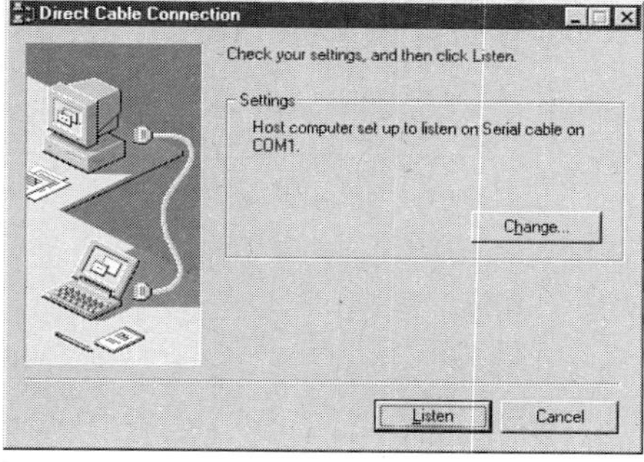

FIG. 8.7 Choose Listen to set up the host for the connection.

If the settings you specified previously are correct, choose Listen to place the host computer in listen mode to listen for a connection by the guest. If you need to change the password or port settings, choose Change.

See "Setting Up a Windows 95 Peer-to-Peer Network" **p. 939**

After placing the host computer in listen mode, start the Direct Cable Connection software on the guest computer. Open the Start menu and choose Programs, Accessories, Direct Cable Connection. Windows 95 displays a dialog box similar to the one shown Figure 8.7, except that the Listen button is replaced by a Connect button. Choose Connect to connect to the host and begin using the connection.

Using Power Management

Most portable PCs (and an increasing number of desktop PCs) support some form of power management that allows the PC's devices to be shut down to conserve power while the computer remains on. Power management, for example, can power down the hard disk when the disk is not being used, conserving battery power. When the system is idle, power management can shut down the display and even CPU to further conserve power. Windows 95 integrates power management into the operating system and adds features to the interface that enable you to easily take advantage of power management.

In order for your PC to use power management, the PC's BIOS must include support for power management, and power management must be enabled in the PC's BIOS.

If you have a newer portable computer that has the APM 1.2 BIOS, you may want to consider installing the Windows 95 OEM Service Release 2 (OSR2) update. OSR2 supports the features of the new APM BIOS, including wake-up on ring for modems, power down of PC Card modems that are inactive, and notebooks with multiple batteries. See Chapter 2, "Installing Windows," for more information on OSR2.

If your portable PC supports power management and power management software (such as MS-DOS's POWER.EXE) is enabled when you install Windows 95, Setup adds support for power management automatically. If power management software was not enabled during Setup, you must enable power management yourself through the Control Panel. The following steps explain how to enable power management:

1. Open the Start menu and choose Settings, Control Panel.
2. Choose the System object.
3. Click the Device Manager tab, and then double-click the System devices item to expand the System devices tree.
4. Select the Advanced Power Management support item and choose Properties.
5. Click the Settings tab to display the Settings page shown in Figure 8.8.
5. Place a check in the Enable Power Management Support check box and then choose OK.
6. Choose OK to close the System properties sheet. Windows 95 prompts you to restart the computer for the change to take effect.

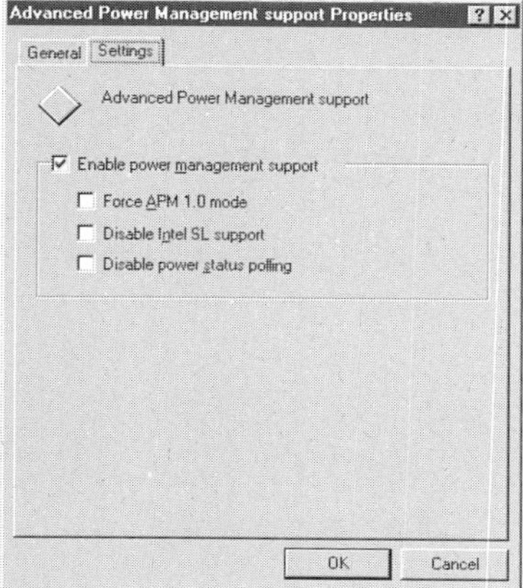

FIG. 8.8
Use the Settings page to control power management.

The other options on the Settings page control the way power management works. These options include:

- **Force APM 1.0 Mode.** Enable this option if your PC's power management features do not work properly. This option causes Windows 95 to use an APM 1.1 BIOS in 1.0 mode, which overcomes problems with some portable PCs.
- **Disable Intel SL Support.** If your computer uses the SL chipset and stops responding at startup, enable this option.
- **Disable Power Status Polling.** Enable this option if your PC shuts down unexpectedly while you use it. This option prevents Windows 95 from calling the APM BIOS to check battery status, consequently also disabling the battery meter in the tray.

Setting Power Management Options

The Power icon in the Control Panel enables you to specify options that control power management features. Double-clicking the Power icon in the Control Panel displays the Power properties sheet shown in Figure 8.9. The large SL button appears on the Power page of the sheet only if your PC uses an SL processor.

▶ **See** "Setting SL Options," **p. 208**

The Power Management list enables you to specify the level of power management your system uses. You can select from the following options:

- **Standard.** Choose this setting to use only the power management features supported by your PC's BIOS. Additional features such as battery status monitoring are not enabled when you choose this feature.
- **Advanced.** Choose this setting to use full power management support, including features provided by Windows 95 in addition to those provided by your PC's BIOS. These include battery status monitoring and power status display on the tray.
- **Off.** Choose this setting to turn off power management.

FIG. 8.9
Use the Power page to set power management options.

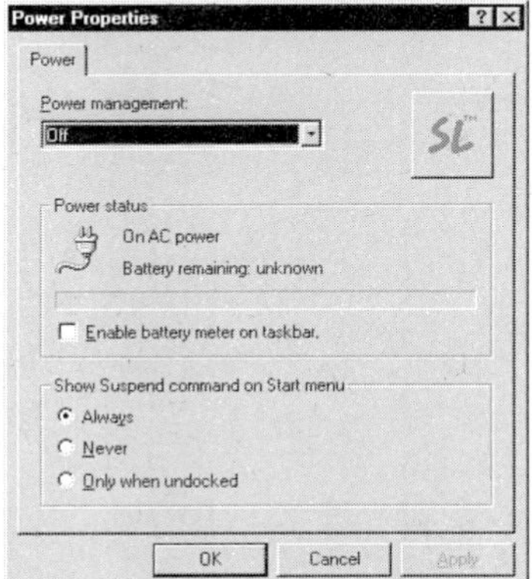

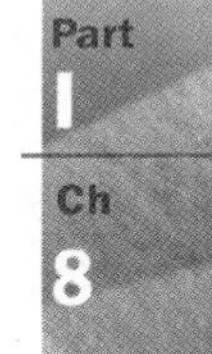

Additional options on the Power page control whether or not the Suspend command appears in the Start menu. Choose Always if you want the Suspend command always displayed on the Start menu. Choose Never if you do not want it to appear on the Start menu, even when the system is undocked. Choose Only when Undocked if you want the Suspend command to appear on the Start menu only when the PC is not connected to a docking station.

When you want to place the PC in suspend mode, open the Start menu and choose Suspend. Windows 95 will immediately place the PC in suspend mode. If you have files open across the network, you should first save or close the files before placing the PC in suspend mode to avoid losing data.

The Power page also displays information about battery status and enables you to turn on or off the power status indicator on the tray. To view the amount of power remaining in your battery, rest the cursor on the power indicator on the tray for a second, and Windows 95 will display a ToolTip listing battery power remaining. Or double-click the power indicator to display a Battery Meter dialog box similar to the one shown in Figure 8.10.

FIG. 8.10
The Battery Meter dialog box shows power remaining.

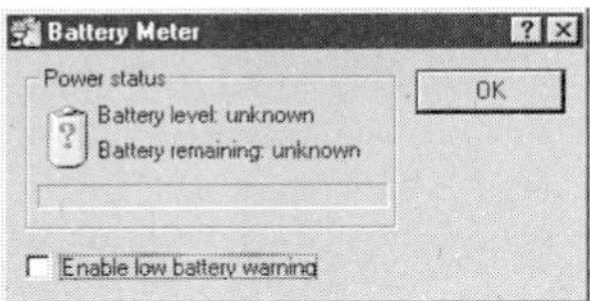

NOTE As you can see in Figure 8.10, Windows 95 cannot always detect the amount of power remaining in the battery. This is often due to the way in which the batteries used in portable PCs drain their charges. The voltage remains fairly steady through the battery's cycle and then begins to drop rapidly as the battery nears the end of its useful charge.

Setting SL Options

If your PC uses an Intel SL processor such as the 486SL, you can use SL-specific options to control additional power management features. As previously explained, an SL button appears on the Power page on systems containing an SL processor. Choosing the SL button displays the SL Enhanced Options dialog box shown in Figure 8.11.

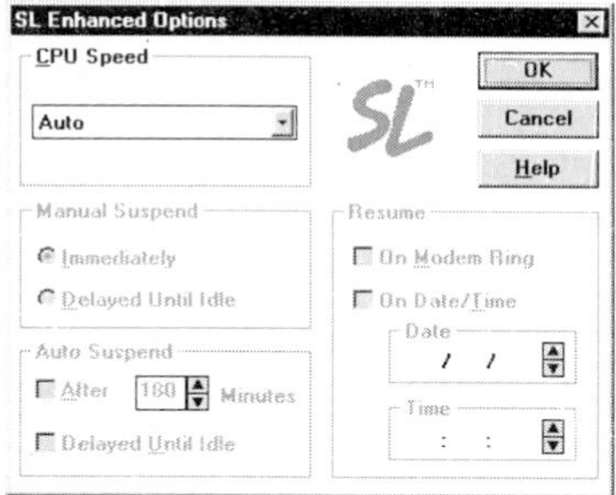

FIG. 8.11 The SL Enhanced Options dialog box controls SL-specific power options.

The following list explains the groups in the SL Enhanced Options dialog box:

- **CPU Speed.** This drop-down list enables you to control how the CPU is managed. Choose Auto to cause the CPU to run at full speed but power down whenever possible to conserve power. Choose 10 percent, 25 percent, or 50 percent to run the CPU at a specific reduced speed. Choose 100 percent to run the CPU at full speed and prevent the CPU from powering down.
- **Manual Suspend.** The two settings in this group control the way the system powers down when you press the Suspend button, close the display (on a notebook PC), or choose Suspend in the Start menu. Choose Immediately in the Manual Suspend group to cause the PC to suspend immediately when you press the PC's Suspend button or close the display. Windows will suspend all applications even if they are currently processing. Choose the Delayed Until Idle option to cause Windows to wait for all applications to finish processing before it powers down the PC. Some applications appear to Windows to be processing when they actually are just waiting for input, so the system might not enter suspend mode if such an application is running and the Delayed Until Idle option is selected.
- **Auto Suspend.** This option controls how the system powers down automatically after a specified period of time with no keyboard or mouse activity. The After option lets you specify an amount of time after which the system powers down automatically. The Delayed Until Idle option causes the system to power down automatically only if there are no active applications. These settings don't affect the screen, hard disk, or other devices individually. Instead, they control shutdown of the entire system, including the CPU.
- **Resume.** These settings control how the system resumes after it has been suspended. The On Modem Ring option, if enabled, causes the system to resume if a call comes in to

a line that is connected to the PC's modem. The On Date/Time option enables you to specify a specific date and time at which the system will resume.

TROUBLESHOOTING

The Windows 95 marketing literature describes more power management features than are available on my laptop computer. Older computers do not have BIOSes that are compatible with APM. Some newer computers have known incompatibilities with the APM 1.1 specifications. Consequently, some or all of Windows 95's Advanced Power Management features might not be available.

Using Dial-Up Networking

Windows 95 expands and improves on the remote access client in Windows for Workgroups, integrating remote access almost seamlessly within the Windows 95 interface. With the remote access features in Windows 95—collectively called *Dial-Up Networking*—you can connect to a remote computer to access its files and printer(s). If the remote computer is connected to a network and you have the necessary access rights on the remote LAN, dialing into the server is just like connecting locally to the network. You can use the shared resources of any computer on the network, send and receive e-mail, print, and perform essentially any task remotely that you can perform with a workstation connected directly to the network.

▶ **See** "Creating a Connection," **p. 212**

NOTE A Windows NT server can act as a TCP/IP gateway, routing TCP/IP traffic for your dial-in PC. If your office network is connected to the Internet, for example, you can dial into a server to gain access to the Internet from home. To use this capability, you must install the TCP/IP network protocol and bind it to the dial-up adapter. The Windows NT server's Remote Access Server service must also be configured to allow TCP/IP dial-in and route TCP/IP traffic.

If you did not install Dial-Up Networking when you installed Windows 95, you must now do so with the following procedure:

1. Open the Start menu and choose Settings, Control Panel, and then click the Add/Remove Programs icon. Then choose the Windows Setup tab to display the Windows Setup dialog box.
2. Double-click the Communications item to display the Communications dialog box.
3. Place a check in the Dial-Up Networking check box, and then choose OK. Choose OK again and Windows 95 installs Dial-Up Networking on your PC.

Before you can begin using Dial-Up Networking, you must install the dial-up adapter and network protocol required by the remote server. The following section explains how to set up Dial-Up Networking.

Setting Up Dial-Up Networking

Setting up Dial-Up Networking requires four steps: installing the dial-up adapter, installing the network protocol(s) used by the remote server, installing a network client, and installing an appropriate file and printer sharing service.

The dial-up adapter is a special driver supplied with Windows 95 that acts as a virtual network adapter, performing much the same function that a typical hardware network adapter performs. Instead of handling network traffic across a network cable, the dial-up adapter handles network traffic through your PC's modem.

To install the dial-up adapter, follow these steps:

1. Open the Control Panel and choose the Network object.
2. In the Configuration page of the Network property sheet, choose Add.
3. Choose Adapter from the Select Network Component Type dialog box, and then choose Add. Windows 95 displays the Select Network Adapters dialog box shown in Figure 8.12.

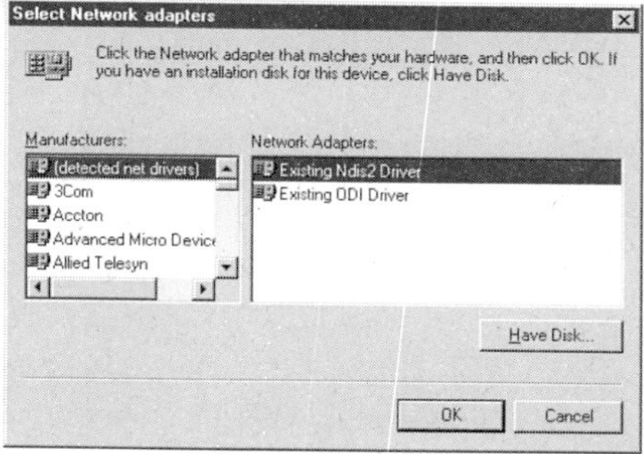

FIG. 8.12 You must install the dial-up adapter before you can use Dial-Up Networking.

4. From the Manufacturers list, choose Microsoft.
5. From the Network Adapters list, choose Dial-Up Adapter, and then choose OK. Windows 95 will add the dial-up adapter to your system.

After you install the dial-up adapter, you must install at least one network protocol to be used for the dial-up connection. The protocol you select depends on the protocol used by the remote server. On Microsoft-based networks, the protocol used typically is NetBEUI. On NetWare-based networks, the protocol typically used is IPX/SPX. If you are connecting to a remote network that uses TCP/IP, you should install the TCP/IP protocol.

To install a protocol and bind it to the dial-up adapter, use the following procedure:

1. Open the Control Panel and double-click the Network icon.
2. From the Configuration page, choose the Add button.
3. Choose Protocol from the Select Network Component Type dialog box, and then choose Add.
4. From the Manufacturers list, choose Microsoft.

5. From the Network Protocols list, choose the appropriate network protocol. Then choose OK.

In addition to a network protocol, you also might need to install a network client. The network client enables your PC to access files and printers on the remote server and network. If you are connecting to a Microsoft network-based computer or network, you should install the Client for Microsoft Networks client. If you are connecting to a NetWare system, you should install the Client for NetWare Networks client.

If you are using TCP/IP to gain access to the Internet through a dial-up server, and do not want to have access to the remote server's files or shared resources on the LAN to which the server is connected, you do not need to install a network client.

To install a network client and bind it to the dial-up adapter, use the following procedure:

1. Open the Control Panel, double-click the Network icon, and then choose Add from the Configuration page.
2. From the Select Network Component Type dialog box, choose Client; then choose Add.
3. From the Manufacturer's list, choose Microsoft, choose the appropriate client from the Network Clients list, and then choose OK.
4. In the Configuration property page, select Dial-Up Adapter from the list of installed network components. Then choose Properties to display the Dial-Up Adapter properties sheet.
5. Choose the Bindings tab to display the Bindings page shown in Figure 8.13.

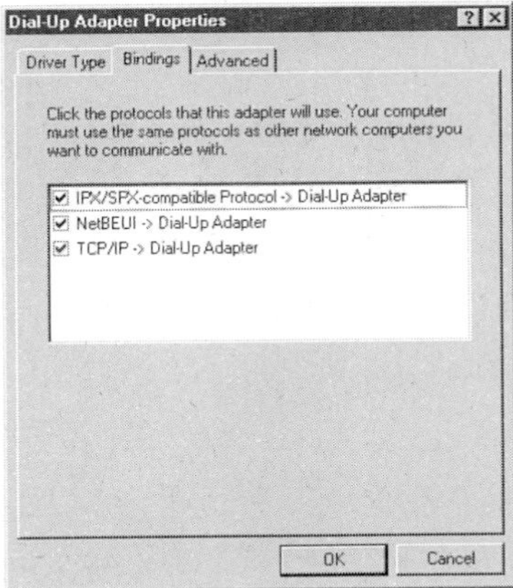

FIG. 8.13 Use the Bindings page to bind a network protocol to the dial-up adapter.

6. Place a check beside the network protocols you want to use with the dial-up adapter, and then choose OK. Choose OK again to close the Network dialog box.

Your PC is now configured to act as a Dial-Up Networking client. Making a connection is explained in the following section.

▶ **See** "Installing and Configuring Your Modem," **p. 76**

NOTE If you have not already installed your modem, do so before continuing. Your modem must be installed in order to use Dial-Up Networking.

Creating a Connection

To create a new Dial-Up Networking connection, first open My Computer, and then choose the Dial-Up Networking folder. The Dial-Up Networking folder contains an object named Make New Connection that starts a wizard to help you create Dial-Up Networking connections. The following steps help you start the wizard and create a Dial-Up Networking connection:

1. Open the Dial-Up Networking folder and double-click the Make New Connection object. Windows 95 displays the Make New Connection Wizard box shown in Figure 8.14.

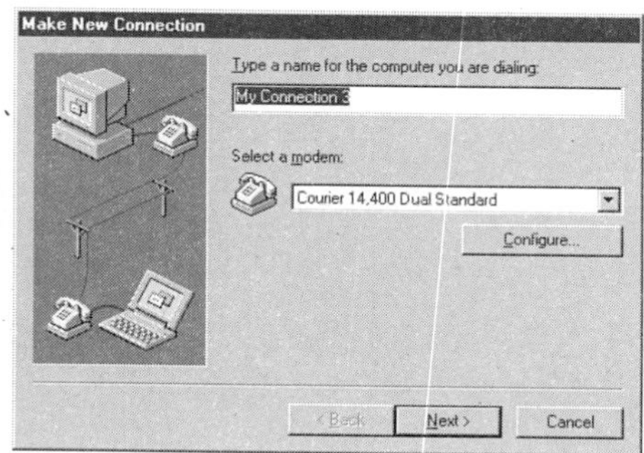

FIG. 8.14 The Make New Connection Wizard helps you create Dial-Up Networking connections.

2. By default, the wizard names the connection My Connection. Highlight the name and enter a name that describes the remote system to which you are connecting. This is the name that will appear under the connection's icon in the Dial-Up Networking folder.
3. Use the Select a Modem drop-down list to choose the modem you want to use for the Dial-Up Networking connection, and then choose Next. The dialog box changes to the one shown in Figure 8.15.

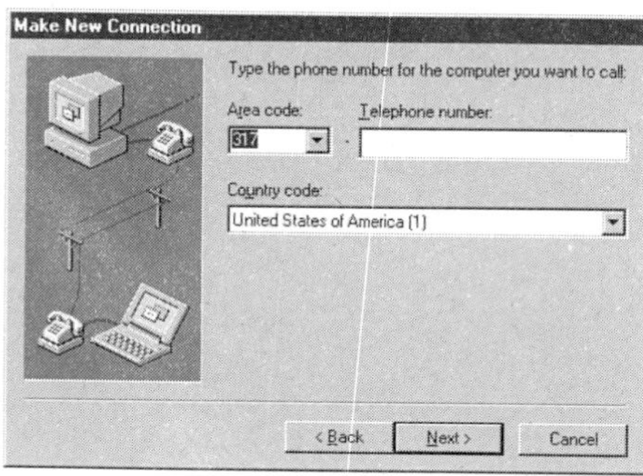

FIG. 8.15 Specify the phone number for the remote connection.

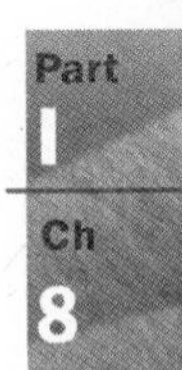

4. Enter the area code and telephone number in the appropriate text boxes.
5. Use the Country Code drop-down list to choose the country in which the remote system is located, and then choose Next.
6. Choose Finish to create the connection and add its icon to the Dial-Up Networking folder.

Connecting to a Remote System

Connecting to a remote system through a Dial-Up Networking connection is simple. Open the Dial-Up Networking folder, and then double-click the icon of the server to which you want to connect. Windows 95 displays a dialog box for the Dial-Up Networking connection similar to the one shown in Figure 8.16.

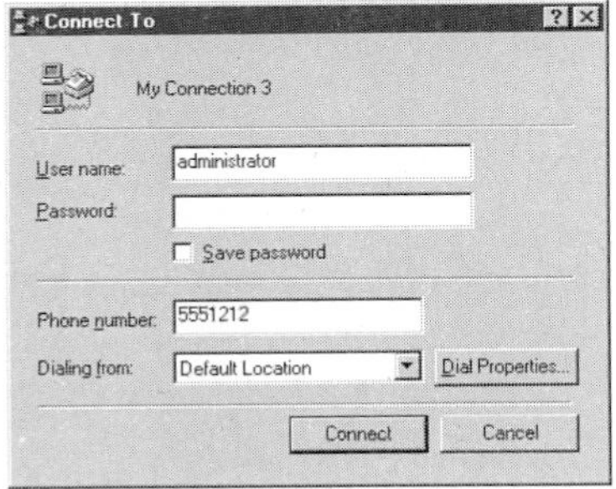

FIG. 8.16 You can verify and change settings prior to making the connection.

In the User Name and Password text boxes, enter the account name and password required by the remote server. If you want Windows 95 to save the password so you don't have to enter it each time you use the Dial-Up Networking connection, enable the Save Password check box.

▶ **See** "Using Network Neighborhood to View Network Resources," **p. 359**

Next, verify that the phone number and dialing location specified in the connection are correct; then choose Connect. Dial-Up Networking dials the remote server and attempts to connect and log on using the name and password you have provided. After the connection is established, you can begin using the shared resources of the remote server and the shared resources of other computers on the remote network as if your PC were connected locally to the network.

A new feature in Dial-Up Networking in the OSR2 release of Windows 95 is *scripting*. Scripts are text files consisting of commands, parameters, and expressions that automate the process of making a connection with a remote system using Dial-Up Networking. The script contains the information that you would normally have to enter manually to make a connection with another computer. Once you create a script, you can assign the script to the appropriate Dial-Up Networking connection in the Scripting tab of the properties sheet for that connection. Once you do this, the script will be executed automatically every time you dial the connection.

To learn how to create a script for automating your Dial-Up Networking connections, open the file SCRIPT.DOC in WordPad. SCRIPT.DOC is located in the WINDOWS folder. A complete description of the scripting language and instructions on how to create a script file are included in this document.

Using Infrared to Communicate with Devices

One of the nuisances you face when moving around with laptop computers is the extra burden of carrying cables, network adapters, and PC Cards. In a temporary office, you have to get out cables, pull out printers, crawl around on the floor routing cables, and install drivers before you can finally print. Then you leave a few hours later.

Most of these nuisances go away if you use a laptop computer with IrDA in an office with IrDA-compatible equipment. IrDA is an abbreviation for the Infrared Developers Association—an industry association that has agreed on communication standards between infrared devices. The IrDA standard ensures that devices from different hardware and software manufacturers will work together.

Infrared communication enables you to communicate between hardware devices without a cable of any type. Instead, a beam of infrared light substitutes for a serial cable that carries data.

CAUTION

Always remove any previously installed infrared drivers before upgrading or changing to a new driver. You will need to do this if you upgrade to a newer infrared driver or if you change IR adapters in your computer.

Installing IrDA Support

Before you go to the effort of downloading the IrDA software upgrade, make sure your computer will support it. After you examine the Device Manager for IrDA software and the IRQ it uses, follow the steps listed in the section "Installing the Infrared Monitor Software" to install the Infrared Monitor.

Checking for IrDA Hardware and Its IRQ Before upgrading your Windows 95 software, check your computer manufacturer's manuals to make sure your computer is IrDA-compliant. If you are unsure, look on the back of your laptop for a small blackish-maroon window approximately 1/2" by 1". It may be next to a wave or signal icon. This is the infrared window.

Check in System Properties for IrDA-compliant hardware by opening the Start menu and choosing Settings, Control Panel. Double-click the System program. Select the Device Manager tab, and then select the View Devices by Type option. Click the Ports (COM & LPT) icon in the hierarchy. Check if there is a Generic IRDA Compatible Device item. This listing will be there if an IrDA device is built in to your computer.

With Generic IRDA Compatible Device selected, click the Properties button. Select the General tab from the Generic IRDA Compatible Device properties sheet. Look at the Device Status check box for the message, "This device is working properly." If you see a message indicating a problem with your IrDA device, check the hardware manuals from your computer's manufacturer for support.

With the properties sheet still displayed, select the Resources tab to check which Interrupt Request (IRQ) the IrDA device uses. Write down the IRQ listed under Resource Settings. COM2 and COM4 correspond to IRQ 3 and are usually assigned to a modem. COM1 and COM3 correspond to IRQ 4 and are usually assigned to a serial mouse.

Installing the Infrared Monitor Software Infrared communication capability was not in the original release of Windows 95 but was added with Service Pack 1 during the first quarter of 1996. For a small shipping and handling fee, you can have Service Pack 1 shipped to you by calling Microsoft at 1-800-426-9400.

ON THE WEB

You can download components of Service Pack 1 for free by visiting this Microsoft software upgrade Web site.

http://www.microsoft.com/windows/software.htm

When you are at Microsoft's software upgrade page, select the hyperlink for Service Pack 1, and then download the file W95IR.EXE into its own folder. This self-extracting file, approximately 300K in size, contains the IrDA installation software.

Since the release of Service Pack 1, Microsoft has released another Windows update, called OEM Service Release 2 (OSR2). Included in this update is a newer version of the IrDA driver, IrDA 2.0. In addition to supporting data transfer between two computers and printing to an IrDA-compliant printer, you can now connect to a local area network (LAN) using an IrDA device. See "Installing the Windows 95b (OSR2) Service Release," in Chapter 2 for more information on OSR2.

You don't have to obtain the complete OSR2 update to take advantage of the newer IrDA driver. You can download the IrDA 2.0 driver from the following Microsoft Web site:

http://www.microsoft.com/windows/software/irda.htm

The newer driver is also called W95IR.EXE, and you can use the following procedure to install either version of the driver.

To install the IrDA upgrade you received from Microsoft, make sure you have uninstalled any previous IrDA drivers. Then follow these steps:

1. Double-click the W95IR.EXE file to expand the files it contains.
2. Double-click RELNOTES.DOC to open it in WordPad. Read the release notes for information that may apply to your computer. Close the release notes when you are done.

3. Double-click the SETUP.EXE file that came from the W95IR.EXE file. Messages will flash while a setup database is built and when Windows detects your infrared hardware. The first Add Infrared Device Wizard appears (see Figure 8.17). Click Next.

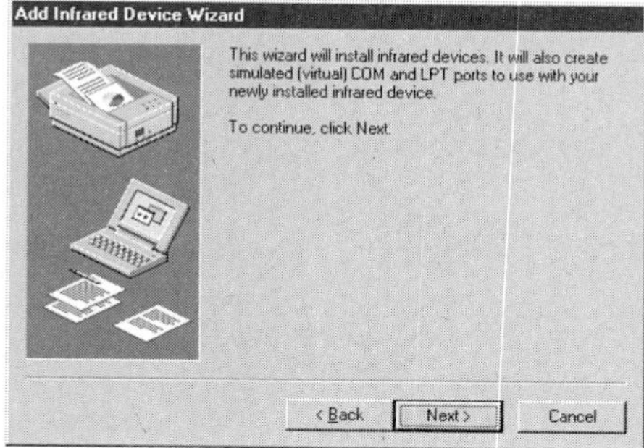

FIG. 8.17
The Add Infrared Device Wizard installs the software for infrared communication.

4. Select the manufacturer and model of your IrDA hardware from the lists in the second wizard dialog box shown in Figure 8.18. If your computer has a built-in IrDA port, choose (Standard Infrared Devices) from the Manufacturers list, and then click Next.

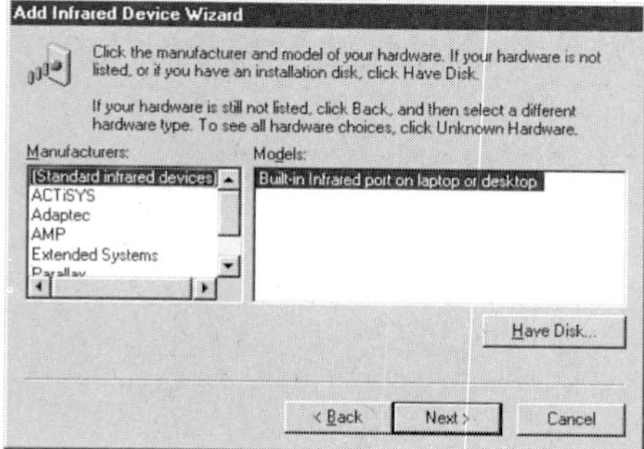

FIG. 8.18
Select the manufacturer and model for your IrDA device.

5. Select the COM port that the IrDA device uses. It may be automatically detected, as shown in Figure 8.19. If not, select a COM port using the IRQ information you saw in the Device Manager. Then click Next.

If you are unsure which COM port to use during installation, take a guess at one that appears unused. If your IrDA communication does not work, uninstall it, and reinstall it using the other COM port.

6. Change the simulated Infrared Serial (COM) port or Infrared Printer (LPT) port if you do not want to use these simulated ports. Figure 8.20 shows the simulated infrared port sheet. Select whether you want to use the default simulated ports or enter new simulated ports, and click Next.
7. Click Finish to complete the installation.

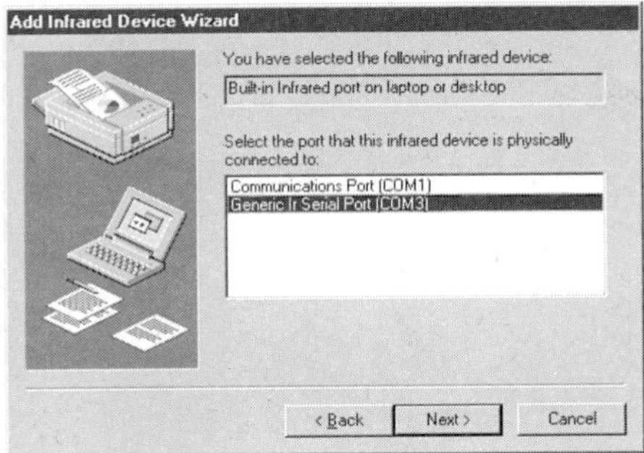

FIG. 8.19 Select the COM port used by your IrDA device.

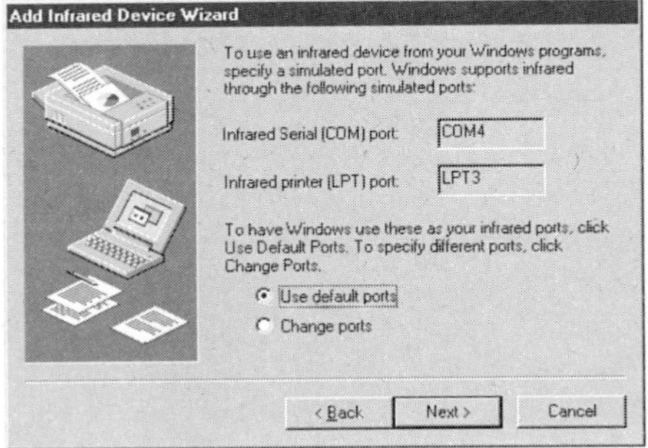

FIG. 8.20 Change the simulated infrared serial and printer ports or accept the defaults.

Starting and Controlling Infrared Communications Support

The Windows 95 Infrared Monitor program must be running if you want your computer to check its surroundings for other IrDA devices, such as printers and network connections. While it is running, the Infrared Monitor sends out an infrared beam and checks for responses every few seconds. If the Monitor gets a response from another IrDA device, it keeps a log that the device is available and indicates whether a driver for that device is loaded.

The Monitor also tracks which devices are currently communicating with your computer and the quality of that communication. You can see the quality level and communication status by opening the Infrared Monitor whenever it is working. Figure 8.21 shows communication in progress with a Hewlett-Packard (HP) printer. Use the Monitor to change the communication rate and enable or disable communication with devices in range.

Starting the Infrared Monitor and Turning On Communication To start the Infrared Monitor, open the Start menu and choose Settings, Control Panel. When the Control Panel appears, double-click the Infrared program. The Infrared Monitor sheet appears.

If you selected the Display the Infrared Icon in The Taskbar option from the Preferences tab of the Monitor, an Infrared icon will appear at the right side of the taskbar. Double-click this icon to display the Infrared Monitor sheet.

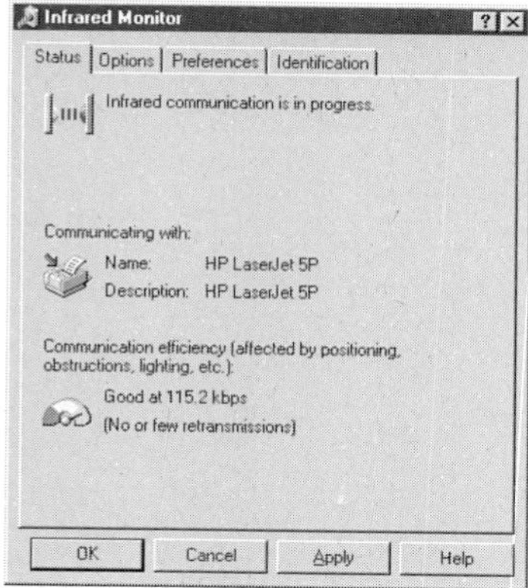

FIG. 8.21
This Status tab shows that data is being sent to an HP LaserJet 5P printer and that the communication rate is good at 115.2 Kbps.

When the Infrared Monitor is running, you can turn communication on and off with a right mouse click. To turn on infrared communication, right-click the Infrared icon on the taskbar, and then check the Enable Infrared Communication On check box. Turn off infrared communication by clearing the Enable Infrared Communication On check box.

The Search For and Provide Status For Devices in Range option and the Enable Software Install For Plug and Play Devices in Range option are turned off when infrared communication is turned off.

Changing the Infrared Monitor Settings To change the Infrared Monitor settings, display the Infrared Monitor by double-clicking the Infrared icon on the taskbar, or by double-clicking the Infrared program in the Control Panel.

Figure 8.22 shows the Status tab when no devices are detected; Figure 8.23 shows the Status tab when an IrDA-compatible printer is within range.

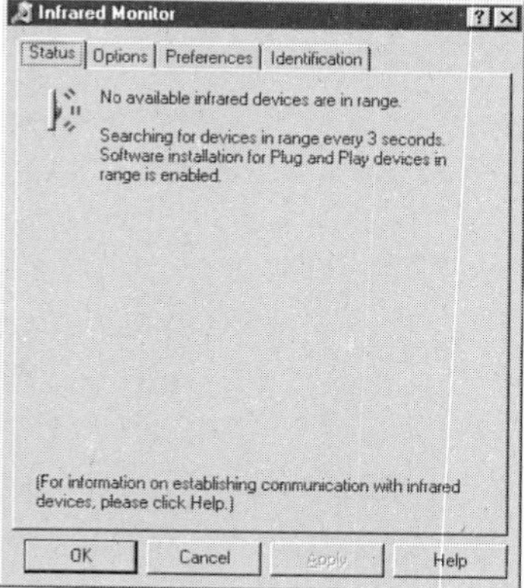

FIG. 8.22
The Status tab shows if devices are in range and the quality of their communication.

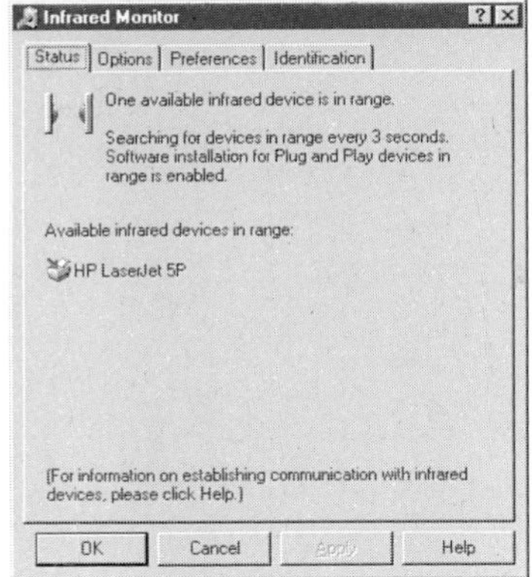

FIG. 8.23
The Status tab shows that an IrDA-compatible printer is in range.

Figure 8.24 shows the Options tab. The following table describes its options.

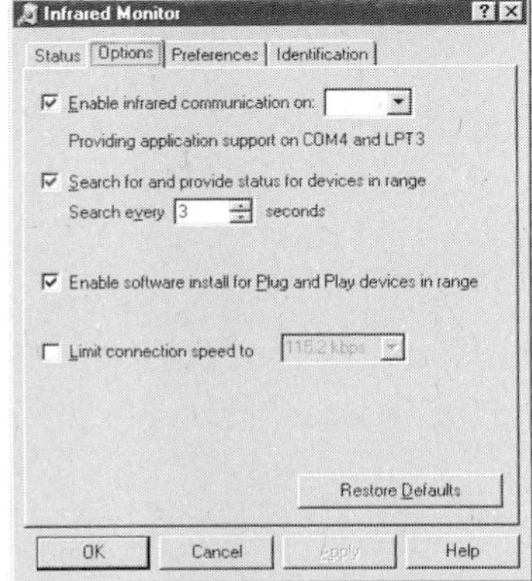

FIG. 8.24
The Options tab enables or disables infrared communication.

Option	**Description**
Enable Infrared Communications On	Enables infrared communication when selected and specifies which physical port is being used. You can choose between the physical COM ports you have available.
Search For and Provide	This must be selected if you want Status For Devices In Range devices to detect one another.
Search Every *x* Seconds	Specifies how frequently devices search for one another.
Enable Software Install for Plug and Play Devices in Range	When selected, Plug and Play devices will automatically install their drivers when the computer is within range. If the driver is already installed, it is not reinstalled. You will probably want to leave this deselected most of the time.

continues

continued

Option	Description
Limit Connection Speed To:	The Infrared Monitor attempts to transmit at the highest possible speed, but this may cause lower effective transmission rates if a large number of retries are required. In some cases, a lower speed may improve the effective transmission rate.

Figure 8.25 shows the options available on the Preferences tab. The following table describes those options.

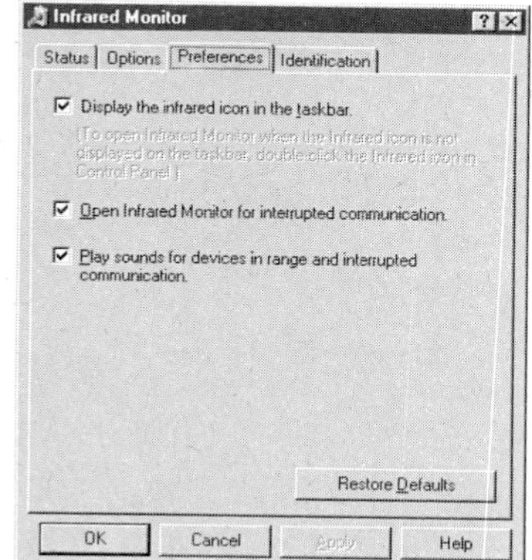

FIG. 8.25 The Preferences tab specifies personal options about how the Infrared Monitor appears.

Option	Description
Display the Infrared Icon in the Taskbar	Select this check box to display a small Infrared icon in the taskbar. Right-click the icon for controls, or double-click it to display the Infrared Monitor.
Open Infrared Monitor for Interrupted Communication	When selected, a warning message displays when infrared communication is interrupted. The message box closes when communication resumes.
Play Sounds for Devices in Range and Interrupted Communication	When selected, a sound plays when communication is interrupted. If you have a sound card, you can customize these sounds by double-clicking the Sounds program in the Control Panel and selecting the sounds to play for infrared events.

Figure 8.26 shows the options available on the Identification tab. The following table describes these options.

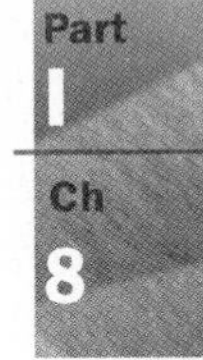

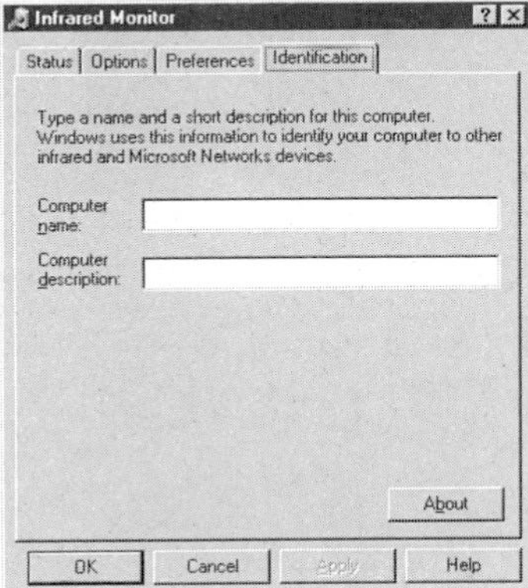

FIG. 8.26
Use the Identification tab to specify a network name and description for your computer.

Option	Description
Computer Name	Specify the name you want for your computer to be identified by on the network.
Computer Description	Specify the description for your computer to help in identifying it on a network.

Finding and Monitoring the Status of Infrared Devices

For infrared devices to communicate, they must be turned on and oriented so they send infrared light to each other. The infrared windows on the devices must be facing each other within an approximate 30-degree cone. They should be from six inches to nine feet apart. Most devices are designed for a range of three to nine feet.

To check the status of communication between two devices, open the Infrared Monitor by double-clicking the Infrared icon on the taskbar, or by double-clicking Infrared in the Control Panel. Select the Options tab. Select the Enable Infrared Communication On check box, select the Search For and Provide Status For Devices In Range check box, and then click Apply.

If the transmission quality is poor, lower the transmission speed by selecting a smaller number from the Limit Connection Speed To: list. Normally, infrared communication occurs at the highest possible speed. In cases of a poor link, a lower transmission rate may actually improve throughput by decreasing retries.

Installing Software for Your Infrared Device

Some Plug and Play IrDA devices will install the appropriate driver on your computer when your computer comes within range. Figure 8.27 shows the dialog box that displays when an IrDA computer comes within range of a Hewlett-Packard 5P printer.

To install software for an infrared device, follow these steps:

1. Right-click the Infrared icon on the taskbar.
2. Select the Enable Plug and Play check box.

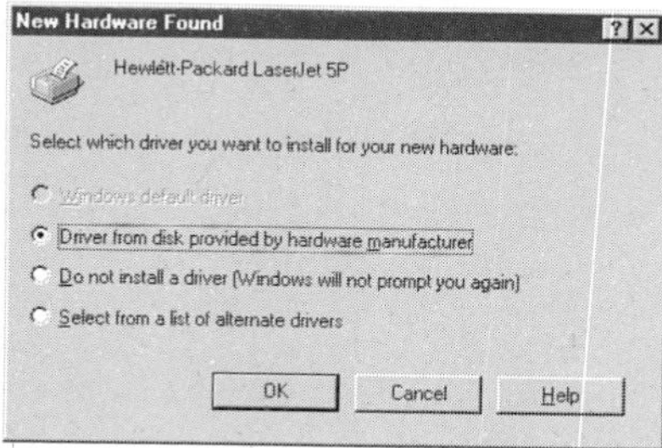

FIG. 8.27
Windows indicates when it is within range of a device for which it does not have a driver.

You also can display the Infrared Monitor sheet and check the Enable Software Install For Plug And Play Devices In Range check box. If you want to prevent unwanted drivers from being installed on your computer, leave this check box clear.

If the IrDA device is not Plug and Play-compliant, you'll need to install the driver for that IrDA device. This driver should be on a disk that came with the device.

If the IrDA device is not Plug and Play-compliant, click Start, Settings, Control Panel; then double-click the Add New Hardware program. Keep the infrared windows of the devices in range and run the Add New Hardware Wizard, or manually install the drivers using manual selections from the Add New Hardware Wizard.

▶ **See** "Installing Legacy (non-PnP) Hardware," **p. 182**

Using Infrared for Direct Cable Connection

You can use infrared to transfer files with Direct Cable Connection. The infrared communication acts the same as communication via a serial or parallel cable. Make sure that infrared is enabled in both devices. Then turn on Direct Cable Connection by opening the Start menu and choosing Programs, Accessories, Direct Cable Connection. Follow the Direct Cable Connection procedures described earlier in this chapter.

Printing with an Infrared Printer

Printing to an infrared printer is the same as printing to any other printer. However, you do need to make sure that the infrared windows on the devices are within an angle of 30 degrees and within six inches to nine feet of the printer.

If you have not assigned the printer to an infrared port, follow these steps:

1. Open the Start menu and choose Settings, Printers.
2. Right-click the Printers icon and choose the Properties sheet.
3. Select the Details tab.
4. Select Infrared from the Print to the Following Port list.

Connecting to a Network Using IR

OSR 2

If you have installed IrDA 2.0, which is the latest version of the infrared driver, you can now connect a computer with an IR device to a local area network (LAN) that is equipped with an IrLan access point device. The IrLan device takes the place of the network adapter that you would normally use in a computer to connect to a network. Check the release notes that come with the IrDA driver for a list of IrDA 2.0-compliant IrLan access devices.

To establish an IR connection with a network equipped with an IrLan device, turn on the IrLan device and run the Infrared Monitor, as described in "Starting the Infrared Monitor and Turning On Communication," earlier in this chapter. Once the IR connection is established, you can double-click the Network Neighborhood icon to view files and folders on the network.

Removing Infrared Support

You must remove infrared support from your computer before upgrading to new or different infrared support. You may need to upgrade if you change the infrared adapter in your computer, or if you upgrade from Infrared Support for Windows v1.0 that was released in Service Pack 1 during the first quarter of 1996.

To remove infrared support, follow these steps:

1. Open the Start menu and choose Settings, Control Panel; then double-click the Add/Remove Programs program.
2. Select the Install/Uninstall tab.
3. Select Infrared Support for Windows 95 Version 1.0 from the list.
4. Click the Add/Remove button.

Troubleshooting When Infrared Communication Fails

If you have trouble with infrared communication and you know the Infrared Monitor is on and the communication is enabled, follow this checklist to search for possible problems:

- Make sure all non-IrDA communication has stopped. Non-IrDA communication prevents IrDA communication.
- Both devices should be IrDA-compliant.
- Check that infrared is on and enabled in both IrDA devices.
- The search option must be turned on by selecting the Search For and Provide Status For Devices in Range check box on the Options tab of the Infrared Monitor.
- Check that the search interval is long enough so the devices can detect each other. Set the Search Every X Seconds box for approximately three seconds on the Options tab. The Search For and Provide Status For Devices in Range check box must be selected.
- Check that the devices are between six inches and nine feet apart and their infrared windows are pointing at each other and within a 30-degree cone. Check that the infrared windows are clean.
- Make sure sunlight is not shining on either infrared window.

http://www.microsoft.com/windows/software/irda.htm

Maintaining Laptop and Desktop Files with Briefcase

Many users of portable PCs also use a desktop system and often need to juggle files between the two systems. You might, for example, have a set of reports you are preparing with your desktop system and you need to move those files to your portable to work on them while you are out of town. Windows 95 includes a Briefcase feature that simplifies the task of synchronizing the files on your desktop and portable PCs, helping you keep track of which copy of the file(s) is most current.

The following is a simplified example of how you might use the Briefcase:

- You create a Briefcase (which appears as a typical folder) on your portable PC.
- You copy one or more files to the Briefcase using a direct cable connection to your desktop PC or through your docking station's network connection.
- You work on the documents contained in the Briefcase while you are away from the office, modifying and updating the files.
- While you are away from the office, a coworker modifies one of the files on your desktop system that you copied to your Briefcase.
- When you return to the office, you reconnect your portable to your desktop PC, and then open the Briefcase on your portable.
- You use the Briefcase to update the files. The Briefcase informs you which files have been modified and enables you to easily copy the files from the Briefcase to their original locations on the desktop PC. The Briefcase also informs you that a file on your desktop PC (the file modified by your coworker) has changed and gives you the option of updating your copy in the Briefcase.

The Briefcase also can detect when the original and Briefcase copies of a file have been changed. The Briefcase then prompts you to specify which copy of the file should be retained. The Briefcase also supports *reconciliation* of the two copies of the file. This means that if the document's source application supports reconciliation, the Briefcase uses OLE to communicate with the source application and merge the two files together, retaining the changes made in each copy of the file.

NOTE Because the Briefcase is a new feature, few applications currently support reconciliation, but the number of applications that support it should grow as developers take advantage of this new feature.

You are not limited to creating a Briefcase on your portable PC. In fact, you can create a Briefcase on a floppy disk or your desktop PC. You might find a Briefcase useful for synchronizing files on which multiple users on the network collaborate. And you are not limited to creating a single Briefcase—you can create as many as you like. For example, you might create a separate Briefcase for each project on which you are currently working.

▶ **See** "Synchronizing Files with a Floppy Disk," **p. 227**

NOTE Placing a Briefcase on a floppy disk is useful if you do not have the necessary cable to connect your desktop and portable PCs using Direct Cable Connection, or your docking station is not connected to the network. Simply create the Briefcase, and then move it to a floppy disk. Drag files from your desktop PC to the Briefcase; then move the Briefcase disk to your portable and begin working on the files.

Creating a Briefcase

If your PC does not already include a Briefcase on your desktop, you can easily create a new Briefcase. To create a Briefcase, follow these steps:

1. Decide where you want the Briefcase to be created (on the desktop, in a floppy disk folder, in a folder on the hard disk, and so on).
2. Right-click in the location in which you want the Briefcase created. If you want the Briefcase created on the desktop, for example, right-click the desktop.
3. From the pop-up menu, choose New, Briefcase. Windows 95 will create a Briefcase and add an icon for it in the location you have selected.
4. If you want to rename the Briefcase, click the Briefcase icon to select it; then click the Briefcase's description. Type a new description and press Enter.

As previously explained, you can create as many Briefcases as you like. By default, Windows 95 creates a Briefcase called My Briefcase on your desktop. You can rename the default Briefcase to suit your preferences.

Placing Files in the Briefcase

Although the Briefcase is a special type of folder, it behaves almost identically to a standard directory folder. You can move or copy files to a Briefcase in the same way you move or copy files to any folder. Simply open the folder in which the files are located, and then drag them to the Briefcase. Hold down the Ctrl key while dragging to copy the files, or hold down the Shift key to move the files. If you prefer, you can open Explorer (open the Start menu and choose Programs, Windows Explorer) and drag the files from Explorer into the Briefcase.

▶ **See** "Copying and Moving," **p. 679**

In addition to using standard file copying and moving techniques to place files in the Briefcase, you also can use Send To to place files in the Briefcase. Locate the file(s) you want to place in the Briefcase; then right-click one of the files. From the pop-up menu, choose Send To, and then choose the Briefcase to which you want to send the selected file(s). Windows 95 will copy the file(s) in the Briefcase.

If you right-drag a document to the Briefcase, the pop-up menu includes an item labeled Make Sync Copy. Choose this option to create a copy of the object in the Briefcase.

Synchronizing Files

If you travel or work at home on your portable with files copied to your Briefcase from your desktop PC, Briefcase can keep your files updated. When your PC is undocked or you are working remotely, use your files as you normally would, opening and saving them in the Briefcase. When you return to the office desktop or remote network, first reconnect your portable to your desktop system or network, or insert the Briefcase floppy disk in your desktop PC. Then simply open the Briefcase and choose Briefcase, Update All. Briefcase displays a dialog box similar to the one shown in Figure 8.28.

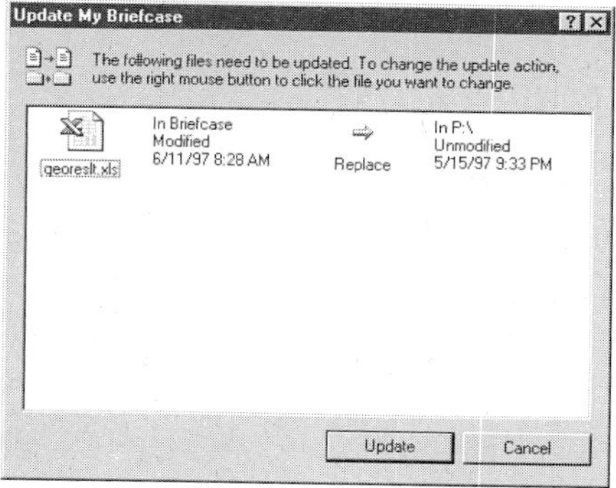

FIG. 8.28
Briefcase prompts you to specify how modified files should be handled.

The left column lists the name of the file, and the second column lists the status of the file in the Briefcase. The third column specifies the update action that occurs if you do not choose a different action. The fourth column indicates the status of the original copy of the file.

If the update actions listed for each file are appropriate, click Update to update the files. To change the update action for a file, right-click the file. Briefcase opens a dialog box as shown in Figure 8.28. Choose the appropriate update action, and Briefcase changes the action for the file. When all of the files are set the way you want them, click Update.

NOTE If you update a file on a network server, you have no guarantee that another user won't modify the file after you have updated it, placing it once again out of sync with your Briefcase copy. If you again update the files in the Briefcase, however, the Briefcase will indicate that the original copy of the file located on the network server has changed.

To select a group of files in the Briefcase, hold down the Ctrl key and click each file you want to update.

If you prefer to update only a few of the files in the Briefcase, simply select the files you want to update, and then choose Briefcase, Update Selection. Briefcase lists in the Update My Briefcase dialog box only those files you have selected.

After your selection of files is complete, choose Briefcase, Update Selection to update the selected files. You also can right-click a file in the Briefcase to open a dialog box, and then choose Update from the context menu to update the selected file(s).

Synchronizing Files with a Floppy Disk

You can move a Briefcase to a floppy disk to simplify transferring files between your portable and desktop PCs. To move your Briefcase to a floppy disk, follow these steps:

1. If you do not yet have a Briefcase on the desktop PC, create one. Right-click the Windows 95 desktop, and then choose New, Briefcase.
2. Open the My Computer folder and position the folder so you can see the Briefcase icon.
3. Open the folder containing the files you want to place in the Briefcase, and then right-drag the files from their folder to the Briefcase icon. From the context menu, choose Make Sync Copy.
4. Place a formatted disk in the desktop PC's floppy disk drive.
5. Right-drag the Briefcase from the desktop to the floppy drive icon in My Computer, and then choose Move Here.
6. Remove the floppy disk containing the Briefcase and insert it in the portable's floppy disk drive.
7. On the portable, work on the files in the Briefcase, opening and saving them in the Briefcase.
8. When you're ready to synchronize the files, place the floppy disk containing the Briefcase in the desktop PC's floppy disk drive. Open My Computer; then open the floppy disk folder. Right-drag the Briefcase from the disk folder to the desktop, and choose Move Here.
9. Open the Briefcase, and then synchronize the files as explained in the previous section.

Synchronizing Files with a Network

You can use a Briefcase to help you synchronize files on a network server on which you collaborate with other users. The process for working with the Briefcase and synchronizing files is the same as for a desktop PC/portable PC scenario. Create the Briefcase on your desktop, and then copy the files from the network server to the Briefcase. Edit the files in the Briefcase. When you're ready to synchronize them again with the original files on the server, open the Briefcase, and synchronize the files as previously explained.

Checking the Status of Briefcase Files

The update status of each file is listed in the Briefcase folder if you use Details to display the contents of the Briefcase as a detailed list. To configure the Briefcase to display a detailed list, choose View, Details.

You also can view the status of files in the Briefcase by selecting the files and choosing Briefcase, Update Selection. You also can view the status of individual files in the same way. In addition, you can use a file's pop-up menu to view its status. With the Briefcase open, right-click the file or folder that you want to check. Choose Properties to display the file's properties sheet. Then choose the Update Status tab to display the Update Status page shown in Figure 8.29.

FIG. 8.29
A file's property sheet shows its update status.

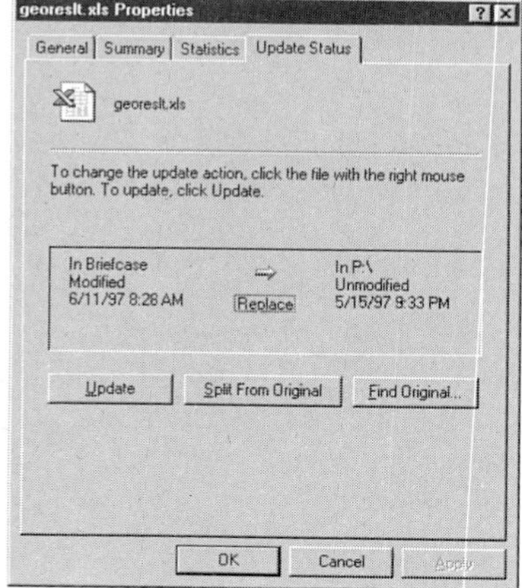

If you want to check the status of all your Briefcase files, choose Briefcase, Update All. A status window pops up, enabling you to view the status of all files in the Briefcase. Choose Update to update the files, or Cancel to close the dialog box without making any changes.

Splitting the Briefcase File from the Original Files

Occasionally, you might want to disassociate (called *splitting*) a file in the Briefcase from its original. Splitting a file removes the link between the two files. To split a file, first open the Briefcase and select the file you want to split. After selecting the file, choose Briefcase, Split From Original. After a file is split from an original, it is labeled an orphan and can no longer be updated.

LCD Screen Mouse Trails

Pointing device features are also enhanced with the mobile user in mind. Switching between integrated pointing devices—track ball or clip-on mouse—to a desktop mouse (Plug and Play-compatible) is now automatically detected and enabled by Windows 95. Installing a serial, Plug and Play mouse amounts to plugging it in, and the system enables its use.

Like Windows for Workgroups, Windows 95 also adds a few special features that make it easier to see the cursor on a passive-matrix LCD panel, which many portable PCs use for their displays (active-matrix panels have much better image quality, and consequently it is much easier to see the cursor on an active-matrix LCD). The following sections explain these features.

Using Mouse Trails

When you move the cursor on a passive LCD display, the display typically cannot update fast enough to adequately display the pointer as it moves across the display. This makes it difficult to see the cursor. To alleviate the problem, you can turn on *mouse trails*. When mouse trails is enabled, a set of "ghost" pointers trail the pointer as it moves across the display. This makes it much easier to locate the cursor.

To enable mouse trails, open the Start menu and choose Settings, Control Panel. From the Control Panel, select the Mouse icon, and then click the Motion tab to display the Motion properties page shown in Figure 8.30.

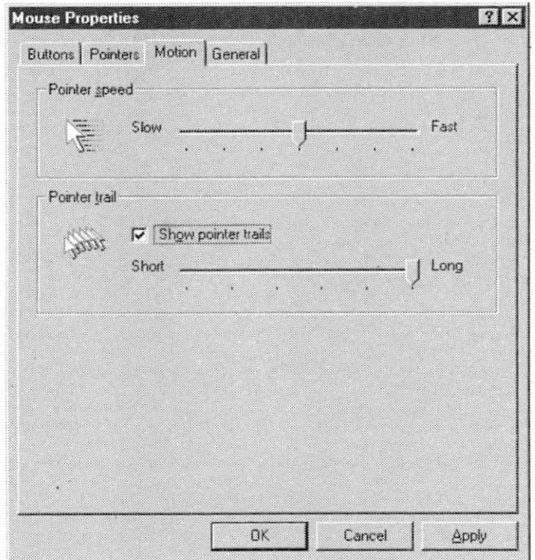

FIG. 8.30
Use the Show Pointer Trails check box to turn on mouse trails.

Place a check in the Show Pointer Trails check box to enable mouse trails. Use the accompanying slider control to specify the length of the mouse trail; then choose OK to apply the changes.

NOTE If you are using the new Microsoft IntelliMouse that came on the market when Microsoft Office 97 was released and have installed the Microsoft IntelliPoint 2.0 software, there is another option that helps you locate the mouse pointer on a laptop screen. The Sonar view, when enabled, produces a series of concentric circles around the mouse pointer when you press and release the Ctrl key. To enable this feature, open the Mouse properties sheet from the Control Panel, select the Visibility tab, and check the Show Location of Pointer When You Press the Ctrl Key option. To locate the pointer, press and release the Ctrl key.

Using Large Pointers

In addition to using mouse trails, you also might want to increase the size of the pointer you use on your portable to make it easier to see. Windows 95 enables you to create pointer schemes much like you create desktop color schemes, saving the pointer schemes by name. Windows 95 includes a small selection of predefined schemes, two of which use large pointers that are much easier to see on a passive LCD panel than the standard Windows 95 mouse pointers.

NOTE If you did not install the optional pointers when you installed Windows 95, you must install them before you can use the large pointer schemes. To do so, open the Control Panel and choose the Add/Remove Programs icon. Double-click Accessories, and then scroll through the Accessories list to find the Mouse Pointers item. Place a check beside Mouse Pointers and choose OK. Choose OK a second time to add the pointers to your system.

To use a large pointer scheme, open the Control Panel and choose the Mouse icon; then choose the Pointers tab to display the Pointers properties page. From the Schemes drop-down list, choose either the Windows Standard (Large) or Windows Standard (Extra Large) scheme. Then choose OK. Windows 95 immediately begins using the new pointers.

TIP To add a new scheme, customize as many pointers as you want; then click Save As on the Pointers property page to identify the new scheme.

In addition to using a predefined scheme, you also can create your own custom schemes. Display the Pointers properties page as described earlier, and then select the pointer you want to change. Choose Browse, and Windows 95 displays a dialog box from which you can select a pointer file. When you select a pointer file, a sample of the pointer appears in the Preview box. When you have selected the pointer you want to use, choose Open to select the pointer and return to the Pointers page. Choose Save As to specify a name for your new pointer scheme.

PART II

Navigation Skills

CHAPTER 9

Understanding Windows 95

by Ron Person

This chapter gives you "the big picture" to help you understand Windows 95. If you're a new user, you'll want to get a feel for the important concepts and see where you are going. If you're an experienced Windows user, you'll want to know what is different and what is the same in this new version of Windows compared to previous versions. And if you are a power user or consultant, you'll want a quick introduction to ways you can customize and troubleshoot Windows 95.

What are the most important elements in a Windows 95 screen?

Learn the different parts of a Windows 95 screen.

How are programs started and documents loaded?

Intermediate and expert users can customize Windows 95 to start programs on startup, from desktop icons or directly from files.

How to customize Windows 95

Learn how to customize Windows 95 by changing Property sheets.

Who should use My Computer and who should use Windows Explorer for their file management needs?

Shows advantages to using both single-pane windows and double-pane windows to manage files.

People who have used previous versions of Windows should read this chapter so that they can quickly grasp what has changed.

After reading this chapter, you should have a good idea what sections to read to start learning about Windows 95. Throughout this chapter, you'll find recommendations for three different approaches to learning more. These three approaches are based on whether you are an inexperienced Windows user, an experienced Windows user, or a power user.

Throughout this chapter, important concepts are broken up by experience level. Rather than repeating basic concepts for each experience level, you should read the concepts from the inexperienced user level up to your level.

This chapter gives you an overview of the most important concepts for controlling Windows 95. It also tells you which book sections are probably appropriate to your experience level.

Understanding the Most Important Screen Elements in Windows 95

The appearance of the Windows 95 screen, shown in Figure 9.1, is completely different from MS-DOS or previous versions of Windows. The backdrop of the screen is the *desktop*. On the desktop, you'll find icons that represent programs or documents, a taskbar containing a Start button and application buttons, and windows that contain programs. If your Windows 95 has been used previously and customized, it may appear slightly different from the figure.

Beginning Users of Windows 95

If you are unfamiliar with previous versions of Windows, the important things to notice are:

- Each graphical item on the screen does something when you put the tip of the mouse pointer on the item and click or double-click the left or right mouse button.
- Icons represent programs, documents, or shortcuts. *Shortcuts* are pointers to a program, document, disk drive, printer, or other resource.
- You use the taskbar and Start button shown at the bottom of Figure 9.1 to start and switch between programs.
- Running programs appear in three ways: as a button on the taskbar, in a window on the screen, or filling the entire screen.

▶ **See** "Learning the Parts of the Windows Display," **p. 253**
▶ **See** "Starting Applications from the Start Menu and Taskbar," **p. 256**
▶ **See** "Creating Shortcut Icons on the Desktop to Start Programs," **p. 261**
▶ **See** "Customizing the Mouse," **p. 881**
▶ **See** "Making Windows Accessible for the Hearing- Sight- and Movement-Impaired," **p. 884**

FIG. 9.1
Microsoft designed the Windows 95 screen to be easier to use for first-time users, yet more powerful and customizable for power users.

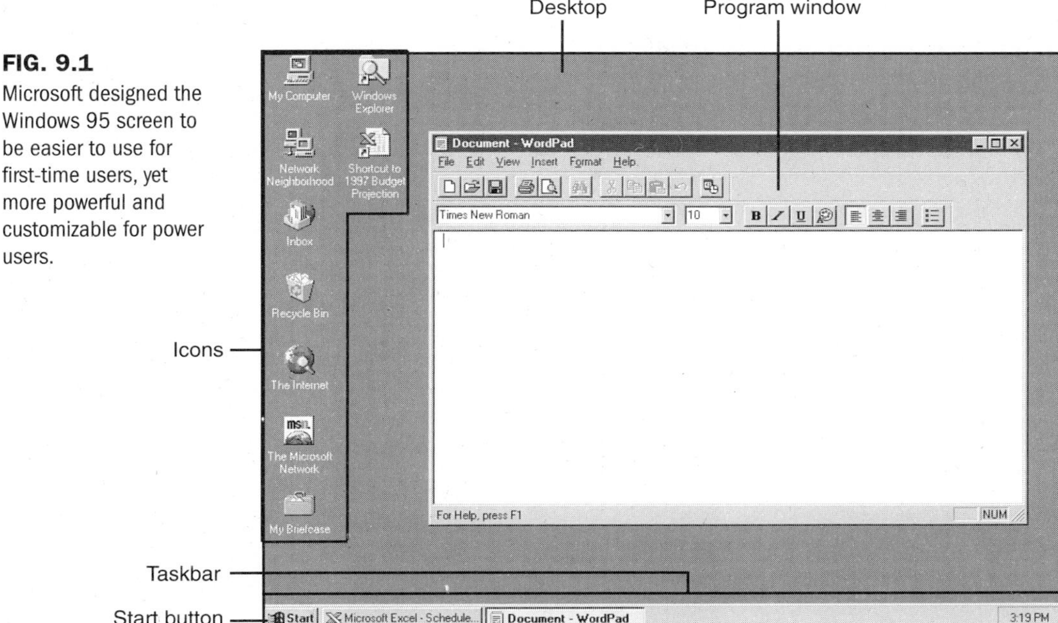

Experienced and Power Users of Previous Windows Versions

If you are familiar with previous versions of Windows or even consider yourself a power user, the important things to notice are:

- You can customize much more of Windows. To customize, click an item with the right mouse button, click Properties, and then change options on the properties sheet for the item.
- The Program Manager is gone. In its place are icons that appear on the desktop and the Start menu that you access with the Start button shown at the bottom of Figure 9.1.
- You can drag icons on the desktop to any location and they will stay there. You can even place folders on the desktop. (*Folders* are the new name for directories.)
- *Shortcut* icons on the desktop act as pointers to programs or documents that you don't want to put directly on the desktop. Shortcuts display a small curved arrow at their lower-left corner. Double-clicking a shortcut icon opens the document or program. Deleting a shortcut icon does not delete the file to which it points.

How to Start Programs and Documents

Microsoft has made it much easier to start programs with Windows 95 than it was in previous versions of Windows. Depending on your experience level and the task, you can start programs or documents in different ways.

Starting from the Start Button

The Start button is a significant enhancement to Windows. Clicking the Start button displays a menu like the one directly above the Start button in Figure 9.2. As you move the pointer over an item on the menu, a submenu appears. When you see the program or document you want to open, click it.

FIG. 9.2
Click the Start button to display the Start menu and your computer's programs and documents.

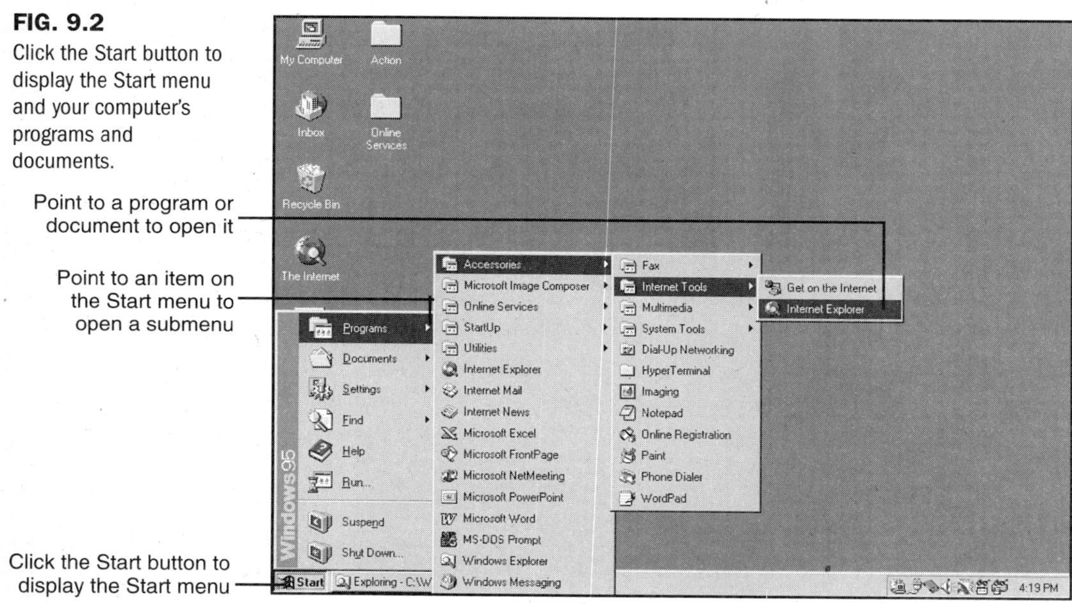

Beginning Users of Windows 95 If you are unfamiliar with previous versions of Windows, the important things to notice are:

- Starting a program or document is easy. Move the mouse pointer over the Start button and click the left mouse button.
- Windows 95 lists your programs on the Start menu.
- Start a recently used document by pointing to the Documents menu item and then clicking the document. The program opens automatically.
- Find documents or programs by pointing to the Find button and clicking Files or Folders. Enter information about the document or program file you want to find.
- Get Help or demonstrations by pointing to the Help button and clicking.
- Shut down Windows by clicking the Start button and then clicking Shut Down.

See "Starting a Program from the Start Menu," **p. 259**

See "Quitting Windows Applications," **p. 270**

Experienced Users of Previous Windows Versions If you are familiar with previous versions of Windows, the important things to notice are:

- You no longer need to open and close Group windows in the Program Manager to find program or document icons.
- Your existing Group windows from the Program Manager in previous versions of Windows now appear as submenus off the Programs item of the Start menu.
- Click the Start button to see your programs and most frequently used documents. Click the item you want to open.
- Go directly to the Control Panel or printer settings from the Settings item on the Start menu.
- Make frequently used programs more accessible on the Start menu by dragging their file icon from the Explorer or My Computer and dropping it on the Start button.

▶ **See** "Running Programs on Startup," **p. 247**

▶ **See** "Specifying Documents to Open at Startup," **p. 249**

▶ **See** "Customizing the Start Menu," **p. 847**

Power Users Very Experienced with Windows If you are a power user and are very experienced with Windows, the important things to notice are:

- At first, the Start menu may seem to slow you down compared to quickly clicking your way through the Program Manager. It will be faster, however, if you customize by adding your own submenus and repositioning programs and documents on the menu.
- Customize the Start menu to include your own submenus by adding a folder to the Start menu.
- Change the properties of programs so that they open as a button on the taskbar, as a window, or maximized to fill the screen.

▶ **See** "Controlling How Startup Programs Appear," **p. 249**

▶ **See** "Managing Windows After an Application Failure," **p. 270**

▶ **See** "Customizing the Taskbar," **p. 844**

Starting from Shortcuts

Shortcuts are icons that point to files, folders, disk drives, and other resources on your computer (see Figure 9.3). Depending on the resource the shortcut points to, when you double-click a shortcut, it starts a program, opens a document, opens a windows showing the contents of a folder or disk drive, and so on. You can put folder shortcuts on your desktop so that when you drag a file onto the folder shortcut, the file is stored in the folder.

FIG. 9.3
Double-click a shortcut icon to open the program or document.

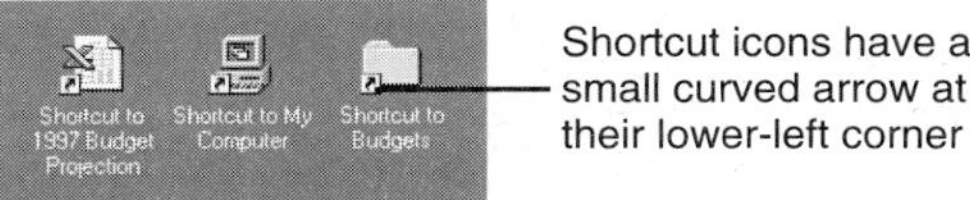

Beginning Users of Windows 95 If you are unfamiliar with previous versions of Windows, the important things to notice are:

- Shortcuts represent documents, programs, or folders.
- Double-clicking a shortcut opens the document or program.
- You can delete a shortcut icon without deleting the file or folder it represents.

▶ **See** "Starting Programs from a Shortcut Icon on the Desktop," **p. 260**

Experienced Users of Previous Windows Versions If you are familiar with previous versions of Windows, the important thing to notice is:

- You can create a shortcut for any program, document, folder, disk drive, printer, or other resource by dragging the icon for the item from the Explorer or My Computer with the right mouse button and dropping it on the desktop.

▶ **See** "Creating Shortcut Icons on the Desktop to Start Programs," **p. 261**

Power Users Very Experienced with Windows If you are a power user and are very experienced with Windows, the important things to notice are:

- You can create shortcuts that automatically run procedures or programs. For example, in Word or Excel, you can create a shortcut to a document or spreadsheet that contains a macro that runs when opened. Another example is the Windows 95 Backup program that enables you to create shortcuts that automatically back up selected files.
- Customize shortcuts by right-clicking the Shortcut icon, clicking Properties, and then clicking the Shortcut tab in the shortcut's properties sheet. You can add shortcut keys, change the file to which the shortcut points, specify how a program runs, and change the icon.

▶ **See** "Modifying and Deleting Shortcuts," **p. 265**

Starting from My Computer or the Explorer

My Computer and the Explorer are windows you can use to manage the program and document files on your computer. Figures 9.4 and 9.5 show My Computer and the Explorer windows.

FIG. 9.4
The My Computer window.

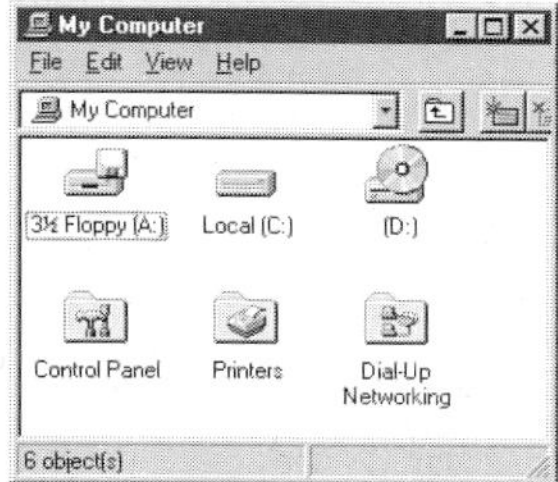

FIG. 9.5
The Explorer window.

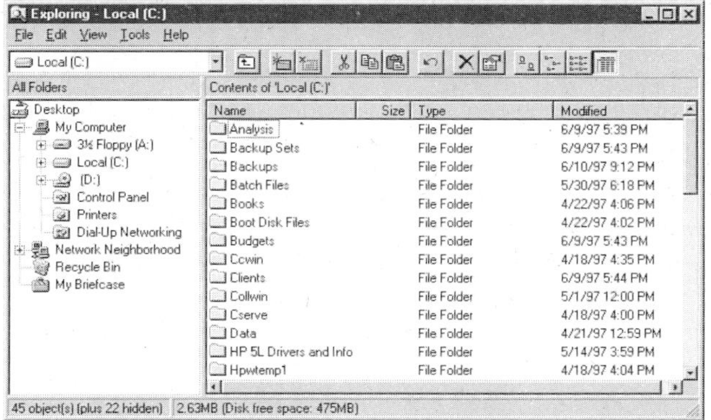

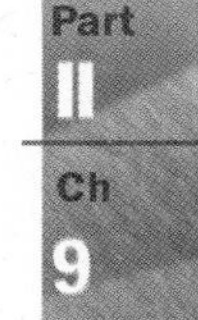

Beginning Users of Windows 95 If you are unfamiliar with previous versions of Windows, the important things to notice are:

- You should use the Start menu to open programs whenever possible. Open documents from within the program. If it is a frequently used document, you may find it on the Documents submenu off of the Start menu.
- If there is a program that you can't find on the Start menu, use a window from My Computer to display program files. When you find the program you want, double-click the program's icon.

▶ **See** "Using My Computer to Open Documents," **p. 268**

Experienced Users of Previous Windows Versions If you are familiar with previous versions of Windows, the important things to notice are:

- If you are familiar with opening program or document files in the File Manager, you'll know how to open programs or documents from within My Computer or the Explorer. Find the file and double-click it.
- You can register a file type with an application so that double-clicking a file of that type opens a specific application and loads the file. Most file types are automatically registered, but you can manually register a file or change a file type's registration by choosing View, Options, and then selecting the File Types tab and either adding a new type or editing an existing type.

▶ **See** "Using Windows Explorer to View Files and Folders," **p. 312**

▶ **See** "Managing Your Files and Folders," **p. 316**

▶ **See** "Opening a Document from Explorer," **p. 329**

Power Users Very Experienced with Windows If you are a power user and are very experienced with Windows, the important thing to notice is:

- Open multiple files at the same time from My Computer or Explorer by selecting the files with Shift+Click or Ctrl+Click, and then right-click one of the selected files. From the shortcut menu, click Open.

▶ **See** "Registering Documents So They Open Applications," **p. 353**

How to Customize and See Properties Sheets

Properties sheets are an important part of Windows 95. Nearly all items you see on-screen have a properties sheet that describes the item. To display a properties sheet, click an item with the right mouse button, and then click Properties from the shortcut menu. Figure 9.6 shows the Taskbar properties sheet.

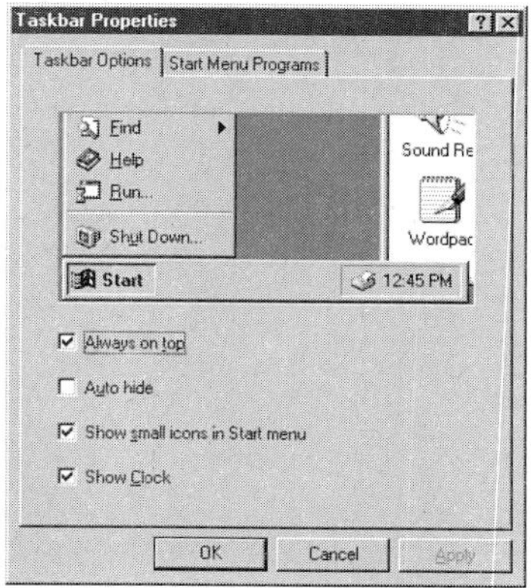

FIG. 9.6
Use properties sheets to get information about an item and change how the item behaves.

Beginning Users of Windows 95

If you are unfamiliar with previous versions of Windows, the important things to notice are:

- You can get a description and change the behavior of many items by displaying the properties sheets.
- Even within some applications, you can see the properties of a document by displaying the file's properties sheet from within the Open dialog box.

See "Changing Settings and Properties with the Right Mouse Button," **p. 673**

Experienced Users of Previous Windows Versions

If you are familiar with previous versions of Windows, the important things to notice are:

- You don't have to go through the Control Panel to customize items anymore. Start clicking with the right mouse button and notice what items have a properties sheet.
- You can customize Windows by right-clicking items you want to change, such as the desktop, and then clicking Properties.

See "Customizing the Desktop Colors and Background," **p. 860**

See "Changing the Screen Resolution, Font Size, and Color Palette," **p. 874**

Power Users Very Experienced with Windows

If you consider yourself a power user and are very experienced with Windows, the important things to notice are:

- You can create logon profiles that change Windows hardware configuration depending on a selection at startup. This is useful for laptops that also serve as desktop computers.
- You can use logon IDs to identify different users on a network or isolated computer. Windows will start up with the customized settings which that user has created.

See "Changing Custom Settings for Each User," **p. 889**

See "Reviewing Your Computer's System Information," **p. 891**

How to Manage Files

Windows 95 has two different approaches to managing files. If you're a new or inexperienced user, you may want to use My Computer. It uses a folder metaphor where files appear as program or document icons (see Figure 9.7). These icons can be moved or copied between folder icons. If you're on a network, examine Network Neighborhood. It shows network files in the same way.

The second way of managing files in Windows 95 is through the Explorer (refer to Figure 9.8). The Explorer displays folders and files using two panes in a window. The left pane shows the hierarchical relationship between folders—which folder is inside another. The right pane displays the contents of the folder that has been selected in the left pane.

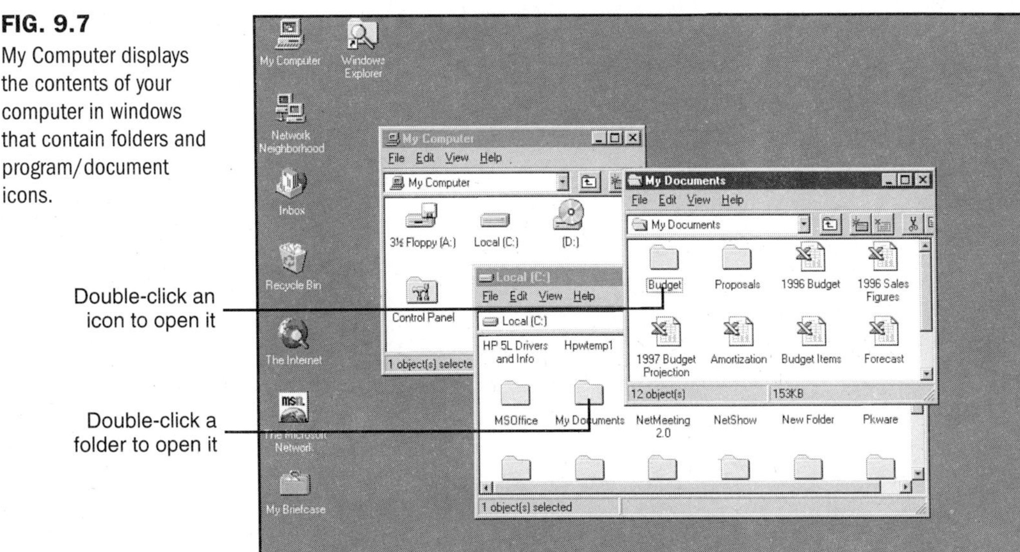

FIG. 9.7
My Computer displays the contents of your computer in windows that contain folders and program/document icons.

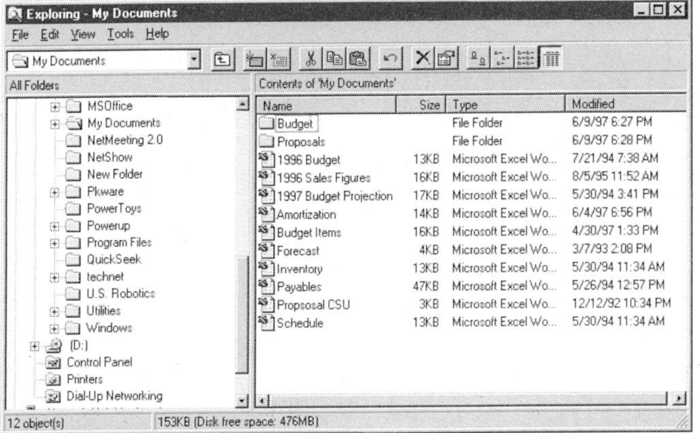

FIG. 9.8
The hierarchical relationship of folders shows in the left pane of the Explorer window.

Beginning Users of Windows 95

If you are unfamiliar with previous versions of Windows, the important things to notice are:

- You should use My Computer to see the contents of your computer. Open disk drives and folders by double-clicking the icon.
- Use My Computer to copy and delete files.
- Create your own folders in a window by clicking File, New, Folder.

See "Managing Files and Folders with My Computer," **p. 301**

Experienced Users of Previous Windows Versions

If you are familiar with previous versions of Windows, the important things to notice are:

- Use either the folder metaphor in My Computer or the hierarchical panes in Explorer to manage your computer's files.
- If you need to see the relationships of folders—how folders are grouped inside other folders—use the Explorer.
- Right-click files in My Computer or Explorer to see the numerous shortcut commands for copying, deleting, printing, and so on.
- At first, you may get frustrated using the Explorer because it doesn't allow multiple windows. You can actually do more in the Explorer than you did in File Manager, but it may take time to figure out how.
- You can change the displays in either My Computer or Explorer to show lists of names with details, and small or large icons.
- My Computer and Explorer also give you access to features such as the Control Panel and Printers. Double-click these folders to change computer and printer settings.

See "Managing Files and Folders," **p. 306**

See "Working with Long File Names," **p. 343**

See "Improving Performance with Disk Defragmenter," **p. 394**

Power Users Very Experienced with Windows

If you are a power user and are very experienced with Windows, the important things to notice are:

- You'll probably prefer to use the Explorer because you can see more file and folder information at a glance.
- If you are used to side-by-side windows from the File Manager, you can re-create them in the Explorer. Open two instances of the Explorer, right-click in a gray area of the taskbar, and then click Tile Vertically.
- All system resources are visible and most are changeable by opening the Control Panel and then System. Click the Device Manager tab. To see properties of any hardware device, click the device and then click Properties. (Select the Computer item to see IRQ and I/O settings for all devices.)

See "Synchronizing Files with the Briefcase," **p. 347**

See "Using Explorer with Shared Resources on a Network," **p. 354**

See "Monitoring Your System," **p. 413**

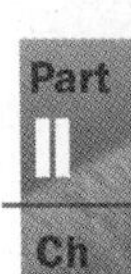

CHAPTER 10

Navigating and Controlling Windows

by Ron Person

What you learn in this chapter will help you operate Windows and any Windows application. This chapter describes the parts of the Windows screen, how to use the keyboard and mouse, and how to start Windows and applications. You learn that there are many different ways to start an application. This chapter not only describes these different methods, it also tells you which ways you might prefer to use depending on your experience and the type of task that you are doing.

Windows control methods

Learn how to operate Windows using keyboard or mouse methods.

Start programs

Start programs using the Start menu or by opening documents.

Manage and troubleshoot problems

Learn how to start Windows after startup problems and how to use safe mode for diagnosis. Create a startup disk.

Create and use shortcut icons

Increase productivity with shortcut icons to start programs or open documents.

Learn how to open and save documents

Open and Save works the same in nearly all Windows programs.

Windows Help can guide you

Use the Help system built into Windows for a little guidance.

Starting and Quitting Windows

If you have not yet installed Windows, turn to Chapter 2, "Installing Windows," to learn how. After you install Windows, you can start Windows simply by turning on your computer. If your computer requires DOS drivers, you may see a DOS-like text screen as the drivers load. Also, if your Windows has multiple configurations installed, as a laptop or desktop version for example, then a text screen will display asking you to choose between the configurations. Once you make your choice, Windows starts.

When Windows starts, you may see a login sheet in which you should type your password. Windows uses the password from the login sheet for two purposes. If the computer is connected to a network, it logs you into the network using your network password. Windows can also use the password from the login sheet to detect which person is using the computer. Because different people may have customized Windows in different ways, the login sheet enables Windows to customize itself to the way you prefer to work with Windows.

Once login sheets are completed, Windows starts and displays the desktop with My Computer, Recycle Bin, and Network Neighborhood icons. You might also see a My Briefcase icon and shortcut icons created by prior users. The *taskbar* usually appears at the bottom of the screen, although it might appear in another location or not at all.

The first time you start Windows, you will see a Welcome to Windows 95 sheet. You can turn this sheet off by clearing the Show this Welcome Screen check box.

CAUTION

Do not turn off your computer until you correctly exit Windows and it displays a message saying that it is safe to turn off the computer. Incorrectly exiting Windows might result in the loss of data.

When you finish running Windows applications and Windows, you must not turn off the computer until you correctly exit Windows. Windows stores some data in memory and does not write it to your hard disk until you shut down. If you turn off the computer without correctly exiting, you might lose this data. To exit Windows correctly, follow these steps:

1. Save the data in the applications in which you are working. If you forget to do so, most applications ask whether you want to save open documents when you exit the application.
2. Exit any DOS applications that you are running.
3. Open the Start menu and choose Shut Down. The dialog box shown in Figure 10.1 displays.

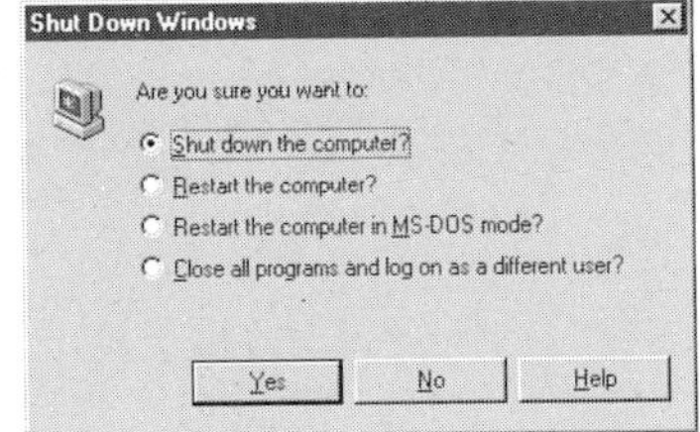

FIG. 10.1
Windows enables you to shut down the computer, restart Windows, restart the computer in MS-DOS mode, or close all applications and log on with another user ID.

4. Choose the Shut Down the Computer? option.

If you share a computer with others, you must restart to use your customized features. Shut down with the Close All Programs and Log On as a Different User? option.

5. Click the OK button.
6. Turn off your computer when you see the message that says that it is safe to do so.

If your computer and Windows are set up to work on a network, you see the Close All Programs and Log On as a Different User? option when you choose the Shut Down command from the Start menu.

Do not turn off the computer hardware until you see a message saying that you can safely do so. This message might take as long as two or three minutes to appear. Turning off the computer before you see this message might result in your losing the data for applications you were working in or not updating the registry if you made changes to applications.

Starting Applications at Startup

If you work with certain programs each time that you use your computer, you can tell Windows to start these programs automatically when you turn on your computer. You can even tell Windows how you want the program to appear at startup—either in a window, maximized, or minimized—so that it appears as a button in the taskbar.

You can also specify that Windows open certain documents at startup. In this case, Windows starts the program associated with the document in addition to opening the document.

Running Programs on Startup tTo specify the programs that you want to run at startup, you add them to the Startup folder. The easiest way to do this is with the Taskbar Properties dialog box, which has a wizard that guides you through the process step by step. Any programs that you add to the Startup folder appear in the Startup menu, which is a submenu of the Programs menu (see Figure 10.2).

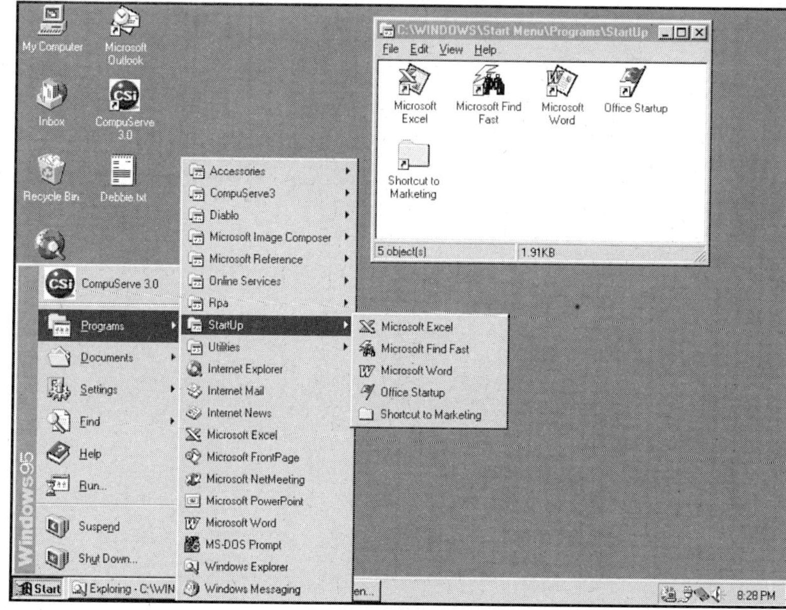

FIG. 10.2
Programs that you add to the Startup folder appear in the Startup menu and run automatically when you start Windows.

To specify programs that you want Windows to run at startup, follow these steps:

1. Open the Start menu and choose Settings; then choose Taskbar.
2. Select the Start Menu Programs tab, as shown in Figure 10.3.

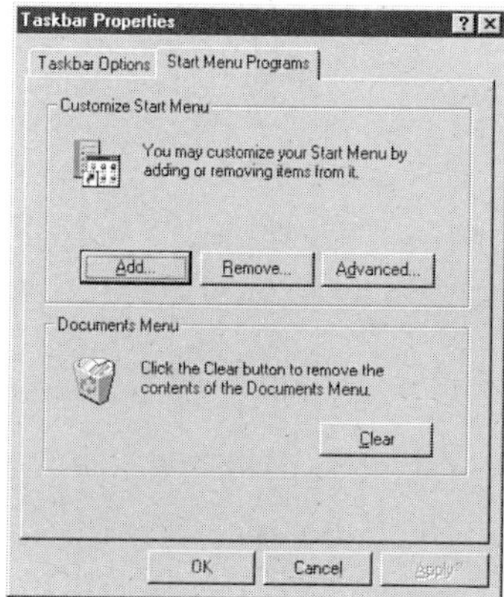

FIG. 10.3
Use the Start Menu Programs page to specify programs to run at startup.

3. Choose Add, Browse.
4. Select the program that you want to add to the Startup folder by double-clicking the folder in which the program is located and then double-clicking the program.
5. Click Next.

6. Double-click the Startup folder.
7. Accept the default title for the program or type a new title in the Select a Name for the Shortcut text box. The name that you enter appears in the Startup menu.
8. Click Finish.
9. Repeat steps 3 through 8 to add more programs to the Startup folder, or choose OK if you are finished adding programs.

NOTE If you frequently change the programs or documents that you want to run on startup, make the Startup folder accessible on the desktop so you can drag program or document files in and out of it. First create a shortcut icon on the desktop for the Startup folder. Use a right-mouse drag and drop to drag program or document files from Windows Explorer or My Computer into the Startup folder. Creating shortcuts is described in the section "Creating Shortcut Icons on the Desktop to Start Programs" later in this chapter.

To remove a program from the Startup folder, follow these steps:

1. Choose Remove on the Start Menu Programs page.
2. Double-click the Startup folder.
3. Select the program that you want to remove and choose Remove.
4. Choose Close.

Specifying Documents to Open at Startup If you regularly work with particular documents each time that you use your computer—for example, if you have a budget worksheet that you work on every day—you can tell Windows to open such documents automatically at startup. For Windows to open a document automatically, the document must be associated with a program. For many programs, Windows automatically associates the documents it creates with the program. This association enables you to open a document and the program that created it simultaneously.

See "Registering a New File Type," **p. 853**

To specify a document to open at startup, you follow the same procedure outlined in the preceding section, "Running Programs on Startup," except that in step 4, you select a document rather than a program. After you do so, the program associated with the document automatically runs at startup and the specified document opens.

Controlling How Startup Programs Appear After specifying that a program run at startup, you can tell Windows how you want the program to display when it starts. By default, Windows runs the program in a normal window. However, you can also choose to have the program run *maximized*, so that it fills the screen, or *minimized*, so that it appears as a button on the taskbar.

To control how a program appears on startup, follow these steps:

1. Add the program to the Startup folder, as described in the section "Running Programs on Startup."

2. Open the Startup folder in either My Computer or Windows Explorer. The Startup folder is located as a subfolder in WINDOWS\PROGRAMS\STARTUP. See Chapter 13, "Managing Files and Folders with Windows Explorer," for detailed instructions on using Windows Explorer to browse files and folders.

See "Viewing Resources in My Computer," **p. 302**

3. Right-click the program that you want to appear on startup. Then choose Properties.
4. Select the Shortcut tab.
5. Select one of the three options from the Run drop-down list, as shown in Figure 10.4.
6. Choose OK.

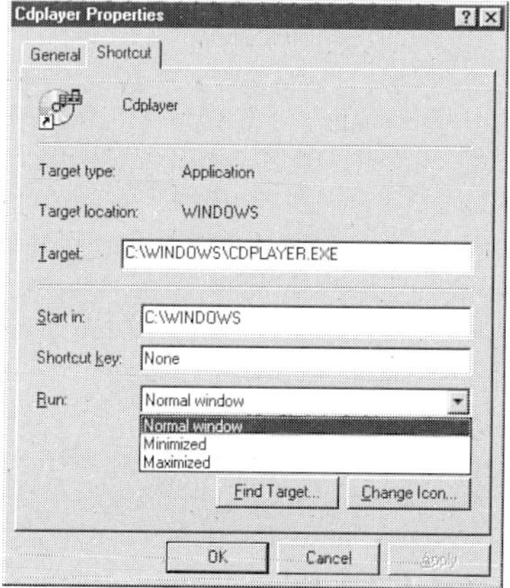

FIG. 10.4
This properties sheet is being used to configure how the CD Player application will run on startup.

Starting Windows After Technical Problems Occur

If you have any trouble starting Windows after you install it, it's good to know some of the avenues that you can take to get out of trouble. In this section, you learn how to create a startup disk, which enables you to start Windows if it doesn't start normally. You also learn how to start Windows in *safe mode*, which can be helpful if you are having certain kinds of problems.

Creating a Startup Disk If you have trouble starting Windows, you might need to use a startup disk to start your computer. For example, if you inadvertently delete a file that Windows needs for startup, you must start Windows with the startup disk in your disk drive and then remedy the problem so that you can start Windows normally.

When you install Windows, you have an opportunity to create a startup disk, which you should label and always keep on hand. If you didn't create the startup disk during installation or have misplaced the disk, you can create one after Windows is installed. Make sure to do so now, before you need the disk. Otherwise, if you have problems starting Windows, you won't be able to get into Windows to create the startup disk. (You might, however, be able to use another computer to create a startup disk.)

To create a startup disk, follow these steps:

1. Open the Start menu and choose Settings; then choose Control Panel.
2. Double-click the Add/Remove Programs button.
3. Click the Startup Disk tab, as shown in Figure 10.5.

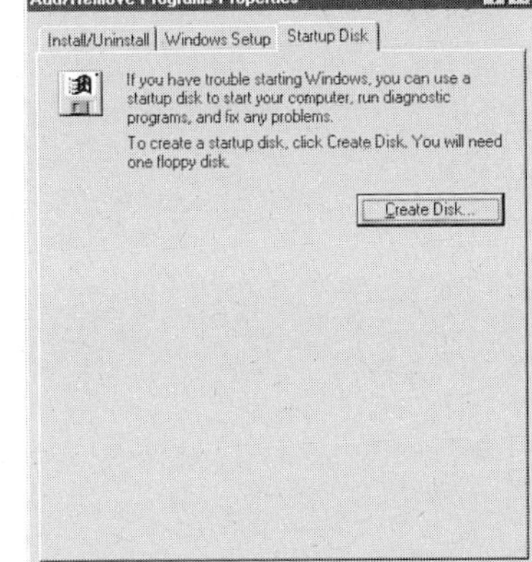

FIG. 10.5
To create a startup disk, click the Startup Disk tab in the Add/Remove Programs Properties sheet.

4. Insert a disk in your disk drive. The contents of this disk will be deleted.

   If you have both a 5 1/4-inch and 3 1/2-inch drive, use the A: drive (usually the 3 1/2-inch drive on newer computers). This is the drive from which your computer attempts to boot if a disk is in the drive.
5. Choose Create Disk and follow the instructions as they appear on-screen.

   To create the startup disk, you must have your original Windows program disks (or CD-ROM) handy.
6. Click OK.

Store your startup disk somewhere safe and easy to remember. If you have a laptop, you should store your startup disk in your laptop case.

To use the startup disk, insert it in the disk drive and reboot the computer. You can now diagnose and correct the problem so that you can start Windows normally. If you are having problems getting Windows started, or it starts but the video or some other piece of hardware does not operate correctly, then read the next section, "Starting Windows in Safe Mode," for instructions on diagnosing and correcting problems.

Starting Windows in Safe Mode Sometimes when you have trouble starting Windows, starting Windows in *safe mode* is helpful. When you do so, Windows uses basic default settings that at least get you back into the Windows environment, where you can fix the problem. For example, if you install the wrong driver for a new monitor, you might not be able to see the

Windows display when you restart Windows. In this case, restarting Windows with the default settings helps because you can see the screen, enter the Control Panel, and set up a different display.

See "Getting Help," **p. 270**

The default settings use a generic VGA monitor driver, no network settings, the standard Microsoft mouse driver, and the minimum device drivers necessary to start Windows. (*Device drivers* are software that enables hardware to work with Windows.) When you start Windows with the default settings, you cannot access any CD-ROM drives, printers, or other extra hardware devices. But you can at least access Windows and then diagnose and correct the problem.

To start Windows in a different mode, follow these steps:

1. Turn on the computer. Make sure that you also turn on the display monitor so that you can see the screen as Windows attempts to start. Be ready to press the F8 key.
2. When the message "Starting Windows" appears on-screen, press F8 to display the Windows 95 Startup Menu. This displays a menu of choices for starting Windows in different modes. Safe Mode is choice 3 or Safe Mode with Network Support is choice 4. Or select one of the other startup modes.
3. Type the selection number for the Safe Mode or Safe Mode with Network Support. Press Enter.

To skip the Startup Menu and start directly in a mode, start your computer and press one of the key combinations in the following table when the message "Starting Windows" appears.

Key Combination	Operating Mode
F5	Loads HIMEM.SYS and IFSHLP.SYS, loads DoubleSpace or DriveSpace if present, and then runs Windows 95 WIN.COM. Start in safe mode.
Shift+F5	Loads COMMAND.COM and loads DoubleSpace or DriveSpace if present.
Ctrl+F5	Loads COMMAND.COM.
F6	Loads HIMEM.SYS and IFSHLP.SYS. Processes the registry, loads COMMAND.COM, loads DoubleSpace or DriveSpace if present, runs Windows 95 WIN.COM, loads network drivers, and runs NETSTART.BAT.

A message informs you that Windows is running in safe mode and that some of your devices might not be available. The words "Safe mode" appear at each corner of the screen.

See "Checking Performance Settings," **p. 896**

Learning the Parts of the Windows Display

Windows computer screens display many graphical elements. Learning the names of these graphic elements or icons is important because you'll see these terms throughout this book. Likewise, you need to be familiar with these elements and icons because you can invoke a command for Windows or a Windows program by clicking the mouse pointer on many of them.

Figure 10.6 shows a Windows desktop that contains multiple applications, each in its own window. The figure identifies the parts of a typical Windows screen.

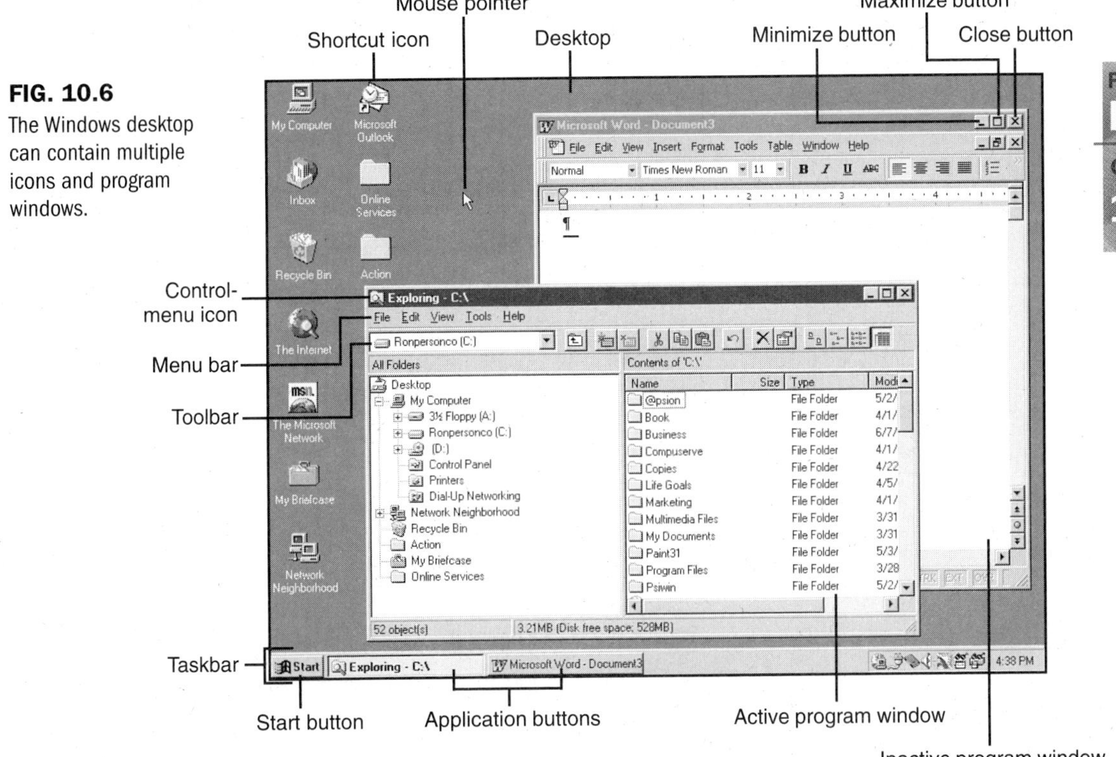

FIG. 10.6 The Windows desktop can contain multiple icons and program windows.

In the desktop shown in Figure 10.6, the Start button appears in the lower-left corner. This button provides one of the easiest ways to start programs or to open documents that you have recently used. (The Start button and taskbar may appear along different edges of the screen if a previous user has moved them.) With the mouse, you can click the Start button to open the Start menu. With the keyboard, you press Ctrl+Esc.

See "Customizing the Taskbar," **p. 844**

Across the bottom of the screen is the taskbar. The taskbar displays all programs currently open and running. You can switch between different programs by clicking the mouse pointer on the program that you want in the taskbar. To use the keyboard, press Alt+Tab to select the program and then release the keys.

TROUBLESHOOTING

Pressing Alt+Tab just seems to alternate between two applications. Hold down the Alt key as you press Tab and you will see a bar displaying icons of all the running applications. As you continue to hold down the Alt key, each press of the Tab key selects the next application icon on the bar. When the application you want is selected, release both the Alt and the Tab keys.

See "Moving the Taskbar," **p. 844**

The taskbar might appear in a different location on your screen. You can move the taskbar by dragging it to another location. You can also hide the taskbar when it is not in use by customizing your screen as described in Chapter 31, "Customizing the Taskbar and Start Menu."

With the mouse pointer, you can control Windows applications quickly and intuitively. The mouse pointer enables you to choose commands, select options, and move on-screen items. When you move the mouse, the mouse pointer moves synchronously. At different locations on the screen, the mouse pointer changes shape to indicate that it has capabilities specific to its current location. To select an item on the screen, you position the pointer on the item and then press or hold down the mouse button. You use four actions to affect on-screen items that are under the tip of the pointer: clicking, double-clicking, right-clicking, and dragging.

Windows enables you to run more than one program at the same time. Each program appears in its own window or as an item on the taskbar at the bottom of the screen. When programs are in windows, the program in the topmost window is the *active* program in the *active* window. Usually, the color of the active window's title bar differs from that of inactive windows. The active window receives your keyboard commands. One of the advantages of Windows is that even while you are working with the active program in the active window, other programs can be working.

The title bar at the top of each window displays the name of the application in the window. After you save a file, the title bar also shows the file name. (The active window is the one on top; it contains the currently running application.)

TIP Throughout this book, the letter that you press in combination with Alt to open a menu command is underlined, as in File.

The menu bar, which is directly under the title bar, displays the menu names. Windows applications use the same menu headings for common functions (such as File, Edit, Window, and Help), which makes it easier for you to learn new applications. To open a menu, click its name with the left mouse button, or press Alt and then the underlined letter in the menu name.

Icons are small, graphic representations. To reduce the clutter of a filled desktop, you can minimize windows so that they appear as icons on the taskbar. Even if not currently displayed in a window, an application is still running if the taskbar displays its icon. The taskbar appears at the bottom of Figure 10.6.

Using the Mouse and Keyboard on the Desktop

With the dominance of the *graphical user interface* (GUI) on today's personal computers, using a mouse has become second nature to most computer users. In Windows 95, you use the mouse even more than in earlier versions of Windows. Although you can still perform most tasks in the Windows environment with the keyboard, you can accomplish them much more quickly with the mouse. Also, many shortcuts are accessible only with the mouse. For example, in Windows 95, you use the right mouse button extensively to access shortcut menus that can significantly reduce the number of steps that it takes to invoke a command. Even if you are a diehard keyboard addict, you should explore the Windows environment with your mouse. You might be surprised by the things that you can now do with the mouse.

See "Customizing the Mouse," **p. 881**

See "Customizing the Keyboard," **p. 882**

This section explains the basic steps that you need to know to perform tasks with the mouse. If you already know how to use the mouse, you might want to skip this section.

Windows users routinely use the mouse to select text, objects, menus and their commands, toolbar buttons, and dialog box options, and to scroll through documents. To perform such tasks, you need to know how to point and click with the mouse.

To click items using the mouse, follow these steps:

1. Move the mouse so that the tip of the mouse pointer, usually an arrow, is on the menu, command, dialog box item, graphics object, or a position within the text. (When moved over editable text, the pointer changes to the shape of an I-beam.)
2. With a single quick motion, press and release the left mouse button.

Throughout this book, this two-step process is called *clicking*. Clicking the mouse button twice in rapid succession while pointing is called *double-clicking*. Double-clicking produces an action different than clicking. In a word processing application, for example, you often click to position the insertion point, but double-click to select a word.

You also can use the mouse for *dragging*. Dragging selects multiple text characters or moves graphic objects such as windows.

To drag with the mouse, follow these steps:

1. Move the mouse so that the tip of the pointer is on the object or at the beginning of the text that you want to select. (When over text, the pointer appears as an I-beam.)
2. Press and hold down the left mouse button.

3. Move the mouse while holding down the mouse button. If you are dragging a graphical object, the object moves when you move the mouse. If you are selecting text, the highlighted text area expands as you move the mouse.
4. Release the mouse button.

A feature in Windows 95 is the extensive use of the right mouse button. Putting the tip of the pointer on many objects on-screen and clicking the right mouse button displays a shortcut menu with commands specific to that object. For example, right-clicking a file name produces a shortcut menu containing commands such as Copy, Delete, and Rename. In some situations such as dragging a file name onto the desktop, you will want to drag using the right mouse button. In this case, you would drag as you would using the left mouse button, but hold down the right mouse key. When you release the item, a shortcut menu will appear.

The mouse is a useful tool, but you can use the keyboard to do nearly everything that you can do with the mouse. The mouse and the keyboard work as a team for controlling Windows applications. You can perform some tasks more easily with the mouse and some more easily with the keyboard. With most Windows applications, you can perform all functions with either. Experiment with the mouse and the keyboard, and use each where it works best for you. The next section gives you detailed information on how to use the mouse and keyboard to accomplish various tasks in the Windows environment.

Starting Applications from the Start Menu and Taskbar

Most of the work that you do on your computer consists of opening a program, using the program to create or modify a document, saving the document as a file, and then closing the program. Windows is designed to make these routine tasks as simple as possible.

One of the most important tasks that you must know how to do is to open or start programs in Windows. This task is very simple to do in Windows. You can open a program in several ways, so you can choose which works best for you. This section describes the different methods for starting programs and for using the Start menu, shortcuts, Windows Explorer, and My Computer. You also learn what to do if a program fails or locks up when you are using it.

Using the Start Menu

The simplest way for a new Windows user to open a program is to use the Start menu. When you install Windows, the installation program usually places each of your programs on a submenu that appears off of the Start menu. You can open the program simply by selecting it from a menu (see Figure 10.7).

NOTE If you are upgrading an earlier version of Windows to Windows 95, the Group windows that appeared within the Program Manager will become submenus that appear off of Programs in the Start menu.

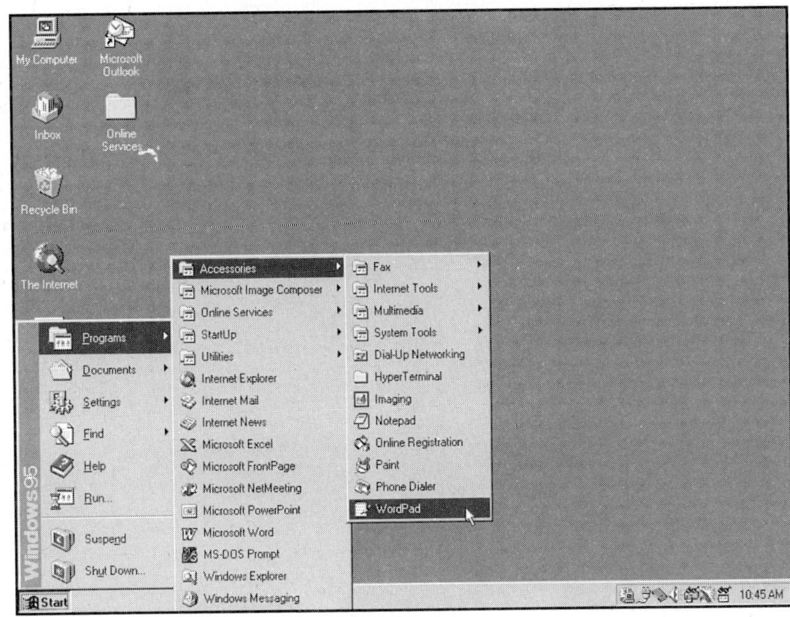

FIG. 10.7
You can select the program that you want to start from one of the menus that cascades from the Start menu. Here the user is choosing to start WordPad.

If you are familiar with Windows and want to make your programs more accessible, you can add the programs that you use most frequently to the Start menu. Then you don't have to move through a series of menus to start these programs. In this chapter, you also learn how to create a shortcut icon on the desktop that starts an application. These powerful features of Windows give you immediate access to your programs. You learn these techniques later in this section.

Understanding the Start Menu

The Start menu is the starting place for many of the tasks that you want to accomplish in Windows. You can open the Start menu at any time, from within any program, with one mouse click. From the Start menu, you can open your programs, customize the look and feel of Windows, find files and folders, get Help, and shut down your computer (see Figure 10.8). While providing all the power of immediate access, the Start menu also is integral to the clean look of the Windows desktop, enabling you to minimize the clutter on your desktop.

Use the Start menu whenever you need to open a program or access other features of Windows. You can open the Start menu at any time, even when you are working in another application such as Microsoft Excel, as shown in Figure 10.9. This is much simpler than in earlier versions of Windows, where you had to switch back to Program Manager to open other programs.

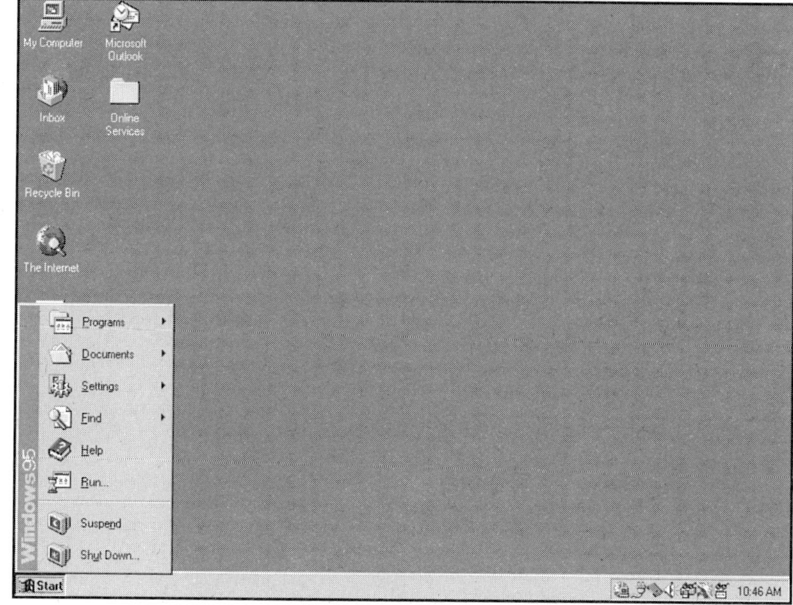

FIG. 10.8
The Start menu is just a mouse click away and gives you instant access to all your programs and many other Windows features.

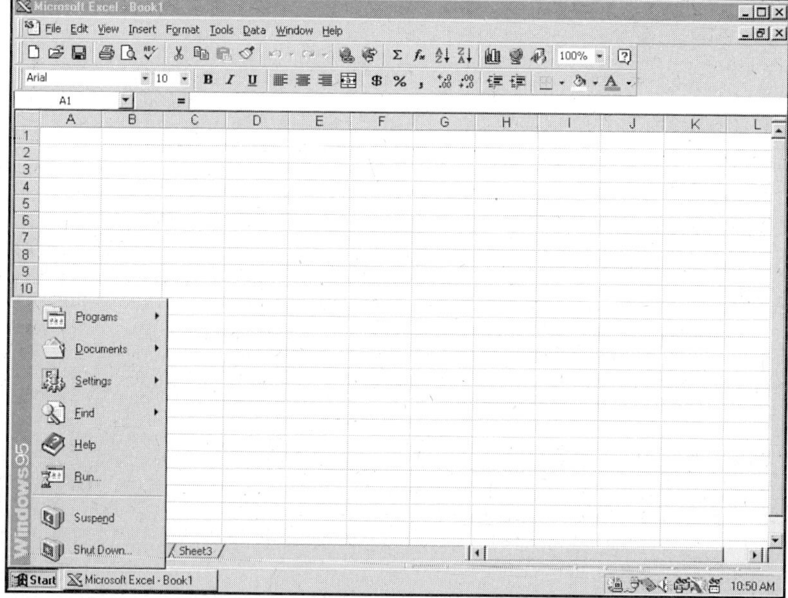

FIG. 10.9
You can open the Start menu without having to leave the program in which you are working. Here the Start menu appears at the bottom of the Microsoft Excel program.

TROUBLESHOOTING

The windows of some programs written for earlier versions of Windows cover the taskbar so it is difficult to switch between applications or click the Start button. Even when you can't see the taskbar, you can switch between applications by holding down the Alt key and pressing Tab. A bar appears with icons for each application. Press Tab until the application you want is selected; then release both keys.

To simultaneously display the taskbar and open the Start menu, press Ctrl+Esc.

Starting a Program from the Start Menu

To start a program from the Start menu, use the mouse to select the program from a menu and then click. It's that easy. You can also use the keyboard, although Windows is definitely designed to work most efficiently with a mouse.

To start a program using the Start menu, follow these steps:

1. Click the Start button in the taskbar to open the Start menu.

   If you have customized your computer, you might not see the taskbar and Start button at the bottom of your screen. If you see a gray line at one edge of the screen, move the pointer to that edge to display the taskbar. With the keyboard, you can press Ctrl+Esc to display the taskbar and open the Start menu.

2. Point to Programs on the Start menu. The Program menu then appears to the right. Then point to the program that you want to start, and click.

   If the Programs menu doesn't list the program that you want to start, click the folder that contains the program. In Figure 10.10, the user has selected WordPad from the Accessories submenu; when the user clicks the mouse, Windows opens that program. To find the program that you want, you might have to move through a series of submenus.

If you are using a keyboard and do not have a mouse available, open the Start menu by pressing Ctrl+Esc, and then use arrow keys to move up and down the menu. Press Enter to select the currently highlighted menu or program.

See "Switching Between Applications," **p. 683**

When you open a program, a button for the program appears in the taskbar. These buttons tell you which programs are open and enable you to move quickly from one open program to another. You learn more about switching between programs later in this chapter.

NOTE Usually you should find the program that you want to open in one of the Start menus' submenus. When you install Windows, the installation program looks for all your applications and puts each in one of the menus. If, however, you can't find your program in the Start menus, you can add a program or folder to the Start menu by following the procedures described in Chapter 5.

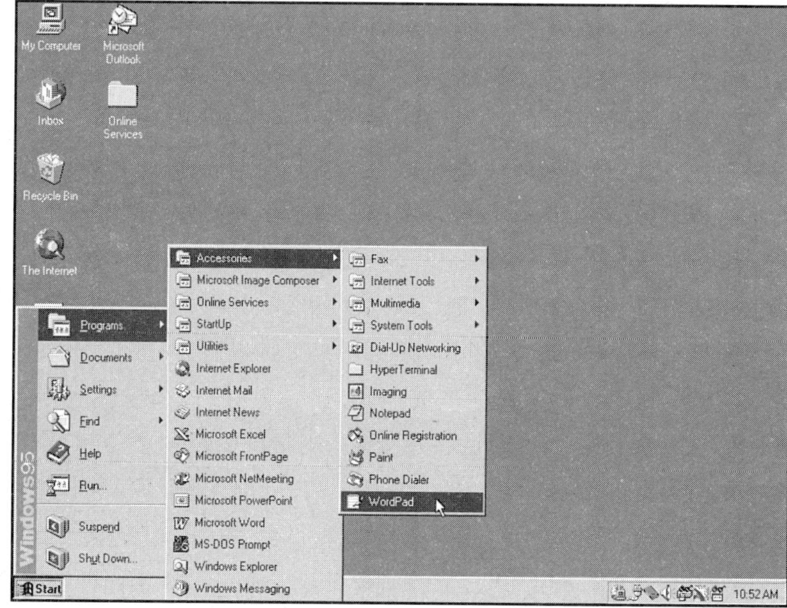

FIG. 10.10
Open the menu that contains the program that you want to start and then click the program.

Starting a Document from the Start Menu

After you click the Start button, you will notice a Documents command in the Start menu. When you choose this command, the Documents submenu appears with a listing of the files that you have worked on recently (see Figure 10.11). To open a document in this list, simply click it. Windows then automatically starts the associated application, if it is not already running, and opens the document.

After a while, the listing in the Documents menu can become quite long and contain documents that you no longer are working with. To clear the list, click the Start button, choose Settings, and then choose Taskbar. Select the Start Menu Programs tab on the Taskbar properties sheet and choose the Clear button (see Figure 10.12). Click OK to close the properties sheet.

Starting Programs from a Shortcut Icon on the Desktop

Another method for starting programs is to create shortcuts for the programs that you use most frequently. These shortcuts can appear as icons on your desktop. To start a program, you simply double-click its icon. If you don't like using menus to start your programs, you might prefer using shortcuts. A drawback to this method, however, is that to access the shortcut icons, your desktop must be visible. If a program is maximized, you cannot see the shortcuts.

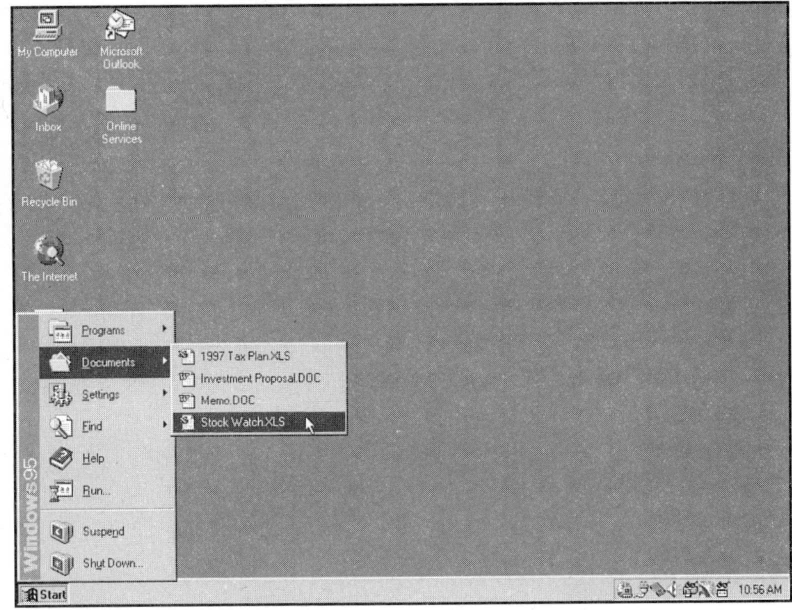

FIG. 10.11
The Start menu maintains a list of the documents that you have worked with most recently. Click one to load it into its application.

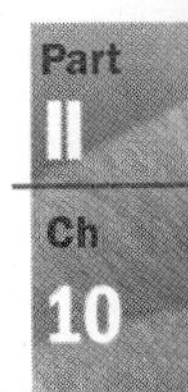

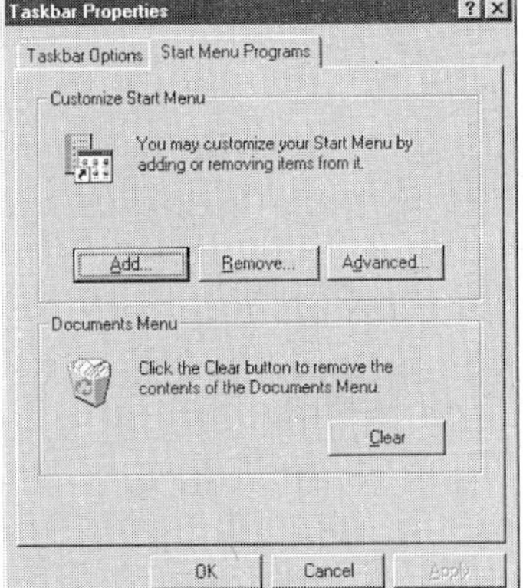

FIG. 10.12
The Start Menu Programs page.

You can always tell if an icon represents a shortcut, because a little arrow appears beneath the icon (see Figure 10.13).

Creating Shortcut Icons on the Desktop to Start Programs

To create a shortcut for a program on your desktop, follow these steps:

1. Using the Windows Explorer or My Computer, locate the program for which you want to create a shortcut.

   See Chapter 13, "Managing Files and Folders with Windows Explorer," to learn how to use the Windows Explorer and My Computer for browsing files and folders.

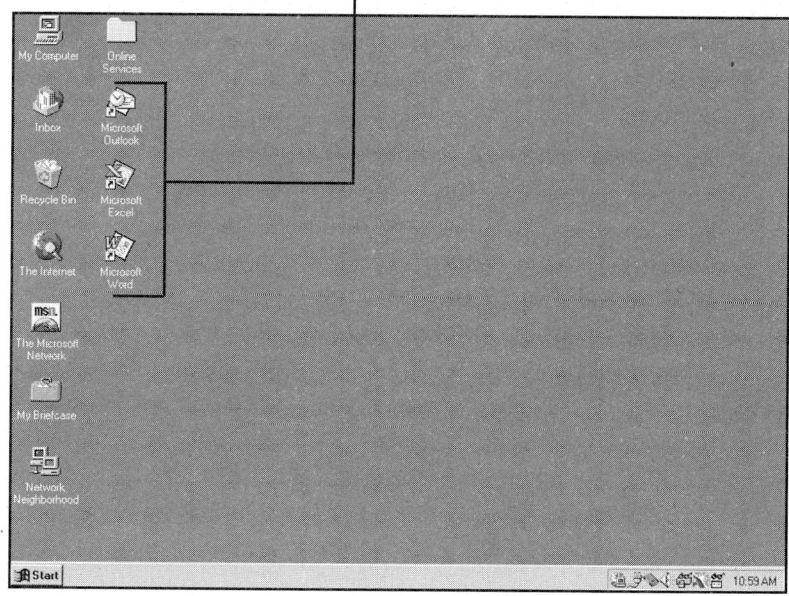

FIG. 10.13
This desktop has three shortcuts, as indicated by the arrows. To start an application, you double-click its icon.

TIP Drag a file from My Computer or Windows Explorer onto the desktop with the right mouse button. Drop the file and select Create Shortcut(s) Here to create a shortcut icon on the desktop.

2. Select the program in the Windows Explorer or My Computer window.
3. Click the program with the right mouse button and choose Copy.
4. Click the desktop with the right mouse button and choose Paste Shortcut.

The icon now appears on your desktop. You can drag the icon to any location. Refer to Figure 10.13, which shows the desktop with three shortcuts.

You also can create a shortcut for a document. Find the document in Windows Explorer or My Computer, and create a shortcut for the document as described in the preceding steps. If the document is associated (or registered) with a program, you can start the program and open the document by double-clicking its shortcut.

See "Registering a New File Type," **p. 853**

TROUBLESHOOTING

Double-clicking a shortcut icon no longer opens the document or program. What may have happened is that the file to which the shortcut pointed was moved or deleted. To correct this problem, you can either delete and then re-create the shortcut, or you can correct its properties sheet. To delete the shortcut icon, right-click the icon; then choose Delete. Choose Yes when asked to confirm the deletion. Re-create the shortcut with the methods described in this section.

To fix a shortcut to a file that has moved, right-click the icon, and then choose Properties. Click the Shortcut tab. Check the file and path name in the Target box; they may be wrong. To find the file, click the Find Target button. This opens a window in My Computer to the file if it is found. If it cannot be found, you can search in My Computer for the correct file and path name.

Setting the Properties for a Shortcut Icon

You can change how a shortcut icon acts and how it appears by opening its properties sheet and changing its properties. On the properties sheet, you can find information such as when a shortcut was created. You also can make a variety of changes such as those listed here:

- Change the file that the shortcut opens.
- Make an application start in a folder you specify.
- Add a shortcut key that activates the shortcut.
- Indicate whether you want the document or application to run minimized, maximized, or in a window.
- Change the icon used for a shortcut.

To display the properties sheet and set the properties for a shortcut icon, follow these steps:

1. Right-click the shortcut icon.
2. Click the Properties command to display the General page of the Shortcut properties sheet shown in Figure 10.14.

   On the General page, you can read where the LNK file for the shortcut is stored, as well as when it was created, modified, and last used. You also can change its file attributes.

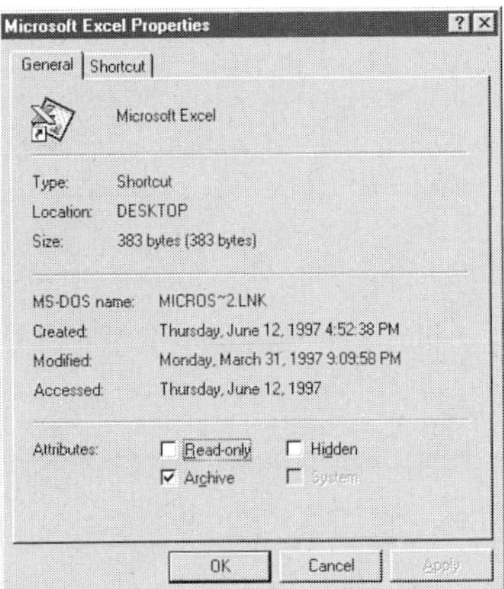

FIG. 10.14
The General page shows you file information about the shortcut icon.

3. Click the Shortcut tab to see the Shortcut page shown in Figure 10.15.

   At the top of the page, you can read the type of shortcut it is and the folder in which it is located. In the figure, the shortcut is to Microsoft Excel application in the Office folder.

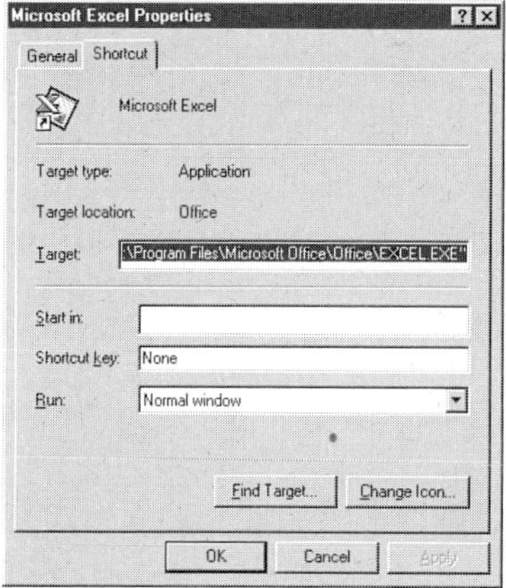

FIG. 10.15
The Shortcut page enables you to specify the file, startup folder, shortcut key, and icon used by a shortcut.

4. If you want a different file to start from the shortcut, click in the Target edit box and type the folder and file name.

   If you are unsure of the location, click Find Target to open a My Computer window in which you can look for the file and folder you want. Once you find the folder and file, close the My Computer windows and type the name in the Target edit box.
5. To specify a folder that contains the file or files necessary for operation, click in the Start In edit box and enter the drive and folders.

TIP You can press a shortcut's key combination to run the shortcut's program or document even when another program is active.

6. To specify a shortcut key that will activate this shortcut icon, click in the Shortcut Key edit box and then press the key you want as the shortcut key. The key must be a letter or a number. You cannot use Esc, Enter, Tab, the spacebar, Print Screen, or Backspace. To clear the Shortcut Key edit box, select the box and press the spacebar.

   To use this shortcut key, press Ctrl+Alt and the key you indicated. Shortcut keys you enter take precedence over other access keys in Windows.
7. To specify the type of window in which the application or document will run, click the Run drop-down list. Select from Normal Window, Minimized, or Maximized.
8. To change the icon displayed for the shortcut, click Change Icon to display the Change Icon dialog box shown in Figure 10.16.

   The Change Icon dialog box displays a scrolling horizontal list of icons stored in files with the extensions EXE, DLL, and ICO.

FIG. 10.16
You can select the icon you want for your shortcut.

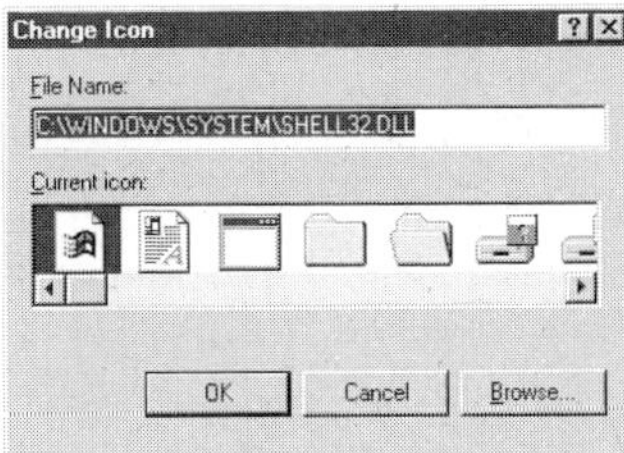

9. Select the icon you want and then choose OK.
10. Click the OK button to make your changes and close the Shortcut properties sheet. Click Apply to make your changes and keep the Shortcut properties sheet open for more changes.

Online computer services and computer clubs maintain large collections of icon files that are available for free.

NOTE When selecting icons for a shortcut, you don't have to restrict yourself to the icons in the file the shortcut points to. You can select an icon from any other DLL, EXE, or ICO file. To see other icon files from the Change Icon dialog box, click the Browse button.

Modifying and Deleting Shortcuts

If you want to modify the name that appears under the icon, click the icon once to select it. Then click the name once to select the text in the name. At this point, the pointer changes to an I-beam. You can press Delete to delete the name or click the pointer where you want the insertion point. After you edit the name, press Enter.

To delete a shortcut, click it with the right mouse button and choose Delete. Choose Yes when the confirmation dialog box appears.

You can arrange icons on the desktop by right-clicking the desktop and then choosing the Arrange Icons command. You are given alternative ways of arranging them.

CAUTION

Be careful when deleting shortcuts from the desktop. When you delete a shortcut for a file, you delete only the shortcut, not the file. However, when you delete an icon that represents a file, you delete the file. You can always tell whether an icon represents a shortcut because an arrow appears beneath the icon.

If, for example, you drag a document from My Computer to the desktop with the left mouse button, the icon actually represents the file; if you then delete the icon, you also delete the file. Make sure that you know what you are doing before you delete an icon on your desktop.

Starting Programs and Documents from Windows Explorer or My Computer

The Windows Explorer is an application that comes with Windows 95. You can use Windows Explorer to view the files and folders on your computer, move, copy, rename, and delete files and folders, and perform other file-management tasks. You can also start programs and open documents from Windows Explorer. The time that you spend learning how to work with this very useful and powerful tool is well invested.

My Computer is similar to Windows Explorer. The main difference between them is that, unlike the Windows Explorer window, the My Computer window does not enable you to view the overall structure of or relationships among all your computer's resources. Typically, when you use My Computer, you view the contents of one folder at a time. For some users, this window is less confusing than Windows Explorer window, which presents a lot of information at once.

This section focuses on starting programs and opening documents. For detailed instructions on using Windows Explorer and My Computer to manage your files, see Chapter 12, "Managing Files and Folders with My Computer," and Chapter 13, "Managing Files and Folders with Windows Explorer."

Opening a Document or Application from Windows Explorer

You can use Windows Explorer to find any file on your computer. After you find the file, you can also use Windows Explorer to start the program or document. If the file is a program file, you can start the program by double-clicking its file in Windows Explorer. If the file is a document, you can start its associated application and open the document simultaneously. If the application is already running, Windows opens the document in that application.

Access Windows Explorer quickly by right-clicking the Start button and then choosing Explore.

To open an application or document in the Windows Explorer, follow these steps:

1. Open the Start menu and choose Programs, Windows Explorer. The Windows Explorer window appears as shown in Figure 10.17.

FIG. 10.17
The Windows Explorer window displays all your computer's resources, including folders and files.

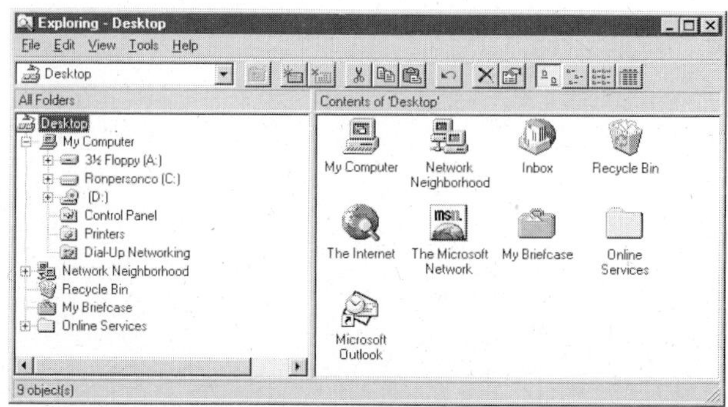

2. In Windows Explorer's left pane, locate and select the folder that contains the program or document that you want to start or open. Click the + sign to open a folder or the - sign to close a folder.

   In Figure 10.18, the user has selected a folder called Marketing, and Windows Explorer's right pane displays the files in that folder.

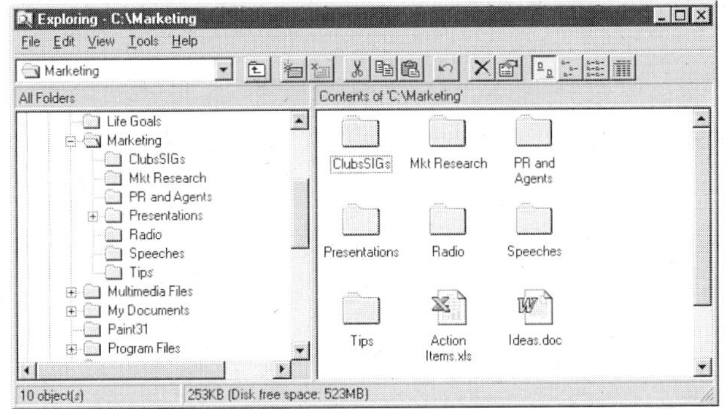

FIG. 10.18 The user has selected the Marketing folder in Windows Explorer's left pane, so the right pane displays that folder's contents.

Each document in the folder is represented by an icon that indicates the application that was used to create the document. The name of the document appears beneath the icon. For more detailed information on each file, choose View, Details. Windows Explorer's right pane then lists the files along with information on the size, type, and the date and time that each file was last modified, as shown in Figure 10.19.

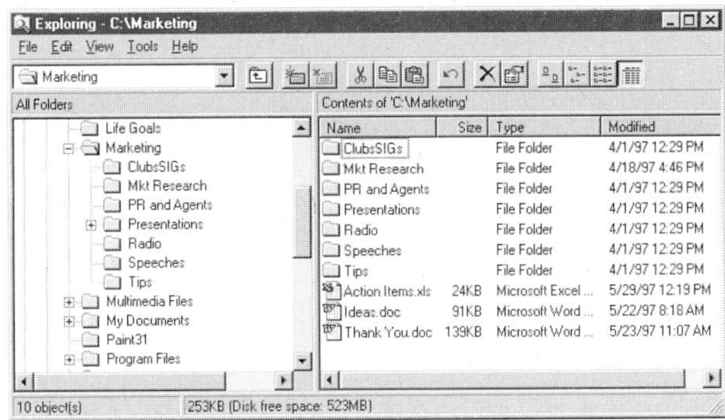

FIG. 10.19 Choose View, Details to display more information for each file in a folder.

3. Double-click the document that you want to open.

   If a document is associated with an application such as a word processor or spreadsheet program, Windows starts the application and opens the document. If the associated application is already running, Windows simply opens the document.

4. To open another document in the same folder, click the Exploring button in the taskbar to redisplay Windows Explorer, and double-click the document you want to open.

5. To open a document in another folder, click the Exploring button in the taskbar to redisplay Windows Explorer, locate and select the folder containing the document in the left pane, and double-click the document in the right pane.

TROUBLESHOOTING

Double-clicking a file in Windows Explorer doesn't open the file. An Open With dialog box displays asking which program should be used to open the file. Windows does not recognize the application to use when opening the document you double-clicked. Windows displays the Open With dialog box so you can select the application to open. Windows records this application so it can open the same application the next time you double-click this type of document. For more information about registering a file with an application, see the section "Registering a New File Type" in Chapter 31.

If you decide to use Windows Explorer routinely to open your documents, you can leave it open on your desktop. When you exit and restart Windows, it automatically opens Windows Explorer window in the same position as you left it.

Figure 10.20 shows how Windows Explorer window might look if a financial consultant organized her documents by client, creating one folder for each client. Within each folder, she would keep all the documents associated with that client and could easily move from client to client, opening documents simply by double-clicking them. With this approach to document management, Windows Explorer, rather than the Start menu, becomes the starting point for your work. You can still use the Start menu to access other Windows applications that you use less frequently or that are not associated with documents. Such applications include the Control Panel, which you use to customize Windows.

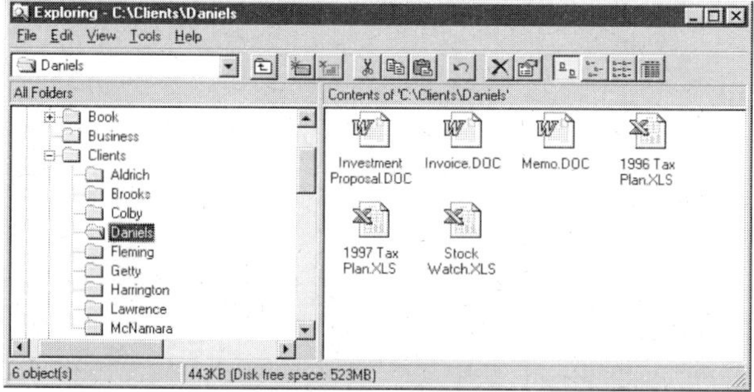

FIG. 10.20
In this desktop, the user has created a folder for each client, and each folder contains all the documents for that client.

Using My Computer to Open Documents

The first time that you start Windows, you will notice a My Computer icon on your desktop. If you double-click this icon, the My Computer window appears as shown in Figure 10.21. You can use My Computer to view your computer's resources, including folders and files. Figure 10.22 shows a window of folders that displays after double-clicking the C: drive icon.

My Computer is a different way of viewing folders, files, and computer resources than that used by Windows Explorer.

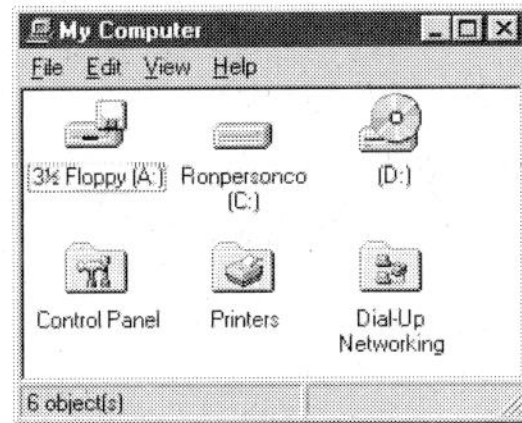

FIG. 10.21 Use the My Computer window to view your computer's resources.

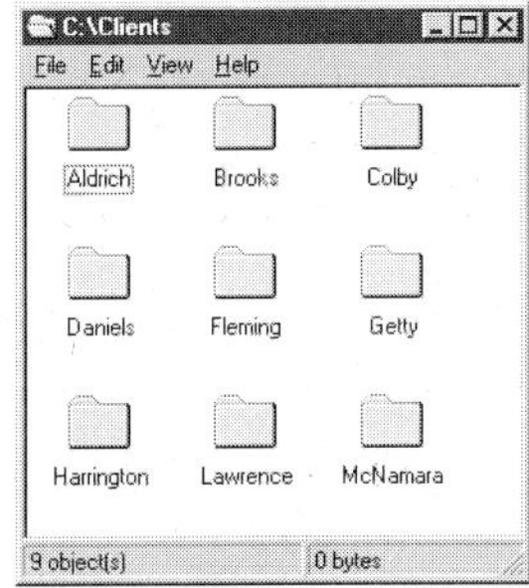

FIG. 10.22 Double-click a folder to display its contents.

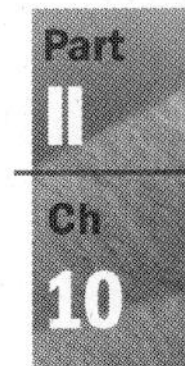

After you open a window for a folder so that you can view its contents, you can open a document (or application) by double-clicking its icon, just as you did in Windows Explorer earlier in this chapter. Figure 10.22 shows the folders within a C: drive. Some users find this window simpler and less confusing than the Windows Explorer window shown in Figure 10.20.

Using Windows 3.1 File Manager or Program Manager

If you upgraded your Windows 3.1 or Windows 3.11 to Windows 95, you still have copies of the File Manager and Program Manager available. Although My Computer and Windows Explorer are more flexible, you may prefer to make the transition slowly and take your time learning the new features of Windows 95.

If you prefer to use File Manager and Program Manager, you can easily do so. Their files, WINFILE.EXE and PROGMAN.EXE, are located in the WINDOWS folder. You can use the procedures described in this chapter to add these programs to your Start menu, create shortcut icons for the desktop, or run them when Windows starts.

Quitting Windows Applications

Most Windows applications operate the same way. To quit a Windows application, follow these steps:

1. Activate the application by clicking the application's window or by pressing Alt+Tab until you have selected the application.

2. Click the Close button, or choose File, Exit.

NOTE Throughout this book, instructions such as "Choose File, Exit" mean that you click the File menu (or press Alt+F) and then click the Exit command (or press Alt+X).

If the application contains documents that you have modified since the last time you saved them, the application prompts you to save your changes before the application quits.

Managing Windows After an Application Failure

Windows 95 significantly improves on how failed or misbehaving applications are handled. Windows 95 continuously polls the applications to see if they are running and responding. When an application fails to respond, Windows 95 displays the [Not Responding] dialog box. In this dialog box, you can click the End Task button to close down the application. You lose all changes to data in the application since the last time you saved. Click Cancel to return to the application.

If the application misuses memory or has a fatal error that causes the application to crash, other applications in Windows will not usually be involved. When an application fails to respond—for example, clicks or keystrokes get no response—press Ctrl+Alt+Del to display the Close Program dialog box.

The application that has trouble will show the phrase "[Not responding]." To continue working in Windows on your other applications, you must shut down this application. Select the application and click End Task. If you click Shut Down or press Ctrl+Alt+Delete again, all applications and Windows 95 will shut down.

Getting Help

Windows applications and accessories have extensive Help screens to help you find information on procedures, commands, techniques, and terms. Many applications even include numbered lists of steps in Help to guide you through complex procedures. The tools in Windows Help enable you to search for topics, print Help information, annotate the Help screens with your own notes, and copy to the Clipboard information from the Help screens for use in other applications.

Many Windows accessories and applications use similar kinds of commands and procedures. Each application's Help screens differ, however. You can learn how to use the application's

Help system by opening the Help menu (from the application's menu bar) and choosing a command similar to How to Use Help.

Understanding Windows Help

You start Windows Help by opening the Start menu and choosing Help. Figure 10.23 shows the Contents tab of the Help Topics window. This is the Help window for Windows 95; other Windows applications provide Help windows that look different, perhaps offering more or fewer Help topics.

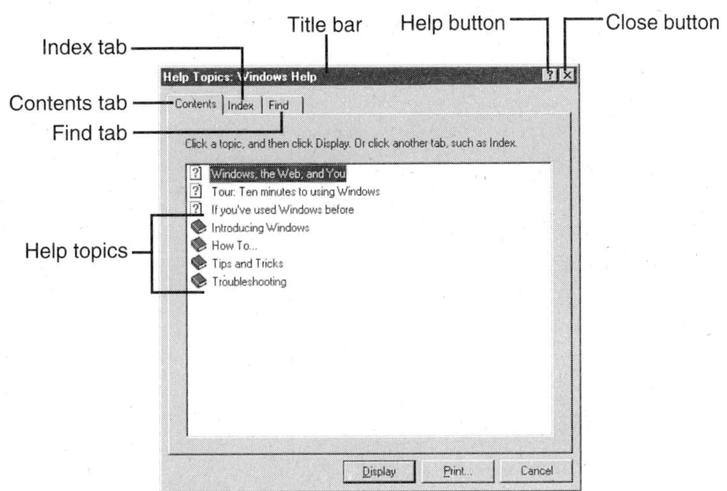

FIG. 10.23
The Windows Help screens offer help regarding all aspects of Windows.

Part II Ch 10

Table 10.1 describes the parts of the Help Topics window.

Table 10.1 Parts of the Help Topics Window

Part	Description
Title bar	Includes the Control-Menu icon at the top left (you can choose either Move or Close), the Help button (use it to display pop-up help, discussed later in the chapter), and the Close button.
Contents tab	Displays the available Help topics.
Index tab	Enables you to search through the available Help topics.
Close	Closes the selected book icon on the Contents page.
Open button	Opens the selected book icon on the Contents page.
Display button	Displays the selected Help item from the Index or Contents page.

continues

Table 10.1 Continued

Part	Description
Cancel button	Closes Help.
Print button	Displays the Print Current Topic dialog box, from which you can print the selected topic.

The Help Topics window uses the standard Windows controls: scroll bars (as needed), the Close button, and the application Control-menu button in the upper-left corner.

NOTE To start Help from within a Windows application, you can press the F1 key. Help then displays for the active application or window.

Using Pop-Up Help In most Windows applications, a question mark button (?) appears in the top-right corner of many dialog boxes and windows. You can use this button to find out information about items on the screen. This information can help you learn how to use the dialog box or window. If you see a data-entry box and are unfamiliar with how it works or what it does, click the Help (?) button; then click the data-entry box. A pop-up window displays Help information about the item you clicked.

For example, you might be interested in learning how to check your hardware devices. To get to the Device Manager, you must open the System application from the Control Panel and then click the Device Manager tab. Once on the Device Manager page, you can learn how the list of hardware devices works by clicking the Help (?) button and then clicking the list. Figure 10.24 shows the pop-up window that tells you about the list in the Device Manager.

FIG. 10.24
To view a pop-up Help window describing a control on a properties sheet or dialog box, click the Help (?) button, and then click any control.

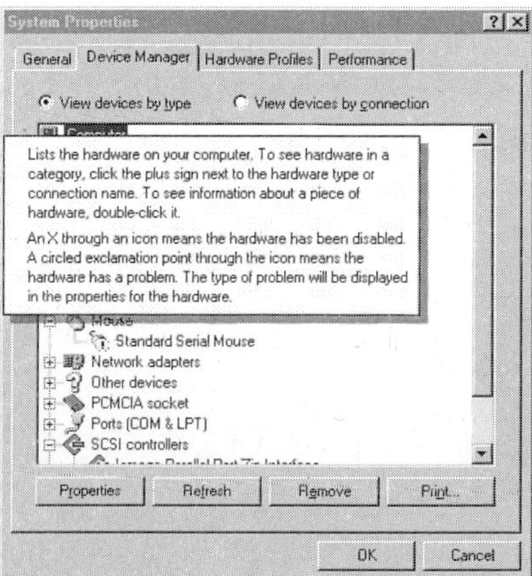

The Help (?) button on the title bar of many properties sheets and dialog boxes enables you to get help on how to use the sheet or dialog box. To use the Help (?) button, follow these steps:

1. Click the Help (?) button. A large question mark attaches to the pointer.
2. Click the control that you have a question about, such as a list or check box. A description box displays adjacent to the control.
3. Click the left mouse button to close the description box.

Using the Contents Page The Contents page of the Help Topics window lists Help topics that are available in the Windows application in which you chose Help (refer to Figure 10.23). Topics are categorized into books. Each Help topic icon first appears as a closed book. When you open a book, you see page icons. Double-clicking a page icon reveals the Help contents for that topic.

Figure 10.25 shows a Help window's contents. In addition to a list of steps, the window also contains a shortcut button. Clicking that button immediately displays the Password Properties dialog box that the Help screen discusses. You can keep the Help window open as you work in the Password Properties dialog box. Many of the topics include tips and tricks that offer shortcuts and other time-saving techniques.

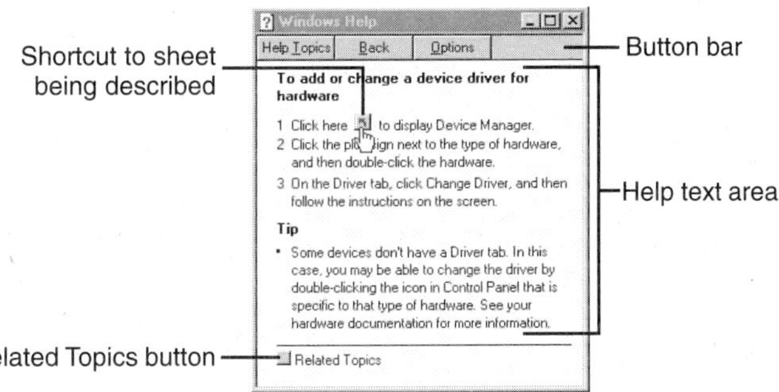

FIG. 10.25
The Windows Help Topics windows display procedural steps and buttons to open dialog boxes described in the procedure.

To display a Help window about one of the topics on the Contents page, follow these steps:

1. Open the Start menu and choose Help.
2. Click the Contents tab.
3. Scroll through the list of topics to locate the topic that you want.
4. Double-click a book to display its contents. The contents of the topic display as page icons.
5. Double-clicking a page icon to display its contents, or select the topic and choose Display. The Help topic displays in a window sized to fit its contents. You can resize the window to make it easier to work in your application.

Using the Help Window After you select a Help topic from either the Contents or Index tab, the Help window appears (see Figure 10.25). Table 10.2 describes the toolbar in the Help window.

Table 10.2 Help Toolbar buttons

Button	Description
Help Topics	Displays the Help Topics window. Options include Copy, Print, and Keep Help on Top.
Back	Moves the Help window back to the previous topic.
Options	Displays a menu of commands enabling you to use the contents of the Help window in different ways. Upcoming sections in this chapter describe these commands.
Related Topics	Displays a list of related Help topics.

Using the Index Page The Index Help page provides a search feature that finds the topic that you want (see Figure 10.26). For example, if you want to learn about adding shortcuts to the desktop, you can type **sho**. The selection bar then moves through the list of index entries to **shortcuts** adding to the desktop. The more letters you type, the closer you get to the topic name.

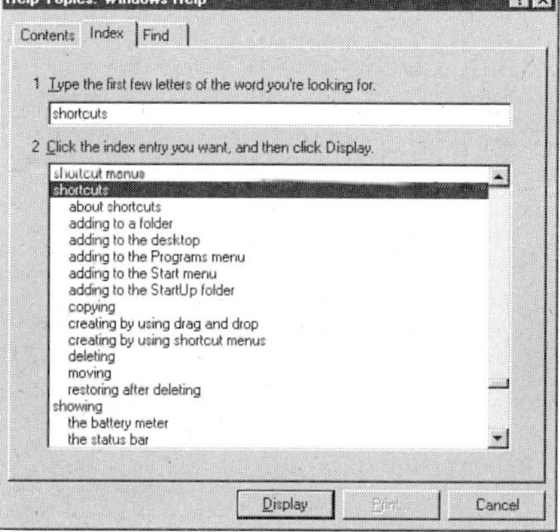

FIG. 10.26
Find a Help topic with the Windows Help Index.

To use the Help Index, follow these steps:

1. Open the Start menu and choose Help.
2. Click the Index tab.
3. Click in the text box and type the name of the subject on which you want Help. As you type, the selection bar moves through the list of topics.
4. When you have selected your topic, double-click it, or click it and choose Display. The Help screen displays.

Jumping Between Topics You can easily jump between Help topics by returning to either the Contents or Index tab. Simply click the Contents or Index button in the Help window. For example, if you finish reading a Help window and want to read about another topic, click the Contents button and the Contents tab redisplays. Then select a new topic from the Contents tab. The Index button redisplays the Index tab.

? When more information related to the topic that you're viewing is available, the Help window includes a Related Topics button. Click the Related Topics button to see a list of related topics. The Topics Found window displays and lists the additional related topics. Click the topic that you want and click Display to view the topic's Help.

Printing a Help Topic Often, having a printed copy of the Help topic in which you are interested can help you understand the topic more clearly. When the topic for which you want information is in the Help window, choose the Options button and then Print Topic to display the Print dialog box. Click OK to print.

NOTE Some of the handiest information that you can print or copy from Help is an application's shortcut keys. If you didn't get a shortcut keystroke template for your application, look in the application's Help contents for a topic similar to Keyboard Shortcuts. Copy these topics (by pressing Ctrl+C) to a word processor, reorganize them, and print them. Alternatively, you can print the topics directly from Help. You can then copy the contents at a reduced size and paste them onto 3-by-5 cards.

Customizing Help

Help is more than just a list of procedures or word definitions. You can print Help screens, copy screens into word processors, and even add notes to Help windows so that Help becomes customized to the kind of work that you do.

Adding Custom Notes to Help Topics You can customize Help information in a Windows application to make Help information more useful to you or to coworkers. You might want to include information about your company's default settings, for example, in a Help window on document formatting, or attach a note that names the templates for mailing labels to a built-in Help window that describes how to create mailing labels. To add such information, you use *annotations.*

To indicate that a Help window has annotated text, Windows displays a paperclip icon next to the topic.

To create an annotation, follow these steps:

1. Display the topic that you want to annotate.
2. Click the Options button and then choose Annotate. The Annotate dialog box, a small notepad, appears.
3. Type the notes that you want to save regarding this Help topic.
4. Click the Save button.

A paperclip icon appears to the left of the topic title in the Help window. Whenever you want to read an annotation, just click the paperclip icon.

To remove an annotation, click the paperclip icon. When the Annotate dialog box appears, choose the Delete button.

Copying Help Information to Another Application You can create a collection of Help topics by copying Help information and pasting this data into a word processor document file. You can copy and paste into another application any information that you see in a Help window. The information transfers as editable text.

See "Using the Windows Clipboard," **p. 902**

To copy the contents of a Help window, choose the Options button and then the Copy command. To paste this information into another Windows application, such as a word processor, open the other application, position the insertion point wherever you want to paste the information, and choose Edit, Paste, or press Ctrl+V.

Finding Help, Support, and Resources

Windows is one of the most popular software applications ever written. Therefore, much support is available for Windows. The following sections describe resources that can help you get the most from Windows.

An extensive listing of telephone, e-mail, and Internet-based help and support is available in Appendix B, "Additional Help and Resources."

See "Additional Help and Resources," **p. 1107**

Getting Telephone Support Use the following telephone numbers to get technical support or product sales information about Windows or Windows applications.

For questions specific to Windows installation, Windows Explorer, or Windows accessories, call Microsoft Corporation's Windows support line at (206) 635-7000. For customer service and product upgrade information, call (800) 426-9400.

If Windows or applications came preinstalled on your computer, your technical support for the preinstalled software will probably be through the hardware vendor who supplied your equipment.

See "Getting Telephone and Fax Support for Windows 95 and Microsoft Products," **p. 1107**

Getting Help over the Internet

See "Navigating the World Wide Web," **p. 482**

See "Storing Favorite Sites," **p. 484**

See "Online Technical Support" **p. 1109**

Microsoft provides two Internet sites that you can access for free software, updates, technical papers, and device drivers. From within your Internet browser, you can access the Microsoft FTP site with this URL:

ftp:\\ftp.microsoft.com

You can access the same information on the World Wide Web by using your browser with this URL:

http:\\www.microsoft.com

Consultants and Training Microsoft Solution Providers develop and support applications written for the Windows environment with Microsoft products. They are independent consultants who have met the strict qualifying requirements imposed by Microsoft.

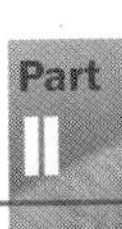

Microsoft also certifies training centers. A certified training center has instructors who have passed a competency exam and use Microsoft-produced training material.

You can find the Microsoft Solution Providers and training centers in your area by calling the following number:

1-800-SOL-PROV

See "Referrals to Consultants and Training," **p. 1114**

CHAPTER 11

Navigating with the Shell Integration Components

by Ron Person

With the introduction of Internet Explorer 4 and integrated shell components, your view of any computer resource, whether local or on the World Wide Web, is the same. You use one Explorer to work with local files and resources as well as Web pages on the World Wide Web. With integrated shell components, the entire *feel* of Windows 95 changes. It works more like a Web application. Procedures like double-clicking take on the Web's single-click. Appearances like the standard file and folder view in Explorer can now be customized to look like Web pages.

Internet Explorer 4 and integrated shell components are the future for Microsoft Windows and its applications. The next release of Windows, code-named Memphis, will incorporate the integrated shell components and its new Web-way of doing things.

This chapter assumes integrated shell components and Internet Explorer 4 have been installed. It also assumes that Windows is operating in single-click mode. To learn how to switch between single- and double-click modes, see "Switching Between Single- and Double-Click Activation" later in this chapter.

Learn a single user interface

My Computer, Windows Explorer, and Internet Explorer have the same appearance and controls. My Computer and Internet Explorer are the same and change to match the resource being viewed.

Switch between single- or double-click activation

If you want Windows to act with an Internet feel you can activate and open files or folders with a single click.

Learn how resources views can appear with a Web look

The new Web View uses an HTML file to control the appearance of folders viewed in My Documents.

Customize toolbars

Use new predefined toolbars or create your own toolbars that contain files, folders, or Web sites.

Use AutoComplete to quickly enter URLs or pathnames

AutoComplete helps you complete long or complex URLs or pathnames.

NOTE This chapter was written with Platform Preview 2 (PR2) of Internet Explorer 4 and integrated shell components for Windows 95. The final release of Internet Explorer 4 and integrated shell components may differ from what is described here.

If you have not installed integrated shell components with Internet Explorer 4, you can learn how to do so by referring to "Adding or Removing Integrated Shell Components" later in this chapter.

NOTE If you have a computer with 16M or less of memory, you may want to forego installing integrated shell components. If you are unsure, you can install integrated shell components to see if there is any performance degradation. Removing them is a simple procedure accomplished with the Add/Remove Programs icon in the Control Panel. Removing integrated shell components is described in a later section, "Adding or Removing Integrated Shell Components."

Use a Single Interface for Local, Network, and Web Information

Microsoft has given Windows a single view from which you can access all computer-based information whether that information is on your local hard disk, your network, or on the World Wide Web. Whether you are looking at your local hard disk, a CD-ROM, the Control Panel, or a Web site, all the information is presented in a similar way through the Explorer window.

Internet Explorer and My Computer are the same program used to view different information. They display their information in a window with a single pane. In contrast, the Windows Explorer also is like Internet Explorer and My Computer, but it uses a left pane to show a hierarchical view of folders and a right pane to show content.

You can prove to yourself that My Computer and Internet Explorer are the same by doing the following experiment:

1. Click My Computer. The My Computer window appears showing either a Web View of the resources on the computer, as shown in Figure 11.1, or a standard view as shown in Figure 11.2.
2. Click in the Address bar and type an URL for a Web site, such as www.microsoft.com, then press Enter. You will be prompted to log onto the Internet. After you log on Figure 11.3 shows how the toolbar and My Computer window change. It has now become the Internet Explorer. Notice that the toolbar has lost buttons such as Up One Level and Properties. In their place are Internet Explorer buttons such as Favorites, Font, and Mail.
3. Click in the Address bar and type a drive and folder, such as **C:\Windows**, and press Enter. In Figure 11.4 you can see the folder-related buttons that appear on the toolbar when viewing a hard drive.

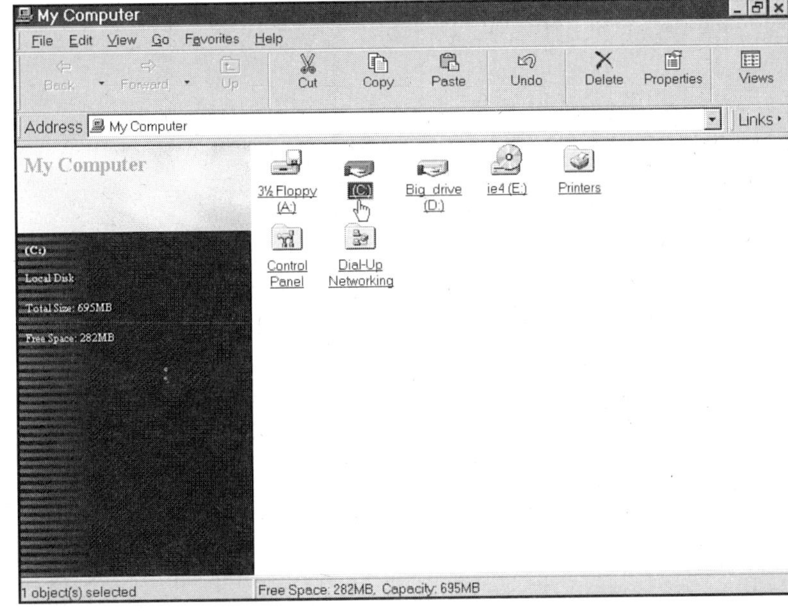

FIG. 11.1
My Computer in the Web View shows the drives and resources on the computer in a Web page-like layout.

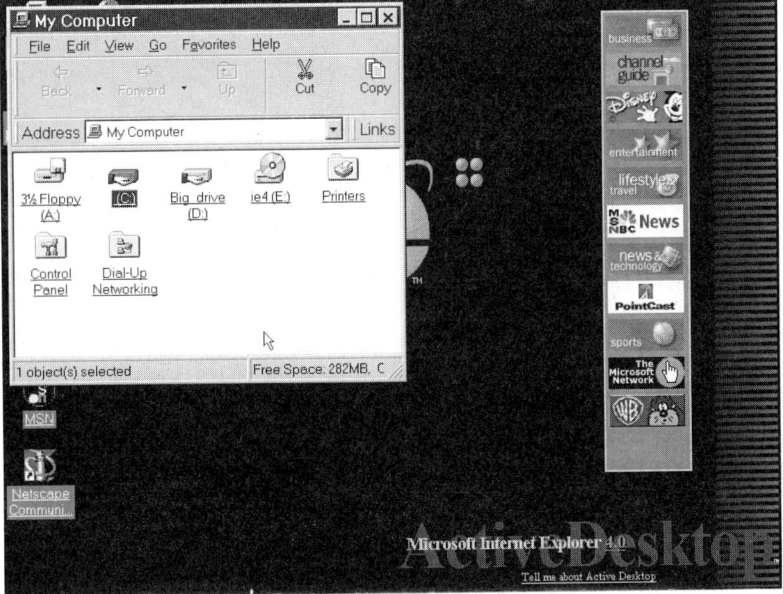

FIG. 11.2
My Computer in a standard view shows the drives and resources on the computer without the additional information from the Web page-like layout.

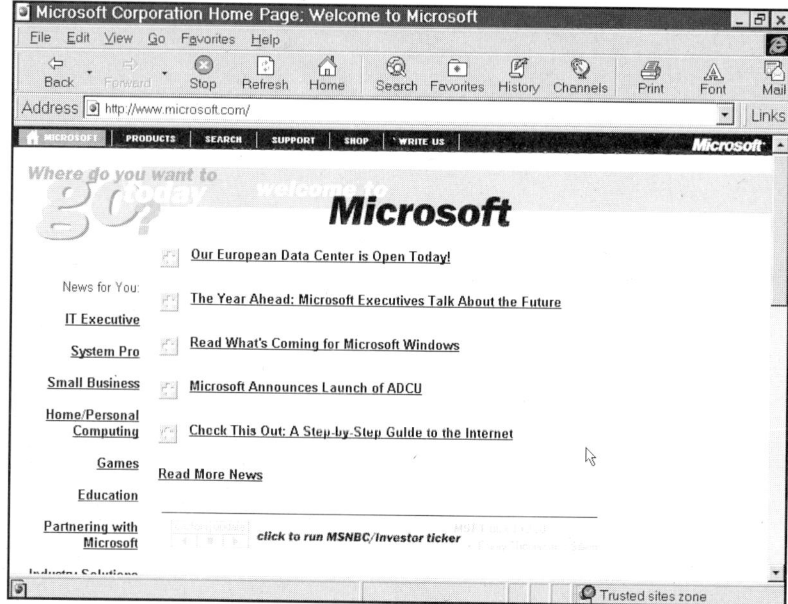

FIG. 11.3
Typing an URL into the Address bar changes My Computer into Internet Explorer 4.

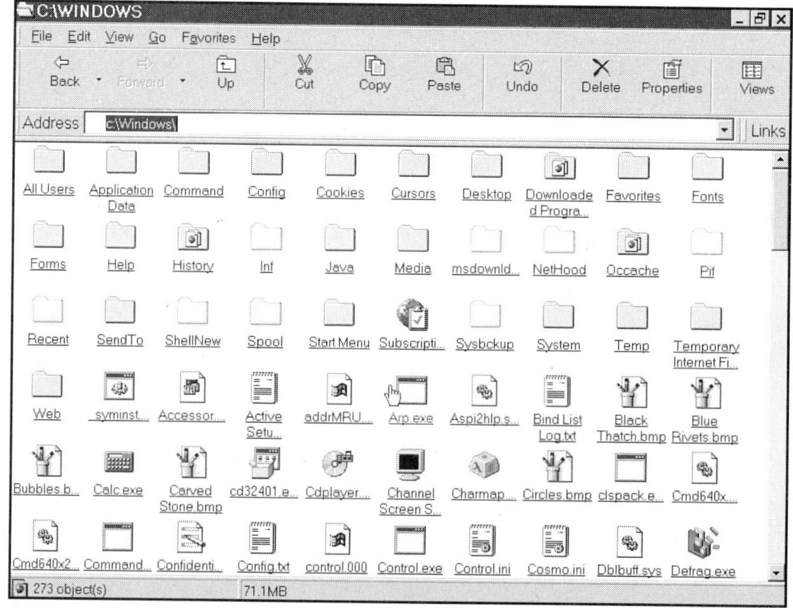

FIG. 11.4
Selecting a drive, folder, or Web site from the Address list changes the display to match the resource being viewed.

Adding or Removing Integrated Shell Components

You don't have to install the integrated shell components. Without them, Internet Explorer 4 still works perfectly fine as an Internet browser, much like the one you're probably accustomed to now. The difference is that the additional user interface enhancements that make Windows act more Web-like are not installed. It's easy to install or remove the integrated shell components, so you can add or remove them when you want.

Follow these steps to remove integrated shell components when they are installed:

1. Click Start, Settings, Control Panel.
2. Activate Add/Remove Programs.
3. Select Microsoft Internet Explorer 4.0.
4. Click Add/Remove to display the Microsoft Internet Explorer 4.0 dialog box.
5. Select the Remove Web Integrated Desktop, but keep the Internet Explorer 4.0 browser option, then click OK.
6. You will be given an opportunity to save changes to features that Internet Explorer 4 may have modified. Click OK.

   Setup will close all programs and reconfigure your system.

After you have installed and then removed integrated shell components you can easily reinstall them with Add/Remove Programs. To reinstall integrated shell components once you have initially installed them follow these steps:

1. Click Start, Settings, Control Panel.
2. Activate Add/Remove Programs.
3. Select Microsoft Internet Explorer 4.0.
4. Click Add/Remove to display the Add/Remove Internet Explorer 4.0 dialog box.
5. Select the Add Web Integrated Desktop, then click OK.

   Setup may need to connect to the Internet to download needed components. When done, setup will close all programs and reconfigure your system.

You also can reinstall the integrated desktop by rerunning the Explorer Installation. It will reinstall only the needed files and leave existing files alone.

Activating and Selecting Files and Folders

If you install integrated shell components, one of the changes you will immediately notice is that objects such as files and folders are activated with a single-click instead of the double-click you are used to in Windows 95. This gives the Windows 95 interface for files and folders in Windows Explorer the same *feel* as working in a Web page in the Internet Explorer. It's another piece in Microsoft's efforts to integrate Windows with the Internet.

Activating a File or Folder

As Figure 11.5 shows, the focus or selection moves to files or folders over which you pause the pointer. When you first begin using this new method it is both more convenient and more frustrating depending on the task you are trying to complete. If you move the pointer quickly over a file or folder the items passed over are not selected. Pausing over the top of an item selects it. To open a folder, program, or document that you have selected, click once. Don't click twice as you did in previous versions of Windows.

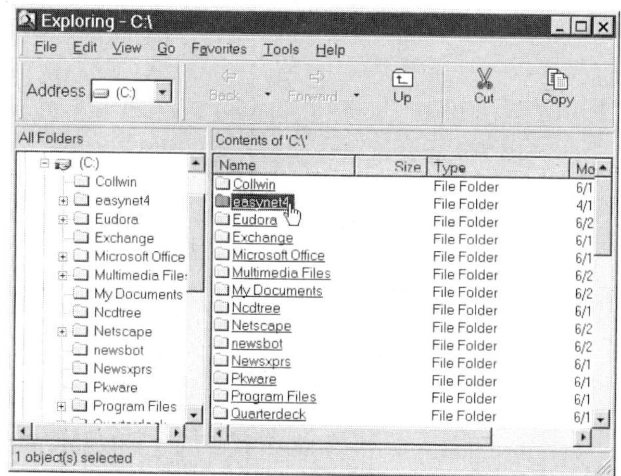

FIG. 11.5
Pausing the mouse pointer over a file or folder changes the focus to the item underneath.

Renaming Files and Folders

When Windows is in double-click mode, you can edit or rename a file or folder by clicking once on the name to select it, pausing, and then clicking a second time where you want to place the insertion point. If you try to edit or rename this way when in single-click mode, the first click opens the file or folder. You never get a chance to edit. Instead you can rename by moving the pointer over a file or folder to select it, then pressing the F2, edit key. You also can right-click the name, then choose the Rename command.

Switching Between Single- and Double-Click Activation

You may find the transition from double-clicks to single-clicks frustrating. If you decide you want to go back to the tried and true double-click method, you can turn this feature off and still use other features of integrated shell mode. To switch between single- or double-click activation follow these steps:

1. Click View, Options in My Computer.
2. Select the General tab as shown in Figure 11.6.
3. Select Classic Style to return your Windows click options to pre-Internet Explorer 4 style. This also changes the interface so that Web view is used only when you select it and folders in My Computer are browsed in seperate windows (the Windows 95 default).

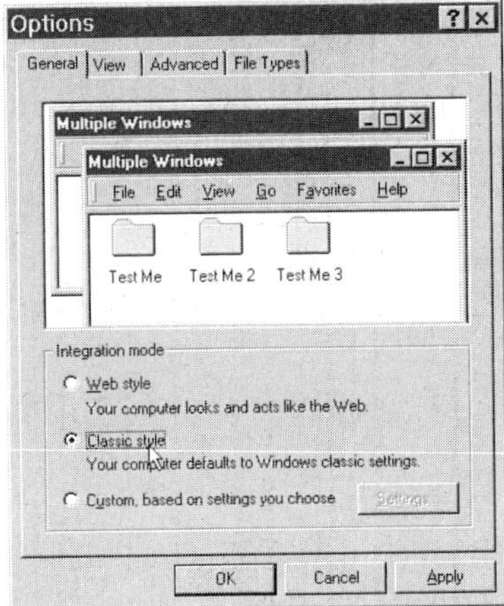

FIG. 11.6
If you don't like single-click activation it's easy to switch back to using a double-click.

4. You can also change any of these settings individually. To do this, select Custom and click Settings. This opens the dialog box shown in Figure 11.7, where you can change any of the Web-related interface settings individually.
5. Click OK.

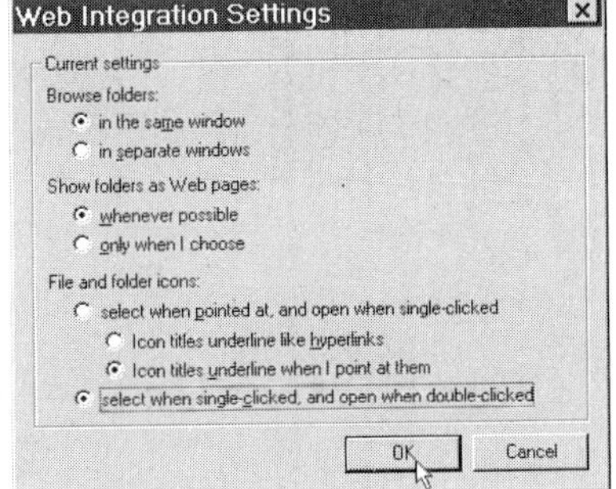

FIG. 11.7
You can control window behaviors and click settings here.

Selecting Multiple Files

When you first begin using a single click, you run into the problem of handling multiple file selections. In previous versions of Windows, you could make a contiguous selection of files by clicking on the first file, then Shift+clicking the last file in a list. Similarly, you could make non-contiguous selections by clicking one first file and Ctrl+clicking additional files.

If you try either of these methods with integrated shell components installed, you'll find that clicking the first file in your multiple selection opens the file immediately, and you'll never get a chance to make additional selections.

To select multiple files or folders while using integrated shell components, move the pointer over the first file you want to select and pause long enough for that file to be selected. Do not click. Now look for the last of the contiguous files or folders. After you've found it, hold down the Shift key as you move the pointer smoothly until it pauses over the last file or folder. All the files in between the first and last pause will be selected.

Selecting contiguous and noncontiguous files or folders is much easier to learn in Large Icons view. It takes practice to move and pause selectively in the Small Icons, List, or Details view.

Select noncontiguous files or folders, like the selections in Figure 11.8, by pausing the pointer over the first file or folder until the file is selected. Look for the next file or folder to select. Once you see it, hold down the Ctrl key and move the pointer over that file or folder and pause until the second file or folder is selected. Continue selecting by moving and pausing as you hold down the Ctrl key.

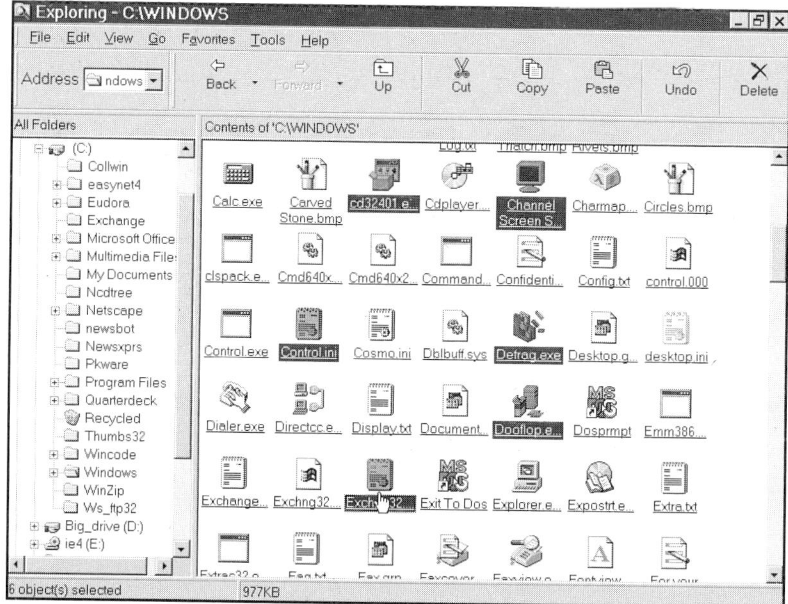

FIG. 11.8 Select noncontiguous items by pausing the pointer over items as you hold down Ctrl.

Activate or run multiple selected files by right clicking one of the selected files and selecting Open or Open With from the context-sensitive menu.

Unselecting files works the same way. Avoid the old habit of clicking a selected file to unselect it. When you have noncontiguous files selected and need to deselect one of them, just move the mouse point over it then hold Ctrl and put the pointer on it again until it unselects.

Looking at Everything with a Web View

Another way in which the appearance of Windows and the Web has merged is the way in which folder contents can be viewed. The Web view presents resources such as the Control Panel or folder contents with an appearance more like a Web page. In fact, the Web view is a Web page created in HTML. Figure 11.9 shows the Web view for the Control Panel.

FIG. 11.9
The Web view of the Control Panel displays information about the selected icon.

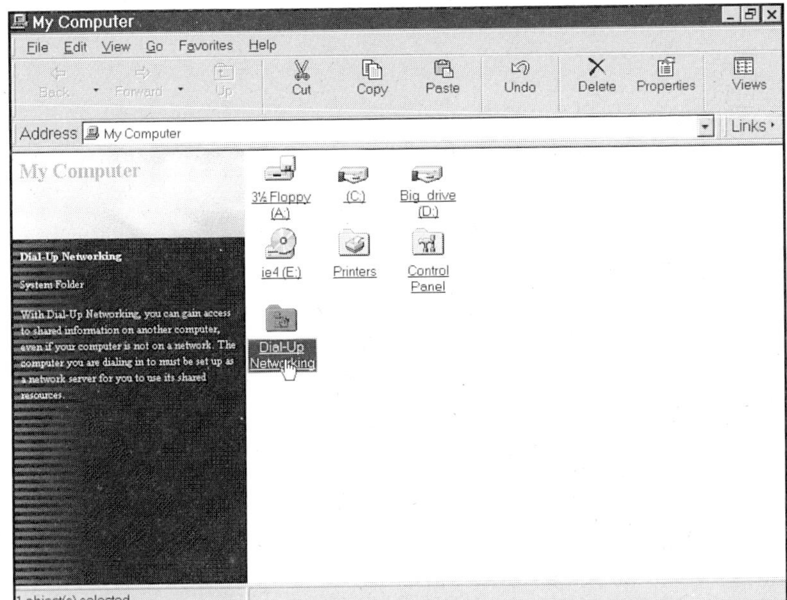

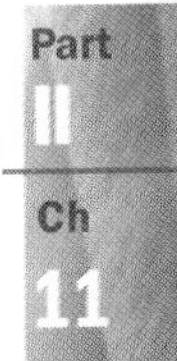

To turn the Web view on or off, click View, Web View. If the Web View menu item is not shown, then the currently selected folder or resource does not have a Web view. A custom Web view for a folder is shown in Figure 11.10.

An Improved Start Menu

Integrated shell components improve the Start menu to make it more useable with the Internet. The Start menu also is easier to customize. You can reorganize items on the menu by dragging them to new locations.

Reorganize Start Menu Items by Dragging

In the previous version of Windows 95, there was no easy way to organize the Start menu. You could use tricks to organize the Start menu such as creating fake names for programs or preceding program names with numbers, but there was no easy way to customize Start.

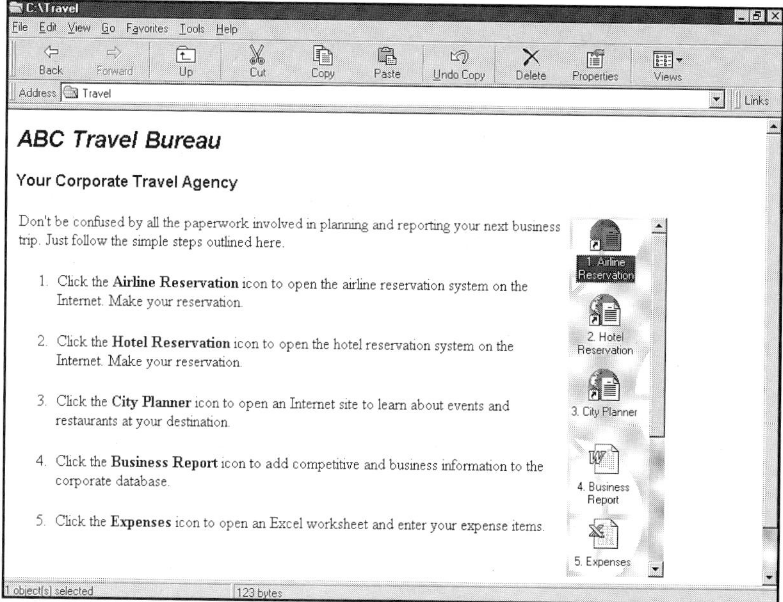

FIG. 11.10
Create your own custom Web views of folders.

Now it's very easy to organize the Start menu. If you want to move an item on the Start menu, just drag it to a new location on the menu. Click Start, then click Programs so the Programs menu will stay open. Drag the menu item you want to a new location as shown in Figure 11.11. As you drag, a heavy black line shows where on the menu the item will be inserted. Drop the menu item in the location you want and Start closes. The next time you open Start, the menu item will be in its new location. Reorganize menu items at the top of the Start menu in the same way. Note that folders, however, do not drag. This also works for any programs you have on the Start menu itself, above the Programs menu.

The Find Menu Item Is Internet Enabled

The Find menu item on Start has been Internet enhanced. Two new menu items, On the Internet and People, have been added. Clicking On the Internet displays the Search page on Microsoft's site. Clicking People brings up the Find People dialog box of the Windows Address Book so that you can quickly search for someone to whom you want to send a message.

Customizing Desktop Toolbars and Taskbar

The taskbar is such a convenient way to switch between applications that Microsoft has added desktop toolbars that function like the taskbar. You can add predefined toolbars to your desktop or create your own desktop toolbars that activate applications, documents, or Web pages.

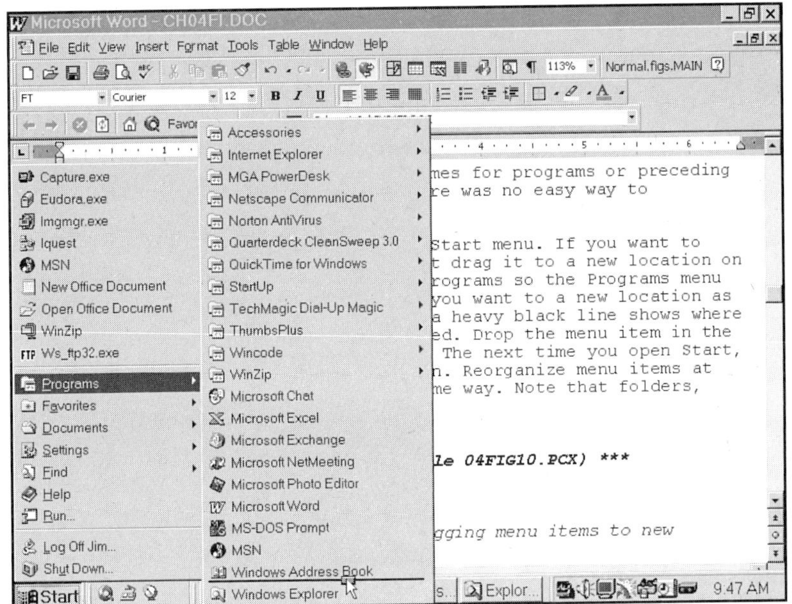

FIG. 11.11
Reorganize the Programs menu by dragging menu items to new locations.

The toolbars are as convenient and productive as the taskbar, but you can customize them. An easy way to think of how to use the toolbars is to imagine them as Explorer windows that you can keep open and dock against the side of the screen. Just like an Explorer window, you can drag and drop shortcuts onto them, move items in and out, start applications or documents from them, or close them.

If you are a systems administrator, don't fret about having a thousand different desktop configurations. You can control desktop customization on all networked desktops using the Internet Explorer 4.0 Administrator's Kit.

The taskbar has a new action as well. Clicking an application's button on the taskbar switches the application between being active in a window and being minimized to a button.

Displaying Built-in Desktop Toolbars

Internet Explorer 4 and the integrated shell components include four predefined toolbars besides the Windows taskbar. Figure 11.12 shows these four toolbars.

To display any of these predefined toolbars, right-click in a gray area of the taskbar or a toolbar, then click Toolbars, and the name of the toolbar you want. To remove a toolbar, right-click the toolbar title, then click Close. You cannot close the taskbar.

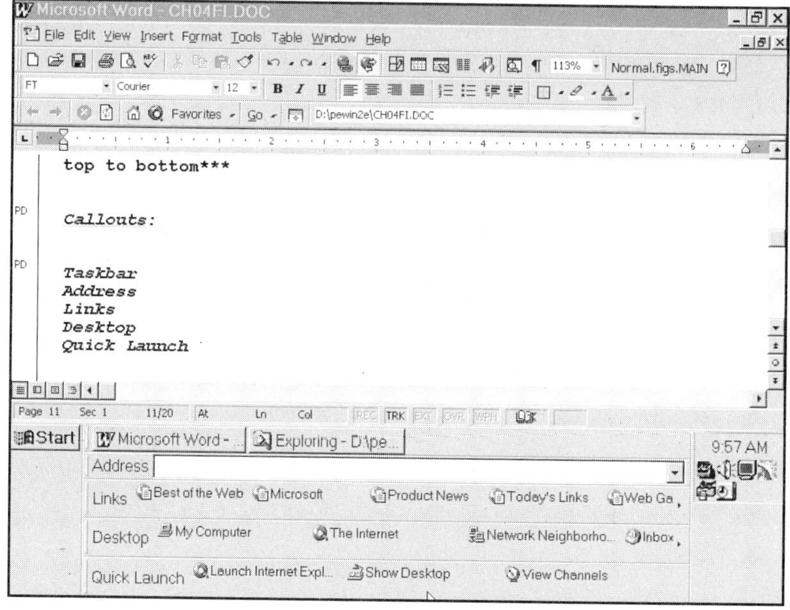

FIG. 11.12
Four new toolbars give you quick access to the Internet Explorer Suite, Address box, Web links, and the Desktop.

The Quick Launch toolbar gives you immediate access to applications in the Internet Explorer suite. The Address toolbar duplicates the address bar at the top of an Explorer window. You can open a Web page by typing in an URL and pressing Enter. The Links toolbar gives you quick access to Web links. The Desktop toolbar displays shortcuts to all the items on your desktop.

The default Links toolbar contains five predefined shortcuts to Web sites. These sites are:

Web Icon	URL	Definition
Best of the Web	**home.microsoft.com/exploring**	Categorized links to some of the most valuable business and personal sites.
Web Gallery	**www.microsoft.com/gallery**	An incredible free gallery of images, sounds, ActiveX controls, Java libraries, and more.
Microsoft	**www.microsoft.com**	Home page for Microsoft's technical site. Access to all the Microsoft technical info you could imagine.
Today's Links	**home.microsoft.com**	Home page for Microsoft. Latest info on new products, press releases, stories, and so on.
Product News	**www.microsoft.com/ie**	Updates and new product information about Internet Explorer.

Changing the Appearance of the Taskbar and Toolbars

Toolbars don't have to be barnacles stuck to the edge of your screen. You can drag them to any location by dragging on a gray area between buttons. Drag them against another edge to dock them in place or create a floating palette in a window by dragging them to midscreen and dropping them.

When you have a lot of toolbars sharing an edge with other toolbars they may all squeeze together so there is no room to see their contents. Zoom a toolbar open or closed by clicking its title or drag handle while it is docked at the top or bottom of the screen. If the toolbars are docked at the top or bottom, you can widen a toolbar by dragging the drag handle left or right. The drag handle is the double vertical bar at the left edge of a toolbar.

Working with Many Toolbars

This procedure will show you how to conveniently arrange multiple rows of toolbars like those shown at the bottom of Figure 11.12. Create as many toolbars as you need. Dock them at the bottom of the screen. Drag the top edge of the toolbars up so the taskbar space has room for as many rows of toolbars as you need. Arrange toolbars in these rows by dragging the toolbar handles up or down to move them between rows or left or right to change their width. Now adjust the toolbar properties so that these toolbars disappear when not in use. To do this right-click in a gray area of the any toolbar and click Properties. On the Taskbar Options tab select Always on Top and Auto Hide. Then click OK. This hides the multiple rows or toolbars when they aren't in use. To display the hidden toolbar drag the pointer to that edge of the screen and the toolbars will display.

Resize toolbars in windows by dragging an edge or a corner. Expand a toolbar to full screen by double-clicking its title bar. Restore it to a window by double-clicking the title bar a second time.

Change the appearance of the Quick Launch, Desktop, or Links toolbar to give yourself more room. Switch between icons only and icons with text labels by right-clicking the gray area on the toolbar and choosing Show Text. Display large or small icons for these three toolbars by clicking in the gray area of the toolbar, then clicking View and choosing either Large or Small. Turn the titles of any of the toolbars off or on by right-clicking the gray area of the toolbar and choosing Show Title. Note that some of these options make more sense for some toolbars than others. For example, the Links toolbar is very hard to use with text labels turned off.

Creating Toolbars to Open Folders, Applications, Documents, and Web Sites

It's easy to set up a toolbar containing folders and shortcuts to applications, documents, and Web links. Figure 11.13 shows a custom toolbar that contains folders and documents. It could also contain a shortcut to an application or Web link. Drag and drop a file onto the folder in the toolbar to drop the document in that folder, or click a folder, application, document, or Web link to open it. Notice that the Explorer window in Figure 11.14 shows the contents of the Project Tools folder. This folder contains the items on the Custom toolbar.

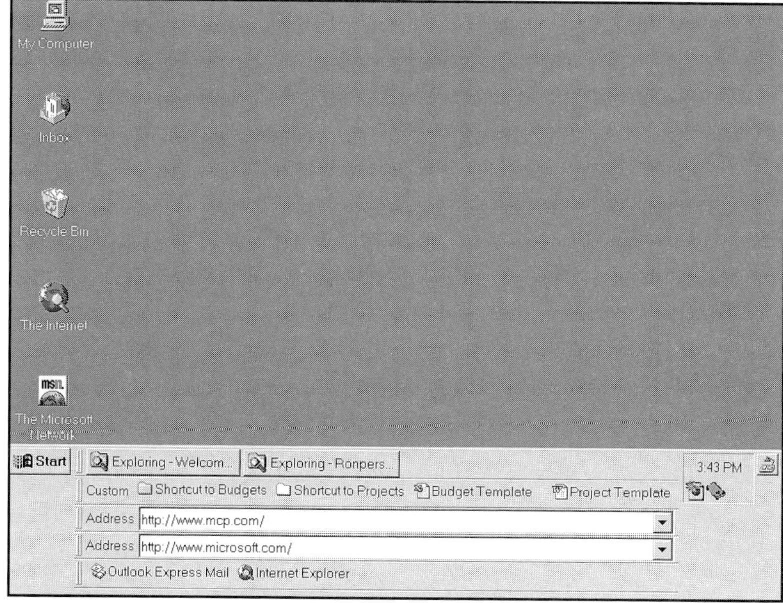

FIG. 11.13 Use multiple rows of toolbars with Auto Hide for quick access to a lot of shortcuts.

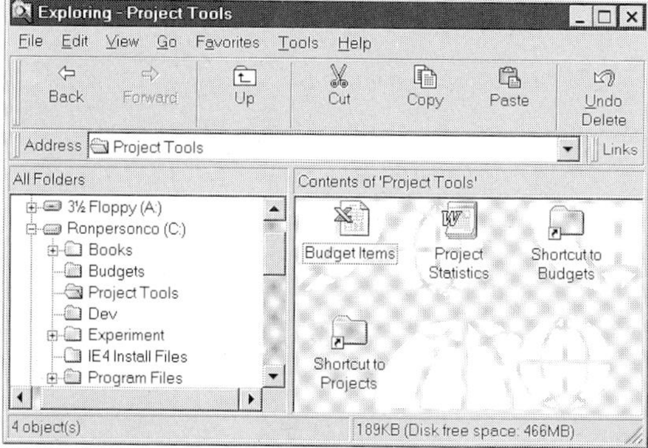

FIG. 11.14 Create a custom toolbar from the contents of a folder.

To create a custom toolbar begin by first creating a folder and giving it a name that will become the name of the toolbar. Keep the name short so it doesn't take up room on the toolbar. Right-drag application files, documents, and hyperlinks into the folder. When you drop them, choose Create Shortcut(s).

Now create the toolbar by right-clicking the title or gray area of any toolbar and clicking Toolbars, New Toolbar. The Browse for Folder dialog box appears as shown in Figure 11.15. Select the folder containing items for your toolbar and click OK.

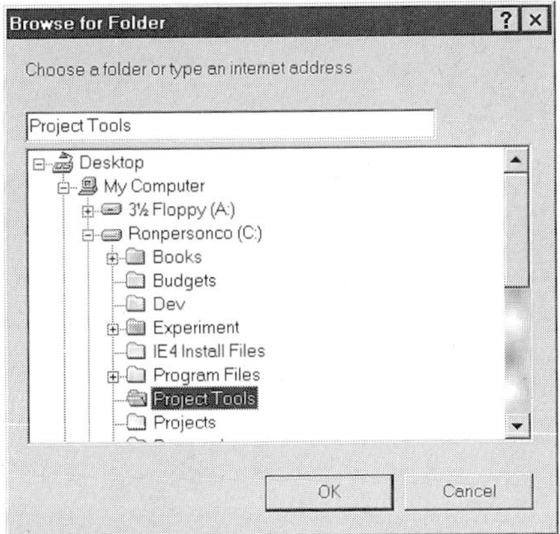

FIG. 11.15
Creating a custom toolbar is as easy as selecting a folder filled with shortcuts.

The custom toolbar you have created docks with the taskbar. Click its shortcut buttons to activate the corresponding application, document, or URL. You can drag or resize the toolbar as you would any other toolbar.

Close the custom toolbar by right-clicking the toolbar title and clicking Close. If you close the custom toolbar you must re-create it to get it back.

If you like to work with a very clean desktop, remove the icons from your desktop so the desktop is clear. To do this right-click the desktop, then deselect Show Icons. You can still have access to your desktop shortcuts by displaying the Desktop toolbar. After you display the Desktop toolbar right-click it, then click Properties. Select the Always on Top and Auto Hide properties so the Desktop toolbar disappears when not in use. If you have folders you use frequently for storage or retrieval, put them on a custom toolbar so you can immediately open them or drop files into them.

Creating Toolbars that Contain Frequently Used Folders

Custom toolbars work well as a way of holding folders in which you frequently work. You can open folders from a toolbar or drag files into a folder on a toolbar.

To reduce the chance of losing folders full of information, you should put shortcuts to folders on toolbars, not the real folders. The same applies to putting folders on your desktop. You reduce the risk of accidentally deleting a folder by putting a shortcut to the folder on your desktop.

The quickest way to create a custom toolbar containing folders is to drag an empty folder from a Windows Explorer window and drop it onto a gray area of the taskbar. The new blank toolbar immediately appears.

Populate this toolbar by dragging files or folders with the right mouse button onto the toolbar and dropping them. Choose Create Shortcut(s) Here from the context menu that appears if you want a shortcut on the toolbar. Choose Move Here or Copy Here to move or copy the file or folder into the toolbar's folder. If you accidentally choose the wrong command, click Edit, Undo in the Explorer window.

Creating Address Toolbars To Display Frequently Used Files and Web Pages

If you have documents or Web pages that you like to use frequently, you can store their addresses in an Address toolbar and dock the toolbar at the side of the screen. Entering or selecting the address you want from the Address toolbar then displays the document or Web page in its application. And because Windows keeps a list of all your recent addresses in the Address drop-down list you can quickly get to other documents or Web pages you have accessed recently.

To create an Address toolbar right-click in the gray area of the Taskbar or a toolbar, then click Toolbars, Address. An Address toolbar will dock with the Taskbar.

To display a document or Web page, click the down arrow in the Address toolbar to select a previously used document or Web page or enter a document or Web page address. The appropriate application will open and load the document or Web page. Figure 11.16 shows the Microsoft Web page displayed in Internet Explorer 4 after selecting the URL from the Address toolbar at the bottom of the screen.

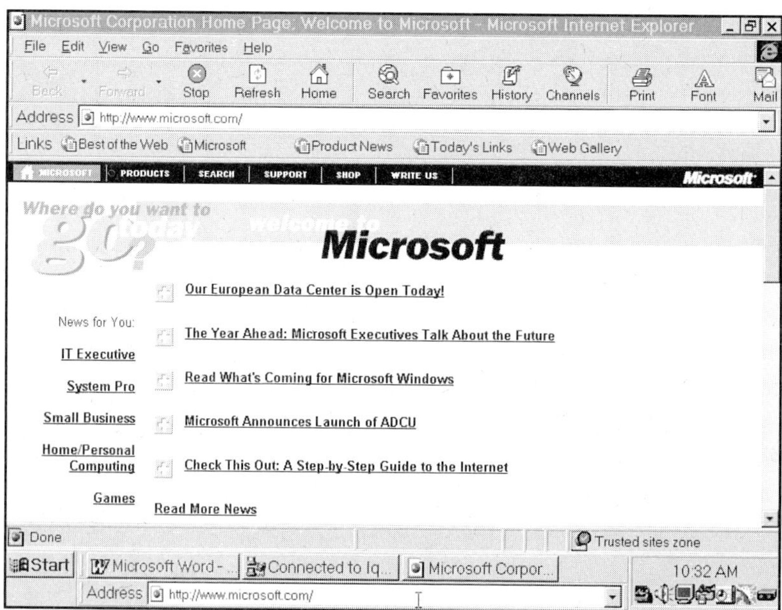

FIG. 11.16 Quickly open documents or Web pages in their appropriate application by selecting them from an Address toolbar.

Creating Documents and Web Pages that Stay Open on the Desktop

If there is a Web page or document that you need open all the time you can create an Address toolbar that displays it. Using this special Address toolbar would let you connect to a Web page or intranet document and easily display and update it whenever you need new data. Links within the document or Web page remain usable and the page can be refreshed. You can even navigate between hyperlinks.

This special Address toolbar can be sized as a window on the desktop or stored as a toolbar against the side of the screen. When it is stored against the side of the screen you can make it hide like other toolbars so it only appears when the pointer moves against the edge where it is stored. Figure 11.17 shows an Address toolbar displaying the Macmillan Computer Publishing Web site in an Internet Explorer 4 window. The right side of the screen shows the Web site for Que, the publishers of this book, in an Address toolbar that has been stored against the right screen edge.

FIG. 11.17
Display documents or Web pages in a specialized toolbar. You can even jump between links and refresh the page.

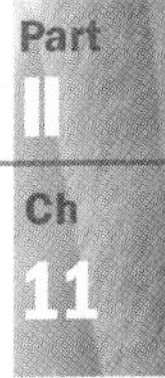

CAUTION

Make sure you drag the document file or hyperlink onto an Address toolbar to display the document in a toolbar. Dragging the file onto another type of toolbar can move the file.

To create a Web page or document in an Address toolbar, follow these steps:

1. Right-click in the gray area of a Taskbar or toolbar, then click Toolbars, Address.
2. If you want to display a Web page, display a Web page in Internet Explorer 4 containing a hyperlink to the page you want displayed.

   Or

   If you want to display a document, display the document's file in Windows Explorer or My Computer.
3. Drag and drop the hyperlink or the file onto the Address toolbar.

   A new toolbar will be created. Its title bar will display the document or Web page's name.

Drag the drag handles of the new toolbar to a clear area of the desktop and release to create a window that shows the Web page or document. Resize the window as you need. Use the scroll bars to move the contents within the window.

To manipulate or refresh the window, right click its title bar to see document appropriate menu items such as Refresh, Open in Window, Always on Top, Auto Hide, and Close.

Create a special Address toolbar that pops into view as shown in Figure 11.16 by docking the special Address toolbar against the side of the screen. Right-click the toolbar's title bar and select Always on Top and Auto Hide. Now click the desktop or another application to hide the special Address toolbar. Any time you want the page to reappear, move the pointer against that side of the screen.

To make a hyperlink jump click the link within the Web page or document as you would for any hyperlink. This will open the link in a new window (not in the address bar window). To manipulate the contents using commands specific to the content, right-click in the Web page or document's background. For example, if the window displays a Web page and you can right-click a link, you will see a context menu displaying Internet Explorer-like commands such as Open and Copy Shortcut.

This special Address toolbar stays at the highest level on the desktop. For example, when you drag it out from the side of the screen it covers all the other objects on the desktop including applications.

Managing Buttons on a Toolbar

The buttons on a custom toolbar are just like files in a My Computer window or in Windows Explorer. Right-click a file or folder button in a custom toolbar and the appropriate context menu displays so you can Open, Quick View, Send To, Cut, Copy, Paste, Create Shortcut, Delete, or see Properties. The menu items will be appropriate to the type of button on which you click.

CAUTION

If you have accidentally moved a file or folder by dragging it onto a toolbar (rather than creating a shortcut) and want to move it to a folder in Windows Explorer, right-click the button and choose Cut. Select the folder where you want the item to go in the Windows Explorer and choose Paste.

Consistent Navigation Between Explorer and My Computer

The navigation buttons for My Computer, Windows Explorer, and Internet Explorer are consistent with Internet Explorer 4 and integrated shell components. Figure 11.18 shows the toolbars for My Computer, Windows Explorer, and Internet Explorer 4. Notice how all three use the Back and Forward buttons to navigate backward or forward along a path of previously selected folders or Web pages.

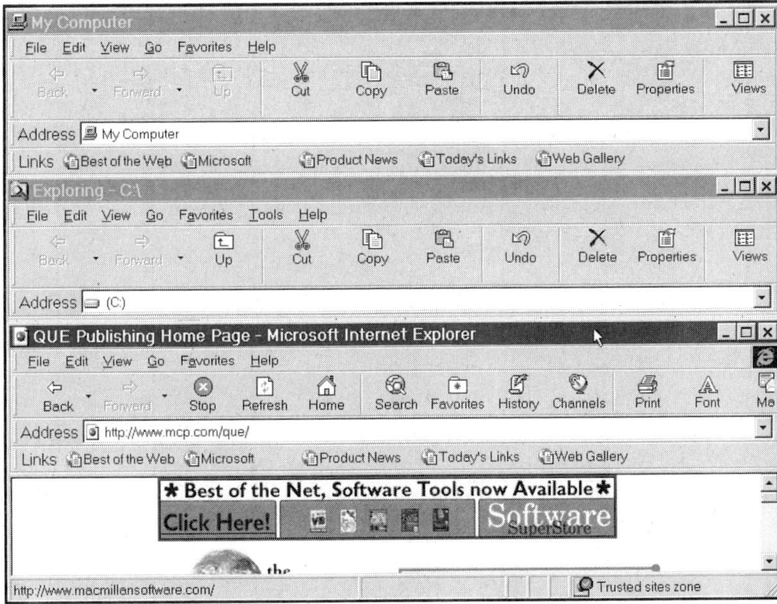

FIG. 11.18 Back and Forward buttons are consistent between the different Explorer views.

My Computer and Windows Explorer have an Up button that displays the next higher level in the hierarchy of resources. For example, if Windows Explorer was currently displaying C:\Reports, then a click on the Up button would display C:\.

A convenient feature of Shell Integration mode is a more accessible history list. A right-click on a forward or backward button displays a short history list of the locations in the direction of that button. Just click the one you want to display. This history list is temporary and is only available for each Windows session.

AutoComplete URLs in Address Bars

Many of us use the same folders and Web sites over and over. This creates a lot of repeat typing. AutoComplete will save you from that repeat typing and reduce your typing errors. As you type a folder location or URL into an Address toolbar, AutoComplete looks through the history list and fills suggestions into the remaining typing area. Just keep typing if you do not like the suggestion. When you see the correct suggestion, just press Enter.

AutoComplete also works in the Run dialog box available when you click Start, Run. You can open a specific folder or Web site by entering the folder's path or the URL in the Open edit box and clicking OK.

The history list that AutoComplete checks against is global. It is built from all the locations you have gone to in My Computer, Windows Explorer, and Internet Explorer. This global history list is stored on hard disk so it is available the next time you start Windows.

Folders Expand Automatically When Dropping Files

Prior to Shell Integration mode, when you wanted to copy or move files in the Windows Explorer, you had to expand folders until you exposed the subfolder into which you want to move or copy a file. Often this added extra steps to moving or copying files.

With integrated shell components installed, moving and copy files into subfolders becomes much easier. Integrated shell components makes this easier by automatically expanding folders while you are moving or copying files.

To see automatically expanding folders work, select a file(s) in Windows Explorer then drag the files over a closed folder that contains subfolders. A folder that contains subfolders displays a + sign to the left. Move the pointer over the folder you want to receive the files and pause. Continue holding down the mouse button. The folder will expand to show all of its subfolders. At that point you can drop the files into a subfolder or pause over other folders you want to expand.

Copying Files and Folders Enhanced

When you copy a file(s), a progress indicator shows the relative length of time for the copy to be completed. In earlier versions of Windows, when you copied a selection containing multiple files, the progress indicator displayed the progress for each file. This gave you no indication of the length of time it would take to copy all the files you selected. In Shell Integration mode, the progress indicator has been improved to show the progress for copying all the files in the selection.

Another improvement made by integrated shell components is that you can work in the folder receiving copied files. For example, if you are copying a large selection of files into a folder named Budgets, you can open the Budgets folder and activate a worksheet in it even while copying continues.

PART III

Working with Files and Folders

CHAPTER 12

Managing Files and Folders with My Computer

by Robert Voss

Viewing the resources on your computer

Learn how to use My Computer to look at the disk drives, folders, files, and other resources on your computer.

Customizing the display in My Computer

You can change how folders and files are displayed, sort folder and file listings, add or remove a toolbar, and customize My Computer in other ways to suit your taste.

Managing Files and Folders

Use My Computer to create new folders, move and copy files and folders from one location to another, and rename and delete files and folders.

Windows 95 offers you several ways to view and manage the resources on your computer. Microsoft has put a lot of effort into creating both a simple and powerful interface between you and the resources on your computer. If you are new to Windows 95, you can jump right into seeing what is on your computer and managing folders and files, using My Computer, the subject of this chapter. As you gain experience, you will discover many powerful tools in Windows 95 for increasing your efficiency and saving time, such as Windows Explorer, which is discussed in the next chapter, the Send To menu, and the shortcut menus you can access with the right mouse button.

My Computer is a folder on your desktop containing all the resources on your computer. If you are accustomed to working with File Manager in Windows 3.1, you may wonder where the hierarchical representation of your hard disk and all its directories and subdirectories went when you first opened My Computer. You can still view the overall organization of your hard disks and other resources on your computer using Windows Explorer (see the next chapter). My Computer offers you a simplified, "up-close" method for viewing files and folders without letting the overall view get in the way. Some users may routinely prefer this approach, and even if you use Windows Explorer most of the time, you may find the single-pane view that My Computer offers handy at times.

Viewing Resources in My Computer

When you first open My Computer by double-clicking its icon on the desktop, the My Computer window appears with an icon representing each of the resources on your computer, as shown in Figure 12.1.

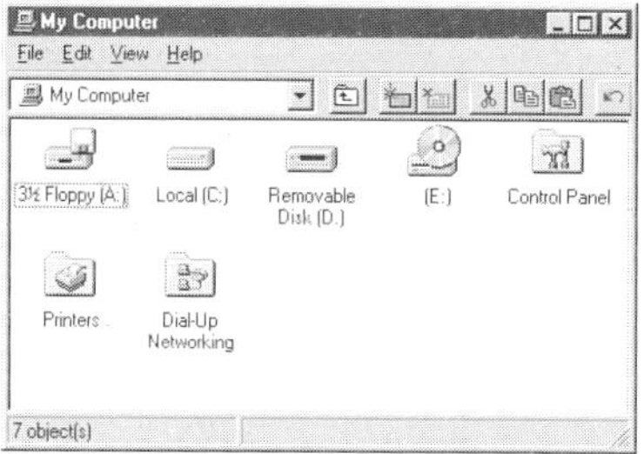

FIG. 12.1 The My Computer window is another way to view the files and folders on your computer.

To look at the contents of a resource, double-click the appropriate folder. To view the folders on your hard drive, for example, double-click the hard disk icon. A new window opens, displaying the folders on your hard drive. You can continue browsing through the folders on your computer by double-clicking any folder whose contents you want to view (see Figure 12.2).

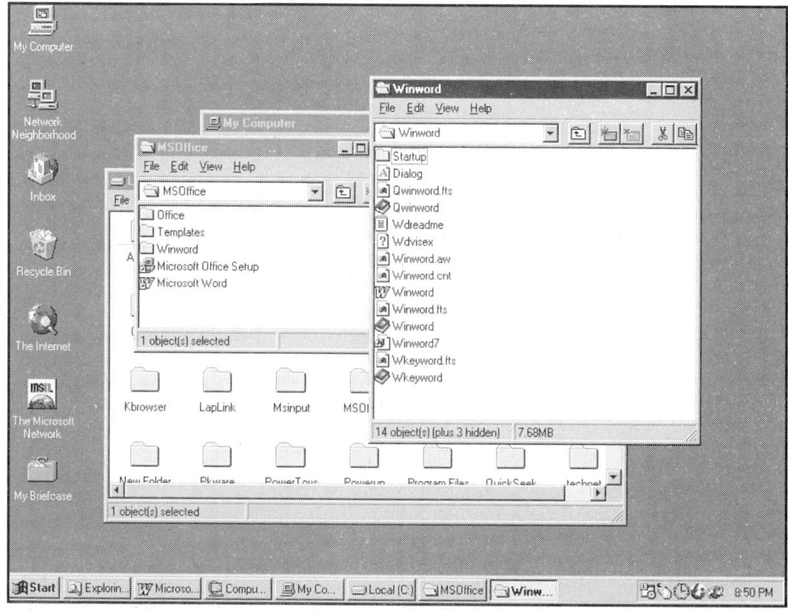

FIG. 12.2 You can browse through the folders in My Computer by double-clicking the folders whose contents you want to see.

As you open up new windows in My Computer to view the contents of the different folders, you won't really have a sense of the hierarchical organization of the folders the way you do in Explorer. In Explorer, you always have a map of the organization of your folders in the left pane. With My Computer, it is more difficult to visualize the hierarchical structure of your folders. If you don't think hierarchically, this may be a relief, as you may prefer to simply think of folders inside other folders that you open up one by one. You can move back through a series of opened folders by clicking the Up One Level button in the toolbar (which is a picture of a folder with an upward-pointing arrow inside it). This is a handy way to retrace your steps.

TIP Move up one level in a folder window by pressing the Backspace key.

Notice in Figure 12.2 that each time you open a new folder, another window appears. If you find it annoying to end up with layer upon layer of folder windows as you open the folders on your computer, you can choose to have the contents of a newly opened folder replace the current contents of the My Computer window, instead of opening a new window. To restrict My Computer to a single window, follow these steps:

1. In the My Computer window, choose View, Options to display the Folder tab in the Options dialog box (see Figure 12.3).

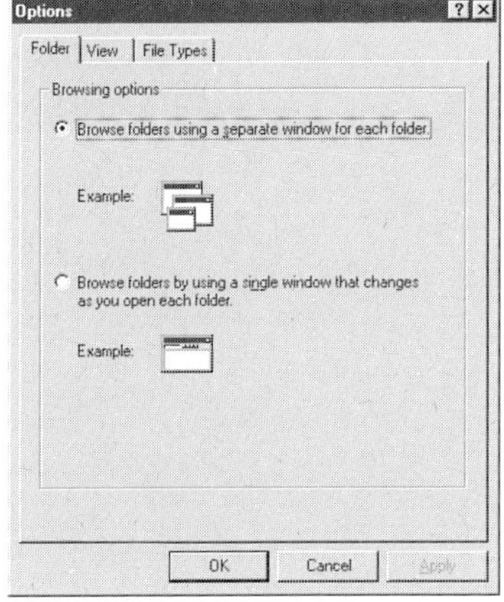

FIG. 12.3
You can select the single windows option in the Options dialog box if you want to use a single window to browse your folders.

2. Select the Browse Folders by Using a Single Window option.
3. Choose OK.

Now when you open a new folder, the folder's contents replace the contents of the current window. You can still use the Up One Level button to move back through a series of folders that you opened.

If Windows currently uses a single window to display the contents of folders you open, but you want a new window to open when you open a folder, hold down the Ctrl key as you double-click a folder. Conversely, if Windows is currently opening a new window when you open a folder but you want to use a single window and replace its contents with the contents of the new folder, hold down the Ctrl key as you double-click a folder.

If you have opened a trail of new single-pane folder windows, you can close them all by holding the Shift key as you click the Close button (X), at the top-right corner of the window.

If you prefer to run your programs from a folder rather than from the Start, Programs menu, here's a shortcut for making a program folder. Double-click the file PROGRAMS.GRP in the Windows folder. This opens a folder window showing a folder for each submenu from the Start, Programs submenu. Minimize this folder so it's always accessible on your taskbar.

You can refresh the contents of My Computer by choosing View, Refresh or by pressing F5. This is necessary, for example, if you are viewing the contents of a disk in the floppy disk drive and you swap disks. You'll have to refresh the window to see the contents of the new disk.

See "Using Windows Explorer to View Files and Folders," **p. 312**

Customizing the My Computer Display

You can change the look and feel of the My Computer window, including how to sort and display files and folders. Once you learn a few techniques, you can customize My Computer to suit your needs.

Changing How Files and Folders Display

When you first opened My Computer, files and folders were represented by large icons (refer to Figure 12.1). You can also display files and folders as small icons, as small icons organized in a vertical list, and as a list with other file details.

To change the way files and folders are displayed, follow these steps:

1. Open the View menu.
2. Choose one of the following commands from the menu:

Command	**Result**
Large Icons	Large Icons
Small Icons	Small icons arranged in columns
List	Small icons arranged in a single list
Details	Small icons in a list, along with size, type, and date modified

A dot appears next to the option that is currently selected. The Details view, shown in Figure 12.4, is very useful for viewing a lot of information about your files in a single window. To change the width of the columns used in the Details view, move the mouse pointer over the line that divides the buttons at the top of each column (the mouse pointer changes to a double-headed arrow), hold down the mouse button and drag the line to the desired width. You can quickly adjust a column to accommodate the widest entry in the column by double-clicking the divider line.

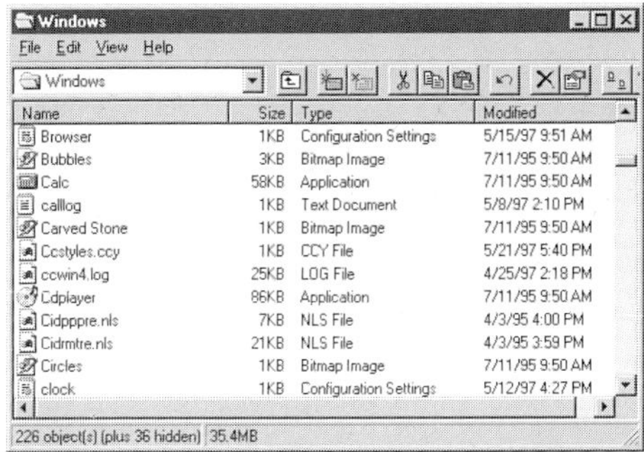

FIG. 12.4
You can view a listing of all the files and folders in a window and the size, type, and date modified for each item using the Details view in My Computer.

You can also switch views using the toolbar. If the toolbar isn't displayed, choose View, Toolbar. There is a tool for each of the four views at the right end of the toolbar.

Two tabs in the View Options dialog box are discussed in detail in Chapter 13, "Managing Files and Folders with Windows Explorer." In the View tab of the Options dialog box, you can control what types of files are listed in My Computer, whether or not the full path name for a file is displayed in the title bar, and whether MS-DOS file extensions are displayed. See "Displaying or Hiding Different File Types," in Chapter 13 to learn more about the View tab.

The File Types tab in the Options dialog box is where you go if you want to register files that have a particular extension. For example, you might want to register the .XLS extension for Microsoft Excel files so that the file is associated with the correct application. Once you register a file type, you can open the file in its application by double-clicking it in My Computer or Windows Explorer. See "Registering Documents So They Open Applications," in Chapter 13 for information on how to register file types.

See "Customizing Explorer's Appearance," **p. 334**

Arranging File and Folder Icons

If you demand order, you will probably want your file and folder icons to always be lined up neatly in My Computer; however, you may prefer to arrange your icons however you want. You can do both in the My Computer window. To arrange your icons automatically, choose View, Arrange Icons, Auto Arrange, or right-click in a blank area in My Computer and choose Arrange Icons, Auto Arrange. Now, as icons are added or removed, they will automatically be rearranged into a regular grid. To turn off automatic arranging, choose the command again.

When the Auto Arrange option is not selected, you can move the icons around to wherever you want. You can also order them into a grid at any time by choosing View, Line Up Icons.

Sorting Files and Folders

There are four additional commands on the View, Arrange Icons submenu that enable you to sort your files and folders. To sort the items in the My Computer window, follow these steps:

1. Choose View, Arrange Icons, or right-click in a blank area in My Computer and choose Arrange Icons.
2. Select one of the following four options from the submenu:

   By Name Sorts the items by name, with folders first, and then files

   By Type Sorts folders and then files by the entry in the type column

   By Size Sorts folders and then files by size

   By Date Sorts folders and then files by date

If you are using the Details view, you can quickly sort your files and folders by clicking the button at the top of the column you want to sort by. To sort by name, for example, click the Name button. The first time you click a button, the items will be sorted in ascending order. Click a second time to sort in descending order.

Managing Files and Folders

Now that you understand the basics of using My Computer to view the files and folders on your computer, you are ready to learn how to manage your files and folders in My Computer. You can rename files, create new folders, move and copy files from one folder to another, and delete files, all from within the My Computer window. In the following sections, you will learn how to accomplish these basic file management tasks. In the next chapter, "Managing Files and Folders with Windows Explorer," you will learn some other techniques that can be used in My Computer as well.

Selecting Files and Folders

The first step in working with a folder or file in My Computer is to select the file. In many cases, you will want to select more than one file at a time. For example, if you are cleaning old files out of a folder, you can save time by selecting all the files you want to delete or archive to a floppy disk at once. This is easy to do in My Computer.

To select a single file, simply click on the file or use the arrow keys to move to the file. You can distinguish a selected file because it is highlighted.

There are a few ways to select multiple files. If the files you want to select are listed contiguously, select the first file, hold down the Shift key and select the last file. The first and last files and all the files in between will be selected.

If the files you want to select are not contiguous, select the first file, hold down the Ctrl key, and then click each of the other files you want to select. To deselect a file that you have already selected, continue to hold down the Ctrl key and click the file again. As long as you are holding down the Ctrl key, you can select and deselect as many files as you want.

Another file selection technique using the mouse is to hold down the mouse button and drag a box around the files you want to select, as shown in Figure 12.5. Of course, to do this the files have to be contiguous, although you can drag the selection around a group of files and then hold down the Ctrl key and click any files in the group that you want to deselect.

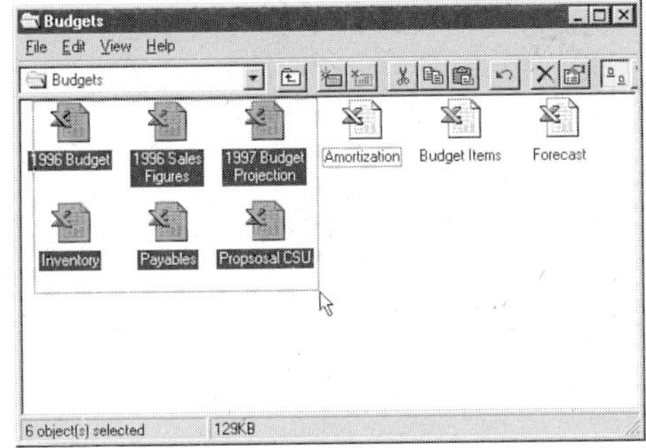

FIG. 12.5
You can use the mouse to drag a rectangle around a group of files to select them. Hold down the Ctrl key and click a file in the group to deselect it.

Although it is easiest to select multiple files using a mouse, you can also use the keyboard. To select contiguous files, use the arrow keys to move to the first file, hold down the Shift key and use the arrow keys to move to the last file in the group. To select nonadjacent files, select the first file, hold down the Ctrl key, use the arrow keys to move to the next file and press the space bar. Repeat this procedure until you have finished selecting the files. You can deselect a file by holding down the Ctrl key, moving the cursor to the file, and pressing the space bar.

To select all the files in a folder, choose Edit, Select All or press Ctrl+A. A clever trick for selecting all but a few files is to select the files and folders you don't want to select and then choose Edit, Invert Selection.

You can cancel a multiple selection at any time by clicking another file or folder.

Renaming Files

You can rename a file in My Computer using either a command or the mouse. To rename a file using the menu command, select the file and choose File, Rename, or right-click the file and choose Rename. An edit box appears around the file name in which you can use the usual editing keys to modify the name. Press Enter or select another file when you are done editing.

You can use the mouse to directly edit the name by clicking the file name once to select it, pausing a second, and then clicking again to open the edit box. Edit the name and press Enter.

Creating New Folders

As you create more and more files with your computer, you will inevitably want to create a filing system using folders. You can create folders and folders within folders to organize your data files however you like. To create a new folder, follow these steps:

1. Open the My Computer window to display the folder within which you want to create the new folder.
2. Choose File, New, Folder.

   or

   Right-click the mouse in a blank area in the window and choose New, Folder from the shortcut menu.
3. Type a name for the new folder that appears and press Enter.

Folders can use long file names, up to 255 characters, but must not contain the following characters:

\?:"<>|

Moving and Copying Files and Folders

Once you get a good filing system set up, you will want to be able to move and copy files and folders. Although you can use the keyboard to move and copy files, it is much easier to use the mouse.

The easiest way to move and copy files is using the drag-and-drop method. However, to do this in My Computer, you need to have two windows open, one displaying the files you want to move or copy, and a second window displaying the destination folder.

To move or copy files using the drag-and-drop method, follow these steps:

1. Display the folder that contains the files or folders you want to move or copy in My Computer.
2. Open a second window to display the folder where you want the files or folders moved or copied.

   If you have selected the option that allows you to browse files and folders using a single window (see "Viewing Resources in My Computer," earlier in this chapter), hold down the Ctrl key and click a folder (or the Up One Level button) in the first window. This will open a second window. Release the Ctrl key and navigate to the destination folder in this second window.
3. Arrange the two folder windows so they are both visible.
4. Select the files or folders you want to move or copy in the first window.
5. To move the selected items, drag and drop them in the new folder in the second window.

   or

   To copy the selected items, hold down the Ctrl key and drag and drop them in the new folder.

   A plus sign (+) appears beneath the mouse pointer when you hold down the Ctrl key, indicating that you are copying the files or folders.

If you drag the selected items with the right mouse button, a shortcut menu appears when you drop the items. You can then choose either Move, Copy or Create Shortcut(s) Here from the menu.

If you make a mistake in a move or copy operation, choose Edit, Undo Move or Edit, Undo Copy right away to reverse the action.

NOTE If you attempt to drag and drop a program file, Windows automatically creates a shortcut for the file. This is to prevent you from inadvertently moving a program file from its original location, which may prevent the program from functioning.

You can also use the drag-and-drop method to move a file to your desktop. If you use the right mouse button, you will have the option of moving, copying, or creating a shortcut for the file on your desktop (see "Creating Shortcut Icons on the Desktop to Start Programs," in Chapter 10). If you don't want to move the actual file from the folder it is currently stored in, but you would like to be able to open the file quickly from the desktop, create a shortcut for the file instead of moving it.

If you want to delete the file, drag and drop it on the Recycle Bin on your desktop (see "Deleting Files," later in this chapter).

You can also use the Edit, Cut (or Copy) and Edit, Paste commands to move or copy files and folders. One advantage to this method is that you don't have to open a second window. You can cut or copy the files in the source folder and then display the destination folder in the same window and paste the files.

To move or copy files and folders using the Edit commands, follow these steps:

1. Display the folder that contains the files or folders you want to move or copy in My Computer.
2. Select the files or folders that you want to move or copy.
3. To move the selected items, choose Edit, Cut or right-click the selection and choose Cut.

   or

   To copy the selected items, choose Edit, Copy or right-click the selection and choose Copy.
4. Display the destination folder in the My Computer window.
5. Choose Edit, Paste or right-click a blank area and choose Paste.

   See "Moving and Copying Files and Folders," **p. 319**

Deleting Files

It is always a good idea to delete files and folders that you do not need anymore to keep your hard disk from getting cluttered. When you delete files in Windows 95, they are sent to the Recycling Bin, where they are temporarily stored. If you need to restore a deleted file, you can open the Recycling Bin, select the file, and restore it.

To delete a file or folder, follow these steps:

1. Select the files or folders you want to delete.
2. Press Delete, choose File, Delete, or right-click the selection and choose Delete.

   You can also drag and drop the selected files or folders to the Recycle Bin icon on the desktop.

3. When the confirmation dialog box appears, choose Yes. You can choose No to cancel the deletion.

CAUTION

Be aware of the fact that if you delete a folder, you also delete all the files and folders in that folder.

See "Restoring Deleted Files," **p. 323**

CHAPTER 13

Managing Files and Folders with Windows Explorer

The first part of this chapter explains how to use the Windows Explorer to work with and manage the files on your computer. You also learn how to carry out many file management tasks using My Computer. The last part of the book describes how you can customize Explorer, synchronize files between different computers, and associate new document files with an application.

How to use the Explorer and folders windows from My Computer to manage files and folders

This chapter contains many tips and some undocumented tricks that will improve your productivity.

Manage the Recycle Bin so you can undelete files

Learn how to restore deleted files or permanently delete files.

View and change file attributes

Using the Windows Explorer, change hidden, system, and read-only file attributes.

Learn to synchronize files between laptop and desktop computers

You can work off your desktop with a laptop and then have the Briefcase update files between the desktop and laptop.

Learn to register file types

Associate documents with applications so that double-clicking the document opens the application.

How to use Explorer on a network

Windows Explorer and My Computer show you the resources that are shared across the network.

Understanding Files and Folders

If you are familiar with the MS-DOS Windows system for organizing files, a folder is analogous to a directory, and a folder within a folder is a subdirectory of a directory. If you like to think hierarchically, you can continue to visualize the organization of your files in exactly the same way as you did with DOS and earlier versions of Windows. The only difference is that instead of directories and subdirectories, you have folders and folders within folders. And, as you see in the next section, you can view the hierarchical arrangement of your folders using Explorer.

Should you misplace a file, use the Find command (Start, Find, Files or Folders) to search for the file by name, type, date saved, or content.

This capability to have folders within folders enables you to refine your filing system by categorizing your files in a way that makes it easy for you to locate a file even if you haven't used it for a long time. If you prefer to use the folder metaphor, you will want to use folder windows created from My Computer, the topic of the preceding chapter, "Managing Files and Folders with My Computer."

Folder windows created from My Computer are like single pane Explorer windows—the left pane that contains a hierarchical structure is not shown in folder windows. Many of the tips and techniques described in the Explorer section of this book work in folder windows, which you learned about in Chapter 12.

Using Windows Explorer to View Files and Folders

Use the *Windows Explorer* to see how the files and folders on your computer are organized. With Windows Explorer, you can view the hierarchical arrangement of the folders on your computer, and you can look into each folder to see what files are stored there. You also can use Windows Explorer to reorganize and manage your files and folders. You can create new folders; move and copy files from one folder to another, to a floppy disk, or to another computer (if you are on a network); rename and delete files and folders; and perform other file management tasks.

The File Manager used in Windows 3.x is still available in Windows 95. Open the file WINFILE.EXE located in the Windows folder to see the new File Manager. Be careful: The File Manager does not support long file names. If you use it, you will lose long file names you have created with Windows 95 applications or the Windows Explorer. Once you learn a few of the Explorer tips described in this chapter, you'll see that Explorer is more powerful.

To open the Windows Explorer, right-click Start, then choose Explorer. When you start Windows Explorer from the Start menu, Explorer opens the Windows\Start Menu folder. The Explorer also can be found in Programs in the Start menu or by right-clicking My Computer.

Figure 13.1 shows the Explorer with the left pane showing system resources and the right pane showing the folders in the Local C drive.

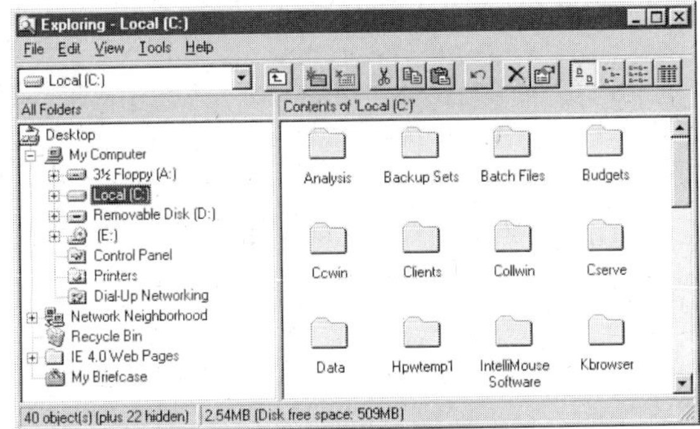

FIG. 13.1
Use Windows Explorer to view the files and folders on your computer. This view shows the Windows Explorer with large icons and a toolbar.

You'll use Windows Explorer frequently to work with your files and folders. If you need to open Windows Explorer to display frequently used folders, you should create Explorer shortcuts. Make these shortcuts readily accessible by adding them to the Start menu.

See "Starting Explorer at Specific Directories or Files," **p. 338**

See "Customizing the Start Menu," **p. 847**

Viewing Your Computer's Resources

The Windows Explorer window is divided into two panes (refer to Figure 13.1). Move between different panes in the Explorer by pressing the Tab key. The left pane displays a hierarchical view of the organization of the folders on your computer. At the top of the hierarchy is the Desktop icon. This represents all the hard disks and resources available to your computer. Just beneath desktop is My Computer, represented by an icon of a computer. Under My Computer are listed all the resources on your computer. These resources include floppy drives (represented by a floppy drive icon) and local hard drives (represented by a hard drive icon). Three special folders, the Fonts, Control Panel, and Printers folders, are used for managing the fonts and printers on your computer and for customizing your computer's settings.

Two other folders that are branches off the Desktop icon are *Network Neighborhood* and the *Recycle Bin.* NetworkNeighborhood appears on your desktop if you installed a network adapter. Open this folder to browse the computers in your workgroup or on your entire network. The Recycle Bin temporarily holds files when you delete them from a folder, so you have the opportunity to recover them if you change your mind.

Depending on the resources on your computer, you may see other folders displayed underneath My Computer. If you have a CD-ROM drive or a removable media drive installed on your computer, for example, you will see their icons under My Computer. You may also see an icon for the *Briefcase* folder. The Briefcase is a special folder used for working on the same files at two locations and keeping them synchronized. If you have installed Dial-Up Networking, which is used to make connections with other computers, you will see the Dial-Up Networking folder under My Computer.

Just beneath the menu bar is the toolbar. If the toolbar is not displayed, choose View, Toolbar to see it. You can use the drop-down list at the left end of the toolbar to open the main folders in the Desktop and My Computer folders. This drop-down list shows all the drives on your computer, including network drives. If you scroll through the list, you'll also find your Control Panel, Briefcase (if installed), printers, Network Neighborhood, and Recycle Bin at the bottom of the list. This list also displays the folder hierarchy of the currently open folder, as shown in Figure 13.2. You can, for example, quickly select the Recycle Bin folder without having to scroll to the bottom of the list in the left pane of the Explorer. To select from the list, click the down arrow next to the text box and click the folder you want to open.

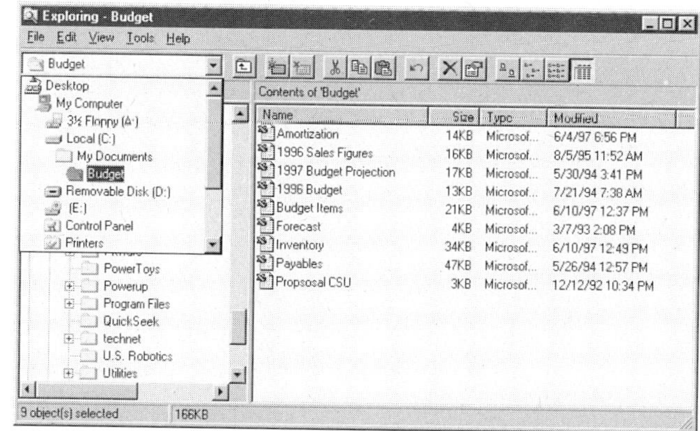

FIG. 13.2
The folders in the hierarchy above the current folder (Budgets) are shown in addition to the list of drives and other main resources. The rest of the folder hierarchy is collapsed for quick access.

▶ **See** "Managing Print Jobs," **p. 145**

Browsing the Contents of a Folder

The right pane of the Explorer window displays the contents of whatever folder is selected in the left pane. If you select the local C drive under My Computer, for example, you see a list of all the resources on your computer, including the floppy and hard drives (see Figure 13.3). To display the contents of your hard disk, click its icon in the left pane. To see the contents of a folder, select the folder on the left and its contents are listed on the right. You can select a folder by clicking it with the mouse or by using the up and down arrow keys on the keyboard.

You can open a specific folder without wading through the Explorer hierarchy by selecting Tools, Go To. Enter the path of the folder you want to open and then click OK.

You can expand and collapse the hierarchical view to display more or less detail. If a plus sign (+) appears next to an icon in the left pane of Explorer, additional folders are within this folder. To display these folders, click the plus sign or double-click the folder. All the folders within this folder are displayed. Some of these folders, in turn, may have folders within them, which you can view using the same procedure. To hide the folders within a folder, click the minus sign (–) next to the folder or double-click the folder. By collapsing and expanding the display of folders, you can view as much or as little detail as you want. Figure 13.3 shows an expanded view of the local C drive folder, which is collapsed in Figure 13.1. Notice that some of the folders on the C drive have plus signs next to them, indicating that they contain additional folders.

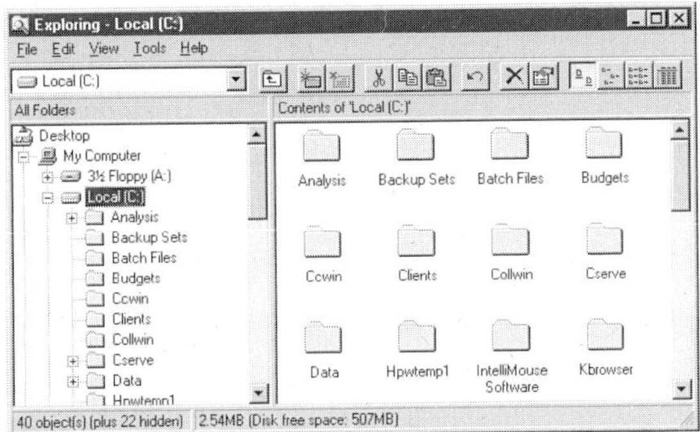

FIG. 13.3
An expanded view of the local C drive in the My Computer folder, showing its folders.

Understanding the File Icons in Windows

Windows uses various icons to represent folders and different types of files. In Figure 13.4, folders within the Windows folder are represented with a folder icon. You can quickly display the contents of a folder within a folder by double-clicking its icon in the right pane of the Explorer. The easiest way to redisplay the original folder is to click the Up One Level button on the toolbar. The Up One Level button is a picture of a folder with an up arrow in it. You also can redisplay the contents of the original folder by clicking its icon in the left pane of the window.

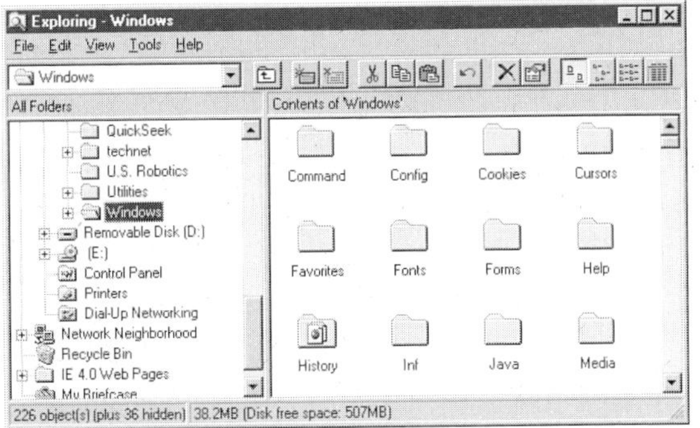

FIG. 13.4
Folder icons in the right pane of the Explorer represent folders within the folder selected in the left pane.

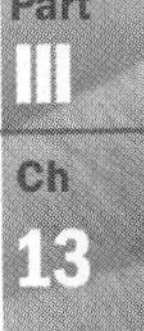

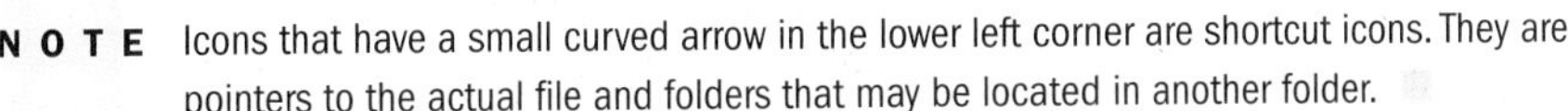

NOTE Icons that have a small curved arrow in the lower left corner are shortcut icons. They are pointers to the actual file and folders that may be located in another folder.

In addition to folders, many types of files can appear in the list of contents. Each type is represented by its own icon. Calendar files, for example, are represented by a calendar icon, and Bitmap files have their own special icon, as shown in Figure 13.5. These icons are helpful for visually associating a file with its program. You can, for example, readily distinguish a file created in the Notepad program from a file created in Paint (see Figure 13.5). You can open a file in its program by double-clicking the file's icon in Explorer.

FIG. 13.5
Different icons are used to represent different file types.

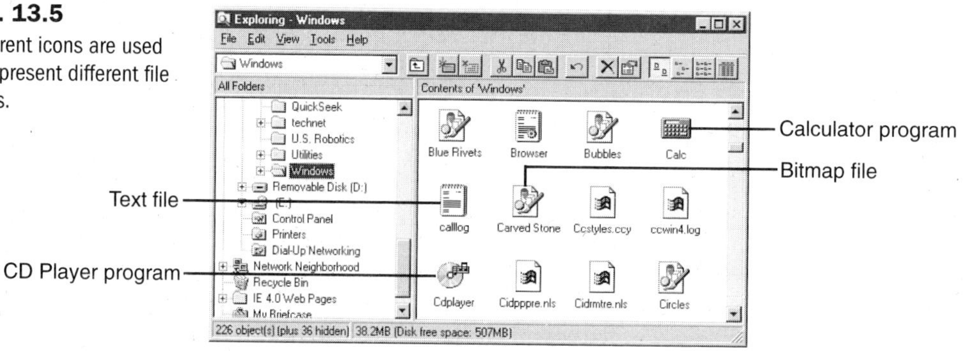

Unlike in the Windows 3.1 File Manager, you don't need to refresh the Explorer to see changes to the disk contents that were made from the DOS prompt.

You may need to update the display of files and folders in the right pane of the Explorer. If you are viewing the contents of a floppy disk and you switch disks, you won't see the contents of the new disk unless you *refresh* the window. To refresh the window, click the icon for the folder you want to refresh (in this case, the icon for the floppy drive) in the left pane of the Explorer. You also can refresh by choosing View, Refresh or by pressing the F5 key.

Managing Your Files and Folders

Explorer is an essential tool for managing the files and folders on your computer. You can use the Explorer to create new folders, move folders from one location to another, copy and move files from one folder to another, and even move files from one disk drive to another. You also can use the Explorer to delete and rename files and folders.

Selecting Files and Folders

To select a file or folder, click it and the selected file becomes highlighted. If another file in the right pane of the Windows Explorer is already selected, you can use the up and down arrow keys on the keyboard to move to a different one.

To select multiple files at once, click the first file and hold down the Ctrl key and click each additional file you want to select. To deselect a file, continue holding down the Ctrl key and click a second time on the file. To quickly select a group of contiguous files, select the first file in the group, hold down the Shift key and select the last file in the group. All the files between the first and last file will also be selected.

If files are in one of the icon views, you can select a group of contiguous files by dragging a box around the group of files with the mouse.

If your files are arranged freeform, you may find it convenient to select groups of files by dragging a rectangle around them using the pointer. Figure 13.6 shows how you can click and drag a rectangle around multiple icons. All the icons within the rectangle will be selected. Once they are selected, you can deselect or select additional files by holding down Ctrl and clicking icons.

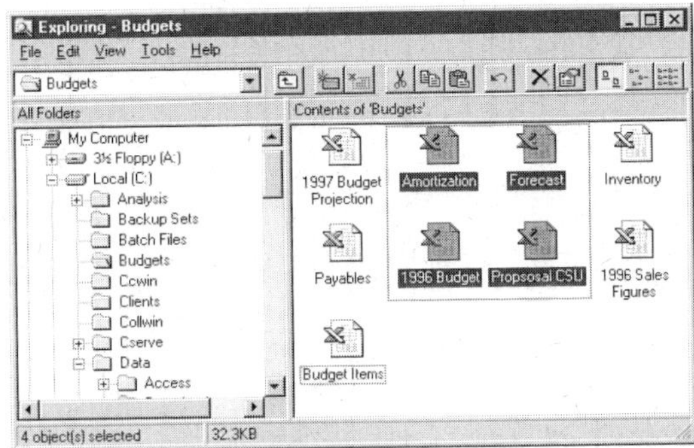

FIG. 13.6
Drag a rectangle around the group of file icons you want to select.

You also can select multiple files with the keyboard. To select multiple adjacent files, select the first file by tabbing into the right pane, press and hold down the Shift key while moving to the last file by pressing the down arrow key. To select nonadjacent files, select the first file, hold down the Ctrl key, use the arrow keys to move to the next file to be selected, and press the spacebar. While you continue to hold down the Ctrl key, move to each file you want to select and press the spacebar. To deselect a file and retain the other selections, hold down the Ctrl key, use an arrow key to move to the file, and press the spacebar.

To select all the files and folders displayed in the right pane, choose Edit, Select All (or press Ctrl+A). If you want to select all but a few of the files and folders in the right pane, select the files and folders you don't want to select; then choose Edit, Invert Selection.

To cancel the selections you have made, simply select another file or folder with the mouse or keyboard.

Renaming Files

Renaming individual files is much easier in Windows 95 than in Windows 3.x. To rename a file, click the file name, pause, then click the file name again. You can also right-click the file name and choose Rename. The name will be selected and the pointer changes to an I-beam to indicate you can edit the text underneath. Click the pointer in the name where you want the insertion point and rename the file. To undo your edits, press the Escape key. To accept your edits, press Enter or click another file.

Renaming Multiple Files

Unlike MS-DOS or Windows 3.x, the Explorer has no facility for renaming multiple file names with a single command. However, you can preserve long file names while renaming multiple files by going to a DOS window and using the RENAME command to rename multiple files. You can even rename long file names.

CAUTION

Using the Windows 3.x or Windows 95 File Manager to rename one or more files converts the long file names for those files into their 8.3 equivalents.

To rename long file names in multiple files using MS-DOS, follow this procedure:

1. Click Start, Programs, MS-DOS Prompt to open an MS-DOS window.
2. At the DOS prompt, type **CD path name** to switch to the directory containing the files you want to rename.
3. Type **RENAME originalname.ext newname.ext**. If the original name or new name are long file names or include spaces, enclose the name and extension in quotes. Press Enter.

When you use the DIR command to see the file names in a DOS window, remember that file names using 8.3 format will be on the left and long file names will be on the right of the listing.

The following list of file names will be used as examples:

Jun Forcast 01.xls
Jul Forcast 12.xls
Aug Forcast 05.xls
Sep Forcast 07.xls

To correct the spelling of "forecast," use the ? wild card to match against any single letter in that character position. Use this MS-DOS command line:

```
rename "??? forcast ??.xls" "??? forecast??.xls"
```

This renames the files to:

Aug forecast05.xls
Sep forecast07.xls
Jul forecast12.xls
Jun forecast01.xls

Match against any number of characters by using the * wild card, even within the quotes needed for long file names. For example, this MS-DOS command line:

```
rename "??? Forcast???.*" "??? Forcast.xls"
```

renames the original collection of files to:

Jun Forcast.xls
Jul Forcast.xls
Sep Forcast.xls
Aug Forcast.xls

Creating New Folders

You can use Windows Explorer to create new folders.

Create a new folder by right-clicking in the blank area of the right pane in Explorer. Choose New, Folder. Type a name for the folder and press Enter. In Windows 95 applications that use the common Save As dialog box, you can create new folders using this same process before you save a file.

To create a new folder, follow these steps:

1. Select the folder in the left pane of Windows Explorer in which you want to create a new folder.
2. Choose File, New, Folder. A new folder appears in the right pane of the Explorer, ready for you to type in a name.
3. Type a name for the folder and press Enter.

Folders can use long names just like files. Folder names can be up to 255 characters and can include spaces. Folders can't use these characters:

\ ? : " < > |

Moving and Copying Files and Folders

Moving and copying files and folders is an essential file management task. Using the Explorer and the mouse, you can quickly move and copy files and folders without ever touching the keyboard.

You can use two approaches for moving and copying files and folders. You can either use the Cut or Copy commands or use the mouse to drag and drop the files.

To move or copy files using the menu, follow these steps:

1. Select the files or folders you want to move in the right pane of the Windows Explorer.
2. Perform one of the following actions to cut the file so it can be moved:

Choose Edit, Cut.

Right-click, choose Cut.

Press Ctrl+X.

Click the Cut button on the toolbar.

Or, perform one of the following actions to copy the file:

Choose Edit, Copy.

Right-click, then choose Copy.

Press Ctrl+C.

Click the Copy button on the toolbar.

3. In either pane of the Explorer, select the folder in which you want to paste the cut or copied file, then follow one of these methods:

    Choose Edit, Paste.

    Right-click, then choose Paste.

    Press Ctrl+V.

    Click the Paste button on the toolbar.

To move or copy files using the drag-and-drop method, follow these steps:

1. Select the files or folders you want to move in the right pane of the Windows Explorer.
2. If the folder where you want to move the selected items is not visible in the left pane of the Explorer, use the scroll bar to scroll it into view. If you need to display a subfolder, click the plus (+) sign next to the folder containing the subfolder.
3. To move the selected items, drag the selected items to the new folder in the left pane of the Explorer.

    or

    To copy the selected items, hold down the Ctrl key and drag the selected items to the new folder in the left pane of the Explorer. A plus sign (+) appears beneath the mouse pointer when you hold down the Ctrl key, that indicates you are copying the files. Make sure that the correct folder is highlighted before you release the mouse button.

Drag and drop selected items onto the destination folder with the right mouse button. When the shortcut menu appears, click Move Here to move items or Copy Here to copy items to the new location.

If you attempt to drag and drop a program file to a new folder, Windows creates a shortcut for that program in the new location. This is to prevent you from inadvertently moving a program file from its original folder. When you attempt to drag a program file, an arrow appears beneath the mouse pointer, indicating that you are about to create a shortcut for that program.

To quickly move selected items to a floppy disk, click the selected items with the right mouse button. Click Send To and then click the disk drive to which you want to send the selected files. Add other drives or folders to the Send To menu through customization.

NOTE If you routinely copy or move files to particular folders or a disk drive, you can create a shortcut for the folder or drive on your desktop. You can then quickly drag and drop files onto the shortcut icon instead of having to scroll to the folder or drive in Explorer. To create a shortcut for a folder or drive, select it in the Explorer, drag it with the right mouse button onto your desktop, and release the mouse button. Choose the Create Shortcut(s) Here command. You can now drag and drop files onto this shortcut icon to copy or move files to this folder or drive.

Copying Disks

At times, you may want to make an exact copy of an entire floppy disk. This is easy to do in either Explorer or My Computer.

You can copy from one floppy disk to another using the same drive, but both disks must have the same storage capacity. The disk you copy onto will be erased in the process.

To copy a disk, follow these steps:

1. Insert the floppy disk you want to copy.
2. Right-click the disk in My Computer or in the left pane of the Explorer window.
3. Choose Copy Disk from the shortcut menu. This opens the Copy Disk dialog box shown in Figure 13.7.

   If you have only one drive of this size, that drive is highlighted for both the Copy From and Copy To areas of the dialog box. If you have another drive of this same size, it is also listed so you can select it to copy from drive to drive.

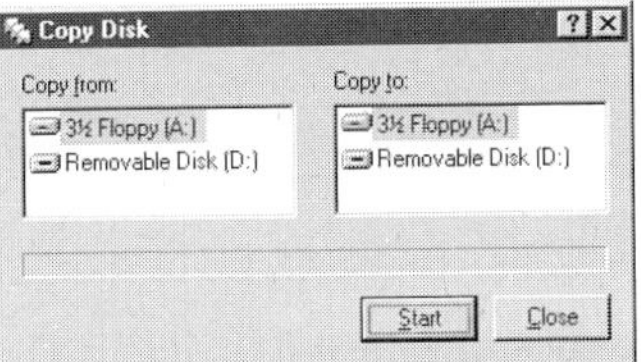

FIG. 13.7
The Copy Disk dialog box shows the selected drives for the copy operation.

4. Choose Start.
5. If you are using the same drive for the master and the copy, you are prompted to switch floppy disks when necessary.
6. When the disk is duplicated, you can copy another disk by choosing Start, or choose Close if you are done.

Copying disks is much faster in Windows 95 than in prior versions of Windows. This is due to the addition of a high-speed floppy driver. If you frequently copy disks, you will notice the speed improvement.

Deleting Files and Folders

Windows now has a folder called the Recycle Bin where deleted files are temporarily stored. The Recycle Bin empties on a rolling basis with the oldest files in the Recycle Bin actually being removed to make room for more recently deleted files. You can restore files from the Recycle Bin if you change your mind or accidentally delete a file.

See "Formatting Disks," **p. 382**

If you realize right away that you have accidentally deleted a file or folder, choose Edit, Undo Delete to restore the files. Press F5 to refresh the file listing and see the restored file or folder.

To delete a file or folder, follow these steps:

1. Select the file or folder you want to delete.

   You can select multiple files or folders using the techniques described in "Selecting Files and Folders," earlier in this chapter.

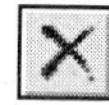

2. Click the selection with the right mouse button and click Delete.

   or

   Choose File, Delete, or press the Delete key or click the Delete button on the toolbar.

   or

   Drag and drop the file onto the Recycle Bin icon on the desktop.

To change whether a confirmation is required to delete a file, right-click the Recycle Bin, choose Properties, and select the Display Delete Confirmation dialog box.

3. Click Yes when the Confirm File Delete dialog box appears (see Figure 13.8), or click No if you want to cancel the file deletion.

   If you are deleting multiple files, Explorer displays the Confirm Multiple File Delete dialog box.

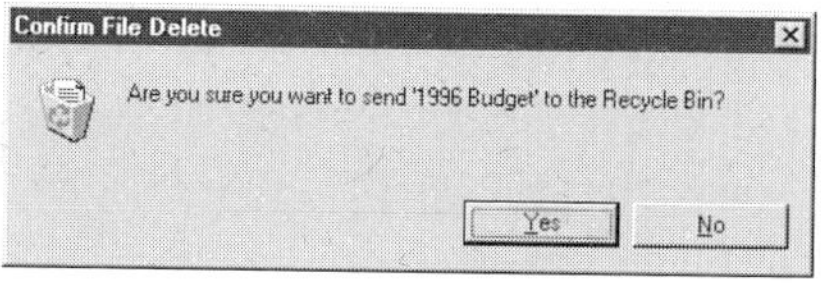

FIG. 13.8
The Confirm File Delete dialog box gives you a chance to check your decision before deleting a file.

CAUTION

If you delete a folder, you also delete all the files and folders contained in that folder. The Confirm Folder Delete dialog box reminds you of this. Be aware of what you are doing before you delete a folder.

You also should be careful not to accidentally delete a program file. If you attempt to delete a program file, the Confirm File Delete message box warns you that you are about to delete a program. Click No if you don't mean to delete the program, but want the other selected files to be deleted. Click Cancel to stop all deletions.

CAUTION

Files deleted from the MS-DOS prompt or from a floppy disk or network drive are not saved to the Recycle Bin. If you delete them, they are gone. You can use utilities such as Norton Utilities for Windows 95 from Symantec to give a broader range of undelete capabilities.

See "Viewing and Changing the Properties of a File or Folder," **p. 327**

Permanently delete files without sending them to the Recycle Bin by holding down the Shift key as you delete them.

When deleting some files, you may see a message warning you that the file is a system, hidden, or read-only file. System files are files needed by Windows 95 to operate correctly and should not be deleted. Hidden and read-only files may be needed for certain programs to work correctly, or they may just be files that you have protected with these attributes to prevent accidental deletion. Before deleting any of these file types, you should be certain that your system does not need them to operate correctly.

Restoring Deleted Files

You can open the Recycle Bin folder just as you do any other folder and select a file and restore it to its original location. You also can move or copy files from the Recycle Bin to a new location, in the same way you learned how to move and copy files from other folders.

To restore a deleted file or folder, follow these steps:

1. Double-click the Recycle Bin icon on the desktop to open the Recycle Bin window, as shown in Figure 13.9.

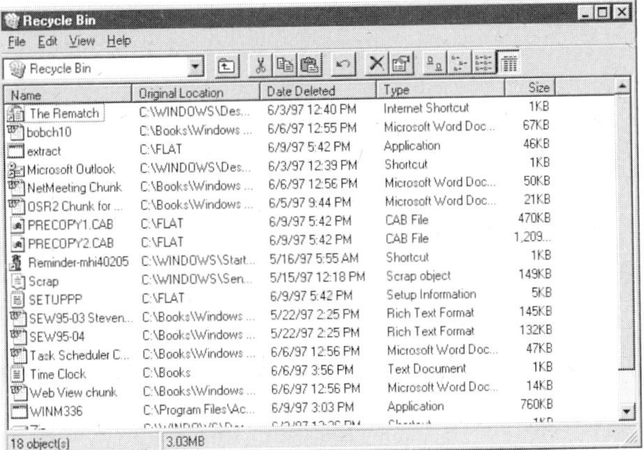

FIG. 13.9
Select files to restore in the Recycle Bin.

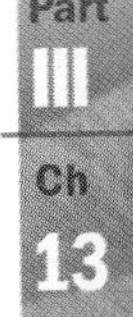

2. Select the file or files you want to restore.

   You can use the techniques described in the earlier section, "Selecting Files and Folders," to select multiple files.

3. Click the selected files with the right mouse button and click Restore, or choose File, Restore. The files are restored in the folders from which they were deleted. If the folder a file was originally in has been deleted, the folder is also restored.

   ▶ **See** "Moving and Copying Files and Folders," **p. 319**

You also can restore a file to a different folder than the one from which it was originally deleted. Open the Recycle Bin folder in Explorer, select the files you want to restore, and use one of the techniques discussed earlier in this chapter to move the file where you want it.

Emptying the Recycle Bin Periodically, you may want to empty the Recycle Bin to free up space on your hard disk. To empty the Recycle Bin, follow one of these procedures:

- Click the Recycle Bin icon on the desktop with the right mouse button and click Empty Recycle Bin.
- If the Recycle Bin is already open, choose File, Empty Recycle Bin.

Once you have emptied the Recycle Bin, you can no longer recover the deleted files and folders that were stored there.

You also can delete selected files from the Recycle Bin. To delete selected files from the Recycle Bin, follow these steps:

1. Open the Recycle Bin and select the files you want to delete.
2. Click the selected files with the right mouse button and click Delete.
3. Choose Yes to confirm the deletion.

CAUTION

The Recycle Bin can be a lifesaver if you accidentally delete a critical file, but don't forget to delete confidential files from the Recycle Bin so that others can't retrieve them.

Changing the Size of the Recycle Bin You might prefer having more free disk space rather than storing a large history of deleted files. If so, you can change the amount of disk space used for the Recycle Bin.

To change the size of the Recycle Bin, follow these steps:

1. Right-click the Recycle Bin icon on the desktop or in the Explorer and click Properties. The Recycle Bin Properties sheet appears, as shown in Figure 13.10.
2. Select the Configure Drives Independently option if you want to change the Recycle Bin size separately for each drive. Or, select the Use One Setting for All Drives option if you want to use the same size Recycle Bin for all drives.

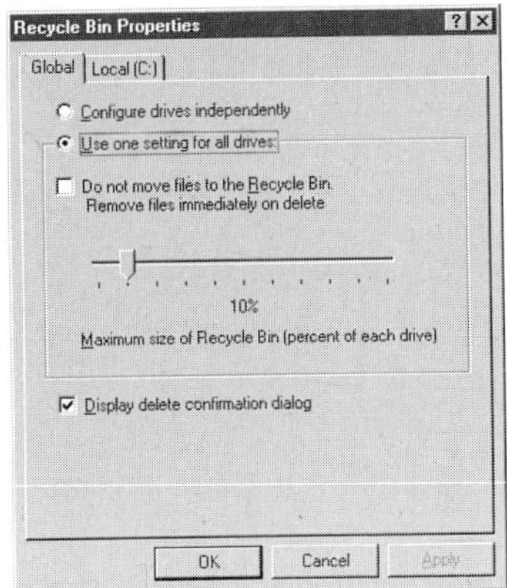

FIG. 13.10
Change the size of the Recycle Bin on the Recycle Bin properties sheet.

3. Drag the slider to change the maximum size of the Recycle Bin to be a percentage of the total disk size.
4. Click OK.

Deleting Without Using the Recycle Bin If you don't want to use up disk space storing deleted files, you can tell Windows to purge all files when they are deleted instead of storing them in the Recycle Bin. To purge all files when deleted, follow these steps:

1. Right-click the Recycle Bin icon on the desktop or in Explorer and click Properties.
2. Select the Purge Files Immediately on Delete option.
3. Click OK.

When you select this option and delete a file, the Confirm File Delete dialog box warns you that the file will not be moved to the Recycle Bin.

NOTE You can turn off the confirmation message for the Recycle Bin by clearing the Display Delete Confirmation Dialog check box on the Recycle Bin properties sheet.

Previewing a Document with Quick View

As you manage the files on your computer, you may want to look at the contents of a file before you make decisions about opening, moving, copying, deleting, and backing up the file. It can be very tedious and time-consuming to open each file in the program that created the file. Windows has a tool called *Quick View* for previewing many types of files without having to open the original program. You can access Quick View from the Explorer or from any folder window.

NOTE A worthwhile product to add to your toolkit is Quick View Plus from the people who wrote Quick View for Microsoft. Quick View Plus extends the Quick View that comes with Windows. It works with over 200 file formats from Windows, DOS, and Macintosh applications. It works with Microsoft Exchange so you can view e-mail and their attachments no matter what their source. It replaces the Quick View command on the context menu so it's easy to access. Quick View Plus sets its viewing screen side by side with Explorer so the two act almost like one program. Quick View Plus also enables you to find documents, print, and copy. Quick View Plus is inexpensive. For more information or trialware software contact:

Inso Corporation
401 North Wabash, Suite 600
Chicago, IL 60611

Phone: (312) 329-0700
Web: **http://www.inso.com**

TIP Preview documents by right-clicking the file and choosing Quick View.

To preview a file using Quick View, follow these steps:

1. Select the file you want to preview.
2. Choose File, Quick View. The Quick View item does not appear on the menu if the file type you select does not have a viewer installed.

   or

   Click the selected file with the right mouse button and click Quick View.

   or

   Drag the file into an existing Quick View window.

   The Quick View window opens, displaying the contents of the file, as shown in Figure 13.11.

You can scroll through the document using the scroll bars or keyboard. If you decide you want to edit the file, choose File, Open File for Editing (or click the Open File for Editing button at the left end of the toolbar).

TIP If you want to compare the contents of two files, you should have a new window opened for each file.

By default, Quick View opens a new window for each file. If this default has been changed, or you need to change it back, choose View and look at the menu. If a check mark appears next to Replace Window in Quick View, choose that option to deselect it and have a new window opened for each file. If you want the contents of the current Quick View window to be replaced when you select a new file for previewing, choose View, Replace Window to select this option. You can use the Replace Window button on the toolbar to activate or deactivate this option.

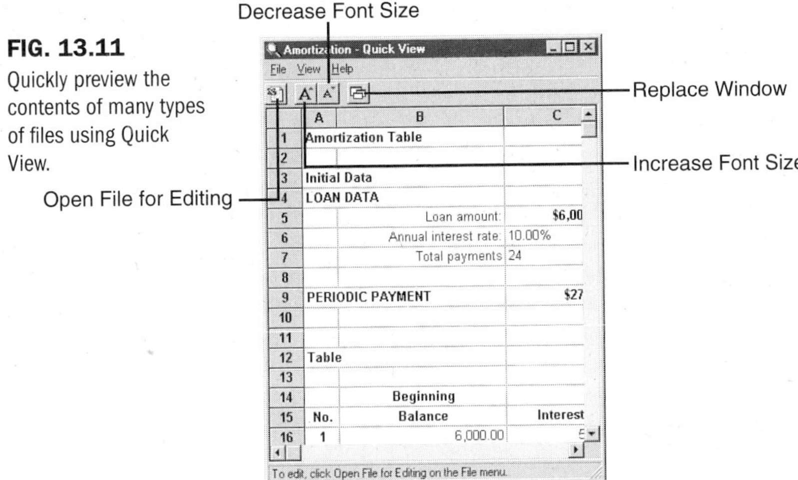

FIG. 13.11
Quickly preview the contents of many types of files using Quick View.

When you first open Quick View, you see a portion of the page of your document. To view whole pages, choose View, Page View. A check mark appears next to the command when it is activated. When you are in page view, you can click the arrows in the upper-right corner of the page to scroll through the document. To return to viewing portions of a page, choose the command again.

When you are in page view, you can rotate the display to preview the file in landscape orientation by choosing View, Landscape. Choose the command again to return to portrait orientation.

You also can change the font and font size used in the display by choosing View, Font and selecting a new font or size. To quickly increase or decrease the font size, click the Increase Font Size or Decrease Font Size tools on the toolbar. When you change the font and font size, it affects only the display in Quick View and does not alter the original file. It's handy to be able to increase the font size if you can't easily read the contents of the file, especially when you are in Page view.

To exit Quick View, choose File, Exit, or double-click the Quick View icon at the left end of the title bar.

Viewing and Changing the Properties of a File or Folder

In Windows, it is easy to check the properties of a selected file or folder. You can find out the type of a file; the location and size of the selected item; the MS-DOS name; and when the file or folder was created, last modified, and last accessed. Each file and folder on a disk also has a set of *attributes,* or descriptive characteristics. Attributes describe whether the file has been backed up, is a Windows system file, is hidden from normal viewing, or can be read but not written over. With Windows Explorer, you can display these attributes and change them.

To display the properties of a particular file or folder, follow these steps:

1. In Explorer (or any folder), select the file or folder whose properties you want to check.
2. Right-click and choose Properties, or choose File, Properties. Windows opens a properties sheet (see Figure 13.12).

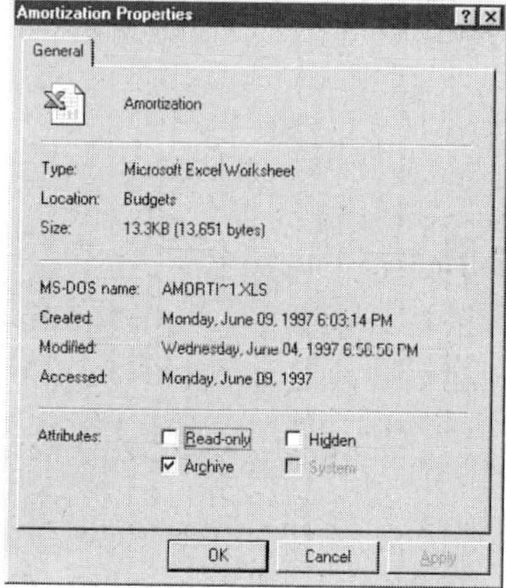

FIG. 13.12 You can check the properties of a file or folder on its properties sheet.

3. View the file or folder's properties.
4. If you want, change the attributes for the file or folder, as described in the following table:

Attribute	**Description**
Read Only	Sets the R or Read-Only attribute, which prevents a file or folder from being changed or erased. Set this attribute for a file or folder when you want to prevent someone from accidentally changing a master template or erasing a file that is critical to system operation.
Archive	Sets the A or Archive attribute. Marks with an A any file that has changed since being backed up using certain backup programs (including Backup, which comes with Windows). If no A appears, the file has not changed since you backed it up.
Hidden	Sets the H or Hidden attribute, which prevents files from displaying in Explorer and My Computer.
System	Sets the S or System attribute, which prevents files from displaying. System files are files that your computer requires to operate. Deleting a system file could prevent your computer from working. Folders cannot have the System attribute set.

5. Click OK.

CAUTION

Read-only files can still be deleted from within Explorer. You will see one additional warning dialog box prompting you if you attempt to delete a read-only file, so setting this attribute does not entirely protect a read-only file from deletion.

NOTE If you want to reduce the odds of accidentally changing or erasing a file, set the attributes to Read-Only and Hidden or System. Remember that Read-Only and System files require only one additional confirmation to delete so be careful when confirming the messages that prompts you to delete files.

To display files with the Hidden or System attribute, choose View, Options. Click the View tab and select the Show All Files option. Now hidden and system files are displayed in the list of files. You can carry out these steps in either Explorer or My Computer.

Opening a Document from Explorer

You can open documents directly from Explorer. In fact, if you like to think in terms of opening documents rather than opening programs and then opening documents, you can use Explorer as your primary interface with your computer, doing all your viewing, opening, and printing of files from Explorer.

To open a document from Explorer, the file type for that document must be registered with a program in order for Windows to know what application to use to open and print the document. Windows automatically registers file types when you install an application.

To open a document in Explorer, double-click the file icon in Explorer or in a folder window. Explorer starts the program for the file and opens the file. If the program is already running and it works with a multidocument interface, the document will load into the program.

▶ **See** "Registering Documents So They Open Applications," **p. 353**

Opening an Unrecognized File Type If Windows does not recognize the file type of the file you double-click, it displays the Open With dialog box shown in Figure 13.13. This dialog box enables you to tell Windows which application should be used to open the file. Choose the program you want to open the file from the Choose the Program list. If you want the program to always be used to open a file of this type, make sure the Always Use this Program to Open this File check box is selected.

You may want to open a file with a program different than the program it has an association with. To do that, hold the Shift key as you right-click the file. Choose Open With, and then choose the program with which you want to open the file.

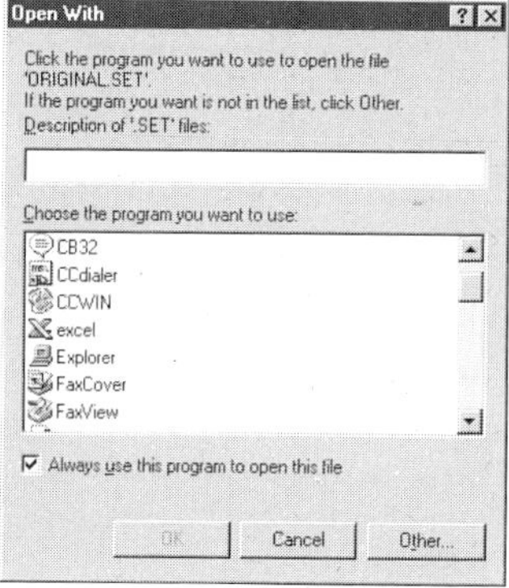

FIG. 13.13
Double-clicking a file that is not recognized produces the Open With dialog box so you can tell Windows which program to use to open the file.

Printing Files

You can send files directly to the printer from Explorer. When you print with Explorer, you send the file to the default printer. To change the default printer, use Control Panel.

To print a file with Explorer, the file must be registered with a program. To print a file using Explorer, follow these steps:

1. Open the folder that contains the file or files you want to print.
2. Select the file or files you want to print.
3. Choose File, Print.

   or

   If you have created a shortcut for your printer on your desktop, drag and drop the selected file or files onto the Printer icon on the desktop.

Quickly print files by right-clicking the file, choosing Send To, and then selecting the printer. To add a printer to the Send To menu, right drag a printer icon from the Printer folder in My Computer into the Windows\SendTo folder. Choose Create Shortcut(s) Here.

See "Drag-and-Drop Printing from the Desktop," **p. 150**

See "Registering a New File Type," **p. 853**

Finding Files

If you are familiar with the Search command from the Windows 3.1 File Manager, you should be impressed by the new features added for finding files in Windows 95.

The Find tool enables you to look for a specific file or group of related files by name and location. When searching by name, it's no longer necessary to use "wild cards" to specify your search, although you can still use them to fine-tune a search. In addition to this improvement, you can search by date modified, file type, and size. The most powerful new feature allows you to search by the text contained in the file or files. If you ever need to look for a file and you can remember a keyword or phrase in it, but don't know the name of the file, this will be a real timesaver.

To find a file or group of related files, follow these steps:

1. Open the Start menu, choose Find and then choose Files or Folders.

   or

   In Explorer, choose Tools, Find, Files or Folders, or right-click in the left pane and choose Find, Files or Folders.

   The Find dialog box appears (see Figure 13.14).

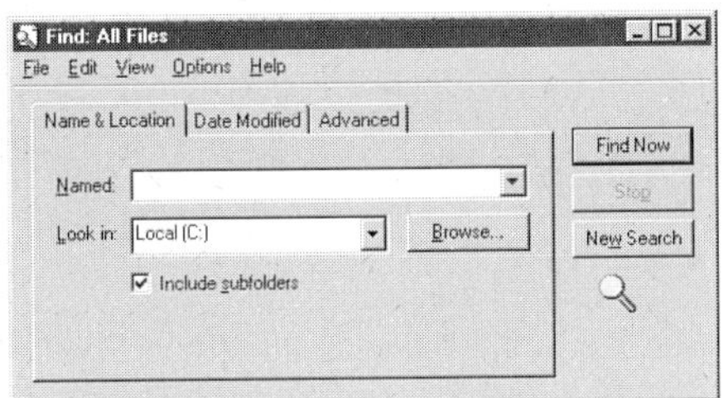

FIG. 13.14 Specify information about files you are searching for in the Find dialog box.

2. Type an entry in the Named text box. If you know the name of the file, type it in the text box. If you don't know the complete name of the file, just type whatever portion of the file name that you do know. Windows 95 finds all files that have these characters anywhere in the name.

   You also can use wild cards to look for all files of a particular type. (You could also use the Type criteria discussed in step 5 to limit files by type.) The following are some examples of how to use wild cards to look for groups of related files:

Entry	What It Finds
*.xls	Files with XLS extension (Excel worksheet files)
d*.xls	Excel worksheet files with file names beginning with the letter d (for example, DRAFT1.XLS)
report??.txt	TXT files beginning with file names starting with *report*, followed by two more characters (for example, REPORT23.TXT)

   To reuse the same search criteria as one used previously, click the arrow at the end of the Named text box and select the name search criteria you want to use from the list.

3. Specify where Find should look for the file in the Look In text box.

   You can type a path name in the text box, select from the entries in the drop-down list, or click the Browse button to select the location to which you want to restrict the search.

   Select the Include Subfolders option if you want to include the subfolders of whatever folders you selected in the search.

TIP To search an entire drive, select the drive letter from the drop-down list and select Include Subfolders.

4. To limit the search to files created or modified within a specific time period, click the Date Modified tab (see Figure 13.15).

   You can restrict the search to files created or modified between two specified dates, or you can search for files created or modified during a specified number of months or days prior to the current date.

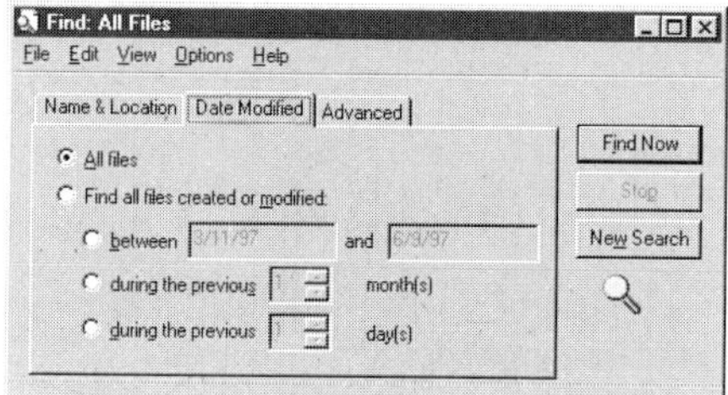

FIG. 13.15 You can narrow your search to a specified time period using options on the Date Modified page.

5. Click the Advanced tab to refine your search even more (see Figure 13.16).

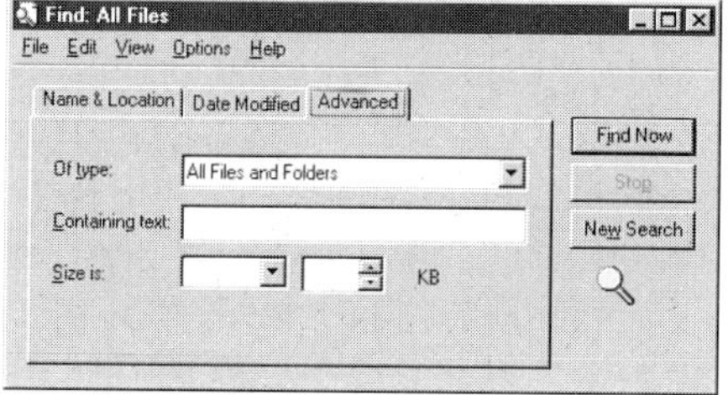

FIG. 13.16 Restrict your file search to files containing specific text or files of a specific size on the Advanced page of the Find dialog box.

6. Select a file type from the Of Type drop-down list to restrict the search to a specific type of file. The types listed here are the registered file types discussed in "Registering Documents So They Open Applications" later in this chapter. These include document types created by application programs, as well as various types of files needed by Windows such as icons, control panels, and fonts.
7. Enter a text string in the Containing Text text box to search for files containing a specific string of text. If you enter several words separated by spaces, Windows treats the entry as a phrase and finds only documents containing those words in that order.
8. Specify the size of the file in the Size Is box. You can specify that the file be exactly a particular file size, or at least (or at most) a specified size. Select from the drop-down list to select which of these options to use; and then specify a size in the Size Is box.
9. When you have finished setting up your search parameters, click the Find Now button.

The Find dialog box expands at the bottom to show the results of the search (see Figure 13.17). If your search parameters were very specific, the search may take a few moments, especially if you told Find to look for files with a specific text string. All files matching the search specifications are listed, along with their location, size, and file type.

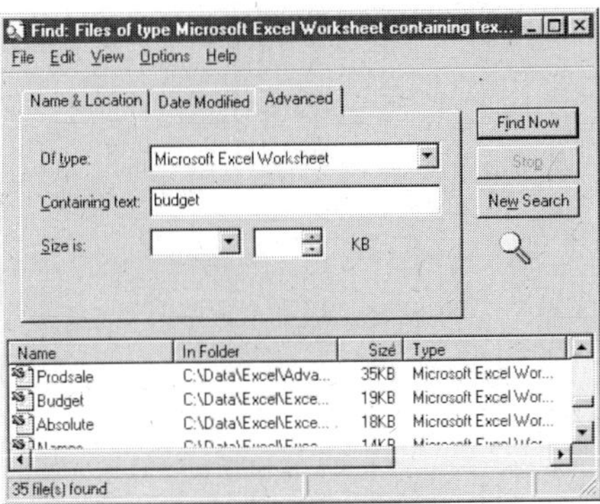

FIG. 13.17
The results of a search are listed at the bottom of the Find dialog box.

Use Find to do large scale or disk-wide file deletions. You can use a search parameter that searches for a specific file type, such as *.XLS, or search for all old files prior to a specific date. When the files display in the bottom of the Find window, use Quick View or view the file's properties to decide which files you want to delete.

At this point, you can perform all the same operations on any of the found files that you can on a file in Explorer. To work with a file in the Find dialog box, select the file and choose the File menu, or click the file with the right mouse button to open the shortcut menu. You can open, print, preview, move, copy, delete, rename, or view the properties of the file. You also can drag and drop the file to any folder in Explorer. This is handy if the file you located is in the wrong folder and you want to quickly move it to the correct folder. The Edit menu contains commands for cutting and copying files for all or just the selected files.

Searching Through Compressed Zip Files

Find will search for file names within files compressed with PKZIP or a PKZIP-compatible compression program. This can be very useful if you archive files in zip format and later need to find a specific file that is within a zip file.

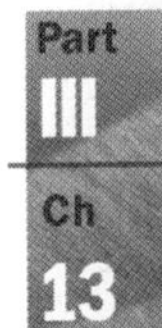

The reason Find can do this is that the file names within a zip file are not compressed. The file names are stored in the zip file as text. You can use Find to search through the contents of the zip files for specific names.

To search for a file name within a zip file, follow these steps:

1. Click Start, Find, Files or Folders.
2. Choose the Options menu and make sure that Case Sensitive is not selected.
3. Select the Name & Location tab. Specify the drive to search and select the Include Subfolders check box. Type ***.ZIP** in the Named edit box.
4. Select the Advanced tab. Type the file name in the Containing Text edit box. Wild cards will not work.
5. Click the Find Now button.

When Find displays a list of zip files containing the file name, you can use Quick View Plus to view all the files in the zip file. Utilities such as Norton Navigator can selectively unzip a single file from the zip file you found.

See "Previewing a Document with Quick View," **p. 325**

Saving the Search Criteria

You can save the search criteria as well as the results in an icon on your desktop. You also can save just the search criteria without saving the results. If you want to save the results with the search criteria, put a check mark in the Options, Save Results check box. To save the criteria, and any results that you specify, choose File, Save Search. The saved criteria, and the results if you specified them, will appear on your desktop as a document icon. You can label the icon by changing its name.

To open the Find dialog box using the saved criteria and result, double-click the icon. The Find dialog box will show the criteria and results as they were when saved. To redo the search, click Find Now.

The View menu has the same commands as Explorer for selecting how you want the files to be displayed in the results pane and for sorting the list of files.

The Options menu has two commands for fine tuning your search. Choose the Case Sensitive command if you want Find to distinguish between upper- and lowercase characters in any text you specified in the Containing Text text box.

If you want to set up a new search, click New Search to clear the criteria for the current search. You can now enter the criteria for the new search.

See "Changing How Folders and Files Are Displayed," **p. 335**

Customizing Explorer's Appearance

Windows offers many options for changing how the Explorer window looks. You can change how folders and files are listed; hide or display the toolbar and status bar; sort the folder and file icons by name, type, size, or date; hide the display of certain types of files; and make other changes to the Explorer window. Any changes you make remain in effect until you make new changes, even if you close and reopen Explorer.

NOTE If you're used to opening multiple Windows in File Manager, take note of the fact that you can't do that in the Explorer. For most work, you don't need to open multiple windows in Explorer because you can drag from any file or folder in the right pane into any drive or folder in the left pane. You can display drives or folders in the left pane by clicking their plus (+) signs without disturbing the contents of the right pane. Should you ever need to have multiple windows in Explorer, just open additional copies of Explorer. You can then copy or move files between them.

See "Opening Side-by-Side Folder Windows from a Desktop Shortcut," **p. 341**

TIP Most of the settings and preferences you choose for viewing a folder will remain with that folder. The next time you open that folder, it will have the same settings it did the last time you opened the folder.

Changing the Width of Panes

Use the mouse to change the size of the left and right panes of Explorer. To change the width of the two panes of the Explorer window, move the mouse pointer over the bar dividing the two panes (the mouse pointer changes to a double-headed arrow), hold down the left mouse button and drag the bar left or right to adjust the size of the two panes to your liking. However, you can't hide one pane or the other completely as you could in Windows 3.1 File Manager.

Changing the Status Bar

The status bar at the bottom of the Explorer window provides information on the item you select. If you select a folder, for example, you see information on the number of items in the folder and the total amount of disk space used by the folder. You can hide the status bar to make more room for displaying files and folders. To hide the status bar, choose View, Status Bar. Choosing this command again displays the status bar.

Hiding the Toolbar

The tools on the toolbar are shortcuts for commands you otherwise access with menu commands. These tools are discussed in the appropriate sections in this chapter. If you don't use the toolbar, you can hide it by choosing View, Toolbar. To display the toolbar, choose the command again.

Changing How Folders and Files Are Displayed

When you first start using Explorer, notice that folders and files are represented by large icons in the right pane of the window, as shown earlier in Figures 13.4 and 13.5. You also can display files and folders as small icons, as a list, or with file details.

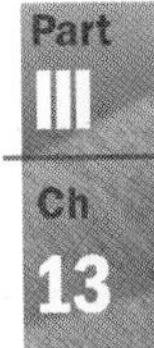

To change the way folders and files are displayed, follow these steps:

1. Open the View menu.
2. Choose one of the following commands:

Command	Result
Large Icons	Large icons
Small Icons	Small icons arranged in multiple columns
List	Small icons in a single list
Details	Size, type, and date modified

The currently selected option appears in the View menu with a dot beside it. Figure 13.18 shows files displayed using small icons.

FIG. 13.18
You can view more files and folders in Explorer when you use small icons.

If the toolbar is displayed, you also can click one of the four tools at the right end of the toolbar to change how items are displayed.

To automatically adjust column widths in the Detail view of Explorer to show the full content width, double-click the line between the column heads.

When you select the Details option, information on the size, type, and date the folder or file was last modified appears in columns next to the item in the list, as shown in Figure 13.19. You can change the width of these columns by moving the mouse pointer over the line that divides the buttons at the top of each column (the mouse pointer changes to a double-headed arrow), holding down the left mouse button, and dragging the line to change the width.

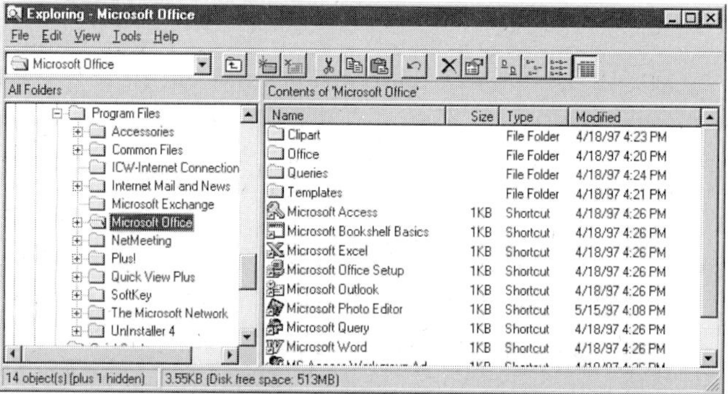

FIG. 13.19
To see information on the folders and files in the Explorer window, choose the Details view. Resize columns by dragging the line between header titles.

Arranging File and Folder Icons

If you select either the Large Icons or Small Icons option for displaying your files and folders, you can choose to let Windows automatically arrange the icons, or you can move the icons around to locate them wherever you want. To arrange the icons automatically, choose View, Arrange Icons. If a check mark appears next to the Auto Arrange command in the submenu, the command is already selected. If not, select Auto Arrange. The icons are now automatically arranged in a grid. If you want to arrange icons at any location in the right pane, deselect Auto Arrange. Some people prefer to have their files and folders arranged in an order of priority, frequency of use, or some other creative arrangement. Figure 13.20 shows files grouped by usage. Some are forecasting files and others are budgetary files.

FIG. 13.20
When Auto Arrange is off, you can arrange icons any way you want.

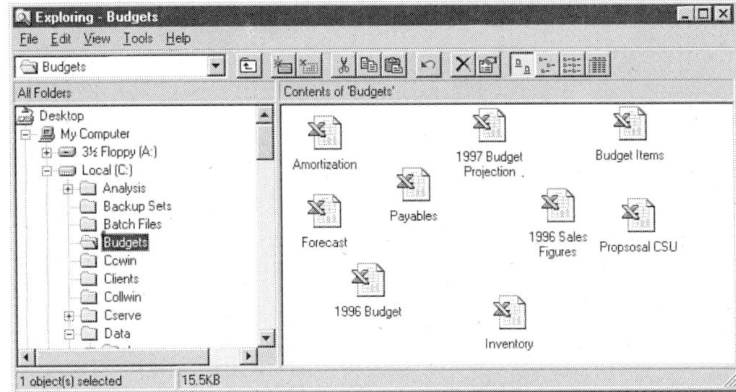

If the Auto Arrange command is not enabled, you can quickly arrange your icons in a grid by choosing View, Line Up Icons.

Sorting Files and Folders

You can sort the files and folders in the right pane of Explorer by name, type, size, and date. To sort the items in the Explorer display, follow these steps:

1. Choose View, Arrange Icons.
2. Select one of the four options from the submenu.

Command	Result
By Name	Sort folders and then files by their name
By Type	Sort folders and then files by the type column (this may not be the same as file extension)
By Size	Sort folders and then files by their size
By Date	Sort folders and then files by their date

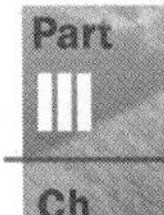

If you selected the Details option for displaying your folders and files, you can quickly sort the list of items by name, size, type, and date modified by clicking the button at the top of the specific column. Click Size, for example, to sort the list of items by size.

When you see a list in Windows 95 and the list headings appear to be buttons, try clicking them to sort the information according to the column on which you click. Each click toggles between ascending or descending order.

Displaying or Hiding Different File Types

You can change several other options in the View Options dialog box. To change these options, follow these steps:

1. Choose View, Options to display the Options dialog box (see Figure 13.21).

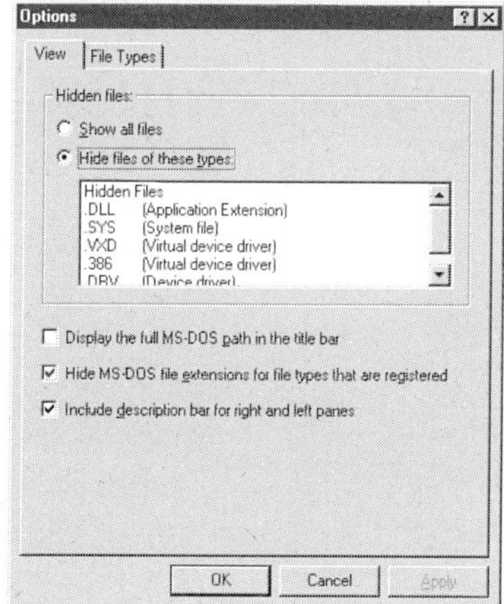

FIG. 13.21 You can change several options on the View page of the Options dialog box.

2. Select Show All Files to list all file types in the Explorer window.

   or

   Select Hide Files of These Types to hide the display of several types of system files.

   Hiding these files shortens the list of items displayed for some folders and also prevents you and other users from accidentally deleting or moving crucial system files.
3. Select the Display the Full MS-DOS Path in the Title Bar option if you want to see the full DOS path for the folder selected in the left pane.
4. Select the Hide MS-DOS File Extensions for File Types that Are Registered option if you don't want the extensions for files associated with a particular program to be displayed.

   (In Windows, a file's icon indicates what program it is associated with, if any; so you may have no reason to see file extensions.)
5. Select the Include Description Bar for Right and Left Panes option to display a descriptive bar at the top of the right and left panes of the Explorer window. The Description Bar shows you such information as the drive letter and path name for the current view.
6. Click OK when you have finished making the selections you want.

Starting Explorer at Specific Directories or Files

One of Explorer's potentially annoying features is that when it opens, it displays the directory or resource of the object from which it was opened. For example, if you right-click Start and choose Explore, Explorer opens and displays the contents of the Start menu folder. If you right-click the My Computer icon on the desktop and choose Explore, Explorer opens displaying the contents of My Computer. Although this design is understandable, many of us expect or would like Explorer to open in a folder we designate or in the last folder in which it was used. Use the following tips and you'll be able to create shortcuts that open Explorer the way you want.

Opening Explorer at Specific Folders or Files

Opening Explorer from a command line enables you to use switches that control how Explorer opens. The command line can be entered in the Target box of a shortcut's Property sheet, entered from an MS-DOS prompt, or typed within an MS-DOS batch file. Understanding how these switches work enables you to open Explorer in the following ways:

- In a single pane, Open view, or with the double pane in the Explorer view.
- With full access to all folders or restricted to a *root* folder or a UNC (Universal Naming Convention) folder.
- With a folder open and no file selected or with a specific file selected.

NOTE Be sure that you type a comma between each switch. Long file names or UNC names entered in the Target line of a shortcut's property sheet do not need to be enclosed in quotes.

The syntax for using switches with Explorer is as follows:

```
Explorer /e,/root,<object>,/select,<sub object>
```

These switches are described here.

Switch	Description
/n	Opens a new window even when a window is already open in the same folder.
/e	Without /e Explorer opens in the single pane Open view seen from My Computer. With /e Explorer opens with two panes.
/root,<object>	Specifies the highest level folder shown in Explorer and then opens in this folder. Explorer is restricted to the root folder and its subfolders. Use a local path or UNC name. If no root is specified, the Desktop is used.
/select,<sub object>	The object specified by <sub object> is selected when Explorer opens. The object can be a file, folder, or resource. Specify the path or UNC unless it is specified by /root.

Opening Explorer and Restricting It to a Folder Much file management time is spent scrolling up and down through the left pane of Explorer looking for the same two or three frequently used folders. With the following trick, you can create shortcuts that open Explorer to the specific folder you want. Two or three of these shortcuts on your desktop or Start menu will save a lot of time.

The *root* switch opens Explorer to the folder or UNC path that you specify, but it also restricts the user to that root and all its subfolders.

Follow these steps to create a shortcut that opens in the folder you want:

1. Create a desktop shortcut to EXPLORER.EXE in the Windows folder.
2. Right-click the shortcut icon and choose Properties.
3. Select the Shortcut tab.
4. Modify the Target line to read:

   ```
   C:\WINDOWS\EXPLORER.EXE /e,/root,C:\my documents
   ```

   This opens Explorer in the double pane window like the one shown in Figure 13.22. Notice that the `/root` switch forces Explorer to display only the My Documents folder and its subfolders. Use the following command line to open a single pane folder window.

   ```
   C:\WINDOWS\EXPLORER.EXE /root,C:\my documents
   ```

FIG. 13.22
Open Explorer in a double pane view with unlimited scope or restricted to a folder as shown here.

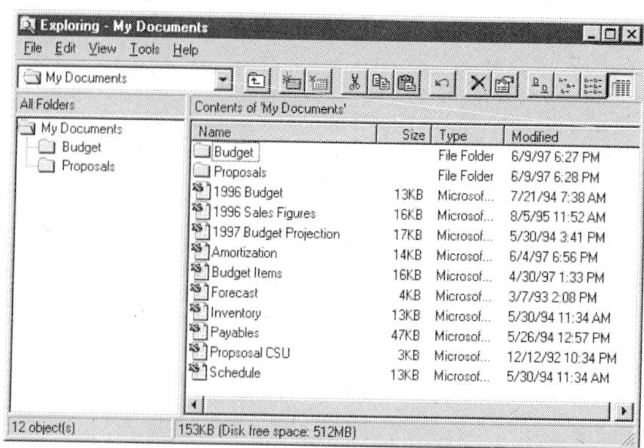

5. Change the icon by clicking the Change Icon button, and then click OK.
6. Rename the shortcut icon to indicate the view that it opens.

When you want to open Explorer to the folder designated by the root switch, just double-click the shortcut. To copy a file or folder into that folder, drag and drop the file or folder onto the shortcut.

Opening Explorer and Selecting a File To open an Explorer window and display a specific file, create a shortcut icon as described in the previous section. Open the shortcut's Property sheet and select its Shortcut tab.

In the Target line enter a line similar to:

```
C:\WINDOWS\EXPLORER.EXE /select,C:\my documents\schedule.xls
```

If you have restricted Explorer to a root folder with a dual pane view, your command line might look something like this:

```
C:\WINDOWS\EXPLORER.EXE /e,/root,C:\my documents,/select,schedule.xls
```

The resulting windows look like Figure 13.23.

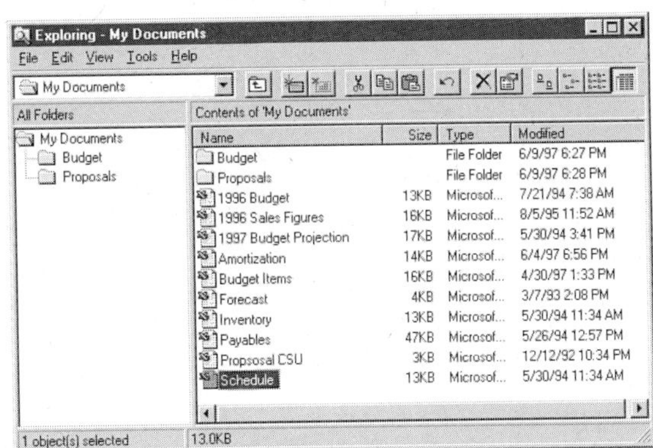

FIG. 13.23
Explorer windows can be restricted to a folder and have a specific file or folder selected when they open.

Customizing Explorer for Side-by-Side Views or Program Groups

Although Explorer is very powerful, some people still miss a few things about the old File Manager and Program Manager. One of the nice features of the Windows 3.x File Manager was its capability to display side-by-side windows. This enabled you to quickly drag and drop files between widely separated folders. Although you can drag and drop between folders in Explorer, it's sometimes more awkward to do so. The following section shows you how to use Explorer switches and a batch file to create a shortcut that opens side-by-side Explorer windows.

Opening Side-by-Side Folder Windows from a Desktop Shortcut

The following procedure creates an MS-DOS batch file that opens two folder windows and positions them side by side, as shown in Figure 13.24. A shortcut to the batch file enables you to rerun it anytime. To use this batch file you won't need to minimize the other programs that are running.

To create the side-by-side folder batch file, follow these steps:

1. Double-click My Computer to open a single pane window. Choose View, Options then select Browse Folders by Using a Single Window and choose OK.
2. Create an MS-DOS batch file by clicking Start, Accessories, Notepad and entering two Explorer command lines that open folder windows into the drives or folders you want. If you want the windows to open side by side, the initial folder for each window must be

different. If the folders are the same, they will open on top of each other. Save this batch file with the extension BAT.

For example, to open two folder windows with one showing "C:\" and the other showing "C:\MSOffice" you would use:

```
Explorer C:\
Explorer /n,C:\MSOFFICE
```

In this example, the first line opens a folder window at the C drive. The second line opens a new folder window at C:\MSOffice.

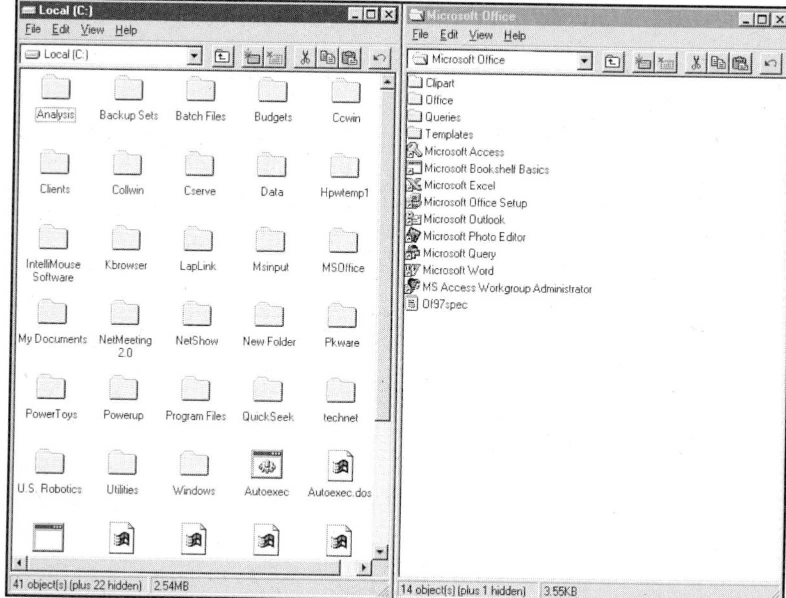

FIG. 13.24
Run side-by-side folder windows from a batch file whenever you want.

3. After you have saved the batch file, you can create a shortcut directly from the batch file by right-clicking the batch file and choosing Properties. Select the Program tab and change the name at the top of the sheet. This name is a descriptive name to help you—it does not appear as the file name. Select Minimize from the Run drop-down list. Select the Close on Exit check box. These actions prevent the batch file window from displaying. Choose OK.

   Windows automatically creates a shortcut because you modified the batch file's properties. The shortcut is stored in the same folder as the original batch file.

4. Drag the shortcut onto the desktop if you want it available from the desktop or add it to the Start menu.
5. Close or minimize all programs and run the batch shortcut by double-clicking it.
6. When the two folder windows appear, click the window you want on the left, then right-click the taskbar in a clear area and choose Tile Vertically. Set any viewing options for

the windows, such as column widths, and then close each window. If these windows display different folders the next time they are opened, they will open in the same position and with the same viewing options.

To run your batch file, double-click the shortcut you created. If you opened both windows into the same folder, the windows will open using the position and viewing options of the last window you closed in step 6.

See "Customizing the Start Menu," **p. 847**

Creating Windows 3.1-Like Program Groups

Some people who used Windows 3.1 liked the way the Program Manager visually grouped their programs and documents. If you prefer this method of starting and visualizing your programs and documents, follow these steps to quickly create a folder window displaying groups of programs and document files that are in your Start menu. Figure 13.25 shows the window which duplicates the contents of the Programs menu.

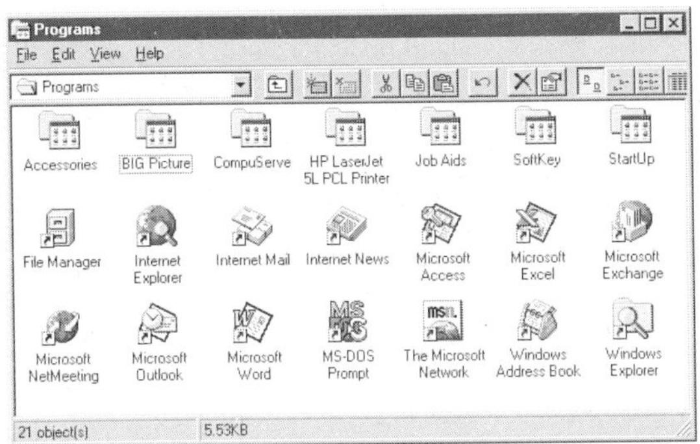

FIG. 13.25
Put the contents of your Start, Programs menu in a window with a single click.

To create a window duplicating the contents of the Programs submenu of the Start button, double-click the PROGRAM.GRP file in the Windows folder. A Group Conversion window displays while the group file converts into a folder window. When it's done, you see a single pane window displaying the contents of the Start, Program menu. Adding or removing programs or documents to the Start, Program menu automatically updates the contents of the window.

Another way to get a window displaying the contents of the Start, Programs menu is to click Start, Run, type **PROGMAN.EXE** in the Open text box of the Run dialog box, and then choose OK.

Working with Long File Names

Windows 95 gives you the capability to type file and folder names up to 255 characters long and include spaces. This makes understanding file and folder names much easier than older versions of Windows or DOS.

CAUTION

Although a file name can be up to 255 characters long and the maximum path length is 260 characters, you shouldn't make them longer than 50 to 75 characters. From a usability standpoint, file names that are too long are difficult to type and difficult to read in a list.

TIP You can display or hide the three-character file extension by choosing View, Options, and then clicking the View tab and clearing the option Hide MS-DOS File Extensions for File Types that Are Registered.

Both of these improvements do not restrict your ability to use Windows files with older Windows or DOS systems that do not use long file names. An abbreviated version of the long file names enables files to be backward compatible.

Renaming Files and Folders

As part of your efforts to keep the files and folders on your computer organized, you may want to rename a file or folder. This is easy to do in Explorer.

TIP If you're using a keyboard, you can rename a file or folder by selecting it and then either choosing File, Rename, or pressing F2.

To edit or rename a file or folder, follow these steps:

1. Click the file or folder name to select it.
2. Pause the pointer over the text in the name until the pointer changes to an I-beam and click where you want the insertion point in the text.

CAUTION

If you accidentally double-click the file name, the program for that file opens and loads the file. To return to naming the file, close the program and click the file name.

3. Edit using normal Windows editing methods. Press Enter to complete your edit.

If you should change your mind while typing in a new name, just press the Escape key to return to the original name. If you have already pressed Enter and the file has been renamed, click the Undo button in the toolbar, choose Edit, Undo, or press Ctrl+Z.

CAUTION

If you change the three-letter DOS file extension to a name, you will see a Rename alert box with this message: "If you change a file name extension, the file may become unusable. Are you sure you want to change it?" This box warns you that by changing the extension you will not be able to double-click the file and open its program. You can still open the file from within the application by choosing File, Open.

Using Long File Names with Older Windows and DOS Systems

Folders and files with long names can be used on older Windows and DOS systems. The *FAT (File Allocation Table)*, an area on the disk that stores file information, has been especially modified to store both old-style 8.3 file names as well as long file names.

CAUTION

Beware of using MS-DOS-based or previous Windows versions of hard disk utilities, file management software, or file utilities with Windows 95. In most cases, long file names will be destroyed and you may lose data.

Some programs that will cause problems with Windows 95 are the Windows 3.x versions of:

Norton Utilities™ by Symantec
PC Tools™ by Central Point Software, Inc.
Microsoft Defragmenter for MS-DOS versions 6.0, 6.2, 6.21, or 6.22
Stacker 4.0 by STAC Electronics

These companies have released Windows 95-compatible upgrades for their utilities. Check with these companies for the correct version to use with Windows 95.

If you must run an old backup or disk management utility with Windows 95, use the LFNBK utility to remove long file names from the disk. After using the old utility, you can restore long file names. LFNBK is described in the troubleshooting section at the end of Chapter 16, "Backing Up and Protecting Your Data."

CAUTION

Long file names cannot use the following characters:

/ \ : * ? " < > |

When you use a long file name, Windows automatically creates a file name fitting the 8.3 convention. This 8.3 file name is saved in its normal location in the FAT so that older Windows and DOS systems can still use the 8.3 file name.

You can see the MS-DOS file name that will be used for a file by right-clicking the file name, choosing Properties, and selecting the General tab. Figure 13.26 shows the File Properties sheet. The long file name is shown at the top of the box and the MS-DOS name appears near the middle.

The rules used to convert long file names to 8.3 file names are:

1. Remove the special characters: \ ; * ? " < > | <space> and any period except the rightmost period.
2. Create the first portion of the name by taking the first six characters in the long file name and adding a *numeric tail* by adding a tilde (~) followed by the number one (1). If a

file in the same directory already uses that number, increase the number to 2. Continue trying numbers through number 9. If that does not yield a unique name, take the first five characters and create a unique numeric tail using numbers from 10 to 99.

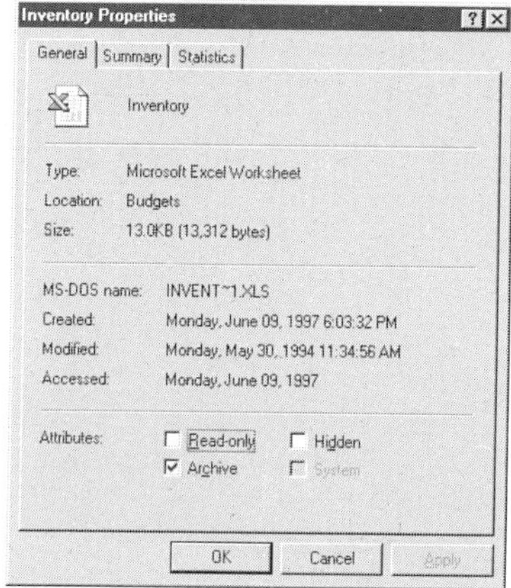

FIG. 13.26
Find out about a file by right-clicking its name and then choosing Properties.

3. Create the file extension by taking the first three characters after the last period. If the long file name does not have a period, there won't be a file extension.

Working with Long File Names in MS-DOS

If you use a DOS command from the command prompt, such as DIR to list a directory containing files with long names, you see the normal file information as well as the long file names. The long file name is displayed in the far right column when using the DOS DIR command.

When working from the MS-DOS command line in Windows 95, you can use either the 8.3 or the long file name assigned to each file. Use long file names in MS-DOS command lines as you would 8.3 names. If the name includes spaces, put quotes around the entire path.

From the MS-DOS prompt, the default command-line character limit is 127 characters. Command lines cannot be longer than 127 characters. To enable longer command lines add the following line to CONFIG.SYS:

```
shell=c:\windows\command.com /u:255
```

If your computer already has the SHELL command in the CONFIG.SYS file, change the /u switch to a value of 255.

If your computer does not have a CONFIG.SYS file in the root, create one by opening Notepad, typing the line as shown, then saving the text file to your boot disk root folder with the name CONFIG.SYS.

The command line will now be limited to 255 characters. This limit includes the MS-DOS command, switches, spaces, quotes, and long file name. You will be able to use 255-character command lines in all MS-DOS virtual machines running in Windows 95. Making this change will not enable MS-DOS on non-Windows 95 computers to use long file names.

Synchronizing Files with the Briefcase

With the proliferation of home computers, laptop computers, and networks, you may often find yourself working on the same file on different computers. The inherent difficulty in working with the same file at more than one location is keeping the files synchronized—that is, making sure that the latest version of the file is at both locations. This used to be a daunting and dangerous task. It is not too difficult to accidentally copy the older version of a file on top of the newer version, rather than the other way around. A new feature in Windows, *Briefcase*, makes the task of synchronizing files in different locations much easier.

NOTE If you frequently transfer files between computers, must maintain synchronized files, or want to control one computer from another, consider using LapLink for Windows 95. Its features are more robust, it updates files faster, and it operates over more communication media than Briefcase.

Briefcase is really a folder with some special features. When you want to work on files at a different location—for example, on your laptop while you are away from your office—you first copy the files from your desktop computer into Briefcase. You then transfer Briefcase to your laptop and work on the files in Briefcase. When you return to the office, you transfer Briefcase back to your desktop and issue a command that automatically updates any files on your desktop that were modified while they were in Briefcase. The files on your desktop are then synchronized with the files in Briefcase.

The Briefcase procedure works whether you transfer Briefcase using a floppy disk, keep Briefcase on one of two computers that are physically connected, or use Briefcase to synchronize files across a network.

See "Maintaining Laptop and Desktop Files with Briefcase," **p. 224**

Installing the Briefcase

Unless you chose the Portable option when you were setting up Windows, or specified the installation of Briefcase in a custom installation, you will not have the Briefcase feature. One way to check to see if you do have the Briefcase feature installed is to look for a Briefcase icon on your desktop. However, the Briefcase icon may have been moved or deleted, so a second way to check is to right-click in a folder or on the desktop. Choose New and if the Briefcase appears as an item, choose Briefcase. If a new Briefcase appears, the Briefcase feature is installed.

CAUTION

If Briefcase is already installed in your Windows 95, Briefcase will not appear in the Accessories portion of the Components list in Add/Remove Programs as described in step 4 of the following instructions. Briefcase will only appear if it has not been previously installed. Once Briefcase is installed, it cannot be uninstalled with Add/Remove Programs. This is to prevent the accidental loss of data from a Briefcase.

To install Briefcase, follow these steps:

1. Open the Start menu, then choose Settings and Control Panel.
2. Double-click the Add/Remove Programs icon.
3. Click the Windows Setup tab.
4. Select Accessories in the Components list and click Details.
5. Select Briefcase in the Components list and click OK.

NOTE Briefcase will only be listed in these options if it isn't installed. Unlike the other accessories, which are listed here regardless of whether they are currently installed, Briefcase disappears from the list once you install it. If you delete your Briefcase, it will not appear in the list and you won't be able to reinstall it without rerunning the Windows setup.

6. Click OK again and insert the Windows disk specified in the Insert Disk message box that appears. Click OK again.
7. Click OK to close the dialog box.

Creating a New Briefcase on the Desktop

If your PC does not already include a Briefcase on your desktop, you can easily create a new Briefcase. To create a Briefcase, follow these steps:

1. Decide where you want the Briefcase to be created (on the desktop, in a floppy disk folder, in a folder on the hard disk, and so on).
2. Right-click in the location in which you want the Briefcase created. If you want the Briefcase created on the desktop, for example, right-click the desktop.
3. From the pop-up menu, choose New, Briefcase. Windows 95 will create a Briefcase and add an icon for it in the location you have selected.
4. If you want to rename the Briefcase, click the Briefcase icon to select it, then click the Briefcase's description. Type a new description and press Enter.

As previously explained, you can create as many Briefcases as you like. By default, Windows 95 creates a Briefcase called My Briefcase on your desktop. You can rename the default Briefcase to suit your preferences.

Synchronizing Files with a Laptop or Another Computer on the Network

You can use Briefcase to keep files synchronized between a laptop and a desktop computer. This is useful because you may update files on the laptop while it is disconnected from the desktop. Upon reconnecting the two computers, you can ask Windows to synchronize the files between the two computers—comparing and updating files between the two computers. The most up-to-date file replaces the unchanged file. If files on both computers have been changed, you will be asked to choose which file should replace the other.

CAUTION

Be sure that the times and dates are correctly set on any computer on which you use synchronization. Incorrect dates or times could cause the wrong file to be overwritten.

Keeping synchronized files between your laptop and desktop computers is most convenient if they can be physically connected by a cable or network. Physically linking two computers is a much faster way to transfer files than by using a floppy disk. Using Briefcase helps you keep the files you are using on both computers synchronized. You can work on either the file on the original computer or the file in Briefcase, and use the Update command to keep the files synchronized.

The recommended approach is to put Briefcase on the computer you use less often.

You may have two computers on which you need to keep synchronized files, but you don't have the computers connected. You can still keep files synchronized by putting Briefcase on a floppy disk and using the disk to move the Briefcase between computers. You can use this method to synchronize files between your work computer and your home computer or between your desktop and laptop computers. Although it's not as fast as synchronizing files between two connected computers, it works well if you are not working with a large number of files and don't have the means to physically connect the computers.

To synchronize files on two computers that are connected by cable or network or that use a floppy disk to transfer the Briefcase, follow these steps:

See "Moving and Copying Files and Folders," **p. 319**

1. Copy the files and folders you want to use on both computers into Briefcase.

   The simplest way to copy the files to Briefcase is to drag and drop them on the My Briefcase icon on the desktop.

The fastest way to move the Briefcase is to right-click the My Briefcase icon, click Send To, and then click the floppy drive where you want to move Briefcase.

See "Sharing Local Resources via Parallel or Serial Connection," **p. 202**

2. Move Briefcase to the computer on which you will be working with the Briefcase files. If your computer is not connected to the other computer, move the Briefcase to a floppy disk.

   Once you move the Briefcase, it will not be located on the original desktop—it can only be at one place at a time.

   The idea is to move, not copy, Briefcase onto the other computer, so that it exists in only one location. An easy way to move Briefcase is to select the My Briefcase icon with the mouse, drag it to the new location with the right mouse button, and choose Move Here from the shortcut menu that appears.

3. If you are using a floppy disk, transfer the floppy disk to the other computer you want to work on.
4. Open and edit the files in Briefcase, as you normally would.

   If Briefcase is on a floppy disk and the other computer you are working on has Windows installed on it, you can transfer the files to the hard disk on that computer to speed up editing. Drag the files to the hard disk, and after you edit them, drag the files back to Briefcase.

   If you are working on computers that are physically connected, open and edit the files from Briefcase. You can work on the files on your portable or laptop even when it is not connected to the desktop.

CAUTION

If the other computer you are working on does not have Windows, you shouldn't transfer them to the hard disk. Open and edit them in the Briefcase on the floppy disk. Otherwise, you'll defeat the purpose of using Briefcase for keeping the files synchronized.

5. Once you are finished editing the files and you need to synchronize the files between the two computers, reconnect the computers if a cable or network connects them.

   If Briefcase was on a floppy disk, you can open Briefcase from the floppy disk or move Briefcase back to the desktop of the original computer. Then open Briefcase.

   Double-click the My Briefcase icon to open it (see Figure 13.27).

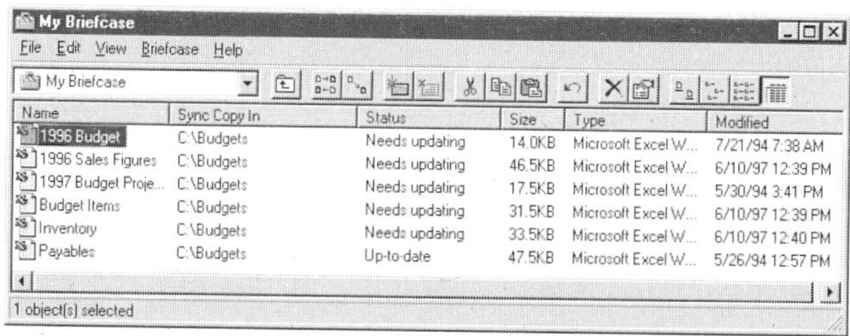

FIG. 13.27 Use Briefcase to keep files in different locations synchronized.

NOTE By default, My Briefcase displays files in the Details view. This view is much like the Details view in Explorer with two additional columns. The Sync Copy In column lists the location of the original file. The Status column indicates whether the file is up-to-date or whether it's older or newer than the original. Like the other columns in the Detail view of a folder, you can sort the list by clicking the column headings.

6. Choose Briefcase, Update All.

   or

   Select only those files you want to update and choose Briefcase, Update Selection.

   The Update My Briefcase dialog box appears, as shown in Figure 13.28.

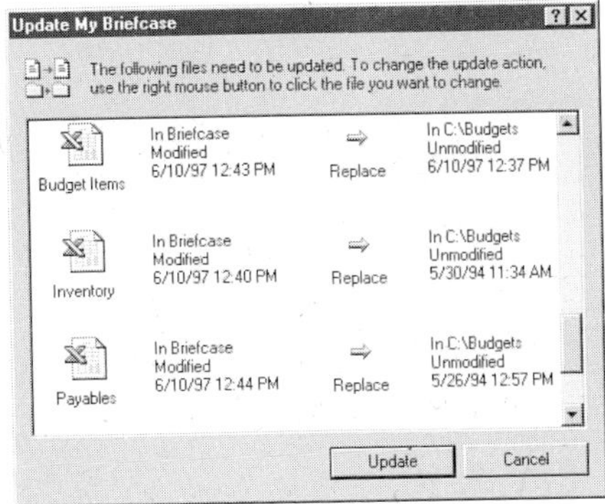

FIG. 13.28
All files that need to be updated are listed in the Update My Briefcase dialog box.

7. Check the proposed update action for each file as it is synchronized with its corresponding file on the other computer.

   The default update action is to replace the older version of the file with the newer version. If you want to change the update action for a file, right-click the file name and change the action using the pop-up menu that appears (see Figure 13.29).

8. Click the Update button to update the files. (The computers must be connected for you to update the files.)

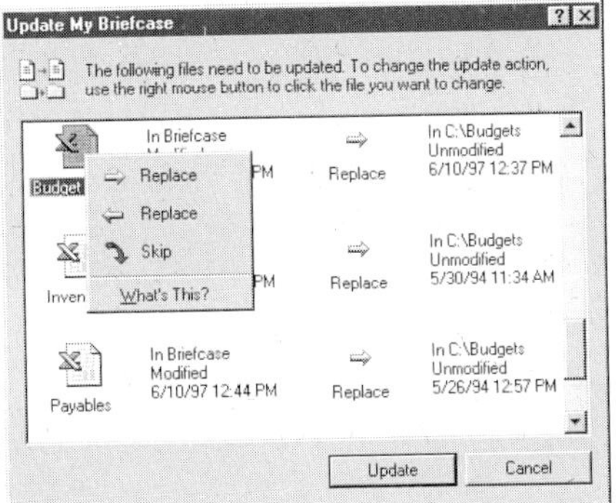

FIG. 13.29
Change the update action that will be applied to a file by right-clicking it and selecting the desired action.

Checking the Status of Briefcase Files

You can check the update status of the files in the Briefcase at any time. To check the status of a file or folder in Briefcase, open My Briefcase by double-clicking it. Examine the Status column in the window.

If you have the Briefcase files displayed in a view other than Details, you won't see this Status column. To check the status, you can choose View, Details to switch to Details view, or you can select the file and choose File, Properties; then click the Update Status tab (see Figure 13.30). The middle portion of the Update Status page shows the status of the file in the Briefcase on the left and that of the original file on the right. If the files are the same, "Up to Date" is indicated in the center. If the files are not the same, "Replace" is shown in the center along with an arrow. The arrow points to the file that is outdated and should be replaced.

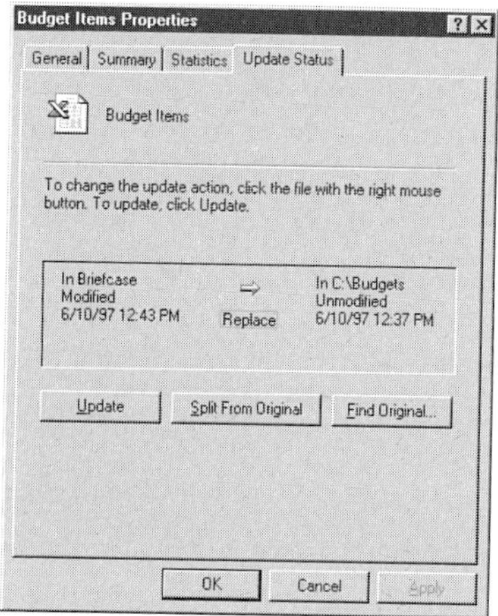

FIG. 13.30 In this figure, the copy of Budget Items in the Briefcase is newer than the copy in C:\Budgets, so Windows indicates that the copy in C:\Budgets should be replaced.

From within this Properties sheet, you can update the file (as described in the preceding section) by choosing Update. You also can prevent a file from being updated (which is discussed in the next section) by choosing Split from Original.

You can choose Find Original to open the folder with the original file, without having to work your way through the hierarchy of folders in Explorer or My Computer.

TROUBLESHOOTING

I modified the original of a file in My Briefcase, but the status still shows "Up to Date." If you have Briefcase or the folder with the original open, the status may not be updated immediately. Choose View, Refresh both in My Briefcase and in the folder containing the original file. This ensures that the status indicates any recent changes.

Preventing a File from Synchronizing

You may want to break the connection between a file in Briefcase and its original file so that when you issue the Update command, the two copies of the file are not synchronized. You may want to do this to preserve the original file or if the portable file is now a file that has changed into a document unrelated to the original.

To split a file from its original, follow these steps:

1. Open Briefcase and select the file you want to split.
2. Choose Briefcase, Split From Original. Notice that the file is now referred to as an orphan in the Status field of the Briefcase window.

You also can split a file by clicking the Split from Original button on the Update Status page of the Properties sheet.

Registering Documents So They Open Applications

When you register a file type with Windows, you tell Windows that the file type has a certain MS-DOS extension and that a particular program should be used to open the file. The most useful reason for registering a file type is that you can double-click any file of that type and the file opens by using the program you have instructed Windows to use.

TIP If you want to open a file with a program other than the program it's associated with, hold down the Shift key and right-click the file. The context menu displays an Open With command. Choose this command to see a list of programs you can use to open the file.

NOTE If you learn how to create and edit your own file types, you can customize the context menu that appears when you right-click a file.

See "Customizing the Shortcut (Right-Click) Menu," **p. 852**

If you double-click a file and the file opens in a program, then the file is registered with that program. If Windows does not have a program associated with the file you double-clicked, the Open With dialog box shown in Figure 13.31 appears.

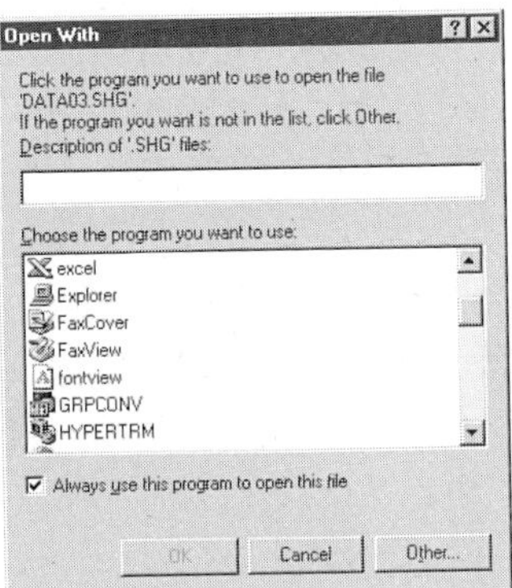

FIG. 13.31
Double-clicking an unassociated file type displays the Open With dialog box which prompts you for the program to run.

To register the file type with a program, follow these steps:

1. Type a description of the file type in the Description edit box. The description displays under the Type column in Explorer for all files with this extension.
2. Scroll through the Choose the Program list to the program you want to open the file in and click the program. If the program is not shown in the list, click the Other button and select the program's EXE file from an Open dialog box.

3. If you want to open other files of this type with the same program, check the Always Use This Program To Open This File check box.
4. Choose OK.

TROUBLESHOOTING

After double-clicking a file, it opens in a different program other than what I expected. You need to change the program to which this file type is registered. To do this, open the Options dialog box from Explorer, select the File Type sheet and edit the association for that file type.

Using Explorer with Shared Resources on a Network

If you are using Windows on a network, you can share resources with other users in your workgroup and use shared resources of other users. You can open the files in any folder that has been designated as shared by another user, and you can share any of your folders so that the files in that folder can be used by other users. You can use Explorer to designate resources on your computer as shared and to browse the shared resources in your workgroup or on your entire network.

See "User-Level versus Share-Level Security," **p. 950**

See "Sharing Workstation Drives," **p. 961**

Browsing Shared Folders

You browse a shared folder using Explorer in the same way you browse a folder on your computer.

To browse a shared folder, follow these steps:

1. Under Network Neighborhood in the left pane of Explorer, find the computer on your network where the folder you want to browse is located.

   If a plus sign (+) appears next to the name of the computer, click the plus sign (+) to display the shared resources on that computer (see Figure 13.32).

   Shared resources can include folders, entire drives, CD-ROM drives, and printers, as you can see in Figure 13.32.
2. Select the shared folder to display its contents in the right pane of Explorer, as shown in Figure 13.33.
3. To open a shared file from Explorer, double-click the file name in the right pane.

Sharing Resources on Your Computer

You can designate any folder on your computer as shared. When you share a folder, you can assign a *share name* and *password* to that folder. You also can specify what type of access users have to the shared folder. Once you have shared a folder, other users have access to the files in that folder. The computers that have the folders you want to share must be on and logged into the network.

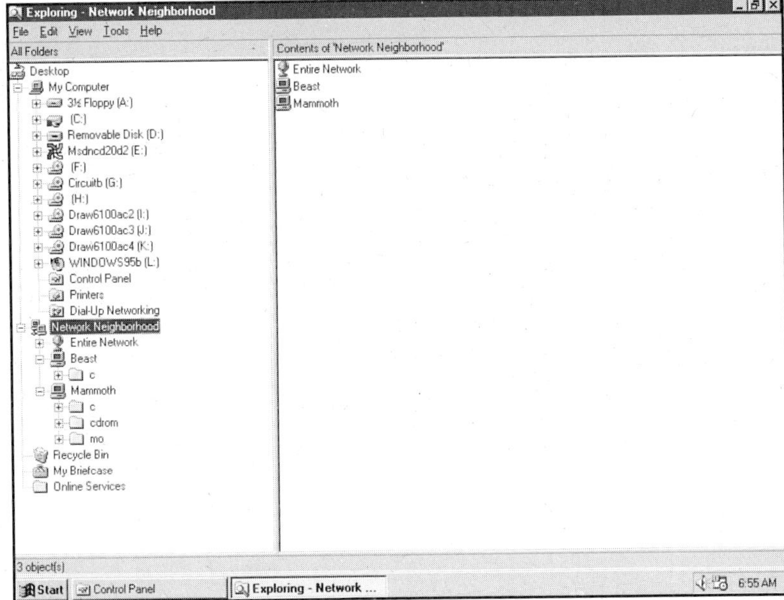

FIG. 13.32
View the shared resources on another user's computer in Explorer.

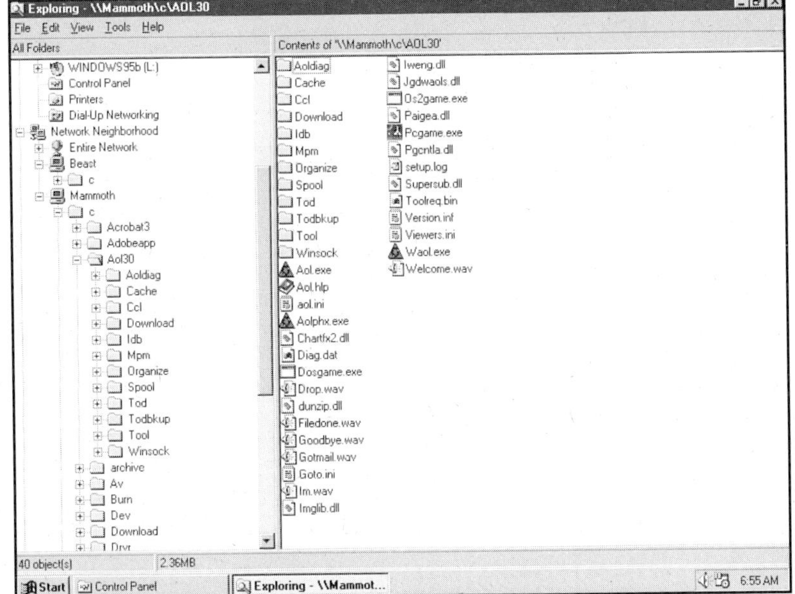

FIG. 13.33
View the contents of a shared folder by selecting it in Explorer.

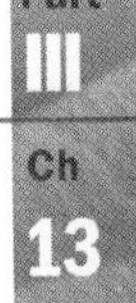

To share a folder, follow these steps:

1. In Explorer, select the folder you want to share.
2. Right-click the folder and then click Sharing to display the Sharing page on the properties sheet.
3. Select the Shared As option, as shown in Figure 13.34.

FIG. 13.34
Designate a folder as shared on the Sharing page of the properties sheet.

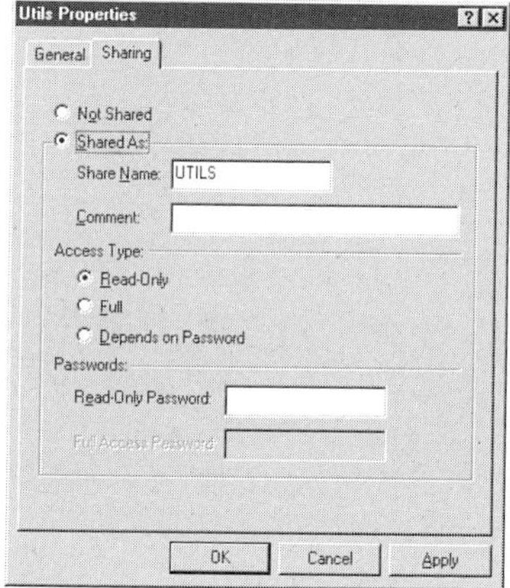

4. You can accept the default share name for the folder or type a new name in the Share Name text box.
5. Enter a comment in the Comment text box, if you want. The comment appears in the Details view of your computer when other users select it in Explorer or Network Neighborhood. Comments can help users locate shared information.
6. Select one of the Access Type options to specify the access for the shared resource.

   You can grant users two levels of access to a shared folder. If you want users to be able only to read files and run programs in a folder, select the Read-Only option. If you want users to be able to read, modify, rename, move, delete, or create files and run your programs, select the Full option. If you want the level of access to depend on which password the user enters, select the Depends on Password option.

   If you want to limit access to the files in the shared folder to certain users, assign a password to the folder and give the password to only those users. If you select the Depends on Password option, you need to enter two passwords—one for users who have read-only access to your files and one for users with full access. If you want all users to have access to your files, don't assign a password.
7. Click OK.

You can share an entire disk drive by selecting the drive and following the preceding steps.

You can quickly tell if you have designated a folder as shared by looking for a hand beneath its folder icon in Explorer or Network Neighborhood, as shown in Figure 13.35.

To change the properties of a shared folder, right-click the folder and change the share name, comment, access privileges, or password for the shared folder.

FIG. 13.35
Shared folders are indicated by a hand at the bottom of their folder icons in the Explorer.

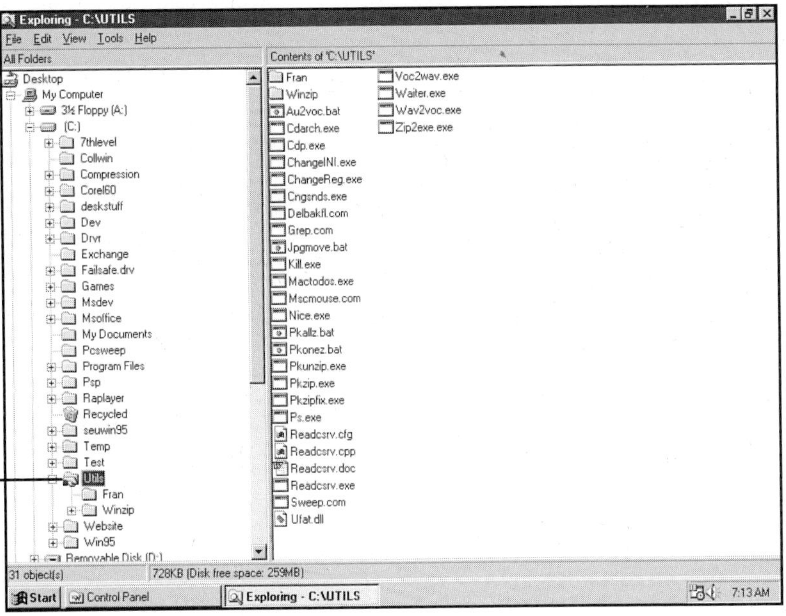

The hand shows this is a shared folder

> **CAUTION**
>
> If the Sharing tab is not visible when you open the properties sheet, you must enable file and printer sharing services.

- **See** "Creating Workgroups," **p. 947**
- **See** "File and Printer Sharing for NetWare Networks," **p. 988**
- **See** "Mapping Drives," **p. 1002**

Stop Sharing a Folder

To stop sharing a folder, follow these steps:

1. Select the folder you want to stop sharing.
2. Right-click the folder, and then click Sharing.
3. Select the Not Shared option and click OK.

Mapping a Network Drive

Windows has greatly simplified working with networks by listing all shared resources in Explorer and Network Neighborhood. You no longer have to map a drive to the shared folder.

However, if you prefer to map a drive to a shared resource on another computer, you can still do it. The mapped drive appears under My Computer, just like any other drive. This makes it easy for you to access files on another computer, while making it obvious that the files are in a drive on the network.

To map a drive to a shared folder, follow these steps:

1. Select the shared folder you want to map in Explorer or Network Neighborhood.
2. Right-click the folder and click Map Network Drive. The Map Network Drive dialog box appears, as shown in Figure 13.36.

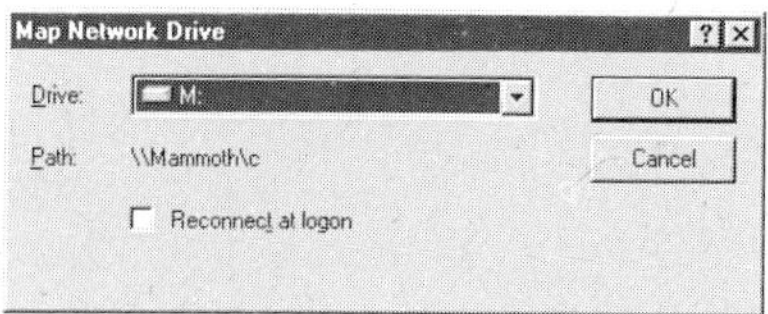

FIG. 13.36
You can map a shared folder to a drive letter in the Map Network Drive dialog box.

3. By default, Windows assigns the next available drive letter on your computer to the folder you select to map. To assign a different letter, click the drop-down arrow and select a letter from the list.
4. If you want to automatically reconnect to this shared folder at logon, select the Reconnect at Startup option.
5. Click OK.

To remove the mapping for a shared folder, click the Disconnect Network Drive button in Explorer or Network Neighborhood, select the network drive you want to disconnect, and click OK. You also can select the drive in the left pane of Explorer, click the right mouse button, and click Disconnect.

Finding a Computer on Your Network

If you know its name, you can quickly find a computer on your network by using the Find Computer command. To find a computer on your network, follow these steps:

1. Open the Start menu and choose Find, Computer.

   or

   In Explorer, choose Tools, Find, Computer.
2. Enter the name of the computer you want to find in the Named text box of the Find: Computer dialog box, as shown in Figure 13.37.
3. Click the Find Now button.

   The dialog box expands, listing the location of the specified computer if it is found on the network, as shown in Figure 13.38.

FIG. 13.37
Find a computer on your network using the Find: Computer dialog box.

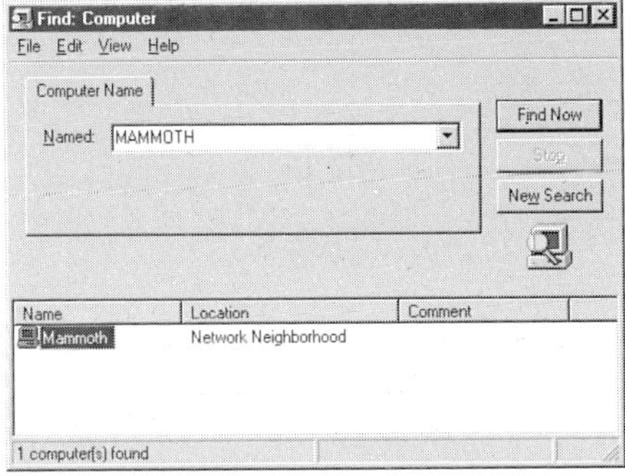

FIG. 13.38
The location of the found computer is listed at the bottom of the Find: Computer dialog box.

4. To open a browse window displaying the shared files and folders on the found computer, double-click the name of the computer at the bottom of the dialog box, or right-click the name and click Open.

See "Creating Workgroups," **p. 947**

Using Network Neighborhood to View Network Resources

When you install Windows and you are connected to a network, you see an icon for Network Neighborhood on your desktop. When you first open Network Neighborhood by double-clicking its icon on the desktop, the Network Neighborhood appears, as shown in Figure 13.39.

FIG. 13.39
The Network Neighborhood window displays all the resources on your network.

To view the shared resources on a particular computer on your network, double-click the icon for the computer to open a new window. You can continue this process to open shared folders and view the contents. Many options discussed in the sections on using Explorer earlier in this chapter are also available in Network Neighborhood. You can, for example, change the way files are displayed; add or remove the toolbar; and move, copy, and delete files.

NOTE If you have file-sharing enabled for your computer, it will appear in Network Neighborhood. However, you can't access your own computer from within Network Neighborhood. Use Explorer or My Computer to access your computer.

By default, each time you open a folder, a new window appears. This can result in a desktop full of windows and lots of confusion. If you prefer to have a single window open for browsing files, with the contents of that window changing as you open new folders, choose View, Options. Next click the Folder tab, select the Browse Folders by Using a Single Window option, and click OK.

When browsing folders using a separate window for each folder, you can hold the Ctrl key while double-clicking the subfolder and prevent a new window from opening. The original window becomes the subfolder. This can help to minimize desktop clutter.

Whether you use Explorer or Network Neighborhood to work with the files on your network depends on your style of working. Try them both and see which works better for you.

CHAPTER 14

File Management Using the Shell Integration Components

by Ron Person

In previous versions of Windows, you used the Windows Explorer or My Computer to manage files and folders. With the introduction of Internet Explorer 4 and integrated shell components, your view of any computer resource, whether local or on the World Wide Web, is the same. You use one Explorer to work with local files and resources as well as Web pages on the World Wide Web. Depending upon how you start it and what you are viewing the Explorer might look like My Computer, the Windows Explorer, or Internet Explorer.

Learn how folders expand automatically when dropping files

When you drag items from the right pane of Explorer over a folder in the left, the receiving folder automatically opens and makes subfolders visible.

See how copying files and folders is easier

Changes to the progress indicators and folder locking make copying a large number of files easier.

How to display folders and resources in a Web view

Web views can increase the information available when viewing resources and folders while making them easier to use.

How to create a default Web view for folders

Learn how to start the Web View Wizard and create FOLDER.HTM and DESKTOP.INI needed to see a folder's Web view.

See examples of simple and robust Web views

Web views can be simple instructional interfaces that help users open files. But they can also be robust fronts for complex business processes such as document management.

NOTE The following chapter was written using the developer's prerelease of integrated shell components for Windows 95. The final release of integrated shell components may differ from what is described here.

Internet Explorer 4 and integrated shell components are the future for Microsoft Windows and its applications. The next release of Windows, code-named Memphis, will incorporate the integrated shell components and its new Web way of doing things.

NOTE The following chapter assumes integrated shell components and Internet Explorer 4 have been installed. It also assumes that Windows is operating in single-click mode. To learn how to switch between single- and double-click modes, see the topic "Switching Between Single- and Double-Click Activation" in Chapter 11, "Navigating with the Shell Integration Components."

If you have not installed integrated shell components with Internet Explorer 4, you can learn how to do so by referring to "Adding or Removing Integrated Shell Components" in Chapter 11, "Navigating with the Shell Integration Components."

There Is a Single Interface to Local, Network, and Web Information

Microsoft has given Windows a single view from which you can access all computer-based information whether that information is on your local hard disk, your network, or on the World Wide Web. Whether you are looking at your local hard disk, a CD-ROM, the Control Panel, or a Web site, all the information is presented in a similar way, through the Explorer window.

Internet Explorer and My Computer are the same program used to view different information. They display their information in a window with one single pane. In contrast, the Windows Explorer is also like Internet Explorer and My Computer, but it uses a left pane to show a hierarchical view of folders and a right pane to show content.

You can prove to yourself that My Computer and Internet Explorer are the same by doing the following experiment:

1. Click My Computer. The My Computer window will appear showing either a Web View of the resources on my computer, as shown in Figure 14.1, or a standard view as shown in Figure 14.2.
2. Click in the address bar and type an URL for a Web site, such as www.microsoft.com; then press Enter. Figure 14.3 shows how the toolbar and My Computer window changes when an URL is entered. It has now become the Internet Explorer. Notice that the toolbar has lost buttons such as Up One Level and Properties. In their place are Internet Explorer buttons such as Favorites, Font, Mail, and Edit.

3. Click in the address bar and type a drive and folder, such as **C:\Windows**, and press Enter. In Figure 14.4, you can see the folder-related buttons that appear on the toolbar when viewing a hard drive.

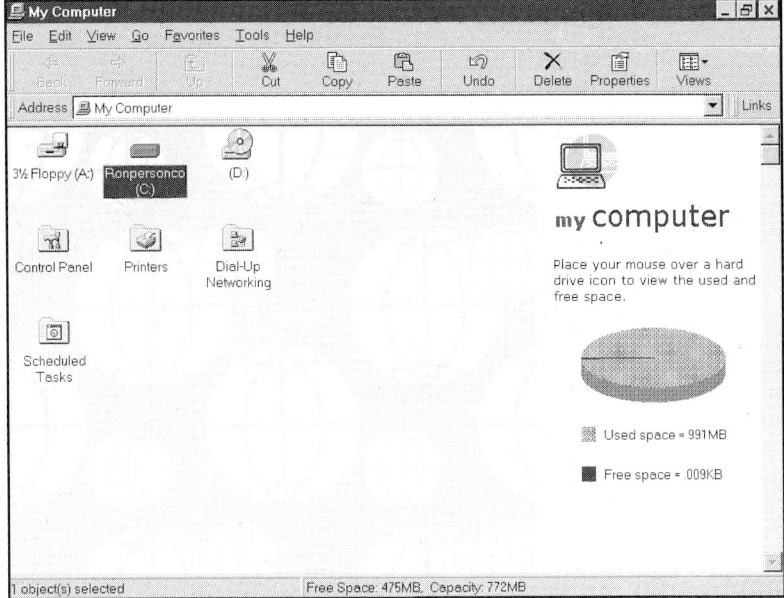

FIG. 14.1
My Computer in the Web View shows the drives and resources on the computer in a Web page-like layout.

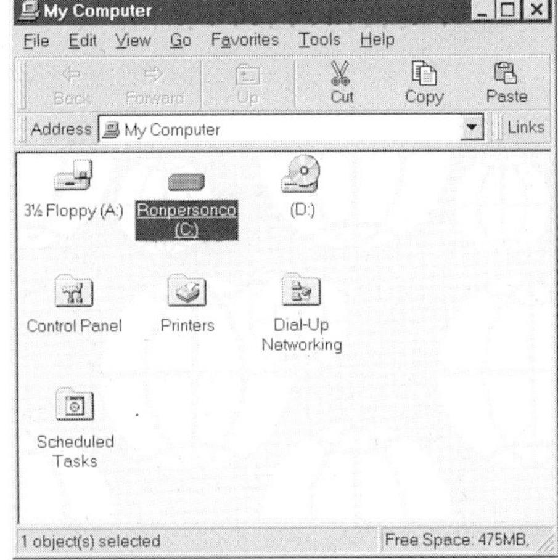

FIG. 14.2
My Computer in a standard view shows the drives and resources on the computer without the additional information from the Web page-like layout.

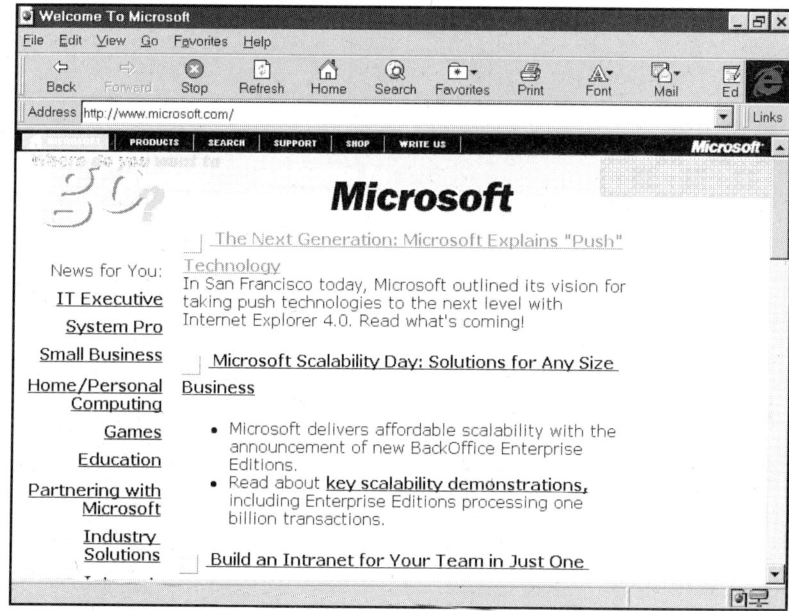

FIG. 14.3
Typing an URL into the Address bar and pressing Enter changes My Computer into Internet Explorer 4.

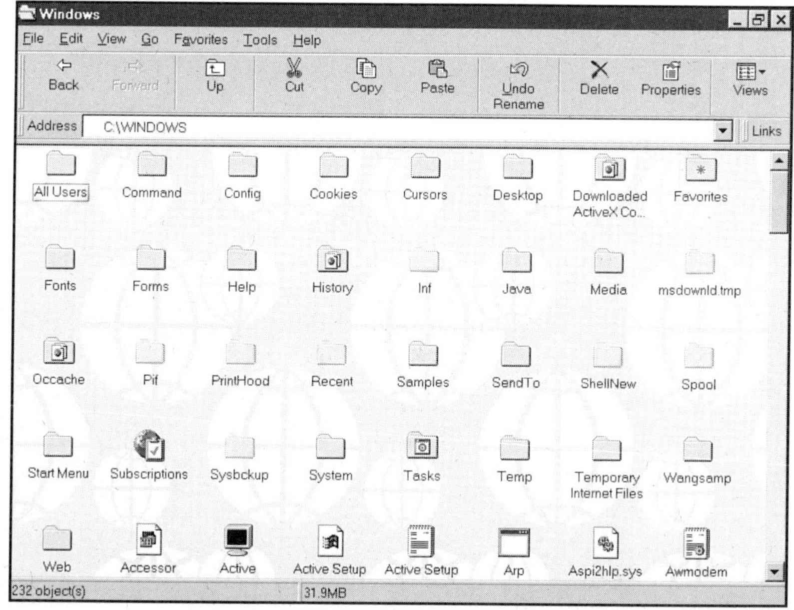

FIG. 14.4
Selecting a drive, folder, or Web site from the Address list changes the display to match the resource being viewed.

Folders Expand Automatically When Dropping Files

Prior to integrated shell components, when you wanted to copy or move files in the Windows Explorer, you had to expand folders until you exposed the subfolder into which you want to move or copy a file. Often this added extra steps to moving or copying files.

With integrated shell components installed, moving and copy files into subfolders becomes much easier. Integrated shell components makes this easier by automatically expanding folders while you are moving or copying files.

To see automatically expanding folders work, select a file in Windows Explorer; then drag the file over a closed folder that contains subfolders. A folder that contains subfolders displays a + sign to the left. Move the pointer over the folder you want to receive the file and pause. Continue holding down the mouse button. The folder will expand to show all of its subfolders. At that point, you can drop the file into a subfolder or pause over other folders you want to expand.

Copying Files and Folders Enhanced

When you copy files, a progress indicator shows the relative length of time for the copy to be completed. In earlier versions of Windows, when you copied a selection containing multiple files, the progress indicator displayed the progress for each file. This gave you no indication of the length of time it would take to copy all the files you selected. With integrated shell components, the progress indicator has been improved to show the progress for copying all the files in the selection.

Another improvement made by integrated shell components is that you can work in the folder receiving copied files. For example, if you are copying a large selection of files into a folder named Budgets, you can open the Budgets folder and activate a worksheet in it even while copying continues.

Viewing Files and Folders with Web Views

Most Windows users are familiar with the four views in My Computer or Windows Explorer that display files and folders: Large Icons, Small Icons, List, and Details. In keeping with Microsoft's push to make Windows 95 more Web-centric, a new view has been added, Web view.

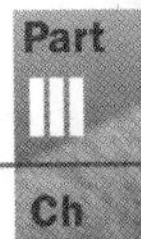

When you first see a Web view, it appears to be nothing more than yet another way to view files and folders. It doesn't appear to have any advantages. Figure 14.5 shows the default Web view of a folder containing files and folders.

The real power of Web views becomes apparent when you understand that the view in the right pane is created from an HTML (Web) file stored in the folder you are viewing. That HTML file can be any HTML file, including one you create. The files and folders in the right pane do not even need to appear.

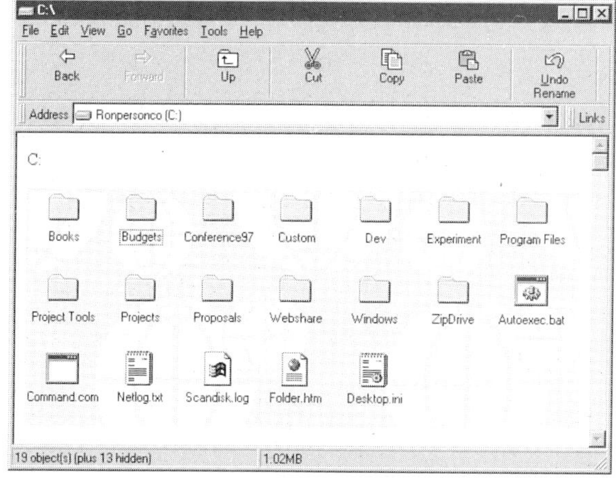

FIG. 14.5
The default view of a newly created Web view shows little advantage over existing views in My Computer or Windows Explorer.

You can create your own Web view with an HTML file that contains text, graphics, objects, and links to applications, documents, templates, or Web sites. Click a link and the application, document, or Web site opens. To see examples of custom Web views designed to meet specific user needs, see "Sample Custom Web Views" later in this chapter.

Web views appear in My Computer or Windows Explorer. Windows comes with three different Web views. The Web view for a disk drive and for the Control Panel window are built in and will display as soon as Web view is enabled. To see a Web view of a folder, you must have the Web view enabled, and there must be a DESKTOP.INI and FOLDER.HTM file for the folder you are viewing. A DESKTOP.INI and FOLDER.HTM file are created in a folder when you run the Web View Wizard as described in "Running the Web View Wizard" found in this chapter.

You can customize any folder's Web view by using any HTML editor to modify the FOLDER.HTM for that folder. (Internet Explorer 4 Internet Suite comes with a free copy of FrontPage Express, an excellent HTML editor.) In fact, any HTML file can be used in the Web view for a resource or folder. FOLDER.HTM and DESKTOP.INI are created initially by running the Web View Wizard.

See "Using FrontPage Express," **p. 612**

See "Creating Advanced Custom Web Views," **p. 376**

Displaying the Graphical and HTML Background

Before you can see the Web View command or a Web view of a folder or resource, you must choose to display a graphical or HTML background. To switch from the standard Windows background to a graphical or HTML background, follow these steps:

1. Open My Computer or the Windows Explorer.
2. Click View, Options, and select the View tab.
3. Click the Display Background Graphics and Custom HTML option to select it. You can have either the Single-Click or Double-Click option selected.
4. Click OK.

   The background in Windows Explorer's right-pane and the full background in My Computer's window will display a graphical background like that shown in Figure 14.6.

It's very easy to change the graphic used as a background. See the section later in this chapter titled "Changing the Predefined Web View Graphics and HTML Backgrounds."

Enabling the graphical or HTML background affects both My Computer and the Windows Explorer. With the graphical background displayed, you still see folders and resources as you would in a standard Windows 95 view. In order to see a Web view or the HTML background, you must turn on the Web view.

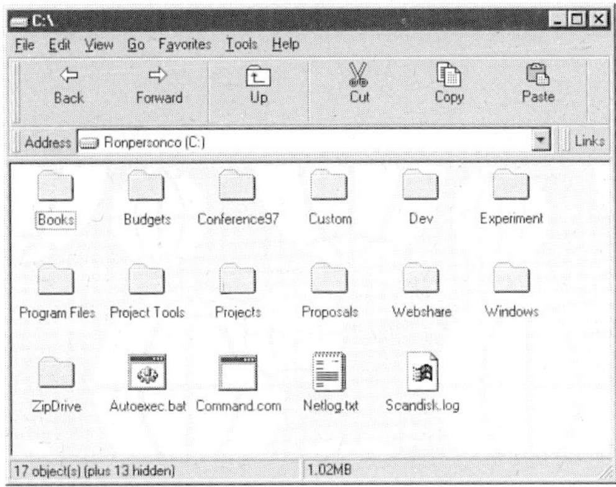

FIG. 14.6
You must display the graphical and HTML background before Web view is available.

Turning Web View On or Off

Once you have turned on the graphical or HTML background as described in "Displaying the Graphical and HTML Background," a new menu item appears under the View menu.

If the folder is configured for a Web view, then the Web View menu item appears. The Web View menu item turns Web view on or off. When the Web view is on, there is a check mark next to the Web View menu item.

If the folder has not been configured for a Web view, the Customize This Folder menu item appears under the View menu. This command will help you configure a folder for a Web view. It is described later in the topic titled, "Running the Web View Wizard," in this chapter.

To immediately see a Web view, select My Computer or Control Panel in the left pane of the Windows Explorer. These resources can display a Web view by default. You cannot display a Web view of a folder until you have created an HTML and DESKTOP.INI file for that folder.

TROUBLESHOOTING

There is no Web View menu item under the View menu. You must enable the graphical and HTML background option before the Web View menu item will appear. See "Displaying the Graphical and HTML Background" section to learn how to do this. If the graphical and HTML background is enabled and there is no Web View menu item, then there is no HTML file and DESKTOP.INI file for that folder. See the "Creating Simple Custom Web Views" to learn how to create the HTML and DESKTOP.INI files needed to show the Web view. By default, the Web View is normally available if you display the Control Panel or My Computer.

Viewing Default Web Views: Control Panel, My Computer, and Folder

Windows 95 with Internet Explorer 4 comes with three default Web views. Two of these Web views are available as soon as you enable Web view: Control Panel and My Computer. To see a Web view of My Computer in the My Computer window, enable Web view; then select My Computer in the Address bar. The Web view looks like Figure 14.7 in My Computer.

FIG. 14.7
An advantage to the default My Computer view is your ability to check disk drive usage.

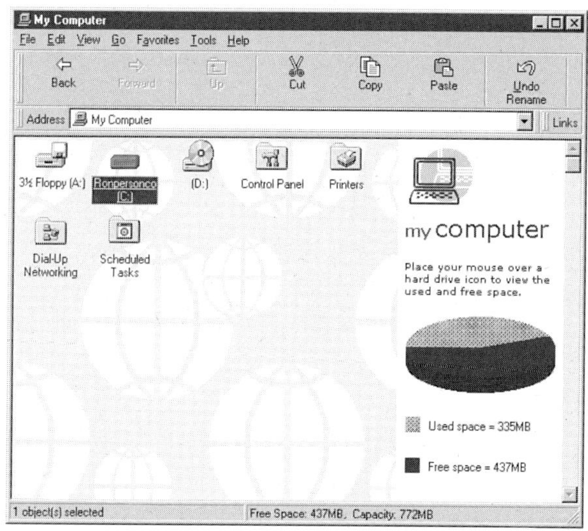

The other default Web view, Control Panel, is also visible as soon as you enable Web view. Figure 14.8 shows a Web view of the Control Panel displaying in the right pane of Windows Explorer. Notice that this Web view displays instructions about the icon under the pointer. The right side of the right pane even includes a button that connects you to the Microsoft Technical Support page on the Web.

The third default view appears when viewing folders with the Web view enabled. This view does not occur automatically. You must create an HTML and DESKTOP.INI file in the folder before you can see a change of appearance. It is very easy to create a default Web view for a folder. In fact, just opening and closing the Web View Wizard in a folder will create these files and enable you to see a folder's Web view. The default Web view created by a blank HTML file from the Web View Wizard is shown in Figure 14.9.

▶ **See** "Creating Simple Custom Web Views," **p. 373**

Sample Custom Web Views

When you initially see a custom view, it's like looking at a blank canvas. What to do? What to do? It's hard to even imagine the possibilities. Once you begin to understand that a Web view can have all the potential of a Web page, your mind begins to open to hundreds of productive opportunities. All the elements you see on a Web page can be included in your folder's Web views: text, graphics, animated graphics, video, audio, VBScript, Java Script, ActiveX controls, Java applets, and links that open documents or connect you to Web sites.

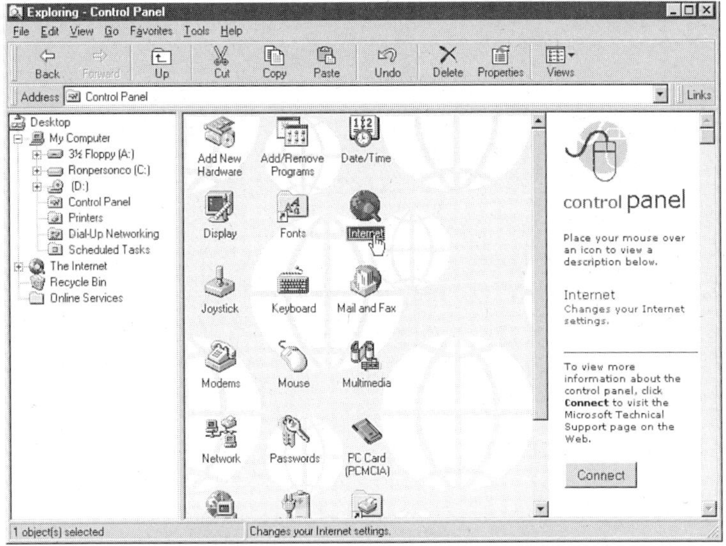

FIG. 14.8
The default Control Panel view displays the icons in the control panel and instructions.

FIG. 14.9
Completing the Web View Wizard creates the files necessary to display a folder's Web view.

One thing to keep in mind as you create custom Web views is that creating custom HTML pages to build these Web views takes a lot more work and skill than adding shortcut icons to your desktop. While a simple Web view is not much work, a truly robust Web view might involve graphic art, technical documentation, and programming.

You don't need to be overwhelmed if you want to create a Web view. You can make one by simply running the Web View Wizard and accepting the default page it creates. Your next step might be to add text that explains what specific files and folders do. After experimenting with FrontPage Express, the free HTML editor, or FrontPage 97, you can modify the FOLDER.HTM file created by Web View Wizard to include text, graphics, and hyperlinks to files you want to open. You only need programming if you want to create a page that involves decision making or file manipulation. The following subsections show some samples and ideas for Web views you can create.

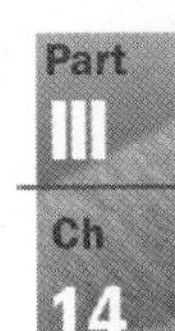

Providing Simple Instructions for Files and Folders The Web view in Figure 14.10 illustrates how adding a little text to a Web view can decrease the confusion for new users about which files to open. In this example, the Web View Wizard was used to create the initial FOLDER.HTM that showed only the "Projects" title and the folder contents. The default HTML editor was then used to add text and assign formats to the lines of text.

The list of file names with indented description was created in FrontPage Express on the FOLDER.HTM file by moving the insertion point to a new line and choosing the Defined Term style. The file name was then typed. Pressing Enter at the end of the file name moves the insertion point to the next line and formats that line with the Definition style, which is indented. The definition for the file was then typed. Each time you press Enter the styles alternate between Defined Term and the indented Definition style. Return to a normal style by selecting the Normal style. After all the text was typed, bold and font sizes were applied. The modified FOLDER.HTM file was then saved back to the folder in which it had been created.

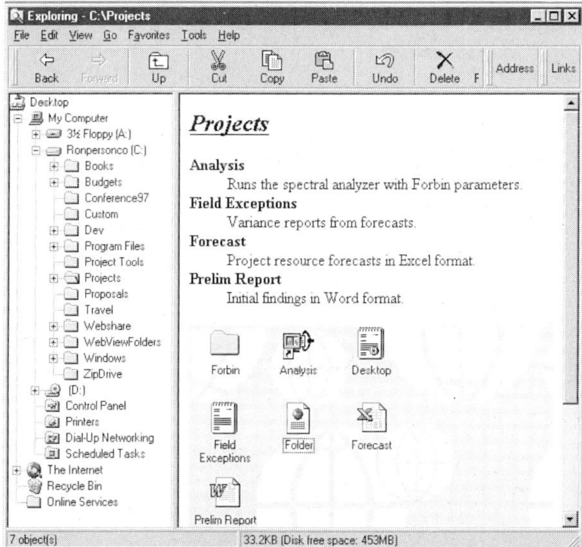

FIG. 14.10
Just adding text to a Web view can make folders and files more understandable.

Instructions Combined with Scrolling File Icons If you need to give users an explanation of files, yet give them access to a lot of files in an organized layout, you might use a Web view like the one shown in Figure 14.11. A table was inserted into FOLDER.HTM with text in the left column and folder contents in the right. The display is in a Web View of My Computer with View, Large Icons selected and icons arranged by name.

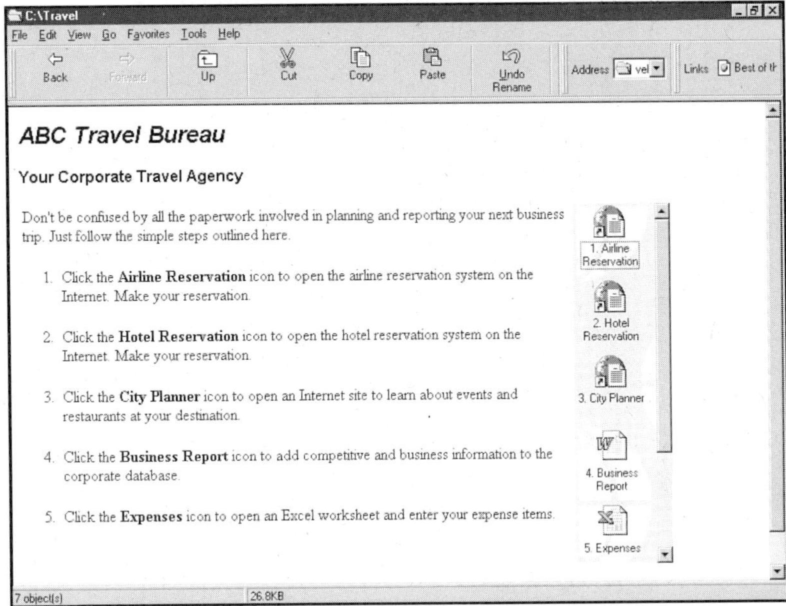

FIG. 14.11
Everyone hates to plan for trips and fill out the expense reports when they return, but a folder with this Web view might make it a little less painful.

In this example, the first two lines were typed as normal text. The list of text explanations and the scrolling window of files were created by inserting a table in FOLDER.HTM that had two columns and one row. All the text was typed in the left cell. The WebView Folder component, the object that displays the folder contents, was dragged and dropped into the cell on the right. The WebView Folder component must be resized so that it fits in the cell or it will not display. In this example, the line:

{position absolute left=0 width=100 top=250 height=360}

was inserted directly after the "<object" tag that opened the WebView Folder component.

In addition to corporate documents related to travel, a folder for business travelers might contain links to Web sites having airline guides, hotel reservations, exchange rates, travel plans, city guides, and more.

Installing Software Installing software is always a little confusing for novices. They need instructions about how to run the Add/Remove Software program and which configurations to choose. You might be able to make it easier for them by creating a FOLDER.HTM that resides in the root directory of the installation disk. Figure 14.12 shows a simple installation Web view that is a little friendlier to beginners. You can put this HTML file and its DESKTOP.INI in the root directory of a floppy disk so that this view appears when the user displays the Web view.

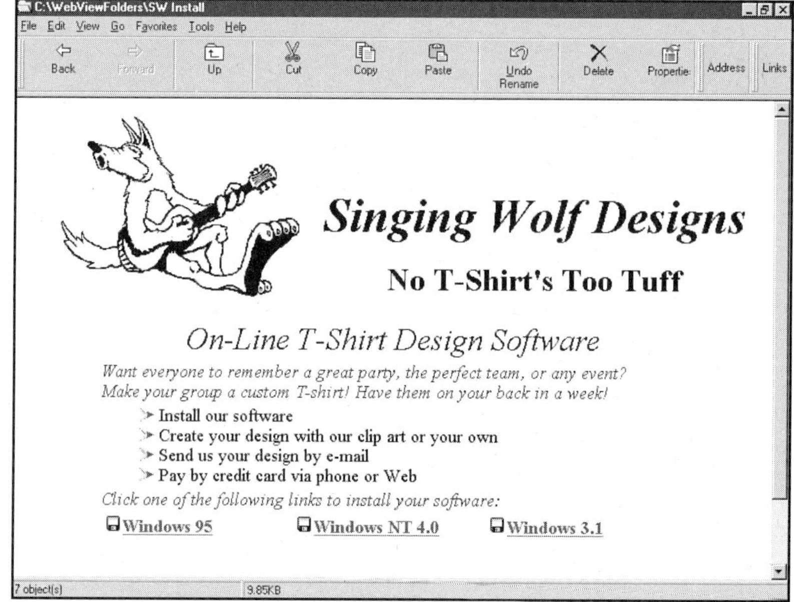

FIG. 14.12 Installing software is always confusing for novices. FOLDER.HTM could make installation easier with hyperlinks to the appropriate EXE files.

The links at the bottom of the Web view are to the EXE files that install each of the different hardware configurations. Clicking a hyperlink to a file will open a registered document or run an application. You might also consider having a link to your Web site or to your e-mail address. Scripts or components in the FOLDER.HTM could display a table showing the software system requirements and the configuration of the current system.

TIP If you do not want users to have access to files through the Web view, delete the Folder component from the HTML page created by the Web View Wizard. As the examples shown here demonstrate, you can use hyperlinks to open specific files.

Creating a Web View with Links to Key Documents and Resources The Web view shown in Figure 14.13 makes project management easier by displaying in a single view all the links to key files, project statistics, and information about the key people. The Search WebBot makes it easy to find HTML and Office 97 information on the company intranet. Across the bottom of the page are hyperlinks that open the group scheduling program, e-mail, and NetMeeting, for collaborative work.

This Web view was created using a three-column table to hold the links to files, project statistics, and people's files. The links are just hyperlinks to document files inserted with FrontPage Express or FrontPage. The Search area is created by using a Search WebBot inserted with FrontPage 97. The Search WebBot runs on any intranet or Internet site that supports FrontPage 97 extensions.

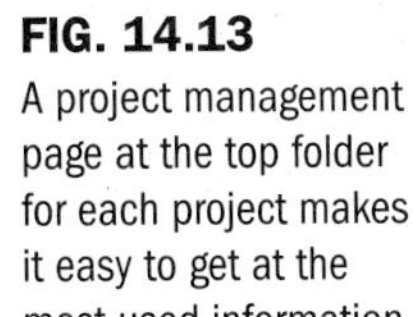

FIG. 14.13
A project management page at the top folder for each project makes it easy to get at the most used information.

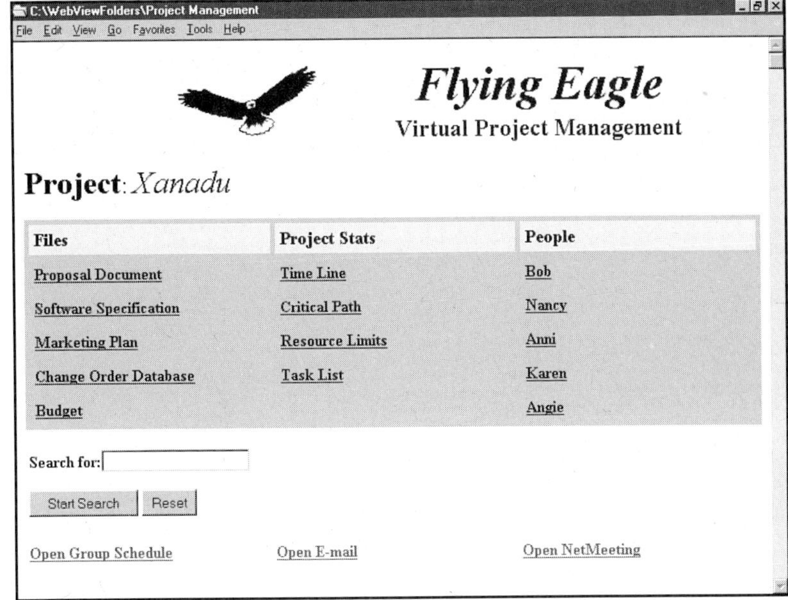

Personal Web View for Frequently Used Resources Create a personalized Web view for your computer that displays the documents, Web links, and other resources that you use most frequently. The Web view in Figure 14.14 is a simple table with a graphic and large fonts at the top. The hyperlinks have been formatted with a Bullet style so they stand out. The two buttons at the bottom are links to a personalized Web news service and to Microsoft Bookshelf. The buttons are free graphics available at www.microsoft.com/gallery.

Creating Simple Custom Web Views

Web views of folders can be very simple involving nothing more than a few lines of explanatory text in addition to the files and folders. Or they can be complex HTML pages involving all the elements of Web design including WebBots, VBScript, Java Script, Visual Basic or Java components, and Dynamic HTML.

Understanding FOLDER.HTM and DESKTOP.INI Before Web views will appear in a folder, the folder must contain two files, DESKTOP.INI and an HTML file that DESKTOP.INI points to. The default DESKTOP.INI points to the file FOLDER.HTM that is created when you first customize a folder's Web view with the Web View Wizard.

The FOLDER.HTM that Web View Wizard initially creates contains a folder component that displays the folders and files in the Web view. The DESKTOP.INI file contains information about this folder component as well as a pointer that specifies which HTML file should be used for the Web view.

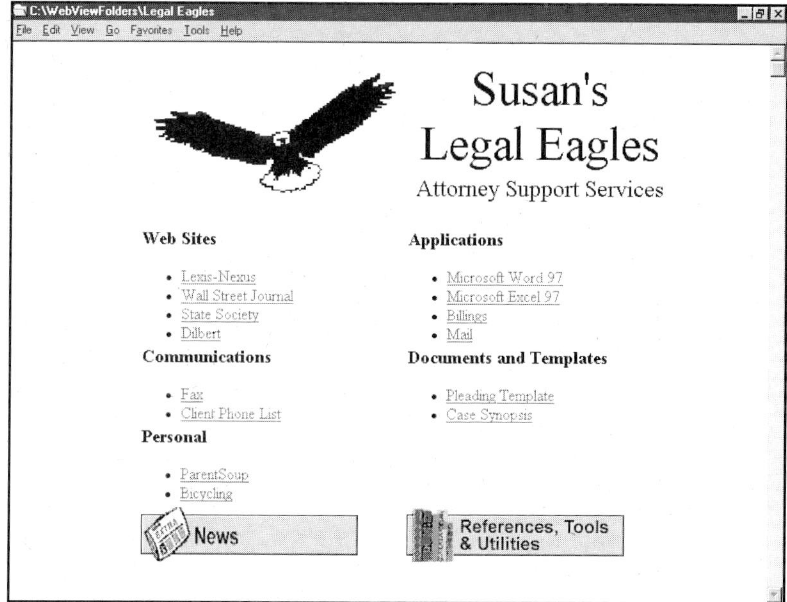

FIG. 14.14 Creating a simple Web view with your most frequently used resources for home or small office.

Running the Web View Wizard To run the Web View Wizard and create the FOLDER.HTM and DESKTOP.INI files, follow these steps:

1. Enable graphical and HTML backgrounds as described in "Displaying the Graphical and HTML Background."
2. Open the folder in which you want to create a Web view.
3. Click View, Customize This Folder or right-click in the folder's view; then click Customize This Folder. The first window of the Web View Wizard appears as shown in Figure 14.15.

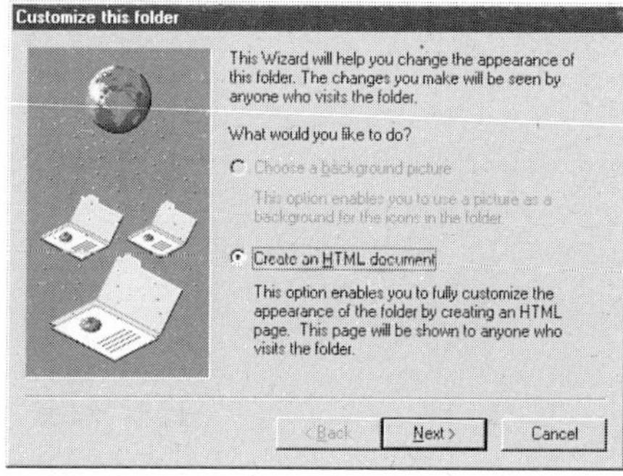

FIG. 14.15 Use the Web View Wizard to create FOLDER.HTM and DESKTOP.INI.

4. Click the Create an HTML Document option; then click Next.

5. The second window, shown in Figure 14.16, explains that an HTML editor will be started. You should follow these steps:
   1. Edit the HTML file to include text and graphics you want.
   2. Save it using the given file name.
   3. Close the HTML editor.

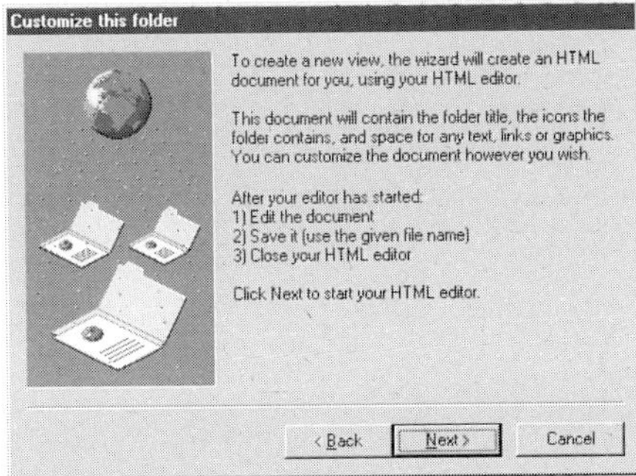

FIG. 14.16
The Web View Wizard will open your HTML editor or Notepad so you can edit the HTML file.

6. Click Next and edit the HTML file being used as a Web view. Chapter 22, "Using FrontPage Express and IE 4 Components" gives an introductory description of how to use the FrontPage Express HTML editor.
7. Save the HTML file with the name proposed by the wizard, and then close the HTML editor. The final Web View Wizard window, shown in Figure 14.17, will display a list of changes you have made. In the figure, the default FOLDER.HTM has been accepted with no changes.

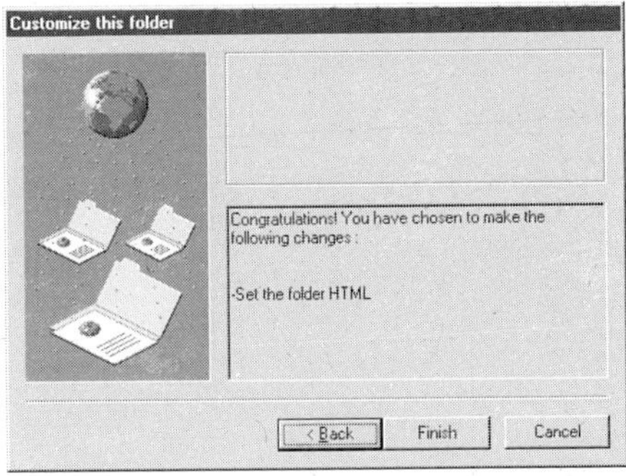

FIG. 14.17
The Web View Wizard summarizes changes you have made to the HTML file.

8. Click Finish.

   If you have created an unmodified FOLDER.HTM file, then your Web view for the folder will appear when viewed through a My Computer window.

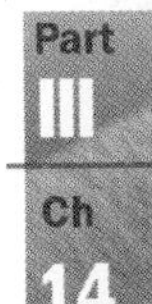

You can edit the HTML files that define Web views using any HTML editor. DESKTOP.INI is easily edited using Notepad.

Put Notepad, the text editor, on the Send To menu as described in "Customizing the Send To Menu" in Chapter 31. Having Notepad on the Send To menu enables you to edit an INI file by right-clicking the file and then choosing Send To, Notepad.

Quickly edit an HTML file by right-clicking on the file in My Computer or Windows Explorer, then choosing Edit.

Creating Advanced Custom Web Views

Once the DESKTOP.INI and FOLDER.HTM have been created by the wizard, you can modify them manually. Modifying these files manually enables you to resize or move the objects in a Web view and move Web views to other folders. You also can add WebBots, ActiveX components, Java applets, scripting, Dynamic HTML, and other elements that comprise HTML pages.

As you customize these two files, remember that FOLDER.HTM can be any HTML file. DESKTOP.INI must be in the folder where the Web view will display. It contains information describing any objects such as WebBots or folder components contained on the HTML page. It also contains a reference to the HTML file that will be displayed as the Web view.

Figure 14.18 shows a default DESKTOP.INI file that has been created with the Web View wizard. The PersistFile line points to the HTML file that will display in the Web view. Edit this line to point to any HTML file you want to appear as the Web view.

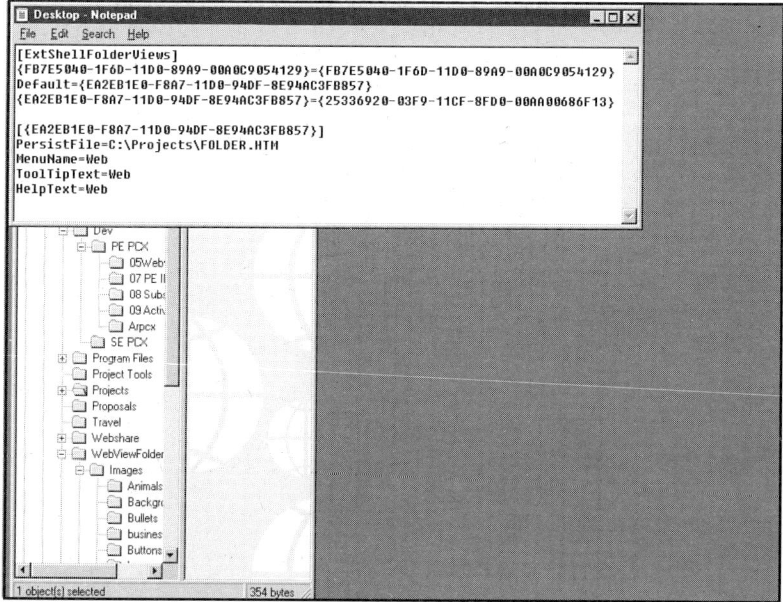

FIG. 14.18
DESKTOP.INI describes the HTML file used for the folder containing DESKTOP.INI.

Changing the Predefined Web View Graphics and HTML Backgrounds In the "Displaying the Graphical and HTML Background" section, you learned how to display a background graphic and custom HTML file that is the default for all Web views. The files used for these defaults are stored in the Windows\Web folder. Modifying the appropriate files in this folder changes the default graphic and HTML backgrounds.

CAUTION

Before changing any of the default HTML files or graphics stored in Windows\Web, make a backup of these files. This will enable you to restore Web views that work, in case your modifications do not work properly.

Some of the default files you can modify are:

Control Panel background	CONTROLP.HTM
Desktop background	DESKTOP.HTM
My Computer background	MYCOMP.HTM
My Computer graphic	MYCOMP.GIF
Watermark behind default Web views	WMARK.GIF
Folders default background and positioning for the Folder object	USEREXP.HTM

Moving Web Views to Another Location

You can create an HTML file and its corresponding DESKTOP.INI file in one folder and move them to another folder. In fact, only the DESKTOP.INI file needs to be in the folder which will display the view. If the HTML file contains a Folder component, to display files and folders, the Web view will display the files and folders for the folder containing the DESKTOP.INI file. To do this, the PersistFile line in DESKTOP.INI must give the pathname to the HTML file that will be used as the Web view.

If you want to move or copy the HTML and DESKTOP.INI files to other folders without regard for path references, then use a relative path reference to describe the location of the HTML file in the PersistFile line. For example,

```
PersistFile=MYVIEW.HTM
```

will refer to the MYVIEW.HTM file located in the same folder as DESKTOP.INI. As long as you copy the two files together into a folder, they will work. ●

CHAPTER 15

Working with Disks and Disk Drives

by Ron Person with Jerry Cox

Before you can start organizing files on a computer, you need to learn how to work with and maintain your floppy disks and hard disks. For example, before you put data on a floppy disk, you usually have to format it to get it ready to receive data. If you want, you can also name your drives to make them easier to identify. Periodically, you also may need to repartition and reformat your hard drive.

Windows 95 comes with several disk utilities that are invaluable for helping you maintain your hard drives and floppy disks and for optimizing the performance of your system. ScanDisk is a utility for checking your disks for file errors and physical damage. Use the Disk Defragmenter to optimize the storage of files on your hard disk, which can noticeably improve file access. The System Monitor is a utility for monitoring the performance of your computer, which can help you fine-tune your system. And if you are running out of hard disk space, try using DriveSpace, the disk compression utility that comes with Windows 95, to squeeze more capacity out of your hard disk.

The Windows 95 file system

Look here for a basic overview of how files are stored on your hard disk.

Format and partition disks

Learn how to prepare your hard disks and diskettes for receiving files.

Compressing your hard disk

Turn to this section to find out how to use the DriveSpace utility to increase the storage capacity of your hard disks.

Optimize the performance of your hard disk

Learn how to use Disk Defragmenter to optimize the storage of files on your hard disk and ScanDisk to check for and repair disk errors.

Monitor your system's performance

If you like fine-tuning your system, look here to find out about the System Monitor.

If you have installed Microsoft Plus! on your system, you have access to DriveSpace 3, an enhanced disk compression utility, and Compression Agent, a companion utility to DriveSpace 3 that provides even higher levels of disk compression. Another Microsoft Plus! add-on is the System Agent, a tool for scheduling all of your disk utilities to run automatically when you are not using your system. This is invaluable for doing routine maintenance on your system and keeping it in top running form.

Understanding What Your Disk Drive Does

You use *magnetic storage* to store applications and data for long periods of time or when the computer is turned off. Magnetic-storage media include *floppy disks* and *hard disks*. Floppy disks are removable and don't contain much space. Hard disks are internal to the computer and have much larger amounts of space.

The hard disk you store your data and programs on does not have to reside in the computer at your desk. If you are connected to a network, you can access information stored on the hard disk in the *file server*, the computer that serves the *clients* on the network. When you start an application or open a data file, the computer places a *copy* of the information stored in magnetic storage (on floppy disks or a hard disk) into electronic memory (RAM). If power is lost, the magnetic copy still is available.

See "Understanding Files and Folders," **p. 312**

You save the work you do in your programs in magnetic *files*, which are stored on a floppy disk or hard disk. Over time, you may have hundreds or even thousands of files. Searching for a specific file among the thousands of files can be very time-consuming.

See "Using Explorer with Shared Resources on a Network," **p. 354**

Large computers and network file servers have multiple hard disks, each disk with its own drive letter. Figure 15.1 shows a hard disk drive (see the icon for drives C), a floppy disk drive (see the icon for drive A), a removable disk drive (drive E), and a CD-ROM drive (drive F). Each disk acts as a separate filing cabinet and can have its own unique folder organization.

NOTE Some drives may have more than one letter, depending on the controller versus drive size. If the drive is larger than the controller or BIOS can read, it can be partitioned as two drives. It is still only one piece of hardware, but software sees it as two drives. It also is possible for a drive to have more than one letter if it is compressed. In this case, the software doing the compression addresses the drive with one letter, and all other software accesses it using another drive letter, which is controlled by the compression software.

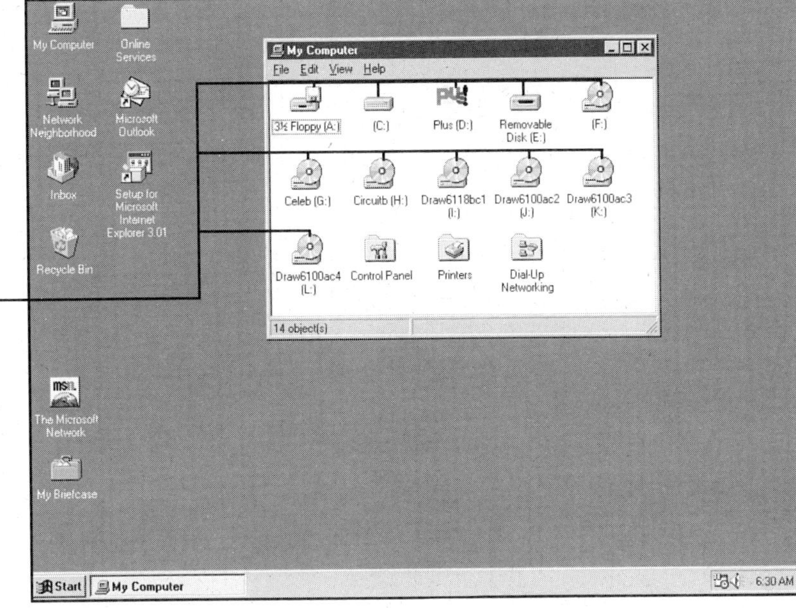

FIG. 15.1
The My Computer window displays all the resources on your computer, including all the floppy disk drives and hard drives.

Drive icons

The FAT32 File System

The FAT file system is the system used by DOS to keep track of the storage of files on disks. Files are stored in units called *clusters*, which in turn are made up of sectors. Each sector is 512 bytes, but the size of a cluster varies, depending on the size of the hard disk. The FAT or File Allocation Table is used to keep track of which clusters belong to which files. Thus, although a file may be made up of many clusters scattered across your hard disk, the FAT table keeps track of the clusters so your applications will "see" the clusters as one file.

The original version of Windows 95, as well as DOS, uses a file system called FAT16, a 16-bit file system. There are two major drawbacks to the FAT16 file system in this age of larger and larger hard disks. First, FAT16 can only support single disk volumes (partitions) of up to 2G. With larger hard disks, you are forced to partition your drive into 2G or smaller volumes. Second, the cluster size increases dramatically as you increase partition size. A 2G partition, for example, uses 32K clusters, which means a small file, such as a shortcut on your desktop that is typically around 1K in size, will use 32K of disk space. This results in very inefficient use of hard disk space, especially if there are many small files on your hard disk. This storage waste is called *slack*. The smaller the cluster size, the less *slack* there is.

Microsoft has introduced a new file system called FAT32 with the Windows 95 OEM Service Release 2 (OSR2). The FAT32 file system supports single disk volumes (partitions) up to 2 terabytes in size and uses much smaller clusters. For partitions up to 8G, FAT32 uses 4K clusters, resulting in much more efficient file storage.

A drawback to the FAT32 file system is that FAT32 disks can only be accessed by the OSR2 version of Windows 95. FAT32 partitions are not recognized by MS-DOS, Windows 3.x or the original release of Windows 95. At this time, Windows NT is also unable to access a FAT32 disk, although Microsoft states that they are still determining if Windows NT will support FAT32 in the future. The upshot of this limitation is that you cannot dual-boot from a FAT32 disk using any of these operating systems.

For more information on how to obtain OSR2 and install FAT32 on your computer, see Chapter 2, "Installing Windows."

The Windows 95 File System

A major architectural change in Windows 95 is the installable file system, which has a new 32-bit, protected-mode Virtual File Allocation Table file system (VFAT) as its primary file system. With the installable file system, Windows 95 can manage multiple files systems, which makes it easy to connect to network computers using different file systems, such as HPFS (OS/2's file system) and NTFS (the Windows NT file system). Note that Windows 95 will not handle HPFU and NTFS on a local hard drive.

VFAT, the primary file system in Windows 95, was actually an optional file system introduced in Windows for Workgroups 3.1. VFAT in Windows 95 has been improved and has many advantages over the original FAT file system used in MS-DOS:

- Faster file accessing and improved multitasking because of the 32-bit, protected-mode data path.
- Improved, dynamic, protected-mode disk caching (VCACHE) for improved performance and stability. Also works with CD-ROMs and network drives.
- No conventional memory used by disk cache driver (VCACHE versus older SmartDrive).
- Cache memory is allocated dynamically, based on available free memory and read/write activity.
- Support for long file names (up to 255 characters).
- Capability to read and write long file names supported by other file systems, such as NTFS and HPFS.
- Support for FAT partitions and short (8.3) file names for backward compatibility.

Formatting Disks

You usually cannot use new disks until you format them (but some disks come already formatted). *Formatting* prepares disks for use on a computer. Formatting is similar to preparing a blank book for use by writing in page numbers and creating a blank table of contents. If a disk contains data, formatting it completely erases all existing data. Part of the process of formatting is checking for bad areas on the disk's magnetic surface. All bad areas found are identified so that data is not recorded in these areas.

The 32-bit multitasking environment in Windows 95 makes it possible to format disks in the background as you go about your work in other applications. This capability is a real time-saver.

Formatting a Floppy Disk

If you attempt to open an unformatted floppy disk in My Computer or Windows Explorer, you will be asked if you want to format the disk. The Format dialog box immediately displays.

To format a floppy disk, follow these steps:

1. Insert the floppy disk to be formatted in the disk drive.
2. Right-click the icon for the drive in a folder window or in the Windows Explorer, and then choose Format. The Format dialog box appears (see Figure 15.2).

   In a folder window, you also can select the drive icon and choose File, Format.

NOTE If you are working in the Windows Explorer, there is no File, Format command; instead, right-click a floppy disk drive icon in the left pane of the Explorer, and select Format from the shortcut menu.

To bypass having to open the Explorer or My Computer, create a shortcut to your floppy disk drive on the desktop. To format a floppy disk, right-click the disk icon, and choose Format from the shortcut menu. You also can copy a floppy disk using the Copy Disk command on the shortcut menu.

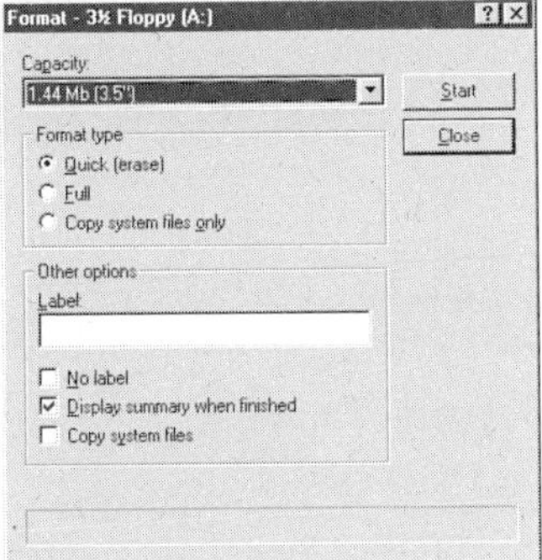

FIG. 15.2
Set up a formatting operation in the Format dialog box.

3. Select the size of the floppy disk from the Capacity drop-down list.
4. Select the type of format you want from the Format Type options:

Quick (Erase)	Formats the disk without scanning it for bad sectors first. Speeds up formatting, but you should be sure that the disk is undamaged.

continues

continued

Full	Checks for bad sectors on the disk before formatting and marks them so that these areas are not used.
Copy System Files Only	Adds the system files to the disk without formatting it so that the disk can be used to start the computer.

5. If you want to assign a label to the disk, type the label in the Label text box. Otherwise, select the No Label option.
6. Select the Display Summary When Finished option if you want to see a screen of information about the disk after it is formatted (see Figure 15.3).

FIG. 15.3
You can get information about a formatted disk in the Format Results message box.

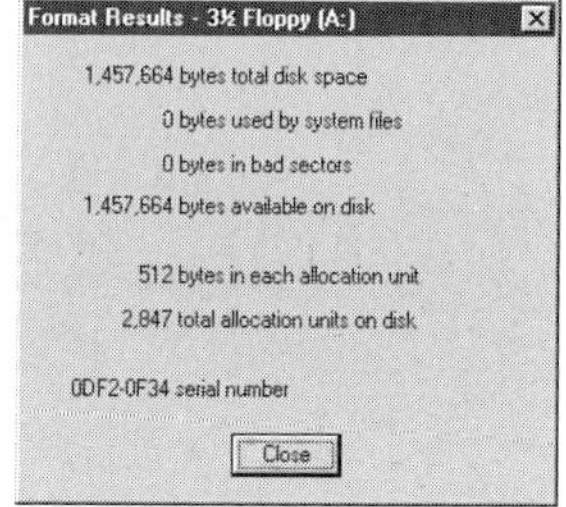

The Format Results message box tells you how much total disk space there is, how many bytes are used by system files and bad sectors, and how many bytes are available.

If you want to switch to another application while formatting a disk, select the Display Summary option so the Format Results dialog box will notify you when the formatting is completed.

7. If you want to use the disk to start the computer, select the Copy System Files option. Do not use this option unless you need to, because system files use storage space on the disk that can otherwise be used for data.
8. Choose Start. The progress of the formatting operation appears at the bottom of the Format dialog box.
9. To format another disk, insert a new disk and repeat steps 3 through 8.
10. When you finish formatting disks, choose Close.

CAUTION

When you format a disk, you remove all the information from the disk. You should check a disk for important files before formatting.

TROUBLESHOOTING

Windows will not format a disk drive. A dialog says there are files open but all applications and documents on the drive are closed. Windows 95 prevents you from formatting a disk that has a file open or a disk that is open in My Computer or the Windows Explorer. Close any documents or applications that are open on that disk, and close any My Computer or Windows Explorer windows open into the disk.

CAUTION

Drives that have been compressed with DriveSpace or another compression software must be formatted from DriveSpace or the appropriate compression software.

Formatting Your Hard Disk

Before you can use a new hard drive, you need to format it as if it has not been formatted before. You also may want to format a hard drive that has been used and is cluttered with data or other operating systems. Formatting does more than just erasing old data, it magnetically scrubs the disk so that the files do not exist.

If you purchased a preassembled computer that contains a hard disk and the computer starts and runs Windows or DOS, then you do not need to format the hard disk. If, however, you install additional hard disks in your computer, you may need to format them before you can use them.

CAUTION

You should format a disk that contains confidential or secret information before giving the computer to someone who should not have access to that data. The erase or delete commands only remove a file's name and location from a disk's table of files. The data still exists on the disk until it is overwritten by another file. Formatting erases the name and location table and magnetically erases the actual data.

Using FDISK to Partition a New Hard Drive An essential part of formatting a hard drive for data is *partitioning*. You must create at least one partition on your hard disk, but you can create more than one partition. You can define these additional partitions as DOS partitions or as non-DOS partitions on which you can install other operating systems. To run Windows 95, you need to create at least one DOS partition, and if want to start Windows 95 from this disk, you must also define this partition as a primary DOS partition and as the active partition. If you don't use the entire disk for the primary DOS partition, you can create an extended DOS partition from the remaining space and divide this partition into logical drives. Use the FDISK program that comes with DOS and Windows 95 to accomplish all these tasks.

If you are installing a new hard disk as your primary drive, place the Windows 95 Startup disk in the drive A and turn on your computer. Windows sees the new drive and asks if you want to allocate all of the unallocated space on your drive. Answer "yes" and it will run FDISK behind the scenes and restart your computer. After the restart, it formats the new partition automatically.

Your other alternative is to boot to DOS Mode by pressing F5 during startup and running FDISK from the DOS Prompt. When you type FDISK at the DOS prompt, it puts a menu on the screen. Be sure to check to see that the drive that you want to partition is the selected drive. Option 5 on the menu allows you to select a different drive. After you confirm that you have the correct drive selected, choose option 1 from the menu. This option creates a DOS partition on your drive and asks if you want to use the entire drive for your DOS partition. The most common answer is "yes." Once the DOS partition is created, your computer will restart and be ready for the formatting of the drive.

As you can see by the two choices of partitioning a hard drive, Windows 95 has made this step much easier.

Formatting an Uncompressed Hard Drive from MS-DOS To format an uncompressed drive from the MS-DOS prompt, type **Format *d:***, where *d*: is the drive letter of the drive that you want to format.

Formatting an Uncompressed Hard Drive from Windows Before you format an uncompressed hard drive, make sure you have backed up or copied any file that you may need again. Once the formatting process begins, you cannot retrieve previous data from the drive.

To format a hard drive, follow these steps:

1. Close all documents and applications on the drive you want to format. Close any windows from My Computer that look at that drive. Collapse all folders in Windows Explorer for the hard drive you want to format.
2. Open My Computer and select the icon for the drive you want to format. Choose File, Format.

   or

   Open Windows Explorer, and right-click the hard drive icon you want to format. Choose Format.

   The Format dialog box displays as shown in Figure 15.4.
3. Select the option you want for formatting your disk:

Capacity	Click the drop-down list arrow to select a different capacity for the drive.
Format Type	
Quick (erase)	Erases all the files, but does not use ScanDisk to check for bad areas of the disk. The disk must be formatted to use this command. If you think your disk may have bad areas or has shown erratic behavior, be sure to run ScanDisk after the Quick format.

Full	Prepares a disk for use. All files are completely removed. Diskettes are checked for bad sectors, but hard disks are not. If this is a new hard disk or a disk that has shown erratic behavior, be sure to run ScanDisk after the Full format.
Copy System Files Only	Does not format the disk but it does copy system files to the disk so the floppy or hard disk can be used to start the computer.
Other Options	
Label	Creates a magnetic label on the disk, which appears in the title bar of My Computer and Windows Explorer.
No label	Disables the label so the disk will not have a label.
Display Summary When Finished	Displays a report when formatting is complete that shows the space available on the disk, the room taken by system files, and the number of bad sectors.
Copy System Files	Copies system files onto the disk after formatting. Select this check box if you need to use this floppy or hard disk to start the computer.

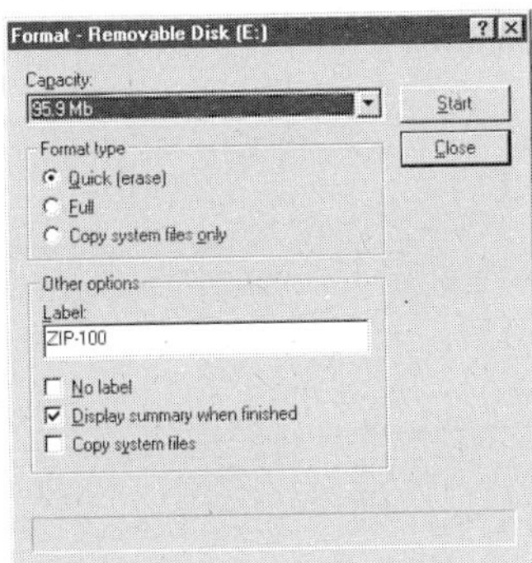

FIG. 15.4
You can use the Format dialog box to do a full format, erase files, and copy system files onto a disk.

4. Choose OK. A dialog box displays telling you that all files on the disk will be destroyed. Are you sure you want to format this drive? Choose OK to format or Cancel to stop.
5. If you choose OK, you will see the Format dialog box showing you the progression of the file format, as shown in Figure 15.5.
6. When formatting is complete, the Format Results dialog box displays the properties of the formatted drive (see Figure 15.6).
7. Choose Close to close the Format Results dialog box; then choose Close to close the Format dialog box.

▶ **See** "Using FDISK to Partition a New Hard Drive," **p. 385**

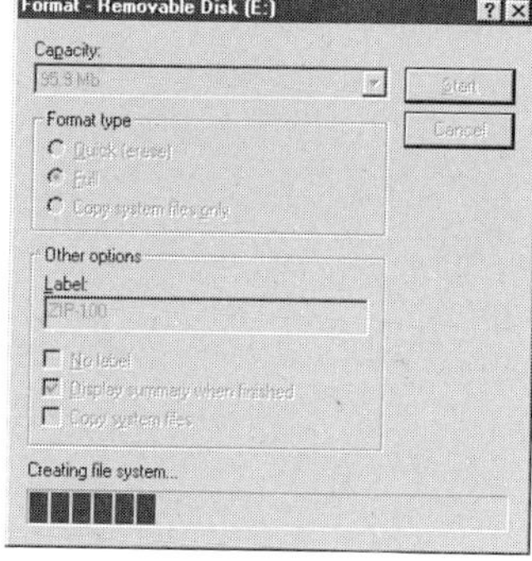

FIG. 15.5
A progression bar at the bottom of the dialog box shows you the progress of disk formatting.

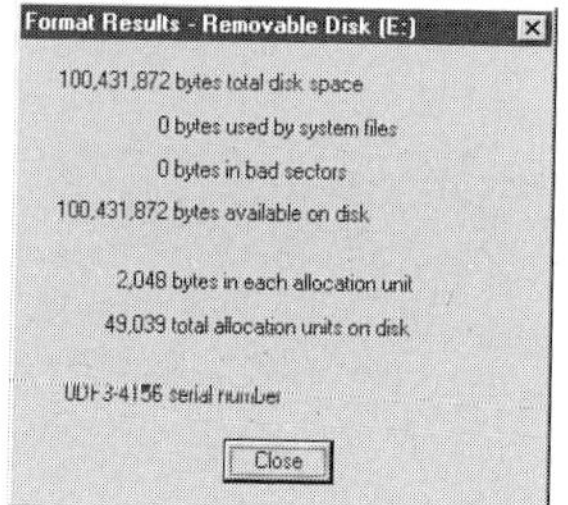

FIG. 15.6
The Format Results dialog box displays a report on disk statistics when formatting is complete.

If My Computer or Windows Explorer does not display the icon for the hard drive you want to format, then you may need to recheck the drive connections to the drive adapter, or partition the hard drive using the FDISK command. You also need to check setup to be sure the proper drive type is selected.

See "Using ScanDisk to Check for Disk Damage," **p. 390**

CAUTION

You cannot format the hard disk containing Windows while Windows is running. If you need to format the hard disk containing Windows, you will need either a disk copy of MS-DOS with the FORMAT command or a set of the Windows 95 upgrade disks that contains a disk for formatting hard disks.

The system files, FDISK, and Format are created on the Startup disk that Windows 95 asks if you want to create during the install. It is *highly* recommended that you create the Startup disk.

Formatting an Uncompressed Drive from the Windows Startup Disk If you want to reformat the drive that has Windows 95 installed on it, you must use the Windows startup disk. Reformatting the drive that has Windows 95 on it is an extreme measure, since it will erase everything on the drive and you will have to reinstall Windows 95 and all your applications. In some cases, this may be necessary, for example, if your installation of Windows is corrupted beyond repair. Also, some users like to periodically back up their entire system and then reformat their hard drive and reinstall Windows 95 and their applications. This "spring-cleaning" can rid your hard disk of files you are no longer using and often improves the performance of your system.

To format the drive that has Windows 95 installed on it, follow these steps:

1. Insert the startup disk in drive A and restart the computer.
2. Type **format *drive_letter*** at the command prompt.

   If you are formatting the boot drive (drive C), type **format C: /s**. The /s parameter will add the system files to the disk.
3. Press **Y** when the warning message appears.
4. When the formatting is completed, you can add a volume label if you want. Then press Enter to complete the formatting.
5. Remove the startup disk and restart the computer.

When you restart your computer, drive C: will have only the files needed to boot the computer. You will then have to reinstall Windows 95 and all your applications. See Chapter 2, "Installing Windows," to learn how to install Windows 95.

Naming Your Drive with a Volume Label

Although you may be accustomed to putting a paper label on disks, both hard disks and floppy disks can have magnetically recorded labels, known as *volume labels*. Volume labels can help you identify disks. You can read the volume label for a disk by looking at the disk's properties.

In the preceding section, you learned how to create a volume label when you format a disk. If you want to create or change a volume label on a previously formatted disk, follow these steps:

1. Open the Explorer or the My Computer window.
2. Select the drive with the volume name you want to change.
3. Choose File, Properties. Alternatively, right-click the drive and choose Properties from the shortcut menu. The Properties sheet appears, as shown in Figure 15.7.

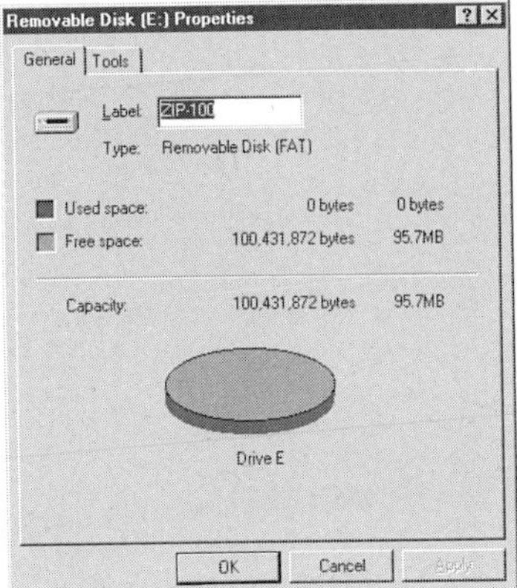

FIG. 15.7
Enter a volume label for a disk in the Properties sheet.

You can view the name of a disk by right-clicking the disk icon in the My Computer or Explorer window and selecting the Properties command.

4. Type the name you want to give the disk in the Label text box and click OK.

   If there is already a name in the box, select it first and then type a new name. The Properties sheet also gives you information on the total size of the disk (in bytes), how much space is used, and the amount of remaining space.

Using ScanDisk to Check for Disk Damage

In an ideal world, you would never have to worry about errors occurring on your hard disk or floppy disks. This not being the case, Windows 95 comes with a program called ScanDisk you can use to check for, diagnose, and repair damage on a hard disk or floppy disk. Part of your routine hard disk maintenance, along with defragmenting your hard disk as described in the next section, should be to periodically run ScanDisk to keep your hard disk in good repair.

In its standard test, ScanDisk checks the files and folders on a disk for logical *errors*; if you ask it to, ScanDisk also automatically corrects any errors it finds. ScanDisk checks for *cross-linked* files, which occur when two or more files have data stored in the same *cluster* (a storage unit on a disk). The data in the cluster is likely to be correct for only one of the files and may not be correct for any of them. ScanDisk also checks for *lost file fragments*, which are pieces of data that have become disassociated with their files. Although file fragments may contain useful data, they usually can't be recovered and just take up disk space. You can tell ScanDisk to delete lost file fragments or save them in a file.

You also have the option of having ScanDisk check files for invalid file names and invalid dates and times. When a file has an invalid file name, you may not be able to open it. Invalid dates and times can cause problems when you use a backup program that uses dates and times to determine how current a file is.

You can run a more thorough test, in which ScanDisk checks for both logical errors in files and folders and also scans the surface of the disk to check for physical *errors*. Physical errors are areas on your disk that are damaged and shouldn't be used for storing data. If ScanDisk finds bad sectors on your hard disk, any data in them can be moved to new sectors, and the bad sectors are marked so that data is not stored in them in the future.

To check a disk for errors, follow these steps:

1. Open the Start menu and choose Programs, Accessories, System Tools, and ScanDisk. The ScanDisk window appears, as shown in Figure 15.8.
2. Select the drive you want to check in the Select the Drive(s) You Want to Check for Errors box.
3. To check only for logical errors in the files and folders on the selected disk, make sure to select the Standard option.

To check for logical errors and to scan the disk for physical errors, select the Thorough option.

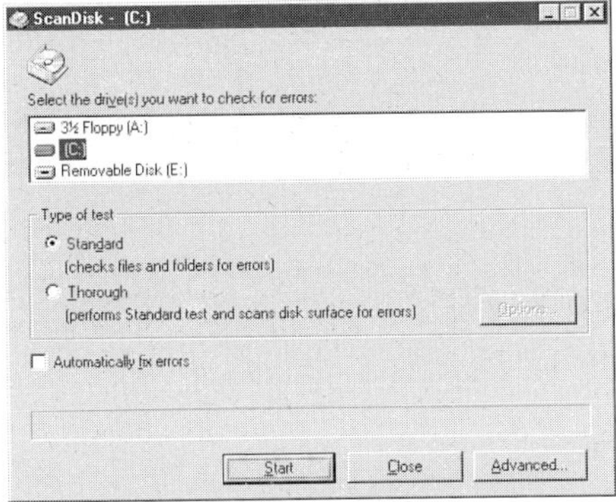

FIG. 15.8
Use ScanDisk to check your hard disk for logical and physical errors and repair any damage.

4. Click the Advanced button to change the settings used for checking files and folders for logical errors. The ScanDisk Advanced Options dialog box appears (see Figure 15.9). Use this dialog box to change the options in Table 15.1.

Table 15.1 ScanDisk Advanced Options

Option	Function
Display Summary Options	
Always	A summary with information about your disk and any errors found and corrected appears whenever you run ScanDisk.
Never	A summary never appears when you run ScanDisk.
Only If Errors Found	A summary shows only if Windows detects errors.
Log File Options	
Replace Log	Saves the details of a ScanDisk session in a log file named SCANDISK.LOG in the top-level folder on drive C. Replaces any existing file with the same name.
Append to Log	Saves the details of a ScanDisk session, appending the information to the end of SCANDISK.LOG.
No Log	The results of the ScanDisk operation are not saved to a log file.
Cross-Linked Files Options	
Delete	Deletes cross-linked files when such files are found.
Make Copies	A copy is made of each cross-linked cluster for each of the cross-linked files.

continues

Table 15.1 Continued

Option	Function
Ignore	Cross-linked files are not corrected in any way. Using a cross-linked file may lead to further file damage and may cause the program using it to crash.
Lost File Fragments Options	
Free	Deletes lost file fragments, freeing up the space they use.
Convert to Files	Converts lost file fragments to files, which you can view to see whether they contain data you need. Files are given names beginning with FILE (for example, FILE0001) and are stored in the top-level folder of the disk.
Check Files For Options	
Invalid File Names	Checks files for invalid file names. Files with invalid file names sometimes cannot be opened.
Invalid Dates and Times	Checks files for invalid dates and times, which can result in incorrect sorting and can also cause problems with backup programs.
Check Host Drive First	If the drive you check has been compressed using DoubleSpace or DriveSpace, ScanDisk checks the host drive for the compressed drive first. Errors on the host drive often cause errors on the compressed drive, so it is best to check it first.

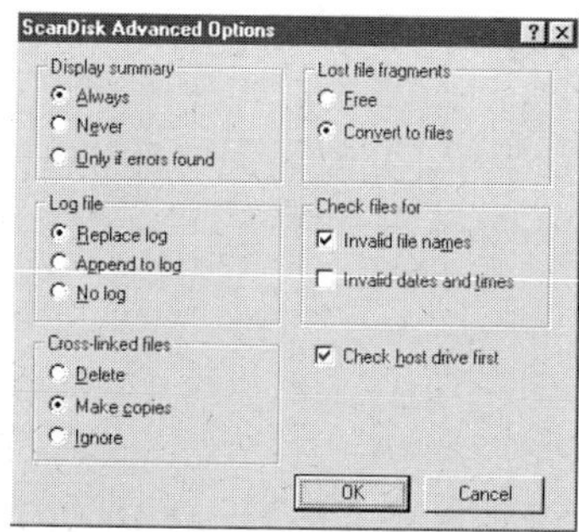

FIG. 15.9
You can change the settings ScanDisk uses to check files and folders for logical errors in the ScanDisk Advanced Options dialog box.

5. If you selected the Thorough option, choose Options to change the settings used to scan the disk for physical errors. The Surface Scan Options dialog box appears (see Figure 15.10). Use this dialog box to change the following options:

Option	Function
System and Data Areas	Scans the entire disk for physical damage.
System Area Only	Scans only the system area of the disk for physical damage. This is the disk area that contains files used to start the computer and hold the operating system.
Data Area Only	Scans only the data area of the disk for physical damage. The data area contains application and data programs. Use this if Windows behaves erratically, even if you have reinstalled it.
Do Not Perform Write-Testing	If this option is not selected (the default), ScanDisk reads and writes every sector to verify both read and write functions. If you select this option, ScanDisk does not write-verify the sectors.
Do Not Repair Bad Sectors in Hidden and System Files	ScanDisk will not move data from bad sectors in hidden and system files. Some programs look for hidden system files at specific locations and will not work if data in these files is moved.

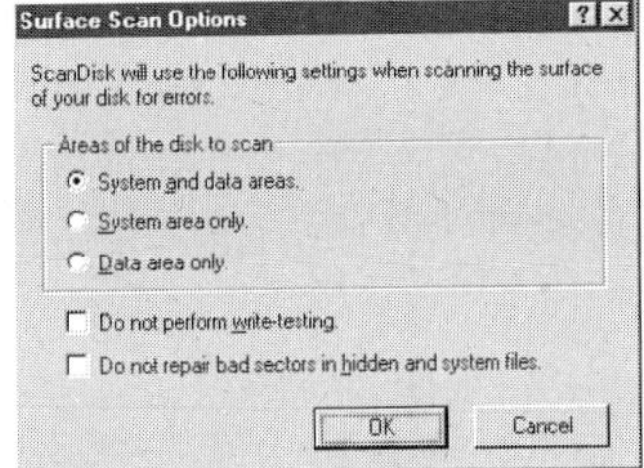

FIG. 15.10
You can change the settings ScanDisk uses to scan the disk for physical errors.

6. Select the Automatically Fix Errors option if you want ScanDisk to automatically fix any errors it finds without first reporting the errors.

   If you don't select this option, ScanDisk informs you when it finds an error, and you can determine how ScanDisk fixes it.

7. Choose Start to begin the test. The progress of the test appears at the bottom of the ScanDisk dialog box. You can halt the test by choosing Cancel. If you told ScanDisk to scan your disk for physical errors, the test can take several minutes. When the test is complete, a summary report like the one in Figure 15.11 may appear, depending on the options you selected in the ScanDisk Advanced Options dialog box. Click Close to close the Results dialog box.

8. Choose Close to exit ScanDisk.

See "Improving Performance with Disk Defragmenter," **p. 394**

FIG. 15.11
The results of a ScanDisk operation appear in the ScanDisk Results dialog box.

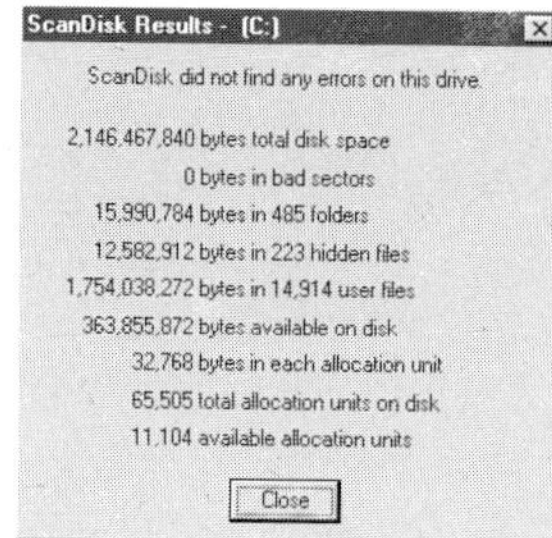

TROUBLESHOOTING

Whenever Windows retrieves a file, the hard disk light seems to come on a lot. It even sounds like the hard disk is chattering. The more we use the computer, the worse this problem gets. ScanDisk didn't show any problems with the disk. The problem is probably not with the physical quality of your hard drive's magnetic surface, which is what ScanDisk checks. The problem is more likely that files on the hard disk are fragmented. Fragmented disks have pieces of files scattered all over the disk. Rather than reading a file at one location in one quick continuous movement, the read-head on the drive must skitter around on the disk searching for all the pieces that belong to a file. Once fragmenting is bad, it gets worse which is why your computer seems to be slowing down the more you use it. Windows comes with a defragmenting utility that will reorganize your files on the disk so they are contiguous and can be read quickly.

Improving Performance with Disk Defragmenter

Information written to a hard disk is not necessarily stored in a *contiguous* (adjacent) block. Rather, fragments of information are more likely spread across the disk wherever the system can find room. The more you use the hard disk, the more fragmented the disk becomes. Obviously, the drive takes more time to hunt for information located in several places than it takes to fetch the same information from a single location. Because of this extra time, disk fragmentation can slow the computer's operation considerably.

The Windows Disk Defragmenter can significantly improve file access time by restructuring files into contiguous blocks and moving free space to the end of the disk.

To optimize the performance of your hard disk, use Disk Defragmenter on a regular basis to defragment your hard disk.

To defragment a disk, follow these steps:

1. Open the Start menu and choose Programs, Accessories, System Tools, and Disk Defragmenter. The Select Drive dialog box appears (see Figure 15.12).

FIG. 15.12
Select the drive you want to defragment in the Select Drive dialog box.

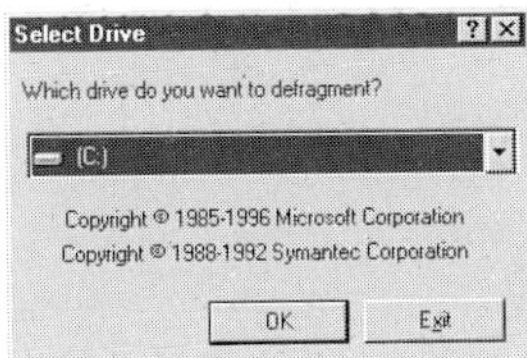

2. Select the drive you want to defragment from the Defragment Which Drive drop-down list and choose OK. The Disk Defragmenter dialog box appears, as shown in Figure 15.13. The percent fragmentation of the selected drive appears in the dialog box. You are also informed whether defragmentation will improve performance.

FIG. 15.13
The Disk Defragmenter dialog box tells you how fragmented your drive is and whether defragmenting it will improve its performance.

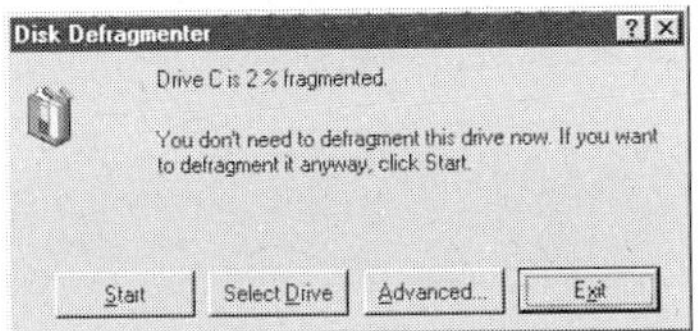

3. To change the Disk Defragmenter options, choose Advanced. The Advanced Options dialog box appears (see Figure 15.14). Use this dialog box to change the following options:

Option	**Function**
Full Defragmentation (Both Files and Free Space)	Defragments all the files on the selected disk.
Defragment Files Only	Defragments only the files on your hard disk, without consolidating the free space.
Consolidate Free Space Only	Only consolidates the free space on the selected disk without defragmenting the files.
Check Drive for Errors	Checks the files and folders on the drive for errors before defragmenting.
This Time Only. Next Time, Use the Defaults Again	Uses the selected options for this defragment operation only.
Save These Options and Use Them Every Time	Saves the selected options and uses them each time you run Disk Defragmenter unless you change them again.

Select the desired options and click OK. You return to the Disk Defragmenter dialog box.

4. Choose Start. The progress of the defragmentation operation appears in the Defragmenting dialog box (see Figure 15.15).

FIG. 15.14
Change the way Disk Defragmenter works in the Advanced Options dialog box.

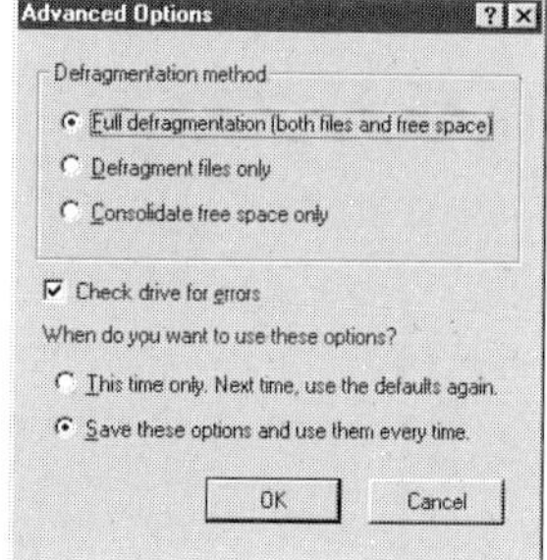

5. When the defragmentation operation is complete, choose Exit to close the Disk Defragmenter, or choose Select Drive to defragment another drive.

Defragmenting a hard disk can take a long time. Although you can continue working on your computer during the defragmentation operation, you will notice a significant slowdown in your computer's operation. Also, every time you make a change that affects the FAT, the defragmenting process has to be restarted. For these reasons, try to run the Disk Defragmenter during a time when you do not need to use the computer, for example, before you leave work for the day.

FIG. 15.15
Monitor the progress of the defragmentation operation in the Defragmenting dialog box.

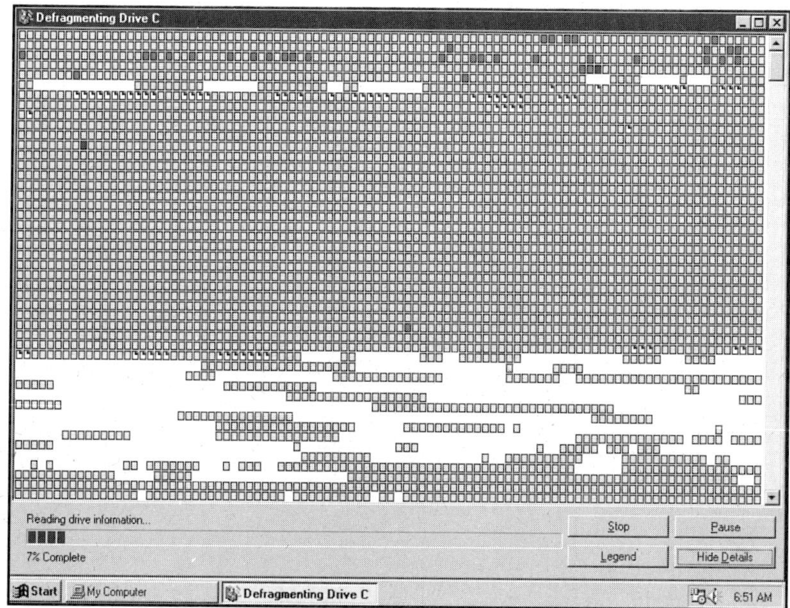

You can pause the defragmentation operation if you need to use your computer before defragmentation is completed and you don't want performance slowed down. Choose Pause from the Defragmenting dialog box to pause Disk Defragmenter. To resume defragmentation, choose Pause again. You can also cancel the defragmentation operation by choosing Stop. Choose Show Details to open a window that displays the details of the defragmentation operation. To close the window, choose Hide Details.

Compressing a Disk

If you are like many computer users, you may reach the limits of the storage space on your computer as you install new programs and generate more and more data files. You've probably also discovered that new releases of Windows programs seem to take up more and more room on your hard disk. One solution is to install a new hard disk in your computer. But if you have limited finances, or you work with a laptop in which it is not possible to add another hard disk, you have another option. Windows 95 comes with a program called DriveSpace that enables you to squeeze more storage space from your existing hard drive. DriveSpace is a software solution to your hardware problem. DriveSpace works by compressing the files on your hard disk so that they take up less room. When you need to use a file, DriveSpace automatically decompresses it. The compression and decompression of files happens transparently—you are not even aware that it is happening. You will notice very little delay in file access when you use DriveSpace.

Microsoft Plus!, the companion software released at the same time as Windows 95, comes with DriveSpace 3, an enhanced version of DriveSpace. DriveSpace 3 offers superb disk compression that improves on Windows 95 DriveSpace in several ways:

- Handles disks up to 2G (versus 512M for the original DriveSpace).
- Works with smaller units of data (512-byte sectors versus 32K byte clusters), improving storage efficiency.
- Supports two new higher levels of compression (HiPack and UltraPack).
- Has settings for specifying what type of compression to use and when to use it.
- Adds a Compression tab to the Properties sheet for floppy and hard disks.

In this section, we assume you have installed Microsoft Plus! on your computer and will use DriveSpace 3.

DriveSpace 3 is included with the OEM Service Release 2 (OSR2) version of Windows 95, so if you have OSR2 installed on your computer, you do not have to install Microsoft Plus! to have access to DriveSpace 3. However, if the hard drive you want to compress has the FAT32 file system installed (see"The FAT32 File System," earlier in this chapter), you cannot compress the drive. FAT32 drives cannot be compressed using DriveSpace3.

NOTE The Windows 95 DriveSpace is compatible with both DoubleSpace, which was included with MS-DOS 6.0 and 6.2, and DriveSpace, which was included with MS-DOS 6.22. You can work with compressed drives of either type, and the two types of compressed drives can coexist on the same computer.

Disk Compression

Despite the name, disk compression doesn't actually compress your hard disk, which is a physical entry, nor does it increase the physical capacity of your disk. What it really does is use software magic to increase the capacity of your hard disk in two ways.

First, disk compression software increases the capacity of your hard disk by reducing the smallest storage unit to 512 bytes, rather than the much larger clusters (8–64K) used in the native DOS environment. This improvement in storage efficiency goes a long way toward reducing the wasted space that occurs when you save a lot of small files.

The second component of disk compression involves the use of a software algorithm that looks for patterns in a data file and codes repeating patterns in a way that takes up less space. Many types of files have lots of repeating information and can be compressed to less than 60 percent of their original size.

The Facts About Disk Compression

DriveSpace 3 is an optional program that you can install when you install Microsoft Plus! or you can install it at a later time. To see if you have DriveSpace 3 available, open the Start menu and choose Programs, Accessories, System Tools. If DriveSpace 3 is not listed in the System Tools menu, you will need to install it using your Microsoft Plus! software (or your Windows 95 CD-ROM if you are using the OSR2 version of Windows 95).

When you run DriveSpace 3, it creates a compressed drive on your existing hard disk. The compressed drive is actually a file, not a physical hard drive, called a *compressed volume file* (CVF). The CVF is stored on a physical, uncompressed drive, called the *host drive*. The CVF is assigned a drive letter, just like a physical drive and can be accessed like any other drive. The file that DriveSpace creates on your hard drive is a hidden, read only, system file, thus is it not acted upon by most normal DOS commands. From the user's point of view, the only difference after running DriveSpace is that the original drive has a lot more free space and there is a new drive, the host drive.

As a rule of thumb, DriveSpace 3 will add 50 to 100 percent more capacity to your disk. The amount of actual compression depends upon the types of files stored on the disk. Some files such as text files or certain graphics files compress significantly, while other files such as an application's EXE file may barely change.

You can run DriveSpace 3 in one of two ways. Typically, you use DriveSpace 3 to compress your entire existing drive to free up more storage space. You can run DriveSpace 3 to compress your C drive, for example, which then becomes a compressed volume file on the host drive H. You also can use DriveSpace 3 to compress a specified amount of the free space on your hard drive to create a new, empty compressed drive. The rest of the hard drive is not compressed. If, for example, you have 80M of free space on your drive C, you can use DriveSpace 3 to compress 25M of the free space to create a new drive D with roughly 50M of free space. You then have 55M free on drive C and 50M on drive D for an effective 105M of free space.

NOTE If you have installed the FAT32 file system on your computer using the Windows 95 OEM Service Release 2 update, you cannot compress your hard disk. DriveSpace 3 does not support compression of FAT32 partitions.

See "Changing the Estimated Compression Ratio for Your Compressed Drive," **p. 406**

TROUBLESHOOTING

Large files will not copy onto the compressed drive. The available free space displayed for compressed drives is only an estimate. It is based on the average compression for all files on your disk. If the file you try to save does not compress as much as the average, then it may not fit in the available space.

Compressing a Drive with DriveSpace 3

Remember that compressed disks can be slow—the greater the compression, the slower your system's performance is likely to be. Also, compressing your system's primary hard disk can take a long time, during which you can't work with your system.

Use the following steps to compress a disk with DriveSpace 3:

1. Open the Start menu and click Programs, Accessories, System Tools, and DriveSpace. The DriveSpace 3 window appears (see Figure 15.16).

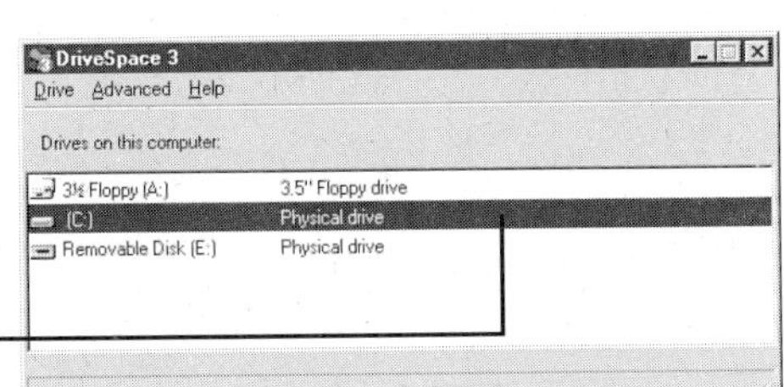

FIG. 15.16
The DriveSpace 3 window displays the available drives on your system.

2. Click the drive that you want to compress.

NOTE If you previously compressed a hard disk with DoubleSpace or DriveSpace (for Windows 95 or for earlier DOS versions), you can select the disk and then choose Drive, Upgrade to convert the disk to DriveSpace 3 format.

3. Choose Advanced, Settings. The Disk Compression Settings dialog box appears (see Figure 15.17).
4. Click the option button for the compression method you want to use:

   No Compression does not compress the disk.

No Compression, Unless Drive Is at Least X% Full only compresses the disk after it's more full than the percentage you specify.

Standard Compression compresses the disk contents by approximately a 1.8:1 ratio.

HiPack Compression compresses the disk contents by up to 2.3:1.

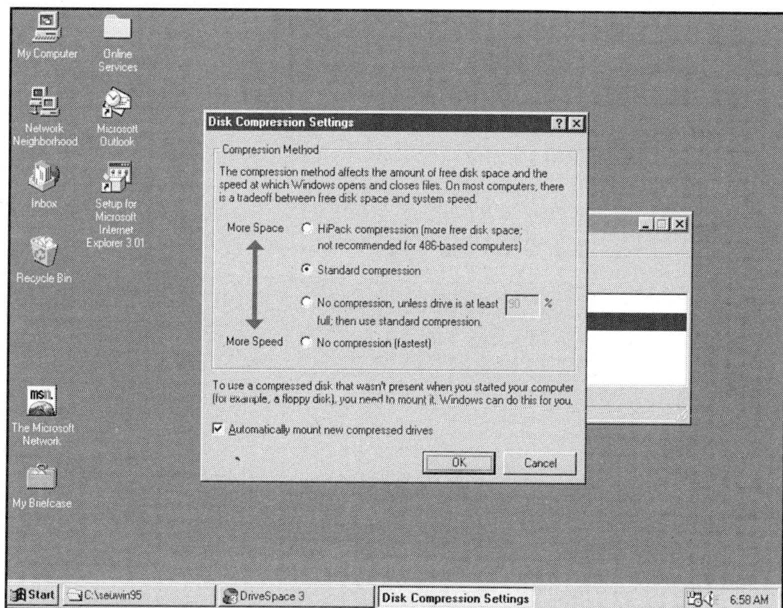

FIG. 15.17 Choose your preferences for compression settings.

NOTE As always, the compression ratio on your hard drive depends on the type of files being compressed. Leave the Automatically Mount New Compressed Drives option checked, especially if you are compressing a floppy disk. This will ensure that the compressed disk is automatically mounted when you insert it in the disk drive. Mounting establishes a connection between a drive letter and the CVF, so the files in the CVF can be read.

5. Click OK to close the Compression Settings dialog box and accept the specified compression method.
6. Choose Drive, Compress. The Compress a Drive dialog box appears (see Figure 15.18), informing you of the estimated results of the compression operation—that is, how much free space and used space the disk will have after compression.
7. Click Options. The Compression Options dialog box appears (see Figure 15.19). Use it to specify a drive letter and free space for the Host drive where DriveSpace 3 will store compressed information about the drive.

   You should only need to change these first two options if your system connects to a network that uses drive H for another purpose. If you compress a floppy disk you might use on another computer that doesn't have DriveSpace 3, click to select the Use

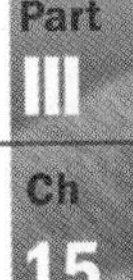

DoubleSpace-Compatible Format check box; note that you do need to select this option for Windows 95 systems without DriveSpace 3 or for systems using DriveSpace from a DOS 6.X version. Click OK to accept the Compression Options you set.

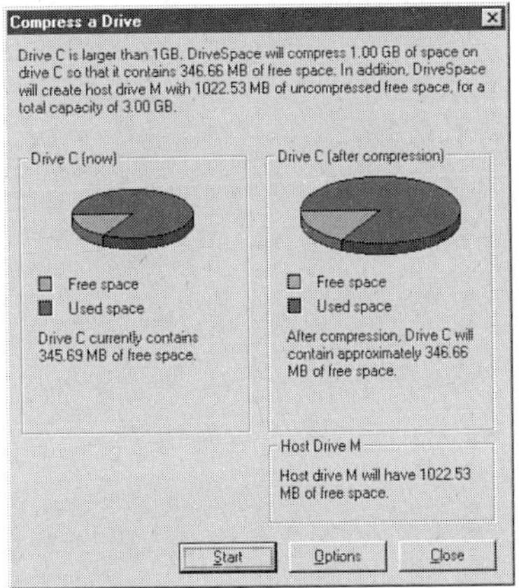

FIG. 15.18
The Compress a Drive dialog box displays information on the size of the selected disk and how much space there will be after running DriveSpace.

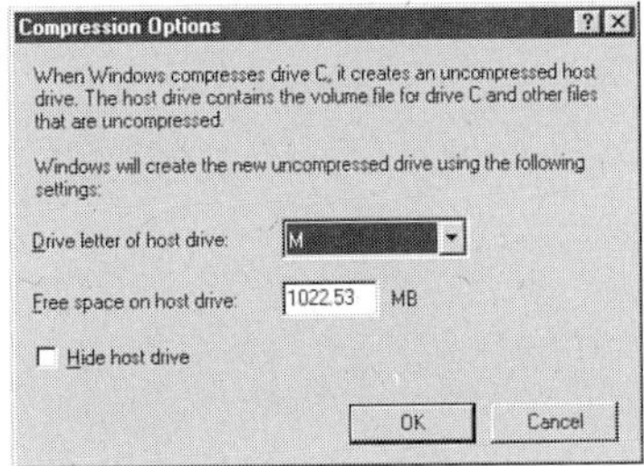

FIG. 15.19
Change the options used for compressing a drive in the Compression Options dialog box.

8. Click the Start button in the Compress a Drive dialog box. The Are You Sure? dialog box appears, asking you to confirm the compression operation (see Figure 15.20).

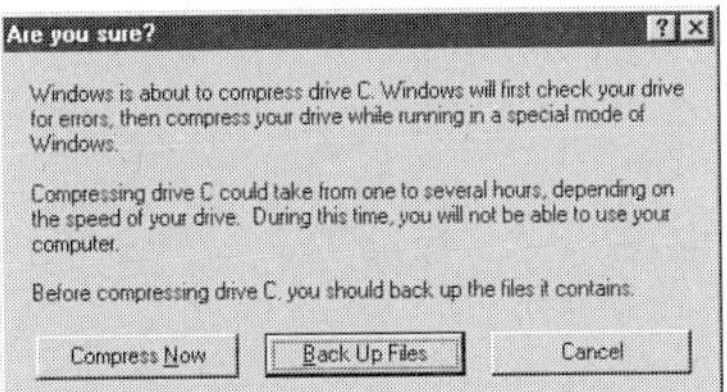

FIG. 15.20
Back up your files before you run DriveSpace by choosing the Back Up Files button.

9. Click the Back Up Files button to make a backup copy of the files on the disk before you compress it. This is an important safety measure; skipping it isn't recommended.
10. DriveSpace 3 runs the backup utility installed to work with your system. Follow any on-screen instructions to complete the backup process.

11. When the backup finishes, click Continue to compress the disk. DriveSpace 3 compresses the disk and then redisplays the Compress a Drive dialog box to report on the compression results.
12. Click Close to complete compressing the disk.
13. A Restart Computer dialog box appears asking if you want to restart your computer. Choose Yes to restart, No to continue working.

    Do not set up new software, change system settings, or run MS-DOS programs until you restart your computer.

Returning a Drive to Normal Compression

DriveSpace also enables you to decompress a drive. Before you decompress a drive, make sure that there will be enough space on the drive to hold all the files on the drive after it is decompressed.

When you choose to decompress a drive and there is not enough room, you get an error dialog box that tells you how much data you have, how much free space you need, and how much data you need to delete or move off of which drive.

To decompress a drive, follow these steps:

1. Open the Start menu and choose Programs, Accessories, System Tools, and DriveSpace 3. The DriveSpace 3 window appears.
2. Select the drive you want to decompress from the Drives on This Computer list.
3. Choose Drive, Uncompress.
4. Choose Start. A confirmation dialog box appears.
5. If you haven't backed up your files, choose the Back Up Files button to open Backup. See Chapter 16, "Backing Up and Protecting Your Data," for detailed information on how to back up your files.
6. Choose Uncompress Now to start the decompression operation. The progress of the decompression operation appears at the bottom of the Uncompress a Drive dialog box.
7. When the message box informing you that the drive has been decompressed appears, choose OK.

Setting Up Your Floppy or Hard Disk to Read Compressed Files

When you work with compressed, removable storage media (such as floppy disks), you must mount the compressed drive if it wasn't present when the computer started. Mounting a drive links a drive letter with a compressed volume file (CVF) and enables your computer to access the files on the compressed volume files.

To mount a compressed drive, follow these steps:

1. Open the DriveSpace 3 window and select the drive you want to mount in the Drives on This Computer list. For example, if you want to read a floppy disk in drive A and the floppy disk has DriveSpace or DoubleSpace compression, then you would select the A drive.

2. Open the Advanced menu and choose Mount.
3. Select the compressed volume file you want to mount. Once you mount a drive, it shows up in the Drives on This Computer list as a compressed drive.

You can select an option so that newly compressed devices automatically mount. Choose Advanced, Settings. Select the Automatically Mount New Compressed Devices option and choose OK. Windows now automatically mounts new compressed devices so that you don't have to mount the compressed device each time you insert it in the computer.

To unmount a compressed drive, follow these steps:

1. Open the DriveSpace 3 window and select the compressed drive you want to unmount from the Drives on this Computer list.
2. Choose Advanced, Unmount.
3. When the message box appears informing you that the operation is complete, choose OK.

Compressing Part of Disk

You don't have to compress your entire hard disk; you can compress some or all of the free space on your hard disk to create a new compressed drive. To create a new compressed drive from part of a hard disk, follow these steps:

1. Open the DriveSpace 3 window and select the drive with the free space you want to use to create a new compressed drive. You cannot select a compressed drive.
2. Choose Advanced, Create Empty. The Create New Compressed Drive dialog box appears, as shown in Figure 15.21.

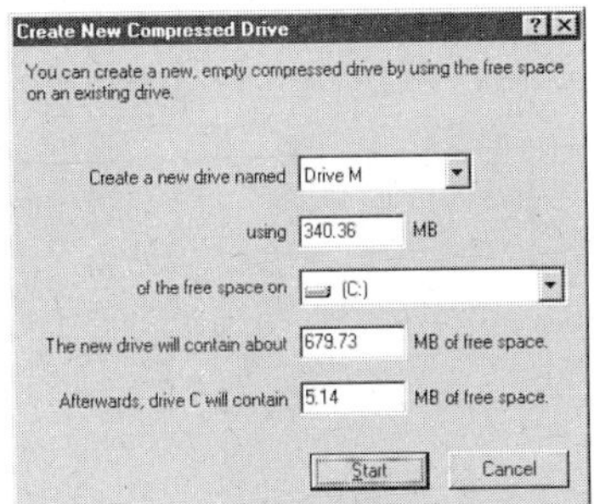

FIG. 15.21 Create a new compressed drive using the free space on your hard disk.

3. Accept the default name for the new drive or select an alternative name from the Create a New Drive Named drop-down list.
4. Enter the amount of free space (in megabytes) you want to use to create the new drive in the Using text box. If you enter a value here, the amount displayed in the new drive will contain about...MB of free space text box changes to reflect how much free space will be created in the new drive.
5. Select the drive that has the free space you want to use to create the new drive from the Of the Free Space On drop-down list.

6. If you know how much free space you want the new drive to have, enter that figure in the New Drive Will Contain About...MB of Free Space text box. If you enter a value here, the amount displayed in the Using text box automatically adjusts to show how much free space on the selected drive will be used for the new drive.

   The amount of free space that will be left on the uncompressed drive is displayed in the Afterwards, drive *letter* will contain...M of free space text box.
7. Choose Start.
8. When the message box appears informing you that the operation is complete, choose OK.

Deleting a Compressed Drive

Deleting a compressed drive is something you want to think seriously about before doing. Deleting a compressed drive removes all the data from the compressed drive returning the drive to a blank decompressed state. One reason for deleting a compressed drive is so that you can remove the physical drive from your computer and have it accessible by any MS-DOS computer. If you only want to return the compressed data to its decompressed form and retain the data on the drive, then use the decompress feature.

See "Returning a Drive to Normal Compression," **p. 402**

When you delete a compressed drive, Windows 95 deletes the compressed volume file (CVF) that contains all the compressed data and application files. (The contents of the CVF file are what looks like a compressed disk drive.) The CVF has the name DRVSPACE.000 and is located on the Host drive. You can't manually delete the DRVSPACE.000 file because it has a system attribute. (You can remove the system attribute and then manually delete the file, but deleting the compressed drive is better.)

In addition to deleting the CVF file, deleting a compressed drive also removes from the DRVSPACE.INI file the line ACTIVATE DRIVE= for the drive represented by the CVF. If you have only one compressed drive on your hard disk, then you will also be asked whether you want to delete the DriveSpace driver, DRVSPACE.BIN. You can delete this driver if you do not have other compressed drives on this drive.

CAUTION

When you delete a compressed drive, you lose all the information stored on that drive, so be sure that you have backed up or moved any files you need on this drive before deleting it.

TROUBLESHOOTING

An overzealous novice removed the system attribute from the DRVSPACE.000 file and deleted it. Is there a way to recover the data that was on the compressed drive? If the user has not saved files to that disk after deleting DRVSPACE.000, you may be able to recover the drive. Use an undelete utility to restore the deleted DRVSPACE.000 file, and then exit Windows and restart.

To delete a compressed drive, follow these steps:

1. Open the DriveSpace 3 window and select the compressed drive you want to delete from the Drives on This Computer list.
2. Choose Advanced, Delete.
3. When the confirmation message box appears, choose Yes.
4. A message box appears asking if you want to delete the DriveSpace driver. Choose Yes if this is the only compressed drive on your computer and you will not be using compressed floppy disks. Choose No if you have other compressed drives or if you will be using compressed floppy disks.
5. When the message box appears informing you that the operation is complete, choose OK.
6. You will be prompted to restart Windows 95 or continue. Switch to any open applications and save the documents; then choose Yes. If you choose No, you cannot change system settings, install applications, or use MS-DOS until you restart.

See "Setting Up Your Floppy or Hard Disk to Read Compressed Files," **p. 402**

If you are in doubt about whether to delete the driver for DriveSpace, remember that it is much easier to reinstall than it is to deinstall the driver. You can remove it now and add it back at any time using the procedure to mount a compressed drive.

Adjusting the Size of the Free Space on a Compressed Drive

You can adjust the distribution of free space between a compressed drive and its host. When you increase the free space on the compressed drive, you decrease the free space on the host drive, and vice versa. To adjust the free space on the compressed and host drives, follow these steps:

1. Open the DriveSpace 3 window and select either the compressed drive or its host from the Drives on This Computer list.
2. Choose Drive, Adjust Free Space; the Adjust Free Space dialog box appears (see Figure 15.22).

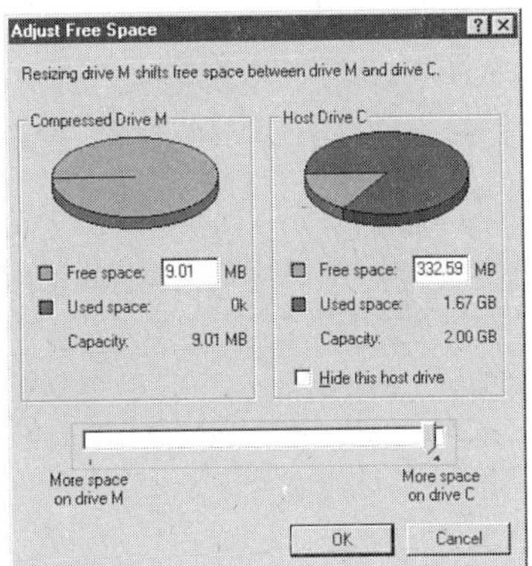

FIG. 15.22
Adjust the distribution of free space between a compressed drive and its host in the Adjust Free Space dialog box.

3. Drag the slider to change the distribution of free space between the compressed and host drives. The pie charts will reflect the amount of free space and used space.
4. Choose OK.

   A message box shows you the amount of free space on the compressed and host drives when the operation is complete.
5. A Restart Computer dialog box appears asking if you want to restart your computer. Choose Yes to restart, No to continue working.

   Do not set up new software, change system settings, or run MS-DOS programs until you restart your computer.

TROUBLESHOOTING

There seems to be enough space on the hard disk to store some very large video and sound files, but even after resizing the compressed drive there still isn't enough space. Some files, such as application, video, and music files, may not compress very much. The estimated free space on a compressed drive, however, is calculated from the average amount of compression for all files on the drive. As a consequence, files that look like they may fit, may not.

Changing the Estimated Compression Ratio for Your Compressed Drive

DriveSpace 3 contains a command that enables you to change the estimated compression ratio. This does not change how tightly data is compressed on your hard drive. It is just an estimate used by Windows 95 to calculate how much free space remains on your hard drive. The remaining free space, as calculated by the estimated compression ratio, is then used in Windows 95 dialog boxes to give you an estimate of how much drive space remains. Changing the compression ratio to a larger number would not compress files tighter but would give you a very misleading idea of how much free space remains.

In general, do not change the compression ratio to more than a two-to-one, 2:1, ratio.

You may want to change the estimated compression ratio in order to see a more accurate calculation of the free space available on your compressed drive. There is a reason that you can calculate this number more accurately than Windows 95. Windows 95 calculates the estimated compression ratio from an average of the actual file size and the compressed file size for all files on the drive. Every time a file is saved or erased, Windows 95 recalculates the estimated compression ratio and then uses that number to calculate the estimated free space remain.

The problem with accepting the estimated compression ratio is that Windows 95 has no idea what types of files you store on the hard disk. Since you are familiar with the types of files you store, you can estimate a better compression ratio. This gives you a better idea of the amount of free space available.

To understand the problem, you must know that different files compress by different amounts. Files such as text files and some graphics files contain a lot of repetitive information that can be tightly compressed into a small space. Other files such as an application's EXE files or a video's JPEG or MPEG files have little room for compression and may not change significantly in size.

If you have just installed many application files on a compressed drive with few data files, then Windows 95 will calculate a low compression ratio. Conversely, if your compressed drive has few application or multimedia files, then the estimated compression ratio will be higher. As long as you continue saving and removing the same type of files, Windows 95 will report a fairly accurate estimated free space. But if you change the type of files you save, the estimated free space will be wrong because the new files compress to a different amount.

If you will not be adding more application or multimedia files to your compressed drive, but you will be adding a lot more data files, then you may want to increase the estimated compression ratio to get a more accurate reading of free space. Conversely, a drive that has stored word processing files may have much less space available than it appears to have when you begin storing sound, video, and application files on it.

CAUTION

What you see is not necessarily what you get when dealing with compression ratios. Some files such as EXE application files or JPEG and MPEG video files compress very little. This means that even though the estimated free space may be 15M, it's doubtful that 12M of JPEG, MPEG, or EXE files would fit because they do not compress as tightly as other files have.

To adjust the compression ratio, follow these steps:

1. Open the DriveSpace 3 window and select the compressed drive whose compression ratio you want to adjust from the Drives on This Computer list.
2. Choose Advanced, Change Ratio; the Compression Ratio dialog box appears (see Figure 15.23).

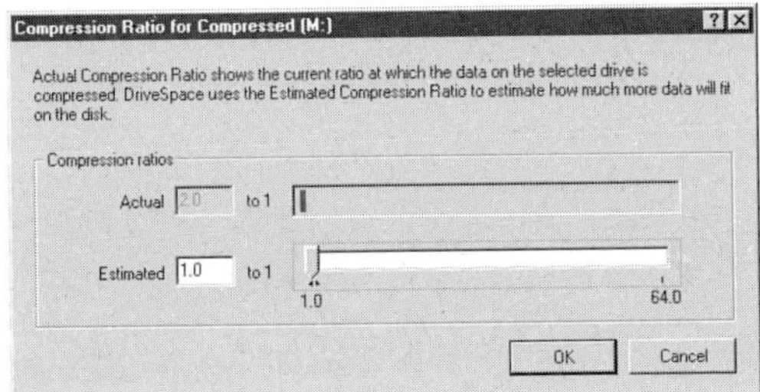

FIG. 15.23 Adjust the compression ratio of a compressed drive in the Compression Ratio dialog box.

3. Drag the Estimated Compression Ratio slider to adjust the compression ratio.
4. When the message box appears informing you that the operation is complete, choose OK.

Viewing the Properties of a Compressed Drive

You can view the properties of a compressed drive or its host using the Drive Properties command. You can find out the name of the compressed volume file and what drive it is stored on, the amount of free and used space on the drive, and the compression ratio if it is a compressed drive.

To view the properties of a drive, follow these steps:

1. Open the DriveSpace 3 window and select the drive whose properties you want to view from the Drives on This Computer list.
2. Choose Drive, Properties. The Compression Information dialog box appears, as shown in Figure 15.24.

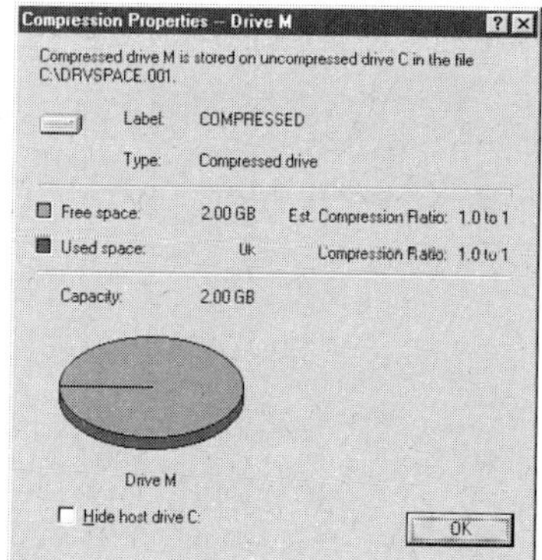

FIG. 15.24
View the properties of a compressed drive or its host in the Compression Information dialog box.

3. You can select the Hide Host Drive option to hide the display of this drive when the drive contents display in the Explorer or My Computer window and in some dialog boxes such as Open and Save As. If you select this option, a message box informs you that you cannot use the data or free space on the drive. Choose Yes to confirm that you want to hide the drive.

   You can use the DriveSpace Properties dialog box to unhide the host drive if you change your mind at a later time.
4. Choose OK.

Improving Compression with the Compression Agent

Compression Agent is a tool that comes with Microsoft Plus! that provides even higher levels of compression and, used in conjunction with DriveSpace 3, allows you to optimize the balance between maximizing disk space and performance. You can specify that particular files and folders are compressed using one of two high compression formats (UltraPack or HiPack) or not at all.

Compression Agent, unlike DriveSpace, doesn't compress files as they are used. Instead, it compresses your files when you run the program. Because it can take a long time to compress your files using the Compression Agent, it is best to run the program when you are not working. You can use the System Agent, discussed in the next section, to schedule the Compression Agent to run after work hours.

To run the Compression Agent, follow these steps:

1. Open the Start menu and click Programs, Accessories, System Tools, and Compression Agent. The Compression Agent dialog box appears (see Figure 15.25).

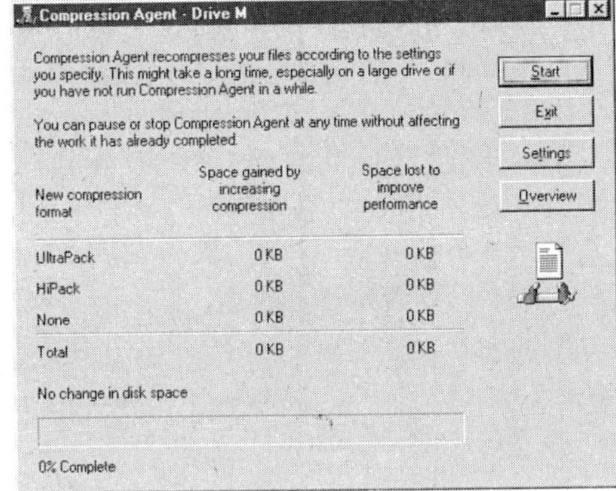

FIG. 15.25
The Compression Agent dialog box is used to set up and run Compression Agent.

2. Click Start to run Compression Agent using the default settings. Compression Agent will recompress the drive file by file, using the best compression method for each file.
3. To change the settings used by Compression Agent, click the Settings button. The Compression Agent Settings dialog box appears (see Figure 15.26).

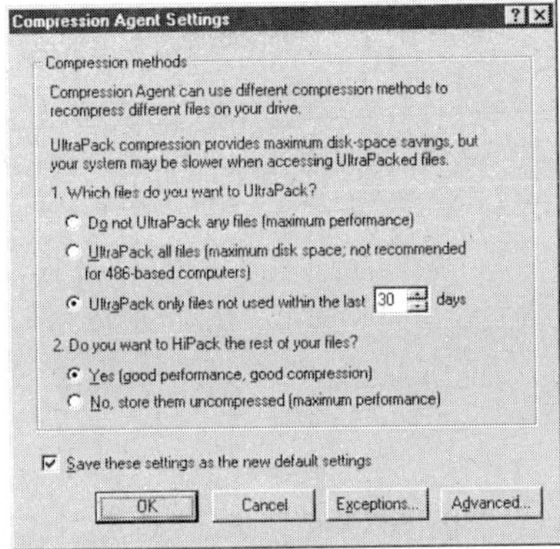

FIG. 15.26
You can specify which compression method you want used on which files in the Compression Agent Settings dialog box.

4. Specify which files you want to UltraPack in the first set of options:
   - Select the Do Not UltraPack Any Files option to maximize performance.
   - Select the UltraPack All Files option to maximize space. Packing and unpacking files using this method is slow, so it is recommended for Pentium systems only.

- Select the UltraPack Only Files Not Used Within the Last Days option to specify that only those files that have not been modified in a specified number of days be UltraPacked.

5. Specify whether or not to HiPack the remaining files in the second set of options:
   - Select Yes to HiPack the remaining files. This option yields a good balance between performance and space-savings.
   - Select No to leave the remaining files uncompressed. Use this option if you want to maximize performance.
6. The Compression Agent can reduce the compression method used for files you have used recently (as specified in step 4). You can override this option when disk space starts to get low by clicking Advanced and specifying a setting in the Advanced Settings dialog box.

   Select the Leave all UltraPacked files in the UltraPack format option if you want files UltraPacked even if you have used them recently.
7. If you want to specify different compression settings for particular files or folders, click the Exceptions button and specify which compression method you want to use for which files and folders.
8. Click Start to run the Compression Agent using your settings.

By manipulating the settings used in both DriveSpace 3 and in Compression Agent, you can fine-tune the balance between performance and disk space, depending on your priorities. For example, to maximize performance while still gaining the benefits of disk compression, you can turn off compression in DriveSpace's Disk Compression Settings dialog box and run the Compression Agent at night to compress your files.

After you choose the settings you want in the Compression Agent, use the System Agent as described in the section "Running Disk Performance Utilities with the System Agent" to run the Compression Agent and recompress the specified disk.

Even when you tell DriveSpace not to compress files, you save space. This is because DriveSpace 3 uses sectors (512 bytes) instead of clusters (32K in size on a 1G drive) as the minimum storage unit. This significantly improves storage efficiency.

Running Disk Performance Utilities with the System Agent

Microsoft Plus! for Windows 95 provides the System Agent, a program that enables you to schedule when to run the system maintenance utilities discussed in this chapter. The System Agent can run other programs, as well, and notify you when your hard disk is low on space.

By default, the System Agent is enabled after you install Plus! This means that each time you start Windows 95, the System Agent starts automatically and runs in the background, only becoming active when it needs to start a scheduled program or notify you of low disk space. Even though System Agent is active by default, it isn't fully set up. After you install System Agent, it automatically places Low Disk Space Notification, ScanDisk for Windows (Standard Test), Disk Defragmenter, and ScanDisk for Windows (Thorough Test) programs in the System Agent. You need to manually tell the System Agent which other programs to run, when to run them, and which program features to use.

To schedule programs with the System Agent, use the following steps:

1. Open the Start menu and choose Programs, Accessories, System Tools, System Agent. The System Agent window opens (see Figure 15.27).

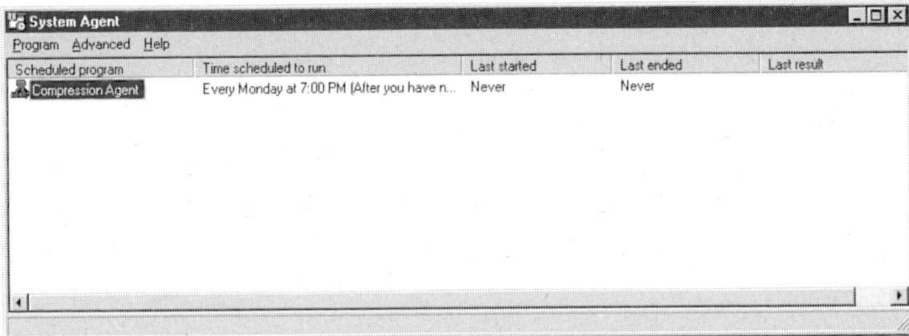

FIG. 15.27 The System Agent window lists the currently scheduled programs.

2. Choose Program, Schedule a New Program. The Schedule a New Program dialog box appears (see Figure 15.28).

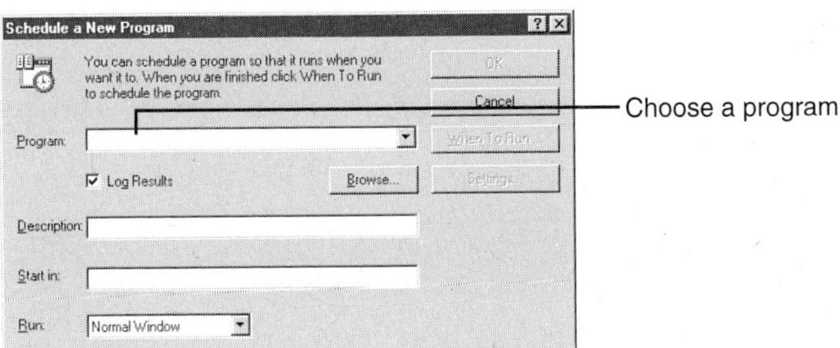

FIG. 15.28 Use the Schedule a New Program dialog box to select programs for System Agent to run according to the schedule you set.

3. Click the drop-down list arrow to open the Program list. Choose a program from the list that appears. You can choose ScanDisk for Windows, Disk Defragmenter, Compression Agent, or Low Disk Space Notification. If you want to run a program other than one of these, click Browse, select the program to run in the Browse dialog box, and then click OK. No matter what method you use, the selected program appears as the Program choice.
4. If you want, you can edit the Description for the program and the Start In folder, which specifies the folder containing files the program needs to run.
5. Open the Run drop-down list and specify whether you want the program to run in a Normal Window, Minimized, or Maximized.

Schedule time-consuming programs such as Disk Defragmenter for a time you won't normally use your computer. Then, leave your computer on during that time, and System Agent will handle the task for you.

6. To specify the schedule for the program, click the When to Run button. The Change Schedule of... dialog box appears (see Figure 15.29).

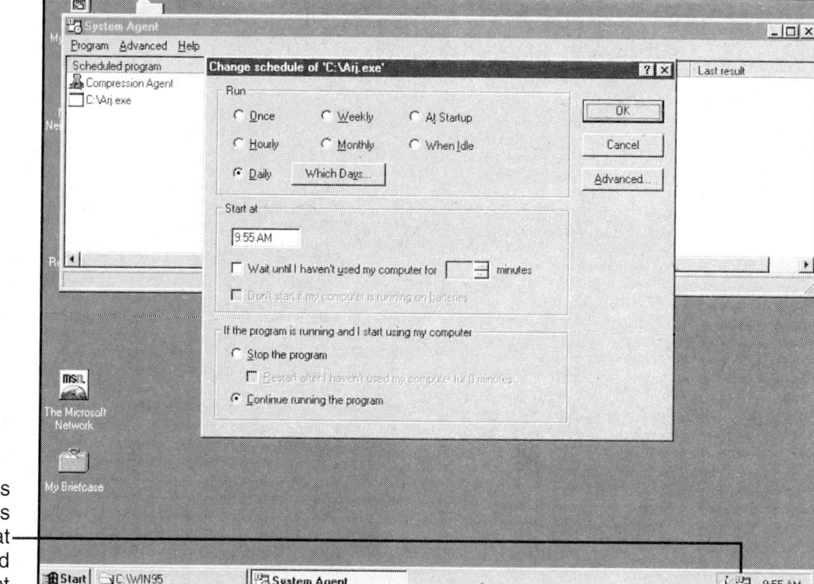

FIG. 15.29 Use the Change Schedule dialog box to set up a schedule for the selected program.

This icon in the status area of the taskbar lets you know that Windows 95 loaded System Agent

7. Click a Run option, such as Weekly or Monthly. Your choice here affects the options available in the Start At area of the dialog box.
8. Specify the options you want in the Start At area. Although there might be other options depending on your choice in step 7, you always need to enter a starting time. Also, you can specify a number of minutes to tell System Agent to wait if you're using your computer when the scheduled program runtime occurs.
9. Choose whether System Agent should Stop the Program or Continue Running the Program should you start using your computer when the scheduled program is running. Stopping the program can protect against data loss while running system utilities.
10. Click Settings to accept your changed schedule of options and to control which features the selected program uses when the System Agent runs the program. The Scheduled Settings dialog box that appears varies depending on the selected program.
11. Specify the settings you want for the selected program; then click OK to close the Scheduled Settings dialog box.

12. Click OK again to finish scheduling the program. System Agent adds the program to the list of scheduled programs.

NOTE Remember that you can schedule the same program to run at different times with different settings. For example, you can schedule a standard ScanDisk check once a week, plus a thorough check once a month.

Although you can use the Program menu choices to make changes to the schedule and settings for one of the listed programs, it's faster to simply right-click the program you want to make changes for. A shortcut menu appears, from which you can choose the following:

- Choose Properties to change things such as the program startup folder and settings (click the Settings button in the dialog box that appears).
- Use the Change Schedule option to adjust how often System Agent runs the program.
- Choose Run Now to run the program immediately, using the settings you specified.
- Choose the Disable option to prevent the listed program from running at the designated time but leave the program on the list; choose Disable again to reinstate the program's schedule.
- Choose Remove to delete the selected program from the System Agent list; confirm the deletion by clicking Yes at the warning that appears.

The Advanced menu in System Agent offers two commands for controlling System Agent itself. Toggle the Suspend System Agent option off whenever you want to stop all your regularly scheduled programs from running; then toggle this choice back on when you need to. The Stop Using System Agent choice completely stops the System Agent operation; after you use this option, System Agent no longer loads when you start Windows, and you have to select System Agent from the System Tools Shortcuts to start using it. To close System Agent after setting it up, choose Program, Exit.

If you have installed Internet Explorer 4.0, you will not find System Agent in your System Tools menu. System Agent is upgraded to the Task Scheduler when you install Internet Explorer 4.0, and the System Agent item in the System Tools menu is replaced with the Scheduled Tasks folder icon. To learn how to use the Task Scheduler, see Chapter 22, "Using FrontPage Express and IE 4 Components."

Monitoring Your System

Windows 95 comes with an application called System Monitor that enables you to monitor the resources on your computer. You can see if you have the System Monitor installed by opening the Start menu, clicking Programs, Accessories, System Tools, and checking for the System Monitor item. If you do not see it on the menu or if it does not start, then you need to rerun Windows 95 and reinstall the System Monitor. Chapter 2 describes how to install and reinstall Windows 95.

You can see information about the 32-bit file system, network clients and servers, and the virtual memory manager, among other things. Most of this information is highly technical in nature and useful only to advanced users. You can display the information in either bar or line charts or as numeric values. To open the System Monitor, open the Start menu; choose Programs, Accessories, System Tools, and System Monitor. The System Monitor window appears, as shown in Figure 15.30.

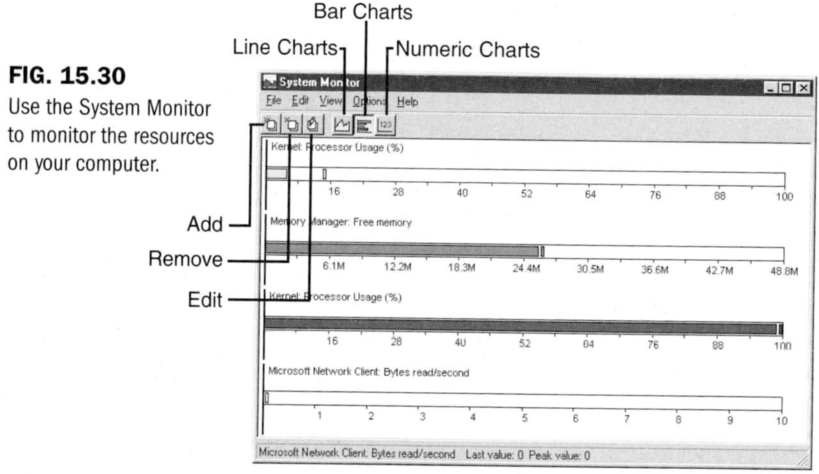

FIG. 15.30
Use the System Monitor to monitor the resources on your computer.

To monitor an item in System Monitor, follow these steps:

1. Select the item you want to monitor by choosing Edit, Add Item; alternatively, click the Add tool. The Add Item dialog box appears (see Figure 15.31).

   You can obtain information on what an item is by selecting the item and clicking Explain. When you select an item in the right box, the explain button becomes an option.
2. Choose OK.
3. Repeat steps 1 and 2 to add additional items to the window.

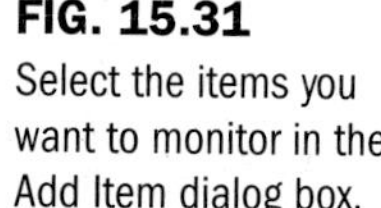

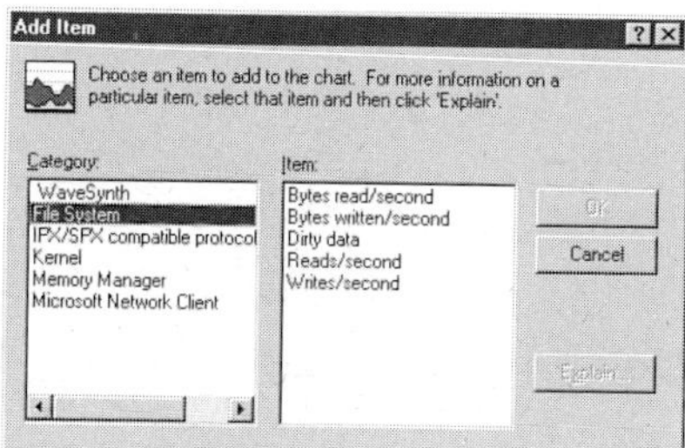

FIG. 15.31
Select the items you want to monitor in the Add Item dialog box.

To remove an item from the window, follow these steps:

1. Choose Edit, Remove Item; alternatively, click the Remove tool.
2. Select the item you want to remove and choose OK.

You can edit an item that is being monitored, changing its display color and the scaling used in its chart. To edit an item, follow these steps:

1. Choose Edit, Edit Item, or click the Edit tool, to display the Edit Item dialog box.
2. Select the item you want to edit and choose OK. The Chart Options dialog box appears, as shown in Figure 15.32.

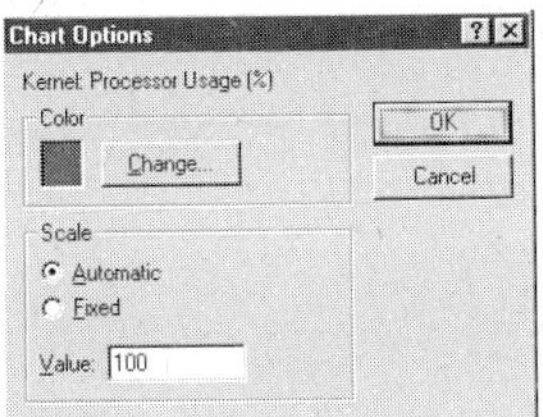

FIG. 15.32
Change the display of an item being monitored in the Chart Options dialog box.

3. Choose Change to change the color of the item.
4. Select Automatic to let System Monitor set the maximum value on the Y-axis.

   or

   Select Fixed and type a value in the Value text box to set your own maximum value for the Y-axis.
5. Choose OK.

You can display the items being monitored as either a line or bar chart or as a numeric value. To change the display, open the View menu and choose Line Charts, Bar Charts, or Numeric Charts; alternatively, click the appropriate tool on the toolbar.

If you want the System Monitor window to stay on top of other windows, even when you work in another program, open the View menu and choose Always on Top. This is handy if you want to monitor some resource as you work in a program. You can shrink the window so that it doesn't take up too much room. Choose the View, Always on Top command again when you don't want the System Monitor window to stay on top of other windows. You can also hide the title bar so that all the System Monitor window is devoted to displaying the chart: Choose the View, Hide Title Bar command. To redisplay the title bar, double-click the chart or press Esc.

TIP Pressing Esc also will hide the title bar if pressed when the title bar is visible.

You can adjust the frequency at which the chart updates by choosing the Options, Chart command and moving the slider to change the update interval. If you are on a network, choose File, Connect to connect to a different computer.

NOTE You can quickly find out how much free disk space there is on a hard disk or floppy disk. Select the disk you want to check in either the Explorer or My Computer, and choose the File, Properties command (alternatively, right-click the desired disk and choose Properties from the shortcut menu). The amount of free space on the disk appears in the Properties dialog box.

Improving Memory Use with Virtual Memory

Your computer has a certain amount of physical memory (RAM) installed. Typically, computers running Windows have at least 4M of RAM, and often 8M or more. The more memory you have, the more programs you can run at the same time and the faster your system operates. However, with Windows 95, you can use a special area of the hard disk as an extension of RAM, called *virtual memory*, to increase the amount of memory available to programs. Using virtual memory, you can run more programs at the same time than is normally possible using only the RAM on the system.

When RAM is tight, Windows begins to move *pages* of code and data from RAM to the hard disk to make more room in RAM. Windows uses a *least-recently used* technique to move pages of memory to the disk, selecting first the pages of code and data not recently accessed by a program. If a program requires a piece of data no longer in physical memory, Windows retrieves the information from disk, paging other information from memory to disk to make room. To programs running in Windows, no difference exists between RAM in the system and virtual memory on the disk.

When you install Windows 95, it automatically determines how much hard disk space to use for virtual memory, depending on the amount of free disk space. In most cases, you should let Windows determine the settings used for virtual memory on your computer. Unless you know what you are doing, changing the settings manually can adversely affect the performance of your computer. If you do want to specify your own virtual memory settings, follow these steps:

1. Open the Start menu and choose Settings, Control Panel.
2. Double-click the System icon to display the System Properties dialog box; select the Performance tab.
3. Click the Virtual Memory tab to display the Virtual Memory dialog box shown in Figure 15.33.
4. Select the Let Me Specify My Own Virtual Memory Settings option.
5. If you want to use a different hard disk for virtual memory than already specified, select a new disk from the Hard Disk drop-down list. The amount of free space on the hard disk appears next to the drive letter.

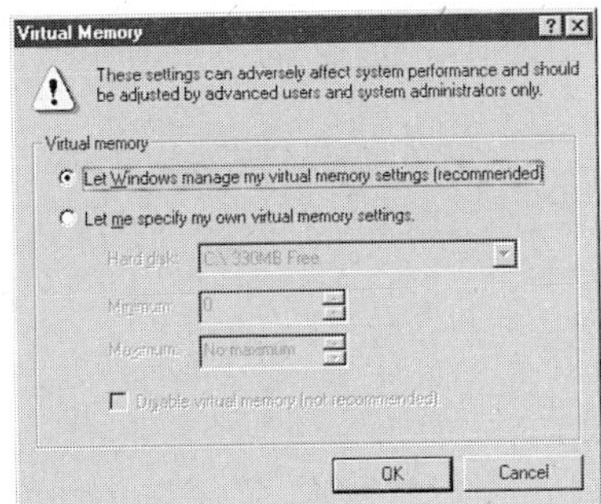

FIG. 15.33
You can let Windows manage your virtual memory settings or specify your own in the Virtual Memory dialog box. Microsoft recommends you let Windows manage virtual memory settings.

6. Specify the minimum amount (in megabytes) of hard disk space you want Windows to use for virtual memory in the Minimum text box.
7. Specify the maximum amount of memory (in megabytes) you want Windows to use for virtual memory in the Maximum text box.
8. Choose OK.

The Virtual Memory dialog box contains a Disable virtual memory (not recommended) check box at the bottom. This turns off all use of virtual memory and is not recommended. ●

CHAPTER 16

Backing Up and Protecting Your Data

by Ron Person

Managing your files means more than just your daily work of creating, naming, and deleting files. If you consider your work valuable, part of your file management routine should be to back up your data by creating a duplicate copy. You will also want to protect your data and system from viruses. *Viruses* are computer programs written for the purpose of interrupting or destroying your work.

The backup program that comes with Windows enables you to create backups onto a removable storage device, such as floppy disks, a tape, or a removable hard disk. Windows does not include a virus protection program at this time, so you need to find a reliable third-party program that will protect your system from this modern-day scourge. ■

How to back up your files

Look here to learn how to copy one or more files from your hard disk to another disk (usually a floppy disk, a tape drive, or another computer on your network).

How to verify that files are backed up correctly

This chapter explains how to compare files on your backup disks with the original files to ensure their validity.

How to use your backup files

Learn how to restore your backed-up files to any location you choose (including their original locations).

How to protect your system from viruses

This section discusses viruses and ways you can protect your system against them.

Backing Up Your Files

As you know, there is more information stored on your hard drive than you can possibly fit on a single floppy disk. The Windows Backup program automatically overcomes this problem by creating a duplicate image of your hard disk's data on a magnetic tape or by spreading an image across multiple floppy disks—as many as necessary to back up your data. During the backup operation, Windows fills each disk in the set to capacity before requesting the next disk. The collection of all these duplicate files and folders is the *backup set.*

As hard disks grow in capacity, it becomes more and more laborious to use floppy disks to back up your data. A much more convenient method is to use a tape backup system. You can fit much more data on a magnetic tape and may be able to back up your entire hard drive with one tape. With tape backups, you also avoid the inconvenience of having to sit at your computer swapping floppy disks. In fact, you can initiate the backup when you leave for lunch; when you return, it will be done.

CAUTION

You put the entire concept of having secure data at risk if your backups are not kept in a safe location, physically separate from the original data. For a small company, the physical location for the backup set can be a safe deposit box or the president's house. For a large company, there are services that pick up tapes and store them in disaster-proof vaults. I know of two instances in which the backups were lost along with the original system. In one case, a thief stole the backup floppy disks that sat next to the computer. In the other case, the fire that destroyed the legal firm's computers also destroyed their backups, which were in a closet in an adjacent room.

NOTE In the last few years, several new options for backing up large amounts of data have appeared on the market. The ubiquitous Iomega Zip Drive is a very convenient way to back up moderate amounts of data (a Zip disk can hold 100M of data). Iomega's Jaz Drive disks can hold up to 1G, ideal for today's large-capacity hard drives. Removable disk media such as these are much faster than tape drives and more convenient to use. Software for backing up your hard drives come with both of these products. For more information, visit Iomega's Web site:

http://www.iomega.com/

NOTE Backup does not install as part of a typical or minimum installation. If Backup is not installed and you want it, refer to Chapter 24, "Installing, Running, and Uninstalling Windows Applications," on how to add programs. On the Windows Setup page of the Add/Remove Programs Properties sheet, look for Backup in the Disk Tools items in the Components list.

To start the backup program, open the Start menu and click Programs, Accessories, System Tools, and Backup. When you first start Backup, you may see a Welcome to Microsoft Backup dialog box that describes the process of making backups. You can select the Don't Show This Again check box if you do not want to see this dialog box again. Backup will also try to detect a tape backup device when you first run it. And you may see a message box that says "Backup has created a Full System Backup file set for you." This means that until you specify otherwise, Backup marks all files and folders to be part of the backup. It is a very good idea to do a Full System Backup at least once a week or once a month, depending on the value of your data and how often program configurations change.

Create a Full System Backup occasionally. It has all the configuration and registry files necessary to rebuild your system from a disaster.

Once you are past these initial dialog boxes, the Backup dialog box appears, as shown in Figure 16.1.

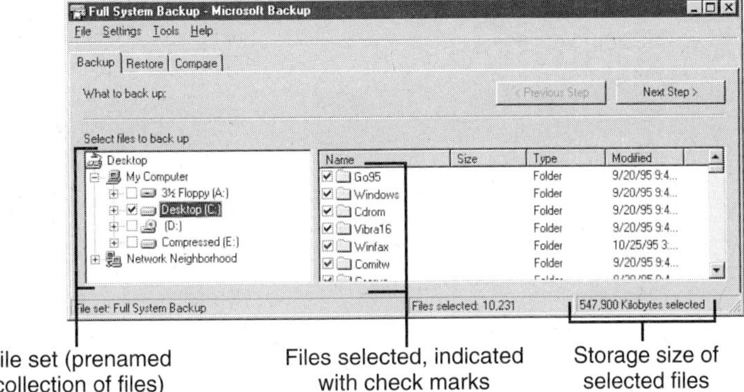

FIG. 16.1
Windows Backup creates duplicate copies of files and folders, compares backups to original files, and restores duplicate files and folders.

Windows divides the three basic functions of Backup into tabs in the Backup dialog box:

- **Backup.** Copies one or more files and folders from your hard disk.
- **Compare.** Compares the files in a backup set to make sure that they match the source files on the hard disk.
- **Restore.** Copies one or more files from your backup set to the hard disk or to another floppy disk.

In addition to these major functions, you can access several other operations from the pull-down menus:

- The File menu enables you to load and save setup files that define settings to be used when backing up and restoring files. The File menu also enables you to print a list of files contained in a backup set.
- The Settings, File Filtering command enables you to filter the folders or file types you want to include in a backup set (this command is discussed in detail later in this chapter). Using the Settings, Options command, you can set various options for each of the major functions, as well as options that affect the program generally.
- The Tools menu contains commands for working with tapes.

Understanding Backup

Before you implement a backup strategy, you need to understand the difference between *full* and *incremental* backups, the two types of backups that you can perform with Windows Backup. When you carry out a full backup, all files and folders on the selected drive are backed up. With a full backup set, you can completely restore your system to its original state in the event of a catastrophe. The disadvantages to a full backup are that it can take a lot of time and storage space if you have many files on your hard drive. The first step of your backup strategy, however, should include a full backup.

With an incremental backup, only those files that have changed since the last full or incremental backup (whichever was last), using the same backup set, are backed up. Typically, you start a backup cycle with a full backup and then periodically perform an incremental backup, using a different set of floppy disks or a new tape, for each incremental backup. Each incremental backup set will contain only those files that have changed since the previous backup. If you need to completely restore your hard disk, you need the full backup set and all the incremental backup sets. The advantage of using incremental backups is that it takes much less time and less space than a full backup. The disadvantages are that you must use a new set of disks (or a new tape) each time you perform an incremental backup and restoring your hard disk is more complicated, since you need to use each of the incremental backup sets, in addition to the full backup set, to be sure that you get the most recent version of a file.

CAUTION

To back up all the files you need to completely restore your system, including essential system files used by Windows 95, you need to use the *Full System Backup Set.* This is the only way to safely back up all the files you need to rebuild your system after a catastrophe. Selecting the drive you want to back up in the Select Files to Back Up pane *will not* back up important system files needed to fully restore your system.

An Overview of How to Back Up Your Hard Disk

Backup makes it easy to name different sets of backup files so that you don't have to select the files and folders each time. When you aren't using your computer (at lunch time, when you return phone messages, or when you leave work), you can start a backup.

Here is the general procedure for creating a backup:

1. Have enough formatted floppy disks or tapes to store the backup.
2. Start Windows Backup.
3. Select the name of a backup set you previously created. Alternatively, manually select the drives, files, and folders you want to back up.
4. Select the Next Step button; then select the destination to which you want to back up. This can be to a tape, to a floppy disk drive, or to another hard disk.
5. Start the backup.

When Backup finishes, you should store the backup media in a safe location physically separate from the computers.

For an extensive list of tape drives compatible with Backup, choose Help, select the Contents tab, and then select the Using Tapes for Backup item. You will also find a list of drives that are not compatible with Backup.

Windows Backup supports the following tape drives and backup devices:

- Hard disks
- Network drives
- Floppy disks
- QIC 40, 80, and 3010 tape drives connected to a primary floppy disk controller
- QIC 40, 80, and 3010 tape drives, manufactured by Colorado Memory Systems and connected to a parallel port

Backup supports compression using the industry standard QIC-113 format. It can read tapes from other backup programs that use the same format with or without compression. Full backups can be restored to a hard disk of another type.

Preparing a Backup Schedule

When you back up important or large amounts of data, it's important to have a backup schedule and a rotation plan for the backup tapes.

Creating a full backup is important to preserving your entire system. Full backups take care of merging Registry settings and the file replacements necessary when restoring a Windows system.

Basically, the backup schedule for most businesses should consist of a full system backup followed by partial or differential backups spread over time. Should your computer ever completely fail, you can rebuild your system using the full backup (which restores Windows, the system Registry, all applications, and their data files as they existed on a specific date). You can then use the partial or differential backups (which store only changed files) to bring the restored system back to its current status. Do a full system backup once a week and a differential backup daily.

Some companies create a full system backup every day. At the end of the week, the tapes are taken to an off-site vault and a new set of tapes are started. Multiple sets of backup tapes are used and rotated between the on-site and off-site storage locations.

CAUTION

Never use one set of tapes for all your backups. If you have only one set of tapes, composed of a full backup and partials, creating another backup means that you overwrite one of the previous backups. Should the

continues

continued

tape fail or the computer fail during backup, you might be left with no backups capable of restoring your system.

Backing Up Files

Whenever you frequently work with the same files and settings, save them as a file set.

Running a backup operation consists of selecting the files you want to backup, specifying the destination for the backup files, and starting the backup. The files that you select for backup will be stored in a single backup file with the extension QIC. To perform a backup, follow these steps:

1. Open the Start menu, click Programs, Accessories, System Tools, and Backup.
2. Select the drive containing the files you want to back up. To select the drive, click the check box for the drive in the left pane of the Backup window.

   In Figure 16.1, local drive C is selected. The files and folders on the drive appear in the right pane. You can expand and collapse the hierarchical display in the left pane by clicking the plus (+) and minus (–) signs next to the folders.
3. Select the files and folders you want to back up. If you want to back up using a file set you have previously named, choose File, Open File Set and select the file set you want to back up.

   See "Saving File Sets," **p. 428**

   You can select all the files in a folder by clicking the check box next to the folder's name in the left pane of the Backup dialog box.

   To view the files and folders inside a folder, in the left pane, open the folder containing the folders or files you want to view, and then in the left pane click the name of the folder whose contents you want to see; its contents appear in the right pane. You can then select individual files or folders inside that folder.

   To select the entire drive, click the box next to the drive in the left pane.

   If you select a folder with many files, a File Selection dialog box momentarily appears, notifying you that file selection is in progress; the box displays the number of files and their total size as the selection progresses.

   The total number of files currently selected and their cumulative size appears in the status bar at the bottom of the window.
4. When you finish selecting the files and folders you want to back up, click the Next Step > button.
5. Select the destination for the backup files (see Figure 16.2).

   If you select a tape drive, the volume name for that tape appears in the Selected Device or Location box. If you select a disk drive, this box shows the drive letter or path, such as A:\.

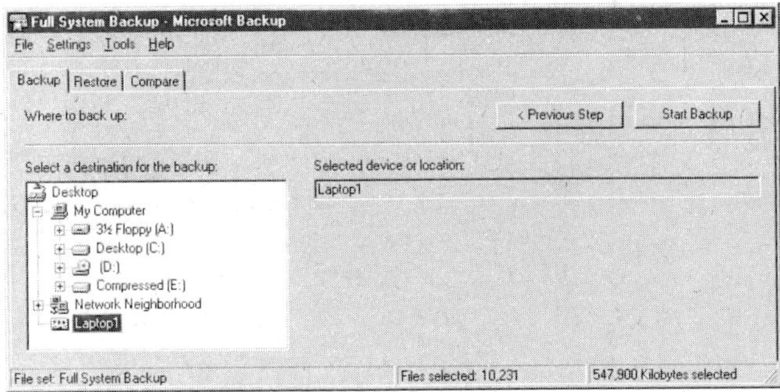

FIG. 16.2
Select the destination for the files you want to back up.

6. Save the file settings for this backup set if you will be doing this backup frequently (see "Saving File Sets," later in this chapter, for more information on saving backup sets).
7. Click the Start Backup button.
8. Type a name for the backup set in the Backup Set Label dialog box that appears (see Figure 16.3). This will be the name of the file containing all the files you have selected for backup.

   If you want to prevent unauthorized people from restoring the backup and stealing your data, click the Password Protect button in the Backup Set Label dialog box and enter a password.

   The name you enter for the backup set is used by you and the computer to identify the data if you ever need to restore or compare it. You can use meaningful names that include spaces, symbols, and numbers. You may want to use a name such as *Accounting, full backup 5/10/95.*

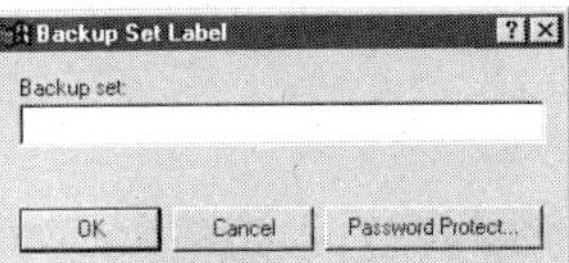

FIG. 16.3
Name the backup set in the Backup Set Label dialog box.

CAUTION

Do not forget the password you assign to your backup set. Without it, there is no way to use your backup.

When you have specified a backup label and an optional password, choose OK. The Backup message box appears (see Figure 16.4), showing you the progress of the backup operation. You can cancel the operation by choosing the Cancel button.

If you are backing up to floppy disks, a message box prompts you when you need to insert the next disk, if necessary.

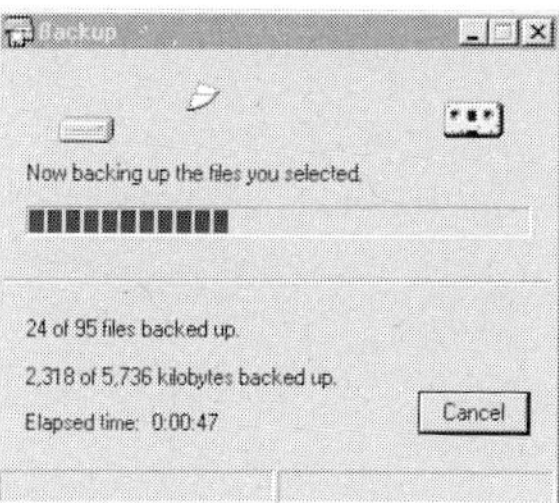

FIG. 16.4
You can monitor the progress of a backup operation in the Backup message box.

9. When the message box appears informing you that the backup operation is complete, click OK. Click OK again to return to the Backup dialog box.

TROUBLESHOOTING

I tried to back up my hard disk on to my Iomega Zip drive with no success. Is there a way to use Windows Backup with my Zip drive? Windows Backup does not support disk spanning with the Zip drive. In other words, if your backup set requires more than one Zip disk, Backup won't work. You can use the backup software that comes with your Zip drive to back up an entire disk onto Zip disks.

The Task Scheduler, available with Internet Explorer 4, will run single copy commands or batch files of copy commands at times that you schedule. To learn more about the Task Scheduler see "Using the Task Scheduler," in Chapter 22.

Using Backup to Create an Archive The Backup program is a handy way to archive files. Suppose that you want to make room on your hard disk by deleting some files you are not currently using but want to use at a later date. Use Backup to archive the files to floppy disks or a tape; then delete the files from the hard disk. If you need the files later, use the restore function to put them back on your hard disk.

See "Restoring Files," **p. 434**

Using Backup to Copy Files to Another Computer Another use for Backup is for transferring folders and files to another computer. The benefit of using Backup for this task is that it takes care of spreading the files across multiple floppy disks when necessary, and it preserves the arrangement of folders, so that you can duplicate your folder organization on another computer. If you purchase a laptop, for example, you can use Backup to transfer the information on your desktop computer to the laptop, including the arrangement of your folders.

Scheduling Backups Using System Agent

You can schedule your backups to run automatically when you are not working with your computer using the System Agent that comes with Microsoft Plus! for Windows. The System Agent has a default schedule for running some of the disk utilities that come with Windows 95, so you

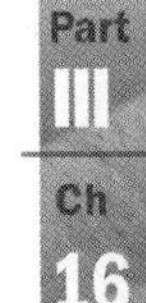

can schedule additional programs to run at specified times. To schedule Backup to run automatically, follow these steps:

1. Create a backup set following the steps outlined in "Saving File Sets," later in this chapter.

   Before you save the backup set, choose Setting, Drag and Drop, and clear the Confirm Operation Before Beginning and Quit Backup After Operation is Finished options. Choose OK.
2. Exit Backup.
3. Click Start, Programs, Accessories, System Tools, and System Agent.
4. Choose Program, Schedule a New Program.
5. Type the following in the Program text box:

   "C:\Program Files\Accessories\Backup.exe" C:\Program Files\Accessories*setname.set*

   Setname.set is the name of the backup set you created.
6. Choose the When to Run button and schedule when you want Backup to run.
7. Exit System Agent.

Be sure to leave your computer running if you have scheduled Backup to run after you leave work. You can create two different schedules, one that does a full backup, perhaps once a week, and another that does daily incremental backups.

Changing Backup Settings and Options

You can change several settings and options that affect your backup operations. To change the settings and options for the backup operation, follow these steps:

1. Open the Settings menu and choose Options.
2. Click the Backup tab to display the Settings–Options dialog box shown in Figure 16.5.

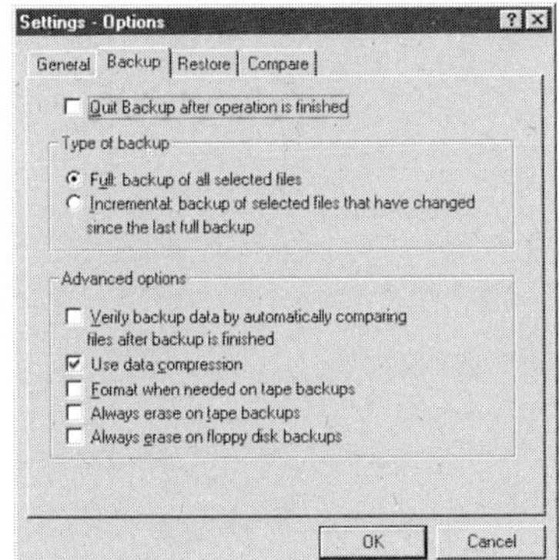

FIG. 16.5
Use the Backup tab in the Settings–Options dialog box to change the settings and options that affect the way backup operations work.

3. Change or select from the following options and then choose OK.

Option	Function
Quit Backup After Operation Is Finished	Closes Backup when the backup operation is completed.
Full: Backup of All Selected Files	Backs up all selected files, regardless of whether file has changed since the last backup.
Differential: Backup of Selected Files that Have Changed Since the Last Full Backup	Only backs up selected files that have changed since the last full backup.
Verify Backup Data by Automatically Comparing Files After Backup Is Finished	Compares each file that is backed up with the original file to verify accurate backup.
Use Data Compression	Compresses files as they are backed up to allow more files to be backed up on a tape or floppy disk.
Format when Needed on Tape Backups	Automatically formats an unused tape before backup operation. This only works on tapes that have not already been formatted.
Always Erase on Tape Backups	Erases the tape on backup. When this option is not selected, backups are added to the tape if there is room.
Always Erase on Floppy Disk Backups	Automatically erases floppy disks before they are used in a floppy disk backup operation. When this option is not selected, backups are added to the floppy disk if there is room.

Saving File Sets

If you back up the same set of files regularly, you can save the settings for that file set. Saving backup settings saves you the trouble of reselecting the files and destination each time you want to back up the files. To save a file set, follow these steps:

1. Open the Backup dialog box and in the Backup tab, select the files you want to back up, as described earlier in this chapter. Click the Next Step > button.
2. Select the destination for the backup files from the Select a Destination list.
3. Choose File, Save As. The Save As dialog box appears (see Figure 16.6).
4. Type a name for the backup set in the File Name text box.
5. Choose the Save button.
6. Choose the Start Backup button if you want to continue the backup operation and create a backup using the file set you just specified.

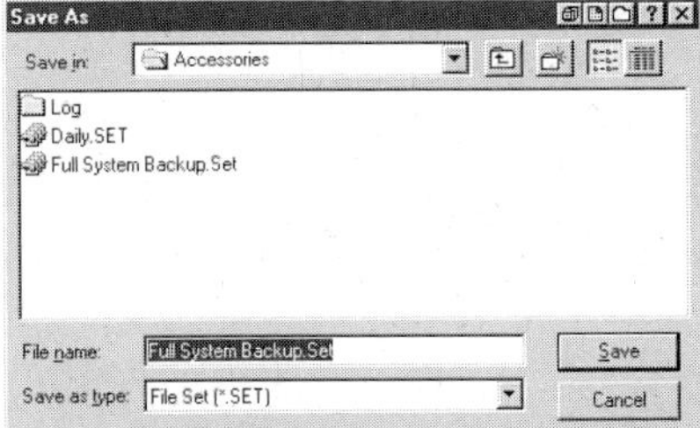

FIG. 16.6
Name your file set with a recognizable name for what it contains and when it was created.

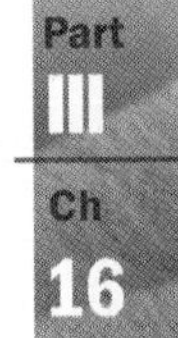

If you make changes to an existing file set, choose the File, Save command to save the file set with the same name without opening the Save As dialog box.

To open a file set for use in a backup operation, follow these steps:

1. Open the Backup dialog box; then click the Backup tab. Choose File, Open File Set to display the Open dialog box shown in Figure 16.7.

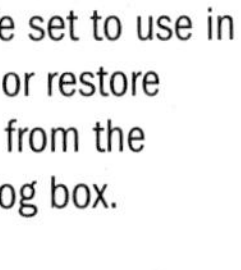

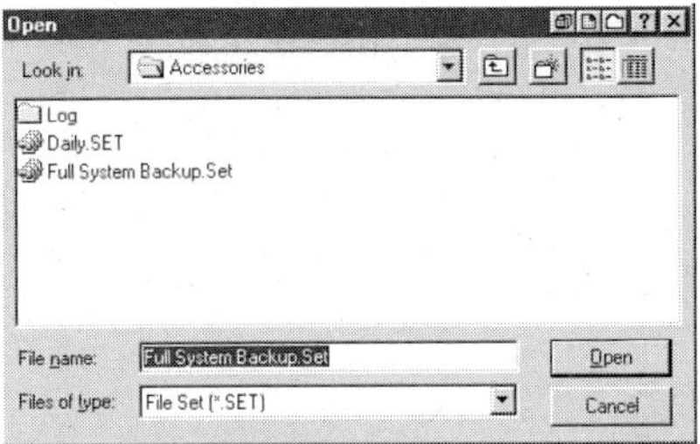

FIG. 16.7
Open a file set to use in a backup or restore operation from the Open dialog box.

2. If you cannot see the file set you want to open, open the folder that contains the file set.
3. Select the file set and choose Open.

The file set is opened, and the files named in this file set are selected in the Backup dialog box.

Filtering Folders and File Types Included in Backup Operations

Backup's file-filtering commands enable you to filter out specific folders and types of files so that they are not included in the backup set. These commands can save you a lot of time when you create a file set to be backed up.

You may not want to include all the files on your hard disk in a backup operation. In some cases, you may want to back up all but a few folders; it is easier to specify the folders you *don't* want to include in the backup set than to select all the folders you do want to include. You may not want to include program files in your daily backups because you can always reinstall your programs if your system crashes. You can dramatically reduce the number of disks you use in a backup if you limit the file set to data files only.

To exclude from a backup files of a specific type or date, follow these steps:

1. Choose Settings, File Filtering. The File Filtering—File Types dialog box appears, as shown in Figure 16.8.

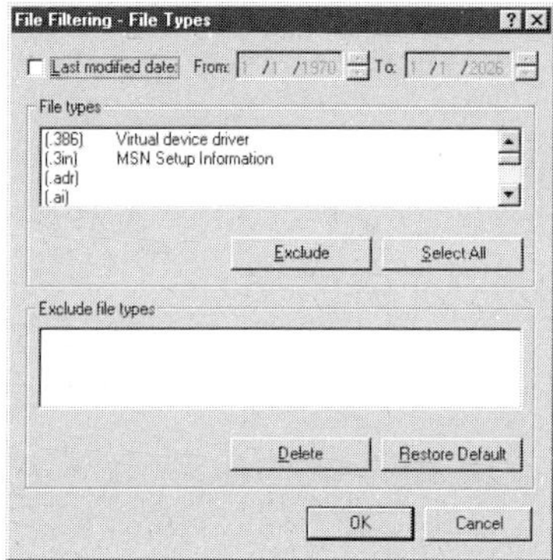

FIG. 16.8
You can exclude files of a specific type or files with specific dates.

2. To exclude files modified between two dates, select the Last Modified Date check box. Enter From and To dates that *exclude* the files you do not want copied. Click the insertion point in the date segment you want to change, and then click the up or down spinner arrow to change the date.

   For example, if you want to exclude files before November 30, 1995, enter a From date of **1/1/1970** and a To date of **11/30/95**.

If you want to exclude all but a few of the file types in the File Types list, click Select All, hold the Ctrl key, and click the types of files you don't want to exclude.

3. To exclude specific file types from the backup operation, select the types of files you want to exclude from the File Types list and click Exclude. Continue to select file types and click the Exclude button until all the file types you want to exclude appear in the Exclude File Types list at the bottom of the dialog box.

   To select all of the file types in the list, click Select All.
4. To delete a file type from the list in the Exclude File Types box, select the file type and click Delete.
5. To clear the Exclude File Types box, click Restore Default.
6. When you finish making your selections, choose OK.

Changing the General Settings in Backup

You can change two options in Backup that affect the backup, restore, and compare functions. To change these options, choose Settings, Options. Select the General tab to display the Settings—Options dialog box shown in Figure 16.9.

- Select the Turn on Audible Prompts option if you want to hear beeps from your computer's speaker during backup, compare, and restore operations.
- Select the Overwrite Old Status Log Files option to replace the old status log with the new one generated by the current backup. The status log records errors and completions of file backups.

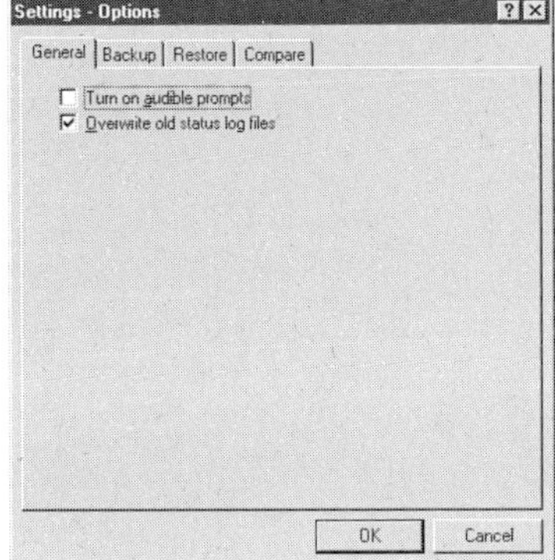

FIG. 16.9 Use the General tab in the Settings–Options dialog box to change the settings and options that affect the way Backup's operations work.

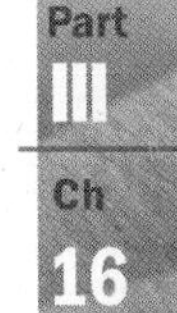

Backing Up with a Simple Drag and Drop

Once you understand the importance of backing up files and see how easy it is to do, you will back up frequently. There is an easy way to back up your files if you created file sets (as described earlier in this chapter). You can drag a file set and drop it onto the Backup icon, or you can double-click a file set name. Either of these actions immediately starts the backup. With the appropriate settings, the entire backup operation can go on in the background, and you can continue to use the computer for other tasks.

Backing up data is so important that if you are an experienced Windows user, you may want to set up other users' computers with drag-and-drop backup so that they can easily protect their data.

To prepare Backup for drag-and-drop operation, follow these steps:

1. Choose Settings, Drag and Drop to display the Drag and Drop dialog box shown in Figure 16.10.

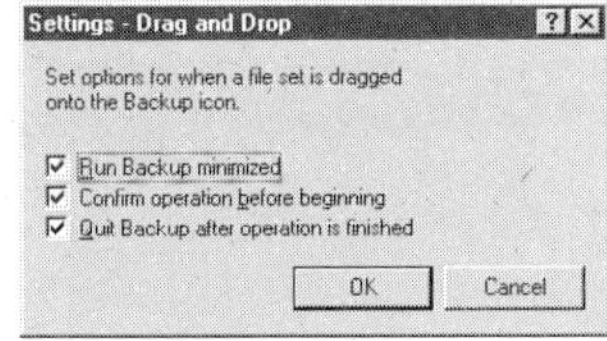

FIG. 16.10 Change the Backup settings to make drag-and-drop backup operate in the background while you work.

2. Change or select from the following options and then choose OK.

Option	Function
Run Backup Minimized	After dragging a file set onto the Backup icon, the Backup window minimizes.
Confirm Operation Before Beginning	Displays a message showing which files will be backed up. Asks you to confirm that you want the files backed up.
Quit Backup After Operation Is Finished	Quits Backup after the file set is backed up.

If Backup is operating in the background, you don't see it as a window on-screen. If you need to stop a backup that is in the background, display the title bar and click the Backup button. A dialog box displays the current backup status and gives you the opportunity to cancel the backup.

NOTE If you have multiple file sets, but you don't want them all as Shortcuts on your desktop, you can still start them quickly to do a backup. In the Windows Explorer or My Computer window, double-click the name of the file set you want to back up. You are prompted whether you want to make a backup; the backup runs with the settings specified for that file set.

Before you can create backups with a drag-and-drop procedure, you must display the Backup program icon. You can open the Program Files/Accessories folder in a window in the Windows Explorer or My Computer. A more convenient method is to create a shortcut to BACKUP.EXE and display it on your desktop.

If you also want a quick way to find and display the SET files that specify your file sets, create a shortcut to the directory containing the SET files. You can do this by using the Find command (available on the Start menu) to find all files that end with SET. Create a new folder and drag the SET files into the new folder. Now create a shortcut to this folder and put that shortcut on the desktop (see Figure 16.11). (Creating shortcuts is described in Chapter 9, "Understanding Windows 95.")

See "Starting Programs from a Shortcut Icon on the Desktop," **p. 260**

FIG. 16.11 Once drag and drop is enabled, backing up is as easy as dropping a file-set icon onto the Backup shortcut.

NOTE Normally, Windows stores the file sets in the Program Files\Accessories folder. If you are unsure where your backup file sets are stored on your hard disk, open the Start menu and choose Find. Search for all files ending with .SET by entering ***.SET** in the Named box.

To back up a file set, you only need to double-click the shortcut to the folder containing the file sets. This opens the folder containing the file sets as a Window on your desktop. Figure 16.11 shows such an open folder. Now drag the file set you want to back up onto the shortcut to BACKUP.EXE and drop it. You are prompted whether you want to continue with the backup operation. Respond by clicking Yes or No.

Formatting and Erasing Tapes

If you use tapes to do your backups, Backup includes two tools for working with tapes. When you purchase a new tape, you must format the tape before you can use it, just as you format a floppy disk. The Format Tape command formats a tape for you. If you want to erase the contents on a tape before you use it for a new backup operation, you can use the Erase Tape command.

To format a tape, follow these steps:

1. Insert the tape in the tape drive.
2. Open the Backup dialog box and choose Tools, Format Tape. If the Format Tape command is grayed out, choose the Redetect Tape command, which enables Backup to detect the tape.
3. When the Format Tape dialog box appears (see Figure 16.12), type a name for the tape and choose OK. You use this name to identify the tape relative to other tapes you use.

Formatting begins. The progress of the formatting operation appears in the Format Tape dialog box. Formatting a tape can take a long time; you may want to start the formatting operation when you are going to be away from your desk for an extended period.

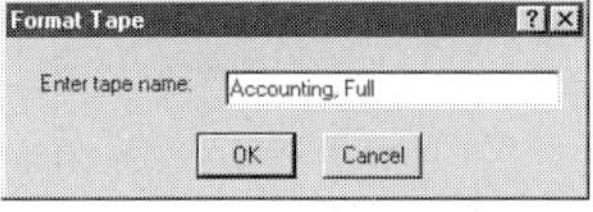

FIG. 16.12
Enter a name for the tape you want to format in the Format Tape dialog box.

4. When the message box appears telling you the operation is complete, choose OK; choose OK again to return to the Backup dialog box.

To erase a tape, follow these steps:

1. Insert the tape in the tape drive.
2. Open the Backup dialog box and choose Tools, Erase Tape. If the Erase Tape command is grayed out, choose the Redetect Tape command, which enables Backup to detect the tape.
3. Choose Yes when the confirmation message box appears. The progress of the erase operation appears in the Erase dialog box.
4. When the message box appears telling you the operation is complete, choose OK. Choose OK again to return to the Backup dialog box.

Restoring Files

If you're lucky, you may never have to use Backup's restore function. When you do need it, however, it's as easy to use as the backup function. You can restore all the files from a backup set or select specific files or folders to restore. You can also choose where you want to restore the files.

To restore files, follow these steps:

1. Open the Backup dialog box and click the Restore tab (see Figure 16.13).
2. Select the drive containing the backup files from the left panel of the window. In Figure 16.13, the tape drive has been selected as the backup source.

FIG. 16.13
In the Restore tab of the Backup dialog box, select the files you want to restore.

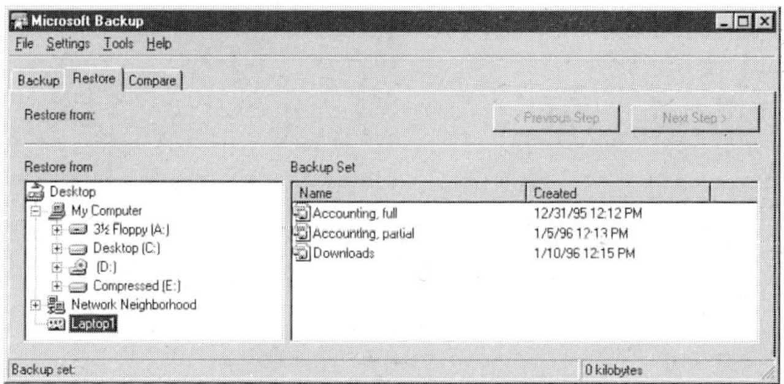

3. Select the backup set containing the files you want to restore from the right pane. If you have more than one backup file on a floppy disk or tape, select the one containing the files you want to restore. A single backup file, with the extension QIC, contains the files you backed up.
4. Click the Next Step > button.
5. Select the folders or files you want to restore as shown in Figure 16.14.

FIG. 16.14
You can select all or part of a backup set when you restore.

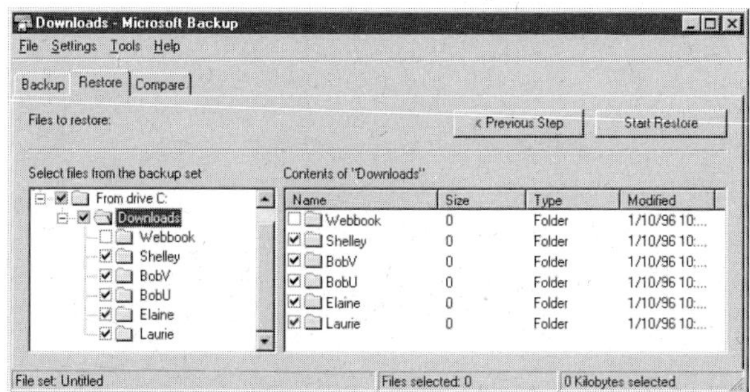

6. Click the Start Restore button. The Restore message box appears, showing you the progress of the restore operation (see Figure 16.15).

By default, the files are restored to their original location. You can choose to restore the files to another location by changing one of the restore options, as described next.

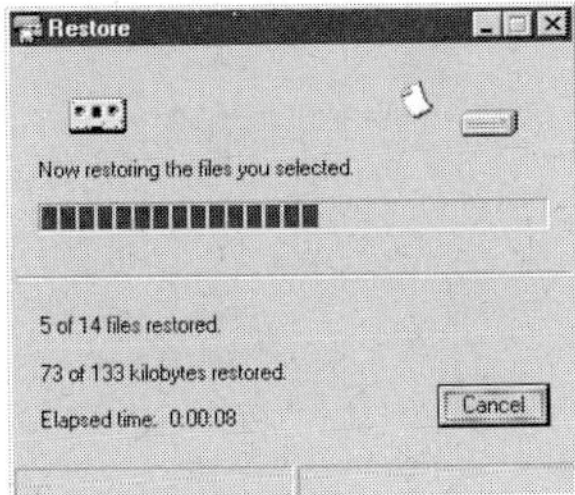

FIG. 16.15 The Restore message box informs you about the progress of the restore operation.

7. When the Operation Complete message box appears, choose OK.

Restoring Files to Other Locations You can restore files to a locations other than their original location (the location from which they were initially backed up). To restore files to an alternate location, follow these steps:

1. Choose Settings, Options.
2. Click the Restore tab.
3. Select the Alternate Location option and choose OK.
4. Perform steps 1 through 6 of the restore procedure described in the preceding section (stop just before you have to click the Start Restore button).
5. Click the Start Restore button. The Browse for Folder dialog box appears (see Figure 16.16).

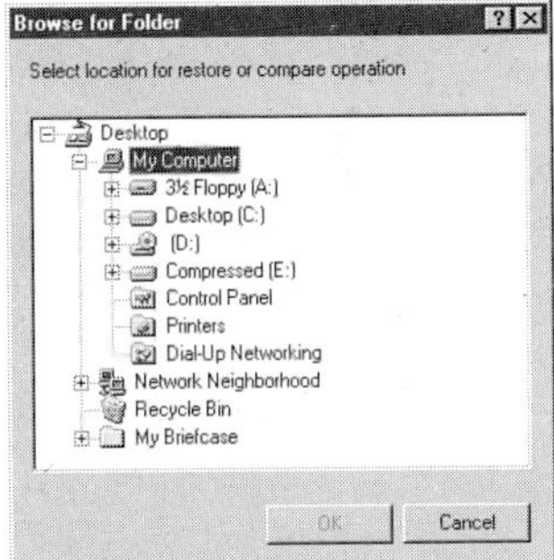

FIG. 16.16 Select the location to which you want to restore files from the File Redirection box.

6. Select the location to which you want to restore the files and choose OK.
7. When the Operation Complete message box appears, choose OK.

Changing Restore Settings and Options You can change several settings and options that affect your restore operations. To change the settings and options for the restore function, follow these steps:

1. Choose Settings, Options.
2. Click the Restore tab to display the dialog box shown in Figure 16.17.

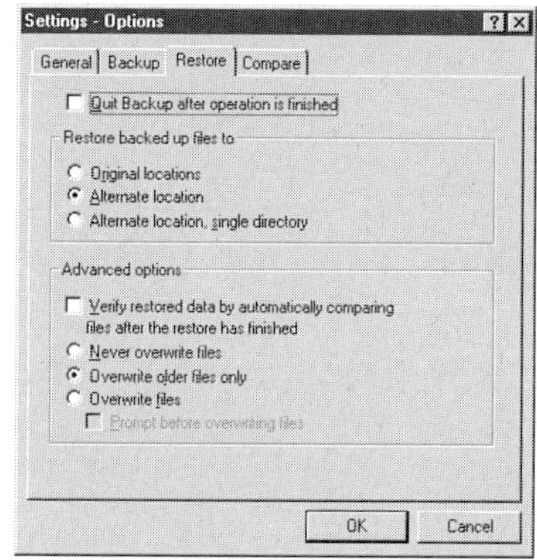

FIG. 16.17 Use the Restore tab in the Settings–Options dialog box to change the settings and options that affect the way restore operations work.

3. Change or select from the following options and then choose OK.

Option	Function
Quit Backup After Operation Is Complete	Closes Backup when the restore operation is completed.
Original Locations	Restores files to their original locations.
Alternate Location	Restores files to an alternate location. (See "Restoring Files to an Alternate Location" earlier in this chapter.)
Alternate Location, Single Directory	Restores files to a single directory at an alternate location. Doesn't duplicate original folder structure.
Verify Restored Data by Automatically Comparing Files After the Restore Has Finished	Compares each file to the file on disk or tape after it is restored to check for accuracy of restore.
Never Overwrite Files	Files that are already on the destination location are not overwritten during a restore operation.
Overwrite Older Files Only	Only files that are older than the files in the backup set are overwritten during a restore operation.
Overwrite Files	All files are overwritten during a restore operation. Use the Prompt Before Overwriting Files check box to specify whether you want to be prompted before a file is overwritten.

Verifying Backup Files

The first time you use a series of disks or a tape for a backup, or any time you want to be absolutely sure of your backup, you should do a comparison. When you compare backups to the original files, you verify that the backup copies are both readable and accurate. To perform a compare, follow these steps:

1. Open the Backup dialog box and click the Compare tab.
2. From the left pane of the dialog box, select the device containing the backup files you want to compare (see Figure 16.18).

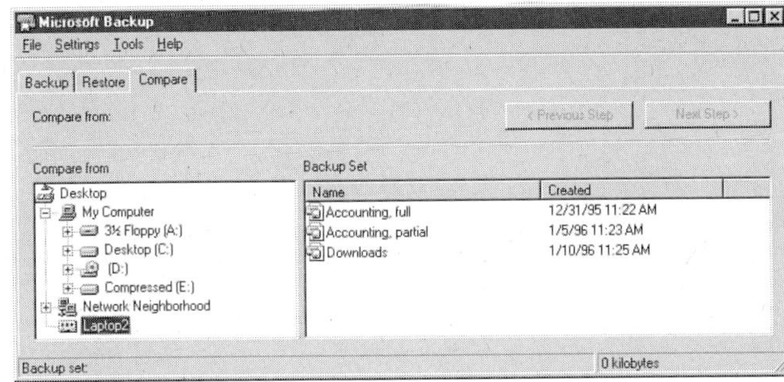

FIG. 16.18
Use the Compare function to verify the accuracy of your backup operations.

3. From the right pane, select the backup set containing the files you want to compare.
4. Click the Next Step > button.
5. Select the files or folders you want to compare to the original files.
6. Click the Start Compare button. The Compare message box informs you of the progress of the compare operation.
7. Choose OK when the Operation Complete message box appears; choose OK again to return to the Backup dialog box.

Changing Compare Settings and Options

You can change several settings and options that affect your compare operations. To change the settings and options for the compare function, follow these steps:

1. Choose Settings, Options.
2. Click the Compare tab to display the dialog box shown in Figure 16.19.
3. Change or select from the following options and then choose OK.

Option	Function
Quit Backup After Operation Is Finished	Closes Backup when the compare operation is completed.
Original Locations	Compare files to files at their original locations.

continues

continued

Option	Function
Alternate Location	Compares files to files at an alternate location.
Alternate Location, Single Directory	Compare files to files in a single directory at an alternate location. Doesn't look for duplicates of the original folder structure.

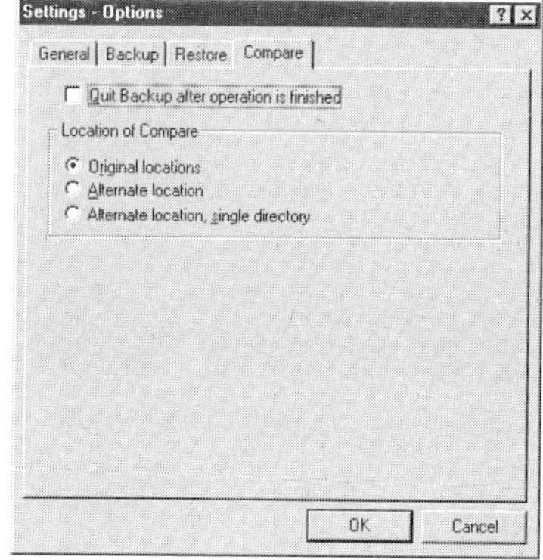

FIG. 16.19 Use the Compare tab in the Settings–Options dialog box to change the settings and options that affect the way compare operations work.

Protecting Your Files from Viruses

You need to take measures to protect your computer from viruses, a scourge of the modern day computer world. In addition to backing up your system regularly, you should obtain an antivirus program and make a habit of using it on a regular basis to protect your files against infection, especially if you frequently introduce files onto your hard disk from outside sources.

Understanding How Viruses Damage Your Computer

A computer virus is a program designed to do damage to either your computer or your computer's data. Viruses make copies of themselves and spread from one computer to another.

There are three ways in which viruses can be transmitted between computers:

- Loading and running infected software
- Booting up with an infected floppy disk
- Opening a document or template file that has a macro virus attached to it

It used to be the case that viruses were only transmitted by one of the first two routes. With the arrival of macro viruses, it has become much more difficult to insulate your system from viruses. Now you can get a virus by simply opening an infected Word for Windows or Excel document or template file. If there is a macro virus attached to the document, all the documents you open from that point on will become infected with the virus. If you commonly exchange documents with other users, you must take precautions against this new type of virus.

The best approach for protecting against viruses is to install one of the available antivirus programs. Used correctly, a good antivirus program can protect against the vast majority of known viruses before they damage your computer. Symantec's Norton Anti-Virus for Windows and McAfee Associates VirusScan are well-respected virus protection programs.

ON THE WEB

Both Symantec and McAfcc Associates provide virus-definition updates that you can download from their Web sites to protect your system against the many new viruses that are constantly arriving on the computing scene. Visit the following Web sites for more information on these products.

http://www.symantec.com

http://www.mcafee.com

PART IV

Working with the Internet

CHAPTER 17

Getting Connected to the Internet

by Brad Lindaas

What is the Internet and how can you benefit from it?

The chapter explains the concept of the Internet, how it came about, and the benefits for business, researchers, and individuals.

What is the means of communication and protocol for the Internet?

TCP/IP is the networking protocol used by many corporate networks as well as the Internet.

How to find a service that can connect you to the Internet and its services

There are many decisions you need to make before deciding how to connect to the Internet.

How to connect Windows 95 to the Internet

Wizards in Windows 95 make connecting to the Internet very easy. If you use an Internet service provider, you will need to know some Internet access information. This chapter explains what you need to complete the Wizards dialog boxes.

Windows 95 provides a flexible and technically robust means of connecting to the Internet, whether you are connecting from a stand-alone computer or from a network. Windows 95 has built-in support for TCP/IP dial-up access, and it supports 16-bit and 32-bit Windows Internet applications. ■

Understanding the Internet

The Internet is an aggregation of high-speed networks, supported by almost 6,000 federal, state, and local systems, as well as university and commercial networks. It spans worldwide to networks in Canada, South America, Europe, Australia, and Asia, with more than 30,000,000 users. The Internet began with about 200 linked computers; today, there are several million linked computers all over the world. The Internet is growing so fast that no one can say how big it is today, or how large it will grow tomorrow.

The main functions of the Internet are:

- *E-mail* (electronic mail). You can send a message to anyone, anywhere in the world (as long as they have access to the Internet), almost instantaneously and for less than the cost of a regular letter, or "snailmail."
- The *World Wide Web* (the Web, or WWW). The fastest growing part of the Internet, the Web provides access to files, documents, images, and sounds from thousands of different Web sites using hypertext, which links you to other documents anywhere on the Internet.
- File transfer using *File Transfer Protocol* (FTP). FTP is an older, but still popular tool for file transfer between computers linked to the Internet. You use FTP to access the hundreds of archives of Windows shareware and freeware software.
- *UseNet newsgroups*. These are open forum discussion groups on topics ranging from science, current events, music, computers, "alternative" issues, and many others. There are currently more than 20,000 newsgroups, and the list grows daily.
- *Gopher*. Named after the mascot of the University of Minnesota, Gopher allows you to burrow through the Internet to find files. Gopher displays lists of documents and links to other gopher sites.
- *WAIS*. When connected to the Internet, you need a way to search for the information you want. The Wide Area Information Server (WAIS) protocol provides a way to search databases of indexed documents, and return pointers to the documents themselves.
- *Telnet*. Telnet provides an alphanumeric terminal window that allows you to login to Internet hosts and access character-based programs.
- Internet Relay Chat (IRC) is an open forum for people to come together and have text based, real-time communications with each other. Based on channels, each one with a different, sometimes specific, topic.

Electronic Mail

The most widely used service on the Internet is e-mail. With e-mail, you are in almost instantaneous contact with anyone else on the Internet, no matter where they live or work.

How do you send an e-mail message? On the Internet, everyone has a unique e-mail address that looks something like this:

username@anynet.com

Businesses, Internet organizations, and services such as Listserv (a program that keeps track of mailing lists) also have addresses. Your address is composed of your user name (such as *jsmith*) and your provider's domain. When Jane Smith subscribes to America Online for her Internet access, she may want to have an e-mail address like this one:

jsmith@aol.com

But, if Joe Smith is already using the "jsmith" login name on America Online, Jane has to pick another one, such as "janesmith" or "jane_s."

The Internet also has *mailing lists*, or e-mail discussion groups, on many topics (such as writing, pets, running a small business, and so on), comprised of members who subscribe to that mailing list. It usually costs nothing to subscribe to most mailing lists.

NOTE To *subscribe* to a mailing list, send an e-mail message to the *listserver* who manages that mailing list. Usually, to subscribe, you send a message with only the word "subscribe" in the message body.

To *send a message* to the members of a mailing list, after you have joined, post a message to the mailing list itself. You respond to messages in the mailing list in the same way you answer an e-mail message from an individual.

The World Wide Web

The World Wide Web, also called the Web or WWW, is the fastest growing and most exciting part of the Internet. It was developed in 1989 at CERN (which stands for *Centre Européen de Recherche Nucléaire*, but which most people call the Particle Physics Research Laboratory) at the University of Bern in Switzerland. Although the rest of the Internet is text oriented, the World Wide Web is graphics and sound oriented. Clicking a *hypertext* or *hypermedia link* (a specially encoded text or graphic image) takes you to other documents, called *Web pages*, where you can view images from the Hubble telescope, visit an art museum, watch a video clip of skiers or read about NBC's hit show, *ER*—all on your computer.

Unlike other Internet file-retrieval systems, which are hierarchical in nature (you wend your way through descending layers of menus or directories to find what you are looking for), the Web is distributed, offering links to other parts of the same document or other documents, which are not necessarily at the same Web site as the current document. With a *browser*, such as Microsoft's Internet Explorer, you can connect to a location referred to as a Uniform Resource Locator (URL), such as:

http://www.mcp.com

and jump directly to the Web page of Macmillan Publishing USA, as shown in Figure 17.1.

After you install Internet Explorer, you can configure it to view and interact with graphical images on many Web sites, listen to music and voice clips, watch videos, and use hypertext links to jump to other World Wide Web sites around the world.

FIG. 17.1
The Macmillan Publishing USA page, as viewed from Internet Explorer. Click elements in the graphic to move to the Web pages for those sites.

Web authoring tools, such as Microsoft's FrontPage Express (included with Internet Explorer 4.0), allow anyone with an Internet account to create his or her own *Home page* (a kind of display you create that anyone on the Web can see). FrontPage Express and other Internet components are discussed in Chapter 22, "Using FrontPage Express and IE4 Components."

FTP

File Transfer Protocol (FTP) was one of the first functions of the Internet. FTP lets you copy files from the many file repositories, or archives, on the Internet. Computers that permit you to log in to them and download files are called *FTP servers*. You use Internet Explorer to access FTP servers. FTP servers that allow you to login using the account "anonymous" are called *anonymous-FTP servers*.

There are thousands of anonymous FTP servers all over the globe, each with thousands of files. *Archie servers* index the files available on anonymous FTP sites. Without going to each site and browsing, you can go to an Archie server and search for files by their names. Of course, if the file is about drug use in ancient Egypt, for example, but is named dr3aeg91.txt, Archie has no clue about what the file contains. After you scan through an index on an Archie server, you can select files from the index you want to download to your computer.

UseNet Newsgroups

Newsgroups are another important service on the Internet. Where e-mail is a one-to-one communication, newsgroups are many-to-many discussions, forming global user communities organized by topics. There are over 20,000 newsgroups currently on the Internet, dealing with every imaginable—and unimaginable—topic. You can read messages from a newsgroup to see whether you want to subscribe. Subscribing to newsgroups is free.

ON THE WEB

UseNet Info Center

http://sunsite.unc.edu/usenet-i/

UseNet Newsgroup listing on the Yahoo! search engine

http://www.yahoo.com/News/Usenet/Newsgroup_Listings/

Gopher

Gopher servers are computers on the Internet that maintain lists of the files residing on their own as well as other computers. With Internet Explorer you can connect to gopher locations and search files. Gopher allows descriptive comments to be attached to file names. Like the World Wide Web, you can click a file name, and download a file to your computer.

Veronica (Very Easy Rodent-Oriented Netwide Index to Computerized Archives) servers allow you to search menu items on Gopher servers. Veronica servers compile databases of Gopher menus and provide information about the files, in addition to the file names and their locations.

ON THE WEB

Gopher listing on the Yahoo! search engine

http://www.yahoo.com/Computers_and_Internet/Internet/Gopher/

Index of Veronica Servers

gopher://gopher.scs.unr.edu/11/veronica

WAIS

Let's say that you are looking for as many documents as you can find about drug use in ancient Egypt, but you do not know the names of the files. *WAIS* (Wide Area Information Server) is the most useful search tool for this kind of search. WAIS has an index of keywords contained in all the documents on servers all over the world. Using WAIS, you can type **drugs** and **Egypt** to get information on your topic, even if the file names of the documents containing that information are obscure.

Telnet

Telnet allows users to log in to a remote computer and interact with it using a terminal emulation window. Telnet provides a way for participants in *MUD* (Multiple User Domain) games to play one another online.

TIP Because Telnet uses short keystroke commands to interact with computers, it can be difficult to use. If you have a better way to access a remote site, use that method instead.

Understanding TCP/IP

TCP/IP stands for Transmission Control Protocol/Internet Protocol. TCP/IP is the method used by every computer on the Internet to transfer files. As the name indicates, it is actually two protocols. The first part developed was the Internet Protocol (IP), developed in the days of ARPANET (the Advanced Research Projects NETwork, the original Internet, formed in the 1960s) to send data in *frames* (self-contained units of information, sometimes also referred to as packets) from one computer network to another. The weakness of IP is its inability to deal with poor transmissions. If a frame gets garbled or interrupted, the receiving IP-based machine just removes it from the transmission.

The TCP protocol envelops the IP. The TCP protocol makes sure every frame is delivered to the receiving network reliably, in the same order it was sent. An error detection system verifies that the frame received is identical to the one sent. Also, TCP ensures that frames have not been garbled during transmission. If a frame arrives that has been garbled, TCP requests the transmitting system to resend the frame.

Every network and every computer on the Internet uses TCP/IP to communicate. Versions of Microsoft Windows after version 3.x have encouraged the development of a Windows TCP/IP standard, called the Windows Sockets Library, or *Winsock*. All manufacturers of Windows-based TCP/IP programs have accepted this standard, which means that, ideally any Windows mail reader you choose will work with the WINSOCK.DLL in your \Windows directory.

But still some problems remain. A version of Winsock bundled with one software manufacturer's application may conflict with another version. Each application may install a version of Winsock in its own directory, causing conflicts with another manufacturer's version. Or an Internet provider may customize its version of Winsock, causing conflicts with Internet applications that cannot recognize the new version. Internet jockeys running Windows must periodically comb their hard drives for mismatched Winsocks.

With Windows 95, such conflicts are less of a problem. Microsoft has created two Winsock libraries, one for 16-bit applications and another for 32-bit applications. In addition, a Virtual Device Driver (VxD), called WSOCK.VXD, manages the TCP/IP interface. Most Windows 3.x-based Internet applications work seamlessly with the Windows 95 Winsock.

NOTE By default, Windows 95 installs the 16-bit WINSOCK.DLL in your Windows folder; it installs a 32-bit version, WSOCK32.DLL, in your \Windows\System folder. If you are using a 32-bit Internet application, Windows 95 knows to use the 32-bit version.

Choosing an Internet Service Provider

As the Internet grows, more and more businesses, called *Internet Service Providers (ISPs)*, are springing up to provide access. Typically, a local provider offers three or more computers, called *servers*, which are linked directly to the Internet. In turn, they provide a pool of high-speed modems connected to local telephone lines. In most cities, a service called *Integrated Services Digital Network* (*ISDN*) is available, offering speeds up to 128Kbps. Unless you live in a remote part of the world, finding a service provider should not be a problem.

Here are some ways to access the Internet:

- If you attend a college or university, or work at a business of any size, you might already have Internet access. See your supervisor, the computer science department, or an administrator for more information.
- Subscribe to a commercial online service, such CompuServe, America Online, or Prodigy. These services handle the connectivity problems for you; it is just a matter of "pointing and clicking" your way to the Net. Windows 95 is beneficial because of its improved high-speed serial port support.
- Sign up with a national Internet provider, such as NETCOM, SPRYNET, or IDT Corp. If you live in a rural area, travel a lot, or want to get many offices online, this may be your best bet. National providers have access phone numbers in major cities and usually offer toll-free numbers for a slightly higher price.
- Sign up with a local Internet provider. This is often the most economical way to get on the Net: many services cost as little as $15 to $25 per month. Every major city in the U.S. and around the world has at least one local provider. Look for advertisements in computer magazines, the newspaper, or your telephone directory.

CAUTION

This listing offers some useful questions to ask when evaluating Internet service providers. More important, before deciding on an Internet service provider, check with your local Better Business Bureau. Before you enter a long-term relationship with the provider the BBB can confirm that the provider has an ethical business.

You can also receive help selecting an Internet service provider online. As you will see in the section "Using the Internet Connection Wizard from Internet Explorer 4.0" later in this chapter, Internet Explorer will perform a search of national service providers in your area, and give you information on each one it finds. If you find a service provider that meets your needs, you will be allowed to register with that company online as well.

Understanding ISDN

Sometimes ordinary modems just are not fast enough. Corporate or academic users who are accustomed to fast, high-bandwidth connections at work find that, even at 33.6Kbps, file transfers and Web browsing via a modem can be annoyingly slow. If you use the Internet for your daily business, or if you are a dedicated Internet surfer, you might want to take advantage of a new way to get much faster connections: the Integrated Services Digital Network, or ISDN for short.

NOTE Even though you can get a 56Kbps modem today, regulation restrictions in the U.S. limit them to 53K. In the real world, a more typical connection seems to be about 40Kbps. An ISDN connection always gets its full-rated speed because it's all digital.

ISDN offers three channels over a standard two-wire phone circuit. The two *B channels* run at 64Kbps, and the *D channel* carries 16Kbps of data. 64Kbps is the amount of bandwidth required to make a standard analog voice call, so each of the B channels can be used interchangeably for data or voice. You can even talk to ordinary analog phones, modems, and fax machines with your ISDN line. With the right equipment, you can also tie the two B channels together to get 128Kbps of bandwidth. Another feature is that ISDN circuits take about a half-second to complete a call rather than the 45 seconds of modems screaching at each other to make a connection, so dial-on-demand service is pleasingly fast.

ISDN sounds like a net surfer's dream, but you may never have heard of it. It was originally developed by Bell Communications Research (Bellcore) as a cheap way to move video-on-demand over existing copper cabling, but local phone companies were slow to adopt the technology because they saw little consumer demand for it. The explosion of interest in the Internet has convinced all seven regional Bell companies to offer ISDN to consumers. Most metropolitan areas, and many smaller communities, now offer residential ISDN service for a reasonable fee.

TIP To find out if ISDN is available in your area, call the Bellcore National ISDN Hotline at (800) 992-ISDN. Give them your address and phone number, and they will search your local phone company's database to see if service is available in your area. You may also want to call your local phone company, or check out their Web site.

ON THE WEB

Microsoft's home page

http://www.microsoft.com/windows/getisdn

As with most other peripherals, you will have to make some decisions before purchasing your ISDN hardware. The key questions to ask are listed here:

- Do you want a serial, parallel, PCMCIA, or bus *terminal adapter* (or TA, the ISDN equivalent of a modem)?
- Do you want to use analog modems or phones on your ISDN line?

Similar to conventional analog modems, ISDN *terminal adapters* (TAs) come in internal and external models, with serial, parallel, Ethernet, ISA, EISA, MicroChannel, PCMCIA, and PCI versions available. Which you choose will depend on your existing hardware configuration and your personal preferences. As ISDN continues to become more popular, more vendors are getting into the ISDN hardware business. Make sure that whatever TA you buy is compatible with your decision to use analog phone equipment on your ISDN line, and make sure the vendor has Windows 95 drivers available if it is a PCMCIA or bus device.

NOTE Terminal Adapters that use the serial port need to operate as fast as the line speed. You need a fairly fast computer and a 16,550 UART to take full advantage of ISDN speed. You might be better off with a parallel port, Ethernet, or PCMCIA TA.

When your ISDN line installation is complete, you will have a special jack called a *U interface*. Most TAs and other ISDN devices (like ISDN telephones and fax machines) require the *S/T interface*. The U interface requires a terminating device called an *NT-1*, which electrically terminates the ISDN line and converts the U interface into an S/T interface.

Some ISDN TAs include a built-in NT-1; that is a valuable feature, because an NT-1 can cost as much as $200. On the other hand, some "super" NT-1s include not only the NT-1, but standard phone jacks for connecting analog devices and even RS-232 ports which eliminate the need for a separate TA. If you want to combine your two B channels into one 128Kbps virtual channel (known as *bonding*), be sure that your selected TA supports this feature.

Although ISDN lines can communicate with regular analog lines, ISDN TAs cannot communicate with regular modems. This incompatibility can pose problems if you need to dial into a BBS, a commercial service like America Online, or a remote-access server at work that does not support ISDN. One way around this is to select a TA (or "super" NT-1) that has one or two ports for analog devices. You can still use one B channel for data while you use the other for your analog phone, modem, or fax machine.

ISDN telephones are becoming more popular too, because they offer conference calling, advanced caller ID, and other features which either cost more or do not exist on standard phones. Some makers include RS-232 ports or phone jacks to make it easier to use your ISDN telephone with your computer and your analog equipment.

NOTE ISDN lines do not carry a dial tone. Don't be alarmed when you pick-up your ISDN phone receiver and do not hear a dial tone; just dial the number as you would on an analog phone.

Using the Internet Connection Wizard from Internet Explorer 4.0

The Internet Connection Wizard from Internet Explorer 4.0 makes it easy to setup your Internet dial-up connection. If you do not have Internet Explorer 4.0, you can still setup your Internet connection; refer to the section "Setting Up Internet Access Manually," later in this chapter.

NOTE The Internet Connection Wizard simplifies setting up dial-up access to the Internet. If your Windows 95 system is connected to a network with Internet access, see the section "Connecting to the Internet with a LAN," later in this chapter.

1. To use the Internet Connection Wizard simply double-click the Internet icon located either on your Desktop or on your taskbar or click Start, Programs, Internet Explorer, Connection Wizard. Click Next in the introductory first step of the wizard.

2. The Setup Options dialog box appears, as shown in Figure 17.2. Select one of the following choices, and then choose Next:

   I want to choose an Internet service provider and set up a new Internet account. Select this option if you do not have an Internet service account. Setup will ask for your area code and telephone number prefix. It will then dial-in to a toll-free number and uses that information to locate a nearby Internet service provider.

   I want to set up a new connection to my existing Internet account using my phone line or local area network (LAN). Select this option if you already have an account with an Internet service provider, but have not configured Windows 95 to dial-in to it.

   I already have a connection to the Internet and I do not want to change it. Select this option if you already have an account with an Internet service provider, and have already configured Windows 95 to use it.

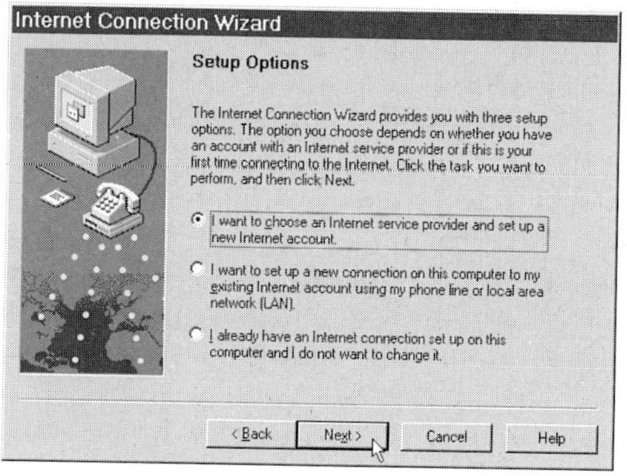

FIG. 17.2
The Internet Connection Wizard asks you to specify how you will connect to the Internet.

Now your installation process branches depending on which option you select. The following three sections detail the steps required for each option.

Completing the Internet Installation Letting Setup Locate a Service Provider

If you selected to use an existing Internet service account, skip this section. If you selected to choose an Internet service provider and open a new account, follow this procedure:

1. After selecting this option, the Begin Automatic Setup dialog box appears warning you that installation media may be needed. Make sure this is handy, and then select Next.
2. The next screen asks for your Location Information, as shown in Figure 17.3. Enter your area code and prefix to help setup locate the nearest Internet service provider. Press Next to continue.
3. Setup will then dial a toll-free number and use your area code and prefix to determine the closest Internet service providers. Information is downloaded to your computer, and the connection is terminated.

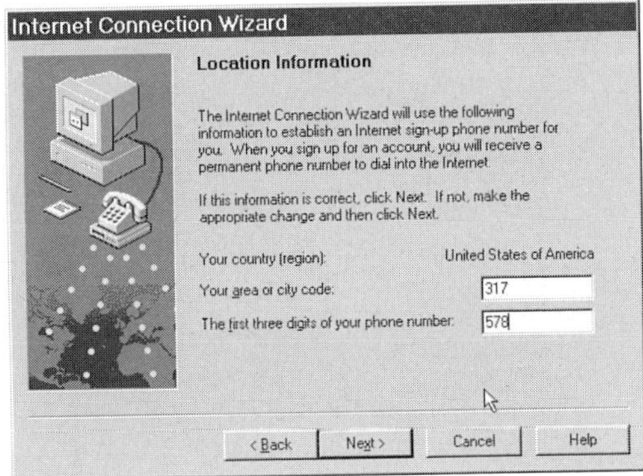

FIG. 17.3
The Internet Connection Wizard needs your telephone information to locate the nearest Internet service provider.

4. Next, the Microsoft Internet Referral Service (see Figure 17.4) presents a list of providers. Information can be found regarding services and rates. If you find one that meets your needs, click on Sign Me Up.
5. Depending on which service provider you select, you will be prompted for user information and a credit card number.
6. Once the registration process is completed, setup will let you finish the process by letting you use your new account by simply pressing the Explore Now! Button on the last screen of the Internet Connection Wizard, as shown in Figure 17.5. Selecting this will dial the number of the selected Internet service provider.

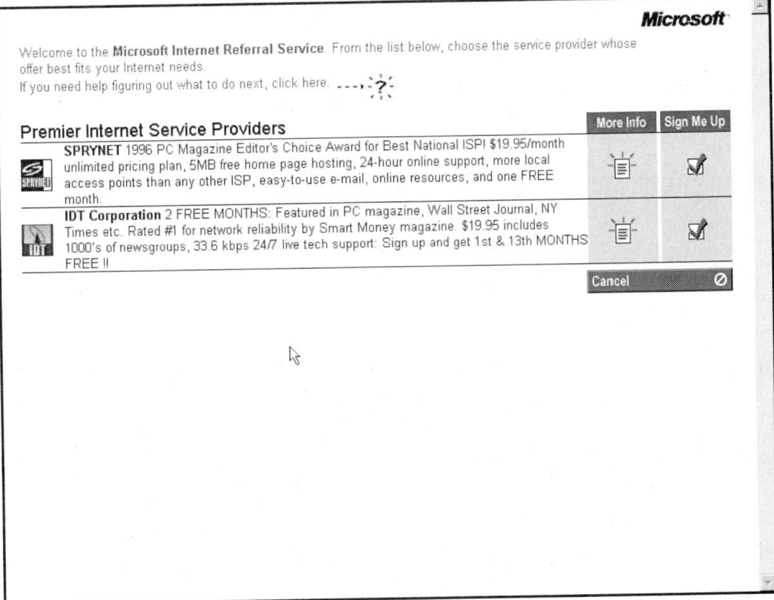

FIG. 17.4
The Microsoft Internet Referral Service displays information about local Internet service providers.

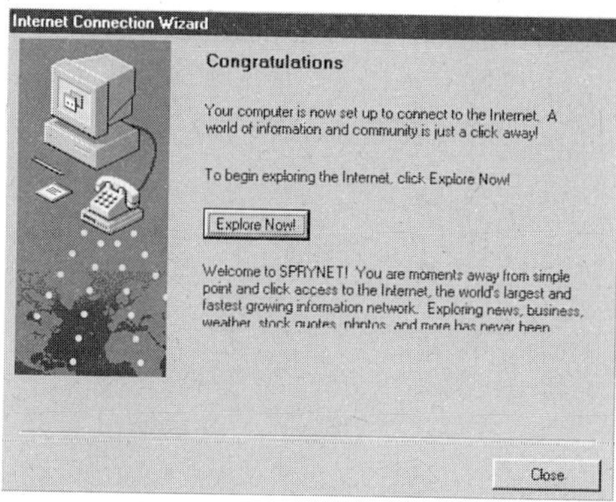

FIG. 17.5
The Internet Connection Wizard gives you the option to use the newly registered Internet account.

Completing the Internet Installation Using an Existing Unconfigured Account

If you selected to use an existing Internet service account that has already been configured for use in Windows 95, skip this section. If you selected to use an existing Internet service account that has not been configured in Windows 95, follow this procedure:

1. After selecting this option, Setup asks if you will be connecting via phone line or local area network, as shown in Figure 17.6. If you will be using a LAN, see the section "Connecting to the Internet with a LAN" later in this chapter. To use a modem, select Next.

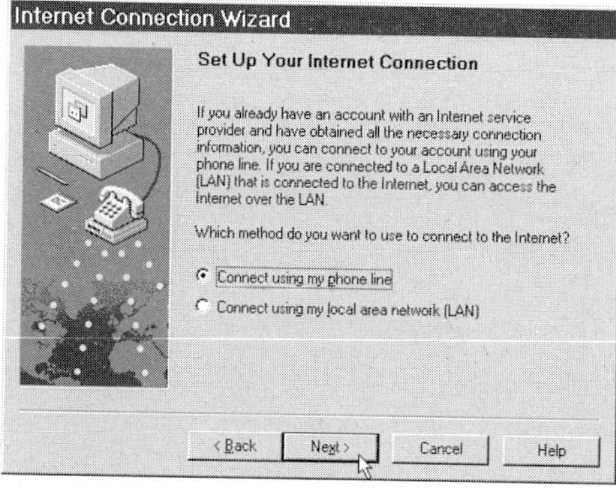

FIG. 17.6
The Internet Connection Wizard gives you the option to use a modem or a LAN.

If you have not setup your modem yet, the Internet Connection Wizard will guide you through the process. Simply respond to each Wizard dialog box, providing information such as your modem model, maximum speed, and manufacturer. Click Next after you provide each item of information the Wizard requests.

2. If you already have other connections set up on the computer, the next dialog box asks if you want to set up a new connection or configure an existing connection. To configure an

existing connection, select it in the list and click Next. Otherwise, for a new connection click Next.

3. You must next provide the telephone number of your Internet service provider, as shown in Figure 17.7. Enter this information and press Next.

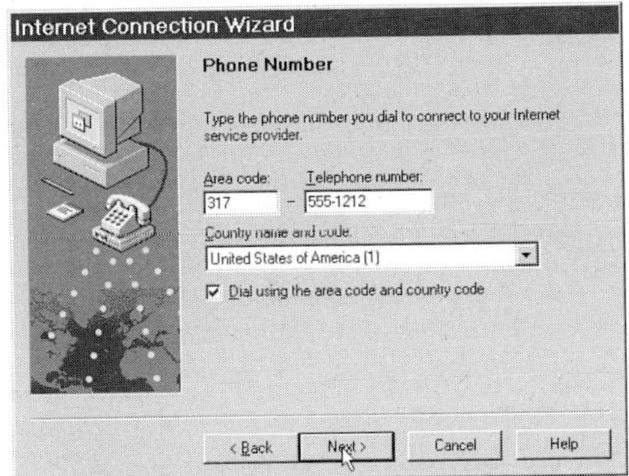

FIG. 17.7 The phone number of your Internet service provider is required to set up your connection.

4. The next screen asks you for the user name and password of your Internet service account. Enter the information and click Next to continue.
5. You are then asked if you would like to configure the Advanced Properties. The default selection is No. Click Next to continue.

NOTE The Advanced Properties include parameters such as PPP or SLIP, logon scripts and static IP and DNS addressing. Most Internet service providers do not require these parameters. Consult your provider if are having trouble connecting, they will walk you through their entries.

6. The next screen asks you to name your Internet connection. Type in a name in the Connection name box.
7. The next screen asks if you want to set up your Internet Mail account. Most providers include Internet mail, so choose Yes, and then Next.
8. If you have previously installed e-mail software on your PC, the wizard will prompt you to use it or configure a new account. To use this existing software select Use an Existing E-Mail Account, select the software from the list, and click Next. Otherwise, select Create a New Internet Mail Account and click Next.
9. Next, enter your name, as you would like other Internet users to see you. This is usually your full name. Click Next to continue.
10. You must next provide your e-mail address, as shown in Figure 17.8. Enter this information and press Next.
11. The next dialog box asks how to configure Internet Mail servers for your account. Use the information provided to you by your Internet provider to describe how your e-mail account is accessed. In most cases, there will be separate e-mail servers for incoming and outgoing e-mail. Be sure to get both addresses and to be clear which is which. Enter the addresses and click Next.

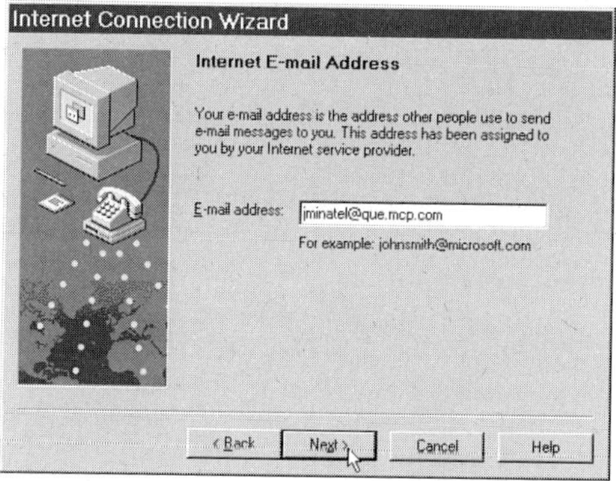

FIG. 17.8
Enter the e-mail address your Internet service provider gave you.

12. In the next dialog box, enter your user name and password for you e-mail account. If your service provider uses Secure Password Authentication, check this option. Then click Next.
13. In the next dialog box, enter a name for the mail account, such as the name of the service provider.
14. The last option to configure is Internet News, or an NNTP newsfeed. This feature should be selected only if your provider supports NNTP newsfeed. Consult your provider for details. To set up a new account, click Yes and click Next.
15. You can create new news account or select an existing one and use it. Then click Next.
16. The next two dialog boxes prompt you for your name and e-mail address for this news account.
17. Next, enter the address of your news server and click Next.
18. In the next dialog box, enter a name for the news account, such as the name of the service provider.
19. If you have access to an LDAP server, you can click Yes in the next dialog box to set up an LDAP directory account. Several public sites with LDAP directories are preconfigured.
20. Finally, the Internet Connection Wizard is ready to finish your configuration. Select Finish to complete the installation.

Once the setup is complete, you can use this Internet icon to use Internet Explorer. If you double-click Internet Explorer, you will be asked to connect to the Internet with the information you just provided.

While connected to the Internet, you can find information about your modem connection by double-clicking the connection icon in the System Tray. The System Tray is located next to the clock on your Taskbar. Once activated it will give you connection information including duration of call, bytes sent and bytes received, as shown in Figure 17.9. Clicking details will give you additional information including your IP address.

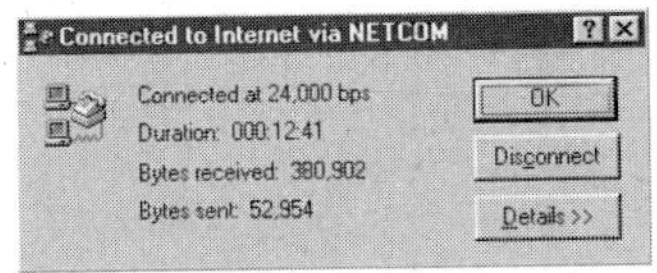

FIG. 17.9
The Internet Connection icon located in the System Tray will show you connection statistics.

Completing the Internet Installation Using an Existing Configured Account

If you instruct the Internet Connection Wizard to use an existing Internet account that has already been configured, in Step 2 of the section "Using the Internet Connection Wizard from Internet Explorer 4.0," there is no additional information needed. Internet Explorer will use the existing connection to dial into the Internet.

Setting Up Internet Access Manually

If you are not using the Microsoft Internet Explorer 4.0, you can set up Windows 95 access to your Internet service provider manually.

Windows 95 Dialup Networking supports two kinds of dial-up Internet connections: SLIP and PPP. SLIP stands for Serial-Line Internet Protocol; PPP means Point-to-Point Protocol. Both are implementations of the TCP/IP Internet protocol over telephone lines. Unless you access the Internet through a LAN and Ethernet cabling, you will probably use telephone lines and SLIP or PPP.

There are both technical and practical differences between the two protocols: technically, SLIP is a *network-layer protocol*; PPP is a *link-level protocol.* Practically, this means that PPP is more fail-safe than SLIP. Windows 95 Dialup Networking is optimized for PPP, which is the protocol to choose if your provider offers a choice.

ON THE WEB

Frequently Asked Questions about PPP

http://cs.uni-bonn.de/ppp/faq.html

If you chose an Internet connection only service, you need the following information from your Internet service provider:

- *Connection type.* The kind of connection provided: SLIP or PPP.
- *User name.* Your user name (you can usually choose your own, such as jsmith).
- *Your password.* A password again, you select your own. The most secure passwords have six or more uppercase and lowercase letters, numbers, and punctuation.
- *Provider's phone number.* The provider's local access phone number. Be sure to use a phone number that is both local and has the appropriate modem speeds.

- *Domain and host name.* Your host and domain name are text names that make identification easier.
- *Domain IP.* Your Domain Name Server's IP address (briefly, DNS is the method the Internet uses to associate unique names for each of the servers on the network).

If your Internet service provider gives you a dedicated IP address to use every time you dial in, you may also need the following:

- *IP address for you.* This is your computer's unique address.
- *IP subnet mask.* This is used when your computer communicates to other network devices located at your Internet service provider.
- *Gateway IP address.* The address of your Internet service provider's network router.

Here is an example of the setup requirements for an Internet provider:

IP Address:	127.8.23.61
Subnet Mask:	255.255.255.0
Host Name:	the name of your Internet host
Domain Name:	anynet.com
Dial:	555-0000 (your provider's dial-up networking phone number)
Login:	jsmith
Password:	pAss-WoRd5
Domain Server:	127.8.23.254

Most of the time you won't need this information, your system will automatically get it from the host when you dial in. However, your provider might configure your system for you or they might help you over the phone while you enter the information in the correct Windows 95 Dial-Up Adapter dialog boxes.

▶ **See** "Installing Plug and Play Hardware," **p. 176**

Installing Dial-Up Networking

The first step when manually setting up Internet access is to install the Dial-Up Networking component. You may have installed Dial-Up Networking when you first set up Windows 95. Here is how you can tell:

1. Double-click My Computer to see whether Dial-Up Networking is installed. If it is, you see a folder named Dial-Up Networking, as shown in Figure 17.10.
2. If you have Dial-Up Networking already installed, go to the section titled, "Installing TCP/IP," later in this chapter. If you do not have a Dial-Up Networking folder, install it now. Open the Start menu, choose Settings, Control Panel.
3. Select the Add/Remove Programs option. The Add/Remove Programs Properties sheet appears.

FIG. 17.10
A view of My Computer with Dial-Up Networking installed.

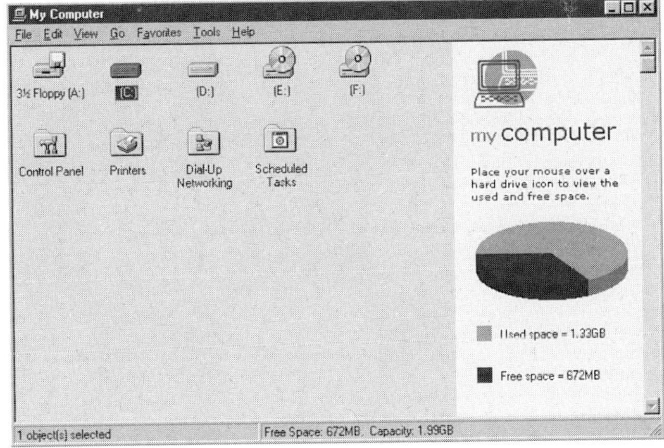

4. Click the Windows Setup tab.
5. Select the Communications option and click the Details button. The Communications dialog box in Figure 17.11 appears.

FIG. 17.11
The Communications dialog box, from which you install Dial-Up Networking.

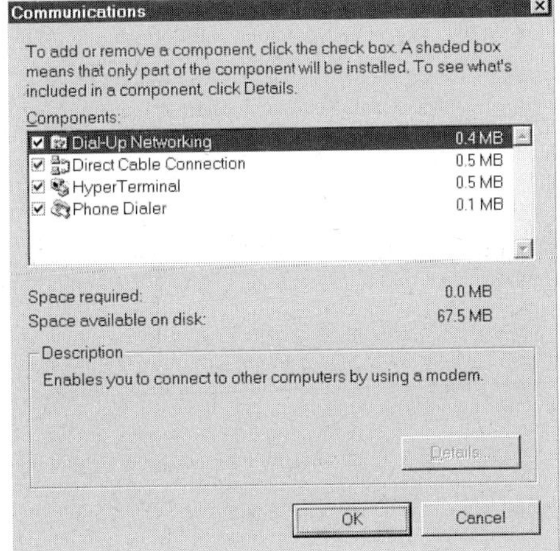

6. Select the Dial-Up Networking option.
7. Click OK in the Communications dialog box; click OK in the Add/Remove Programs Properties sheet to complete the installation.

Installing TCP/IP

Next you have to install the TCP/IP protocol. If you installed the Dial-Up Networking Adapter during the Windows 95 installation, you may have also installed TCP/IP. Here is how you can tell:

1. Open the Start menu and choose Settings, Control Panel. Double-click the Network program icon. If you do not see the TCP/IP protocol listed, install it now.

   Click the Add button, select Protocol, and click the Add button. The Select Network Protocol dialog box appears, as shown in Figure 17.12. Select Microsoft from the Manufacturers list, select TCP/IP from the Network Protocols list, and click OK.

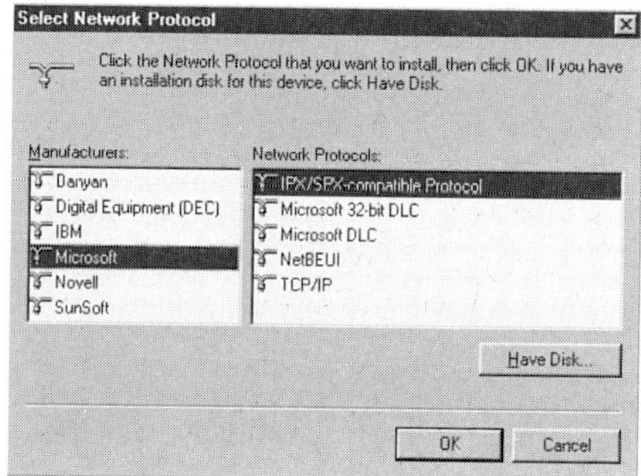

FIG. 17.12 The Select Network Protocol dialog box; select Microsoft from the Manufacturers list and TCP/IP from the Network Protocols list.

2. Now make sure your dial-up adapter is using (the term is, *is bound to*) the TCP/IP protocol. In the Network dialog box, select the Dial-Up Adapter and then click Properties. Click the Bindings tab, as shown in Figure 17.13. Make sure the check box next to the TCP/IP Dial-Up adapter is selected. Click OK to return to the Network dialog box.

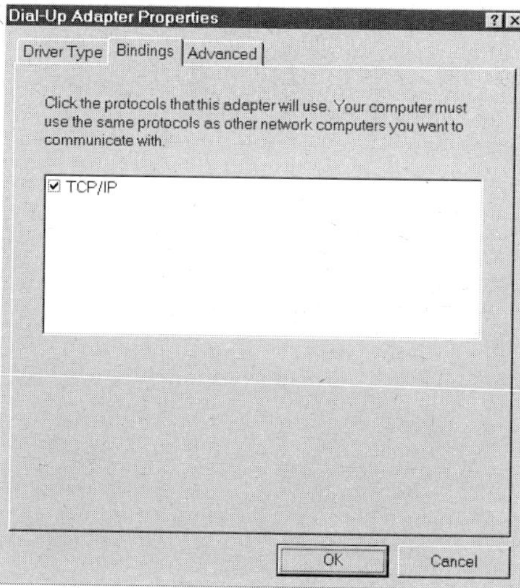

FIG. 17.13 The Bindings tab in the Dial-Up Adapter Properties sheet, showing TCP/IP bound to the adapter.

3. Select TCP/IP from the Network list in the Network dialog box and click Properties. Select the IP Address tab and make sure the Obtain An IP Address Automatically check box is selected. This check box sets your IP address to 0.0.0.0 (this is not visible because

the check box is grayed-out), which means your Internet provider will dynamically assign you an IP address when you call in.

NOTE If your Internet service provider assigns you a permanent IP address, enter that address manually on the IP Address tab: in the IP Address box, check the Specify an IP Address option and enter the assigned address in the IP Address field. You must also type the subnet mask address for your provider in the Subnet mask field.

When you connect using PPP, the permanent IP address is used instead of the Internet service provider dynamically assigning one to you. When you connect with SLIP, the permanent IP address shows up in the Specify an IP address box to confirm your IP address for your SLIP connection.

If the address you are typing has less than three numbers before the period, use the Right Arrow key to jump to the next area between the periods in the field, or type a period. If you type three numbers before the period, the cursor moves to the next area automatically.

4. In the TCP/IP Properties sheet, click the DNS Configuration tab. Instead of defining the DNS addresses here, you define them as part of the Dial-Up Networking connection in the following section, "Creating a Configuration for Your Internet Service Provider." Select Disable DNS. Click OK to close the TCP/IP Properties sheet.
5. Click OK to close the Network control panel. Exit and restart Windows 95.

Installing SLIP

If you are using a SLIP account, you need to install the SLIP software. Follow these steps to install it:

1. Open the Start menu and choose Settings, Control Panel. Double-click Add/Remove Programs. Select the Windows Setup tab; then select Have Disk.
2. Click Browse. Select the drive and directory where the file RNAPLUS.INF is located. On the Windows 95 CD-ROM, you can find the file in the ADMIN/APPTOOLS/DSCRIPT folder. When you have selected the file, click OK.
3. The Have Disk dialog box appears. Select the SLIP and Scripting for Dial-Up Networking check box (see Figure 17.14). Click Install.

Creating a Configuration for Your Internet Service Provider

In the preceding sections, you configured Windows 95 for TCP/IP connections. Now you need to tell it about the connection you will be making to your Internet service provider. To do this, you create and configure a new connection using the following steps:

1. Open the Dial-Up Networking folder from the My Computer window. If this is the first time you have opened it, a Connection Wizard runs to help you enter all the information necessary for a dial-up connection.

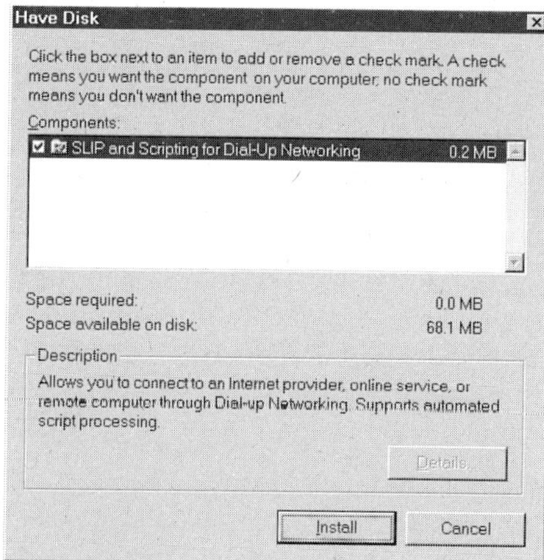

FIG. 17.14 To use SLIP, select the SLIP and Scripting for Dial-Up Networking check box.

2. Double-click the Make New Connection icon to display the Make New Connection Wizard shown in Figure 17.15. Type the name of your Internet service provider in the Type a Name for the Computer You Are Dialing text box. If you have not already configured Windows 95 for your modem, click Configure to do so now.

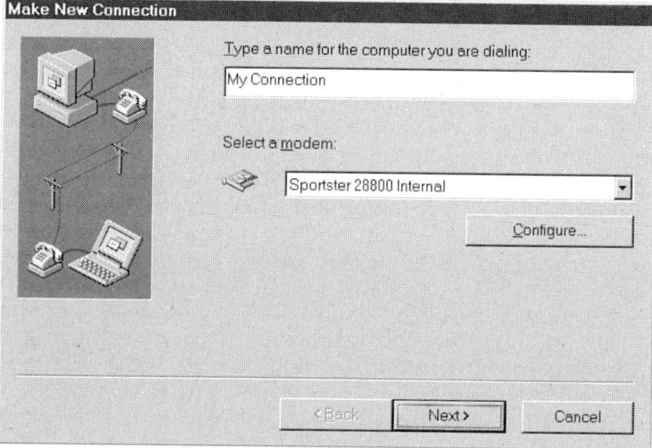

FIG. 17.15 Clicking Configure opens the Modem Properties sheet.

3. If you have configured your modem, continue by clicking Next; then enter the area code and telephone number for your Internet service provider. Select your country code and area code from the drop-down menus. Click Next, and then click Finish to complete the installation. Now you have a new icon in your Dial-Up Networking Box specific to this connection. For easier access, right-drag the icon to your desktop and choose Create Shortcut(s) Here to create a shortcut.
4. If your provider requires you to log on by means of a terminal window, you must enable that function. In the Dial-Up Networking window, right-click the connection icon you just created and choose Properties. In the Connect Using area of the dialog box, click

Configure. Now choose the Options tab (see Figure 17.16). In the Connection Control section, make sure the Bring Up Terminal Window After Dialing check box is selected. Choose OK. This returns you to the first box of the Property sheet.

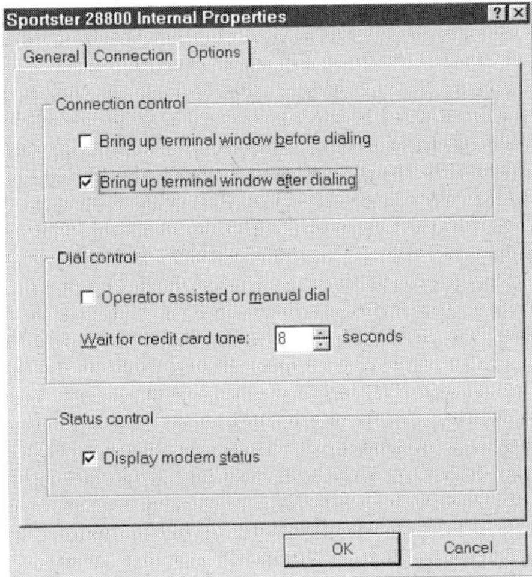

FIG. 17.16
Check the Bring Up Terminal Window After Dialing option to enable this function.

5. In the Property sheet, click Server Type in the Connect Using section. This displays the Server Types dialog box (see Figure 17.17). Use the Type of Dial-Up Server drop-down menu to select the type of connection, PPP, SLIP, or CSLIP. Your Internet service provider can tell you what type of account you have.

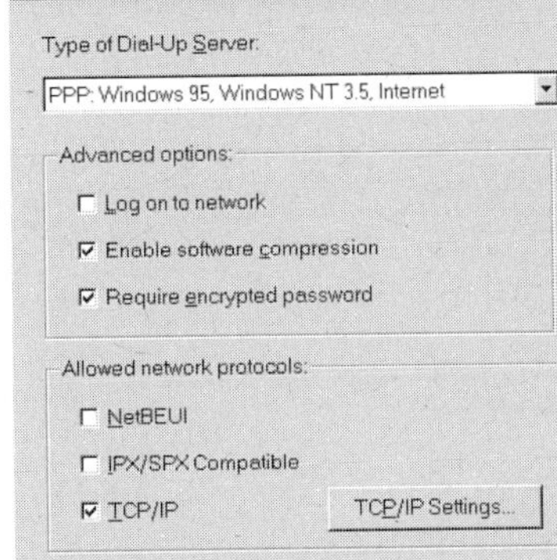

FIG. 17.17
If you are using a PPP connection, your Server Types dialog box should look like this.

6. In the Advanced Options group, select the Enable Software Compression check box. This improves throughput of your connection, but is only used when both sides of the connection support it.

Select the Require Encrypted Password check box if you do not want your password to transmit in clear text when you connect. Your Internet service provider must support CHAP for this to work. If it only supports PAP, and you select this option, the connection will fail.

The Log On To Network option is not used for Internet access.

NOTE *PAP* stands for Password Authentication Protocol. *CHAP* stands for Challenge-Handshake Authentication Protocol. Both protocols allow you to log in without typing your user name and password in a terminal window. CHAP provides additional security, as it prevents your password from being transmitted in clear text over the connection.

7. From the Allowed Network Protocols group, select the TCP/IP check box. This option provides quicker connect time after dialing the Internet provider. The NetBEUI and IPX/SPX Compatible check boxes are not relevant to connecting to the Internet. Make sure they are unselected.
8. Click the TCP/IP Settings button. The TCP/IP Settings dialog box displays. Figure 17.18 shows a completed TCP/IP Settings dialog box. Any values entered here will override those specified in the Network Control Panel TCP/IP properties.

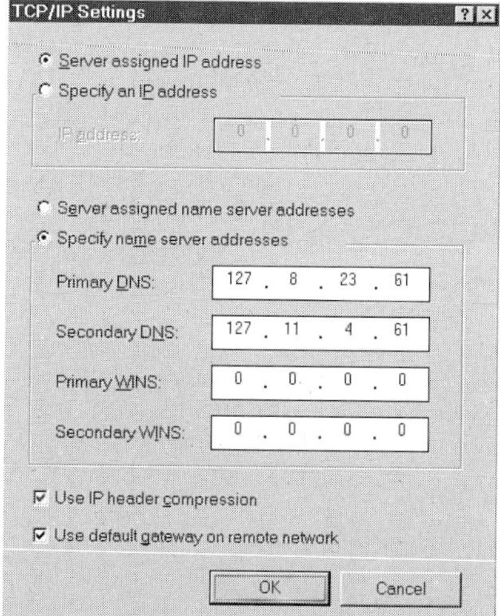

FIG. 17.18
Use the TCP/IP Settings dialog box to define parameters only for this connection.

CAUTION

Be careful when entering server address numbers. Depending on the edit movement keys you use, the zero (0) placeholders might not be replaced by numbers you enter. Make sure inappropriate zeroes do not remain.

Select the Server Assigned IP Address option if your Internet service provider uses dynamic IP addressing. If your Internet service provider gave you a permanent IP address, check the Specify an IP Address option and enter the number in the IP address field.

9. When you make a connection to your Internet service provider, addresses for the Domain Name System (DNS) servers can be automatically assigned. If your Internet service provider supports this capability, select the Server Assigned Name Server Addresses option.

   Sometimes, your Internet service provider must give you addresses for their DNS servers. In this case, check the Specify Name Server Addresses option, and enter the addresses into the Primary DNS and Secondary DNS fields. The Windows Internet Naming Service (WINS) addresses do not apply to Internet connections. Leave the Primary WINS and Secondary WINS fields blank.

10. Select the Use IP Header Compression check box. This improves throughput at low modem speeds, but must be supported by your Internet service provider.

11. Select the Use Default Gateway on Remote Network check box. This ensures that all IP traffic is routed through your Dial-Up Internet connection.

12. Click OK. Click OK again. Finally, click OK to close the dialog box for your Dial-Up Connection.

Connecting to Your Internet Service Provider

You are now ready to dial your Internet service provider. Follow these steps:

1. Double-click your New Connection icon (either on the desktop if you have created a shortcut, or in the Dial-Up Networking folder). The Connect To dialog box displays the phone number for your Internet service provider.

2. Enter your user name and password in the Connect To dialog box (see Figure 17.19). If desired, you can check Save Password to avoid having to enter your password each time you dial in.

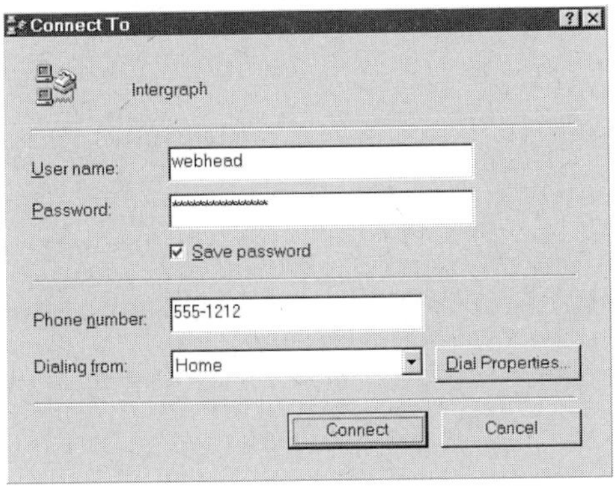

FIG. 17.19
Click Connect in the Connect To dialog box to dial your Internet service provider.

If your Internet service provider requires you to login using a terminal window, you do not have to enter your user name and password here because you enter that information in the terminal window that appears after the modem connects.

3. Click Connect. The modem dials and connects.

   If your Internet service provider requires you to login using a terminal window, the Post-Dial Terminal Screen appears, as shown in Figure 17.20. Enter your user name and password, and then click Continue or press F7.

CAUTION

If you share files or printers from your system using File and Print Sharing, be aware that Internet users can gain unauthorized access to your shared resources. You can use the Internet Control Panel to perform a security check before your system dials the Internet. See the section "Using the Internet Control Panel" later in this chapter.

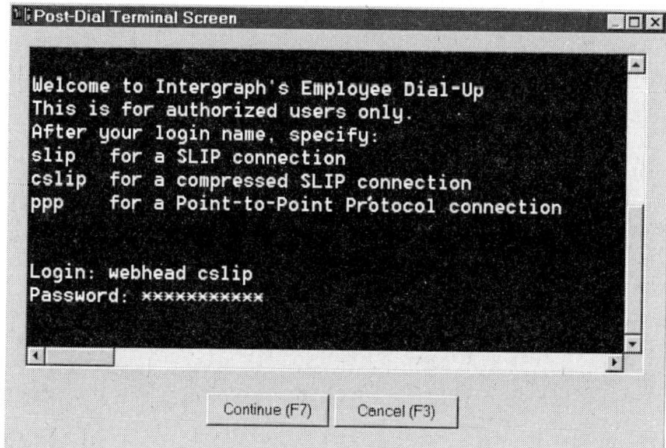

FIG. 17.20
Use the Post-Dial Terminal Screen to enter your user name and password when your Internet service provider does not support PAP or CHAP with PPP.

NOTE Unless you configured Windows 95 to require a password at the start of each day's session, you will have to retype your password here the first time each day, or after you reboot.

If you are using a SLIP connection, follow these steps to connect:

1. After you enter your user name and password in the terminal window, you should get a message from your provider telling you your IP address for this session. Most providers tell you what your IP address is with a message like `Your IP address is` or `SLIP session from ###.###.###.### to ###.###.###.###`. The second address is usually your IP address. Write down your IP address and click the Continue button.
2. You should see a dialog box like the one in Figure 17.21, asking you to confirm your IP address. Type the IP address you just wrote down and click OK. You should be connected in a few seconds.

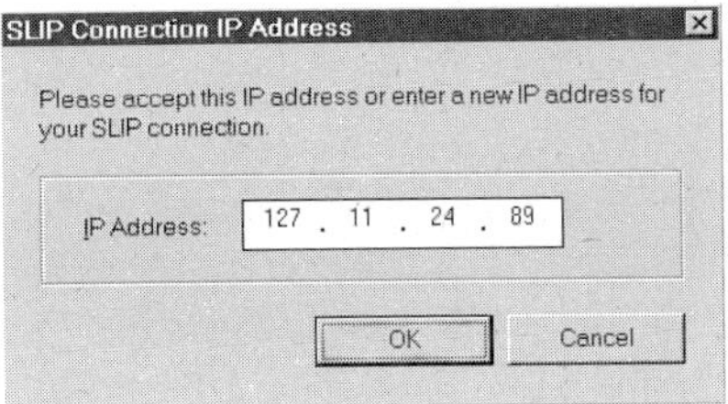

FIG. 17.21
Use this dialog box to enter your IP address. If you are not sure of the address, ask your Internet provider what your address is for SLIP.

NOTE Most Internet providers can switch your account from SLIP to PPP for no charge. PPP offers better error correction than SLIP. Additionally, PPP accounts may not require you to use the terminal window to log in and do not require you to enter your IP address manually. If you do decide to use a SLIP account, you may want to copy all of the settings down just in case there are some problems later and your configuration gets deleted.

TROUBLESHOOTING

I entered all the information in the Property sheet for my connection, and I configured my modem correctly, but I still cannot connect. If you are having problems connecting with your service, make sure that your server type is correct. In the Dial-Up Networking folder, right-click your Connection icon; then select Properties. Click Server Type. Make sure that the server type in the connection properties is set to PPP, not SLIP or CSLIP. Deselect the Enable Software Compression check box in the Advanced Options section of the page.

If you have a SLIP account, make sure that you have changed the server type to SLIP or CSLIP (PPP is the default). Make sure that you type the correct IP address when prompted during the login process.

Testing Your Connection

Use Ping (a program that comes with Windows 95) to test if a connection is working. When executed, Ping requests the remote computer you designate to send back a response to let you know you are connected.

To use Ping to test your connection to the Internet, follow these steps:

1. After you are connected to your Internet service provider, open a DOS window.
2. At the DOS prompt, type **ping ftp.microsoft.com**. If the Microsoft server is busy, it may not answer right away. If so, ping your Internet provider's host computer by name. The name may be mail or mach1. Or ping 128.95.1.4, a DNS server. The remote host replies:

```
Pinging ftp.microsoft.com [198.105.232.1] with 32 bytes of data:
Reply from 198.105.232.1: bytes=32 time=180ms TTL=18
Reply from 198.105.232.1: bytes=32 time=185ms TTL=18
Reply from 198.105.232.1: bytes=32 time=176ms TTL=18
Reply from 198.105.232.1: bytes=32 time=181ms TTL=18
```

This tells you that your computer is talking to the server. Unless you have on-going problems connecting, you will only need to use the Ping command once.

NOTE After you make a connection to your Internet service provider, you can use the Winipcfg program to display the TCP/IP configuration of the Dial-Up Adapter. To run Winipcfg, Open the Start menu and choose Run. Type **winipcfg** in the Open text box and click OK. Click More Info to display the detailed information, as shown in Figure 17.22.

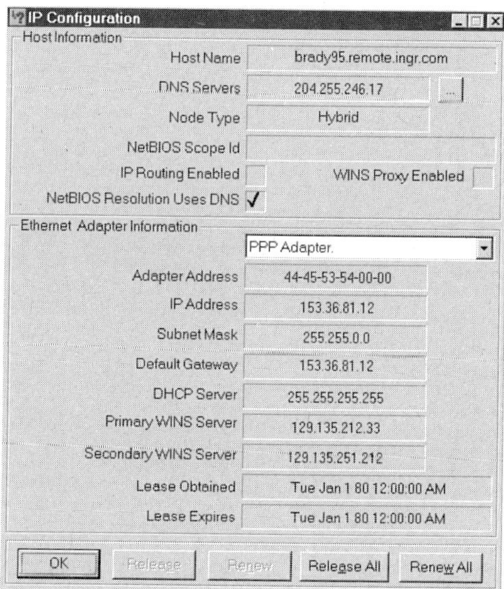

FIG. 17.22 Use Winipcfg to display the TCP/IP parameters of your connection.

TROUBLESHOOTING

After connecting with my SLIP account, I can ping the server, but still cannot use Winsock applications to connect to a resource. You may have to switch the server type. From My Computer, open the Dial-Up Networking folder. Right-click your connection to open the Properties sheet. Select Server Type; then try changing the server type in the connection properties from SLIP to CSLIP or CSLIP to SLIP, depending on what it is currently set for.

I can run Internet Explorer, but other network applications will not work. What is wrong? If you have a Winsock application that is not working properly, check to see whether that application requires a specific WINSOCK.DLL file. Some Winsock applications come with their own WINSOCK.DLL, which may not work with Windows 95. First, try renaming the application-provided WINSOCK.DLL to ensure that you are using the WINSOCK.DLL in your Windows directory. If the application does not work with the Windows 95 WINSOCK.DLL, replace it with the application's WINSOCK.DLL file.

Exercise caution, because renaming your Windows 95 WINSOCK.DLL might cause other Winsock applications not to work and is not recommended. Contact the application vendor to see whether they have an updated version that will work with the Windows 95 WINSOCK.DLL.

Everything seems to be configured properly, but I still cannot connect to my Internet service provider. If you are having trouble connecting, open the Networks icon in the Control Panel, select the Dial-Up Adapter, select Properties, select the Advanced tab, and set Record a Log File to Yes. This action writes a file called PPPLOG.TXT to your Windows directory that contains information recorded during the connecting process. You can use this information when you talk to your provider to find a solution.

I have a PPP connection and sometimes cannot connect to my provider. If you are having problems when connecting with Internet service providers offering PPP accounts, it may help if you turn off IP header compression. To do so, open Control Panel, double-click Network, click Dial-Up Adapter to select it, and click Properties. In the Properties sheet, select the Advanced tab and deselect the Use IP Header Compression option.

Using the Internet Control Panel

Windows 95 includes the Internet Control Panel to provide additional control over your Windows 95 Internet connection. With the Internet Control Panel, you can do the following:

- Configure Windows 95 to automatically dial-up your Internet service provider when an application needs access to the Internet.
- Configure Windows 95 to automatically disconnect from the Internet after a specified time of no activity.
- Perform a security check before you connect, to warn you if Internet users may gain access to your File Sharing or Printer Sharing resources.
- Setup and manage your proxy server location, if your organization uses one to control access to the Internet.

NOTE When Internet Explorer 4.0 is installed, many configuration options relating to Internet Explorer are added to the Internet Control Panel. This section deals only with configuration options for the Internet connection, and those are found on the Connection tab.

Configuring Automatic Connection and Disconnection

Use the Connection property sheet to configure Windows 95 to automatically dial-up your Internet service provider when an application needs access to the Internet. You can also configure Windows 95 to disconnect after a period of inactivity. If your Windows 95 system has access to the Internet through a LAN, do not enable the auto connect feature.

To configure automatic connection and disconnection, follow these steps:

1. Open the Start menu and choose Settings, Control Panel. Double-click the Internet icon. The Internet Properties sheet appears. Choose the Connection tab, as shown in Figure 17.23.
2. Select the Connect to the Internet as needed check box.

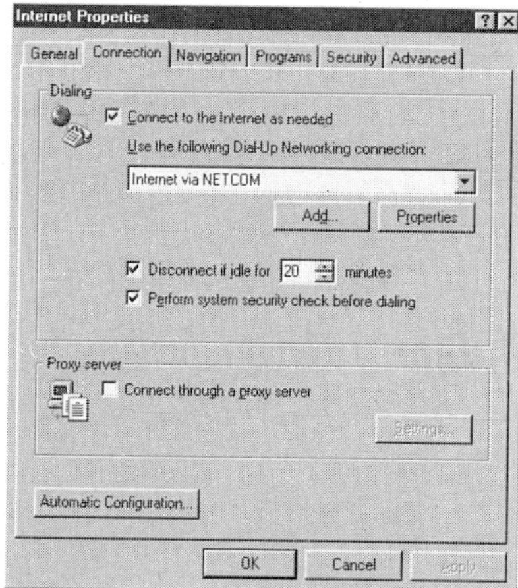

FIG. 17.23 Use the Internet Control Panel Connection property sheet to automatically dial-up your Internet service provider when an application needs access to the Internet.

3. In the Use the following Dial-Up Networking Connection list, select your Internet service provider. Alternatively, you can create a new entry by clicking the Add button. If you add a connection, refer to Step 2 in the section "Connecting to Your Internet Service Provider," earlier in this chapter.

   If you want to review or modify the properties of the Dial-Up Networking connection, click the Properties button.

4. If your Internet service provider charges connection time fees, check the Disconnect if Idle box to save money when you accidentally leave your system online. Enter the number of minutes of inactivity before the disconnect occurs. Windows warns you one minute before the disconnect occurs, and allows you to remain online if desired.
5. To help prevent Internet users from gaining access to your File Sharing and Printer Sharing resources, check the Perform System Security Check Before Dialing box. When you dial your Internet service provider, the system will check for shared folders and printers, and warn you if Internet users can access them.

Using a Proxy Server

A proxy server acts as a gateway between some Internet applications, like Internet Explorer, and the Internet. Normally, proxy servers are setup as a security barrier between your LAN and the Internet. If your Windows 95 system is not on a LAN, you do not have to configure the proxy server settings. Proxy servers perform the following functions:

- Setting up a security barrier between your LAN and the Internet, preventing access of Internet users to information and shared resources on your LAN.
- Auditing and filtering of outgoing requests, to prevent employee access to non-work related sites.
- Caching of Internet information to improve the performance of your Internet connection. The first employee to access a Web page, such as the Wall Street Journal home page, waits the longest because the proxy server fetches the page and stores it in cache. But

thereafter, every employee who accesses the same page fetches the page from the proxy server cache instead of over the Internet, and perceived performance is much faster. Algorithms within the proxy server assure that the cache is kept up-to-date and that users always get the correct information.

To configure Windows 95 to use a proxy server, follow these steps:

1. Open the Internet Control Panel, open the Start menu, and choose Settings, Control Panel. Double-click the Internet icon.
2. Select the Connection tab
3. Select the Connect through a proxy server check box. The Settings button becomes active; select this button. The Proxy Settings property sheet appears, as shown in Figure 17.24.

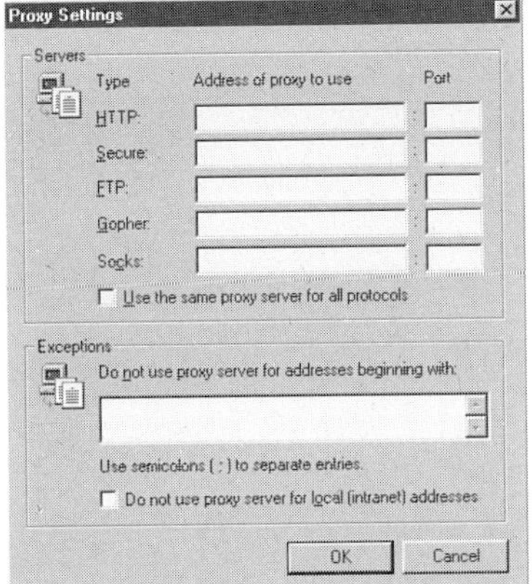

FIG. 17.24
Use the Internet Control Panel Proxy Settings property sheet to configure your Internet Connection to use a proxy server.

4. The options available on this property sheet should be verified by your network administrator. Please consult with him/her before entering information here.

Connecting to the Internet with a LAN

If your computer is part of a local area network (LAN), connecting to the Internet with Windows 95 is as easy as connecting a single user. The difference is that instead of getting the information you need from an Internet service provider, you obtain it from your network administrator.

To connect to the Internet with a LAN, follow these steps:

1. Open the Start menu and choose Settings, Control Panel. Double-click the Network icon. If you followed the procedures to install Dial-Up Networking, you will now have both Dial-Up Adapter and TCP/IP installed. Select the TCP/IP protocol and click Properties. If you do not see the TCP/IP protocol in the Network Components list, refer to the section "Installing TCP/IP," earlier in this chapter.

2. Select the IP Address tab. If your LAN has a Dynamic Host Configuration Protocol (DHCP) Server, click the Obtain an IP Address Automatically button.
3. If your LAN does not have a DHCP server, obtain an IP address from your network administrator. Click the button marked Specify an IP address and fill in the address. Use the arrow key to move between the fields separated by periods. You should also enter the Subnet Mask address at this time.
4. Now click the Gateway tab. This is the address of the connection point between your LAN and the Internet. Enter the address provided by your network administrator.
5. Now select the DNS Configuration tab (see Figure 17.25). Select Enable DNS. Obtain your Host and Domain names from your network administrator and enter them in the spaces provided. If you are part of a smaller organization, you may not have a Domain Name Server of your own, but have a domain name provided by your service provider.

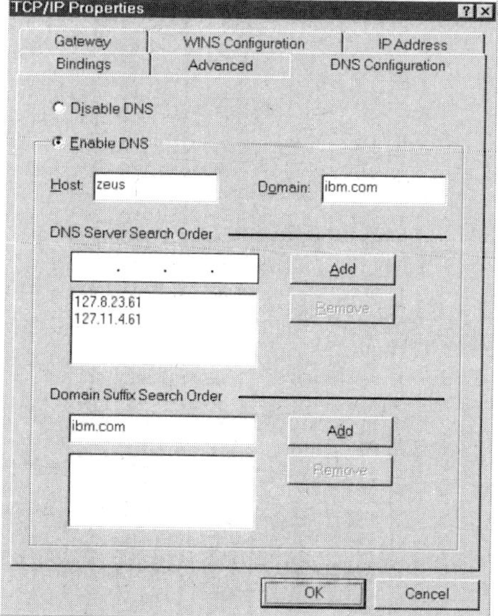

FIG. 17.25
Use the DNS Configuration tab to identify the DNS servers on your LAN.

6. In the DNS Server Search Order text box, enter the numeric address of the DNS server your network administrator gives you.
7. If your LAN is running Windows NT, you might have to set up the Windows Internet Naming Service (WINS). Click the WINS Configuration tab and follow your network administrator's instructions.
8. Click OK to close the Network control panel. Exit and restart Windows 95.

TROUBLESHOOTING

I do not run TCP/IP on my LAN and I experience occasional system pauses. How do I fix this? If you are using TCP/IP for your Internet connections and the protocol is bound to both your LAN and dial-up adapter but no DHCP server is present on the LAN, your system may pause for a few seconds every once in a while. The system pauses as it attempts to identify other TCP/IP hosts on your LAN. To avoid this, unbind TCP/IP from your LAN adapter.

Open the Network icon in Control Panel. Select the Network Card; then click Properties. Click the Bindings tab, and deselect the TCP/IP option in the dialog box.

CHAPTER 18

Browsing the Internet with Explorer

by Ron Person, Francis Moss, Paul Robichaux, and Brady P. Merkel

The World Wide Web, designed by researchers at CERN in Geneva, Switzerland, is a collection of hypertext documents served from computers throughout the world. Web documents, or pages, can contain pictures, text, sounds, movies, and links to other documents. Web pages can—and usually do—contain links to documents on other computers. The name "Web" comes from the interlinked nature of the pages.

Internet Explorer is a Web browser. Designed to take advantage of the full range of Windows 95's features, Internet Explorer uses the productive Windows 95 user interface and supports shortcuts and long file names. Figure 18.1 shows Internet Explorer 4.0's main window and the default page that ships with the software. Internet Explorer 3 is part of Microsoft's Plus! Pack for Windows 95. If you purchased a new computer with Windows 95 installed, the Internet Explorer 3 or 4 might be installed as well. Also, Microsoft offers the most current version of Internet Explorer as a free download from their Internet site and The Microsoft Network.

How to install Internet Explorer and integrated shell components

Learn which of the installation methods best meets your needs.

About the Internet and World Wide Web

Understand the terminology and use of Internet Explorer with the Internet and World Wide Web.

Navigating through the Web most efficiently

With or without integrated shell components, there are time saving tips that can help you find what you want faster.

How to customize Internet Explorer

Many features in Internet Explorer are customizable to improve its performance, security, and your personal tastes.

How to control content access, security, and the Microsoft Wallet

Internet Explorer 4 has new features to control access to rated sites as well as the capability to use credit cards online.

NOTE The following chapter was written using Platform Review 2 (PR2) of integrated shell components for Windows 95. The final release of integrated shell components may differ slightly from what is described here.

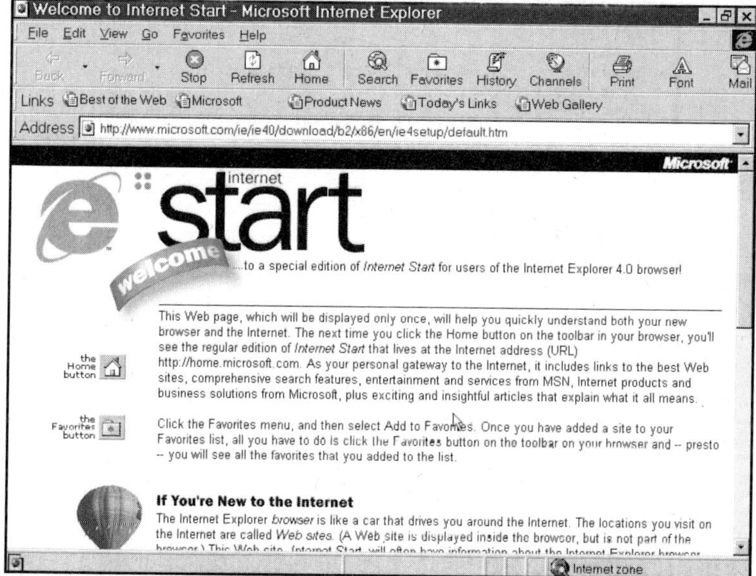

FIG. 18.1
Internet Explorer 4.0's main window includes a toolbar for quick access to common functions.

NOTE This chapter describes both Internet Explorer 3 and Internet Explorer 4. While these applications have a similar appearance Internet Explorer 4 has additional features that make it easier to use as well as increasing its security and performance. Features available only in Internet Explorer 4 are indicated with an icon. All figures are shown are of Platform Review (PR2) release of Internet Explorer 4.

Internet Explorer shares a common look and feel with Microsoft's other applications and includes Windows 95 features like ToolTips and the common file and print dialog boxes. It also has many similarities to other Web browsers. If you are already accustomed to another browser, you will find the Internet Explorer both comfortably familiar and excitingly different.

Some of the areas Internet Explorer 4 has improved over previous versions are the following:

- User interface through integrated shell components
- Integrated collaboration software—NetMeeting can build collaborative works over the Web
- Integrated communication software: Outlook Express Mail and Outlook Express News
- WebCasting that pushes information you request to you over the Web when the information needs updating
- Subscriptions to any Web site so you are notified of site changes or can update images of the site stored locally

- Control over features and customization by the network administrator
- Security and e-cash enhancements

Installing Internet Explorer 4

Your computer might have Internet Explorer 4 already installed. You can check to see the version of Internet Explorer you have by clicking Help, About Internet Explorer and reading the About Internet Explorer dialog box. If the version number starts with 4, then you have version 4 and do not need to install Internet Explorer 4. (You may still need to install Internet Explorer 4 Suite components such as NetMeeting that can be installed separately.)

If you do not have Internet Explorer 4 installed, you should probably install it, unless it is against your company policy. Internet Explorer 4 operates at the same speed or better as Internet Explorer 3 under the same system requirements. (This is not true of integrated shell components, which can degrade the performance of computers with less than 16M.)

When you install Internet Explorer 4, you have the option of installing suites of Internet applications that come with Internet Explorer 4. Your choices of components to be installed are listed in Table 18.1.

Table 18.1 Internet Explorer 4 Suite Installation Types

Installation Type	Contents of Installation
Minimal Installation	Internet Explorer 4 and multimedia enhancements.
Standard Installation	Internet Explorer 4, Microsoft Outlook Express, Microsoft Web Publishing Wizard, and multimedia enhancements.
Full Installation	Internet Explorer 4, Microsoft Outlook Express, NetMeeting, Microsoft FrontPage Express, Microsoft NetShow, Microsoft Web Publishing Wizard, and multimedia enhancements.

The components that compose the contents of the three different Internet Explorer 4 installations are:

Internet Explorer 4	The Web browser that also acts as a file and resource manager
Outlook Express	An integrated mail and newsreader application
Microsoft NetMeeting	Collaborative software that enables application sharing, voice, whiteboard, and chat over the Internet
Microsoft FrontPage Express	An easy-to-use Web page editor
Microsoft NetShow	A player for audio/animation files broadcast over the Internet
Microsoft Web Publishing Wizard	Provides an easy way to transfer Web files from your PC to a server on the Web

Multimedia enhancements	Multimedia extensions such as ActiveMovie, DirectX, and Interactive Music Control

ON THE WEB

You can install each of the components separately by downloading them from Microsoft's Web site at:

http://www.microsoft.com/ie/ie40

This setup also gives you the option of installating the integrated web functionality as part of your desktop. This option can be installed through the IE 4 setup or uninstalled through the Add/Remove Applications Control Panel at a later time.

See "Adding or Removing Integrated Shell Components," **p. 283**

Installing from Desktop Icon

Some computer manufacturers might ship their computers with Internet Explorer 3 or Internet Explorer 4 available for setup. In that case, you will see an icon on the desktop with a label similar to Internet Explorer 4 Setup. Double-click this icon to set up Internet Explorer 4. You are prompted as to what components you want to install.

Installing from CD-ROM

The smallest installation option for Internet Explorer 4 is well over 10M. If this is too large for you to download, you might want to install Internet Explorer 4 from CD-ROM. Some computer manufacturers might ship their computers with Internet Explorer 3 on hard disk and Internet Explorer 4 available on CD-ROM.

Free downloadable upgrades that are very large are usually available from Microsoft for a nominal fee of approximately $15. Check with the Microsoft Upgrade Service at 800-426-9400 for information on ordering a copy of Internet Explorer 4 and integrated shell components on CD-ROM.

To install from CD-ROM, insert the CD-ROM in its drive, then click Start, Settings, Control Panel. Double-click Add/Remove Programs, select the Install/Uninstall tab, and click the Install button. Follow the directions when prompted.

Installing from the Microsoft Web Site

Internet Explorer 4 Suite is free if you download it from Microsoft's Web site. The smallest installation takes approximately 11M. This takes over an hour by 28.8 modem so a good strategy is to download the smallest Internet Explorer 4 suite and then return later for additional components as you need them.

ON THE WEB

Find Internet Explorer 4 on Microsoft's Web site at:

http://www.microsoft.com/ie/ie40

Look for and read the download instructions. You need to decide whether you want to install Internet Explorer 4 with Browser Only or Browser with Shell Integration. The integrated shell components are described in Chapter 4, "Operating with Integrated Shell Components." (You can load or unload shell integration components at any time using Add/Remove Programs from the Control Panel.)

The download is in two steps. You first will download the Active Setup Wizard. You can save this wizard to hard disk and run it later or you can start it immediately and begin Internet Explorer 4 installation. The wizard is approximately .4M. When you run the Active Setup Wizard, IE4SETUPW.EXE, you are given the choice of downloading the Standard, Enhanced, or Full installation. You can install these components as they download or download them to hard disk and install them at a later time by double-clicking the downloaded file to decompress it. Once decompressed install the suite using Add/Remove Programs from the Control Panel.

Starting Internet Explorer 4

The quickest way to start Internet Explorer 4 is to double-click the Internet Explorer 4 icon on the desktop. (Click it if you have single-click activation enabled.) You also can go the long way around and click Start, Programs, Internet Explorer Suite, Internet Explorer. With this long route, you at least get to see all the applications that are part of the Internet Explorer Suite you have downloaded.

The first time you start Internet Explorer 4, it will connect to a special setup site that tells you the Internet news about IEU. After that, when you start, you will connect to your normal home page.

If you have integrated shell components installed, an easy way of starting Internet Explorer 4 is by moving the pointer against the taskbar's edge to activate the Quick Launch toolbar. Click the Internet Explorer icon to start it.

See "Customizing Desktop Toolbars and Taskbar" **p. 288**

Understanding World Wide Web URLs

Uniform Resource Locators (URLs) specify the location of resources on the Internet that are part of the World Wide Web. You use URLs with Internet Explorer to identify where to retrieve information from the Internet. URLs are also used within World Wide Web documents to link to other resources. Figure 18.2 illustrates the makeup of an URL. The first part of an URL defines the Internet protocol used to get the resource. Use a colon to delimit the protocol from the remainder of the URL. The number of supported protocols is growing, and you might find protocols that are not listed below.

Specifier	Protocol
ftp	File Transfer Protocol
http	HyperText Transfer Protocol
https	Secure HTTP

continues

continued

Specifier	Protocol
gopher	Gopher Protocol
telnet	Telnet Terminal Session
news	UseNet News, uses NNTP
mailto	Electronic mail address

ON THE WEB

Information about Internet Protocols on the Yahoo search site

http://www.yahoo.com/Computers_and_Internet/Software/Protocols/

As shown in Figure 18.2, the protocol is http, which indicates that this resource is retrieved using the HyperText Transfer Protocol. The rest of the URL includes the Internet host name (www.w3.org) and the path to the document on the host.

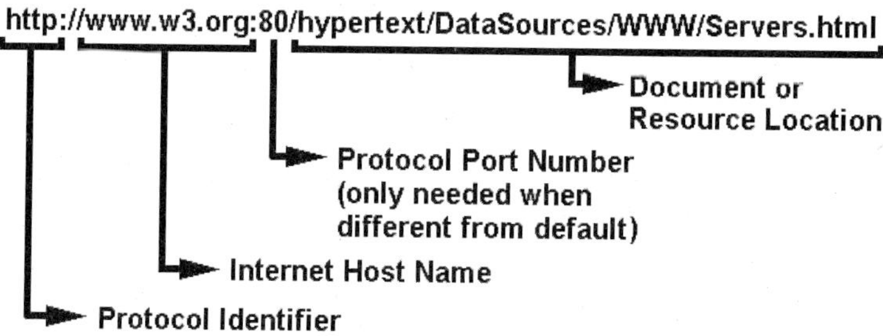

FIG. 18.2 URLs serve as simple identifiers to resources on the World Wide Web.

What follows the protocol depends on which protocol is used. Most URLs introduce a server host name by double slashes. If an application protocol is running on a non-standard TCP/IP port (a virtual network location on a host), the TCP/IP port number can follow the server name, delimited by a colon. If no TCP/IP port number is defined, the standard TCP/IP port number for that protocol is used instead.

Paths to specific files, directories, or programs on the server follow the server host name. Finally, arguments or parameters to server programs may be passed at the end of the URL. Consider the following examples of URLs:

- **http://www.intergraph.com/index.html**

  This http: URL identifies a document named index.html on the www.intergraph.com server, using the HyperText Transfer Protocol. Internet Explorer fetches the document and displays it in the window.

- **http://www.intergraph.com/ics/**

  When a directory is specified with no document, an HTTP server usually returns a default file or a listing of the files in the directory, depending on how the HTTP server is configured.

- **https://www.intergraph.com/catalog/order.pl**

  This https: URL identifies a secure HTTP server, which communicates with Internet Explorer in a trusted way. Using these URLs, you prevent Internet hackers from getting the information you submit, such as your credit card number.

- **ftp://ftp.intergraph.com/help/FAQ**

  This ftp: URL identifies a file named FAQ in the help directory on the ftp.intergraph.com anonymous-ftp server. Note that no user name and password are supplied. In this case, the FTP connection is established using the user name `anonymous`, and your e-mail address as the password.

  You can download files from an FTP site directly if you know the file location and name. Use the following syntax:
  ftp://anonymous:your-userid@ftp.intergraph.com/help/FAQ

  If an HTML page has a link to an anonymous FTP file, you only need to click the link to download the file.

- **gopher://gopher.intergraph.com:70/pub/win32**

  Named after the mascot of the University of Minnesota, Gopher allows you to list and find files on the Internet. The gopher: URL requests a listing of the /pub/win32 directory on the gopher.intergraph.com server. The additional :70 after the server name identifies the port number to connect to. Port numbers are optional in URLs and default to the standard port number for the particular protocol.

- **news:news.answers**

  The news: URL identifies a UseNet newsgroup. In this case, Internet Explorer connects to your Network News Transfer Protocol (NNTP) server, configured in the View Options News Property sheet.

- **mailto:info@intergraph.com**

  The mailto: URL identifies an e-mail address. When you click a mailto: URL, Internet Explorer brings up Microsoft Exchange, which allows you to fill in a subject, return address, and message. The message is sent to the address in the URL.

- **file:c:\htdocs\default.htm**

  To reference local files, as opposed to those on the network, use a file: URL. When you drag and drop a file onto Internet Explorer, the document appears with a file: URL. In general, URLs always use forward slashes, but Internet Explorer allows backslashes as well.

- **telnet://ausername:apassword@archie.sura.net**

  The telnet: URL identifies a host to invoke a terminal session, including the user name and password. When you click a telnet: URL in Internet Explorer, the Telnet application is used to handle the request.

Navigating the World Wide Web

There are several ways to open a Web page. The most common way is also the simplest: just click a hyperlink to jump to the page. Hyperlinks are usually shown as underlined and colored text. There are other ways to jump to another page or Web site:

- Type an URL into the Address toolbar and press Enter.
- Select an URL from the drop-down list on the Address toolbar.

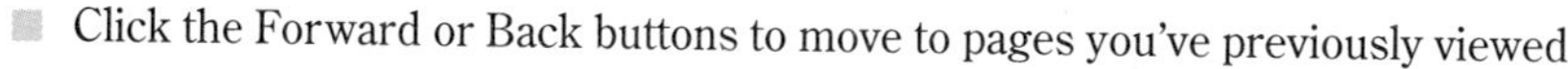

- Click the Forward or Back buttons to move to pages you've previously viewed.

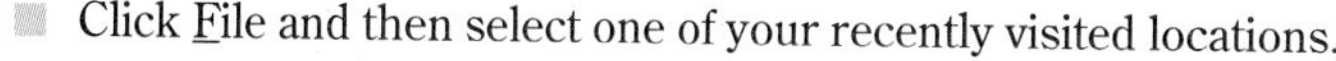

- Click File and then select one of your recently visited locations.

- Click the Favorites button and choose from a stored URL.
- Click View, Options, Navigation tab, View History to see a list of all sites you've visited, then double-click a site.

- At any time, you can jump back to your Home page (the initial page loaded when you launch the Internet Explorer) by clicking the Home icon or choosing Go, Home Page.

- Jump directly to a favorite site by choosing a site from the Favorites list. Click the Favorites toolbar button or choose Favorites, then select the site you want to visit. If you see a folder at the bottom of the Favorites list, pause the pointer on the folder to see its contents.

If you know the URL for the Web site you want to visit, it's easy to just type the URL into the Address bar and press Enter. For example, click in the Address bar, type

```
www.mcp.com/que
```

then press Enter to visit the Que publishing site and its huge array of computer books.

The History list that appears at the bottom of the File menu is cleared after each session. To see Web sites you have visited during previous sessions, click View, Options, and select the Navigation tab. Click View History to see a list of sites, then double-click the site you want to open.

TIP **IE4**

A convenient feature that is added when integrated shell components are installed is a more accessible history list. Right-clicking a Forward or Back button displays a short history list of the locations in the direction of that button. Just click the one you want to display. This history list is temporary and is only available for each Windows session.

Type an URL in the Address box and press Enter to display the contents at that site.

TIP

If you have integrated shell components installed you can type an URL into any Address toolbar on the desktop, even if Internet Explorer 4 is not running. You also can click Start, Run and type the URL into the Run dialog box. When you press Enter, Internet Explorer starts and displays the contents at that URL.

▶ **See** " Customizing Desktop Toolbars and Taskbar," **p. 288**

To open an HTML document from a drive on your computer, just double-click the HTML file to open Internet Explorer and load the document. From within Internet Explorer you also can click File, Open, Browse to select an HTML file from disk. HTML files appear with an HTM extension in Windows.

Right-click a picture or background texture in Internet Explorer to save the picture to your disk, copy it to the Clipboard, or set it as your desktop wallpaper. You can also drag images from a Web page to the My Computer window or the Explorer to copy them onto your disk, or into Exchange to mail them.

Using AutoComplete URLs for Faster Entry

A new feature with Internet Explorer 4 and integrated shell components is AutoComplete. This feature takes some of the guesswork and keystrokes out of entering obscure URLs or path names. AutoComplete works in any Address toolbar as well as the Run dialog box.

See "Customizing Desktop Toolbars and Taskbar," **p. 288**

There are a couple of different ways AutoComplete can help you enter an address. You might notice one way as you begin to type an URL or path name into an Address toolbar. If you have previously entered the address you are typing, Windows attempts to complete the address as you type it. For example, if, during a previous session, you had entered **www.microsoft.com**, you would see the entire address appear as you reached a point where Windows could tell the address was unique to Microsoft. For example, you might type

www.m

and the rest of the Microsoft URL would fill in automatically as shown in Figure 18.3. If this is not the URL you want, just keep typing. If you want to move to the end of the AutoComplete URL, press the right arrow key and continue typing. If you want to access the URL as it exists, press Enter.

Windows compares your typing in the Address toolbar and Run box to all the URLs and path names you have previously entered. These are stored in the Windows\History folder.

Some URLs to specific pages can be very complex. In this case, AutoComplete can help you with a scrolling list of possibilities. To see a list of possible matching sites, type as much of the URL as you can—for example, **www.micros**—then press Ctrl+down arrow. Each time you press Ctrl+down arrow the URL changes to another alternative from the list. To see a full list of matching URLs, hold Ctrl and click the down-arrow at the right side of the Address bar.

AutoComplete also helps you complete an URL as you type it by wrapping the site's name inside of www and com. For example, if you type *mcp* and then press Ctrl+Enter, the *mcp* becomes

http://www.mcp.com

You can then press Enter to go to the Macmillan SuperLibrary of books.

FIG. 18.3
When Windows recognizes an URL or path name you have previously entered, it attempts to complete it for you.

Stopping Downloads and Refreshing Pages

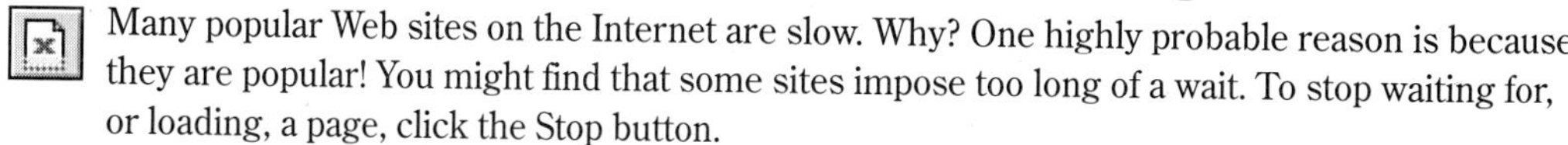

Many popular Web sites on the Internet are slow. Why? One highly probable reason is because they are popular! You might find that some sites impose too long of a wait. To stop waiting for, or loading, a page, click the Stop button.

When you stop loading a page, you might change your mind and want to reload it. You might also need to reload pages that didn't completely load the first time. To reload a page, click the Refresh button on the toolbar, or select View, Refresh. The Internet Explorer reloads and redisplays the page you are on.

Storing Favorite Sites

You probably have some favorite sites that you visit frequently. The Internet Explorer supplies easy ways to keep track of your favorite sites: the Favorites list and the Create Shortcut command. Putting a shortcut to a Web site on your desktop is most useful for no more than a few Web sites that you want to get to quickly. If you have more than a few sites to save, put them in the Favorites list.

TIP If you frequently need up-to-date information on specific Web sites, make sure you read Chapter 20, "Subscribing to Web Sites and Offline Browsing."

TIP Right-click a link to open a new window to the link, create a shortcut to the link, copy a shortcut to the link to the Clipboard, save the linked document to a file, or add the link to your Favorites list.

Create Shortcut creates a shortcut to the currently displayed page and puts it on your desktop. To create a shortcut, follow these steps:

1. If you are not already there, go to the page for which you want a shortcut.
2. Create the shortcut by choosing File, Send Shortcut.
3. You are asked to confirm that you want to create a shortcut on the desktop. Choose OK to create the shortcut.

When you need to store a large number of frequently visited Web sites, use a Favorites list. Shortcuts to your favorites are stored in the Windows\Favorites folder. To add a Web site to your Favorites list, follow these steps:

1. Display, in the Internet Explorer, the Web site you want to add to the Favorites list.
2.  Click Favorites, Add to Favorites. The Add to Favorites dialog box appears as shown in Figure 18.4.
3. IE4 Select Subscribe if you want this favorite to be updated when other subscribed sites are updated to your disk.
4. Click OK if you want to store this page directly under the Favorites menu.

   or

   Click Create In if you want to keep your sites organized by storing them in folders. The Add to Favorites box expands, as shown in Figure 18.5. Select the folder in which you want to store your Web site, and click OK. If you want to create a new folder, select the folder in which you want the new folder to reside, click New Folder, type its name, and choose OK. Choose OK again to store the Web site in the new folder. You can create folders within folders.

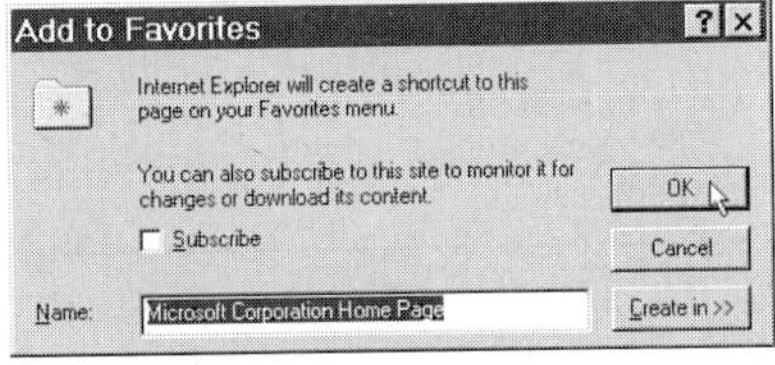

FIG. 18.4
Store the link to a favorite Web site by adding it to your Favorites list.

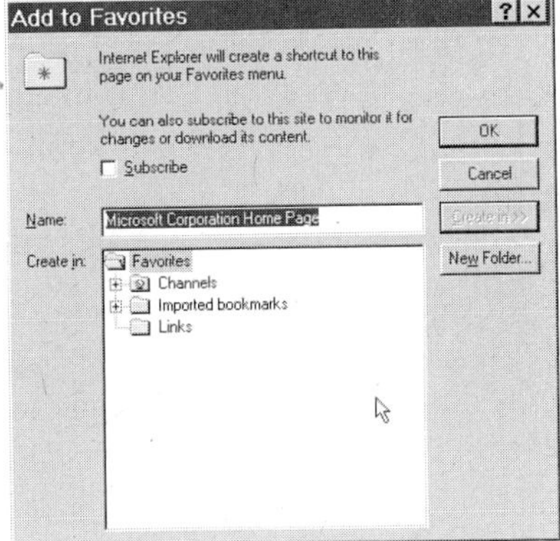

FIG. 18.5
In the expanded Add to Favorites dialog box, you can store your favorite in an existing folder or a new folder you create.

It takes a lot of research to find sites that are valuable. You wouldn't want to lose your Favorites list. Maintain a backup copy of your Favorites list by copying the files in the Windows\Favorites folder to disk or tape.

Reorganizing Favorites List with Drag and Drop

A new feature in Internet Explorer 4 with integrated shell components is the capability to reorganize your Favorites list by dragging favorites within the list to new locations. This enables you to organize your Favorites list the way you want rather than sticking with alphabetical order.

To organize your Favorites list, click Favorites, then drag the site or folder to a new location on the list. A black horizontal bar shows where the item's new location will be when you drop it. Figure 18.6 shows a favorite being dragged to a new location. Note the black horizontal bar. The black box around the item's name shows its original location.

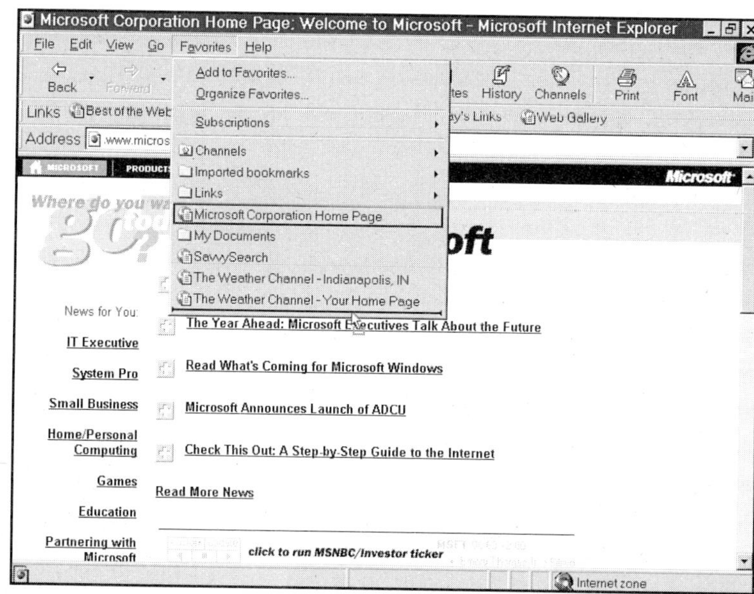

FIG. 18.6
In Internet Explorer 4, you can drag favorites to a new location on the menu.

As you view Web pages, you might see a link that you want on your Start menu. Drag the link over Start and drop it. The next time you click Start the link will be at the top of the Start menu. This really gives you quick access.

Managing Your Favorites List

One of the tough things about the Web is that the information is so intriguing. It's easy to find more information than you can immediately digest. So you add the site to your Favorites list in hopes that you'll come back someday. The problem is that the Favorites list builds so quickly it's soon unmanageable, unless you know about the Organize Favorites dialog box.

Begin by clicking Favorites, Organize Favorites. The Organize Favorites dialog box appears, as shown in Figure 18.7.

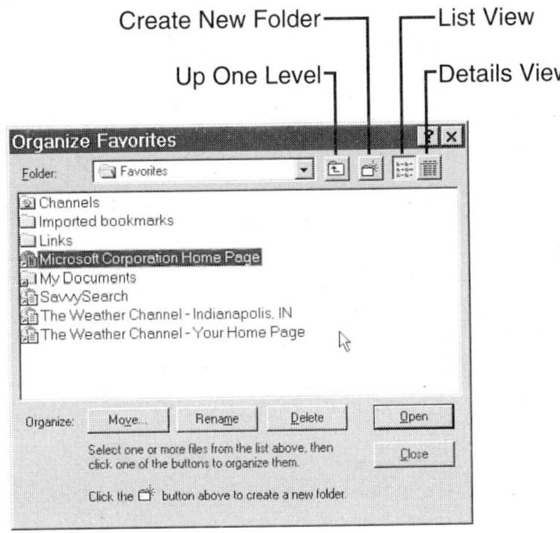

FIG. 18.7
Manage your list of favorites from within the Organize Favorites dialog box.

Use one of the following procedures to manage the URL shortcuts stored in Favorites:

Move an item	To put it in a folder at its same level, drag it and drop it on the folder. If the move is more complex, select the item, then click Move. Click the folder where you want to move the shortcut. Click OK.
Rename	Use editing methods the same as in Windows Explorer or select the item, click Rename, and type the new name.
Delete	Select the item and press Delete or click Delete. Click Yes in the confirmation dialog box.
View the shortcut	Select the URL shortcut and click Open to display the Web page in a new window.
Open a Favorite folder	Double-click the folder.
Move to the higher	Click the Up One Level button.
Create a new folder	Open the folder in which you want a new folder, then click the Create New Folder button.
Change views	Click the List or Details View button.

Many commands for managing favorite sites are available by right-clicking a shortcut within the Organize Favorites dialog box.

Previewing Favorite Sites as Thumbnails

Some names used by Web sites or pages are pretty inscrutable. One way to make your lists of sites more understandable is to show thumbnail pictures of each page in addition to a name. Figure 18.8 shows a view of a folder's contents in Windows\Favorites.

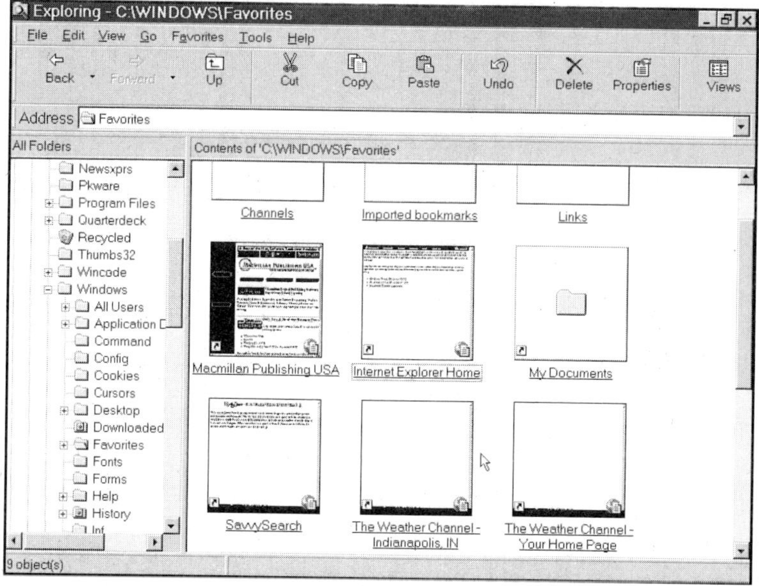

FIG. 18.8
Thumbnail views of folder contents make it easier to remember your favorites.

To show a thumbnail sketch of the contents of a folder, you must first enable thumbnails for files in a folder. After enabling thumbnails for a folder, you can select the Thumbnail view from the View menu.

To enable thumbnail views for the Web sites stored in your Favorites folder, open Windows Explorer and right-click the Windows\Favorites folder. Select Properties. In the General tab, select the Enable Thumbnail View check box. (This selection applies only to the selected folder, not to subfolders in it.)

Viewing Favorites While Browsing

In IE 4, you can view your Favorites on screen while continuing to browse the web. To do this, choose View, Explorer Bar, Favorites or click the Favorites button. This opens a two-paned view with the favorites in the left pane. You can click any Favorite links on the left to browse on the right.

Select a folder in which you want to view thumbnails, in this case the Windows\Favorites folder, then click View, Thumbnails. The Thumbnails menu item only appears when thumbnail view has been enabled. When you open a folder, you now see thumbnail views of file contents.

Searching for Web Sites

There are more than 100,000 Web servers available, with millions of files. Finding what you need can be impossible if you don't know where to start. Internet Explorer makes it easy for you to get started.

To search for Web documents with Internet Explorer, click the Search button on the toolbar or choose Go, Search the Web. Internet Explorer displays the search page, where you can type key words and ask for links to related documents. Some Web search sites are faster than others, while others serve to index different sets of documents.

Moving the mouse pointer over a search link displays a ToolTip with a description of the page for the link. The description comes from the page's META tag or from the first few lines of text on the page.

Searching Is Easier with Internet Explorer 4's Dual Pane Search Window

While the Internet is an amazing repository of information, it can be incredibly time consuming to search. One of the little annoyances of searching with most browsers is that search engines create index-like pages of links to pages that might have the information you want. You must repeatedly click backward and forward moving between the index of links and the pages it references. Sometimes this involves hundreds of links, which means at least two hundred clicks.

Internet Explorer 4 has a better way of working with searches. It creates two panes in the Internet Explorer window, as shown in Figure 18.9. The left pane continuously displays the links that result from your search. The right pane displays the contents of the link you select from the left pane. This enables you to quickly find which link contains the information you need.

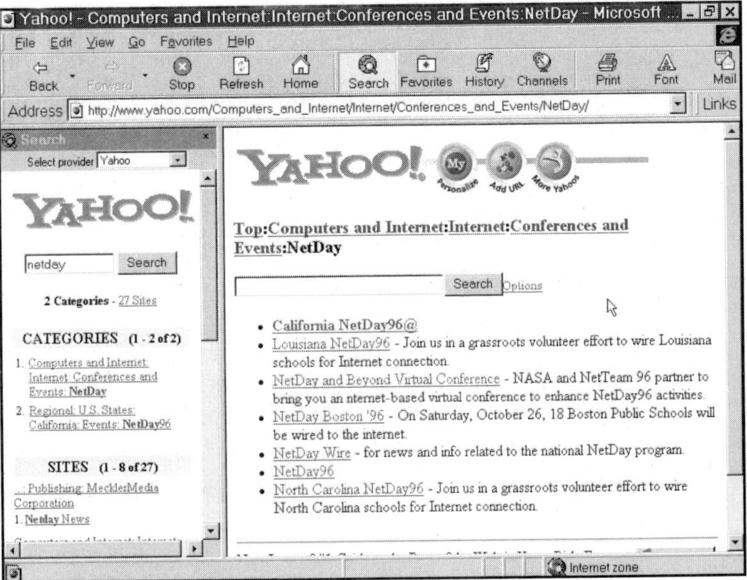

FIG. 18.9
The left pane continues to list search results while the right pane shows a Web site you have clicked.

When you find a page that contains information you need to frequently track, you might want to subscribe to the page. When you subscribe, Internet Explorer 4 checks at a frequency you specify to see if the page has changed. Windows 95 can even send you e-mail to notify you when a change occurs. See "Subscribing to Any Web Site" and "Subscribing to Web Sites and Offline Browsing " in Chapter 20.

If you are not connected to the Internet when you click the Search button, you are given the opportunity to connect to your service provider, then Internet Explorer 4 connects to the search page at **home.microsoft.com**.

To view the search page in a single window instead of in frames, right click the Search title bar in the Search pane and choose Open in Window. This opens a separate Explorer window with the search page. To close the search page in the original window, click the Search button again in that window.

Searching for Text on a Page

Web page designers are learning to keep their pages no longer than one or two screens, so it's usually easy to scan a page for the information you want. In some cases, though, you'll want to search within a Web page for a word or phrase. Usually this occurs when a search has found a page that doesn't look like it matches your criteria. By searching the page's text, you can find the word or phrase you used as a criteria. Another instance where text search is useful is when you're faced with conference proceedings that are very long and all in one Web page. You can use a text search to find specific topics out of the proceedings.

Searching a Web page for text is the same as in most word processors; click Edit, Find (on this page) or press Ctrl+F to display the Find dialog box. Type in the Find What dialog box the word or phrase you want to find. Select whether you want matching case and whole word matches. Select the direction in which you want to search the page. Click Find Next. The dialog box remains on-screen until you click Cancel.

Printing HTML Pages

Even with the offline browsing capabilities of Internet Explorer 4, it is still occasionally useful to have a printed copy of Web pages. Printing a Web page involves two parts. Before you print, define how you want the page set up with margins, orientation, headers and footers, and so forth. When you print, specify the printer, the number of pages, number of copies, and so forth.

Defining the Page Setup

To define how the Web page prints to paper, click File, Page Setup to display the Page Setup dialog box shown in Figure 18.10.

While most of the elements in the Page Setup dialog box are like other page setup dialog boxes you have used, the Header and Footer boxes are probably unique. By typing codes in these two boxes, you can specify information and formatting for headers and footers.

Type text in upper- and lowercase as you want it to appear in the header or footer. Do not enclose the text in quotes. To insert information or formatting in the header or footer, use the codes from Table 18.2.

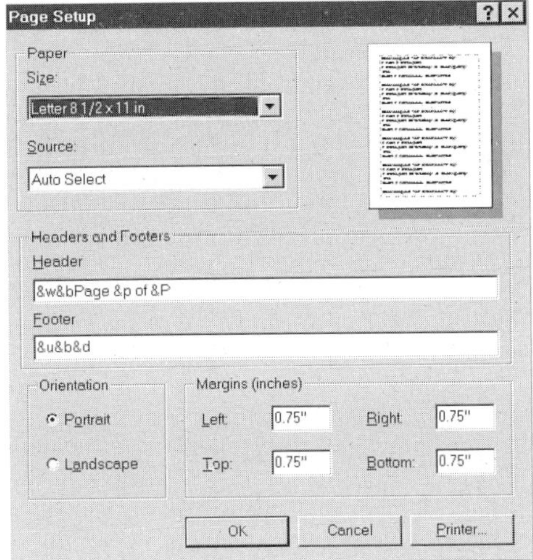

FIG. 18.10
Specify the page layout, headers, and footers in the Page Setup dialog box.

Part IV Ch 18

Table 18.2 Codes Used in the Header and Footer Box for Formatting and Positioning

Code	Description
&b	Breaks the header or footer into left- and right-aligned portions
&w	Title shown in Internet Explorer 4 window
&u	URL of the page
&d	Date in the short format—for example, 8/1/97—specified by Regional Setting in the Control Panel
&D	Date in the long format—for example, Monday, May 26, 1997—specified by Regional Setting in the Control Panel
&t	Time in the format specified by Regional Setting in the Control Panel
&T	Time in 24-hour format
&p	Current printed page number
&P	Total number of pages
&&	Single ampersand (&)

When you are ready to print the current page, click Print in the toolbar or click File, Print. With the exception of the Print frames and Linked Documents areas, the Print dialog box, shown in Figure 18.11, is the same as other common print dialog boxes in Windows.

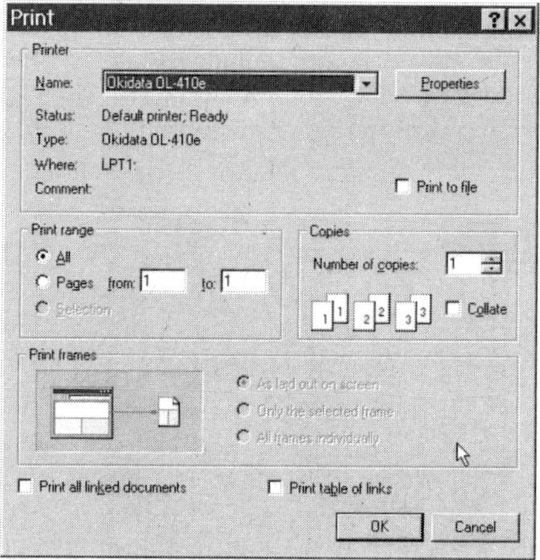

FIG. 18.11
Select the Print All Linked Documents to print all pages linked to the page displayed.

The Print Frames options are only available when the web page you are printed is laid out with frames. The options:

As laid out on screen	Prints the page with the frames laid out as close as possible to the screen layout
Only the selected frame	Only the frame that you are currently in will print; if you have not clicked in a frame, this will print the default frame defined in the page
All frames individually	Each frame will be printed beginning on a new printed page

Selecting the Print All Linked Documents check box prints all pages linked to the page being displayed. In some cases, printing all linked documents could deforest acres of woodlands.

If you decide you need to pause or stop a print job, stop the printer by clicking Start, Settings, Printers. Right-click the icon for the printer, then click Pause Printing. To clear all the pages, click Purge Print Documents.

If you are unsure how many pages will print when you select Print All Linked Documents, use the following safe procedure. It pauses the printer before printing starts and collects all the pages. You can then inspect the pages to see the quantity and their URLs before printing. You even can delete pages you don't want to print.

To collect Web pages to a paused printer, examine them, and then print, follow these steps:

1. Click Start, Settings, Printers to display the Printers dialog box.
2. Click the icon for the printer to which you are printing.
3. Click Printer, Pause Printing so it is selected. When this item is selected, the printer will not print until Pause Printing has been cleared.

4. Activate Internet Explorer 4 and click File, Print.
5. Select options as necessary and select Print All Linked Documents; then click OK.
6. Click the printer button on the taskbar to activate the printer window. Figure 18.12 shows a list of pages to be printed.

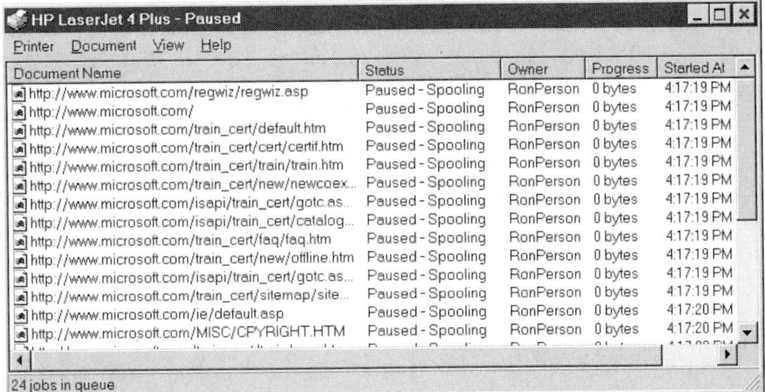

FIG. 18.12
Collecting all pages to a paused printer saves a lot of paper and time.

7. Scroll through this list of pages and delete pages you don't want printed. To delete a page, select its name, then click Document, Cancel Printing. To delete all the pages, click Printer, Purge Print Documents.
8. Print the documents remaining in the list by clicking Printer, Pause Printing to remove its check mark.

The Print Table of Links option prints a list of the links in the page and their Web addresses in tabular format at the end of the printed Web page.

Sending Shortcuts to Web Pages via E-Mail

If you find a Web page that has information someone else needs, you can send them a shortcut to the page by e-mail. To transmit a shortcut to a Web page, follow these steps:

1. In Internet Explorer, display the page you want to transmit.
2. Click File, Link by E-mail. Your mail program appears, similar to the Outlook Express mail window shown in Figure 18.13.
3. Complete the mail program addressing and send the message.

The recipient of the e-mail receives an e-mail that includes a shortcut to the page you had displayed. (This is only available in e-mail programs that are compatible with OLE embedded objects such as Outlook and Outlook Express.) Double-clicking the shortcut icon starts the recipient's browser and accesses the Web page.

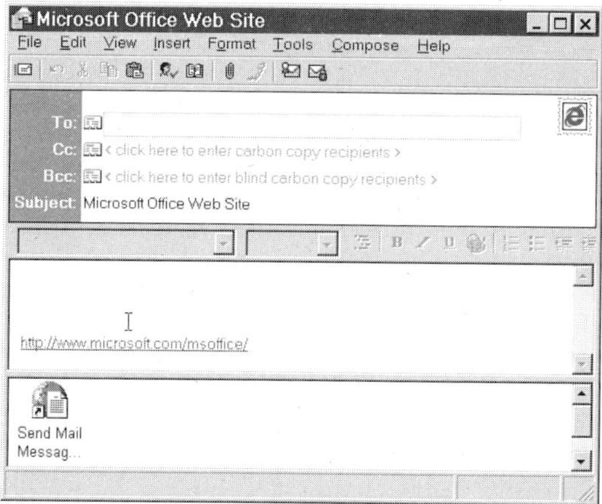

FIG. 18.13 Embed a shortcut to a Web site in your e-mail.

Customizing Internet Explorer

Although the Internet started with the intent of having a common communication, it took very little time for market forces to differentiate Internet browsers from different companies. Each browser has different features and ways of being customized. You can customize Internet Explorer to change little things like how hyperlinks display as well as more serious changes such as security and how it behaves with add-in programs and applets. The Internet Explorer lets you control its behavior with the Options dialog box, displayed when you choose View, Options.

NOTE Customization tabs and features are different between Internet Explorer 3 and Internet Explorer 4. Many of the same custom display and appearance options are the same, but they are located in different positions in the Options dialog box. Features that are only in Internet Explorer 4 are indicated by the Internet Explorer 4 icon.

Changing How Addresses Display

You can control settings used for displaying Web pages with the General tab in the Options dialog box. To open this dialog box, click View, Options. You can change how hyperlinks appear, whether pictures display, the text and background color for pages, and more. Figure 18.14 shows the General tab of the Options dialog box.

Controlling Graphics, Sound, and Video

Graphics, sound, and video enliven Web pages at the cost of slowing down your searches and burdening the already overloaded Internet. You have the option of turning these features on or off. All of these options are controlled in the Advanced Tab of the options dialog box shown in Figure 18.15.

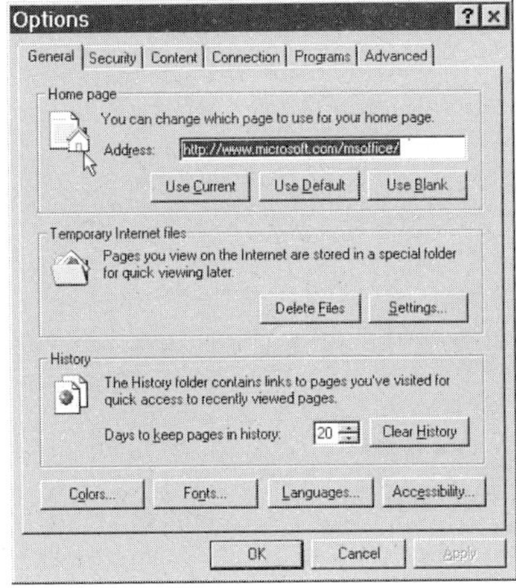

FIG. 18.14
The Appearance page gives you control over how Web pages and links appear on your screen.

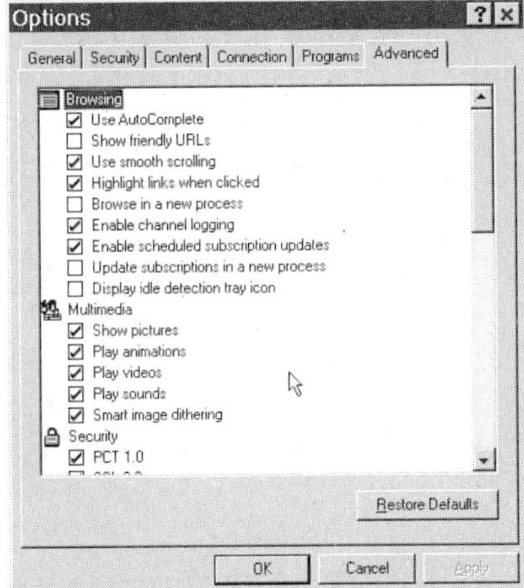

FIG 18.15
The Multimedia section controls where animation, sounds, pictures, and video are downloaded in the pages you view.

By default, all of these multimedia options are on so all of these types will be downloaded and displayed. To speed up page viewing time and do your part to reduce traffic on the internet, turn these off when you don't need them. The following table describes what each option controls:

Show Pictures	Controls embedded pictures including JPEG, GIF, and PNG. This is the most common multimedia type you will come across
Play Animations	Controls animated GIFs, Shockwave, and other animation types
Play Videos	Controls AVI, MPEG, and MOV movies
Play Sounds	Controls WAV, MIDI, Real Audio, and other sound types

Smart Image Dithering	This controls how images are displayed if the number of colors and color palette on your PC differs from the colors in the web image. There is no performance benefit to turning this off

All of these options control only multimedia embedded as part of a web page. When you click a link to a file of one of these types, it will still download or display. You can also still display embedded files individually. This way, only the ones you want to view (or hear) are downloaded. To do this, right click the missing image icon for the image you want to view and choose Show Picture.

Changing Text and Background Colors

In Internet Explorer, you control the text and background colors of some Web documents. However, some Web pages might define their own colors. To set your color preferences, click View, Options, select the General tab, then click the Colors button. Select custom colors as follows:

- Click the Text button to bring up the Color dialog box. Choose a color from the selected palette or mix a custom color, then choose OK. Internet Explorer uses that color for displaying text on Web pages when the text color is not predefined.
- Click the Background button to bring up the Color dialog box. Choose a color from the selected palette or mix a custom color, then choose OK. Internet Explorer uses that color for displaying the background on Web pages when the background color is not predefined.
- To use the text and background colors defined in your windows desktop settings, click Use Windows colors.

Changing Fonts

Internet Explorer lets you control which fonts are used when it displays proportional or fixed-width text. Most Web documents use proportional text, because it is easier to read. To change fonts, click View, Options, select the General tab, then click the Font button. From the Fonts dialog box, select the character set, proportional and fixed-width font, and font size.

Some Web authors use different fonts than those you prefer. In that case, the author's fonts are displayed instead.

Serif fonts are easier to read for large amounts of text. The small wings, or *serifs,* on each character help the eye follow the text quickly. A commonly used serif font is Times New Roman.

Standard HTML lets page authors set the font sizes in a document. If the author uses *relative* font sizes, you can control the size displayed. Enlarge or reduce the font size by clicking the Font toolbar button and selecting a new size or by selecting View, Fonts, then choosing a font size from the submenu.

Changing Hyperlink Appearance

Internet Explorer lets you control how hyperlinks display. Some users prefer their links underlined, while others like them to appear as plain text. You can set your preference for how hyperlinks appear by clicking View, Options, selecting the General tab, and then clicking the Colors button. In the Underline links drop down list, you can select to have links underlined always, never, or when you are hovering over a link.

Internet Explorer also lets you choose what colors to use for links you have visited or not visited. To specify a color for links you have visited, click View, Options, select the General tab, click the Colors button. Click the Visited color button to control the color of links to pages you have seen that are still in your history file. Unvisited controls the color of the links that you have not seen or that have expired from your history.

When you click the color button, select from one of the predefined colors or create a custom color by clicking the Define Custom Colors. Choose OK or Apply to see the result on Web pages.

The Use hover color option changes the color of links when you hover the pointer over them. To use this, select the option then choose a hover color the same way you choose colors for visited and unvisited links. This is most beneficial if your hover color is different than your visited or unvisited color.

Changing the Home Page Links on the Links Bar

You might prefer Internet Explorer to start with a page you have defined. It might be a Web page you use most frequently, or it could be a page you have created on your local hard drive so that Internet Explorer opens more quickly.

Here is how to change the home page:

1. Display the page you want to use as your home page.
2. Click View, Options, then select the General tab shown in Figure 18.16.
3. If you have the correct page displayed in step 1, then click the Use Current button to fill in the Address box. You can type in a path name or UNC to a file on your local or networked drive. To start IE with a blank page, click the Use Blank button.
4. Click OK.

If you want to return to the original Home page, that was predefined when you installed Windows, select the page you want to reset from the Page drop-down list, then click the Use Default button.

The Links buttons displayed on the links toolbar are controlled by a special Links folder in Favorites. To add or change the links on this toolbar, use the techniques described in sections relating to Favorites in this chapter to add or remove favorites in this folder

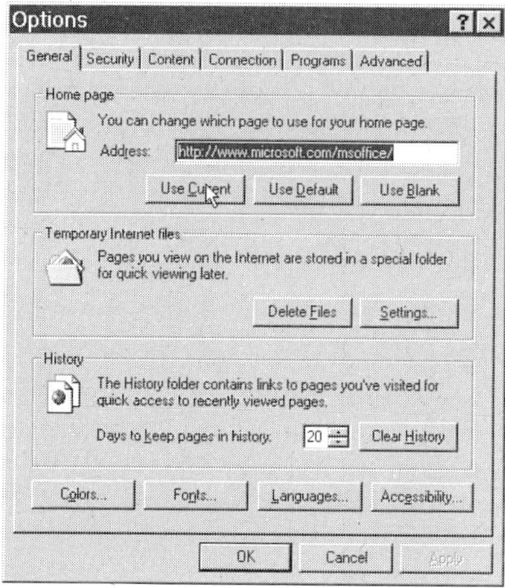

FIG. 18.16
You can define your own home page.

Adjusting the History List Size

Internet Explorer saves a shortcut in the Windows\History folder for each Web page you visit. You can adjust how many days shortcuts are kept. To adjust this, click View, Options, and select the General tab from the Options dialog box. Change the number in the Days to keep pages in history box.

If you want to see a history of Web sites visited, click View, Explorer Bar, History or click the History button. This displays the history list in a two paned view with the history on the right as shown in Figure 18.17.

To display a Web page from the history list, just click it. The page will display if it is still in temporary storage or Internet Explorer 4 will attempt to reconnect to the site to display the page. Empty the history list by clicking the Clear History button in the General tab. To delete individual pages or sites (and all of the pages in history from that site) right click the site or page and choose Delete Local Copy.

Managing Internet Explorer's Temporary Storage

Internet Explorer caches Web pages and their graphics in the Windows\Temporary Internet Files folder on your hard disk. Internet Explorer stores recently used HTML pages and graphics locally so the browser doesn't need to download text and graphics as you move backward and forward through pages you have previously accessed.

You can see the files in the Windows\Temporary Internet Files folder in the Windows Explorer or by clicking View, Options, selecting the General tab, clicking the Settings button, and clicking the View Files button.

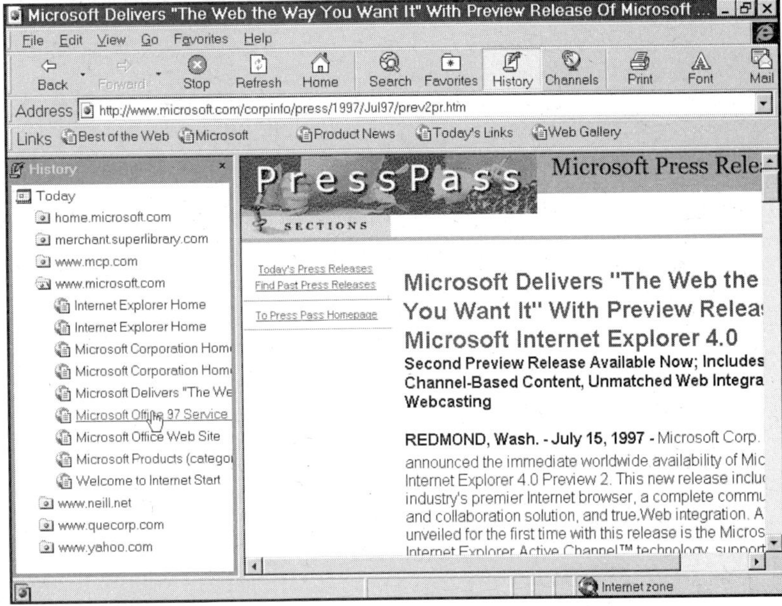

FIG. 18.17
Click any link in the history in the left pane to open that page in the right pane.

Internet Explorer can automatically check for updates to the cached pages when you return to them or only when you refresh them. To configure Internet Explorer to automatically check for new pages that have been cached, click View, Options, select the General tab, and click the Settings button. The Settings dialog box displays as shown in Figure 18.18. Select Every Visit to the Page if you want the page updated whenever you display it. This slows down performance but ensures you are always seeing the most current page. Select Every Time You Start Internet Explorer to update the temporary files only when you first display the page after starting Internet Explorer. If you want to have fast access but only see information that is in the Temporary Internet Files folder, then select Never.

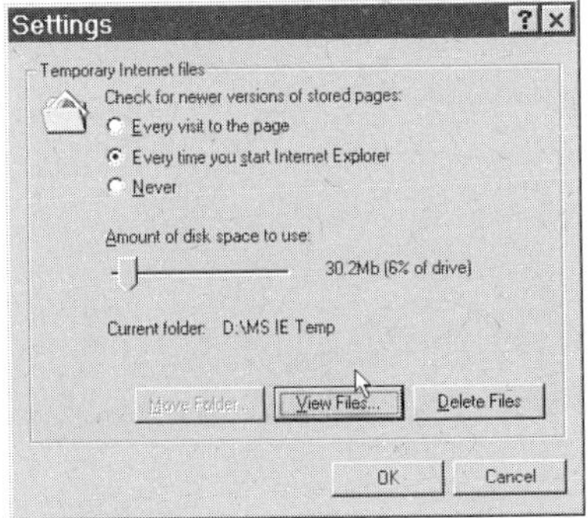

FIG. 18.18
Use the Settings dialog box to specify how frequently pages update and how much disk storage is used.

To adjust the amount of disk space Internet Explorer uses to cache Web pages, use the slider for Amount of Disk Space to Use. Making this amount smaller gives you more available hard disk space, but can slow the performance of Internet Explorer 4 because it must go to the Internet more frequently to refresh pages. If you are continually low on hard disk space you will probably want to use a smaller Web page cache.

TROUBLESHOOTING

When I navigate to Web sites that update frequently, the documents look the same as when I last read them. Why? It is possible you are actually viewing documents that Internet Explorer found in cache, instead of the latest version available from the Web. Select the Every Visit to the Page option from the Settings dialog box if you want to ensure you are always viewing the most current page. This will cause Internet Explorer to seem slower because it has to refresh over the Internet. You may want to subscribe to the Web site and have Internet Explorer 4 automatically update the cache. This not only ensures up-to-date pages, but it enables you to browse Web sites off line. See Chapter 20, "Subscribing to Web Sites and Offline Browsing."

Setting Internet Explorer as the Default Browser

Sometimes you might install other Internet browsing software on your system, and that software registers itself as your default browser. If you want to keep Internet Explorer as your Internet browser, click View, Options, select the Programs tab, and select the Internet Explorer Should Check to See Whether It is the Default Browser option. When this box is checked and you start Internet Explorer, it checks to see if Internet Explorer is the default browser; if it is not you are asked if Internet Explorer should be restored as the default browser.

Installing Add-Ins and New Document Types

Internet Explorer comes preconfigured to accommodate and use many common file types, including Microsoft Office documents, JPEG and GIF images, WAV and AU sounds, AVI videos, and various other file types. When you install most Windows 95 applications, they register themselves and their file type so you can automatically view their files when accessed from the Internet. You might need to add new file types for some documents types, such as CAD drawings, files compressed on UNIX machines, or MIDI files. You might also want to change the application associated to view a certain file type.

For example, if you frequently edit JPEG graphic files, you might want to double-click a JPG file in the Windows Explorer and have it load in a photo editor program; but the registration is currently set up so that the JPG file loads in Internet Explorer.

Internet Explorer uses the file type settings in Windows to determine which programs to use. To see how to register a new file type in Windows, see "Registering a New File Type," in Chapter 31.

Using Certificates to Identify People, Sites, and Publishers

The Internet is a public network. When two computers communicate, data is visible on all the network equipment between them. Internet hackers use this fact to access information that you might want kept private. To thwart hackers from accessing private information, such as business information, banking or credit card data, Internet Explorer and many Internet sites employ different types of security software to encrypt the data so only the authorized receiver can read it. You can use Internet Explorer to view and send private information to secure sites, knowing that Internet hackers cannot view the information.

TIP To view the security certificate information for a Web page, right-click a blank area on the page and select Properties; then click the Security tab to read the Certificate Information.

You can configure Internet Explorer to warn you when you are about to send information to a site that is not considered secure. Follow these steps to define the level of security you want:

1. Click View, Options and select the Content tab shown in Figure 18.19.

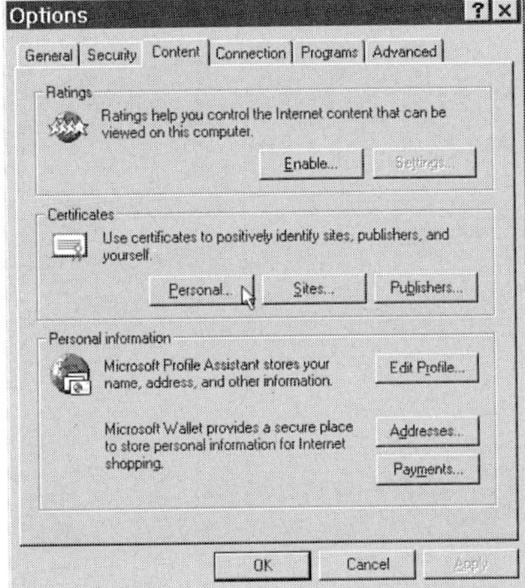

FIG. 18.19 Use the Content tab to positively identify sites, publishers, and yourself.

2. Click Personal to display the Client Authentication dialog box, which lists certificates you own that identify you to other sites. (This is like showing your photo ID when cashing a check.) To view a certificate, select it, then click View Certificate. Click Close.
3. Click Sites to display lists of certificates whose sites have sent to Internet Explorer, see Figure 18.20. These certificates identify the site and the length of time the certificate is valid. They enable Internet Explorer and the site to communicate securely when transmitting information such as credit card or financial data. To see detailed information about any of the certificates listed, select it and click the View Certificate button. Click Close when you are done.
4. Click Publishers to see a list of all software publishers and certificate granting companies that you believe are trustworthy, see Figure 18.21. For example, Microsoft might appear on this list if you have previously selected an option to allow immediate download of any software from Microsoft. Click OK.
5. Click OK.

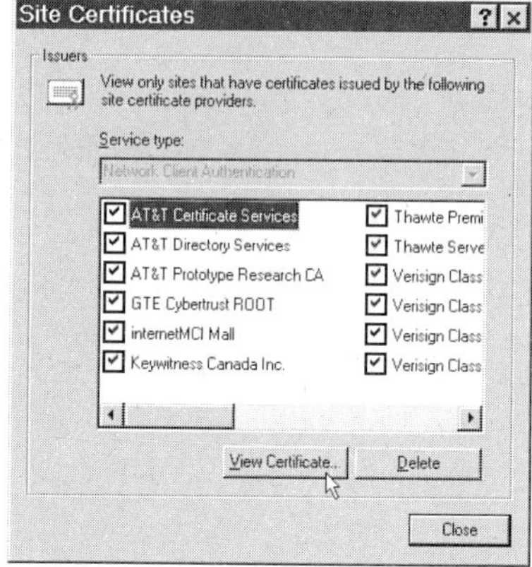

FIG. 18.20
View lists of Web sites with which you have exchanged a certificate to ensure security.

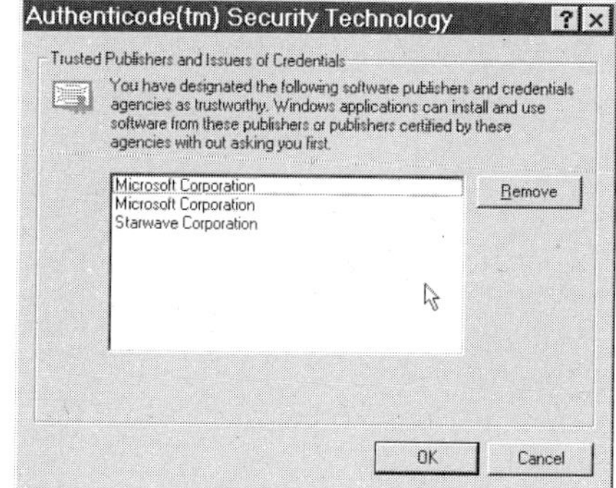

FIG. 18.21
View lists of software publishers that you want to specify as trustworthy. Software from trustworthy certificates downloads without your intervention.

To get a certificate that identifies you or your business, go to **http://www.microsoft.com/ie/ie40/oe/certpage.htm** for a list of security certificate providers. Currently, Verisign is the only provider. You can go directly to their site at **https://digitalid.verisign.com/**.

Setting Internet Security Zones

New to Internet Explorer 4 is the ability to set your security preferences according to *zones.* Zones are groups of sites that you define so that some sites can have different security preferences associated with them. For example, you may completely trust sites on your own corporate intranet so you can put them in a "trusted" zone. The higher your level of trust, the more type of applications Explorer will run and the fewer warnings you will see about potentially dangerous file types.

You select zones in the Options dialog box Security tab shown in Figure 18.22.

There are four different defined zones. They are described in Table 18.3.

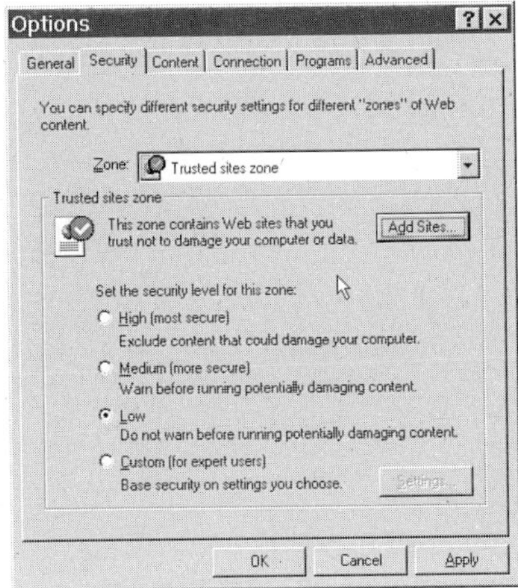

FIG. 18.22
The security tab is used to assign security for each zone and assign sites to a zone.

Table 18.3 Internet Explorer 4 Security Zones

Zone	Description	Default Security Level
Local Intranet	Assign web servers that are part of your intranet (and therefore supposed trusted to this)	Medium
Trusted Sites	For sites that you trust that are outside of your intranet	Low
Internet	Any site not listed in one of the three other groups is assigned to the Internet Zone by default	Medium
Restricted Site	Assign sites that you know to have potentially dangerous file types (viruses, trojan horse scripts, etc) to this zone	High

There are three types of security predefined. These are:

- High: Prevents any type of executable file from downloading without warning you first. Active Content is not downloaded or displayed
- Medium: You are warned before any executable file or Active Content is downloaded
- Low: Any files and active content from a site with a valid ID is downloaded and run with no warnings

To change the security level for an entire zone, select the different level. If you choose to set the Restricted zone to anything other than High security, you will be prompted with a warning that this could allow dangerous content to be downloaded without warning.

To add a site to the Local Intranet, Trusted, or Restricted zones, select the Zone and click the Add Sites button. Type the address of the site in the Add this web site to zone box as shown in Figure 18.23 and click Add. You must type the full site address here including the protocol (usually http:// for Web sites).

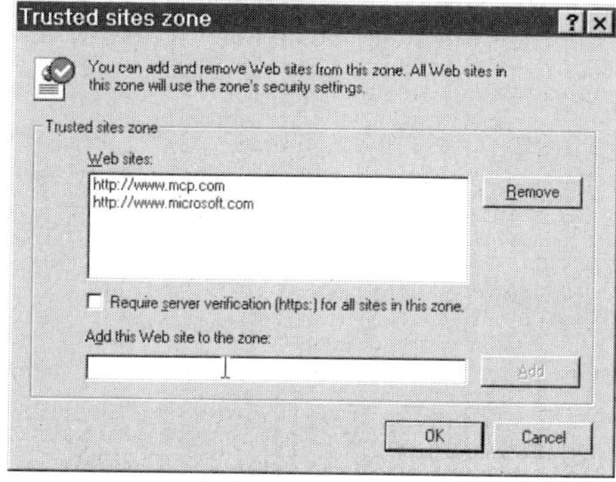

FIG. 18.23
The sites in this zone are listed at the top and you add sites by typing the full site address at the bottom.

Defining Your Own Security Settings

In addition to using the three predefined security settings (high, medium, and low) described in the previous section, you can also define your own custom settings to define to any of the zones. It is suggested that you do this only if you have a good understanding of the types of file content on the web and the risks they pose. To define a custom set of security preferences, in the Security tab:

1. Select the Zone you want to define custom settings for.
2. Select the Custom and then click Settings. This opens the Security Settings dialog box in Figure 18.24.

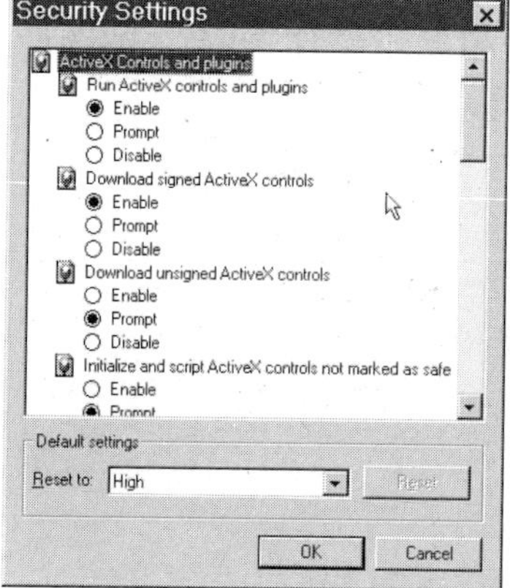

FIG. 18.24
The Security Settings dialog box has options for security preference for each class of executable file.

3. Select whether you want the content class enabled, prompted, or disabled for each type of content. The main types are:

   ActiveX and Plug-ins: These can be set differently depending on whether you are just downloading them or running them and whether or not they are signed or come from a "safe" site

   Java applets

   Scripting: Controls JavaScript, VBScript, and Jscript languages

   File downloads

   Miscellaneous: A few other categories that don't fit elsewhere

4. When you are done customizing, click OK.

Controlling Access to Violent or Sex-Oriented Sites

The Internet and World Wide Web contain vast amounts of information, but its very quantity and uncontrolled nature means that some of the information is repugnant to some people. While the continual mayhem and violence on television far exceeds violence on the Web, the same is not true for sexual content. Some of the most profitable and frequently visited Web sites publish explicit sexual content.

The Web is such a valuable source of information for children that many parents limit their children's access to the Web, but do not restrict it entirely. While it is not mandatory, many sexually explicit sites subscribe to a rating system. You can use this rating system to prevent Internet Explorer from viewing sites that exceed ratings you specify.

NOTE One form of child endangerment on the Web is from pedophiles. A 1993 FBI investigation in online pedophilia led to 96 arrests that resulted in 89 convictions as of May 1997. Pedophiles often work by posing as children and building trust through online chat. After they build trust, they collect personal information and then request a meeting with the child. They can only do this if you do not monitor your child's e-mail and online use.

The danger from pedophiles shouldn't cause you to keep your children from the Web any more than you would keep them from school or the library. It should cause you to set up rules for computer use and to be aware of your child's online activity.

Some tips from the National Center for Missing and Exploited Children and other sources are the following:

- Post a copy of online rules by the computer.
- Never reveal personal addresses or phone numbers.
- Never display or transmit a photo. A request for a photo should be of immediate concern.
- Never allow meetings with online friends unless they are supervised by a parent.
- Use a family e-mail address that is accessible to all members of the family.

continues

continued

- Children should be taught to notify a parent at the first sign of suggestive information or requests to meet.
- Install rating software and use the access settings in Internet Explorer 4 to control access.
- Put the computer in a family area so it is easy to see your child's online activities.
- Never give children unlimited time online. This is just as bad as unlimited television.

The Web is a tremendous educational source for parents and children. For more information on children's safety, visit the following sites:

Child Safety on the Information Highway by School District 4J, Eugene Oregon
www.4j.lane.edu/InternetResources/Safety/Safety.html

Parent Soup, a large site dedicated to helping with all aspects of parenting
www.parentsoup.com

National Center for Missing and Exploited Children
www.missingkids.org

For Piece of Mind, an organization to aid parents and child safety
www.csoftinc.com

To prevent your Internet Explorer browser from accessing rated sites, follow these steps:

1. Click View, Options and select the Content tab shown in Figure 18.25.

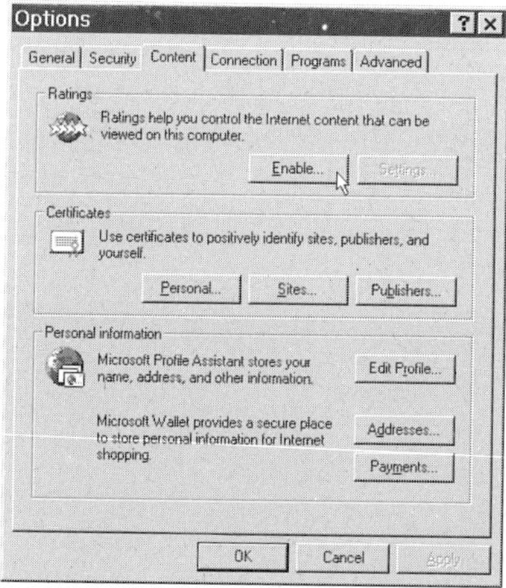

FIG. 18.25
The Content tab has the controls for accessing Web pages based on their ratings.

2. Click the Enable Ratings button to display the Create Supervisor Password dialog box. Enter a password you can remember and reenter it as a cross-check. Click OK. This installs the Content Advisor and displays the Content Advisor dialog box.

3. Select the Ratings tab, then select one of the categories to rate. Slide the Rating control to the rating level you will allow. Figure 18.26 shows level 3 for the Sex category. Adjust the rating for each category you want to limit.

FIG. 18.26
Restrict access by adjusting the rating level for each category.

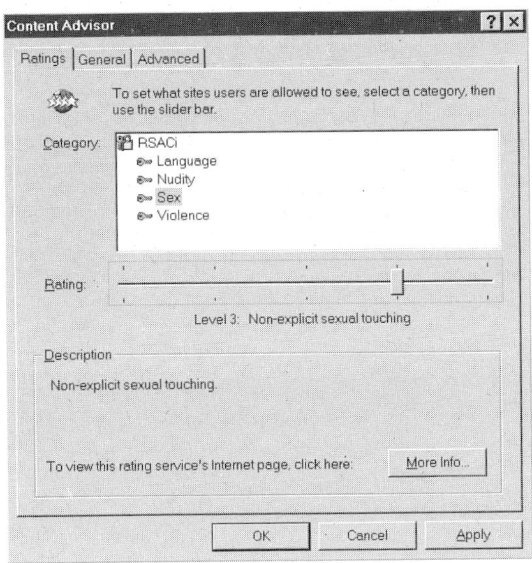

4. Select the General tab shown in Figure 18.27. Prevent access to unrated sites by clearing the Users Can See Sites that Have No Rating option. If you want to use a password to view each unrated site as it is accessed, then select the Supervisor Can Type a Password option.

FIG. 18.27
If a site doesn't have a rating, you can make it inaccessible to Internet Explorer.

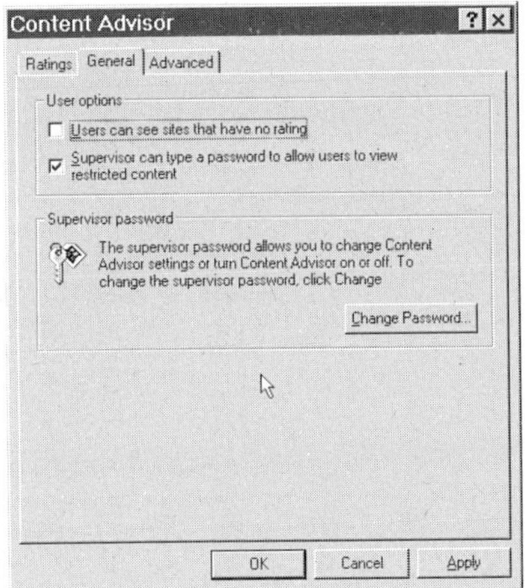

5. Click OK.

To change ratings at a later time, click the Settings button on the Security tab. Change passwords by clicking the Change Password button in the General tab. You need the original password to change settings or passwords. It's a good idea to change passwords frequently. Disable ratings by clicking the Disable Ratings button on the Security tab.

NOTE While many sexually explicit sites subscribe to one or more rating systems, some do not. If you are concerned about your child's access to the Web, set the ratings on the Ratings tab, then select the General tab and clear the Users Can See Sites That Have No Rating option and select the Supervisor Can Type a Password option. These options restrict your child from sites that are not rated. However, your child can still access unrated sites by asking you to type the password. The password needs to be typed each time the child attempts to enter an unrated site.

Internet Explorer 4 comes with a rating system developed by the Recreational Software Advisory Council (RSAC). There are other rating systems in use that can be added to Internet Explorer. Sites that subscribe to other rating systems usually include a link on their home page that downloads the add-in for their rating service. You also can check with the following sites for software that controls access.

NOTE There are many filtering and access control software systems. Some of the filtering software enables you to limit access to more than just Web sites. Some packages enable you to limit offensive materials found in news groups, IRC chat sessions, FTP sites, AOL, Compuserve, and more. You can find out more at the following sites:

SafeSurf—**www.safesurf.com**

CyberPatrol—**www.microsys.com**

CYBERSitter—**www.solidoak.com**

SafeSearch—**www.teachersoft.com**

Net Nanny—**www.netnanny.com**

SurfWatch—**www.surfwatch.com**

If you suspect someone has downloaded offensive photos, you can search for them on the hard disk and remove them. Downloaded pictures from sex sites are usually in JPEG or GIF format and use the JPG or GIF file extension. You can search a hard disk for JPG files by clicking Start, Find, Files or Folders. Type ***.JPG** or ***GIF** in the Named box and select the hard drive from the Look In drop-down list. Click OK. You can view files by double-clicking the file in the Windows Explorer. Permanently delete them by selecting the file and holding down the Shift key as you press the Del key. (If you do not hold down the Shift key when deleting files they can be restored from the Recycle Bin at a later time.)

Making Online Purchases with Microsoft Wallet

The Microsoft Wallet helps you make online financial purchases. The Microsoft Wallet stores your personal and confidential information such as addresses and credit and debit card information so that you don't have to repeatedly reenter the same information when you make online purchases. When you use the wallet to make online financial payments, you only need to enter a password to release your financial data to the online vendor.

Microsoft Wallet protects its financial information by password. This password also identifies whose financial information should be used in a transaction because the Microsoft Wallet can hold information for multiple people. The wallet includes industry standard Secure Socket Layer (SSL) protocol for transmission of credit card information. In addition, other software developers can create add-ins using Secure Electronic Transaction (SET).

Addresses used in the Wallet are shared with the Windows Address Book. This makes it easy to enter ship-to-addresses for family, friends, or businesses by clicking a name you already have in the Windows Address Book.

ON THE WEB

To learn more about Microsoft Wallet or to download Microsoft Wallet as an Internet Explorer 3 ActiveX control or as a Netscape plug-in, go to:

www.microsoft.com/commerce/wallet

Microsoft Wallet is extensible. This means that vendors can add additional functionality and payment methods over time. Its initial release included payment information for Visa, Mastercard, American Express, and Discover cards. In the future, you might see the Microsoft Wallet used with ATMs, digital certificates, proprietary systems, and more.

At the time this book went to press, the following online financial transaction companies had announced they would support the Microsoft Wallet:

CyberCash Inc.

CyberCharge

DigiCash

GC Tech Inc.

GlobeSet, Inc. (formerly Interval, Inc.)

IC Verify®

Paylinx Corp.

Tellan Software Inc.

Trintech Inc.

VeriFone® Inc.

Entering Addresses in the Microsoft Wallet

To enter a new address or select an existing ship-to address from the Windows Address Book, follow these steps:

1. Click View, Options and select the Content tab.
2. Click the Addresses button to enter a ship-to address or select a ship-to address from the Windows Address Book. The Address Manager dialog box appears.
3. Click Add to add a ship-to address. The Add a New Address dialog box appears as shown in Figure 18.28.

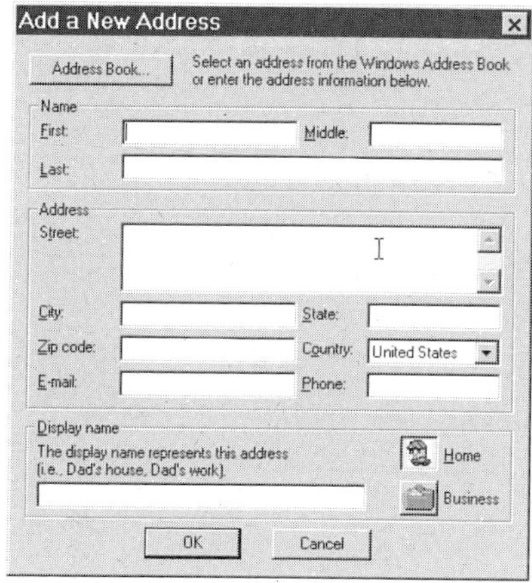

FIG. 18.28
Enter new ship-to addresses or select an existing address from the Windows Address Book.

4. Click the Home or Business buttons as appropriate, then enter ship-to address information.

   or

   Click Address Book, select an address from the Windows Address Book, click the Home or Business button, then click OK.
5. Names you add or edit are changed in the Windows Address Book. Click Close.

You can edit or delete names in the Address Manager by selecting the name, then clicking the Edit or Delete buttons.

If you want to be notified before sending an address over the Internet, select the Warn Me Before Sending Addresses Over the Internet check box in the Address Manager.

See "Using the Windows Address Book," **p. 789**

Entering Financial Data in Microsoft Wallet

To enter new financial information into the Microsoft Wallet, follow these steps:

1. Click View, Options and select the Contents tab.
2. Click the Payments button to enter financial payment information. The Payment Manager window appears.

3. Click Add and click a payment method, such as Visa. The introductory window of the Add a New Credit Card Wizard explains the steps you will follow. Click Next.
4. Enter your credit card information in the Wizard shown in Figure 18.29. Click Next.

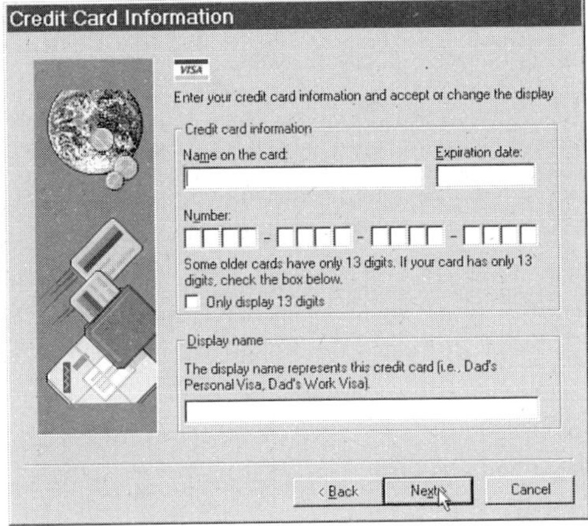

FIG. 18.29 Enter credit card information and a name that identifies the card in the wallet.

5. Select a billing address from the Billing Address drop-down list or enter a new address by clicking New Address in the Wizard. Click Next.
6. Enter a password for this card, then reenter it a second time for confirmation. The two must match exactly, including upper- and lowercase. Store this password in a secure location. You will need the password to use this information from the Microsoft Wallet. Click Finish.
7. Click Close, then click OK to close the Options dialog box.

Internet Explorer 4 with Dynamic HTML

Dynamic Web pages that animate or update interactively intrigue and entertain. They are more vibrant and attractive, but they are also more expensive to develop in time and resources. To make dynamic Web pages more attainable, Microsoft has developed Dynamic HTML.

Dynamic HTML is a new technology that is built in to Internet Explorer 4. Because Microsoft intends for Dynamic HTML to be compatible with other browsers, it is working with the World Wide Consortium (W3C) so that it will be part of the open standard usable on other operating systems and different browsers.

Developers take advantage of Dynamic HTML when creating their pages. There is nothing that you as a Web reader need to do other than enjoy faster performance and more interactive Web pages.

Dynamic HTML works by providing a complete object model for the HTML language. Every element on an HTML page becomes an object that can be manipulated by programs such as Java, JavaScript, C++, Visual Basic, and Visual Basic, Scripting Edition. Dynamic HTML also includes an event model to trap keyboard and mouse events. Dynamic HTML is based on current HTML so that browsers that are not Dynamic HTML-compatible default to usable HTML pages. For example, in Internet Explorer 4, developers can create expandable/contractable outlines. In a browser that is not compatible with Dynamic HTML, that outline would appear as a static text outline.

When combined with straightforward programming, the object model of Dynamic HTML provides Web pages with the following enhancements:

- Dynamic Content — Text and graphics can be under program control. For example, selecting an option button changes graphics on the same page. When the graphic changes, the text reflows.
- Dynamic Styles — Cascading Style Sheets (CSS) are under program control. For example, text colors or formatting can change when the mouse passes over text formatted by cascading style sheet.
- Absolute Positioning — Text or graphic elements can be controlled to the smallest screen unit in their x, y, and z position. Changing the x and y coordinates while the page displays makes items move on screen. The z position determines front-to-back placement so that you can order overlapping objects.
- Multimedia — Multimedia controls that you are familiar with in PowerPoint, such as transitions and filters, are built in to Internet Explorer 4.
- Data Binding — Dynamic HTML pages can contain databases of information. This is very useful when the person reading the page wants to make changes to the data. For example, a query to a sales database might bring back information about product sales for a region. The reader can then sort, filter, or reorganize the table of information without having to requery the online database.

ON THE WEB

As Dynamic HTML becomes pervasive, you will see its results without being aware it is Dynamic HTML. To see demonstrations of specific Dynamic HTML capabilities, check the following Web sites:

Microsoft's SiteBuilder Gallery–

www.microsoft.com/gallery

Internet Explorer 4 Components–

www.memphis97.com/ieindex.htm

Joel Carley's Internet Explorer 4 Page–

www.icomnet.com/~jcarley/links.htm

CHAPTER 19

Working with the Active Desktop

by Ron Person

Adding Internet Explorer 4 and integrated shell components to Windows 95 can change the way you work and think. Instead of working from your computer's desktop, you can work from the Webtop. Imagine your world of information and applications expanding outward. Your computer screen is no longer a window to the data and applications in your office, but it becomes a window to all the data and applications on the Web. It's a heady and perhaps frightening thought, but it also can expand the way you think and the way your company works.

Learn how the Active Desktop can help you work

With the Active Desktop the Windows desktop becomes a view of Web pages—your own custom Web pages or active Web pages from the World Wide Web or your corporate intranet.

Add Web pages to your desktop

Use your own custom Web page as a desktop so frequently used links are immediately available.

Add Desktop components to your desktop

Put free custom applications on your desktop that display live data from the Internet.

Change the order in which components display

Learn how to change which components appear on top of others.

What Is Active Desktop?

The *Active Desktop* is one of the most important aspects of the Webtop metaphor. The Active Desktop displays live Web pages, ActiveX components, and Java applets. Information that you need to monitor or small applications that help you work are always available and current on your desktop. Figure 19.1 shows an Active Desktop with multiple active components on the desktop. The Active Desktop becomes an active part of your work instead of just a holding place for icons.

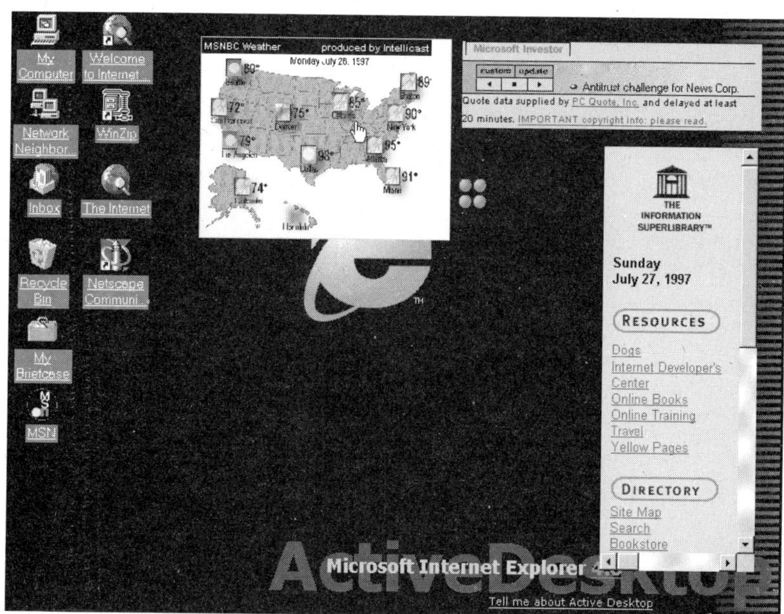

FIG. 19.1
The Active Desktop can transform your work from desktop computing to Webtop computing.

Switching Active Desktop On and Off

The Active Desktop can be either enabled or disabled. When it is disabled, the desktop has the appearance of standard Windows 95. When the Active Desktop is enabled, it displays the active components you specify. To enable or disable Active Desktop, right-click the desktop, then click Active Desktop. There are three Active Desktop options on the Active Desktop menu. A check mark to the side of the View as Web Page menu item indicates that the Web view of the Active Desktop is enabled.

Using a Web Page as Your Desktop

Internet Explorer 4 can make your personal computing even more Web-centric by using your own custom HTML (Web) page as the desktop background. Figure 19.2 shows an Active Desktop containing graphics, links that start applications, links to connect to Web sites, and links to open local folders and drives.

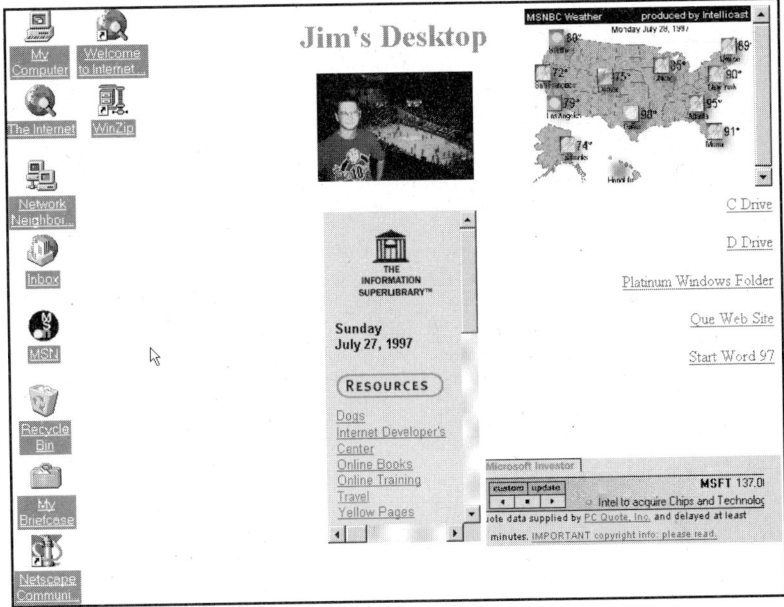

FIG. 19.2
Use an HTML page to make your desktop even more Web-centric.

With earlier versions of Windows 95 you could add shortcut icons to the desktop to open frequently used documents or Web sites. These shortcuts are easy to create. Although creating a Web page that becomes your desktop is not as easy as creating shortcut icons, there is far more you can do with a Web page. Consider some of the following ideas for using Web pages on your Active Desktop:

- Having your custom Home page as your desktop so your favorite links, news, sports, and weather are always visible
- Having a graphical background that personalizes the screen for you or your company
- Having rapidly changing data, like news, stocks, and weather from subscription sites, immediately visible so you are always aware of changes
- Displaying organized tables of links to applications, documents, and Web sites so you can quickly start application, load documents, or access sites
- Displaying help information and links to create a kiosk-like display for untrained users
- Creating Webtops for a workgroup, division, or corporation that can be updated by the network administrators

▶ **See** "Creating Simple Custom Web Views," **p. 373**

▶ **See** "Using FrontPage Express," **p. 612**

Creating an HTML page that acts as your desktop is not as interactive and instantaneous as adding shortcut icons to a standard desktop. To create a useful desktop requires knowledge of what work you want to do and how you want to organize the links and information on the page. Once you've planned how you want your HTML desktop to look, you will then need to use an

HTML editor such as Microsoft FrontPage Express or Microsoft FrontPage to create the HTML page. (Microsoft FrontPage Express is included as a free program with Internet Explorer 4.)

See "Using FrontPage Express," **p. 612**

Once you have created an HTML page you want to use as the Active Desktop, follow these steps to use the HTML page as your Active Desktop:

1. Right-click the desktop and then choose Active Desktop, Customize my Desktop. The Display Properties dialog box appears with the Background tab selected (see Figure 19.3).

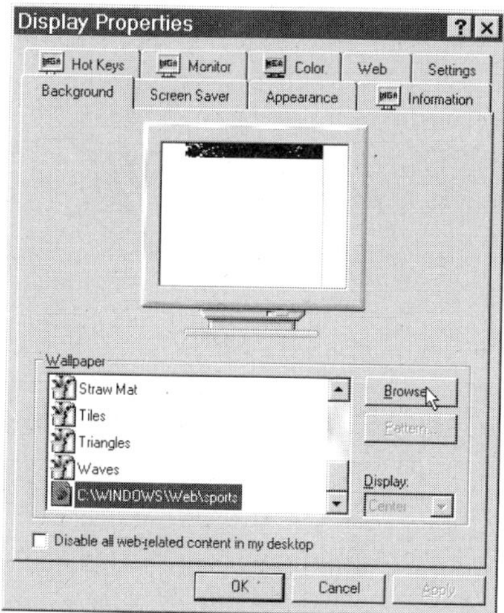

FIG. 19.3
The Desktop tab enables you to specify that you want an HTML page as the desktop background.

2. Click Browse to display the Browse dialog box. Select the HTML file you want to use as a desktop, then click Open.
3. Click OK.

If you want to return to a standard Windows 95 desktop, right click on the desktop, choose Active Desktop and deselect, View as Web Page. If you want to disable Web items in the active desktop, select the Disable all web-related content in my desktop option in the Background tab of Display properties.

Displaying Components on the Active Desktop

Your active desktop can contain many different components. They can be simple graphics, Web pages linked to a Web site, Active Channels of push information, and objects created from ActiveX controls or Java applets. Many companies are creating desktop components. They range from entertaining animated graphics to scrolling stock-market tickers to live news feeds.

When you need to see the Active Components on your desktop and it's covered with open application windows it's easy to minimize all the open windows. Click the Show Desktop icon in the Quicklaunch Toolbar. Click once to minimize all windows. Click again to restore all windows.

Displaying Components

Before you can display components on the desktop, you must have the Active Desktop enabled as described earlier in the section titled "Switching Active Desktop On and Off." Objects will not appear on the desktop unless you select to display objects on the desktop background.

To display components on the desktop background, follow these steps:

1. Right-click the desktop, then click Properties. The Display Properties dialog box appears. Select the Web tab shown in Figure 19.4.
2. In the list of objects, select the objects you want displayed.
3. Click OK.

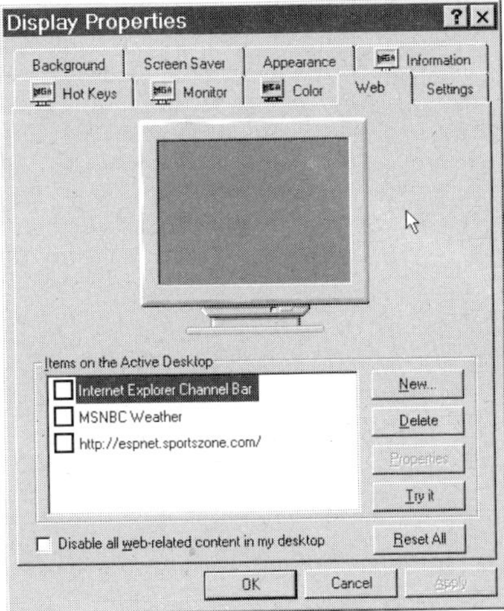

FIG. 19.4
The Web tab controls the individual Active Desktop icons.

Components do not automatically appear in the list of objects. You must make these components available to Windows. The following sections describe how to make Web pages, graphics, and Active Components appear in the objects list.

TROUBLESHOOTING

After adding components to the Active Desktop, they don't appear on screen. Make sure you have enabled Active Desktop. Right-click the desktop, then click Active Desktop and select View as Web Page so there is a check mark next to it.

Adding a Picture to the Active Desktop

Pictures on your desktop could be for pleasure or for information. They could be photos of your children or favorite vacation area. Or they could be satellite weather maps that update over the Internet every hour.

If the picture you want on your desktop is on the Web, connect to the Web before adding the picture. This enables the Internet Explorer to refresh the picture as soon as it is added.

To add a picture to the Active Desktop, follow these steps:

1. Right-click the desktop or the desktop icon on the right end of the taskbar, then click Properties. The Display Properties dialog box appears. Select the Web tab.
2. Click New to display the New dialog box shown in Figure 19.5 (You will also be prompted to connect to the Microsoft Web site to see a gallery of Active Desktop components. If you want to use any of these, follow that prompt.)

FIG. 19.5
You can add pictures or entire Web pages to your desktop.

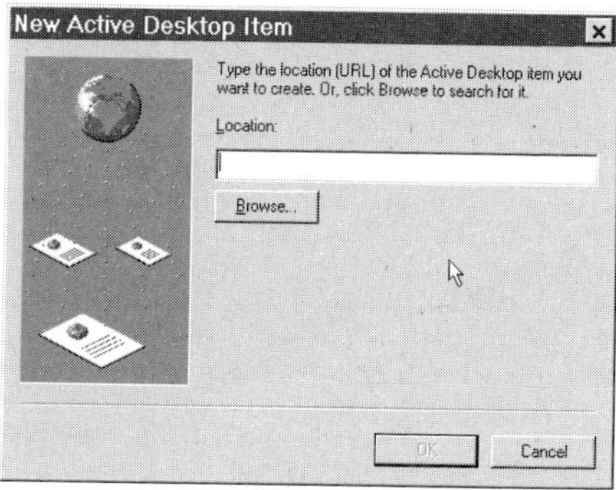

3. If you know the address of the item to add, enter it. Otherwise, click Browse.
4. If you want a picture on the desktop, select Picture in the Files of Type box.
5. This is a standard open file dialog box. Select the picture file to be added, click Open, then click OK.
6. The Picture appears selected in the list of objects on the Desktop tab. Click OK to add the picture to your desktop.

Picture files can include BMP, GIF, and JPG (JPEG) files. GIF and JPEG files are the most common picture format on the Internet.

Unless it is your Web site that contains the picture you want displayed it is best to save the picture to your local drive instead of linking to a graphic file on someone's Web site. Web sites change structure and content so frequently that your link may not remain valid for long.

TIP The easiest way to capture an image from the Web is to right-click the image when it appears in a Web page in the Internet Explorer. Click Save Picture As. Save the picture to a name and directory where you can locate it. Do not violate copyrights by using graphics that are not free. Using a copyrighted graphic in your commercial Web site could cost you a legal suit.

Move pictures on the Active Desktop by moving the pointer over the top-left corner. Drag the two double bars to move the entire picture. Resize a picture by moving the pointer over the lower-left corner and dragging the corner.

Adding a Web Site to the Active Desktop

Windows 95 really becomes Web-top computing when you use Web pages as your desktop. The Web pages you use as desktops can be linked to live Web sites or can be updated by a scheduled subscription. You also can create your own HTML pages that you can use as the desktop.

The following are a few of the reasons you might want Web sites on your Active Desktop:

- Having Web sites with rapidly changing data, like news, stocks, and weather, immediately accessible.
- Displaying multiple individual Web pages that cover your desktop. When you see a piece of information you want to know more about, just expand that Web page and click the hyperlink to open Internet Explorer and access the information.
- Displaying helpful information in a scrolling window. Users can click a hyperlink or graphic to jump to a page with more specific information.
- Displaying a scrolling list of hyperlinks to the most frequently used applications or documents. Click a link and the application or document opens.

Web sites added to your desktop can be like Web sites you subscribe to for offline browsing. Desktop Web sites can have multiple levels of pages and be updated on a schedule, and you can be notified when updates occur. For more information on working with subscriptions, read Chapter 20, "Subscribing to Web Sites and Offline Browsing."

Before you add a Web site to your desktop, connect to the Internet. This enables Internet Explorer to refresh the Web site as soon as it is added to the Active Desktop. To add a Web site to the Active Desktop, follow these steps:

1. Right-click the desktop, then click Properties. The Display Properties dialog box appears. Select the Web tab.
2. Click New to display the New Active Desktop Item dialog box shown in Figure 19.5.
3. Enter the address of a Web site or click Browse.
4. If you click Browse, select Internet Shortcut in the Files of Type box and then select any of the shortcuts listed. This is a standard open dialog box so click Open when you have selected the item to use.
5. If you want to display an HTML file on your local drive, click Browse, select HTML Documant in the Files of Type box, and select the file, then click Open, OK. You will return to the Web tab of the Display Properties dialog box. Skip to Step 9 to finish.

6. If you want to display a Web site, type the URL of the Web site using the full syntax, including protocol, such as **http://www.microsoft.com**, then press enter. The Subscribe dialog box, shown in Figure 19.6, appears.
7. In the Subscribe dialog box, click Customize if you want to set a custom schedule for updating the content of this active desktop item. Chapter 20, "Subscribing to Web Sites and Offline Browsing," describes in detail how to set subscription properties. Click OK after changing properties.

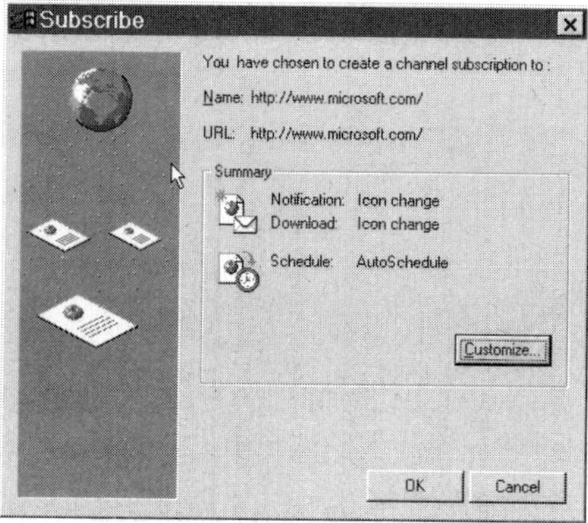

FIG. 19.6 When you add a Web site to your desktop, you can schedule the site for updates.

8. The Web site downloads and becomes a desktop component. It will appear in the list of objects in the Desktop tab.
9. Click OK in the Display Properties dialog box. The local HTML page or Web site you specified will appear on the Active Desktop.

Once you have added a Web site to your Active Desktop, you can treat it much like browsing an offline Web site. To manipulate the Web site, right-click it to display the context menu shown in Figure 19.7. Note that you can Refresh (Update) the Web site, open links in new windows, and print the current page. Click Properties if you want to see the site's URL and the date of its last update.

Move Web sites on the Active Desktop by moving the pointer over the top-left corner. Drag the two double bars to move the entire Web site. Resize a Web site by moving the pointer over the lower-left corner. Scroll through a Web site that is larger than its container using the scroll bars.

Adding a Component to the Active Desktop

Components can include ActiveX objects and Java applets that are written to run on your Active Desktop. Components can be very simple such as animation, or they can be very robust and complex, handling tasks such as time and billings or document management.

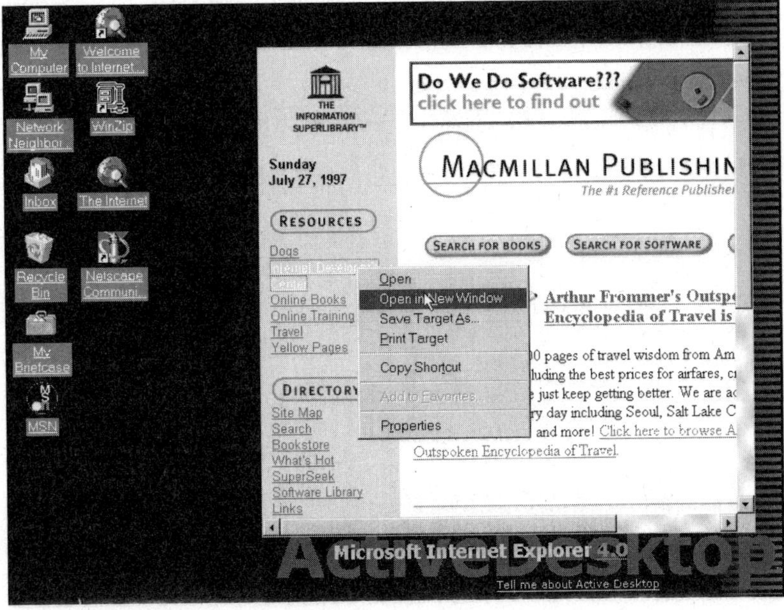

FIG. 19.7
Right-click a Web site in the Active Desktop to refresh, print, or navigate through the site.

NOTE ActiveX components are programs written in Microsoft Visual Basic or Microsoft C++ that can be downloaded over the World Wide Web and run within Internet Explorer. Java applets are programs written in Java that can be downloaded over the World Wide Web and run within Internet Explorer and Netscape Navigator. Both types of components add a lot more intelligence and functionality to a Web page than is available through HTML, but decrease page performance and increase the probability of browser crashes.

During Internet Explorer 4's initial release period, sample components were available primarily at Microsoft's Desktop Component Gallery Web site. As desktop components become more pervasive, you will find them at many commercial sites. For example, financial institutions and stock brokers might have components available at their sites, which give easy access to portfolio information or online trading.

ON THE WEB

One place to look for useful Active Desktop components is the Internet Explorer 4 gallery:

http://www.microsoft.com/ie/ie40/gallery

Adding Active Components to your Active Desktop is simple on your part—the work is done by the Web site developer. In most cases, like the example shown in Figure 19.8, you can click a hyperlink or an Add to my Desktop button on a Web page and the Web site will download and install the component on your Active Desktop. (See the section later in this chapter titled "Hiding, Removing, and Editing Objects" to remove a component you do not want.)

When you add a component to your desktop, you may be taken through the New Web Site procedure described in the section in this chapter titled "Adding a Web Site to the Active Desktop" and given an opportunity to schedule frequency of updates.

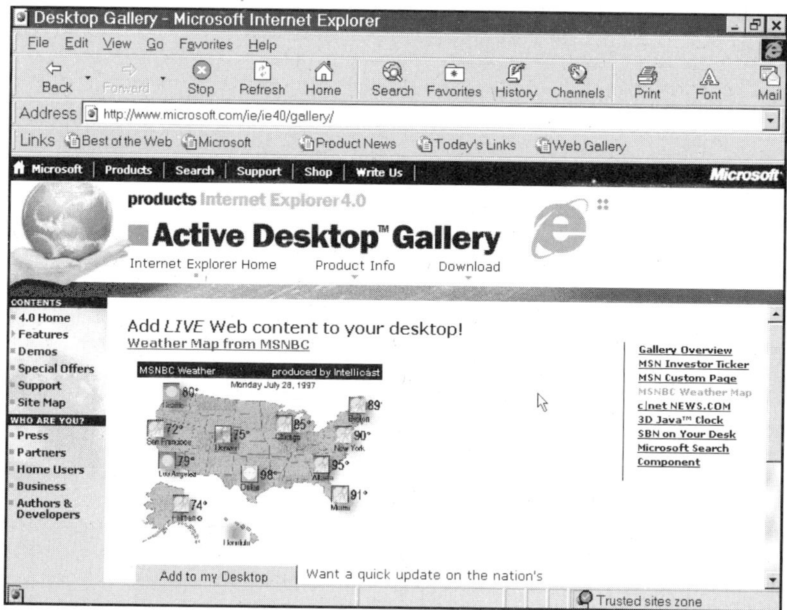

FIG. 19.8
Click a hyperlink or a button to download and install a component on your Active Desktop.

Hiding, Removing, and Editing Objects

You don't have to have all your components, pictures, and Web sites visible at the same time on your Active Desktop. You can keep them available, but hidden.

To display, hide, remove, or edit objects on the desktop background, follow these steps:

1. Right-click the desktop, then click Properties. The Display Properties dialog box appears. Select the Web tab.
2. To hide an object, clear the object's check box in the list.

   or

   To remove an object from the list, select the object, then click Remove. If you ever want the object back, you will need to repeat the procedure to add an object.
3. Click OK to accept the changes.

Customizing a Component

Some objects can be customized after you add them to your Active Desktop. Customizing may change their appearance, their behavior on your computer, or their interaction with their target Web site. Each component will have different properties that can be customized.

Figure 19.9 shows the Microsoft Investor component in the upper portions of the screen. This component displays a ticker of stocks in your portfolio as well as headline news that fits categories you specify.

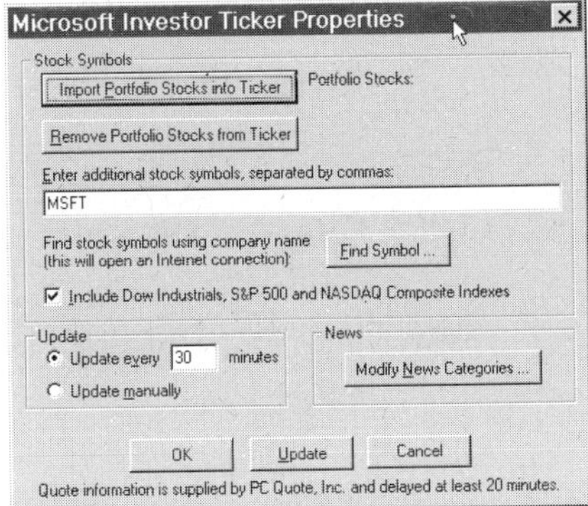

FIG. 19.9
Some components can be customized to change their behavior or appearance.

Clicking the banner takes you to **http://investor.msn.com** for more information about your portfolio and Microsoft Investor. Clicking the Update button updates information in the ticker.

CHAPTER 20

Subscribing to Web Sites and Offline Browsing

by Ron Person

Using the Web, you soon discover that there probably is useful information out there, but it's difficult to find and there are too many sites to search. When you do find the information you want, it's hard to keep track of all sites where it's located and time-consuming to follow changes and updates. And, of course, many of us use modems, so even after finding information it takes a long time to download. And then you have to stay logged on to the Internet while you read the information you've found.

Microsoft has attacked these problems with an approach built into Internet Explorer 4. Internet Explorer 4 incorporates something called *Webcasting*, a new model for automating the delivery of online information and Web site content.

Understand how Webcasting and offline browsing work

Webcasting automatically pulls information off a Web site according to your schedule. Once a site is downloaded, you can browse it without being online.

Subscribe to any Web site and schedule updates

Subscribe to any Web site and specify when and how much of the site will be downloaded automatically to your computer.

Understand the advantages of Channel Definition Format and Premier Channels

Channel Definition Format enables you to subscribe to specific content within a Web site. Premier Channels may give you access to high-quality restricted information that is tailored to your needs.

Use offline browsing as a real time and money saver

Offline browsing is easy and more convenient than online browsing.

NOTE The following chapter was written using Platform Preview (PR2) of Internet Explorer 4 for Windows 95. The final release of Internet Explorer 4 may differ from what is described here.

Understanding the Types of Webcasting

The first approach in Webcasting is to *subscribe* to any Web site. When you subscribe, Internet Explorer 4 searches through the site for pages that have changed. You can be notified of pages that have changed or have the pages downloaded so you can read them offline (which means you don't have to be connected). You can specify the amount of information to download from the site and how you want to be notified. The first approach's advantage to you is that you can monitor any Web site for changes and browse it offline. The advantage to Web site developers is that they don't have to modify their site for the Web crawler to work. (The other two types of Webcasting require a little to a lot of programming.) The disadvantage to using this method is that you still get a lot of information you don't want or need. Even if you specify that Internet Explorer should return pages three levels of hyperlinks into a site, it will probably include many topics you don't want and not go deep enough on topics you do want. You may still be inundated by infoglut.

The second approach has greater advantages to you and to Web site developers. In fact, it has received rousing endorsements from site and content developers. In this approach, a Web site developer adds to the Web site a single page that acts like a table of contents or index and a schedule of when updates occur. The page is created using a simple text file with the Channel Definition Format (CDF). Microsoft is proposing this format to the industry as an open standard and has placed it before the World Wide Web Consortium for approval. When Internet Explorer 4 accesses a site that has a CDF file, it presents you with a list of topics or contents within the site to which you can subscribe. You can then subscribe to a topic within a site and disregard what you don't want. The advantage to you is faster updates of just the information you want. The advantage to developers is that it is easy to create without modifying their existing site. (Future versions of Microsoft FrontPage will include the ability to create CDF files.) Site owners can tailor their content and advertising to the requests of subscribers. Corporate MIS departments will also like it because it should reduce network traffic.

Subscribing to Any Web Site

This first approach of Webcasting operates with any Web site. Although the term Webcasting implies that the pages are cast or *pushed* from the Web site to the browser, in fact, they are requested or *pulled* by the browser from the Web site. Some software companies refer to this approach as a *push,* but in reality the browser works with a scheduler to pull selected information from a Web site.

You will want to subscribe to any Web site you want to stay current with. Internet Explorer 4 checks the pages on the sites to which you subscribe to see if the content has changed. (It doesn't actually match every page; it just checks the date they were last changed.) You have a choice of being notified of changes or having the changed pages downloaded to your computer for later viewing. This handy feature is known as offline browsing.

CAUTION

A few Web sites do not allow Web utilities that automatically update pages to traverse their sites. These can drain a site's responsiveness while they examine all the links in the site. Because of this, it's ineffective to subscribe to a site that prohibits automatic updating browsers and utilities.

Internet Explorer 4 checks Web sites or pages to which you subscribe according to a schedule you set. Of course, you can manually update a site at any time—a couple of clicks and Internet Explorer 4 connects to the Internet and updates the site you specify.

Subscribing to Web Sites

To subscribe to any Web site, follow these steps:

1. Display the Web site in Internet Explorer 4.
2. Click Favorites, then click Subscriptions, Subscribe to display a Subscription dialog box similar to the one shown in Figure 20.1.

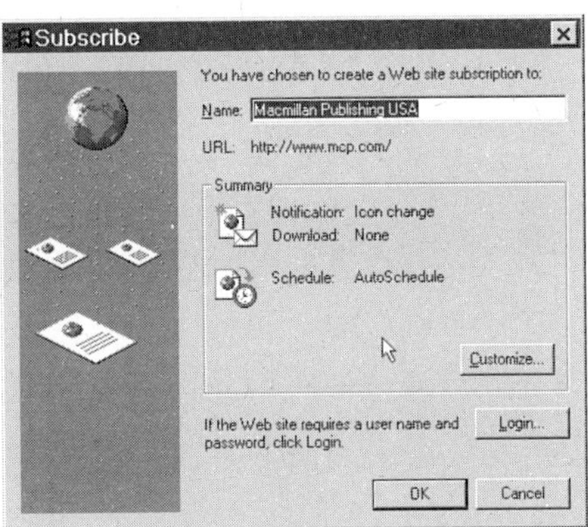

FIG. 20.1
The Subscription dialog box shows you the site you are subscribing to, how you will be notified of updates, and the update schedule.

3. Click OK to accept these settings or click Customize to customize the subscription.

If you want to change the subscription settings as you create a new subscription, you can change a few of them by clicking Customize in the Subscribe dialog box. This will start a Subscription wizard that will walk you through:

How you want to be notified when a page changes

Whether or not to download pages linked to the site

How many levels of pages to download (this site only)

Selecting a schedule or making a custom schedule

You'll probably find it easier to use the Properties dialog box to change these settings than to use this Wizard, especially since not all of the possible settings are available in the Wizard. Procedures for customizing a subscription are in the topics following "Customizing Subscriptions" later in this chapter.

Managing Subscriptions

Once you have subscribed to Web sites, you will need to be able to manage them so you can edit update schedules, change the depth of hyperlinks updated, or delete sites to which you no longer want to subscribe. Managing your subscriptions is very straightforward. It's very similar to managing files in the Windows Explorer.

To open the Subscriptions window and manage subscriptions, follow these steps:

1. Click Favorites, Subscriptions, Manage Subscriptions. The Subscription window shown in Figure 20.2 appears. This window displays the files in WINDOWS\Subscriptions.

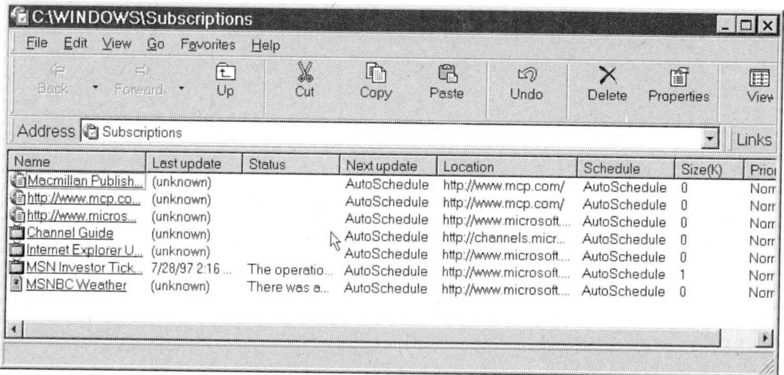

FIG. 20.2
Manage your subscriptions in the Subscriptions window.

2. Right-click a site you want to change. Select one of the following menu items:

Open	Opens the site in an Explorer window so you can view the site with its current update.
Update Now	Update selected site(s) by connecting to the Internet and updating files.
Copy	Copies selection. Use Paste in receiving application.
Delete	Delete selected site(s).
Properties	Open the property sheet for the site so you can change a file's Schedule, Delivery, or Notification properties.

3. Close the Subscription window by clicking the Close icon or clicking File, Close.

Column headings, such as Name, Status, and Location can be dragged left or right to new positions so you can view information the way you want.

It's easy to switch from the Subscription window to the Internet Explorer 4 if you remember that all the Explorer windows are really the same. Just type an URL into the Address bar of the Subscription window and press Enter. Or double-click one of the subscription icons. The Subscription window will access that site, either online or offline, and change appearance to become the Internet Explorer.

Customizing Subscriptions

In most situations, you will want to customize some or all of your subscriptions. The properties you will most likely want to customize is when the subscription updates and how much information downloads. When you initially create a subscription, you customize the subscription by clicking the Customize button (refer to Figure 20.1).

You might need to edit an existing subscription to change its properties. To change a subscription, open the Subscription window as described in the preceding section, "Managing Subscriptions." Right-click a site, then click Properties. Select the Subscription, Receiving, or Schedule tabs and make the changes you need as described in the following topics.

Scheduling Automatic Updates Internet Explorer 4 will schedule updates for your subscriptions. If your computer is turned on, Internet Explorer 4 will start, connect to the Internet, and check your subscriptions for changes. Of course, you also can manually update a subscription at any time or specify that a subscription will only be updated manually.

To schedule an update, follow these steps:

1. Right-click the subscription and click Properties.
2. Select the Schedule tab shown in Figure 20.3.

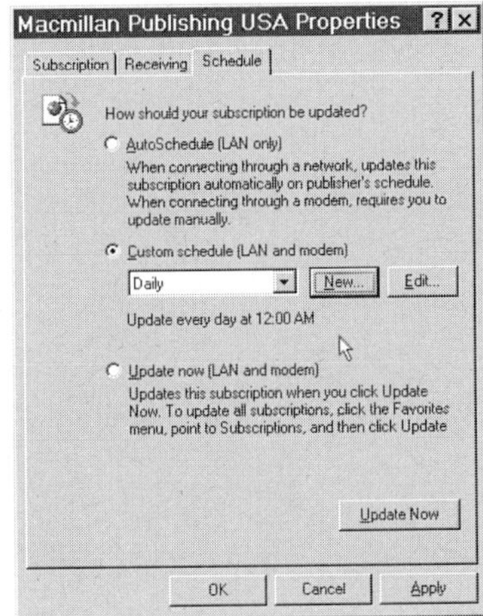

FIG. 20.3
Schedule when you want this Web site checked for changes and updates downloaded.

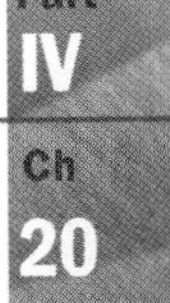

3. Select either:

   AutoSchedule to have the site updated whenever the Web site publisher determines (should only select this if you have a permanent Internet connection via a LAN) or

   Custom Schedule which allows you to determine the frequency and time of updates or

   Update now and the site will only be updated when you select to update it manually

4. Select when you want Internet Explorer 4 to automatically login and check for updates.

Daily	Update at approximately the time shown in the dialog box. Learn how to set the default daily time by reading "Setting Daily and Weekly Defaults" in this chapter.
Weekly	Update each week on the day shown and at approximately the time shown. Learn how to set the default daily time by reading "Setting Daily and Weekly Defaults" in this chapter.
Monthly	Update on the specified day of each month at approximately the time shown.

5. Change additional options or click OK.

If you are a system administrator, you might freak out at the thought of 10,000 users all requesting Web updates on the hour. Actually, a time range is used and each Internet Explorer 4 generates a random time within that range. For even more network control over subscriptions with Internet Explorer 4, make sure you check the Internet Explorer Administrator's Kit 4.0 (IEAK) available from Microsoft. Find the most current release of IEAK by searching Microsoft's site at:

http://www.microsoft.com/

If you want to create a custom schedule for updates, follow these steps:

1. Select the Schedule tab.
2. Click the Custom option, then the Edit button to display the Custom Schedule dialog box. The dialog box that displays depends upon whether you choose daily, weekly, or monthly updates.
3. Select one of the following periods for updates:
   - *Daily.* Select Daily as shown in Figure 20.4 to update on daily at a time specified in Update At. Internet Explorer 4 will also update at repeat intervals during the day if you select the Repeat every option.
   - *Weekly.* Select Weekly as shown in Figure 20.5 to update on weekly intervals on specific days during each week. Internet Explorer 4 will update at repeat intervals during the day if you select the Repeat every option.
   - *Monthly.* Select Monthly as shown in Figure 20.6 to update on a specific day of the month at monthly intervals. You can specify the day of the month by its ordinal

position in the month, for example, 2nd day in the month, or by the day's name, second Tuesday. Internet Explorer 4 will update at repeat intervals during the day if you select the Repeat every option.

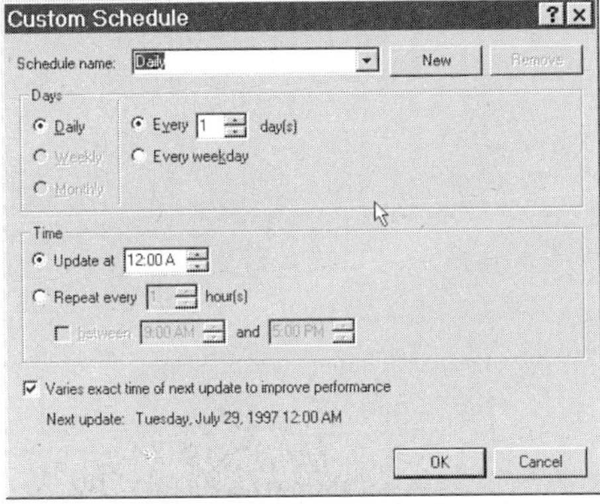

FIG. 20.4
Updates can be once daily or repeat at intervals during the day.

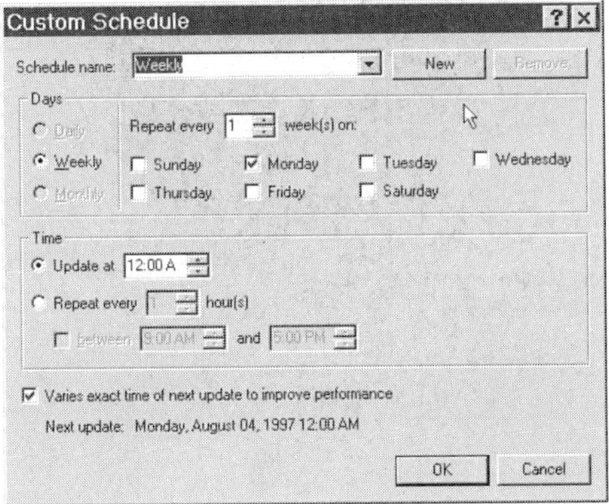

FIG. 20.5
Weekly updates can be made.

4. Click OK to return to the Custom Schedule dialog box. Click OK again or select another tab to customize more.

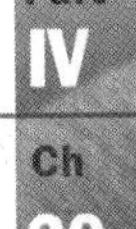

While sites are updating, the Update Progress window appears on screen as shown in Figure 20.7. To See the full view shown here, click the Details button (which changes to No Details). In it you can read the names of the sites that are being updated. If you want to cancel an update, click Stop. To skip over one site's update and proceed with the next site, click Skip. Notice that Internet Explorer 4 does not have to be open while files are updating.

The bottom part of this status box shows the progress and results for each site. While your computer is waiting to connect to a site, the status is Pending. During the update itself the status is Updating. When the Update is done, the status will be Succeeded. If your computer is not able to retrieve updated pages from the site, the status will be Failed.

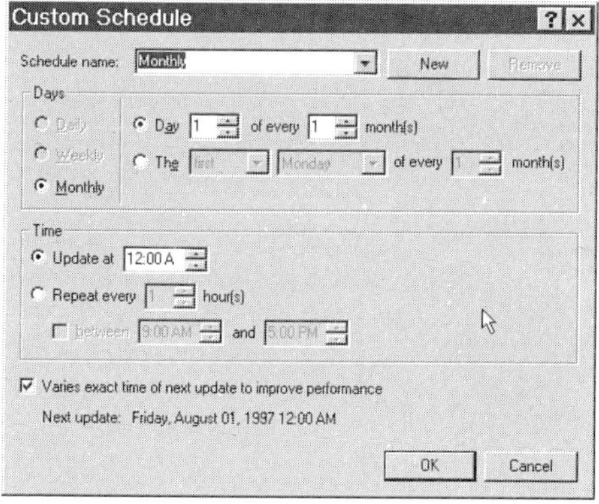

FIG. 20.6
Monthly updates also is a feature.

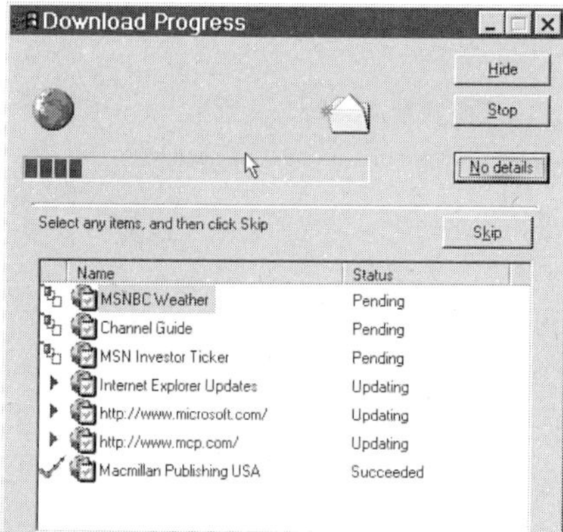

FIG. 20.7
The Update Progress indicator shows you the portions of the Web site being updated.

Entering Username and Password for Restricted Sites Sites such as the *Wall Street Journal* (**www.wsj.com**) or the *Visual Basic Programmer's Journal* (**www.windex.com**) have high-value content for which you must pay a subscription fee. For that fee you receive a password that gives you access to the content-laden depths of their sites. Internet Explorer 4's subscription service can also use this password to gain access so your computer can have a fresh *Wall Street Journal* or *Visual Basic Programmer's Journal* waiting for you to browse as you sip your morning coffee.

You do not have to subscribe to the specific page that has the login screen. You can subscribe to a page above the login screen and specify a depth of delivery that reaches below the login screen. When Internet Explorer 4 reaches the page that requests your user ID and password, it supplies them and then continues updating.

To enter a password for use by a subscription, follow these steps:

1. If you are initially creating the subscription, click the Login button. If you are editing an existing subscription, right-click the subscription in the Subscription window, then click Properties.

Select the Schedule tab and click Login to display the Login Options dialog box shown in Figure 20.8.

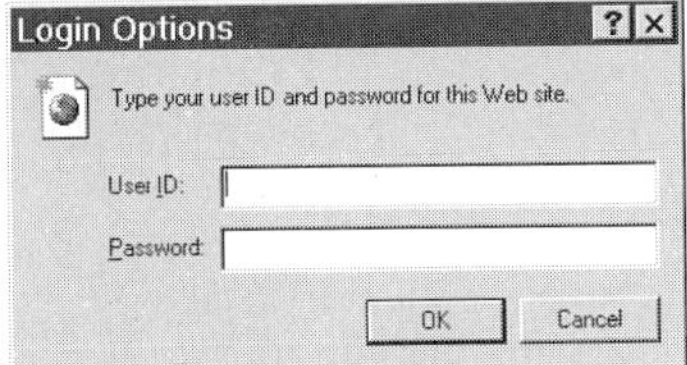

FIG. 20.8
Internet Explorer 4 requires a user name and password to update sites such as the *Wall Street Journal.*

2. Enter in the User ID box the name you use to log in to the site. Use the same spelling with upper- and lowercase exactly the same as when you registered at the site.
3. Enter in the Password box the password you use for the site. Use the same spelling with upper- and lowercase exactly the same as when you registered at the site.
4. Click OK to return to the Schedule tab. Click OK again or select another tab to customize more.

Check your subscription with a password after you create it by opening the Subscription window, right-clicking the site you have just created and then clicking Update. If the subscription fails because of the user ID or password, try a manual login for that site and check your use of upper- and lowercase letters. Edit the subscription's user ID and password to match those you've tested.

Controlling the Size and Depth of Subscription Wouldn't it be great if you had all the information you needed on your computer? While computer capabilities are growing at an incredible rate, you probably can't fit all the information you want because there are limits on storage space, access time, and bandwidth. If you don't set some limits on the storage size of downloads, your hard disk will fill up. And if you don't set some limits on the time or types of downloads, you may get a call from the MIS staff for hogging the network.

On Web sites that have not been optimized for a scheduled pull of information, you will probably find that going beyond a depth of three layers brings down far too much unwanted information because of the site width at three levels deep. Site developers can optimize their sites for scheduled pull so that you can start your subscription from a point within the site such that all the layers below have a narrow content focus. Another option for you and site developers is to subscribe to and use the Channel Definition Format (CDF).

Before you subscribe to a site, you may want to wade into it and explore how many layers deep you need to go for the information you need. The number of pages needing updating increases exponentially with each additional layer of depth.

If you know the exact portion of the site that you need to subscribe to, don't start at the site's home page. On sites with discrete HTML pages, you can subscribe to a page that is already deep within the site. You may not be able to do this with an active server page or a page that was created in response to your query.

CAUTION

If you select the Follow Hyperlinks option, the update will include pages outside the subscribed site to the depth you have indicated. This can create a very large download.

To put limits on the resources spent in updating your subscription, follow these steps:

1. Right-click the subscription in the Subscription window, then click Properties.
2. Select the Receiving tab.
3. Click the Yes, download this site option. Then click the Advanced button.
4. The Advanced Download Options dialog box is shown in Figure 20.9. To set a limit on the number of kilobytes downloaded for this site per session, select Maximum Download size and enter a limit in kilobytes.

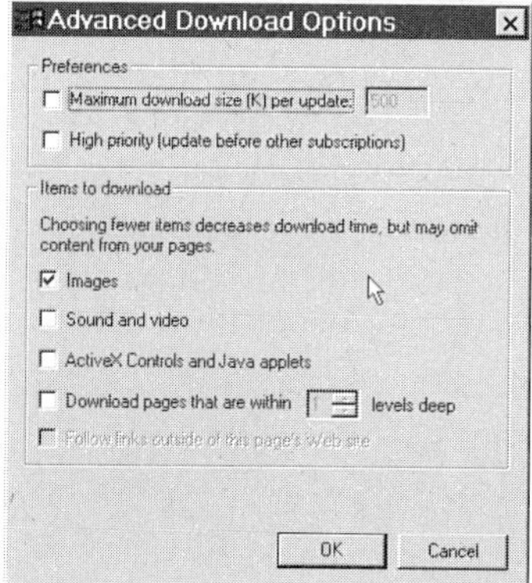

FIG. 20.9
This dialog box controls how much content and what type of files will be downloaded.

5. To download ActiveX, Java, sound, and video, select any of the options for those types of files. Note that these files are usually very large so if you set a limit in Step 4, set it with these file sizes in mind.
6. By default, you are only subscribed to the main page at the address you entered. To download pages linked from it, select Download pages that are within n levels deep and set the number of levels. It's a good idea to start with 1 or 2 levels and work your way up if needed. With this selected, you can also select to download links that lead off of this site.

7. If you have several site subscriptions, you can choose one to be downloaded first by selecting High Priority.
8. Click OK or select another tab to further customize the subscription.

Getting Notified of Updates You will probably want to know about changes to Web sites to which you have subscribed. There are two different ways you can be notified when updates occur. The first method is always enabled. With this method a *red gleam* appears at the top left corner of Web page icons in the Subscription window shown in Figure 20.2.

The second way you can be notified of an update is through e-mail. When an update occurs Windows 95 sends you an e-mail message containing an update notice or copy of the HTML page. This can be useful if you are traveling or need to notify others of changes that occur. It also works as an "in-your-face" notice of an update that is very hard to ignore.

To specify how you want to be notified of updates, follow these steps:

1. Right-click the subscription in the Subscription window, then click Properties.
2. Select the Receiving tab.
3. Click Yes, Send a Message to the Following Address to receive an update notification by e-mail. If your e-mail address is not there or you need to change it, click Change Address and enter the address and server. Click OK in the Address dialog box.
4. Click OK or select another tab to further customize the subscription.

Manually Updating Subscriptions You can manually update individual subscriptions or all subscriptions. You might want to manually update all subscriptions if you are about to leave on a trip or develop a report and you want to be sure that all the Web sites you subscribe to are current. You'd want to update an individual site if the scheduled update won't be soon enough to meet your needs. If you know you don't need scheduled updates on a site, you can specify that a subscription will only be updated manually.

If you want a sheet to only be updated manually, then select the Now Update check box on the Schedule tab of the site's properties sheet. Figure 20.3 shows the Schedule tab.

To manually update all subscriptions, you will need to have your modem or Internet access line connected. Click Favorites, Subscriptions, Update All. If you have many sites to update or the sites involve large files such as sound and video, the update process may take a long time. You can continue work in other programs while subscriptions update.

To update an individual subscription, follow these steps:

1. Click Favorites, Subscriptions, Manage Subscriptions. The Subscriptions window opens as shown in Figure 20.2 displaying the site name, date of last update, success or failure of update, and more.
2. Right-click the name of the site you want updated and click Update Now. (You also can update all subscriptions from here by selecting File, Update All.) The Update Progress window opens during Internet connection, and the subscription updates.

Subscribing to Sites that Use the Channel Definition Format

A limitation to the *scheduled pull* type of Webcasting is that subscribing to even three levels of pages on most Web sites brings back a lot of unwanted information that clogs your hard disk. Microsoft has developed the *Channel Definition Format* (CDF) to prevent this problem.

CDF creates a table of contents or index for a Web site. You can subscribe to topics within that table of contents rather than having to download a broad cross-section of the site. The CDF can also include scheduling information describing when different topics will update so you can be assured of having the most recent information as it comes available.

Prior to CDF, *push publishing* over the Internet involved many proprietary formats from many different server vendors with push servers and many different content providers. This fragmented the market, requiring clients to buy in to many different proprietary push servers. It was like having to buy part of a radio station just to get the news. And once you bought it, you couldn't listen to other channels. With CDF, you aren't tied to a specific content publisher or server vendor.

For you as a client, Web sites that support CDF will be much more efficient to use. You can look in a left pane on the browser to see the topics and structure of information on the site. You can subscribe to just the information topics you want rather than subscribing to geographic portions of a Web site's tree-like structure. Your information will also be more current because updates can be synchronized with scheduled updates on the site.

The major push software vendors are supporting Microsoft's efforts to create a standard. Some of the major push software vendors who have committed to publishing with CDF are:

- PointCast
- BackWeb
- AirMedia
- FirstFloor
- Torso
- UserLand Software
- DataChannel
- Lanacom
- NetDelivery
- NCompass
- Diffusion
- Wayfarer

Some of the major content providers that have already committed to supporting CDF are:

- CNN
- *Wall Street Journal*
- Ziff-Davis
- *New York Times*
- *Los Angeles Times*
- *Chicago Tribune*
- 30 other major media companies

Web site developers will appreciate CDF because it means they do not have to redevelop their existing sites. They only need to create a single CDF file that defines the content, structure, and update schedule of their site. This CDF file is basically a text file that contains categories of URLs within the site.

Subscribing to a CDF site should be much easier than a basic Webcasting subscription, yet give you better results. Open a Web site that incorporates CDF, then click a button or hyperlink that subscribes you to the Web site (as shown in Figure 20.10). In the Add to Channel wizard, you can choose between monitoring changes or downloading updates for use offline. You will also have the capability to choose the update schedule and other options. There will also be an option so that you or someone else can be notified by e-mail whenever an update occurs.

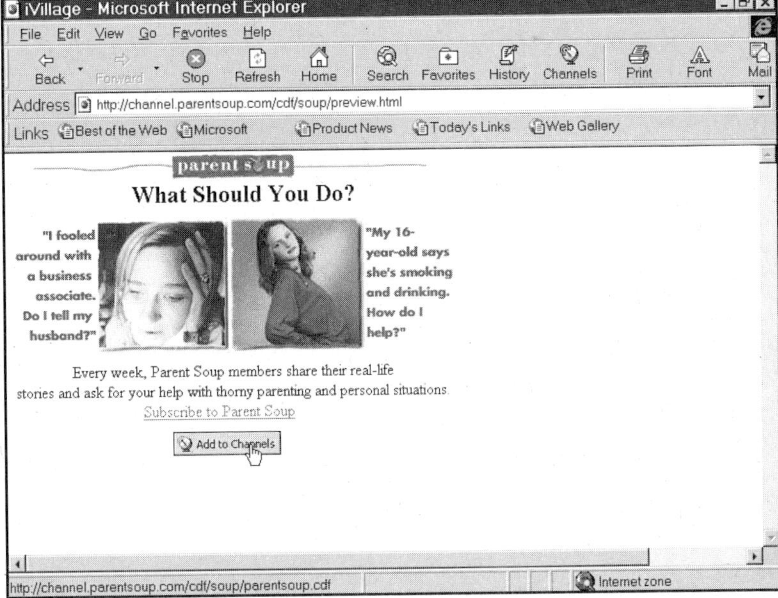

FIG. 20.10 Clicking the Add to Channels button starts the Channel Subscription wizard.

When you complete the Channel Subscription Wizard, the logo for the channel appears in the Channel Pane of the browser and in the Channel Bar on the Active Desktop. The Channel Pane appears as a pane on the left side of Internet Explorer 4. Clicking a channel button in the Channel Pane opens a list of available topics within that channel. The Channel Bar appears on the right side of the Active Desktop and displays buttons. Clicking a button gives you access to that button's channel of information. You will be able to subscribe to channels for offline browsing.

Browsing Offline When You Can't Stay Connected

The Web is full of great information, but did you ever try taking any of it with you? Ever wish you could access the Web without logging on? Like that time when you and the resident teenager had the long discussion over who has priority on the house phone. Or that time your body was 37,500 feet over the Rockies, your mind was back in the office trying to remember the last Web site you saw, and your toes were being cramped by a momentarily worthless laptop under the seat in front of you. When you learn how to browse offline, you can take the information with you without being connected to the Internet.

If you used an earlier version of Internet Explorer or Netscape Navigator, you might have tried saving individual pages as HTML files to disk.

With Internet Explorer 4's offline browsing capabilities, all those Web sites you've subscribed to are available with their graphics and hyperlinks intact. If you click a hyperlink and the linked page is available from the hard drive, it opens in Internet Explorer 4. If it isn't available, Internet Explorer 4 displays a dialog box asking if you want to reconnect to the Internet and open that page.

Before you can browse offline, you must have previously subscribed to and updated the Web sites you want to browse. Doing this stores as much of the Web site as you specify on your hard disk.

When you want to browse offline, click File, Work Offline. Now you can access a Web site you have subscribed to just as you would if you were online. You can type an URL into the Address bar, select a Favorite you've subscribed to, or click the Updated Subscriptions icon in the taskbar and select an updated Web site from the list.

If you want to see a list of the sites to which you have subscribed, start Windows Explorer or Internet Explorer 4, then click Favorites, Subscriptions, Manage Subscriptions. The sites you have subscribed to and their status will be listed in the Subscription window.

While you are browsing offline, you can click hyperlinks. If the target page for that hyperlink is available for offline browsing, it opens immediately just as it would if you were online, but it opens a lot faster. If you move the pointer over a hyperlink to a page that has not been stored, the pointer changes to the pointing finger with an international NOT symbol. If you click the hyperlink with this NOT pointer, a dialog box like that in Figure 20.11 displays. Clicking Connect will connect you to the Internet and display the linked page. Clicking Stay Offline will keep you disconnected and browsing offline, and the page will remain unavailable.

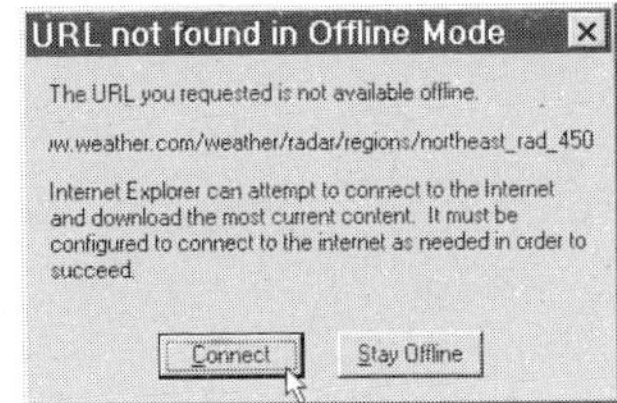

FIG. 20.11
Clicking an unavailable hyperlink displays this dialog box so you can connect to the Internet.

If you're rushing to go on a trip and don't have time to update all your subscriptions, open the Subscription window by clicking Favorites, Subscriptions, View All. In the Subscription window, right-click the sites you do want to update and click Update.

To get the fastest updates, right-click sites in the Subscription window, click Properties, and select the Delivery tab. Clear the Download Images, Download Sounds and Videos, and Follow Hyperlinks options. Do this for all the sites you need. Use a Ctrl+click to select the ones you have just modified, then right-click and choose Update. Web sites update very quickly when they only need to update text.

If you are online and want to browse offline, just click File, Browse Offline.

Browsing Previously Viewed Sites

If you've viewed a Web page in the recent past, you may be able to view it again without going online even if you haven't subscribed to that Web site. Internet Explorer 4 stores recently viewed pages and their graphics in the Windows\History folder. To see a page, open the Windows\History folder and double-click the Web page you want to view.

CHAPTER 21

Using Outlook Express Mail and News

by Brady P. Merkel

Outlook Express is Microsoft's Internet e-mail and UseNet news client. Although it shares the same name as its bigger cousin Outlook 97 from the Microsoft Office 97 suite of tools, Outlook Express is quite different, and especially streamlined to work with the Internet.

Create and send Internet messages

Outlook Express provides the core functionality to send mail messages to other Internet recipients.

View and organize your received mail

Use Outlook Express to read your messages and organize them into folders. Outlook Express also provides an Inbox assistant to organize messages when they arrive.

Secure your messages

Outlook Express provides a way to encrypt your messages such that only the intended readers can read them.

Participate in UseNet community forums

Use Outlook Express News to post and read articles that millions of other users can see.

Customize Outlook Express

Personalize Outlook Express to make you more productive.

Understanding Outlook Express

The mail portion of Outlook Express provides many features:

- Connect to multiple Internet mail accounts and manage all of your messages in one consistent interface.
- Connect to Internet Mail Access Protocol (IMAP) as well as Post Office Protocol (POP) mail accounts.
- Work offline to save connection fees.
- Read and send HTML-formatted messages that include graphics, text, animation, or multimedia files.
- Send and receive secure messages.
- Use the Address Book for managing your contacts and finding people on the Internet.

▶ **See** Using Outlook Express Mail," **p. 543**

If you want to participate in the exciting world of UseNet News (a network of distributed discussion groups), you use the news capabilities of Outlook Express. Like Outlook Express Mail, there are several noteworthy features:

- Connect to several news servers to read news from several locations, including Microsoft's public news site.
- Search and locate interesting newsgroups.
- Browse through newsgroup articles quickly and easily.
- Download news articles to read them offline.
- Check your articles for spelling errors before posting them.
- Apply automatic filters to avoid seeing articles that do not interest you.

▶ **See** "Using Outlook Express News," **p. 584**

Outlook Express is a trimmed-down version of Microsoft Outlook 97. See Table 21.1 for a comparison of Outlook Express with Outlook 97 and Microsoft Exchange, the original Windows 95 messaging client. Outlook Express was designed for small-office and home-office users who only need core Internet functionality. If you decide to upgrade to Outlook 97, Outlook Express provides tools to export your message folders and Address Book records into a format that Outlook 97 can import.

Table 21.1 Comparing Messaging Clients

Feature	Exchange	Outlook 97	Outlook Express
Rich Text Formatting	Yes (RTF)	Yes (RTF)	Yes (HTML)
Embedded Object Support	Yes	Yes	No
Inbox Assistant	Yes	Yes	Yes

Feature	Exchange	Outlook 97	Outlook Express
Out-of-Office Assistant	Yes	Yes	No
Supports POP	Yes (Internet Mail)	Yes (Internet Mail)	Yes
Supports IMAP	No	No	Yes
Supports FAX	Yes	Yes	No
Microsoft Mail and CompuServe	Yes	Yes	No
Public Folders	Yes	Yes	No
Security	Yes	Yes	Yes
Scheduling	Yes (Schedule+)	yes	No
Journal	No	Yes	No
Tasks	Yes (Schedule+)	Yes	No

See "The Universal Inbox," **p. 733**

Using Outlook Express Mail

Outlook Express Mail provides a comprehensive easy-to-use Internet mail tool. Within minutes, you can configure Outlook Express Mail with your mail account, and start exchanging messages with other Internet users. Outlook Express Mail supports HTML-formatted messages, secure messages, an inbox assistant for automatically filtering your incoming mail, a highly customizable interface, and the following Internet standards:

- *HTML.* For rich HyperText Markup Language content in mail
- *POP3.* Post Office Protocol 3, for fetching new messages from the mail server
- *IMAP4.* The Internet Mail Access Protocol which allows messages to remain stored on the mail server
- *SMTP.* The Internet workhorse for mail transport, the Simple Mail Transfer Protocol
- *MIME.* Multipurpose Internet Mail Extension for richer messages beyond plain text
- *S/MIME.* Secure-MIME, which allows you to digitally sign and encrypt your messages

ON THE WEB

Microsoft's newsgroup for Outlook Express Mail can be accessed from Internet Explorer by using the following URL:

news://msnews.microsoft.com/microsoft.public.internet.mail

Part IV Ch 21

TROUBLESHOOTING

When I try to start Outlook Express, I receive the error "There was an error starting Microsoft Outlook Express," or the error "The ordinal 508 could not be located in the dynamic link library Rasapi32.dll." I reinstalled Outlook Express, but it still fails to start. How can I get Outlook Express to run again? In early versions of Outlook Express, there are three potential causes for the problem: 1. a name you gave to one of your mail or news accounts may have leading spaces; 2. an Outlook Express registry key is damaged; or 3. one of the files for the Internet Connection Wizard is missing or corrupted.

To check for case 1 and 2, open the registry editor to the HKEY_CURRENT_USER\Software\Microsoft\Internet Account Manager\Accounts key. Analyze each account name referenced there, looking for names that begin with a space. If there appears to be missing information in the HKEY_CURRENT_USER\Software\Microsoft\Internet Account Manager key, delete the key and reenter your accounts in Outlook Express.

For case 3, verify that the following Internet Connection Wizard files exist and have the right version, or later:

File	Version
\Program Files\Internet Explorer\Connection Wizard\ Icwconn1.exe	4.71.0.7629
Windows\System\Inetcfg.dll	4.71.0.7629
Windows\System\Icfg95.dll	4.71.0.7629
Windows\System\Inet16.dll	4.71.0.7628

If any of the files above are missing or the wrong version, reinstall Outlook Express.

Connecting to a Mail Server

Outlook Express allows you to configure multiple mail servers for incoming mail. For instance, if you have a mail account with an Internet Service Provider and another with your company, you can use Outlook Express to accept messages from both locations.

To define a new mail server for Outlook Express, follow these steps:

1. Open the Start menu and choose Programs, Internet Explorer Outlook Express. When you start Outlook Express for the first time, the Internet Connection Wizard displays. The Internet Connection Wizard steps you through the configuration for a mail server entry.

   If you already have a mail server defined in Outlook Express and want to add another, launch Outlook Express and choose Tools, Accounts, then click Add, and Mail. This starts the Internet Connection Wizard to add an additional mail server.

2. The first step of the wizard is the Your Name dialog box appears, as shown in Figure 21.1. Enter your full name in the Display name text box. This name will appear in mail

you send to others. When others save your mail address in their Address Book, it will save under this name.

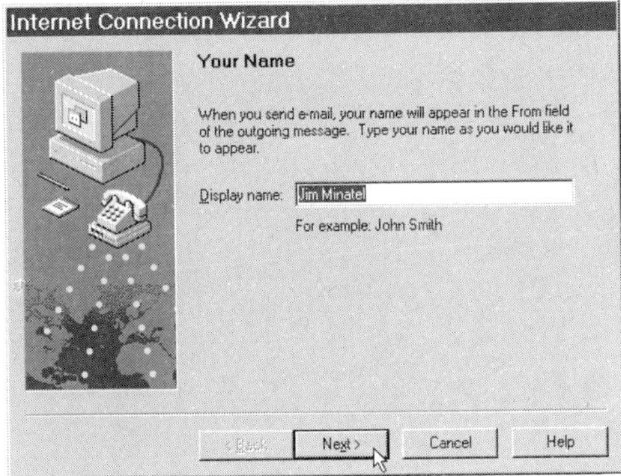

FIG. 21.1
Specify your full name in the Display name text box.

3. Click Next. The Internet E-Mail Address dialog box appears, as shown in Figure 21.2. Enter your mail address in the E-mail Address text box. Your Internet Service Provider assigns your e-mail address. Mail addresses usually take the format of your username followed by an @ symbol, then the Internet Service Provider's domain name, such as johndoe@server.com. When others send you messages, or reply to messages you send, this address is what they use.

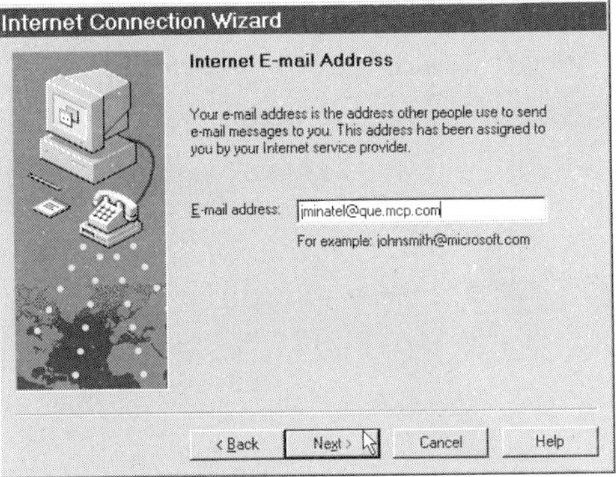

FIG. 21.2
Define your e-mail address in the E-mail Address text box.

4. Click Next. The E-mail Server Names dialog box appears, as shown in Figure 21.3. In the Mail Server drop-down, choose the type of mail server your Internet Service Provider uses. Choose POP3 if your mail server uses the Post Office Protocol 3 method to download messages. Choose IMAP if your mail server uses the Internet Mail Access Protocol.
5. In the Incoming Mail Server text box, enter the hostname of the mail server. Your Internet Service Provider will supply this hostname. This host serves to store your incoming messages. When you connect to the host with Outlook Express, you can

download and view your messages. An IMAP server allows you to store and organize your messages on the server, while a POP3 server requires that you download the messages first.

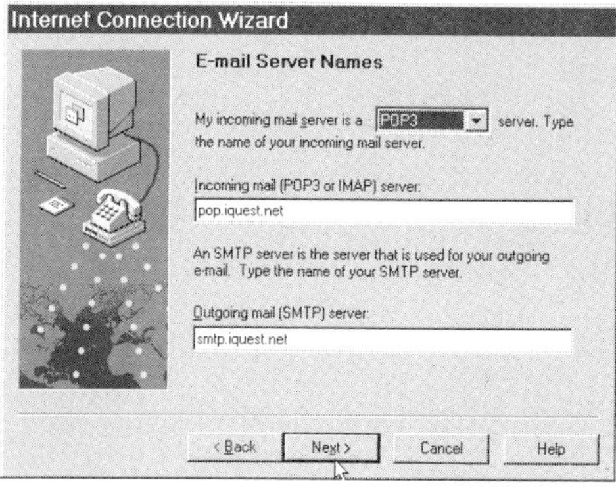

FIG. 21.3 Specify your mail server type in addition to your incoming and outgoing mail server addresses.

6. In the Outgoing Mail (STMP) Server text box, enter the hostname of the server used to process outgoing messages. The outgoing mail server uses the Simple Mail Transfer Protocol to accept messages you send and forward them to the recipients.
7. Click Next. The Internet Mail Logon dialog box appears, as shown in Figure 21.4. If your Internet Service Provider offers Secure Password Authentication, choose the Log On Using Secure Password Authentication (SPA) option button. In this case, Outlook Express will logon to the mail server using the username and password you use to logon to Windows 95.

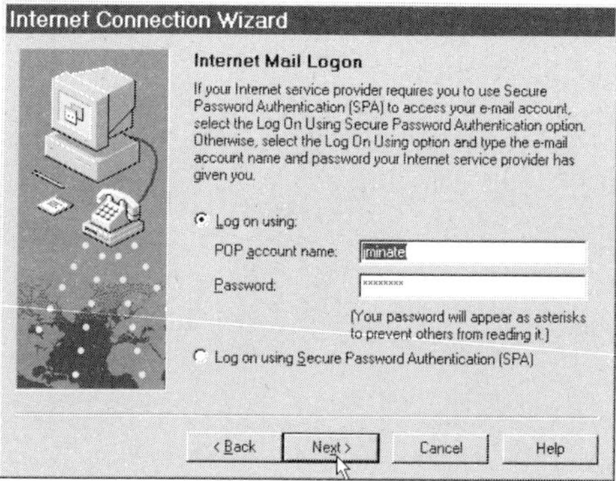

FIG. 21.4 Enter the username and password required to access the mail server.

If your Internet Service Provider requires that you use a specific username and password to access mail, choose the Log On Using option button. Enter the username in the POP Account text box, and the associated password in the Password text box.

8. The next step of the Internet Connection Wizard asks you to name your new mail connection (see Figure 21.5). Choose a name that best describes your mail server.

For instance, if you have a POP3 mail account with your company, you may want to name the connection "Work" or something similar. The mail account name you choose can be completely arbitrary, just choose a name you will recognize.

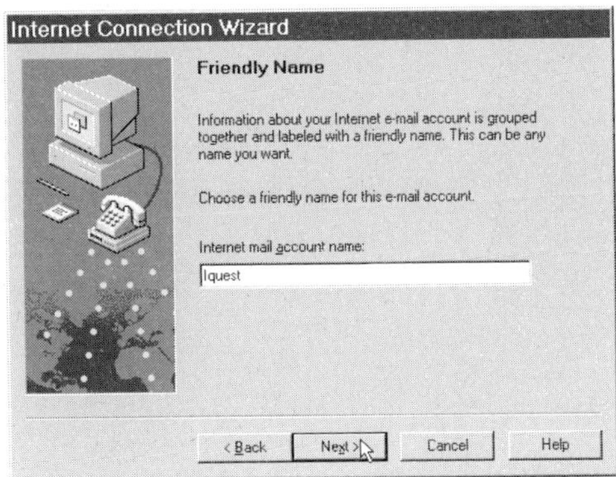

FIG. 21.5
In the Friendly Name step, choose a meaningful name for your mail account.

9. Click Next. The Choose Connection Type dialog box appears, as shown in Figure 21.6. If you will use a modem connection to access this mail account, choose the Connect Using My Phone Line option button. Otherwise, if you can access the mail server using a Local Area Network (LAN), choose the Connect Using My Local Area Network (LAN) option button.

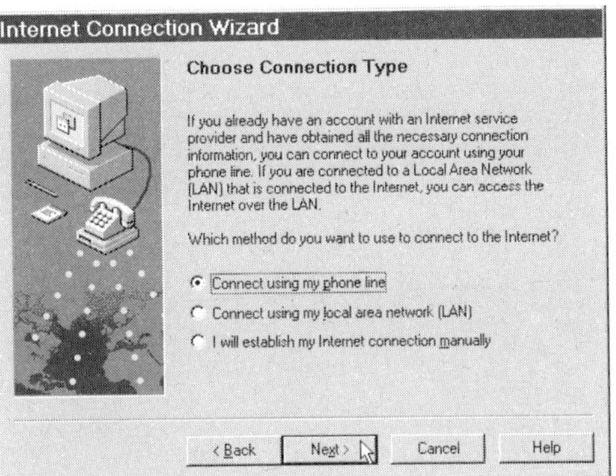

FIG. 21.6
If you dial-in to access mail, choose the Connect Using My Phone Line option button.

If you chose Connect Using My Phone Line, click Next to see the Dial-Up Connection dialog box, as shown in Figure 21.7. Here you can create a new dial-up networking connection, or choose a dial-up configuration you already have. If you created a dial-up configuration for your Internet Service Provider, choose the Use An Existing Dial-Up Connection option button, and select the connection in the list.

If you want to create a new dial-up connection, choose the Create A New Dial-Up Connection option button and click Next. The Internet Connection Wizard steps you through creating a new dial-up networking connection.

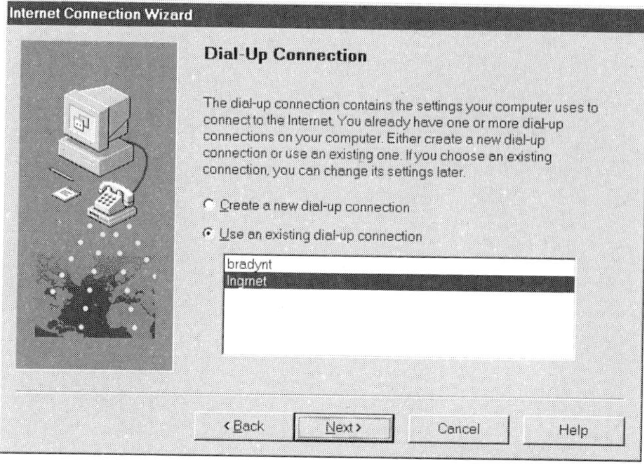

FIG. 21.7
Choose the appropriate dial-up connection to access your mail server.

10. Click Next. The Complete Configuration dialog box appears, as shown in Figure 21.8. At this point, you have defined all of the information you need to use Outlook Express. If you want to change any settings, click Back. Click Finish to accept your new Mail settings.

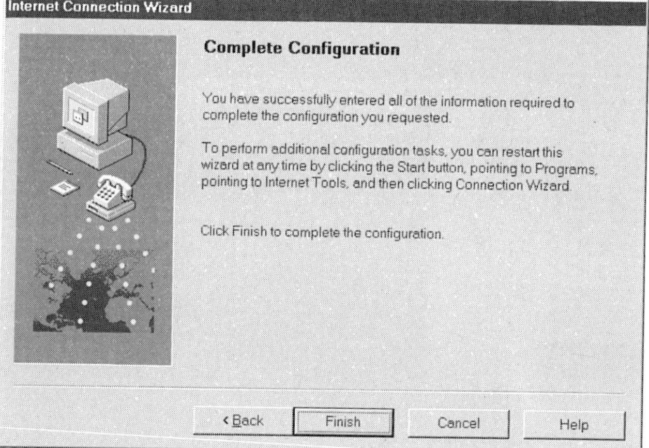

FIG. 21.8
Click Finish to accept your entries.

Reviewing Your Mail Account Settings

The Internet Connection Wizard only asks for the basic configuration information needed to establish a connection to your mail server. You should review the mail account settings and fill in the details that the Internet Connection Wizard missed. To review your Outlook Express account settings, follow these steps:

1. Choose the Tools, Accounts menu. The Internet Accounts dialog box displays, as shown in Figure 21.9.

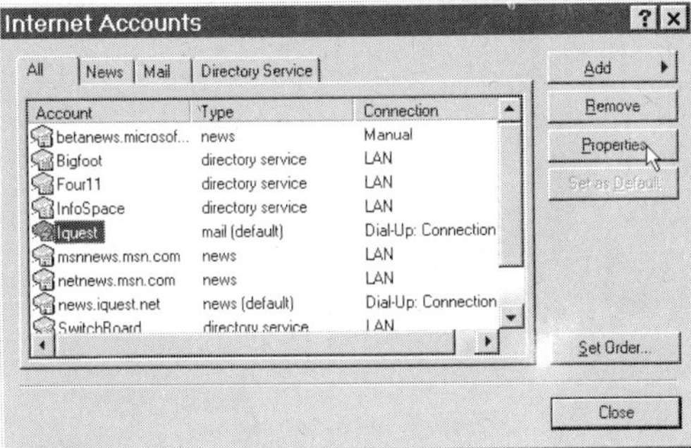

FIG. 21.9
Choose the mail account you want to review.

TIP To see only mail accounts, click the Mail tab.

2. Choose the mail account you want to review and click Properties. The Mail Account Properties dialog box displays, as shown in Figure 21.10.

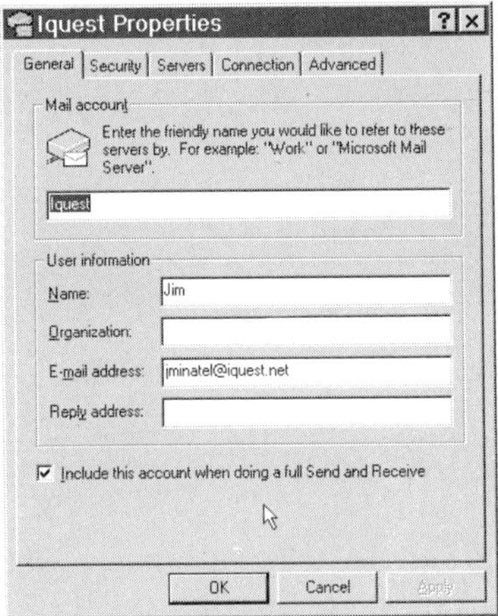

FIG. 21.10
Use the Mail Account Properties General tab to change your full name, e-mail address, organization, or mail account label.

3. Review the settings in the Mail Account Properties General tab. The Internet Connection Wizard should have defined many of the text boxes for you. One text box that the Internet Connection Wizard does not define is the Organization text box. Type the name of your company or organization name into the Organization text box.
4. If there is no e-mail address in the Reply Address text box, Outlook Express will use the one defined in the E-mail Address text box to stamp outgoing messages with a return address. If you want recipients of your messages to send replies to a different e-mail

address, type the preferred e-mail address in the Reply Address text box. This is useful when you have multiple e-mail accounts, but you want all replies to go to a single account.

5. If you want this account to be polled when Outlook Express does a full send and receive, check the Include This Account When Doing a Full Send and Receive check box. Otherwise, leave the check box blank, and Outlook Express will process messages on this account only when you explicitly ask for it, using the Tools Retrieve menu.
6. The Mail Account Properties Servers tab (see Figure 21.11) shows the server settings for your mail account. The Internet Connection Wizard defines these values when you add your mail account, but you can change them here if desired.

FIG. 21.11
Use the Mail Account Properties Servers tab to change your server addresses and login information.

7. Use the Mail Account Properties Connection tab (see Figure 21.12) to specify how you connect to your mail server, via a LAN, automatic dial-up connection, or manually.

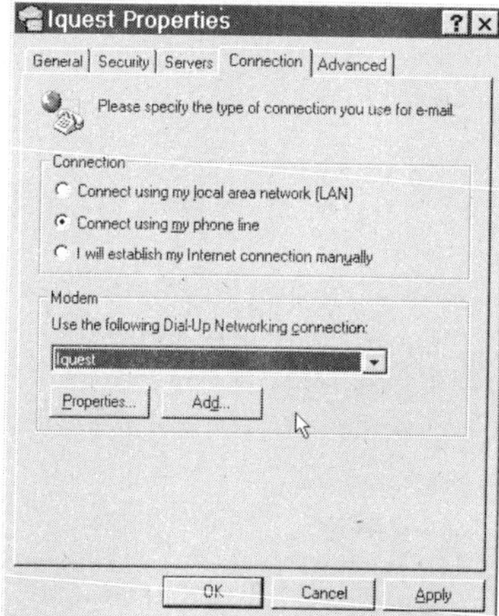

FIG. 21.12
Use the Mail Account Properties Connection tab to change your type of network connection.

8. If you prefer to dial up to the Internet manually, choose the I Will Establish My Internet Connection Manually option button. If you choose Connect Using My Phone Line, Outlook Express will dial up for you.
9. The Mail Account Properties Advanced tab (see Figure 21.13) allows you to change certain settings that you do not normally need to adjust. For instance, if your mail server requires you to use a different TCP/IP port number for outgoing SMTP mail, other than the default port number of 25, type the new port number in the Outgoing Mail (SMTP) text box. If the server requires you to connect via the Secure Sockets Layer (SSL), check the This Server Requires a Secure Connection (SSL) check box.

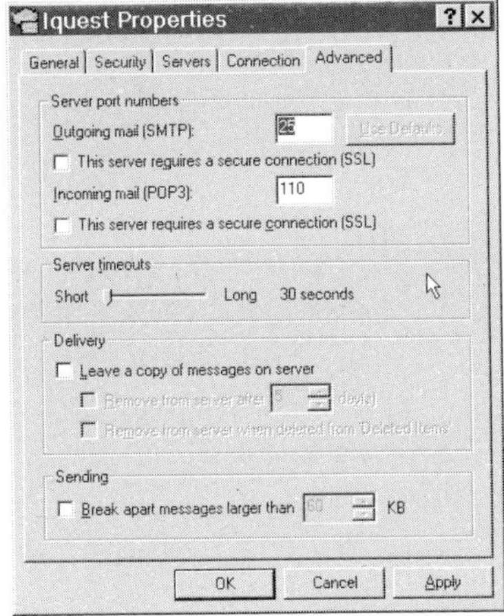

FIG. 21.13
Use the Mail Account Properties Advanced tab to adjust mail server settings you do not normally need to change.

Similarly, if your mail server requires you to use a different TCP/IP port number for incoming POP3 or IMAP mail, type the new port number in the Incoming Mail (POP3) text box. If the server requires you to connect via the Secure Sockets Layer (SSL), check the This Server Requires a Secure Connection (SSL) check box.

10. If you experience timeout errors when connecting to your mail server, increase the Server Timeouts slider to a longer duration. By default, 30 seconds should be adequate for most connections, but your mail server may be excessively busy processing other requests. There is no harm in adjusting the slider to a longer timeout value, but you may grow impatient as Outlook Express waits the length of time for a server response when the server is down for any reason.
11. If your mail server uses the POP protocol to download new messages, you can adjust when messages are removed from the server. Check the Leave a Copy of Messages on Server check box if you prefer to keep copies of messages on the server. This is particularly useful when you use Outlook Express on more than one computer to access the same POP mail account.

    To remove messages automatically on the server after they download to Outlook Express, check the Remove From Server After N Day(s) check box and adjust the number of days to your preferred duration. If you want to remove messages from the server when you empty the Outlook Express Deleted Items folder, check the Remove From Server When Deleted From 'Deleted Items' check box.

12. If your mail server uses the IMAP protocol to manage messages, enter the server path to your messages in the Root Folder Path textbox. If you do not know this value, ask the mail server administrator.
13. Some mail servers do not allow large messages. To automatically break apart large outgoing mail messages into multiple smaller messages, click the Break Apart Messages Larger Than N KB check box. Ask your mail server administrator for the limits they recommend. This parameter is most useful when sending large attachments. When messages are broken apart, recipients will get multiple message fragments and must reassemble the original message upon receipt.
14. Click OK to dismiss the Mail Account Properties dialog box.
15. If you use Outlook Express to connect to multiple mail servers, and you want this account to server as your preferred mail server to process outbound messages, click the Set As Default button in the Internet Accounts Dialog box. If you are undecided of which account to use as your preferred mail server, choose the one that is fastest, least expensive, or offers fewest busy signals when dialing in.
16. When you are done changing properties for accounts, click Close.

NOTE The Security settings tab and e-mail security in general are discussed later in this chapter in "Understanding Message Security."

Working with Mail Folders

Outlook Express stores messages in folders. If your mail server is an IMAP server, the folders actually reside on the server. By default, there are five folders, but you can add others. The five default folders are listed in Table 21.2. To see your folders, choose View, Folder List. If you prefer to work in Outlook Express without the folder list, choose Go, Go To Folder to jump from folder to folder.

Table 21.2 Default Folders

Folder	Used For
Inbox	Default location for new messages.
Draft	Stores messages you have not addressed or sent yet.
Outbox	Temporary location for pending outgoing messages.
Sent Items	Stores messages you sent.
Deleted Items	Temporary location for messages you want to discard.

When there are unread messages in a folder, Outlook Express displays the folder name in **boldface** text, and includes the number of unread messages in parentheses after the folder name. This way, you can quickly see which folders have unread messages.

Messages in the Deleted Items folder will remain there, undeleted, unless the folder has been configured to delete them. To configure Outlook Express to delete messages in the Deleted Items folder, choose Tools, Mail Options, and then select the Read tab. Select the box next to Empty messages from the 'Deleted Items' folder on exit. Messages will be deleted every time Outlook Express is closed.

You can move and copy messages between folders, and you can configure Outlook Express to automatically file incoming messages into your folders for you using the Inbox Assistant.

Adding Folders To better organize your messages, you can create your own folders. To create a new folder, choose File, Folder, New Folder. Alternatively, you can right-click any Outlook Express folder, and choose New Folder. The Create Folder dialog box displays. Type the name of your new folder in the Folder Name text box, and select the folder where you want your new folder to appear. For instance, if you want to create a new top-level folder named Work Documents, type the name and select the Outlook Express icon. Click OK.

To better organize your messages, you can create your own folders. To create a new folder, follow these steps:

1. Choose File, Folder, New Folder.

   Alternatively, you can right-click any Outlook Express folder, and choose New Folder. The Create Folder dialog box displays, as shown in Figure 21.14.

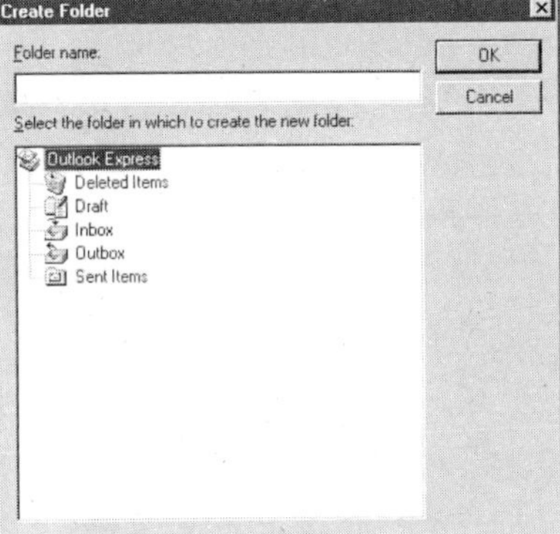

FIG. 21.14
You can create your own Outlook Express folders.

2. Type the name of your new folder in the Folder Name text box, and select the folder where you want your new folder to appear.

   For instance, if you want to create a new top-level folder named Work Documents, type the name and select the Outlook Express icon.

3. Click OK.

Moving or Copying Messages to Another Folder To move a message from one folder to another, drag the message from the message list into the destination folder. Also, you can choose Edit, Move to Folder and use the Move dialog box to choose the destination folder.

If you want to copy the message, you can Ctrl-drag it from the message list to the destination folder. Or, choose Edit, Copy to Folder and choose the destination folder in the Copy dialog box.

Moving Folders to Another Folder If you want to reorganize your folder layout, you can drag a folder to be nested within another folder. Also, you can select the folder and choose File, Folder, Move To, or choose Edit, Move To Folder and use the Move dialog box to choose the destination folder.

CAUTION

If you move, rename, or delete a folder and have Inbox Assistant rules established to automatically file messages into the folder, you will need to edit the rules to reflect the new location or name.

Renaming Folders To rename a folder, click on its name in the folder list, wait a second, then click again. You can edit the name directly in the folder list. Alternatively, right-click the folder and choose Rename, or select the folder and choose File, Folder, Rename and type or edit the new name in the Rename dialog box. You cannot rename the default folders: Inbox, Outbox, Deleted Items, Draft, or Sent Items.

Compacting Folders Outlook Express stores folders, and all of the messages within the folder, on your local disk drive. In time, after you have added and deleted several messages within a folder, the associated disk file can become fragmented and waste valuable disk space. You can compact the disk file to recover the unused space. To compact a folder, select it in the folder list, and choose File, Folder, Compact.

Deleting Folders To delete a folder and all of its contents, select the folder and press the Delete key. Outlook Express will ask you to confirm the removal. Click Yes. When you delete a folder, you will lose all of its contents. Deleted mail folders do not appear in the Recycle Bin or in the Deleted Items folder.

Reading Messages

Once you have defined a Mail Account, Outlook Express can connect to the mail server and download the messages available. To initiate the download, choose Tools, Send and Retrieve. The Logon dialog box appears. Provide the password to your mail account in the Password text box. If you want Outlook Express to remember your password for subsequent connections, check the Remember Password check box. Click OK.

If you dial in via modem to connect to your mail server, the Connect To dialog box displays to confirm your connection. Click OK.

Once the connection has been established, Outlook Express retrieves the messages into the Inbox folder. You can watch the status of the download in the Getting Mail dialog box. To see your Inbox folder, choose View, Folder List, then select the Inbox folder in the folder list.

See "Working with Mail Folders," **p. 552**

Outlook Express provides two ways to read the message: You can view it in a preview pane, or view it in a separate window.

TROUBLESHOOTING

I received an HTML-formatted message and the pictures do not display. Why? The images are not linked from a publicly available location. Ask the author to send the message again with the images linked from a Web server or shared network drive to which the recipient is connected. If the author is using Outlook Express, there is also an option in Outlook to send the picture itself instead of just a link. See "Inserting Images in a Message," and "Customizing How You Send Mail" later in this chapter.

Using the Preview Pane The Preview Pane provides a way to read your messages without having to open a new window. The selected message simply appears in the pane and allows you to scroll through the message, as shown in Figure 21.15. The Preview Pane does not prevent you from opening a message in a separate window (see the next section).

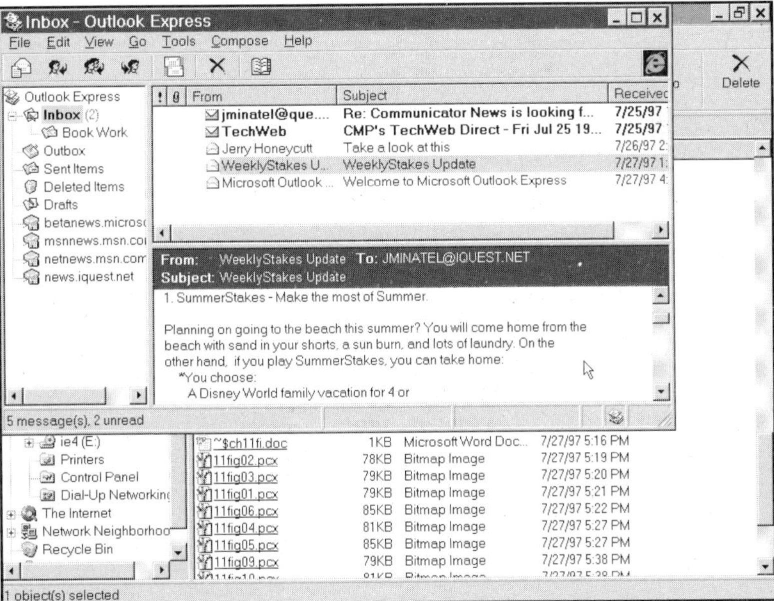

FIG. 21.15
Use the Preview Pane to read your messages quickly.

To change the settings for the Preview choose View, Layout. This opens the Layout dialog box. To turn off the Previews Pane, uncheck Use Preview Pane. With the Preview Pane on, you can select to see it Below Messages or Beside Messages. With Show Preview Pane Header selected, the sender and subject of the message are shown in the divider bar of the preview pane. When done, click OK.

You can adjust the size of the Preview Pane by dragging the border splitter bar. If the message has attachments, you will see a paperclip icon in the top-right corner of the Preview Pane. Click the paperclip icon and choose the attachment to open.

Reading Your Messages in a Separate Window To read a message in a separate window, select the message in the message list and choose File, Open. You can also double-click the message, or right-click it and choose Open. This opens the message in a separate window, as shown in Figure 21.16.

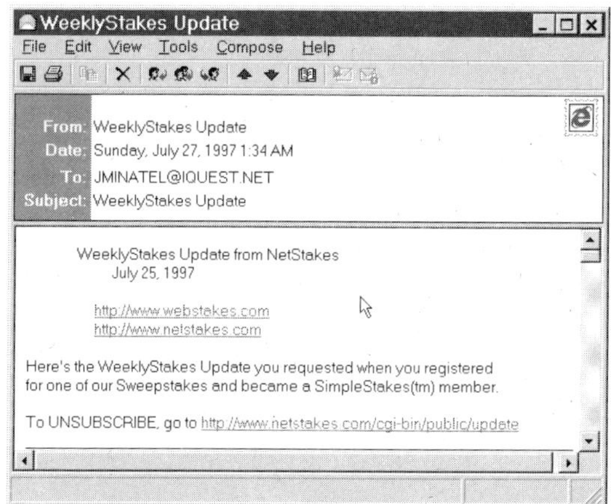

FIG. 21.16
Open a message in a separate window to see additional headers and message priority.

Scroll through the message to read it. In the header of the message you can see the date the message was sent, the subject line, and who sent the message, as well as any other recipients. The message priority, as assigned by the sender, is indicated in the top-right corner of the header.

To display the properties of the sender or other recipients, double-click the name in the header. You can also add a message sender or recipient into your Address Book. Choose Tools, Add to Address Book, then select which name to add.

See "Using the Windows Address Book," **p. 789**

If there are any attached files to the message, you see them in a pane at the bottom of the window. Right-click the pane and choose View to change the appearance of the attached files to Large Icons, Small Icons, or List view. The file size in bytes is indicated in parentheses after the name of the file.

To read the next message without going back to the main Outlook Express window, click the Next toolbar button, or choose View, Next, Next Message. To read the next unread message, choose View, Next, Next Unread Message. To jump to the next unread folder, choose View, Next, Next Unread Folder. Similarly, you can view the previous message by clicking the Previous toolbar button, or choosing View, Next, Previous Message.

Viewing Headers of Messages Occasionally, you may want to see the mail headers that accompany a message. You can inspect the mail headers to learn how a message was sent to you.

To see a message's headers, double-click the message to open it in a separate window. Then, choose File, Properties to display the Message Properties dialog box. Click the Details tab (see Figure 21.17) to see the headers. If you want to see the raw, unformatted message source, click Message Source.

FIG. 21.17
Read the message headers for some clues as to the message origin.

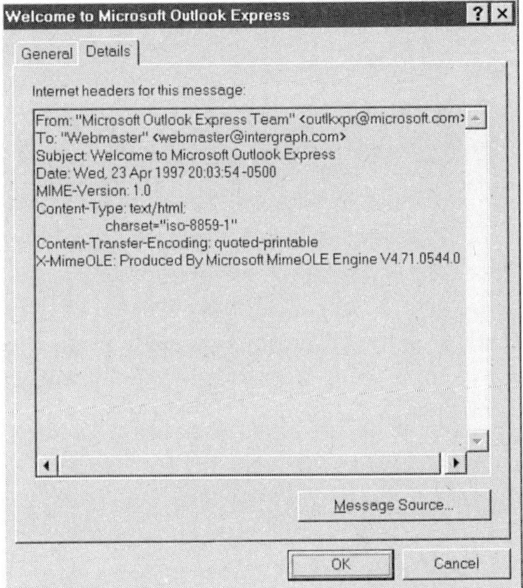

The message's header includes items such as the Return-Path to let Outlook Express know who sent the e-mail and the Date of the message. These headers are used by Outlook Express to process your mail.

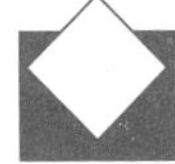

TROUBLESHOOTING

I received a message from someone using a Geocities account and I cannot view the message. How can I see the message? Geocities sends the message with an incorrect MIME header. To read the message, you can view the message source. Open the message and choose File, Properties, then click the Details tab and click Message Source.

Viewing File Attachments When you read a message with attached files, you'll see the paperclip icon in the preview pane, and icons for each file in the bottom of the message window.

To view file attachments from the preview pane, click the paperclip icon and choose the file name to open. Outlook Express will open the attachment in an application associated to view the file type. For example, if someone sends you a Microsoft Word document as an attachment, Outlook Express will open Microsoft Word (if you have it installed, WordPad will open .DOC files if Microsoft Word is not installed) to view the document. If you do not have an application installed that can view an attached file type, Outlook Express will allow you to choose one, or save the file to disk. If you know you want to save an attached file to disk from the preview pane, press the Ctrl key while choosing the file name.

To view file attachments from a message window, double-click the file name in the attachment pane at the bottom of the window. Outlook Express will open the file in an associated application. If there is no association for that file extenstion, Outlook will not open the file. An error message will instruct you to create a file association in My Computer. If you want to save the attachments, choose File, Save Attachments.

Using Inbox Assistant to Filter Incoming Messages One of the most powerful features of Outlook Express is the Inbox Assistant. The Inbox Assistant can automatically process incoming messages for you. As messages arrive from your mail server, the Inbox Assistant can perform custom actions based on the criteria you define. For example, it can help your productivity by automatically moving messages to specific folders. It can also serve as an auto-responder tool to automatically reply to messages with a prepared response.

Choose Tools, Inbox Assistant to show the Inbox Assistant dialog box, as shown in Figure 21.18. As you add custom rules to Inbox Assistant, they are listed in this dialog box. Since some rules may affect others, it is important to pay attention to the rule ordering. Inbox Assistant processes rules in the list from first to last.

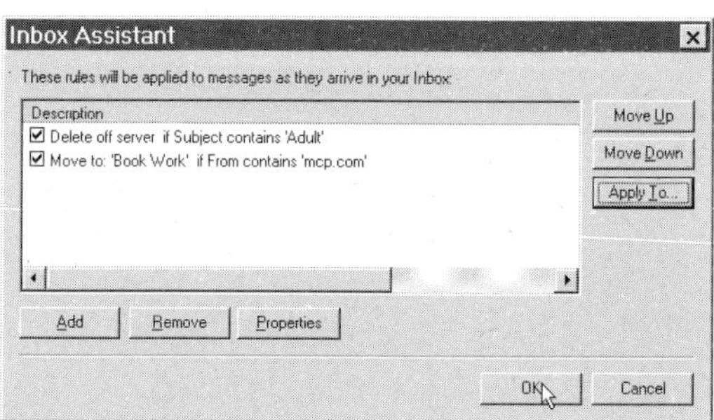

FIG. 21.18
Inbox Assistant processes messages from top to bottom fashion.

Click Add to add a new rule. The Properties dialog box displays, as shown in Figure 21.19.

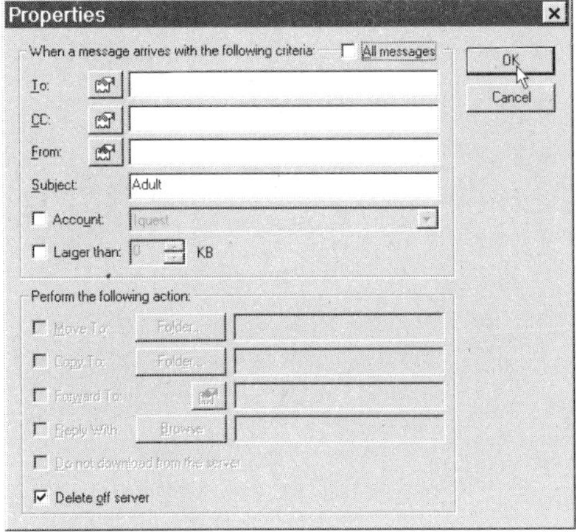

FIG. 21.19
Use the Properties dialog box to define the rule criteria and the action.

Specify the criteria for the new rule. You can combine criteria to be more specific. The following is a list of the allowed criteria:

- *All Messages.* Check this if you want the rule to apply to all messages. This is useful when you want to forward all messages to another mail account, or move them all to a specific folder.
- *To.* Type an address or name in the text box, or use the Address Book to select a name. When a message's recipient matches the text entered, Inbox Assistant will act on the message.
- *CC.* Like the To box, type an address or name in the text box, or use the Address Book to select a name. When a message's Carbon Copy recipient matches the text entered, Inbox Assistant will act on the message.
- *From.* Like the To box, type an address or name in the text box, or use the Address Book to select a name. When a message's sender matches the text entered, Inbox Assistant will act on the message.
- *Subject.* Type the text that a message subject must match. If any part of a message subject matches the text you provide, Inbox Assistant will act on the message.
- *Account.* To apply this rule only to messages from a chosen mail account, check the check box and choose the account to match against. Typically, you would combine the Account criteria with another, such as To, or Subject.
- *Larger Than N KB.* If you want to perform an action only on large messages, check the check box and adjust the message size required.

Once you define the message matching criteria, specify the action you want to occur for this rule. If desired, you can perform multiple actions. The following is a list of the actions supported:

- *Move To.* Check the check box and select the folder. Messages that match your criteria are moved to the folder selected.
- *Copy To.* Check the check box and select the folder. Messages that match your criteria are copied to the folder selected.
- *Forward To.* Check the check box and type an e-mail address or select one from the Address Book. Messages that match your criteria are forwarded to the recipient(s) defined.
- *Reply With.* Check the check box and browse for a prepared e-mail response. Senders of messages that match your criteria will receive the response.
- *Do Not Download From Server.* Check the check box to prevent Outlook Express from downloading the matching messages from the mail server.
- *Delete Off Server.* Check the check box to remove the matching messages from the mail server.

If you have your own Internet domain, ask your Internet Service Provider or network administrator to alias the sales@yourdomain.com e-mail address to your personal address. Then, use Inbox Assistant to send automatic e-mail responses to messages sent to that address. In the prepared response, provide information on how to contact you, as well as information about your products and services. If you have a Web site, be sure to include the URL, too.

Searching for Messages in Your Folders After several weeks or months, you can collect a lot of messages. Not to worry, Outlook Express provides a comprehensive tool for finding messages that you have stored in your folders. To locate messages that match your criteria, select a folder and choose Edit, Find Message. The Find Message dialog box appears, as shown in Figure 21.20.

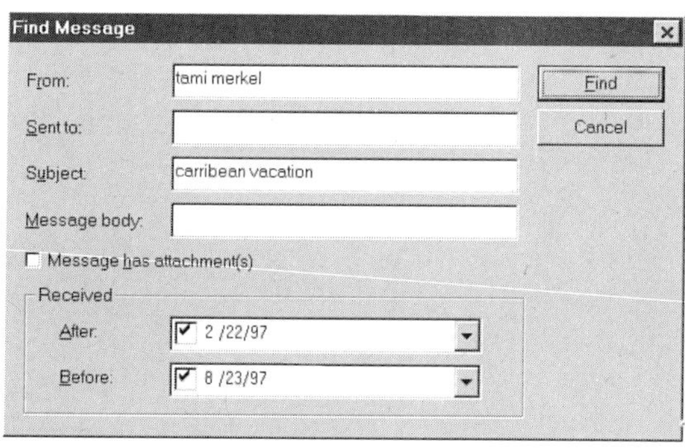

FIG. 21.20
Use the Find Message dialog box to locate that hard-to-find message from long ago.

Specify the criteria for your search. You can combine criteria to be more specific. The following is a list of the criteria supported:

- *From*. Type the message sender's name or address in the text box.
- *Sent To*. Type the message recipient's address or name in the text box.
- *Subject*. Type some text of the message subject to find.
- *Message Body*. Type some text to find within the message body.
- *Message Has Attachment(s)*. Check the check box to find only those messages with attached files.
- *Received After*. Check the check box and specify the date of when you think the message arrived. Outlook Express will save time by not searching for messages earlier than the date defined.
- *Received Before*. Check the check box and specify the latest date you think the message arrived. Outlook Express will save time by not searching for messages later than the date defined.

Once you specify the search criteria, click Find. Outlook Express will search the folder for the first message that matches. Press F3, or choose Edit, Find Next to locate the next matching message.

Sorting Messages You can sort the message listing in the order you prefer. The easiest way to sort the list is to click the column heading at the top of the message list. For example, to sort the list by date received, click the Received column heading. Click the column heading again to reverse the direction. Alternatively, choose View, Sort By and select the sorting order you want.

Deleting Messages If you no longer need a message, or do not want to store it in a folder, you can delete the message. To delete a message, select it in the message list and press the Delete key, or choose Edit, Delete. If you want to delete a message while reading it in a message window, press Ctrl-D.

Outlook Express temporarily stores deleted messages in the Deleted Items folder. If you want to restore a deleted message, find it in the Deleted Items folder and move it to another folder.

To empty the Deleted Items folder, right-click its icon in the folder list and choose Empty Folder. If you want to empty the folder when you exit Outlook Express, choose Tools, Options and click the General tab, as shown in Figure 21.21. Check the Empty Messages From The Deleted Items Folder On Exit check box.

Sending Messages

With Outlook Express, you can compose new messages, or reply to or forward messages you have received. When addressing your messages, you can use the Address Book to select names, or enter e-mail addresses manually. Outlook Express tries to prevent sending messages with invalid or incorrect e-mail addresses, so it checks the addresses to make sure they conform to Internet e-mail address format.

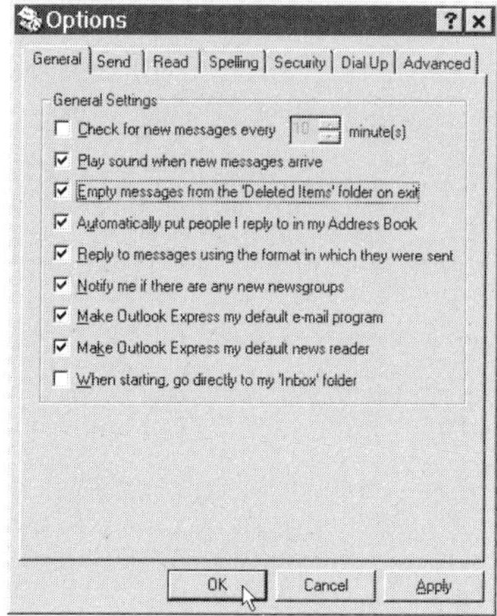

FIG. 21.21 The Mail Options dialog box allows you to specifiy that Deleted Items should be deleted at exit.

Sending a Message To compose a new message and send it, follow these instructions:

1. Click the New Message toolbar button. Alternatively, you could choose Compose, New Message.

   The New Message window appears, as shown in Figure 21.22.

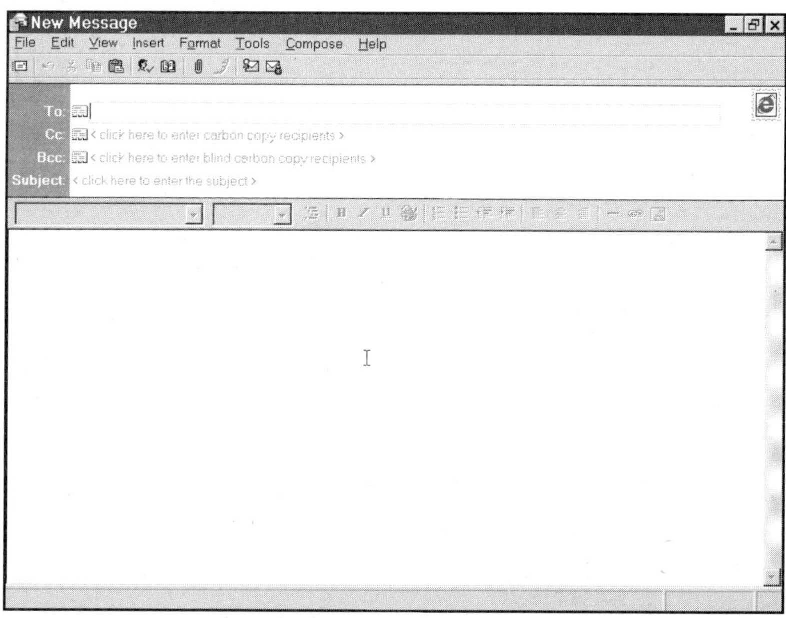

FIG. 21.22 Use the New Message window to compose and send your messages.

2. Enter the main recipient's name or e-mail address in the To box. Alternatively, you can click the Address Book icon next to the To box and select your message recipients there.

   If you enter a partial name, Outlook Express will help you look-up the correct name in the Address Book by pressing Ctrl-K. You can also enter multiple recipients in the To box—simply separate their names with semicolons.

3. If you want to send a carbon copy, or courtesy copy, to other recipients, type their names or e-mail addresses in the Cc box.

   Again, you can use Address Book to select the recipients. To send a copy of the message to another person, hidden from the recipients listed in the To and Cc boxes, enter their name or e-mail address in the Bcc box. *Bcc* is short for Blind carbon copy.

4. Type the message subject in the Subject box.

5. Press the Tab key to move the pointer to the body of the message and type your message.

   If you want to include the text of a file as your message (but not as an attachment), choose Insert, Text From File and browse for the file to include.

6. Click the Send toolbar button when you are finished composing your new message. Or, choose File, Send Message Using, then select the mail account to use for sending the message.

   If you haven't finished the message, all is not lost—you can close the window and save the message in your Draft folder. Simply double-click the message there when you are ready to finish it and send it.

If you have multiple preferred message layouts–such as one that looks like an inter-office memorandum, another that you send to customers, and perhaps another you use to send to strategic partners–you can compose the different layouts and save them in your Draft folder as message templates. Then, when you want to send a message with any of these formats, right-click the preferred template in the Draft folder and choose Forward. Outlook Express will copy the template and open a new message where you can address it, give it a pertinent subject, type your message, and send it.

Depending on your Mail Options, Outlook Express may not send the message until you connect to the mail server. Instead, the outgoing message is temporarily stored in the Outbox folder, awaiting your next connection to the mail server.

See "Customizing Outlook Express Mail," **p. 573**

TROUBLESHOOTING

I cannot type spaces at the beginning of lines of outgoing messages. How can I insert spaces there? Since leading spaces are not defined in HTML, Outlook Express ignores any spaces at the beginning of lines. If you really need to insert spaces, you can insert nonbreaking spaces. Press the ALT key while typing 0160 on the number pad for each space you need. Remember the NUMLOCK key

continues

continued

must be ON. Or you can choose Tools, Options, click the Send tab and choose Plain text as your mail sending format instead of HTML.

When I press tab within a new message, Outlook Express moves the focus away from the message content area. Why? Since tabs are not defined in HTML, Outlook Express defaults to standard Windows behavior, where pressing the tab key cycles to other fields and panes within the window.

I tried to use Send Current Document in Internet Explorer 4.0, and received a general protection fault in MSIMNUI.DLL. How can I correct the problem? You have encountered a bug in Internet Explorer 4.0 with how it integrates with Outlook Express Mail. To work around the problem, disable the option to empty your Deleted Items folder on exit.

See "Customizing Outlook Express Mail," **p. 573**

Inserting a Signature in Outgoing Messages When sending mail messages, it is useful to attach a concise footer, or *signature*, to every message. The signature serves to identify the message author, as well as other useful information about the author. To customize your own signature for outgoing messages, choose Tools, Stationery, and click the Signature button to open the signature dialog box, as shown in Figure 21.23.

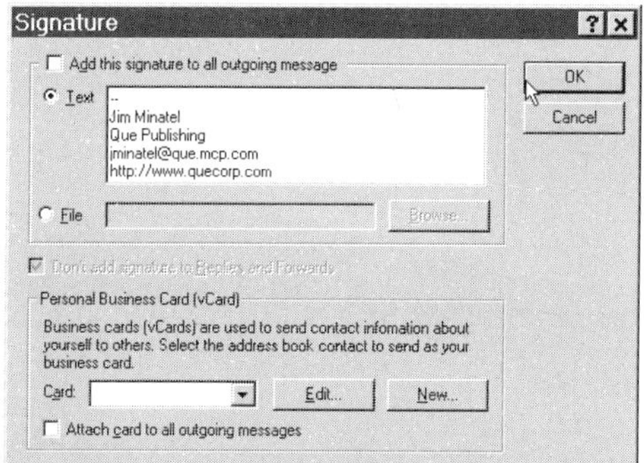

FIG. 21.23
Specify your name and contact information in the Signature dialog box.

It is usually sufficient to simply state your name and e-mail address as your e-mail signature. Many Internet users include phone numbers, Web site addresses, and even postal addresses in their signature. Others include quips in their signature. Your choice of signature is completely up to you.

CAUTION

Large signatures are disdained. If your signature typically exceeds the length of your article content, you may be flamed, or involved in a mail bomb.

See "A Note About 'Netiquette'," **p. 609**

- To define a small amount of signature text, choose the Text option button and type your signature into the text box provided.
- If you want to include a file as your signature, choose the File option button and locate the file path and name in the box provided. Using a file as your signature is especially useful when using HTML as your message format.
- If you want your signature to append to your outgoing messages, check the Add this Signature to All Outgoing Message check box.

  You can always add you signature to a new message using the Insert Signature toolbar button, or by choosing Insert, Signature.

Another new way to send something like a signature is the Personal Business Card or vCard. The advantage of a vCard is that it defines a more standardized way of presenting the contact information. You can create a vCard from the same Signature dialog box shown in Figure 21.23. To create the vCard, click New. This opens the dialog box shown in Figure 21.24.

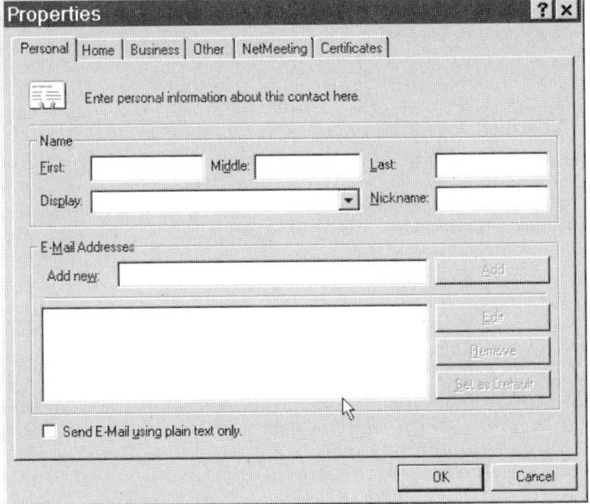

FIG. 21.24 Create your vCard with in the tabs in this dialog box.

Your vCard should include at least your name and e-mail address. Beyond that, it can include home or business contact information, NetMeeting Settings, and security certificates. When you have entered everything you want to, click OK. In the Signature options, you can choose to Attach card to all outgoing mail messages. Or, you can leave this unselected and attach to individual messages by selecting Insert, Business Card in the new message composition window.

When someone with Outlook Express or another vCard-compliant mail reader receives a message from you with the vCard attached, they will be able to look at it to see the information about you and use it to add you to their address book.

TROUBLESHOOTING

I received a warning about my signature file being too large. Why? Outlook Express limits signature files to 1K in size and truncates any signatures larger than 1K. Make the file smaller or use the text option.

Sending Attachments To attach files to your outgoing messages, click the Insert File toolbar button, or choose Insert, File Attachment. Browse to the file, select it, and click Attach. Repeat the process for additional attachments.

Each attached file appears in a pane at the bottom of the message window. Right-click the pane and choose View to change the appearance of the attached files to Large Icons, Small Icons, or List view. The file size is indicated in parentheses after the name of the file.

To remove an attached file from the message, select it in the pane and press the Delete key, or right-click the file's icon and choose Remove.

When you send the message, Outlook Express will automatically encode the attachments so they will transmit properly through the Internet. Each recipient must then decode the attachments to see them properly. If one of your recipients encounters problems decoding your attached files, change your file-encoding method.

Changing the Priority of an Outgoing Message You can mark a message as high, normal, or low priority. The message priority actually doesn't affect the message delivery speed—it simply changes how it appears to the recipients. In the case of Outlook Express, the message priority displays as an exclamation point icon for high priority, as the Internet Explorer *e* icon for normal priority, and as a down-arrow icon for low priority.

By default, Outlook Express sends messages as normal priority. To send the message as high priority, right-click the priority icon in the top right of the message window and choose High Priority, or choose Tools, Set Priority, High. To send the message as low prority, right-click the priority icon and choose Low Priority, or choose Tools, Set Priority, Low.

Forwarding a Message To send a message to another recipient, and optionally add comments to the message, select the message, click the Forward toolbar button, or choose Compose, Forward. Alternatively, you can right-click the message in the message list and choose Forward.

If you want to forward a message as an attachment, so the recipient can see the original headers, choose Compose, Forward as Attachment instead.

Outlook Express opens the message and adds the text Fw: to the beginning of the subject to indicate that it is a forwarded message. Enter the new recipients in the To, Cc, or Bcc boxes. Add your comments to the top of the message and click the Send toolbar button. The message is on its way.

Replying to a Message To send a reply to the sender of a message, select the message and click the Reply To Author toolbar button or choose Compose, Reply to Author. If you want to reply to all the recipients of the original message, click the Reply All toolbar button, or choose Compose, Reply to All.

Outlook Express opens the message and adds the text Re: to the beginning of the subject to indicate that it is a reply to a previous message. Add any new recipients in the To, Cc, or Bcc boxes. Type your responses in the message and click the Send toolbar button.

Formatting Outgoing Messages in HTML You can use Outlook Express to create messages with HTML content, including different font typefaces and sizes, background colors, hypertext links, and even embedded images.

Outlook Express sends a plain text version of the message, and the HTML formatted message as an attachment. Thus, if a recipient cannot view HTML messages, they can read the plain-text version.

To format a message in HTML, open a new message and choose Format, Rich Text (HTML). If you prefer to send HTML formatted messages all the time, you can set Outlook Express to always enable HTML formatting mode.

When you enable HTML formatting mode, the HTML formatting bar appears above the message area. Use the new toolbar to modify your message text.

▶ **See** "Using FrontPage Express and IE 4 Components," **p. 611**

Changing the Font Typeface, Size, Style, and Color HTML supports formatting text in different typefaces, sizes, styles (such as bold, italic, and underline), and colors. To change the typeface of text, select the text and choose the desired typeface name in the Font option list on the left of the HTML formatting bar. The text will display in the typeface selected.

Standard HTML supports seven relative font sizes, ranging from smallest (1) to huge (7). The reasons for this is to give the reader ultimate control on how large text should display. Some readers are comfortable with small text size because they have a large screen, or acute vision. Other readers may prefer larger text sizes because they have vision problems, or want to show the message to a large audience on-screen. To change the size of text, select the text and choose the desired size in the Font Size option list on the HTML formatting bar. The text will display in the size selected.

To change text to bold, italic, underline, or all three styles, select the text and click the desired style buttons in the HTML formatting bar. The text will display in the styles selected.

To color your text, select the text and select a color in the Font Color option list in the HTML formatting bar. The text will display in the color selected.

You can also use the Format, Font dialog box to change text formatting.

TIP Press the F2 key to see the source of your HTML formatted message.

Aligning Paragraphs In HTML, there is a limited ability to align text. You can left justify, center, or right justify the text. By default, text you type in the new message window is left justified. To center text within the window, select the text and choose Format, Align, Center, or click the Align Center button on the HTML formatting bar. To right justify text, select the text and choose Format, Align, Right, or click the Align Right button on the HTML formatting bar. To restore text to the left margin, select the text and choose Format, Align, Left, or click the Align Left button on the HTML formatting bar.

To type a new line, but not enter a new paragraph, press Ctrl-Enter.

HTML has no notion of tab stops, nor sophisticated left-right columnar text alignment. To indent text, Outlook Express exploits a feature in HTML called the BLOCKQUOTE tag. Each time you indent a paragraph, Outlook Express creates a nested BLOCKQUOTE, which displays the desired appearance of indented text.

NOTE Because HTML does not support tabs, pressing the Tab key in HTML mode moves the focus to the next input box. In addition, HTML does not recognize leading spaces at the beginning of a paragraph, however, you can enter nonbreaking spaces by holding down the Alt key while you type 0160 on the numeric keypad. Remember to have the NUMLOCK key ON.

To indent text, select the text and choose Format, Increase Indent or click the Increase Indentation button on the HTML formatting bar.

To decrease the text indentation, select the text and choose Format, Decrease Indent or click the Decrease Indentation button on the HTML formatting bar.

NOTE When working with right-justified text, the Increase Indentation and Decrease Indentation functions work relative from the right margin.

Creating a Numbered or Bulleted List If you want to display a number of paragraphs as a bulleted or numbered list, select the paragraphs and click the Formatting Bullets button, or Formatting Numbers button on the HTML formatting bar. Alternatively, you can choose Format, Bullets, or Format, Numbers.

To return a paragraph to a non-bulleted or non-numbered list, simply select the paragraph and click the respective toolbar button again.

NOTE You can nest bulleted and numbered lists. Use the Increase Indentation and Decrease Indentation toolbar buttons to promote and demote list items.

Adding a Horizontal Line and Vertical Spacing To add horizontal dividers in your message, use the HTML Horizontal Line feature. Move the pointer to the location where you want a horizontal line and click the Insert Horizontal Line button on the HTML formatting bar, or choose Insert, Horizontal Line.

Once you have a horizontal line in your message, select it and drag the edge markers to change the width and height of the line. This is a useful way to add vertical spacing in your message.

Inserting Images in a Message You can insert images in your message, but the images must be available at a Web site or shared network folder. You actually insert HTML links to the images, and when the recipient views the message, their mail tool will fetch and display the image from the shared location.

To insert an image, first make sure it is in a shared location that your recipient can access, then follow these steps:

1. Move the pointer to the location where you want the image, and click the Insert Image button on the HTML formatting bar, or choose Insert, Picture. The Picture dialog box displays, as shown in Figure 21.25.

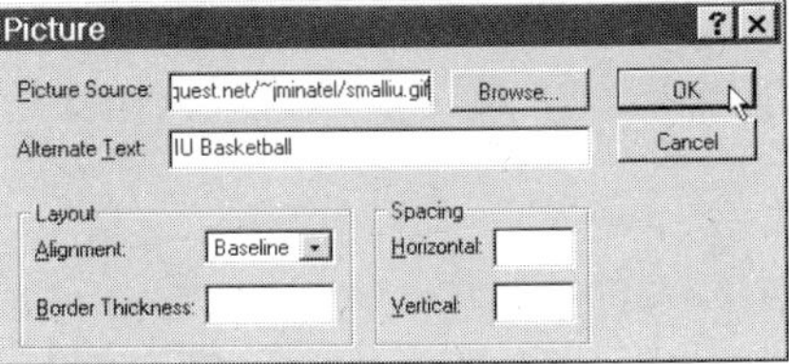

FIG. 21.25
Use a shared location when linking to an image.

2. In the Picture Source text box, type the location of the image in such a way that it would be recognized when the recipient gets the message. If the image is on a Web server, type the full URL to the image, such as http://www.intergraph.com/ingrlogo.gif. If the image is on a shared drive within your organization, use the UNC path, such as \\ntserver\images\brady.jpg. If the image is not on a public server, be sure you have selected to send pictures with the message.
3. In the Alternate Text text box, type in a brief description of the image. The description will be shown while the image is loading when the recipient displays the message.
4. Select the way you want the image aligned with your message text in the Alignment option list. For an alignment which allows text to flow around the image, select Left or Right.
5. If you want a border around the image, enter the pixel width desired in the Border Thickness text box.
6. If you want additional spacing around the image, to set it away from any text, enter the pixel amount of spacing in the Horizontal Spacing and Vertical Spacing text boxes.
7. Click OK. The image should appear in the message window.
8. To change the size of the image, select it and drag the image edge markers.

If you want to review or adjust the image information, right-click the image and select Properties to see the Image dialog box again.

Changing the Message Background Outlook Express allows you to change the color of a message background, as well as select an image to be tiled on the message background.

To change the color of the message background, choose Format, Background, Color and select a color.

To use an image as the background, choose Format, Background, Picture. The Background Image dialog box appears. Similar to inserting images into the message, the background image must exist on a shared location that your recipient can access or you must select to send the picture with the message in your sending options. Type the URL to the shared location in the Enter the URL of the Background Image text box. For Web locations, use an *http:* URL, for shared folders, use a *file:* URL, such as file://\\ntserver\images\tami-bg.jpg.

Inserting a Link in a Message If you want to link some text to a Web site, select the text and click the Set Link button on the HTML formatting bar, or choose Insert, HyperLink. The Link dialog box displays, as shown in Figure 21.26.

FIG. 21.26
Link any text to an Internet Web site in the Link dialog box.

Select the link type in the Hyperlink Type option list. For Internet Web sites, the link type is usually *http:*. Use *file:* for files on shared drive locations. Type the resource location in the URL text box.

A quick and easy way to insert links in a message is to type the URL or e-mail address, followed by a space. Outlook Express will automatically recognize the format and make a hypertext link for you.

Understanding Message Security

Outlook Express employs sophisticated public/private key security technology to allow you to encrypt your messages such that only your intended recipient can read the message (you will need the recipient's personal certificate to do this). In addition, you can attach a digital signature to your outgoing messages such that your recipients can verify that the message really came from you, and not an impostor. You must have a personal certificate to digitally sign your messages.

Similarly, armed with your personal certificate, other e-mail users can send encrypted messages to you, which only you can read. Also, if you have their personal certificate, you can authenticate their digitally signed messages, to be confident that they actually sent the message, and that the message wasn't altered en route to you.

Getting a Digital Certificate Personal certificates are acquired from a trusted third-party Certificate Authority. Most Certificate Authorities charge a fee for their services. If you are interested in acquiring a personal certificate and you use Microsoft Internet Explorer 4.0, you can get a free evaluation certificate from VeriSign.

ON THE WEB

VeriSign's Digital ID Center

http://digitalid.verisign.com/

You can also get a certificate by clicking Tools, Options, selecting the Security tab and clicking Get Digital ID. This will take you to a Web site that will begin walking you through the process of getting a digital ID. During this process, you will enter your name and e-mail address. Outlook Express will step you through generating a private key that is stored on your computer. Without this key, the certificate is useless. With VeriSign, the will send you back an e-mail message with links in it to install your ID. Be sure to open the message in Outlook Express and not another mail reader. You should get the message almost instantly.

After getting the ID installed, you have to configure an account to use the ID.

1. Select Tools, Accounts, and selct the e-mail account to use the ID with (this should have the same address that you used to register for the ID).
2. Click the Properties button and select the Security tab.
3. Select Use a digital ID when sending secure message from.
4. Click the Digital ID button.
5. Select your ID in the list as shown in Figure 21.27. To see more about the ID, click Properties or Fine Print. When you are done, click OK in the properties dialog box then close in the accounts dialog box.

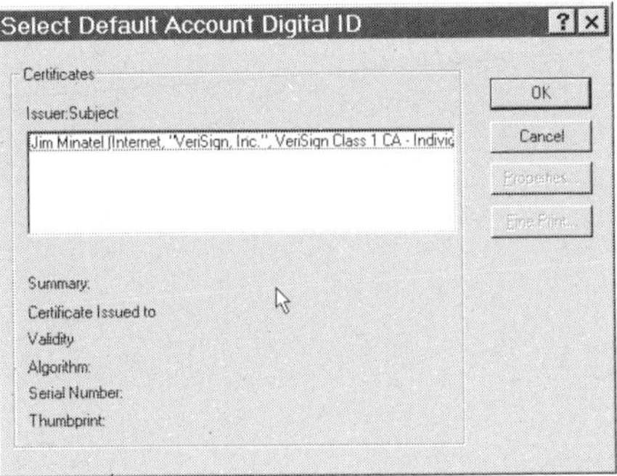

FIG. 21.27
If you have more than one ID, they will be listed here.

Reading Digitally Signed Messages You read digitally signed messages the same way you read other messages. When you receive a digitally signed message, Outlook compares the address that it came from with the address contained in the certificate. Equipped with that information, Outlook Express will analyze the sender's digital signature and verify that it fits the certificate. In addition, Outlook Express validates that the message was not modified during its transmission to you (it examines the message body and compares it with a special code in the digital certificate). If the sender's e-mail address does not match the digital signature and certificate, you will see a warning message, as shown in Figure 21.28.

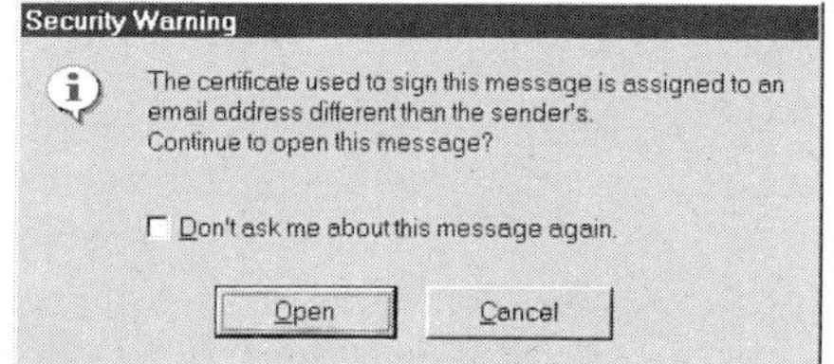

FIG. 21.28 Outlook Express warns you when someone pretends to be someone they are not.

Any security warning you get from Outlook Express can indicate that someone is trying to pull a fast one. Do not take the warning lightly—someone may be trying to pretend to be someone else, or they might be trying to intercept and modify an official message. So, if you receive a message indicating that the head of engineering wants you to change the specs of your project, but the digital signature does not agree, you can probably assume that someone is trying to pull a practical joke. Nonetheless, in this case I would follow up to see if it really was true.

If a digitally signed message checks out okay, you will get no warning, but Outlook Express will display an icon in the header area of the message to indicate that the digital signature is valid.

There are currently three classes of IDs available from VeriSign. A class 1 ID only verifies that the person applying for it has the e-mail address they are applying to use. It does not identify the user's real identity. So when you get a message with a class 1 ID attached, you can be sure that it was sent from the address it claims, but the sender could have made up any name they wanted.

A class 2 ID also verifies the sender's name. This is done by requesting more information about the user during registration and comparing it to a large database of personal and business information.

Class 3 IDs are currently used for server applications only.

Reading Encrypted Messages You read encrypted messages the same way you read other messages. In order for someone to send you an encrypted message, they must have a copy of your personal certificate. When you receive an encrypted message, Outlook Express will use your own private key portion of your personal certificate to decrypt the message. If all goes well, Outlook Express displays a small lock icon in the header part of the message, to indicate that the message was sent encrypted. When you see the lock icon, it is very unlikely that someone else has intercepted and read the message.

If an encrypted message arrives and Outlook Express cannot decrypt it, you will not be able to read the message. When this occurs, send your personal certificate to the sender and tell them to use it when encrypting messages to you. It is possible that the sender is using an incorrect certificate.

Sending Digitally Signed Messages To send a digitally signed message, compose the message like you normally do, then click the Digitally Sign Message toolbar button or choose Tools, Digitally Sign. That's all there is to it! When you send the message, Outlook Express will compute a verification code for the message and embed it in the digital signature. This allows the recipient to validate that the message was not modified after you sent it, as well as have confidence that you sent it, and not an impostor.

You can configure Outlook Express to digitally sign your outgoing messages automatically. To do this, select Tools, Option, and select the Security tab. Select Add digital signiture to all outgoing messages.

Sending Encrypted Messages You must have a recipient's personal certificate in order to send encrypted messages to them. If you do not have a person's personal certificate, ask them to send it to you. They should also digitally sign the message such that you can trust it was really them who sent the message and it didn't get modified on its way to you.

When you receive the sender's personal certificate, store it in your Address Book so you can encrypt messages sent to them.

See "Using the Windows Address Book," **p. 789**

To send an encrypted message, compose it as you would any message, and click the Encrypt Message toolbar button, or choose Tools, Encrypt. When you send the message, Outlook Express will use each recipient's personal certificate to encrypt the message content. When a recipient receives the message, they will use the private key portion of their personal certificate to decrypt and read the message.

You can configure Outlook Express to encrypt your outgoing messages automatically.

E-Mail Security Zones With the advent of HTML mail, there is a new danger lurking in e-mail. The same types of files that could transmit viruses or damage your computer in Web pages can now be part of e-mail messages. Outlook Express allows the use of security "Zones" to set protection for the messages you receive. The zones setting are changed in the Security tab of the Options dialog box. The two available zones are Internet and Restricted sites.

To learn more about these zones and their settings, see "Setting Internet Security Zones" in Chapter 18. The settings described for Internet Explorer these are the same as for Outlook Express.

Customizing Outlook Express Mail

You can customize Outlook Express Mail to be more productive when reading and sending e-mail. To customize Outlook Express Mail, choose Tools, Mail Options. The Mail Options dialog box displays, as shown in Figure 21.29.

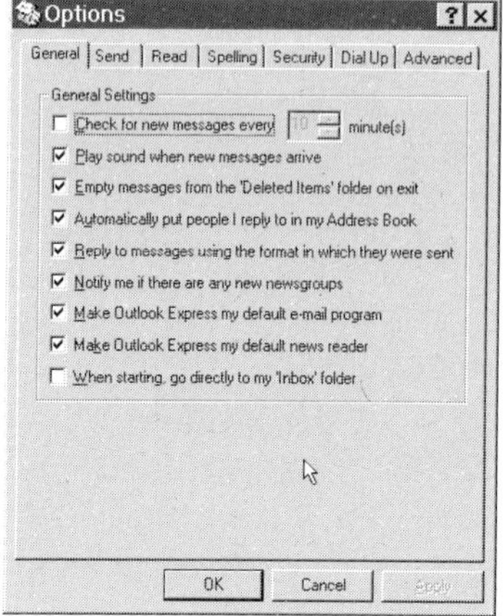

FIG. 21.29 This General preferences tab controls settings that don't fit into the other categories.

Setting Outlook's General Reference The settings in General preference that pertain to mail are:

- To force Outlook Express to check the mail server for new messages at specified intervals, check the Check for New Messages Every N Minute(s) check box and define the amount of time desired.
- Check the Play Sound When New Messages Arrive check box to sound the system beep when a new message arrives.
- Check the Empty Messages from the 'Delete Items' Folder On Exit check box to permanently remove deleted messages when you leave Outlook express. If you leave the check box unchecked, deleted messages will stay in the Deleted Items folder until you remove them manually by selecting them and pressing the Delete key, or right-clicking the Deleted Items folder and choosing Empty Folder.
- If you want Outlook Express to record recipient addresses when you send messages to them, check the Automatically Put People I Reply to in My Address Book check box. Saving recipient addresses in your Address Book allows you to send future messages without typing in the addresses manually.
- Reply to Messages Using the Format in Which They Were Sent specifies that messages sent to you in HTML will be replied to in HTML and messages sent plain text will be sent plain text. This makes it easier for the recipient to read your reply in their mail program.
- Check the Make Outlook Express My Default E-Mail Program check box if you prefer to use Outlook Express, instead of other mail programs such as Microsoft Exchange or Microsoft Outlook 97. Therefore, the next time you need to send an e-mail message from Windows 95, Outlook Express will automatically display, as opposed to another e-mail program you may have installed.

The other options relate to reading news with Outlook and are discussed later in this chapter.

Customizing How You Send Mail The Mail Options Send tab (see Figure 21.30) allows you to customize what Outlook Express does when sending an e-mail message.

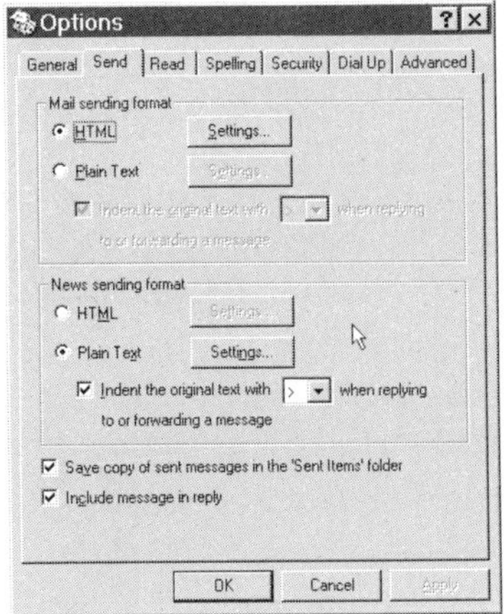

FIG. 21.30
Use the Mail Options Send tab to adjust your sending settings and preferred outgoing message format.

- Check the Save Copy of Sent Messages in the 'Sent Items' Folder check box to retain a copy of each message you send. This is useful in the instance when you need to find when or what you sent to a specific recipient. Be forewarned that if you send many messages, your 'Sent Items' folder can become quite large and use up valuable disk space.
- Check the Include Message In Reply check box to copy a message's content into your reply. This way, recipients can the read the original message that prompted your reply.

You also can configure your preferred format for outgoing messages.

- Choose the HTML option button if you want your outgoing messages to use the rich capabilities of the Hypertext Markup Language.

  Click the Settings button to adjust the HTML settings, as seen in Figure 21.31. In the Encode Text Using option list, choose Quoted Printable or Base64 as your preferred MIME (Multipurpose Internet Mail Extension) format for sending HTML messages. Quoted Printable will allow users to read and decode your message without the need for a special browser, although the message will appear to run together and have HTML tags embedded in it. Use Base64 if you are confident that the recipient has a tool that can decode Base64 messages. If a recipient does not have a Base64-capable mail tool, the message appears as a long string of letters and digits.

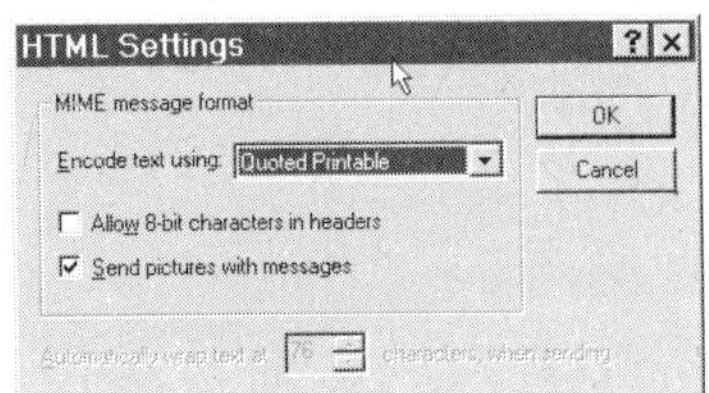

FIG. 21.31
Define the MIME encoding type in the HTML Settings dialog box.

Check the Allow 8-Bit Characters in Headers check box to send foreign characters (such as a cedilla or umlaut), multi-byte characters, or high-ASCII characters in the header of the message. Do this only when you are sure that the mail server can process 8-bit headers (most Internet systems do not). If you are unsure whether your mail server can handle 8-bit headers, uncheck this check box. In this case, any 8-bit characters are encoded, and recipients must use a capable mail tool to decode them and display them properly.

Check Send Pictures with Message if you want to attach picture files with the message. This way, your messages can include pictures from your local hard drive that are not available publicly on the Web sites or shared network drives.

- To send your messages with no rich formatting, choose the Plain Text option button. Click Settings to adjust the Plain Text settings, as seen in Figure 21.32. You have the choice of sending Plain Text messages using MIME or Uuencode. Most Internet mail tools understand MIME, but some still use the older Uuencode encoding method. Uuencode was invented for encoding UNIX-to-UNIX message attachments, and is still used by older UNIX systems and early Windows mail tools (such as Microsoft Mail). MIME is a replacement for the nonstandard Uuencode format. Choose MIME unless you are sure your recipients require Uuencode formatted messages.

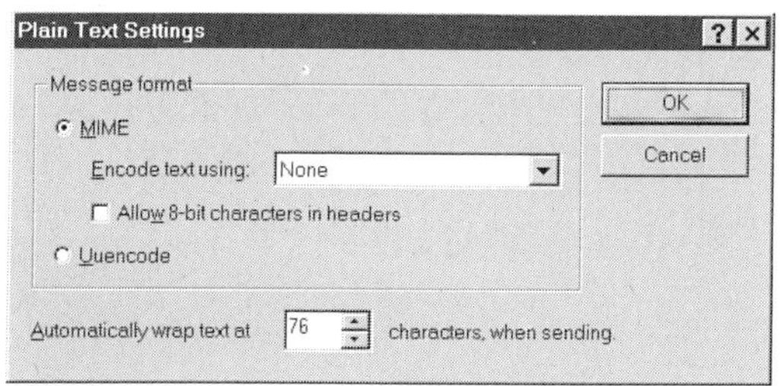

FIG. 21.32
Choose your preferred message encoding format when using Plain Text.

If you choose MIME, you can choose no encoding, or encode messages using Quoted Printable or Base64-formats. In the Encode Text Using option list, choose None to avoid encoding the message at all. Choose Quoted Printable to allow users to read and decode your message without the need for a special browser. Choose Base64 if you are confident that the recipient has a tool that can decode Base64 messages. If a recipient does not have a Base64-capable mail tool, the message appears as a long string of letters and digits.

Check the Allow 8-bit Characters in Headers check box to send foreign characters, multi-byte characters, or high-ASCII characters in the header of the message. Do this only when you are sure that the mail server can process 8-bit headers (most Internet systems do not). If you are unsure whether your mail server can handle 8-bit headers, clear this check box. In this case, the 8-bit characters are encoded, and recipients must use a proper mail tool to decode them and display them properly.

Adjust the Automatically Wrap Text At N Characters, When Sending counter where you want your messages to wrap. Outlook Express will insert carriage returns into your message at the right location so that message recipients can see your entire message without having to scroll horizontally in their mail tool. The default setting of 76 characters is acceptable in most situations, as it allows your message to be indented when a recipient replies.

- If you include original messages in forwards and replies, it is useful to indent the original message using some character before each line. This way, recipients can easily see which parts of the message are from the original message, separate from your own comments. To prefix each original line with a special character, check the Indent the Original Text with > When Replying to or Forwarding a Message check box. If you want to use a different prefix character, such as a pipe or colon, choose the character from the option list provided.

Customizing How You Read Mail The Mail Options Read tab, as shown in Figure 21.33, allows you to customize how Outlook Express behaves when you read mail.

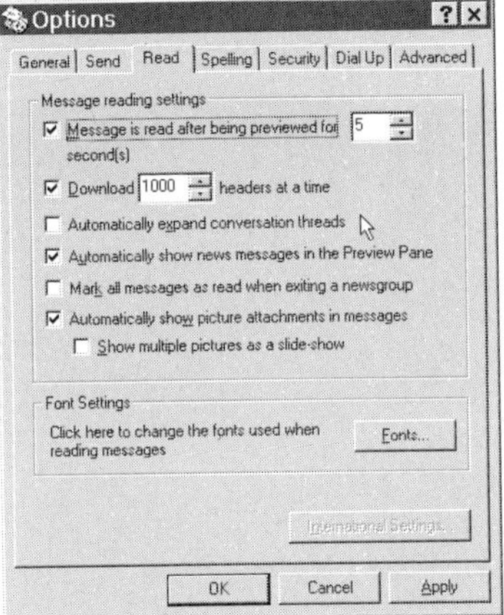

FIG. 21.33 Use the Mail Options Read tab to choose your preferred mail reading settings.

- If you use the Preview Pane to read messages without opening them in a separate window, you can command Outlook Express to mark the message as read when it has been previewed for a certain duration. To enable this feature, check the Mark Message as Read After Previewed for N Second(s) check box, and adjust the number of seconds preferred.
- Click Font Settings to indicate your preferred language, font typefaces, and sizes for reading and sending messages (see Figure 21.34).

Customizing the Spell Checker Outlook Express can save you a lot of embarrassment when sending messages that contain spelling errors by performing a spell check. Use the Mail Options Spelling tab, as shown in Figure 21.35, to customize how Outlook Express will check your messages before you send them.

FIG. 21.34
Customize the language, font typefaces, and sizes for Outlook Express in the Fonts dialog box.

FIG. 21.35
Tailor the spelling checker to your preferences in the Mail Options Spelling tab.

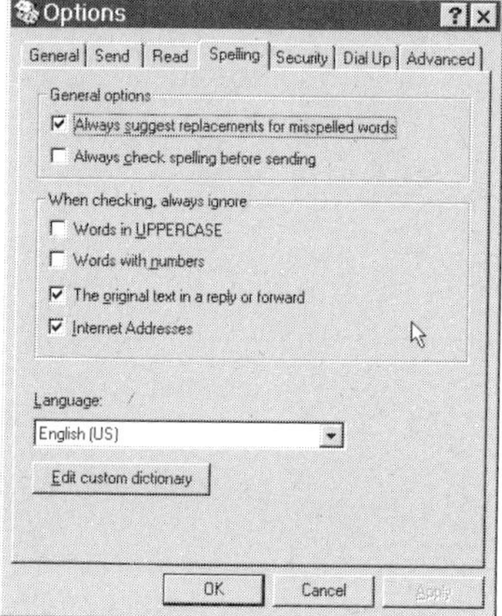

- If you want the spelling checker to offer suitable replacements when it finds spelling errors, check the Always Suggest Replacements For Misspelled Words check box.
- To scan for spelling errors in your outgoing messages before sending them, check the Always Check Spelling Before Sending check box.
- Sometimes the spelling checker indicates misspelled words where there are none. To tune the behavior of the spell checker to avoid some common occurrences, choose your preferred settings.

  Check the Words in UPPERCASE check box to avoid words you type in all uppercase letters (such as acronyms).

TIP Avoid typing long messages completely in uppercase letters, as recipients view it as shouting.

Check the Words with Numbers check box to avoid spell checking terms with letters and words combined, such as ISO9000 or Intense 3D-100.

It is generally considered disrespectful to correct spelling of other people's messages. Check the The Original Text in a Reply or Forward check box to avoid spell checking and correcting text in an included message.

Check the Internet Addresses check box to avoid spell checking Internet e-mail and Web site addresses. Internet addresses often contain unconventional sequences of characters, and correcting the addresses could result in invalid links.

- Choose your preferred spelling check language in the Language option list. This can help the spelling checker identify atypical use, such as the spelling of centre versus center.
- If you want to modify the dictionary of custom words that the spelling checker compares words to, click Edit Custom Dictionary.

Customizing Mail Security Use the Mail Options Security tab, as shown in Figure 21.36, to customize your message security preferences.

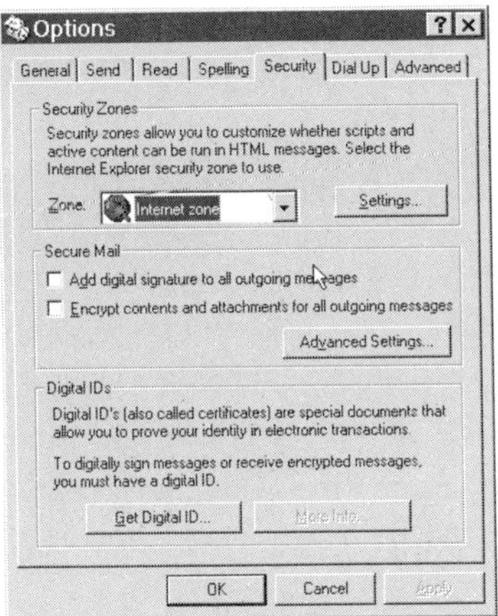

FIG. 21.36
Use the Mail Options Security tab to secure or authenticate your outgoing messages.

- To set preferences for security zones, click Settings and see "Setting Internet Security Zones" in Chapter 18. The settings described for Internet Explorer there are the same as for Outlook Express.
- If you want to digitally sign every outgoing message, check the Add Digital Signature to All Outgoing Messages check box. Digitally signing a message provides two benefits: Recipients can verify the digital signature and prove that you sent the message, as opposed to an impostor, and recipients can verify that the message is genuine and was not altered by someone after you sent it.
- To send messages that can only be read by your intended recipient, check the Encrypt Contents and Attachments for All Outgoing Messages check box. Outlook Express will encrypt outgoing mail with the recipient's personal certificate, and thus prevent others from reading the message.
- Click Advanced Settings to change your security preferences (see Figure 21.37).

  To include your personal certificate when sending signed messages, check the Include My Digital ID with Signed Messages check box. Recipients can use the information in the personal certificate to encrypt messages they send to you, as well as authenticate your messages.

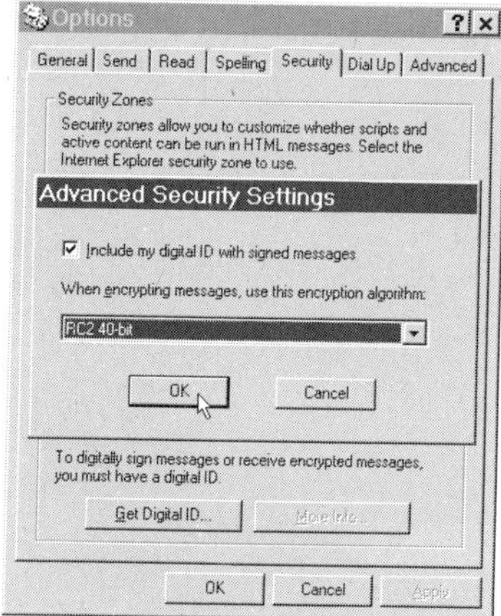

FIG. 21.37 Indicate your security settings in the Advanced Security Settings dialog box.

There are many encryption algorithms from which to choose. Each algorithm provides a tradeoff between performance and security. Generally, algorithms that use larger bit counts provide the better security. Identify which encryption algorithm you want to use in the When Encrypting Messages, Use This Encryption Algorithm option list. The available algorithms may be limited by encryption regulation or the version of Explorer you use.

Customizing Dial-Up Preferences Outlook Express is capable of initiating an Internet connection if it needs to connect to send or receive messages. The preferences related to this are shown in Figure 21.38.

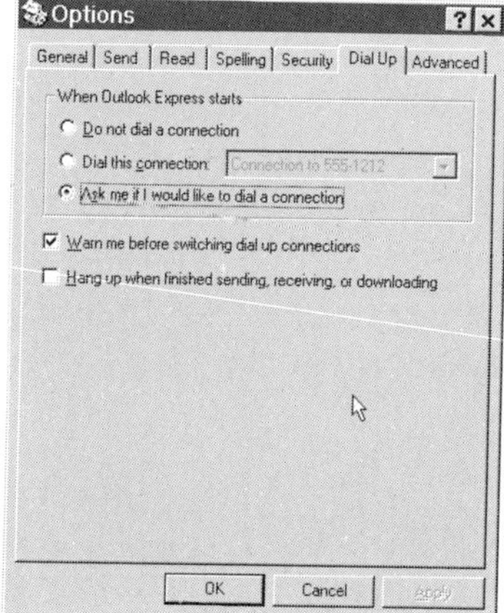

FIG. 21.38 Outlook Express connects to the Internet through existing Internet settings.

To control whether Outlook Express connects to the Internet each time you start it, select:

- Do Not Dial a Connection will start Outlook Express without starting a connection. You will need to start a connection manually to send or receive mail
- Dial this Connection and choose a connection from the list
- Ask Me If I Would Like to Dial a Connection will prompt you each time

The other options are:

- Warn Me Before Switching Dial Up Connections: You should select this if you let Outlook dial a connection and you have more than one defined connection. Otherwise, Outlook may hang up a connection you have open to dial another one
- To minimize online time, select Hang Up When Finished Sending, Receiving, or Downloading

Configuring Advanced Settings There are a few final settings shown in Figure 21.39 that relate to mail. The others are related to news only.

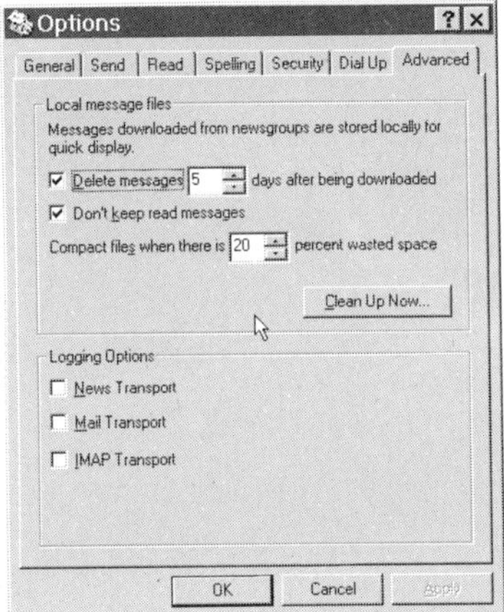

FIG. 21.39 Two of the logging options here relate to mail.

The Mail Transport and IMAP Transport options here can be turned on to create a log and troubleshoot mail server problems. IMAP only applies if you have an IMAP server instead of POP3.

Customizing the Toolbar Outlook Express provides a toolbar for quick and easy access to the most useful mail functions. To display the toolbar, choose View, Toolbar.

If you prefer to move the toolbar to one side, bottom, or top of the window, choose Tools, Layout and select Left, Right, Top, or Bottom. Also, you can right-click the toolbar and choose Align, then Left, Right, Top, or Bottom to achieve the same results.

If you are unfamiliar with the Outlook Express toolbar buttons, choose Tools, Layout, and select Show Text on Toolbars. Alternatively, you can right-click over the toolbar and choose Text Labels. Read the toolbar text labels and associate them with the toolbar icons. In time, you will become familiar with the button meanings, and can turn the text labels back off to reduce the size of the toolbar.

You can quickly see the text labels on the toolbar by clicking and dragging the border of the toolbar to expand it. Similarly, you can hide the text labels by dragging the toolbar border in the opposite direction.

Outlook Express allows you to customize the toolbar with your most needed buttons. Choose Tools, Layout, Customize, Buttons or right-click the toolbar and choose Buttons. The Customize Toolbar dialog box appears, as shown in Figure 21.40. Use this dialog box to display the toolbar functions you need. Select the buttons you want to display in the Available Buttons list, and click Add. Alternatively, select the toolbar buttons you want to hide in the Toolbar Buttons list and click Remove. You can also drag and drop the buttons to change their location. See Table 21.3 for the available toolbar buttons and their descriptions.

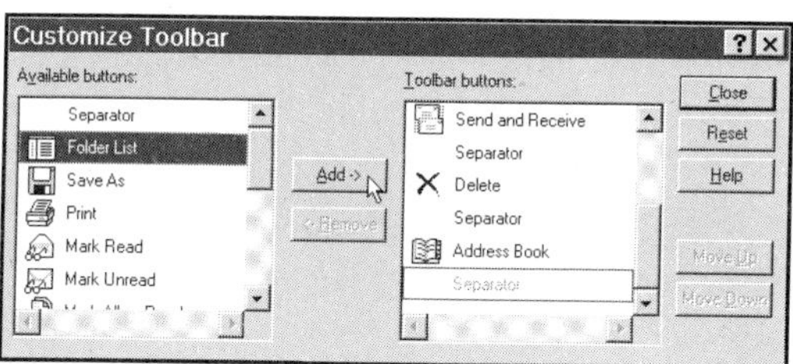

FIG. 21.40 You can customize your toolbar in Outlook Express.

Table 21.3 Available Toolbar Buttons in Outlook Express Mail

Button	Action
Compose Message	Compose a new message.
Find	Locate a message.
Folder List	Display the list of your message folders.
Go to Inbox	Display the contents of your Inbox folder.
Go to Outbox	Display the contents of your Outbox folder.
Go to Sent Items	Display the contents of your Sent Items folder.
Help	Get Help.
Save As	Save the selected message to a file.
Move To	Move the selected message to a folder.
Copy To	Copy the selected message to a folder.
Print	Print the selected message.
Delete	Delete the selected message.
Send and Retrieve	Connect to the mail server and send all outgoing messages and download any new messages.
Address Book	Open the Windows 95 Address Book.

Language	Choose the preferred language.
Mark Read	Mark the selected message as read.
Mark Unread	Mark the selected message as unread.
Mark All As Read	Marks all messages in the folder as read.
Reply to Author	Compose a response to author of the selected message.
Reply to All	Compose a response to all recipients and the author of the selected message.
Forward Message	Send the selected message to another recipient.

Once you have the toolbar buttons you need in the Toolbar Buttons list, select the functions and click Move Up and Move Down to organize the toolbar buttons into related groups. For additional visual organization, add a separator icon in between grouped functions.

If you want to start all over and return the toolbar to the default layout, click Reset. Click Help if you need help customizing your toolbar.

When you are finished, click Close. Outlook Express will remember your settings.

Adding or Removing Columns in the Message List Like the toolbar, you can choose which columns to display in Outlook Express' list of messages. Choose View, Columns to display the Columns dialog box. Use this dialog box to display the columns desired. Select the columns you want to see in the Available Columns list, and click Add. Alternatively, select the columns you want to hide in the Displayed Columns list and click Remove.

To change the order of the column appearance, select a column in the Displayed Columns list and click Move Up or Move Down appropriately. Columns are listed in left-to-right fashion. See Table 21.4 for the available columns and their descriptions.

Table 21.4 Available Columns in Outlook Express Mail

Column	Description
Account	The Mail account from which the message was received.
Sent	The date and time when the message was sent.
From	The sender of the message.
Subject	The subject of the message.
Received	The date and time when the message was received.
Size	The size of the message, in kilobytes.
Priority	The message's priority (urgent, normal, and so on).
Attachment	Whether or not there is an attachment.
To	The intended message recipient(s).

Once you choose the headers you want to show, you can drag them in the message list laterally to change their location.

When viewing a list of messages, click a column header to display the list in that column's ascending or descending order. For example, to list the messages from largest to smallest, click the Size column header. Click it again to reverse direction. Alternatively, you can right-click over a column header and choose Sort Ascending or Sort Descending.

If you want to start all over and return the column layout to a default layout, click Reset. To discard your changes, click Cancel. When you are finished, click OK. Outlook Express will remember your settings.

Using Outlook Express News

You can use Outlook Express to participate in UseNet News. One of the most popular services on the Internet, UseNet News serves as user forums, or virtual communities, on just about every topic imaginable. Topics range from zero-dimensional geometry (alt.0.d), to the wi.* hierarchy, consisting of groups with articles about Wisconsin. Participating in UseNet News is free, excluding your connect-time charges.

UseNet News is arranged into individual groups called *newsgroups*. All of the newsgroups are organized into a hierarchy that orders related topics with a mostly logical naming scheme. Each newsgroup name starts with a three- or four-letter prefix, followed by a newsgroup name. Here are the most common prefixes:

- *alt.* Alternative topics, everything from alien invasions to xenophobia
- *biz.* Covers business affairs, commerce, and commercial products
- *comp.* Computers and computer-related topics
- *news.* News of interest to the Internet community, such as announcements of new groups
- *rec.* Recreation, hobbies, and sports
- *sci.* Scientific interests
- *soc.* Social issues
- *talk.* Discussions and debates
- *misc.* Everything that won't fit elsewhere

Individual regions, countries, and states have hierarchies too, identified by their postal ID prefix. For example, the **ca.general** group is for general discussion about California, and in **hsv.jobs,** you can find job postings for the city of Huntsville, AL. You can find a list of all of the newsgroups in **news.groups**, complete with descriptions.

Group names move from the general to the specific as you read them. For example, the **comp.infosystems.www.announce** and **comp.infosystems.www.servers.ms-windows** groups are both about the World Wide Web. The first has announcements about the Web, and the second is about Web server software for Microsoft Windows platforms.

Newsgroups are created using a closely watched balloting mechanism, involving impartial people to solicit and count votes by e-mail. And, some newsgroups are *moderated*, meaning that when someone posts an article to that group, the article is forwarded to an individual who approves the article for distribution. Moderated newsgroups usually have high-quality information, at the expense of minor delays for the approval cycle. Conversely, *unmoderated* newsgroups allow anyone to post articles without approval.

The most unruly newsgroups are those in the alt hierarchy (alt is an abbreviation for *alternative*), on topics from **alt.0.d** to **alt.zine**, a newsgroup about alternative magazines. Anyone is allowed to create a newsgroup in the **alt** area. This untamed nature causes many organizations to avoid participation in the **alt** hierarchy. If you do not see the **alt** hierarchy, contact your Internet service provider or Network Administrator—he or she can explain the policy.

To use Outlook Express to participate in the fascinating world of UseNet news, you must configure Outlook Express with your news server and preferences. To do that, you need the address or host name of a news server. Outlook Express connects to the news server to post and receive the newsgroup articles. If you do not know the address of a news server, consult your Internet service provider or Network Administrator.

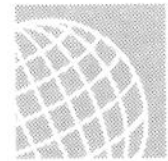

ON THE WEB

Microsoft's newsgroup for Outlook Express News can be accessed from Internet Explorer by using the following URL:

news://msnews.microsoft.com/microsoft.public.internet.news

Connecting to a News Server

Outlook Express allows you to configure multiple news servers. For instance, if you have a news account with an Internet Service Provider and another with your organization, you can use Outlook Express to accept articles from both locations.

To define a news server for Outlook Express, you follow a process similar to "Connecting to a Mail Server" earlier in this chapter :

1. Open the Start menu and choose Programs, Outlook Express. When you start Outlook Express News for the first time, the Internet Connection Wizard displays. The Internet Connection Wizard steps you through the configuration for a mail and news server entry.

   If you already have a news server defined in Outlook Express and want to add another, choose the Tools, Accounts menu, then click Add, and News. This starts the Internet Connection Wizard to add an additional news server.

2. Click Next to proceed with the setup. The Internet News Display Name dialog box appears. Enter your full name in the Display name text box. This name will appear in news you send to others. When others save your address in their Address Book, it will save under this name.

3. Click Next. The Internet News E-Mail Address dialog box appears. When you *post,* or submit, articles to a newsgroup, Outlook Express News will automatically put your name and e-mail path at the top of the article. This way, other UseNet News users can know that you submitted the article and how to contact you. Type your mail address in the E-mail address text box. Your Internet Service Provider assigns your e-mail address. Mail addresses usually take the format of your username followed by an @ symbol, then the Internet Service Provider's domain name, such as johndoe@server.com. When others send you messages, or reply to messages you send, this address is what they use.
4. Click Next. The Internet News Server Name dialog box appears. In the News (NNTP) Server text box, enter the hostname of the news server. Your Internet Service Provider will supply this hostname. This host serves to store your newsgroup articles. When you connect to the host with Outlook Express News, you can subscribe to newsgroups and view, respond to, and post articles.
5. If your Internet Service Provider does not require you to use a specific username and password to access news, go to the next step.

   To define the username and password to use news, choose the My News Server Requires Me to Log On option button and click Next. The Internet News Server Logon dialog box displays.

   If your Internet Service Provider offers Secure Password Authentication, choose the Log On Using Secure Password Authentication (SPA) option button. In this case, Outlook Express will logon to the news server using the username and password you use to logon to Windows 95.

   If your Internet Service provider requires that you use a username and password to access news, choose the Log On Using option button. Enter the username in the News Account text box, and the associated password in the Password text box.
6. The first step of the Internet Connection Wizard asks you to name your new news connection. Choose a name that best describes your news server. For instance, if you have a news account with your company, you may wish to name the connection "Work" or something similar. The news account name you choose can be completely arbitrary; just choose a name you will recognize.
7. Click Next. The Choose Connection Type dialog box appears. From here, the Wizard follows steps 9 through 21 of "Connecting to a Mail Server" earlier in this chapter.

Reviewing Your News Account Settings

It is useful to review your settings and fill in any other details that the Internet Connection Wizard did not fill in for you. To review your Outlook Express News account settings, follow these steps:

1. Choose the Tools, Accounts menu. The Internet Accounts dialog box displays, as shown in Figure 21.41.
2. Choose the news account you want to review and click Properties. The News Account Properties dialog box displays, as shown in Figure 21.42.

FIG. 21.41
Choose the news account you want to review.

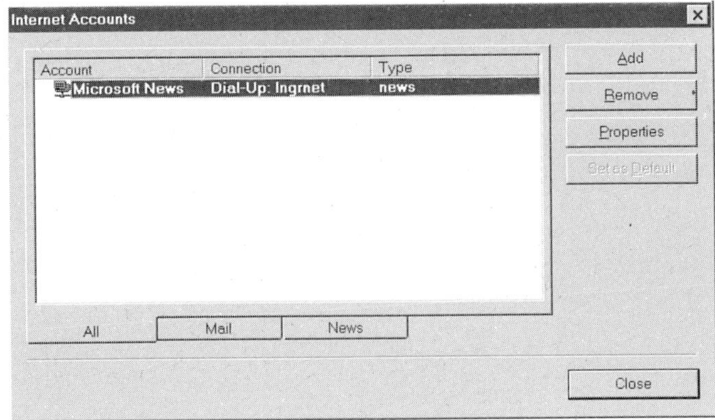

FIG. 21.42
Use the News Account Properties General tab to change your full name, e-mail address, organization, or news account label.

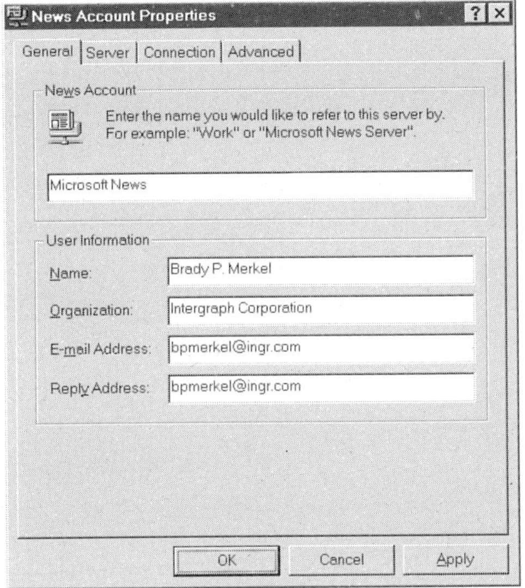

3. Review the settings in the News Account Properties General tab. The Internet Connection Wizard should have defined many of the text boxes for you. One text box that the Internet Connection Wizard does not define is the Organization text box. Type the name of your company or organization name into the Organization text box.
4. If there is no e-mail address in the Reply Address text box, Outlook Express News will use the one defined in the E-mail Address text box to stamp outgoing articles with a return address. If you want readers of your articles to send replies to a different e-mail address, type the preferred e-mail address in the Reply Address text box. This is useful when you have multiple e-mail accounts, but you want replies to all go to a single account.

5. The News Account Properties Server tab (see Figure 21.43) shows the server settings for your news account. The Internet Connection Wizard defines these values when you add your news account, but you can change them here if desired.

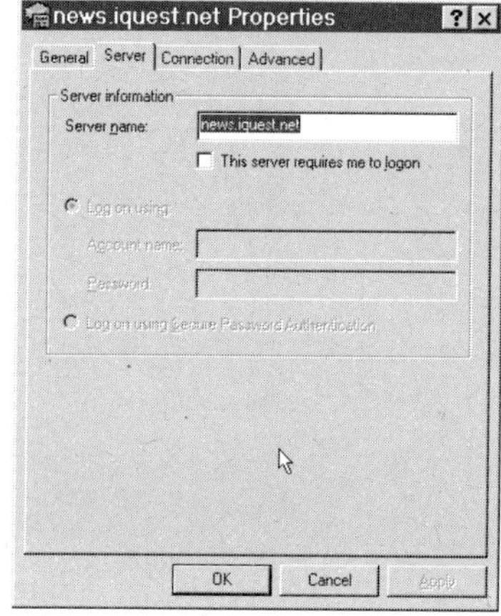

FIG. 21.43 Use the News Account Properties Server tab to change your news server address and login information.

6. Use the News Account Properties Connection tab (see Figure 21.44) to specify how you connect to your news server, via a LAN, automatic dial-up connection, or manually.

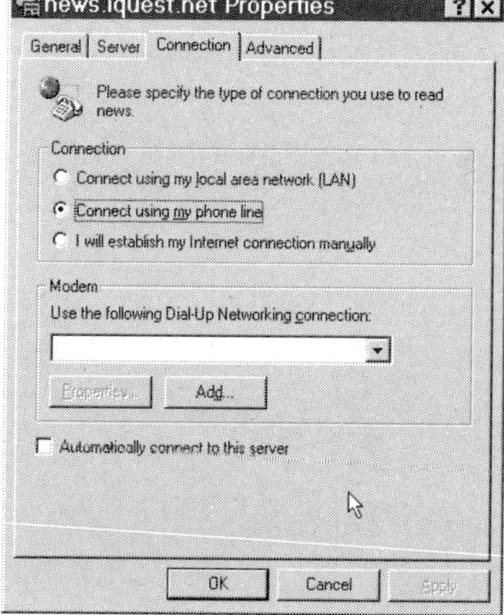

FIG. 21.44 Choose how you connect to your News server in the News Account Properties Connection tab.

7. If you prefer to dial up to the Internet manually, choose the I will Establish My Internet Connection Manually option button. If you choose Use the Following Dial-Up Networking Connections, Outlook Express News will dial up for you.
8. If you want Outlook Express News to automatically connect to the server when you choose to read a newsgroup (such as when selecting a *news:* URL in Internet Explorer), check the Automatically Connect to This Server check box.

9. The News Account Properties Advanced tab (see Figure 21.45) allows you to change certain settings that you do not normally need to adjust. For instance, if your news server requires you to use a different TCP/IP port number for accessing news, other than the default port number of 119, type the new port number in the News Server text box. If the server requires you to connect via the Secure Sockets Layer (SSL), check the This Server Requires a Secure Connection (SSL) check box.

FIG. 21.45
Use the News Account Properties Advanced tab to adjust news server settings you do not normally need to change.

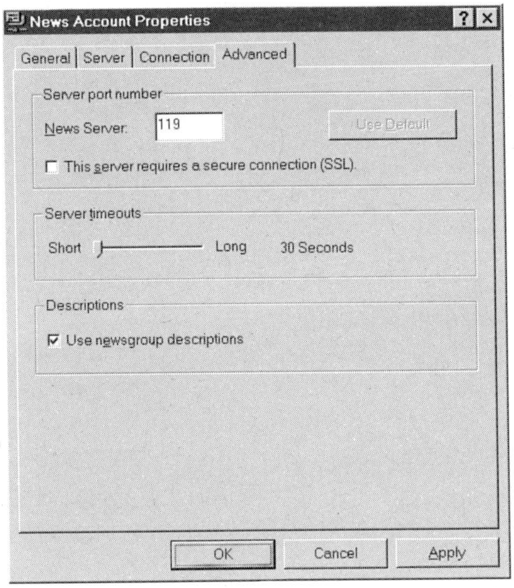

10. If you experience timeout errors when connecting to your news server, increase the Server Timeouts slider to a longer duration. By default, 30 seconds should be adequate for most connections, but your news server may be excessively busy processing other requests. There is no harm in adjusting the slider to a long timeout value, but you may grow impatient as Outlook Express waits the length of time for a server response when the server is down for any reason.
11. If you are unfamiliar with UseNet News newsgroups, check the Use Newsgroup Descriptions check box. When checked, Outlook Express News will download a description file from the news server and use it when displaying newsgroup names. The descriptions are more informative when searching for newsgroups covering a desired topic. Be warned, however, as the description file can be quite lengthy and take a long time to download.
12. Click OK to dismiss the News Account Properties dialog box.

Viewing and Subscribing to Newsgroups

To begin your UseNet News experience, you start with the list of available newsgroups. To download and display the list of newsgroups from the news server, select the newsgroup account and choose Tools, Newsgroups or click the News Groups toolbar button (if you haven't downloaded groups for a server, you will be prompted to download them when you select the news group account). With more than 10,000 newsgroups, the download might take a few minutes. You can watch the status of the download in the Downloading Groups dialog box, as shown in Figure 21.46.

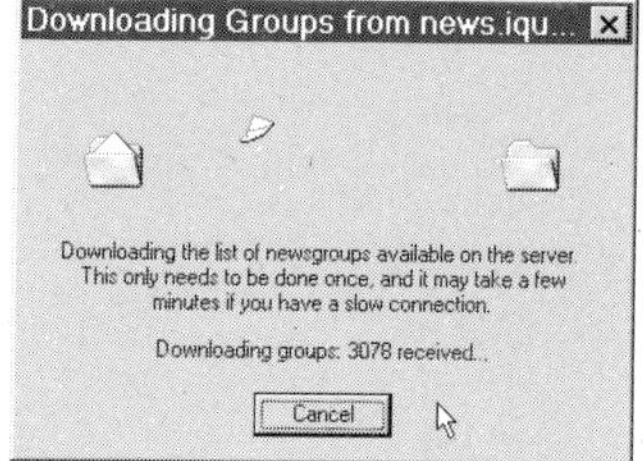

FIG. 21.46
Monitor the download of newsgroup information.

Fortunately, you do not have to download the list of newsgroup each time you participate in UseNet News—Outlook Express will watch for new groups automatically and notify you when they become available (new newsgroups are created every week). If you need to force Outlook Express to redownload the newsgroup list, click Reset List. Once loaded, Outlook Express displays the list in the Newsgroups dialog box, as shown in Figure 21.47.

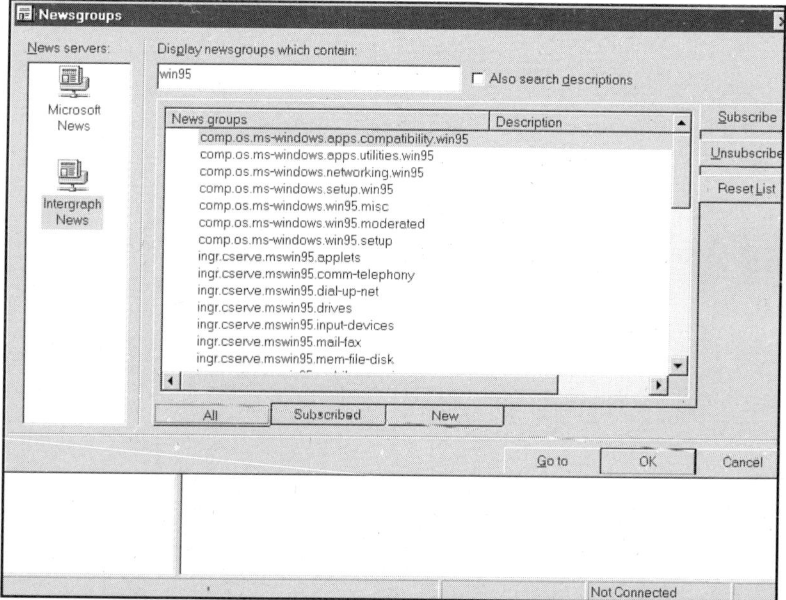

FIG. 21.47
Use the Newsgroups dialog box to find the topics in which you are interested.

TIP If you have difficulty understanding which newsgroups cover which topics, you can configure Outlook Express to download newsgroup descriptions, too, but this requires support from your news server.

In the Newsgroups dialog box, you can choose to see all the newsgroups available, only the new ones since you last connected, or the newsgroups to which you have *subscribed.* When you subscribe to a newsgroup, you simply mark it so that Outlook Express will monitor it for you. Also, Outlook Express will remember which newsgroups you have subscribed to between sessions, so you can return to your favorite discussions quickly.

Finding and Subscribing to a Newsgroup In the early days of UseNet, reading through the long list of newsgroups and locating one for a particular topic was a daunting task. To make your search easy, Outlook Express provides a capability to filter through the newsgroup list and descriptions. Follow these steps:

1. Click the News Groups toolbar button or choose Tools, Newsgroups to open the Newsgroups dialog box.
2. Choose the All tab in the Newsgroups dialog box.
3. Type a search keyword in the Display Newsgroups Which Contain text box. Outlook Express displays the newsgroups that match your keyword. Check the Also Search Descriptions check box to also search the newsgroup descriptions—if your server provides them—for your keyword. To change the list sorting, click the News Group or Description column header.
4. To subscribe to a newsgroup, select it in the News Groups list and click Subscribe. When you subscribe to a newsgroup, it appears with a small newspaper icon next to it. You can see a shortened list of only your subscribed-to newsgroups on the Subscribed tab. To unsubscribe from a newsgroup, select it in the list and click Unsubscribe.
5. Once you are finished selecting your newsgroups, click OK to dismiss the Newsgroups dialog box.

If you turn on View, Folder List, Outlook Express will list each newsgroup you subscribe to under the news account name. You can also select the news account and see a listing of each subscribed newsgroup, as well as the state of each. Like most of the Outlook Express views, you can change the columns listed.

If you are unfamiliar with UseNet News, start with the following newsgroups. They are purposely set up for new users, and can help you understand how to use the UseNet:

- *news.announce.newusers.* Learn about the UseNet
- *news.newusers.questions.* Ask basic UseNet questions
- *misc.test.* Practice posting your own articles

Other popular newsgroups include:

- *news.answers.* View the Frequently Asked Questions (FAQ) articles of all newsgroups
- *comp.windows.ms.* For Microsoft Windows information
- *rec.humor.funny.* A moderated newsgroup with jokes and funny stories

Viewing a Subscribed Newsgroup Once you have subscribed to a newsgroup, you can see the available articles by selecting the newsgroup in the folder list. Within seconds, Outlook Express will connect to the news server and retrieve the list of available articles (see Figure 21.48).

FIG. 21.48
Select a newsgroup to see the available articles.

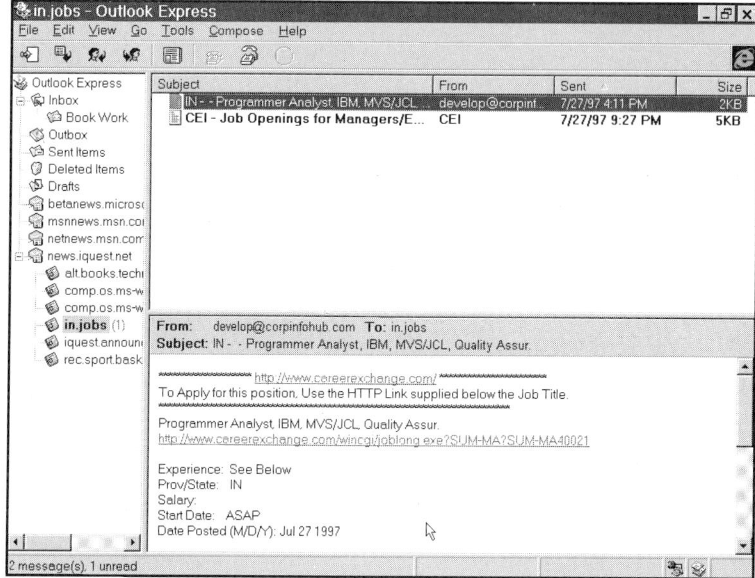

To sort the article list, click a column header, or choose View, Sort By and select Subject, From, Sent, or Size. If one of these columns is not visible, you can configure Outlook Express to show it.

Outlook Express can also group articles into *threads*, where articles are listed together with their related responses. Threads allow you to follow a discussion without having to read unrelated articles in between. To turn on thread organization, choose View, Sort By, Group Messages By thread.

You expand or collapse threads by clicking the plus (+) or minus (-) sign next to the first article. Alternatively, select the message and choose View, Expand or Collapse. If you prefer to see threads always expanded, you can configure Outlook Express to never collapse them (see "Customizing How You Read News," later in this chapter.)

NOTE Outlook Express tracks threads by the subjects of articles. If you post a response to an article and change the subject line, you will start a new thread.

Viewing a Newsgroup Without Subscribing Outlook Express allows you to view the articles in a newsgroup without actually subscribing. To do so, follow these steps:

1. Open the Newsgroups dialog box by clicking the News Groups toolbar button, or choosing Tools, Newsgroups.
2. Click the All tab and locate a newsgroup you want to see in the list.
3. Select the newsgroup and click Go To.
4. Outlook Express adds the newsgroup to the folder list, but uses a dim icon to indicate that you have not subscribed to it.
5. View the articles in the list as you would normally.
6. If you decide to subscribe to the newsgroup, right-click the newsgroup name in the folder list and choose Subscribe to this Group, or choose Tools, Subscribe to this Group.

When you close Outlook Express, any newsgroups you have viewed but have not subscribed to will be forgotten.

Unsubscribing from Newsgroups If you have grown disinterested in a newsgroup, you can unsubscribe from it. To unsubscribe from a newsgroup, right-click it in the folder list and choose Unsubscribe from This Group, or select the newsgroup and choose Tools, Unsubscribe from This Group.

Alternatively, click the News Groups toolbar button or choose Tools, Newsgroups to display the Newsgroups dialog box. Click the Subscribed tab and select the newsgroup you want to unsubscribe from and click Unsubscribe.

Viewing News Articles

Outlook Express displays the articles in the order that they arrived at the news server. Sometimes this can be confusing, because you may see a response to an article that has not appeared yet. The reason for this is that UseNet News works in a store-and-forward manner. Articles hop from news server to news server along the Internet, and often arrive out of sequence. For example, if you are in Florida, you will likely see articles posted by users in Georgia well before articles posted by users in California.

To read an article, double-click it in the article list, or select it and choose File, Open. The article displays in a separate window. The subject of the article appears in the title bar of the window.

Newsgroup articles have a format similar to e-mail messages. You can see the article subject, the author's name, the newsgroups in which the article was posted, and the date the article was posted.

To view the previous article in the list, click the Previous toolbar button, or choose View, Next, Previous Message. Click the Next toolbar button to read the next article in the list, or choose View, Next, Next Message. If you want to jump to the next unread article, unread thread, or unread newsgroup, choose View, Next, and click Next Unread Message, Next Unread Thread, or Next Unread Newsgroup.

TIP Outlook Express identifies World Wide Web links and e-mail addresses in UseNet articles. Use the links to jump directly to a Web site (using your default Web browser) or send e-mail to other users.

Using the Preview Pane For fast and efficient reading of newsgroups, you can use the Preview Pane, rather than displaying each article in a separate window. The Preview Pane does not prevent you from opening a message in a separate window.

To change the settings for the Preview choose View, Layout. This opens the Layout dialog box. To turn off the Preview Pane, uncheck Use Preview Pane. With the Preview Pane on, you can select to see it Below Messages or Beside Messages. With Show Preview Pane Header selected, the sender and subject of the message are shown in the divider bar of the preview pane. When done, click OK.

You can adjust the size of the Preview Pane by dragging the border splitter bar. If the article has attachments, you will see a paperclip icon in the top-right corner of the Preview Pane. Click the paperclip icon and choose the attachment to open.

Decoding News Articles Occasionally, you may encounter an article that looks completely like gibberish—the text of the message is a jumble of alphanumeric characters which do not seem to follow any known language constructs. Well, you may have downloaded a specially coded article, encoded using *ROT13*. ROT13 is short for Rotated by 13 letters—all **A**s became **M**s, **B**s became **N**s, and so on. The entire alphabet is rotated by 13 letters. The author purposely encoded the article this way to prevent someone from *accidentally* reading it—the article may include some offensive wording, for instance. Read the subject line first to see if you want to read the article—it will provide some clues as to the decoded content.

If you encounter a ROT13 article, and agree that you want to read it, double-click the article to open it in a separate window, then choose Edit, Unscramble (ROT13). Outlook Express will reverse the ROT13 encoding such that you can read the article as you normally do.

Viewing News Attachments Sometimes an article includes a file attachment. You can view file attachments in news the same manner you can in mail.

However, some large files are split up in smaller parts and posted in several articles. If you find a group of articles, each referencing Part 1, Part 2, and so on, in the subject line, Outlook Express can automatically combine them and decode the large attachment. Select each of the articles (all must be present) in the article list using the Shift-click and Ctrl-click procedure, then choose Tools, Combine & Decode. Outlook Express will combine the messages into one large message, then decode the file attachment and allow you to save it or open it.

Sorting News Articles The easiest way to sort the article list is to click the column heading at the top of the list. For example, to sort the list by date sent, click the Sent column heading. Click the column heading again to reverse the direction. Alternatively, choose View, Sort By and select the sorting order you want.

Searching for Newsgroup Articles Outlook Express provides a simple tool for finding newsgroup articles. To locate articles that match your criteria, choose Edit, Find Message. The Find Message dialog box appears, as shown in Figure 21.49.

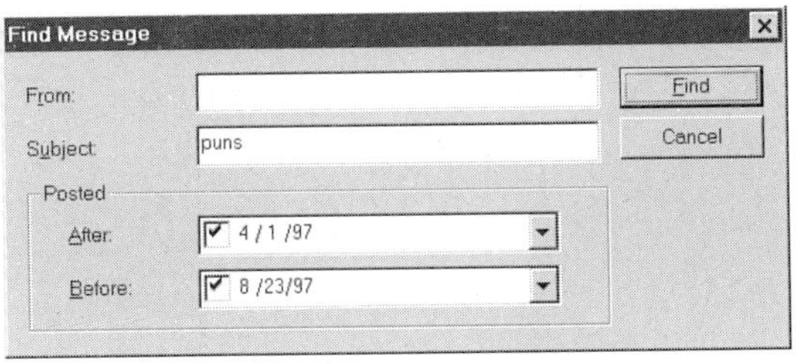

FIG. 21.49
Use the Find Message dialog box to locate interesting articles.

Specify the criteria for your search. You can combine criteria to be more specific. The following is a list of the criteria supported:

- *From*. Type the author's name or address in the text box.
- *Subject*. Type some text of the article subject to find.
- *Posted After*. Check the check box and specify the date of when you think the article was posted. Outlook Express will save time by not searching for articles earlier than the date defined.
- *Posted Before*. Check the check box and specify the latest date you think the article was posted. Outlook Express will save time by not searching for articles later than the date defined.

Once you specify the search criteria, click Find. Outlook Express will search the newsgroup for the first article that matches. Press F3, or choose Edit, Find Next to locate the next matching article.

Viewing Headers of News Articles Sometimes it is useful to see the full set of news headers that accompany a message. There is actually some interesting information there, such as the author's organization, and the path the article took through the Internet to arrive at your news server.

To see the article headers, double-click the article to open it in a separate window. Then, choose File, Properties to display the article properties dialog box. Click the Details tab (see Figure 21.50) to see the article headers. If you want to see the raw, unformatted article source, click Message Source.

The messages' header includes items such as the Return-Path to let Outlook Express know who sent the e-mail, and the Date of the message. These headers are used by Outlook Express to process your mail.

Using Newsgroup Filters Once you become familiar with UseNet News, you may want to configure Outlook Express to avoid showing you articles that you do not want to see. Having fewer articles to wade through makes your UseNet News sessions more productive, and allows you to read more newsgroups in the same amount of time. In Outlook Express, you use Newsgroup Filters to prevent the display of articles that meet your criteria. You can filter articles by author, subject, length, or the age of the article. Outlook Express will not download or display filtered articles.

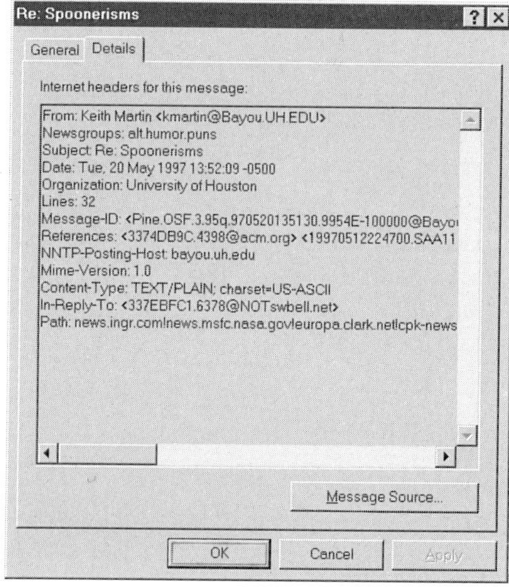

FIG. 21.50 Article headers can reveal interesting information, such as the path the article took through the Internet.

To filter newsgroup articles, follow these steps:

1. Choose Tools, Newsgroup Filters. The Group Filters dialog box displays, as shown in Figure 21.51.

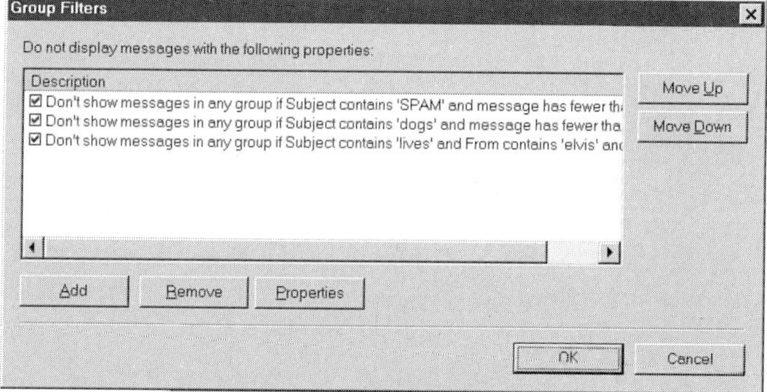

FIG. 21.51 Group Filters let you avoid articles that do not interest you.

2. Click Add. The Properties dialog box displays, as shown in Figure 21.52.
3. In the Group(s) option list, select the newsgroups to which you want this filter to apply. Alternatively, you can select All Servers, or make your criteria match only certain news servers if you have multiple servers defined.
4. In the From text box, type an author's name or e-mail address that you want to avoid. If you have the author's name and e-mail address recorded in the Address Book, you can click the Address Book button to select the author's record.

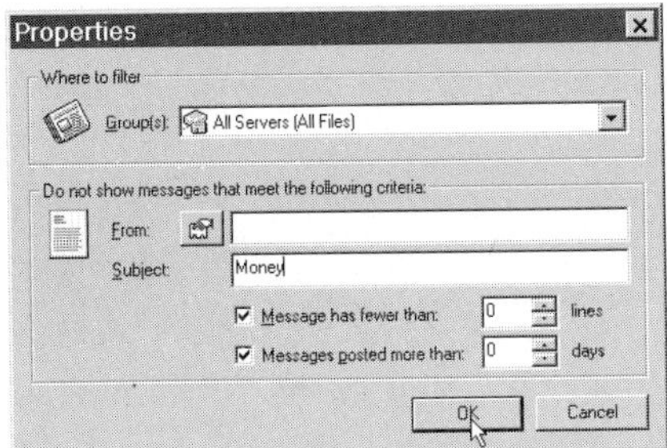

FIG. 21.52
Define your criteria of which articles to skip.

5. In the Subject text box, type some text of article subjects that you want to avoid. Be sure to choose specific text, as Outlook Express will not download articles that match the text. You probably would not want to use commonplace words, such as *the*, *of*, and so on.
6. If you want to avoid small articles, check the Message Has Fewer than N Lines check box, and select the minimum number of lines you want to read.
7. To avoid old articles, check the Messages Posted More than N Days check box, and select an acceptable article age. Outlook Express will avert articles not posted in the time frame chosen.
8. Click OK to dismiss the Properties dialog box and add your new criteria to the filter list.

Since some filters may affect others, it is important to pay attention to the ordering. Newsgroup filters process in a top-down fashion. Select a filter description and click Move Up or Move Down to change the processing order.

If you want to disable a filter without deleting it, uncheck the check box beside the filter description. To delete a filter, select it and click Remove. To edit a filter, select it and click Properties.

When you encounter a newsgroup that includes articles that are filtered, Outlook Express will notify you with a warning, as shown in Figure 21.53.

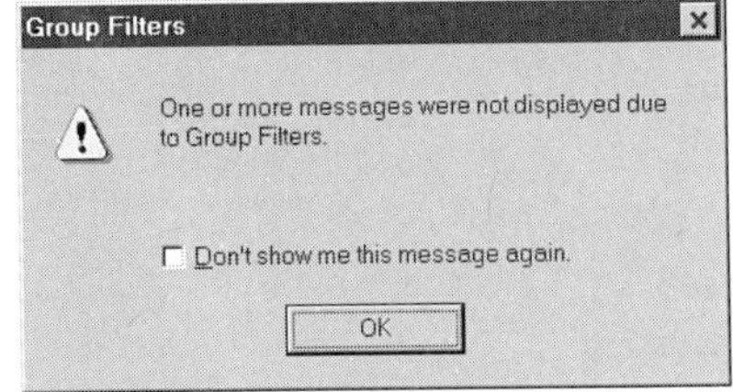

FIG. 21.53
Outlook Express notifies you when your filters are at work.

Reading News Articles Offline

If you pay for your time online, or you will be off the Net for a while (such as when you travel), you may want to read newsgroups offline. You can command Outlook Express to download article headers, whole newsgroups, or only specific articles. Then you can disconnect from the network and read the articles offline, saving you money for access time, or filling the time as you wait to reach your destination. There are several ways to identify the articles you want to read offline, as follows:

- If you only want to mark a newsgroup such that only new headers are downloaded, select the newsgroup in the newsgroup list and choose Tools, Mark for Retrieval New Headers. Outlook Express displays a single down-arrow icon next to the selected newsgroup.
- To mark an entire newsgroup for download, select the news server in the folder list. Then, select the newsgroup you want to download in the newsgroup list and choose Tools, Mark for Retrieval All Messages. A double down-arrow icon appears next to the selected newsgroup.
- To download only new articles in a newsgroup, select the newsgroup in the newsgroup list and choose Tools, Mark for Retrieval New Messages. A starred down-arrow icon appears next to the selected newsgroup.
- To unmark a newsgroup, select it and choose Tools, Mark for Retrieval, Unmark.
- To mark an individual article for download, right-click the article in the article list and select Mark Message for Download, or choose Tools, Mark for Retrieval, Mark Message.
- To mark an entire thread for download, select the original article and choose Tools, Offline, Mark Thread for Retrieval.
- Choose Tools, Mark for Retrieval, Mark All to download all of the articles in the article list.
- To unmark an article, select it and choose Tools, Mark for Retrieval, Unmark.

Once you have marked the newsgroups and articles you want, you must instruct Outlook Express to download them. First, get connected to the network if you are not already. You can choose Tools, Offline, Dial to initiate the connection to your server. Next, *synchronize* with your news server to download the marked items. There are several choices of synchronization, as follows:

- Choose Tools, Download All to download everything you have marked.
- Choose Tools, Download '*news server name*' to download the items marked for download on that specific server or account.
- If you are in an article list, choose Tools, Download This Newsgroup to download marked items in this newsgroup only.
- If you have limited the number of headers downloaded to a finite number to save time, choose Tools, Get Next N Headers, where N is the number of headers to download, as defined in your News Options.

Posting News Articles

As you wind your way through UseNet newsgroups, you will encounter many opportunities to offer your own opinions, ask a question, or help a fellow reader with an answer. To actively participate in a newsgroup, you must send, or *post,* your opinions, questions, or answers to the news server.

Posting New Articles in Newsgroups When you post an article, you identify which newsgroup in which to post the article. In fact, you can post an article to several newsgroups at once. This is called *cross-posting.* Be careful when cross-posting articles to newsgroups that do not relate to your article, otherwise you may be *slammed, flamed,* or chastised, for wasting bandwidth.

To post a new article, follow these steps:

1. Select the newsgroup to which you want to post a new article and click the Compose Message toolbar button, or choose Compose, New, Message. The New Message window opens, as shown in Figure 21.54.

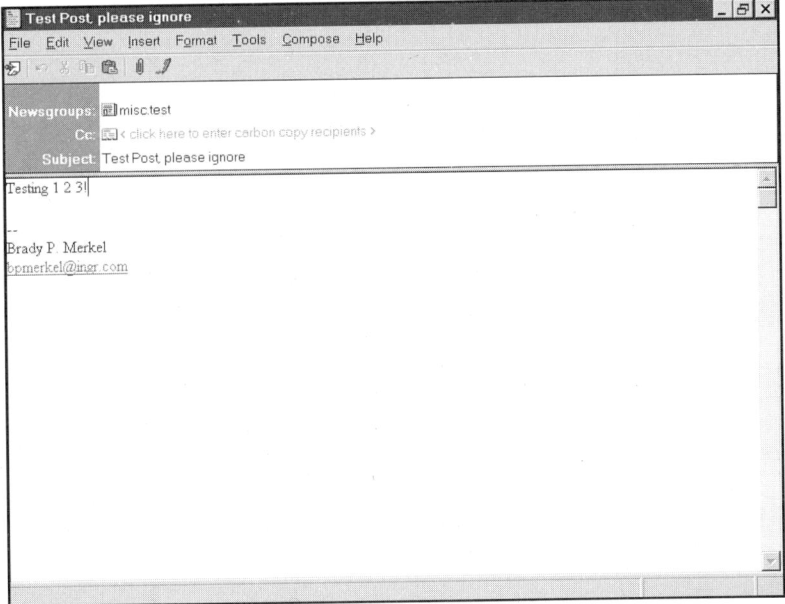

FIG. 21.54
Type a newsgroup, a distinct subject, and compose your new article.

2. Type the name of the target newsgroup in the Newsgroups text box. If you want to post your message to multiple newsgroups, type in the newsgroup names, separated by commas. If you are unsure of the newsgroup names, click the newspaper button beside the Newsgroup text box. This displays the Pick Newsgroups dialog box, as shown in Figure 21.55.

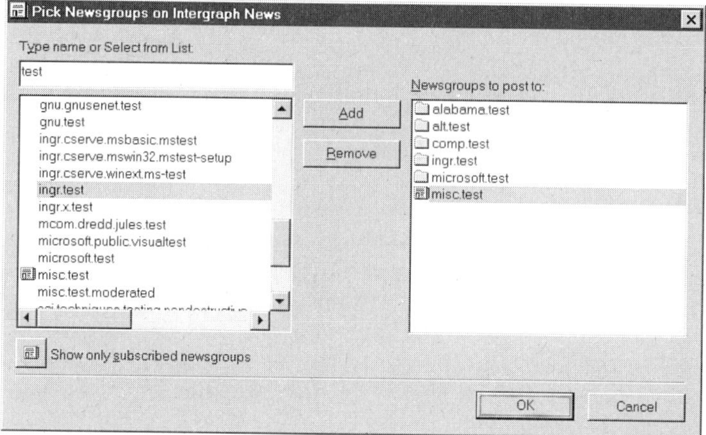

FIG. 21.55
Choose the newsgroups to which you want to post your article.

In the Pick newsgroups dialog box, select the newsgroup names from the list on the right and click Add. If you want to see all of the newsgroups and not just those that you subscribe to, click Show Only Subscribed Newsgroups. To remove a newsgroup from your Newsgroups To Post To list, select it and click Remove. Click OK once you have chosen the newsgroups to which you want to post your new article.

3. If you want to send a Carbon Copy of the article to an e-mail recipient, enter the name or e-mail address in the Cc text box. You can also select recipients from the Address Book by clicking the button beside the Cc text box.
4. Enter the subject of your article in the Subject text box. For new articles, select a subject that is brief and distinct. UseNet users are more likely to read your article if they notice your subject.
5. Type the text of your article in the area provided. You can also compose your article with HTML formatting, but that is not recommended as many news readers cannot view HTML-formatted articles.
6. If you want to attach files to your article, click the Insert File toolbar button, or choose Insert, File Attachment. In addition, you can include the text from a file—choose Insert, Text From File and browse for the file you want.
7. Choose Tools, Spelling to check your spelling, then click the Post Message toolbar button to submit your article to the world.

NOTE Many news servers have a limitation on the allowed size of an individual article. If your article is long, or you attach a large file to your article, you can configure Outlook Express to split it into multiple smaller articles.

In a few minutes, your news server will list your article along with others in the same newsgroup. To see your article, go to the newsgroup you posted to Tools, Get Next N Headers. When your article appears in the list, double-click it and read it as others would.

NOTE It is a good idea to "lurk" (Netspeak for reading articles but not posting any) in a newsgroup for a while before posting. Think of it as being at a party where you do not know anyone. You might prefer to stand around and observe before joining in a conversation. Also, before asking a question in a newsgroup, consult the group's Frequently Asked Questions (FAQ) article. You may find your answer there.

TIP To practice posting articles, use the **misc.test** newsgroup. Do not expect a reply from other users, though—no one reads that newsgroup regularly. It is used only for practice and testing news software.

Replying to Newsgroup Articles As you read an article, you will likely want to post a response back to the newsgroup, e-mail a response directly to the author, or forward the article to another e-mail recipient.

To respond to an article, first make sure you open the article in a separate window. Then, click the Reply To Group toolbar button. Outlook Express opens a new article window and automatically copies the original article into your article. To avoid wasting bandwidth, remove any of the original text that does not pertain to your response. Compose your response, check your spelling, and click the Post Message toolbar button.

TIP When you post a response to an article back to a newsgroup, keep the subject the same, prefixed with the letters "Re:". Some UseNet users employ news software that orders related articles by subject into threads. If you change the subject, they may miss your article.

Canceling an Article After You Have Posted It to a Newsgroup Sometimes you may post an article to a newsgroup and want to go back and remove the article from circulation. A good example of this is if you post something for sale, and you want to remove, or cancel the article after you have sold the item.

As you read articles, Outlook Express knows when you read one you posted. If you want to cancel an article you posted, right-click the article in the article list and choose Cancel, or select the article in the article list, and choose Compose, Cancel Message. Outlook Express will inform the news server that you want the article removed. The news server will, in turn, inform all subsequent news servers to remove the article. Within a few days, your article will have been removed from every news server the world over.

Compacting News Folders to Reclaim Disk Space Outlook Express stores all downloaded headers and articles in cache files on your PC. After a while, especially if you read many newsgroups, the local disk usage can become quite high. Since most news servers expire articles frequently, Outlook Express will automatically rebuild your cache files when you connect, and keep the headers and articles that are still available on the server. Still, you can reclaim valuable disk space if you remove newsgroup headers and articles that you have read already. Follow these steps:

1. Select a news server and choose File, Clean Up Files to display the Local File Clean Up dialog box, as shown in Figure 21.56.

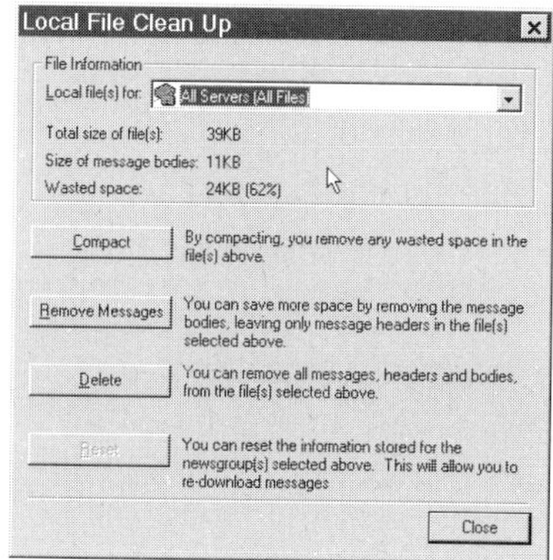

FIG. 21.56 Force an immediate purge of unneeded news cache files in the Local File Clean Up dialog box.

2. Select a news server, or newsgroup you want to clean up in the Local File(s) For option list. To help you understand which server or newsgroup is using the most space, read the file sizes below the option list. Select All Servers (All Files) to clean up all of the cache files.
3. Click one or all of the following buttons, depending on how much disk space you want to reclaim:
    - Click Compact to eliminate any wasted space in the cache files selected.
    - Click Remove Messages to dispose the article bodies, but keep the headers, in the cache files selected.
    - Click Delete to purge all articles and headers from the cache files selected. Use this option to regain the most space.
4. To configure Outlook Express to automatically clean up the cache files as you use Outlook Express, see "Customizing the Article Disk Cache," later in this chapter.

Customizing Outlook Express News

You can customize Outlook Express News to be more productive when reading and sending UseNet news. To customize Outlook Express News, choose Tools, Options.

NOTE Outlook Express Mail and News share many settings. The settings relating to mail were covered earlier in this chapter in "Customizing Outlook Express Mail."

Setting General News Options The General options that apply only to news are:

- Notify me if there are any new newsgroups that alert you when new groups are available on the server.
- Make Outlook Express my default news reader. This will cause Outlook to be launched when you click a news link in Explorer.

Customizing How You Post News Articles The News Options Send tab allows you to customize what Outlook Express does when sending a news article (see Figure 21.57).

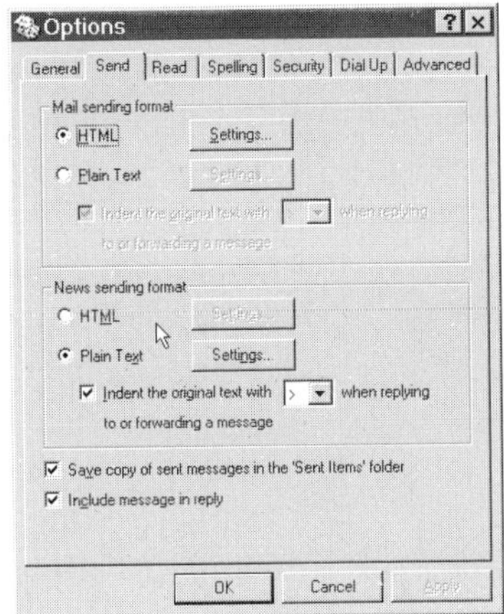

FIG. 21.57 Choose your preferred news-sending format in the Options Send tab.

- Check the When Posting, Save a Copy in 'Sent Items' Folder check box to retain a copy of each article you send. This is useful in the instance when you need to find when or what you posted to a specific newsgroup. Be forewarned that if you post many articles, your 'Sent Items' folder can become quite large and use up valuable disk space.
- Check the Include Message In Reply check box to copy an article's content into your post or e-mail reply. This way, news readers and mail recipients can the read the original article that prompted your reply.

You can also configure your preferred format for new articles you post.

- Choose the HTML option button if you want your articles to use the rich capabilities of the Hypertext Markup Language. Some of your readers may not be able to read HTML articles, as described in the warning in Figure 21.58. If you are sure you want to use HTML, click Yes. To avoid the warning again in the future, check the Don't Ask Me This Again check box before clicking Yes.
- If you include original articles in article responses, it is useful to indent the original article using some character before each line. This way, recipients can easily see which parts are from the original article, separate from your own comments. To prefix each original line with a special character, check the Indent With This Character > When Replying to a Newsgroup check box. If you want to use a different prefix character, such as a pipe or colon, choose the character from the option list provided.

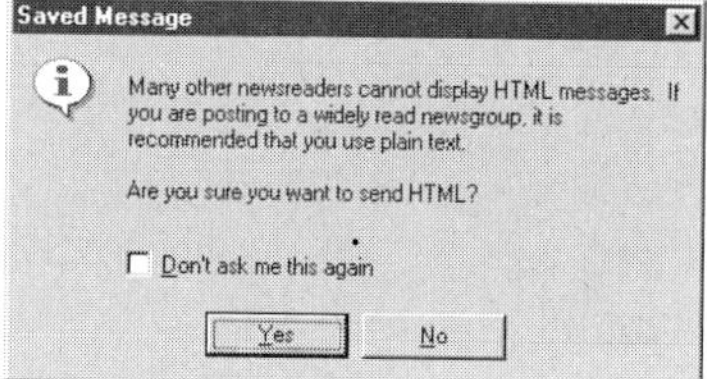

FIG. 21.58
Consider that many news readers cannot read HTML formatted messages.

Customizing How You Read News The News Options Read tab, as shown in Figure 21.59, allows you to customize how Outlook Express News behaves when you read news.

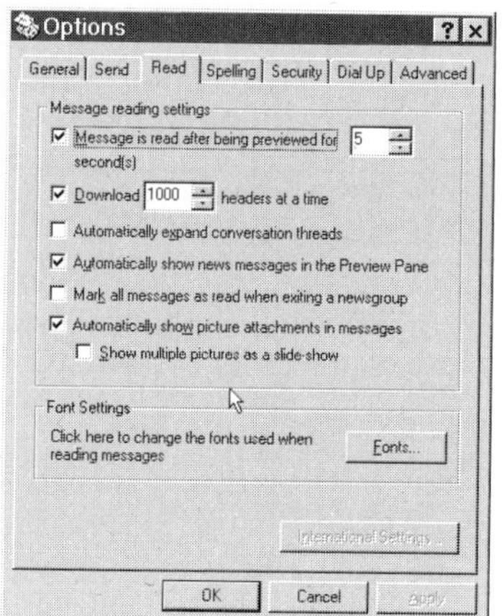

FIG. 21.59
Set your news reading preferences in the News Options Read tab.

- If you connect to your news server over a modem connection, you may prefer to limit how many news article headers Outlook Express will download. Some newsgroups may have thousands of articles in them, and downloading all of the article headers could take several minutes over a slow connection. Instead, check the Download N Headers At A Time check box, and adjust the number of headers preferred. If you enable this feature, Outlook Express News limits the maximum number to 1,000.

  If you prefer to download all article headers, uncheck the check box.
- Outlook Express can organize the list of available articles by *threads*. Each thread starts with an original article, and follows with each reply. Organizing the articles by thread allows you to quickly see an article and all of its replies without jumping to other topics in between. If you want Outlook Express News to display all article headers in each thread, check the Auto Expand Conversation Threads check box. Otherwise, you will only see the first article of each thread, and must open it manually to see the replies.
- If you use the Preview Pane to read articles without opening them in a separate window, you can ask Outlook Express News to mark the article as read when it has been previewed for a certain duration. To enable this feature, check the Message Is Read After Being Previewed for N Second(s) check box, and adjust the number of seconds preferred.

- Sometimes, you may quickly skim through a newsgroup reading only interesting articles, then jump to another newsgroup. When you leave a newsgroup, Outlook Express can automatically mark all articles in that newsgroup as being read, such that the newsgroup no longer displays in bold to signify unread articles. Check the Mark All Messages As Read When Exiting A Newsgroup check box if you want Outlook Express to enable this feature. Otherwise, Outlook Express News will continue to display the unfinished newsgroups and articles in bold until you explicitly read them, or manually mark them as having been read.
- Outlook Express News can fetch and display an article in the Preview Pane when you move the cursor onto it in the list. Unfortunately, this can result in unnecessary network traffic when you may not really want to read a specific article. If you connect to the news server by a modem, you may want to uncheck the Automatically Show Messages In The Preview Pane check box. Then, to preview an article, move the cursor to the article desired and press the spacebar to fetch and display it.
- Click Font Settings to indicate your preferred language, font typefaces and sizes for reading and posting articles.

Customizing the Spell Checker All of the spell checking options are identical to those for mail covered earlier in this chapter.

Customizing Your News Signature When posting news articles, it is useful to attach a concise footer, or signature, to every article. The signature serves to identify the article author, as well as other useful information about the author. To customize your own signature, select Tools, Stationery and select the News tab.

Here, you can add a news signature. This is identical to adding a signature for e-mail as discussed in, "Inserting a Signature in Outgoing Messages" earlier in this chapter. You can also add a vCard discussed in that same section.

Customizing the Article Disk Cache Outlook Express News saves newsgroup and article information on your local hard disk to improve performance when downloading and reading news. You can tune Outlook Express News to optimize disk space usage in the News Options Advanced tab, as shown in Figure 21.60.

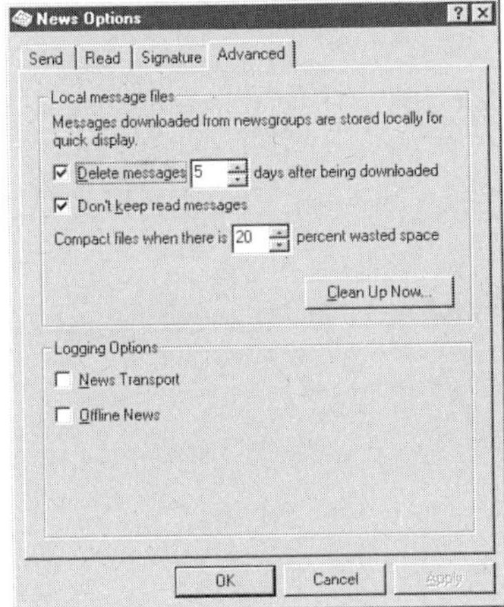

FIG. 21.60
Manage local disk usage of Outlook Express News in the News Options Advanced tab.

- To automatically remove locally cached articles, check the Delete Messages N Days After Being Downloaded check box, and adjust the number of days to your preferred duration. The number you choose depends on your news activity, as well as disk space availability.
- Check the Don't Keep Read Messages check box to remove locally cached articles once you have read them.
- Since Outlook Express News caches newsgroup headers and articles on your local disk, and some of this information is no longer needed, the result can be large files with unused areas, or wasted space within them. Outlook Express News can automatically compact the cache files and eliminate the wasted space. You can tune the level of wasted space that triggers Outlook Express News to compact the files. Adjust the percentage of wasted space allowed in the Compact Files When There Is N Percent Wasted Space counter. The default value of 20 percent is okay for typical usage.

  If you want to force Outlook Express to clean up the cache files immediately, click Clean Up Now.
- If you are experiencing problems when connecting to your news server, or downloading articles, check the Logging Options News Transport check box. You can use the resulting log session to share with your network administrator to debug the news transactions.

Customizing the Toolbar Like Outlook Express, Outlook Express News provides a toolbar for quick and easy access to the most useful news functions. To display the toolbar, choose View, Toolbar. The options for where to display the toolbar and text labels are the same as in the toolbar settings for mail.

Outlook Express allows you to customize the toolbar with your most needed buttons. Choose Customize, View, Layout, and click Buttons or right-click the toolbar and choose Buttons. The Customize Toolbar dialog box appears. Use this dialog box to display the toolbar functions you need. Select the buttons you want to display in the Available Buttons list, and click Add. Alternatively, select the toolbar buttons you want to hide in the Toolbar Buttons list and click Remove. You can also drag and drop the buttons to change their location. See Table 21.5 for the available toolbar buttons and their descriptions.

Table 21.5 Available Toolbar Buttons in Outlook Express News

Button	Action
Folder List	Display the list of your message folders.
Next Unread Message	Jump to the next unread article.
Next Unread Newsgroup	Jump to the first unread article in the next unread newsgroup.
Next Unread Thread	Jump to the beginning of the next unread thread.
Print	Print the selected article.

Button	Action
Save As	Save the selected article to a file.
Copy To	Copy the selected article to a folder.
Dial	Connect to your news server.
Hang Up	Disconnect from your news server.
Mark as Read	Indicate that the selected article is read.
Mark Thread as Read	Indicate that the whole thread of the selected article is read.
Mark All as Read	Indicate that all articles and newsgroups are read.
Mark Unread	Indicate that the selected article is unread.
Find	Locate an article.
News Groups	Display the Newsgroups dialog box.
Go to Outbox	Display the contents of your Outbox folder.
Go to Sent Items	Display the contents of your Sent Items folder.
Help	Get Help.
Language	Choose the preferred language.
Reply to Author	Compose a mail response to the author of the selected article.
Reply to Group	Compose a news article response to post to the newsgroup of the selected article.
Reply to All	Compose a mail response to all recipients and the author of the selected article.
Get Next Headers	Download the next batch of article headers in the current newsgroup.
Stop	Stop any current activity.
Mark for Download	Tag the selected newsgroup or article for downloading.
Unmark	Indicate that you do not want to download the selected newsgroup or article.
Download All	Download all of the articles you have marked for offline reading.
Download Account	Download the articles and groups marked for offline reading on this account.
Download Newsgroups	Download the articles in this group for offline reading.
Combine and Decode	Assemble a multipart article into one article and decode the attached file.

continues

Table 21.5 Continued

Button	Action
Unscramble	Display an article that has been scrambled.
Compose Message	Compose a new article.
Cancel Message	Indicate to the news server that you no longer want one of your articles to be posted.
Forward	Send the selected article to a mail recipient.

Once you have the toolbar buttons you need in the Toolbar Buttons list, select the functions and click Move Up and Move Down to organize the toolbar buttons into related groups. For additional visual organization, add a separator icon between grouped functions.

If you want to start all over and return the toolbar to the default layout, click Reset. Click Help if you need help customizing your toolbar.

When you are finished, click Close. Outlook Express will remember your settings.

Adding or Removing Columns in the Newsgroup List Outlook Express News provides an alternate set of column headings when you view the list of newsgroups on a news server. Customize the column headings in the same manner as you customize the article column headers. See Table 21.6 for the available columns and their descriptions.

Table 21.6 Available Newsgroup Columns in Outlook Express News

Column	Description
Name	The name of the newsgroup.
Description	The description of the newsgroup, if available.
Total	The total number of articles available in the newsgroup.
Unread	The number of articles you have not read yet in the newsgroup.
New	The number of new articles since you last read the newsgroup.
Last Updated	The date when the newsgroup was updated.

Adding or Removing Columns in the Article List Like the toolbar, you can choose which columns to display in Outlook Express News' list of articles. Choose View, Columns to display the Columns dialog box. Use this dialog box to display the columns desired. Select the columns you want to see in the Available Columns list, and click Add. Alternatively, select the columns you want to hide in the Displayed Columns list and click Remove. To change the order of the column appearance, select a column in the Displayed Columns list and click Move Up or Move Down appropriately. Columns are listed in left to right fashion. See Table 21.7 for the available columns and their descriptions.

When viewing a list of articles, click a column header to display the list in that column's ascending or descending order. For example, to list the articles in the order that they were posted, click the Sent column header. Click it again to reverse direction. Alternatively, you can right-click over a column header and choose Sort Ascending or Sort Descending.

If you want to start all over and return the column layout to a default layout, click Reset. To discard your changes, click Cancel. When you are finished, click OK. Outlook Express News will remember your settings.

Table 21.7 Available Article Columns in Outlook Express News

Column	Description
Subject	The subject of the article.
From	The sender of the article.
Sent	The date and time when the article was posted.
Size	The size of the article, in kilobytes.
Lines	The number of lines in the article.

A Note About "Netiquette"

In most newsgroups, there are no rules except those enforced by the opinion of group members. However, there are certain community standards for UseNet newsgroups that are generally agreed upon. These standards are referred to as *Netiquette,* short for Network Etiquette:

- Do not *spam*. This refers to the wholesale unsolicited posting of advertisements or self-aggrandizing announcements to many groups. The term *spam* comes from a Monty Python comedy skit that repeats the product name incessantly, in an attempt to make a sale.
- Do not post sexist, racist, or demeaning messages. Doing so will usually bring down the newsgroup's wrath on the poster, whose later postings will be ignored or *flamed.* To be flamed is to be disparaged in public, and is often accompanied with a barrage of e-mail that will fill your disk drive, or that of your Internet service provider.
- Avoid excessive crosstalk or chatting between two posters. Keep private discussions in e-mail.
- Do not post private e-mail to a newsgroup without permission of the original author.
- Keep articles short, without overly long quoting of the message to which you are responding. In Netspeak, long, rambling postings are flamed for wasting bandwidth.

CHAPTER 22

Using FrontPage Express and IE 4 Components

by Barry Gross, Ron Person, and Bob Voss

FrontPage Express

Learn how to use FrontPage Express, the easy-to-use HTML editor, to create and edit Web pages.

Task Scheduler

Find out how to use the Task Scheduler to schedule tasks to run automatically at predefined times.

NetMeeting 2.0

Find out how to use NetMeeting 2.0 to meet with other NetMeeting users to exchange data and communicate verbally or visually over a network.

NetShow

Learn how NetShow can enhance your experience on the Web, enabling you to view multimedia files as they download.

Microsoft has made integration with the World Wide Web a major part of their software strategy. They have made the Internet browser, My Computer, and Windows Explorer a single entity. The Active Desktop brings Webtop computing to your personal computer just as personal computers brought desktop computing. To make it even easier for your work to integrate with the Web, Microsoft has included several other software applications with the Internet Explorer 4 Suite.

FrontPage Express is a good HTML editor you can use to create or edit Web pages. It may become just as important to your future work as a word processor.

Those of us who work with virtual teams, who telecommute, or who do technical support over the phone will be glad to see the introduction of NetMeeting 2.0. NetMeeting enables you to share data, applications, and a chat session over the Internet. You can collaborate on documents even when team members are across the continent. And if you have the correct hardware, you can even include voice and video.

Anyone who has had to interrupt their work to go to a seminar will appreciate the third application, NetShow. It promises the ability to get training or seminars on demand. NetShow can be used for broadcasting audio, video, and illustrated audio (sound combined with sequenced images) over the Web or an intranet. Microsoft is already using it on their Web site to deliver multicast videos and on demand training.

NOTE This chapter was written using Platform Preview 2 (PR2) of Internet Explorer 4, FrontPage Express, NetMeeting 2, and NetShow for Windows 95. The final releases may differ from what is described here. At the time of this printing, Microsoft has announced that the final product name for "FrontPad" will be "FrontPage Express." Throughout this chapter, we will refer to the product by its final name, FrontPage Express, even though the screens in the book show the old name that was used in PR2.

Using FrontPage Express

Integrating Windows with the World Wide Web is a very important part of Microsoft's long-range strategy. As part of that strategy, the Internet Explorer 4 Suite and integrated shell components have made Windows very *Web-centric*. Even if you never plan on creating your own Web site as a computer user in this Web-centric system, you may need to create and edit Web pages as well as read them.

One situation where you may want to edit a Web page is if you are reading a Web page in Internet Explorer 4 and want to edit or annotate the page and then save it to your local drive or post it to the Web server. Just select Edit, Page in the Internet Explorer 4 toolbar and your HTML editor opens so you can edit the page.

Another situation that may become more common involves Web views, a new feature in Windows Explorer, installed when integrated shell components are installed. Web views display Web pages within Windows Explorer. These pages can even contain file, folder, and resource information. To customize how these Web pages appear, you will need an HTML editor.

Everyone may not have or need the power of a robust HTML editor like FrontPage 97 so Microsoft has included a free copy of FrontPage Express as part of the Internet Explorer 4 Suite. Based on the editor portion of Microsoft's FrontPage 97, FrontPage Express features a WYSIWYG (what-you-see-is-what-you-get) document display that makes document creation and editing simple and fast.

What Is FrontPage Express?

FrontPage Express is an HTML (Hypertext Markup Language) editor that enables you to create or modify Web pages. It includes tools for entering and editing text, images and hyperlinks, and for formatting the elements on your Web page. It also includes commands to help you insert tables useful for organizing data and links. You can also create forms with edit boxes, drop-down lists, and so forth to collect and then transmit data.

While you create Web pages visually, FrontPage Express handles all the underlying HTML coding automatically. FrontPage Express also provides a dialog box that allows you to view and edit the HTML code of your documents directly. FrontPage Express includes a Personal Home Page Wizard that helps you create your own home page. If you are familiar with Microsoft Word, it isn't much of a leap to start using FrontPage Express to create your own Web pages.

If you are familiar with Microsoft FrontPage 97 you will be able to use FrontPage Express immediately. Many people who do not need the extra features in FrontPage 97 will be able to create and edit simple Webs using FrontPage Express. FrontPage Express does not include the following major features found in FrontPage 97:

FrontPage Explorer	Manages Web connections and resources to help you manage and post an entire Web of pages.
ToDo List	A task list to help you manage the project of creating a Web.
Preview in Browser	Displays the page being edited in the current browser.
Advanced toolbars	Toolbars used for advanced features.
Image Editor	A graphics editor.
Clip art	A collection of clip art useful for images, buttons, and backgrounds.

To learn more about Microsoft FrontPage 97, read a copy of *Special Edition, Using FrontPage 97*, published by Que Corporation.

Starting FrontPage Express

FrontPage Express can be started from within Internet Explorer 4.0 or from the Start menu. To start FrontPage Express from the Windows 95 desktop, open the Start menu and choose Programs, Internet Explorer Suite, then FrontPage Express. The FrontPage Express window appears, as shown in Figure 22.1.

FrontPage Express can also be started by selecting Edit, Page in Internet Explorer 4.0. This opens Internet Explorer's current document in FrontPage Express for editing.

Creating a New Web Page

When you start FrontPage Express, it begins with a blank untitled normal page. You are given the opportunity to insert a title. The title appears in the browser's title bar when the Web page is active. It helps people identify the page's contents and purpose when they are searching for pages. Assign a title to your new HTML document by following these steps:

1. Choose File, Page Properties or right-click in the document window and choose Page Properties.
2. Select the General tab.
3. Enter your title in the Title text box (see Figure 22.2).

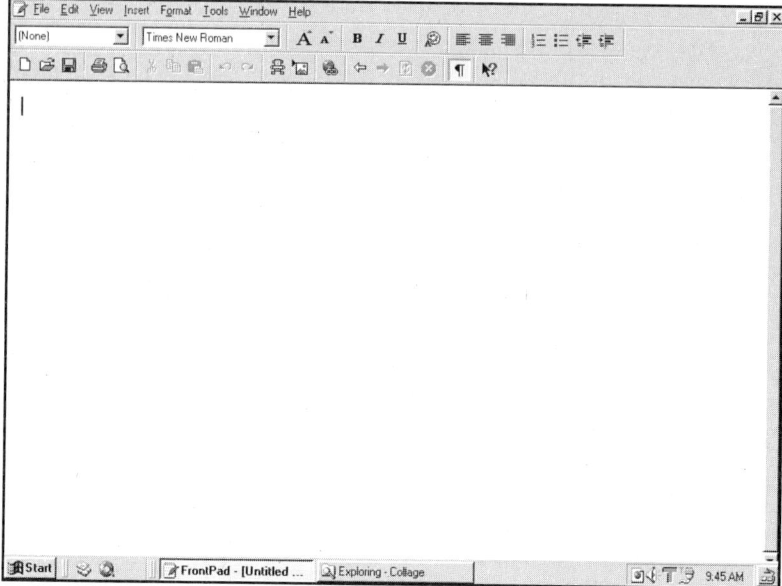

FIG. 22.1
FrontPage Express starts with a new blank document ready for you to begin editing.

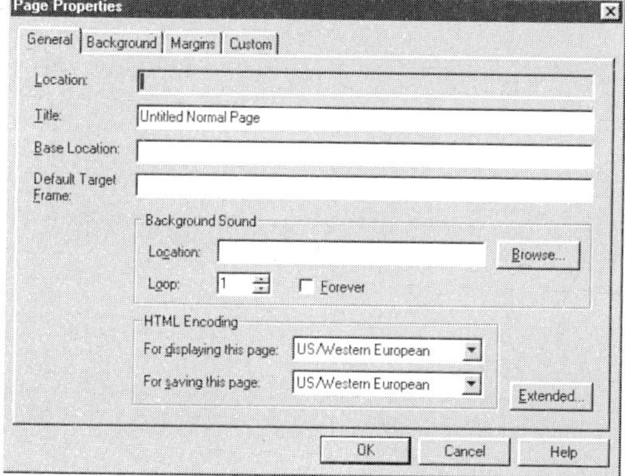

FIG. 22.2
Specify a title for your HTML document in the General tab of the Page Properties dialog box.

4. Click OK.

Once you have titled your new Web page, you can begin building the Web page by entering text, inserting images, tables, hyperlinks, and all the other components that make up a Web page. You can then format your page to give it the look and feel that you want it to have. The following sections guide you through the specific tasks that go into creating a Web page using FrontPage Express.

Formatting Text

Type text or copy and paste it from another document. Text in your HTML document can be formatted similarly to formatting text in a word processing document. To specify the font characteristics for your text, follow these steps:

1. Select the text that you want to format.
2. Choose Format, Font to open the Font dialog box (see Figure 22.3).

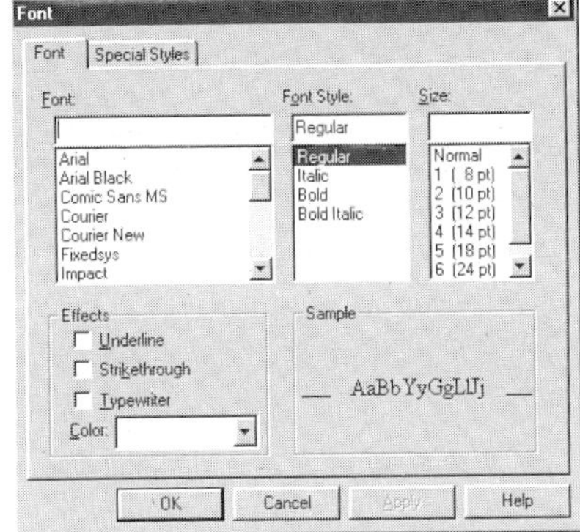

FIG 22.3
Use the Font dialog box to select the font, font style, and size of the selected text.

3. Select the font you want to use from the Font list box.
4. Select a font style in the Font Style box.
5. Select the size for the font in the Size list box.
6. If you want to format your text with additional effects, check the Underline, Strikethrough, or Typewriter boxes in the Effects group.

   The Typewriter option formats your text with a fixed-width font.
7. Select a color for your text from the Color drop-down list.

   You can preview all your selections in the Sample box and make changes before you close the dialog box.
8. When you have finished making your selections, click OK.

You can also do most of your text formatting using the FrontPage Express Format toolbar. The toolbar includes tools for selecting a font, increasing and decreasing font size, applying font styles, and choosing a font color.

In addition to the text formatting that you are used to using in word processing, there are several special styles that are unique to HTML documents. Each browser displays an HTML style using its own format settings. To access these styles, choose Format, Font and select the Special Styles tab (see Figure 22.4). There are nine options to assign special HTML text formatting, as described in the following table:

Table 22.1 Special Styles for Formatting HTML Text

Option	Function
Citation	For titles of books, films, and so on; typically displayed in italic.
Sample	For a sequence of literal characters; displayed in a fixed-width font.
Definition	For a word being defined; typically displayed in italic.
Blink	For creating text that blinks on and off.
Code	For computer code; displayed in a fixed-width font.
Variable	For displaying a variable. Instructs the reader to replace the variable with specific information; typically displayed in italic.
Bold	Displays bold text.
Italic	Displays italicized text.
Keyboard	For user keyboard entry; typically displayed in plain fixed-width font.
Vertical Position	Specifies superscripted or subscripted text. Set the amount to move text up or down in the By box. The Sample preview pane indicates the relative position of the text above or below a normal baseline.

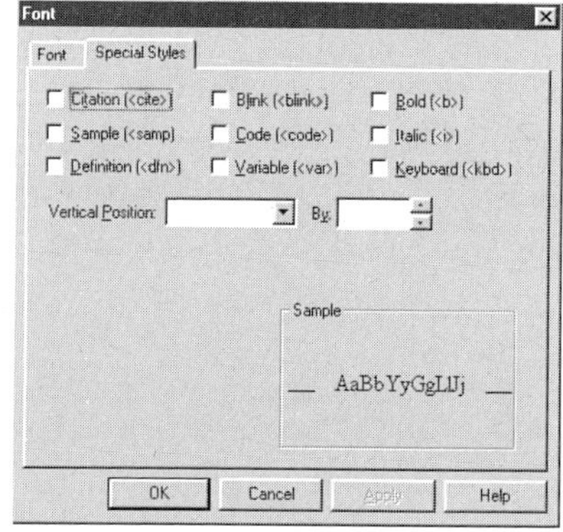

FIG. 22.4
Use the Special Styles tab of the Font dialog box to apply various HTML styles to the text in an HTML document.

Formatting Paragraphs

The HTML code used to create Web pages includes specific styles used for paragraphs. Each style appears in the way predefined by the browser displaying the Web page. These styles are used for different types of paragraphs ranging from body text, to definitions, to bulleted lists, and heading levels.

Each of these styles displays text as defined in the browser. Browsers do produce similar results, though. For example, Normal is used for body text; Bulleted List indents paragraphs and precedes them with a bullet; Numbered List indents paragraphs and numbers them; and Heading formats each line appropriate to its topic level.

To set the paragraph format, choose Format, Paragraph or right-click the paragraph and choose Paragraph Properties. The Paragraph Properties box, shown in Figure 22.5, appears.

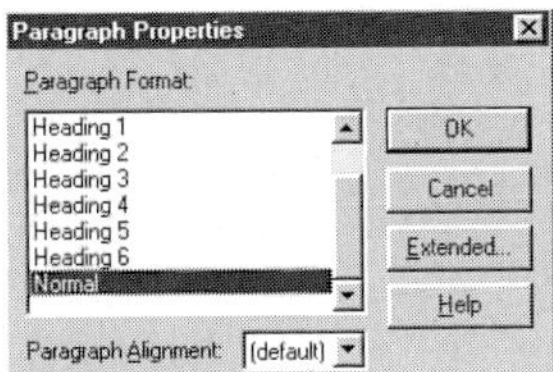

FIG. 22.5 The Paragraph Properties dialog box sets the predefined style for a paragraph.

You can select a paragraph format and set the paragraph alignment in the Paragraph Properties dialog box. Select one of the following paragraph formats from the Paragraph Format list box. (Not all of these options are always available. If you want to format a paragraph with a format that is not listed in the Paragraph Properties dialog box, use the drop-down style list on the formatting toolbar as described after the table. This drop-down list on the toolbar always lists all available styles.)

Paragraph Formatting Styles Format	Use
Address	Generally used to specify the author of a document, a way to contact the author (e.g., an e-mail address), or a revision date. It is usually the last item in an HTML document.
Bulleted List	Displays paragraphs with left indentation. Each paragraph preceded by a bullet. Bullet type can be changed.
Defined Term	Creates a left-aligned title line for the term being defined. Pressing Enter at the end of the defined term creates a new line with the Definition style.
Definition	A left-indented paragraph that follows a line with the Defined Term style. Pressing Enter creates the next paragraph with the Defined Term style.
Directory List	A form of bulleted list that is intended for use with short entries.
Formatted	The HTML "preformatted" style generates text in a fixed-width font and displays spaces or tabs that you enter. Use this style to create columns of numbers when you can't use a table.
Headings 1 through 6	Headings appear in different size and prominence. These are usually used to indicate a topic heading level in the document.

continues

continued

Paragraph Formatting Styles Format	**Use**
Menu List	A bulleted list for use with short entries.
Normal	Standard text in the body of your document.
Numbered List	Paragraphs display with left indentation and are sequentially numbered. Numbering style can be changed.

The Paragraph Alignment pull-down menu at the bottom of the Paragraph Properties dialog box enables you to set paragraph alignment of left, center, or right to display that paragraph in the corresponding screen location.

The FrontPage Express Format toolbar, shown in Figure 22.6, speeds the paragraph formatting process. Display the toolbar by clicking View, Format Toolbar if it is not already selected. Set paragraph alignment by clicking one of the three alignment icons immediately to the right of the color palette icon. Paragraph formatting can be set using the drop-down style menu at the far left of the Format toolbar. Format paragraphs with line numbering or bullets by clicking the Numbered List or Bulleted List buttons on the Format toolbar.

FIG. 22.6
Quickly change paragraph styles by choosing new styles from the Format toolbar.

Remove Bulleted List or Line Numbering format by reformatting the paragraphs with Normal style or clicking the bulleted list or numbered list button again.

Customizing the Bullet or Numbering Style

To change the numbering or bulleting of lists, choose Format, Bullets and Numbering to open the List Properties dialog box (see Figure 22.7). You can also open the dialog box by right-clicking a list in your HTML document and choosing List Properties.

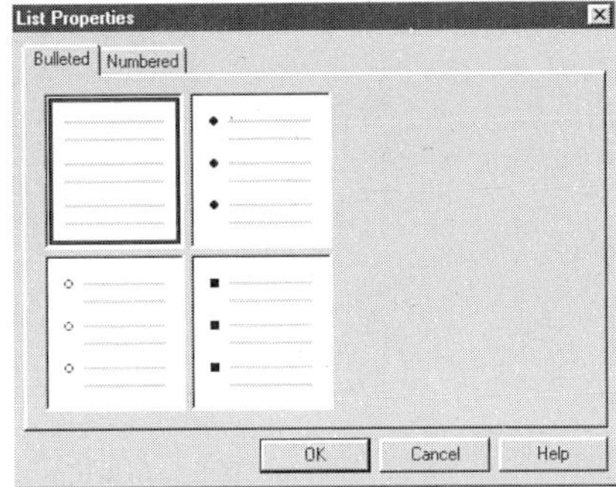

FIG. 22.7 Change the formatting of a list in the List Properties dialog box.

Selecting the Bulleted tab allows you to choose various bullet styles, while selecting the Numbered tab allows you to specify various numbering or lettering schemes as well as the number or letter to start from.

Trying to insert a normal paragraph in the midst of a numbered list can be frustrating. If you format the inserted paragraph as Normal, then the rest of the numbered list starts its numbering from 1, rather than the next number in the sequence. Prevent this by inserting your paragraph and giving it the Normal style. Format the paragraph where you want numbering to restart by clicking Format, Bullets and Numbering, select the Numbered tab, choose the number where you want the list to restart from the Start At box, and click OK.

Two additional tools on the Format toolbar are the Decrease Indent and Increase Indent tools, located at the far right of the toolbar. Each time you click one of these tools, you increase or decrease the indentation for the selected paragraph.

Creating Color or Image Backgrounds

You can add a color to the background of your Web page in FrontPage Express. If you don't specify a background, the viewer's browser will display your page with the default background (usually plain gray or white if someone hasn't changed the default). By specifying an image as your background, the browser will "tile" or repeat the image to fill the background area. The background image file should be in either the Graphical Interchange Format (GIF) or the Joint Photographic Experts Group (JPEG) file format. These are the formats widely supported by graphics-capable Web browsers.

Follow these steps to specify a color as your document's background:

1. Choose Format, Background or right-click in the document and choose Page Properties. Select the Background tab.
2. Click the Background color drop-down list to select a color. You can select one of the 16 standard colors (see Figure 22.8) or select Custom (from the bottom of the color drop-down list) to open the Color dialog box (see Figure 22.9).

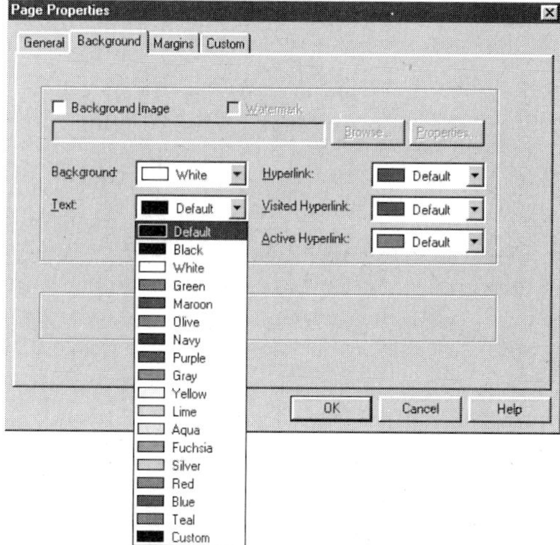

FIG. 22.8 Specify a background color for your HTML document in the Background tab of the Page Properties dialog box.

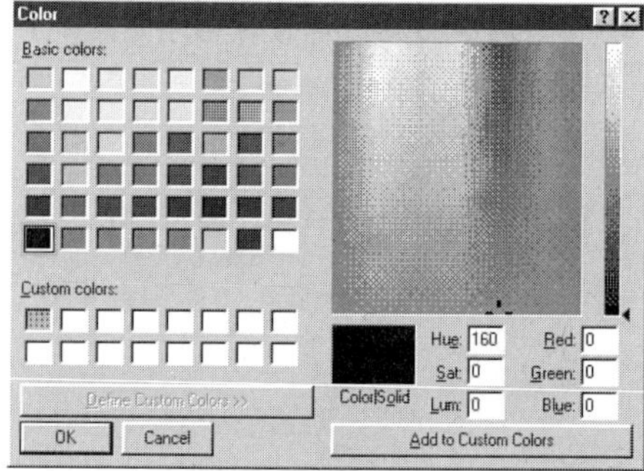

FIG. 22.9 You can create a custom color for your page background using the Color dialog box.

3. Click OK when you have finished your color selection.

Many Web pages use an image as their background. Images create a very custom impression behind the contents of a page. Be careful that you do not select a background image that makes reading difficult—most readers will not work to read the page. To specify an image as your document's background, follow these steps:

1. Choose Format, Background or select the Background tab in the Page Properties dialog box.
2. Select the Background Image checkbox.
3. Choose Browse to open the Select Background Image dialog box.
4. Select the Other Location tab to use a graphics file on your local drive or network. Select the From File option button and specify the path to your local background image file or choose Browse to locate the file on your hard disk. Select From Location and enter the URL to use a graphic file on your intranet.

   or

   Select the Clip Art tab to use backgrounds that come with FrontPage Express. Select Backgrounds from the Category list. Select the background you want.
5. Click OK to return to the Background tab.
6. If want the background to appear to stay fixed as the viewer scrolls down the page, select the Watermark check box.
7. Click OK.

You will now see your document set against the tiled image as a background.

You can copy background images from Web pages viewed in Internet Explorer by right-clicking the background and choosing Save Background As and specifying a file path on your hard disk. Copyright laws may apply so you should obtain permission from the Web site's owner before copying any images.

Adding Images to Your Web Page

FrontPage Express supports a wide range of image file formats for insertion into your Web page. Strictly speaking, there are only two image formats, GIF (.gif) and JPEG (.jpg), that are in wide use on the Web. However, FrontPage Express will automatically convert images from the following file formats:

- Bitmap (.bmp)
- TIFF (.tif)
- Windows metafile (.wmf)
- Sun Raster (.ras)
- PostScript (.eps)
- PCX (.pcx)
- Targa (.tga)

You can also resize images in the FrontPage Express document window by clicking the image to select it and then moving your mouse cursor over one of the resizing points at the borders of the image, where the mouse pointer changes to a two-sided arrow. Click and drag the mouse to change the dimensions of the image.

When you insert an image that is not in the GIF or JPEG format, FrontPage Express first converts it to the GIF format (for images with 256 or fewer colors) or the JPEG format (for images with more than 256 colors). When you save your HTML document, FrontPage Express will prompt you to save your image file in the new format if a conversion took place.

Generally speaking, the GIF format (technically GIF87a or GIF89a) is the appropriate format for simpler images that don't require more than 256 colors. The GIF89a format also has the ability to display images against a transparent background. The JPEG image format supports full 24-bit ("true") color and is required for more complex images and digitized photographs.

To insert an image into your HTML document from a file, follow these steps:

1. Choose Insert, Image or click the Insert Image icon in the center of the Standard toolbar to open the Image dialog box (see Figure 22.10).

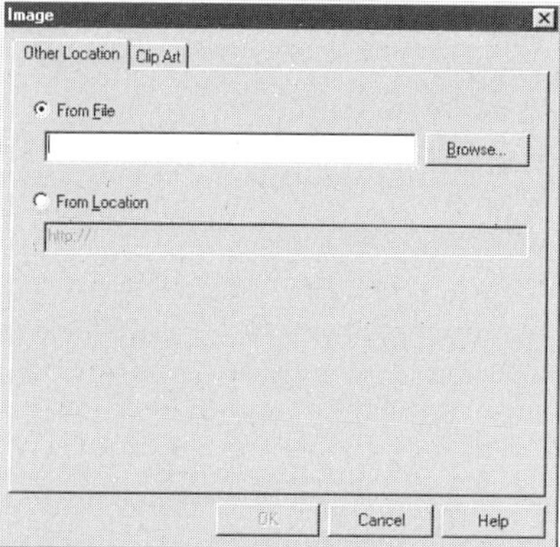

FIG. 22.10
Use the Image dialog box to insert images into your Web page.

2. Enter the path to the image file in the From File text box or choose the Browse button to locate the file on your hard disk.
3. Click OK.

Images that are objects in other open Windows applications can be inserted into a FrontPage Express document using drag-and-drop or copy-and-paste methods. When you save your HTML document, you will be prompted to save these image files along with your document.

You can insert clip art images from Microsoft Office into your HTML documents as follows:

1. Open Excel, Word, or PowerPoint.
2. Choose Insert, Picture, Clip Art.
3. Choose the desired category and picture and choose Insert.
4. While the image is selected, choose Edit, Copy to copy the image to the clipboard.
5. Open your FrontPage Express document window, position the insertion point, and choose Edit, Paste.

There are extensive resources on the Web where you can find artwork for your HTML documents. Following is a list of some of the better art sites that allow free downloading of image files. To save an image to your local drive from a Web page, right-click the image in Internet Explorer and choose Save Picture As and then specify a path on your hard disk.

ON THE WEB

Web resources of free art:

http://www.microsoft.com/gallery

http://www.clipart.com

http://the-tech.mit.edu/KPT/bgs.html

http://www.barrysclipart.com/mdex.html

http://sunsite.unc.edu/gio/iconbrowser/

http://home.eurocontrol.fr/~christin/index.html

http://www.hq.nasa.gov/office/pao/Library/photo.html

Controlling the Properties of an Image

Once an image is inserted into your Web page, you can customize its properties using the Image Properties dialog box. To customize an image, click the image to select it and choose Edit, Image Properties or right-click the image and choose Image Properties. The Image Properties dialog box appears (see Figure 22.11). There are three tabs in the Image Properties dialog box. The two tabs relating to graphics are summarized in the following sections.

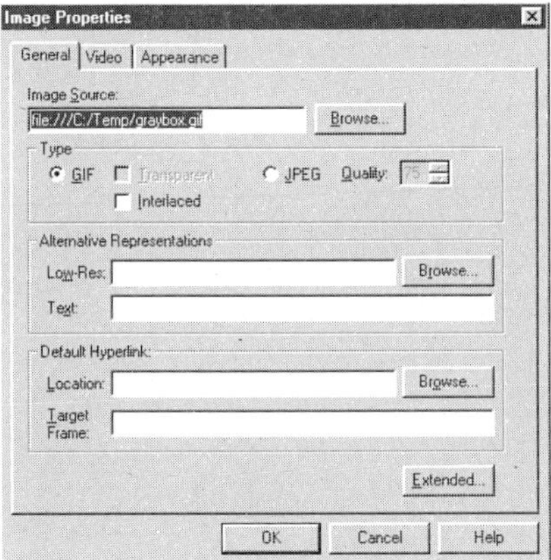

FIG. 22.11 The General tab in Image Properties dialog box.

General Tab The General tab enables you to change the path to a graphic, the graphics file type, or the resolution of the display. The Image Source field shows the file name of the image or its URL if the image is from the Web. Local file names are preceded by "file:///", while files located on a Web are preceded by "http://". If you pasted an image file from the clipboard that

FrontPage Express had to convert from a format other than GIF or JPEG, it will be assigned a temporary file name until you save your document at which time FrontPage Express prompts you to supply a file name for the image.

The GIF or JPEG radio buttons indicate the image's file type. You can easily convert between GIF and JPEG by merely selecting the other button. When you save an image in the JPEG format, you can specify a Quality setting in the range 1–99. The JPEG file format compresses the image file and a lower Quality setting will result in the image being saved with more compression, smaller file size, and a resulting loss of image detail.

For a GIF format image, the Transparent box will be checked if the image was created with a transparent background, an optional feature of the GIF89a format type. The Interlaced check box indicates that the image features *interlaced* loading, which directs Web browsers to load and display the image in four stages. This is especially useful for large image files that you include in your HTML document that may take a long time to download from the Web. The viewer will see the image load slowly in stages rather than having to wait for the entire image to download before seeing anything. You can check the Interlaced box and FrontPage Express will automatically convert your image to the GIF interlaced format.

You may want to specify a Low-Res Alternative Representation if the image file is large and you want the viewer's browser to display a smaller size image file while it waits to download the full-size image. Simply enter the path to the smaller size image file in this field. If the viewer's browser does not display images or has the image display disabled, it will display whatever text you enter in the Text Alternative Representation field in place of the image. Also, some browsers will display the text while the image is loading.

Appearance Tab Control the layout and size properties of your images in the Appearance tab of the Image Properties dialog box (see Figure 22.12).

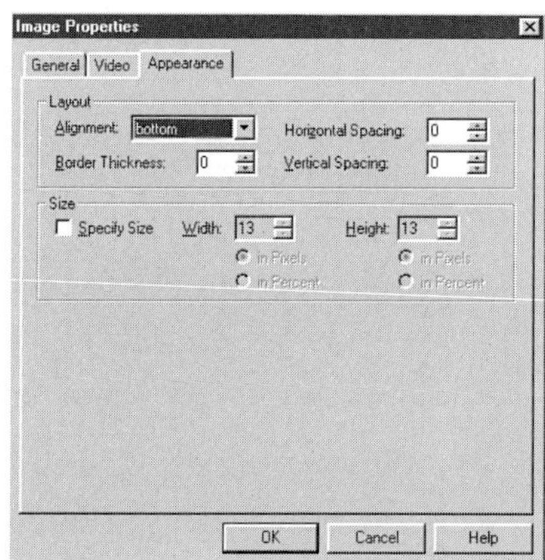

FIG. 22.12
Set the Layout and Size properties of your images in the Appearance tab of the Image Properties dialog box.

The pull-down Alignment menu enables you to specify how text placed next to your image will be aligned:

bottom	Align the text with the bottom of the image.
middle	Align the text with the middle of the image.
top	Align the text with the top of the image.
absbottom	Align the image with the bottom of the current line of text.
absmiddle	Align the image with the middle of the current line of text.
texttop	Align the top of the image with the top of the tallest text in the current line.
baseline	Align the image with the baseline of the current line of text.
left	Place the image in the left margin and wrap the text that follows down the image's right side.
right	Place the image in the right margin and wrap the text that follows down the image's left side.

Border Thickness allows you to specify the thickness in pixels of a black border to be applied around the image.

Horizontal and Vertical spacing allow you to specify the spacing in pixels between the image borders and the nearest text or adjacent image.

The Height and Width of the image is specified in pixels in the options in the Size box. You can select Specify Size to direct the viewer's browser to scale the image dimensions either in Pixels or in Percent of the browser window size.

Select Specify Size when you have large images with text that wraps around the image. This causes a viewer's browser to reserve the indicated space for the image and properly formats adjacent text while the image downloads. This prevents the surrounding text from jumping into place after the image downloads.

Inserting Horizontal Lines

You can easily create horizontal lines of various sizes and colors to provide separation between sections of your document. Choose Insert, Horizontal Line to add a horizontal line to your document. To adjust the properties of the line, right-click the line and choose Horizontal Line Properties to open the Horizontal Line Properties dialog box (see Figure 22.13). You can specify the line width either as a Percent of the browser window or as an absolute length in Pixels. The height of the line can be set in increments of one pixel. The alignment of the line can be set to Left, Center, or Right. The color of the line can be specified using the pull-down color menu, in a manner similar to setting Background color described previously. The last check box will direct the browser to display a Solid line rather than a shaded line if the default color is selected.

Early in the history of Web page design, horizontal lines or rules were used to separate sections of Web pages. Now most Web designers try to stay away from using horizontal lines. Instead, they attempt to structure content and reader-flow using tables and columnar structure.

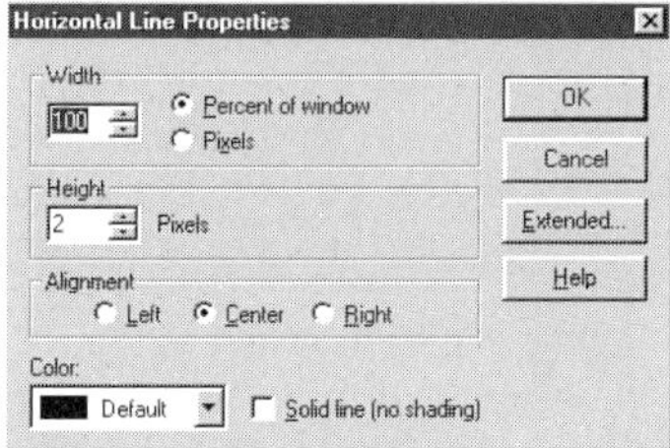

FIG. 22.13
Set Horizontal Line Properties in the Horizontal Line Properties dialog box.

Adding Scrolling Text

A marquee is a region of scrolling text that your document can use to draw the viewer's attention. Marquees are normally located in the top or bottom portion of documents. To add a marquee, follow these steps:

1. Choose Insert, Marquee to open the Marquee Properties dialog box (see Figure 22.14).

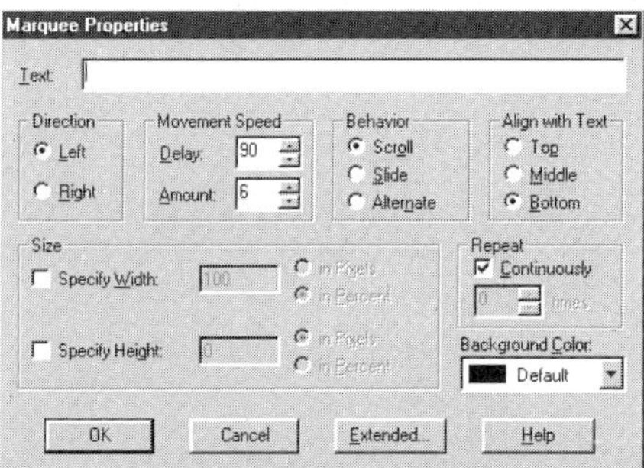

FIG. 22.14
Set Marquee Properties in the Marquee Properties dialog box.

2. Enter the line of text that you want to scroll across the screen in the Text field of the dialog box.
3. Select either Left or Right as the Direction for scrolling.
4. Set the Movement Speed Delay time in milliseconds.

   The Delay time sets the time between each successive step in the direction that the text is moving.
5. Set the Amount setting to specify the amount of movement in pixels of each step that the text takes on the screen.

6. Select Scroll in the Behavior box if you want the text to move across the screen and then start scrolling again.

   or

   Select Slide if you want your text to move across the screen and then remain in place after it reaches the opposite side.

   or

   Select Alternate to cause your text to reverse directions each time it reaches the opposite side of the screen.
7. Select one of the options in the Align with Text box to specify how text around the marquee is aligned.

   Adjacent text can be aligned with the Top, Middle, or Bottom of the marquee.
8. Select Specify Width to specify the width of the marquee as an absolute number of pixels or as a percentage of the browser window size.
9. Select Specify Height to specify the height of the marquee as an absolute number of pixels or as a percentage of the browser window size.
10. Select Continuously to repeat the marquee motion continuously or specify a number of times for the motion to be repeated.
11. Select a Background Color for the marquee area from the drop-down list.
12. Click OK.

You can also resize a marquee in the FrontPage Express document window by clicking the marquee to select it and then moving your mouse cursor over one of the resizing points at the borders of the image, where the mouse pointer changes to a two-sided arrow. Click and drag the mouse to change the dimensions of the marquee.

The actual scrolling action of a marquee cannot be previewed within FrontPage Express. FrontPage Express simply denotes the marquee text within a dashed box, set against the marquee background color. You will need to view your document in Internet Explorer to preview the animated effects. First save your file in FrontPage Express and then open it in Internet Explorer to preview the actual text motion within your marquee.

Adding Background Sound

You can add background sound to your Web page so that it plays when the Web page opens, providing your computer has sound capability. To add background sound, follow these steps:

1. Choose Insert, Background Sound to open the Background Sound dialog box shown in Figure 22.15.

FIG. 22.15
Insert sounds that play when a user opens the Web page.

2. Select the From File option button and specify the path to the sound file on your hard disk or choose Browse to locate it.

   The following sound file formats are supported: *.wav, *.mid, *.midi, *.aif, *.aifc, *.aiff, *.au, and *.snd.

3. Click OK.

ON THE WEB

To download free sound files for use in your Web pages, check out:

http://www.microsoft.com/gallery

Adding Hyperlinks

Perhaps the most powerful aspect of HTML comes from its ability to link text or images to another document or resource anywhere on your local drive, intranet, or the World Wide Web. A viewer's browser may highlight the designated text or image with color or underline to indicate that it is a hypertext link.

The destination of a hyperlink is entered as a Uniform Resource Locator (URL). An URL gives the address of a resource on the World Wide Web and also identifies the protocol that will be used to transfer the resource, such as HTTP (Hypertext Transfer Protocol) or FTP (File Transfer Protocol). The general format for an URL is *protocol://hostname/path_to_resource.*

An URL can be either absolute or relative. An absolute URL specifies the full Internet address of the resource, including the protocol, host name, and path. For example, http://www.microsoft.com/ie/default.asp is an absolute URL.

A relative URL normally omits the *protocol* and *hostname* specification and may omit part of the absolute path to the resource as well. The browser will fill in the missing information of the protocol, hostname, and any missing file path information and locate the new resource relative to the Web document that contains the referring hyperlink. For example, if only a file name is specified as an URL, the browser will search for that file in the same folder on the same host machine as the Web document containing the hyperlink.

By using relative URLs to link to other files on your Web site, it will be easy to move your file folders under other directories on your Web server or even to another Web server entirely, without needing to go through and change the URL of each to reflect the change that you made to the absolute address. Documents addressed relatively can be located more quickly and thus load faster than documents with absolute addresses.

To add a hyperlink from your document to a resource on the World Wide Web, follow these steps:

1. Enter the text or insert the image that will serve as the *anchor* for the link.

   This anchor contains the hyperlink in the viewer's browser. The reader clicks the anchor to activate the link.

2. Select the anchor and choose Insert, Hyperlink to open the Create Hyperlink dialog box (see Figure 22.16).

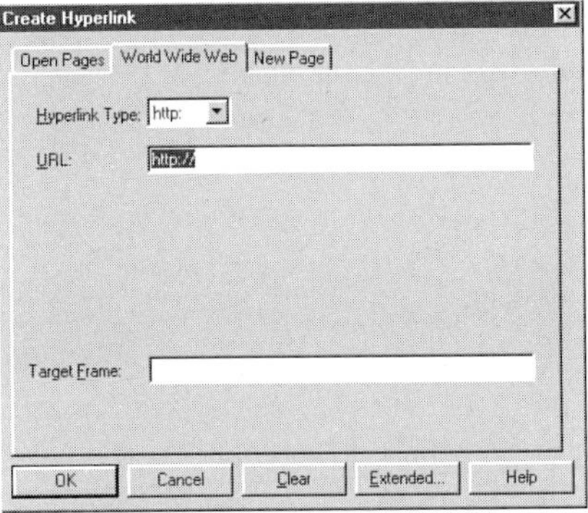

FIG. 22.16 Insert a Hyperlink into your document using the Create Hyperlink dialog box.

3. Select the World Wide Web tab to insert a link to a resource on the Web.
4. Select the type of hyperlink from the Hyperlink Type drop-down list:

Type	Explanation	Format of Path Designation
file:	file on local hard disk	file://drive_designator/path_to_file
ftp:	File Transfer Protocol	ftp://ftp.hostname/path_to_resource
gopher:	Gopher protocol	gopher://gopher.hostname/path_to_resource
http:	Hypertext Transfer Protocol	http://www.hostname/path_to_resource

continues

continued

Type	Explanation	Format of Path Designation
https:	Secure Hypertext Transfer Protocol	https://www.hostname/path_to_resource
mailto:	Electronic mail	mailto:mailbox_name@host
news:	UseNet news	news:newsgroup_name
telnet:	Telnet login	telnet://hostname
wais:	Wide Area Information Server	wais://hostname/path_to_resource

5. Enter the path to the Web resource serving as the destination for the hyperlink in the URL text box.

   You can also specify a relative URL by omitting the "*protocol://*" designator and part of the path (see the previous discussion of relative and absolute paths).

6. Click OK.

FrontPage Express automatically retrieves the URL of the open Web page on your browser when the Create Hyperlink dialog box opens. Before inserting a hyperlink in your FrontPage Express document, open Internet Explorer and go to the destination you want as a target for the link. Switch to your FrontPage Express document. Select the anchor for the link and choose Insert, Hyperlink and notice that the URL field will automatically be filled in the Create Hyperlink dialog box. Click OK to finish.

If you used a text anchor for your hyperlink, notice that the text appears blue and underlined. This is the default format for a hyperlink. Text that serves as a hyperlink is normally displayed in a special color to alert the viewer that it is a hyperlink. You can control how your hyperlinks will be colored via the Background tab of the Page Properties dialog box (see Figure 22.17). Choose File, Page Properties or right-click anywhere in your document window and choose Page Properties to open the Page Properties dialog box.

There are three categories for setting the way a hyperlink will be displayed in a viewer's browser:

Hyperlink	A hyperlink the viewer has never activated before.	Default color blue
Visited Hyperlink	A hyperlink the viewer has previously activated.	Default color purple
Active Hyperlink	A hyperlink the viewer is currently pointing to (i.e., a hyperlink changes to this color when the user moves the mouse over it).	Default color red

Use the drop-down color menus to set colors for the three types of links and click OK.

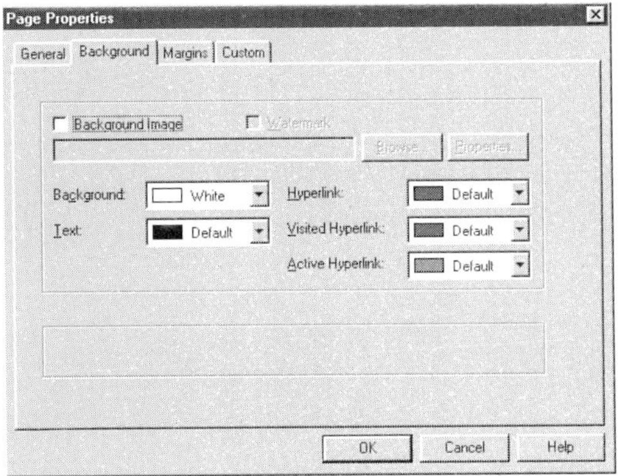

FIG. 22.17 Set the display colors for your hyperlinks in the Background tab of the Page Properties dialog box.

Create Hyperlinks to a Location Within a Web Page Bookmarks enable you to create hyperlink targets at specific places within a Web page. For example, if you want the viewer to skip to a section at the bottom of the Web page or to the middle of another Web page, you can set bookmarks at these places. The hyperlink can then specify the target Web page and the target bookmark on that Web page.

To insert a bookmark into a FrontPage Express document, follow these steps:

1. Move your cursor to the place in the Web page where you want to create the bookmark.

   You may select some text that will serve as the bookmark location.
2. Choose Edit, Bookmark to open the Bookmark dialog box (see Figure 22.18).

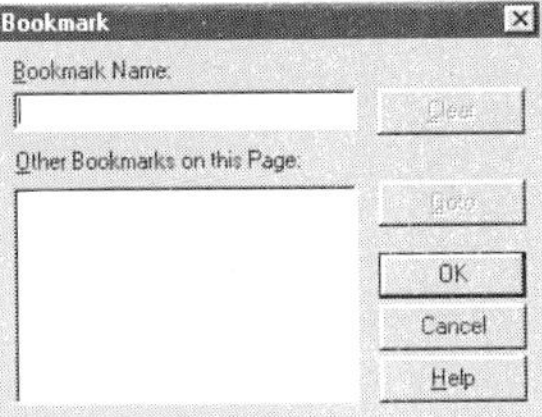

FIG. 22.18 Add a bookmark to your document in the Bookmark dialog box.

   Any previously defined bookmarks on the current page will be displayed under Other Bookmarks on this Page.
3. Fill in the Bookmark Name field with a short descriptive phrase for the new bookmark.

   If you selected text as the bookmark location in Step 1, it will be filled in as the default name for the bookmark.
4. Click OK.

FrontPage Express displays the bookmark in your document window with dashed underlines if Format Marks is selected in the View menu. Also, a bookmark flag icon will be displayed in your document to denote the bookmark location if you didn't select some text to serve as the bookmark location before naming the bookmark.

To add a hyperlink to a bookmark in a document, follow these steps:

1. Open the page with the bookmark if it is on a different page than the one that will contain the hyperlink.
2. Enter the text or insert the image that will serve as the anchor for the hyperlink and select it.
3. Choose Insert, Hyperlink to open the Create Hyperlink dialog box and select the Open Pages tab (see Figure 22.19).

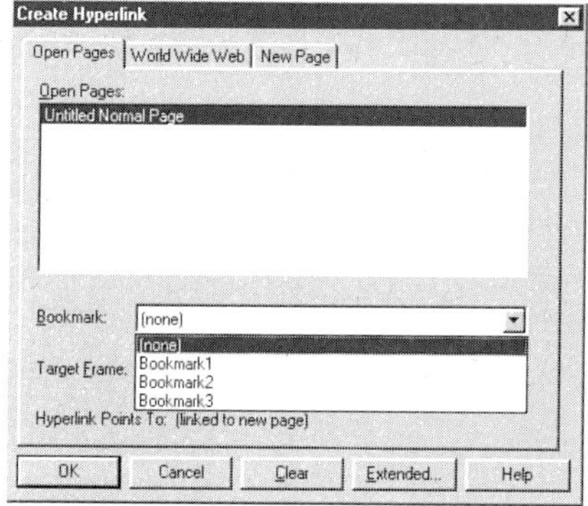

FIG. 22.19
Create a hyperlink to a target within a Web page using the Open Pages tab in the Create Hyperlink dialog box.

4. Select the title of the page containing the bookmark from the Open Pages listing.
5. Select the bookmark you want to link to from the Bookmark drop-down list.
6. Click OK.

To change the properties of a bookmark, first position the cursor in the bookmark and then either choose Edit, Bookmark Properties or right-click and choose Bookmark Properties to open the Bookmark dialog box. You can remove the bookmark by selecting Clear or rename it by changing the text in the Bookmark Name field.

Adding Tables

One of the most important design features available in an HTML editor is the ability to create and manipulate tables. Tables are rows and columns that create a grid of cells. If you use Microsoft Office, they are the same as tables in Word or a spreadsheet in Excel. Figure 22.20 shows a Web page containing text and graphics laid out in a table. The table has four columns, only two of which are used. The inner two columns contain the text and graphics, while the outer two columns are used to center the content of the table on the page and create a border of “white space.” To make room for the eagle logo, two cells in adjoining rows are merged. Although you can format borders around tables, the dashed lines shown here are invisible when the page appears in the browser.

FIG. 22.20 Tables are an important tool in designing your Web page.

Tables solve one of the tough design problems in Web page design, positioning text and graphics accurately. Tables are an easy way to create ordered rows and columns of graphics, text, and hyperlinks. Tables can even be used to create newsletter-like column formats. If you have browsed the Web very much, you are familiar with how many sites arrange material in three columns—left column links, middle column text content, and right column advertisements or graphics. This type of layout is nearly impossible without the use of tables.

While the new Cascading Style Sheets (CSS) allow very accurate positioning of text and graphics, CSS is not supported by a wide base of browsers. (Internet Explorer 3 supports a limited range of the CSS standard, Internet Explorer 4 should support all of CSS, and Netscape Communicator supports a few parts of CSS.) However, nearly all browsers support tables, so you can be assured your Web page will appear approximately the way you want in most browsers.

Many of the examples in Chapter 5, "Customizing Folders with IE4," were created using tables as design grids in which text, graphics, and hyperlinks were placed.

See "Creating Simple Custom Web Views," **p. 373**

To create a table in your Web page, follow these steps:

1. Move the insertion point to where you want the table.
2. Click Table, Insert Table to display the Insert Table dialog box shown in Figure 22.21.
3. Enter the number of rows and columns you want in the Rows and Columns boxes.

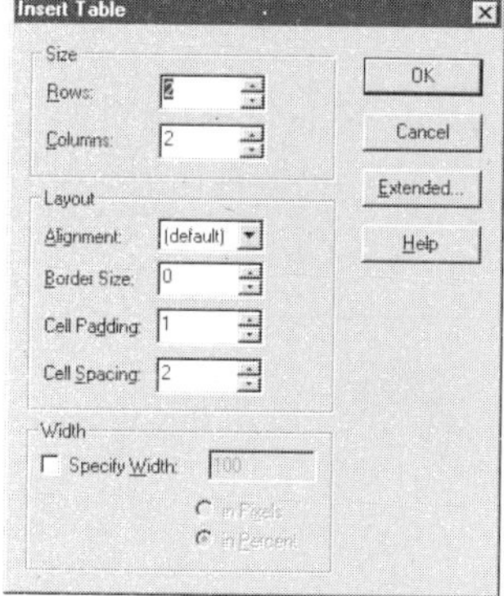

FIG. 22.21 Insert a table with a specific size, alignment, and border spacing with the Insert Table dialog box.

4. Select the Layout of the table using the following options:

Alignment	Select the horizontal alignment of the entire table on the page. Default is the original alignment.
Border Size	Border width in pixels. Use 0 to create an invisible border in most browsers.
Cell Padding	Sets the padding in pixels between the cell contents and the left edge of the cell. This applies to the entire table and cannot be set for one cell. Default padding is one.
Cell Spacing	Sets the spacing in pixels between cells in a table. The default is two.

5. If you want to specify a width for the entire table, select the Specify Width box and enter the width measured in pixels or percent of the page width. In most cases, you should use 100 percent so the table will resize for the browser displaying the page.
6. Click OK.

FrontPage Express will insert a table at the insertion point in the Web page. If you used zero pixels for the border width, the border will appear as a dashed line so you can see it. It will not appear in the browser.

You can also quickly create a small table (up to 4 rows by 5 columns) from the Insert Table button on the Standard toolbar. To do this, click the Insert Table button. Drag the cursor to highlight the number of rows and columns you want in the table in the drop-down table menu as shown in Figure 22.22.

To insert items such as text, graphics, or hyperlinks in a cell within a table, click the cell in which you want the element, then type or choose a command from the Insert menu. You can format one or more cells within a table by dragging across the cells, rows, or columns you want to format and then clicking a command from the Format menu.

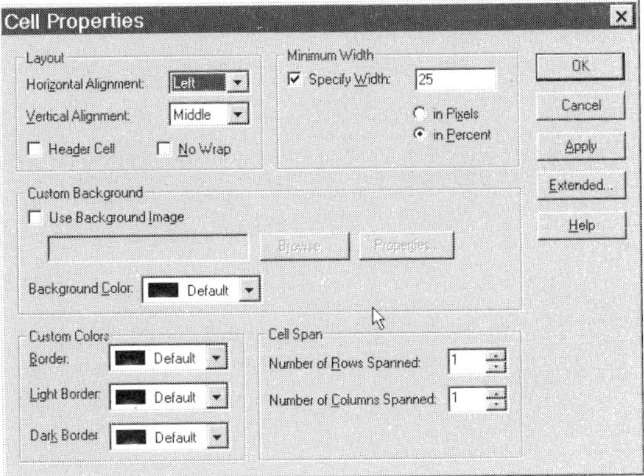

FIG. 22.22
Highlight the number of rows and columns to quickly create a table.

Format individual cells or rows or columns of cells by selecting the cells, then clicking Table, Cell Properties. The Cell Properties dialog box appears as shown in Figure 22.23. Select the formatting changes you want. To adjust the widths of columns, it is usually easiest to set the table width to 100 percent, then adjust the column widths so the total percentage of all column widths equals 100 percent. If the column widths do not total 100 percent, it is difficult to predict the appearance.

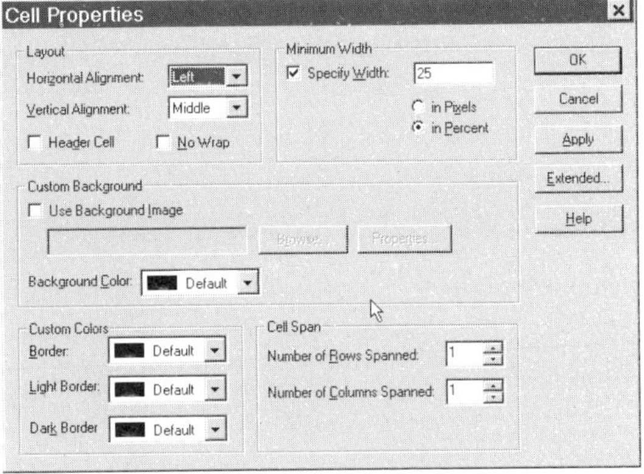

FIG. 22.23
Format the properties of single or groups of cells with the Cell Properties dialog box.

Format the entire table by moving the insertion point inside the table, then clicking Table, Table Properties. The Table Properties dialog box appears as shown in Figure 22.24. Select the formatting changes you want, then click OK.

Adding Form Fields

NOTE FrontPage 97 server extensions must be installed on the server hosting the Web page containing form fields. If you are interested in running or maintaining a server with FrontPage 97 server extensions, you should consider reading *Special Edition Using Microsoft FrontPage 97* from Que.

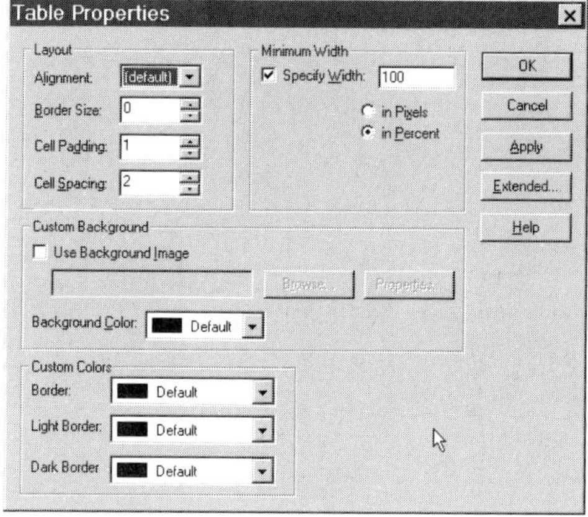

FIG. 22.24
Modify or format an entire table with the Table Properties dialog box.

You can gather information from people using your Web pages by creating form fields on the page. These enable you to put text boxes, check boxes, option buttons, drop-down lists, and more on your Web page. When someone enters data in these fields and then clicks the Submit button, the data they entered is returned to the server hosting the Web page. The FrontPage extensions on the server then create a data file containing the responses.

With the addition of scripting or programming, you can also use these fields to control how a Web page responds. For example, a user might select an option button that indicates they are a novice user. This lets the server know to return a Web page that includes complete directions on how to use a file. Another example might be a Web view that doesn't display file names. Instead, the user selects the type of work they want to do from a drop-down list. The server receives that selection and returns the appropriate document template or file.

To insert a form field in a Web page, follow these steps:

1. Move the insertion point to where you want the form field inserted.
2. Click Insert, Form Field, then select from one of the following choices to immediately insert the field:

One-Line Text Box	A single-line text entry box.
Scrolling Text Box	Multiple line text entry box. Text scrolls when the text fills the box.
Check Box	Square check box. Check boxes have on or off properties.
Radio Button	Round option buttons. Only one option button within a group can be selected.
Drop-Down Menu	Drop-down list.

Push Button	Rectangular buttons selectable for Normal, Submit, or Reset functionality.
Image	Inserts a graphic image that can act as a button to submit form fields.

There is also a forms toolbar with buttons for inserting several form fields. If the toolbar is not displayed, select View, Forms Toolbar to display it. The forms toolbar has buttons for all of the form fields listed except Image.

When you insert a form field in a blank area of a Web page, you will see dashed horizontal lines above and below the field. These lines indicate the start and end of a Form area on the Web page. Form fields must be in a Form area. You can put multiple fields within a Form area.

Option buttons, also known as radio buttons, are usually used to force the user to make a single exclusive choice from a group of options. To make option buttons behave so that only one can be selected from a group, place all of the option buttons for a group within the same Form area.

Each form field has its own unique set of properties that specify information such as the variable name returned to the server to identify that field's data and the field's initial value. To change the properties of any field, right-click the field, then click Form Field Properties. The field's property dialog box displays. Figure 22.25 shows the Text Box Validation dialog box. Figure 22.26 shows the Check Box Properties dialog box.

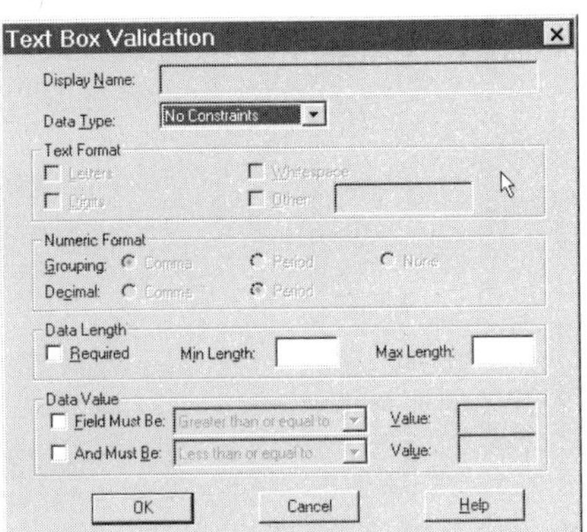

FIG. 22.25
Set the text box variable name, width, and initial values in the Text Box Validation dialog box.

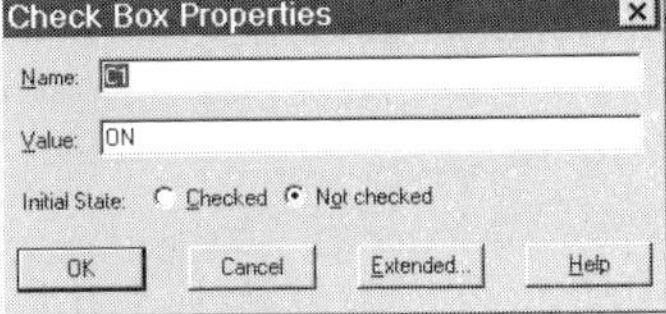

FIG. 22.26
Set the check box variable name, the value returned to the server, and its initial value in the Check Box Properties dialog box.

Inserting WebBots to Add Special Features

FrontPage Express includes WebBots, components that add special features to your Web page. You can insert these WebBots and gain features that might normally require writing a CGI program. For WebBots to work, the server hosting your Web page must include FrontPage server extensions.

Installing FrontPage Express and FrontPage 97 on the same computer makes the FrontPage Express WebBots available to FrontPage 97 under the Insert menu.

FrontPage Express comes with WebBots that include the following features:

WebView Folder Title	Displays the name of the folder containing the Web page.
WebView Folder Contents	Displays the files and folders of the folder containing the Web page.
WebView Shortcut to Mail	Activates the mail client.
WebView Shortcut to News	Activates the news client.
Include	Includes a file, image, or Web page within the current page. Store this included file locally and use a relative URL to specify its location.
Search	Creates a form in which you can type key words. Searches your Web and creates a list of hyperlinks to pages where the word or phrase is found.
Timestamp	Displays the date and time the page was last changed.

For additional information on WebBots and FrontPage server extensions, please read *Special Edition Using FrontPage 97*, published by Que Corporation.

To insert a WebBot in a Web page, follow these steps:

1. Move the insertion point to where you want the WebBot inserted.
2. Click Insert, then select WebView Component where component is the name of one of the FrontPage Express WebBots.

   or

   Click Insert, WebBot Component, then select Include, Search or Timestamp and click OK.

See "Creating Simple Custom Web Views," **p. 373**

Viewing the HTML Code in Your Web Page

Up to now, you have been using FrontPage Express as a visual editor. You can, however, view and edit the HTML code for a document in FrontPage Express. To see the HTML code behind the Web page, follow these steps:

1. Choose View, HTML to open the View or Edit HTML dialog box (see Figure 22.27).

   The HTML code for the active FrontPage Express page displays.

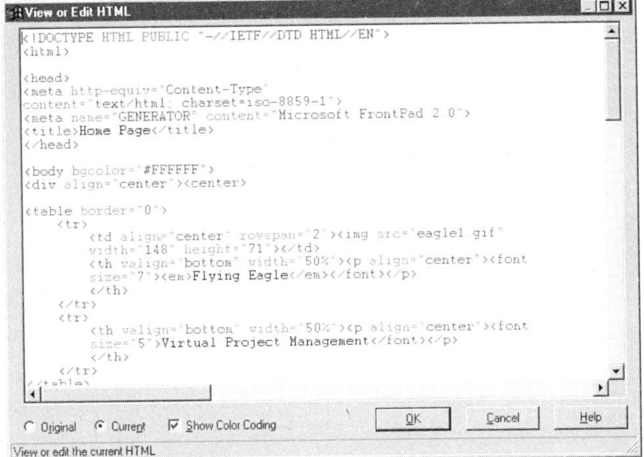

FIG. 22.27 You can view and edit the HTML code for a Web document in FrontPage Express.

2. Select the Original option to view the page as it was last saved.

   or

   Select the Current option to view the page in its current state.
3. To view the text of the HTML tags, parameter names, parameter values, and document content in different colors, check the Show Color Coding box.
4. When you are finished viewing or editing the text, click OK.

You can directly edit the HTML code in the dialog box, but if you plan to do a significant amount of HTML coding (rather than relying on FrontPage Express's visual interface), there are a multitude of HTML editors available that are more suited to this task than FrontPage Express.

ON THE WEB

If you want to learn HTML programming, there are extensive resources on the World Wide Web that will help. Here are a few that should give you a good start:

http://www.w3-tech.com/crash/HTMLMenu.html

http://www.netusa1.net/~jbornema/html.html

http://www.davesite.com/webstation/html/

http://www.w3.org/pub/WWW/MarkUp/MarkUp.html

http://www.ncsa.uiuc.edu/General/Internet/WWW/HTMLPrimer.html

http://scholar.lib.vt.edu/reports/soasis-slides/HTML-Intro.html

http://www.woodhill.co.uk/html/html.htm

http://www.stars.com/Vlib/Authoring/HTML.html

Using the Task Scheduler

Task Scheduler is a new application that comes with Internet Explorer 4.0 that can be used to schedule particular tasks to run at regular intervals. You might, for example, schedule Disk Defragmenter and ScanDisk to run every evening after you've finished work as part of your routine disk maintenance. Task Scheduler starts every time you start Windows and runs in the background, so you don't even have to think about a task once it is scheduled. You can easily change the schedule for a task or temporarily suspend all scheduled tasks if you are busy on your computer during times when tasks are scheduled to be completed.

The Task Scheduler consists of a folder, called Scheduled Tasks, which you can view in My Computer. Each scheduled task is an object in the Scheduled Tasks folder and as with any object in Windows 95, a task has a property sheet. You use the property sheet to set up and schedule a task and to set other parameters for the task. The folder/property sheet paradigm, which is so familiar in Windows 95, makes it easy to create and define a task in Task Scheduler.

If you have been using System Agent, the program that comes with Microsoft Plus! that is used for scheduling tasks, you will discover that System Agent is upgraded to Task Scheduler when you install Internet Explorer 4.0. Any tasks that you had scheduled in System Agent are automatically converted to tasks in Task Scheduler. You can use Task Scheduler the same way you used System Agent to schedule tasks.

NOTE If Task Scheduler was not installed as part of your Internet Explorer 4.0 installation, you can download and install it as an additional component from the Microsoft Web site.

Starting Task Scheduler

There are two ways to open Task Scheduler, either from the Start Menu or in My Computer. To open Task Scheduler from the Start menu, click Start, then Programs, Accessories, System Tools, Scheduled Tasks. From My Computer, click the Scheduled Tasks folder. Either way opens the Scheduler Tasks folder, shown in Figure 22.28. As with any folder window, you can select different views to show more or less detail.

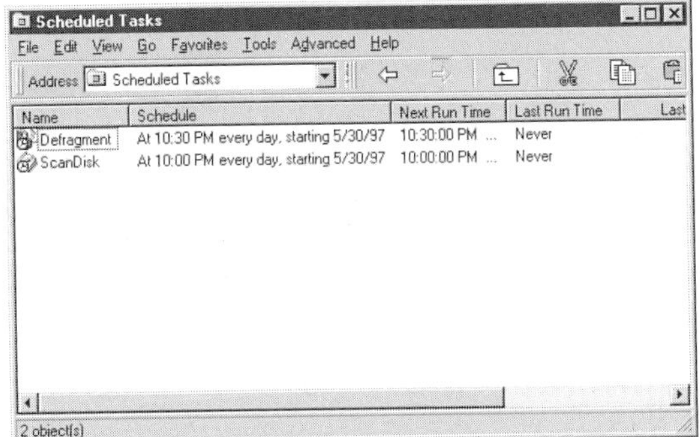

FIG. 22.28 Tasks scheduled in Task Scheduler are found in the Scheduled Tasks folder.

Once you have opened the Scheduled Tasks folder, you should check to make sure Task Scheduler is actually running. To do this, choose Advanced, Start Using Task Scheduler. If the command Stop Using Task Scheduler appears in the Advanced menu, then Task Scheduler is already running. When Task Scheduler is running, the Task Scheduler icon will appear in the lower-right corner of the taskbar.

Scheduling a New Task

Adding a new task to the Scheduled Tasks folder consists of adding a task object to the Scheduled Tasks folder, just as you would add a new folder to a folder window, and then defining the task using the property sheet for the task.

To schedule a new task, follow these steps:

1. Open the Scheduled Tasks folder in My Computer or click Start, then Programs, Accessories, System Tools, Scheduled Tasks.
2. Click the Add Scheduled Task item in the scheduled task window to start the schedule Task Wizard.
3. Click Next in the first introductory screen of the Wizard.
4. The Wizard opens a dialog box (shown in Figure 22.29) listing all of the programs from your start menu. If the task is one of these programs, select it and click Next. If it isn't one of these, click Browse and find the program to schedule.

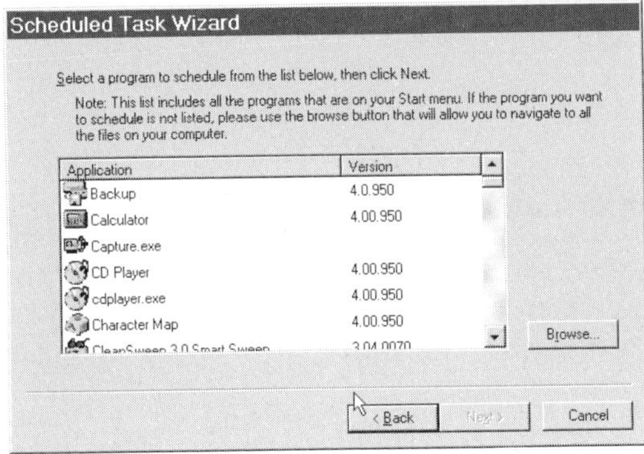

FIG. 22.29 Select the program you want to schedule as a task from this list.

5. Type a name for the new task. As a default the name of the program will be entered as the task name.
6. Choose a schedule for running the task from the options shown in Figure 22.30. Click Next.

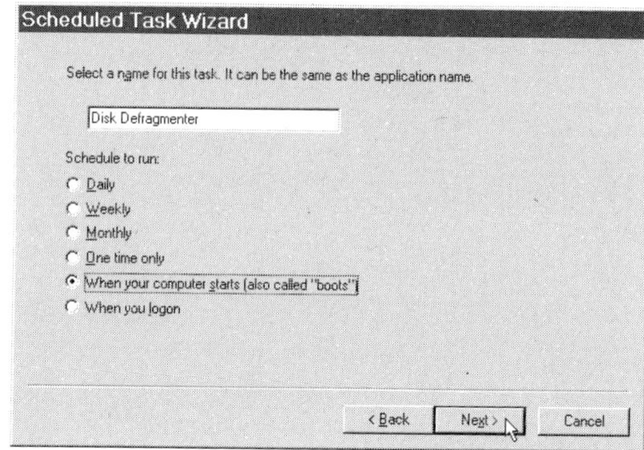

FIG. 22.30 Daily, weekly, monthly, when the computer boots, and when you logon are the options for scheduling repeating tasks.

7. To add command line options to the program, set a customized schedule, or to control other advanced properties select Open Advanced Properties of the task bar then click Finish. If you don't need to do any further customization, just click Finish.
8. If you choose to modify advanced properties, the Task Scheduler displays the Task sheet.
9. On the Task tab (Figure 22.31), you can add command line parameters after the pathname for the task in the Run box, if needed, to specify how the task application will run.

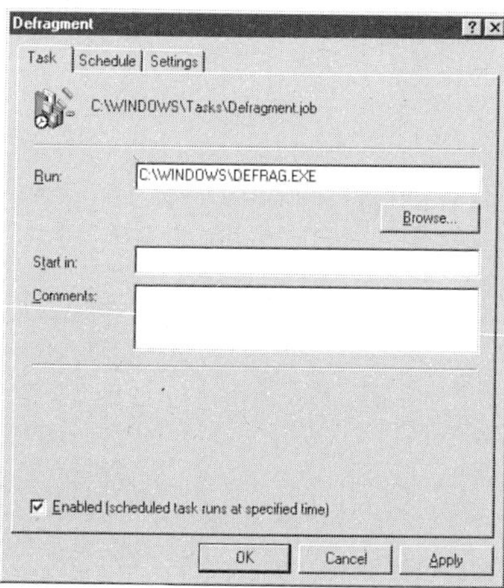

FIG. 22.31 Enter the command line for the task you are scheduling in the Run box of the Task sheet.

10. If the application you are scheduling needs to run from a specific folder, type the path for the folder in the Start In text box.

11. Add comments to the Comments box, if desired.
12. To customize the schedule, click the Schedule tab (see Figure 22.32).

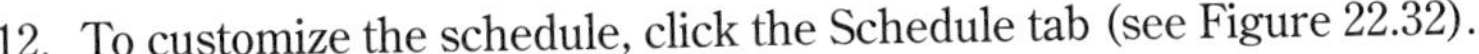

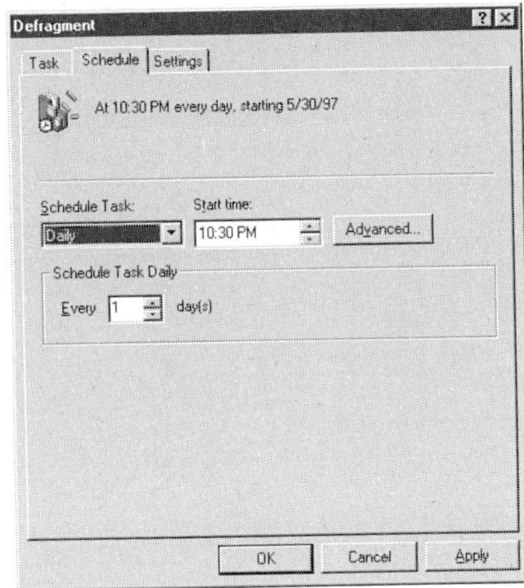

FIG. 22.32 Refine the schedule for a task in the Schedule sheet.

13. Select the interval at which you want the task to run from the Schedule Task drop-down list.
14. If you scheduled the task to run daily, weekly, monthly, or just once, select a time of day for the task to run from the Start Time drop-down list.
15. Depending on what interval you selected in Step 12, the dialog box will change to give you selections for fine-tuning your schedule.

    Figure 22.32 shows how the dialog box will appear if you scheduled the task to run daily. If you scheduled the task to run monthly, the dialog box will appear as shown in Figure 22.33.

    Select the desired settings for the task.

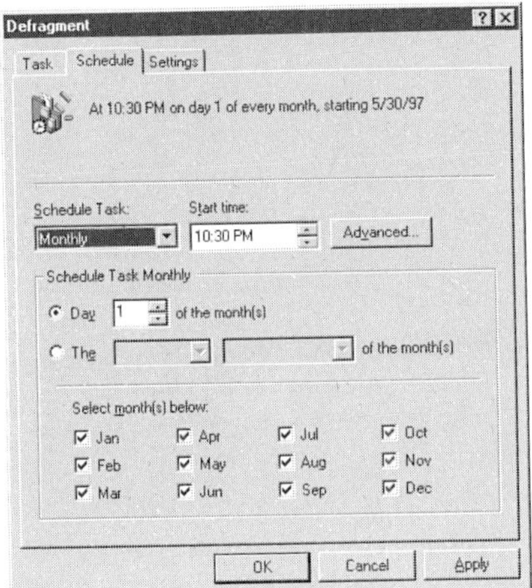

FIG. 22.33 When you schedule a task to run monthly, you can select which months you want the task to run in.

16. You can define other scheduling options by choosing the Advanced button to open the Advanced Schedule Options dialog box (see Figure 22.34).

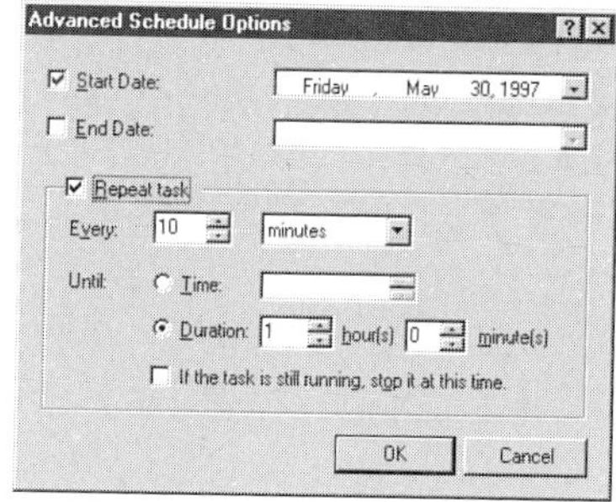

FIG. 22.34 Set the starting and ending dates and other scheduling options in the Advanced Schedule Options dialog box.

17. When you have finished scheduling the task, click OK.

You can modify a scheduled task by opening the property sheet for the task and changing the settings in Task, Schedule, and Settings tabs.

Customizing a Scheduled Task

The Settings property sheet allows you to customize a scheduled task in several ways. To change the settings for a scheduled task, follow these steps:

1. Right-click the task in the Scheduled Task folders and choose Properties.
2. Click the Settings tab to display the Settings property sheet (see Figure 22.35).

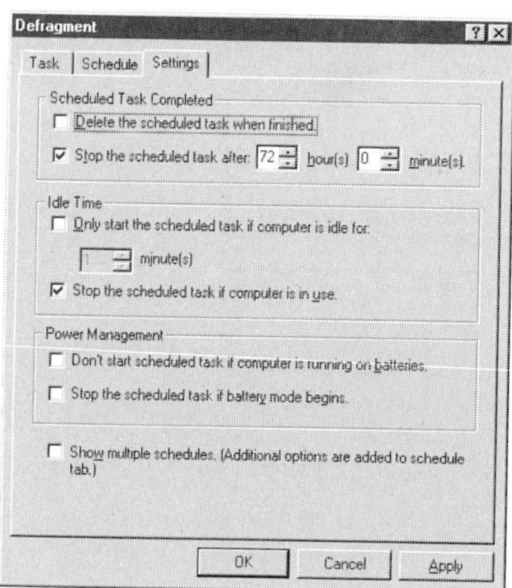

FIG. 22.35 The Settings tab offers many ways to customize how a task will run.

3. Make selections in the Settings tab to customize your task. The following table describes each of the settings:

Option	Action
Delete the scheduled task when finished:	Deletes the task item when the task has finished running.
Stop the scheduled task after:	Stops the task application after a specified time period.
Only start the scheduled task if the computer is idle for:	Specifies that a scheduled task should not start unless the computer has been idle for the specified time period.
Stop the scheduled task if the computer is in use:	Stops a task that is running if you start using the computer.
Don't start the scheduled task if the computer is running on batteries:	If you are using a laptop and it is on battery power, the scheduled task will not be started.
Stop the scheduled task if:	Stops a running task if a battery mode begins. Laptop switches to battery power.
Show multiple schedules:	Adds more scheduling options to Schedule tab.

4. When you have made your selections, click OK.

You can also charge any of the task or schedule settings while you have this dialog box open.

Scheduling Batch Files to Run Automatically

Remember batch files? These little programs that are remnants from the days of DOS can still come in very handy for automatically completing tasks for you. As an example, suppose you want to back up a folder and all of its subfolders to an Iomega Zip Disk without getting involved in using a dedicated backup program. This is a simple task using the venerable DOS command, XCOPY. You can then use Task Scheduler to run this batch file automatically at the end of the day to back up your day's work.

The first step in creating this automated backup is to create an MS-DOS prompt shortcut that runs the XCOPY command when it is executed. To do this, follow these steps:

1. Create a copy of the MS-DOS shortcut.

   To do this, open the Windows\Start Menu\Programs folder, right-click the MS-DOS icon, and choose Copy. Right-click again and choose Paste. A copy of the MS-DOS prompt icon appears.
2. Rename the icon you just created. For example, you may name it "Backup of Books Files to Zip Disk."
3. Right-click the icon and choose Properties.
4. Select the Program tab.

5. Enter the XCOPY command in the Batch File text box.

   For example, if you want to back up a folder called Book Chapters and all of its subfolders to a Zip Disk in drive D, the command would be:

   XCOPY "C:\Book Chapters\" D:\ /s

   Note that if the folder name contains spaces, you should include the entire pathname in quotes. The /s parameter specifies that Book Chapters and all of its subfolders should be copied. XCOPY has other parameters that can refine your backup procedure:

   /m Copies only files whose archive attribute is on and then turns it off. Good for limiting backup to files that have changed since the last backup.

   /d <date> Copies only files with a creation date that is the same as or later than the date specified.

6. Click OK.

Now that you have created the MS-DOS prompt with its associated batch file, you can use the procedure described in "Scheduling a New Task," earlier in this chapter. In step 4 of the procedure, use the Browse button to locate the MS-DOS prompt you just created. Next, schedule the DOS session to run whenever you want. Be sure to leave the correct Zip Disk in the Zip drive before you leave your computer. When you come back later, your files will have been backed up automatically.

You are not limited to running simple one-line batch files as in the example just given. You can enter the name of any batch file you have created in the Batch File text box of an MS-DOS prompt shortcut and that batch file will be executed when you run the MS-DOS prompt.

Try using Task Scheduler to run your Microsoft Office applications automatically when you need to carry out a lengthy operation that you would prefer to do when you are not around. For example, if you have a complex Excel worksheet that takes a long time to recalculate, you could schedule Excel to start and open and recalculate the worksheet, using an AutoOpen macro. Or, you could schedule Word to open and run a mail merge operation while you sleep!

Suspending Task Scheduler

Suppose you need to put in extra hours to catch up on your work and you don't want to be interrupted by tasks scheduled to run at night. You can temporarily suspend Task Scheduler so that all scheduled tasks are put on hold.

To pause Task Scheduler, follow these steps:

1. Open the Scheduled Tasks folder, using My Computer or the Start menu.

2. Choose Advanced, Pause Task Scheduler.

   The Task Scheduler icon will appear with an X through it in the taskbar when it is paused.

   If a task misses its scheduled time while the Task Scheduler is paused, it won't run until its next scheduled time.

3. To resume the Task Scheduler, choose Advanced, Continue Task Scheduler.

To suspend a specific task without suspending other scheduled tasks, open the property sheet for the task and clear the Enabled check box on the Task sheet.

Turning Off Task Scheduler

When you turn off Task Scheduler, scheduled tasks will not be run and Task Scheduler will not start up when you start Windows. To turn off Task Scheduler, follow these steps:

1. Open the Task Scheduler folder from My Computer or by clicking Start, then Programs, Accessories, System Tools, Scheduled Tasks.
2. Choose Advanced, Stop Using Task Scheduler.

Group Collaboration with NetMeeting 2.0

The interconnectivity that the Internet has brought to computer users around the world has given birth to a new type of software called collaboration software. Collaboration software enables multiple users to work together in real-time from disparate locations, communicating by voice, video, and data exchange using a local area network (LAN) or the Internet. NetMeeting 2.0 is the latest version of Microsoft's contribution to this arena. NetMeeting 2.0 has many powerful features that allow users to "meet" over the Net to exchange ideas, make joint decisions, collaborate on editing a document or refining a budget, and just stay in touch.

NetMeeting 2.0 allows you to conference with other NetMeeting users using data, audio, and video exchange. NetMeeting gives priority to audio communication, so that, depending on the available bandwidth, the speed of data and video exchange will be varied as necessary to maintain a high-quality audio connection.

Figure 22.36 shows a NetMeeting conference in progress. The Current Call tab lists the two participants in the conference. In Figure 22.37, you can see Microsoft Excel being used as a shared application. In this case, because the person who is sharing the application is not collaborating, the person viewing the application cannot work in the application.

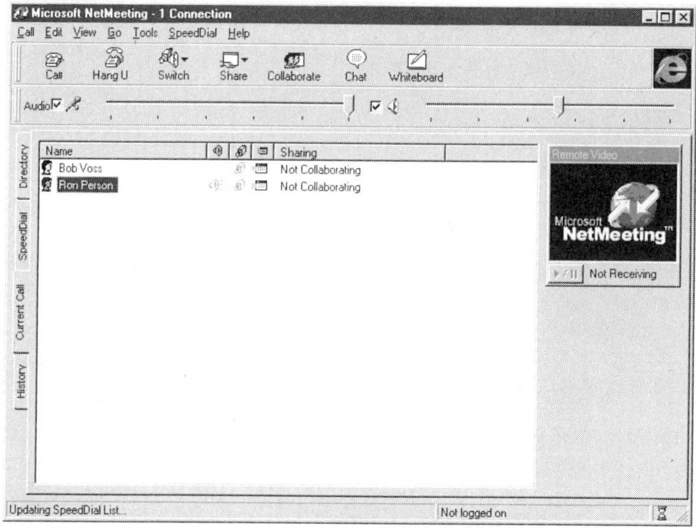

FIG. 22.36
The Current Call tab in NetMeeting lists the participants who are currently involved in a call.

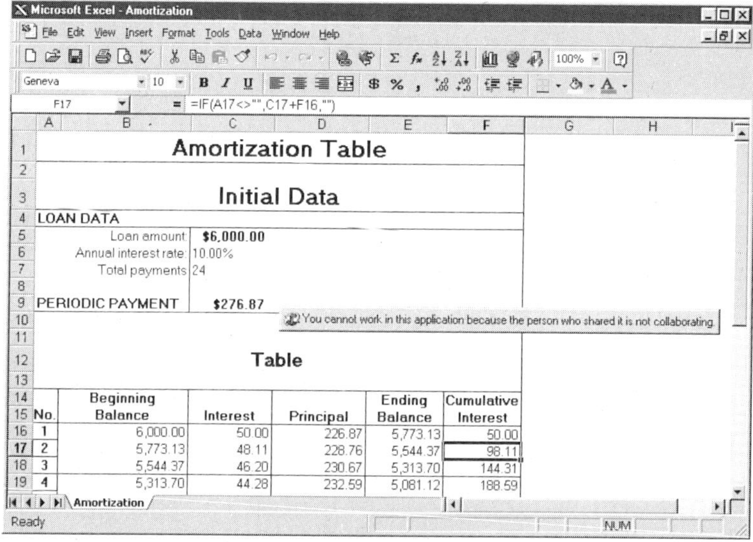

FIG. 22.37
You can share an application in a NetMeeting conference so that multiple users can view and work on a document.

NOTE NetMeeting 2.0 incorporates two important industry standards for communications, T.120 and H.323. T.120 is the standard for multipoint data conferencing, which defines how applications are shared and data exchanged over a data network. H.323 is the standard for low-bandwidth audio and video conferencing, which includes the codecs used to compress and decompress audio and video data. Conforming to these worldwide telephony standards enables NetMeeting to cooperate with other products that are T.120- and H.323-compliant, regardless of what platform they are on. In the confusing world of telecommunications, this capability is vitally important.

Data Conferencing

NetMeeting 2.0 is capable of multipoint data conferencing, meaning that multiple users can exchange data with one another simultaneously. With NetMeeting, you can exchange data with other participants in a conference in several ways:

- **Shared applications:** Participants can share an application that resides on the computer of just one of the participants. All participants can watch as one person works in the application, editing data, highlighting important aspects of a document, or demonstrating a feature of the application. At any time, the person sharing the application can opt to collaborate with other participants so that they can work in the application as well, even if they don't have the application on their computers.
- **Shared clipboard:** Participants in a conference can share data via a common clipboard, so that information from an application on one participant's computer can instantly be copied and pasted to an application on another participant's computer. One participant, for example, could contribute data from a document on her computer to the document being worked on in a shared application.
- **Whiteboard:** Imagine an electronic whiteboard that you could "walk up to" at any time during a data conference to use just as you would use a whiteboard in an ordinary conference room. This is exactly what the Whiteboard in NetMeeting allows you to do. Use the Whiteboard to sketch out an idea, draw a diagram, or make a list of points for a meeting. Essentially a drawing program, Whiteboard has tools for drawing, moving objects, pointing to or highlighting areas on a page, or turning to a new page. All participants in a conference can view and work on the Whiteboard.
- **Chat:** This feature allows participants to exchange text messages. This is useful for jotting down shared meeting notes or for communicating when one or more of the participants in a conference lacks audio capability. You can even exchange private messages with selected participants in a conference.
- **File transfer:** Transferring data files is a mode of data exchange that we are all familiar with. NetMeeting 2.0 enables you to transfer data files in the background while you are in conference. You can transfer a file to a selected participant or to all the participants in the conference, who can then choose to accept or reject the file. You could, for example, work collaboratively on a document in a data NetMeeting session, using a shared application on your computer, and then send each participant a copy of the edited file at the end of the conference.

NOTE Although you can transfer files in the background during a NetMeeting data conference, be aware that file transfer is slow in comparison to normal file transfer using a regular communications package. The reason for this is that NetMeeting is working with a limited bandwidth and has to divide up that bandwidth with the other forms of exchange that are happening simultaneously. File transfer is not given the highest priority. If you know you want to transfer a file to the participants in a planned conference, you can save time by sending them the file ahead of time via e-mail or making the file available online so they can download it prior to the conference.

Video Conferencing

If two or more of the participants in a NetMeeting conference have video hardware that is compatible with video for Windows, you can exchange visual data. You can see one another as you carry on a meeting or use your video capabilities to show another participant a prototype of a product you are working on, a diagram or schematic, or the view from your corner office window. Video and audio conferencing in NetMeeting 2.0 are point-to-point, meaning you can see and talk to only one person at a time. In a meeting with several participants, you can decide at any time who you want that person to be by selecting the person's name from the list in the Current Call window.

NOTE Although you can see and speak with only one participant with NetMeeting as this is written, H.323 conference servers and gateways are currently being developed that will enable multiple users to exchange audio and video data.

You can dynamically resize the My Video window during a video conference to change the size of the image being sent to the other user. You can also move the My Video and Remote Video windows, which normally reside in the Current Call window, to any location on your desktop, and pause and resume the transmission of video data using buttons in the video windows. And even if you don't have the hardware needed to send video images, you can still receive them from other participants in a conference.

Audio Conferencing

You may not need to or have the capability for transmitting video images but would still like to enhance your NetMeeting sessions with real-time voice exchange. NetMeeting allows you to do this with ease. You can engage in point-to-point voice communication with other NetMeeting users (or users of H.323-compliant voice applications). NetMeeting supports both half-duplex (one person speaking at a time) or full-duplex (both people speaking simultaneously) calls, and allows you to adjust the sensitivity of your microphone, tune your audio using the Audio Tuning Wizard, and turn off your microphone if you want to interrupt audio transmission.

System Policies

Administrators can control how NetMeeting works by using system policies. Many NetMeeting features can be controlled, including the default directory server, which customization options are available to users, and the amount of bandwidth that can be used for audio and video transmission. This can prevent users from tying up resources unnecessarily using the video and audio features of NetMeeting.

ON THE WEB

For more information on system policies in NetMeeting, refer to the NetMeeting Resource Kit or visit the following Web site:

http://www.microsoft.com/windows95/

Ways to Use NetMeeting

NetMeeting 2.0 opens up limitless possibilities for cooperating over the Internet:

- **Technical support:** Use your intranet and NetMeeting to provide remote technical support to end users in your company. The user can call the technical support person, establish a NetMeeting connection, and watch as the support person diagnoses the problem. In many cases, this may save technical support staff a visit to the person needing help. The regular telephone can be used for verbal communication during the support session.
- **Meetings:** You can host a meeting with one or more participants. Once you have all established a connection via an ILS, you can exchange data using a shared application, the shared Clipboard, the Whiteboard, and Chat. You can also exchange audio and video data to liven up the meeting.
- **Collaborative Editing:** Several people can work together editing a document that appears in a shared application. You could, for example, involve people from several locations in the editing of an annual report or a budget. Each participant would be able to work on the actual document, using the shared application that resides on one of the participants' computers.
- **Remote Parenting:** You promised your kid to help him with his project, but got called away unexpectedly to a meeting. Well, back at the hotel room you can set up a NetMeeting session with your child, using your laptop computer, and keep that promise.

ON THE WEB

For a complete overview of the features of NetMeeting 2.0 and to download NetMeeting to your computer, visit the following Web site:

http://www.microsoft.com/netmeeting/corp/corpfeatures.htm

How NetMeeting Works

This section is only meant to give you an overview of how NetMeeting works. To learn more about the details of how to use NetMeeting, refer to the Help topics in NetMeeting.

The first step in establishing a connection in NetMeeting is to find the people you want to meet with. This is done by using a directory server called the Microsoft Internet Locator Server, or ILS. The ILS helps you find the people you want to communicate with, and once that is accomplished and a connection is established, the ILS drops out of the picture. The ILS is not involved in the communication between callers. Microsoft currently has several directory servers online that you can use to link to other users or you can set up your own ILS by using the software that is part of the Microsoft Internet Information Server package. If your company has its own intranet, for example, you would benefit by having your own ILS for users of the intranet.

When you first start NetMeeting, it will start a Wizard that walks you through selecting an ILS, your usage preferences, connection speed, and audio settings. After you have been through this Wizard once, you can select a different server or change any of your other setup information by choosing Call, Change My Information.

Figure 22.38 shows the listing for one of Microsoft's directory servers. In this case, the list has been filtered to show only those users who have categorized their user information for business use only. The list shows everyone who is currently connected to that server and running NetMeeting. A red asterisk next to a name indicates that the person is currently involved in a call. To call someone on the list, double-click the name. The person receiving your call will see a dialog box on his screen and have the choice of accepting or rejecting your call (see Figure 22.39). If you are called by someone, you will see the same dialog box and also can reject or accept the call.

CAUTION

The first time you connect to one of Microsoft's directory servers, you may be in for a shock. You will quickly discover that many NetMeeting users are looking for a different kind of meeting than you are and you may be offended by the remarks you see in the Comments field of the Directory window. Normally, you can avoid pornographic material on the Web by picking and choosing what sites you link to. NetMeeting is a different story. When you connect to a directory server in hopes of finding someone to hold a NetMeeting session with, you are entering a strange world that reflects a wide range of human behavior. Prepare yourself!

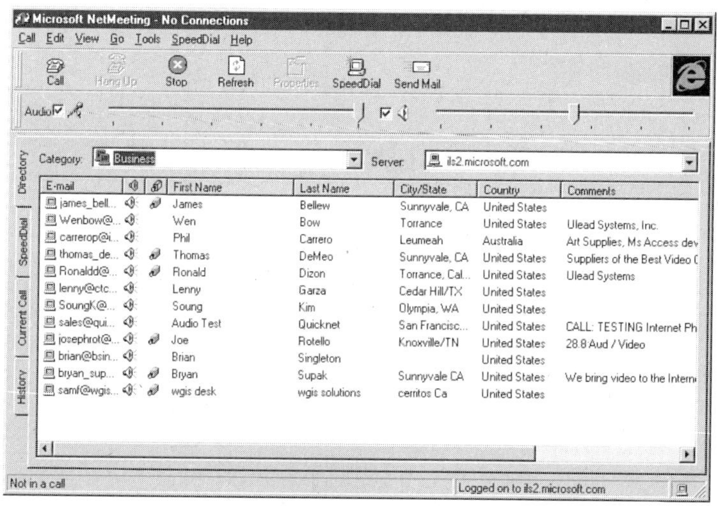

FIG. 22.38 The Directory tab displays a listing of everyone connected to a selected directory server.

FIG. 22.39 You are notified when someone is trying to call you. You can accept or reject the call.

Once you have established communication with another NetMeeting user, you can use all of the features of NetMeeting to conference with the other user. Even if you are not capable of audio and video communication, you can still share applications, exchange data using the shared clipboard, exchange messages using Chat, and transfer files. To find out how to use the features of NetMeeting, refer to the Help topics in the Help menu.

Introducing NetShow 2.0

Another new component of Internet Explorer 4.0 is the latest version of NetShow, Microsoft's application for broadcasting multimedia content over the Internet and intranets. Some Web sites are already taking advantage of NetShow to broadcast entertainment clippings as shown in Figure 22.40.

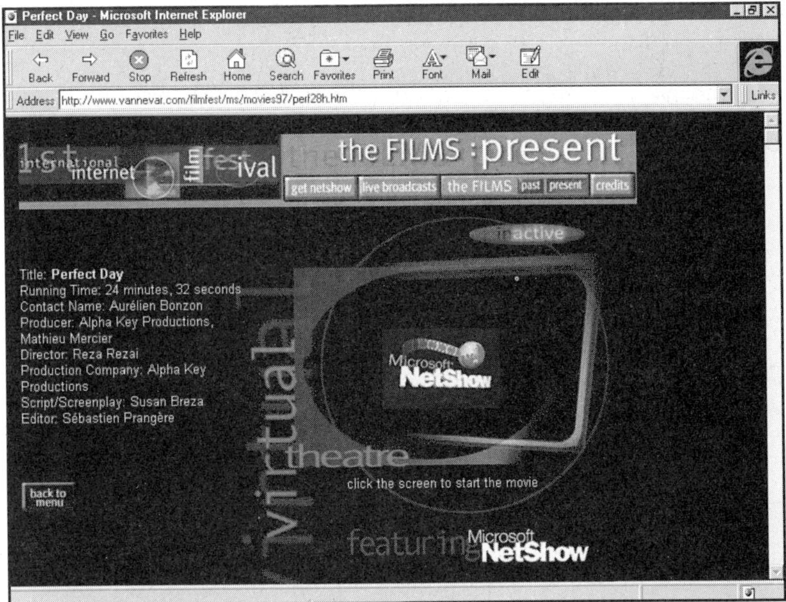

FIG. 22.40
Companies can use NetShow to broadcast entertainment or training over the Web.

NetShow 2.0 incorporates some exciting new technologies that take the broadcasting of rich multimedia presentations to a new level. NetShow can be used to multicast multimedia content, which means a single multimedia file can be sent to multiple users, rather than the same file being sent multiple times to reach the same users. This cuts down the amount of data traffic on a network.

From the user's point of view, the most exciting development is the use of media streaming technology. Instead of having to first download a multimedia file before it can be played back, NetShow delivers a continuous stream of data that can be played back almost immediately. The data isn't actually stored on the computer; it is simply played back as it arrives and then discarded. The benefit of media streaming is obvious. You no longer have to suffer through the interminable wait as a large multimedia file downloads before you can view the file. You start viewing the file right away and stop viewing the file if it is not what you are looking for.

NetShow can be used for broadcasting audio, video, and illustrated audio (sound combined with sequenced images). NetShow has three components: NetShow server, NetShow client, and the NetShow authoring and production tools. NetShow server resides on a Windows NT 4.0 server and does the job of broadcasting multimedia files to clients, either live or on demand (from stored content). NetShow client is the player the allows the user to play multimedia content sent by the server. As soon as a user clicks a link to a file, the player starts and the file is played back.

The NetShow authoring and production tools are used to create multimedia content that takes advantage of NetShow's technologies, including tools for creating ASF files, which are files that use the new Active Streaming Format standard that allows media streaming.

ON THE WEB

To find out more about NetShow, visit the following Web site:

http//www.microsoft.com/netshow/

PART V

Working with Applications

CHAPTER 23

Application Management Fundamentals

by Ron Person

The information that you learn in this chapter carries over to all Windows applications. This "learning carry-over" is important: After you learn how to use one Windows application, you understand most of the concepts necessary to operate other applications. The skills that you acquire in this chapter will help you operate such control features as menus and dialog boxes and learn how to control such display aspects as the size and position of the windows in which different documents or applications display. ■

Open menus and choose commands

Learn how to open application menus and choose commands from the menus.

Change the location and size of windows

Find out how to change the size of application windows and arrange them on your screen.

Display the properties of the desktop, file, or taskbar

Learn how to use the right mouse button to view and change the properties of objects.

Work in applications

Learn the fundamentals of working in applications, including how to open and save files, navigate within a document, select and edit text and objects, and switch between application and document windows.

Working in the Windows Environment

Windows uses concepts that, for many people, make computers easier to use. The basic organizational concept is that all applications run on a desktop and that each application runs in its own window. Windows can run multiple applications, just as you might have stacks of papers on your desk from more than one project. You can move the windows and change their size just as you can move and rearrange the stacks of papers on your desk.

See "Making Windows Accessible for the Hearing-, Sight-, and Movement-Impaired," **p. 884**

See "Understanding Data Linking," **p. 913**

See "Cutting, Copying, and Pasting Data," **p. 903**

Just as you can cut, copy, and paste parts between papers on your real desktop, Windows enables you to cut or copy information from one application and paste the information into another. Some Windows applications even share live information; when you change data in one application, Windows automatically updates linked data in other applications.

The process for making entries, edits, and changes to text, numbers, or graphics is similar in all Windows applications. The basic procedure is as follows:

1. Activate the window that contains the desired application.
2. Select the text, number, or graphics object that you want to change. You can select items with the mouse or the keyboard.
3. Choose a command from the menu bar at the top of the application.
4. If a dialog box appears, select options to modify how the command works. Then execute the command by choosing the OK button.

An *application window* is the window that contains an application. *Document windows* appear inside application windows and contain documents. In many (but not all) applications, you can have several document windows open at a time. You switch between them by pressing Ctrl+F6 or by selecting from the Window menu the document that you want.

The Control menu contains commands to control a window's location, size, and status (open or closed). Each application and each document window within the application window has its own Control menu. The application Control menu appears at the left edge of the application's title bar. The document Control menu appears at the left edge of the document's title bar (if the document window is smaller than a full screen) or at the left edge of the menu bar (if the document window is a full screen). To open an application Control menu, click the application Control-menu icon (the icon at the top-left corner of the program window), or press Alt+spacebar. To open a document Control menu, click the document Control-menu icon (the icon in the upper-left corner of a document window) or press Alt+hyphen (-).

To maximize a window so it fills the screen, click the Maximize button, a square window icon in the window's top-right corner (see Figure 23.1). You can also minimize a window and place it on the taskbar. To do so, you click another icon in the window's upper-right corner, the Minimize button, which looks like an underline representing the taskbar (see Figure 23.1).

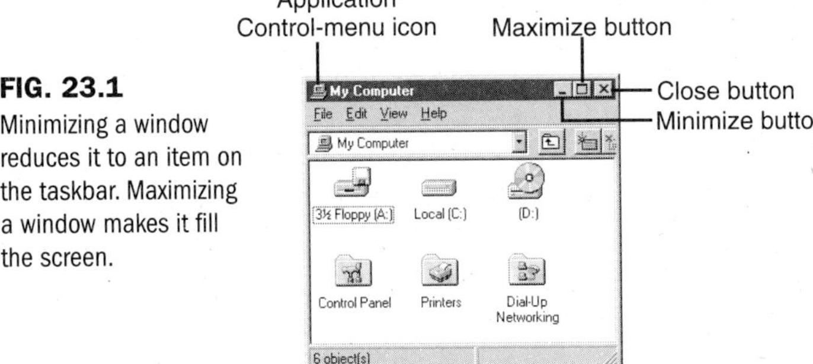

FIG. 23.1
Minimizing a window reduces it to an item on the taskbar. Maximizing a window makes it fill the screen.

TIP To minimize all windows with one command, click a clear area in the taskbar with the right mouse button and choose Minimize All Windows.

TIP To restore all minimized windows with one command, click a clear area in the taskbar with the right mouse button and choose Undo Minimize All.

When you minimize a program, its window shrinks to become an icon and name on the taskbar. The program still runs even though it is not in a window. To make a program on the taskbar appear in a window, click the program in the taskbar. (To use the keyboard to activate a program, press Alt+Tab repeatedly until you have selected the appropriate program, and then release the keys.)

You can resize a window by dragging its window border with the mouse, or by choosing the Size command from the Control menu. You can move a window without resizing it by dragging its title bar with the mouse, or by choosing the Move command from the Control menu.

▶ **See** "Customizing the Mouse," **p. 881**

▶ **See** "Customizing the Keyboard," **p. 882**

Table 23.1 introduces keystrokes that perform certain actions. You may want to refer to this table as you read through the book or begin working with Windows 95.

Table 23.1 Keystrokes to Control Windows

Keystroke	Action
Alt+Esc	Activates the next application window.
Alt+Tab	Displays a program bar showing open programs as icons. Each press of Alt+Tab selects the next icon. Releasing Alt+Tab activates the program selected in the program bar.

continues

Table 23.1 Continued

Keystroke	Action
Alt+Shift+Tab	Moves the selection through the program bar in the opposite direction of Alt+Tab. Releasing Alt+Shift+Tab activates the selected program.
Ctrl+F6	Activates the next document window (if an application has multiple document windows open).
Ctrl+Esc	Displays the Start menu. Press the up or down arrow keys to select from the menu.
Alt+spacebar	Displays the Control menu for the active program icon or window. Use the Control menu to change the location, size, and status of the program window.
Alt+hyphen (-)	Displays the Control menu for the active document window within the program. Use this Control menu to change the location, size, and status of the document window.

Using Menus and Dialog Boxes

Every properly designed Windows application operates in a similar way. As you will learn, you can move and resize all windows the same way in every Windows application. You can also execute commands the same way in all Windows applications.

You can choose a command from a menu by using the mouse or the keyboard (also, many time-saving shortcuts exist for choosing commands). If a command requires information from you before executing, a dialog box appears when you choose the command. In the dialog box, you use the mouse or the keyboard to choose options or enter values that control the command.

See "Making Windows Accessible for the Hearing- Sight- and Movement-Impaired," **p. 884**

Choosing Menus and Commands

When you click a menu, a list of commands drops down under the menu, as shown in Figures 23.2 and 23.3. If you're not sure where to find a command, try browsing through the menus by clicking them until you find the command that you want. Many applications use similar commands for similar actions—a practice that makes learning multiple Windows applications easier.

To choose a menu or command with the mouse, move the tip of the pointer over the menu or command name and click the left mouse button. To choose a menu or command with the keyboard, press Alt+*letter* where *letter* is the underlined letter in the menu. When the menu appears, press the key for the underlined letter in the command (you don't have to hold down the Alt key while you do this). For example, to choose the File menu's Open command, hold down the Alt key, press F, and then press O.

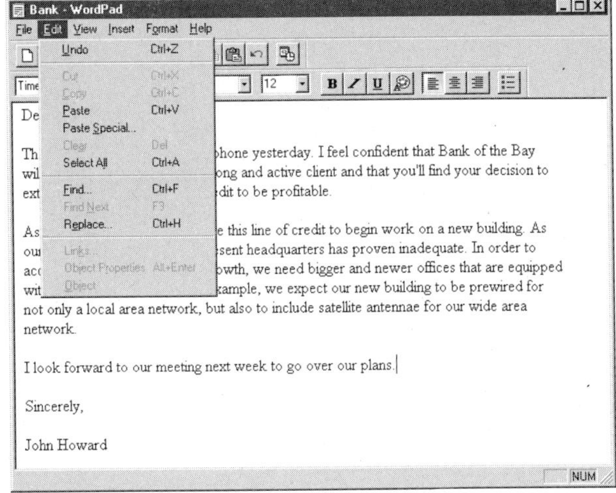

FIG. 23.2
WordPad's Edit menu displays shortcut keys.

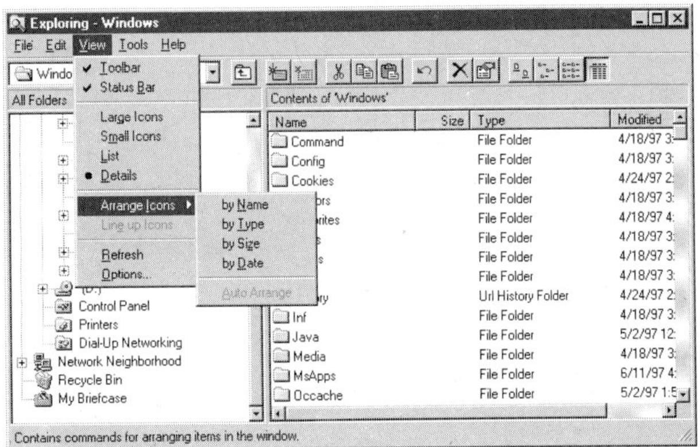

FIG. 23.3
In the Explorer, when you choose View, Arrange Icons, you see a submenu that displays additional commands.

TIP To change the colors of the text in menu commands, see "Creating Custom Color and Text Schemes" in Chapter 32.

You can choose commands that appear in a menu in solid black (bold) type. You *cannot* choose commands that appear in gray in a menu, even though you can see them. Gray commands or options are *disabled*. Commands or options appear in bold only when they are available, or *enabled*. For example, the Edit menu's Copy command appears in bold type only when you have selected something to copy.

Command names followed by an ellipsis (...) display an additional dialog box or window from which you can choose options or enter data. If you choose Edit, Find... from a Windows application, for example, a dialog box appears in which you type the word that you want to find.

Commands with a check mark to the left are commands that toggle on and off. A check mark indicates that the command is on; no check mark indicates that the command is off.

Commands with key combinations listed to the right have shortcuts. In Windows Explorer, for example, the Edit menu lists a shortcut for the Copy command, Ctrl+C. Therefore, to copy a file, you can choose Edit, Copy or press Ctrl+C.

Commands with an arrowhead next to them, as in Figure 23.3, have submenus that list additional commands. In the Explorer, the Arrange Icons command in the View menu has an arrowhead to its right, indicating that a submenu will show the ways in which you can arrange icons.

If you don't want to make a choice after displaying a menu, click the pointer a second time on the menu name or click outside the menu. If you are using the keyboard, press Esc to exit a menu without making a choice. Continue to press Esc until no commands or menus are selected.

NOTE If a dialog box appears on screen and you aren't sure what to do, you can escape without making any changes. Click the Cancel button or press the Esc key to cancel the current dialog box and ignore any changes to options.

Most Windows applications have an Undo command. If you complete a command and then decide that you want to undo it, check whether the Edit menu includes an Undo command.

Selecting Options from Dialog Boxes

Commands that require more information before they work, display a *dialog box*—a window similar to those shown in Figures 23.4 and 23.5. Dialog boxes like the one in Figure 23.4 have areas in which you enter text (such as the File Name text box) or select from a scrolling list of choices (see the Save In list of disks and folders in Figure 23.4). Many applications also include drop-down list boxes with lists that appear only when you select the box and press the down arrow key, or click the down arrow on the right side of the text box.

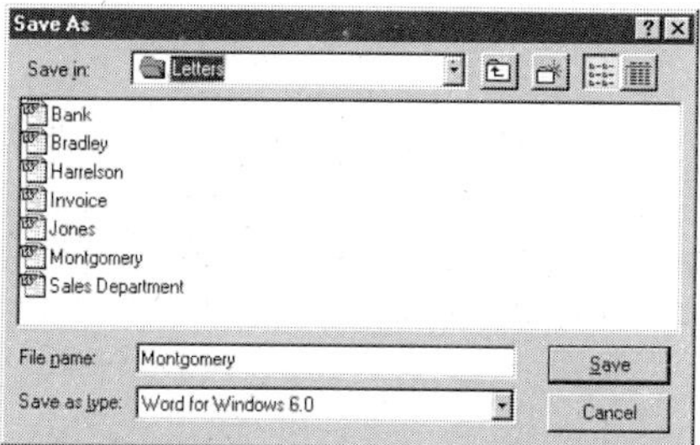

FIG. 23.4 The Save As dialog box is similar among Windows programs.

Figure 23.5 shows that dialog boxes can have round *option* buttons and square *check boxes*. The option buttons are clustered in a group labeled Hidden Files. When options are in such groups, you can choose only one of them. Check boxes act independently of other check boxes so you can select as many of them as you want. After you select options or make text entries, you accept the contents of the dialog box by choosing the OK button or cancel them by choosing the Cancel button.

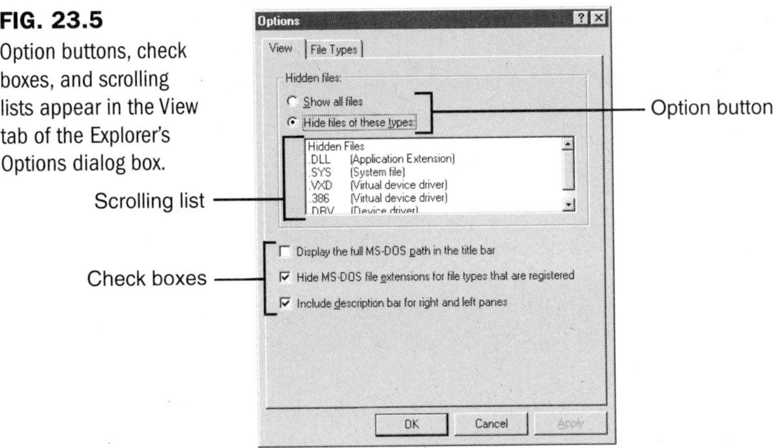

FIG. 23.5
Option buttons, check boxes, and scrolling lists appear in the View tab of the Explorer's Options dialog box.

If a dialog box hides something that you want to see on-screen, you can move the dialog box with the mouse by dragging the dialog box by its title bar to a new position. With the keyboard, press Alt+spacebar to open the dialog Control menu and then choose Move. A four-headed arrow appears. Press any arrow key to move an outline of the dialog box. Press Enter when the outline of the dialog box is where you want to place the dialog box. (Before you press Enter, you can cancel the move by pressing Esc.)

Figure 23.6 shows other types of controls used in dialog boxes, and Table 23.2 summarizes them.

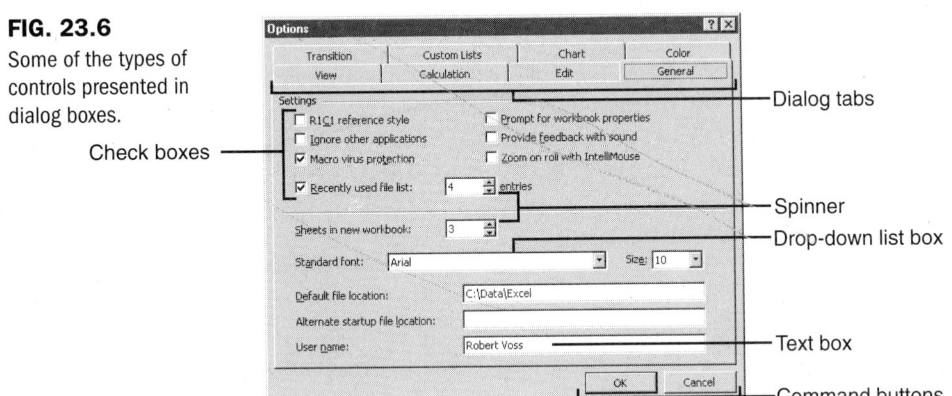

FIG. 23.6
Some of the types of controls presented in dialog boxes.

Table 23.2 Types of Dialog Box Controls

Control	Use
Text box	Move the pointer over the text box until it changes to an I-beam shape, then click. Type text entries manually. If you make a mistake, press the Backspace or Delete key to erase characters.
List box	You will see two types of lists. *Scrolling lists* show a columnar list of choices (refer to Figure 23.5). Click the up or down arrow on the right side of the list to scroll through the list, and then click the item that you want. The selected item appears in highlighted text (and might also appear in the text box above the list). The second type of list, a *drop-down list*, like the one shown in Figure 23.6, displays its scrolling list after you click the down arrow.
Option button	Click one option from within a group of option buttons. (You can select only one option button in each group.) The selected option button has a darkened center. To remove a selection, select a different option in the same group.
Check box	Click a check box to turn it on or off. Check boxes are square and contain an X when selected. You can select more than one check box at a time.
Spinner	Click the up or down arrow on the right side of a spinner to make the number change in increments of one.
Command button	Click a command button to complete the command, cancel the command, or open an additional dialog box for more alternatives.
Dialog tab	Click a dialog tab to see another grouping of options.

Using the Mouse in Dialog Boxes To select an option button or check box, click it. Clicking a blank check box selects it by putting an X in it. Clicking a check box that already has an X removes the X. To turn off an option button, click one of the other option buttons in the group.

To choose command buttons such as OK, Cancel, Yes, or No, click them.

See "Editing Text in Text Boxes," **p. 667**

To select from a scrolling list box, click in the list box and then scroll through the list by clicking the up or down arrow in the scroll bar at the right side of the list box. To jump through large sections of the list, click in the scroll bar's shaded area. For long moves, drag the scroll bar's square to the new location. When the desired selection appears in the list box, click that selection.

Some Windows applications use drop-down list boxes. When closed, these list boxes look like the Printer list box shown in Figure 23.7 when closed; when open, they look like the same list box as shown in Figure 23.8. To select from a drop-down list box, click the down arrow on the text box's right side. When the scrolling list appears, select from it the same way that you select from any scrolling list box: Click the item that you want.

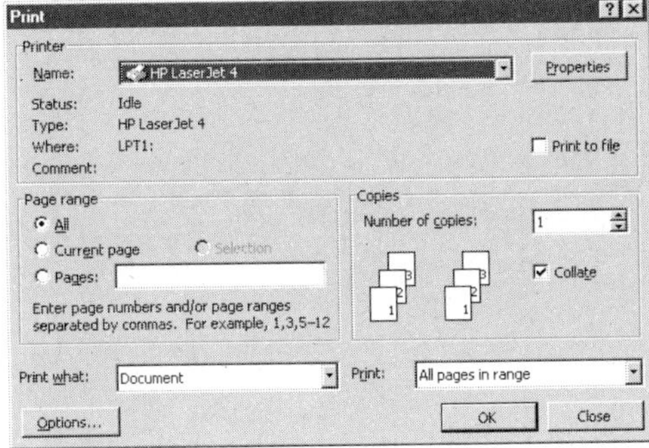

FIG. 23.7
The Printer drop-down list box when closed.

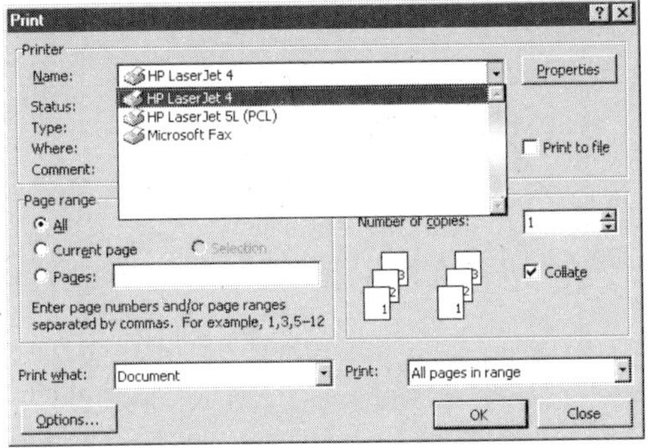

FIG. 23.8
The Printer drop-down list box when open.

NOTE In some dialog boxes, double-clicking an option button or an item in a list selects that option and simultaneously chooses the OK command button. In the Open dialog box, for example, you can double-click a file name to select and open the file. Experiment with the dialog boxes in your applications to determine whether double-clicking is a viable shortcut.

Using the Keyboard in Dialog Boxes Some drawing or graphics applications require that you use the mouse. In most Windows applications, however, you have the same functionality available from either the keyboard or the mouse. You might find that in some situations using the keyboard to control Windows is faster or more convenient.

To access a group of option buttons with the keyboard, you press Alt+*letter*, where *letter* is the underlined character that appears in an option's label. If the individual options do not have an underlined letter, press Alt+*letter*, where the underlined *letter* is in the title of the option group; then use the arrow keys to select an option.

To select a check box, press Alt+*letter*, where *letter* is the underlined character in the check box's label. Each time that you press Alt+*letter*, you toggle the check box between selected and deselected. An X appears in the check box when the box is selected. You also can toggle the active check box between selected and deselected by pressing the spacebar.

To make an entry in a text box, select the text box by pressing Alt+*letter*, where *letter* is the underlined character in the name of the text box. Press Alt+N, for example, to select the File Name text box in the Save As dialog box shown in Figure 23.9. Type a text entry or edit the existing entry by using the editing techniques described in the upcoming section "Editing Text in Text Boxes."

FIG. 23.9
The Save As dialog box's File Name text box when selected.

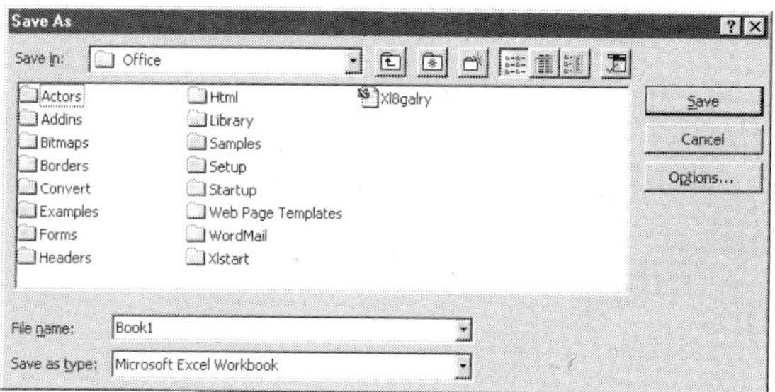

To select from a list of alternatives in a scrolling list box, select the list box by pressing Alt+*letter*, where *letter* is the underlined character in the name of the list box. When the list box is active, use the up or down arrow key or Page Up or Page Down to move through the list. The text is selected and displayed in reversed type. (To use the keyboard to display a drop-down scrolling list, press Alt+*letter* to activate the list and then press Alt+down arrow to drop the list. Then select items by pressing the up or down arrow keys.)

To select a command button, press Alt+*letter*, or if no letter is underlined, press Tab or Shift+Tab until a dashed line encloses the name of the button that you want. Press the spacebar to select the active button indicated by the dashed enclosure. At any time, you can select the command button that appears in bold type (usually the OK button) by pressing Enter. Press Esc to choose the Cancel button and escape from a dialog box without making any changes.

Changing Folders in Save As and Open Dialog Boxes When you save a file on your hard disk, Windows places the file in a folder in your hard disk. Folders are analogous to the file drawers and file folders that you use in your office to help you organize and locate your papers. You can locate files more easily if you store related files together in a folder. For example, you can store all the business letters that you create with your word processor in a folder named LETTERS and all your proposals in a folder named PROPOSALS.

Don't store the files that you create in the folders that store your program files. If you ever have to reinstall or upgrade a program, you might lose files that you store in the program folders. Also, these folders are already full of files, and it is difficult to find yours. Create your own folders, and folders within folders, to store your files.

The first time that you use the File, Open, or File, Save As command in a program, the application usually assumes that you want to open or save a document in that program's folder. Usually, however, you want to open or save a file in one of your own folders. You must tell the program where the file that you want to open is located or where you want to save a file—whether that location is a different folder, a different drive on your hard disk, or a disk inserted in Drive A or B. To switch folders or drives, use the appropriate list boxes in the Open and Save As dialog boxes, as discussed in the following paragraphs.

See "Using Windows Explorer to View Files and Folders," **p. 312**

See "Working with Long File Names," **p. 343**

The selected folder appears in the Look In drop-down list (see Figure 23.10). You can display this list to select another drive.

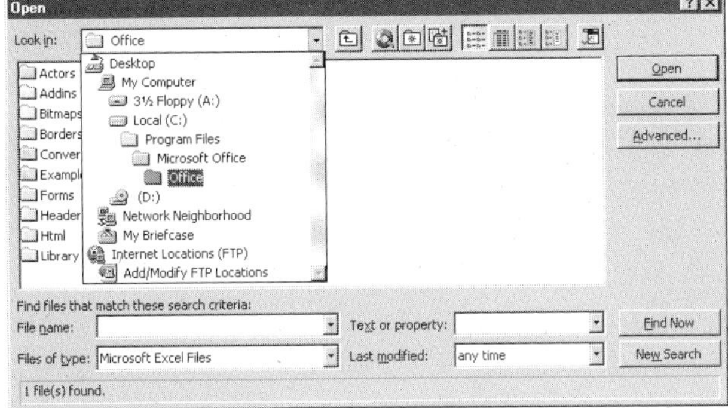

FIG. 23.10
Open the Look In drop-down list to select a different drive in the Open and Save As dialog boxes.

The list box includes all the folders in the current folder. An icon that resembles a file folder represents each folder. If you want to open a file in a folder contained within another folder, you first must open the folder containing the folder with the file. You can do so by double-clicking the folder icon.

To change disk drives or folders in the Open or Save As dialog boxes, follow these steps:

1. Display the Look In drop-down list by clicking its drop-down arrow, and then select the drive that you want.
2. To select a folder, double-click the folder icon. You can also click the Up One Level button to move up one level in the folder structure.
3. Select the file from the list, or type the file name in the File Name text box.
4. Choose Open or Save.

Editing Text in Text Boxes You can use the text-editing techniques that you learn in this section in all Windows applications. Although the editing techniques described are specifically for the text boxes that appear in dialog boxes, they also apply to editing text in other locations in Windows applications.

To use a mouse when editing text in a text box, you position the pointer over the text where you want to place the insertion point, and then click. When moving over editable text, the pointer changes from an arrowhead to an I-beam shape. To select multiple characters, drag across the characters.

While positioned in a text box, you can press left or right arrow keys to move left or right, End to move to the end of the text, and Home to move to the beginning of the text.

To delete a character to the right of the flashing insertion point, press Delete. Press Backspace to delete a character to the left of the insertion point.

Replace existing text with new text by selecting the text that you want to replace and then typing the new text. Select text with the mouse by dragging the I-beam across the text as you hold down the mouse button. To select text with the keyboard, move the insertion point to the left of the first character that you want to select, press and hold down Shift, and press the right arrow key.

NOTE When editing text in an application, you usually can use Edit menu commands such as Undo, Copy, and Paste. Although these commands often do not work in dialog boxes, the keystroke equivalents Ctrl+C (to copy), Ctrl+X (to cut), and Ctrl+V (to paste) frequently do work.

Controlling the Size and Position of Windows

Just as you move papers on your desktop, you can move and reorder windows on-screen. In fact, you can resize windows, expand them to full size, shrink them to a small icon to save space, and restore them to their original size.

The easiest way to resize and reposition application or document windows is with the mouse. As you will see, you can simply drag title bars or edges to move windows or change their size.

As you move the mouse pointer over edges of application or document windows, the pointer changes shape. Each shape, shown in Table 23.3, indicates the type of window change that you can make by dragging that edge or corner. Before you can move a window, it must be active—that is, the window must be on top. To activate a window, you can click it or press Alt+Tab until you select the application.

Table 23.3 Pointer Shapes Used When Moving or Resizing Windows

Shape	Pointer	Mouse Action
↔	Left/right	Drag the edge left or right
↕	Up/down	Drag the edge up or down
↘	Corner	Drag the corner in any direction

Using Taskbar Shortcuts to Arrange Windows

There are times when you want to quickly arrange a few applications on your desktop so that you can compare documents, drag and drop between documents, and so on. Manually moving and resizing each window is a tedious job, so Windows 95 has a few shortcuts that can make this type of work easier.

When the taskbar has a lot of application buttons, the titles may be too truncated to read. Pause the pointer over a button to see a pop-up title.

First, you can make your desktop easier to work on by minimizing all applications so that they appear as buttons on the taskbar. To do this quickly, right-click a blank area of the taskbar. When the shortcut menu appears, click Minimize All Windows.

If you want to compare documents in two or three applications, minimize all applications except the two or three you want to work with and then right-click a gray area of the taskbar. When the shortcut menu appears, click either Tile Horizontally or Tile Vertically. Your applications will appear in adjacent windows that fill the screen as shown in Figure 23.11.

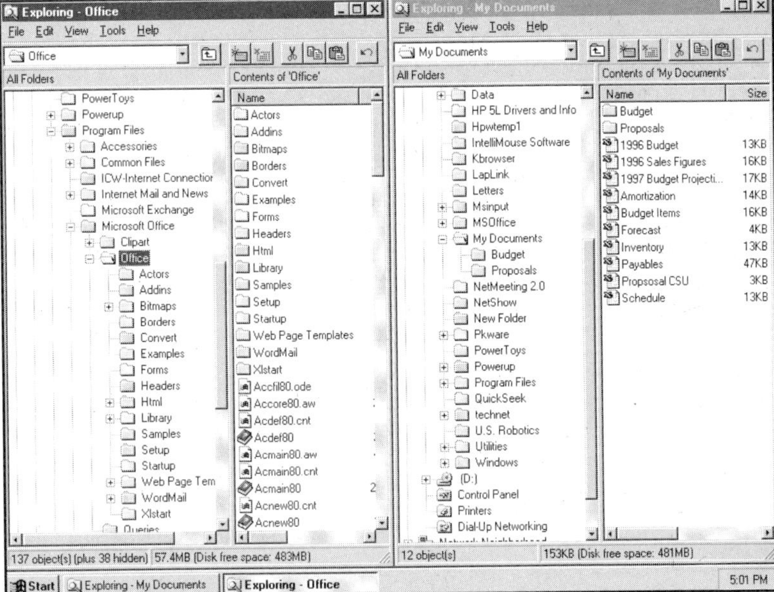

FIG. 23.11 Tiling application windows horizontally or vertically makes it easy to compare documents or to drag and drop contents.

If you want to be able to quickly see all the application title bars so that you can click title bars to switch between many application windows, right-click in the gray area of the taskbar. When the shortcut menu appears, click Cascade. The windows will arrange as shown in Figure 23.12.

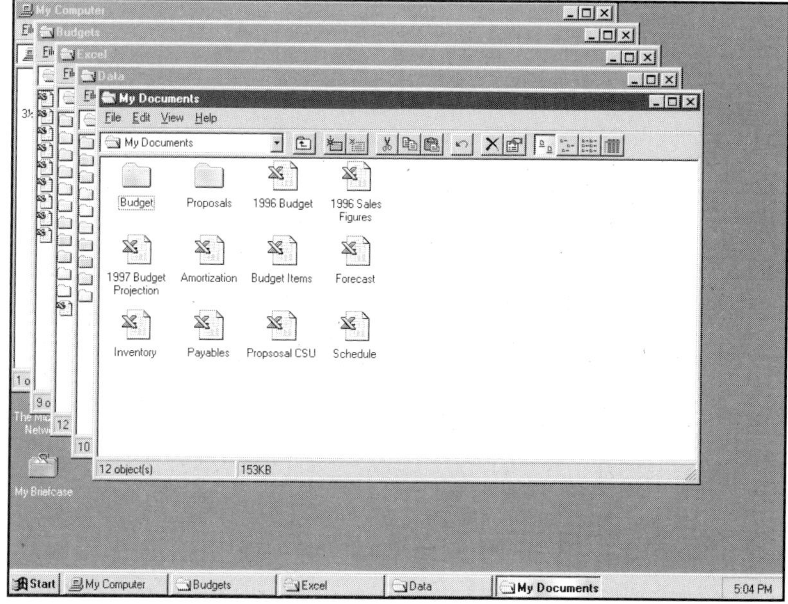

FIG. 23.12
Cascading application windows overlays them so that you can see each title bar. It is then easy to move among windows by clicking the title bars.

Moving a Window or a Desktop Icon

If an application window is not maximized (does not fill the screen), you can move the application's window. Move the pointer over the application's title at the top of its window, hold down the left mouse button, and drag the window to its new location. Windows displays an outline that indicates the application's position. When you release the mouse button, the window moves to its new position.

To drag document windows within the application, you use the same technique. As long as the document is within a window, you can drag its title bar. You can more easily arrange some documents within the application by choosing Window, Arrange All. This command puts document windows in predefined layouts.

Changing the Size of a Window

You cannot size a maximized window—a window that fills the screen—because you cannot make it any larger.

To change the size of a window with the mouse, you first activate the window by clicking it. Move the pointer to one edge or corner of the window until the pointer changes to a two-headed arrow (refer to Table 23.3). Press and hold down the mouse button, and then drag the double-headed arrow to move the edge or corner of the window to resize it. The moving edge appears as an outline until you release the mouse button.

To move two edges at once with the mouse, move the pointer to the corner of a window so that the pointer becomes a two-headed arrow tilted at a 45-degree angle. Drag the corner to its new location and release the mouse button.

Learning About Drag and Drop

After becoming proficient at operating Windows and its programs with commands, you will want to learn some of the faster, but less obvious, methods of controlling Windows and its programs. One of the most powerful methods is *drag and drop*.

The term *drag and drop* specifies exactly the action that the method uses. You click an object, such as a folder, and then hold down the mouse button as you drag the object to a new location. You drop the object by releasing the mouse button.

▶ **See** "Drag-and-Drop Printing from the Desktop," **p. 150**

▶ **See** "Backing Up with a Simple Drag and Drop," **p. 431**

For drag-and-drop methods to work, each Windows object has to know how to behave when dropped on other Windows objects. For example, if you drag the icon of a file in Windows Explorer and drop it on the icon for a program, the program starts and loads that file.

Figure 23.13 illustrates how you can use drag and drop to make frequently used folders more accessible. Instead of tediously having to find the folder each time in Windows Explorer, you can put a shortcut icon on the desktop that enables you to open the folder directly. To create a shortcut icon with drag and drop, follow these steps:

1. Double-click the My Computer icon to open its window. Make sure that the window does not fill the screen.
2. Double-click the local drive icon for your computer.
3. Click a folder that you frequently use, then hold down the right mouse button and drag the folder out of the window and over the desktop.

   In Figure 23.13, the user has dragged the Budgets folder to the desktop.
4. Release the right mouse button. A menu appears over the folder on the desktop as shown in Figure 23.13.
5. Choose the Create Shortcut(s) Here command.

TIP You can tell at a glance that an icon is shortcut by the small arrow at the lower-left corner.

The Shortcut to Budgets icon, shown in Figure 23.14, remains on the desktop even after you close the My Computer windows. You can open the folder at any time by double-clicking the shortcut icon.

FIG. 23.13
The user has dragged the reverse-colored Budgets folder (by holding down the right mouse button) and dropped the folder to the desktop. When you release the mouse button, a shortcut menu appears.

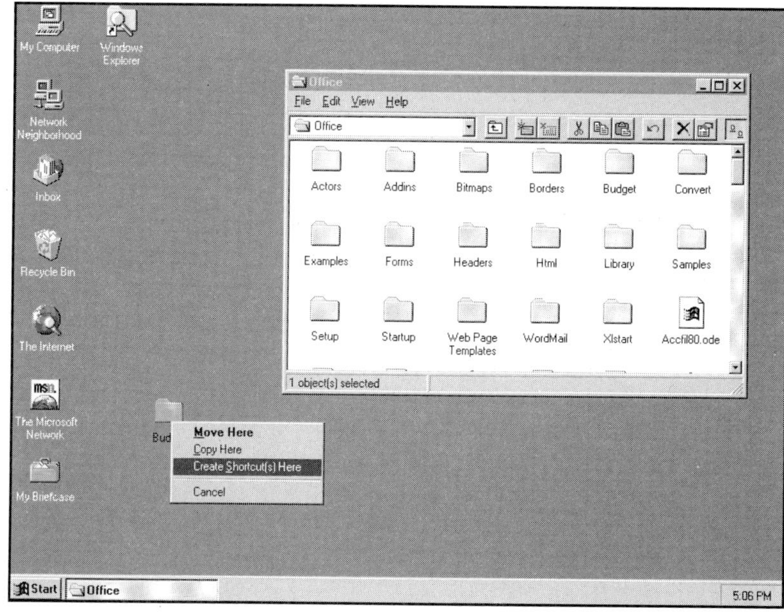

FIG. 23.14
Choosing the Create Shortcut(s) Here command produces a shortcut icon on the desktop that you can click to start the application.

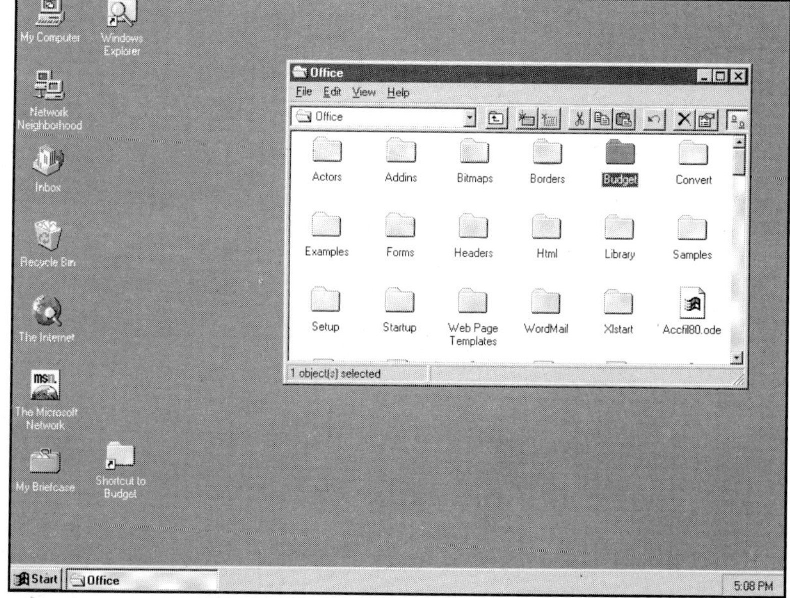

CAUTION

When dragging and dropping a file or folder, make sure that you use the right mouse button and choose Create Shortcut(s) Here from the shortcut menu. This creates a shortcut icon while leaving the original file or folder in its original location. If you delete the shortcut icon, the original file or folder remains intact. If you delete an original icon (which you create by dragging with the left mouse button) from your desktop, Windows deletes the original file or folder along with the icon. If the file is important, this causes a disaster and a lot of interoffice panic.

NOTE Drag-and-drop features are available only with Windows applications that are compatible with Object Linking and Embedding (OLE).

You can use the drag-and-drop method to save time in many ways. You can move and copy files and folders, which makes reorganizing the contents on your computer easy. You can drag a shortcut for your printer onto your desktop, drag documents from My Computer or Windows Explorer, and then drop them onto the printer icon, which prints the documents. With applications compatible with the OLE 2 specifications, you can even drag and drop objects from one application to another. For example, you can drag a table from a spreadsheet into a word processing document.

Throughout this book, you accomplish your computer tasks by using drag-and-drop methods. Always look for ways to use these methods for saving time and trouble.

Changing Settings and Properties with the Right Mouse Button

One important Windows concept is that most objects that you see on-screen have *properties* related to them. Properties can include such characteristics as an object's appearance and behavior.

You can change some properties, but others are *read only*—you can view them, but cannot change them. For example, changeable properties of the Windows desktop include the types of patterns and wallpapers used as backgrounds and the color of different screen elements. Read-only properties that you can see but not change include a file's size or a program's version number.

You can experiment to find properties in Windows, the Explorer, and most Windows 95 applications. To see an object's properties, point to the object and click the right mouse button (that is, you *right-click* the object). A properties sheet appears, or a menu displays a Properties command. For example, you can place the pointer's tip on most objects, such as the desktop or a file, and then click the right mouse button. From the menu that appears, select the Properties command.

NOTE Don't be afraid to experiment when you look for properties. To discover how you can customize Windows, right-click files, taskbars, and so on. If you do not want to change the object's properties, press the Esc key or click the Cancel button in the properties sheet that appears.

To see the properties that you can change on the desktop, right-click the desktop and then choose the Properties command. The Display properties sheet shown in Figure 23.15 appears. In this dialog box, you can change the display's background, color, and screen saver, as well as display adapter settings. To learn how to change these settings, see Chapter 32, "Customizing the Desktop Settings." Click the Cancel button to remove the dialog box without making changes.

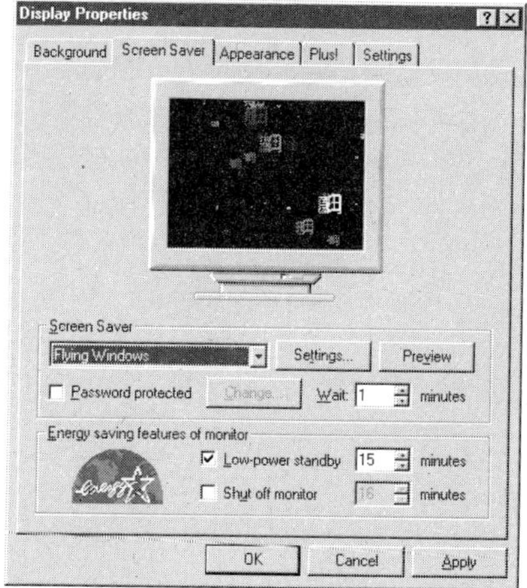

FIG. 23.15
Right-click the desktop and then choose Properties to see the desktop properties. The Screen Saver page, shown here, enables you to choose one.

If you want to change how the taskbar operates, right-click a blank area of the taskbar and then choose the Properties command. The Taskbar properties sheet is displayed. On this sheet, you can add or remove applications from the Start menu, or change when and how the taskbar is displayed. Chapter 31, "Customizing the Taskbar and Start Menu," describes this properties sheet and how to customize the taskbar. Click the Cancel button to remove the dialog box without making changes.

Working with Applications

Many operations are similar among Windows applications. Nearly all Windows applications, for example, start with the File and Edit menus. The File menu includes commands for opening, closing, saving, and printing files. The Edit menu includes commands for cutting, copying, pasting, and other editing actions specific to the application. The procedures you use to control menus and select items in dialog boxes are the same in nearly all Windows applications.

Opening, Saving, and Closing Documents

When you create or edit a document and then save the document, you create a *file* that Windows stores in a magnetic recording on disk. The file contains all the information necessary to re-create the document in your program. When this book uses the term *file*, it usually refers to the information stored on the computer's hard disk or on a removable disk.

When first started, many applications present a new, empty document: It's a blank page if the application is a word processing, graphics, or desktop publishing application; it's an empty worksheet if the application is a spreadsheet application. If you finish working on one file, you can start a new file by choosing File, New. Your application might ask you for information about the type of new file to start.

To open an existing file, choose File, Open. An Open dialog box similar to the one shown in Figure 23.16 appears. In the Look In drop-down list, select the drive that contains your file. The Look In drop-down list displays your computer's drives as icons. Click the drive you want to look in. In the Look In box, select the folder that contains your file and then choose OK to display the list of files in that folder. From the files presented, select the one that you want to open and then choose OK or press Enter.

FIG. 23.16
The Open dialog box is common to many Windows applications.

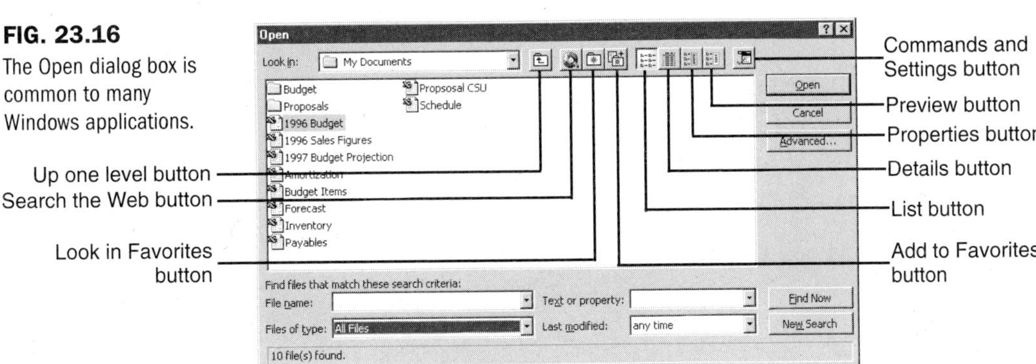

TIP Double-click a file name in the Open dialog box to open that file.

You can do far more in a Windows 95 Open dialog box than meets the eye. Click a button at the top of the dialog box to get the result you want. Table 23.4 lists the buttons and their results.

Table 23.4 Open Dialog Box Buttons

Button	Result
Up One Level	Moves up to the next higher folder
Search the Web	Opens the Search page of your Internet browser

continues

Table 23.4 Continued

Button	Result
Look in Favorites	Displays a list of favorite or frequently used files
Add to Favorites	Adds the selected file to the Favorites list
List	Displays files in a list view
Details	Displays files with all file details shown
Properties	Displays a file or folder's properties
Preview	Displays the contents of a file using QuickView
Commands and Settings	Displays a shortcut menu from which you can print, sort, or search for files and map to a network drive

Explore with your right mouse button by clicking files or folders to see some of the things you can do to files and folders. When you right-click a file or folder, a shortcut menu appears with various commands from which you can choose. The specific commands on the menu can vary, depending on the file type. Table 23.5 lists the basic options that are available for most file types.

In some applications, you can open multiple documents by selecting the files with Ctrl+click and then clicking the Open button.

Table 23.5 Shortcut Commands for Files and Folders

Command	Result
Open	Opens the file.
Open Read Only	Opens the file as a read-only document that must be saved to a different file name.
Print	Prints the file.
Quick View	Displays a preview of the file.
Send To	Copies the file to a shortcut folder, floppy disk, or mail or Fax address.
Cut	Removes the file or folder from its location in preparation to paste it elsewhere.
Copy	Copies the file or folder in preparation to copy it elsewhere.
Paste	Pastes a file or folder that has been cut or copied. (This command appears only when a file or folder has been cut or copied to the Clipboard.)

Command	Result
Create Shortcut	Creates a shortcut to the file or folder.
Delete	Deletes the selection(s).
Properties	Displays the file or folder's properties.

The File menu contains two commands for saving files: Save As and Save. Choose one of these commands the first time that you save a file. They tell Windows where to save the file and enable you to name your file. If you choose File, Save As, you can create a new version of an existing file by specifying a new name for the file. The Save As dialog box is often similar to the Open dialog box shown in Figure 23.16. In the Save As dialog box, you must specify the drive and folder to which you want to save your file and name the file.

After you type the file name in the File name text box, choose Save or press Enter to save the file. After you name your file, you can choose File, Save to save it without changing its name or location. The File, Save command replaces the original file.

To close a document, you often can choose File, Close. If you choose File, Exit, you exit the application. When you close or exit a Windows application, you might be prompted to save any changes that you made since you last saved your document.

Scrolling in a Document

Most applications include scroll bars at the right and bottom edges of the screen, as shown in Figure 23.17. You can use the vertical scroll bar at the right to scroll up and down in your document. You can use the horizontal scroll bar to scroll left and right. To scroll a short distance, click the arrow at either end of a scroll bar, and you will scroll in the direction that the arrow points. To scroll a longer distance, click in the gray area next to the arrow or drag the scroll bar box to a new location. In many applications, the scroll bars are optional; if you want more working space, you can turn them off.

FIG. 23.17
To scroll through a document, use the scroll bars on the window's right and bottom sides.

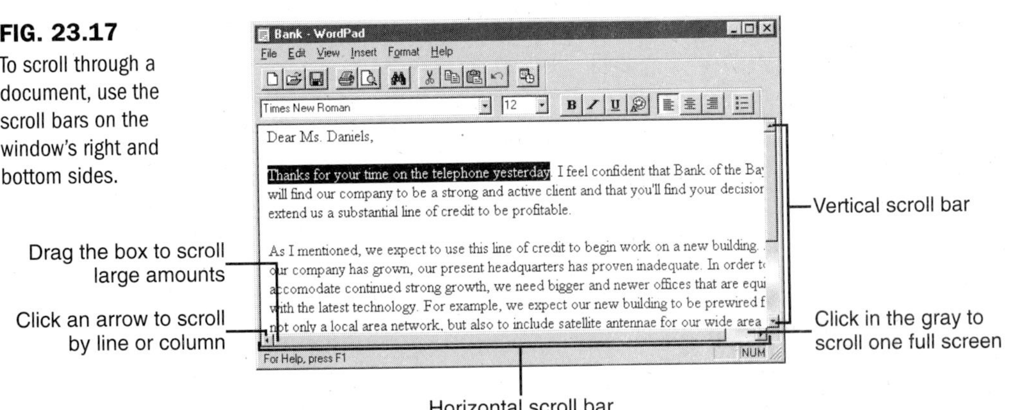

To scroll with the keyboard, you can press the arrow keys to move a character or line at a time, or press the Page Up or Page Down keys to move a screen at a time. With most applications the Home key scrolls you to the left margin, and the End key takes you to the end of the line or the right side. Holding down the Ctrl key while pressing any other scrolling key extends the scroll: Ctrl+Home, for example, takes you to the beginning of your file; Ctrl+End takes you to the end of the file; Ctrl+left arrow or Ctrl+right arrow moves you a word at a time rather than a character at a time. Most applications have many shortcuts for scrolling.

If you use the scroll bars to scroll, the insertion point does not move—it remains where it was before you scrolled. If you use the keyboard to scroll, the insertion point moves as you scroll.

Using Simple Editing Techniques

Editing text and objects is similar in all Windows applications. When you work with text, in your document or in a dialog box, the mouse pointer turns into an I-beam when you move it over editable text. You can use the I-beam to move the insertion point and select text. The flashing vertical insertion point is where the text that you type appears. (The insertion point is equivalent to the cursor in DOS applications.)

Although the pointer changes to an I-beam over editable text, you cannot edit at the location until you click the mouse button.

You can use the mouse or the keyboard to move the insertion point. To use the mouse, position the I-beam where you want the insertion point in the text and click the left mouse button. (If you cannot see the insertion point, it might be under the I-beam. Move the mouse a little to move the I-beam.) To use the keyboard to move the insertion point, press the arrow keys.

See "Cutting, Copying, and Pasting Data," **p. 903**

See "Understanding Data Linking," **p. 913**

See "Embedding Information in Your Documents," **p. 922**

To insert text at the insertion point, you simply type. Most applications push existing text to the right to make room for the new text (although some applications enable you to select an overtype mode, which replaces existing text as you type). To delete text to the left of the insertion point, press the Backspace key. To delete text to the right of the insertion point, press the Delete key.

Most applications contain an "oops" function: the Edit, Undo command. This command undoes your most recent edit (or more edits, depending on the program).

CAUTION

If you accidentally press the Insert key, you turn on Overtype mode, which types new text over existing text. If this happens, press the Insert key again. Some applications display "OVR" or a similar indicator in the status bar to show when they are in Overtype mode.

Selecting Text and Objects

You can sum up one of the most important editing rules in all Windows applications with three simple words: select, then do. You must select text or an object before you can do anything to it. If you don't select first, the application doesn't know where to apply your command.

To select text and objects, you can use the mouse or the keyboard. To select text with the mouse, position the I-beam at the beginning of the text that you want to select, click and hold down the left mouse button, drag to the end of the text that you want to select, and release the mouse button. To select text with the keyboard, position the insertion point at the beginning of the text that you want to select, press and hold down the Shift key, use arrow keys to move to the end of the text that you want to select, and then release the Shift and arrow keys. The selected text appears in reverse type, as shown in Figure 23.17.

Many shortcuts exist for selecting. Some of the following shortcuts apply to text in many Windows documents and dialog boxes:

- To select a word with the mouse, double-click the word.
- To select a word using the keyboard, hold down Ctrl+Shift while pressing the left or right arrow key.
- To select a length of text with the mouse, you can drag until you touch the end of the screen, which causes the screen to scroll.

  To select a length of text with the keyboard, position the I-beam where you want to start the selection, hold down the Shift key, and scroll to the end of the selection by using any keyboard scrolling technique.

After you select a word, you can change its appearance. For example, you might make the word bold or change its font. In most applications, typing replaces the selection, which enables you to replace text by selecting it and typing the new text. If you select a graphic, you can resize it or apply formatting.

To use the mouse to select an object such as a picture, click the object. (To select multiple objects, hold down Shift while you click each one in turn.) To select an object with the keyboard, position the insertion point beside the object, hold down Shift, and press an arrow key to move the object in the direction indicated by the arrow key. Selected objects, such as graphics, usually appear with *selection handles* (small black boxes) on each side and corner. These handles are used to resize and move objects.

Copying and Moving

After selecting text or an object, you can use the Edit menu to copy or move the selection. The Edit menu commands, that all Windows applications use to copy and move, are Cut, Copy, and Paste. The Edit, Cut command removes the selection from your document, and Edit, Copy duplicates it. Both commands transfer the selection to the Clipboard, a temporary holding area. The Edit, Paste command copies the selection from the Clipboard and into your document at the insertion point's location. Your selection remains in the Clipboard until you replace it with another selection.

To copy and paste between documents and dialog boxes, try using the shortcut keys described in this section.

To copy a selection, choose Edit, Copy; then move the insertion point to where you want to duplicate the selection, and choose Edit, Paste. To move a selection, choose Edit, Cut; then move the insertion point to where you want to move it, and choose Edit, Paste. Many shortcuts exist for copying and moving. Ctrl+X usually cuts a selection, Ctrl+C copies a selection, and Ctrl+V usually pastes the Clipboard's contents. Many Windows applications also take advantage of the Windows drag-and-drop feature, which enables you to use the mouse to drag a selection to its new location and drop it into place.

Because all applications running under Windows share the Clipboard, you can move or copy a selection between documents and between applications as easily as you can move and copy within a file. The next two sections explain how to switch between documents and applications.

Switching Between Document Windows

In many (but not all) Windows applications, you can easily open more than one document and switch between the documents in the same application. Use these techniques when you want to copy or move information from one document to another. To open multiple documents, choose File, Open each time for a different document. If your application doesn't support multiple documents, it closes the current file, asking whether you want to save any changes that you made since you last saved.

If your application supports multiple documents, each document opens in its own document window as shown in Figure 23.18. Multiple document windows have a document Control menu to control the active document window's size and position.

The document Control menu appears to the left of the document title bar, or if the document is displayed as a full screen, to the left of the menu bar. You can click the document Control-menu icon to display the Control menu. This menu enables you to change the window's size or close the document. If you are using the keyboard, press Alt+hyphen (-). There is, however, an easier way to control document windows than through the document Control menu.

A faster way to control documents in Windows is to use the buttons that appear at the top right corner of each document, as shown in Figures 23.19 and 23.20. If the document fills the application window, the Restore Document button appears to the right of the menu bar as shown in Figure 23.19.

If a document is in its own window, three buttons appear at the top right corner of the document's title bar, as shown in Figure 23.20. Click one of these buttons to reduce the document to an icon, enlarge the document to fill the application window, or close the document.

Reducing a document window creates an icon in the application window such as that shown in Figure 23.21. Notice that this icon has three buttons that you can click to restore the document to a window, enlarge it to full screen, or close it.

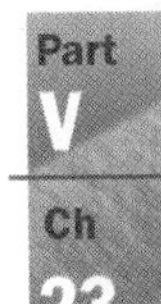

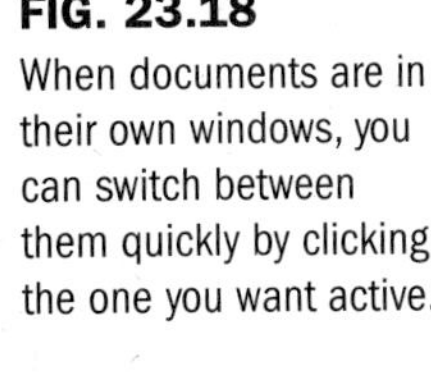

FIG. 23.18
When documents are in their own windows, you can switch between them quickly by clicking the one you want active.

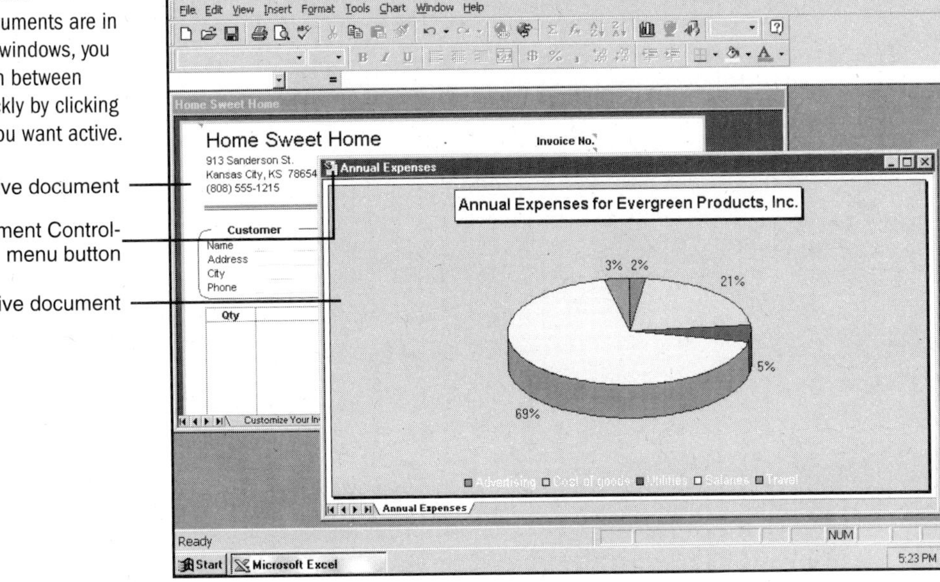

FIG. 23.19
Maximized documents fill the entire program window.

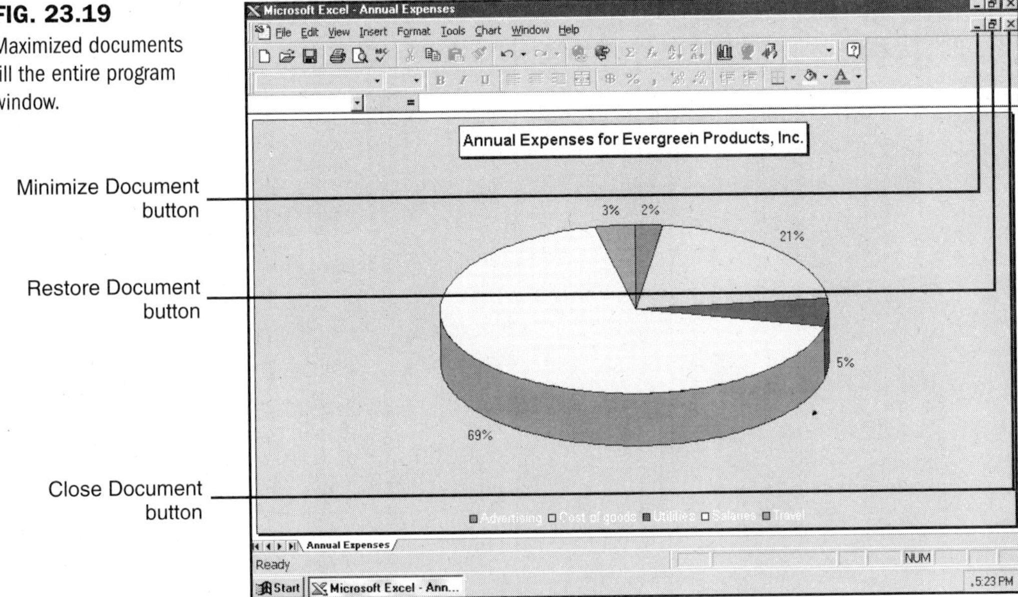

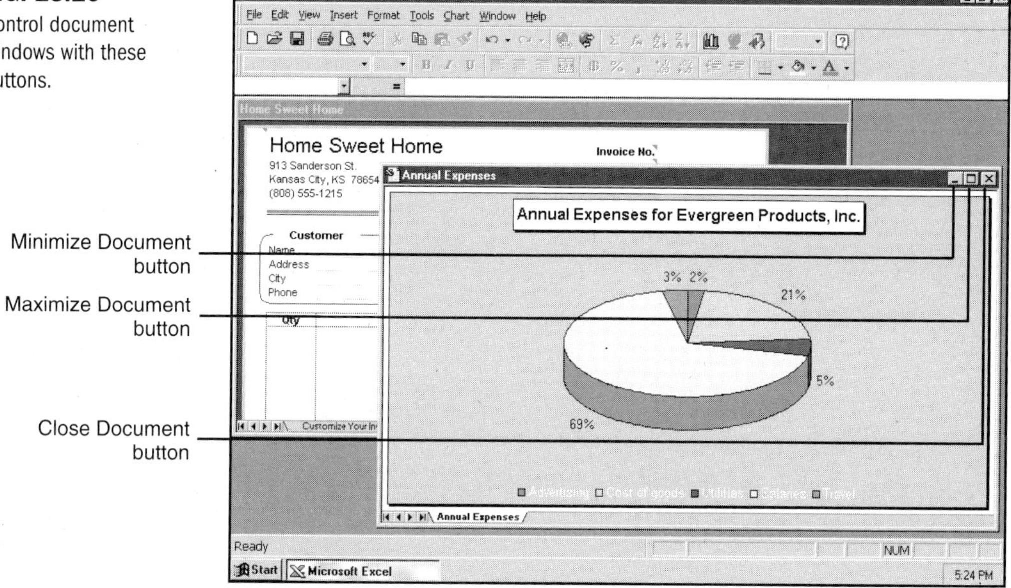

FIG. 23.20
Control document windows with these buttons.

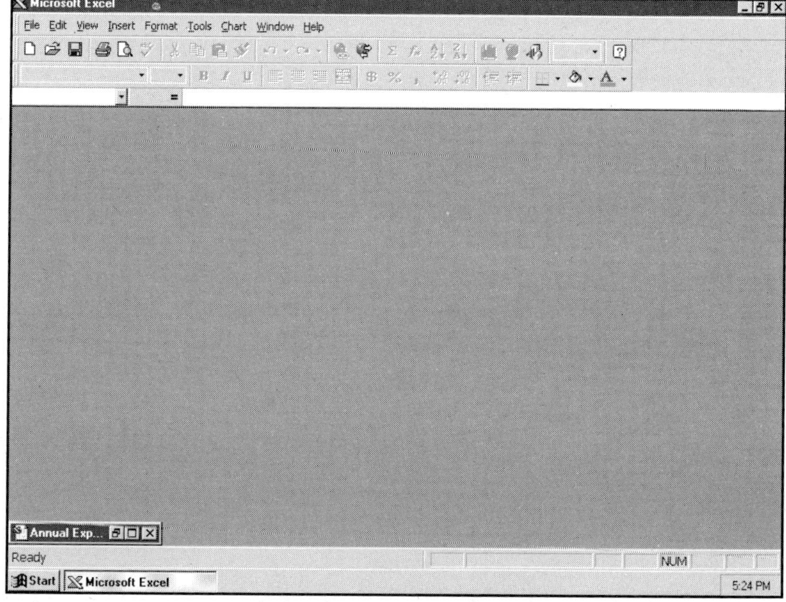

FIG. 23.21
Documents reduced to icons require less space in the program's window.

Switching Between Applications

When you run several applications, you need an easy way to switch between them. If the taskbar is visible, you can switch to another application by clicking the application's button in the taskbar. If you cannot see the taskbar, press Ctrl+Esc to display it and open the Start menu.

Another way to switch between applications is to hold down the Alt key and press Tab. When you first press Alt+Tab, a bar with open applications appears, as shown in Figure 23.22. Continue holding the Alt key to keep the bar on screen. Each time you press Alt+Tab, the next application on the bar is selected. A box encloses the icon of the active application. Press Shift+Alt+Tab to move the selection to the application to the left. Release Alt+Tab when you have selected the application that you want to activate.

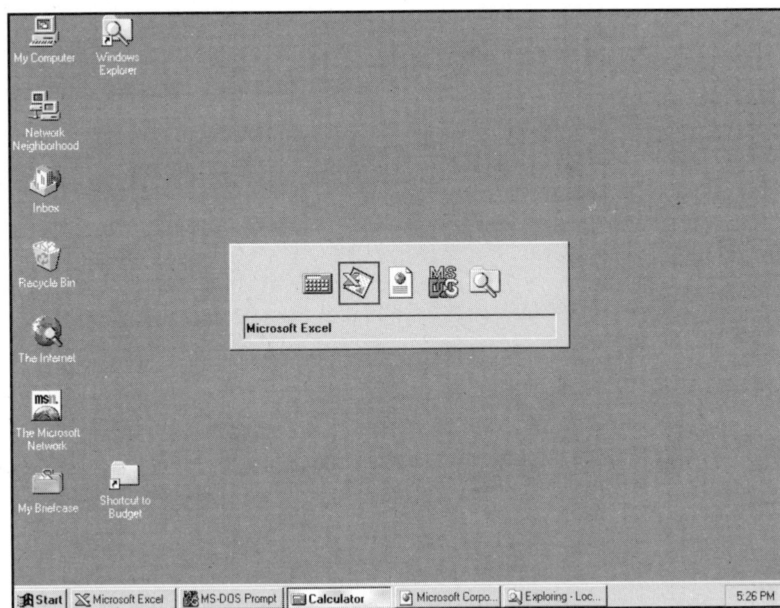

FIG. 23.22
Press Alt+Tab to switch to another open application.

To switch between document windows with the mouse, click the window that you want to activate. If the window that you want to activate is not visible, you might have to move or size the active window on top. (To move a window, drag its title bar; to size a window, drag its border.) To use the keyboard to switch between document windows, open the Window menu and select from the list of open windows the document that you want.

CHAPTER 24

Installing, Running, and Uninstalling Windows Applications

by Michael O'Mara

Install 16-bit applications in Windows 95

Look here to find out how to install applications that were written for the Windows 3.x environment.

Install Windows 95 applications

This is where you learn how to use Setup to install Windows 95 applications.

Add and remove Windows component applications

Refer to this section to learn how to use the Add/Remove Programs icon in Control Panel to install and uninstall individual components of Windows 95 without having to reinstall Windows 95 from scratch.

Uninstall applications

Find out how to uninstall a Windows application in Windows 95 automatically, using the Add/Remove Programs icon, or manually, if Windows 95 can't do it automatically.

An operating system provides the foundation for applications such as word processors, spreadsheets, and graphics programs. The applications don't come with the operating system; you must purchase and install your applications separately.

In the old days of DOS-based applications, installing a new program was fairly simple. Usually you just copied files into a directory on your hard disk. Efforts to integrate the application into your system seldom went beyond adding a couple of lines to your AUTOEXEC.BAT or CONFIG.SYS file. Each application stood alone with minimal interaction with the operating system and no interaction with other applications.

Now things have changed. Applications are bigger, more powerful, and much more complex. They've become so intertwined with the operating system that it's hard to tell where the dividing line is between Windows and an application. And nearly every Windows application has the potential to interact with any other Windows application on your system.

Not surprisingly, the process of installing and removing applications has grown more complex as well. Fortunately, as application installation grew more complicated, application developers turned to automated setup programs to handle most installation chores. And Windows 95 adds new features to further automate adding and removing applications.

Not long ago, the typical PC user worked with only a couple of applications, and never used more than one program at a time. Now, multitasking is a way of life. The average Windows user probably works with a dozen applications regularly, several of which are likely to be open and running simultaneously. To juggle all those concurrent tasks effectively, you need to understand how Windows manages tasks behind the scenes.

Understanding How Windows Runs Applications

Windows 95 can run applications designed specifically for Windows 95. It also can run most older Windows 3.1 applications, DOS-based applications, and applications designed for Windows NT. Windows 95 no longer requires the traditional CONFIG.SYS, AUTOEXEC.BAT, and INI files for configuration information. However, for backward-compatibility, Windows 95 can use settings from INI files and can maintain its own versions of CONFIG.SYS and AUTOEXEC.BAT in order to support loading real-mode device drivers.

Although Windows 95 can run various kinds of applications successfully, it provides different kinds of support for each category of application. Windows applications fall into one of two general categories: 32-bit applications (designed for Windows NT and Windows 95) and 16-bit applications (designed for Windows 3.1 and earlier versions). This section describes how Windows 95 runs these programs. Chapter 25, " Installing, Running, and Uninstalling MS-DOS Applications," discusses DOS-based applications.

Support for Win32 Applications

Windows 95 offers several significant advantages over Windows 3.1. Some advantages such as preemptive multitasking and multithreading support are available only to 32-bit applications.

See "Working with Long File Names," **p. 343**

Support for long file names is one feature of Windows 95's 32-bit operating system that is available to any application designed to make use of it. Of course, all Windows 95 applications will let you create file names containing up to 255 characters, allowing you to assign files names such as "First Quarter Sales Results" instead of "1QSALES." Theoretically, program developers can adapt 16-bit applications to use long file names as well. However, don't expect many older Windows applications to add long file name support; the programmers are likely to concentrate on converting the application to full-fledged 32-bit status instead of spending time on minor upgrades.

Most applications benefit from Windows 95's 32-bit architecture, which makes memory addressing more efficient. In addition, Windows 95 runs each 32-bit application in its own memory space. Ordinarily, such details are of interest only to programmers. However, these advantages have a side effect that all users will appreciate. If a 32-bit application hangs or crashes, the problem is isolated, confined to the application's own address space, and thus unlikely to affect other running applications. You can simply exit the problem application and, without even rebooting, have Windows 95 clean up the affected memory.

See "Managing Windows After an Application Failure," **p. 270**

Advantages of Preemptive Multitasking and Multithreading Despite appearances, our computers can't really perform multiple tasks from several different applications all at the same instant. Generally, computers perform only one or two tasks at a time, but it can do so very fast. Therefore, if the applications are designed to break operations into small tasks, the operating system can switch between tasks from several applications so quickly that it seems that all the applications and their processes are running simultaneously.

Programmers had to design Windows 3.1 applications to surrender control of the CPU voluntarily at various points of execution, enabling Windows to switch to another task. This scheme is called *cooperative multitasking*. However, some applications were more cooperative than others. If an application was reluctant to share CPU capacity with other applications, Windows 3.1 couldn't do much about it.

Preemptive multitasking, on the other hand, enables the Windows 95 operating system to take control away from one running task and pass it to another task, depending on the system's needs. The system doesn't have to wait for an application or process to surrender control of the CPU before another application can take its turn.

With preemptive multitasking, Windows 95 doesn't depend on the foresight of application programmers to ensure that an application performs multitasking successfully. Windows 95 has more power to arbitrate the demands of various running applications.

Multithreading enables an application to create and run separate concurrent *threads* or processes and thus handle different internal operations. Each process gets its own share of Windows 95's multitasking resources. For example, a word processing application might use one thread to handle keyboard input and display it on-screen. At the same time, a separate thread can run in the background to check spelling while another thread prints a document.

Some Windows 3.1 applications implement their own internal multithreading, with varying degrees of success. Now, Windows 95 makes multithreading an integral feature of the operating system, available to all 32-bit applications.

Increased System Resources Windows 95 doesn't remove the limitation on System Resources that was common in Windows 3.1, but the improvement is dramatic. The system limits on some kinds of programming information that Windows 3.1 severely restricted are now unlimited. Windows 95 still limits other kinds of programming information, but those limits are significantly higher than in Windows 3.1. As a result, you can run more applications, create more windows, use more fonts, and so on—all without running out of system resources. For instance, as I write this, I have two very large, resource-hungry applications running, plus a communications program, a personal organizer, Explorer, and CD Player. That's more than enough to exhaust system resources in Windows 3.1 and precipitate a flurry of error messages. But in Windows 95, I still have more than 80 percent of the available system resources free.

NOTE With 32-bit applications in Windows 95, rarely will you have the "Not Enough Memory" error (which occurred frequently in Windows 3.1).

Support for Windows 3.1 Applications

Most Windows 3.1 applications run in Windows 95 without modification or special settings. Microsoft claims that 16-bit Windows applications run at least as well in Windows 95 as in Windows 3.1.

Windows 3.1 applications continue to use cooperative multitasking; they cannot use Windows 95's preemptive multitasking and multithreading. However, 16-bit applications can benefit from the advantages Windows 95 derives from 32-bit device drivers and improved printing throughput due to multitasking at the operating system level.

▶ **See** "Managing Windows After an Application Failure," **p. 270**

Windows 3.1 applications running in Windows 95 all run in the same virtual machine and share the same address space—just as they do when running in Windows 3.1. As a result, they don't share the same crash protection as Windows 95 applications. If one 16-bit application hangs or crashes, it's likely to affect other 16-bit applications that are running at the same time. In other words, any application failure that would have required rebooting or restarting Windows 3.1 will require you to shut down all the 16-bit applications you're running. However, a failure of a 16-bit application should not affect 32-bit applications, and Windows 95 probably can clean up after an errant 16-bit application without requiring a reboot to recover System Resources and clear memory.

Installing Applications in Windows 95

To install any Windows application, you usually use a setup program or install utility. Installing DOS-based applications is a different matter (and the subject of Chapter 25, "Installing, Running, and Uninstalling MS-DOS Applications"). These setup programs for Windows applications take care of all the details of installing the application. You don't have to concern yourself with creating directories, copying files, and integrating the application into Windows. That's good, because installing sophisticated applications can be complex. A manual installation of a major software suite is beyond the capabilities of the average user, and a dreaded chore for even the most advanced user.

▶ **See** "Installing MS-DOS Applications," **p. 720**

What Does Setup Do?

A typical setup or installation program begins by prompting you for some information and then installs the application automatically. The better setup programs provide feedback during installation to keep you informed of what it's doing to your system and the progress of the installation. Depending on the complexity of the application you are installing, the setup program might give you an opportunity to select various options and customize the installation. The program might limit your input to accepting or changing the path where you install the application, selecting whether to install various optional components, or specifying configuration settings for the new application.

After receiving your input, the setup program proceeds to perform some or all of the following steps automatically:

- Search for an existing copy of the application it's about to install and switch to upgrade mode if appropriate.
- Scan your system to determine whether your hard disk has enough room for the necessary files and perhaps check for the existence of special hardware or other system requirements.
- Create directories and copy files. Often, the setup program must expand files that are stored in a compressed form on the distribution disks.
- Create a shortcut that you can use to launch the application.
- Add a folder and/or shortcuts to your Start menu.
- Update Windows' configuration files.
- Update the Windows Registry.
- Register the application as an OLE server.
- Register the application's file types so Windows can recognize the file-name extensions for the application's document and data files.
- Install fonts, support utilities, and so on.
- Configure or personalize the application.

What If There's No Setup Program?

A few Windows programs don't include a setup utility to install the application—the developer just didn't supply one. Such an application is probably a small utility program for which installation consists of copying a couple of files to your hard disk and perhaps adding a shortcut to your Start menu to launch the application. You'll probably find instructions for installing the application in an accompanying manual or README file.

The installation instructions may assume that you're installing the program in Windows 3.1, not Windows 95. Fortunately, this isn't a serious problem. Most of the procedures for installing an application in Windows 3.1 work equally well in Windows 95. For instance, although Windows 95 supplies new tools for managing files, the underlying process of creating directories (folders) and copying files is the same in both versions of Windows. Also, for backward-compatibility, Windows 95 includes full support for WIN.INI and SYSTEM.INI files, so any additions that you're instructed to make to those files should work as expected.

▶ **See** "Adding and Removing Programs in the Start Menu," **p. 847**

▶ **See** "Registering Documents So They Open Applications," **p. 353**

There are two common manual installation procedures that you must adapt for Windows 95. First, if the Windows 3.1 installation instructions require that you create a file association in File Manager, you must substitute the Windows 95 equivalent of registering a file type. See "Registering Documents So They Open Applications," in Chapter 13 to learn how to register file types. Second, instead of creating a program item in Program Manager, you add a program to the Start menu.

See "Adding and Removing Programs in the Start Menu," **p. 847**

Using Windows 3.1 Applications in Windows 95

According to Microsoft, Windows 95 features full backward-compatibility with 16-bit Windows 3.1 applications, and thus you can install and use your Windows 3.1 applications in Windows 95 without modification. And in fact, with only rare exceptions, Windows 3.1 applications do indeed run successfully in Windows 95.

For a current list of programs with known incompatibility problems with Windows 95 and suggested fixes or workarounds, read the file PROGRAMS.TXT in the Windows folder. You can also search for compatible software programs at the following site on the Internet:

http://www.microsoft.com/windows/thirdparty/compat.htm

If you encounter a compatibility problem with a legacy application—an older application designed for a previous version of DOS or Windows—running in Windows 95, check with the application's developer for a patch or workaround for the problem. In some cases, perhaps the only solution is an upgrade to a new, Windows 95 version of the application.

Installing Windows 3.1 Applications

You install Windows 3.1 applications in Windows 95 the same way that you do in Windows 3.1. You simply insert the first disk of the program's installation disks in your floppy disk or CD-ROM drives, run the Setup program, and follow the prompts and instructions.

The installation instructions for most Windows 3.1 applications direct you to use the Run command to start the setup program and begin installing the application. The instructions might mention that you can find the Run command on the File menu in either Program Manager or File Manager. However, in Windows 95, you find the Run command on the Start menu.

NOTE You might prefer a different technique for launching the Setup program. Open the My Computer window and double-click the drive icon for the drive that contains the installation disk. Then locate the Setup program's icon and launch the program by double-clicking it.

When you use this technique, you need not type the command in the Run dialog box to start the Setup program. The technique also lets you scan the disk for README files before installing the application.

Of course, the setup program for a legacy application will be tailored to Windows 3.1 instead of Windows 95. For example, the installation program will probably offer to create Program Manager groups (see Figure 24.1) and update INI files. Fortunately, you can just accept those options when the program offers them. Windows 95 will intercept Program Manager updates and automatically convert them to Start menu shortcuts. Windows 95 also transfers WIN.INI and SYSTEM.INI entries into the Registry.

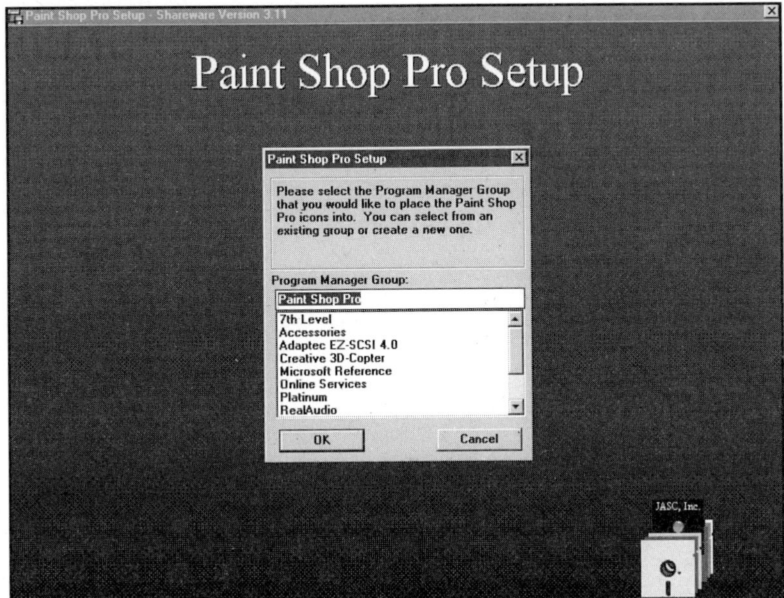

FIG. 24.1
Windows 95 translates some actions of a Windows 3.1 application's Setup program into their Windows 95 equivalent.

If you install Windows 95 as an upgrade to Windows 3.1, the Setup program should take care of such issues. The Windows 95 Setup program automatically transfers information about your existing applications to the Registry when you install Windows 95 into your existing Windows 3.1 directory. As a result, you shouldn't have to reinstall applications.

Running Windows 3.1 Applications

After installing a Windows 3.1 application in Windows 95, you can launch and run the application just like any other Windows application. Windows 95 changes the application's appearance automatically, giving it the new Windows look (see Figure 24.2). The application window's title bar will have the new format, complete with the new style of Minimize, Maximize, and Close buttons, and most buttons and other window elements will take on the new three-dimensional look.

▶ **See** "Starting and Quitting Windows," **p. 246**

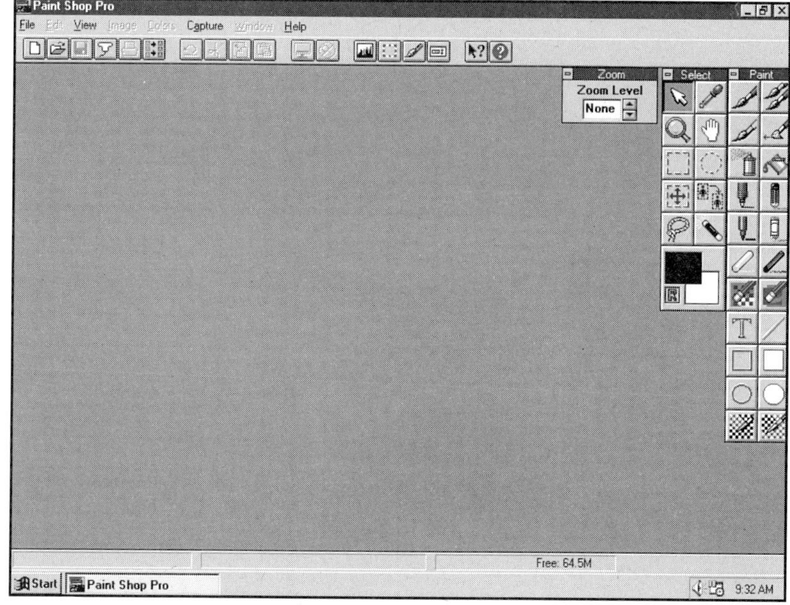

FIG. 24.2
Running a Windows 3.1 application in Windows 95 gives the program an automatic facelift. However, despite the change of appearance, the application performs the same as in Windows 3.1.

Beneath the superficial appearance changes, the application works the same as it did under Windows 3.1. The application might benefit from some Windows 95 performance improvements, such as more efficient printing. However, to take maximum advantage of the features and capabilities of Windows 95's 32-bit operating system, you must upgrade to a new version of the application. In the meantime, you should be able to continue using your 16-bit Windows 3.1 applications effectively and efficiently.

Installing Windows 95 Applications in Windows 95

The basic technique for installing Windows 95 applications is essentially the same as installing other Windows applications; you run Setup (or Install) and follow the prompts. The Setup program takes care of all the details of installing the application. However, the Run feature is located in the Start menu in Windows 95.

One new feature of Windows 95 is an optional way to start an application's setup program: a new Install Programs Wizard accessible via the Add/Remove Programs icon in the Control Panel. The Add/Remove Programs dialog box provides a common starting point for adding and removing Windows applications and Windows system components and accessories.

When you're ready to run the Install Programs Wizard and use it to install a Windows application, follow these steps:

1. Open the Start menu and choose Settings, Control Panel. This opens the Control Panel window shown in Figure 24.3.

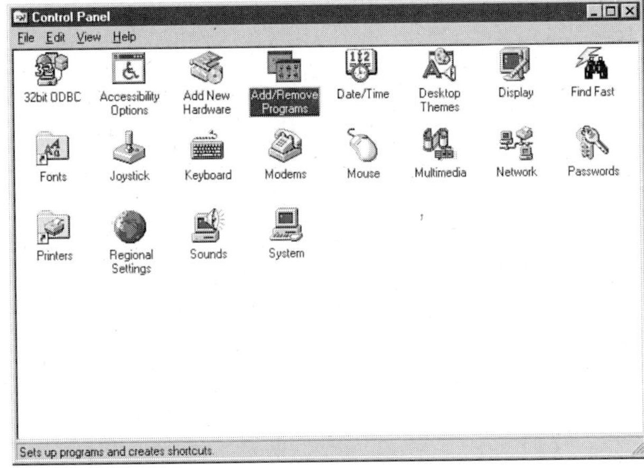

FIG. 24.3 The Windows 95 Control Panel contains a new wizard to make installing applications easier.

2. In the Control Panel window, double-click Add/Remove Programs to open the Add/Remove Programs properties sheet shown in Figure 24.4. By default, the Install/Uninstall tab should be active.

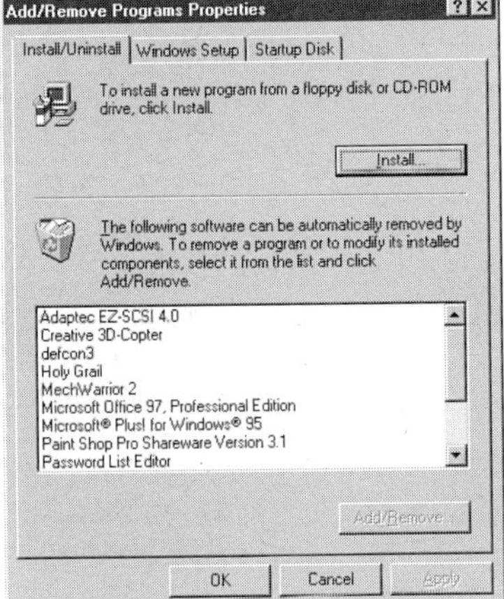

FIG. 24.4 The Add/Remove Programs Properties dialog box is the master control for adding and removing applications.

3. To start the Install Program Wizard, choose Install.
4. When the Install Program from Floppy Disk or CD-ROM dialog box appears, insert the application's distribution disk (the first floppy disk or compact disc) in the appropriate drive and click Next.
5. The wizard searches the disk's root directory for an installation program (usually named SETUP.EXE or INSTALL.EXE) and displays the command line in the Run Installation Program dialog box (see Figure 24.5).

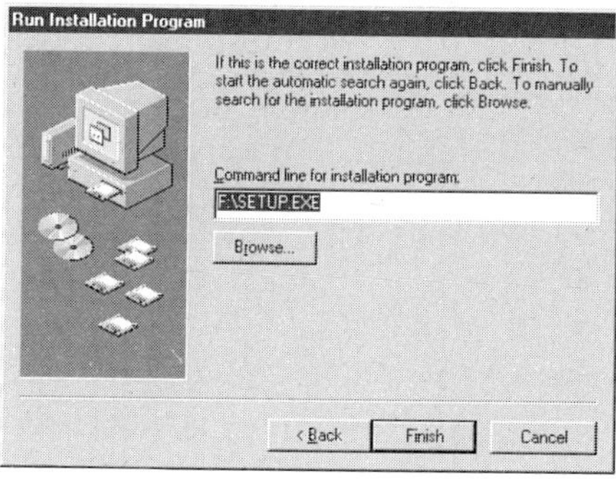

FIG. 24.5
Usually the wizard finds the application's setup program on the disk.

6. If the wizard fails to find the setup program (perhaps because it is in a subdirectory) or you want to run a different setup program (perhaps from a network drive), you can choose Browse and select a different file in the Browse dialog box (see Figure 24.6). Choose Open to insert the selected file name in the wizard.

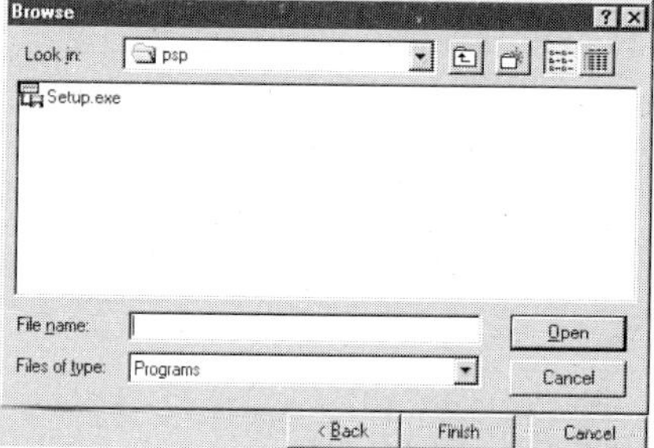

FIG. 24.6
If the wizard needs help locating the setup program, you can browse for the correct file.

7. After the correct command line for the setup program appears in the Run Installation Program dialog box, click Finish to start the setup program and begin the application installation.

The application's setup program then proceeds to install the application. You'll probably need to respond to several prompts during the installation process. If the setup program includes a Windows 95-compatible uninstall feature, the wizard notes this and adds the new application to a list of programs that you can remove automatically. (The section "Removing Windows Applications," later in this chapter, discusses this new feature in more detail.)

NOTE You also can use the Install Programs Wizard to install Windows 3.1 applications. However, using the wizard for this purpose yields no significant advantage. Windows 3.1 setup programs lack the special features that let you use the Add/Remove Programs control panel to remove the applications later.

Adding Windows' Component Applications

The Add/Remove Programs icon in Control Panel lets you install and remove Windows components and accessories as well as applications. Therefore, you can reconfigure your copy of Windows 95 without reinstalling it. The feature is a more powerful version of the Windows 3.1 Setup utility.

Adding and Removing Windows Components

To use the Windows Setup feature to add or remove a Windows components, follow these steps:

1. Open the Start menu and choose Settings, Control Panel.
2. Open the Add/Remove Programs properties sheet by double-clicking the Add/Remove Programs icon.
3. Click the Windows Setup tab to display a list of Windows components as shown in Figure 24.7.

   In the Components list box, a check mark next to an item indicates that the component is already installed on your system. If the check box is gray, the Windows component is composed of more than one subcomponent and some (but not all) subcomponents are currently installed. For instance, in Figure 24.7, only some of the subcomponents (accessories such as Calculator, Paint, and WordPad) of the accessories component are installed. To see what's included in a component, choose Details.

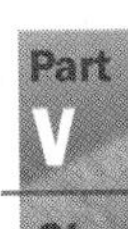

FIG. 24.7
The Windows Setup tab of the Add/Remove Programs properties sheet lets you add and remove parts of Windows.

4. Select a component in the Components list box. When you do, the Description box in the lower portion of the dialog box displays a description of that component.

5. If the component you selected consists of more than one subcomponent, choose Details to open a dialog box listing the subcomponents. (For example, Figure 24.8 shows the Accessories dialog box listing the subcomponents of the main Accessories component.) Sometimes in this dialog box, you can choose Details to narrow your selection further.

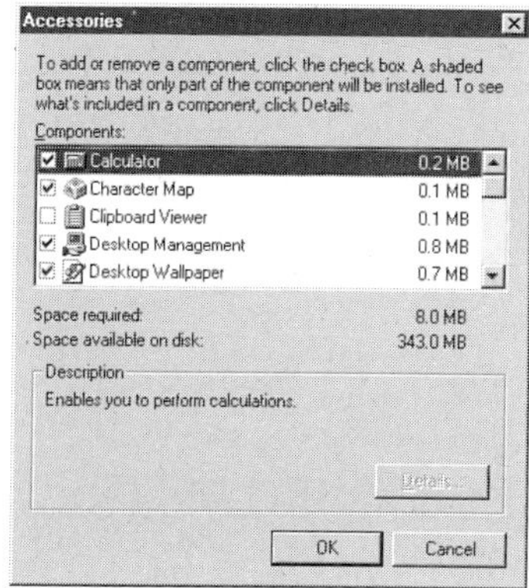

FIG. 24.8
The Accessories dialog box lists a component's parts. By choosing Details, you can narrow your selections.

6. Mark components for installation or removal by clicking the check box beside that item in the Components list. Adding a check mark to a previously blank check box marks that item for installation. Conversely, clearing a previously checked box instructs Windows to uninstall that component.
7. If you're selecting subcomponents in a dialog box you opened by choosing a Details button, click OK to close that dialog box and return to the Add/Remove Programs properties sheet.
8. When the check marks in the Components lists specify the components that you want composing your Windows system, choose Apply in the Add/Remove Programs properties sheet. You'll need to supply the Windows Setup disks or CD when prompted.

TROUBLESHOOTING

When I use the Windows Setup feature to add new components, it adds those components, but it also removes other components. Why? If you clear a check box for a component that was checked when you run Windows Setup, this tells Windows to remove the component, rather than to not install it. This can be confusing the first time you run Setup again to add new components. Leave those components that are already installed checked unless you want to remove those components.

Installing Unlisted Components

Eventually, you might want to install a Windows component that doesn't appear on the Components list in the Windows Setup tab of the Add/Remove Program properties sheet. For example, you might want to install one of the system-management utilities from the Windows 95 Resource Kit.

To install a Windows component not listed in the Components list box, open the Add/Remove Program properties sheet, click the Windows Setup tab, and choose the Have Disk button at bottom of the dialog box. This opens the Install From Disk dialog box. When adding Windows components from a supplemental disk, you must supply the full path to the correct INF file.

In the Copy Manufacturer's Files From field, specify the path to the setup information file (INF) for the Windows component that you want to install. (The setup information file tells Windows Setup what is available to install and how to do it.) You can either type the path and file name or choose Browse and select the file in the Browse dialog box. After specifying the correct path, click OK. Windows opens the Have Disk dialog box (see Figure 24.9), which lists the components available for installation. Check the ones that you want to install, and then choose Install. You might have to supply disks and browse for needed files when prompted.

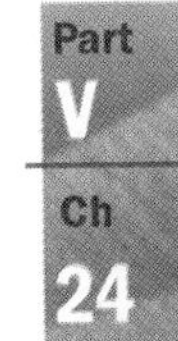

FIG. 24.9
The Have Disk dialog box lists the Windows components available on the supplemental disk, or at least the components described in the INF file that you selected.

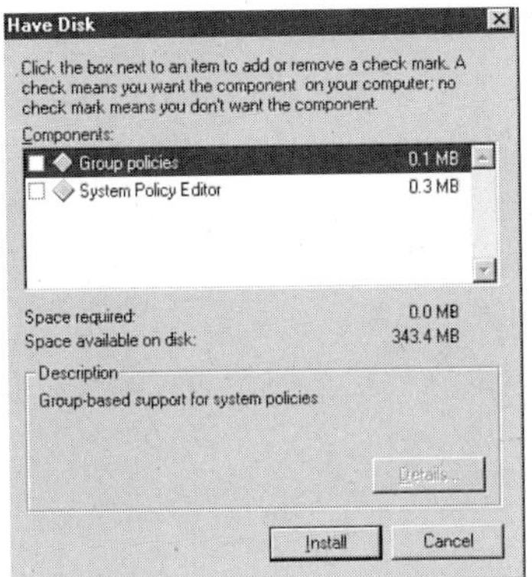

Windows not only installs the component, but also adds the component to the Components list in the Windows Setup tab. Later, you can remove the component just like any other in the list.

See "Installing MS-DOS Applications," **p. 720**

Installing components for DOS applications is different than the procedure used with Windows. In most cases, installing many of the major DOS applications requires suspending Windows 95 and switching to the "exclusive" DOS mode. This procedure is described in detail in Chapter 25 in the section "Working with DOS Applications in Windows 95."

Running Applications

After you install your application's and Windows' accessories, Windows 95 gives you many options for launching them. You can use any of the methods to run any application. The technique that you choose depends on your personal preferences, working style, and what you're doing at the time.

The various methods for launching applications are discussed in more detail in Chapter 10, "Navigating and Controlling Windows," and Chapter 13, "Managing Files and Folders with Windows Explorer." The following is a summary of the techniques:

- Choose the application's shortcut from the Start menu.
- Create and use a shortcut on the desktop.
- Right-click the application's icon in Windows Explorer or the My Computer window; then click Open in the context menu.
- Double-click the application's icon in the My Computer window or Windows Explorer.
- Choose the Run command from the Start menu, and then type the path and file name of the application's executable file.
- Choose the Run command from the Start menu. Then drag an EXE file from My Computer or Network Neighborhood, and drop the file into the Run dialog box.
- Use the Windows 3.1 Program Manager, and then run the application by double-clicking its program item.

NOTE Windows 95 includes updated versions of both Program Manager and File Manager. The optional 3.1 interface will add applications to the Program Manager during installation. If you opt for the Windows 3.1 interface, you also can add program items to the Program Manager manually.

If you want to start Windows 95 in the Program Manager, you need to install Window 95 using the Custom option. Choose User Interface in the Computer Settings dialog box and then choose Change. Select Windows 3.1 (Program Manager) and choose OK. If you have already installed Windows 95, add a shortcut to PROGMAN.EXE to the \WINDOWS\STARTUP folder. PROGMAN.EXE is located in the \WINDOWS\ folder.

▶ **See** "Registering Documents So They Open Applications," **p. 353**

- Open a document or data file associated with the application. When you open a file, Windows launches the application automatically and then opens the file in that application. There are as many ways to open files as there are ways to launch applications. For instance, you can open files in Explorer, by choosing a recently used file from the Documents submenu on the Start menu, or by double-clicking a shortcut on your desktop.
- Finally, for a bizarre twist, try this method of launching a Windows application. You can open a MS-DOS window and type the command to start the application at the DOS prompt. You would expect to get an error message saying the program requires Windows to run. But, instead, Windows 95 launches the Windows application for you.

Removing Windows Applications

Installing a Windows application can be a complicated venture. Windows applications are often tightly integrated with the operating system. Installing such applications not only requires copying the application's files into the application's own directory, but also adds numerous support files to your Windows directory and changes Windows' settings. Fortunately, nearly all applications provide setup programs to automate the installation process.

Removing an application can be similarly complicated. Finding all the support files and settings added or changed during the application's installation can be nearly impossible. Fortunately, many application setup programs now offer an uninstall option to automate the process when you need to remove the application from your system.

Windows 95 takes this welcome trend a step further by adding a facility to remove applications. That facility is in the same Control Panel dialog box that you use to install applications and Windows components.

Removing Applications Automatically

Windows 95's Add/Remove Programs Wizard adds to the capability of individual setup programs by tracking an application's components in the Registry. This lets Windows delete an application's files and settings but still identify and retain any files that another application might share and use.

NOTE Only applications that provide uninstall programs specifically designed to work with Windows 95 appear in the list of applications that Windows 95 can remove automatically.

To uninstall an application automatically, start by opening the Control Panel and double-clicking the Add/Remove Programs icon. This opens the Add/Remove Programs properties sheet—the same sheet you used to install the application (see Figure 24.10).

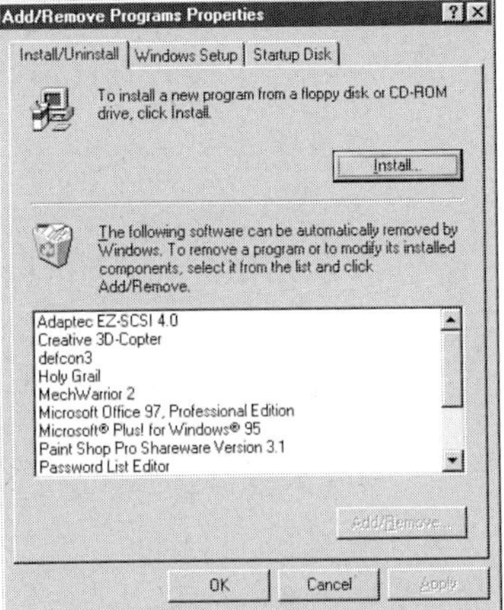

FIG. 24.10
In the Add/Remove Programs properties sheet, you can remove applications as well as install them.

The lower portion of the dialog box lists applications that you can remove. To remove an application, select it from the list and choose Remove. After you confirm that you want to remove the program, Windows runs the selected application's uninstall program.

Removing Applications Manually

If you want to remove an application from your system, just hope that it's one that Windows can remove automatically. Removing an application manually can be difficult, and possibly dangerous.

Remove Files from the Application Directory Getting rid of the files in an application's own directory is fairly straightforward. In fact, that should probably be the first step in removing an application manually.

Many applications install support files in the Windows directories. It's nearly impossible to tell what application added which files, and to make matters worse, several applications can share the same files. If you ignore the files in the Windows directories when you remove an application, you can leave numerous orphaned files on your system needlessly consuming hard disk space. However, if you make a mistake and delete the wrong file or one that another applications also uses, you might render the other application unusable.

If you find support files in your Windows directory that you think are unnecessary, copy them to a separate folder before you remove them. If you don't encounter any problems after a few months, you can delete that folder.

Remove Shortcuts and Folders from the Start Menu After you remove an application's files from your hard disk, you want to get rid of any shortcuts that pointed to the application. To delete a shortcut icon from your desktop, simply drag and drop the shortcut onto the Recycle Bin icon on your desktop. The Recycle Bin is like a trash can that stores deleted files until the Bin reaches a certain capacity.

See "Understanding the Most Important Screen Elements in Windows 95," **p. 234**

See "Managing Your Files and Folders," **p. 316**

See "Emptying the Recycle Bin," **p. 324**

To remove the application from the Start menu, click the Start button and choose Settings, Taskbar. Then in the Taskbar properties sheet, click the Start Menu Programs page. Next, choose Remove to open the Remove Shortcuts/Folders dialog box (see Figure 24.11).

The Remove Shortcuts/Folders dialog box, like the Windows Explorer, displays a hierarchical list of folders and files. To expand the display and show a folder's contents, you can click the plus sign beside the folder. Select the folder or shortcut that you want to delete, and then choose Remove. To remove other items, repeat the process as necessary. When you finish removing items, click Close.

Remove File Associations After you remove an application, you can remove any associations that might have existed between file extensions and the defunct application. After all, you don't want Windows to try to launch the nonexistent application when you double-click a document file.

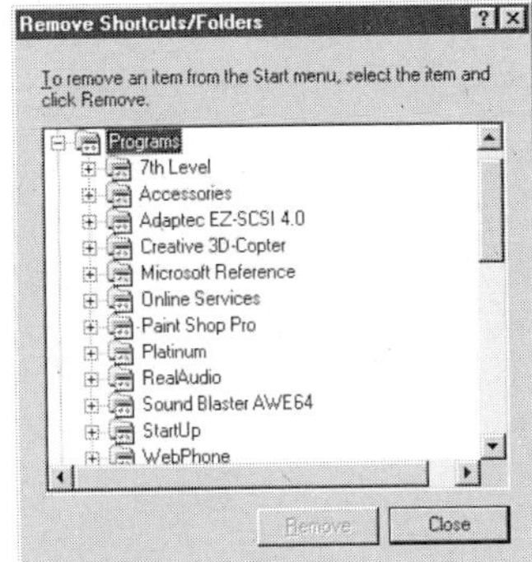

FIG. 24.11
After removing an application, you open the Remove Shortcuts/ Folders dialog box to remove the application's folder and shortcuts from your Start menu.

To remove the link between a file extension and an application, start by opening the My Computer window. Next, choose View, Options to open the Options dialog box; then click the File Types tab. You then see the screen shown in Figure 24.12. Scroll down the Registered File Types list and select the file type that you want to delete; then choose Remove. Windows asks you to confirm your choice. If you answer Yes, Windows abolishes the registration of that file type.

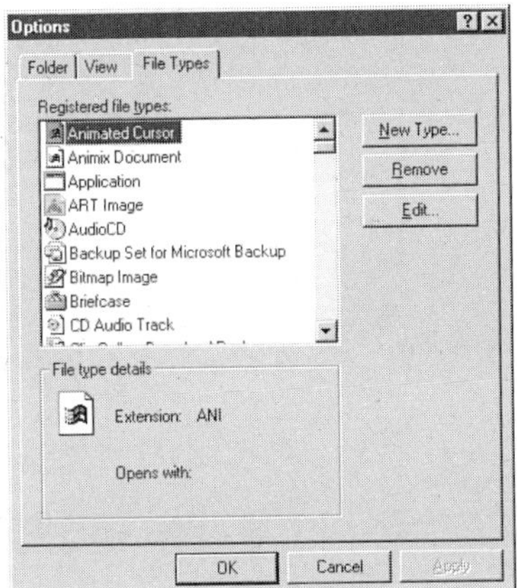

FIG. 24.12
Using the Options dialog box to remove a file type registration is easier and safer than editing the Registry directly.

There are several commercial utilities available for helping you uninstall applications, including MicroHelp's UnInstaller, Quarterdeck's CleanSweep 95, and Vertisoft's Remove-It for Windows 95. Be sure to get the Windows 95 versions of these programs that are designed to modify the Registry when you uninstall a program. These utilities will also uninstall Windows 3.x programs.

CHAPTER 25

Installing, Running, and Uninstalling MS-DOS Applications

by Dick Cravens

What's new in MS-DOS for Windows 95

Find out about the many improvements in Windows 95 for supporting MS-DOS applications.

How Windows 95 works with MS-DOS applications

Turn here to learn to start, end, and control an MS-DOS session.

Using MS-DOS mode

Learn how to use MS-DOS mode to work with DOS applications that won't work in the Windows environment.

Installing, configuring, and uninstalling MS-DOS applications

In these sections, you learn how to install a DOS program, then how to alter the default settings using the Properties sheet. You also learn how to remove a DOS program from your computer.

Starting and running MS-DOS programs

Find out how to start your DOS programs from a command prompt and by using the standard Windows 95 methods for starting applications.

Although Windows 95 is designed from the ground up to shield the user from the often confusing world of the command line, AUTOEXEC.BAT, CONFIG.SYS, and memory management practices, it offers surprisingly rich support for those users who still desire or need to work in the MS-DOS environment. If you have a favorite MS-DOS application, utility, or game, there's absolutely no need to give it up or suffer performance loss. In fact, Windows 95 offers greatly enhanced MS-DOS support compared to earlier versions.

None of this comes without a small price—you must learn a few new concepts and controls to master Windows 95 MS-DOS operations. The reward is far greater control over MS-DOS application environments under Windows 95 than under previous versions.

If you're currently using another brand of DOS other than Microsoft MS-DOS, have no fear—Windows 95 MS-DOS support is so compatible and configurable, you can easily adjust for any minor variations between DOS versions from other vendors such as IBM's PC-DOS, or Novell/ Digital Research DR-DOS.

Understanding How Windows 95 Works with MS-DOS Applications

Applications that simply would not run under earlier versions of the Windows MS-DOS Prompt now perform admirably. For applications that still won't run under the new Windows, a special mode helps you run them quickly and easily from within Windows, and then automatically returns you to your Windows session when you're finished.

The following are some of the improvements in Windows 95 for supporting MS-DOS applications:

- Better local reboot support
- Zero conventional memory usage for protected-mode components
- Consolidated setup for MS-DOS-based applications
- Toolbar support for windowed MS-DOS applications
- Graceful shutdown for windowed MS-DOS sessions
- Long file name support, with full backwards compatibility for "8.3" format file names
- Execution of Windows programs from the MS-DOS session
- The ability to open documents from the command line
- Better control over MS-DOS window fonts
- User-scalable MS-DOS session windows
- Improved Cut, Paste, and Copy commands for integrating MS-DOS and Windows application information
- Universal Naming Convention (UNC) path name support
- Spooling of MS-DOS-based print jobs

Windows 95 makes dealing with MS-DOS/Windows integration quicker and easier than ever and makes working with MS-DOS applications similar to working on a machine running only MS-DOS. In addition, MS-DOS emulation under Windows 95 gives the user many of the other benefits of Windows 95: the graphical user interface, multitasking, enhanced printing support and networking support.

Conventional Memory in Windows 95

An added bonus of the overall design of Windows 95 is the greater conservation of conventional memory (that below the 640K mark). Windows 95 replaces DOS-based drivers, which cannot be loaded above the first 1M of memory, with virtual device drivers (VxDs). VxDs are protected-mode drivers that can be loaded above 1M, thereby freeing up space in the conventional (up to 640K) and upper memory areas (between 640K and 1M). You can then use HIMEM and EMM386 to load any real-mode device drivers and TSRs (terminate-and-stay resident) programs into the upper memory area to free up conventional memory for DOS applications. Some MS-DOS applications simply couldn't run under Windows 3.1. By the time mouse, network, SCSI, and other necessary drivers were loaded, there simply wasn't enough RAM below 640K. Windows 95 alleviates this situation by checking each driver specified in your installation against a "safe list" of known drivers, and loading approved ones in extended memory, or substituting equivalent drivers.

For example, if your PC is on a NetWare network and uses a SCSI CD-ROM drive, the SMARTDrive disk cache, DriveSpace disk compression, and an MS-DOS mouse driver, you can save more than 250K in conventional memory using the MS-DOS system in Windows 95.

CAUTION

Don't run MS-DOS or Windows 3.1 file system utilities in a Windows MS-DOS session or you may corrupt files or lose long file names. Examples of this type of software are MS-DOS disk defragmenter and unerase or undelete utilities. Windows comes with many of these utilities, so use the Windows versions instead (don't just boot to MS-DOS to use your older utilities; some of them will corrupt the Windows 95 long file name system).

Starting the MS-DOS Prompt Session

Getting started with MS-DOS under Windows is as simple as selecting a menu item. To begin a session, follow these steps:

1. Open the Start menu and choose Programs. Windows displays a submenu.
2. Choose the MS-DOS Prompt menu item. Windows opens the MS-DOS Prompt window, as shown in Figure 25.1.

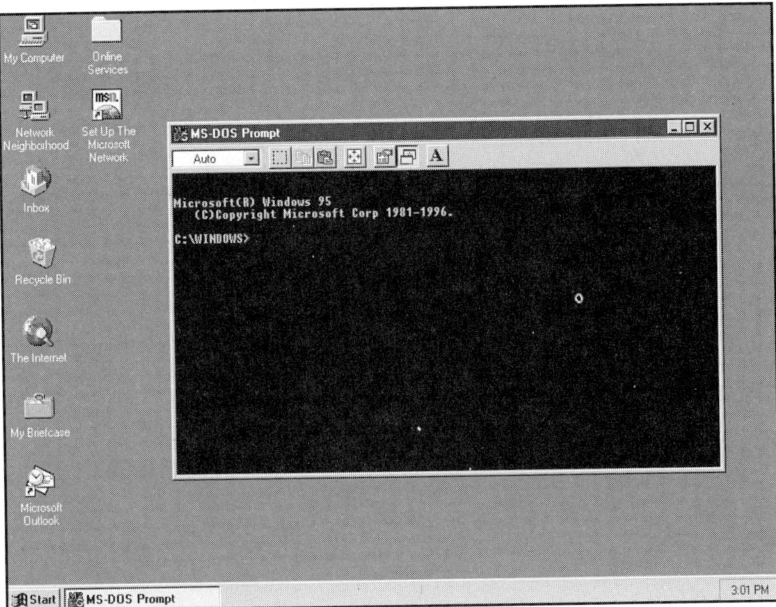

FIG. 25.1
The MS-DOS Prompt window where you can execute DOS commands.

Ending MS-DOS Prompt Sessions

You can still run DOS batch files, either from the command line, the Run command in the Start menu, or from within Windows, using a shortcut. In Windows 95, you can modify the properties of the BAT file using the properties sheet. Right-click the shortcut and select the Program tab. You can select what mode you want the DOS session to run in (normal window, maximized, or minimized) and assign a shortcut key. You also can specify that the DOS window be closed when the batch file is finished running.

You also can specify a batch file that will be run whenever you start a particular DOS program. Open the properties sheet for the DOS program, select the Program tab, and type the full path and name for the batch file in the Batch File text box.

Now that you've started an MS-DOS Prompt session, practice closing it before you move on to the finer points of operation. To close the MS-DOS Prompt window, follow these steps:

1. Click in the MS-DOS Prompt window to bring it to the foreground.
2. Find the flashing cursor near the MS-DOS command prompt. At the flashing cursor near the MS-DOS command prompt, type **exit**.
3. Press Enter, and Windows closes the MS-DOS Prompt session window.

Don't leave MS-DOS Prompt sessions open any longer than necessary. Every session takes a big chunk out of available CPU time, slowing down your entire Windows performance in all applications.

NOTE As with most other procedures under Windows, several other ways to close an MS-DOS Prompt session are available. As alternatives, try each of the following:

- Double-click the MS-DOS icon in the top-left corner of the MS-DOS Prompt session window.
- Click the MS-DOS icon; then choose Close from the menu.
- Click the Close icon in the upper-right corner of the MS-DOS Prompt window.
- Right-click anywhere in the MS-DOS Prompt window title bar. Windows displays a menu from which you can choose Close.

Ending Sessions with Running Applications

Windows also allows you to close sessions that have applications open; but by default, it warns you if the application is running or has open files.

Besides giving you options for more gracefully ending a session, Windows 95 improves on previous versions by performing better session cleanup, releasing memory, and deallocating system resources much more consistently.

To close an active session, simply follow the same procedures for closing a session with just an MS-DOS Prompt that you used earlier. This time, however, Windows displays the warning dialog box shown in Figure 25.2.

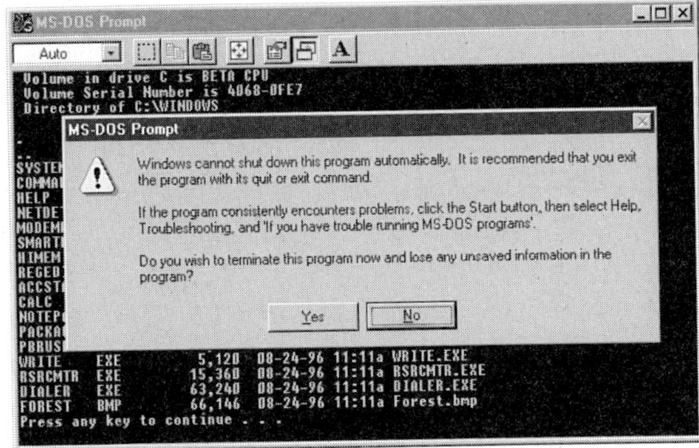

FIG. 25.2
Windows warns you if you try to exit an MS-DOS session while an application is active.

If you choose No, Windows returns you to the MS-DOS Prompt session, and you can exit the program before you close the MS-DOS session.

Otherwise, choose Yes and Windows shuts down the MS-DOS session and terminates the running application. It's not recommended that you close sessions this way, since you will lose any information that was not saved in the program, but you can do it in an emergency (for example, if the application is hung and simply won't *let* you exit gracefully).

TROUBLESHOOTING

My MS-DOS application simply won't respond and none of the close procedures you list are working. What can I do to shut down this unresponsive application and get back to work? Will I lose all my data in other applications? Use the classic "three-fingered salute," Ctrl+Alt+Del, after which Windows 95 displays the Close Program dialog box. Windows 95, however, does a good job of recovering from application failure because it gives you a choice of which task to shut down instead of assuming the one in the foreground is the culprit. After you select the application task to deal with, you have the choice of ending the errant task, shutting down the entire computer, rebooting using Ctrl+Alt+Del again, or canceling.

You learn a way to override the Windows warnings about closing an active MS-DOS Prompt session later in this chapter.

See "Miscellaneous Properties," **p. 725**

Controlling the MS-DOS Prompt Session

Now that you know the basics for working in a DOS window, you are ready to learn about the ways you can work with and control your DOS sessions.

Change the MS-DOS session from full screen to windowed and back again by pressing Alt+Enter.

Using the MS-DOS Prompt Toolbar

Windows MS-DOS sessions have a variety of interface controls. The toolbar will be familiar to you if you've been using the Windows Explorer. Figure 25.3 shows the MS-DOS Prompt toolbar and its controls.

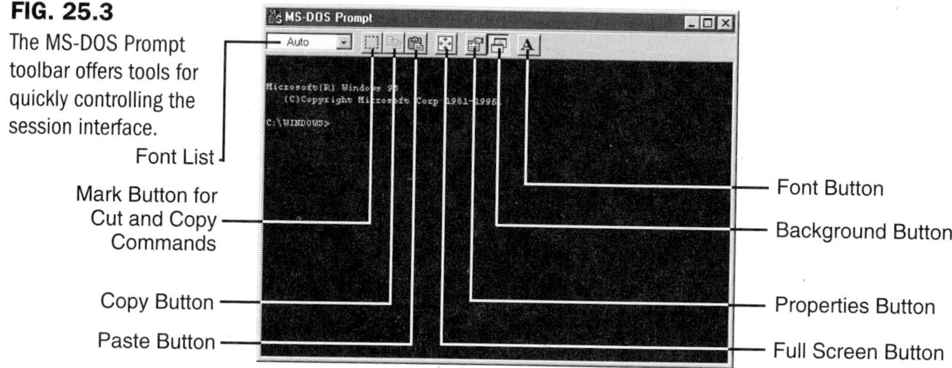

FIG. 25.3
The MS-DOS Prompt toolbar offers tools for quickly controlling the session interface.

To continue running a DOS application in the background when you switch to another application, click the Background button on the Prompt toolbar. If you are downloading a file using a DOS-based communications application, for example, you will want to enable background operation. Normally, you will not want to run the DOS application in the background, so that you free up all system resources for the foreground application.

Controlling the MS-DOS Prompt Interface

Windows offers TrueType scalable fonts in addition to the familiar system fonts, allowing on-the-fly resizing of the entire session window. To try the new font features, open an MS-DOS session and perform the following steps:

1. Click the toolbar's Font list, then choose TT7×14 (the TrueType font for TT7×14 resolution). The window should now appear as shown in Figure 25.4 (assuming you're using 800×600 Super VGA display resolution).
2. Grab the window borders in the lower-right corner and resize the window. Notice that the vertical and horizontal window scroll bar controls appear on the window, but the text in the window remains the same, as shown in Figure 25.5.

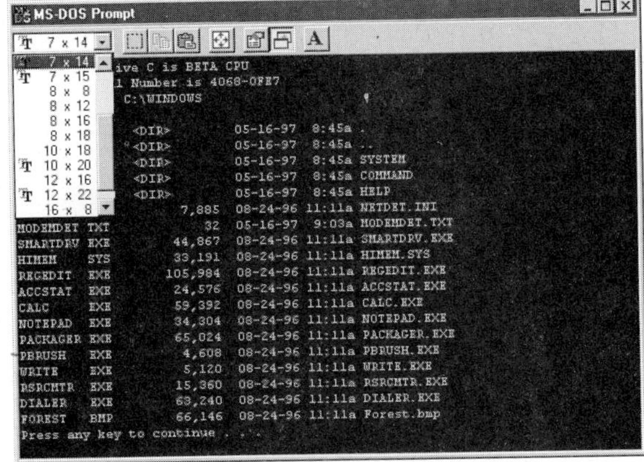

FIG. 25.4
You can use the toolbar to control TrueType fonts in your MS-DOS Prompt session.

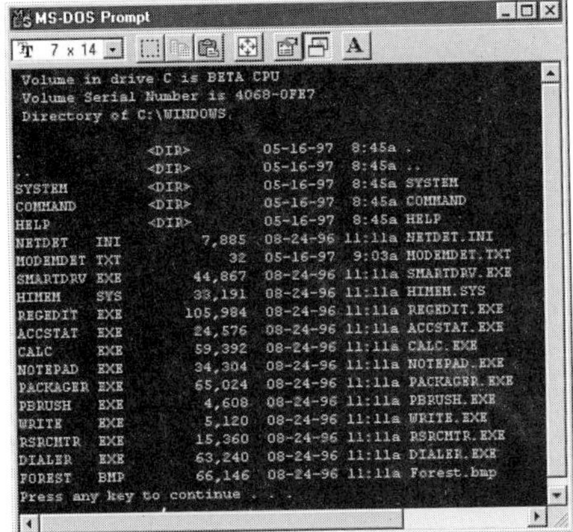

FIG. 25.5
Windows supports dynamic resizing of the MS-DOS Prompt window. You can access any hidden areas of the session using standard scroll bar controls.

Part V Ch 25

3. Repeat the procedure in step 1 to select the 4×7 font mode. Notice that the text in the window is much smaller, and the window has shrunk to match (see Figure 25.6). Grab the window borders again and try to enlarge the window; notice how it is limited to a maximum size.

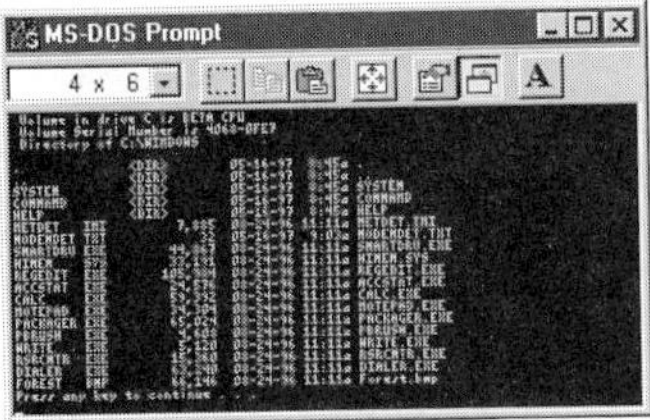

FIG. 25.6
If you choose a font that allows full viewing of the MS-DOS Prompt session, Windows won't let you resize the window larger than the session.

4. Repeat the procedure in step 1 to select Auto mode. The window does not change.
5. Grab the window borders in the lower-right corner and resize the window. Notice how Windows alters the font on-the-fly. When you change the window size again, the font adjusts automatically to the nearest available size.

Using the Windows Clipboard with the MS-DOS Prompt

Windows offers even easier access to the data in your MS-DOS session, via the toolbar. Copying information from your session into a Windows application is quick and easy. Follow these steps to try it out:

1. Using the mouse, click the Mark tool and select text in your MS-DOS application.
2. Click the Copy tool on the MS-DOS Prompt toolbar. Windows places a copy of the text in the Clipboard.
3. Using the mouse, click your Windows application (for example, Notepad) to make it active. Position the cursor where you want to insert the text and then choose Edit, Paste from the Notepad menu. Notepad displays the text copied from your MS-DOS session window.

TROUBLESHOOTING

I used to be able to use the mouse to highlight text in an MS-DOS session and then press Enter to copy the text to the Clipboard, but now it doesn't work. This still works under Windows 95, but it simply isn't enabled by default. You can use the mouse to select and copy text if the application you're running supports it (for example, EDIT), but the MS-DOS Prompt itself won't (for example, you can't mark and copy the results of the dir command that MS-DOS writes to your window). If you use the toolbar on your MS-DOS sessions, just click the Mark tool on the toolbar before you select the text. If you've set up your MS-DOS sessions so the toolbar doesn't show, then you can tell Windows 95 to enable the QuickEdit feature.

To enable this feature, simply click the window system icon (the MS-DOS icon in the upper-left corner) and choose Properties and then choose the Misc tab when the properties sheet appears. Check the QuickEdit box under the Mouse section, click OK, and you're ready to go.

TIP To copy information from a Windows application to an MS-DOS application, select and copy the information in the Windows application and then choose the Paste tool on the Prompt toolbar. You also can right-click the MS-DOS window title bar and choose Edit, Paste if you don't have the toolbar displayed. You can use this method to paste information into a DOS application or onto the DOS command line.

Using Long File Names

One of the most bothersome limitations of the MS-DOS environment has been the 8.3 file name format. Windows 95 supports longer file names, and the MS-DOS Prompt offers support for them, too. To see how this works, follow these steps:

1. Using My Computer, create a new folder called Incredibly Long Folder Name on the root of Drive C, as shown in Figure 25.7.

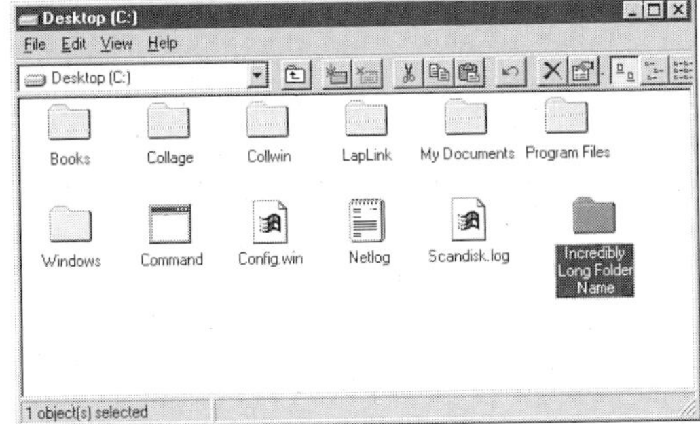

FIG. 25.7
You can use up to 255 characters in a file or folder name.

2. Using the Start menu, open an MS-DOS Prompt. At the prompt, type **dir c:***. The MS-DOS window displays the folder listing for the root of Drive C (an example is shown in Figure 25.8).

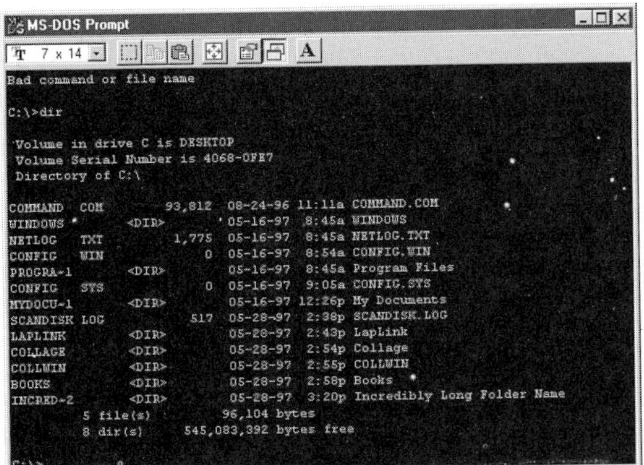

FIG. 25.8
The MS-DOS Prompt session supports and displays both long and short file and folder (directory) names.

Notice the dual display of both the 8.3 format and long format folder names. Windows and MS-DOS coordinate both naming systems, but not without a price—the 8.3 format name uses the tilde character (~) to show the inevitable truncation. Even under Windows, some long names may be shortened using the ellipsis characters (...) when space is at a premium.

To ensure complete backwards compatibility, Windows still uses file extensions, even though they are not displayed in the Windows Explorer or on the Desktop. If you rename a file from the Windows environment, it does not change the hidden file name extension. Windows still uses the extension for file associations with applications and viewers.

NOTE Not all applications support long file names just because Windows does. It's doubtful that any MS-DOS application will support long file names because most were written prior to this version of Windows. Most 16-bit Windows applications won't support longer file names until their first release after Windows 95, if then. Some software companies will probably wait for the first release of their application as a true 32-bit program to include this feature.

Many of the native MS-DOS commands in Windows 95 have been enhanced to provide support for long file names. For example, the dir and copy commands both support long file names.

You can use long file names at the DOS command prompt if they don't include spaces. If they do include spaces, enclose the file name in quotes. For example:

```
CD "MSOFFICE\WINWORD\BUSINESS LETTERS"
```

Using Universal Naming Convention Path Names

More and more PCs are on *local area networks* (*LANs*). Most shared resources on a LAN are stored on *servers*, or PCs dedicated for a particular network task, such as printing, file storage, or database storage.

Gaining access to other PCs on the network, whether server or workstation, can be a tiresome process of mapping the other machine to a virtual drive letter on your system. The Windows 95 MS-DOS Prompt offers a way around this with *Universal Naming Convention (UNC)* support. This is a fancy way of saying that you can view, copy, or run files on another machine without having to assign it a drive letter on your computer. It also means that if you are running short of logical drive letters, you can get to servers that you use only intermittently, with a simple command from the MS-DOS Prompt.

For example, if you want to run an application called SHARED.EXE in the folder STUFF on server FRED1, you can enter the following at the command prompt:

```
\\fred1\stuff\shared.exe
```

You also can use this feature with any legal MS-DOS command. For example, to see the contents of the folder STUFF, use the familiar dir command as follows:

```
dir \\fred1\stuff
```

This yields a standard folder listing of the contents of that area of the server.

NOTE Although the MS-DOS prompt in Windows 95 supports UNC names, be aware that some DOS and Windows 3.1x applications do not support UNC.

Printing from the MS-DOS Prompt

The biggest change in printing support for MS-DOS applications comes in the form of better conflict resolution and print job queuing. Windows handles printer port contention between MS-DOS and Windows applications by shuttling all MS-DOS print tasks to the same printer management utility used by Windows applications.

▶ **See** "Printing from MS-DOS Applications," **p. 152**

Understanding MS-DOS Mode

Although you will be able to run most DOS applications without any difficulties from within Windows, you may run into problems with some poorly designed MS-DOS applications—some MS-DOS applications demand total control over system resources and access hardware in the most direct way, bypassing "standard" Windows methods.

Windows 95 accommodates a poorly behaved application to the best of its capability, via *MS-DOS mode*. This mode is the equivalent to the Real mode present in older versions of Windows, with some "real" improvements.

MS-DOS mode works by giving the errant MS-DOS application the entire system for the duration of the session. Windows removes itself from memory, and leaves only a small "stub" loader in preparation for its return to control of your system.

▶ **See** "Advanced Program Settings," **p. 722**

To use this mode, the user sets a property in the Advanced Program Settings dialog box. When the MS-DOS application runs, Windows literally shuts down, loads the application, and then returns automatically when the application is finished. This process can be slow and cumbersome, but it's faster and more convenient than exiting Windows manually, using the dual-boot option, and reloading Windows.

Knowing When to Use MS-DOS Mode

Before you decide to enable MS-DOS mode for an application, try these other options:

- Confirm that you've optimized the MS-DOS session settings for that application. Check the program's documentation for special memory requirements or other unusual needs. You may be able to adjust MS-DOS support in Windows to make the application work in a standard MS-DOS session.
- Try running the application in full-screen mode, using the Alt+Enter key sequence.

If either of the preceding methods works, you will have a faster, more convenient alternative, allowing you the full benefit of multitasking and other features in Windows, all of which disappear during the MS-DOS mode session.

Setting Up an Application to Run in MS-DOS Mode

Whenever possible, Windows 95 determines that an application needs to run in MS-DOS mode and closes down all other applications and switches to this mode automatically. Unless you specify otherwise, you'll be warned when Windows is about to switch to MS-DOS mode.

In some cases, you may have to manually configure an application to run in MS-DOS mode. If you try to run such an application, you get an error message telling you that you can't run the application in Windows. If this happens, you should manually configure the application to run in MS-DOS mode, using the following steps:

1. If you haven't created a shortcut for the application, create one now. You can only modify the settings of a DOS application using a shortcut.
2. Right-click the shortcut for the application and choose Properties.
3. Select the Program tab and choose Advanced to display the Advanced Program Settings dialog box.
4. Select the Prevent MS-DOS-based Programs from Detecting Windows option.
5. Choose OK.

Double-click the shortcut icon to try running the application. If the application still doesn't run, follow these steps:

1. Open the Advanced Program Settings dialog box again, as covered in the last steps.
2. Select the MS-DOS Mode option.
3. Choose OK.

Try running the application again. If it still doesn't run, you have to modify the configuration for the MS-DOS mode, using the following steps:

1. Open the Advanced Program Settings dialog box. The dialog box appears as in Figure 25.9.
2. Select the Specify a New MS-DOS Configuration option.

   Selecting this option allows you to override the default settings for the MS-DOS-mode session.
3. Modify the lines in the CONFIG.SYS for MS-DOS Mode and AUTOEXEC.BAT for MS-DOS Mode windows as needed to allow this application to run.

   The changes you make here affect only this application. In this way, you can customize each application that must run in MS-DOS mode.
4. If necessary, choose the Configuration button and select from the options in the Select MS-DOS Configuration Options dialog box and choose OK.

   Be aware that when you choose from among the options in this dialog box, you remove the entries that already appear in the CONFIG.SYS and AUTOEXEC.BAT text boxes.

FIG. 25.9
Windows allows you to override the default settings for MS-DOS mode support. You can even run a special CONFIG.SYS and AUTOEXEC.BAT file for each application.

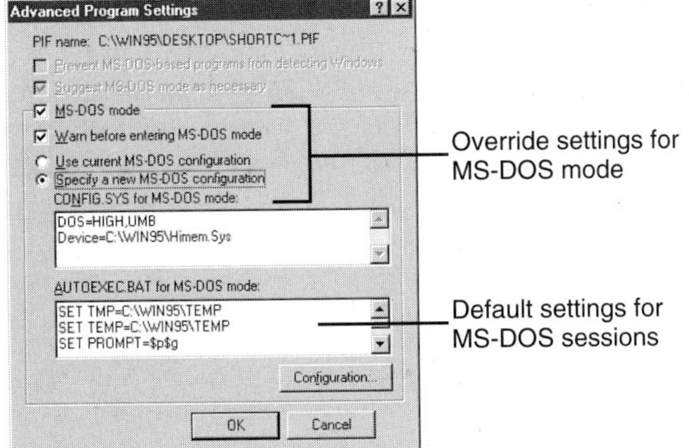

CAUTION

Use the Direct Disk Access option with great care. It is possible for an MS-DOS application to destroy long file name support when you select this option.

5. Choose OK twice to close the dialog boxes.

If there are programs or drivers that you want to load for all your MS-DOS mode sessions, edit the file named DOSSTART.BAT that is located in your \Windows folder. For example, if you want to have access to your CD-ROM drive in your MS-DOS sessions, include a line that will enable the CD-ROM. For example:

```
MSCDEX.EXE /D:MSCD0001 /M:12
```

MSCDEX is included with Windows 95 and is located in the \Windows\Command folder. You also need to include a line in your CONFIG.SYS file that loads the CD-ROM real-mode driver. This driver is not loaded into memory when you're running Windows 95.

TROUBLESHOOTING

I set my main MS-DOS Prompt to run in MS-DOS mode, and now whenever I start it, Windows shuts down completely! How can I set it back if I can't get to the properties? You can access the properties of any program or file from the Windows Desktop without running the program or opening the file. When Windows restarts after the MS-DOS Mode session, locate the icon for the MS-DOS Prompt program (in the WINDOWS\START MENU\PROGRAMS folder) with the Windows Explorer and right-click the icon to get the menu that offers the Properties function.

When the properties sheet opens, go to the Program page and choose the Advanced button, which opens the Advanced Program Settings dialog box, as shown earlier in Figure 25.9. Simply uncheck the MS-DOS Mode box and choose OK twice to close the properties sheet and return to the Desktop. See "Configuring Your MS-DOS Application" later in this chapter.

Using PIF Files

Some MS-DOS applications running in Windows 3.1 required special settings kept in a Program Information File (PIF). Creating PIFs required a lot of knowledge and time as well as a modicum of luck. Windows 95 reduces that mess by using the same mechanism for MS-DOS applications and data that's now used for Windows files: the properties sheet. With a simple right-click of the mouse, you can directly view and alter the entire gamut of controls for your MS-DOS application. No separate editor, no hunting for the PIF, and then confirming that it's the correct one. Although Windows 95 still uses PIF files, the properties sheet provides a unified means of viewing the PIF properties for a given application.

One of the more confusing issues under Windows 3.1 was the need to create a PIF file for each MS-DOS application that required custom settings. Windows 95 takes care of that chore automatically—all you need to do is view the properties for your MS-DOS application.

To view an example properties sheet for an MS-DOS application, follow these steps:

1. Using the Windows Explorer, find the Windows folder and then open the Command folder.
2. Select EDIT.COM in the file list in the right pane of Explorer.
3. Right-click to open the shortcut menu and choose Properties. Windows displays the Edit properties sheet, as shown in Figure 25.10.

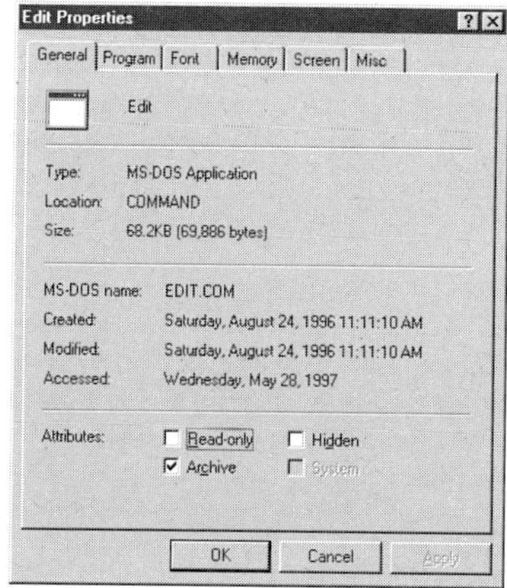

FIG. 25.10
The properties sheet for MS-DOS applications has several tabs unique to the needs of the MS-DOS environment.

If you're mystified by some of the terms and control types you see here, don't worry. The section "Configuring Your MS-DOS Application," later in this chapter, shows examples of how these controls can help you maximize the performance of Windows when you run MS-DOS applications.

Graphic-Intensive Applications

One great example of the enhanced MS-DOS support available under Windows 95 is the capability to run some applications in graphics mode in a window. Although this doesn't sound like a big trick, remember that earlier versions of Windows don't support this at all—you are forced to run MS-DOS graphics-mode applications full screen.

Why would you want to take advantage of running MS-DOS applications in a window? For some of the same reasons you like Windows applications: the capability to quickly and easily move back and forth between applications and the capability to easily cut and paste information between programs.

Also, in earlier versions of Windows, moving from a full-screen MS-DOS application in graphics mode back to Windows involves a time lag during which the display has to reset for a completely different video mode and resolution; some monitors handle this gracefully, but most don't. Running your MS-DOS program in a window avoids this altogether.

NOTE Windows 95 contains the capability to self-configure for many popular MS-DOS programs. These configurations are derived from research with the applications used the most and are stored in a file called APPS.INF. When you install an MS-DOS application, Windows checks to see if it's registered in the APPS.INF database. If the application is listed in the APPS.INF file but no PIF file exists, Windows uses the information to create a PIF for future use.

Although this new capability is wonderful, be aware that not all MS-DOS applications are supported. Not all applications follow the "official" guidelines for MS-DOS hardware access. (Some programmers break or bend the rules to gain faster performance; for example, writing directly to the video hardware versus using the MS-DOS service calls for video.) Hence, Windows 95 can't support them in a windowed, virtualized MS-DOS environment. The same application may run perfectly full screen because there are fewer layers of virtualization for Windows to provide. Game programs are a great example of this scenario, which constantly attempt to use the system timer, video, and sound resources as directly as possible.

How do you know if your application will run in graphics mode in a Windows 95 window? The best test is to try it. Follow these steps to test your program:

1. Locate the icon for the MS-DOS graphics program you want to test and double-click it to start the program. Windows starts the program in full-screen mode unless you've configured it otherwise or if the program was installed with a windowed default. If the program opens in a window, press Alt+Enter to return to full-screen mode.
2. If the program supports both Character and Graphics modes, activate the program feature that requires graphics mode (such as Page or Print Preview).
3. When the screen has reformatted for graphics display, press Alt+Enter to return to windowed display mode.
4. If Windows can't support the application in this mode, you will see the warning box displayed in Figure 25.11.

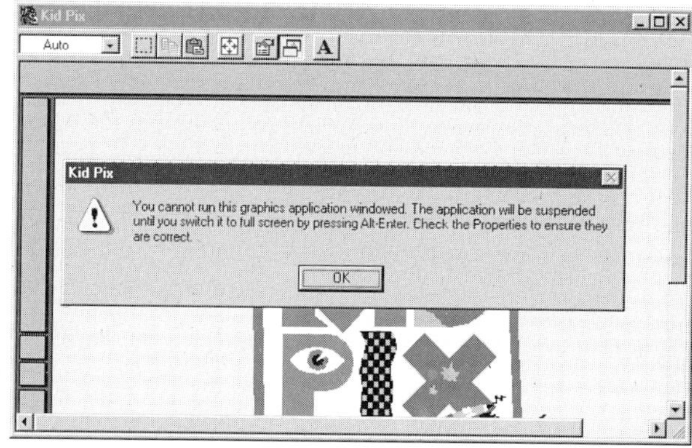

FIG. 25.11 Although Windows now offers improved support for MS-DOS graphics mode, some applications still don't work in a window.

Improved Memory Protection

Windows 95 offers a higher level of memory protection for the entire system and specifically for MS-DOS applications. This reduces the chance of programs writing to each other's memory space. You can specify special protection for conventional system memory by checking the Protected check box on the Memory property page, as shown in Figure 25.12.

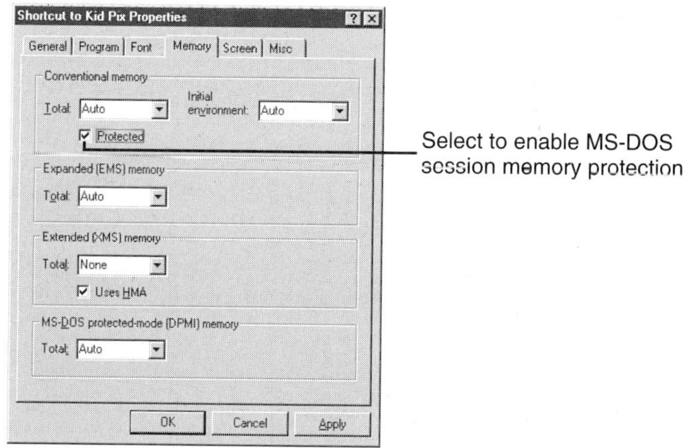

FIG. 25.12 Windows 95 allows you to protect conventional memory from errant applications via the Protected setting on the Memory property page.

Although it might seem logical to enable this option by default for all MS-DOS applications, enough overhead is involved in tracking this for each session that it's really best to turn it on only for those applications that have proven that they require it.

Enhanced Virtual Machine Support

MS-DOS application support requires the presence of a virtual MS-DOS environment, or *virtual machine.* Windows 95 offers many improvements over the virtual-machine model used in previous versions of Windows.

The virtual-machine support in Windows 3.1x required an existing real-mode MS-DOS environment. The method Windows 3.1x used to create this environment, although it worked, had two major shortcomings: It wasted system memory and restricted the customization of individual virtual MS-DOS sessions. Program Information Files (PIFs) allowed the user to alter some parameters of the memory model for each successive virtual-machine session, but the overall settings could not be altered once Windows 3.1 was started.

Windows 95 offers many improvements over this model. Because Windows 95 doesn't require a complete, existing real-mode MS-DOS environment before it runs, you can control almost every aspect of the virtual MS-DOS environment because it is more "truly" virtual. You can even run batch files within the session to customize the environment for your application's needs.

Windows 95 also offers better management of MS-DOS session closings. Under Windows 3.1, not all system memory and resources were released when a virtual-machine session ended. This resulted in a slow erosion of performance with the eventual inability to open additional applications and requiring the user to restart Windows.

Enhanced Local Reboot Support

Windows 95 improves over Windows 3.1 in how it handles programs that do not respond (or *hang*). In Windows 3.1, a program that did not respond was handled with a local reboot that theoretically affected only the errant program and its data. Under Windows 3.1's local reboot, the Ctrl+Alt+Del key sequence didn't restart the machine; it closed the misbehaving application and theoretically left Windows and all other applications fat and happy.

Local reboot had two main problems:

- Users didn't always know which application was hung, so when they used Ctrl+Alt+Del, Windows often closed the wrong one (sometimes offering to shut itself down!).
- Windows 3.1 didn't always respond quickly to the Ctrl+Alt+Del command, and the user "sat" on the keys, resulting in a complete machine reset. (A single Ctrl+Alt+Del would bring up a blue screen warning that a second Ctrl+Alt+Del would reset the system; often this screen would flash by as the system crashed and restarted, making history of any unsaved data.)

Windows 95 improves on this scenario by putting a menu between you and data loss. A single Ctrl+Alt+Del displays the Close Program dialog box.

If an application creates a problem or freezes, Windows now indicates that it is "not responding," and you have the choice of ending that task or completing an orderly shutdown of the entire system. Although this doesn't totally insulate your computer from errant applications, it does drastically improve your ability to control otherwise disastrous circumstances.

Installing MS-DOS Applications

Now that you have explored the basic concepts, tools, and techniques behind MS-DOS Prompt session support under Windows 95, look at the steps required to install and configure an MS-DOS application.

NOTE You can install any application in the following two ways:

- Locate and run the installation program for the application.
- Create a folder for the application and copy the files to that folder.

Although Windows can handle complete installations of true Windows applications, it relies on structures and capabilities that are simply not present in most MS-DOS applications. Thus, you need to set up application shortcuts and Start button menu items manually.

Using MS-DOS Application Installation Programs

Most professionally written MS-DOS applications have an installation or setup program that handles the details of installation for you. Besides simply creating a storage area for the application and moving the files to it, these installation programs perform the additional operating system configuration chores that may be necessary for successful operation.

NOTE MS-DOS installation programs that are Windows-aware may handle some of the preceding tasks for you, but most won't—you'll have to handle some of the tasks yourself. How do you know what alterations to make? Look for the documentation for the manual program installation instructions in the program folder. Often this is a simple text file, labeled README.TXT or INSTALL.TXT.

See "Installing Applications in Windows 95," **p. 688**

Installing MS-DOS Applications from the MS-DOS Prompt

You can find and run your MS-DOS application installation program from the Windows Explorer or the Start button Run command. However, you should, instead, go directly to the MS-DOS Prompt session and install your application directly or else your application may not have a structured installation program. In either case, Windows certainly allows you this level of control.

Using an Installation Program from the MS-DOS Prompt Running the installation program from an MS-DOS Prompt is just like doing it on a machine that's running only MS-DOS. Follow these steps to begin:

1. Open a new MS-DOS session from the Start menu.
2. At the MS-DOS Prompt, enter the command to start the installation program (for example, **a:\install.exe**) and press Enter.
3. When the installation program is finished, close the MS-DOS session manually or run the application.

See "Ending MS-DOS Prompt Sessions," p. 706

Installing MS-DOS Programs Manually from the MS-DOS Prompt Some MS-DOS applications don't have installation programs at all. This is most common with shareware applications or small utility programs.

To install your application manually, follow these simple steps:

1. Open a new MS-DOS session from the Start menu.
2. At the MS-DOS Prompt, enter the command to create a folder for your program (for example, **md c:\myprog**) and press Enter.
3. Enter the command to copy the program to the new folder, such as **xcopy a:*.* c:\myprog**. MS-DOS copies the files to the new folder.

NOTE You may need to alter the preceding routine slightly if your application comes as a compressed archive (such as a ZIP or an ARJ file). Usually, all this means is an additional step for decompression once the files are copied.

Configuring Your MS-DOS Application

Before you explore the myriad options for customizing the MS-DOS environment for your application, there's one point that needs to be stressed: The odds are very good that your program will run perfectly without any reconfiguration at all. Microsoft has done a truly admirable job in observing the reality of how people use MS-DOS applications under Windows, and it is reflected in the design of Windows 95 MS-DOS defaults. Preset configurations for the most popular MS-DOS applications are stored in Windows, awaiting your installation of the program. So before you begin messing around with all the options, be smart and run the program a few times. The old adage truly applies: If it ain't broke, don't fix it. See "Graphic-Intensive Applications," in this chapter about the APPS.INF file.

Understanding and Configuring MS-DOS Application Properties

You've already been introduced to the Windows properties sheet. Now you should take a closer look at specific property options and how they relate to your application.

General Properties The General properties page is primarily informational, with minimal controls other than file attributes (see Figure 25.13).

The only real controls exposed in the General properties page are the file attribute settings. These are used mainly to protect documents (by setting the read-only attribute), and you shouldn't alter them unless you have a specific reason.

NOTE A running MS-DOS application displays only six properties tabs. (The General tab is not shown when the program is in use.)

Program Properties The Program properties page gives you control over the basic environment your application starts with (see Figure 25.14).

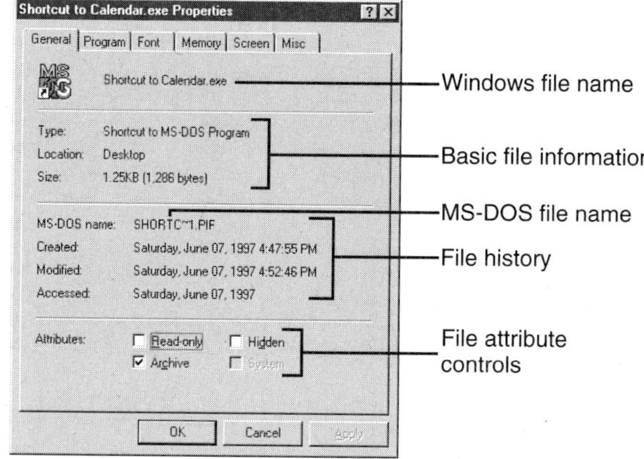

FIG. 25.13
The General properties page gives you most of the basic information about the file and easy access to control of the file attributes.

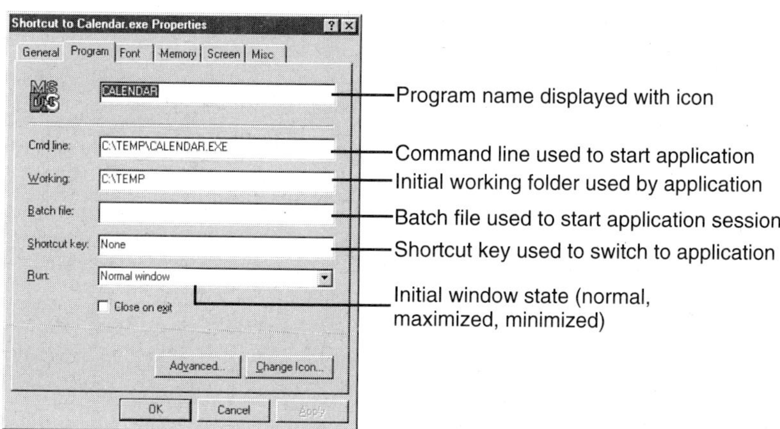

FIG. 25.14
The Program properties page allows you to alter the variables used to name and start the application.

Advanced Program Settings Clicking the Advanced button in the Program properties page opens the Advanced Program Settings dialog box, shown in Figure 25.15.

If you need to run your application in MS-DOS mode, here's where you can enable it. You can even set up custom CONFIG.SYS and AUTOEXEC.BAT values for your session. If you click the Specify A New MS-DOS Configuration option button, you can edit the special CONFIG.SYS and AUTOEXEC.BAT values right in this dialog box.

If you click the Configuration button, you will see the dialog box displayed in Figure 25.16.

All the settings under the Advanced dialog box should be altered only if your MS-DOS application simply won't run in a standard session with the default settings. For that matter, don't even enable MS-DOS mode unless your application demands it.

See "Knowing When to Use MS-DOS Mode," **p. 713**

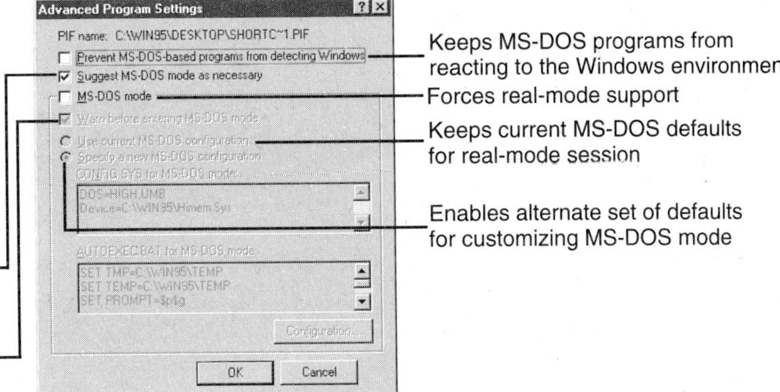

FIG. 25.15
The Advanced Program Settings dialog box enables you to define the precise mode and environment for your MS-DOS session.

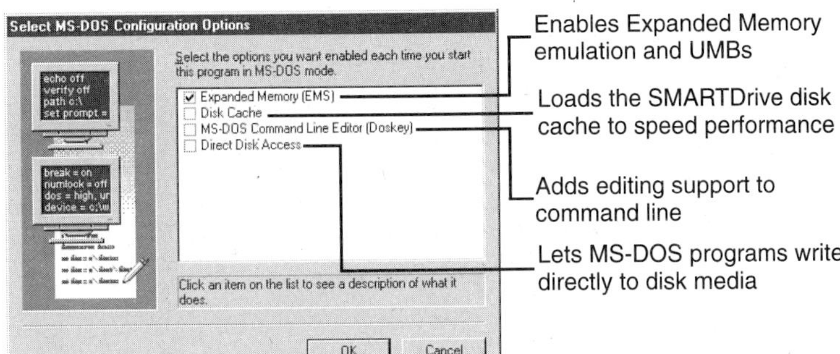

FIG. 25.16
The Select MS-DOS Configuration Options dialog box lets you control expanded memory, disk caching, disk access, and command-line editing.

Changing MS-DOS Application Icons If you click the Change Icon button shown in Figure 25.14, the Change Icon dialog box appears (see Figure 25.17).

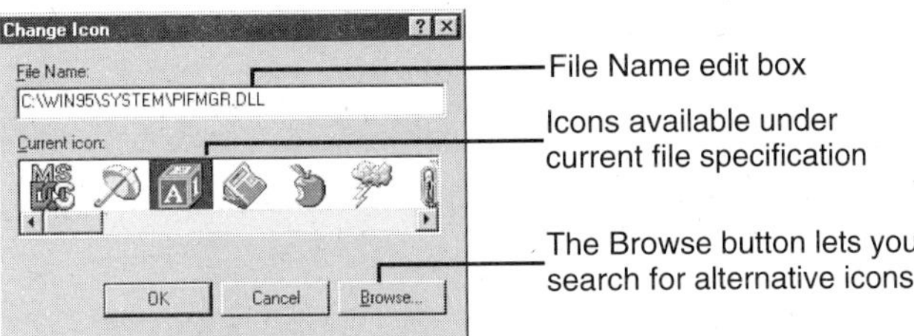

FIG. 25.17
The Change Icon dialog box lets you customize the icon for your MS-DOS application.

It's likely that your MS-DOS application won't come with any icons. Windows 95 shows you the icons in the file PIFMGR.DLL when you choose Change Icon. You can choose icons from other applications simply by specifying them in this dialog box.

Font Properties The Font properties page is primarily informational with minimal controls other than file attributes (see Figure 25.18). It works just like the Font list control on the MS-DOS session toolbar.

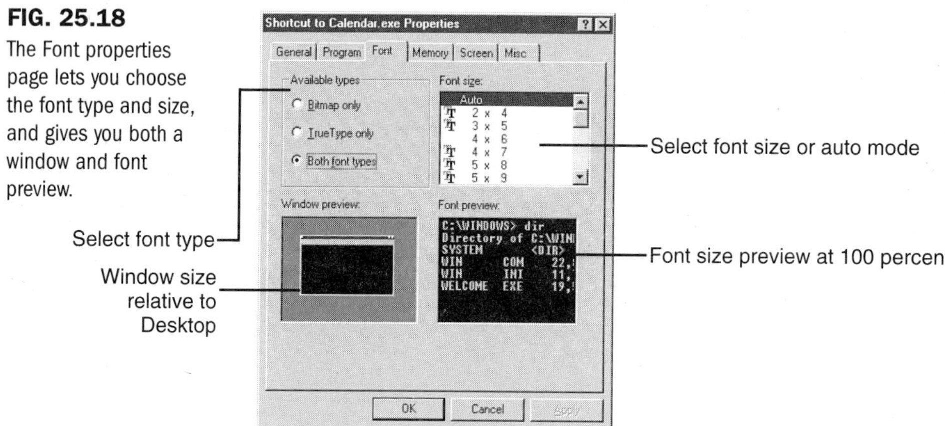

FIG. 25.18
The Font properties page lets you choose the font type and size, and gives you both a window and font preview.

TROUBLESHOOTING

When I selected a TrueType font for the display in an MS-DOS window, the font did not change on the screen. If you are running a DOS application in graphics mode, you cannot change the font because DOS graphics applications handle fonts directly. If the application supports text mode, you can switch to text mode (from within the application) and then you will be able to switch screen fonts. The other alternative is to run the application in full-screen mode (press Alt+Enter) and then change the fonts.

Memory Properties The Memory properties page makes simple work of the traditional maze of MS-DOS memory management (see Figure 25.19). With a few mouse clicks, you can configure your application memory precisely as needed.

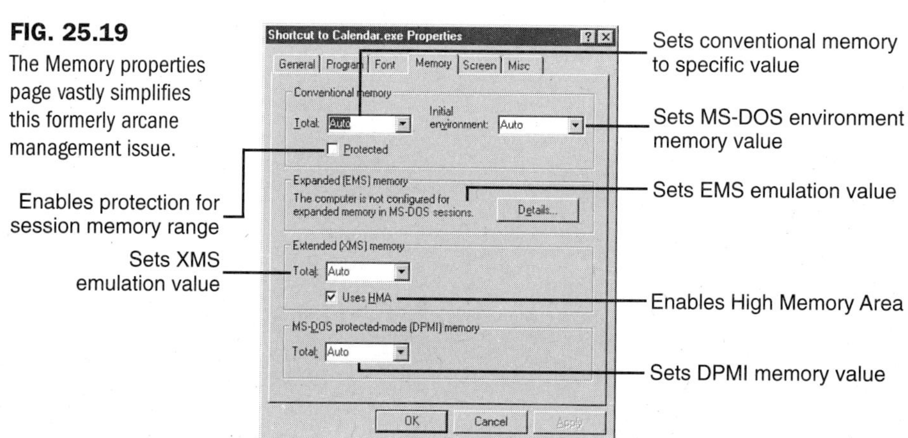

FIG. 25.19
The Memory properties page vastly simplifies this formerly arcane management issue.

Several dozen books have been written on the subject of MS-DOS memory management. Let's keep it simple: If your application works without altering these values, *do not change them.* If your application doesn't work with the default settings, *consult the documentation* to determine what the appropriate settings are. *Then* you can alter the values in this dialog box. Proceeding in any other way, unless you have considerable experience with the techniques involved, can severely inhibit the performance of your system.

See "Improved Memory Protection," **p. 718**

Screen Properties The Screen properties page lets you control the appearance of the MS-DOS session (see Figure 25.20).

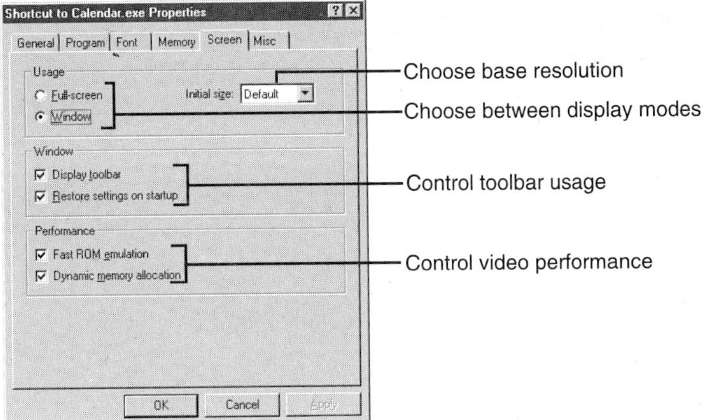

FIG. 25.20
The Screen properties page gives you control of the size, type, and performance of the MS-DOS interface.

You may find that certain MS-DOS programs (especially those running in graphics mode) respond poorly to the video emulation used in windowed mode. If so, try defeating the performance defaults by unchecking the Fast ROM Emulation and Dynamic Memory Allocation options. Fast ROM Emulation tells the Windows 95 display driver to mimic the video hardware to help display MS-DOS programs faster. Dynamic Memory Allocation releases display memory to other programs when the MS-DOS session isn't using it. If you experience strange display problems with your MS-DOS programs, try changing these settings.

Miscellaneous Properties The Misc properties page covers the remaining configuration items that don't fit under the other categories (see Figure 25.21).

- The *Allow Screen Saver* control lets your default Windows screen saver operate even if your MS-DOS session has the foreground.
- *Always Suspend* freezes your MS-DOS application when you bring another application (either MS-DOS or Windows) to the foreground. If you have an application that must perform time-sensitive operations (such as a communications program), make sure to disable this option.

- *Idle Sensitivity* tells your MS-DOS program to yield the system to other applications if it really isn't doing anything important. A word processor, for example, won't have a problem letting go of the system clock when you're not using it. A communications program, however, may need to respond quickly, so you want to set its idle sensitivity to Low.
- The *Mouse* controls enable *QuickEdit* mode (letting you mark text using just the mouse) and *Exclusive Mode* (the MS-DOS application has control of the mouse cursor when the application is in the foreground, even if you try to move the mouse out of the MS-DOS window).
- The *Warn If Still Active* item in the Termination box tells Windows to notify you before the MS-DOS session is closed. It's really best to leave this enabled, unless you are absolutely certain that the MS-DOS program will never, ever have open data files when you close it.
- The *Fast Pasting* setting simply tells Windows that your MS-DOS program can handle a raw data stream dump from the Windows Clipboard. Some MS-DOS programs clog at full speed, so if you paste to your MS-DOS application and you consistently lose characters, turn this one off.
- *Windows Shortcut Keys* allows you to override the standard quick navigation aids built into the Windows environment, just for your MS-DOS session. (Some MS-DOS programs think they can get away with using the same keys, and something has to give—Windows!) By default, Windows "owns" these shortcuts, but you can lend them to your MS-DOS application by unchecking them here.

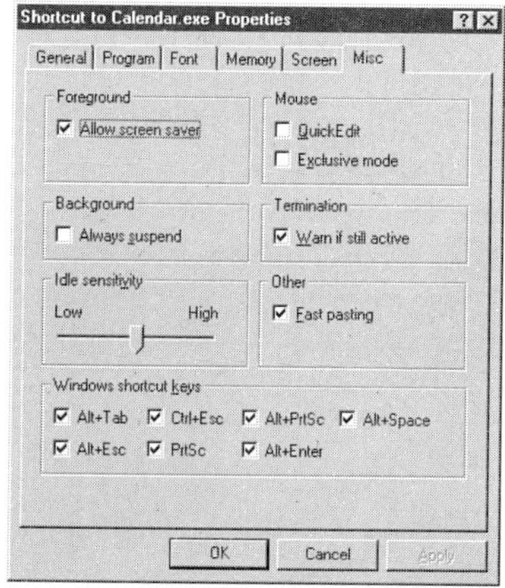

FIG. 25.21
The Misc properties page controls screen saver, mouse, background operation, program termination, shortcut key, and editing options.

Running Installed MS-DOS Applications

Windows comes set up with a default MS-DOS Prompt configuration designed to run the vast majority of applications. Although your application may have special needs, odds are it will work fine if you start it from within a running MS-DOS Prompt session.

To start your application from an MS-DOS Prompt session, follow these steps:

1. Open a new MS-DOS Prompt session from the Start menu.
2. At the MS-DOS Prompt, enter the command to move to the folder of the program you want to start (for example, **cd \wp60**) and press Enter. The MS-DOS Prompt now shows the current folder, as shown in Figure 25.22.
3. At the MS-DOS Prompt, enter the command to start your application (for example, **wp**) and press Enter. The MS-DOS Prompt window now displays the application you've started, as shown in Figure 25.23.

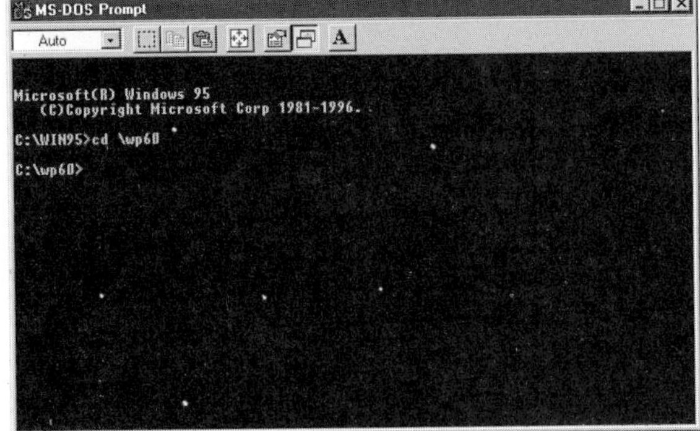

FIG. 25.22 Once you're in the MS-DOS Prompt session, all the basic MS-DOS commands can be used to start your application.

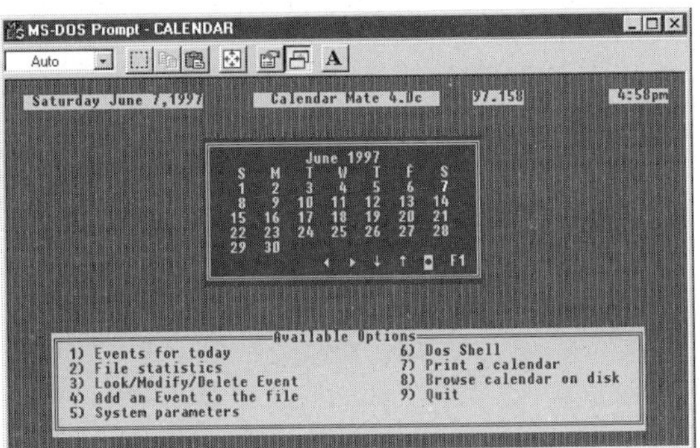

FIG. 25.23 Once your application starts, Windows displays it in the MS-DOS Prompt window space. Note that the window title reflects the command name of the program running.

Although running an application from within the MS-DOS Prompt window works well and seems familiar to the veteran command-line user, it's not really the most convenient method under Windows.

In addition to the default Windows MS-DOS Prompt, Windows 95 offers four other ways to start an application:

- Windows Explorer
- The Start button Run option

- The Start button Programs menu
- The Application shortcut

If you want the opportunity to enter optional (or even required) command-line parameters when you run a DOS application, follow these steps:

1. Right-click the shortcut icon for the application and choose Properties.
2. Select the Program tab and add a question mark to the end of the path in the Cmd Line text box.
3. Choose OK.

Now when you double-click the shortcut, a text box will appear in which you can input the startup parameters for the application.

These startup methods work just like they do for their Windows counterparts.

See "Starting from My Computer or the Explorer" **p. 238**

Removing MS-DOS Applications

If you decide to remove your MS-DOS application from your computer, there are two easy ways to do it:

- Use the MS-DOS Prompt dir and deltree commands
- Use the Windows Explorer and Recycle Bin

CAUTION

Regardless of which technique you use, make sure that you don't have any data stored with the application you're removing. Some applications allow you to store your documents or data files in the same folder as the application code itself. Although this is inherently poor design, it still happens; and if you don't tell the application to save your files to another folder or directory, you may be very sorry after you've deleted the program itself.

Using MS-DOS Commands to Remove an MS-DOS Application

Perhaps the most straightforward way to remove an MS-DOS application is to use the MS-DOS tools themselves. To do this, follow these steps:

1. Open MS-DOS Prompt session from the Start menu.
2. At the MS-DOS Prompt, type the command **dir c:*appdir* /p** (where *appdir* is the folder in which your doomed application awaits its final moments). In this example, you'll use **c:\wp60 /p**. The MS-DOS Prompt session displays a folder listing similar to that shown in Figure 25.24.

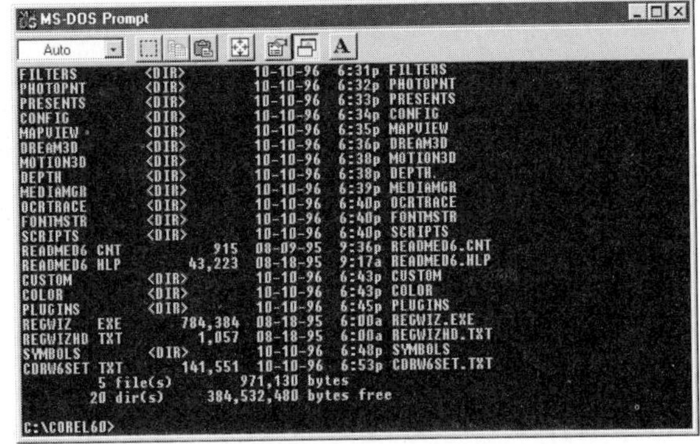

FIG. 25.24
The `dir` command shows the contents of the folder you want to delete. The `/p` switch displays the listing one page at a time. Simply press any key to continue through the listing.

3. Look for any files that contain your personal data (be sure to check in any subfolders). If necessary, copy or move these files to another location.
4. After you've saved any personal data, delete the application. At the MS-DOS Prompt, type **deltree c:*appdir*** (where *appdir* is the folder containing the application to be deleted) and press Enter. MS-DOS displays a message asking you to confirm the deletion. If you're absolutely sure, type **y** and press Enter. MS-DOS deletes the application folder and all subfolders.

See "Moving and Copying Files and Folders," **p. 319**

Part V
Ch 25

Using the Explorer to Remove an MS-DOS Application

An even simpler way to remove an MS-DOS application is to use the Explorer and the Recycle Bin. It's really as simple as locating the application folder, checking it for your personal data, and then dragging it to the "trash."

For complete instructions on using the Explorer to remove an application, see Chapter 13, "Managing Files and Folders with Windows Explorer."

See "Deleting Files and Folders," **p. 321**

Cleaning Up Shortcuts and the Start Menu

Be sure to remove shortcuts to applications after you've removed the application itself. If you don't, Windows will still try to load the application and ask you to help find it when it can't—a real hassle. If you've placed the shortcut on your Desktop, simply drag it to the Recycle Bin.

If you used the Control Panel Add/Remove Programs feature discussed in Chapter 16 to add the shortcut to the Start menu, just follow the removal steps outlined in that chapter.

See "Removing Windows Applications," **p. 698**

ON THE WEB

Check out a shareware utility called Start Clean, written by Firas El-Hasan, which is available at the following Internet site:

http://users.aol.com/felhasan/startcln.htm

This utility scans your system and removes any items in the Start menu folder that are no longer linked to programs.

CHAPTER 26

Using Microsoft Exchange and Messaging

by Brady P. Merkel, Gordon Meltzer, Peter Kent, and Ken Poore

Windows Messaging, previously known as Microsoft Exchange, is a central communications client that organizes the electronic mail and faxes that you receive in one convenient location. Windows Messaging operates not only as your Universal Inbox but also includes tools that you can use to compose, store, organize, and send messages via e-mail and fax.

In its basic configuration, Windows Messaging coordinates communication among members of your local area network (LAN) workgroup or enterprise and handles communications via the Internet, yet still finds time to send and receive faxes in several formats. In more advanced configurations, Windows Messaging handles communications with other message services such as CompuServe and Microsoft Mail.

Install Windows Messaging

Windows Messaging is comprised of a core set of programs and utilities for e-mail. Other components, called Services, are added and configured based on what you need.

Create a Personal Address Book

The Address Book keeps all your contacts and correspondents in a single, organized list.

Choose and install messaging services

Each service provides a particular function, adding in capabilities such as connecting to an Internet mail account or accessing e-mail on CompuServe. The modular design of Windows Messaging enables it to grow with your needs.

Create and send messages

Windows Messaging provides a rich set of features and tools to make it very easy.

Work with and organize received messages

Use Personal Folders to sort and manage all your incoming mail messages in organized folders. You can customize each folder by grouping the messages by subject, sender, or other information.

Overview of Windows Messaging Features

So that you know how to set up Windows Messaging during the installation process, you should have some detailed information about what Windows Messaging can do. Knowing about the capabilities will help you to make the right installation and setup choices.

NOTE When Microsoft originally released Windows 95, the messaging component was named Microsoft Exchange. Since Microsoft used that same name to identify their server product, they decided to rename the client component *Windows Messaging*. For the purpose of simplicity, the term *Windows Messaging* is used to refer to the original Microsoft Exchange and the recent name change. Where appropriate, an icon in the margin identifies new features in Windows Messaging.

You call on Windows Messaging when you want to compose a fax. You visit Windows Messaging again when you want to send a message to a colleague down the hall, to anyone in your enterprise, or possibly, anyone connected to the Internet. When one of those folks replies, the message will appear in your Inbox, no matter where it originated. Faxes sent to your fax card head for the Windows Messaging Inbox, too.

Your messages do not have to be just plain text, either. Because Windows Messaging supports rich text format, you can view and create messages using any font on your system, at any size, in any color. The first time you see a mail message that has made it around your workgroup, and each member has contributed his thoughts in a different color, you will begin to appreciate the power of Windows Messaging.

More important than rich text is the ability to work with Object Linking and Embedding (OLE). Your messages can contain OLE documents created in applications that are OLE servers, such as Microsoft Word for Windows, Microsoft Excel, or any of the many OLE server applications.

The inclusion of Windows Messaging in Windows 95 confirms the notion that e-mail is now a standard feature of personal computing. Integration with the operating system and applications enables you to easily take full advantage of all the usefulness of e-mail in increasingly complex networked environments.

Clients and Servers

The introduction of this chapter noted that Windows Messaging was a central communications client. The word *client* is so important in Windows Messaging, and in Windows 95 generally, that it needs to be explained along with its complementary counterpart, the *server*.

For the purposes of programs such as Windows Messaging, a server is a program, running on a network, that holds information accessible by users on the network. These users employ programs called clients to get at the server-based information.

If the server is a mail or fax server, it provides a place to store mail and fax messages for all the clients (users) on the network. This is the kind of server to which the Windows Messaging client connects.

The Universal Inbox

Discussions of Windows Messaging have commonly referred to the "Universal Inbox." The Inbox function is a very important part of Windows Messaging, as this section explains.

You use Windows Messaging to communicate, and a large part of communication is finding out what others have to say. You may receive messages by fax or e-mail. In Windows 95, these received messages are directed to Windows Messaging, where they can be conveniently read. Windows Messaging is called a *universal* Inbox because all messages, both fax and e-mail, no matter where they come from, go to your Windows Messaging Inbox.

Windows 95's designers decided that collecting all these messages in one place would be more convenient for users. All of those messages can now be set up to communicate through the universal inbox of Windows Messaging, eliminating the need to use different messaging packages to read your e-mail and faxes.

Microsoft Workgroup E-Mail

If your computer connects to a local area network (LAN), Windows Messaging is the program you will use to send and receive e-mail with your workgroup colleagues. Windows 95 contains a Microsoft Mail Postoffice so you can set up an e-mail system on your workgroup network.

Once you have a Postoffice installed, Windows Messaging collects all e-mail addressed to you. You can then read, reply to, and forward them, all while using the Windows Messaging program. Other accessory programs, installed on your network, will let Windows Messaging send and receive e-mail over networks wider than your workgroup LAN.

See "Installing the Workgroup Postoffice," **p. 766**

Online Service Mail Systems

The Microsoft Network (MSN) is an online service, similar in concept to CompuServe and America Online. Each of these provides e-mail to its members as a service.

Windows Messaging provides a way to dial into online services and quickly retrieve any e-mail waiting for you. You also can use Windows Messaging to send e-mail to other service members.

Rich Text Format

Windows Messaging supports rich text format (RTF). This means you can create messages using any font on your system. You also can change the text's size and use different colors. These text-formatting capabilities let you personalize your messages, and they can be quite useful when messages route to various people for comment. Individuals can use different colors, typefaces, and type sizes to help set off each set of comments.

OLE Support

OLE allows you to put part of one document into another. Every major Windows applications publisher has used this capability. You can highlight a section of a document, copy it into the Windows Clipboard, and paste-link or paste-embed it into another program. The original program might be a spreadsheet, and the target program might be a word processor. It does not matter, as long as the source program is an OLE server, and the target program is an OLE client. Most major programs are both.

NOTE The data you copy and paste-link or paste-embed is called an *OLE object*. Often in Windows 95, OLE objects have an associated icon. You can drag the icon into other programs, or drop it on the Windows desktop. In other cases, the OLE object simply appears in its original format, such as rows from a spreadsheet.

Windows Messaging extends your powers to work with OLE objects by allowing you to drop them into mail messages you compose.

Most Windows applications are OLE-enabled. Although Microsoft Word and Excel were mentioned in the section "Overview of Windows Messaging Features," any OLE object can be embedded in a message and sent with that message. For more information on using OLE, see Chapter 35, "Advanced Ways of Sharing Data Between Applications with OLE."

Installing and Configuring Windows Messaging

If your computer arrived with Windows 95 already installed on it, you may have Windows Messaging already available. If you are upgrading a previous version of Windows to Windows 95, you can install Windows Messaging during your initial installation or afterward. After the first few steps, however, the process is the same. The following sections explain how to install and configure Windows Messaging.

NOTE Windows Messaging requires a minimum of 6M of memory in your system to run. For good performance, plan to have at least 8M. Windows Messaging also takes 10M of space on your hard drive for required files. The basic program files take 3.7M of disk space. Because Windows Messaging can work with all sorts of data, you should allow a few megabytes for your incoming messages, too. It is easy to end up with 5M or more of faxes and e-mail.

Deciding Whether to Use Windows Messaging

Before you load Windows Messaging, you must first determine whether you really need it. Just because you use e-mail does not mean that you will always benefit from using Windows Messaging. Windows Messaging has powerful features and integrates into Windows 95; however, Windows Messaging can require some detailed configuration and maintenance, and it does occupy some of your system resources.

To help you make your decision, consider these questions:

- Do you want to share e-mail with others in your workgroup?
- Do you have more than one e-mail address on different online services such as CompuServe or an Internet service provider?
- Does your current e-mail program poorly manage received messages or have an inadequate address book?
- Do you read e-mail on a laptop computer that is occasionally connected to the network?
- Does more than one person use your computer to read e-mail?
- Do you have a fax modem and want to send and receive faxes?

If you answered *yes* to any of these questions, chances are you will benefit from using Windows Messaging. Conversely, if you are happy with your current e-mail program and only connect to one online service to send and receive e-mail, then you might want to skip loading Windows Messaging altogether. Of course, the choice is still yours, and you can always load Windows Messaging, try it, and delete it later if you don't seem to get much out of it.

Installing Microsoft Exchange During Windows 95A Setup

When upgrading a previous version of Windows to the initial release of Windows 95 (not OSR2), you can install Microsoft Exchange during the Windows 95 setup. The Windows 95 Setup Wizard displays the Get Connected dialog box, shown in Figure 26.1. In this dialog box, you can choose to install The Microsoft Network online service, Microsoft Mail for use on workgroup networks (LANs), and the Microsoft Fax service.

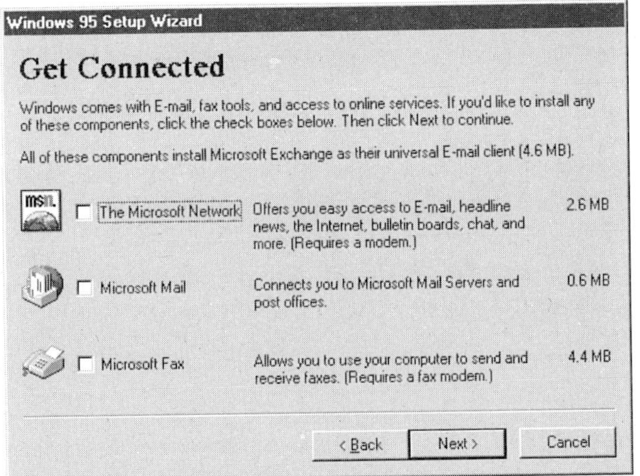

FIG. 26.1
The Get Connected dialog box is the first step to installing Microsoft Exchange.

You can install any or all of these three connectivity components. (You can always add them later, too.) MSN, Microsoft Mail, and Microsoft Fax all require Microsoft Exchange to work, so when you choose any of them, Microsoft Exchange is installed for you.

See "Using Custom Setup Mode," **p. 41**

It is also possible to install Microsoft Exchange without installing any of these items; for instance, if you want to use Microsoft Exchange for Internet e-mail. To do so, you must choose a Custom installation—you can then select Microsoft Exchange from a list of optional components.

Adding Microsoft Exchange After Windows 95A Is Installed

If you did not install any of the connectivity components during your Windows 95 installation, or your computer did not arrive with Windows Messaging already installed, you can still add Windows Messaging.

If you are upgrading to the original version of Windows 95, you can install Microsoft Exchange.

Follow this procedure to install Microsoft Exchange:

1. Double-click the Inbox icon on your desktop. You will see the Inbox Setup Wizard.

NOTE If you have installed a Microsoft Exchange service and now want to install one or more other services, you will not be able to use this procedure. This procedure works only when no Windows Messaging services have been installed. To install Microsoft Fax or The Microsoft Network, open the Start menu and choose Settings, Control Panel. Then double-click the Add/Remove Programs icon, click the Windows Setup tab, and select the item from the list of components. To install Microsoft Mail or Internet Mail, right-click the Inbox icon, choose Add, and select the service you want to install.

2. Choose one or more of the information services offered to you. The services are The Microsoft Network, Microsoft Mail, and Microsoft Fax. (To make this example most useful, what happens when you choose all three will be covered, too.)
3. After selecting the information services you want, choose OK.
4. The Inbox Setup Wizard asks you to insert your Windows 95 CD-ROM or floppy disk. Insert the CD or disk and choose OK. Windows then installs the needed files.
5. The Inbox Setup Wizard asks whether you have used Microsoft Exchange before. Because you are setting up Microsoft Exchange for the first time, choose No. Then choose Next. Windows displays the message box shown in Figure 26.2.
6. The services you selected in step 2 are checked, along with Internet Mail. If you plan to use Microsoft Exchange for receiving e-mail from an Internet service provider (other than The Microsoft Network), leave this check box checked. If you are not going to use Internet e-mail, deselect this check box.

NOTE The Microsoft Network has a level of service that provides full Internet access, and it also allows users at *all* levels to send and receive e-mail across the Internet. However, the Internet Mail service referred to by the Inbox Setup Wizard is intended for use with other Internet service providers, not with The Microsoft Network.

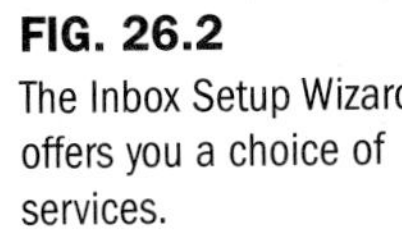

FIG. 26.2
The Inbox Setup Wizard offers you a choice of services.

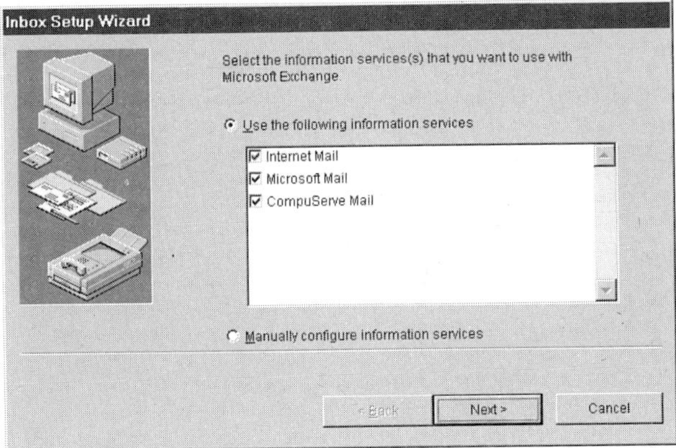

7. Choose Next to begin configuring your services.

The basic setup of Microsoft Exchange is done, but the Inbox Setup Wizard continues, setting up each of the services you have selected. Read the following sections to configure the individual communications services you just chose to use with Microsoft Exchange.

TROUBLESHOOTING

I followed the procedure in the section, "Adding Microsoft Exchange After Windows Is Installed" but could not get Windows Messaging to install correctly. The Inbox Setup Wizard may run into problems—it may even "crash" while setting up your information. For instance, you may get a message telling you that the wizard was unable to complete something and to click the Finish button to end the procedure. If this happens to you, double-click the Inbox icon and the wizard should start again.

Upgrading to OSR2 Windows Messaging

OSR 2

If you run the initial release of Windows 95 with Microsoft Exchange, you can upgrade to Windows Messaging. The update is available for free from Microsoft's Web site (connect time charges may apply). In Windows Messaging, Microsoft improved the client startup time, includes the Microsoft Mail service, and fixed several problems with the Internet Mail service.

Follow this procedure to upgrade to Windows Messaging:

1. Connect to Microsoft's Web site and download the Windows Messaging self-installer. The self-installer is available **http://www.microsoft.com/windows95/info/updates.htm**. Download the update file and save it into a temporary folder. If you want the United States version, download **exupdusa.exe**, which is a little over 3M in size.

2. Run the file you downloaded. A dialog box appears and asks you to review the license agreement. Click Yes to accept the terms of the agreement.
3. A dialog box appears welcoming you to the Windows Messaging installation program. The dialog box warns you that the installation may fail if shared files are currently in use. Close all other running applications and then click Continue.
4. In the next dialog box, enter your name and organization. Click OK.
5. Windows Messaging Setup checks for required disk space and copies files. If all goes well, you should see the dialog box indicating that the installation was successful. Click OK. The upgrade to Windows Messaging is done.

If you used Microsoft Exchange before, you should see that Windows Messaging is very similar. In fact, Windows Messaging should automatically inherit your Microsoft Exchange profile settings. To check your settings or add new services, right-click the Inbox icon on the desktop and select Properties.

Configuring Microsoft Mail

If you chose to install Microsoft Mail or if you add Microsoft Mail after upgrading to Windows Messaging, you see the dialog box shown in Figure 26.3. (If you did not choose to install Microsoft Mail, you can skip this section.)

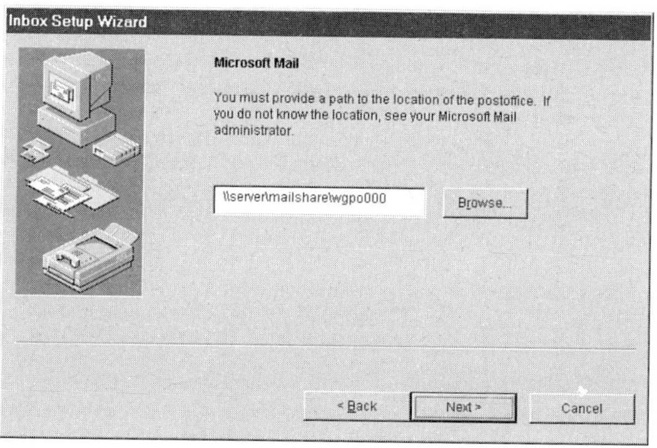

FIG. 26.3 You need to specify a Postoffice location to use Microsoft Mail.

Microsoft Mail requires that one of the computers on the workgroup LAN be set up as a Postoffice. You may have a network administrator who has already done this. If so, ask the administrator for the path to the Postoffice. Then put the path to the Postoffice in the text box shown in Figure 26.3 (click the Browse button and search for the path if necessary), and choose Next.

When the administrator creates a Postoffice, a folder called WGP0000 is created. For example, if the administrator creates a folder called Mail and tells the Microsoft Workgroup Postoffice Admin Wizard to place the Postoffice there, the wizard places the WPG0000 folder inside the Mail folder. You must specify where the WPG0000 folder is. In this example, you would enter **C:\MSMAIL\WGP0000**, not C:\MSMAIL.

If you don't have an administrator to set up your Postoffice, turn to the "Installing the Workgroup Postoffice" section later in this chapter. Then return to this section.

You are shown a list of people who have been given access to the Postoffice. Select your name from this list (if it's not on the list, ask the administrator to add it). The Inbox Setup Wizard then asks for your password. Again, ask your administrator what password he used when creating your account, and carefully type that into the text box. Then choose Next.

The wizard has finished setting up Microsoft Mail, and you are ready to use it on your workgroup LAN.

Configuring Internet Mail

If you chose to install Internet Mail, you see the dialog box shown in Figure 26.4. (If you did not choose to install Internet Mail, skip this section.) The first step is to specify your Internet access method.

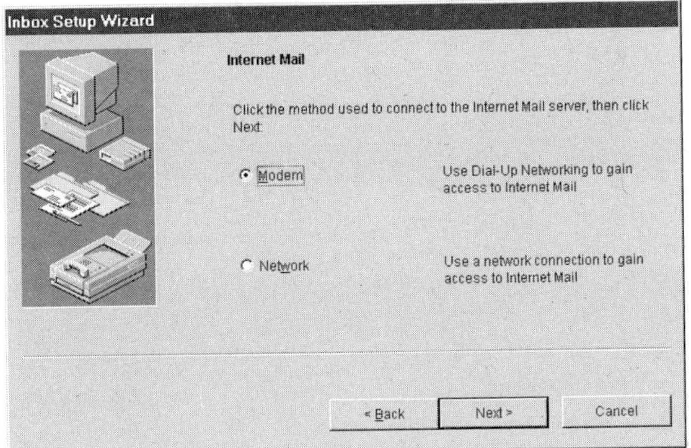

FIG. 26.4
Choose an access method to the Internet for your Internet Mail.

NOTE In order to use Internet Mail, you must have the TCP/IP protocol installed on your computer. If it is not, you will see a message reminding you to install it. To install TCP/IP, open the Start menu and choose Settings, Control Panel; double-click the Network icon and choose Add; select Protocol and choose Add; select Microsoft and TCP/IP, and then choose OK. See Chapter 17, "Getting Connected to the Internet," for more information.

Internet Access Method The wizard offers Modem and Network options for Internet access. If you connect to the Internet by modem and Dial-Up Networking, follow these steps:

1. Choose Modem, and then choose Next.
2. Now select the connection you created in Dial-Up Networking that dials your Internet service provider.

   If you have not created a connection yet, choose New and create a connection. (Chapter 17, "Getting Connected to the Internet," provides detailed instructions for creating a connection.)

NOTE If you have not yet installed the TCP/IP software, the Wizard skips step 2; it doesn't ask you which service provider to use. Later, you can specify a service provider by choosing Tools, Services on the main Windows Messaging menu, clicking Internet Mail, choosing Properties, and clicking the Connection tab.

3. Choose Next.

If you connect to the Internet via your LAN, choose Network and then choose Next.

Selecting Your Internet Mail Server Now tell the wizard about your Internet Mail server. Either you can tell the wizard the Name of the server where your Internet mail is stored, or you can tell the wizard its IP Address. Figure 26.5 shows an example, with a mail-server name filled in. When you are finished, choose Next.

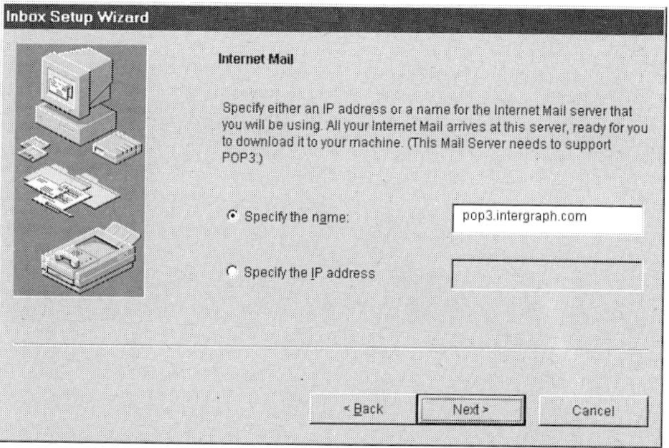

FIG. 26.5 Enter your Internet Mail server information.

Internet Mail Transfer Method You can choose Off-line or Automatic mail transfers:

- Off-line lets you use Remote Preview to view only incoming mail headers. You selectively decide which messages to download to your inbox, based on the header contents.
- Automatic instructs Windows Messaging to connect to your Internet Mail server and retrieve all new mail into your inbox automatically. The Automatic option also automatically sends any outbound Internet mail you have created.

Make your choice, and then choose Next.

Your Internet E-Mail Address Next, the wizard wants you to fill in your e-mail address in the form *user@domain*. Enter this in the text box called E-Mail Address. Also, put your full name in the text box called Your Full Name. When you are finished, choose Next.

Internet Mailbox Information The Inbox Setup Wizard needs the Mailbox Name and Password you use to access your account in your Internet Mail server. Enter them in the text boxes provided and then choose Next.

Internet Mail is now set up and ready to use with Windows Messaging.

Completing Your Microsoft Windows Messaging Installation

Now that you have set up the various services you selected, the Wizard finishes off the more general Windows Messaging settings. First, it asks you which Personal Address Book it should use.

You probably have not created a Personal Address Book (assuming that you are installing Windows Messaging for the first time), so simply choose Next.

You see a similar dialog box, this time asking where your Personal Folder file is. This file stores all your messages. Choose Next to accept the file that the Wizard is suggesting.

NOTE It is common for network-based e-mail users (especially if you are using the Microsoft Mail service) to have personal folders exceeding 50M. When backing up your system, be sure to specify the directory in which you have placed your files containing your address book and personal folders (see Chapter 16, "Backing Up and Protecting Your Data"). Also, be sure to exit Microsoft Windows Messaging before running the backup; otherwise, the backup may skip your personal folders file because Windows Messaging has it open.

Next, the wizard may ask whether you want to run Windows Messaging automatically every time you start Windows. This choice requires some thought; Windows Messaging uses many system resources and can affect performance in low-memory configurations. If you are going to use Windows Messaging only on a dial-up basis, such as with The Microsoft Network or an Internet service provider, choose No.

TIP If you connect to a LAN, start Windows Messaging automatically every time you start Windows so that you will not miss any e-mail from workgroup members.

Running Windows Messaging at Windows startup wastes system resources if you do not need to use Windows Messaging services constantly. If you do not expect much e-mail and use Windows Messaging and its communications services infrequently, select the Do Not Add Inbox to StartUp Group check box.

If your messaging needs require constant connectivity or periodic automatic logon to an online service to check for new mail, choose to Add Inbox to the StartUp Group.

To complete the installation, choose Next. The Inbox Setup Wizard displays a final dialog box confirming that Windows Messaging is set up to work with all the communications services you selected (see Figure 26.6).

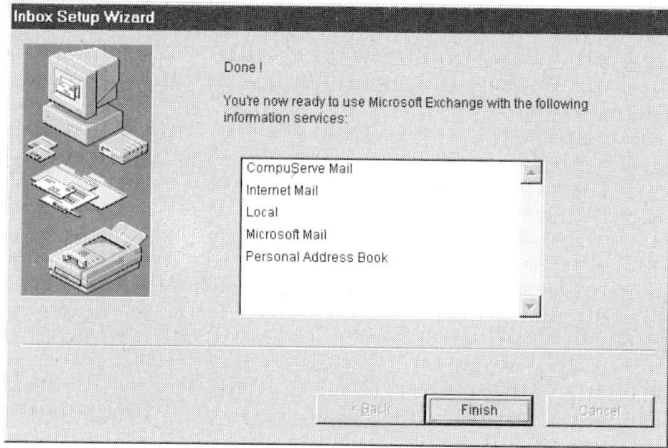

FIG. 26.6
The Inbox Setup Wizard confirms that the setup of services is complete.

Choose Finish. After this long setup and configuration process, you are ready to start using Microsoft Windows Messaging. (The Windows Messaging window opens automatically immediately after the wizard closes.)

Using the CompuServe Mail Service

The universal inbox of Windows Messaging is designed to be a flexible, modular mail system, able to access many different mail services across many different networking and dial-up connections. Earlier in this chapter, you read how to install the service that allows you to send and receive mail over the Internet. CompuServe has a similar add-in module that allows Windows Messaging to be the inbox for CompuServe mail as well.

Installing the CompuServe Mail Service

You must first add the service to Windows Messaging in order for you to use it. Follow these steps:

1. The CompuServe mail connector is not included with Microsoft Windows Messaging, so you first need to obtain the latest version of CompuServe Mail for Windows Messaging from CompuServe. After logging into CompuServe, use **GO CISSOFT** and select CompuServe Mail for Microsoft Windows Messaging (Win 95). Then choose to download the file (CSMAIL.EXE)—it's a free download.
2. CSMAIL.EXE is a self-extracting archive. Once downloaded, copy it into its own directory and run CSMAIL.EXE to extract the setup files. Next, run the extracted SETUP.EXE to start the installation.

3. Follow the instructions provided by the setup program. When the program asks if you would like the service to be installed into your default profile, select Yes. After the service is installed, you are prompted to enter your Name, CompuServe ID, and Password.

Configuring the CompuServe Mail Service

Once installed, you may never need to change how the service is configured. However, if your password changes, or if you would like to set up the service to connect to CompuServe on a scheduled basis, you have to reconfigure it.

Follow these steps to change your CompuServe Mail settings:

1. Open the Start menu and choose Settings, Control Panel.
2. In Control Panel, double-click the Mail icon.
3. Choose the CompuServe Mail Service and select Properties. You will see the tabbed dialog box shown in Figure 26.7. The tabs contain the following configuration settings:
   - **General.** Choose this tab to update your Name, CompuServe ID, or Password.
   - **Connection.** Choose this tab to change the Phone Number to access CompuServe, the modem you use to connect, or the Network type (such as Tymnet or SprintNet). You also can select what type of connection you have to CompuServe. Choose Windows Modem Settings if you are using a modem to connect to CompuServe. Choose Winsock Connection if your computer is connected to the Internet. Choose Direct Connection if you have a communications port (for example, COM1) directly wired into CompuServe.
   - **Default Send Options.** Choose Send Using Microsoft Exchange Rich-Text Format if you want to preserve all the rich text formatting (fonts, colors, and so on) in your e-mail message. Setting the Release Date holds outgoing messages in your outbox until the date specified; if not set, all mail is sent as soon as possible. The Expiration Date is the date that mail is deleted in your recipient's mailbox.
   - **Advanced.** The Create Event Log option generates a mail message in your inbox each time you connect to CompuServe. The log details how many messages were retrieved and sent, and notifies you if there was a problem connecting. Setting Delete Retrieved Messages removes messages from your CompuServe mailbox when Windows Messaging successfully retrieves them. The Change CompuServe Dir option tells the service where your CompuServe access program (for example, WINCIM) resides on your system. Use Schedule Connect Times to set up when Windows Messaging should automatically connect to CompuServe and retrieve and send mail messages.

FIG. 26.7
Use the General tab on The CompuServe Mail Settings property sheet to configure your CompuServe account information.

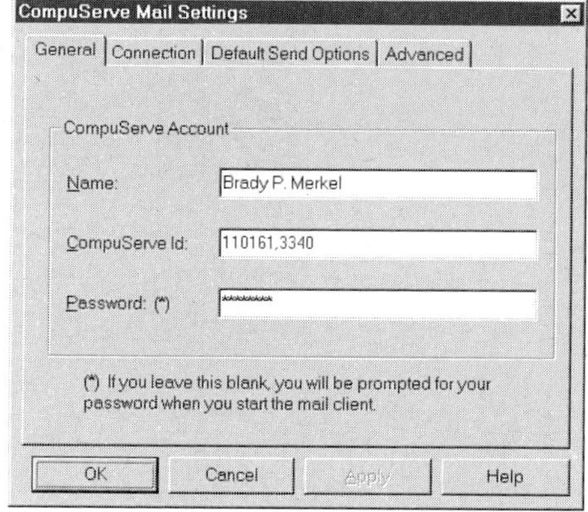

Creating and Sending Mail Messages

After you configure one or more information services, you can create and send a message with the Windows Messaging client. If Windows Messaging were perfect, it would have a universal composition screen in which you could compose any type of message for any type of recipient and for any delivery method. Because of the differences between fax recipients and electronic-mail recipients, however, you have to decide whether to compose a mail message or a fax.

This section explains how to create and send an e-mail message to members of a work-group LAN.

Creating a Mail Message

How to send an e-mail message to a member of your workgroup LAN will be explained first. You'll be working with the message form discussed earlier in this chapter. Remember that you'll have all the power of rich text formatting and OLE available when you create your e-mail message.

TIP To quickly e-mail a file from within Explorer, right-click the file name and select Send To, Mail Recipient.

If the Windows Messaging window is not open, start the Windows Messaging program by double-clicking the Inbox icon on the desktop. Then choose Compose, New Message. If you prefer to use the toolbar, click the New Message button. Windows Messaging opens the New Message window.

Figure 26.8 shows the initial blank composition window, which is the New Message form, or window. You will see this form frequently while you work in Windows Messaging. Now you can work on your message.

FIG.26.8
Use the New Message window to compose messages.

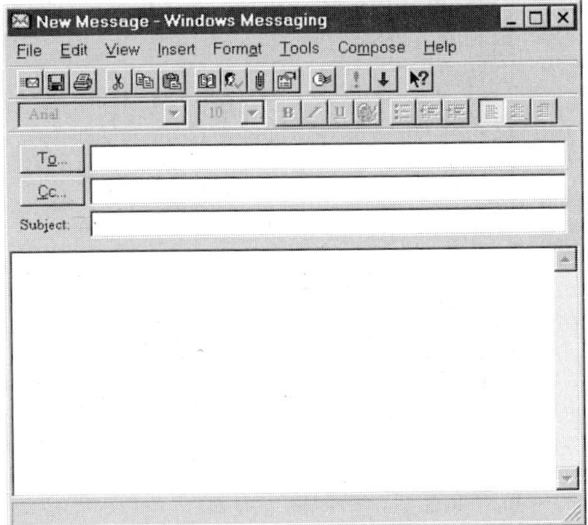

TIP You also can get to the New Message window by pressing Ctrl+N in the main Windows Messaging window.

Choosing a Recipient

When you click To in the New Message window, your Personal Address Book pops up, showing the list of recipients that you have created. Select the names of the people to whom you want to send your message; you can select names for the To box and names for the Cc box.

You may want to send a blind carbon copy, called a Bcc. The blind copy will be sent to any recipients on the Bcc list. The recipients of the original message and any Cc recipients will not know a copy has gone to the Bcc recipient. The New Message form does not show the Bcc text box by default. You can display this text box by choosing View, Bcc Box.

Entering Text

Start with the Subject box and type the subject of the message.

Pressing Tab takes you to the main message-entry space, where you can write what you have to say. Start entering text now.

TIP Enter your text for the message first and format it later.

Formatting Message Text

If you use a word processor, you should see a remarkable similarity between the word processor and the menus and toolbars of the New Message form. The toolbars and menus give you the option of choosing the following formatting options for your message text (the options are listed as they appear on the toolbar, from left to right):

- Font (limited to the fonts on your system)
- Font Size (as small or large as the TrueType font scaler can handle)
- Bold
- Italic
- Underline
- Text Color
- Bullets
- Indents
- Text Alignment (left-align, center, and right-align)

You can combine these options to create messages in rich text format. Whenever you use fonts in varying sizes, colors, and alignments, or other formatting options, you add depth to your communications.

Sending Files and OLE Objects with Windows Messaging

You are not limited to text messages, or even rich text format messages. One of the most useful capabilities is including files and objects in messages. When you use files and objects in your messages, you can add a lot of extra content to those messages with very little work.

Practically any file on your system can be included in a message. You can send text files, graphics files, and files created by the applications you have. However, if you do send an application file (such as a spreadsheet or database file), be sure that your recipients also have the same applications so they can read what you send them.

NOTE If you want to send a file to a user who retrieves mail from an online service such as CompuServe and who may not be using Windows Messaging to read mail, you should not send the file as an OLE object. Send it as a file instead. Few e-mail programs other than Windows Messaging can interpret an embedded OLE object in an e-mail message. On the other hand, most e-mail programs, including those on nearly all online services, have no difficulty detecting an attached file and can deliver it properly to your recipient.

Follow these steps to insert a file (also known as an *attachment*) into a mail message:

1. After opening up a New Message window by choosing Compose, New Message, choose your recipients and type in the subject of the message. Go to the body of the message and choose Insert, File. A file selection dialog box appears (see Figure 26.9).

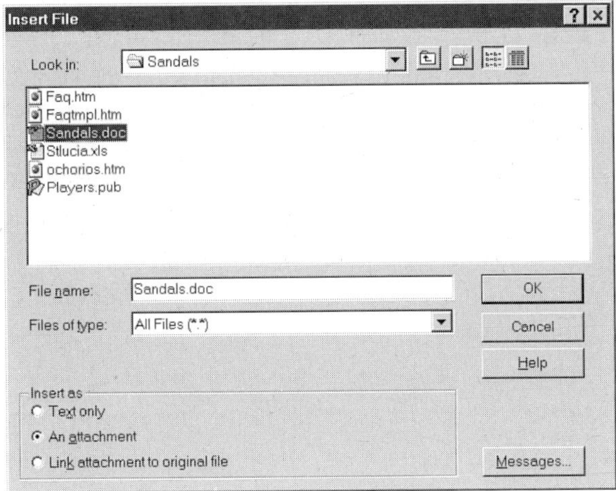

FIG. 26.9
Use the Insert File dialog box to insert files into mail messages.

2. Browse through your file system and select the file you want to include inside the message.
3. Use the options in the Insert As section at the bottom of the dialog box to choose how you would like to insert the file into your message:
   - If your message is a straight text file, you can insert the file directly into the mail message, dumping the contents of the file right into the body of your message. Select the Text Only option in the Insert As section at the bottom of the dialog box. Press the OK button to import the text file's content into your mail message.
   - If you are inserting a file containing something other than straight text, you must insert it as an attachment. This preserves the file as a separate item in your mail message. The recipients of the message can save the file to their disk when they read your message, or they can choose to double-click the File icon in the mail message and launch the application associated with the type of file you sent them.
   - Related to the previous method of attaching the file and using the mail message as a means to transfer it around, you can choose to send the recipients a link to the file. This only works, however, if you and all your recipients are on a network that can access the file through Network File sharing. To learn how to send links, continue reading the next section.

Sending File Links with Windows Messaging

Windows 95 introduced a powerful feature called *shortcuts*, which are simple links to files elsewhere on the system or network. You can place shortcuts on your desktop, in other directories, or on the Start menu so you can have quick access to what the shortcut points to. You also can send shortcuts in mail messages.

The benefit of doing this is that you are not actually inserting the entire file into your mail message: you are merely inserting a link, or shortcut, to the file. When your recipients receive your mail message and double-click the inserted link, their application resolves the shortcut to the file on your system, connects to your machine, and accesses the file directly over the network. Sending a link is useful if the file to send is very large or may be accessed by several people simultaneously, like a Microsoft Access database file (.MDB file).

Follow these steps to send a file link in a mail message:

1. Verify that the file you want to send is on a shared drive, accessible to all the recipients to whom you want to send the file link.
2. Choose Insert, File from the New Message window's menu. Browse through the file system and locate the file you want to send. Select the file—its name will appear in the File Name field.
3. In front of the file name, type in the UNC name of the network share containing this file. If the file is in a subfolder of the share, be sure to include it in the UNC (see Figure 26.10).

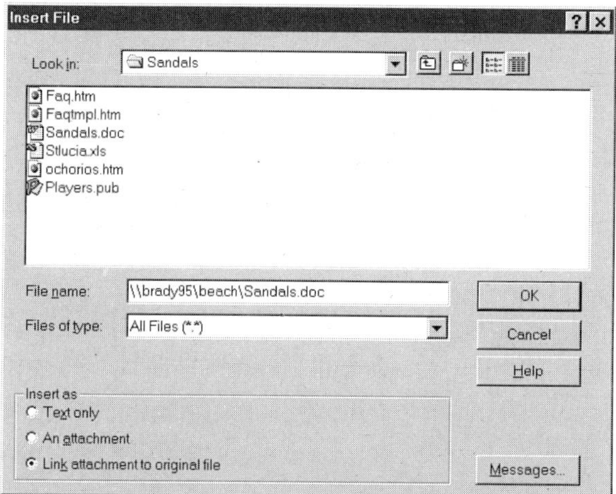

FIG. 26.10
Instead of embedding large files in messages, send links.

4. In the Insert As box at the bottom of the dialog box, choose to insert the file as Link Attachment To Original File.
5. Choose OK.

NOTE You can send links to Internet sites in mail messages. In Internet Explorer, choose File, Create Shortcut, when displaying the page you want to mail to someone else. Then in your mail message, choose Edit, Paste to insert the link.

If you are only going to send types of files that are common and built into Windows 95, you should send them as embedded OLE objects. This way, the recipient only has to double-click the object and Windows 95 automatically knows how to view it.

You can insert the following types of Windows 95 objects into your messages:

- Audio Recorder
- Bitmap images
- Media clips
- Microsoft Word documents or pictures
- MIDI sequences
- Packages
- Paintbrush pictures
- QuickTime movies
- Video clips
- Wave sounds
- WordPad documents

Each application on your system that is an OLE server can create OLE objects that you can place in your messages, so the preceding list is not exhaustive.

Follow these steps to insert an OLE object in a mail message:

1. In Windows Messaging, choose Insert, Object. The list of available object types appears (see Figure 26.11).

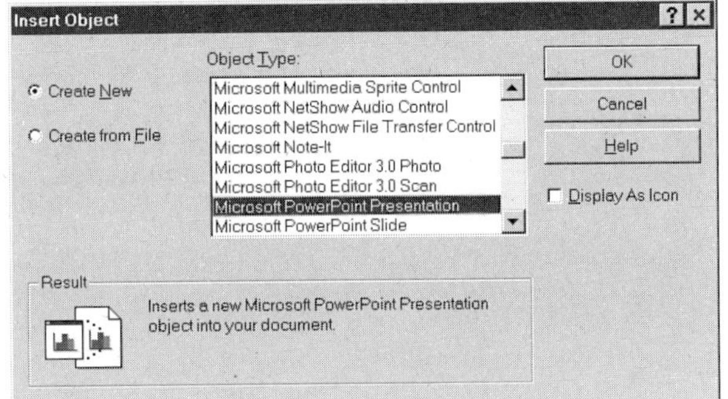

FIG. 26.11
Use the Insert Object dialog box to choose an OLE object type to insert in a message.

TIP If you want your OLE option to appear as an icon, select the Display As Icon option while in the Insert Object dialog box. Leave this check box cleared if you want the data—the spreadsheet rows, word processing text, picture, or whatever—displayed rather than the icon. (Some objects—sounds, for instance—can't be displayed, so their icons display automatically.)

2. Select the type of object you want to include in your message, and then choose OK. Select Wave Sound, for example, to insert a sound recording in the message. The application used to create the object starts. In the case of a Sound Wave object, the Sound Recorder applet starts.

NOTE Notice that the OLE server application that opens has a special kind of title bar. Instead of saying Sound Recorder, for instance, the title bar would say Sound Object in Mail Message. The OLE server applications also have slightly different menus and options from when they run normally. The File menu in Sound Recorder, for example, has a new option: Exit & Return to Mail Message.

3. Use the application to create the object that you want to mail. In this case, record the audio that you want to send with your mail, and then choose File, Exit & Return to Mail Message. The application disappears, leaving the Wave Sound icon in your message.

If you are inserting a form of data that can be displayed, and if you didn't choose the Display As Icon check box in the Insert Object dialog box, you see the actual data rather than the icon. You can move this data, or the icon, around in your message, and you can give the icon a more useful name than the default name (Bitmap Image).

When recipients get a message containing an icon, they must double-click the icon. This starts the application that created the OLE object. The object is then played or displayed (see Figure 26.12).

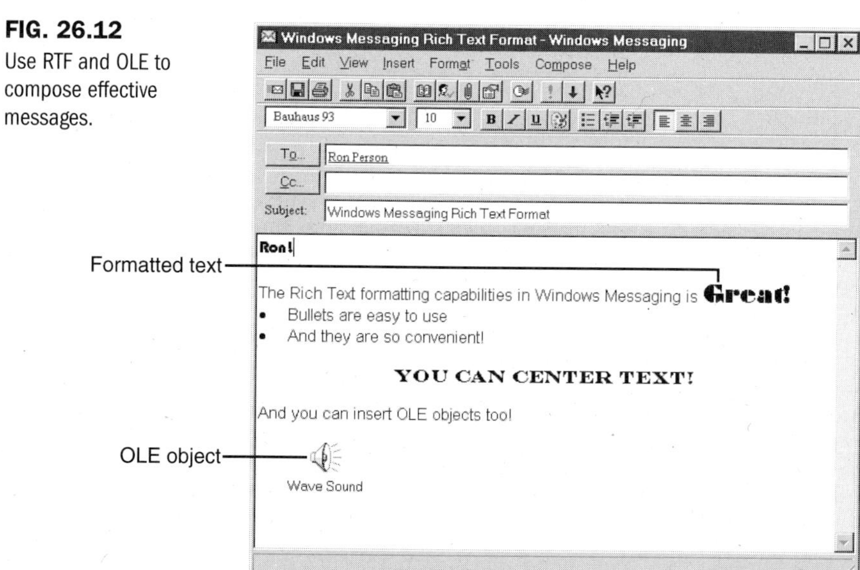

FIG. 26.12
Use RTF and OLE to compose effective messages.

When you insert objects in messages, rename the icon, including text such as "Click here to play," to make the icon's intended function obvious to the receiver. To rename the icon, right-click it, choose Rename, and then type the new name in the text box over the old name. Press Enter when you finish.

Embedding an object or file in a message is an example of OLE at work in Windows Messaging.

TIP

Many applications today have a File, Send command that creates a new e-mail message and automatically embeds the document you are working on in the new e-mail message.

Finishing and Sending Your Mail Message

Once you have written your message and added any formatting or OLE objects that you want, there are a few more options you may want to select.

Choose Tools, Options, and then click the Send tab. The following list describes the items on the Send page:

- **Font.** Select the font typeface and size you prefer for new messages.
- **Read Receipt and Delivery Receipt.** Request that a receipt be sent back when the message has been delivered to or read by the recipient.
- **Sensitivity.** Set the sensitivity ranking such as Normal, Personal, Private, or Confidential to your message.
- **Importance.** Choose whether you want High, Normal, or Low priority for your message. You also can choose the High/Low icons to perform this task.
- **Save a Copy in 'Sent Items' Folder.** Saves a copy of all of your outgoing messages in the Sent Items folder.
- **Use Simplified Note on Internet mailto: and file.send.** Use a simple compose window when sending quick messages from a Web browser.

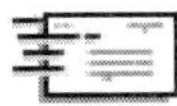

Close the Properties box. To send your message, choose File, Send, or click the Send button.

TROUBLESHOOTING

I sent a Microsoft Mail message on my workgroup network, but the message was not received.
Make sure that only one Postoffice is installed for your workgroup and that the Postoffice is located in a shared folder that everyone in the workgroup can access.

Using Remote Mail

When you are not connected to a network or your online service and need to read your e-mail, Remote Mail can help you download specific mail messages and optimize your modem connect time. Remote Mail is best used when you expect either a large number of messages to be waiting in your inbox, or you anticipate large messages with attachments that you don't want to download all at once. Remote Mail enables you to connect to your e-mail service, look at the headers of all the mail in your inbox, and choose which mail messages you want to download and read. This section shows how easy Remote Mail is to use.

Setting Up Remote Mail

Most add-in mail services for Windows Messaging support using Remote Mail in addition to the usual way Windows Messaging transfers mail. Some Windows Messaging add-in services require more configuration than others to set up Remote Mail. Some services, such as the CompuServe Mail Service for Windows Messaging, require no set up at all—you can use Remote Mail any time without any additional configuration. The Microsoft Mail service, however, has several options important to configuring Remote Mail.

To use Remote Mail with a Microsoft Mail Postoffice, you need to configure the connection and delivery options of Microsoft Mail. However, you must first have a Dial-Up Networking connection established to connect you to the machine where the Postoffice resides.

See "Using Dial-Up Networking," **p. 209**

To set up Remote Mail for Microsoft Mail, follow these steps:

1. Open the Start menu and choose Settings, Control Panel.
2. Double-click the Mail icon.
3. Choose the Microsoft Mail service and click Properties.
4. On the Connection page, select which type of connection you use to access your Microsoft Mail Postoffice:
   - If you are sometimes connected to a LAN and sometimes using a modem to read mail (if you are using a laptop, for instance), choose Automatically Sense LAN or Remote. Windows Messaging figures out how you are connected and uses the right connection type.
   - If you are always on the LAN, select Local Area Network (LAN). You will probably not use Remote Mail if you are always connected to the LAN where your Microsoft Mail Postoffice resides. However, you can still use Remote Mail if you have a slow network connection to the mail server or do not want mail to be automatically delivered to your inbox.
   - If you always use a modem to send and receive mail, choose Remote Using a Modem and Dial-Up Networking.
   - If you do not want to connect via a LAN or a modem, choose Offline. You can compose mail while not connected and reconnect later, if needed.

5. Choose the LAN Configuration page.
6. If you are connected to the LAN and still need to use Remote Mail, choose the Use Remote Mail option. Mail will only be delivered and sent when you use Remote Mail.
7. Choose the Remote Configuration page. These settings are used only when you use a modem to read mail remotely (see Figure 26.13).

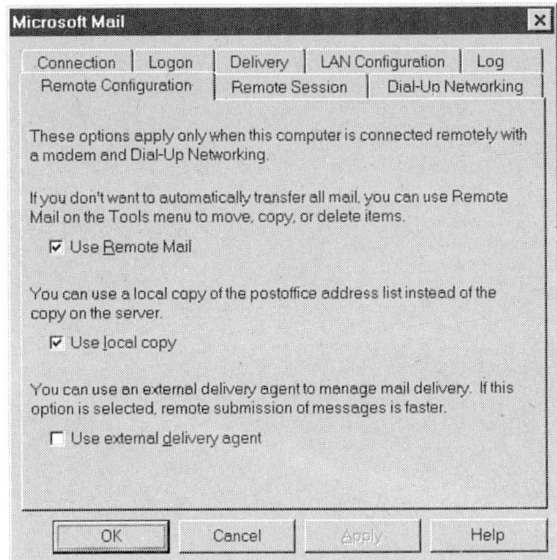

FIG. 26.13
The Remote Configuration Page sets up your Microsoft Mail Service to use Remote Mail.

8. Choose the Use Remote Mail option. This enables Remote Mail for the Microsoft Mail Service.
9. If you want to keep a local copy of the Postoffice's Address List on your machine so you can select Postoffice mail addresses while not actually connected to the Postoffice, choose the Use Local Copy option. You can later download a copy of the Address Book and store it locally.
10. If you want to connect to your Postoffice automatically during your Windows Messaging session, choose the Remote Session page and choose When This Service Is Started. You can set up scheduled connections to your Postoffice by clicking the Schedule Mail Delivery button. Otherwise, by default, you will only connect to your Postoffice when you choose.
11. If you use Dial-Up Networking to connect to your Postoffice, on the Dial-Up Networking page, select which Dial-Up Networking Connection you use to connect to your Postoffice.

Once configured, Remote Mail is very easy to use. The next section explains how to use Remote Mail after it's configured.

Sending and Receiving Mail Using Remote Mail

Once you configure your mail services to use Remote Mail, the process of connecting to your e-mail service, sending, selecting, and downloading mail is very easy.

Remote Mail uses a separate window for viewing the headers of mail messages waiting on the remote e-mail service. When you initially connect to your mail service, you will usually have Remote Mail retrieve the headers of all your new mail, as well as send out what is in your outbox. After completing that and disconnecting, you will review the headers of all your new messages, choosing which ones you would like to download and read. Finally, you reconnect to your mail service and retrieve the messages you have selected. Here are the steps you would typically take to access your mail using Remote Mail:

1. From the Windows Messaging menu, choose Tools, Remote Mail, Microsoft Mail. This displays the dialog box shown in Figure 26.14.

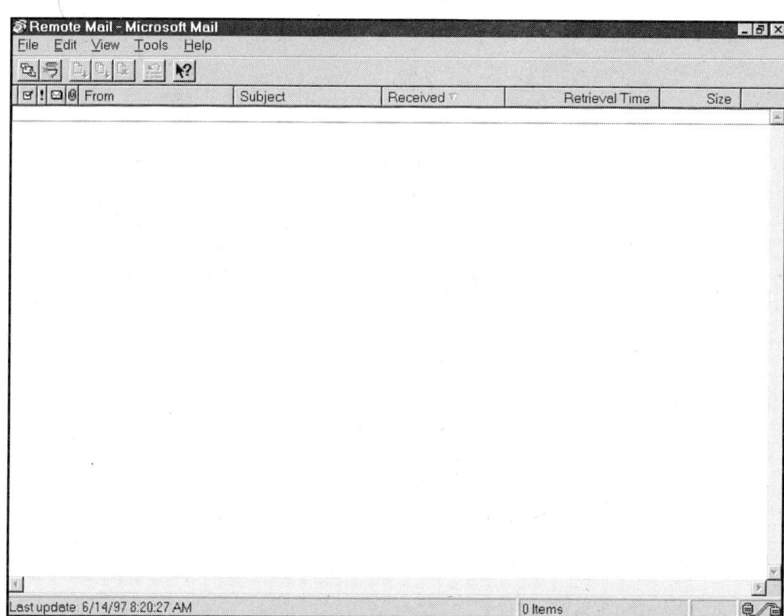

FIG. 26.14 Use the Remote Mail window to select which messages you want to receive from your Postoffice.

2. Click the Connect icon or select Tools, Connect. The Connect to Server dialog box in Figure 26.15 appears.

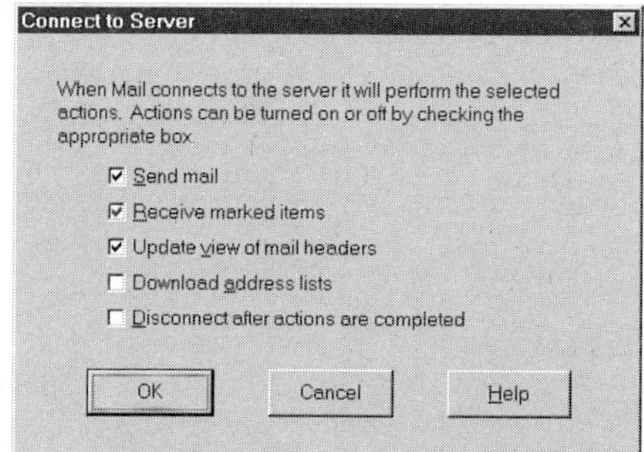

FIG. 26.15 You can do several different tasks when updating the list of message headers.

3. While retrieving the waiting message headers, you also can choose the following options:
   - Send Mail takes any messages in your outbox addressed to a mail recipient in the Postoffice and sends them.
   - Receive Marked Items retrieves the messages you have selected from your header list. The first time you enter the Connect dialog box, you will probably not have chosen to retrieve any messages.
   - Update View of Mail Headers checks for new messages.
   - Download Address Lists downloads a local copy of the Postoffice's Address List. This will enable you to select Postoffice mail recipients when you are not connected to the Postoffice. If you think your copy of the address list is out-of-date, you should choose this option. Depending on the number of people in your Postoffice, this could add several minutes to your connection time.
   - Disconnect After Actions Are Completed terminates your modem connection after your headers are downloaded.
4. Click OK to start the transfer. A dialog box with a gauge will keep you informed of what is transpiring during your connection. After a few moments, depending on how many options you've selected, the Remote Mail dialog box will display the headers of the messages waiting in your Postoffice inbox (see Figure 26.16).

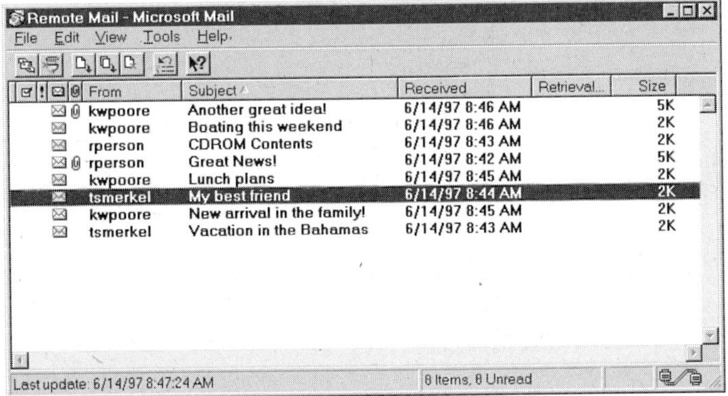

FIG. 26.16
The list of waiting messages appears after updating the message headers.

5. Now you can select which messages you need to retrieve from your Postoffice inbox. When you select which messages to retrieve, you have three options from which to choose (each of these options is also available by right-clicking the message header and choosing it from the pop-up menu):
   - Click the Mark to Retrieve button, or choose Edit, Mark to Retrieve, from the menu to retrieve the message and remove it from the Postoffice. The next time you update the message headers, you will not see this message in your Postoffice.
   - Click the Mark to Retrieve a Copy, or choose Edit, Mark to Retrieve a Copy, to retrieve a copy of the message, but also keep it in your Postoffice. The message will be marked as "read" and will not be bolded when you update your headers again.

If you use both a notebook computer and a computer that is connected to your Postoffice over a LAN, choose to Retrieve a Copy of your mail messages. Messages will stay in your Postoffice inbox so you can access them from your LAN-based computer later.

- Click the Mark to Delete button or choose Edit, Mark to Delete to delete messages without reading them (see Figure 26.17).

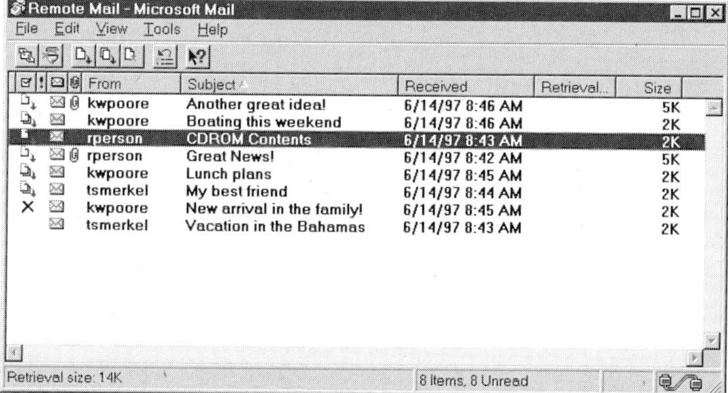

FIG. 26.17
Choose the messages to retrieve from your Postoffice using Remote Mail.

6. Click the Transfer Mail button or choose Tools, Transfer Mail. A dialog box similar to the Update Headers dialog box seen earlier appears; only this time with the Send Mail, Receive Marked Items, and Update View Of Mail Headers selected by default.
7. Click OK to process your marked items and refresh your view of the waiting message headers. All messages marked for retrieval are placed in your Windows Messaging Inbox where they can be accessed as usual.
8. If you did not choose to disconnect from the Postoffice automatically and you're finished with Remote Mail for now, you should click the Disconnect button or choose Tools, Disconnect to end your connection with the Postoffice.
9. You can either close the Remote Mail window by selecting File, Close, or select your main Windows Messaging window and continue working with both windows open.

Using Remote Mail with Other Mail Services

The Microsoft Mail service's Remote Mail capabilities are very robust and configurable. Other Windows Messaging services such as CompuServe require no special configuration at all. To use Remote Mail to access your CompuServe Mail, select Tools, Remote Mail, CompuServe Mail from the Windows Messaging menu. Similar dialog boxes appear as in Remote Mail for Microsoft Mail explained in the previous section, and they all work the same way.

Viewing Received Mail

To view and work with your received mail, you must have the Microsoft Windows Messaging program running. This section explains how you can see your received mail and how to keep the Windows Messaging window organized at the same time.

How Things Are Organized in Windows Messaging

Windows Messaging contains, by default, four Personal folders, each of which holds a different kind of message. The folder names show the function of the folders:

- **Inbox.** Where messages that come in to you are initially stored.
- **Deleted Items.** Stores messages that you have deleted from other folders.
- **Outbox.** Stores messages you are sending until you actually send them.
- **Sent Items.** Stores messages you have sent after they are successfully sent.

It is very useful to see all four Windows Messaging folders on your screen. If you display all four folders, you can tell what kind of message you are seeing.

To display all four folders described earlier, choose View, Folders on the Windows Messaging menu bar. You also can click the Show/Hide Folder List icon on the toolbar.

When you choose to display the folder list, your Windows Messaging window divides into two parts. On the left side of the window, you see the list of the four folders. When you highlight a folder on the left side of the window, the contents of that folder appear on the right side of the window.

For example, if you highlight the Inbox folder, you see the contents of your Inbox folder on the right side of the window. The contents of the Inbox folder are your received messages and faxes. If a message in the inbox appears in **boldface**, the message is new and has not yet been read.

The types of messages that you can see in your inbox depend on the Windows Messaging services that you installed. If you installed Microsoft Fax, for example, you can see faxes. If you installed The Microsoft Network, you can see mail from MSN members and from the Internet. If you have Microsoft Mail installed for your workgroup network, you can see workgroup Mail messages. With Internet Mail installed, you can see mail from your own Internet mailbox.

Figure 26.18 shows an inbox that contains several types of messages. You can manipulate these messages in several ways. You examine how to manipulate and work with those received messages in the next sections.

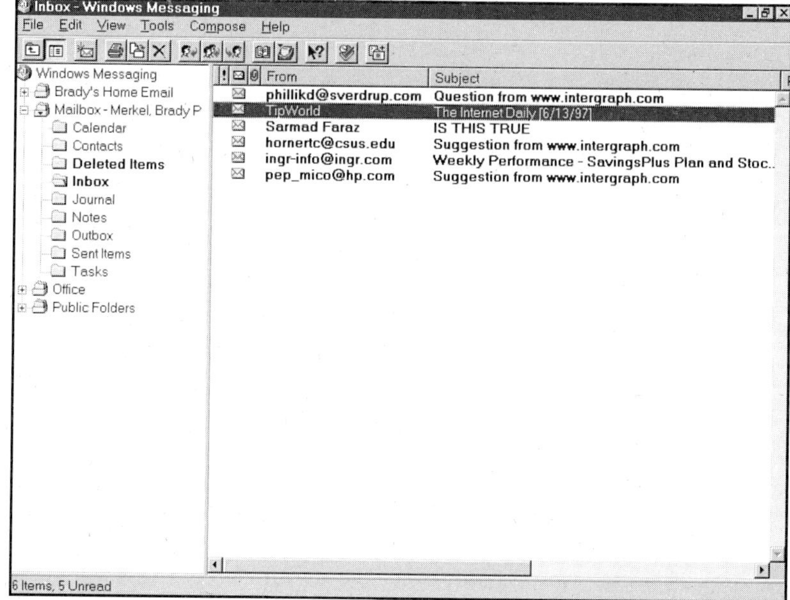

FIG. 26.18
The Windows Messaging inbox is where all your new messages are placed.

Reading Mail Messages

To read a mail message, double-click the message in your inbox. The standard message form opens, displaying the message. The Subject appears in the message form title bar. Figure 26.19 shows a received mail message.

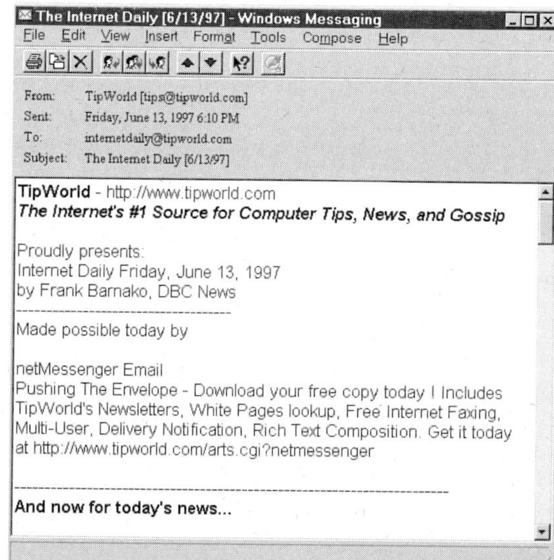

FIG. 26.19
Opening a mail message in your inbox displays the message.

Editing, Replying to, and Forwarding Messages

The standard message form (refer to Figure 26.8) is an important place where a great deal of messaging action takes place. Notice that the form looks very much like a Windows word processor, complete with Formatting toolbar. All the Rich Text tools are available, just as they are when you compose a message. In fact, the standard message form for composing a message is identical to the form for viewing, editing, replying to, and forwarding mail messages.

As a shortcut to send, reply to, forward, or edit a message without displaying it first, select the message in your inbox and then right-click.

While you are working with a received mail message, you can edit it if you want. Add text, files, or OLE objects; then use the tools in the Compose menu to whisk your reply on its way (see Figure 26.20).

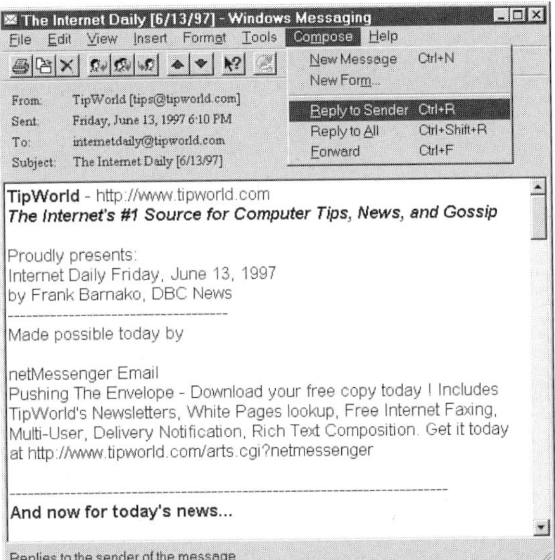

FIG. 26.20
The Compose menu has Reply and Forward options.

Sorting Messages

Above the messages in any of the Windows Messaging folders are column headings. These headings indicate the following:

- The importance of the message (according to the sender)
- The item type
- Whether files are attached to the message
- The sender's name

- The subject
- The date and time the message was received
- The size of the message (in kilobytes)

You can sort the messages in any of the Windows Messaging folders in the following ways:

- Click the column heading to sort the messages in the folder by the value in that column, in ascending order.
- Right-click the column heading to change the sort from ascending to descending order.
- Choose View, Sort in the main Windows Messaging window to access more elaborate sorting functions. Figure 26.21 shows these functions.

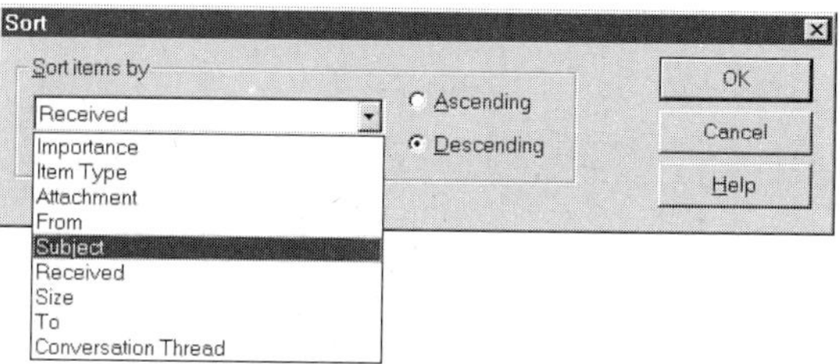

FIG. 26.21
You can use these advanced options to sort your messages.

NOTE The default From, Subject, Received, and Size columns in Windows Messaging are only the tip of the iceberg. You can display many more columns if the column headings are relevant to your work. You will find loads of column options, many of which are rather obscure. The options available depend on the message services you have installed. What works for one service may not work for another.

Deleting Messages

When you finish working with a message in your inbox and you want to delete it, highlight it and press the Delete key. The message is removed from the inbox, but it is not really deleted. Rather, it is moved to the Deleted Items folder.

CAUTION

Deleting a message from the Deleted Items folder completely removes it from your system. It is not placed in the Recycle Bin.

Using the Message Finder

You can use Windows Messaging to search through all of your folders, looking for messages that match certain criteria. You can choose among many options, shown in the following list. You can find items matching the following:

- The name of a sender you specify with the From option
- A message you sent to a certain recipient with the Sent To option
- A message sent Directly to you, or Copied (Cc) to you
- A message with a particular subject, by choosing the Subject option
- Certain text in the message with the Message Body option

To use Message Finder, choose Tools, Find in the main Windows Messaging window, and then choose the search option you want to use. For example, if you are looking for messages sent to John Jones, enter **John Jones** in the Sent To text box. Windows Messaging displays a list of messages matching the criteria you have chosen.

Working with User Profiles in Windows Messaging

When you installed Windows Messaging, you worked with the Inbox Setup Wizard. You gave the wizard information about yourself, and you installed one or more communications services. You also gave the wizard information about the services you chose, such as User ID and Mailbox Name.

When you finished installing Windows Messaging, the wizard saved all the information you gave it. The wizard saved your information in something called a *user profile.*

The user profile in Windows Messaging is where all your personal information and the information on all your communications services are stored. The name of the user profile created by the wizard for you is Default Settings. Default Settings becomes the default user profile for your computer.

You can add as many user profiles as you need by following the steps in the following section.

This default profile is fine for one user. If your computer has more than one user, however, you may want to create a special user profile for everyone who uses your machine.

Suppose that you share a computer with coworkers who work the second shift. If you do not use The Microsoft Network, but your coworkers do, they may want to set up their own user profiles. Then they can configure and personalize Windows Messaging to suit their needs without disturbing the settings that you use during your shift.

Adding Multiple User Profiles in Windows Messaging

To create an additional user profile, follow these steps:

1. Open the Start menu and choose Settings, Control Panel.
2. In Control Panel, double-click the Mail and Fax icon.
3. Choose Show Profiles. You see the list of existing Windows Messaging profiles.
4. Choose Add to create a new user profile. The Inbox Setup Wizard starts to run.

5. Select the communications services that you want to use with the new user profile you are creating (see Figure 26.22). Then choose Next.

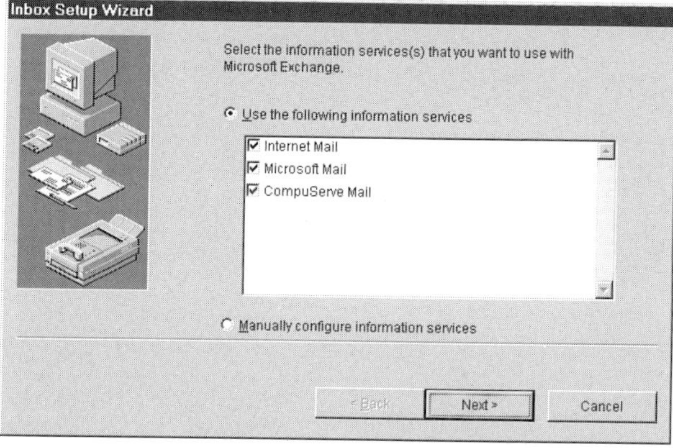

FIG. 26.22 Choose the services to use with your new user profile.

6. Type the name for your new user profile in the Profile Name text box (see Figure 26.23). Then choose Next.

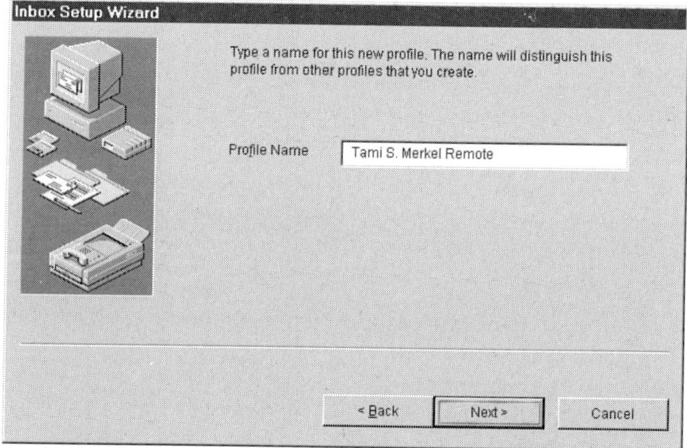

FIG. 26.23 Choose an appropriate name for a new user profile.

7. You now work with the wizard to set up the communications services you chose in step 5. This works the same way it did when you first installed Windows Messaging.

See "Installing and Configuring Windows Messaging," **p. 734**

When you finish the Inbox Setup Wizard, your new user profile is ready to use. Your screen returns to the Mail dialog box you saw in step 3. Your new user profile is added to the list of profiles (see Figure 26.24.)

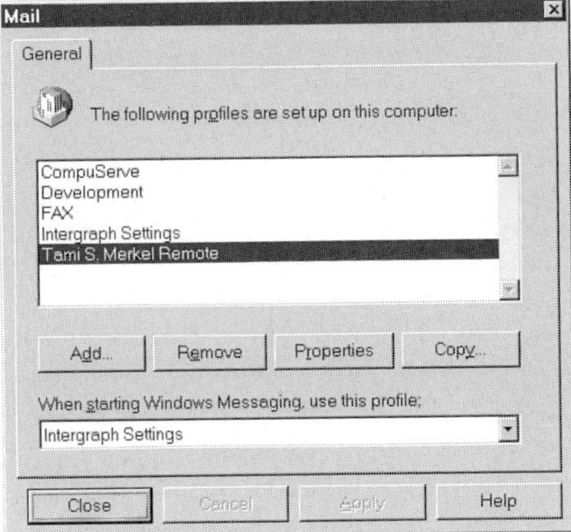

FIG. 26.24
Your new user profile has been added to Windows Messaging.

When you have more than one user profile installed, you will want Windows Messaging to ask you which profile to use each time Windows Messaging starts. Follow these steps to set up Windows Messaging so that it asks which user profile to use:

1. Start Windows Messaging by double-clicking the Inbox icon on your desktop.
2. Choose Tools, Options. The Options dialog box appears.
3. In the When Starting Windows Messaging area of the General page, check the Prompt for a Profile to Be Used box (see Figure 26.25).
4. Choose OK.

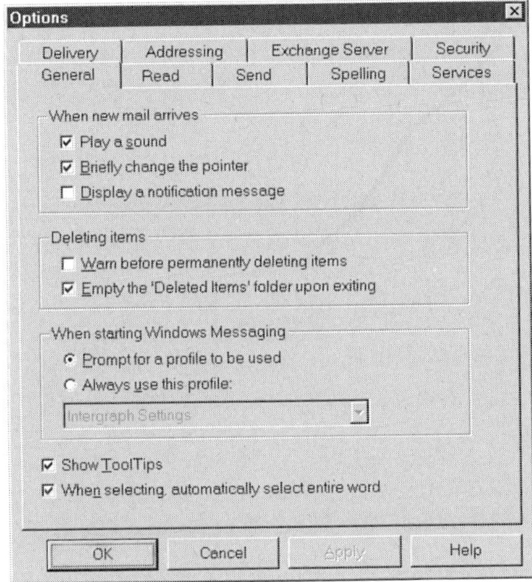

FIG. 26.25
When you tell Windows Messaging to prompt you for a user profile, you ensure that each user of your computer has the opportunity to pick their own Windows Messaging user profile.

TROUBLESHOOTING

I want to use Microsoft Fax, The Microsoft Network, and Microsoft Mail, but I do not see any references to those services in my Windows Messaging menus. Install the desired services in Microsoft Windows Messaging. In the Windows Messaging main window, choose Tools, Services, Add, and select the desired service from the list. A wizard guides you in setting up the service, if necessary.

NOTE If you have set up your computer with a different session profile for each user—so the user has to log on when Windows starts—you can ensure that each person's profile starts automatically. Each user should log on to Windows; open Windows Messaging; choose Tools, Options; and then click the Always Use This Profile option button and select the appropriate profile.

Enabling Mail and Message Security

Normally, when you run Windows Messaging, your mail folders display immediately in the Windows Messaging window. You can see and work with Inbox, Deleted Items, Outbox, and Sent Items as soon as Windows Messaging is running. This means that anyone who starts Windows Messaging on your computer can access all your mail in these four folders.

To make your mail secure, you must set a password for access to your mailbox so that nobody else can open your mailbox and read or work with your messages without your permission. Follow these steps to set up password security for your mail folders:

1. With Windows Messaging running, choose Tools, Options. The Options dialog box appears.
2. Click the Services tab, highlight Personal Folders, and choose Properties.
3. When the Personal Folders Properties sheet appears, choose Change Password. The Microsoft Personal Folders dialog box opens (see Figure 26.26).

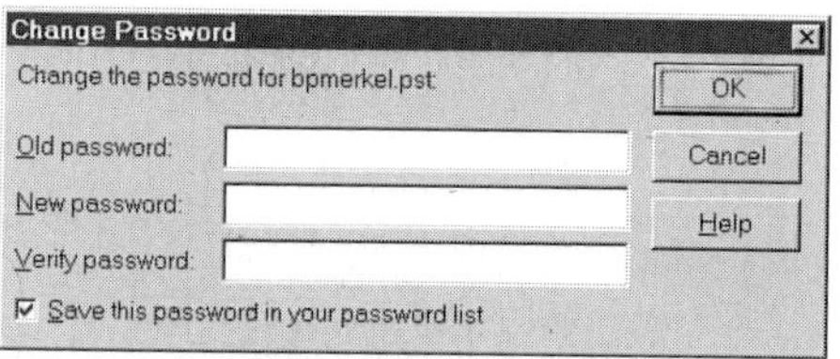

FIG. 26.26
Set a password for your mail folders for security.

TIP Don't select the Save This Password in Your Password List option unless you've set up Windows for different users and each user has to log on using a password. If you select this option, you lose password security, because Windows enters the password for you whenever you start Windows Messaging.

4. Enter the password of your choice in the New Password text box. Then repeat the password in the Verify Password text box.
5. Choose OK.

The next time you run Windows Messaging, you have to enter your password to see the contents of your mail folders.

CAUTION

If you forget your mailbox password, you cannot access the contents of your mailbox again. You have to delete your personal folders and set up Windows Messaging again.

If you want to get rid of your mailbox password, follow steps 1 and 2. Then in step 3, type your current password in the Old Password text box. Leave the New Password and Verify Password text boxes blank. This means that you have changed back to having no password security for your mailbox folders. Then choose OK.

Working with the Workgroup Postoffice

Microsoft Mail requires that one of the computers on the workgroup network be set up as a Postoffice. This is usually a job for the network administrator or manager. If this is your function, this section is important for you.

The Postoffice machine is the place where all mail messages are stored for the workgroup. You can choose your machine for Postoffice duties or select a different machine.

The Postoffice must be installed somewhere on the network, in a shared folder that all members of the workgroup can access. Windows 95 comes with the Postoffice and a wizard that helps you install it.

You have to make the following decisions about your Postoffice:

- Which machine to install the Postoffice on (choose a machine that has a shared folder that everyone in the workgroup can access)
- Who will manage and maintain the Postoffice

If you're sure there is no Postoffice installed on your workgroup LAN, and if you're sure that you are the right person to set it up, the process is simple.

Installing the Workgroup Postoffice

When you are ready to install the Postoffice, follow these steps:

1. Open the Start menu and choose Settings, Control Panel.
2. Double-click the Microsoft Mail Postoffice icon.
3. Select Create a New Workgroup Postoffice, as shown in Figure 26.27. Then choose Next.

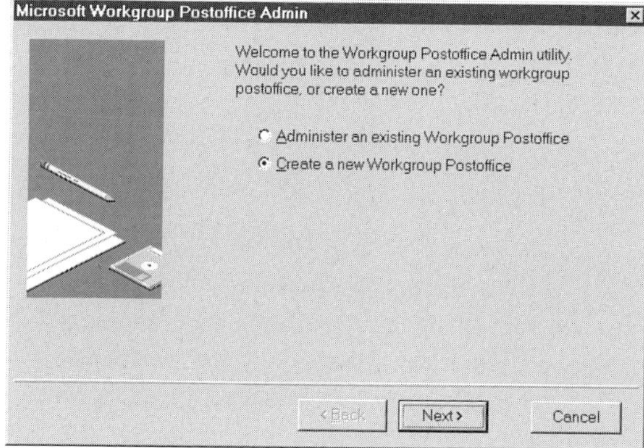

FIG. 26.27 Use the Microsoft Workgroup Postoffice Admin utility to create a new Workgroup Postoffice.

4. Type the full path to the folder you have chosen for the Postoffice in the Postoffice Location text box. Remember, this needs to be a shared folder that everyone on the Workgroup LAN can access. You can click the Browse button to find the folder.
5. Choose Next. The folder you have selected for the Postoffice displays for your approval. Choose Next again.
6. The next dialog box that appears requests administration details. Type your name in the Name text box, your mailbox name in the Mailbox text box, and your mail password in the Password text box (see Figure 26.28). Choose OK.
7. You'll see a message box reminding you to allow other users access to the Postoffice—which can be done from Windows Explorer. Choose OK. You have finished creating your Postoffice.

See "Sharing Workstation Drives," **p. 961**

NOTE The other text boxes shown in Figure 26.28 may be filled in as you prefer, but are not required to set up the Postoffice.

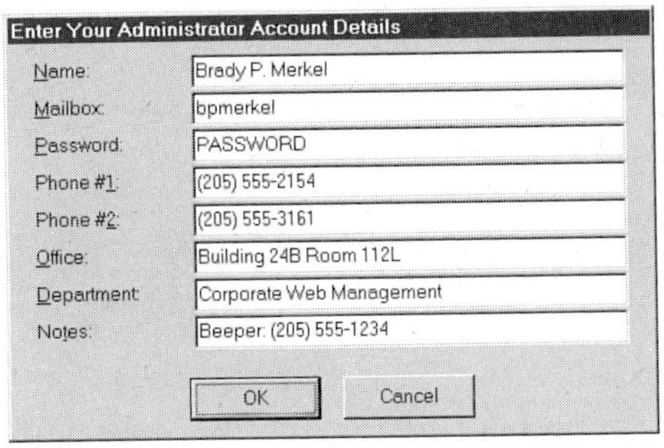

FIG. 26.28
Enter Postoffice Administrator information in this dialog box.

CAUTION

Create only one Postoffice on your workgroup network. If you create more than one, the mail system won't work properly.

CHAPTER 27

Using Fax, Address Book, and Phone Dialer

by Ken Poore and Brady P. Merkel

This chapter covers three topics that are not all directly related, but require coverage because they are all tools you may use every day. ■

How to create, send, and receive faxes

The first section in this chapter shows how to use Microsoft Fax, a service that you can install into Microsoft Exchange that enables you to send and receive faxes.

How to manage and use all your e-mail and fax addresses

The next section explains the Address Book, an integral part of Microsoft Exchange and Fax that maintains all your fax and e-mail recipient addresses and information, including phone numbers and other personal contact information.

How to set up a speed dialer to dial frequently used numbers

The final section shows how to use the Phone Dialer, a useful accessory that mimics and improves upon a phone speed dialer many of us already use today.

Overview of Microsoft Fax

Microsoft Fax works within Microsoft Exchange's Universal Inbox to provide a convenient place to compose, attach, or embed documents, and address a fax. Exchange gives you several ways to create faxes. You can use the Compose New Fax Wizard to send a simple typed message or an attached file. (Yes, you can transfer computer files using Fax, as you'll find out later.) You can use the same New Message window that you use to compose e-mail, or you can create your fax in another application and send or print it to the fax system. Your faxes can include text, pictures, OLE objects, and files. This richness of function is one of the key benefits of using the fax capabilities within Microsoft Exchange.

Installing and Configuring Microsoft Fax

If you chose to install Microsoft Fax while using the Inbox Wizard, you see the Location Information dialog box shown in Figure 27.1. The wizard asks you to enter information about your telephone number: your area code, the number (if any) that you dial to get an outside line, and whether you are using pulse or tone dialing.

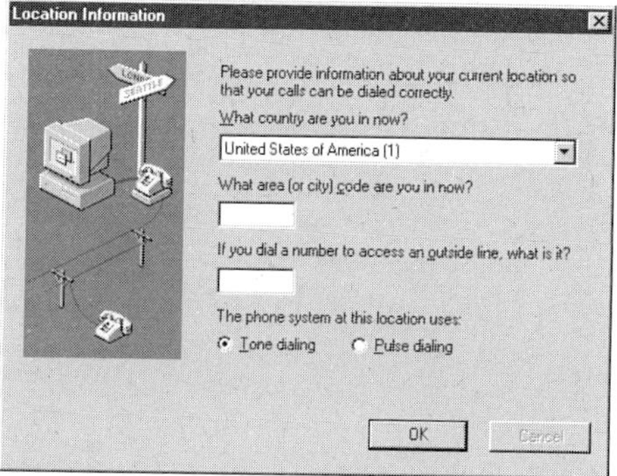

FIG. 27.1
The wizard's Location Information dialog box.

You are then asked whether you want to use a modem or a network-fax service (you can choose only the latter if you have installed network software; if you haven't, the wizard ignores your selection and assumes that you want to use a modem). Select the appropriate option button and choose Next.

The wizard now asks for information about the modem or network-fax service. If you have already installed a modem, you see something like the Microsoft Fax dialog box in Figure 27.2. (If you haven't yet installed a modem, the Install New Modem Wizard starts.)

See "Installing and Configuring Your Modem," **p. 76**

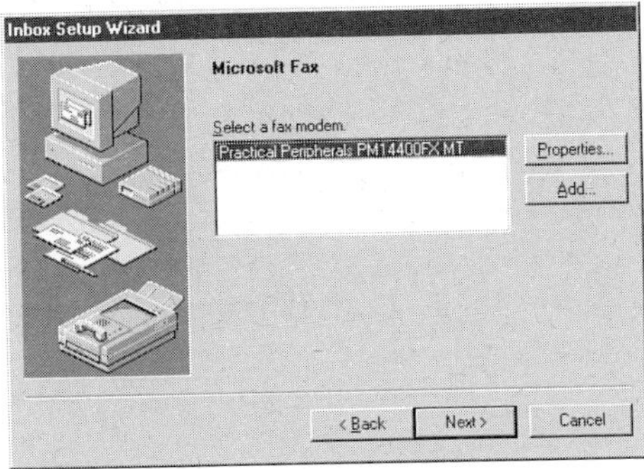

FIG. 27.2
The Inbox Setup Wizard's Microsoft Fax dialog box lets you specify the kind of device you want to use for sending and receiving faxes.

Select which modem you want to use for your fax messages—in the illustration, there is only one choice. You can add another fax modem—or a Network Fax Server—by clicking the Add button. Or modify the selected fax modem's properties by choosing Properties. When you've selected the fax modem (or added a Network Fax Server), choose Next.

TIP If you want to be prompted to receive a fax when the phone rings, select Properties, Manual Answer mode. You can still pick up the phone and talk, too.

If you select a modem rather than a Network Fax Server, the wizard asks you whether you want Microsoft Fax to answer each incoming call on the phone line the modem is connected to. Choose Yes or No. (If you choose Yes, you may also want to change the Answer After *n* Rings value—you'll probably want the smallest value, two rings.) Then choose Next.

The Inbox Setup Wizard now asks for the information that will be used on any fax cover sheets you send along with your outgoing faxes, so people will know who sent them and how to fax back to you.

Enter your name and other information as requested in the dialog box shown in Figure 27.3. You must enter the fax number or you will be unable to continue. Then choose Next.

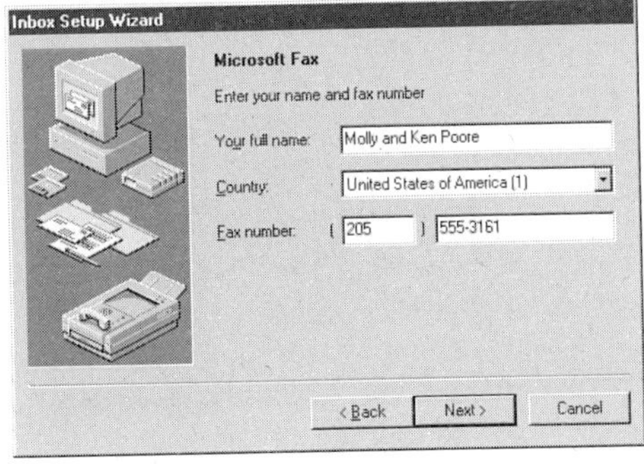

FIG. 27.3
Enter the personal information you want included on your faxes in this dialog box.

The Fax service is now installed. If you selected another service to install, the Inbox Setup Wizard now asks for information about that service.

Faxing a Quick Message or a File

You can also send a quick text message, or "fax" a file. This method lets you type a quick note (you cannot format the note) or transmit a file attached to the fax using the BFT fax technology. If you want to do more—such as send a nicely formatted fax message, put pictures inside it, or fax from your word processor—see "Sending a More Complete Message," later in this chapter. In the main Exchange window, choose Compose, New Fax. The Compose Fax Wizard appears.

A quick way to fax a file from within Explorer is to right-click the file and select Send To, Fax Recipient.

See "Working with Phone Dialer," p. 797

The wizard first verifies the location from which you are sending the message, as shown in Figure 27.4. If you have created other dialing locations and moved your portable computer to one of them, choose I'm Dialing From and specify the new location. (Notice also that you can click the check box at the bottom of the dialog box to tell the wizard not to display this next time.) Then choose Next.

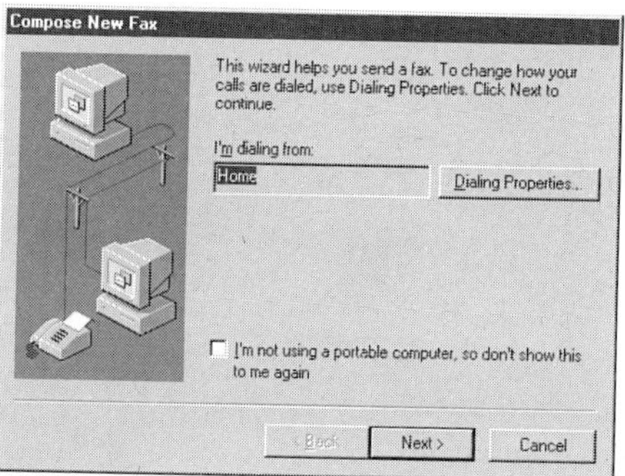

FIG. 27.4
The Compose New Fax Wizard confirms your dialing location.

Addressing a Fax

The wizard next prompts you for a recipient and offers to show you your Personal Address Book. If you want to choose a name from the address book, choose Address Book to display the address book (see Figure 27.5). Select a recipient and choose OK.

You also can type the recipient information in the text boxes named To and Fax #, without using the Personal Address Book. Use the Add to List button if you want to send the fax to several different numbers. Select the first and choose Add to List; select the second, and choose Add to List; and so on. Choose Next when you are ready to continue.

See "Working with the Exchange Address Book," p. 785

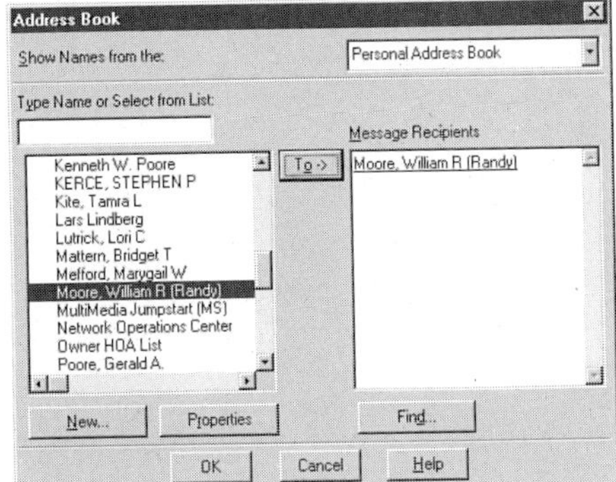

FIG. 27.5
Choose a fax recipient from your Personal Address Book.

Selecting a Cover Page

If you don't like any of the predesigned cover pages, use the Cover Page Editor to customize one of them or to create your own. See "Using the Fax Cover Page Editor," later in this chapter.

Next, the wizard asks whether you want to send a cover page with your fax. Windows has the following built-in cover pages:

- Confidential
- For your information
- Generic
- Urgent!

To use a cover page, select the page you want from the displayed list. Click the No button if you don't want to send a cover page.

Options for Fax Transmission

There are a variety of fax options that you can set before you move on. Choose Options to display the Compose New Fax Wizard's Send Options dialog box (see Figure 27.6). Use these options to control when your fax is sent, the format you use to send it, the paper size, and the security applied. In this dialog box, you also can choose the Dialing Location via the Dialing button, or you can choose a cover page to send with your fax as you did in the preceding section.

The following sections explain these options and how to use them.

Time to Send You can select a time to send your fax. Your choices are these:

- As Soon as Possible
- Discount Rates (night and weekends)
- Specific Time (which you can choose)

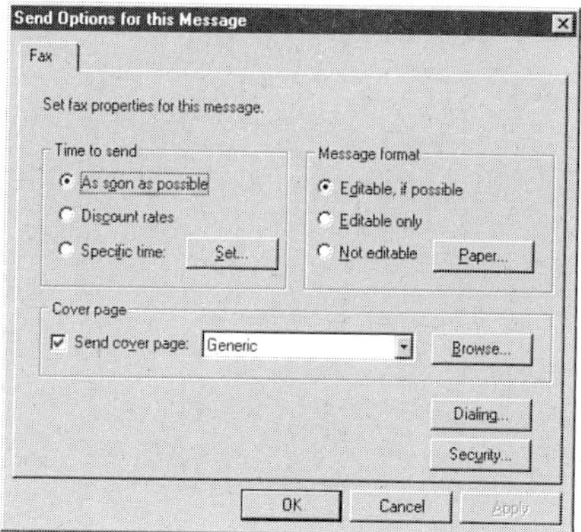

FIG. 27.6
This dialog box lets you specify various fax-sending options.

To set up the times for your discount phone rates, from the main Exchange menu, select Tools, Microsoft Fax Tools, Options, and choose the Set button next to the Discount Rates option.

Message Format The Message Format section deals with the *editable faxes* technology. A traditional fax is a single graphics image. Editable faxes are more like file transfers between computers, with the optional addition of a cover page. In fact, editable faxes are so much like file transfers that the technology behind them is called BFT, for *Binary File Transfer.*

An editable fax can be edited by the recipient in the application that created it or in any application that can open its file type. If you send a document created in Word for Windows (a DOC file), the recipient can open it in Word, WordPad, AmiPro, or WordPerfect, using import filters if necessary.

Sending editable faxes is very convenient, because the receiver's options are increased. The recipient can view or print the fax as you sent it, or edit the fax first.

You have three choices with the Message Format option:

- **Editable, If Possible.** Editable faxes can be exchanged only between computers using Microsoft Exchange and Microsoft Fax. This is the optimum way to send a fax.

  If the receiver is using a traditional fax machine, using editable format is not possible, so the fax is sent the old-fashioned way, as a graphic. If the recipient has a fax card in a computer but doesn't have Microsoft Exchange installed, the fax is delivered as a graphic. Exchange automatically determines which way to send the fax when it connects to the receiving machine.

NOTE In the near future, other systems may implement *Binary File Transfer* (BFT) in a way that is compatible with the Microsoft system. When that happens, you will be able to exchange editable faxes with those systems, too.

Editable faxes can be exchanged between Microsoft Exchange systems very quickly, because the format used is much more compressed than the format that regular fax machines use.

- **Editable Only.** This option works only for transfers between two Microsoft Exchange systems. If the receiving system is not a Microsoft Exchange system, the fax will not go through.
- **Not Editable.** You use this option when you want all your faxes to be sent as a single graphic image in traditional fax format.

Message Security Choose the Security button to see the Security options. Security works only with editable faxes. You have two basic choices: None and Password-Protected. If you choose None, your fax can be read immediately upon receipt. Choosing Password-Protected requires the recipient to type the password that you applied to that fax transmission in order to see it.

CAUTION

If you activate password security on a fax that is sent to a non-Microsoft Exchange recipient or fax machine, your fax will not go through.

Paper Size and Orientation, and Image Quality Choose Paper to access the Paper Size and Orientation options. These options are usable with noneditable faxes. You can choose letter or legal paper. You also can choose Portrait (vertical) or Landscape (horizontal) page orientation.

You also can change the Image Quality in this dialog box. This determines the resolution at which Exchange prepares the fax. As with a laser printer, the higher the resolution, the crisper and cleaner your fax will be when printed.

Pick one of the following three Image Quality options based on your need for a high-quality fax balanced against the additional time it takes to send the fax at a higher resolution:

- **Best Available.** This setting is recommended; it makes your fax look as good as possible on the receiving end.
- **Fine** (200 dots per inch, or dpi). Fine mode can result in incompatibilities if the receiving side doesn't support it. If it works with your recipient's hardware, it will look as good as possible.
- **Draft** (200×100 dpi). Draft mode looks coarser than Fine or Best Available, but transmits faster.

Cover Page To send a cover page with your fax, select the Send Cover Page option and choose which type of cover page to send.

When you finish selecting all the options you want to use, choose Next, and the Compose New Fax Wizard moves on to let you enter the Subject of the fax, and, if you want, a Note to put on the cover page.

See "Using the Fax Cover Page Editor," **p. 777**

Fax Subject and Note When you finish working with all the options described in the preceding sections and you choose Next, the Compose New Fax Wizard displays a dialog box where you can enter the subject of the fax and add a note to accompany your fax.

Type the subject in the Subject text box. Optionally, you can type a note in the Note text box to go along with your fax. Click the Start Note on Cover Page check box to start your note on the cover page. If you leave the box unchecked, the note will start on a new page in your fax. Choose Next.

Adding Files to Your Fax

After the Compose New Fax Wizard finishes with the fax subject and note (covered in the preceding section), it offers you a dialog box where you can select files to include with the fax.

To include a file, choose Add File. You can use Explorer to browse and find the file you want to send with your fax.

After you choose the file, or files, to send with your fax, the wizard shows the files you selected in the Files to Send text box. When you finish selecting files to add to your fax, choose Next.

CAUTION

The files you choose can be sent only if the fax is sent in editable format. If you use any other format, Microsoft Fax will not send the fax or cover sheet.

For this reason, choose to add files to your fax only if you are certain that the recipient's system can support editable format, and that both your sending system and the recipient's receiving system are configured for editable faxing. (Configuring your fax in editable format was covered in "Options for Fax Transmission," earlier in this chapter.)

After you add any files you want to send with your fax, choose Finish, and Microsoft Fax sends your fax.

See "Configuring Your Modem," **p. 85**

TROUBLESHOOTING

I'm trying to send a fax, but it won't go through. Do you hear the modem dial the fax? If not, make sure that you have a fax modem selected and that the settings are correct for your modem type. In Exchange, choose Tools, Services, Microsoft Fax, Properties; then click the Modem tab. You should see your fax modem displayed; if not, click Add to configure your modem.

If you can hear the modem dial the phone, but the modem disconnects just after dialing, repeat the preceding procedure. When you see your modem, select it and then click Properties. Make sure that the modem is set to allow enough time to connect after dialing (60 seconds is a good choice). This parameter often is set to 1 second by Windows for no apparent reason.

Sending a More Complete Message

There are a couple of other ways to send fax messages. First, you may want to use the same window you used to create an e-mail message. The only difference between creating a fax message and an e-mail message is in the way you address it. If you address the message to a fax "address," the message will be a fax message.

If you don't already have the fax address in your Address Book, you need to add it first. Then use the To button in the New Message window to add this address to the To line of your message.

Choose File, Send Options to modify fax options while working in the New Message window.

The advantage of sending a fax using this method is that you have all the New Message window's tools available. You can write a message, using all the text-editing capabilities. You can also attach files and insert pictures into your fax.

The other way to fax is directly from an application. For instance, you can fax from your word processor. Many applications have a Send option on the File menu. If an application you want to use *doesn't* have such an option, you can "print" to Microsoft Fax on the FAX print driver.

See "Adding Names to Your Address Book," **p. 786**

Using the Fax Cover Page Editor

The Fax Cover Page Editor is a miniature word processor that allows you to work with graphics as well as rich text. Use the Fax Cover Page Editor to create custom-made cover pages or to modify one that is supplied with Exchange. You can do the following things with cover pages that you create or edit:

- Insert data from the Personal Address Book into your cover page.
- Paste items from the Clipboard into your cover page.
- Import text or graphics (such as a logo) into your cover page.

To use the Cover Page Editor, open the Start menu; choose Programs, Accessories, Fax; and then click Cover Page Editor. The Cover Page Editor program starts up.

When you first start the Cover Page Editor program, there is no cover page file loaded. From here, you can design a new cover page. If you start designing a new cover page and then decide you want to start over again, choose File, New, or click the New File icon on the toolbar.

Fax cover pages have a file name extension of CPE. The cover pages that come with Exchange are located in the C:\WINDOWS folder.

To edit and customize an existing cover page, choose File, Open. Then select the cover page you want to work with.

The most useful feature of the Cover Page Editor is the ability to insert information from your Personal Address Book into your cover sheets. You do this by choosing Insert from the menu bar and then choosing from the options on that menu and successive submenus (see Figure 27.7). Information you can insert includes:

- Recipient's or Sender's Name
- Recipient's or Sender's Fax Number
- Recipient's or Sender's Company

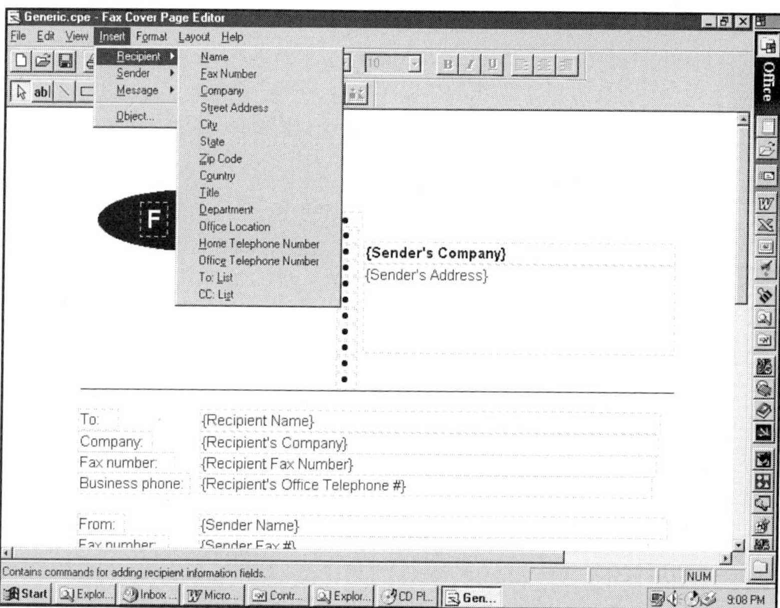

FIG. 27.7 Insert Address Book information into your fax cover sheet.

Viewing Received Faxes

The Exchange Inbox can display both e-mail and faxes that you've received (see Figure 27.8). You can see the fax sender's phone number as well as the date and time the fax was received.

When you double-click a normal, noneditable fax, the Fax Viewer opens and displays the fax. When you double-click a received editable fax, though, or a fax that has attached files, the message window opens. Inside this window, what you see depends on what you received. If you received a fax that the author created in the New Message window, you see exactly what the author saw; the text looks the same, any icons representing attached files look the same, and so on. If, however, you are receiving a fax from another application (sent using the File, Send option), you see an icon representing the fax. Double-click this icon to open the application associated with that type of file. For instance, if you double-click a DOC file that you've received, the program associated with it opens: Word or WordPad.

FIG. 27.8
The Exchange Inbox shows a received fax.

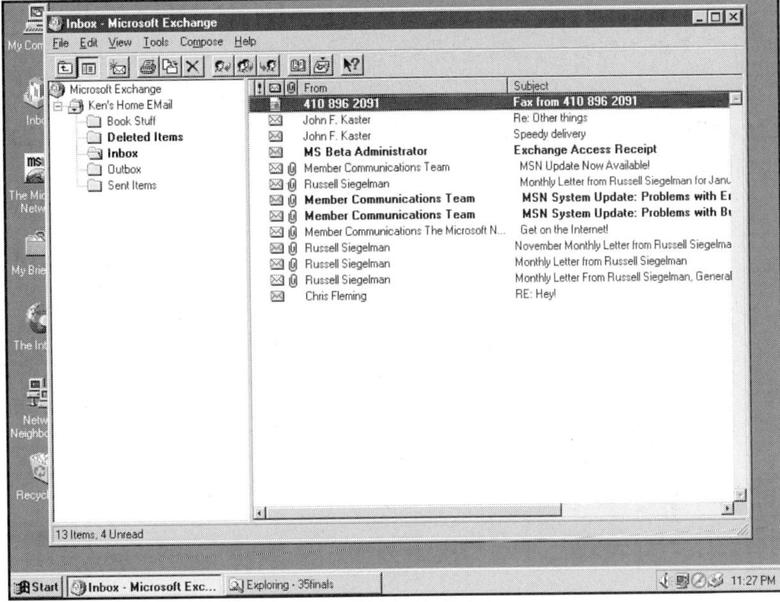

NOTE If you receive a fax that the author "printed" to Microsoft Fax on the fax driver, it comes through as if it were a normal fax from a fax machine. Double-clicking the fax in the Inbox opens the Fax Viewer, not the Message window.

For instance, Figure 27.9 shows a fax received from Notepad. Notice the Notepad icon in the message form to the left of the Notepad window. When the icon was double-clicked, Notepad opened and displayed the fax text. You can edit the text just as though you created the file on your own computer.

TROUBLESHOOTING

Someone is trying to send me a fax, but I'm not receiving it. Make sure that your fax modem is installed. From the Exchange window, choose Tools, Services. Select Microsoft Fax and choose Properties. Then click the Modem tab and make sure your modem is shown in the list of Available Fax Modems. If it is, click the Properties tab and check to see whether the modem is set to answer automatically. If not, select the Answer After check box, and set the number of rings to wait before your fax modem answers calls.

Using Other Fax Options

In addition to the options available when using the Compose New Fax Wizard, there are a few other very useful features that you can enable whenever a fax is sent.

▶ **See** "Options for Fax Transmission," **p. 773**

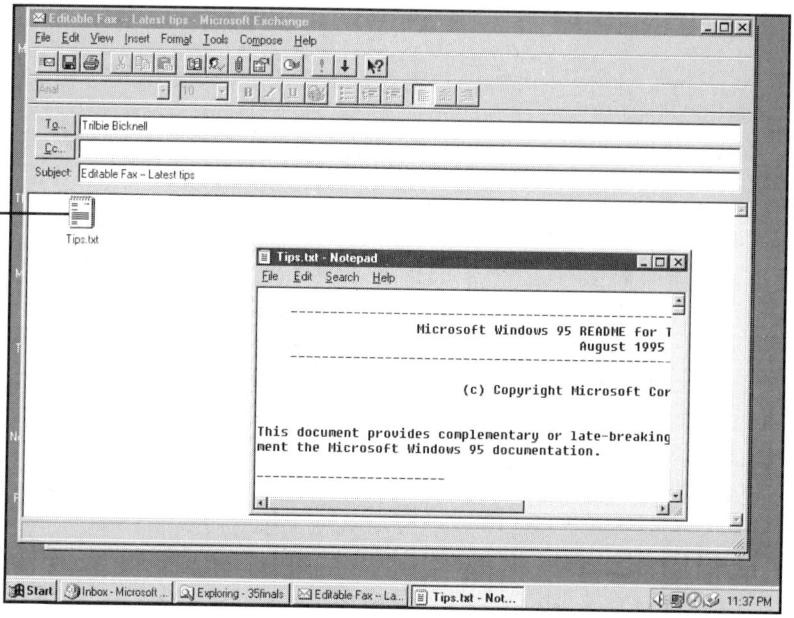

FIG. 27.9
Viewing an editable fax in the application that created the fax.

Notepad icon

Using Advanced Fax Security

Security for ensuring that nobody else can view the contents of your faxes is built into Microsoft Fax; by default, however, it is not enabled. To enable the advanced security, select Tools, Microsoft Fax Tools, Advanced Security from the Exchange menu. This type of security is based on key encryption, which is different from the password-based security mentioned earlier. As you would guess, password-based security is based only on a single password; a recipient on the other end must know that password to unlock your fax.

Key encryption is more advanced and more secure, requiring more setup. It works by sending a "public" version of your key to all the people from whom you will eventually receive encrypted faxes. They keep this public key on their systems and use it when they only want you to decrypt whatever they send. Likewise, you must get their public keys and store them on your system so that you can send them encrypted material that only they can decrypt. Whenever you send them a secure fax, it is encrypted using the public key they already sent to you. When they receive the encrypted fax, their system uses their own private version of the key to decode the message.

Setting Up Your Encryption Keys The first steps in using Advanced Fax Security for Microsoft Fax are the creation of your key encryption set and establishing yourself in the encryption "system." For the encryption system to maintain its integrity, the system itself must be protected by your own password; otherwise, anyone else who logs on to your computer might access your encryption system. This is the first line of defense. All of your subsequent key encryption is based on this same password, so you must keep this to yourself or the entire scheme is compromised. Click the New Key Set button to establish your keys (see Figure 27.10).

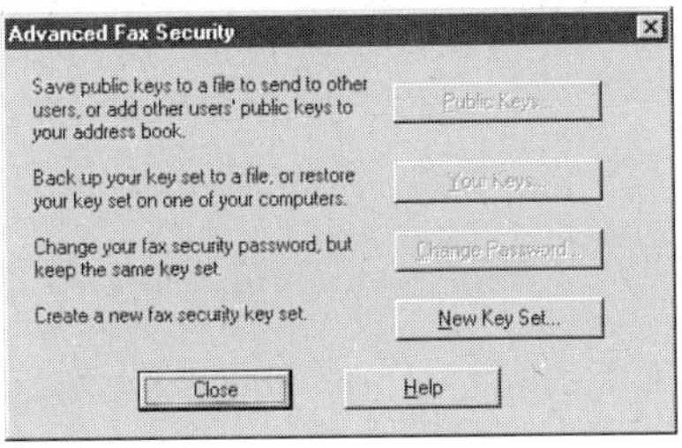

FIG. 27.10
Setting up Advanced Fax Security involves the creation of encryption keys.

Figure 27.11 displays the dialog box in which you enter your password to build your encryption keys. This same password is used to lock the encryption system. Type in your Password and Confirm it by typing it in again. Checking the Save the Password in Your Password List option saves you from typing in your password each time you receive an encrypted fax, but it also leaves your faxes wide open to anyone who can sit down at your computer and get into your e-mail. If you need the maximum available security, do not select this option. If you keep your password secure, you probably won't have to regenerate your keys in the future. Click OK to return to the Advanced Fax Security dialog box.

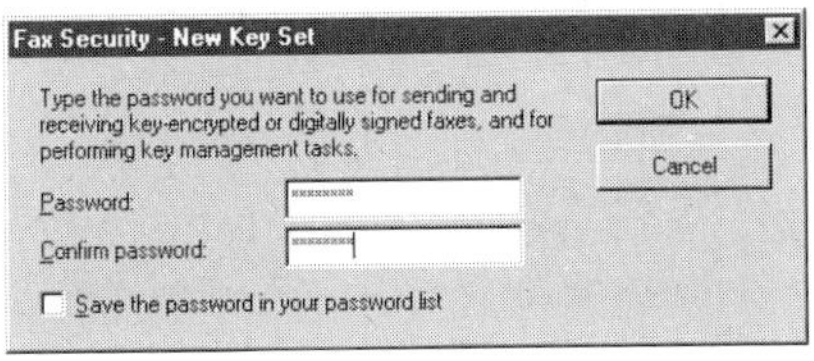

FIG. 27.11
You must first establish your password within the key encryption system.

NOTE Your encryption keys are *not* the same as your password; your keys are made up of an encrypted mixture of your password and your user information. The resulting keys themselves are totally unrecognizable (they're a mish-mash of bits) and virtually unbreakable.

Sharing Your Public Keys To send your public keys to the people who will be sending you encrypted faxes, you must first write your public key to a file so you can later send it via e-mail. Click the Public Keys button on the Advanced Fax Security dialog box, and then click the Save button (see Figure 27.12).

The next dialog box appears, this time asking whose public keys you want to save to the public-key file (see Figure 27.13). If you had other public keys available in your Address Book, they would be listed on the left next to your public key. During the first run through this, only your public key is likely to be available, so click your name and add it to the To: list, then click OK.

FIG. 27.12
There are several options to help you manage your public keys.

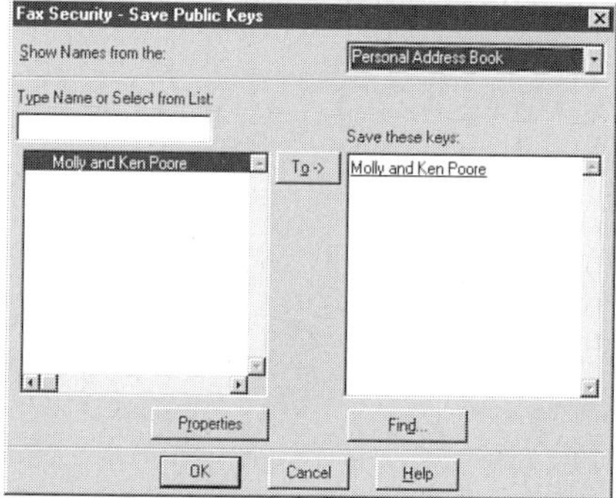

FIG. 27.13
Selecting your public key.

A Save Public Keys dialog box appears (see Figure 27.14), prompting you to write your public key to a file. Choose a folder and click Save.

All public key files end with an .AWP extension. It's a good idea to put these files in a folder other than your main Windows directory so you can easily keep track of them.

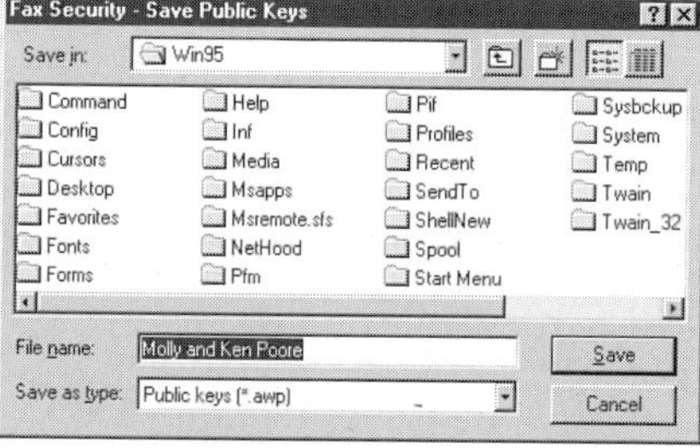

FIG. 27.14
Writing your public key to a file.

Now you should send this file in a mail message to those whom you will receive encrypted faxes from (you can send it to them on a floppy, too). Go back to the main Exchange Window and select Compose, New Message. Select those who will be sending you encrypted faxes, attach the file containing your public keys, and then send it. Be sure to ask them to send you their public keys as well.

When you receive a message from someone containing a public key as a file attachment to an e-mail message, save the attached file. Then, from the Exchange menu, choose Tools,

Microsoft Fax Tools, Advanced Security; then select Public Keys from the Managing Public Keys dialog box (refer to Figure 27.12). Click Add and choose the file you just extracted from the e-mail attachment. You will then see the dialog box shown in Figure 27.15.

Choose the names of the users you want to add to your Address Book's public key list by selecting them from the list and clicking OK.

FIG. 27.15
Adding public keys to your system.

Sending a Secure Fax Now that all your public keys are set up, you can send a key-encrypted secure Fax. Choose Compose, New Message. When the New Message dialog box appears, choose File, Send Options, and click the Fax tab. Click the Security button and you can now choose Key-Encrypted Security. If you didn't save your password by using the Save the Password in Your Password List option when you first created your keys, you will have to type in your password next. Close the options dialog boxes and return to composing your fax. Select the recipients, being careful to only choose those recipients for whom you've received a public key. Complete your fax and send it.

Changing Fax Dialing Options Most fax machines have the capability to continually redial the destination fax if the line is busy—Microsoft Fax does, too. Other options such as making toll calls within your area code and various dialing settings are also available. All these options are available by choosing Tools, Microsoft Fax Tools, Options (see Figure 27.16). The following list describes the options in the Microsoft Fax Properties dialog box.

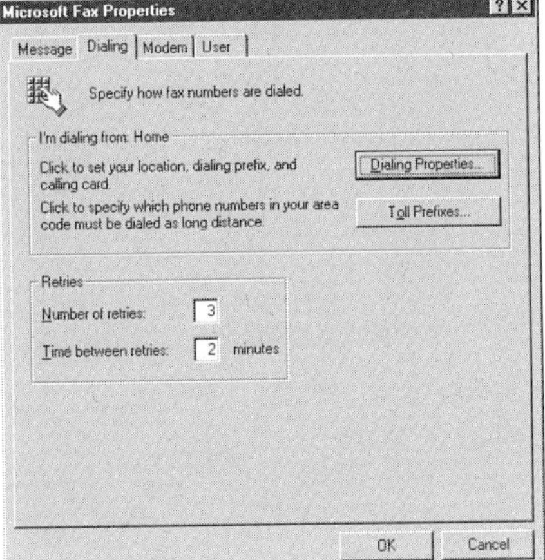

FIG. 27.16
Fax dialing options.

- On the Dialing page, the Toll Prefixes option allows you to select which exchanges in your area code are toll calls requiring the fax to dial 1 and the area code before dialing the number (see Figure 27.17).

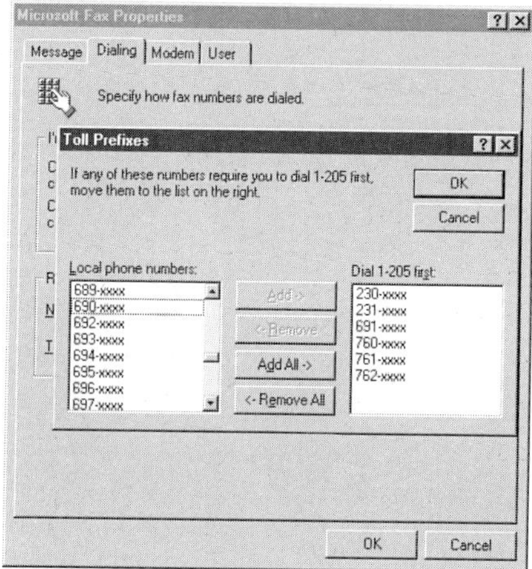

FIG. 27.17
Choosing phone exchanges that are toll calls.

- Choose Dialing Properties to configure your location and to enter the codes needed to block call waiting and other dialing options.

  ▶ **See** "Configuring Your Modem," **p. 85**

- You can change how your modem redials after getting a busy signal by setting the Number of Retries and the Time Between Retries.
- Your user information is inserted into cover pages. If you would like to change your user information, click the User tab and modify it (see Figure 27.18).

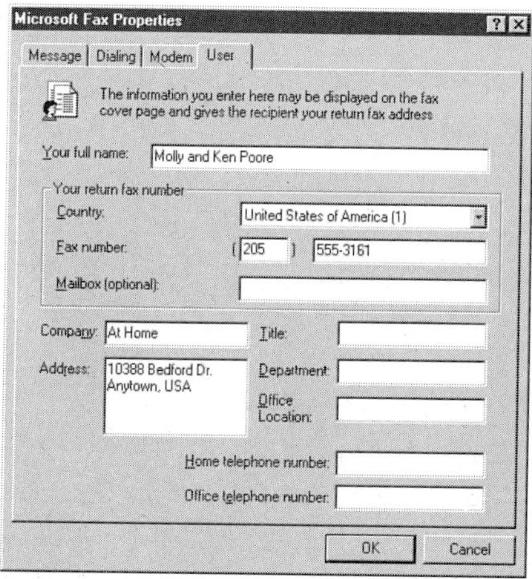

FIG. 27.18
Setting up user information for your fax cover pages.

Working with the Exchange Address Book

The Exchange Address Book can help you keep track of how to contact your correspondents. You enter names into the Address Book and specify the type of communications to use (fax, Internet mail, Microsoft LAN Mail, CompuServe Mail, and so on). The Exchange Address Book makes sure that your messages are addressed properly.

The entire Exchange Address Book is built from several different modular, building-block address books. The number of these building-block address books is determined by the communications services you installed when you set up Exchange.

Some of the services you installed come with their own building-block address book modules. For example, if you installed The Microsoft Network online service, a building-block address book for MSN was installed in your address book. The MSN Address Book is configured by Microsoft to contain the names and e-mail addresses of all the members of The Microsoft Network.

Microsoft Mail for your workgroup LAN has a building-block address book—built by the network administrator—that is part of your Exchange Address Book. In Exchange, the Microsoft Mail Address Book is called Postoffice Address List.

The final module making up your address book is called the Personal Address Book. Here, you can store the names and addresses you use most often. You can transfer names into your Personal Address Book from the other address books.

The Exchange Address Book also has options you can use to control how it displays the names you store.

Now, to display and work with the address book from the Microsoft Exchange window, choose Tools, Address Book; or press Ctrl+Shift+B.

Setting Display Preferences

By default, names appear with the first name followed by the last name (John Jones). If, however, you have a rather long list or know several men called John, you may find viewing the list sorted by last names to be faster.

You can use the Personal Address Book Properties settings to change the order in which first and last names display. To change the order, follow these steps:

1. From the Exchange main window, choose Tools, Address Book. The Address Book opens.
2. Select Personal Address Book from the Show Names From The: drop-down list. The names in your Personal Address Book appear.
3. Choose Tools, Options. The Addressing dialog box appears.
4. In the When Sending Mail list, select Personal Address Book.

5. Click Properties. The Personal Address Book properties sheet appears.
6. Now you can choose to show names by first name or last name. Click First Name or Last Name on the Personal Address Book page, as shown in Figure 27.19.

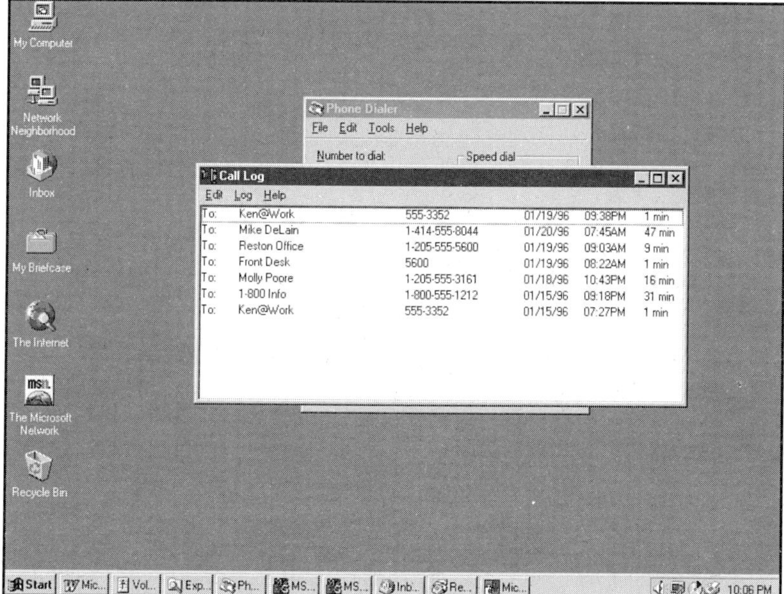

FIG. 27.19 Use this properties sheet to select how to display names in the Personal Address Book.

7. You also can give the Personal Address Book a more descriptive name. You might want to call it Business Contacts, for example. Type the name you want to use for the Personal Address Book in the Name text box.
8. Click the Notes tab, and type any information you want to record about your Personal Address Book in the text box.

Adding Names to Your Address Book

You want to use Exchange as the powerful communications tool it can be. Part of harnessing the power of Exchange is as simple as keeping a well-organized address book so that you have all the mail addresses and fax numbers you need conveniently at hand.

1. Open the Exchange Address Book by choosing Tools, Address Book. You also can click the Address Book button on the toolbar.
2. In the Show Names From The: drop-down list, select Personal Address Book.
3. Choose File, New Entry. You can also choose the New Entry button on the toolbar. The New Entry dialog box appears (see Figure 27.20).

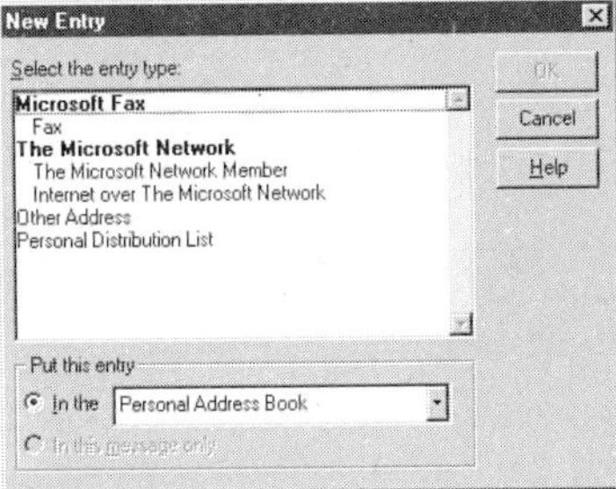

FIG. 27.20
The power of Exchange is evident in the range of address types to which you can send messages.

4. Select the type of address you want to add to your Personal Address Book. In this example, you're adding a Microsoft Fax entry to the book. Then choose OK. The New Fax properties sheet appears.
5. The properties sheet that you see in Figure 27.21 has text boxes for all the names and numbers required to reach your recipient. Type the pertinent information in each page. Then choose OK. The properties sheet closes, and the new entry appears in your address book.

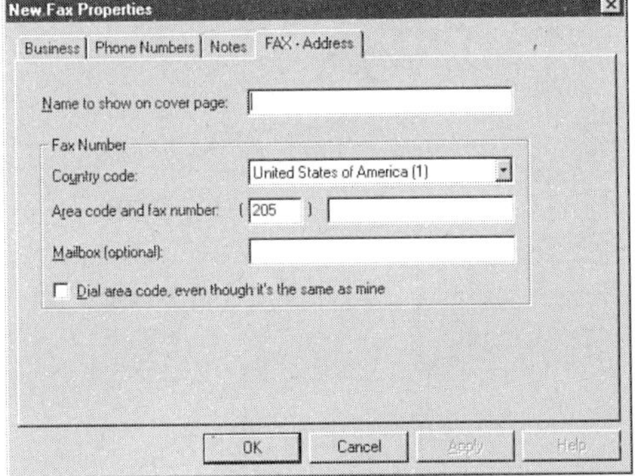

FIG. 27.21
The New Fax properties sheet is typical of the properties sheets you fill out when adding entries to your address book.

You follow the same steps as those for a Microsoft Fax entry to add different types of addresses such as Microsoft Network addresses or Internet Mail addresses.

The difference between adding the fax address you illustrated and the other possible address types is that after you select the entry type from the New Entry dialog box (step 4 in the previous list), the New Properties sheet that appears is different.

Adding Groups to Your Address Book

To send a message to a group of recipients, create a Personal Distribution List. Once you have a Personal Distribution List, you only have to create a message once, and you can send it to all the members of the list with one click.

Follow these steps to create your Personal Distribution List:

1. Open the Address Book by choosing Tools, Address Book.
2. Choose File, New Entry. The New Entry dialog box appears (refer to Figure 27.20). The New Entry dialog box contains a scrolling list of address types.
3. The last entry in the scrolling list is the Personal Distribution List entry type. Select Personal Distribution List at the bottom of the list.
4. In this example, you're putting your Personal Distribution List in your Personal Address Book. At the bottom of the New Entry dialog box is a setting that says Put This Entry In The. Make sure Personal Address Book shows in the text box. If it doesn't, click the drop-down arrow and scroll to select Personal Address Book.
5. Choose OK. The New Personal Distribution List Properties sheet appears.
6. Name your list. Type the name for your list in the Name text box. In this example, you name your Personal Distribution List **Staff Members on Project X**.
7. If you want to make some notes about the list, click the Notes tab and type your comments in the text box. You might use this space to document how the group members were chosen. You can enter anything that's useful in this text box.
8. Click the Distribution List tab.
9. Build the Distribution List now. You do this by adding members to the list. Choose Add/Remove Members. A dialog box appears, titled **Edit Members of** (name of your Distribution List), as shown in Figure 27.22.
10. Perhaps one of the people you want to add to the Personal Distribution List is already in another of your building-block address books. If so, choose the proper address book by selecting it from the scrolling list, which is shown in Show Names from The: list. When you choose an address book in Show Names from The:, all the address entries in that address book become visible. In this example, choose to Show Names from The Microsoft Network. Next, add some addresses from The Microsoft Network online service to your Personal Distribution List.

NOTE You can only use the Microsoft Network address book while online. If you select this address book while offline, the Connect dialog box appears so you can log on.

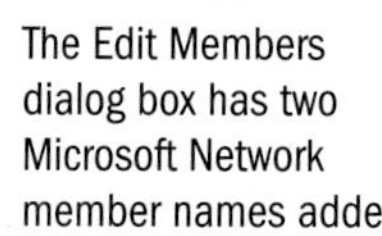

FIG. 27.22 The Edit Members dialog box has two Microsoft Network member names added to the Personal Distribution List.

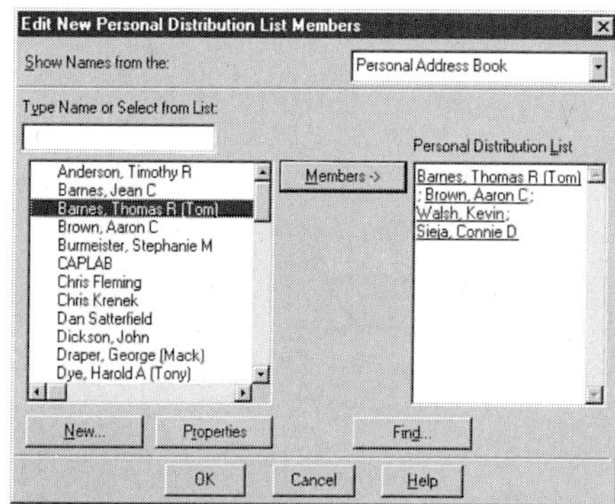

To add other names from existing address books, select Show Names From The:, and select the next address book from the scrolling list. Then repeat the preceding steps from step 10.

You also can put people on your Personal Distribution List who are not already in any of your address books. However, you have to put that person into your Personal Address Book first.

See "Adding Names to Your Address Book," **p. 786**

Choose New. Then follow the steps discussed earlier for adding a name to your Personal Address Book. Once you make the addition to the book, that name is added to the Personal Distribution List automatically. When you finish adding members to your Personal Distribution List, choose OK.

Your Personal Distribution List appears in your Personal Address Book, along with any individual addresses you have stored there. By choosing the list as a recipient in a message you create, the message is sent to all members of the Personal Distribution List.

Using the Windows Address Book

When you install Outlook Express, you also install a new and improved Windows Address Book. The new address book is fully integrated with Outlook Express but can also run as a stand-alone contact management application. In Windows Address Book, you can store home and business addresses, e-mail addresses, telephone numbers, fax numbers, security certificates, and other contact information. Some of the features of the Windows Address Book enable you to do the following tasks:

- Manage your personal contacts
- Create distribution lists for your e-mail messages
- Search for people on the Internet
- Manage security certificates
- Print your address book to keep with you
- Import or export contact information for other address books
- Import or export vCards

To start Address Book, choose Start, Programs, Windows Address Book. You can also start Address Book from within Outlook Express: choose Tools, Address Book, or click the To, Cc, or Bcc buttons in a new message window. Outlook Express also uses the Address Book to resolve names to an e-mail address.

TIP Use the Start, Find, People to search for people in your address book or on the Internet using Directory Services.

Adding and Editing Contacts in Your Address Book

The Windows Address Book allows you to quickly and easily manage your personal contacts. To add a contact to your address book, follow these steps:

1. In the Address Book, click the New Contact toolbar button, or choose File, New Contact. The new contact properties sheet displays, as seen in Figure 27.23.

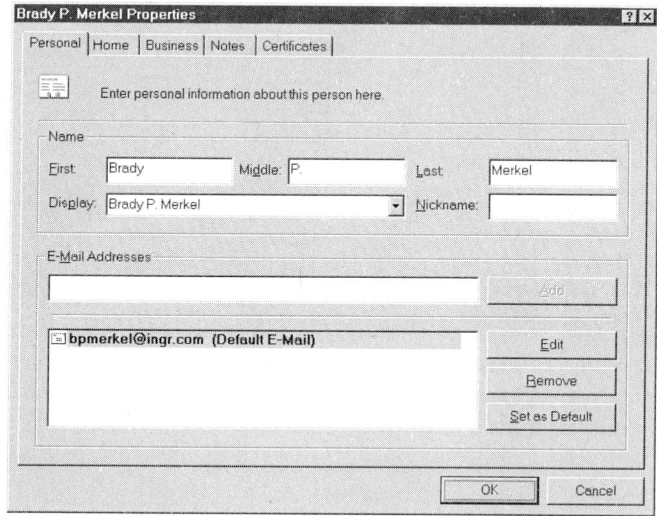

FIG. 27.23 Enter your contact information in the new contact properties sheet.

2. On the Personal tab, type the contact name, display name, and e-mail addresses.

Each contact requires a display name. If you do not enter one, Address Book will create one for you using the first, middle, or last name, nickname, or company name.

3. On the Home and Business tabs, type the addresses of the contact, in addition to the phone, fax, and cellular numbers. If your contact has an Internet Web site, type the URL.
4. On the Notes tab, type other important information about your contact that might come in handy, such as their spouse's and children's names, birthdays, and so on.
5. Use the Certificates tab to import and manage security certificates for your new contact. You use security certificates when you send encrypted messages to a contact, or you want to verify a contact's digital signature.

   Once you import a certificate, select it and click Properties. In the Certificate Properties dialog box, you can review the validity, expiration dates, and issuing institution, and determine whether you trust the certificate. If you do not trust a certificate, indicate so in the Trusted option list.
6. Click OK to add the new contact.

TIP In Outlook Express, you can quickly add names to your Address Book. Simply right-click a recipient's name and choose Add to Address Book.

Once you add a contact to your Address Book, you can use it in other applications such as Outlook Express.

If you ever need to go back to an Address Book entry to update the contact information, simply double-click the entry in the address book and modify the information as needed. Alternatively, you can select the contact in the list and click the Properties toolbar button, or choose File, Properties.

To delete a contact from your address book, select the contact in the list, and click the Delete toolbar button; or choose File, Delete. If the contact is a member of any of your groups, it is removed from each of the groups as well.

Creating a Group

Suppose you frequently invite several of your contacts to a weekly meeting, and you want an easy way to address the whole group in each invitation message. The way you do that is by using a *group*, or distribution list. You create a group and add the invited contacts to it. Then, when you send a message to the group, you address it to the group name, rather than each contact. Address Book allows you to create as many groups as you need, and each contact can be in more than one group, if desired. To create a group, follow these steps:

1. In Address Book, click the New Group toolbar button, or choose File, New Group.
2. In the Group Properties dialog box, give the group a meaningful name such as **Staff**.
3. Click Select Members to add your contacts to the group distribution list.
4. In the Select Group Members dialog box, select each contact you want in the group (you can even select other groups you have defined) and click Select.
5. Click OK when you have identified the members of the group.
6. Click OK again to save your new group. It should appear in your Address Book with a group icon next to the name.

If you no longer need a group, you can delete it. Deleting a group removes only the group collection and does not remove the contact members from the Address Book. To delete a group, select it in the Address Book list, and click the Delete toolbar button, or choose File, Delete.

Adding and Removing Contacts in a Group

If you want to add new members to a group, you can open the group and choose additional members. In addition, you can remove contacts you no longer want included in the group.

To add new contacts to a group, follow these steps:

1. Double-click the group you want to modify in the address book list. Or select the group name and click the Properties toolbar button, or choose File, Properties.
2. Click Select Members, and then select each additional contact from the Select Group Members dialog box.
3. Click OK to add the new members to the group.
4. Click OK again to save your new group membership.

To delete contacts from a group, follow these steps:

1. Double-click the group you want to modify in the address book list. Or select the group name and click the Properties toolbar button, or choose File, Properties.
2. For each contact in the Members list that you want to remove, select the contact and click Remove. Note: Removing a contact from a group does not remove it from your Address Book.
3. Click OK to save your changes.

Sorting Names in the Address Book List

As your address book begins to grow, you may find it difficult to locate contacts in the Address Book list. To make it easier to locate a contact, you can sort the Address Book list by any of the column headings. Simply click the appropriate column heading that interests you. To sort in the reverse direction, click the column heading again.

If you want to sort by first name or last name, use the View menu. Choose View, Sort By and select First Name or Last Name.

Searching for Names in Your Address Book or a Directory Service

If you are trying to locate someone, the Windows Address Book provides an easy way to find them in your Personal Address Book, or on the Internet.

To search for names in your address book or through a Directory Service, follow these steps:

1. In the Address Book, click the Find toolbar button, or choose Edit, Find. The Find People dialog box displays.
2. In the Search list, select the location to search: your personal Windows Address Book, or an Internet Directory Service.
3. Type the name you want to search for in the Name text box. If you know additional information such as the E-mail address, enter it as well to reduce the number of potential responses (especially when searching an Internet Directory Service).
4. Click Find Now.
5. The search results display at the bottom of the Find People dialog box, as shown in Figure 27.24. When searching a Directory Service, you can configure the number of responses and the time allowed for the search.

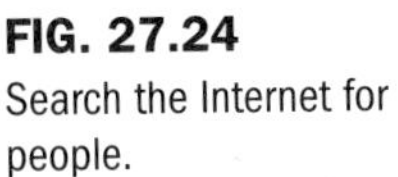

FIG. 27.24
Search the Internet for people.

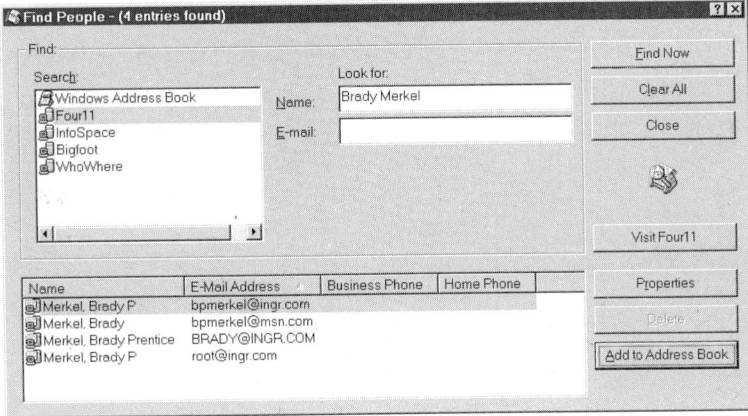

6. If you get multiple responses to your search, select each entry that looks promising, and click Properties to see additional information about the person. Click a column heading to sort the list.

   If you found a person from a Directory Service that is not in your Windows Address Book, and you want to add it, select the entry and click Add to Address Book. If you want to visit a Directory Service's Web site, select the Directory Service in the Search list and click the Visit Directory Service button. Some Directory Services allow you to add or update your own entries.

You can also use Tools, Check Names within Outlook Express to resolve names to your Windows Address Book and Internet Directory Services. See the next section for details on choosing which services should be searched.

Understanding Directory Services

The Windows Address Book uses a new and exciting capability to search Internet sites for people: *Directory Services*. Windows Address Book uses a technology known as the Lightweight Directory Access Protocol (LDAP) to search for the information.

When you install the Windows Address Book, it comes configured with four Internet Directory Service providers. If you prefer, you can add others, edit their properties, or delete the ones you no longer need.

NOTE Unlike the Address Book, you cannot view the entire contents of a Directory Service. In addition, Directory Service searches limit the number of responses, so you may need to provide additional information to reduce the search results.

To add a Directory Service entry, follow these steps:

1. In the Windows Address Book, choose File, Directory Services.
2. Click Add to add a Directory Service. Type the name of the Directory Service in the Friendly Name text box.

3. Type the Internet address of the Directory Service in the Directory Server text box.
4. Choose the required server authentication type, and provide the user name and password if needed.
5. If you want this Directory Service to be searched when you check names in Outlook Express, check the Check Names Against This Server When Sending Mail check box.
6. Click the Advanced tab. Type the maximum number of seconds you want to wait when searching this Directory Service in the Search Time-Out text box.

   Type the maximum number of responses you are willing to wait for in the Maximum Number of Entries to Return text box.

   If you are not getting any search results from a Directory Service, try increasing the time-out value and decreasing the maximum number of responses value.
7. If your Directory Service requires an LDAP base identifier, type it into the Search Base for this Directory Service text box. Contact the Directory Service administrators for this value.
8. Click OK. Your new Directory Service is added to the list.

To review or edit a Directory Service entry, follow these steps:

1. In the Windows Address Book, choose File, Directory Services.
2. Select a Directory Service in the list and click Properties. The Directory Service's properties sheet appears, as shown in Figure 27.25.

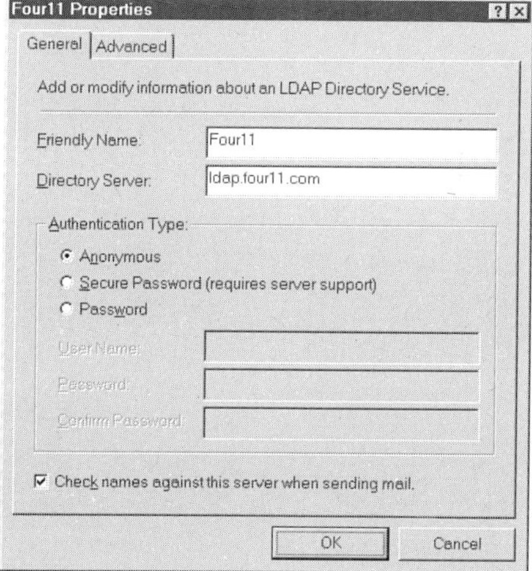

FIG. 27.25 You can review or edit the Directory Service's properties.

3. On the General tab, review the Directory Service connection settings and edit the values if you need to. If you want this Directory Service to be searched when you check names in Outlook Express, check the Check Names Against This Server When Sending Mail check box.
4. On the Advanced tab, as shown in Figure 27.26, you can tune the amount of time and number of responses you will wait for when searching the Directory Service.

FIG. 27.26
Adjust the time-out and maximum response values to tune the amount of time it takes to perform a Directory Service search.

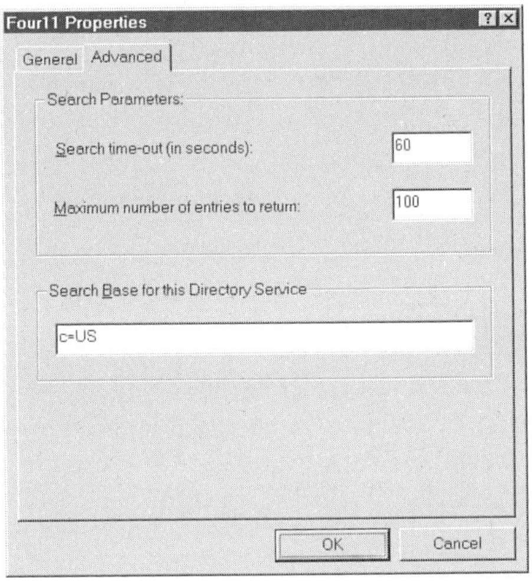

5. Click OK to save your settings and dismiss the dialog box.

When you check names while composing a new message in Outlook Express, first, your Personal Address Book is checked and then the Directory Services you have enabled. To define the order of Directory Services to search when checking names, follow these steps:

1. In the Windows Address Book, choose File, Directory Services.
2. Click the Options tab. If you see no Directory Services in the list, you need to enable one or more to be searched when you check names. See the previous text on editing a Directory Service entry.
3. Select a Directory Service and click Up or Down to change the order. Directory Services are searched in a top-down manner.
4. Click OK to save your settings and dismiss the dialog box.

To delete a Directory Service, follow these steps:

1. In the Windows Address Book, choose File, Directory Services.
2. Select a Directory Service in the list, and click Remove.
3. Click OK to save your settings and dismiss the dialog box.

Printing Your Contacts

If you are traveling, you can print your Address Book for easy reference. Choose File, Print, and select from the choice of printing in three different formats:

- **Memo.** For all address book information.
- **Business Card.** For only business-related information.
- **Phone List.** For only contact names and telephone numbers.

Importing Other Address Books

The Windows Address Book supports importing contact and group information from other address books, such as from Microsoft Exchange, Netscape Navigator, or Qualcomm Eudora. To import contacts from other address books, follow these steps:

1. Within Windows Address Book, choose Tools, Import, Address Book.
2. In the Windows Address Book Import Tool dialog box, select the type of address book you want to import and click Import.
3. The Import tool will attempt to locate the address book to import. Follow the prompts to facilitate locating the desired address book. For example, if you are importing a Microsoft Exchange Personal Address Book, you may need to log in to the specific Exchange profile. If the Import tool cannot locate the address book file, it will offer you the opportunity to locate the file manually.
4. As the Import tool reads each new contact and group, it compares it with the contacts you already have in your Windows Address Book. The Import tool will ask you to replace any contacts where the names are the same.
5. You should see a confirmation box that informs you that the import was successful. Click OK and click Close to dismiss the address book Import tool.

Exporting to Other Address Books

You can export your Address Book if you need to upgrade to a mail system that uses its own Address Book (such as Microsoft Exchange or Outlook 97). Alternatively, you can export your Address Book into a comma-separated format so you can import it into a database or spreadsheet. To export your Address Book, follow these steps:

1. In Windows Address Book, choose Tools, Export, Address Book.
2. In the Windows Address Book Export Tool dialog box, select the type of address book you want to export and click Export.

   If you selected Comma Separated Values, locate the folder where you want to create the .csv file, and type the name of file.

   If you are exporting to a Microsoft Exchange Personal Address Book, you may need to log in to the specific Exchange profile.

3. As the Import tool writes each contact and group, it compares it with the contacts you already have in your address book. The Export tool will ask you to replace any contacts where the names are the same.
4. You should see a confirmation box that informs you that the export was successful. Click OK and click Close to dismiss the address book Export tool.

Exporting your contacts and groups does not remove them from your Address Book.

Exporting vCards

A *vCard* is an electronic business card. vCards use an industry-standard format for exchanging business card information between different types of programs such as e-mail and address books. vCards are exchanged as files with the .VCF file name extension. To export a contact to a vCard, follow these steps:

1. Select a contact in your Address Book and choose Tools, Export, vCard..
2. Navigate to the folder where you want to create the vCard and type the file name.
3. Click Save.

Once you save a vCard to a file, you can attach it to e-mail messages or transfer them to your personal data assistant. Exporting a contact to a vCard does not remove it from your Address Book.

Importing vCards

If someone sends you a vCard, you can import it directly into your Windows Address Book. To import a vCard, follow these steps:

1. In Address Book, choose Tools, Import, vCard.
2. Locate the vCard on your local system or network drive.
3. Click Open.
4. In the Properties dialog box, review and modify any of the contact attributes.
5. Click OK to save the new contact in your address book. If the vCard contact name matches one that already exists in your address book, you will be prompted to replace it.

Working with Phone Dialer

The Phone Dialer is a handy accessory built into Windows 95 that acts as a speed dialer, remembering up to eight phone numbers. This may seem a bit redundant if you already have a speed dialer built into your existing phone, but this one is very easy to program and change, plus it can do the more intricate dialing needed to navigate voice-mail systems and make credit-card calls. Phone Dialer can even keep a log of your outgoing and incoming calls. You can access the Phone Dialer from the Start menu by choosing Programs, Accessories (see Figure 27.27).

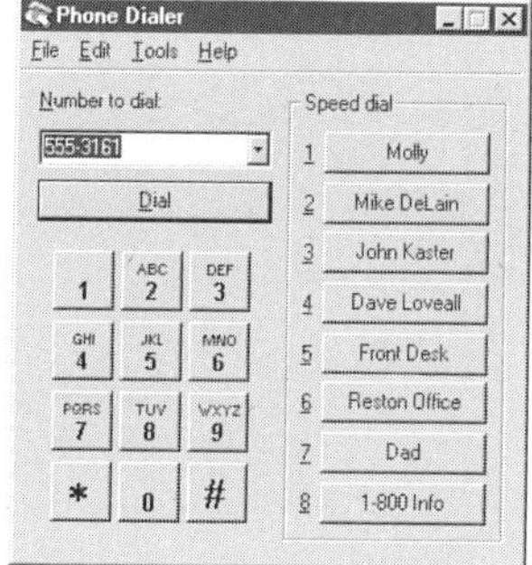

FIG. 27.27
Use Phone Dialer to make calls with your modem.

NOTE If you don't see the Phone Dialer on the Accessories menu, open the Start menu and choose Settings, Control Panel. Then double-click the Add/Remove Programs icon, click the Windows Setup tab, and select the Communications component. Select Details and be sure the Phone Dialer is selected. Click OK twice to save your changes.

Adding Phone Dialer Entries

When it's first started, your Phone Dialer has no speed-dial entries set. Your first task is to add names and phone numbers to the eight blank dial memories. Click any blank entry and type in the Name and Number you want to save (see Figure 27.28).

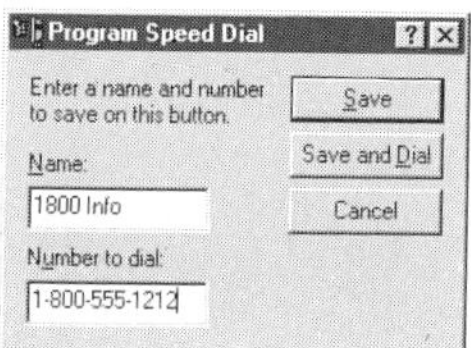

FIG. 27.28
You can enter a short name for each Phone Dialer entry.

Both the Save and the Save and Dial buttons are now available. You can immediately use your new entry to dial the phone by clicking the Save and Dial button or use the Save button to program your speed-dial entry and exit the dialog box.

TIP If you have a phone number that contains letters (555-FOOD or 1-800-555-SNOW), just put quotes ("") around the letters, for example, 1-800-555-"SNOW."

Once your number is entered and saved, clicking the speed-dial entry immediately starts the phone dialing and opens the Dialing dialog box shown in Figure 27.29. While waiting for your call to be answered, you can type in a description of the call as you want it to appear in the phone log.

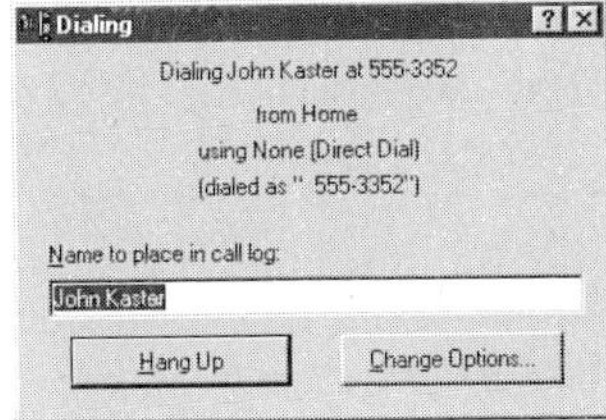

FIG. 27.29
Enter a log entry while the phone is dialing.

Click the Hang Up button if you want to abort the call immediately. The Change Options button gives you a chance to stop the call and redial with a number you type into the Number to Redial field (see Figure 27.30). This allows you to specify exactly what you want the modem to dial, ignoring any properties (such as your calling card number) set in the Dialing properties sheet. After typing in your number, click the Redial Number button to dial your new entry. If you click the Dialing Properties button, any changes you made in the Number to Redial text box are discarded, and your original speed-dial number appears with your current Dialing properties applied to it.

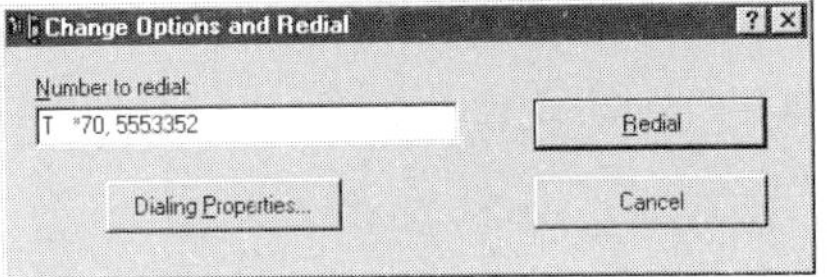

FIG. 27.30
You can make a temporary change to a Phone Dialer number when dialing.

Using Complex Phone Number Sequences

The convenience of voice-mail has an annoying side effect: All those voice menus prompting you to "Press one to leave a message, Press two to talk with an operator" can drive you crazy and waste a lot of your time. Likewise, credit cards and various long-distance carriers have required us to use dozens of numbers and procedures to make connections. A few built-in extras in your modem can handle things such as credit-card dialing, long-distance service connections, and navigation through many voice-mail hierarchies.

- To wait for the prompts within a voice-mail system, you can use the comma (,) to insert a two-second pause within your dialing sequence. Use more than one comma for a longer pause.
- If you need to wait for a secondary dial tone, use the letter **W**.
- If you need to wait for silence on the line, you can insert an @ sign.
- If you are making a credit-card call and need to wait for the tone from your long-distance carrier, insert a dollar sign ($) followed by your card number.
- You can also use * and # characters within the phone number to make those voice-mail menu selections.

For example, let's say you want to make a personal long-distance call from your office and charge it to your AT&T calling card. You know that your company's long-distance carrier is MCI, so you'll have to access the AT&T network to get the cheapest rates. Here's how to build your Phone Dialer sequence:

1. Type a **9** followed by a **W** to access the outside line, and wait for the dial tone.
2. Type the AT&T network access code: **10"ATT"** followed by a zero (**0**) to start the credit-card call.
3. Type the phone number you're trying to reach, such as **(205)-555-3161**.
4. To wait for AT&T to give their signal for you to enter your calling card number, type **$**.
5. Type in your credit-card number, such as **314-555-222-4321**.

Putting all these pieces of your dialing sequence together, it would read:

9W10"ATT"0(205)-555-3161$314-555-222-4321

That would be a definite candidate for saving in the Phone Dialer!

Using the Phone Dialer Log

The Phone Dialer comes with a log in which it will keep a record of your outgoing and incoming calls (see Figure 27.31). Each time you connect a phone call, an entry is placed in this text file. You can cut, copy, and delete from this log using the Edit menu commands, and you can redial an entry in your Log by double-clicking it or by selecting Log, Dial.

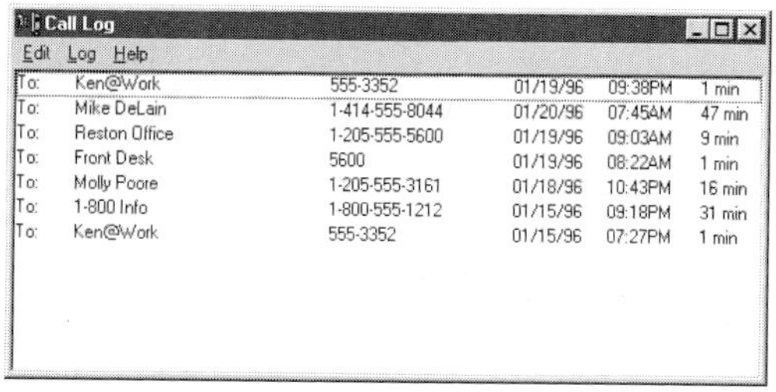

FIG. 27.31
Log entries can be used to redial or copy and paste into other documents.

Call Log

Edit Log Help

To:	Ken@Work	555-3352	01/19/96	09:38PM	1 min
To:	Mike DeLain	1-414-555-8044	01/20/96	07:45AM	47 min
To:	Reston Office	1-205-555-5600	01/19/96	09:03AM	9 min
To:	Front Desk	5600	01/19/96	08:22AM	1 min
To:	Molly Poore	1-205-555-3161	01/18/96	10:43PM	16 min
To:	1-800 Info	1-800-555-1212	01/15/96	09:18PM	31 min
To:	Ken@Work	555-3352	01/15/96	07:27PM	1 min

CHAPTER 28

Using WordPad and Paint

by Ron Person

Windows 95 comes with several accessory programs that are useful additions to your usual suite of full-featured applications. WordPad is a simple word processor that can be used to create, edit, and format documents. For many, WordPad may be all you need for your word processing tasks. Paint is a simple graphics program that will serve the needs of many users for creating, viewing, and editing graphics files. In this chapter, you learn how to use these two very useful Windows 95 accessories. In the next chapter, you will learn how to use some of the other Windows 95 accessory programs.

How to prepare simple word processing documents

You learn to use WordPad for simple, everyday word processing tasks such as creating letters and reports.

How to create and edit bit-mapped images

You learn to use Paint to create and edit pictures that can be inserted into other applications.

Using WordPad

WordPad is a simple but powerful word processor that comes with Windows 95. WordPad offers many of the editing and formatting capabilities—such as cut, copy, and paste— commonly found in more advanced applications, along with the ability to share information with other applications and files using OLE.

WordPad is easy to use. The techniques and features you've learned to use in other word processors—such as how to select commands and how to enter, format, and print text—also work here. Because the margins, a font, and tabs are already set, you can actually begin a new WordPad document as soon as you start the application. WordPad's Help command can assist you if you run up against something new.

Starting WordPad

To start WordPad from the desktop, follow these steps:

1. Open the Start menu and choose Programs and then choose Accessories.
2. Choose WordPad. WordPad starts up and displays the WordPad window (see Figure 28.1).

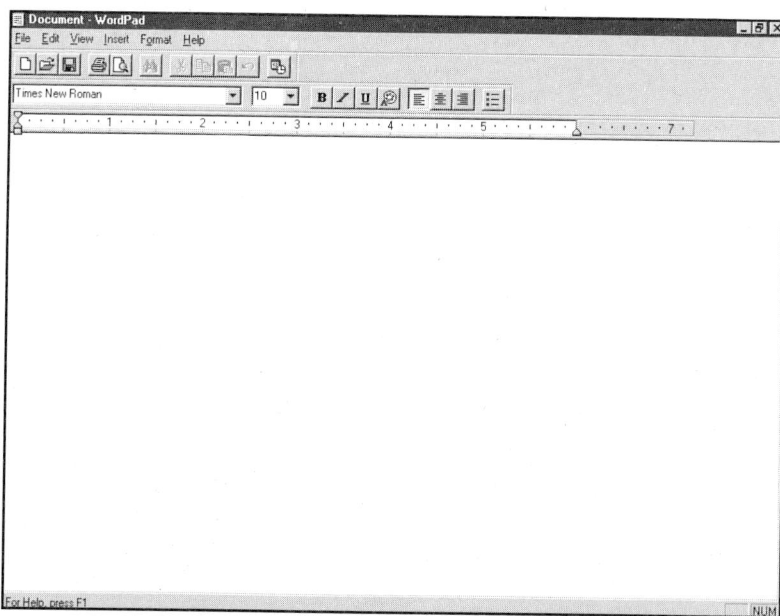

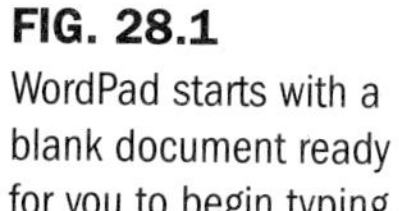

FIG. 28.1
WordPad starts with a blank document ready for you to begin typing.

Unlike more robust Windows applications, WordPad does not support MDI (Multiple Document Interface) and therefore can contain only one document at a time. When you open a new blank document, you will be asked if you want to save the current document.

Because WordPad is not as resource-hungry as "more robust Windows applications," you can open multiple instances of WordPad to edit multiple WordPad documents of different formats, including Word, ASCII, RTF, and Windows Write.

You can create new documents in any one of three formats in WordPad. When you choose the File, New command, the dialog box shown in Figure 28.2 appears. Select one of the following document types:

- **Word 6 Document.** This format can be opened and edited in Microsoft Word 6.0 or Microsoft Word 97. This is handy if you use WordPad on your laptop and Word 6 or Word 97 on your desktop. If you save a Word document from WordPad, you will lose advanced features such as columns that were created in Word.

CAUTION

If you're working in Word 97, and you open a document created in WordPad and then save it as a Word 97 document, you will not be able to reopen it in WordPad. If you want to be able to work with the document in WordPad, save the document as an .RTF file in Word 97.

- **Rich Text Document.** This format (RTF) is compatible with several word processing programs and includes fonts, tabs, and character formatting. RTF files are also used to create Windows Help files using the Microsoft Help compiler.
- **Text Document.** This format includes no text formatting and can be used in any word processing program. Use this format for creating DOS batch files.

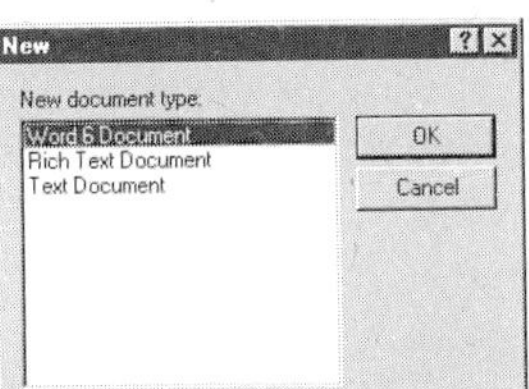

FIG. 28.2
You can create new documents in any one of three formats.

WordPad is an OLE 2-compliant application, so you can insert objects from other OLE applications into a WordPad document or insert all or part of a WordPad document into an OLE application. You can, for example, insert a graphic created in Windows Paint as an object into a WordPad document and then double-click the Paint object and edit the graphic in place. The WordPad menus and toolbars are replaced with the Paint menus and toolbars while you edit the object. Use the Insert, Object command or the drag-and-drop method for exchanging information with other OLE applications.

See "Using Embedding to Link Information," **p. 922**

WordPad also is MAPI-enabled, which means you can use it with Microsoft Exchange to send mail and faxes. To mail or fax a document from WordPad, choose the File, Send command.

You can drag and drop files and folders from any common File Open dialog box (including WordPad's) into Explorer, onto the desktop, or into any OLE-compliant application such as Word 97. You can, for example, insert a WordPad document into a Word document by dragging it from the File Open dialog box in WordPad and dropping it into the Word document where you want it to be inserted.

TROUBLESHOOTING

When I try to save a file in WordPad with a non-default extension, WordPad appends the file name with the DOC extension. When you save a file with an extension that is not associated with an application in the Registry, WordPad appends the default DOC extension to the filename. In Notepad, the default extension TXT is appended to the filename. To avoid this, enclose the file name in quotation marks.

I am unable to print multiple or collated copies from WordPad. These features are unavailable in the File Print dialog box. WordPad does not support multiple or collated printing. Unless these features are supported with the printer driver for your printer, you cannot print multiple or collated copies from WordPad.

I selected a block of text in a WordPad document and tried to print just the selection, but the Selection option is unavailable in the File Print dialog box. Although this option is shown in the File Print dialog box, the capability to print selected text is not supported in WordPad. To work around this limitation, copy the text to a new WordPad document and print that document.

Using WordPad to Create and Edit System, Batch, and Text Files

WordPad is very useful for creating and editing TXT and system files (that is files with the extension BAT, SYS, INI, and so on), especially when the file in question is too large for Notepad. When you open a SYS, INI, BAT, or TXT file in WordPad, edit or view it, and then save it again, it is saved with its original file extension. This feature eliminates any worry about inadvertently saving a system file with the wrong extension, as can happen in a regular word processing program. And, WordPad provides more features (such as the replace command) for editing your files than does Notepad.

To create a new text file in WordPad, choose File, New and select Text Document in the New dialog box. When you save the document, it is given the TXT extension automatically. If necessary, change the extension, for example, to BAT for a DOS batch file.

Create a shortcut for WordPad in the SendTo folder so you can quickly open any file with WordPad from Explorer or a folder window.

See "Adding Items to the Send To Menu," **p. 850**

You can change the association for TXT files so that they open in WordPad instead of Notepad when you double-click them or choose Open in the context menu in Explorer or My Computer. To change the association, follow these steps:

1. Choose View, Options in Explorer or My Computer and select the File Types tab.
2. Select Text Document from the Registered File Types list.
3. Choose Edit, select open in the Actions list of the Edit File Type dialog box and choose Edit.
4. Choose the Browse button and locate and select WORDPAD.EXE, which is located in the Program Files\Accessories folder.
5. Choose OK and make sure that .txt is selected in the Default Extension for Content list.
6. Choose Close twice.

Creating Post-It Notes on Your Desktop

Because WordPad is an OLE 2-compliant application, you can drag and drop selected portions of a WordPad document into other OLE applications or onto the desktop. When you drag a selection onto the desktop, you create a scrap; double-click the icon for the scrap, and WordPad opens up and displays the information in the scrap. You can use these scraps as electronic Post-it notes; bits of information you might otherwise lose track of, secured to your desktop.

If you create desktop notes frequently, for example, while on the phone, you can add WordPad to your StartUp folder so that it is immediately available or simply create a shortcut on the desktop to WordPad.

To create a note on your desktop, follow these steps:

1. Open WordPad and create the note.
2. Select the note and drag and drop it on the desktop. The scrap appears as a desktop icon, labeled with the first few words of the note. The data is saved as a file in the desktop folder.

You can rename the scrap. Note that you don't have to save the note in WordPad. Whenever you double-click the scrap icon, the note is opened in WordPad. If you make changes, however, you do need to save the changes because the scrap file isn't saved automatically.

If a Word for Windows file will not open, try opening it in WordPad. If it opens, you may see symbols and characters you do not recognize. Start a new instance of Word for Windows and open a blank document. Base this new document on the same template as the document that would not open. Now return to WordPad and copy the entire document. Switch to the blank document in Word for Windows and paste. Reapply paragraph styles as necessary. WordPad seems to be able to open documents that contain file errors that make Word balk.

Using Windows Paint

Paint is simple and easy to use, but it also may be as powerful a graphics application as you will ever need. You can use your creations in other Windows applications, such as WordPad or Word for Windows.

Here are some of the graphic effects you can create with Paint:

- Lines in many widths, shades, and colors
- Brush strokes in a variety of styles, widths, shades, and colors
- Unfilled or filled shapes with shades or colors
- Text in many sizes, styles, and colors
- Special effects such as rotating, tilting, and inverting

Because Paint is a bitmap graphics application, the shapes you create are painted on screen in one layer. Although you can't layer objects, you can move, flip, and tilt them. You also can change the color of your painting, or erase it completely and paint something new.

Starting Windows Paint

To start Paint, Click Start, Programs, Accessories, Paint. Paint starts up and opens a new, empty Paint file (see Figure 28.3).

FIG. 28.3 When you start Paint, a new file opens.

To open a previously saved Paint file, choose File, Open. Select the file from the Open dialog box.

Selecting Tools and Colors

To paint, draw, fill, color or shade, write, and edit in Paint, you first must select the appropriate tool and shade or color. Figure 28.4 shows the individual tools in the toolbox located on the left side of the screen.

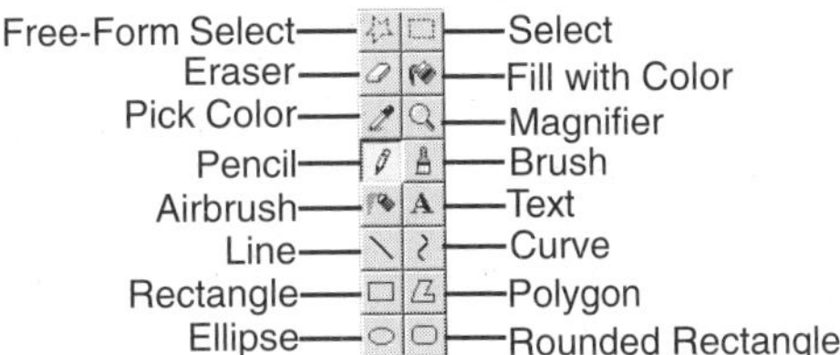

FIG. 28.4
The Paint toolbox provides the tools you need to create and modify a picture.

The palette offers two choices: foreground and background shade or color. At the left end of the palette (see Figure 28.5) is a box overlaying a box. The *top* box is the *foreground* color; the *bottom* box is the *background* color. The color you use depends on which mouse button you use to draw lines, brush strokes, and shapes. The left mouse button draws with the foreground color; the right mouse button draws with the background color. For example, when you draw a shaded box with the left mouse button, the foreground color borders the box and the background color fills the box. If you draw with the right mouse button, the foreground and background colors are reversed. (Drawing is discussed in the next section, "Using the Paint Toolbox.")

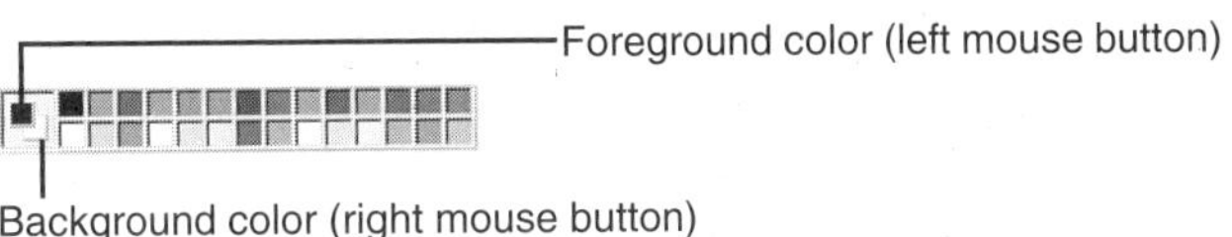

FIG. 28.5
Choose foreground and background colors from the Paint palette.

To select a tool or color, position the pointer on the tool or foreground color that you want and click the left mouse button. To select a background color, point to the color you want and click the right mouse button. You must use the left button when selecting a tool—the right mouse button can't be used to select a tool.

Using the Paint Toolbox

The Paint toolbox includes tools for selecting areas, airbrushing, typing text, erasing, filling, brushing, drawing curves or straight lines, and drawing filled or unfilled shapes. Most of the tools operate using a similar process, as described in the following steps.

To draw with the tools in the Paint toolbox, follow these steps:

1. Click to select the tool you want to use.
2. Position the pointer where you want to begin drawing, then press and hold down the mouse button as you draw with the mouse.
3. Release the mouse button to stop drawing.

Three exceptions to this process are:

- The Text tool, that you first click to select the text location, then type the text.
- The Paint Fill tool, which works by pointing and clicking.
- The Curve tool, which works by clicking, dragging, and clicking.

Aligning Drawn Objects When you want lines or shapes to line up accurately on screen, refer to the cursor position indicators in the Status Bar at the bottom of Paint's window. The two numbers that display tell you the position of the insertion point or drawing tool on screen. The position is given in X, Y coordinates, measured in pixels, from the top left corner of the painting. The left number is the X-coordinate (the position relative to the left edge of the painting); the right number is the Y-coordinate (the position relative to the top of the painting). If the numbers in the Cursor Position window read *42, 100*, for example, the cursor is 42 pixels from the left edge of the painting and 100 pixels down from the top of the painting.

Whichever tool you use, Edit, Undo is a useful ally. Use it to undo your most recent action. Undo undoes up to the last three actions. Just continue to select Undo to undo the number of actions you desire.

TROUBLESHOOTING

When I select the Undo command to undo a procedure I am in the middle of completing, the current procedure as well as the previous action are reversed. This is a bug in Paint. If you don't complete an action and you try to undo it, the previous action, as well as the current, incomplete action will be undone. You can reverse the action that was undone by choosing the Edit, Repeat command.

Several tools, including the Selection and Shape tools, use the right mouse button to undo. To cancel the shape you're currently drawing, click the right mouse button *before* you release the left mouse button.

The following sections describe how to use each of the toolbox tools.

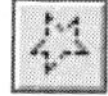

Selecting a Free-Form Area The Free-Form Select tool enables you to select an area by drawing a free-form boundary. Click the Free-Form Select tool, then select either the Transparent (doesn't include the background) or Opaque (does include the background) tool at the bottom of the toolbox. Draw any shape to enclose an area of the drawing. If you make a mistake while using the Free-Form Select tool, click the left mouse button outside the cutout area to cancel the cutout and try again. Once enclosed, an area can be moved, cut, or copied (and then pasted), resized, tilted, flipped, or inverted with the Edit menu commands. If you cut an area, the selected background color shows the color the cleared area will be. With an area selected, press Delete to delete it from the picture.

Selecting a Rectangular Area The Select tool enables you to select an area by dragging a rectangular box. Follow the instructions for the Free-Form Select tool in the previous section to use this tool.

Erasing Parts of Your Picture The Eraser tool erases as you drag it over your picture, just like an eraser on a chalkboard. Click the Eraser tool and then select the eraser size from the bottom of the toolbox. Drag across the picture with the left mouse button pressed to erase.

The selected background color shows the color the erased area will be. Choose Edit, Undo if you want to restore what you have erased.

Filling an Area with Color The Fill With Color tool fills in a shape. Click the Fill With Color tool and select foreground and background colors from the palette. Position the pointed tip of the Fill With Color tool inside the shape that you want to fill. Click the left mouse button to fill with the foreground color, or the right mouse button to fill with the background color.

You can use the Options, Edit Colors command to create a custom color palette from Paint's 48 colors or from colors you define by choosing the Define Custom Colors button in the Edit Colors dialog box.

TROUBLESHOOTING

I created a custom color palette, but when I try to use the colors in this palette to edit a 256-color bitmap, different colors than those I selected from the palette appear in the picture. This is a known bug in Paint with no current workaround. You have to use the standard color palette to edit 256-color bitmaps.

Picking Up a Color from the Drawing The Pick Color tool picks up the color on which you click for use in the current tool. To pick up the color of the spot where you click, click the Pick Color tool and then click anywhere in the painting. You can resume using the previous tool or select another tool and paint with the new color.

Magnifying the View of the Drawing The Magnifier tool magnifies the view of the drawing. Click the Magnifier tool and then select a magnification value at the bottom of the toolbox (1x, 2x, 6x, or 8x). Position the rectangle over the area you want to enlarge and click the left mouse button. You can work with the individual pixels that make up the painting. You can use any of the tools in the magnified view.

Drawing a Free-Form Line The Pencil tool draws a one pixel-wide, free-form line in the currently selected color. Draw with the left mouse button pressed to use the foreground color; draw with the right mouse button pressed to draw with the background color.

Painting with a Brush The Brush tool provides a selection of brush shapes with which you can paint lines of various widths and shapes. Click the Brush tool button and select from the brush shapes that display at the bottom of the toolbox. Paint with the left mouse button pressed to use the foreground color; paint with the right mouse button pressed to use the background color.

Painting with an Airbrush The Airbrush tool paints with a mist of color; the more densely you spray, the heavier your coverage. Click the Airbrush tool and select from the sprayer sizes that display at the bottom of the toolbox. Select a color from the Color palette: the left mouse button sprays with the foreground color; the right mouse button sprays with the background color. Hold the tool in one position longer to spray more densely.

Adding Text to a Picture Use the Text tool to add text to your painting. Click the Text tool and, in the area below the toolbox, select Opaque (the background color fills the text box behind the text) or Transparent (the picture appears behind the text). Next, in the picture area, drag to determine the size of the text box. Choose View, Text Toolbar to turn on display of the Font toolbar (only required the first time you use the Text tool). Select a font, point size, and bold, italic, or underline options. Click in the text box and type. Use the limited set of editing tools, including word-wrap and Backspace. Text appears in the foreground color.

If your painting includes a lot of text, type the text in Word or WordPad, select and copy it, and then paste it into Paint.

TROUBLESHOOTING

The Text Toolbar is not available from the View menu. You must click the Text tool and drag a text area before the Text Toolbar is available from the View menu.

An error message appears saying that I need to resize the text box. The text box isn't large enough to hold the text you are pasting into it. Enlarge the box and try again.

I was in the middle of typing text into a Paint picture and I opened Help. The text disappeared and did not reappear when I closed Help. There are a few problems that occur when you open Help in Paint:

- If you open Help when you are using the Text tool, the text disappears.
- If you have selected a portion of a picture with the Select or Free-Form Select tools, the selection is lost when you open Help.
- If you are using the Curve or Polygon tools to edit a picture, you will lose what you have created with the tools when you open Help.

One workaround for these problems is to save the picture before you open Help and reopen the saved image after you've closed Help. You also can click elsewhere in the picture or select another tool to set the element you were working on before you open Help. Selections made with the selection tools cannot be preserved when you open Help.

Drawing a Straight Line The Line tool draws a straight line. Click the Line tool and select a line width from the display at the bottom of the toolbox. To draw a straight line, click the mouse where you want to start the line and then drag the mouse. To cancel the line that you're drawing, click the right mouse button before you release the left mouse button. If you're drawing with the right mouse button, click the left button to cancel the line. To draw a line that is perfectly vertical, horizontal, or at a 45-degree angle, press and hold down the Shift key as you draw.

Drawing Curves The Curve tool draws a curve. To draw a curve, follow these steps:

1. Click the Curve tool.
2. Select a line width from the display at the bottom of the toolbox.

3. Draw a straight line and release the mouse button.
4. Click the left mouse button and drag away from the line to pull the line into a curve.
5. When you've achieved the shape you want, release the mouse button to complete the line. Repeat the process on the other side of the line to create an *s*-shaped curve.

Drawing Rectangles and Squares The Rectangle tool draws a rectangle or square with different borders or fill color. Click the Rectangle tool and select Border Only, Border and Fill, or Fill Only from the bottom of the toolbox. To create the size box you want, press and hold down the mouse button and drag to that size. Release the mouse button when you have the size you want. Use the left mouse button to border with the foreground color and fill with the background color; use the right mouse button to border with the background color and fill with the foreground color. The size of the border is determined by the last line size you selected.

TIP To draw a square, select the Rectangle tool, then press and hold down the Shift key as you draw.

Drawing Objects with Many Sides (Polygons) The Polygon tool draws a multi-sided shape. Each side on the shape is a straight line. To draw a polygon, follow these steps:

1. Click the Polygon tool and select Border Only, Border and Fill, or Fill Only from the bottom of the toolbox.
2. Click and drag to draw the first side of the polygon. As with the Line tool, you can use the Shift key to draw a straight line segment for the polygon.
3. Release the mouse button and click to draw other sides of the polygon.
4. Double-click at the next-to-last vertex point to finish and close the polygon to its first point.

Drawing Ellipses and Circles The Ellipse tool draws an *ellipse* (an oval) or circle. Click the Ellipse tool and select Border Only, Border and Fill, or Fill Only from the bottom of the toolbox. To draw a circle, press and hold down the Shift key as you draw.

Drawing Rectangles with Rounded Corners Use the Rounded Rectangle tool to draw a rectangle with rounded edges. Click the Rounded Rectangle tool and select Border Only, Border and Fill, or Fill Only from the bottom of the toolbox. Press and hold down the mouse button and drag to create the size rectangle you want. Release the mouse button when you have the size you want.

Editing a Painting

As you edit, be aware that completed objects cannot be edited, only erased or painted over and replaced. You can edit any object while creating it, but not after you complete the object. The method that you use to complete an object depends on the object. To complete a straight line, for example, you *release* the mouse button; to complete text, you *click* the mouse button or select another tool. You can cancel a line or curve before you complete it, for example, by clicking the opposite mouse button; you can change the appearance of text *before* you complete it by making a selection from the Text Toolbar.

TROUBLESHOOTING

I tried to clear my screen of the current contents, but the Image, Clear Image command is unavailable. The Clear Image command is unavailable if the Text tool is selected. Select any other tool and the command is available.

Moving a Selection

You can move an object or area on screen after you select it. (The object is still selected if you just pasted it.) Paint has several tricks for moving selections.

To move a selection, follow these steps:

1. Use one of the Select tools to select an object or area of the drawing. Select either Transparent (to leave the background showing) or Opaque (to hide the background). A dashed line encloses the selection.
2. Move the crosshair over the selection. The crosshair becomes an arrow.
3. Press and hold down the left mouse button to drag the selection to its new location. To copy the selection to a new location rather than moving it, hold down the Ctrl key as you drag the object to its new location.
4. Release the mouse button to place the selection, then click outside the selection to fix it in its new location.

Getting Different Views of the Painting You can zoom in to get a closer look at your painting or zoom out to see the whole page. Use either the View, Zoom command or the Magnifier tool.

The larger magnifications of the picture display the *pixels*, or tiny squares of color, which make up your painting. You can paint pixels in the selected foreground color by clicking the dots with the left mouse button and in the background color by clicking the right mouse button.

To zoom in for a close-up view of your painting, follow these steps:

1. Choose View, Zoom. Select Normal Size (Ctrl+Page Up), Large Size (Ctrl+Page Down), or Custom. If you select Custom, the View Zoom dialog box appears. Select 100%, 200%, 400%, 600%, or 800%.
2. Use the scroll bars to display the part of the painting you want to see.

To zoom back out to regular editing view, choose View, Zoom and select Normal Size or click the Magnifier tool and then click in the picture.

Select the area you want to flip, rotate, stretch, or skew. Place the pointer over it, and click the right mouse button to display a shortcut menu.

To use your painting or part of your painting as wallpaper, follow these steps:

1. Display the painting you want to use as wallpaper.
2. If you want to use only part of the painting on the desktop, select that part.
3. Choose File, Set as Wallpaper (Tiled) to repeat the painting as a pattern over the desktop, or Set as Wallpaper (Centered) to display the painting in the center of the desktop.

Saving Paint Files

When you save a Paint file, Paint assigns the extension .BMP to the file name and saves the file in Windows bitmap format.

To save a Paint file, click File, Save As. Type the name in the File Name text box. Click the Save As Type box to select one of the following file formats:

Format	File Extension Assigned
Monochrome Bitmap	BMP
16 Color Bitmap	BMP
256 Color Bitmap	BMP
24-bit Bitmap	BMP

Then click Save.

TROUBLESHOOTING

Many graphics files seem to use PCX format, but Paint won't save this format. Paint saves only with the BMP format. You can open PCX files with Paint, but if you want to make any changes and save the file again, you will have to save it as a BMP file. One way you can work around this is to use Microsoft Paintbrush from Windows 3.1 within Windows 95. You can copy the files PBRUSH.EXE, PBRUSH.DLL, PBRUSH.HLP, and PBRUSHX.CDX from the WINDOWS directory in Windows 3.1 into a Windows 95 folder. You can create a new folder within the PROGRAMS folder called Paintbrush. With Paintbrush, you can open and save PCX files.

You may want to convert your PCX files to BMP format. Microsoft has a graphics converter available and there are many free converters available through bulletin board services.

CHAPTER 29

Using Calculator, Calendar, and Other Accessories

by Ron Person

Some of the simplest of the accessory programs that come with Windows 95 may turn out to be the most useful to you. If you do a lot of calculations, the calculator that comes with Windows will come in handy. The clock on the taskbar gives you the time at a glance and the date when you move the mouse pointer over it. Notepad is great for taking simple notes and editing text files, such as an AUTOEXEC.BAT or CONFIG.SYS file. When you need to insert a special character, such as a copyright symbol, into a document, the Character Map will serve that need.

How to use the calculator to do calculations

Find out how to use the built-in calculator for completing everything from simple to complex scientific calculations.

How to use the clock

Learn how to use the clock that is part of the Windows 95 taskbar.

How to use Notepad

Learn how to use this simple text editor for taking notes and working with text files.

How to use special characters in your documents

Here you learn to insert special characters into any Windows document with the Character Map.

Calculating with Calculator

Like a calculator you keep in a desk drawer, the Windows Calculator is small but saves you time (and mistakes) by performing all the calculations common to a standard calculator. The Windows Calculator, however, has added advantages: You can keep this calculator on screen alongside other applications, and you can copy numbers between the Calculator and other applications.

The Standard Windows Calculator, shown in Figure 29.1, works so much like a pocket calculator that you need little help getting started. The Calculator's *keypad*, the on-screen representation, contains familiar number *keys*, along with memory and simple math keys. A display window just above the keypad shows the numbers you enter and the results of calculations. If your computational needs are more advanced, you can choose a different view of the Calculator, the Scientific view (see Figure 29.2).

FIG. 29.1
The Standard Calculator.

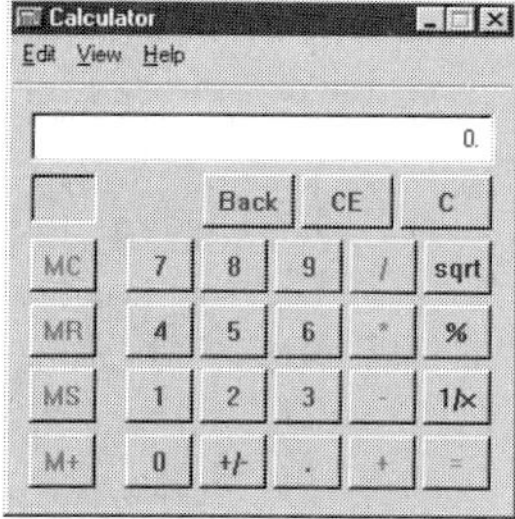

FIG. 29.2
The Scientific Calculator.

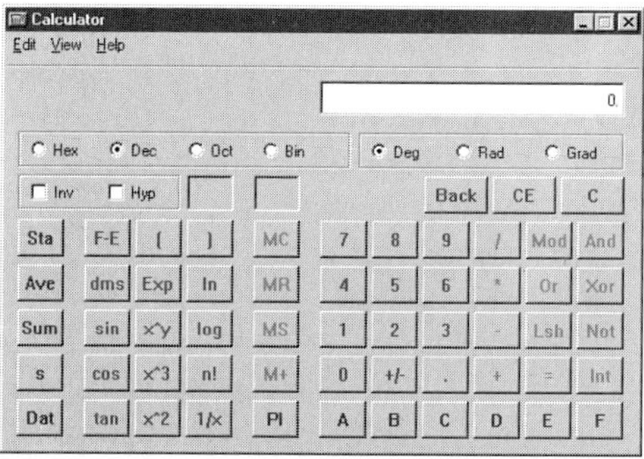

To display the Calculator, open the Start menu and click Programs and then click Accessories. Finally, click Calculator. The Calculator opens in the same view (Standard or Scientific) that was displayed the last time the Calculator was used.

To close the Calculator, click the Close button in the title bar. If you use the Calculator frequently, however, don't close it; click the Minimize button to minimize the Calculator to a button on the taskbar.

The Calculator has only three menus: Edit, View, and Help. The Edit menu contains two simple commands for copying and pasting; the View menu switches between the Standard and Scientific views; and the Help menu is the same as in all Windows accessories.

Operating the Calculator

To use the Calculator with the mouse, just click the appropriate numbers and sign keys like you would press buttons on a desk calculator. Numbers appear in the display window as you select them, and the results appear after the calculations are performed.

To enter numbers from the keyboard, use either the numbers across the top of the keyboard, or those on the numeric keypad (you first must press the NumLock key if the NumLock feature is not enabled). To calculate, press the keys on the keyboard that match the Calculator keys. Table 29.1 shows the Calculator keys for the keyboard.

Table 29.1 Keyboard Keys for Using the Calculator

Calculator Key	Function	Keyboard Key
MC	Clear memory	Ctrl+L
MR	Display memory	Ctrl+R
M+	Add to memory	Ctrl+P
MS	Store value in memory	Ctrl+M
CE	Delete displayed value	Del
Back	Delete last digit in displayed value	Backspace
+/–	Change sign	F9
/	Divide	/
*	Multiply	*
–	Subtract	–
+	Add	+
sqrt	Square root	@
%	Percent	%
1/x	Calculate reciprocal	R
C	Clear	Esc
=	Equals	= or Enter

NOTE To calculate a percentage, treat the % key like an equal sign. For example, to calculate 15 percent of 80, type **80*15%**. After you press the % key, the Calculator displays the result of "12."

You can use the Calculator's memory to total the results of several calculations. The memory holds a single number, which starts as zero; you can add to, display, or clear this number, or you can store another number in memory.

Copying Numbers Between the Calculator and Other Applications

When working with many numbers or complex numbers, you make fewer mistakes if you copy the Calculator results into other applications rather than retyping the result. To copy a number from the Calculator into another application, follow these steps:

1. In the Calculator display window, perform the math calculations required to display the number.
2. Choose Edit, Copy.
3. Activate the application you want to receive the calculated number.
4. Position the insertion point in the newly opened application where you want the number copied.
5. From the newly opened application, choose Edit, Paste.

You can also copy and paste a number from another application into the Calculator, perform calculations with the number, and then copy the result back into the application. A number pasted in the Calculator erases the number currently shown in the display window.

To copy a number from another application into the Calculator, select the number in the application and choose Edit, Copy. Next, activate the Calculator and choose Edit, Paste.

If you paste a formula in the Calculator, you can click the equal (=) button to see the result. If you copy *5+5* from WordPad, for example, paste the calculation in the Calculator, and click the = key, the resulting number 10 appears. If you paste a function, such as @ for square root, the Calculator performs the function on the number displayed. If, for example, you copy @ from a letter in WordPad and paste it into Calculator while it is displaying the number 25, the result 5 appears.

Numbers and most operators (such as + and –) work fine when pasted in the Calculator display, but the Calculator interprets some characters as commands. Table 29.2 lists the characters that the Calculator interprets as commands.

Table 29.2 Calculator Command Characters

Character	Interpreted As
:c	Clears memory.
:e	Lets you enter scientific notation in decimal mode; also the number E in hexadecimal mode.
:m	Stores the current value in memory.
:p	Adds the displayed value to the number in memory.

Character	Interpreted As
:q	Clears the current calculation.
:r	Displays the value in memory.
\	Works like the Dat button (in the Scientific Calculator).

Using the Scientific Calculator

If you have ever written an equation wider than a sheet of paper, you're a good candidate for using the Scientific Calculator. The Scientific Calculator is a special view of the Calculator.

To display the Scientific Calculator, activate the Calculator and choose View, Scientific.

The Scientific Calculator works the same as the Standard Calculator, but adds many advanced functions. You can work in one of four number systems: hexadecimal, decimal, octal, or binary. You can perform statistical calculations, such as averages and statistical deviations. You can calculate sines, cosines, tangents, powers, logarithms, squares, and cubes. These specialized functions aren't described here but are well documented in the Calculator's Help command.

See "Getting Help," **p. 270**

Using the Taskbar Clock

It's convenient to have a clock always on the screen, and Windows includes one in the taskbar. If yours isn't displayed, you can turn on the clock, adjust the time, and even select a time zone. You'll be surprised at how much control you have over that little clock (see Figure 29.3).

See "Changing the Taskbar Options," **p. 846**

FIG. 29.3
The taskbar clock.

The following table describes the taskbar clock options:

Action	Result
Point to time	Displays the date.
Double-click the time	Displays the Date/Time Properties, where you can set the date and time or select a time zone.
Right-click the time, and then click Properties	Displays Taskbar Properties, where you can turn Show Clock on or off.

Using Notepad

Notepad is a miniature text editor. Just as you use a notepad on your desk, you can use Notepad to take notes on screen while working in other Windows applications. Notepad uses little memory and is useful for editing text that you want to copy into a Windows or DOS application that lacks editing capability.

Notepad retrieves and saves files in text format. This feature makes Notepad a convenient editor for creating and altering text-based files. Because Notepad stores files in text format, almost all word processing applications can retrieve Notepad's files.

Starting Notepad

To start Notepad, click Start, Programs, Accessories, and choose Notepad. Notepad starts up and displays a blank document in the Notepad window (see Figure 29.4). You can begin typing.

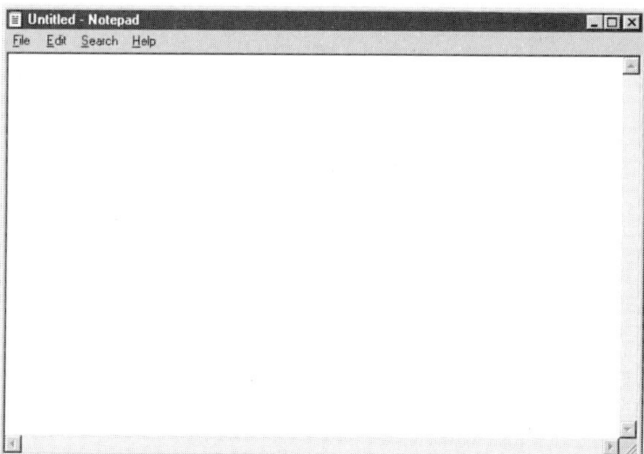

FIG. 29.4
The initial blank Notepad file is ready for text.

Working with Documents in Notepad

Unlike most word processing applications, Notepad doesn't, by default, wrap text to the following line. You must choose Edit, Word Wrap to activate this feature.

You can move the insertion point by using either the mouse or the keyboard. You select and edit text in Notepad the same way you select and edit text in WordPad.

Limited formatting is available from the File, Page Setup command. You can change margins and add a header or footer. You cannot format characters or paragraphs in any way, although you can use Tab, the Space Bar, and Backspace to align text. Tab stops are preset at every eight characters.

With Notepad's Edit commands, you can cut, copy, and move text from one place in a file to another. Text that you cut or copy is stored in the Clipboard. When you paste text, this text is copied from the Clipboard to the document at the insertion point.

See "Using Simple Editing Techniques," p. 678
See "Copying and Moving," p. 679

Creating a Time-Log File with Notepad

By typing a simple entry at the top of a Notepad document, **.LOG**, you can have Notepad enter the current time and date at the end of a document each time you open the file. This feature is convenient for taking phone messages or for calculating the time spent on a project. The text ".LOG" must be entered on the first line of the document and must be uppercase. As an alternative, you can choose Edit, Time/Date or press F5 to insert the current time and date at the insertion point.

Notepad can open binary files, which WordPad cannot. Although most of what you see when you open binary files is unreadable, you can sometimes find helpful information in the header of the binary file. This is a good reason to keep Notepad on your computer, even if WordPad is more suitable for most tasks.

Inserting Symbols with Character Map

The Character Map accessory gives you access to symbol fonts and ANSI characters. *ANSI characters* are the regular character set that you see on the keyboard and more than a hundred other characters, including a copyright symbol, a registered trademark symbol, and many foreign-language characters. One symbol font, Symbol, is included with most Windows applications. Other symbol fonts may be built into the printer. When you set up and indicate the model of the printer, font cartridges, and so on, the printer tells Windows what symbol fonts are available. (Printer fonts appear in Character Map only when they include a matching screen font.)

See "Installing and Deleting Fonts," p. 166

To start Character Map, open the Start menu and click Programs, then click Accessories. Finally, click Character Map. You are presented with the Character Map window shown in Figure 29.5.

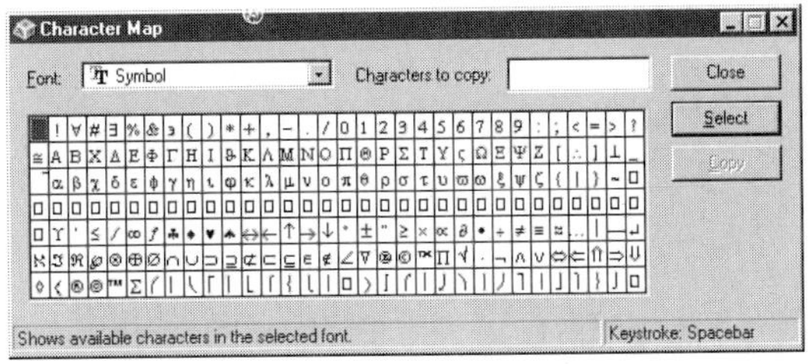

FIG. 29.5 Use Character Map to insert any of hundreds of special characters and symbols into a document.

The Character Map window includes a drop-down Font list box from which you can select any of the available fonts on the system. After you select a font, the characters and symbols for this font appear in the Character Map table. Each set of fonts may have different symbols. Some fonts, such as Symbol and Zapf Dingbats, contain nothing but symbols and special characters.

To insert a character in a Windows application from the Character Map, follow these steps:

1. Start the Character Map accessory.
2. Select the font you want to use from the Font list.
3. View an enlarged character by clicking and holding down the mouse button on a character or by pressing the arrow keys to move the selection box over a character.
4. Double-click the character you want to insert or click the Select button to place the current character in the Characters to Copy text box.
5. Repeat steps 2 through 4 to select as many characters as you want.
6. Click the Copy button to copy to the Clipboard the characters you've selected.
7. Open or switch to the application to which you want to copy the characters.
8. Place the insertion point where you want to insert the characters and open the Edit menu and choose Paste (Ctrl+V).

If the characters don't appear as they did in Character Map, you may need to reselect the characters and change the font to the same font in which the character originally appeared in the Character Map.

If you plan to use Character Map frequently, you may want to create a shortcut for this application so that you can start Character Map directly from the desktop.

See "Creating Shortcut Icons on the Desktop to Start Programs," **p. 261**

CHAPTER 30

Communicating with HyperTerminal

by Jerry Honeycutt

HyperTerminal is a Windows accessory that enables you to connect your computer to another PC or online service. HyperTerminal is a full-featured communications tool that greatly simplifies getting online. With HyperTerminal, you can connect to a friend's computer, a university, an Internet service provider, or even CompuServe.

What is HyperTerminal

Find out what HyperTerminal is and how it compares to the other communications tools provided with Windows.

How to use HyperTerminal

Learn how to use HyperTerminal for completing some common tasks such as creating a connection or downloading a file.

How to configure HyperTerminal

Learn how to configure HyperTerminal to work with your computer and modem and to customize your connections.

Introducing HyperTerminal

Before graphical interfaces to online services such as CompuServe and the Microsoft Network existed, most communications tools were character-oriented. For example, students all over the world used terminal-emulation programs to connect to their schools' computers. They typically used VT-100 terminal emulation, which makes their PC behave like any other display terminal on the system. CompuServe is another example, but instead of emulating a terminal, it displays one line of text at a time. Remember the days before WinCIM?

If you can use the graphical communications tools mentioned here, why do you need a character-oriented tool such as HyperTerminal? The reason is that most bulletin boards, Internet shell accounts, and university connections are still character-oriented. Most bulletin boards do not provide a sleek, graphical interface like the Microsoft Network. HyperTerminal does the following:

- Makes the focal point of your activities the connections you create (documents), which allows you to dial or configure a connection without loading HyperTerminal first.
- Automatically detects the terminal-emulation mode and communications parameters of the remote computer.
- Fully integrates with TAPI and the centralized modem configuration, which provides Windows 95 applications a single interface to your modem for dialing, answering, configuration, and more.
- Supports several popular terminal-emulation modes and file transfer protocols, such as VT100, VT52, and Kermit.
- Enables you to greatly customize each of your connections.

What You Can Do with HyperTerminal

HyperTerminal is a communications tool with many uses. The following list describes many tasks you can do with HyperTerminal:

- Connect to another computer and exchange files.
- Connect to an online service (such as CompuServe) that supports one of HyperTerminal's terminal-emulation modes.
- Connect to a school's computer using VT-100.
- Connect to an Internet service provider using a shell account and even access the World Wide Web using Lynx.

What You Can't Do with HyperTerminal

Although HyperTerminal is a useful communications tool, it is not the only tool you will need for your communications activities. The following list describes some activities you can't do and refers you to other chapters in this book:

- *Connect to another network.* If you need to connect your computer to another network, use Dial-Up Networking as described in Chapter 37, "Sharing Windows 95 Peer-to-Peer Resources."
- *Graphically connect to the Internet World Wide Web.* While many service providers provide Lynx, a character-oriented Web browsing tool, you'll need a graphical browsing tool to take full advantage of the Web. See Chapter 17, "Getting Connected to the Internet."

  See "The World Wide Web," **p. 445**

  See "Using Remote Network Access," **p. 969**

Using HyperTerminal

When you installed Windows, you were given the option to install HyperTerminal as one of your accessories. If you did not install HyperTerminal or you removed it from the Start menu, you can install it at any time by selecting Install/Remove Applications from Control Panel. To load HyperTerminal, click the Start button and choose Programs, Accessories, HyperTerminal.

See "Configuring Your Modem," **p. 85**

See "Adding and Removing Windows Components," **p. 695**

TIP If you have not yet configured your modem, Windows prompts you to set it up the first time you run HyperTerminal.

Figure 30.1 shows the HyperTerminal folder. By default, each connection that you create appears in this folder as an icon.

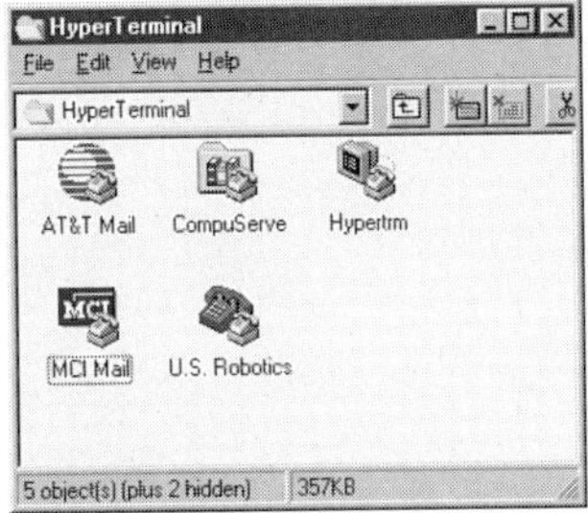

FIG. 30.1 Double-click Hypertrm to create a new HyperTerminal connection, or double-click another icon to open an existing connection.

Creating a New Connection

Before you can connect with HyperTerminal, you need to create a new connection. To do so, follow these steps:

1. Double-click the Hypertrm icon in the HyperTerminal folder. If HyperTerminal is already loaded, choose File, New or click the New button on the toolbar. HyperTerminal prompts you for a new connection description.

2. In the Connection Description dialog box, shown in Figure 30.2, type a descriptive name for your new connection, select an icon, and click OK. HyperTerminal then displays the Phone Number dialog box.

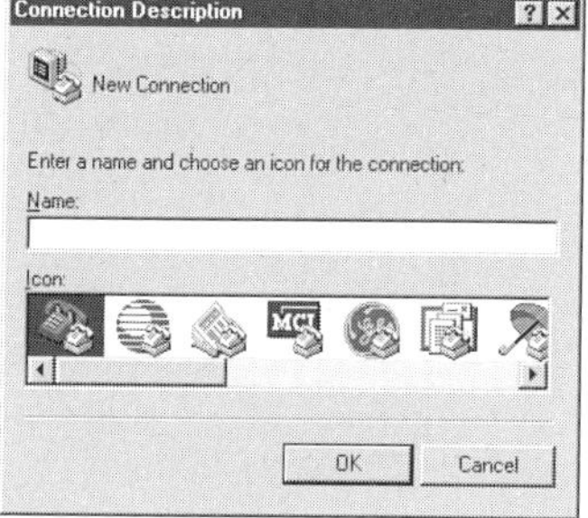

FIG. 30.2 Create a new connection and select an icon to help you easily identify it later.

3. Type the phone number for your new connection. Verify the country code, area code, and modem choice. Click OK. HyperTerminal displays the Connect dialog box, as shown in Figure 30.3.

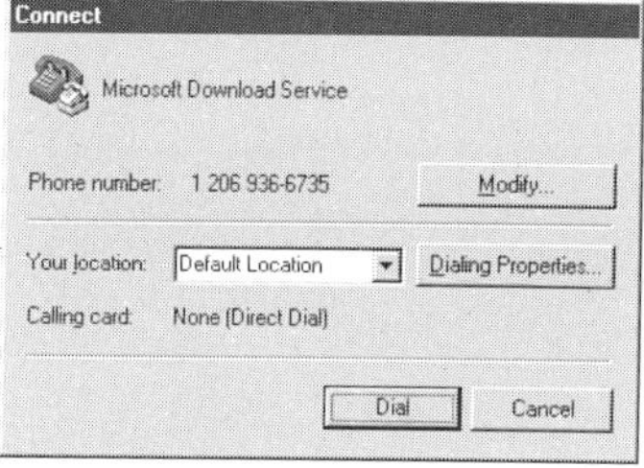

FIG. 30.3 After you set up the connection, simply click Dial to begin.

4. Select your location (usually Default Location) and click Dial if you want to establish your new connection. You can also click Dialing Properties to change the default location, outside line access, and other dialing properties.

Figure 30.4 shows the entire HyperTerminal window with a session in progress. Most of HyperTerminal's features are available on the toolbar. Table 30.1 describes each toolbar button.

Table 30.1 The HyperTerminal Toolbar

Button	Name	Description
	New	Creates a new connection.
	Open	Opens an existing connection.
	Connect	Displays the Connect dialog box.

Button	Name	Description
	Disconnect	Disconnects the current connection.
	Send	Sends a file to the host.
	Receive	Receives a file from the host.
	Properties	Displays the properties sheet for the connection.

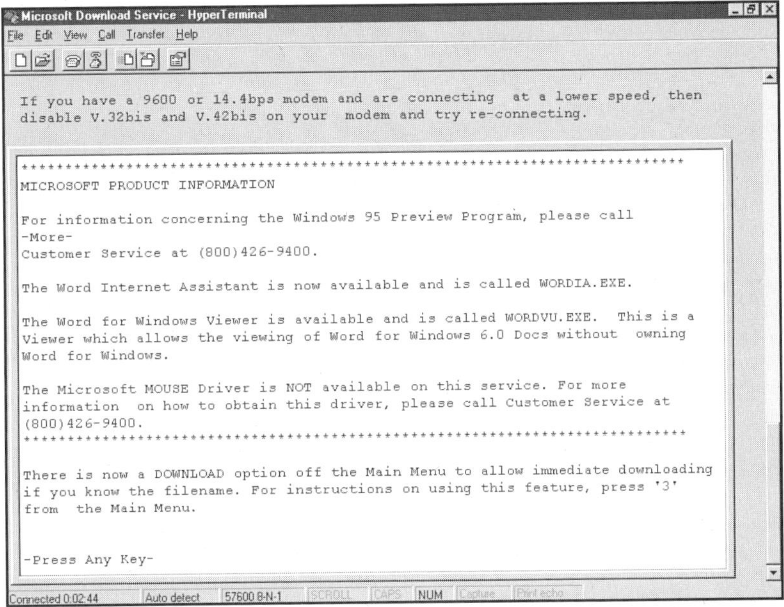

FIG. 30.4
After a connection to the remote computer is established, you interact with it just like a display terminal on the system. Click the scroll bar to review previously displayed text.

To save your new connection, choose File, Save As. HyperTerminal prompts you for a file name. If you want your connections to show up in the HyperTerminal folder, accept the default path. If you quit HyperTerminal without saving your new connection, HyperTerminal prompts you for a file name. To hang up, choose Call, Disconnect, or click the Disconnect button on the toolbar.

TROUBLESHOOTING

I try to dial a connection, but I get an error that says "Another program is using the selected Telephony device." Make sure that you don't have any older Windows communications programs running in the background that might be controlling the modem. Although Windows 95 communications tools can share the modem, older Windows communications programs can't.

continues

continued

I connected to the service fine, but all I see on-screen is garbage—usually at the bottom of the screen. Choose File, Properties to display the properties sheet for your connection; click the Settings tab, and set Emulation to Auto Detect. HyperTerminal automatically determines which terminal emulation your service uses.

Using an Existing Connection

The next time you want to use the connection you previously created, it will appear in the HyperTerminal folder. To establish this connection, double-click the icon in the folder and click Dial.

To make access to your connection quicker, copy a shortcut to the connection onto the desktop or the Start menu.

If HyperTerminal is already running, choose File, Open, or click the Open button on the toolbar.

Capturing Text from the Screen

By capturing text, you can save everything that appears in the HyperTerminal window. You may want to save the information displayed by HyperTerminal for the following reasons:

- You want to review or use it later.
- The information is scrolling by so quickly that you can't read it.

There are two ways to capture text from the remote computer: to a file or to the printer.

If text is scrolling by faster than you can read it, try pressing Ctrl+S to pause the screen and then press Ctrl+Q to resume.

Capturing Text to a File

To capture text received from the remote computer to a file, follow these steps:

1. Choose Transfer, Capture Text from the menu.
2. Type the name for a file in which you want to put the text, or click Browse to select a file. Your screen should look similar to Figure 30.5.
3. Click Start. HyperTerminal stores all text it receives from the remote computer in this file.

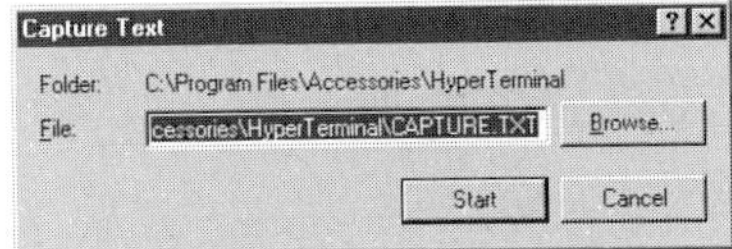

FIG. 30.5
Type the name for a file in which to capture text.

After you start capturing text, you can stop by choosing Transfer, Capture, Stop; pause with Transfer, Capture, Pause; or resume with Transfer, Capture, Resume. Notice that these menu options are available only after you start capturing text to a file. Once you choose Stop, you will be prompted for a file name the next time you choose Capture.

Capturing Text to the Printer

Capturing text to the printer is even easier than capturing to a file. To capture to the printer, choose Transfer, Capture to Printer. All text that HyperTerminal receives will be sent to the default printer. A check mark is displayed next to Capture to Printer, indicating that the option is turned on. To turn it off, choose it again.

TROUBLESHOOTING

I captured text to a text file, but when I view the file, I can read some of the lines, but the rest of them are garbled. If you are using terminal emulation, such as VT-100, this condition is normal. This emulation uses escape codes, which tell HyperTerminal where to put the cursor or how to format text. Escape codes can't be displayed as normal text. However, they are still captured to the file.

Sharing Text with Other Programs

The cut-and-paste process is still one of the most useful features in Windows. With a few keystrokes or mouse clicks, you can transfer data from one program to another. HyperTerminal is no exception. To copy data from HyperTerminal using the mouse, select a block of text in the window and choose Edit, Copy or press Ctrl+C.

Pasting is simple, too. After copying data to the Clipboard from another application such as Notepad, choose Edit, Paste to Host or just press Ctrl+V.

See "Understanding the Data-Sharing Capabilities of Windows 95," **p. 902**

NOTE In applications such as Notepad, pasting text from the Clipboard puts the text in the document, which is then displayed in the window. When you paste text into HyperTerminal, it actually transmits the text to the remote computer.

Exchanging Files with the Remote Computer

You can easily exchange files with another computer using HyperTerminal. For example, you may want to download a program update from the bulletin board of your favorite software vendor. You also can download public domain software from a variety of bulletin board systems (BBSs) around the country.

CAUTION

Before running a program downloaded from a remote computer, run it through a virus scan program to make sure that it's not infected. Otherwise, severe and irreparable damage may occur to your programs and data files if you download a virus.

You also may be asked to upload a data file to a vendor's bulletin board so that the vendor can help you fix a problem. HyperTerminal can do it!

Downloading Files

Before you begin downloading a file, you must make sure that you have a connection with a host computer, as described in the previous section "Using an Existing Connection."

To download a file from a host computer, follow these steps:

1. Start the download process on the bulletin board or host computer. Bulletin boards or other host computers vary in how to start a download; follow the instructions given to you online. Make a note of the file transfer protocol you selected on the host. HyperTerminal supports several popular file transfer protocols. Table 30.2 describes each protocol.
2. If you selected Zmodem as the protocol, you are done. The host computer initiates the file transfer with HyperTerminal. Otherwise, choose Transfer, Receive File from the menu, or click the Receive button. The Receive File dialog box appears.
3. Type a folder name or click Browse to select a folder (see Figure 30.6). Then select a protocol to use for downloading the file. The protocol you use should match the protocol you chose (or the system chose for you) on the host computer.

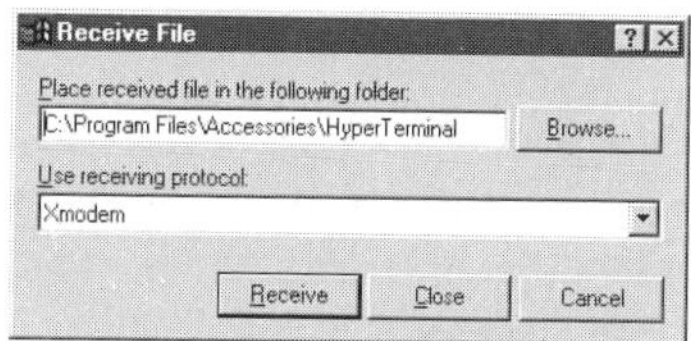

FIG. 30.6 Tell HyperTerminal where you want to store the file; then click Receive to begin the download.

See "Opening, Saving, and Closing Documents," **p. 675**

4. Click Receive, type a file name, and click OK. HyperTerminal starts your download. Figure 30.7 shows the dialog box that displays the status of your download. (You may see a different dialog box depending on the protocol you chose.)

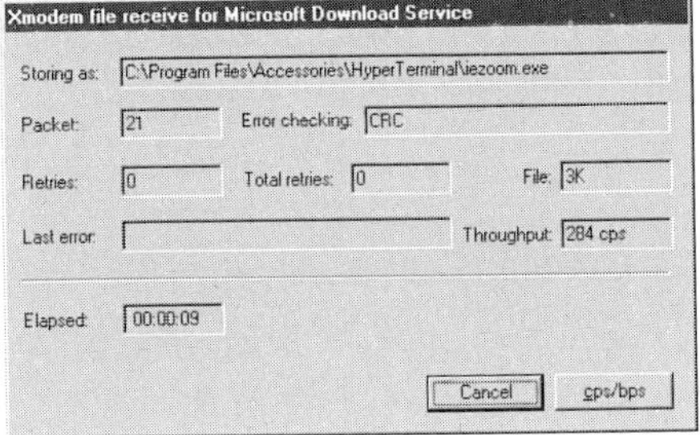

FIG. 30.7
This dialog box shows the status of your download such as the file name and time elapsed. The dialog box used varies depending on which protocol you used for the download.

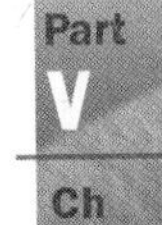

Table 30.2 File Transfer Protocols Supported by HyperTerminal

Protocol	Description
Xmodem	Xmodem is an error-correcting protocol supported by virtually every communications program and online service. It is slower than the other protocols.
1K Xmodem	1K Xmodem is faster than Xmodem, transferring files in 1,024-byte blocks as opposed to the slower 128-byte blocks in regular Xmodem. Otherwise, they are similar.
Ymodem	Many bulletin board systems offer Ymodem, which is another name for 1K Xmodem.
Ymodem-G	Similar to Ymodem, Ymodem-G implements hardware error control. It is more reliable than the first three protocols. However, to use Ymodem-G, your hardware must support hardware error control.
Zmodem	Zmodem is preferred by most bulletin board users because it is the fastest protocol of those listed. Zmodem is reliable, too, because it adjusts its block sizes during the download to accommodate bad telephone lines. Zmodem has two other features that make it stand out from the rest. First, the host can initiate the download; you do nothing beyond step 1. Second, you can download multiple files at one time using Zmodem. The host computer initiates a download for each file you selected.
Kermit	Kermit is extremely slow and should not be used if one of the other protocols is available. Kermit is a protocol left over from VAX computers and mainframes.

Uploading Binary Files

You can upload both binary and text files. Binary files include bitmaps, programs, and word processing documents that contain more than just readable text. For example, a program file contains code and program data that is not readable. On the other hand, text files contain characters that are easily read. This section describes how to upload a binary file. To learn how to upload text files, see "Uploading Text Files" later in this chapter.

Before you begin uploading a binary file, you must establish the connection to the host computer, as discussed in "Using an Existing Connection," earlier in this chapter. To upload a binary file to a host computer, follow these steps:

1. Initiate the upload on the bulletin board or host computer by following the on-screen instructions. The host displays a message indicating that it's waiting for you to start uploading.

NOTE If you are using Zmodem, you may not need to start the upload on the host computer. Zmodem can initiate the upload on the host for you. To try initiating the upload from your computer, skip step 1. However, if the host computer doesn't understand how to initiate an upload this way, you will have to start over from step 1.

2. Choose Transfer, Send File from the menu, or click the Send button on the toolbar. HyperTerminal displays a dialog box similar to the one shown in Figure 30.6 in the previous section "Downloading Files."
3. Type a file name or click Browse to select a file.
4. Select a protocol to use for uploading the file. The protocol you use should match the protocol you chose (or the system chose for you) on the host computer.
5. HyperTerminal starts the upload to the host computer. It displays the status of your upload in a dialog box similar to the one shown earlier in Figure 30.7.

TROUBLESHOOTING

I'm trying to use Ymodem-G as the transfer protocol, but it doesn't work. Your modem probably doesn't support hardware error control. Try using Ymodem instead.

I initiated a Ymodem upload from my computer, but the host doesn't respond. The host computer doesn't understand how to initiate an upload this way. You will need to initiate an upload first on the host computer and then on your computer. Alternatively, you may not be at the correct prompt on the host computer.

After reviewing the preceding suggestions, I still can't download or upload a file. Make sure that you are selecting the exact same transfer protocol the host computer is using. If you continue to have difficulty, contact the sysop (system operator) of the remote computer.

Uploading Text Files

Before you begin uploading a text file, be sure that you're connected to a host computer, as described in the earlier section "Using an Existing Connection." To upload a text file to a host computer, follow these steps:

1. Start the upload on the bulletin board or host computer. The host displays a message indicating that it's waiting for you to start the upload.
2. Choose Transfer, Send Text File from the menu. HyperTerminal prompts you for a text file name.

CAUTION

Don't try to upload a binary file using this feature. You may think that the file transferred okay, but the remote computer will receive a file with garbage in it.

3. Type a file name or click Browse to select a file.
4. Click Open. HyperTerminal starts uploading the text file to the host computer. Note that you do not see a dialog box showing the status of the upload.

Configuring HyperTerminal

HyperTerminal is a flexible communications tool. You can customize all aspects of each of your connections and HyperTerminal automatically saves your settings. For example, you can choose which font a connection uses or which terminal-emulation mode HyperTerminal uses. The next time you use that connection, HyperTerminal uses the settings you previously set. This section shows you how to configure HyperTerminal for each of your connections.

When you change configuration items in HyperTerminal, the changes apply only to the connection you have loaded. Thus, every connection can be customized differently.

Turning Off the Toolbar and Status Bar

You might want to turn off the toolbar or status bar for a HyperTerminal connection, especially if you do not have enough screen space to display the entire terminal area. To toggle the toolbar, choose View, Toolbar from the menu. A check mark beside Toolbar indicates that the option is turned on.

To toggle the status bar, choose View, Status Bar. Likewise, a check mark beside Status Bar indicates that it is turned on.

Changing Fonts

You can choose a specific font and style for your HyperTerminal connection. For example, if you want HyperTerminal to display a full screen in a smaller window, choose a smaller font size and resize the window.

NOTE You can't use a small font size to display 132 columns unless you are using VT-100 terminal emulation. HyperTerminal will always resize the display area to 80 columns.

To choose a different font for this HyperTerminal connection, follow these steps:

1. Choose View, Font from the menu. HyperTerminal displays the Font dialog box, which is common to most applications.
2. Set the font, style, and size. The Font dialog box shows you a preview of your choice.
3. Click OK when you are satisfied with your choice. HyperTerminal immediately resizes the display area for 80 columns, using the font you have chosen.
4. Optionally, click the right button in the display area and choose Snap. HyperTerminal resizes the window to fit the display area. This technique is useful if you want to use a smaller font to have a smaller HyperTerminal window.

▶ **See** "Understanding Fonts," **p. 160**

NOTE If the display area is larger than the HyperTerminal window, you can use the scroll bars to move the display area up, down, left, or right in the window.

Changing a Connection Setup

It is easy to change the properties for a connection after you create it. You can change the connection's icon, name, country code, area code, phone number, and modem in the connection's properties sheet, as shown in Figure 30.8.

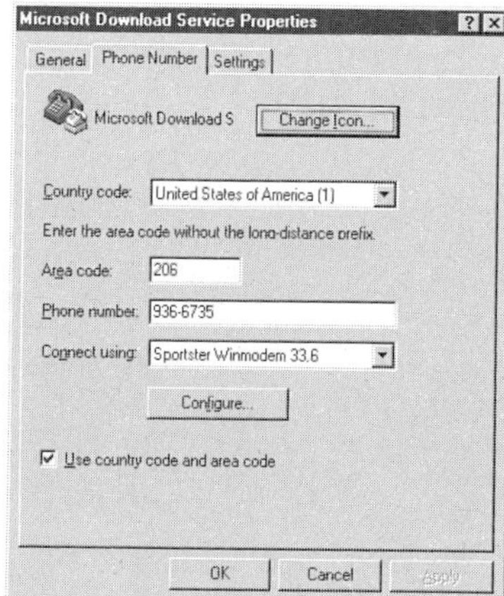

FIG. 30.8
Change the icon, name, phone number, and modem to use for this connection. Click OK to permanently save your settings.

To change the properties of your connection, follow these steps:

1. Choose File, Properties from the menu, or click the Properties button on the toolbar.
2. Click Change Icon, select another icon from the list, and change the connection name.
3. Select a country code.
4. Type the area code and phone number. (If you select the default location when you dial, Windows will not dial the area code if it matches your default area code.)

You can change the HyperTerminal properties sheet without even running HyperTerminal. Right-click the connection you want to change in the HyperTerminal folder, and then choose Properties.

5. Select a modem. Windows displays the modems you currently have installed or enables you to go directly to the port. If you go directly to the port, you can bypass the Windows 95 modem configuration, controlling the modem directly. For normal usage, select a configured modem so that you can take advantage of centralized modem configuration.
6. Click OK to save your settings.

Configuring the Connection Settings

The Settings page of the properties sheet enables you to change the terminal properties of HyperTerminal. For example, you can change the terminal-emulation mode. Figure 30.9 shows the Settings page of this sheet. Table 30.3 describes each terminal emulation available in HyperTerminal.

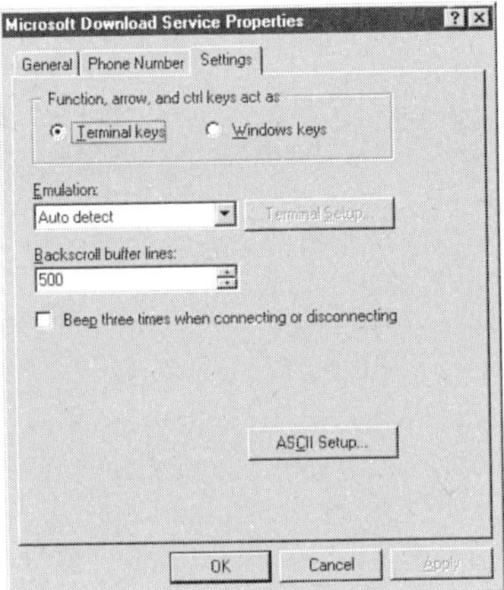

FIG. 30.9
Use the Settings page of the properties sheet to change the terminal emulation and other useful settings.

Table 30.3 Terminal Emulation Supported by HyperTerminal

Protocol	Description
ANSI	A popular, generic terminal emulation supported by most UNIX systems that provides full-screen emulation.

continues

Table 30.3 Continued

Protocol	Description
Auto Detect	Automatically determines which terminal emulation the remote computer is using.
Minitel	An emulation primarily used in France.
TTY	Is actually absent of any terminal emulation. TTY simply displays all the characters it receives on the display.
Viewdata	An emulation primarily used in the United Kingdom.
VT 100	The workhorse of terminal emulations. Many remote systems such as UNIX use it.
VT 52	A predecessor to VT 100 that provides full-screen terminal emulation on remote systems that support it.

To change the settings for this connection, follow these steps:

1. Choose File, Properties from the menu, or click the Properties button on the toolbar. Alternatively, right-click a connection document in the HyperTerminal folder.
2. On the Settings page, choose Terminal Keys or Windows Keys. Terminal Keys sends function keys F1 through F12 and arrow keys to the remote computer instead of acting on them in Windows; Windows Keys causes Windows to act on them. For example, if you choose Terminal Keys and press F1, the key would be sent to the host, and the host would respond to it. If you choose Windows Keys and press F1, Windows would display help.
3. Set Emulation to the terminal emulation you want. HyperTerminal must be using the same terminal emulation the host computer is using.

If you set Emulation to Auto Detect, HyperTerminal automatically determines what emulation the host is using and configures itself appropriately. Use this setting for normal situations.

4. Set the number of lines you want in Backscroll Buffer Lines. In the HyperTerminal main window, the current screen is displayed with a white background. If you press Page Up or use the scroll bar to scroll backward, you see previously displayed text with a gray background. The default value for Backscroll Buffer Lines is 500 lines, which allows you to review about 20 screens and doesn't consume a large amount of memory.
5. Turn on Beep Three Times When Connecting or Disconnecting if you want to be notified when you are making or breaking a connection.
6. Optionally, Click ASCII Setup and set the options for how text files are sent and received. Figure 30.10 shows the ASCII Setup dialog box, and Table 30.4 describes what each option does.

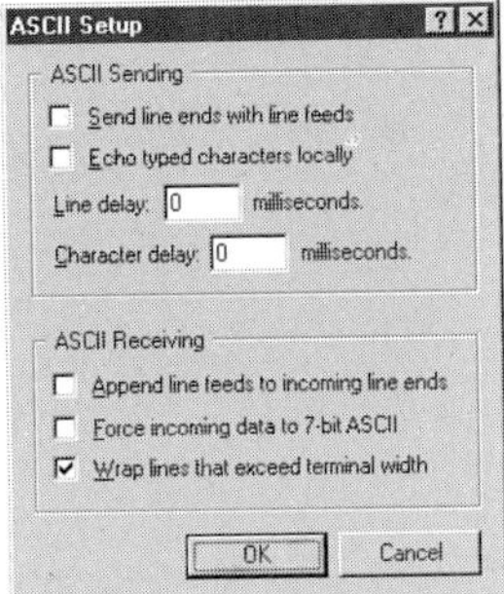

FIG. 30.10
Use the ASCII Setup dialog box to configure how ASCII files will be sent and received. For example, you can choose to send line feeds with line ends.

Table 30.4 ASCII Setup Options

Option	Description
Send Line Ends with Line Feeds	Attaches a line feed to the end of every line that HyperTerminal sends. Turn on this option if the remote computer requires it or you turned on Echo Typed Characters Locally. Pressing Enter moves you to the beginning of the current line instead of starting a new line.
Echo Typed Characters Locally	Displays each character you type on the keyboard instead of depending on the host to echo each character. Turn on this option if you can't see the characters you type. If you see each character twice (ssuucchh aass tthhiiss), turn off this option.
Line Delay	Sets how much time to delay between lines. Increasing the amount of time between lines allows the remote computer time to get ready for the next line. Increase this setting in increments of 100 milliseconds if the remote computer frequently loses portions of each line.
Character Delay	Sets how much time to delay between characters. Increasing the amount of time between characters allows the remote computer time to get ready for the next character. Increase this setting in increments of 5 milliseconds if the remote computer randomly loses characters.
Append Line Feeds to	Incoming Line Ends Attaches a line feed to lines received. Turn on this option if the lines you receive from the host computer are displayed one on top of another.

continues

Table 30.4 Continued

Option	Description
Force Incoming Data to	7-bit ASCII Changes 8-bit characters to 7-bit. Turn on this option if HyperTerminal displays Greek or unrecognizable symbols. This option forces HyperTerminal to stick with readable characters.
Wrap Lines That Exceed	Terminal Width Turns word wrapping on or off. Turn on this option if you want lines that are longer than the terminal width to be continued on the following line.

NOTE If you have selected a particular terminal emulation on the Settings tab, you can further refine the configuration by selecting Terminal Setup. HyperTerminal displays a different dialog box depending on which emulation you have chosen. The following table shows the options available for each emulation mode:

Emulation	Options
ANSI	Cursor: Block, Underline, or Blink
Minitel	Cursor: Block, Underline, or Blink
TTY	Cursor: Block, Underline, or Blink Use Destructive Backspace
Viewdata	Hide Cursor Enter Key Sends #
VT100	Cursor: Block, Underline, or Blink Keypad Application Mode Cursor Keypad Mode 132-Column Mode Character Set
VT52	Cursor: Block, Underline, or Blink Alternate Keypad Mode

Configuring Your Modem for HyperTerminal

You probably configured your modem after you installed Windows. You set options such as the port, speaker volume, and speed. In HyperTerminal, you can override any of these options. For example, if your modem is configured in the Control Panel to connect at 56,000 bps, you can configure your connection to connect at 2,400 bps. However, changing your connection doesn't change your modem's configuration; it is simply overridden by the connection.

Configuring your modem for a particular connection is the same as configuring it in the Control Panel.

See "Installing and Configuring Your Modem," **p. 76**

The first two tabs, General and Connection, are the same as those displayed for configuring the modem in Control Panel.

HyperTerminal automatically detects the configuration of the modem you are calling. Therefore, you don't need to change the data bits, stop bits, or parity settings you might have been familiar with in the past.

The Options tab is added to the HyperTerminal modem properties sheet only when you open it from HyperTerminal. This page enables you to set additional properties for HyperTerminal. To set these options for HyperTerminal, follow these steps:

1. Choose File, Properties from the menu, or click the Properties button on the toolbar. Alternatively, right-click the appropriate connection icon in the HyperTerminal Connections folder and choose Properties.
2. Select the Phone Number tab and choose Configure.
3. Click the Options tab. HyperTerminal displays the page shown in Figure 30.11.

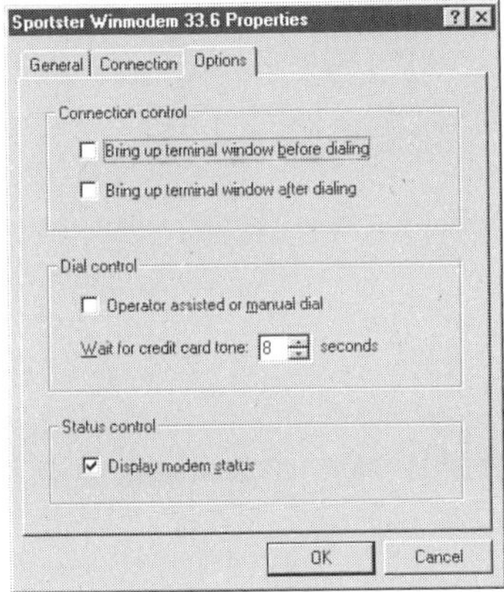

FIG. 30.11 You can refine your modem configuration on the Options page of the Modem properties sheet by choosing to display a terminal window before and after dialing, which gives you more control over how the phone is dialed and the connection is made.

4. Set options as described in Table 30.5 and click OK to save.

Table 30.5 Modem Options

Option	Description
Bring Up Terminal Window Before Dialing	Displays a terminal window (shown in Figure 30.12) before HyperTerminal starts dialing, enabling you to enter modem commands directly. (See your modem's manual for a list of commands.) Bring Up Terminal Window After Dialing Displays a terminal window after HyperTerminal has dialed the phone number, enabling you to enter modem commands directly.

continues

Table 30.5 Continued

Option	Description
Operator Assisted or Manual Dial	Enables you to dial the telephone number directly. HyperTerminal prompts you to dial the telephone number.
Wait for Credit Card Tone	Allows you to specify how many seconds HyperTerminal will wait for the credit- or dialing-card tone.
Display Modem Status	Displays the status of the modem. Turning this option off disables the Modem icon in the taskbar.

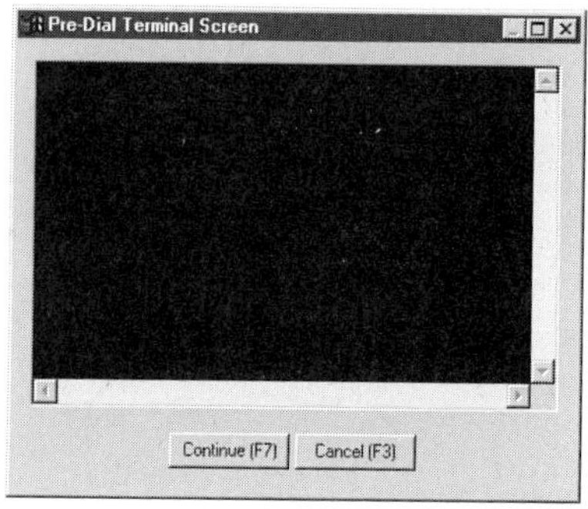

FIG. 30.12 You can use the terminal window to send commands directly to the modem before and after the phone number is dialed.

NOTE HyperTerminal doesn't have a menu option or toolbar button to answer an incoming call. However, you can easily answer an incoming call if you have a Hayes-compatible modem by typing **ATA** and pressing Enter in the HyperTerminal window after the phone rings.

PART VI

Customizing Windows

CHAPTER 31

Customizing the Taskbar and Start Menu

Why should you customize the taskbar?

Here you find ways to resize and move the taskbar as well as ways to modify the taskbar options.

Why you should modify the Start menu

Ways to add and remove programs in the Start menu and clear the documents list are explained.

Why should you customize the Send To menu?

Learn why you should customize the Send To menu, how to add items to the Send To menu, and how to create submenus.

Why you should customize the shortcut menu

You can find out how to register a new file type, edit an existing file type, remove a file type, and more in this section.

The more you use Windows, the more you'll appreciate its customization options. You can save time by setting features so that they normally appear or act in the way that you prefer. You can change the look and feel of almost every component of Windows, from the taskbar, Start menu, and desktop, to the date and time formats, language used, keyboards, mouse settings, and more. Once you have used Windows 95 for a while, you will probably want to modify at least some Windows 95 features to suit your personal taste and needs.

Two features of Windows 95 that you may want to customize right away are the taskbar and Start menu. These are features that you use constantly in Windows, so it makes sense that they look and work the way you want. For example, you can customize your taskbar to appear only when you want it to. That gives your applications more room on-screen. You can also position the taskbar in locations other than at the bottom of the screen. If you frequently use the same applications, you can add them to the Start menu so they are easy to find.

In this chapter, you learn how to do all these things and more. In the following two chapters, you will learn more about customizing the desktop, screen colors, sounds, and many other aspects of Windows.

Customizing the Taskbar

In Chapter 14, "File Management Using the Shell Integration Components," you learned how to use the taskbar to navigate between your open applications. The taskbar is one of the most useful new features in Windows 95; it's a tool you'll use constantly throughout the day. When you first start Windows 95, the taskbar is located at the bottom of the screen and remains visible all the time—even when you maximize an application. In this section, you learn how you can customize the taskbar to give it the look and feel that best suits your needs and preferences.

Resizing the Taskbar

You can change the size of the taskbar to accommodate a large number of buttons or to make it easier to read the full description written on a button. To resize the taskbar, follow these steps:

1. Point to the edge of the taskbar. The pointer becomes a double-pointing arrow.
2. Hold down the left mouse button and drag to the desired size.

The taskbar resizes in full button widths. If the taskbar is horizontal against the top or bottom of the screen, you can change its height. If the taskbar is positioned vertically against a side, you can change its width.

Moving the Taskbar

You can position the taskbar horizontally along the top or bottom (default) of the desktop or vertically along the side of the desktop (see Figure 31.1). To reposition the taskbar, point to a position on the taskbar where no button appears, hold down the left mouse button, and drag to the edge of the screen where you want to position the taskbar. A shaded line indicates the new position. Release the mouse button to place the taskbar.

When the taskbar is positioned at the side of the desktop, it can be so wide that you don't have enough space to work. If so, you can drag the edge of the taskbar to give it a new width. When the taskbar is against a side, you can change its width in pixel increments, not just in full button widths.

Using the Taskbar Menu

As in other Windows screen areas, you can click the right mouse button in a gray area of the taskbar to display a shortcut menu (see Figure 31.2). Use the taskbar menu to rearrange windows on the desktop, to reduce applications to buttons, and to change the properties of the taskbar.

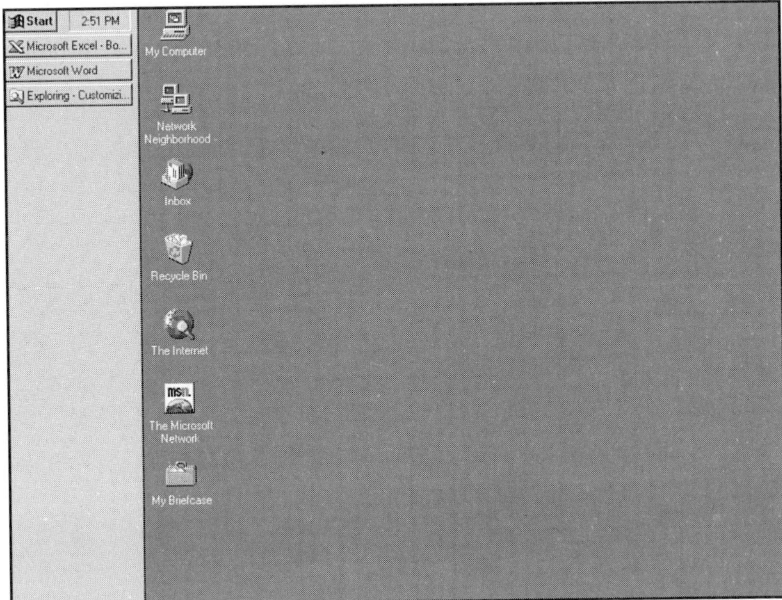

FIG. 31.1
Reposition the taskbar for your convenience.

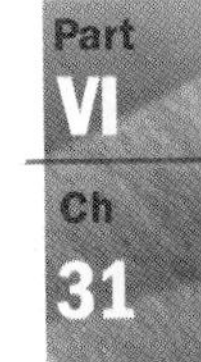

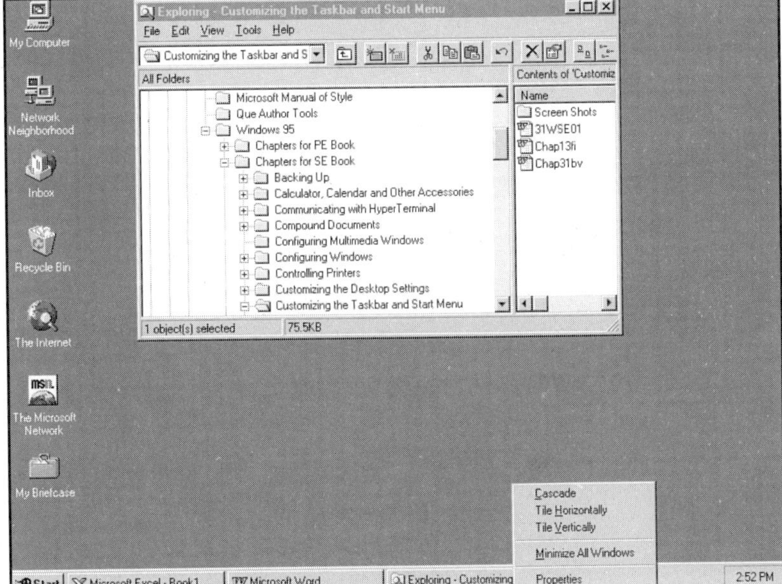

FIG. 31.2
Right-click in the gray area of the taskbar to display the shortcut menu.

The following table describes each of the commands on the taskbar menu.

Command	Description
Cascade	Displays windows one over the other from left to right, top to bottom.
Tile Horizontally	Displays windows top to bottom without overlapping.
Tile Vertically	Displays windows left to right without overlapping.
Minimize All Windows	Reduces all open windows to buttons on the taskbar.
Properties	Displays the Taskbar properties sheet, where you can change the Start menu or taskbar options.

See "Customizing the Start Menu," **p. 847**

Changing the Taskbar Options

You can hide or display the taskbar using the Taskbar properties sheet. Figure 31.3 shows the commands available from the Taskbar Options tab. You also can turn the clock area of the taskbar on and off.

To change taskbar properties, follow these steps:

1. Point to a position the taskbar where no button appears, either below or between buttons, and right-click. Choose Properties.

   or

   Open the Start menu and choose Settings, Taskbar.
2. Click the Taskbar Options tab.
3. Select or deselect a check box to turn an item on or off. The options are explained in Table 31.1.
4. Click OK.

Table 31.1 Options on the Taskbar Options Tab

Option	Description
Always on Top	The taskbar displays over all open windows.
Auto Hide	Hides the taskbar to make more space available on your desktop and in application windows. To see the taskbar, move your mouse pointer to the bottom of the screen (or where the taskbar is if you moved it) and the taskbar reappears. When you move the pointer away, the taskbar disappears again.
Show Small Icons in Start Menu	Displays the Start menu with small icons and without the Windows banner. This enables you to see more of what's on-screen while in the Start menu.
Show Clock	Hides or displays the clock in one corner of the taskbar.

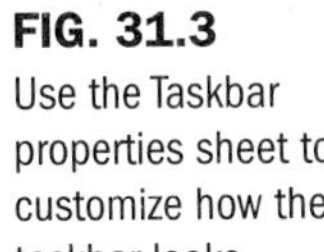

FIG. 31.3
Use the Taskbar properties sheet to customize how the taskbar looks.

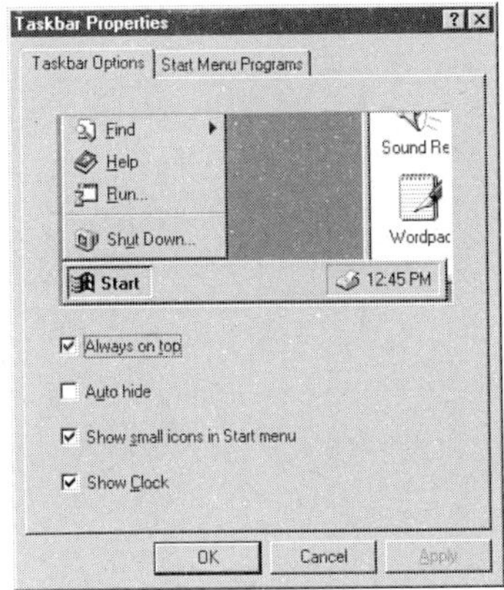

TIP When you select the Auto Hide option, the taskbar is reduced to a gray line at the edge of the screen. When you move the mouse pointer over this line, the taskbar reappears. You can modify the width of this line by right-clicking the desktop and choosing Properties. Select the Appearance tab, and select Active Windows Border from the Item list. Modify the value in the Size text box to the desired width and choose OK. Note that this affects the border width of your application windows as well.

Customizing the Start Menu

You can customize the contents of the Start menu. You can add a list of applications you use frequently and then launch those applications directly from the Start menu. By adding programs to the Start menu, you avoid having to display additional menus.

TIP To quickly add a program to the highest level of the Start menu, drag the program's file from the Explorer or My Computer window and drop it on the Start button.

Adding and Removing Programs in the Start Menu

To add a program to the Start menu, follow these steps.

1. Right-click a gray area between buttons on the taskbar. Choose Properties.

   or

   Open the Start menu and choose Settings, Taskbar.
2. Click the Start Menu Programs tab (see Figure 31.4).
3. Click the Add button to display the Create Shortcut dialog box shown in Figure 31.5.
4. Click the Browse button to display the Browse dialog box. This dialog box looks very similar to an Open File dialog box.
5. Find and click the file for the program or document you want to add to the Start menu. Choose the Open button after you select the file.

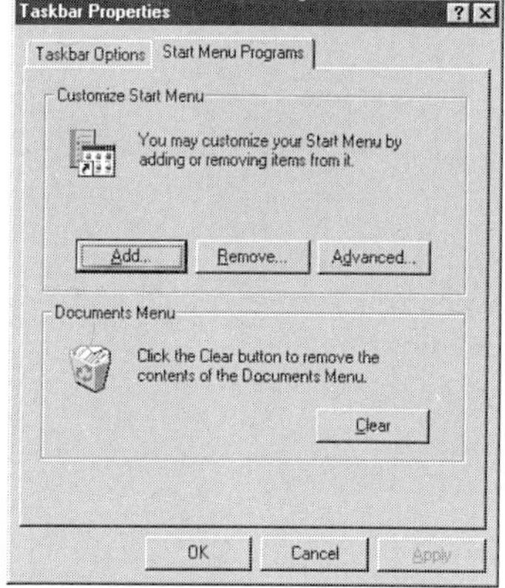

FIG. 31.4
The Start Menu Programs tab enables you to add programs to the Start menu.

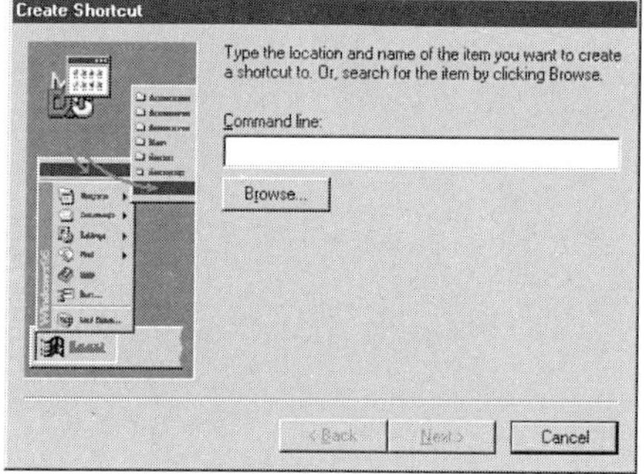

FIG. 31.5
In the Create Shortcut dialog box, type or select the file of the program you want to add to the Start menu.

You can limit the displayed files to program files by selecting Programs from the Files of Type list at the bottom of the dialog box. For example, if you want to start Excel, open the Program Files folder, open the Microsoft Office folder, and finally, open the Office folder. Find and click EXCEL.EXE in the Office folder. Most program files use an EXE extension.

Adding a document's file to the Start menu enables you to open the document in its related application, assuming the document type is registered. See "Customizing the Shortcut (Right-Click) Menu," later in this chapter.

6. Click the Next button to display the Select Program Folder dialog box (see Figure 31.6).
7. Select the folder that corresponds to the location on the Start menu where you want the program to appear. Choose Next.

   For example, if you want the program you selected to appear at the top of the Start menu, select the Start Menu folder. If you want the program to appear as an item on the Programs menu, select the Programs folder.
8. Type the name or words you want to appear on the Start menu in the Select a Name for the Shortcut text box. Choose Finish.

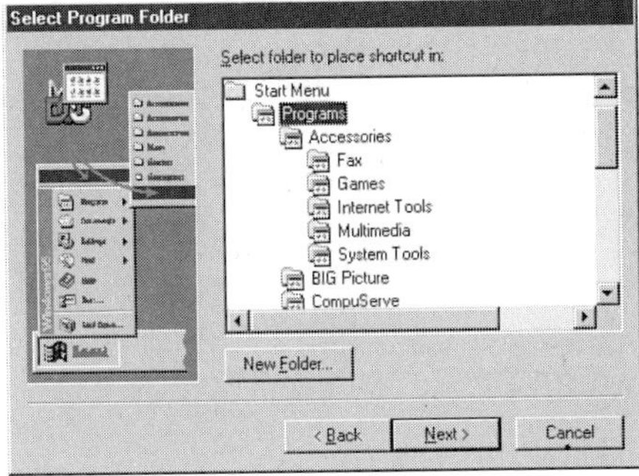

FIG. 31.6
You can position your document or application anywhere on the Start menu.

You can make it easy to launch the applications you added to the top of the Start menu by using the keyboard. Right-click the Start button and choose Open. Rename each application item, adding a number to the beginning of the name. To launch an application from the Start menu, press Ctrl+Esc to open the Start menu, and then type the number for the application you want to start.

To remove a program from the Start menu, you follow a similar process:

1. Display the Taskbar properties sheet as described earlier in this chapter.
2. Click the Start Menu Programs tab.
3. Click the Remove button to display the Remove Shortcuts/Folders dialog box shown in Figure 31.7.

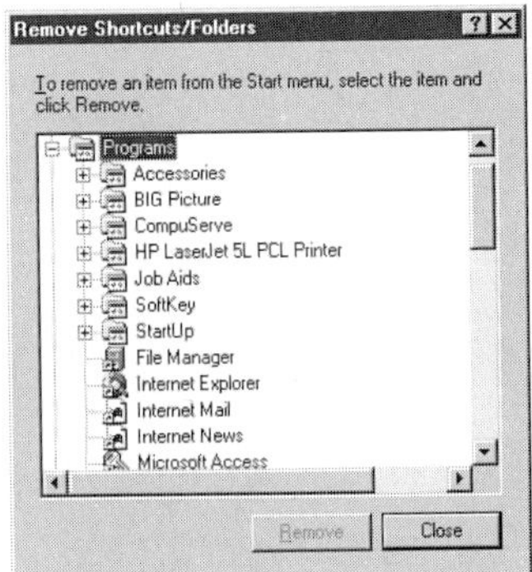

FIG. 31.7
You can easily remove any item from the Start menu using the Remove Shortcuts/Folders dialog box.

4. Select the shortcut or folder you want to remove from the Start menu.
5. Click the Remove button to remove the file or folder.
6. Remove additional items or choose Close. Choose OK when you return to the Taskbar properties sheet.

See "Starting from Shortcuts," **p. 237**

See "Opening a Document from Explorer," **p. 329**

Clearing the Documents List in the Start Menu

The Start menu contains a Documents item that shows a list of recently used documents. At times, this list can become too long, or you might want to clear the list so documents are easier to find. To clear documents from the Documents menu, follow these steps:

1. Display the Taskbar properties sheet.
2. Click the Start Menu Programs tab.
3. Click Clear in the Documents Menu area.
4. Choose OK.

Adding the Control Panel, Dial-Up Network, and Printers Menus to the Start Menu

You can directly access all the items in the Control Panel by adding a special Control Panel folder to the Start Menu folder. To create this folder, follow these steps:

1. Right-click the Start button and choose Open. The Start Menu window appears.
2. Right-click in a blank area of the Start Menu window and choose New, Folder.
3. Name the folder **Control Panel**.

Now, when you click the Start button, you see "Control Panel" at the top of the Start menu. When you select Control Panel, a cascading menu of all the Control Panel items opens.

NOTE It might seem simpler to create a folder named Control Panel in the Start Menu folder, select all the items in the Control Panel window, and then drag and drop them into the new folder to create shortcuts. This works just fine, but the words "Shortcut to" will appear in front of each item. The previous method results in a cleaner-looking menu.

You can create menus on the Start Menu for one other item using this method: printers. For the Printers folder, create a folder in the Start Menu folder with the name "Printers."

Customizing the Send To Menu

The Send To menu is a very useful tool for using the mouse to move, open, print, fax, and perform many other actions with files and folders. The Send To command is instantly available by right-clicking a file or folder in the Explorer, in a folder window, or on the desktop.

Adding Items to the Send To Menu

When you first start Windows 95, there are a few standard items that appear in the Send To menu, such as your floppy disk drive and My Briefcase (if you installed the Briefcase). However, you can add many other items to the Send To folder, including folders, printers, Zip drives, applications, and so on.

To add items to the Send To menu, follow these steps:

1. Open the Send To folder, which is in the Windows folder.
2. Open the folder containing the item you want to add to the Send To menu.
3. Drag and drop the item into the Send To folder using the right mouse button.

   You can also drag items from the desktop into the Send To folder.
4. Click Create Shortcut(s) Here.
5. Edit the file name to remove the words "Shortcut to."
6. Repeat steps 2 through 5 for any other items you want to add to the Send To menu.

Some suggestions for items you can add to the Send To menu are:

- Folders, for moving files to commonly used folders
- External drives, such as a Zip drive
- Printers
- Applications for opening a file (WordPad, for example)

If you have more than one printer, add each one to the Send To menu. That way, you can choose what printer to use to print a file. Or if you set up different configurations for the same printer (such as high and low resolution modes), include both of them in the Send To menu.

Figure 31.8 shows a Send To menu with several items that have been added.

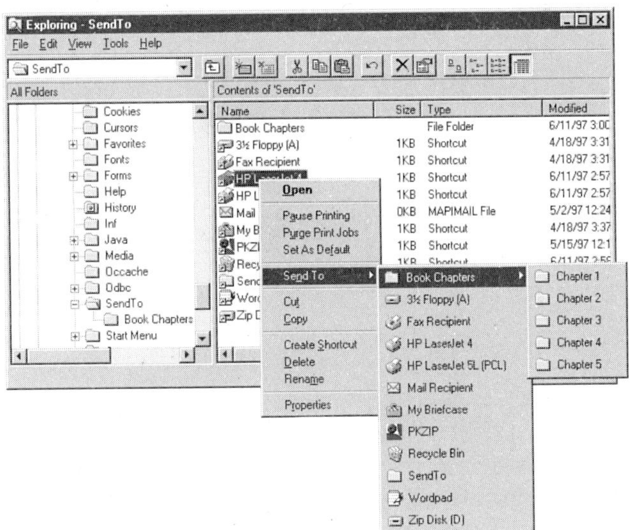

FIG. 31.8
You can add many items to the Send To menu to speed up processing your files.

NOTE When you send a file to a folder on the same disk, the file is moved. If you send the file to a different disk, it is copied. Be careful not to move EXE files using the Send To menu.

Add the Recycle Bin to the Send To menu to quickly delete a file or files. One benefit of using the Send To menu to send files to the Recycle Bin is that you don't have to see the Confirm File Delete message box.

You can even add Send To to the Send To menu. Create a shortcut to the SendTo folder in the SendTo folder. Now, when you want to add an item to the Send To menu, right-click the item and choose Send To, SendTo.

Creating Submenus in the Send To Menu

If you routinely use the Send To menu to move files from folder to folder, you might want to create submenus of folders on the Send To menu. This will keep the main Send To menu from becoming cluttered with a long list of folders. Using this technique, you can categorize your folders, making it easier to find the folder you want to send a file to. For example, you might create a folder named Book Chapters in the Send To folder that contains shortcuts to the folders you create for each chapter.

To create submenus on the Send To menu, follow these steps:

1. Create a new folder in the Send To folder and assign a name indicating what category of folders it will contain.

   Using the previous example, you would name the folder "Book Chapters."

2. Open the new folder and create shortcuts to the destination folders that you want to appear in the submenu.

   In this example, you would create shortcuts for each of the chapter folders.

   You might want to edit the names of the folders to remove the words "Shortcut to."

Now, when you open the Send To menu and select the parent folder (Book Chapters), a submenu will appear with a list of folders from which you can select to move your files (refer to Figure 31.8).

You can use this same procedure to create submenus for other items. If you have several printers, for example, you can create a Printers folder in the Send To folder and create shortcuts to each of the printers inside this folder.

Customizing the Shortcut (Right-Click) Menu

You can add or modify the commands on the shortcut menu that opens when you right-click a file in the Explorer, in a folder window, or on the desktop. You can do this by specifying the application(s) that will act on this type of file. For each application, you can specify different actions the application will take on, such as opening, printing, or running a macro with the file. Applications that have macro languages or startup switches can use those macros or startup switches to control what happens when you start the application using the shortcut menu command.

There are many actions that can occur with a file type. When you double-click a file, the action that has been designated as the default action is executed. Usually, the default action is opening the file, but you can change the default to another action. In this section, you learn how to register a new file type (when the file type is not already registered), and you learn how to customize the actions associated with a file type.

Registering a New File Type

Registering a file type is analogous to associating a file in Windows 3.1, although you now do a lot more than simply tell Windows with what application to open a file. You can associate multiple applications with one file type and specify several actions that can occur with a file type; for example, you can tell Windows to print the document or open a new document of the same type.

To register a new file type, follow these steps:

1. In the Explorer, choose View, Options.
2. Click the File Types tab of the Options dialog box (see Figure 31.9).

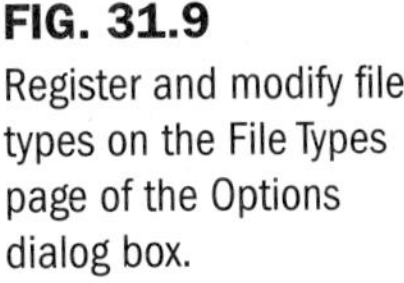

FIG. 31.9
Register and modify file types on the File Types page of the Options dialog box.

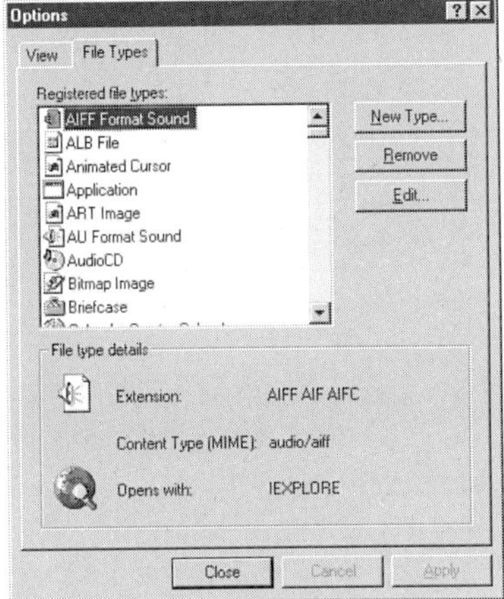

3. Choose the New Type button. The Add New File Type dialog box appears (see Figure 31.10).
4. Enter a description of the file type in the Description of Type text box.

   This description appears in the Registered File Types list on the File Types page of the Options dialog box. For example, if you want to be able to double-click mainframe text files that use commas to separate data and have that file load into Excel, you might use a description similar to Comma Separated Values (CSV).
5. Enter the file extension to be associated with this file type in the Associated Extension text box. This is the three-letter file extension associated with DOS-based files. For example, a comma-separated values file uses the extension CSV.

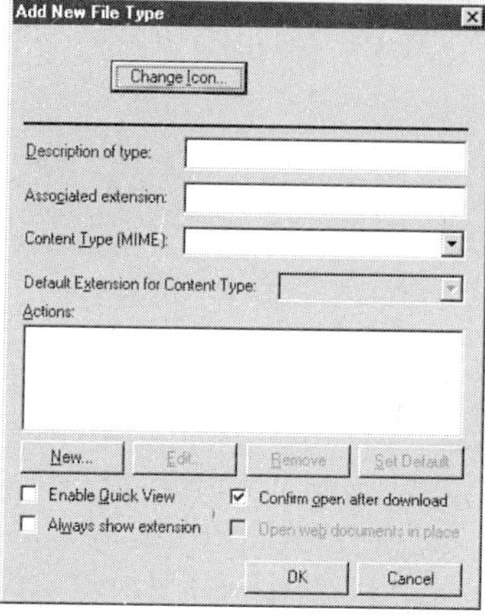

FIG. 31.10
Enter the information for a new file type in the Add New File Type dialog box.

6. Choose New to add a new action to the file type in the New Action dialog box. The action is actually a custom command that appears on the shortcut menu when you right-click the file.
7. Type an action, for example, **Open CSV in Excel**, in the Actions text box. What you type will appear as an item on the shortcut menu for this file type. You can type anything, but commands usually start with a verb. If you want the command to have an accelerator key, precede that letter with an ampersand (&).
8. Select the application to be used to perform the action in the Application Used to Perform Action text box.

   You can enter the path and directory to the EXCEL.EXE file—for example, **"C:\Program Files\Microsoft Office\Office\\EXCEL.EXE."** Include the quotation marks if the file name has spaces in it. You can also choose Browse to find and select the application to use.

   Figure 31.11 shows the completed New Action dialog box.

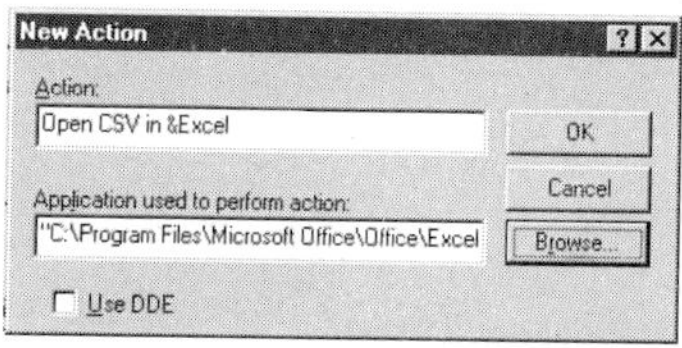

FIG. 31.11
Designate a shortcut menu action and the program used to perform that action in the New Action dialog box.

9. While the New Action dialog box is still displayed, select the Use DDE check box if the program uses DDE (dynamic data exchange).

   If you select the Use DDE check box, the dialog box expands (see Figure 31.12), displaying the DDE statements used to communicate with the DDE application. If you know how to write DDE statements, you can customize the action performed with the associated application.

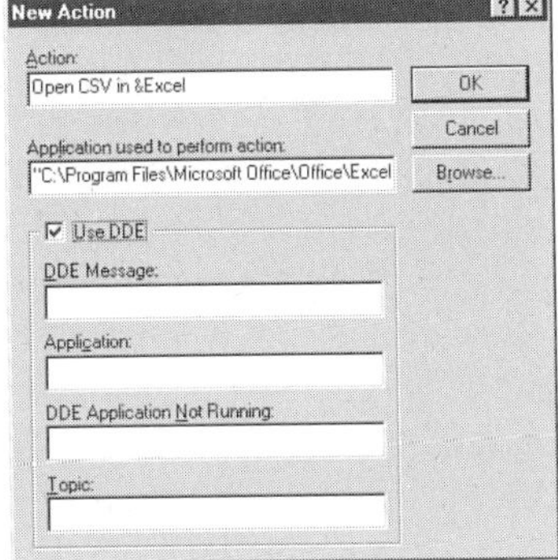

FIG. 31.12
You can enter your own DDE statements to customize the action associated with a registered file type.

10. Click OK.
11. If you have more than one action listed in the Actions box, select the one you want to be the default action, and then choose the Set Default button.

    The default action is the one that is performed when you double-click a file of this type in the Explorer or My Computer.
12. Select the Enable Quick View check box if the file type supports Quick View. Quick View allows you to view a file without opening it.
13. Select Always Show Extension if you want the MS-DOS file extension for this file type to always be displayed in the Explorer and My Computer, even when you have selected the Hide MS-DOS File Extensions option on the View page of the Options dialog box.
14. Choose Close twice.

See "Previewing a Document with QuickView," **p. 325**

Editing an Existing File Type

At times, you might want to change existing file-type options. For example, say you want to change the action that opens BMP files in Paint so they will open in a different image editor. You would edit the BMP open action to include the path and file name for that image editor instead of Paint.

You can also add new commands to the shortcut menu for a registered file type. For example, you might want the option of opening BMP files with either Paint or another image editor. Instead of editing the open action already in place, you would add a new open command associated with the other image editor. You also can change the description, icon, and other aspects.

To edit an existing file type, follow these steps:

1. In the Explorer, choose View, Options.
2. Click the File Types tab to display the File Types page of the Options dialog box (refer to Figure 31.9).
3. Select the file type you want to edit in the Registered File Types list.
4. Click the Edit button.

5. Edit the characteristics for the file type using the same procedures outlined earlier for creating a new file type in the section "Registering a New File Type."

   To edit an action, you must first select that action from the list. Actions for a file type depend on parameters or arguments understood by that file type. Some applications can accept macros names as actions, others accept "switches," and still others accept arguments left over from DOS commands. To learn more about the actions, check the technical reference manual for the application you are starting.

   To add a new action for a file type already registered, click New in the Edit File Type dialog box and follow the procedures outlined earlier for creating a new file type. This is how you customize the shortcut menu for a file type to include new commands for acting on that file type. For example, **Open with CorelDRAW!**.
6. Click OK.
7. Repeat steps 3 through 6 for any other file types you want to edit.
8. Click Close.

You are not limited to one occurrence for a particular action in a shortcut menu. For example, you can have two Open commands in the shortcut menu for a registered file type, each of which uses a different application to open files of that type. The example for opening BMP files with either Paint or CorelDRAW! is such a case. When you name the action in the New Action dialog box, give the command a name that will allow you to distinguish it from the other commands in the menu.

Removing a File Type

If you no longer want a document to start a specific application, you can remove its file type description.

To remove a file type description, follow these steps:

1. In the Explorer, choose View, Options.
2. Click the File Types tab to display the File Types page of the Options dialog box (refer to Figure 31.9).
3. Select the file type you want to remove in the Registered File Types list.
4. Click Remove.
5. Click OK.

Changing the Icon for a File Type or Other Object

You can change the icon used to designate a file type, drive, folder, and other objects on your computer. To change the icon used for a particular file type or object, follow these steps:

1. In the Explorer, choose View, Options.
2. Click the File Types tab to display the File Types page of the Options dialog box (refer to Figure 31.9).

3. Select the file type or other object whose icon you want to change in the Registered File Types list.
4. Choose the Edit button.
5. Click the Change Icon button to display the Change Icon dialog box shown in Figure 31.13.

FIG. 31.13
Use the Change Icon dialog box to select a new icon for a file type or other type of object.

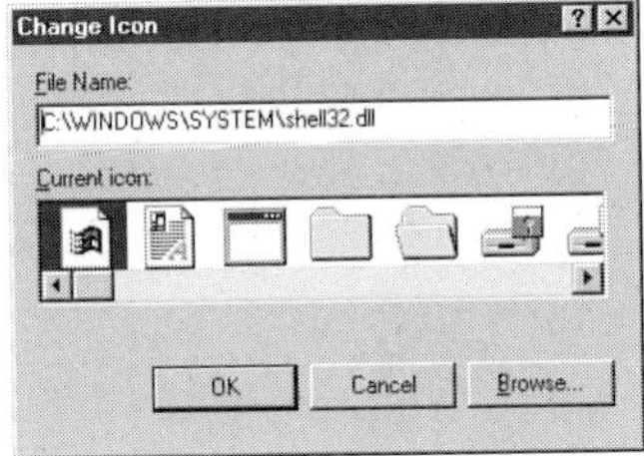

6. Select a new icon from the Current Icon scrolling list.

   The name of the file containing the icons currently shown is listed in the File Name text box. You can use the Browse button to search for a new file containing different icons. All Windows programs come with their own icons, and you can obtain collections of icons from bulletin boards, the Internet, and other sources. Programs are even available that allow you to create your own icons.
7. Click OK three times.

CHAPTER 32

Customizing the Desktop Settings

How to change the colors and patterns on your desktop

Learn how to change the desktop and background colors and color schemes of Windows and to change wallpaper and background patterns.

How to use Microsoft Plus! to add themes and change visual settings

Look here to learn how to use the desktop themes that come with Microsoft Plus! and to change other settings that Plus! enables you to change.

How to use the screen saver

Use the screen saver to liven up your desktop and add privacy to your computer.

How to change the screen resolution, color palette, and font size

Look here to find out how to change the resolution of your screen display and modify the color palette (number of colors displayed) and font size used on-screen.

Many Windows users feel more comfortable with their computers after they customize the Windows screen. Applying a personally selected color, pattern, and background makes the computer seem more like their own. Another way you can customize the screen and even add protection is to enable the screen saver that comes with Windows. In this chapter, you learn about the many ways you can customize your desktop, including using the additional customizing features that come with Microsoft Plus!.

Customizing the Desktop Colors and Background

Changing colors is just one way you can customize the windows you see on-screen. You also can change the pattern used in the desktop background, add a graphical wallpaper as a background, change the border width of windows, and more.

Wallpaper options you select for the desktop background can include graphics that come with Windows—including some wild and colorful ones—and designs you create or modify with Windows Paint. The graphic images you use as wallpaper are nothing more than computer drawings saved in a bitmap (BMP) format. You also can use the Windows Paint program to create your own bitmap drawings to use as screen backgrounds.

You can put wallpaper over just the center portion of the desktop, or you can tile the desktop with wallpaper. When tiling, the wallpaper reproduces itself to fill the screen.

See "Saving Paint Files," **p. 813**

Changing Windows Colors

After working in the drab and dreary DOS or mainframe computer world, one of the first changes many people want to make is to add color to their Windows screens. You can pick colors for window titles, backgrounds, bars—in fact, all parts of the window. Predesigned color schemes range from the brilliant to the cool and dark. You also can design and save your own color schemes and blend your own colors.

Using Existing Color Schemes Windows comes with a list of predefined color schemes. Each color scheme maps a different color and text to a different part of the screen.

You can select from existing schemes, or you can devise your own (described in the next section). To select one of the predefined schemes, follow these steps:

1. Right-click the desktop, choose Properties, and then select the Appearance tab.

   or

   Open the Start menu and choose Settings, Control Panel; then click the Display icon and select the Appearance tab.

   The Appearance tab of the Display Properties dialog box appears, as shown in Figure 32.1.
2. Select the Scheme list; then select a predefined color and text scheme from the list. The sample screen at the top of the dialog box illustrates what this color scheme looks like.
3. Choose OK to use the displayed color scheme, or return to step 2 for other predefined schemes.

Creating Custom Color and Text Schemes You can change all or some of the colors in a scheme, change the color of the text, and even change the color and width of borders. To create new color schemes while the Appearance tab is open, follow these steps:

1. If you want to use an existing scheme as a base (as opposed to using Windows Standard as a base), select the scheme from the Scheme list.

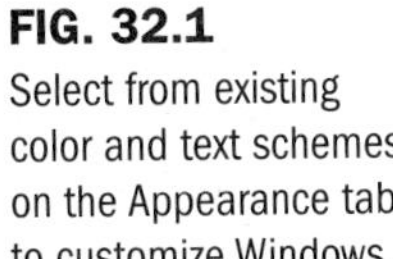

FIG. 32.1
Select from existing color and text schemes on the Appearance tab to customize Windows appearance.

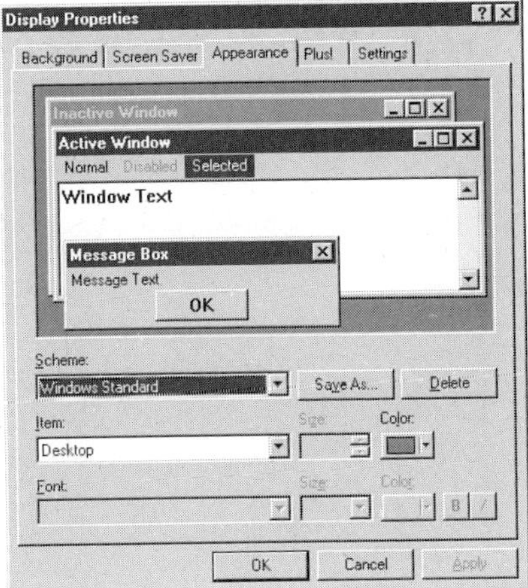

2. Select from the Item list the screen element you want to modify. Or click a screen element in the sample window at the top of the dialog box. You can select elements such as the Menu Bar, Button, Active Border, and so on.
3. Select from the Size, Font, and Color lists how you want to change the selected element. Some options are available only for certain elements.
4. Choose one of these alternatives for the colors you have selected:
   - If you want to color another window element, return to step 2.
   - If you want to use these colors now but not save them for the next time you run Windows, choose OK or press Enter.
   - If you want to save these colors so you can use them now or return to them at any time, choose the Save As button. Then type a name in the Save Scheme text box and choose OK.
   - If you want to cancel these colors and return to the original scheme, select that scheme from the Scheme list if it was saved, or choose Cancel.

To remove a scheme from the list, select the scheme you want to remove from the Scheme list and click Delete.

Wallpapering Your Desktop with a Graphic

Using a graphic or picture as the Windows desktop is a nice personal touch. For special business situations or custom applications, you might want to use a color company logo or pictorial theme as the wallpaper.

Windows comes with a collection of graphics for the desktop. You can modify these images or draw new images for the desktop with the Windows Paint program. For high-quality pictorials, use a scanner to create a digitized black-and-white or color image.

Figure 32.2 shows one of the many wallpaper patterns that come with Windows. Figure 32.3 shows a logo used as a backdrop. Many companies scan and then enhance their corporate logo as a BMP file, and then they use it as the desktop background. Most of the patterns must be tiled to fill the entire screen, which you learn how to do in the following steps.

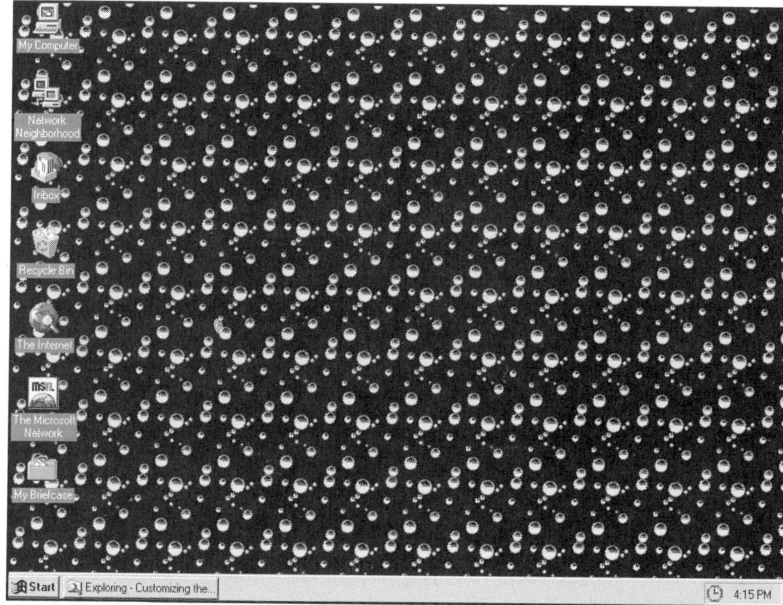

FIG. 32.2 This is Bubbles, one of the many Windows images you can use to wallpaper your desktop.

FIG. 32.3 Edit existing wallpaper files or create your own with Paint.

To select wallpaper, follow these steps:

1. Right-click the desktop, choose Properties, and then select the Background tab.

   or

   Open the Start menu and choose Settings, Control Panel; then click the Display icon and select the Background tab.

   The Background tab of the Display Properties dialog box appears (see Figure 32.4).

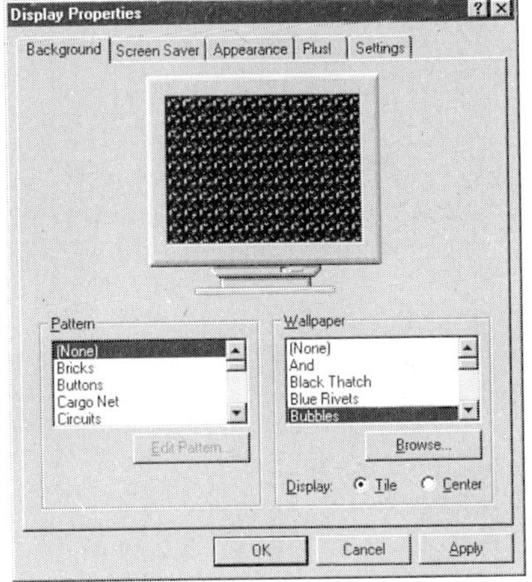

FIG. 32.4 Use the Background tab in Display Properties to select new wallpapers and patterns.

2. Choose a wallpaper from the Wallpaper list box. If the graphic file (with a BMP extension) is located in a folder other than Windows, choose the Browse button to find and select the graphic file.
3. If the graphic is large enough to fill the screen, select Display Center to center the wallpaper in the desktop. If the graphic is small and must be repeated to fill the screen, select Display Tile.
4. Choose OK if you are finished or make other display property changes.

When you choose a wallpaper from the Wallpaper list box, you see a miniature rendition of it in the display shown in the upper part of the Display Properties dialog box. This allows you to preview wallpapers before selecting the one to use. Remember, however, bitmap images displayed as desktop wallpaper use more memory than a colored or patterned desktop.

Wallpaper is created from files stored in a bitmap format. These files end with the BMP extension and must be stored in the Windows folder. You can edit BMP formats with the Windows Paint program. You also can read and edit files with PCX format in Paint and save them in BMP format to use as a desktop wallpaper.

You can create your own desktop wallpapers in one of three ways:

- Buy clip art from a software vendor. If the clip art is not in PCX or BMP format, use a graphics-conversion application to convert the image to one of these formats. Use

Windows Paint to read PCX format and resave the figure in BMP format. Computer bulletin boards, online services, and the Internet have thousands of BMP graphics files.

ON THE WEB

Check out **Anonymous FTP: bongo.cc.utexas.edu** through the path: /gifstuff/ftpsites.

You might also look at **Anonymous FTP: ftp.cica.indiana.edu** through the path: /pub/pc/win3/* for bitmaps for Windows.

- Scan a black-and-white or color picture using a digital scanner. Save the scanned file in BMP format or convert it to BMP format.
- Modify an existing desktop wallpaper, or create a new one with Windows Paint or a higher-end graphics program. Save the files with the BMP format.

Store your new BMP (bitmap) graphics files in the Windows folder so they will appear in the Wallpaper Files list box in the Display Properties dialog box.

To remove a wallpaper file from the Wallpaper Files drop-down list, delete or remove its BMP file from the Windows folder. To remove the wallpaper from the desktop, repeat the preceding steps but select (None) as the type of wallpaper.

Changing the Background Pattern

Wallpapers, while pretty and often amusing, can consume a lot of memory. If you want a simpler background or want to conserve memory, you can use a background pattern. The pattern is a small grid of dots that repeats to fill the screen. In Figure 32.5, the example area shows how one background pattern appears. Windows comes with predefined patterns you can select; you also can create your own. The color of the pattern is the same as the color selected for Window Text in the Color dialog box.

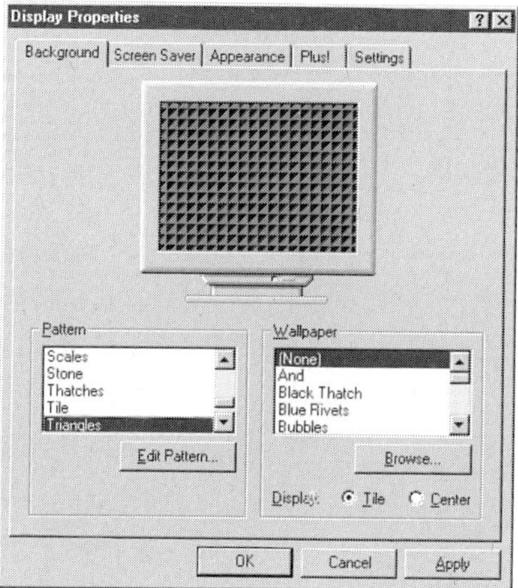

FIG. 32.5
Background patterns are simpler and conserve memory.

To select a pattern, follow these steps:

1. Right-click the desktop, choose Properties, and then select the Background tab.

   or

   Open the Start menu and choose Settings, Control Panel; then click the Display icon and select the Background tab. The Background tab of the Display Properties dialog box appears.
2. Select a pattern from the Pattern list. Some of the built-in repetitive patterns you can select are 50% Gray, Boxes, Diamonds, Weave, and Scottie.
3. Choose OK to add the pattern to the desktop. Alternatively, use the following procedure to edit the pattern just selected.

You can edit or create new patterns only if you have a mouse. To edit an existing pattern or create a new pattern while the Background tab is displayed, follow these steps:

1. Select a pattern from the Pattern list.
2. Click the Edit Pattern button to display the Pattern Editor dialog box, shown in Figure 32.6.

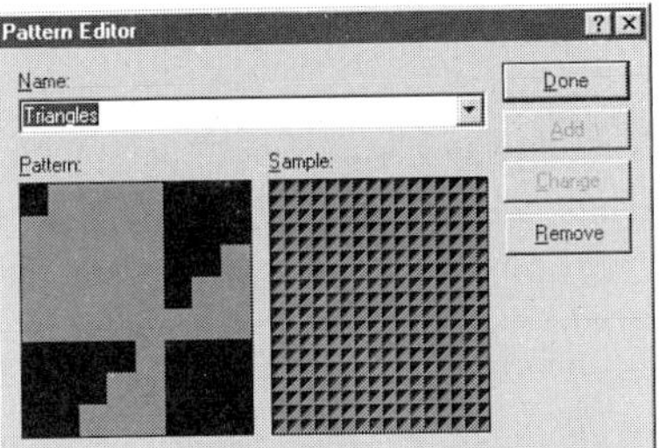

FIG. 32.6 Editing your pattern by using an existing pattern as a base can be easier than working from the (None) pattern.

3. Click in the editing grid in the location where you want to reverse a dot in the pattern. Watch the Sample area to see the overall effect.
4. Continue to click in the grid until the pattern is what you want.
5. When you finish creating or editing, continue with one of the following options:
   - If you want to change an existing pattern, click Change.
   - If you want to add a new pattern, type a new name in the Name list box and choose the Add button.
6. When you finish editing, click Done. Choose OK in the Display Properties dialog box.

To remove an unwanted pattern from the list, select the pattern and click Remove. Confirm the deletion by choosing Yes. The Remove button is available only after you select a new pattern name.

Working with Desktop Themes

The Microsoft Plus! Desktop Themes provide you with appealing graphics and sounds to decorate your desktop and highlight system events (see Figure 32.7). Each Desktop Theme offers a coordinated set of elements, so you can set the appropriate mood for your computing experience. Plus! provides Desktop Theme combinations for computers displaying 256 colors and for computers displaying 16-bit or higher color. If you did not install the high-color Desktop Themes, you can rerun the Plus! Setup at any time to do so. The following are the Desktop Themes provided with Plus!:

256 Color:

Dangerous Creatures

Leonardo da Vinci

Science

The 60's USA

Sports

Windows 95

High Color:

Inside Your Computer

Nature

The Golden Era

Mystery

Travel

When you choose a Desktop Theme, you can specify whether to replace Windows screen elements you specify using the Control Panel. Desktop Themes provides these desktop elements; you can choose which of these you want to use for your system:

- *Screen Saver.* Displays the Theme screen saver when you leave your computer idle.
- *Sound Events.* Assigns the Theme sounds to system events such as Windows startup and exit.
- *Mouse Pointer.* Applies the Theme pointer styles for different types of pointers, such as the pointer used to select text or the one that appears while Windows is busy performing an operation.

NOTE If you need a high degree of accuracy when pointing with the mouse, the Mouse Pointer option for several Themes might make your pointing more difficult because of the pointer shapes assigned by the Theme. If you have trouble with this, clear the Mouse Pointer option for the current Theme.

- *Desktop Wallpaper.* Covers the desktop with the decorative background provided by the Theme.

FIG. 32.7 Make every workday a safari by choosing the Dangerous Creatures Desktop Theme.

- *Icons.* Assigns custom Theme icons to desktop objects such as the My Computer object and Recycle Bin.
- *Icon Size and Spacing.* Makes desktop icons use the icon size and spacing specified by the Theme; remember that larger icons use more computer memory, so if your system is low on memory, don't use this option.
- *Colors.* Applies the Theme colors to windows and other screen elements.
- *Font Names and Styles.* Uses the Theme fonts for screen elements such as window titles.
- *Font and Window Sizes.* Uses the Theme font sizes and default window sizes.

As mentioned earlier, the Theme replaces the desktop elements you specify using the Control Panel. You should note, however, that the most recent element you select using either method (Desktop Themes or the Control Panel) becomes active. For example, if you apply a Desktop Theme but aren't quite satisfied with the screen saver, you can use the Control Panel to choose another screen saver to use.

Selecting and Setting Up a Theme

Plus! Setup! creates an object icon for the Desktop Themes in the Windows 95 Control Panel, which contains other objects for controlling Windows' appearance and operation. Use the following steps to use the Desktop Themes object to select a Theme:

1. Open the Start menu and choose Settings, Control Panel.
2. In the Control Panel window, double-click the Desktop Themes icon (see Figure 32.8). The Desktop Themes dialog box appears, as shown in Figure 32.9. Use this dialog box to select and set up a Theme.

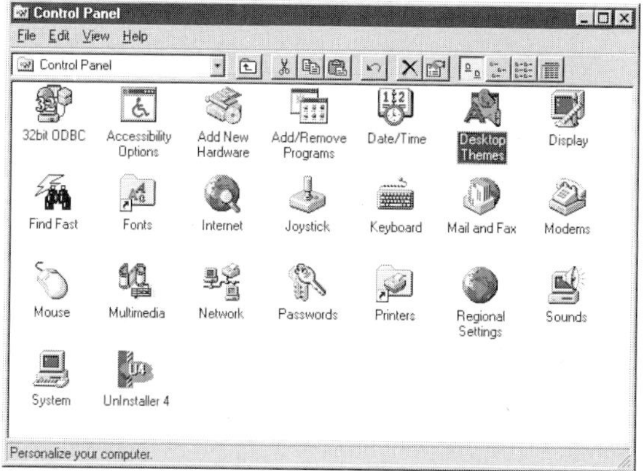

FIG. 32.8
Select a Desktop Theme using the Control Panel.

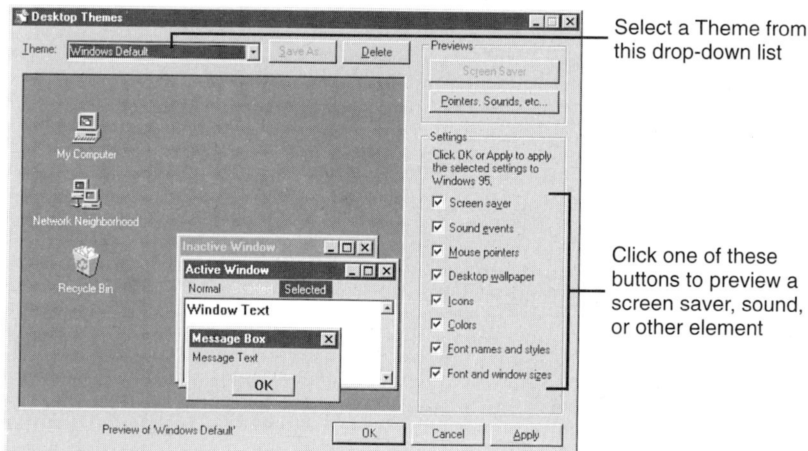

FIG. 32.9
Plus! provides numerous options for setting up the Desktop Theme of your choice.

3. Click the down arrow beside the Theme drop-down list to display the available Desktop Themes. Click the name of the Theme you want to use. A dialog box tells you that the Theme files are being imported. When that dialog box closes, the preview area of the Desktop Themes changes to display the appearance of the Theme you selected, as shown in Figure 32.10.
4. On the right side of the dialog box, choose the Settings to use for the Theme you selected.
5. (Optional) To preview the selected Theme's screen saver, click Screen Saver in the Previews area. The screen saver appears on-screen. Move the mouse or press a key to conclude the preview.

FIG. 32.10
After you select a Desktop Theme, you see a preview of your Windows desktop.

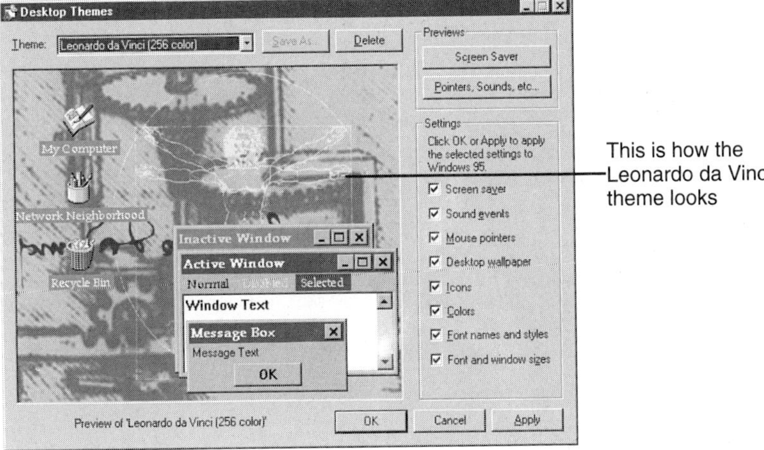

6. (Optional) To preview several of the selected Theme's other elements, click Pointers, Sounds, etc... in the Previews area. A Preview dialog box for the Theme appears; the dialog box has three tabs for Pointers, Sounds, and Visuals. Click the tab you want to view. Each tab offers a list box with the elements for the Theme. For the Pointers and Visuals tabs, simply click an element in the list to see a preview in the Preview or Picture area. For the Sounds tab, click an element in the list; then click the right arrow icon near the bottom of the dialog box to hear the sound. Click Close to conclude your preview.
7. After you select a Theme, choose settings, and preview elements to your satisfaction, choose OK to close the Desktop Themes window. The selected Desktop Theme appears on your system.

Saving a Custom Theme

Any Control Panel changes you make after selecting a Theme take precedence over the Theme settings. In fact, you can make desktop setting changes in Control Panel and save those settings as a custom Theme. To do so, follow these steps:

1. Use Control Panel to change any settings you want, including the wallpaper, screen colors, sounds, and so on.
2. If the Control Panel window isn't open, open the Start menu and choose Settings, Control Panel.
3. In the Control Panel window, double-click the Desktop Themes icon.

TIP To permanently delete a Desktop Theme, select it in the Theme drop-down list; then click Delete. Click Yes in the dialog box that appears to confirm the deletion.

4. Open the Themes drop-down list and choose Current Window settings. The Save As button becomes active.
5. Click the Save As button. The Save Theme dialog box appears.

6. (Optional) Choose another folder in which to save the Theme.
7. Enter a unique name for the Theme in the File Name text box.
8. Click Save to save the Theme and return to the Desktop Themes dialog box. The newly saved Theme appears as the Theme selection.
9. Click OK to accept your new Theme and apply it to Windows 95.

Adjusting Plus! Visual Settings

Plus! adds new features to the display settings available in the Windows 95 Control Panel. These visual settings are designed primarily to make your desktop more attractive. Plus! enables you to specify new icons for My Computer, the Network Neighborhood, and the Recycle Bin desktop icons. You can choose to show the contents of a window (rather than just an outline when you drag the window). Choose whether you want to smooth the appearance of large fonts on-screen. You also can choose to show icons with all possible colors or expand the wallpaper (when centered using the Background tab of the Display Properties dialog box from Control Panel) so it stretches to fill the entire screen.

NOTE Most of the Plus! visual settings require more system resources than the normal display settings. In particular, showing window contents while dragging and using all colors in icons consumes more RAM. Consider all your computing requirements before you use up RAM by selecting any of these features.

To work with the Plus! visual settings, open the Start menu and choose Settings, Control Panel. In the Control Panel window, double-click the Display icon. The Display Properties sheet appears. Click the Plus! tab to display its options, as shown in Figure 32.11. To assign a new Desktop icon, click the icon you want to change in the Desktop Icons area. Click Change Icon. In the Change Icon dialog box that appears, scroll to display the icon you want; then click OK to accept the change.

To enable any of the other Plus! display features, select the feature in the Visual settings area of the Plus! page. If you want more information about a particular feature, right-click the feature, and then click What's This?. A brief description of the feature appears. Click or press Esc to clear the description. To accept your visual settings and close the Display properties sheet, click OK. Close the Control Panel window, if you want.

Changing Icon Size and Spacing

You can change the size of the icons and the spacing around icons on the desktop by using the Appearance tab of the Display properties sheet. Click the Item drop-down list. Choose Icon Spacing (Horizontal) to change the text area available for the text below the icons on your desktop. You can enter a number in the Size box from 0 to 150. Using 0 creates a narrow space for the text, so **Recycle Bin** changes to **Re** on one line and **Bin** on one line. Using 150 enables you to use longer names for your icons; 43 is the default. Choose Icon Spacing (Vertical) to adjust the space above and below an icon from 0 to 150, with 43 being the default.

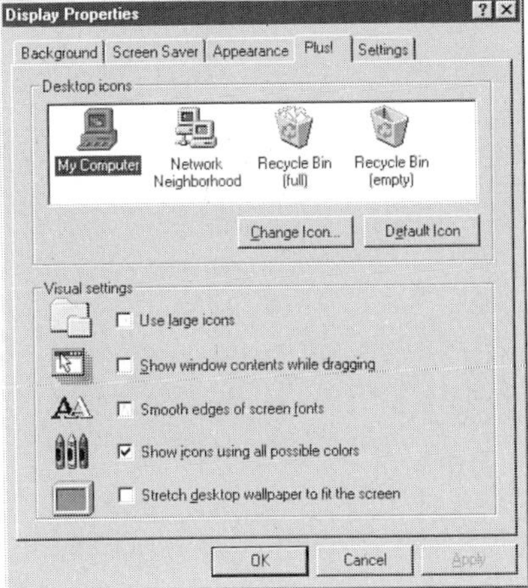

FIG. 32.11
Plus! enables you to make additional adjustments to the Windows Display Properties.

Changing the Name of Desktop Icons

You can change the name of any Desktop icon by clicking the name to select it and then clicking the name again to reveal the Rename text box. Enter the new name and press Enter. Name changes remain in effect until you change them again.

Having Fun with the Screen Saver

Screen savers display a changing pattern on-screen when you haven't typed or moved the mouse for a predetermined amount of time. You can specify the delay before the screen saver activates, and you can set up various attributes—including a password—for most of the screen savers.

To select and set up a screen saver, follow these steps:

1. Right-click the desktop and choose Properties; then select the Screen Saver tab.

   or

   Open the Start menu and choose Settings, Control Panel; then click the Display icon and select the Screen Saver tab.

   The Screen Saver tab of the Display Properties dialog box appears (see Figure 32.12).
2. Select a screen saver from the Screen Saver list.
3. The miniature display shows you a preview of the screen saver. To see a full screen view, click Preview. Click anywhere on-screen to return to the dialog box from the preview.
4. To customize the appearance and properties of your screen saver, click Settings. The options and settings for each screen saver are different. Figure 32.13 shows the options for customizing the Flying Windows screen saver.

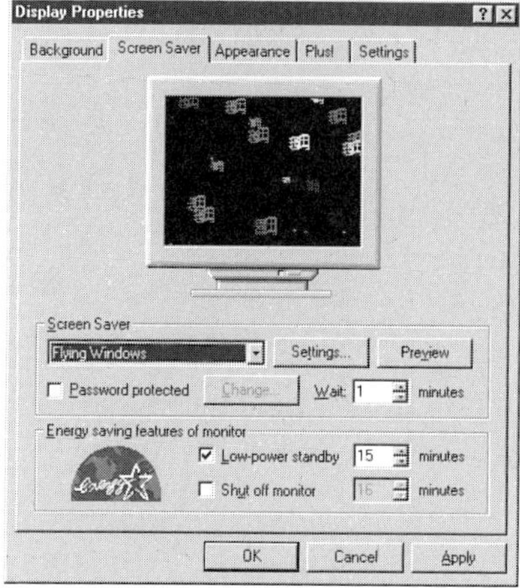

FIG. 32.12 Customizing your screen saver can display information, attract attention, or warn people away from your computer.

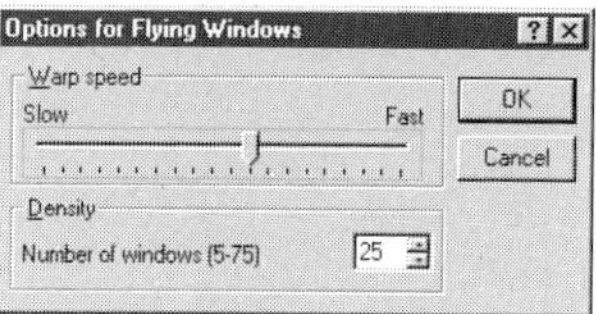

FIG. 32.13 You can customize screen savers so they act differently.

5. In the Wait text box, type or select the number of minutes you want the screen to be idle before the screen saver appears. A range from 5 to 15 minutes is usually a good time.
6. Choose Apply to apply the Display Property changes you have selected so far. You will see the changes take effect, but the Display Properties dialog box stays open. Choose OK to accept the changes and close the dialog box.

Protecting Your Computer with a Screen Saver Password

Although each screen saver has unique settings, all except Blank Screen have an area where you can specify password protection. If you don't want uninvited users to use your computer, you can specify a password that is associated with a screen saver, so only those who know the password can clear the screen saver and use your computer.

To protect your computer by using a password, follow these steps:

1. Right-click anywhere on the desktop; then choose Properties to open the Display properties sheet.
2. Click the Screen Saver tab.
3. Select a screen saver from the Screen Saver drop-down list and set its options.
4. Select the Password Protected check box and choose Change.
5. Type your password in the New Password text box, and confirm your password by typing it again in the Confirm New Password text box.

Asterisks will appear in the text boxes as you type your password to prevent others from seeing it (see Figure 32.14).

FIG. 32.14
Enter a password for the screen saver in the Change Password dialog box.

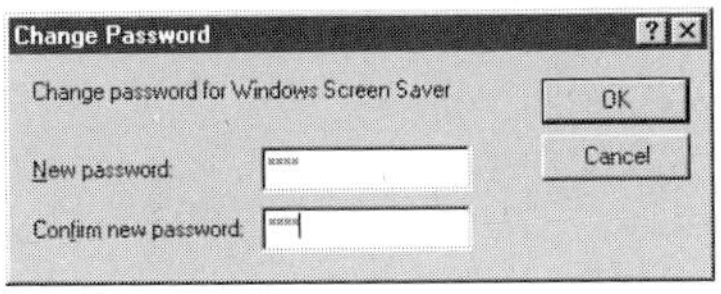

6. Choose OK. When the confirmation message appears, choose OK again.

Now, when the screen saver appears and you press a key on the keyboard or move the mouse, a dialog box appears in which you have to type your password to clear the screen saver.

Using Your Display's Energy-Saving Feature

If you leave your computer on continuously, or if you leave your desk for long periods of time while your computer continues to run, you will want to conserve energy by using the energy-saving features that are built in to many newer monitors. Although the energy used by one monitor might seem small when multiplied by the millions of computers in use across the nation, it is easy to see that selecting this option one time can save a lot of energy and reduce pollution. When you consider the cost of running the tens of thousands of monitors in a single large corporation, the dollar savings can be significant.

Monitors that satisfy EPA requirements usually display an "Energy Star" sticker on the monitor or in the manual. Older monitors do not have the energy-saving feature.

If you have a monitor that is an Energy Star but the Energy Saving Features of Monitor options are not available in the Screen Saver tab, you should install the correct display drivers for your monitor. To check which display driver is installed, open the Display Properties sheet, choose the Settings tab, and then choose the Change Display Type button. From the dialog box that appears, you can install the display driver for your manufacturer and model. After you have the correct driver, select the Monitor Is Energy Star Compliant check box. (Selecting this check box does no good if the monitor is not compliant.)

To set Windows so it takes advantage of the energy-saving features of Energy Star-compliant monitors, follow these steps:

1. Right-click the desktop and choose Properties.
2. Choose the Screen Saver tab (refer to Figure 32.12).
3. Select the Low-Power Standby check box, and select the number of minutes the computer should be idle before the monitor goes into low-power standby. This mode reduces power requirements but keeps the monitor ready to be instantly used.
4. Select the Shut Off Monitor check box, and select the number of minutes the computer should be idle before the monitor shuts down. This mode completely turns off your monitor.
5. Choose OK.

When you return to your workstation, you can press any key or move the mouse to return to normal monitor use from low-power standby. The Shut Off Monitor mode shuts off the monitor rather than putting it in Standby mode. This saves the most energy. The manual for your monitor will describe the best way to turn the monitor on again.

See "Understanding the Device Manager," **p. 191**

See "Using Power Management," **p. 205**

Changing the Screen Resolution, Font Size, and Color Palette

With Windows, you have the ability to change how your application displays, even while you work. This can help if you run applications that operate with different screen resolutions, or if you use programs that look better in different font sizes. Some applications, such as graphics programs or multimedia, work better when they use 256 colors and higher resolution.

The resolution is the number of dots shown on-screen. The more dots on-screen, the more detail you can work with. However, with a high-resolution screen, icons or fonts that appear an adequate size on a VGA screen can now appear small.

Changing the resolution while Windows is running enables you to switch between VGA mode (640 × 480 pixels on-screen) and the more detailed and wider view of SVGA mode (800 × 600 pixels). This can come in handy when you work on different types of tasks. You might, for example, have a laptop computer that displays on its LCD screen in VGA mode. When you work at your desk and have a high-resolution monitor connected to the laptop, you want to work in SVGA mode.

Changing the Screen Resolution

You can change the screen resolution, the number of dots on the screen, if your display is capable of running Super VGA 800 × 600 resolution or better and Super VGA or better is currently set as the monitor type.

You can change the resolution by following these steps:

1. Open the Display properties sheet and click the Settings tab.
2. In the Desktop Area box, drag the slider to the desired resolution.
3. Click OK.
4. When the dialog box appears, informing you that Windows will adjust the resolution, click OK.
5. Click Yes when the message box appears, asking if you want to keep the settings.

If you don't have the correct monitor type selected, you may not be able to change your screen resolution. To find out what monitor type you have selected or to change the monitor type, follow these steps:

1. Open the Display properties sheet and click the Settings tab.

2. Choose the Change Display Type button to display the Change Display Type dialog box.
3. Choose the Change button next to the Monitor Type area.
4. Select the manufacturer for your monitor in the Manufacturers list box and the model for your monitor in the Models list box.

   If you are unsure, choose Standard Monitor Types from the Manufacturers list box and choose a monitor from the Models list box.
5. Choose OK; then choose Close.
6. When you return to the Display properties sheet, you can change other display properties. Choose OK.

When you exit the Display Properties sheet, you might need to restart Windows to implement the new monitor type. You will be asked whether you want to restart at that time.

If you have the OSR2 version of Windows 95 installed, the steps for changing the monitor type are slightly different:

1. Open the Display properties sheet and click the Settings tab.
2. Click Advanced Properties.
3. Click Change.
4. Select Show All Devices in the Select Device dialog box.
5. Select the manufacturer and model for your monitor in the Manufacturers and Models lists.
6. Choose OK and then Close.
7. When you return to the Display Properties sheet, you can change other display properties. Choose OK.

Part VI Ch 32

NOTE Depending on the video card that you have installed in your system, you may find additional tabs in the Display Properties sheet or additional features on the Settings tab. See the documentation that comes with your video card to find out more about the custom features that come with your card.

CAUTION

Changing to an incorrect monitor type that cannot be implemented might cause your screen to be unreadable. If that happens, shut off your computer. Restart your computer and watch the screen carefully. When the phrase "Starting Windows 95" appears, press F8. This displays a text menu that enables you to start Windows in *safe mode.* Safe mode displays Windows on any screen, but many resources will not be available, such as networking and CD-ROM. While in safe mode, repeat the steps described in this section and select either a monitor type you are sure of or a resolution that will work from the Standard Monitor Types list.

After your monitor is in Super VGA mode or better, you can change between screen resolutions by dragging the slider in the Desktop Area section of the Settings tab.

Changing the Number of Colors Available to Your Monitor

Depending on your display adapter and the monitor, you can have the same resolution screen, but with a different palette of colors available. For example, you might have some business applications that use only 16 colors, while most games and multimedia use 256 or more colors.

To change the size of your color palette, click the Color Palette down arrow in the Settings tab. Then click the number of colors you need.

Changing Font Sizes

Need glasses to read the screen? You can enlarge (or reduce) the size of the font Windows uses on-screen. All text on-screen will change size. You have to restart Windows, however, to see the change.

You can select from any of the following font size options:

- Small Fonts scales fonts to 100 percent of normal size.
- Large Fonts scales fonts to 125 percent of normal size.
- Custom displays the Custom Font Size dialog box where you can specify your own size.

To change the size of screen fonts, follow these steps:

1. Right-click the desktop and choose Properties. The Display properties sheet appears.
2. Click the Settings tab. Figure 32.15 shows the Properties sheet.

   The Settings tab has changed in the OSR2 version of Windows 95, as shown in Figure 32.16.

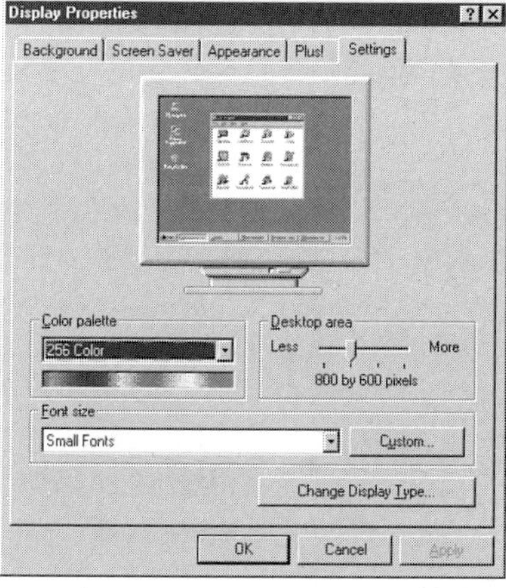

FIG. 32.15
Change your display's appearance in the Settings tab.

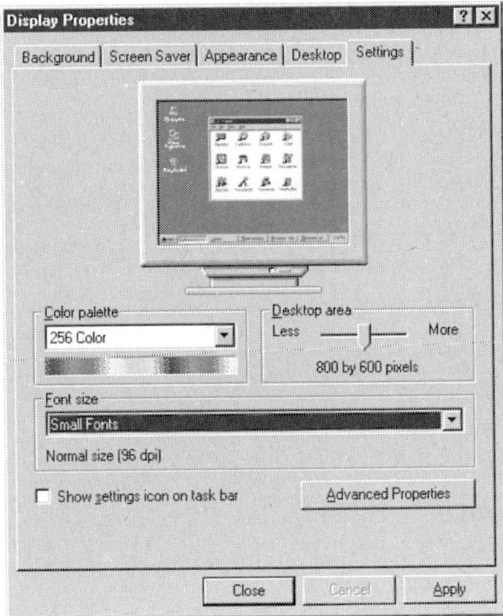

FIG. 32.16
The Settings tab has changed in the OSR2 version of Windows 95.

3. Choose Large Fonts or Small Fonts from the Font Size list box.

   or

   Click Custom to display the Custom Font Size dialog box (see Figure 32.17). Type or select a percentage of normal size in the Scale text box, or drag across the ruler and then release the mouse button to resize. Notice the sample font and its size below the ruler. Choose OK.

   In the OSR2 version of Windows 95, there is no longer a Custom button (refer to Figure 32.16). Select Other from the Font size list to open the Custom Font Size dialog box.

4. Click OK to accept the change and close the Display properties sheet.

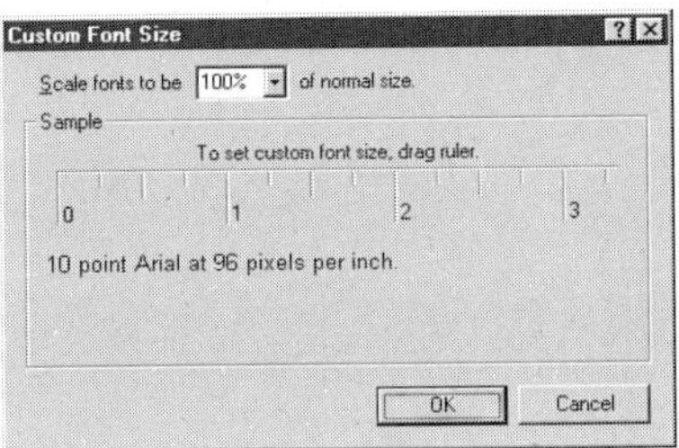

FIG. 32.17
You can create your own custom font size.

CHAPTER 33

Customizing Your System Settings

by Ron Person and Robert Voss

In the previous two chapters, you learned how to customize many elements of the Windows 95 screen to change how Windows looks and operates. In this chapter, you learn how to customize additional settings that affect the way Windows works for you. These settings include customizing the mouse and keyboard settings, enhancing the accessibility of Windows for hearing-, sight-, and movement-impaired individuals, changing the date, time, and language settings, and several other system-related settings. ■

Customizing sounds

Learn how to change the sounds associated with Windows events, such as when you close a window or make an error.

Customizing the mouse

Look here to find out how to change the settings for your mouse, including the functions for the mouse buttons, the speed of the pointer, and the double-click speed.

Customizing the keyboard

Learn how to change the settings for your keyboard, including the delay before a character repeats and the rate of character repeat.

Customizing accessibility options

Learn how to activate the many options that make it easier for those with physical disabilities to operate Windows 95.

Setting the date, time, and other regional settings

Find out how to change the date, time, and other regional settings (such as number and currency formats).

Checking system information

Learn how to use the Device Manager to check the hardware settings on your computer and how to create user profiles.

Changing the Sounds Related to Windows Events

Windows has sounds related to different events such as errors, closing programs, shutting down Windows, emptying the Recycle Bin, and so on. You can change the sounds used for each of these events; you can even use your own sound files.

To change the sounds related to an event, follow these steps:

1. Open the Start menu, and choose Settings, Control Panel.
2. Double-click Sounds to display the Sounds properties sheet shown in Figure 33.1.

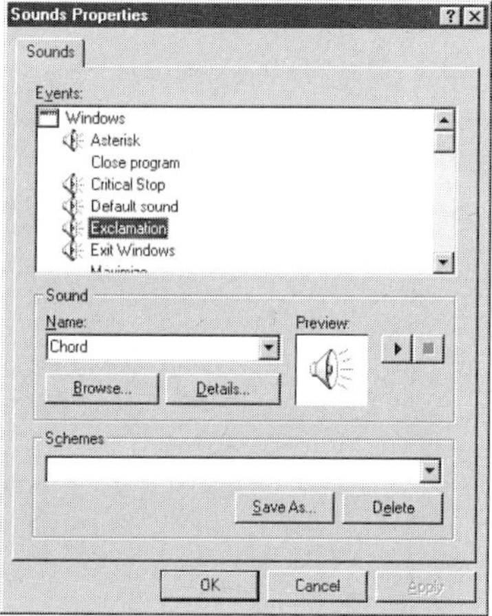

FIG. 33.1
You can assign your own sound files to different Windows events.

3. Scroll through the Events list until you see the event sound you want to change; then click that event.
4. Select the WAV file that contains the sound for that event by clicking the Browse button and selecting a WAV file. Click OK. The Browse dialog box opens in the WINDOWS\MEDIA folder, but you can change to any folder.
5. Preview the sound by clicking the ▶ button to the right of the Preview icon.
6. Click OK.

NOTE You can create your own collection of WAV files by following the procedures described in Chapter 4, "Configuring Multimedia Windows 95." You can also look on public bulletin boards, online services, and the Internet to find thousands of free WAV files.

Entire collections of sounds have been grouped for you as sound schemes. To change all the sounds involved in a sound scheme, select the scheme you want by choosing it from the Schemes drop-down list.

If you create your own scheme of sounds/events, you can save it with a name. Then you can return to it by clicking the Save As button, entering a name, and clicking OK.

Customizing the Mouse

If you are left-handed, or if you like a fast or slow mouse, you need to know how to modify your mouse's behavior. You can change mouse options in the Mouse properties sheet, shown in Figure 33.2.

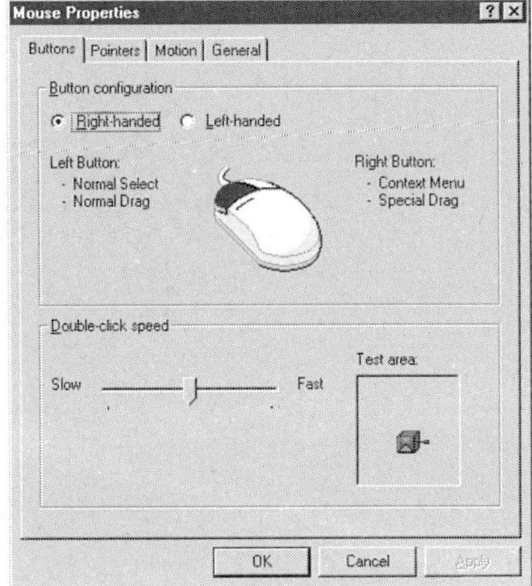

FIG. 33.2 You can change the speed of your mouse and more in the Mouse properties sheet.

To change how your mouse behaves and appears, follow these steps:

1. Open the Start menu and choose Settings, Control Panel; then double-click the Mouse icon. The Mouse properties sheet appears.
2. Click a tab and make the changes you want.
3. Click Apply to accept the change and to continue making changes, or click OK to accept the change and close the Mouse properties sheet.

Mouse options are grouped on four tabs: Buttons, Pointers, Motion, and General. Table 33.1 describes each tab.

Table 33.1 Tabs of the Mouse Properties Sheet

Tab	Description
Button	Select either a Right-Handed mouse or Left-Handed mouse. Set the Double-Click Speed, and then double-click in the Test Area box to determine whether you set a speed you're comfortable with. When you double-click at the right speed in the Test area, you'll be surprised by what appears.
Pointers	Change the size and shape of the pointer. You can select schemes of pointer shapes so all pointer shapes for different activities take on a new appearance.

continues

Table 33.1 Continued

Tab	Description
Motion	You can set the Pointer Speed to make the mouse move more slowly or quickly across the screen. You can add a Pointer Trail to the mouse to leave a trail of mouse pointers on-screen. This feature is especially useful if you have an LCD screen where the mouse pointer can sometimes get lost. This option cannot be shown for video display drivers that don't support it.
General	To add a new mouse to your system, click Change and the Select Device dialog box displays. Make your selection from there. You also can add a new mouse with the Add New Hardware Wizard, available from the Control Panel.

TIP Double-click a pointer shape while in the Pointers tab to replace one shape in a scheme.

See "LCD Screen Mouse Trails," **p. 228**

NOTE Many mouse manufacturers include other options for customizing the mouse. Check the Mouse Properties dialog box for additional options that you can use to customize your mouse.

Customizing the Keyboard

Although changing the keyboard speed doesn't result in a miracle that makes you type faster, it does speed up the rate at which characters are repeated. You also can change the delay before the character repeats.

To change keyboard properties, follow these steps.

1. Open the Start menu and choose Settings, Control Panel; then double-click Keyboard. The Keyboard properties sheet appears (see Figure 33.3).
2. Click a tab and make the changes you want.
3. Click Apply to accept the change and to continue making changes, or click OK to accept the change and close the Keyboard properties sheet.

Keyboard options are grouped on three tabs: Speed, Language, and General. Table 33.2 describes these tabs.

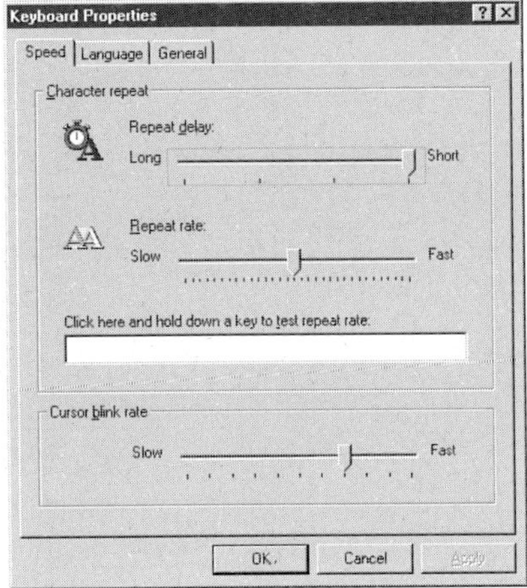

FIG. 33.3 You can change the keyboard repeat and more in the Keyboard properties sheet.

Table 33.2 Tabs of the Keyboard Properties Sheet

Tab	Description
Speed	Change the keyboard repeat speed. Drag the Slow/Fast pointer to change the Repeat Delay Speed (how long before the first repeat) or the Repeat Rate. Click in the Click Here box to test the results. Drag the Slow/Fast Pointer for Cursor Blink Speed to change the speed the cursor blinks.
Language	Use the Language tab to select the language you use. Click Add to display the Add Language dialog box and select a language from the drop-down list. Click Properties to select an appropriate keyboard layout. Click Remove to remove a language from the list. Click the up and down arrows to change the order of the languages you have selected. Changing this option enables your applications to accurately sort words that might contain non-English characters, such as accent marks. However, changing the language setting does not change the language used by Windows. You need to purchase a different language version of Windows to accomplish this.
General	To change keyboards, click the Change button and the Select Device dialog box appears. Make your selection from there. You can also add a new keyboard with the Add New Hardware Wizard, available from the Control Panel.

Making Windows Accessible for the Hearing-, Sight-, and Movement-Impaired

In an effort to make computers more available to the more than 30 million people who have some form of disability, Microsoft has added Accessibility Properties. You can use these properties to adjust the computer's sound, display, and physical interface.

To make accessibility adjustments, follow these steps:

1. Click the Start button and choose Settings, Control Panel.
2. Double-click the Accessibility Options icon. The Accessibility properties sheet appears (see Figure 33.4).
3. Make your selections and click OK.

TROUBLESHOOTING

Accessibility Options does not appear in my Control Panel. Reinstall Windows using a custom installation and select Accessibility Options. Appendix A, "What's on the CD?," describes how to reinstall options in Windows.

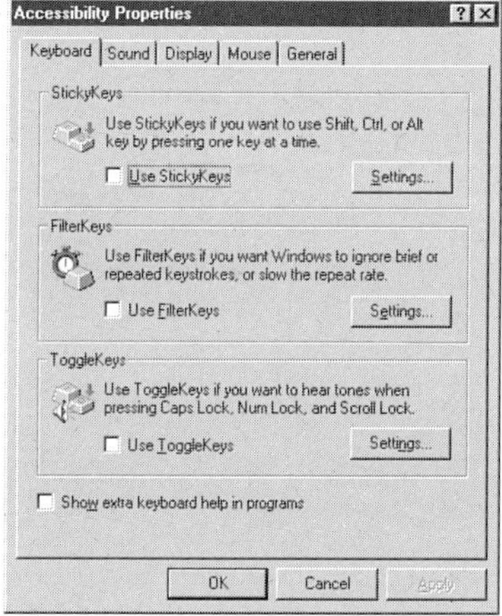

FIG. 33.4
Use the Accessibility properties sheet to make Windows easier for a person with a disability to use.

The Accessibility properties sheet includes the tabs outlined in Table 33.3.

Table 33.3 Tabs of the Accessibility Properties Sheet

Tab	Description
Keyboard	Makes the keyboard more tolerant and patient. Select Use StickyKeys if you need to press multiple keys simultaneously but can press keys only one at a time. Select Use FilterKeys to ignore short or repeated keystrokes. Select Use ToggleKeys to make a sound when you press Caps Lock, Num Lock, and Scroll Lock.

Tab	Description
Sound	Provides visual warnings and captions for speech and sounds. Select Use SoundSentry to make Windows use a visual warning when a sound alert occurs. Select Use ShowSounds to display captions instead of speech or sounds.
Display	Selects colors and fonts for easy reading. Select Use High Contrast to use color and font combinations that produce greater screen contrast.
Mouse	Controls the pointer with the numeric keypad. Select Use MouseKeys to use the numeric keypad and other keys in place of the mouse. The relationship of keys to mouse controls appears in Table 33.4.
General	Turns off accessibility features, gives notification, and adds an alternative input device. Use Automatic Reset to set Windows so accessibility features remain on at all times, are turned off when Windows restarts, or are turned off after a period of inactivity. Notification tells users when a feature is turned on or off. The SerialKey device enables Windows to receive keyboard or mouse input from alternative input devices through a serial port.

Some of these accessibility features may be difficult for a disabled person to turn on or off through normal Windows procedures. To alleviate this problem, Windows includes special *hotkeys*. Pressing the keys or key combinations for the designated hotkey turns an accessibility feature on or off or changes its settings. Table 33.4 gives the hotkeys for different features.

Table 33.4 Hotkeys for Accessibility Features

Feature	Hotkey	Result
High-Contrast Mode	Press left Alt+ left Shift+Print Screen simultaneously	Alternates the screen through different text/background combinations.
StickyKeys	Press the Shift key	Turned on or off five consecutive times.
FilterKeys	Hold down right Shift	Turned on or off key for eight seconds.
ToggleKeys	Hold down Num Lock key	Turned on or off for five seconds.
MouseKeys	Press left Alt+ left Shift+Num Lock	Turned on or off simultaneously.

MouseKeys can be very useful for portable or laptop computer users and graphic artists as well as for people unable to use a mouse. Graphic artists will find MouseKeys useful because it enables them to produce finer movements than those done with a mouse. After MouseKeys is turned on, you can produce the same effects as a mouse by using these keys:

Action	Press this key(s)
Movement	Any number key except 5
Large moves	Hold down Ctrl as you press number keys
Single-pixel moves	Hold down Shift as you press number keys
Single-click	5
Double-click	+
Begin drag	Insert
Drop after drag	Delete
Select left mouse button	/
Select right mouse button	-
Select both mouse buttons	*

CAUTION

Use the numeric keypad with MouseKeys, not the numbered keys across the top of the keypad. Make sure the Num Lock key is set so the keypad is in numeric mode rather than cursor mode.

Setting the Date and Time

Use the Date/Time properties sheet to change the date or time in your system (see Figure 33.5). You also can change the format of the date and time to match another country's standard.

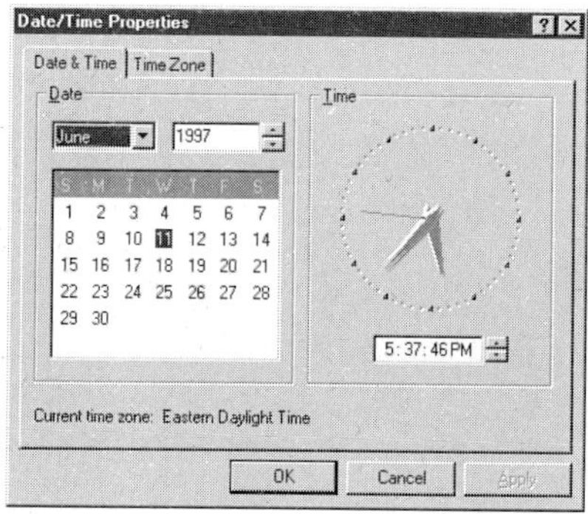

FIG. 33.5
You can change the system date and time in the Date/Time properties sheet.

TIP To display the current date, point to the clock on the taskbar and the date will pop up.

To change date and time properties, follow these steps:

1. Double-click the clock on the taskbar.

   or

   Open the Start menu and choose Settings, Control Panel; then double-click Date/Time.

   The Date/Time properties sheet appears.

2. Click a tab and make the changes you want. See Table 33.5 for a description of things you can change.
3. Click Apply to accept the change and to continue making changes, or click OK to accept the change and close the Date/Time properties sheet.

Date and time options are grouped on two tabs: Date & Time and Time Zone. Table 33.5 describes these tabs.

Table 33.5 Tabs of the Date/Time Properties Sheet

Tab	Description
Date & Time	To change the Date, click the down arrow and select a month, or click the up and down arrows to select a year. Click the day of the month in the calendar. To change the time, click the element you want to change in the digital time display. For example, to change hours, click the first two numbers. Click the up and down arrows next to the time display.
Time Zone	Click the down arrow to select a new time zone (see Figure 33.6). Select the Adjust for Daylight Saving Time check box to have the time automatically adjust for daylight saving time.

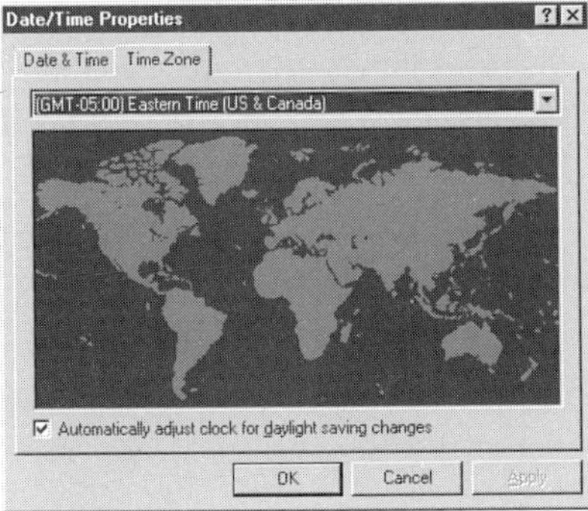

FIG. 33.6 You can change the time zone to reflect the time in any area of the world.

Customizing for Your Country and Language

Windows has the capacity to switch between international character sets, time and date displays, and numeric formats. The international settings you choose in Control Panel affect applications, such as Microsoft Excel, that take advantage of these Windows features.

NOTE Although you can change the language and country formats, doing so does not change the language used in menus or Help information. To obtain versions of Windows and Microsoft applications for countries other than the United States, check with your local Microsoft representative. Check with the corporate offices of other software vendors for international versions of their applications.

The Regional Settings properties sheet provides five tabs (see Figure 33.7). The region you select on the Regional Settings tab will automatically affect the settings in the other tabs.

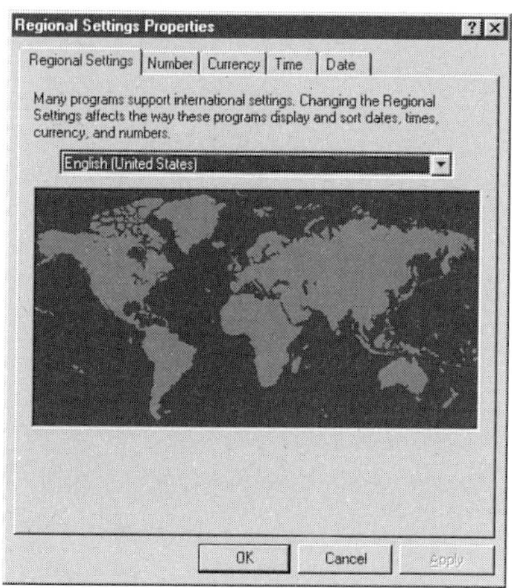

FIG. 33.7 You can change settings, including the formats used for numbers, dates, times, and currencies by selecting a region in the Regional Settings tab.

To change Regional Settings properties, follow these steps:

1. Open the Start menu and choose Settings, Control Panel; then double-click Regional Settings. The Regional Settings properties sheet appears.
2. Click a tab and make the changes you want.
3. Click Apply to accept the changes and to continue making changes, or click OK to accept the change and close the Regional Settings Properties screen.

Table 33.6 describes each tab in the Regional Setting properties sheet.

Table 33.6 Tabs of the Regional Settings Properties Sheet

Tab	Description
Regional Settings	Click the down arrow and select your geographic region, or click your region on the global map. This selection automatically changes other settings in the dialog box.
Number	To make a change to the format, click the down arrow next to the box you want to change and choose what you want, or click in the box and type what you want.
Currency	To make a change to the format, click the down arrow next to the box you want to change and choose what you want, or click in the box and type what you want. To select some currency symbols, you might have to select a different keyboard first. The No. of Digits After Decimal setting can be overridden by some applications, such as spreadsheet programs.
Time	Change the symbols, separator, and style of the time display. To make a change to the format, click the down arrow next to the box you want to change and choose what you want, or click in the box and type what you want.
Date	To make a change to the format, click the down arrow next to the box you want to change and choose what you want, or click in the box and type what you want.

Changing Custom Settings for Each User

Windows accommodates situations where people share a computer or move between computers. Windows enables you to store your custom settings for colors, accessibility features, and so on with your logon name. When you log on to the computer, Windows resets the computer with your settings.

User profiles are stored with your user logon ID, but you must tell Windows that you want to store user profiles for each different logon ID.

To create or remove a custom user profile for each logon ID, follow these steps:

1. Open the Start menu and choose Settings, Control Panel; then double-click Passwords.
2. Click the User Profiles tab. Figure 33.8 shows the User Profiles tab.
3. Select one of the following:
   - Select All Users of This PC if you want all users to use the same settings. Go to step 5.
   - Select Users Can Customize Their Preferences if you want Windows to use the customization setup during the last use of that logon ID. Go to step 4.

4. If you make the second selection in step 3, you can choose from the following:
   - Select Include Desktop Icons and Network Neighborhood Contents in User Settings if the user profile should remember changes to these items.
   - Select Include Start Menu and Program Groups in User Settings if the user profile should remember changes to these items.
5. Click OK.

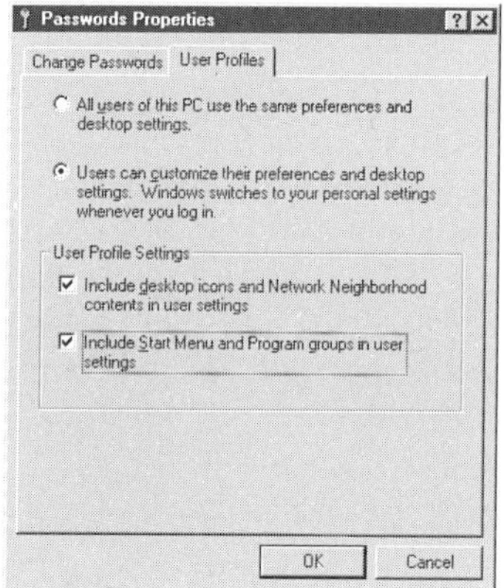

FIG. 33.8
You can create user profiles so people sharing the same computer can save their custom settings.

When you are done with a Windows computer shared by multiple users, log off the computer so others can log on and use their custom user profiles. To log off, click the Start button, and choose Shut Down, Close All Programs and Log On as a Different User?. Choose OK.

If you selected Users Can Customize Their Preferences, whenever a person logs on to Windows and customizes settings, those settings are saved with that logon ID. The next time someone logs on with that logon ID, Windows changes to the settings for that ID.

Preventing Others from Using Windows

You might work in an area where you need to keep your computer secure. For example, your work might involve financial, market, or personnel data that is confidential. One way you can help to protect this information is to require a password before Windows will start.

To create or change your Windows password, follow these steps:

1. Open the Passwords properties sheet as described in the previous section.
2. Click the Change Passwords tab. Then click the Change Windows Password button to display the Change Windows Password dialog box. If you have network passwords, they will be listed so you can change them to match your Windows password.
3. Type your old password in the Old Password text box.
4. Type your new password in the New Password and Confirm Password text boxes.

5. Choose OK, and then choose OK again.

Windows provides security for the network environment from the other tabs on the Password properties sheet.

See "Maintaining Workgroup Security," p. 959

Reviewing Your Computer's System Information

One of the more gruesome aspects of using DOS or earlier versions of Windows was working with configuration files when you wanted to customize or optimize your computer. People who wanted to install sound cards or network adapters, change memory usage, or specify I/O (Input/Output) or IRQ (interrupt request) settings faced immersion in the arcane world of configuration files. Configuration files gave you no help; yet if you made an error, part of your hardware might not be recognized, your system might run slower, or it might not run at all.

Windows 95 makes specifying configurations easier. Now you can select only allowable options from straightforward dialog boxes, and you can see settings from other hardware devices that might cause conflicts.

Reading Your Registration and Version Number

You can see your registration number, the version number of Windows, and the type of processor on which Windows is running on the General page of the System properties sheet. To see this page, follow these steps:

1. Open the Start menu and choose Settings, Control Panel to display the Control Panel window.
2. Double-click the System icon.
3. Click the General tab of the System properties sheet (see Figure 33.9).

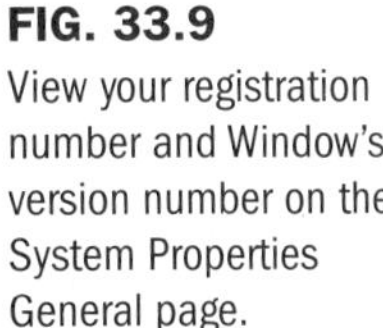

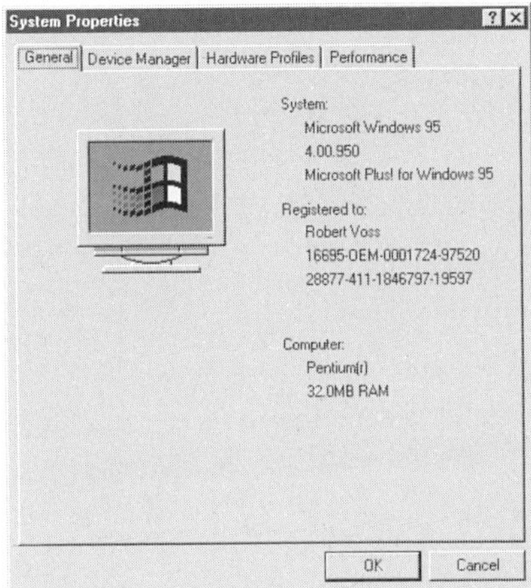

FIG. 33.9
View your registration number and Window's version number on the System Properties General page.

NOTE If you have the OSR2 version of Windows 95 installed, you will see a "B" after the 4.00.950 designation. This is a handy way to determine whether OSR2 is installed on a system.

Examine the Hardware on Your Computer

You might need to examine the configuration settings and drivers for hardware connected to your computer. You can use the System properties sheet to help you troubleshoot hardware. If you need to see a list of IRQ and I/O settings, you need to use the Device Manager.

To display the Device Manager page, follow these steps:

1. Open the Start menu and choose Settings, Control Panel to display the Control Panel window.
2. Double-click the System icon.
3. Click the Device Manager tab of the System properties sheet (see Figure 33.10).

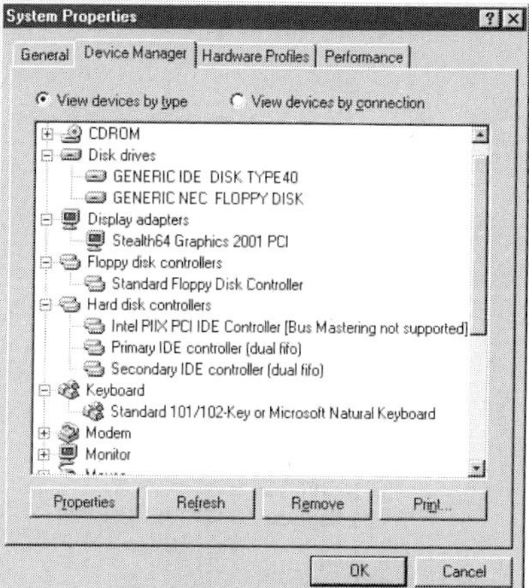

FIG. 33.10 View the hardware devices and their drivers on the System Properties Device Manager page.

4. To see the drivers installed for a device, click the + sign to the left of the device. To see information about a device or to remove the device, select one of the following buttons:

Button	**Action**
Properties	Displays a listing of properties appropriate to the device. Select the Computer item to see IRQ and I/O settings.
Refresh	Windows reexamines the installed hardware and attempts to update the list.
Remove	Removes the selected device or driver.
Print	Prints a report of configuration settings.

5. Choose OK.

▶ **See** "Installing Plug and Play CD-ROM Drives," **p. 133**

▶ **See** "Installing Plug and Play Hardware," **p. 176**

Checking IRQ, I/O, DMA, and Memory Settings Hardware devices each require a unique section of memory (I/O address). Some hardware devices also require an interrupt request (IRQ) or direct memory access (DMA) to operate. If any of these settings conflict with the settings for another device, either or both of the devices might not work.

You can see a list of these settings in your computer by selecting the Computer icon on the Device Manager page of the System properties sheet and then clicking Properties. Select from the option buttons to display the list of settings you want to see. Figure 33.11 shows the list of IRQ settings.

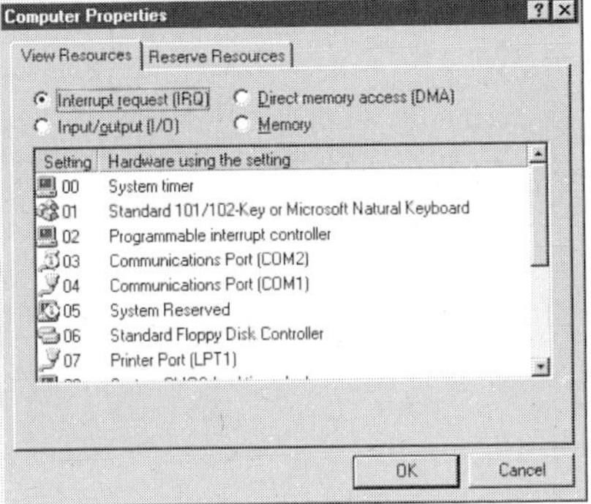

FIG. 33.11
Use the View Resources page to track down conflicts in IRQ and I/O settings.

In MS-DOS and in prior versions of Windows, it was difficult to tell the cause of conflicts between hardware devices. In Windows 95, the Device Manager shows you lists of IRQ and I/O settings. You can scan through the lists and see where you accidentally installed two device drivers for the same device or you set two different devices to the same or overlapping IRQ or I/O settings.

If you find you installed two drivers for the same device, you can delete one of them. If you find a conflict because two hardware devices are using the same memory or IRQ settings, you can resolve the conflict easily through the Device Manager. The approach you might take to resolve a conflict is to look through the lists in the Device Manager to find an open IRQ or I/O setting, check the two manuals for the particular devices to determine what other IRQ or I/O settings they will work with, and change the settings for one of the devices so it doesn't conflict.

TROUBLESHOOTING

One of the hardware devices on a computer is not working. Click the Device Manager tab on the System properties sheet and check for an **X** through a device. This means the hardware has been disabled. Double-click that device to check its settings. If a device icon has a circled exclamation point, the hardware has a problem. Double-click the icon to inspect the type of problem.

It took a couple attempts with different driver selections before some of the hardware would work. Now some of the devices on the system work slowly, intermittently, or incorrectly. Check the Device Manager page of the System properties sheet to see if you have multiple drivers installed for the same hardware device. Delete all the drivers except the driver for your specific manufacturer and model. If there are multiple drivers, but not one specific to your hardware device, keep the generic driver.

The computer works with either a sound card or a network adapter card, but not both. The usual cause of this problem is a conflict between IRQ ports and I/O addresses. Each hardware device must have its own IRQ port and its own I/O address. Sound cards and network adapters are notorious for conflicting with each other over these. To see the IRQ port and I/O address used by each device, display the Device Manager page, select the Computer icon, and choose Properties. On the View Resources page that appears, you can select the Interrupt Request (IRQ) or Input/Output (I/O) option to view a list of settings for each device on your computer. Write down the current settings and watch for conflicts. Then change the settings for devices that conflict with others.

See "Installing a Plug and Play Modem," **p. 77**

See "Installing and Configuring Your Modem," **p. 76**

Creating, Naming, and Copying Hardware Profiles

Hardware profiles are collections of hardware settings; they're useful if you use different collections of hardware on your computer. For example, you might have a laptop computer that uses a VGA LCD monitor on the road but uses an SVGA large-screen monitor on the desktop.

By saving a collection of hardware settings as a profile, you only need to choose the profile you want rather than manually change hardware settings when you want to run a different combination of hardware.

When you start a Windows 95 computer that has multiple hardware configurations, you have the option of choosing the named hardware profile you want to use. From a text screen in Startup, you see something similar to this:

```
Windows cannot determine what configuration your computer is in.
Select one of the following:
1. Original Configuration
2. Multimedia
3. Desktop
4. None of the above
Enter your choice:
```

Type the number of the profile you want to use and press Enter. Windows 95 then starts with that configuration of hardware, only loading the hardware drivers required.

To make use of the distinct hardware profiles, you must first copy the existing default profile. The default profile is named Original Configuration. After you copy a profile, you can edit the devices included in it and rename it to help you recognize it. To copy or rename a hardware profile, follow these steps:

1. Open the Start menu and choose Settings, Control Panel to display the Control Panel window.
2. Double-click the System icon.
3. Click the Hardware Profile tab of the System properties sheet (see Figure 33.12).

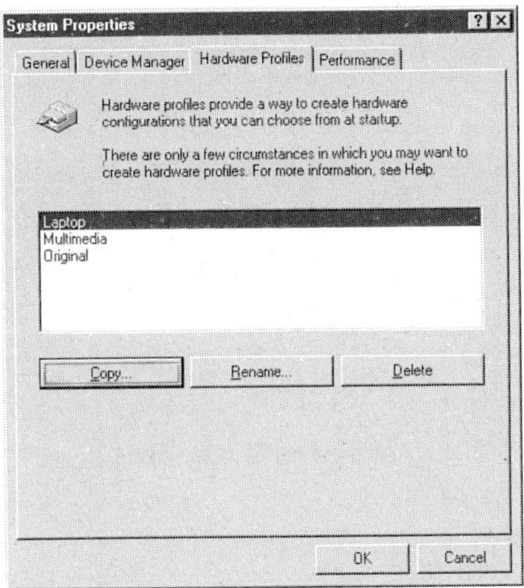

FIG. 33.12 Keep different combinations of hardware devices stored as named hardware profiles.

4. Select the hardware profile you want to work with and then click one of the following buttons:

Button	Action
Copy	Displays a Copy Profile dialog box in which you can enter a new name. Copies the hardware configuration from the selected profile to this new profile.
Rename	Changes the name of a profile.
Delete	Deletes a profile.

5. Choose OK.

To create a new profile or change an existing profile, follow these steps:

1. If you want to create a new profile, copy an existing profile as described in the preceding steps. Use a unique, descriptive name for the profile.
2. Click the Device Manager tab on the System properties sheet.

3. Click the plus sign next to the hardware type you want to change for the configuration; then double-click the specific hardware you want to change. This displays the device's properties sheet.
4. In the Device Usage area of the properties sheet, deselect any hardware profile you don't want to use this device with. By default, all of your devices will be used with all of your profiles until you make changes.
5. Choose OK.
6. Repeat steps 3 through 5 until you have configured all the hardware for this profile.
7. Choose OK.

Depending on the changes you made, you might be prompted to restart your computer.

See "Using Your Laptop with a Docking System," **p. 198**

Checking Performance Settings

You can check the performance parameters of your computer on the Performance page of the System properties sheet. To see this page, follow these steps:

1. Open the Start menu and choose Settings, Control Panel to display the Control Panel window.
2. Double-click the System icon.
3. Click the Performance tab of the System properties sheet (see Figure 33.13).

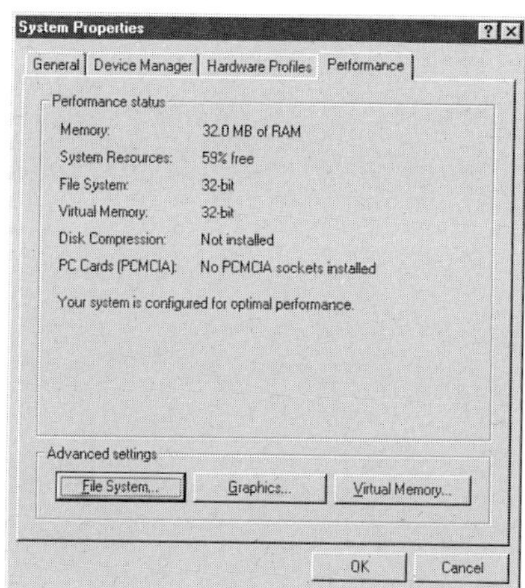

FIG. 33.13
The System Properties Performance page provides information on your computer's performance parameters.

4. View the performance status parameters on the Performance page, or choose File System, Graphics, or Virtual Memory for advanced performance tuning options.
5. Choose OK.

CAUTION

In general, do not change the settings available on the Performance page. Windows 95 usually sets these parameters optimally.

See "Improving Performance with Disk Defragmenter," **p. 394**

PART VII

Sharing Data Between Applications

CHAPTER 34

Simple Ways of Sharing Data Between Applications

by Rob Tidrow with Bob Voss

- **How to use the Windows Clipboard and Clipboard Viewer**

  Learn how to use the Edit, Cut, Copy, and Paste commands, both within and between applications.

- **How to use the Clipboard Viewer**

  Look here to find out how to view and save the information stored in the Clipboard.

- **How to use drag and drop to move text, data, and graphics within an application**

  Learn a second method for moving information by using the mouse instead of the Clipboard.

- **How to transfer data with DOS applications**

  Use the Clipboard to transfer information between DOS and Windows applications and copy text from the DOS command line into the Clipboard.

- **How to transfer data using file converters**

  Learn about a third method for transferring information between applications.

- **How to link information between two locations**

  Learn how to create a link between information located in two documents.

You can share data from one document or application to another because Windows has *data-exchange* capabilities (also called *data sharing*). These capabilities are as simple as cutting or copying a piece of text from one program to another, and as complex as editing a piece of data in one application that you created in another application. The latter operation, known as *in-place editing*, is a component of OLE, which is discussed in Chapter 35, "Advanced Ways of Sharing Data Between Applications with OLE."

Cutting, copying, and pasting are simple operations that make you more efficient in Windows. Although many experienced Windows users are familiar with the data-sharing techniques detailed in this chapter, no discussion of the Windows operating system is complete without mention of them. ■

Understanding the Data-Sharing Capabilities of Windows 95

Windows 95 supports data exchange using Clipboard object linking and embedding (OLE). All Windows applications provide some means of sharing data with another application. All applications, for example, have access to the Windows Clipboard, to which you can copy or cut data. Not all Windows applications, however, have OLE-capability.

Sharing data among applications can help you automate redundant tasks. Data-sharing capabilities also enable users to create more powerful, more informative, and more advanced documents that tap into the abilities of multiple applications. Many applications that adhere to Windows 95 standards let you copy an element from one type of application and use it in another application. You can, for example, create a picture from Paint and use it in a WordPad document, as shown in Figure 34.1.

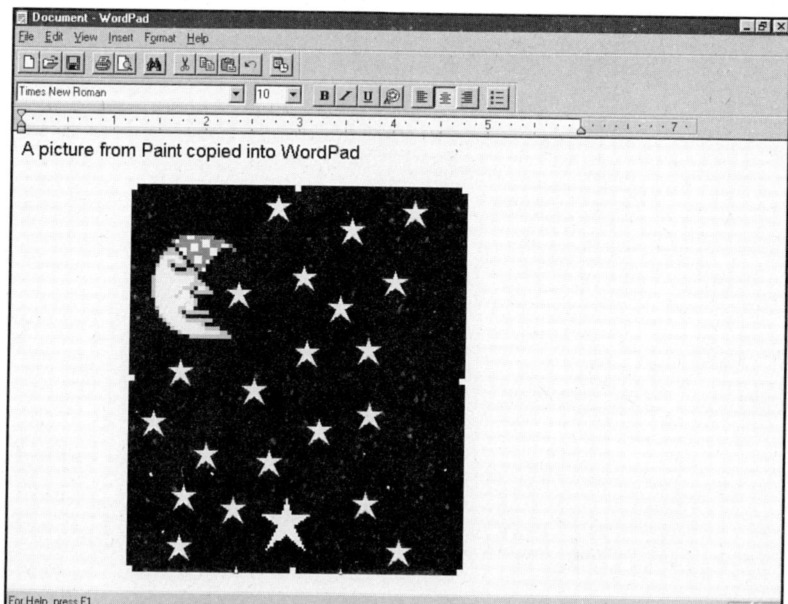

FIG. 34.1 This picture was copied from Paint into WordPad.

Using the Windows Clipboard

The most basic way to exchange data from one source to another is to use the Windows 95 Clipboard, an area in memory that applications can access to share data. When you use the Clipboard, you *cut* or *copy* data to the Clipboard and then *paste* that data in your document.

Copying places a replica of the material that you selected in the Clipboard. Cutting removes the data from your document and places it in the Clipboard. Pasting places the data from the Clipboard into your document.

NOTE When you paste data from the Clipboard, you don't remove it from the Clipboard. You can paste the data from the Clipboard into your document as many times as you like. The Clipboard retains your cut or copied data until you clear the contents manually, or until you cut or copy something else to the Clipboard.

Cutting, Copying, and Pasting Data

Applications that let you access the Clipboard generally use standard menu commands or keyboard shortcuts. In many Windows 95 applications, you can transfer data to and from the Clipboard by choosing commands from the Edit menu.

To cut or copy something from a WordPad document, follow these steps:

1. Select the text in the document that you want to cut or copy, as shown in Figure 34.2.

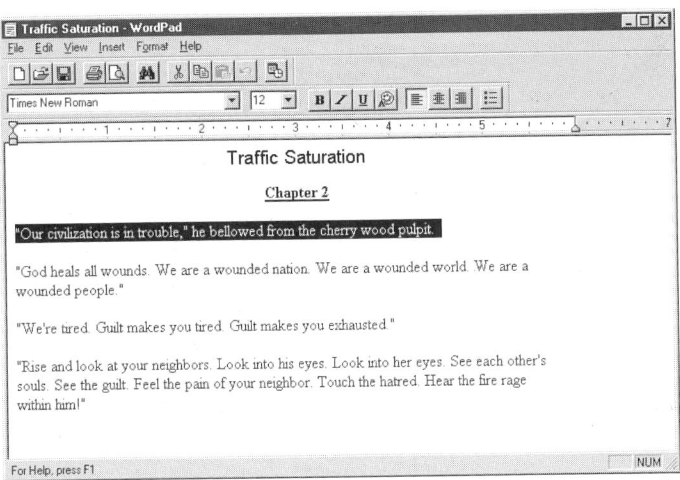

FIG. 34.2 Select the text you want to cut in the source document.

2. Choose Edit, Cut to cut the text to the Clipboard, or choose Edit, Copy to copy the text to the Clipboard.

   In many cases, you also can right-click the selection to display a shortcut menu and choose Cut or Copy from the menu.

Now that you have something in the Clipboard, you can paste it somewhere in the document, or into another document. To paste, follow these steps:

1. Position your cursor at the place in the document where you want to paste the element (if you're copying to a document in another application, open that application and document, then position the cursor).
2. Choose Edit, Paste to paste the contents of the Clipboard into its new location, Figure 34.3 shows WordPad text pasted into a Paint drawing.

Another standard way to use the Clipboard is to use the buttons in an application's toolbar. Figure 34.4 shows the Cut, Copy, and Paste buttons on the WordPad toolbar.

FIG. 34.3
Pasting text from a WordPad document into a Paint drawing.

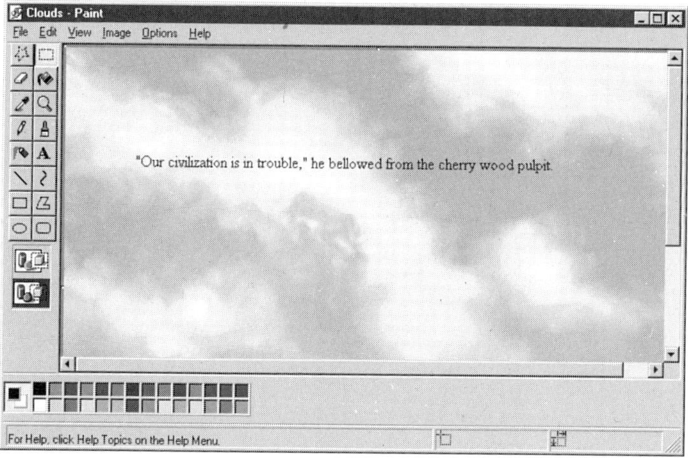

FIG. 34.4
Cut, Copy, and Paste buttons provided in the WordPad toolbar.

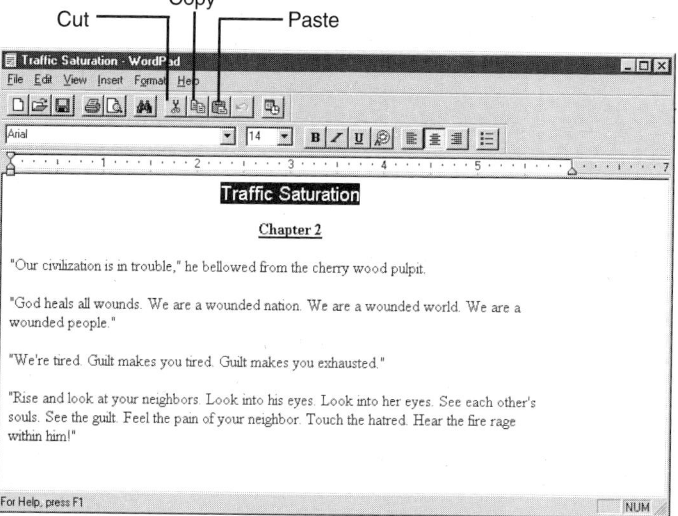

Quick View Plus is an add-on product for Windows 95 created by Inso Corporation. Quick View Plus enhances the Quick View feature that comes with Windows 95 in several ways. These include the capabilities to preview many more types of files, and to copy and paste information from a file that you are viewing. This feature allows you to view a file created by an application you don't have on your computer and then to copy and paste information from that file into another document.

For more information on Quick View Plus, contact Inso Corporation at (312) 329-0700. You can download a trialware version of the program from the Internet at the following address:

http://www.inso.com

Using Keyboard Shortcuts

Windows 95 supports a common set of keyboard shortcuts that, unless the shortcut has been reassigned, you can use in any application that supports data sharing. Table 34.1 shows these shortcuts.

Table 34.1 Cut, Copy, and Paste Keyboard Shortcuts

Action	Windows 95 Shortcut Keys
Cut	Ctrl+X or Shift+Delete
Copy	Ctrl+C or Ctrl+Insert
Paste	Ctrl+V or Shift+Insert

Copying Information to a Dialog Box

You can use a keyboard shortcut to help you fill in a dialog box. The Letter Wizard dialog box in Microsoft Word, which is used to create letters (see Figure 34.5), is requesting the recipient's name and address. You can type the information or copy it from somewhere else. For this example, assume that you have the recipient's name and address stored in a Notepad document and that you want to copy and paste that information into the dialog box.

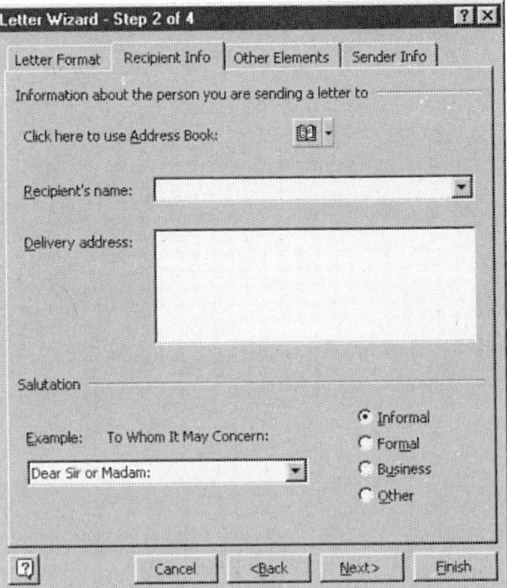

FIG. 34.5
You can cut or copy information to Windows 95 dialog boxes and wizards.

To copy information from the Notepad document to the Word Letter Wizard dialog box, follow these steps:

1. Select the information that you'll replace.
2. Switch to the open Notepad document by clicking the button in the taskbar at the bottom of the screen.

3. In the Notepad window, select the information that you want to copy, as shown in Figure 34.6.

FIG. 34.6
Highlight text in the Notepad document to copy to the Clipboard.

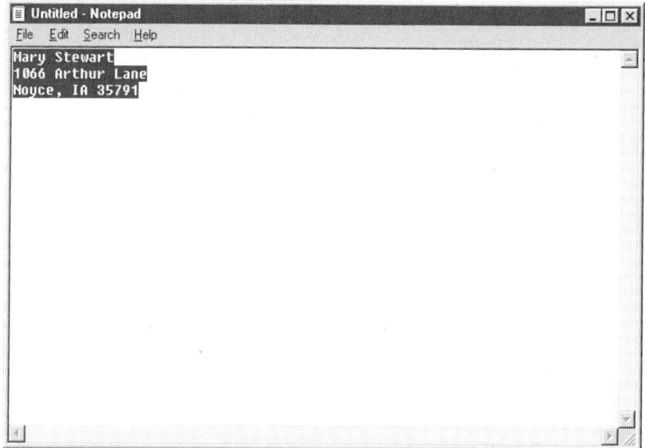

4. To copy the highlighted text, choose Edit, Copy, or press Ctrl+C.
5. Click the Word button on the taskbar to return to the Letter Wizard dialog box in Word. The old entry in the recipient's text box should still be highlighted.
6. Press Ctrl+V to paste the information from the Clipboard to the text box. Figure 34.7 shows the completed text box.

FIG. 34.7
The information from the Clipboard is pasted into the text box.

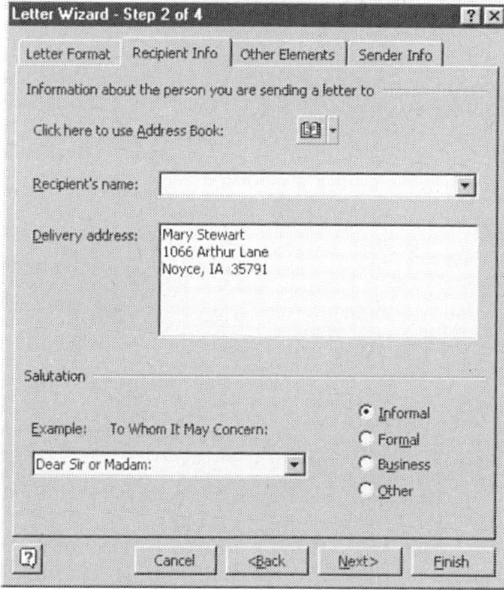

NOTE You can't use the Edit menu or any button on a toolbar while you're in this dialog box. The only way to copy from the Clipboard is to press Ctrl+V or Shift+Insert. The same holds true when you're trying to cut or copy from a dialog box. Press Ctrl+X to cut or Ctrl+C to copy highlighted text in a text box.

Capturing Screens with the Clipboard

Many Windows screen-capturing programs are available, but you also can use the Clipboard to capture the contents of the screen. When the screen image is captured, it's held in the Clipboard in bitmap format.

To capture the entire screen and paste it into a WordPad document, follow these steps:

TIP You also can capture the contents of the active window onscreen by pressing Alt+Print Screen or Shift+Print Screen, depending on your keyboard.

1. Press the Print Screen key to capture the entire screen and place it in the Clipboard.
2. Open or switch to WordPad.

3. In a new or existing document, choose Edit, Paste. The screen image, in bitmap format, is pasted into the WordPad document.

See "Using Windows Paint," **p. 805**

Using Drag and Drop to Move or Copy Information within an Application's Documents

A second method for moving information is to use the mouse to drag and drop selected pieces of information, which can be text, graphics, or data, from one location to another. When you drag and drop information, you are moving or copying it directly from one location to another, without using the Clipboard as a go-between. In this section, you learn how to drag and drop information within an application. In the next chapter, "Advanced Ways of Sharing Data Between Applications with OLE," you learn how to drag and drop objects from one application into another.

NOTE To use drag and drop, you must be working in an application that supports it. Most applications in the Microsoft Office suite, for example, support drag and drop, including Word, Excel, PowerPoint, and Access. Check the manual that comes with your application for information on using drag and drop.

To copy information with drag and drop in WordPad, follow these steps:

1. Open WordPad, and then open a document or create a new document that contains some text.
2. Select the text that you want to move or copy.
3. To move the text, position the mouse pointer over the selected area and drag the text.

   To copy the text, hold down the Ctrl key as you drag the text. A plus sign (+) appears next to the mouse pointer.

Up to the point that you release the mouse button to drop the text, you can press or release the Ctrl button to either copy or move the selection.

The mouse pointer changes as you drag, as shown in Figure 34.8.

FIG. 34.8
The gray dashed line indicates where the text will be placed.

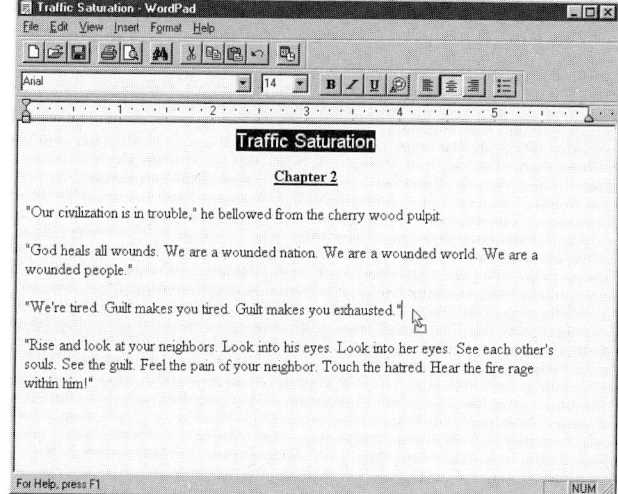

4. Drag the text to the position in the document where you want to place it. The gray vertical bar indicates the position of the new text.
5. Release the mouse button to complete the move or copy procedure.

Some applications, such as Word for Windows, allow you to move or copy text between two documents using drag and drop. To do so, make sure you can see both documents on screen at the same time, and then drag the item from one document to another following the steps just described.

In Chapter 35, "Advanced Ways of Sharing Data Between Applications with OLE," you learn how to use drag and drop to transfer information from one application to another.

TROUBLESHOOTING

When I copy information with drag and drop, the original document loses its information. You used the move feature instead. Make sure that you hold down the Ctrl key throughout the process. Release the mouse button first and then release the Ctrl key. The plus sign (+) next to the box in the mouse pointer indicates that you are copying the selection.

My copied text appears in the middle of existing text. Don't forget to watch the gray dashed line that's part of the mouse pointer. This line shows exactly where the copied text will be inserted.

I get a black circle with a slash through it when I try to copy. The black circle with the slash indicates that you can't drop the item in the area where the mouse is, such as the title bar or status bar. Make sure that you go all the way into the other document before you release the mouse button.

Although most Windows 95 users use Windows-based applications, millions of copies of DOS applications are used on Windows systems. Applications such as Lotus 1-2-3 for DOS, WordPerfect 5.1 for DOS, and the MS-DOS prompt remain very popular. Windows 95 lets you copy information from a DOS application or from a DOS command prompt to a Windows application.

Windows 95 supports the following ways to transfer information from DOS applications to Windows documents:

- You can transfer text from DOS to Windows, from Windows to DOS, and between DOS applications by means of the Clipboard.
- You can transfer graphics from DOS to Windows applications by means of the Clipboard.
- You can copy text from the MS-DOS command prompt to the Clipboard.

Using the Clipboard to Exchange Data

Some DOS applications use their own Clipboard equivalent, but none provide an area that lets you transfer text and graphics between applications. When you want to transfer text between applications, you usually have to use text converters or file-conversion utilities that transform the text into a format that the application can read. In many cases, you have to convert the text to an ASCII text file, which strips out your formatting and special character enhancements.

When you want to share data from a DOS application to a Windows application, you use a process known as *mark, copy, and paste*. The Mark, Copy, and Paste commands are located in the control menu of a DOS window. You also can find the Mark button on the MS-DOS Prompt toolbar.

To copy a list of your files at the DOS command prompt to a WordPad document, follow these steps:

1. Open the MS-DOS Prompt into a window (see Figure 34.9). You can change the way your DOS window looks by going into its properties and then changing the font or screen options.
2. Click the Mark toolbar button, or choose Edit, Mark from the Control menu. A blinking cursor appears at the top of the DOS window, indicating that you're in marking mode.
3. You now need to mark the area that you want to copy by drawing a box around it with your mouse pointer. To do so, place your mouse pointer where you want to start marking, hold down the left mouse button, and then drag the box around the text that you want to copy. Your screen should look something like the one shown in Figure 34.10.

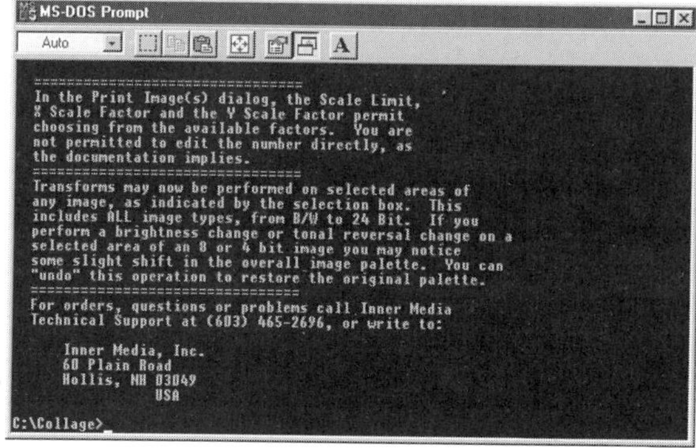

FIG. 34.9
You can copy text from the DOS window to a Windows document.

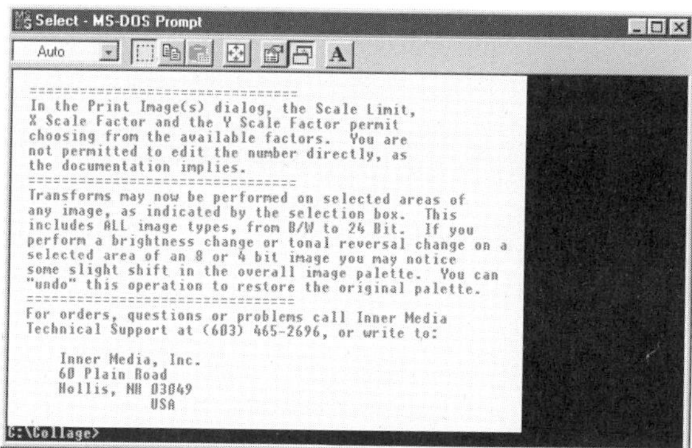

FIG. 34.10
Mark the text that you want to copy.

4. When you're satisfied with the selection, release the mouse button.
5. Click the Copy button in the toolbar; choose Edit, Copy from the Control menu or press Enter to copy the selection to the Clipboard.
6. Switch to WordPad, and place the cursor where you want the text to be placed.
7. Click the Paste toolbar button, or choose Edit, Paste. The text from the DOS window is placed in your WordPad document (see Figure 34.11).

See "Understanding and Configuring MS-DOS Application Properties," **p. 721**

Copying Data from Windows to DOS

You also can copy data from a Windows application to a DOS application by cutting or copying the data to the Clipboard and then pasting the data into the DOS application. When you do this, all the formatting that you placed in the Windows document is lost.

To copy data from Windows to DOS, follow these steps:

1. In your Windows application, such as WordPad, select the text that you want to copy.
2. Choose Edit, Copy, or Edit, Cut.

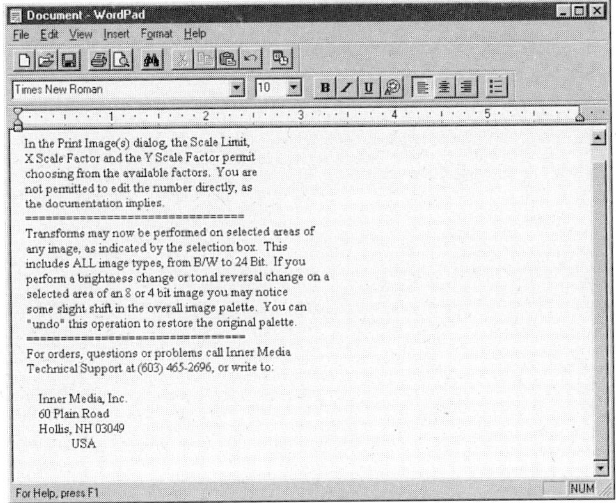

FIG. 34.11
You can insert text you copied from a DOS window into a WordPad document by pasting it from the Clipboard.

3. Switch to the DOS application, such as WordPerfect 5.2 for DOS. (Make sure the application is in a window and not full screen.)
4. Place the text or mouse cursor where you want to paste the text.
5. Choose Edit, Paste from the Control menu of the DOS application. The text now appears in the document.

Transferring Data by Using File Converters

Rather than cut and paste parts of a document into another document, you sometimes need to import an entire file into a different application. You may, for example, want to import a Windows Write file into WordPad. (Write was distributed with Windows 3.x.) Many software companies distribute Write files with their software to announce updates or changes in the software.

To open files that were created in other programs, many Windows applications include built-in file converters. *File converters* take the file format and transform it to a format that the application can read. During a file conversion, text enhancements, font selections, and other elements usually are preserved. Sometimes, however, these elements are converted to ASCII format.

To convert a Write file to WordPad format, follow these steps:

1. Start WordPad and choose File, Open.

TIP Click the Files of Type drop-down list to view the types of files you can open in WordPad.

2. Locate a file with the extension WRI and open it. WordPad starts to convert the file.

You now can edit the file as a WordPad file.

The type of converters you have installed for an application may depend on the installation options you chose at setup. See the application's documentation for specific converters.

Many other Windows applications include file converters to allow you to read and edit file formats that are created in other applications. Depending on the type of installation you perform, Word for Windows, for example, includes the following set of converters:

- Rich Text Format
- Text File
- Unicode Text Files
- Schedule+ Contact List
- Personal Address Book
- Outlook Address Book
- MS-DOS Text with Layout
- Text with Layout
- All Word Documents
- Word (Asian Version) 6.0/95
- Word for Macintosh 4.0-5.1
- Lotus 1-2-3
- WordPerfect 5.x
- WordPerfect 6.x
- Microsoft Excel Worksheet
- HTML Document

Rich Text Format (RTF) files have become the common language for exchanging files between word processors. You can preserve much of the formatting you apply to a document when you save it as an RTF file. If you don't have the correct converter for exchanging a file from one application to another, try creating an RTF file from the document and importing the document into the receiving application.

Another way to convert files is to save the file in a different format during the Save As process. When you need to import a Word for Windows file into WordPerfect or Word for Macintosh, for example, you can select those formats from the Save As Type drop-down list in the Save As dialog box. This list contains the types of formats in which you can save a Word for Windows document (see Figure 34.12).

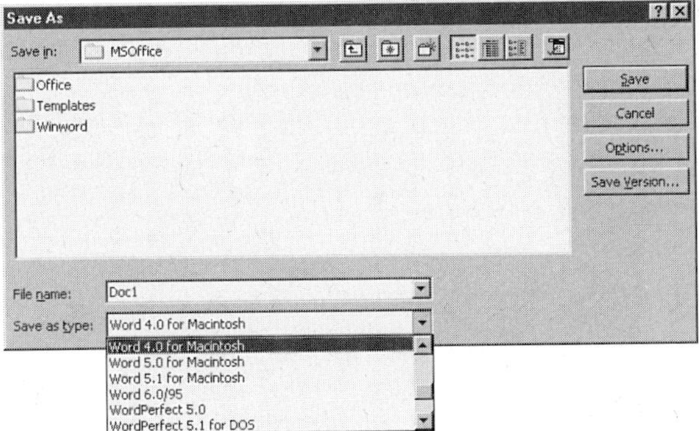

FIG. 34.12
Use the Save As Type list options to transfer files to different applications.

Understanding Data Linking

A more sophisticated way to exchange data in Windows 95 is through the use of linking. Before the arrival of the OLE standard, DDE (dynamic data exchange) was the technology used to link data. Now OLE offers both linking and embedding. OLE allows you to create links from one document or file to another document or file. These links can be between documents that are created in the same application (such as Word) or documents that are created in different applications (such as Word and Excel).

After you establish a link, you can update the information automatically by editing the original source of the information. This procedure lets you use data in various places but updates it in only one place. You must set up a *link* between two applications (or two documents) that support OLE. The application that requests data is called the *client* application. The other application, called the *server* application, responds to the client application's request by supplying the requested data.

See "Using Embedding to Link Information," **p. 922**

With linked documents, you can work in the client application and make changes in data that's linked to the server application. When you change the data in the client application, Windows 95 automatically changes the data in the server application. The advantage to exchanging data by links is that data is kept up-to-date in the client and server applications.

One possible use of linking is taking data from an Excel worksheet and placing it in a Word document. If you need to change the Excel data, you need to change it only in Excel; the data is updated in Word automatically. In Figure 34.13, for example, data for the regional sales of TechTron is shown in an Excel worksheet. Figure 34.14 shows the same numbers in a Word document that can be distributed to the staff in the form of a memorandum.

Suppose that you want to put together a new memo each month to detail sales for the entire year, but you want to create the memo document one time and update the sales data in the Word document automatically. You can do this by using an OLE link. In this example, to change the worksheet data in the Word document, you need to change the data while you're working in Excel.

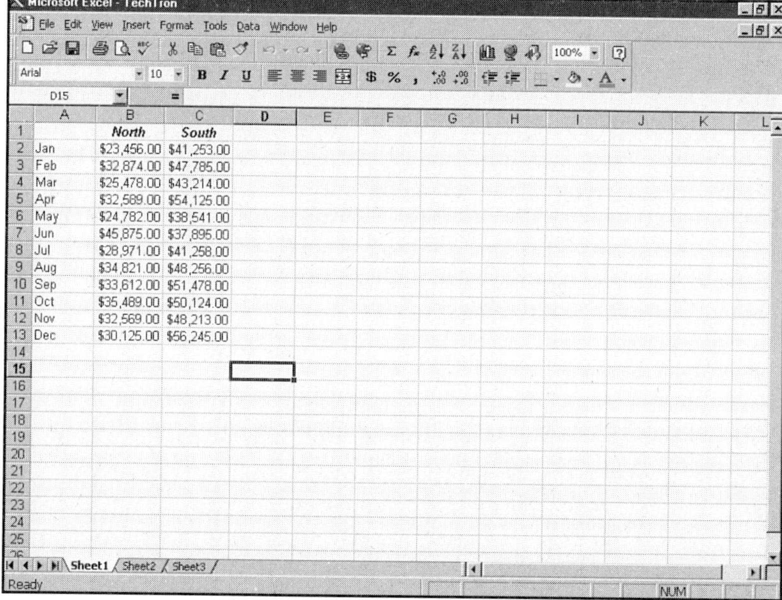

FIG. 34.13
Data from an Excel spreadsheet can be linked to a Word document.

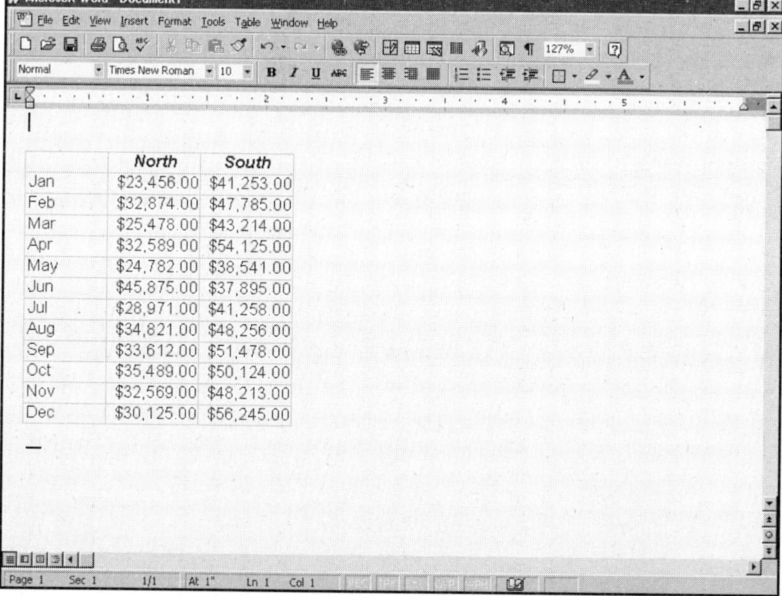

FIG. 34.14
The Word document reflects any changes that you make in the Excel document.

Windows 95 provides two ways to use linking: interactively and through a macro language. The easiest way to use linking is the interactive method, which is based on the Clipboard copy-and-paste method you used earlier in this chapter but has some important differences. The macro method, which involves creating a macro in the application's macro language, isn't discussed in this book. See *Special Edition Using Excel Visual Basic for Applications*, Second Edition, published by Que, for more information on creating links using a macro language.

When you establish a link between applications, you use the Edit menu's Copy and Paste Link or Paste Special commands. If you have an Excel worksheet that you want to link to a Word document, follow these steps:

1. Open an Excel worksheet. You also can create a new worksheet from which you will link data.
2. Select some data in the worksheet, as shown in Figure 34.15.

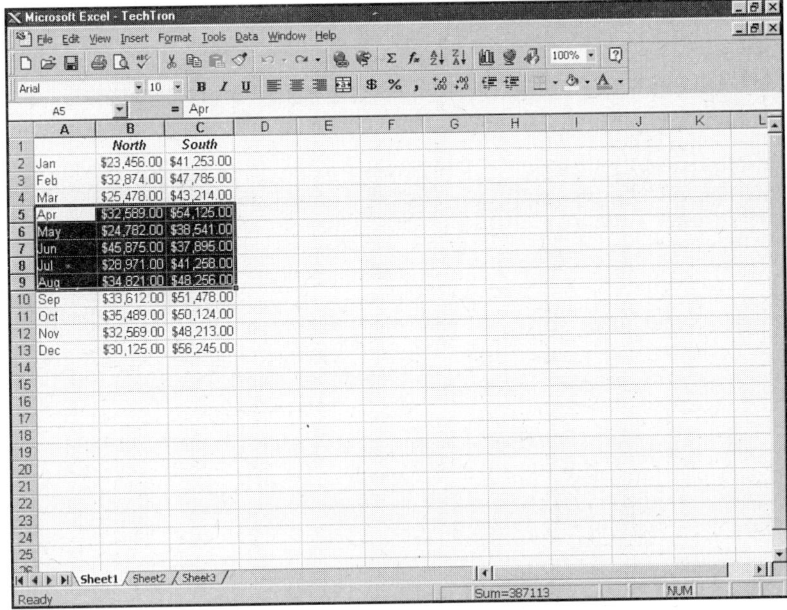

FIG. 34.15
Select data in Excel to link to Word.

3. Choose Edit, Copy to copy the selected data to the Clipboard.
4. Open Word and then open an existing document or start a new document.
5. Choose Edit, Paste Special and the Paste Special dialog box appears.
6. In the Paste Special dialog box, click the Paste Link option (see Figure 34.16). If you don't click this button, Word inserts the data from Excel as a table without linking.
7. Select Formatted Text (RTF) in the As list box.

   If you select Microsoft Excel Worksheet Object, the selected cells are inserted as an object (using OLE) into the Word document, instead of as a linked table. Sharing information by embedding objects using OLE is covered in Chapter 35, "Advanced Ways of Sharing Data Between Applications with OLE."

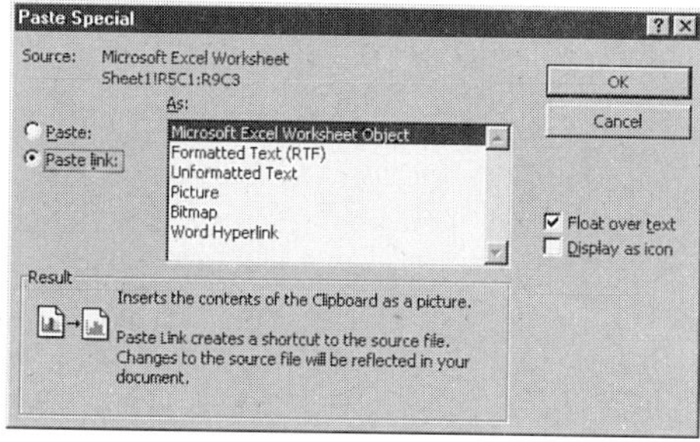

FIG. 34.16
Make sure you click the Paste Link button to establish a link.

8. Choose OK. The Excel data is inserted into the Word document as a table (see Figure 34.17).

When changes are made in the data in Excel, those changes are reflected in the Word document.

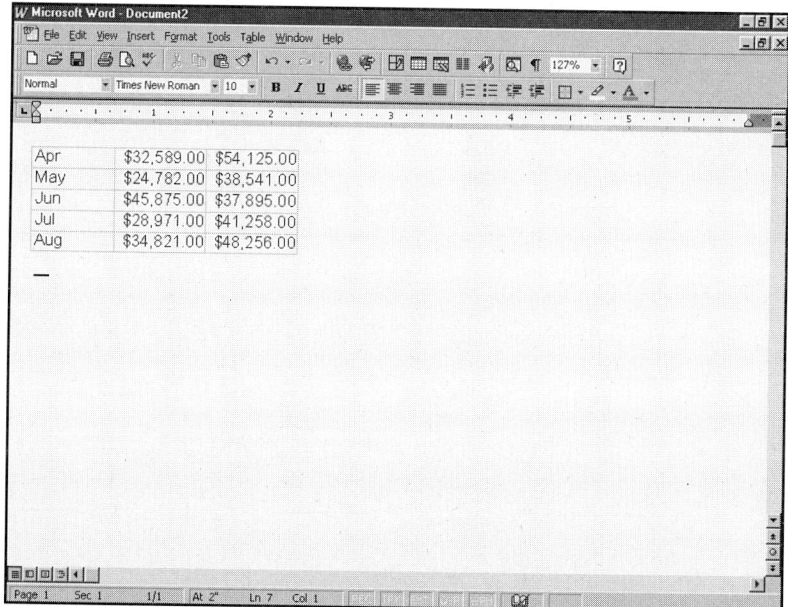

FIG. 34.17
Excel data is now linked to the Word document.

To see changes take place, switch back to the Excel worksheet and then follow these steps:

1. Change some of the data or formatting in the area that you linked to the Word document (see Figure 34.18).
2. Press Enter or click outside the cells that you edited. The data changes in the Word document to reflect your changes.
3. Switch to the Word document to see the updated data (see Figure 34.19).

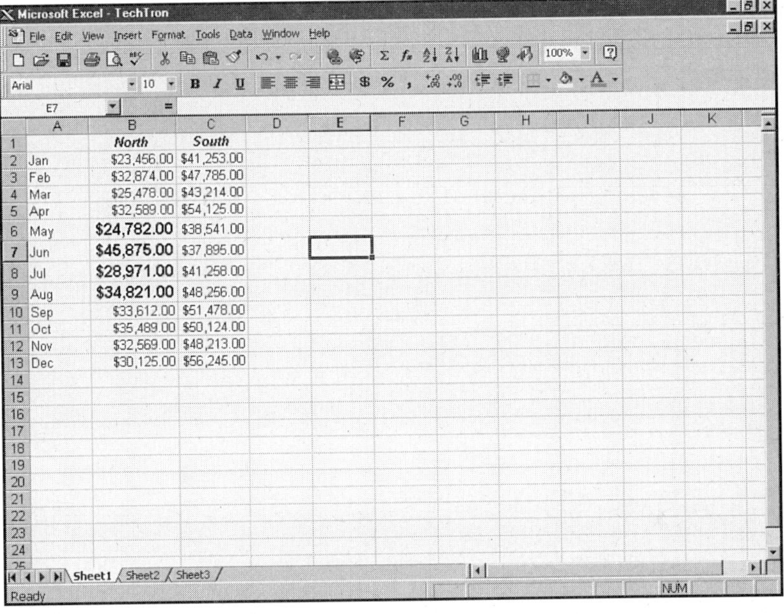

FIG. 34.18
Change some data in the Excel worksheet.

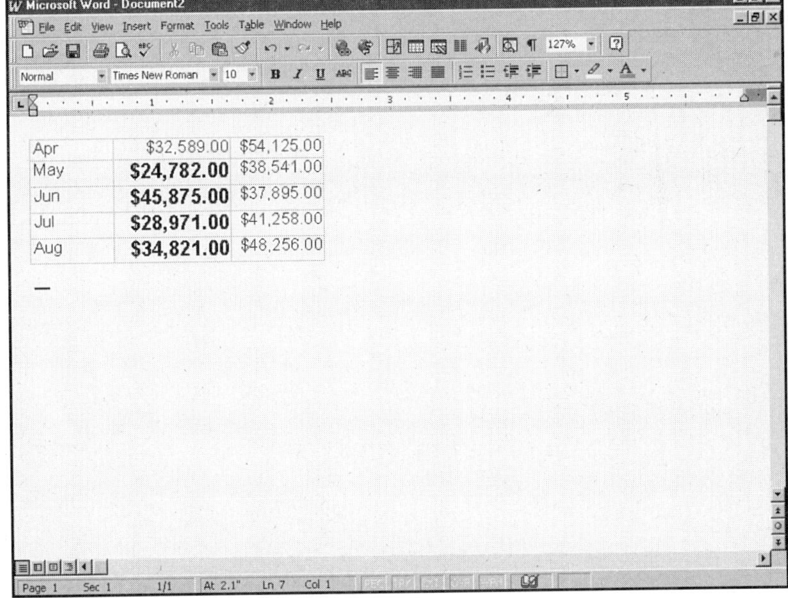

FIG. 34.19
The Word document is updated to reflect your changes.

NOTE If you change the name or path of your client or server documents, you must re-establish your links. You should make a habit of changing or creating file names and directories for your documents before you create a link. Otherwise, your data won't update properly, causing you to work with old data.

CHAPTER 35

Advanced Ways of Sharing Data Between Applications with OLE

by Rob Tidrow with Bob Voss

Understand compound documents and objects

Learn about what a compound document is made up of and the terminology used to describe compound documents.

Embed information within documents

Look here to learn the procedures for embedding objects from one application into a document in another application.

Edit OLE objects in a document

Learn how to edit the objects you have embedded in a document.

Create OLE shortcuts on the desktop

Learn how to use OLE technology to create many kinds of shortcuts on your desktop.

Expanding on the topic of data exchange and information sharing, this chapter introduces you to compound documents and object linking and embedding (OLE). *Compound documents* are documents you create by using multiple types of data. *Object linking and embedding* is a technology invented by Microsoft that allows you to build compound documents. ■

Introduction to Compound Documents

As the personal computer industry matures and more powerful operating systems (such as Windows 95) are developed, users are gaining the ability to create documents that include almost any type of data, from almost any source. When you think about the elements that you place within a document—a sound clip, a picture, a spreadsheet—think about them as objects. An *object* is simply a piece of data that has a characteristic (such as sound) and a behavior (it plays a sound when you click it).

Objects are the basic building blocks of Microsoft's programming interface called object linking and embedding, or *OLE* (pronounced "oh-lay"). OLE allows you to build *compound documents*, which are documents that you create in one application but with objects from several different applications.

One technical definition of a compound document is that it's a data file maintained by a container application, and that it contains one or more embedded objects. If you break this down, it means that you can, for example, use Word as your container application and have an Excel chart be your embedded object. You might be asking, "What's all the fuss about? I've been doing this using the Clipboard and copy-and-paste already."

Well, the major difference between OLE (specifically OLE version 2.0) and simple data exchange (via the Clipboard) is that OLE lets you edit your Excel chart (your embedded object) while still in Word for Windows. You can't do that with a simple Clipboard cut-and-paste operation or with linking. With a linking, you have to return to the original application (in this case, Excel) to edit or modify the drawing. When you want to edit an OLE object in the compound document (in this case, a Word document), you just double-click the object, and elements common to the Excel interface appear on the Word for Windows interface. Figure 35.1 shows an example of this.

The obvious benefit of having the ability to edit an embedded object within a compound document is that you don't have to return to the source application every time you want to change the object. Many times, you just need to change the spelling of a word, the position of a graphical element, or one or two entries of data after you place an element in your document. By using OLE 2.0, you double-click the object, wait a few seconds (or minutes, depending on your system) while your application changes, and then make the necessary changes to the object. On the other hand, when you link data, you must open the application that created the data, open the file that contains the data, change the data, and then update the link.

NOTE Microsoft released a Service Pack 1 Update that includes an OLE 32 update. This update fixes problems that are known to occur with files created by Excel, Word, and PowerPoint, which use OLE for file storage. What can happen with these applications is that information from deleted files can end up in current files. Although this information is not visible within the native application, if you open the file in Windows Notepad, you might be able to see the information. If this information is of a sensitive nature, this might present a security problem.

You can download the Service Pack 1 Update from The Microsoft Network (**GO WINDOWS**), the World Wide Web (**http://www.microsoft.com**), or on CompuServe (**GO WINNEWS**). If you subscribe to Microsoft TechNet, the Service Pack 1 Update was included with the March 1996 CD-ROM.

If you have the OEM Service Release 2 (OSR2) version of Windows, which is installed on most newer computers, the OLE 32 update is incorporated into Windows. See "Installing the Windows 95b (OSR2) Service Release," in Chapter 2 for more information on OSR2.

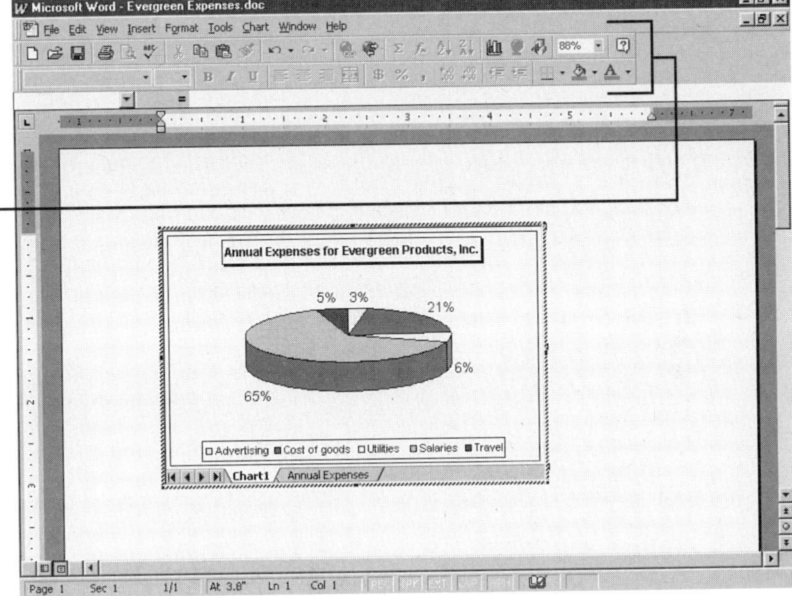

FIG. 35.1
While in Word, you can edit an Excel chart by using OLE 2.0 capabilities.

You're still in Word...
...but these are the Excel menus and tools

OLE Terminology

Similar to linking, OLE uses terms for each part of the embedding and linking stages. Two terms you need to understand are *client* and *server*. The *client* application uses the services of another application through OLE. The *server* application provides OLE services to a client application.

OLE Technology

Some of the advantages of OLE include:

- *OLE objects can be updated dynamically.* Like links, OLE objects can be updated dynamically when the source data changes.
- *OLE enables applications to specialize.* Rather than have one giant application that tries to be everything for everybody, OLE allows applications to do what they do best. A drawing package, for instance, can focus on drawing; spreadsheets can focus on sorting and analyzing data; word processors can focus on creating documents; and so on.
- *OLE lets users get tasks done.* When users use embedded objects, they can focus on getting their task done rather than on the application necessary to get the job completed.

When you embed an Excel chart in a Word document, for example, Excel is the OLE server and Word is the OLE client. You can think of this relationship the same way you think of a relationship with your attorney. The attorney is the *server* because he or she provides a service to you (legal help). You're the *client* because you're requesting services from the attorney (better known as the server). The services you obtain from the attorney can then be thought of as *objects*. You can use these objects, but if you need to update them or expand them (gain more knowledge of incorporating your business, for instance), you must go back and request help from your attorney. This is the same way you can update your embedded objects by using OLE. The client requests services from the server to help update the object.

Other OLE terms you need to understand include in-place editing, drag and drop, container object, and OLE automation. These terms are defined in the following list:

- **In-place editing.** Refers to the ability to modify an embedded object within the client application without leaving the client application.
- **Drag and drop.** Refers to the capability to grab an object, move it across the screen, and place it into a client document. An example of dragging and dropping an object is selecting an Excel chart in Excel, dragging it to Microsoft Word, and dropping it in a document.
- **Container object.** An object that contains another object or several objects. In the preceding example, the Word document is the container object that holds the Excel object.
- **OLE automation.** Refers to the capability of a server application to make available (this is known as *expose*) its own objects for use in another application's macro language. This term is used a great deal among advanced users and software developers. One example of this is Microsoft's Visual Basic for Applications (VBA) programming language. VBA Excel version, for example, can use objects in Microsoft Project's VBA environment, enabling developers to create powerful custom applications.

Using Embedding to Link Information

If you're confused by linking and embedding, keep in mind one major difference between the two: where the information is stored. Linked information is stored in the source document. The destination contains only a code that supplies the name of the source application, document, and the portion of the document. Embedded information is stored in the destination document, and the code associated with OLE points to a source application rather than a file.

In some cases, you can't use the source application by itself; you have to use your destination application to start the application. These applications include WordArt, ClipArt, Microsoft Graph, and others. You generally launch the source application by choosing Insert, Object.

Embedding Information in Your Documents

When you embed an object, the information resides in the destination document, but the source application's tools are available for use in editing. You can embed information from a document in one application into a document in another application. You can, for example, embed a table you have created in an Excel worksheet into a document you are creating in Word. You can accomplish this task using the Edit, Copy and Edit, Paste Special commands or by using the mouse to drag and drop the information. The Paste Special command has more flexibility in that it allows you to link or not link the object with its source. When you drag and drop an object, the object is not linked to its source.

Using the Menu to Embed Information To use the menu to embed information from one document into another, follow these steps:

1. Select the information in the source document.
2. Choose Edit, Copy.
3. Switch to the destination and open the document that will contain the object.
4. Choose Edit, Paste Special to display the Paste Special dialog box. The Paste Special dialog box in Word is shown in Figure 35.2.

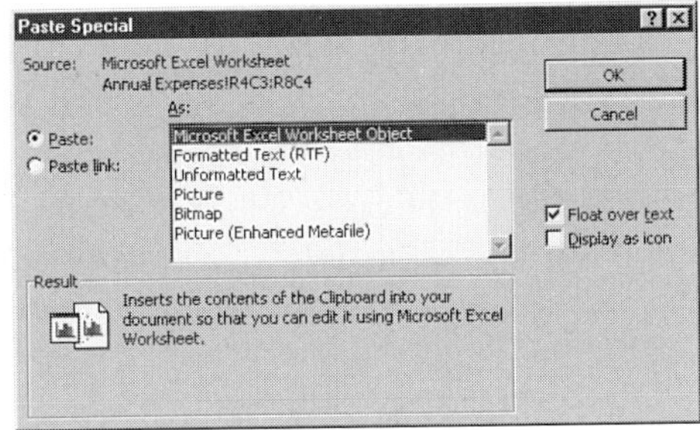

FIG. 35.2 You can select the type of information you want to paste from the Clipboard and whether it is linked to the source in the Paste Special dialog box.

5. Select the object from the As list (in Figure 35.2, Microsoft Excel Worksheet Object).
6. Select either the Paste or Paste Link option.

   If you select Paste, the object is embedded but not linked to the source document. When you double-click the object, the menus and toolbars for the source application appear, allowing you to edit in place.

   If you select Paste Link, the object is linked to the source document. When you double-click the object, the original document is opened and the information you linked is selected.
7. Choose OK.

Using Drag and Drop to Embed Information OLE 2.0-compliant applications fully support drag-and-drop operations. This means you can drag an object from a document in one OLE 2.0 application and drop it into a document in another OLE 2.0-compliant application.

To drag and drop information from one application to another, follow these steps:

1. Open both applications and arrange their Windows side-by-side.
2. Select the information in the source document.

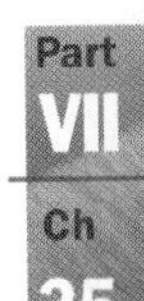

3. Drag the selection and drop it at the desired location in the destination document.

To copy rather than move the object, hold down the Ctrl key as you drag and drop it into the destination. Otherwise, you will move the selected information from the source to the destination. Look for the plus sign next to the mouse pointer when you hold down the Ctrl key. Don't release the Ctrl key until you've released the mouse button.

When you embed information from one application into another by using drag and drop, it is not linked to the original data. Changes in the source document will not be reflected in the embedded object. To link an embedded object, use the menu method just described.

If the application you want to drop an object in is minimized or hidden by other applications, you can drag the object to the application's button on the taskbar, pause for a few seconds until the application window appears, and then drop the object at the desired location in the destination application.

NOTE When you drag and drop information from one application to another, it is embedded as an object in the destination document if the data types for the two applications are different. If the data type is the same, the information is inserted in its native format. When you drag and drop a range of cells from Excel to a Word document, for example, it is inserted as an object. When you drag a text selection from Word to Excel, on the other hand, it is inserted as straight text, since a cell can accept text. To insert a text selection as an object, you must use the Edit, Copy and Edit, Paste Special commands.

If you accidentally move rather than copy data from one application to another using drag and drop, switch back to the source application and choose Edit, Undo to restore the information in the source document. The object in the destination document will not be affected.

If you forget to hold down the Ctrl key as you start the drag-and-drop operation, it doesn't matter. As long as you are holding down the Ctrl key when you drop the object, the object will be copied, not moved. You can cancel the drag-and-drop operation by pressing the Esc key.

See "Using Drag and Drop to Move or Copy Information Within an Application's Documents," **p. 907**

See "Understanding Data Linking," **p. 913**

Inserting a File into a Document

You can insert a file into documents by choosing Insert, File, which allows you to insert an entire file as an object. When you use Paste Special to link a file (as you did in Chapter 34), only the text you select before using the Edit, Copy command is part of the target file. If you later go back and insert text before or after the source-document selection, the target document doesn't include the entire text. Choosing Insert, File alleviates this problem.

To insert a file into a document, follow these steps:

1. Move to the position in the target document where you want to insert the file.
2. Do one of the following, depending on the application you use:
   - In WordPad, choose Insert, Object. Click the Create From File option. The Insert Object dialog box appears (see Figure 35.3).

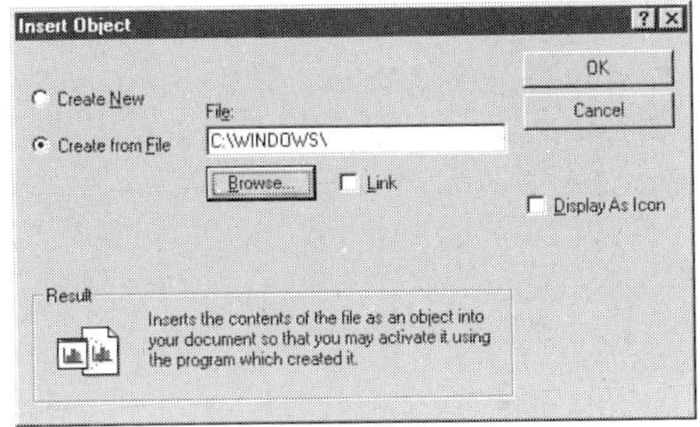

FIG. 35.3 Enter the file name or use the Browse button to indicate the file you want to embed in a WordPad document.

   - In Word, choose Insert, File. The Insert File dialog box appears (see Figure 35.4).
   - In Microsoft Excel, choose Insert, Object. The Object dialog box appears. Click the Create From File tab and choose the application and file.

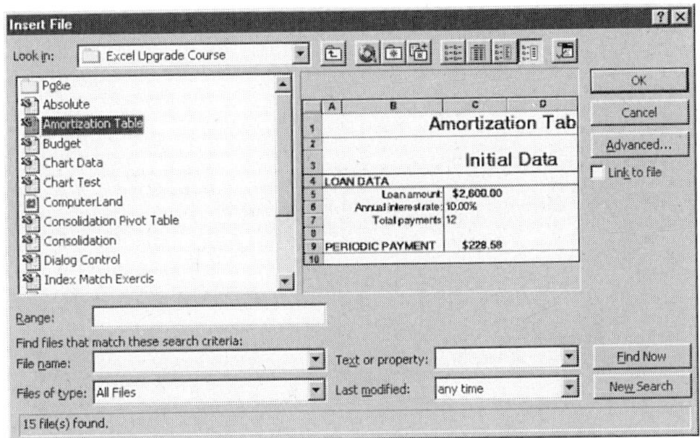

FIG. 35.4 Use Word's Insert, File command to embed a file in a Word document. Here the Preview button was selected to display a thumbnail view of the document.

3. Identify the file you want to insert, including the drive and directory, if necessary.
4. Select the Link or Link To File option.
5. Click OK.

To see that the file you inserted is a linked object, click anywhere in the document to show a gray highlight or to show the object's field codes. In Word, you can press Shift+F9 to toggle between viewing the text of the file and the field code for the inserted object.

If you want to insert several word processing documents into a single larger document, remember that each document will retain its original formatting. You will want to give your documents a consistent appearance by formatting them the same. You can use templates and styles to help ensure consistency among documents.

Inserting a New Object into Your Document

If you want to use the features of another application in your compound documents, you can choose Insert, Object and select an application from the provided list. As pointed out at the beginning of this chapter, many applications now support this feature of OLE 2.0, including the standard Microsoft Office applications, the Windows applications (for example, Paint and WordPad), and other Windows applications. Some Windows applications come with small applications that can only be used from within the main application.

As examples of the types of applications that support OLE as a server application or client application, the following applications come with Microsoft Office. When you install Microsoft Office on your system, these applications are installed in a centralized location that allows many Office applications to access them easily. The WordPad application, which comes with Windows 95, can embed many types of objects, some of which are listed here.

Application	Use
Microsoft Clip Gallery	Inserts clip-art pictures
Microsoft Map	Inserts a map showing different levels associated with data
Microsoft Equation	Creates mathematical expressions
Microsoft Graph	Inserts charts from data in a Word table
Microsoft Organization Chart	Creates organization charts
Microsoft Word Picture	Inserts a picture and the tools associated with the Word drawing toolbar
Microsoft WordArt	Creates logos and other special text effects

To use the tools from another application within your document to create a new object, follow these steps:

1. Position the insertion point in the destination document.
2. Choose Insert, Object. The Insert Object dialog box appears (see Figure 35.5).
3. Select the Create New option button, and then select an application from the Object Type list.
4. If you want to see only an icon for the object, select the Display as Icon check box.
5. When you finish with the Insert Object dialog box, choose OK.

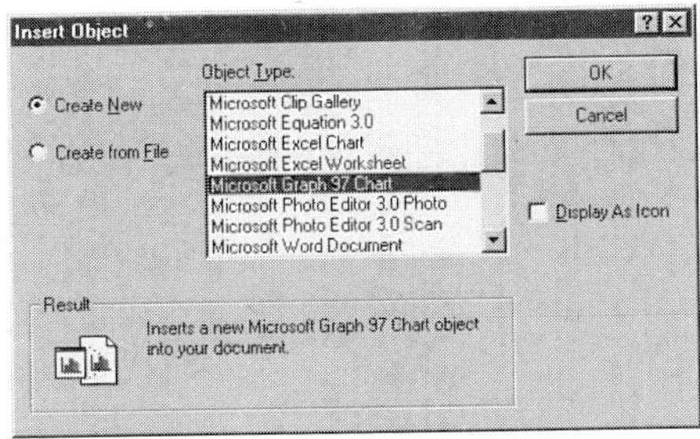

FIG. 35.5
The Insert Object dialog box lists applications as well as Windows applications.

The title bar identifies the application you are viewing. Applications that support OLE 2.0 display the name of the container application. Applications that support OLE 1.0 display the name of the source application.

After you complete these steps, one of two things occurs. A separate window for the application appears with the document active. Or you'll remain in your client document window, but the menu bar and toolbar change to reflect the source application (see Figure 35.6).

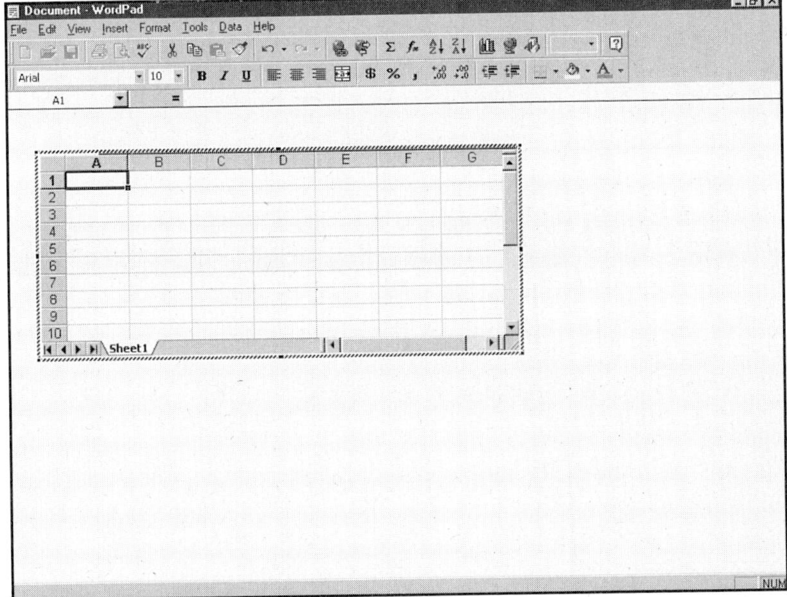

FIG. 35.6
When you choose Microsoft Excel Worksheet, you get in-place editing. The menu bar and toolbar change to Microsoft Excel, enabling you to use Excel features, such as the AutoSum button.

Create the object by using the application's toolbar and menus. When you finish creating the object, you can exit the object in one of two ways:

- If you launched a separate window for the application, choose File, Exit.
- If you stayed in your destination document, click outside the object.

Editing an Embedded Object

Regardless of which method you use to embed information into your document, you can edit the embedded object with the tools of the source application. To edit the object, follow these steps:

1. Click the object. Handles appear around the object, and the status bar tells you to double-click the object (see Figure 35.7).

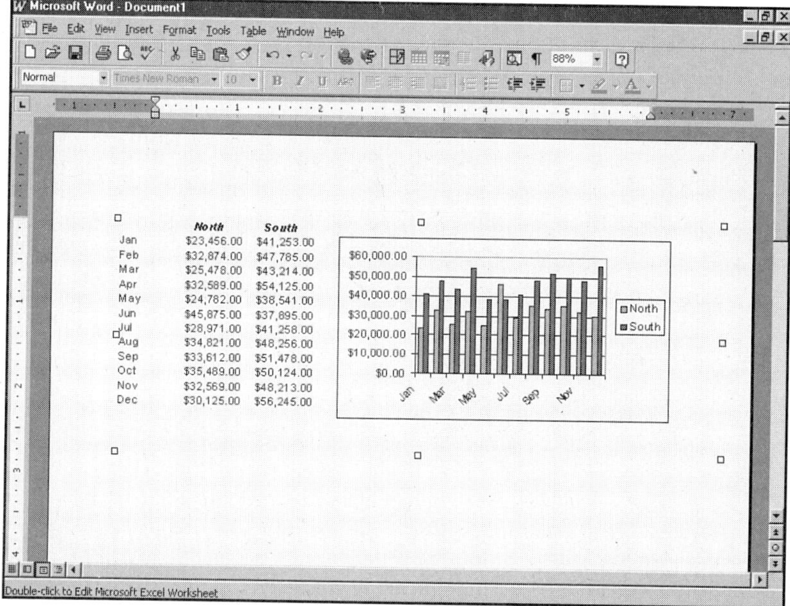

FIG. 35.7 The status bar displays instructions on how to get to the source-application tools.

2. Double-click the object. Depending on the source and destination applications, a separate window for the program appears, or the current window's toolbar and menu bar change to those of the source application.
3. Edit the object, using the application's toolbar and menus.
4. When you finish editing the object, exit the object. If you launched a separate window for the application, choose File, Exit. If you stayed in your destination document, click outside the object.

Creating an Example Compound Document

The best way to learn how to use OLE is to actually use it a few times. This section uses Microsoft Excel and some common Windows 95 applications, such as Paint and Sound Recorder, to show you how to build a compound document. If you don't have Excel and Word, you can use other OLE 2.0-compliant applications to simulate this exercise.

Embedding a Paint Object in Word

To start your document, open Word, which will be the container application where you'll embed server objects. In English, this means you'll use Word as your main program and embed a Paint bitmap, an Excel chart, and a sound file into your Word document.

1. In Word, create some text such as **Let's embed a Paint object first:**.
2. Switch to Paint and open SETUP.BMP, which is located in the WINDOWS folder..
3. Click the Select tool on the Paint tool box. Mark an area on the drawing that you want to embed in your Word document. Choose Edit, Copy.
4. Switch to Word and place the cursor where you want to insert the drawing object. Choose Edit, Paste Special. The Paste Special dialog box appears (see Figure 35.8).

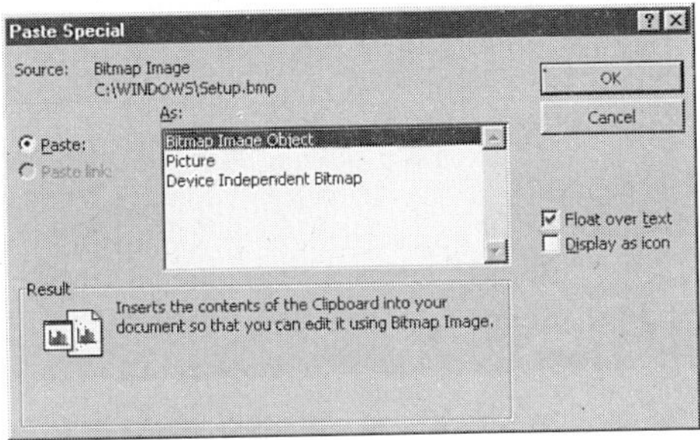

FIG. 35.8
You can embed objects by using the Paste Special dialog box.

5. In the Paste Special dialog box, make sure that the Paste Link check box isn't marked. You don't want to link this object to your document. Also, select Bitmap Image in the As list box. Click OK.
6. After a few seconds, your Word document displays an embedded Paint object. How do you know it's embedded? Click the object, and a thin border surrounds it. This is a frame that Word puts around the object. Double-click the object, however, and the entire Word interface changes to look like Paint (see Figure 35.9).

Embedding an Excel Object by Dragging and Dropping

Another way to embed an object into your Word compound document is by dragging and dropping it from a server application. To drag a chart from Excel into Word, use these steps:

1. Open Excel and create a chart. You don't have to load it with a lot of data, but do a simple one, as shown in Figure 35.10.
2. Arrange your desktop so that you can see Word and Excel at the same time, as shown in Figure 35.11.
3. Select and drag the chart into the Word window. Place the gray box with a plus sign in it at the spot where you want the chart embedded. If you want it in a special place in the document, you should prepare the document for the object before you start the drag-and-drop process.

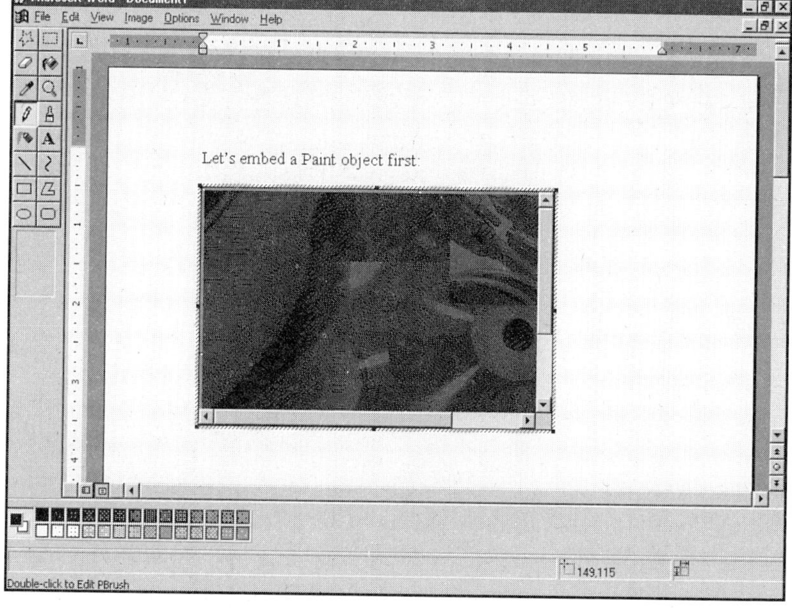

FIG. 35.9
Double-clicking the Paint object changes the Word interface to show Paint tools and menus.

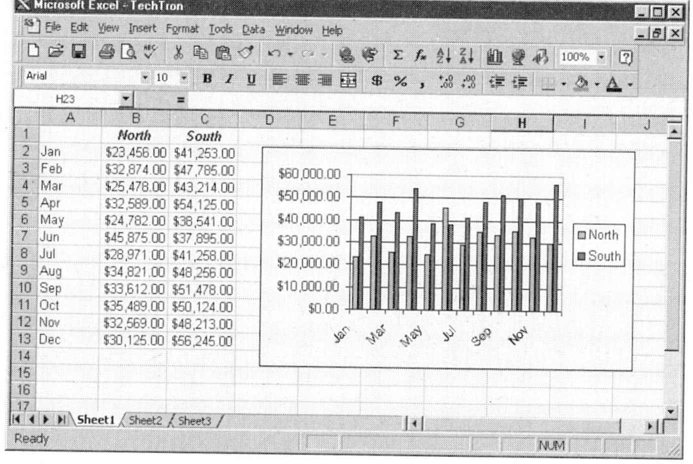

FIG. 35.10
You can drag a chart from an Excel worksheet into a Word document.

4. Release the mouse button. The Excel chart now appears in the Word document as an embedded object.

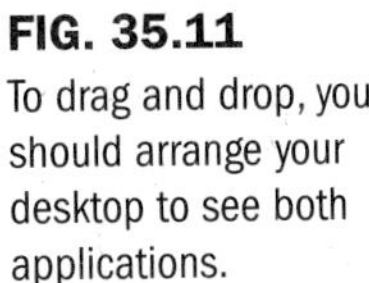

FIG. 35.11
To drag and drop, you should arrange your desktop to see both applications.

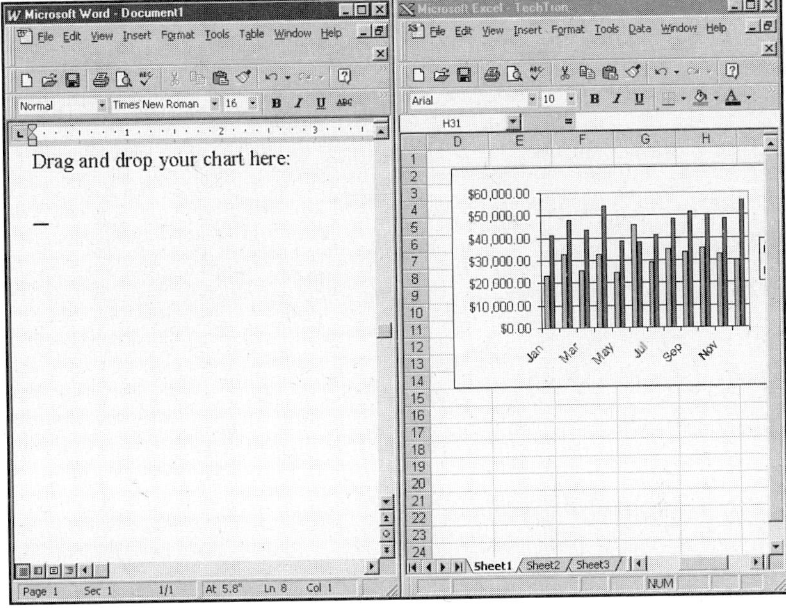

Embedding a Sound Clip in Word

To add a little flavor to your Word compound document, include a sound clip that your readers can click. You need to have a sound card and microphone to create and hear these sounds, but you still can embed the sound clips even if you don't have a sound card installed. To embed a sound clip in your document, follow these steps:

1. In Word, choose Insert, Object.
2. In the Insert Object dialog box, select Wave Sound from the Object Type list.

NOTE If you have a specific sound clip that you want to embed, click the Create from File option and select the file you want to embed. If you don't click this option, the default setting is to create a new sound clip.

3. Click the Display As Icon check box to embed an icon of the sound clip in your Word document. When you use an icon, you reduce the system resources necessary to store the object.
4. Click OK. An icon of the sound object appears in the Word document (see Figure 35.12).
5. Double-click the icon to play back the sound file you recorded. To edit the wave sound object, right-click the wave sound icon and choose Wave Sound Object, Edit from the shortcut menu. The sound recorder will open as shown in Figure 35.13.

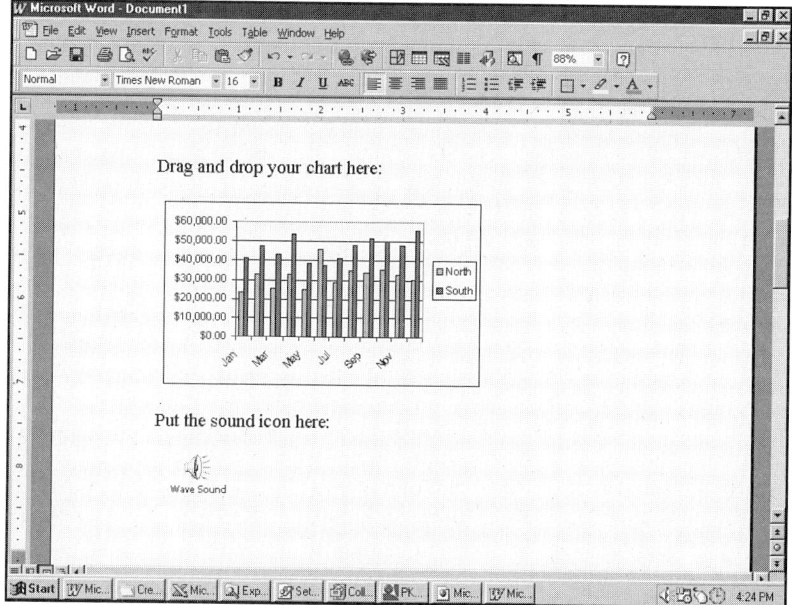

FIG. 35.12
The sound object appears as an icon in your document.

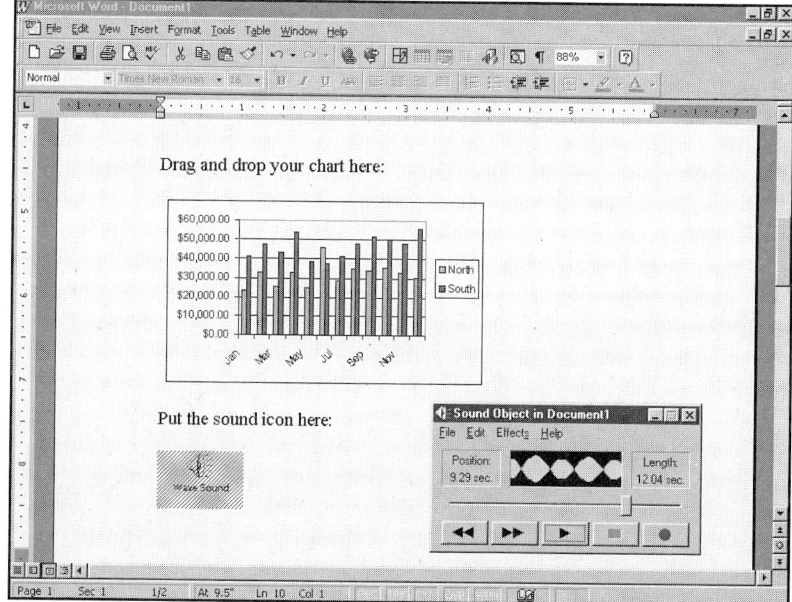

FIG. 35.13
You can activate the sound recorder application to edit the sound object by right-clicking the sound object icon and choosing Wave Sound Object, Edit.

Editing an Embedded Object in Your Compound Document

If your data changes, your taste in art differs now from when you embedded the graphic object, or you want to add something to your sound clip, you can edit each object without leaving Word. This section shows you how to edit the Excel chart that you embedded earlier in the section "Embedding an Excel Object by Dragging and Dropping."

To edit the chart, follow these steps:

1. Double-click the Excel chart in your Word compound document. The Word interface automatically changes to the standard Excel interface (see Figure 35.14).

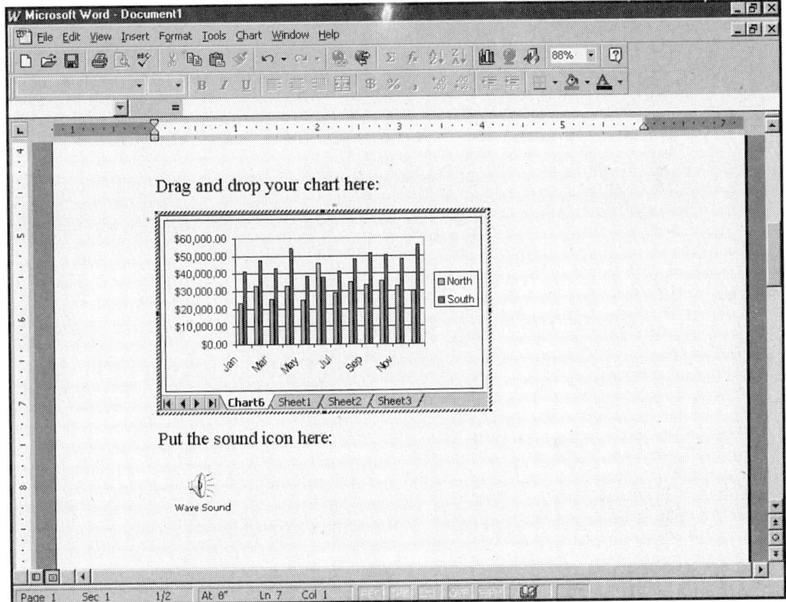

FIG. 35.14
With OLE 2.0, your container application takes on the appearance of the source application.

2. Make changes to the chart by using the toolbars and menu options. When you finish, click outside the chart. This returns the Word interface to its original state (see Figure 35.15).

TROUBLESHOOTING

When I double-click a linked or embedded object, a Cannot Edit error message appears. This means that the source file can't be opened. Make sure that the application needed to edit the file is on your machine. Also make sure that you have enough system memory to run both the container and source applications. Keep in mind that compound documents demand more memory than simple documents.

continues

continued

The margins are 0 (zero) in all my embedded Microsoft Word objects. Word sets the margins at 0 (zero) inches in a document object to eliminate excessive white space around the object. To change the margins, double-click the Word document object to open it for editing. Choose File, Page Setup; click the Margins tab and then enter new margin settings.

When I double-click an embedded Microsoft Excel object, Microsoft Excel doesn't open. You probably have the Ignore Other Applications check box selected, which causes Microsoft Excel to ignore all requests from other applications. In Excel, choose Tools, Options and then click the General tab. Clear the Ignore Other Applications check box.

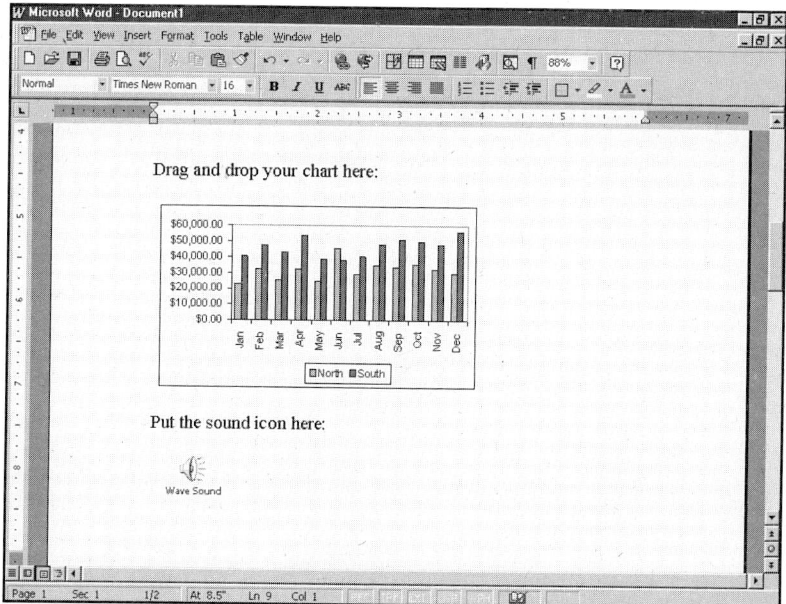

FIG. 35.15 Word's interface returns to its original state, but the Excel chart has changed.

Linking Objects to Shortcuts on the Desktop Using OLE

One of the most useful new features in Windows 95 is the ability to create shortcuts to virtually any object, including files, folders, floppy drives, and printers.

In the following sections, you learn how to link document objects with icons on your desktop. These shortcuts can expand your ability to share and access the information on your computer.

See "Starting from Shortcuts," **p. 237**

Creating Document Shortcuts

Document shortcuts allow you to quickly navigate to a particular location in a document. You can, for example, create a document shortcut on the desktop to a cell in an Excel worksheet, so that when you double-click the shortcut, Excel starts, and the target worksheet opens with the cell selected. You can create a shortcut to a location or selection in any OLE 2.0-compliant application. You can keep these shortcuts on the desktop, or you can place them in a folder on the desktop, if you don't want to clutter up your desktop with shortcuts. Using folders to store your document shortcuts also can help you organize them.

One example of how you can use document shortcuts to save time is if you are working in a document in which you spend a lot of time navigating from one location to another. To ease navigation, you can create document shortcuts to key locations in the document so that you can move to a particular location by simply double-clicking the shortcut for that location. You can collect all the shortcuts for a document in a folder, so that it becomes a computerized table of contents that streamlines navigation.

To create a document shortcut, follow these steps:

1. Make a selection in the document (cells in a worksheet or text in a word processing document).
2. Drag and drop the selection to the desktop by using the right mouse button.
3. Choose Create Document Shortcut Here from the menu that appears when you release the mouse button.

When you double-click the shortcut, the document opens at the original selection. You can move the shortcut to a folder that you create on the desktop.

NOTE Not all OLE-compliant applications allow you to create document shortcuts using drag and drop. In these cases, you can create a document shortcut by making a selection, choosing Edit, Copy, right-clicking the desktop, and choosing Create Shortcut from the menu.

Creating Document Scraps

You also can create document scraps on your desktop. *Scraps* are pieces of information from any OLE document that you store on your desktop or in a folder. At any time, you can drag a scrap into a document in any OLE application to insert it as an embedded object. You can use the scrap as many times as you like in as many different documents as you like.

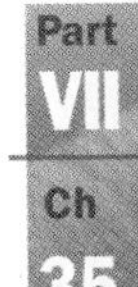

To create a scrap, follow these steps:

1. Select the information you want to create a scrap from.
2. Drag the selection to the desktop or to a folder.

A scrap consisting of the selected information is created. If you double-click the scrap, the information in the scrap appears in the application that created it. You can drag and drop the scrap into any OLE document to embed it as an object in the document.

Use scraps to create Post-it notes on your desktop. When you want to save a bit of information that you don't want to forget on your desktop, open WordPad (click Start; then choose Programs, Accessories, WordPad), type the note, select the text, and drag it to the desktop. You don't have to save the WordPad file. To read the note, double-click the scrap. The name of the scrap is taken from the first sentence of the scrap text. You can rename the scrap to give it a more useful name.

Creating Links to Internet and MSN Sites

In Chapter 17, "Getting Connected to the Internet," you learned how to create shortcuts on your desktop to sites on the Internet and Microsoft Network. This is useful if you routinely access certain sites and want to access these sites by double-clicking a shortcut. You also can embed these shortcuts into any OLE document so that you can access these sites from within the document. Imagine distributing a document to your colleagues loaded with shortcuts to useful sites on the Internet. All they have to do is open the document and double-click the shortcuts.

To embed an Internet or MSN shortcut in a document, drag and drop the shortcut from the desktop into the document. You can then double-click the shortcut to sign on to the Internet or MSN and move to that site.

PART VIII

Networking with Windows

CHAPTER 36

Setting Up a Windows 95 Peer-to-Peer Network

by Craig Zacker with Robert L. Bogue

In addition to its client/server capabilities, Windows 95 also is a peer-to-peer network operating system. A peer-to-peer network is one in which every workstation can directly communicate with every other workstation, without the need for an intervening server. You can therefore share a workstation's resources with other users in the same way that a server's resources are shared on a client/server network.

In the Microsoft Windows networking model, the boundaries between the server and the workstation are far less distinct than they are on a Novell NetWare network. All Windows servers are functional clients as well, allowing a user to run an application or access a remote network resource while the machine continues to perform its server duties. Every client workstation also can function as a server, offering access to its resources to other network users. A peer-to-peer network is one in which all of the computers function as both clients and servers. ■

Build a Windows 95 peer-to-peer network

Learn how a Windows 95 peer-to-peer network can operate as part of a client/server network or function on its own.

Create a workgroup

You can organize your network to accommodate almost any need by creating small teams of workers, called workgroups.

Install Windows 95's peer-to-peer networking components

See how to install components through the Control Panel by using the Network dialog box.

Add peer-to-peer networking into an existing client/server network

In a client/server network environment, Windows 95 can add peer-to-peer functionality to an existing infrastructure.

Establish procedures for securing peer network resources against unauthorized access

In the absence of a server to authenticate logons, it is important to be aware of peer network security.

Learn about user-level and share-level security

Windows 95 supports both levels of security.

Using the Peer Advantage

A Windows 95 peer-to-peer network can operate as part of a client/server network, or it can function on its own, without the presence of a server. A high-powered client/server NOS like NetWare or NT Server greatly increases the efficiency of the file and print services for which the local area network was originally designed. It also provides the potential for the evolution to higher level network services such as shared databases and communication applications. However, despite the added power, there is a basic functional drawback to the client/server model.

With the client/server arrangement, when one user needs access to a file on another user's local hard drive, the only solution is to copy the file to a server drive, so that both users can access it from there. There is no direct communication between workstations, as shown in Figure 36.1. On a peer-to-peer network, the file can be accessed directly, without bothering its owner. When one user needs to briefly use an application installed on another's machine, the user can simply access the application from the other's drive.

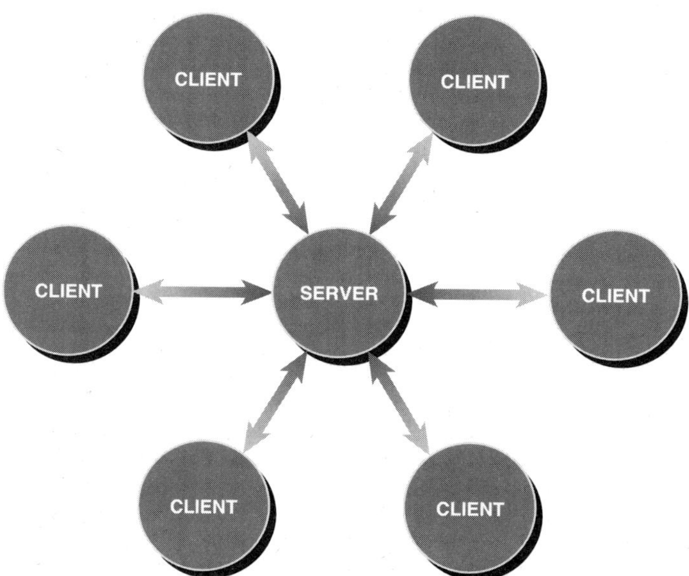

FIG. 36.1
The client/server model allows a workstation to communicate only with host servers.

Thus, it is clear that the peer-to-peer networking model does offer something that the client/server model lacks. Instead of every workstation communicating only with a central point, the server, every machine is theoretically capable of communicating with every other machine, as shown in Figure 36.2.

Peer-to-peer networking also allows users to share their workstations' hardware resources more efficiently. With Windows 95, you can allow other network users to access your CD-ROM drive, printer, or fax modem with little effort beyond the normal installation procedure for the device. On a client/server network, configuring any of these devices for network access is a more complicated undertaking, sometimes requiring additional server hardware or software.

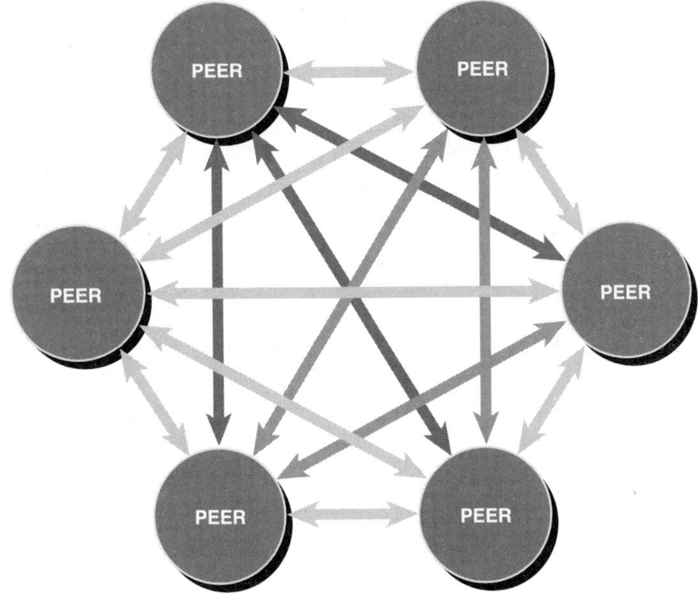

FIG. 36.2
Peer-to-peer networking can allow any workstation to access the resources of any other workstation.

Combining client/server with peer-to-peer networking is easy with Windows 95. You can construct a peer-to-peer network for a small business and add servers later, or add peer functionality to your existing client/server network. In either case, Windows 95 simplifies the conversion because all of the necessary client software is integrated into the operating system. You can therefore have a network that grows with the needs of the organization and offers the best features of both the client/server and peer-to-peer networking models.

Integrating Peer Networking into the Windows Environment

Like Windows for Workgroups and pre-version 4.0 Windows NT before it, Windows 95 incorporates both peer-to-peer and client/server networking functionality into the base operating system package. Windows 95 surpasses its predecessors, however, by automating more of the network configuration process and by providing a user interface in which peer network objects are presented side by side with server resources and those of the local machine.

Whichever organizational model you use in your network—client/server, peer-to-peer, or a combination of the two—your users will be working with the same interface. All other computers on the network appear as icons, with their shared resources displayed hierarchically beneath them.

Interestingly, Windows for Workgroups possesses much of the same basic networking capability that Windows 95 now does; that is, the ability to integrate client/server and peer-to-peer functionality into one operating system. The primary and crucial difference between the two is the ease and efficiency with which this is done.

With Windows 95, the process of adding peer-to-peer networking functionality almost never conflicts with the operation of an existing client/server configuration, as it often does in Windows for Workgroups. This allows you to create a business network that takes the fullest advantage of both network types. When every computer is capable of communicating with every other computer, the working environment is completely flexible.

You can create small teams of workers, called workgroups, that function with a greater amount of autonomy because of the access they are granted to each other's computing resources. You can therefore organize the network to accommodate the needs of the business, rather than organize the business around the constraints of the network.

Creating a New Peer Network with Windows 95

Like Windows for Workgroups and Windows NT before it, you can outfit a group of computers with network interface cards, connect them with cables and, using no software other than Windows 95, have them communicate with each other to great effect. Peer users can share their files, printers, fax modems, and CD-ROM drives without the intervention of a network administrator. You also can provide users with higher-level services, such as e-mail, group scheduling, and remote system administration, just as on a client/server network. Further, the addition of Plug and Play technology eliminates one of the largest stumbling blocks to the do-it-yourself network: selecting, installing, and configuring the hardware.

For a small business or home network of 10 workstations or less, purchase identical thin Ethernet Plug and Play network interface cards, insert one in each machine, connect them with prepackaged 50-ohm coaxial cables, and you have a network. Windows 95 identifies the cards and installs the correct drivers for you, and the basic installation is finished. Configuration and administration of your new network will take a little more effort, but that will be covered in this chapter and those immediately following.

Wiring a Small Network

Whereas Thin Ethernet is not the most recent technology in general use today, it's one of the most inexpensive and the simplest to install (which is why it's also known as *Cheapnet*). The professional standard in office networks is another Ethernet variety, 10BaseT, which uses twisted-pair, or telephone-type cabling. The complicating factor in a 10BaseT network is the need for a concentrator (or wiring hub), to which every workstation must be connected. This incurs additional expense. Thin Ethernet cables can simply be strung from one machine to the next, using the T-connectors supplied with the interface cards, and with a terminator plug installed on both ends. This wiring layout is called a *bus* topology. You must have at least six feet of cable between each pair of machines, and the total bus length cannot exceed 186 yards. The biggest problems with this kind of arrangement are:

- **Grounding problems.** Sometimes buildings will not have good grounds. The result is that the machines each have a different potential voltage (don't worry about what potential voltage actually is) and this can cause problems with machines communicating with one another. The solution is to have an electrician verify all of the outlets that the computers are plugged into.

- **Bad Ts or Terminators.** Just like everything else, there are a few bad Ts and Terminators. If either of these two types of devices fails, you may have some network communication, or no network communication. Review each T and terminator for visible damage, and keep a spare of each on hand to test, one by one, if a problem is discovered.
- **Cabling.** 10Base2 cabling is notoriously sensitive to tight bends. Try to allow 10Base2 cabling to make gentle arcs rather than tight corners. Tight corners can cause the cable to become unreliable.

Installing Peer-to-Peer Services

Manually installing Windows 95's peer networking capabilities is merely an extension to the network client installation procedure. Windows 95's Client for Microsoft Networks allows a workstation to see and access resources on both client and server machines running the Windows NT, Windows for Workgroups, or Windows 95 operating systems.

See "Installing the Client for Microsoft Networks for Windows NT 4.0," **p. 1027**

All machines with a functioning Windows client are visible to all users on the network, even those that are not configured to share any resources. The only step that remains for a Windows 95 machine with the Client for Microsoft Networks already installed is to add a service into the networking configuration that will allow the computer to share its own resources with other users on the network. To install the service, follow these steps:

1. Double-click the Network icon from the Windows 95 Control Panel and click Add.
2. Select Service, click Add again, highlight Microsoft and then File and Printer Sharing for Microsoft Networks. Click OK.
3. Click File and Print Sharing on the Network's Configuration page (see Figure 36.3), and select whether you want to share your drive(s), printer(s), or both. Click OK twice to complete the installation and restart Windows when you are asked to do so.

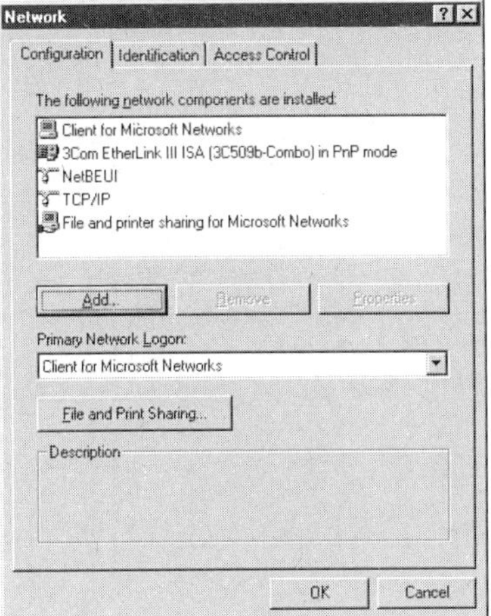

FIG. 36.3
The File and Print Sharing service enables the workstation to share its resources with others.

CAUTION

When installing the service, be sure not to choose the File and Print Sharing for NetWare Networks service by mistake. This is a completely different module that performs roughly the same workstation-sharing tasks, but in a NetWare environment. It uses NCP, the NetWare Core Protocol, instead of SMBs, Server Message Blocks, and makes a workstation appear to the network just as though it were a NetWare 3.12 server. It cannot run at the same time as the File and Print Sharing for Microsoft Networks service. One must be removed before the other is installed.

Windows Networking and Server Message Blocks

The SMB protocol was developed by Microsoft, Intel, and IBM to provide core networking functions between computers running the Windows network operating systems (Workgroups, NT and 95), as well as LAN Manager, LAN Manager for UNIX, AT&T StarLAN, IBM LAN Server, 3Com® 3+Open®, 3+Share®, and DEC PATHWORKS operating systems. Similar in functionality to Novell's NetWare Core Protocol (NCP), SMB provides commands that control four of the most fundamental networking operations: session control, file and print services, and messaging.

Session control is used to establish and break down connections to other machines on the network. File and Print commands initiate communications of the appropriate type for the transmission of data files and print jobs, and messaging commands are used whenever an application sends or receives messages from another workstation.

Whereas the basic Windows 95 Client for Microsoft Networks provides the client-side SMB functionality, the addition of the File and Printer Sharing service adds the capability for the Windows 95 machine to act as a server, by installing the VSERVER.VXD virtual device driver. Windows 95 machines with both of these components installed are peers in that they possess both client and server functionality in the same machine. This is why you may hear a workstation referred to as a "server," when the discussion involves the sharing of its resources.

Configuration Options

The File and Printer Sharing Service has only two configuration options:

- **Browse Master.** Used to designate whether this workstation should be the Browse Master for the workgroup. A Browse Master is a workstation that maintains a list of the other machines in the local workgroup. This arrangement saves time and network traffic by not forcing each machine to search the entire network segment for other machines each time it is browsed. The Windows 95 operating system cooperatively assigns a default Browse Master for each workgroup, but you can use this option to override the assignment. The current workstation can be designated a permanent Browse Master or prevented from ever being assigned Browse Master status.
- **LM Announce.** Used to control whether or not the workstation's presence should be advertised to LAN Manager 2.x workstations on the network. The default value of this parameter is No, and it needs to be set to Yes only if you have clients running LAN Manager 2.x that will be accessing the resources of your workstation.

These options are accessible from the service's properties sheet in the Network.

Integrating Windows 95 Peer Services into a Client/Server Network

In a client/server network environment running Windows NT or NetWare servers, Windows 95 can add the peer-to-peer functionality described at the beginning of this chapter to the existing infrastructure, and it can do it far more easily than Windows for Workgroups ever could. What this means is that, in addition to connecting to servers, workstations also can communicate directly with each other.

Thus, Windows 95 users can easily create their own local peer networking groups within the overall structure of the existing client/server network. Nearby users can share hardware conveniently, and users can perform the bulk of the configuration and administration tasks without the constant intervention of the network administrator.

CAUTION

Always consult with your network administrator before adding peer-to-peer networking to a working environment on any substantial level. You may weaken the performance of the network for other users, and the network administrator may waste a great deal of time trying to track down the cause of the performance degradation.

Users can easily access both client/server and peer networking functions because of Windows 95's improved ability to present and manipulate network entities within a logical, usable interface that fully integrates servers and other workstations into the desktop metaphor. In Chapter 35, you learned how users can access client/server resources, and how the Windows 95 interface can empower network users to achieve a greater level of network understanding than before.

In the rest of this chapter, you see how Windows 95 integrates peer networking entities into the desktop metaphor, how you can organize them into logical groupings, and how to use login and security procedures to grant appropriate access rights to all network users.

Peer Networking and Routability

A large business network is actually more accurately described as an *internetwork*—a network of networks. Individual LANs, or network segments, each containing a limited number of machines, form natural divisions between departments, divisions, or geographical locations within a company. The default transport protocol used in most of the Microsoft networking products is called NetBEUI, and unlike NetWare's IPX and TCP/IP, NetBEUI is a nonroutable protocol. This means that communication between Windows network machines is limited to those within the local segment, as shown in Figure 36.4, unless you take explicit steps to provide routing between networks. This situation is quickly changing, however; NT Server and Workstation 4.0 were the first Microsoft network operating systems to use TCP/IP as their default protocol.

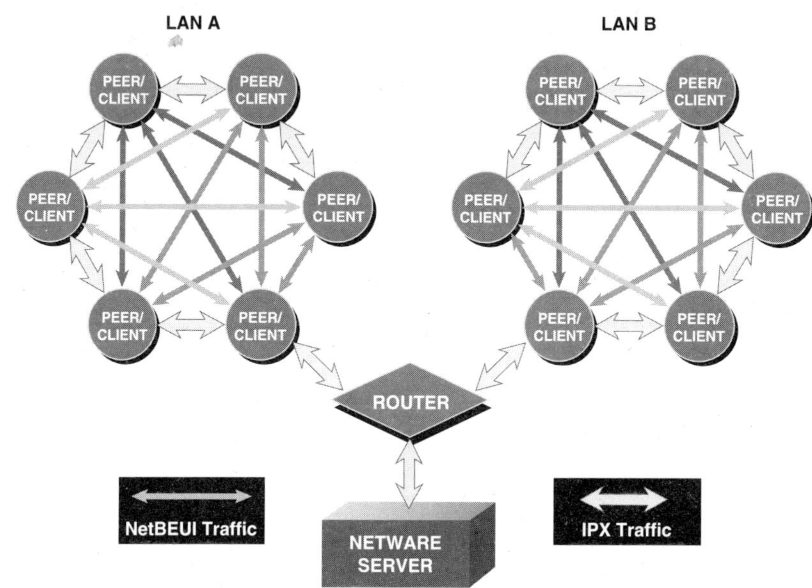

FIG. 36.4 All of the workstations on both LAN A and LAN B can function as clients to the NetWare server, because IPX (the default NetWare protocol) can be routed between network segments.

A workstation on LAN A, however, can enter into a peer networking relationship only with the other workstations on the same segment, because the NetBEUI protocol cannot be routed.

In order to route NetBEUI traffic between network segments, you must configure the Client for Microsoft Networks to utilize a second protocol, in addition to NetBEUI. When you add the Microsoft IPX/SPX-compatible or TCP/IP protocol to the network configuration and bind it to the Client for Microsoft Networks, the new protocol provides the routability that allows users to communicate with workstations on other network segments.

Although perceived by some as a shortcoming, the nonroutable nature of NetBEUI can actually be an advantage on large networks where peer and client/server networking are combined. The NetBEUI protocol operates at peak performance on relatively small network segments. Further, using NetBEUI limits the amount of additional network traffic generated when you add peer-to-peer functionality to an existing network.

Peer Networking and Controlling Traffic Levels

The signal traffic on a local area network consists of a great deal more than just the files, print jobs, and other data being sent from one place to another. Networked computers communicate on a great many levels, and countless transactions are being conducted between machines, even when the computers all seem to be idle. Just the practice of a computer making its presence known to the other machines on the network adds traffic.

On a purely client/server NetWare network, for example, each server periodically sends out communications packets to inform all the other servers of its presence. If a large network has 50 servers and 1,000 workstations, the increase in this type of traffic incurred by having all of the workstations advertise their presence would be enormous. This is why it's usually best to keep peer networking traffic limited to the local segment whenever possible. That way, each LAN is subject only to the additional burden generated by its own machines.

In the networking scenario being presented here, it would not be the responsibility of the average Windows 95 user to monitor traffic levels on the network, even if he or she were to function as a peer network administrator. This is a very complex undertaking, requiring special tools and expertise. It's important, however, to be aware of the consequences of your actions. The object here is to remove some of the burden from the professional network administrator, not add to it.

A network that is already approaching high traffic levels on a regular basis is likely to be pushed into the danger zone by the addition of peer traffic. Users, of course, are not likely to have any knowledge of this, and many other factors affecting network performance throughout the enterprise. It's important to always consult your network administrator before implementing any new services that could negatively impact other users.

Creating Workgroups

A single network segment can contain dozens of machines—far more than a normal user would need to access on a regular basis. Microsoft peer networks are therefore broken up into still smaller collections of machines called workgroups, as shown in Figure 36.5. A *workgroup* is a number of users whose relationship can be defined by any criteria that is convenient to the organization of the company or the network. Workgroup members may be users performing the same task, members of the same department or project team, or simply a group of people that sit near each other. For whatever reason, these users form a logical grouping based on their need to share the resources of each other's machines.

When browsing through the Entire Network display of the Network Neighborhood, workgroups are listed at the top level. Expanding a workgroup icon will display the workstations contained within it. Belonging to a workgroup does not limit the user's access to resources outside of the group.

The workgroup to which a Windows 95 workstation belongs is defined in the Identification page of the Control Panel's Network dialog box, as shown in Figure 36.6. Every Windows machine on a network must have a unique name, and must belong to a logical grouping, either a workgroup or a domain (see the next section for more information on domains). When it's time to create and access shares, these will later be used as part of a UNC name to identify the resources on this machine to the rest of the network (see Chapter 37, "Sharing Windows 95 Peer-to-Peer Resources").

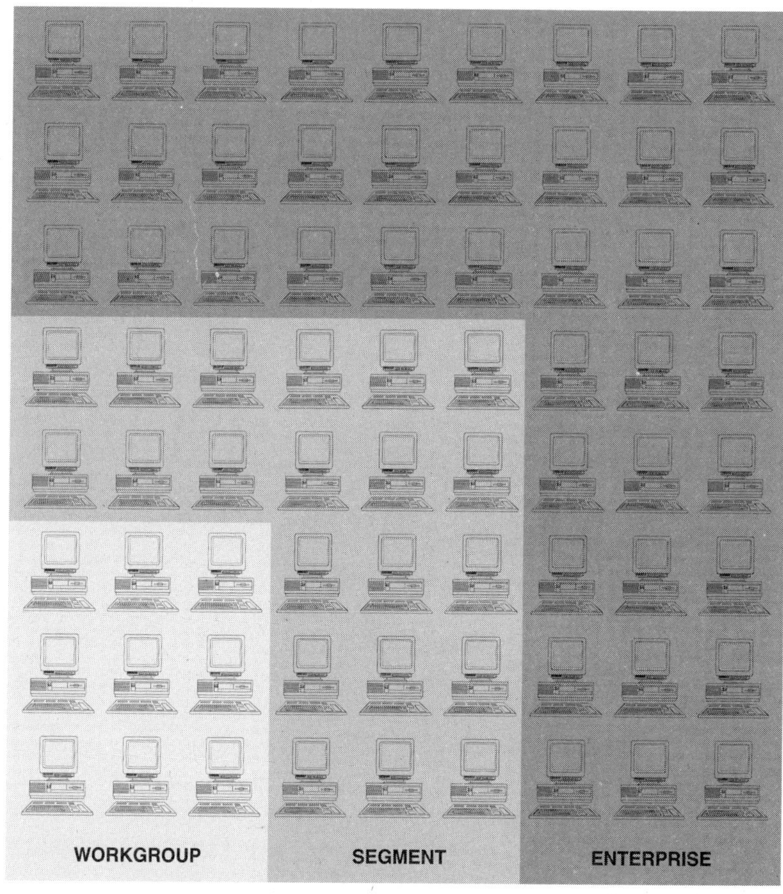

FIG. 36.5
A workgroup is a small collection of users within an existing network that have a regular need for access to each other's machines.

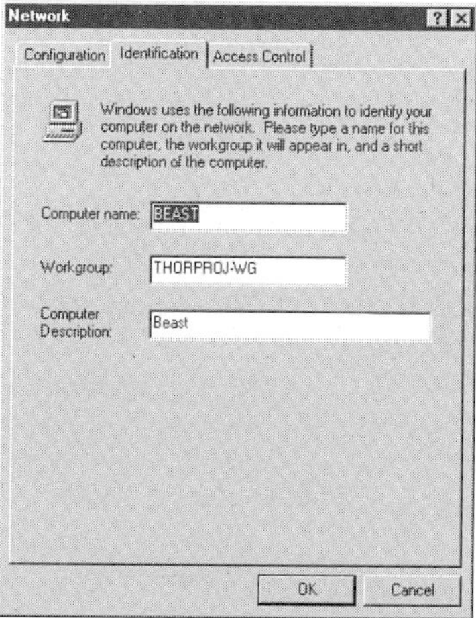

FIG. 36.6
Every networked computer must be identified by name and by a logical grouping.

A workgroup need not already exist for it to be named in the Identification page. Every machine on the network could create its own workgroup simply by entering a unique name in this text box. The Computer Description text box has no function other than to further identify this computer to the rest of the network. It could contain the full name of the user, the machine's purpose, or nothing at all.

CAUTION

Care should be taken not to assign names to workgroups that duplicate existing server names. This may prevent other users from accessing the server.

When a Windows 95 machine is a part of a workgroup, it is solely responsible for maintaining security over its own resources. As described in the next chapter, shares are created to allow other users access to a machine's drives and printers. These shares are, in a workgroup, individually password-protected by each machine. This is one reason workgroup computing should be limited to relatively small groups where security is not a major issue.

Using Domains

On a network that uses Windows NT as its network operating system, users are probably already using a domain login to gain access to client/server network resources. A *domain* is a logical grouping of computers that is entirely controlled and administered from a Windows NT server. Whereas share passwords in a workgroup are stored on the individual machines where the shares are located, passwords and all security information for domain users are stored on a server that has been designated a *domain controller*. In order for one workstation to access a drive on another workstation, both users must have valid accounts on the domain controlling server.

Network Browsing and Using a Domain

When utilizing Windows 95 in a network environment, you can normally only browse peer resources that are on your local network, even though you have access to machines on other networks. This is because the Windows 95 browser is designed to keep information only for local machines.

However, if you set the workgroup name of the Windows 95 machines to be the same as a Windows NT domain name, you will be able to browse all of the resources in this NT domain—including the Windows 95 machines.

This is a result of the additional architecture involved in a domain and is quite useful if you need to browse and share peer-to-peer resources over multiple networks.

Two screens in the Windows 95 Network dialog box are essential to the use of a domain logon. The properties sheet for the Client for Microsoft Networks contains a Login Validation section, as shown in Figure 36.7. To log on, the user must enable this section and specify a domain name. The Access Control page of the main Network dialog box allows the selection of

Share-level or *User-level* access control to the devices on that workstation. You must specify the domain name here if you intend to use the domain's security information to control access to shared devices.

NOTE User-level access control is not limited to Windows NT domains. A NetWare server also can be specified if the File and Printer Sharing service for NetWare networks has been installed.

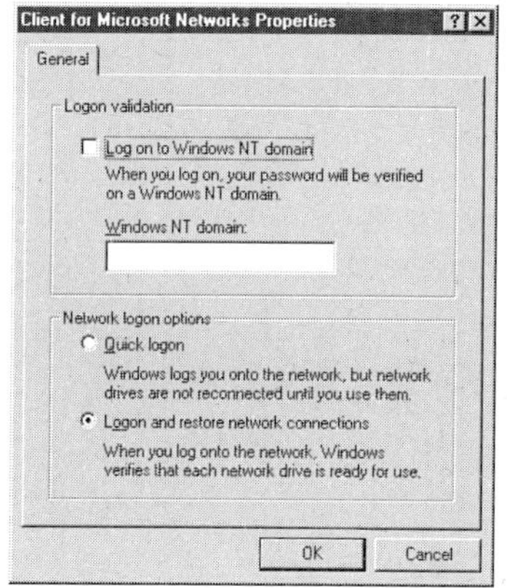

FIG. 36.7 Logon Validation must be enabled and a domain name supplied in order to perform a Windows NT domain logon.

User-Level versus Share-Level Security

When deciding which type of security validation to use, keep in mind the nature of the resources being protected. Traditional network security policies dictate that sensitive data should always be stored on server drives for protection against both intrusion and accidental loss.

Adding peer networking as an adjunct to a client/server arrangement is supposed to be a tool of convenience, and user-based security can sometimes defeat that purpose. If you regularly have a network administrator create user accounts on the Windows NT server in order to grant access to workstation devices, you then defeat the purpose of implementing a peer system, in part. You must, therefore, also consider your network's existing security policies before selecting an access control method.

Share-level security has its drawbacks as well. It is relatively limited in its access rights, allowing only a choice between read-only and full access to a shared drive, whereas user-level access rights can be more specifically customized. Share-level security also is subject to the whims of each workstation's user. If a member changes passwords, for example, without informing the other workgroup members, problems may result.

Situations like this are not insurmountable. Workgroup members can agree on a set of security policies that may involve, for example, the use of the same passwords for all group resources, or agreements on the sharing of particular resources. Remember, peer-to-peer is not just a technology, it's also a philosophy.

Building a Workgroup Administrator

Very often the best run departmental networks are those that have a knowledgeable networker among the regular members of the group. Some corporations are moving heavily toward decentralizing a portion of their MIS personnel. Instead of having specialized people concerned with only one aspect of the enterprise network, such as dedicated wide-area technicians and others who deal only with telephony, they are hiring (or cross-training) people for more general use and assigning them to specific departments.

This practice has two natural results. The corporation develops more well-rounded and generally capable MIS personnel; and, the administrator becomes a member of the department that he or she is dedicated to servicing. A sense of team spirit develops that leads the administrator to fight for the rights of coworkers when it comes to allocation of resources and equipment.

Implementing Windows 95 peer networking within a client/server environment will require at least one person who is familiar with the networking capabilities of the operating system and the administrative tools that are included within it. This workgroup administrator should be responsible for designing and implementing the resource-sharing policies observed by the users in the group. The job description is flexible, based on the needs of the users and the services already provided at the corporate level.

The Role of the Workgroup Administrator

The primary function of the workgroup administrator is to make the computing tasks of the less knowledgeable workgroup members easier. This is most often done by limiting their network environment to the resources they actually need to access regularly. One of the ironic qualities of Windows 95 is that it is easily capable of providing the user with an embarrassment of riches. Unlimited access to the contents of 100 different workstations is not going to make an employee's job easier.

A well-functioning workgroup has policies that limit user access to necessary resources. Such policies include the sensible creation of shares on each machine and a well-designed policy for the storage of files as well.

It is a good idea to create similar directory structures on all of the workgroup's computers. This practice gives users a basic familiarity with the layout all of the machines in the workgroup. Synchronizing directories also makes it easier for users to share applications that have been installed on other machines.

The administrator should also designate specific directories for the location of shared data files. The files may be grouped according to application, by project, or using any system convenient to the operation of the department. By collecting them all on the same place on each machine (such as a directory called \SHARED FILES), the administrator can create a documented standard for his workgroup's organization. With such a standard in place, new users will be able to come up to speed quickly and occasional users of the workgroup's equipment will find themselves in familiar surroundings.

The administrator also works behind the scenes to see that no one computer is carrying too much of the workgroup's weight. One of the primary drawbacks of peer networking is when a computer's background activities as a server detract from its efficiency as a client. If a dozen users are all constantly accessing files on a single computer, the performance level of the machine functioning as the server will suffer. The workgroup administrator must distribute shared hardware and software resources evenly throughout the group, and maintain an even level of traffic for each user so that all of the group members can remain productive.

Windows 95 provides the administrator with the tools that he or she needs to perform these organizational tasks. ●

CHAPTER 37

Sharing Windows 95 Peer-to-Peer Resources

by Craig Zacker with Robert L. Bogue

Sharing workstation resources

How to configure your workstation to share its drives, printers, and fax modems with other network users.

Securing shared resources

How to use Windows 95's security measures to prevent unauthorized access to your workstation's shared resources.

Using remote network access

How to access shared network resources from a remote Windows 95 computer using a dial-up connection.

Using the remote access server

How to configure a Windows 95 workstation to function as a remote access server through which dial-up users can access network resources.

Balancing the load

How to organize a peer workgroup network for convenient and efficient sharing.

Creating a productive working environment isn't the easiest of tasks. You have to consider the mechanics of sharing workstation resources as well as examining the user policies and limitations of these workstations.

It is also important to balance the load between workstations and to consider the security level you want each individual workstation to have. With Windows 95, these issues are easily handled. ■

Creating Shares

Resources on a Microsoft Windows network are called *shares*. A share can be a hardware device, such as a modem or a printer; it can be a storage device, such as a CD-ROM or optical drive; or a share can be a logical entity on a hard disk drive, such as a volume, a folder, a directory, or a file. The owner of the server or workstation must explicitly designate a particular resource in that machine as shared in order for other users to access it over the network.

NOTE Whenever a computer on a Microsoft Windows network shares any device or resource, that computer is considered to be a server. **Peer-to-peer** means that computers can function as both clients and servers at the same time.

Sharing a Drive

To create a shared drive, make sure that the File and Print Sharing dialog box in the Network dialog box has I Want to be Able to Give Others Access to My Files enabled and that you have selected the desired access control method in the Access Control sheet (see Chapter 43, "Network Management and Security," if you're uncertain how to do this). Then do the following:

1. Open the My Computer window or launch the Windows Explorer. Select the local drive or folder you want to share.

NOTE Any storage device attached to the workstation and mounted as a drive letter can be shared with other network users.

2. Choose File, Properties and click the Sharing tab, or click the right mouse button and choose Sharing from the context menu.
3. Click the Shared As button to activate the option fields.
4. Enter a Share Name to identify the device to the network. Any text you enter in the optional Comment field also appears on all share listings.

When assigning share names, remember these things:

- A share name need not describe the exact location of the share on the server—you can use any descriptive name.
- Appending a dollar sign ($) to the end of the share name prevents the share from being advertised to other machines browsing the network. Remote users gain access by specifying the correct UNC name.

The appearance of the rest of the Sharing page depends upon whether you have chosen to use share-level or user-level access control in the Network dialog box. To complete the drive-sharing process, follow the procedure outlined in the following section that is appropriate for the type of access control you have selected.

▶ **See** "User-Level versus Share-Level Security," **p. 950**

Using Share-Level Access Control

When you configure a workstation to use share-level access control, the Sharing page of the properties sheet takes on the appearance shown in Figure 37.1.

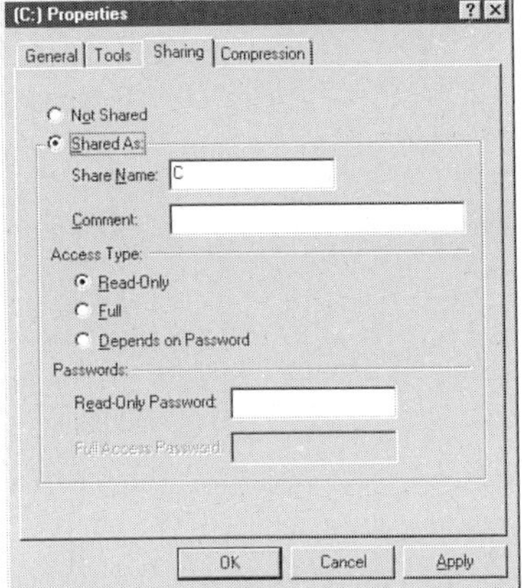

FIG. 37.1
Share-level access enables any user with the correct password to access a shared drive.

Use the following procedure to grant share-level access:

1. Select an Access Type to denote whether users are granted Read-Only or Full access. The Depends on Password option enables users of both levels to access the share, based on the password entered.
2. Enter password(s) for Read-Only and/or Full Access, depending on your Access Type selection.
3. Click the OK button. Confirm your password(s). Click OK again to create the share.

TIP To prevent unauthorized access, always assign a password for all shares.

Using User-Level Access Control

When you configure a workstation for user-level access, a slightly different Sharing page appears in the properties sheet (see Figure 37.2).

To grant access to shares on workstations configured for user-level access control, use this procedure:

1. Choose the Add button and select a user or group from the list presented by the Windows NT validation server (see Figure 37.3). You could also use a NetWare server, but NT will be used throughout this example.

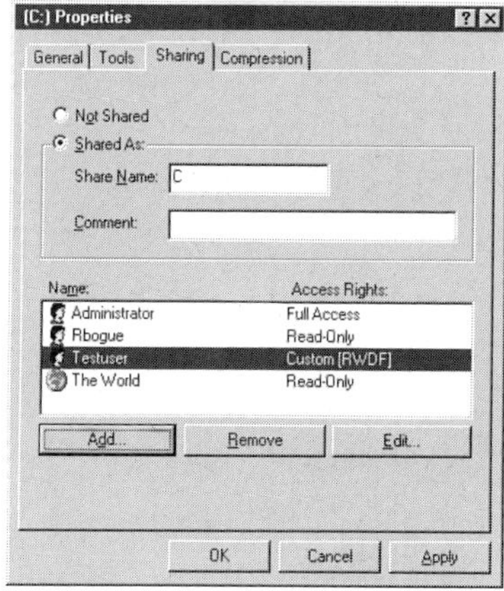

FIG. 37.2
User-level access requires a Windows NT server for user validation.

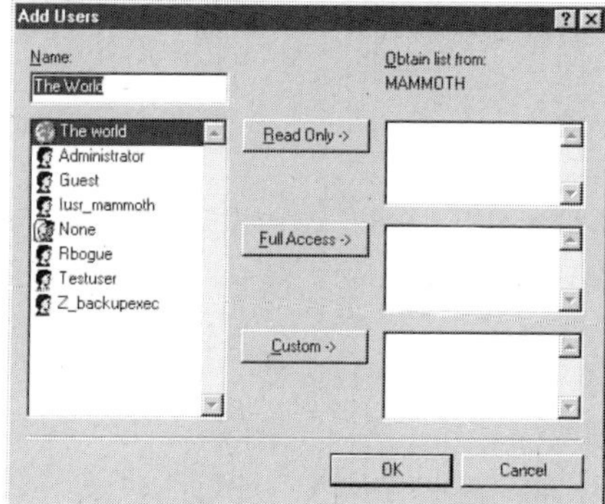

FIG. 37.3
The list of users and groups presented comes from the Windows NT server specified in the Access Control dialog box.

2. Select the level of access for that user: Read Only, Full Access, or Custom. Selecting Custom produces the Change Access Rights dialog box, from which you can select for that user any or all of the rights shown in Figure 37.4.

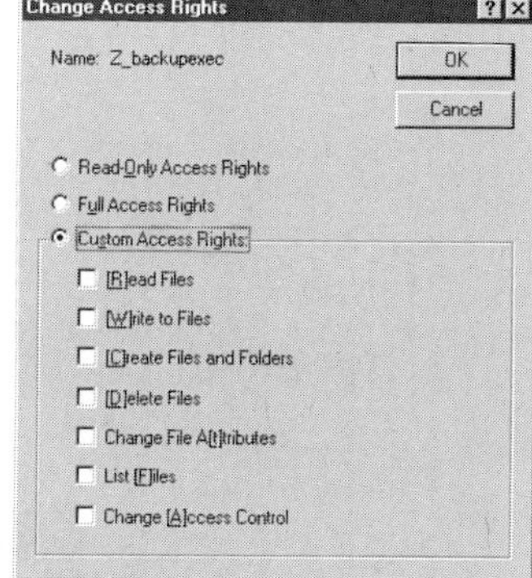

FIG. 37.4
You can grant a custom user any combination of these rights.

3. Click OK to add the user. Repeat the process for additional users or groups, if necessary. Then click the OK button to create the share.

After you have shared a drive or a folder, the icon that displays in the local drive of the My Computer and Explorer windows changes to include an outstretched hand, as shown in Figure 37.5.

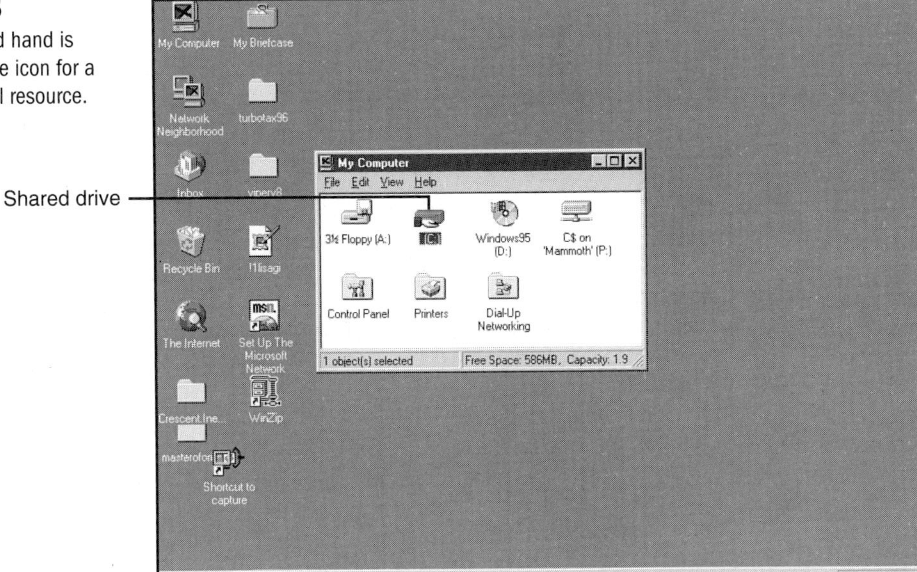

FIG. 37.5
An extended hand is added to the icon for a shared local resource.

NOTE When user-level access control is enabled, each user sharing the drive must be added to the access list, either individually or as part of a group. Individual user and group accounts are maintained on a Windows NT or NetWare machine. If NT is used, this NT machine must be either the primary domain control server for the domain specified in the properties sheet of the Client for Microsoft Networks or a Windows NT machine specified by name in the Access Control screen of the Network dialog box.

Share-level access control enables any network user who furnishes the correct password to access the share.

CAUTION

If you switch your workstation's access control method from share-level to user-level (or vice versa), all of your shares are lost. You must reshare all folders, printers, and fax modems, and assign rights under the new method before users can access them.

Configuring Access Rights

As with most file systems, the permissions for shared drives in Windows 95 travel downward through the directory structure. When you grant a user full access to the root of your C: drive, you also grant that user rights to every folder and file on that drive. In Microsoft networking parlance, these rights are called *implied rights*. NetWare calls them *inherited rights*. When you use share-level access control, these rights, once granted, cannot be rescinded by any processes, other than disconnecting the user or ceasing to share the drive. You cannot grant or deny rights to individual files in Windows 95, as you can in Windows NT and NetWare. If you share a subdirectory of a previously created share and assign it more limited rights, the network user then has access to two different shares, each with its own permissions. The rights of the original share are unaffected by the creation of the new share.

NOTE As a security precaution, you can share only local drives on a Windows 95 workstation. You cannot "reshare" a network drive to provide access to another user who has insufficient rights to the source of the share.

You can effectively overlap shares with different permissions. If you grant read-only access to the root of a drive, and full access to a folder located farther down the tree, you provide the user with both forms of access to that subdirectory, depending on which share the user chooses to access.

You can tell if a folder is already included as part of another share by looking at the very top of the Sharing page of the folder's properties sheet, where the name of any enclosing share is listed.

Filtering Access Rights

When user-level access control is in effect, you can grant users or groups lesser rights to a subdirectory than they have to the parent. This capability adds an important measure of flexibility to the effective creation of shares on Windows 95 machines.

NOTE Windows 95 uses the term **folders** to refer to what the rest of the PC world calls **directories**. The two terms are, in most instances, interchangeable.

For example, suppose that you are sharing a folder called \DATA\IRS and that read-only access has been granted to all users (The World, in Windows NT parlance). If you then create a share of the folder \DATA, granting full access to The World, the Change Security dialog box appears and notifies you that folders within the new share have already been granted different security rights (see Figure 37.6).

You are then given several choices:

- *Apply These Changes to Inside Folders*, causing full access to be granted to the \DATA\IRS folder, in this case.

- *Do Not Change Any Inside Folders*, retaining the read-only access to \DATA\IRS and granting full access to the rest of \DATA.
- *Display Each Folder Name Individually*, causing another dialog box to appear and asking if security changes should be applied to the \IRS folder within the \DATA share. If you select Yes, the \IRS folder in both shares will have read-only access. You answer the same question for any other folders within the \DATA folder that have been shared.

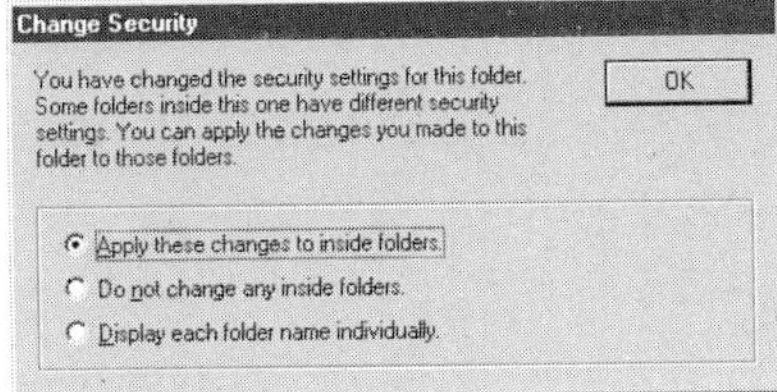

FIG. 37.6 User-level access control enables you to assign individual access rights to folders within a share.

The second or third option is preferable in most situations. You can allow users and groups to have full access to \DATA and yet limit them to read-only access for \DATA\IRS. This arrangement is similar to the Inherited Rights Mask in the NetWare file system.

Accessing the Sharing page of any shared folder's properties sheet displays the **effective rights**, that is, the rights currently in force for that folder.

TROUBLESHOOTING

I've created a user-level share and assigned access rights to a particular user, but he is being denied access. What is wrong? Check the status of the user's account on the Windows NT validation server. The user's access will be subject to any restrictions specified on that server.

Maintaining Workgroup Security

The shortcomings of share-level security and the complexities involved in maintaining user-level access are reason enough for many network administrators to reject peer networking as a viable option on a corporate network. Network operating systems like Windows NT and NetWare are more flexible in enabling rights-allocation; you can grant users access to individual files and restrict access to a particular directory branch at any point. On a peer network contained within a client/server network, however, workstation security is less of a concern because users still have access to server drives where they can store their most highly sensitive files in complete safety.

Even though most workgroups are made up of users who share a certain degree of trust, you must have sufficient network protection to guard against the inadvertent intrusion, as well as the malicious one. If you organize a workstation's directory structure properly from the outset, you best enable effective sharing.

Connecting to Shared Drives

After you have successfully created a share out of a drive or folder, it immediately appears on the network as a subordinate object to its host machine. The Entire Network display in the Network Neighborhood or the Windows Explorer displays the names of all the workstations contained in the workgroup and the names of all the shares on each workstation, as shown in Figure 37.7.

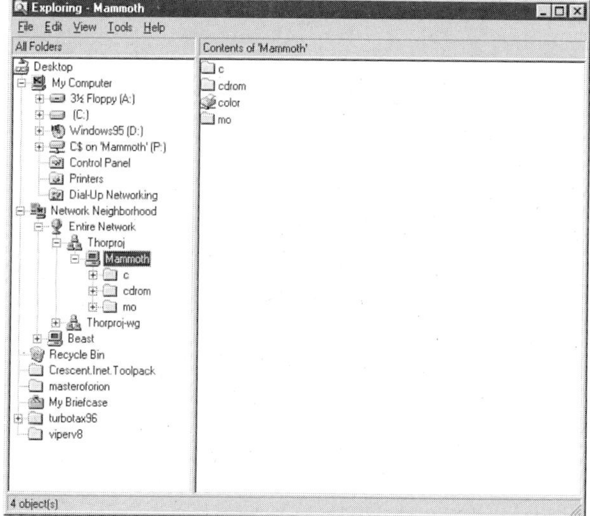

FIG. 37.7 The Windows Explorer shows all the shares available on the workgroup.

Clicking a share for the first time brings up a password validation screen that contains the usual option to save the password to the cache for future access. After access is granted, the folders and files of the share appear on a remote machine like those of a local or a client-server network drive.

You also can map a drive letter to a share on a peer workstation. The procedure is exactly the same as the process for mapping to drives on a client/server network. The UNC name specified in the Map Network Drives dialog box, or the NET USE command line, should appear as follows:

\\WORKSTATION\SHARE_NAME

See "Mapping a Network Drive," **p. 357**

NOTE The NetBEUI protocol, by default, limits a Windows 95 workstation to 10 simultaneous connections to other Windows network machines, including servers. If you work in what is primarily a Microsoft shop, this number may not be sufficient. To increase the limit, open the Network dialog box in the Control Panel. In the Advanced page of the properties sheet for the NetBEUI protocol, raise the number in the Maximum Sessions setting. You can set this value as high as 117, but set it only as high as you need for normal use.

Locating Computers

Despite the emphasis of this chapter on peer networking within the workgroup, Windows 95 is in no way limited to accessing the shared resources of nearby machines. You can access any peer workstation on the local network segment, and depending on the protocols being used, possibly any machine on the entire enterprise network.

See "Peer Networking and Routability," **p. 945**

In a large-enterprise network environment, the sheer number of available machines may make it difficult to locate a particular server or workstation that you don't access frequently. For this reason, Windows 95 includes in its Find feature the capability to search for networked computers, files, or folders.

To locate a computer on the network, follow these steps:

1. Choose Find from the Start menu, or choose Tools, Find in the Explorer or Network Neighborhood window and then choose Computer.
2. Begin entering the UNC name of the machine in the space provided in the Find: Computer dialog box (see Figure 37.8). Entering even a partial name displays all the machines matching your selection.
3. Click the Find Now button to begin the search. The Find utility locates machines of all types: Windows NT servers; Windows NT, Windows 95, or Workgroups workstations; and NetWare servers.
4. Use the File, Explore command or double-click a found machine name to view its contents.

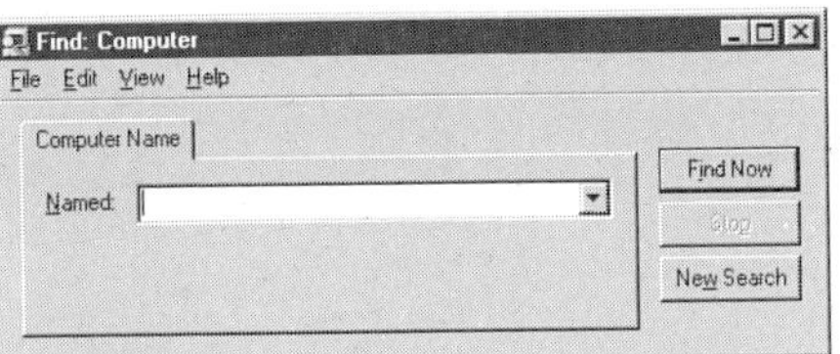

FIG. 37.8
The Windows 95 Find utility can locate any machine visible on the network.

Sharing Workstation Drives

In Chapter 34, "Simple Ways of Sharing Data Between Applications," you learned about enabling users to access files stored on network server drives. Setting up a workstation drive share is a bit different. Whereas a network is a public space, an individual's workstation may seem more like his or her "home."

To make this arrangement work successfully, peer-to-peer networking participants need to follow certain rules of etiquette. Remote users must leave things more or less the way they found them, and the host must keep anything not fit for public display behind closed doors. Establishing specific policies for the workgroup is the best way to ensure that standards are maintained.

Another safeguard is to limit the shared areas of each workstation drive. Allowing a remote user free access to one's entire drive (or *house*) is asking for trouble, no matter how friendly the relationship between coworkers. Unlimited access also makes finding specific items or files harder for the remote user.

You can choose specific directories or files for shared access on NetWare or Windows NT server drives. On a Windows 95 machine, however, you may need to modify the directory structure to accommodate the need for security. In many cases, if you grant access to a folder, you cannot prohibit access to anything contained within that folder.

Sharing Applications

To create an effective file-sharing arrangement, you must first decide exactly what material on each user's drive needs to be shared. This decision isn't as easy as it used to be. At one time, if you just copied the contents of the \WP51 directory from one computer to another, you had a fully functional copy of WordPerfect. You cannot simply copy a directory with today's Windows applications, which often require INI settings and library files located in several different directories. Even users who have become rather adept at modifying Windows 3.1 INI files may be daunted by the prospect of the Windows 95 registry.

To effectively share a Windows 95 application, you usually need to perform a network installation to the machine doing the sharing. This way, remote users can install the program themselves from the share, and add the appropriate settings to their own configuration files but leave the actual executables on the shared drive.

This technique can be an effective means of conserving hard disk space, especially when several people use an application only occasionally. Licensing issues may interfere with this practice, however. Many applications today protect themselves against users installing multiple copies of a single-user product on a network. In other cases, the terms of the license may deem this practice to be perfectly acceptable, as long as only one person is using the application at a time.

You can also effectively share smaller binaries over the network. DOS command-line utilities should cause no problems, and many small Windows utilities will function properly from a remote workstation.

NOTE Even the simpler Windows programs, like small utilities used for managing compressed files or viewing graphics, are comprised of several files in addition to the actual executable. Typically, some of the other files are dynamic link libraries (.DLLs) that are called while the program is running. Many installation programs copy .DLLs to the \WINDOWS\SYSTEM directory, so they are always available for use. (When a program searches for one of its files, it always checks the \WINDOWS\SYSTEM directory before running the PATH.)

Storing a copy of any required DLLs in the actual program directory will, in some cases, allow the program to run from another workstation on the network without installing it, as long as the Working Directory in the remote icon's properties sheet specifies the program directory on the host machine. Other applications cannot be run this way because they may require that their OLE objects be entered into the local machine's registry.

Sharing Data Files

Aside from sharing applications, the other major reason for sharing drives is to access data files. Administrators must take particular care regarding the granting of simultaneous read-write access to such files by multiple users.

Depending on the file type, more than one user may or may not be able to access the file at the same time. Applications usually deal with a second user attempting to open a file in one of three ways:

- **By denying the user any access at all.** The file locks open and any attempt to address it by another process generates an error message.
- **By allowing the user read-only access.** Some applications open a copy of the file, denying write access to the original but enabling the user to save it to another file name, if desired.
- **By sharing the file between the two users.** Only files specifically designed for sharing should be accessible by multiple users. Usually, this method is possible only with some database file types that lock individual records (divisions within the file) rather than the entire file.

When sharing data files, the administrator needs to be conscious of the way that the associated applications deal with simultaneous accesses. If, for example, a workgroup uses a particular Microsoft Excel spreadsheet file to document and track the progress of a project, users may then need only to refer to the file sometimes, and at other times they may need to update it.

Most likely, only one user will have read-write access to the file. Any other users will be in read-only mode, as imposed by the application. However, Microsoft Excel enables a user to explicitly open a file in read-only mode by marking a check box in the Open dialog box. In this case, a conscientious workgroup member who requires only read access to the spreadsheet can leave the read-write access available for another person's use.

Successfully enabling the sharing of single-user files represents the essence of well planned workgroup computing. To construct such a cooperative dynamic, the network administrator must be fully aware of both the system capabilities and the needs of all workgroup members.

Sharing CD-ROMs and Other Removable Drives

Although almost every home computer now sold includes a CD-ROM, this component is not usually standard equipment on the average business machine. One of the outstanding advantages to peer networking is the capability to share a CD-ROM drive among several users without the need to install it on a file server (a complicated process in a NetWare environment).

NetWare and CD-ROM Drives

Loading a CD-ROM onto a NetWare file server requires the use of NLMs devoted to that task. You must allocate memory to support the additional disk space of the CD-ROM, and you must remount

continues

continued

the volume every time the disk is changed. These tasks result in increased expense and aggravation for the network administrator.

On the user side of the equation, a NetWare-mounted CD-ROM appears as a new volume on the server. The name of the volume is taken from the volume label of the CD itself, so each disk creates a different volume. Although this technique provides a good way of knowing what disk is currently in the drive, it also forces users to map a new drive letter whenever they access a different CD-ROM.

When a CD-ROM drive is installed on a Windows 95 workstation, sharing the drive is an easy matter. The procedure is the same as that for sharing a local hard drive.

See "Creating Shares," **p. 954**

Except in rare cases, you should create a CD-ROM share at the root of the drive. Although you can create a share from a specific directory on a CD-ROM, creating a share at the root enables you to use that same share for any disk loaded in the drive. You need only provide read-only access to a CD-ROM.

NOTE Even though a CD-ROM is a read-only device, limiting the CD-ROM share to read-only access provides benefits to the user. When a user with full access attempts to save changes to a write-protected drive, an error message is generated, forcing the user to Cancel or Retry the operation. When a user is granted read-only access to the share, issuing a Save command bypasses the error and automatically produces the Save As dialog box. The user can write the changes to another drive if necessary.

Using Networked CD-ROMs

CD-ROMs are rapidly becoming the preferred method of software distribution for users and manufacturers alike. When installing software from a CD-ROM drive accessed over the network, take note of whether the product is being completely installed to the local hard drive, or if it requires later access to the CD-ROM.

Many informational resource CDs, as well as games, install a viewer or other executable to the local drive and access the bulk of their application files from the CD-ROM itself. In these cases, the application sets up pointers to the original location of the drive so it can easily find the drive later. These pointers are nearly always in the form of drive letters.

Therefore, take the following steps to ensure that applications on CD-ROM are installed properly:

- Map a drive to the CD-ROM when installing software that requires access to the disk to run properly. Do not use the Network Neighborhood to browse the drive, unless the software is expressly designed for use with Windows 95.
- Make the drive mapping a permanent one if you want to access the data on the CD repeatedly.

This latter step is necessary because changing the drive letter of the CD-ROM drive may prevent the application from locating its data files. Some applications (like the Windows 95 Setup program) are well-behaved when this obstacle occurs and prompt you to specify the location of the CD when the application cannot find it. Other applications are more belligerent and refuse to run unless you reinstall the application from the new drive letter.

Using Networked Optical, JAZ, and ZIP Drives

When sharing other types of drives with removable media, follow the same procedure as for a CD-ROM, with the exception of the rights assignment. When you are creating a drive-sharing plan, you must consider the access rights to removable drives with read-write capability (such as magneto-optical drives) just like those of any hard disk. Again, though, create the share at the root of the drive so you can change the media without resharing.

You can share CD-ROM drives mounted on Windows for Workgroups workstations over a Microsoft peer network. To do so, be sure to include the /S switch on the line in the AUTOEXEC.BAT file that loads the Microsoft Windows CD extensions (MSCDEX.EXE).

Networking Tape Drives

Tape drives fall into still another category because you typically don't mount these devices as drive letters on the local machine. Instead, the devices are directly addressed through software specifically designed for that purpose.

Traditionally, network backup software runs on a server and addresses tape devices directly attached to that server. For a tape drive attached to a workstation, you must instead use a stand-alone backup software package. However, many workstation backup products can also back up network drives.

Cheyenne Software and Arcada Software (now owned by Seagate), which also include agent services for their network backup products in Windows 95, have both released workstation backup packages for Windows 95. These products can preserve long file names and back up any device (local or network) that is mapped to a drive letter, including Windows NT and NetWare drives. Thus, you can back up an entire workgroup's data to a single tape, not by sharing the tape drive's functionality with the workstations, but by bringing the workstations' data over the network to the tape.

Sharing Workstation Printers

To allow peer network users to access a printer installed on a Windows 95 workstation, you must first install the printer in the normal manner and enable the I Want to be Able to Allow Others to Print to My Printer(s) feature in the File and Print Sharing page in the Network dialog box. As with drive sharing, be sure to select the desired access control method in the Access Control page of the Network dialog box.

To create a printer share, use the following procedure:

1. Open the Printers window from the Settings option on the Start menu or through the Control Panel.
2. Highlight the printer you want to share and choose Sharing from the File menu or from the printer's context menu (see Figure 37.9).

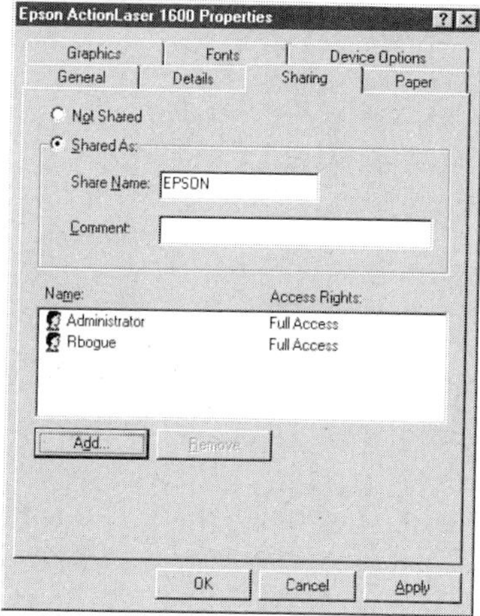

FIG. 37.9
Use the Sharing page to assign the printer a networking name and to provide access control.

TIP Notice that the Sharing dialog box is actually one page of the printer's properties sheet, where you can access it via the Sharing tab.

3. Select the Shared As option button and enter a Share Name. The printer appears with this name to the rest of the network. You also may (optionally) enter further descriptive information for the printer in the Comment field.
4. If you are using share-level access, enter a password to protect access to the printer. For user-level access, select the users or groups who are permitted to use the printer. Click OK to create the share.

Whether your workstation is configured for user-level or share-level access control, a shared printer has only two security options: full access or no access. After you have created the share, an outstretched hand is added to the printer's icon to indicate its status.

Accessing Shared Printers

Configuring Windows 95 to access a shared workstation printer is no different than if the printer were installed on a server. You can launch the Add New Printer Wizard by any of the following methods:

- Open the Printers window and double-click the Add Printer icon.

- Locate the printer share in the Network Neighborhood or Explorer window and choose File, Install.
- Drag the Shared Printer icon from the Network Neighborhood or Explorer window to the Printers window.
- Launch the Add New Hardware icon from the Control Panel and select Printer from the list of devices.

Administering Workstation Print Queues

Windows 95's all-or-nothing printer security limitation affects the administration of print queues on workstations. As with a server-based printer, users can double-click a shared workstation printer's icon and open a window displaying all the pending print jobs in the queue. In Windows 95, all users have equal access to the queue. Any user with permission to access the printer can reorder the pending jobs, as well as pause or cancel any job in the queue.

However, the queue for a server-based printer is located on that network server, and the rights to manipulate the queue are also controlled by the server. NetWare and Windows NT both have a more extensive array of permissions in regard to accessing print queues. You can limit users' access to only the rights that they require, giving them a distinct advantage in the area of printer management. This should not be a significant problem in a cooperative workgroup, but if the resources of a client/server network coexist with the peer network, you may choose one of several alternatives to workstation-based print queues.

The first alternative is to avoid workstation-based printers entirely and run all printers from the client/server network. A unit equipped with a network adapter such as the HP JetDirect can be located anywhere a network connection exists. HP JetDirect also utilizes a server's print queue, providing additional administrative security and lessening the burden on the workstation that would otherwise be servicing the printer. The additional expense of the network card for the printer is negligible when you consider the average company networking budget.

NOTE You must install the additional RPC (Remote Procedure Call) Print Provider service with the Client for Microsoft Networks to provide Windows 95 with the capability to administer print queues on Windows NT servers. The service is installed through the Network protocol by adding a new service, clicking the Have Disk button, and browsing to the ADMIN\NETTOOLS\RPCPP directory of the Windows 95 CD-ROM.

The other alternative to standard Windows 95 printer sharing is to leave the printer attached to the workstation but utilize a NetWare print queue.

Sharing a Workstation's Fax Modem

Windows 95 incorporates fax services into the operating system using its Microsoft Exchange front end. Users can fax documents directly using the File, Print command of any application or the File, Send command of any application that uses the messaging application programming interface (MAPI). When both sender and recipient are using the Microsoft At Work binary file transfer protocol, you can even edit the faxed documents.

Windows 95 also can share the use of a workstation's fax modem, just as easily as it can share a drive or a printer. The workstation essentially becomes a fax server, enabling multiple network users to submit documents to its queue for sequential servicing by the modem.

NOTE Incoming faxes are held at the workstation where the modem is installed. Windows 95 alone does not have the capability to automatically route the faxes to their intended recipients, although this can be accomplished with the inclusion of Exchange Server on the network. In the absence of Exchange Server, the person designated as the fax server administrator must perform this task manually.

Before configuring a workstation for modem sharing, you must install the modem on the fax server workstation. You also must install Microsoft Exchange and Microsoft Fax on both the fax server and the client workstations.

To configure a workstation modem for network sharing, use the following procedure:

1. Double-click the Mail and Fax icon in the Control Panel. Select Microsoft Fax and click the Properties button.

TIP You can access the same sheet from the Microsoft Exchange Inbox window by choosing Tools, Microsoft Fax Tools, Options.

2. Select the Modem tab in the Microsoft Fax properties sheet and enable the option to Let Other People on the Network Use My Modem To Send Faxes (see Figure 37.10).
3. Click the Properties button, and a sharing sheet appears, similar to the sheet box for sharing a drive or a printer.

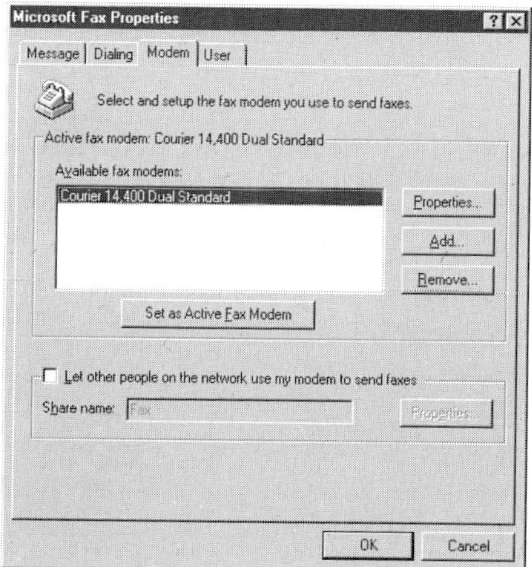

FIG. 37.10 You can install and configure modems through the Microsoft Fax properties sheet.

NOTE When you share a fax modem, a new shared directory is created on the workstation's C: drive. The path to that directory (C:\NETFAX, by default) appears in the title box of the properties sheet. This directory is where queued faxes are stored pending transmission. The seemingly incongruous options for read-only and full access that are provided when you create the modem share are actually referring to the access rights for this directory. You also can control access to network fax services from the directory's own Sharing dialog box. Always assign network users full access rights to the shared directory if they will be using the fax server.

4. Click the Shared As option button and enter a Share Name for the modem. If you are using share-level security, select Full for the access type and enter a password if you want. For user-level security, select users or groups who will have access to the share.
5. Click OK. Verify your passwords, if necessary, and then click OK again to create the share.

Accessing a Shared Fax Modem

After you have completed the preceding steps, any Windows 95 workstation on the network can make use of the shared fax modem. To configure the workstation to utilize the shared modem, use the following procedure:

1. Open the Microsoft Fax properties sheet as you did in step 1 of the preceding section.
2. Select the Modem tab and click the Add button next to available fax modems.
3. Select Network Fax Modem and click OK.
4. Enter the UNC name for the shared modem in the Connect to Network Fax Server dialog box. Click OK to close each dialog box.

NOTE The Connect to Network Fax Server dialog box does not contain a browse feature to facilitate the location of the fax modem. Notice the UNC name of the modem before you begin the procedure.

All of the functionality provided by Microsoft Fax is now available to the remote workstation. In fact, performance will be better than using a local modem, because the remote workstation does not have to process the fax transmission in the background. Windows 95 returns all system resources to the user as soon as the printing operation is complete.

Using Remote Network Access

Windows 95 defines the term *networking* more generally than most other operating systems. The connection of two computers via modems and a telephone line is considered a network interface just like a LAN connection. Windows 95 integrates these functions into the Network protocol along with the other networking components.

The Windows 95 Dial-Up Adapter is a driver like any other adapter driver, except the operating system uses the adapter to direct network traffic to a modem rather than a network interface card. A workstation can use this adapter to connect to an Internet service provider, to another Windows 95 workstation, Netware Communications Server, or to a Windows NT remote access server.

This section teaches you how to configure a Windows 95 workstation to be a dial-up server or a client. With this arrangement, a remote machine can dial into a Windows 95 workstation that is connected to the office LAN, and access not only the workstation's resources, but the LAN's resources as well. The remote machine can attach to the network like any workstation with a direct connection and perform any of the normal network functions, albeit more slowly.

NOTE Do not confuse **remote access** with **remote control**. Some communications products enable an offsite computer to dial into a host workstation and commandeer its interface by redirecting screen, keyboard, and mouse signals to the modem. When the remote user runs a program, all the microprocessing tasks are performed by the host computer. This process is remote control.

With Windows 95, the remote machine literally connects to the host as a peer. The host, despite functioning as a remote access server, continues to operate as a normal network workstation. Both the host and remote users can run different programs, with each machine doing its own microprocessing. This procedure is remote access.

Before configuring Windows 95 to function as a remote access server (or client), you must install a modem and the Dial-Up Networking module from the Windows 95 CD-ROM, as well as the File and Print Sharing for Microsoft Networks service.

See "Configuring Your Modem," **p. 85**

See "Installing Internet Explorer 4," **p. 477**

Using the Dial-Up Server

The Windows 95 dial-up server enables a single computer running any one of the following clients to access its internal resources using a modem connection:

- Windows 95
- Windows NT
- Windows for Workgroups
- The Windows 3.1 Remote Access Server (RAS) client
- Any other Point-to-Point Protocol (PPP) client

The server also functions as an IPX/SPX or NetBEUI gateway, enabling these clients to access other network resources that are available to the dial-up server through these protocols.

NOTE Although the Windows 95 dial-up server included in Microsoft Plus! can route NetBEUI and IPX/SPX traffic to the remote client, it cannot perform this function for TCP/IP. As a result, a remote user cannot access a corporate Internet connection by dialing into a Windows 95 workstation. Such access would require a Windows NT server, which functions as an IP router to its remote access clients.

Configuring the Dial-Up Server

The dial-up server module is available only on the Microsoft Plus! for Windows 95 CD-ROM. You must install the dial-up server during the standard Setup procedure for the package.

After installing the dial-up server, use the following procedure to configure the workstation to be a dial-up server:

1. Open the Dial-Up Networking window from the Start, Programs, Accessories menu.
2. Choose Connection, Dial-Up Server (see Figure 37.11).

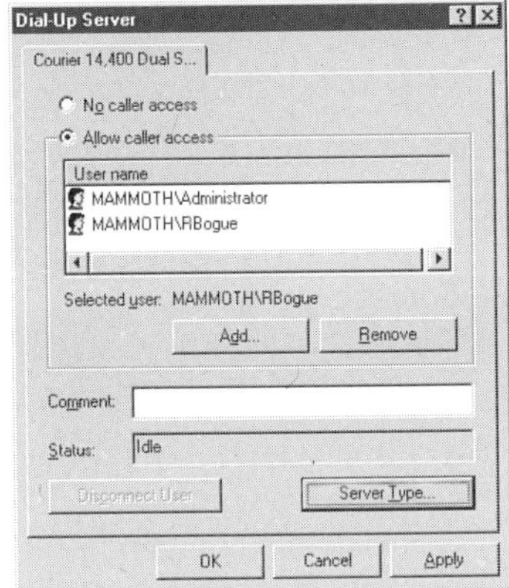

FIG. 37.11
Use the Dial-Up Server dialog box to configure a modem for remote access.

3. Choose the Allow Caller Access option button.
4. Click the Change Password or Add button, depending on your access control method.
    - For workstations configured for share-level security, click the Change Password button. Enter and verify a password for entry to the server, and click OK twice to close the dialog box.
    - For workstations configured for user-level security, click the Add button to select users or groups who are allowed access to the dial-up server. Click OK to close the dialog box.

When you close the dialog box, the dial-up server is ready to receive calls.

NOTE The Server Type button in the Dial-Up Server dialog box contains settings you should not need to alter for a Windows 95-to-Windows 95 connection. The Type of Dial-Up Server, when left at its default setting, causes the server to attempt first to initiate a PPP connection, and then drop to a Remote Access Server (RAS) connection, if necessary. The PPP server defaults to the use of software, not hardware, compression. For a RAS connection, the opposite is true.

The Point-to-Point Protocol (PPP) is a medium-speed Data-link layer protocol used for direct serial communications between two nodes, two routers, or a node and a router. It is most commonly used for Internet communications.

Ensuring Dial-Up Security

Securing a dial-up connection is much more important than the workgroup security considerations covered in "Configuring Access Rights," earlier in this chapter. An unprotected phone line is a gateway not only to your workstation, but possibly to your network. Always require a password for any form of dial-up access to any computer.

Windows 95's access control mechanisms, both user-level and share-level, only provide the means to allow or disallow a remote computer's access to the server. Beyond that, the server's resources are protected by the security measures implemented during the creation of the shares. In short, dial-up users are subject to the same share restrictions as any other network users.

When you implement user-level access control for a dial-up server, requiring a correct user name protects the machine against the risk of intrusion by someone outside the company. For this reason, avoid granting access to Guest accounts, or to groups like Everyone or The World when dial-up access is used.

Installing and Configuring a Remote Network Access Client

For the purpose of connecting to another Windows 95 computer, the following instructions assume that the client computer is not already attached to a local area network. Before you configure a Windows 95 machine to be a Remote Network Access (RNA) client, the following components must be installed on the workstation (all the software is available on the Windows 95 CD-ROM):

- A modem
- The Client for Microsoft Networks
- The Dial-Up Adapter
- The NetBEUI protocol (and the IPX/SPX protocol, if your network uses it)
- The Dial-Up Networking module

With the Windows 95 machine, you must create a new client (and an associated icon) in the Dial-Up Networking window for each different computer or service provider you connect to. Each client maintains its own settings and scripts, if needed, for logging into the host computer. Use the following procedure to create a dial-up client:

1. Open the Dial-Up Networking window from the Start, Programs, Accessories menu.
2. Double-click the Make New Connection icon to activate the Make New Connection Wizard, as shown in Figure 37.12.
3. Enter an identifying name for the new client you are creating, and be sure that the modem you want to use on the client machine is specified. You may click the Configure button to alter the settings for the modem, if needed. Click the Next button to proceed to the next screen.
4. Enter the area code, telephone number, and the country code for the computer you will be calling. Click the Next button to go to the next screen.

5. Click Finish to complete the process and create a new icon in the Dial-Up Networking window.

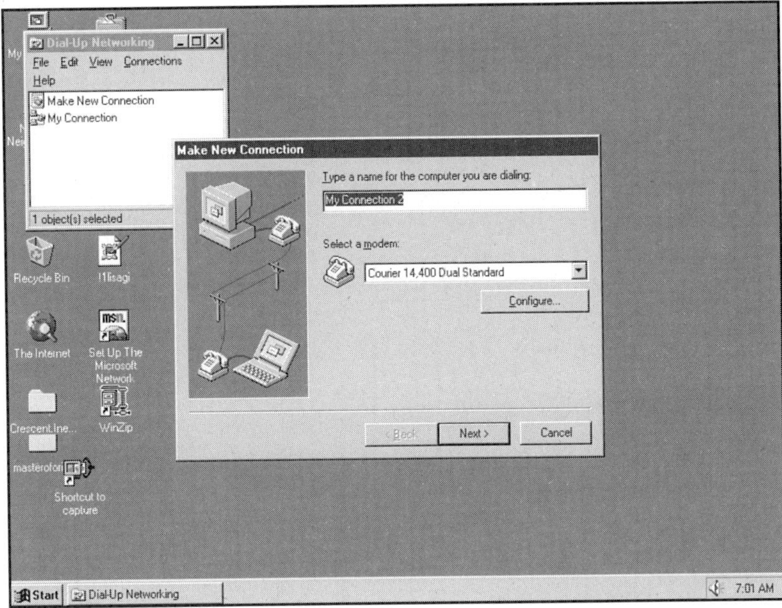

FIG. 37.12 Use the Make New Connection Wizard to configure Windows 95 to dial into a particular host server.

After you have configured the client, double-click the new icon and enter the required password to initiate the call to the host computer. The status of the call attempt appears as you progress through the connection and password-checking sequences. After the computers have successfully established a connection, access to the host computer's resources is available to the remote machine through the normal Windows 95 interface.

The newly created icon in the Dial-Up Networking window has a properties sheet through which you can alter the same modem settings as in Step 7 of the preceding steps as well as additional settings provided through an Options page. One setting you may find useful is on the Connection page of this sheet (see Figure 37.13). After you connect to a host, the remote resources are so completely integrated into Windows 95 that you may find yourself forgetting that a dial-up connection is active. Enabling the call disconnect feature under Call Preferences is a good idea so your connection terminates after the specified period of inactivity.

Clicking the Server Types button in the properties sheet of your new connection icon presents a dialog box that enables you to modify the client for use with a variety of hosts (see Figure 37.14). When you are connecting to a Windows 95 dial-up server, the default settings usually suffice. The sole exception may be the Require Encrypted Password check box under Advanced Options. You must set both the client and the server to either use (or not use) password encryption.

FIG. 37.13
The client's properties sheet contains a number of settings you may alter to suit that particular client.

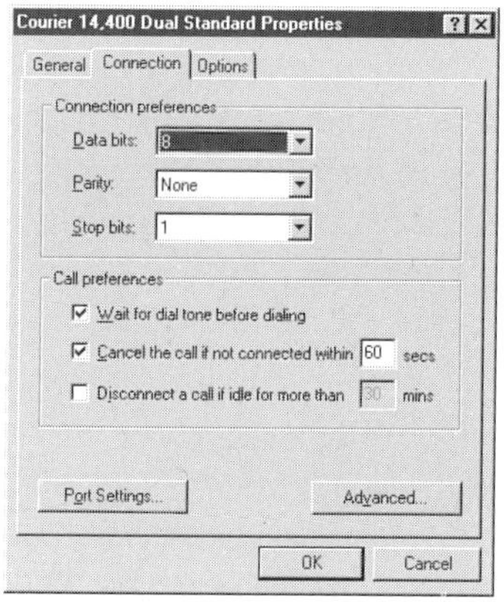

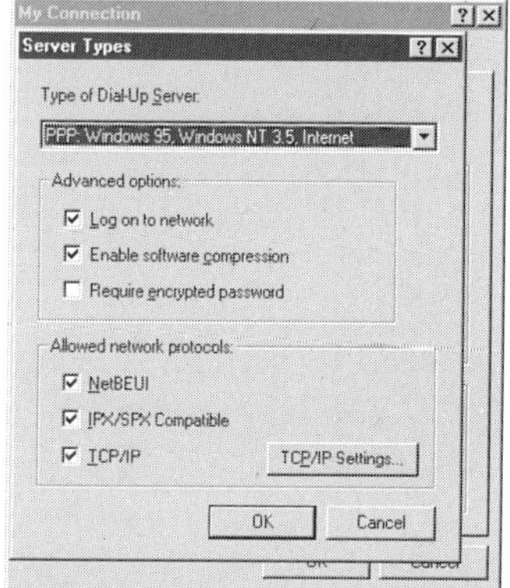

FIG. 37.14
The Server Types dialog box enables you to modify the client for use with various host computers.

Sharing Drives over the Internet

On a client/server network with Windows NT servers, TCP/IP has become a very popular protocol, and is the default on Windows NT 4.0. Windows NT has features that overcome the protocol's primary administrative drawback: the need to assign unique IP addresses to every machine on the network. NT's *dynamic host configuration protocol* (DHCP) dynamically assigns addresses to network workstations. The *Windows Internet naming service* (WINS) maintains host tables for the rapidly changing network more efficiently than a traditional *domain naming service* (DNS).

WINS also performs routing functions for TCP/IP, and one of the WINS's byproducts is its capability to allow Windows NT drives to be shared over the Internet. When you configure a Windows NT server on your network to use the WINS module and give it an external IP address (that is, an address visible from outside the company's firewall), then you can set up any Windows 95 machine with an Internet connection to contact that server through the WINS.

For more information on WINS server, try

http://www.winserve.com

Open the TCP/IP Properties sheet in the Network protocol of a remote Windows 95 machine and enable WINS Resolution in the WINS Configuration tab, specifying the correct IP address for your company's WINS server. Once you have done this, you can connect to any Internet service provider using either a dial-up or a direct connection and access shares on the WINS machine.

Unlike a local area network connection to the Windows NT machine, the shared resources are not browsable. In other words, you cannot open the Network Neighborhood window and see your Windows NT machine there. You must know the address of the server and the UNC names of the shares and have appropriate rights to access them. With this information, you can then map a drive or use the Run command on the Start menu to specify the share name and gain access.

This feature could be an enormous convenience for companies that must provide remote network access to distant users. Instead of maintaining a modem pool on the Windows NT machine and having users incur long distance phone charges to dial into the home office, the company can set up the NT server with WINS and have users call a local Internet provider (wherever they happen to be) and gain virtually the same access to that server. Instead of using a high-priced telephone network to establish a remote connection, telecommuters can use the Internet. The possibilities for increasing the flexibility and economy of remote data communications using this technology are unlimited.

Of course, some users may perceive this capability as a gigantic security hole. Some servers may already be accessible from outside the company, without their administrators even knowing it. When administrators are aware of its capabilities, however, WINS can offer users remote network access, with no additional investment in modems and telephone lines.

NOTE Microsoft has included a protocol in Windows NT called the Point-To-Point Tunneling Protocol (PPTP). This protocol allows communications to be encrypted over the Internet to minimize the security concerns.

Unfortunately, Microsoft has not released a PPTP protocol driver for Windows 95. This effectively limits the usefulness of this technology to connecting two NT networks together, or allowing Windows NT workstations to dial in.

Look for Microsoft to support PPTP in Windows 95 soon.

Balancing the Load

The overall performance of a workstation may degrade significantly if a large number of other users continually access its resources. On a peer network, therefore, the best arrangement is to spread the shared resources of the workgroup evenly among the workstations.

To achieve this balance, you may need to store a shared application on a different computer than its data files, or you may need to distribute files of a similar type among several machines. You also should spread hardware around the workgroup.

Creating a Dedicated Peer Server

There is an alternative approach to the problem of balancing resources within a workgroup. If multiple users rely heavily on Windows 95 to provide fax and print services, you may want to dedicate a computer to duty as a fax or print server.

Windows 95 provides a number of controls that enable the user to adjust the priority allotted to various system activities. You can optimize a machine that is not used as a production workstation to provide peak performance for tasks like printing and faxing, which are usually background processes.

The use of a dedicated machine may seem contradictory on a peer network, and the concept of a peer server is something of an oxymoron, but many different factors contribute to the way in which a network is designed. Modest needs call for modest solutions, and Windows 95 has emerged as the much needed filler of a significant gap between single-user systems and fully realized network systems.

For example, if a limited group of users requires fax services, only two ready solutions were available at one time. You could equip each user's workstation with its own modem and its own dedicated telephone line, each of which would remain idle most of the time. You could also invest a significantly greater amount of time, money, and administrative effort on a network server-based faxing system. Now, for the price of a single modem and phone line, users who need fax services can access them using the operating system software they already possess.

Using Workgroup Applications and Utilities

The Windows 95 operating system's peer networking capabilities are by no means limited to hardware sharing. Workgroup members can use Windows 95 to communicate among themselves at many different levels. If you do not already have a corporate e-mail system in place, Microsoft Exchange provides that capability. The \OTHER directory on the Windows 95 CD-ROM also contains several groupware utilities that have been part of Windows since Windows for Workgroups was first released, but which still may be useful to Windows 95 users.

Chat

Chat enables a Windows 95 user to select another Windows network user from a list and page them for a text-only chat. This feature can be a useful form of intermediate communication, falling somewhere between e-mail and the telephone. Chat is particularly valuable for contacting someone while they are talking on the phone.

Clipbook Viewer

The Clipbook viewer extends the capabilities of the Windows Clipboard, enabling network users to share captured information. Users working with the same data can easily share quotes, excerpts, or boilerplate text between their open applications on different machines.

CHAPTER 38

Connecting Windows 95 to a Novell Network

by Craig Zacker

NetWare is still the most popular network operating system in use today, and Windows 95's ability to function as a NetWare client was a major issue from the very beginning of its development. In attempting to build the ultimate network client, Microsoft knew that it would have to deal with new NetWare client installations, but that the true test would be the workstation upgrade procedure. ■

How to install the Microsoft Client for NetWare Networks to a Windows 95 workstation

You can add NetWare connectivity to the existing configuration with this Windows 95 default.

How the Windows 95 installation program reacts to previously installed NetWare clients

Look here to learn about the many client options for this network operating system.

The various alternative NetWare clients that you may use with Windows 95

Look here for recommendations concerning the alternative clients.

How to connect to a NetWare Directory Services (NDS) database with Windows 95

Look here for detailed information about connecting to an NDS database.

Introducing the Windows 95 Client for NetWare Networks

The arrival of Windows 95 supplied NetWare users with a new client that was immediately heralded as state-of-the-art. With its full 32-bit protected-mode architecture, the Microsoft Client for NetWare Networks uses no conventional memory. Gone are the memory management considerations that have for years plagued the use of DOS terminate-and-stay-resident (TSR) drivers for networking, and in their place are increased performance, simplified configuration, and easy installation.

In addition to the key features discussed in following sections, the Windows 95 Client also provides support for login scripts, global drive mappings, and command-line processing. Service releases of Windows 95 have also added support for NDS support.

NOTE Login script processing, while a major advantage to this client, is not yet completely effective. Although there are no problems with the basic commands such as drive mappings, difficulties have been reported with more complicated scripts, particularly those using IF...THEN loops. It is recommended that you fully test login scripts for successful completion before putting them into regular use.

Key Features of the Windows 95 Client

Microsoft's Client for NetWare Networks provides users with several new features not found in any other NetWare client, as well as enhancements of some existing ones. The following sections describe these key features.

Speed File transfers to and from NetWare drives are noticeably faster under Windows 95. Microsoft claims that its new client is twice as fast on large block transfers as a real-mode client running with Windows 3.1. The client also offers full support for the NetWare Core Protocol Packet Burst protocol as well as Large Internet Packets.

Integrated RAM Caching Windows 95's protected-mode networking is integrated with its file system. The clients are actually file system drivers, allowing network data to be serviced by Windows 95's 32-bit VCACHE, right along with local files. Files cached in memory do not have to be read and reread from the network drive during repeated use.

Plug and Play Networking All of the components of the Client for NetWare Networks are Plug and Play-capable, meaning that they can be dynamically unloaded without disturbing running processes or restarting the machine. You can remove a PC Card network adapter from its slot, and all of the networking components associated with it will be unloaded. Replace the card, and all of the components are reloaded again, without interruption of other processes.

Network Reconnection The NetWare client possesses excellent reconnection capabilities. A temporary detachment from the network doesn't disturb other system processes, either. Connections, drive mappings, and printer support are resumed when the machine is reattached.

Long File Names The protected-mode clients allow Windows 95 long file names to be transmitted over the network and stored on NetWare volumes (if they have been appropriately equipped with OS/2 name space).

Installing the Windows 95 Client for NetWare Networks

The last chapter covered the installation of a new network adapter, the Client for Microsoft Networks, and the NetBEUI protocol. The following procedure adds NetWare connectivity to this equation. Of the components already installed, only the adapter driver is required to attach to a NetWare network. You will be adding an additional client and a second protocol to the configuration. Both clients and protocols will be accessing the same adapter driver, as shown in Figure 38.1.

See "Installing a Network Adapter," p. 1022

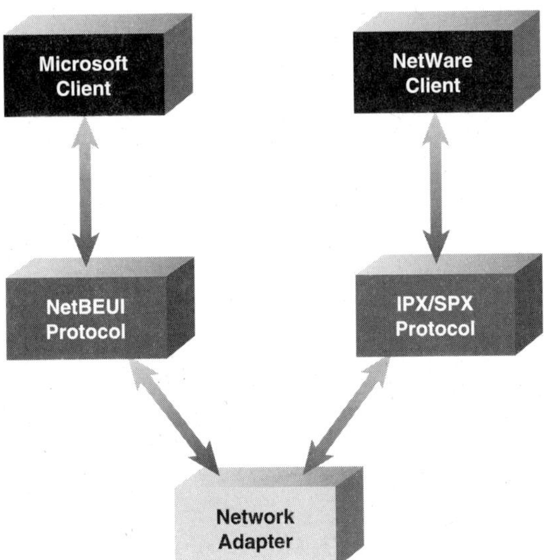

FIG. 38.1 Multiple protocols can be bound to a single adapter, each servicing a different client.

To add NetWare connectivity using the Windows 95 Client for NetWare Networks, use the following procedure:

1. Double-click the Network icon in the Windows 95 Control Panel and choose Add.
2. In the component list of the Select Network Component Type dialog box, double-click Client.
3. Select Microsoft under the Manufacturers listing and Client for NetWare Networks under the Network Clients listing. Click OK.

4. Select the Client for NetWare Networks, which should now appear in the Configuration page of the Network dialog box (see Figure 38.2), and click Properties.

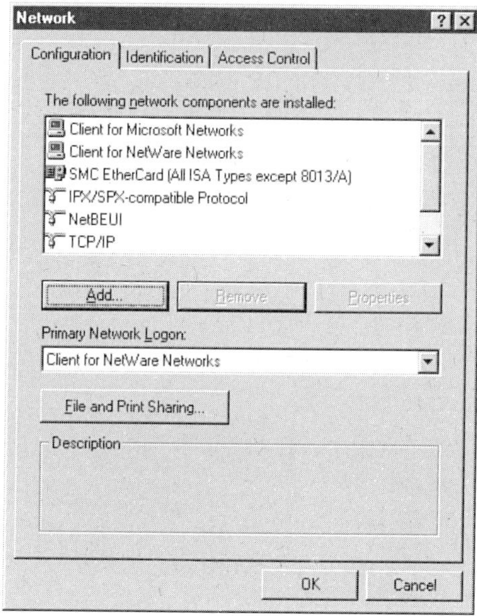

FIG. 38.2 Protected-mode clients for Microsoft and NetWare networks can be installed on the same Windows 95 machine.

TIP The network component listing in the Network dialog box is always sorted by component, in the following order: Clients, Adapters, Protocols, Services.

5. In the properties sheet, click the General tab and supply the name of your preferred NetWare server; this is the server that you always log into first. Your login scripts, if you elect to use them, reside on this server.
6. Click the check box to Enable Login Script Processing, if you want. Click OK.
7. Set the Primary Network Logon selector on the Configuration page to Client for NetWare Networks, if you want the NetWare login screen to appear first, each time you start Windows 95.

TIP NetWare uses the term "login," whereas Microsoft prefers "logon." The terms are interchangeable.

8. Click OK to close the Network applet and complete the installation. You will be prompted to reboot your system. After you reboot, your computer should be capable of connecting to a NetWare server.

Examining the Installation Process

The preceding installation procedure was a very simple one, but it is worth examining more closely to see what actually occurred.

Step 3 of the process was the selection of the client to be installed. After clicking Add, you may have noticed that not only did the Client for NetWare Networks appear in the Network Configuration screen, but the IPX/SPX-compatible protocol appeared as well. The IPX/SPX protocol is essential for NetWare communications, and Microsoft's client automatically installs the 32-bit version that is supplied with Windows 95. If you remove the IPX/SPX-compatible protocol, the Client for NetWare Networks are also removed.

NOTE Novell's own IPX ODI version of the same protocol also ships with the operating system. It is primarily included for use with Novell's real-mode clients, but it will also function with the Microsoft Client for NetWare Networks in cases where the IPX/SPX-compatible protocol cannot be used. Likewise, the IPX/SPX-compatible protocol can be used with Novell's real-mode clients.

Furthermore, if you select the IPX/SPX-compatible protocol, click the Properties button and examine its Bindings. You will see that the protocol has also been bound to the Client for Microsoft Networks. So, what you have at this moment is a network configuration that looks like Figure 38.3. Both the NetBEUI and IPX/SPX-compatible protocols are being used by the Client for Microsoft Networks.

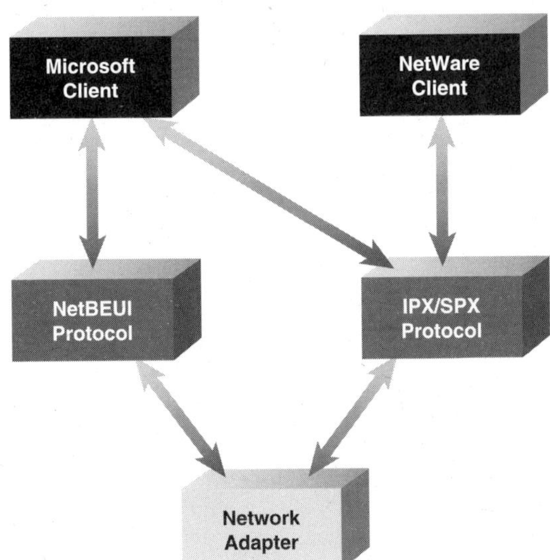

FIG. 38.3
Newly installed protocols are automatically bound to all available clients and adapters that can make use of them.

For many networks, the binding of the IPX/SPX-compatible protocol to both installed clients is a desirable situation because the IPX/SPX-compatible protocol can provide internetwork routing services to the Client for Microsoft Networks that NetBEUI cannot. Notice, however, that NetBEUI has not been bound to the Client for NetWare Networks because NetWare can make no profitable use of the protocol, and Windows 95 knows not to bind it.

If you had multiple adapters installed in the Windows 95 system, both protocols would have been automatically bound to both adapters, resulting in an interwoven network configuration in which all adapters are bound to all possible protocols, which in turn are bound to all possible clients.

Modifying the Default Installation

In some cases, this cross binding of clients, protocols, and adapters may be called for, but some of the automatic bindings may be unnecessary. You should remove unnecessary bindings because they consume system resources and slow down network performance.

In the case of your installation, if you are working on a single segment network, or all of the Windows NT machines that you need to access are located on the local network segment, the binding of the Client for Microsoft Networks to the IPX/SPX-compatible protocol can safely and profitably be removed.

Performing this task is a simple process:

1. Double-click the Network icon in the Control Panel.
2. Select the IPX/SPX-compatible protocol and choose Properties.
3. Click the Bindings tab and remove the check mark next to Client for Microsoft Networks (see Figure 38.4).
4. Click OK twice and the binding is removed as soon as the system restarts.

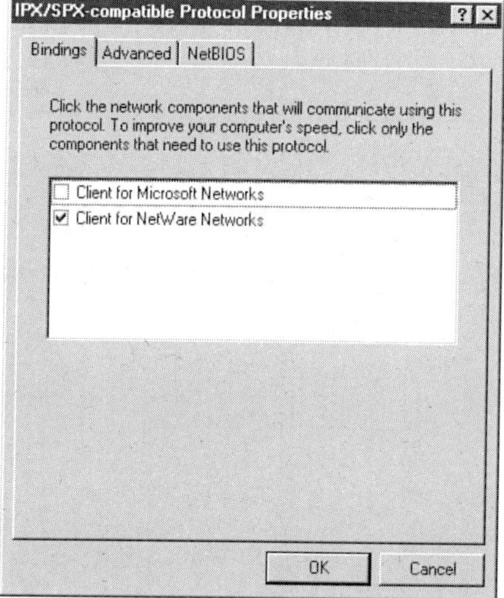

FIG. 38.4
Unbinding a protocol from a client is as easy as clearing a check box.

Another situation in which you should remove extraneous bindings is if a Windows 95 machine is using NetBEUI or the IPX/SPX-compatible protocol to connect to a LAN, but is also using a dial-up connection to an Internet service provider. A second adapter, called the Dial-Up Adapter, would have to be installed, along with the TCP/IP protocol. In this case, it would be beneficial to remove the bindings of the two LAN protocols from the Dial-Up Adapter, as well as that of the LAN adapter to the TCP/IP protocol. You would then have a system in which each adapter was using only the protocols that it needed, conserving system memory and optimizing performance.

Installing Windows 95 on an Existing NetWare Client

The simplest way to gain network connectivity with Windows 95 is to have a functioning network client present when the operating system is installed.

The Windows 95 setup program scans the machine's configuration files and the DOS memory control blocks (MCBs) for the presence of a Microsoft client, as well as a NetWare shell (NETX.EXE or NETX). The program also looks for other network-related TSRs that are running, all in an attempt to ensure that once Windows 95 has been installed, the workstation retains the same level of network connectivity that it had before the process began.

Always keep in mind that while Windows 95 examines the contents of startup files like AUTOEXEC.BAT, CONFIG.SYS, and WINSTART.BAT, it bases its installation decisions primarily on the network drivers that it finds in memory at the time of the installation. If, for example, your system is set up to use the NetWare NETX redirector, but you boot the machine from a floppy using NETX.EXE, the installation routine considers this a NETX machine, and behaves accordingly.

TIP In most cases, the recommended method for installing Windows 95 to a network workstation is to start with the machine in its normal working state, before running **SETUP.EXE**.

In order to maintain the workstation's networking capabilities, Windows 95 modifies its installation routine in accordance with the results of its memory and disk scans. A file called NETDET.INI, located in the Windows directory, contains instructions for the installation program to follow under specific circumstances.

NOTE In networking situations in which you want to upgrade a large number of workstations to Windows 95, you can modify the NETDET.INI file to accommodate the specific needs of the environment. See "Advanced Installation Techniques" in Chapter 2 for more information on this procedure.

In its default configuration, Windows 95 attempts to install the Microsoft Client for NetWare Networks, using the IPX/SPX-compatible protocol and a 32-bit protected-mode adapter driver. This is the optimum arrangement for Windows 95 running on NetWare. The installation program specifies other components only when they are required to maintain the same level of network connectivity as before the installation began.

This installation process remarks out entries in the AUTOEXEC.BAT and SYSTEM.INI files that are not needed in the new network environment and migrates settings found in configuration files like NET.CFG and PROTOCOL.INI to the Windows 95 Registry. The installation may also move the commands to launch required networking TSRs from the AUTOEXEC.BAT file to WINSTART.BAT. Any configuration settings that conflict with the capabilities of the default client installation may cause other actions to be substituted.

Supporting NetWare Directory Services

In the most common exception to this default installation, an existing real-mode NetWare client is retained because SETUP.EXE detects a workstation running VLMs to connect to a NetWare 4.x NDS tree. At the time of the initial Windows 95 release, no protected-mode client with NDS support was available, and retaining the VLMs was the only alternative.

NOTE The most recent release of Windows 95 (OSR2) includes the protected-mode client for NDS, but it is available only on preinstalled computers and cannot be used to upgrade existing Windows installations. The installation procedure has therefore remained the same: If SETUP detects a VLM installation connecting to an NDS tree, real-mode networking is preserved.

As you learn later in this chapter, a choice is now available for clients supporting NetWare Directory Services. The installation routine favors Microsoft's implementation, but after comparing the two, you may prefer to use the Novell client.

NOTE Windows 95 is capable of detecting whether a VLM-equipped workstation is logging in to a NetWare Directory Services database. If you are running VLMs to connect to a NetWare 3.x server, or a NetWare 4.x server in bindery emulation mode, the Microsoft protected-mode client is installed.

Supporting Other Networking TSRs

Aside from an NDS connection, Windows 95's SETUP also attempts to detect any other TSRs that involve network communications. These may include requesters for server-based database engines, network application protocol drivers, or modules providing connectivity to mini- or mainframe computers. When SETUP detects such modules, the installation program may take several different action stops to preserve their functionality:

- TSR load lines may be migrated from AUTOEXEC.BAT to WINSTART.BAT.
- The Client for NetWare Networks may be configured to utilize Novell's IPX ODI protocol, instead of Microsoft's IPX/SPX-compatible protocol.
- A real-mode client may be retained, but the IPX/SPX-compatible protocol substituted for Novell's IPX ODI protocol.
- A real-mode client may be retained in its entirety.

WINSTART.BAT and Windows 95

WINSTART.BAT is a Windows convention that dates back to version 3.1 and before, but has acquired new significance for Windows 95 users. WINSTART.BAT is simply a batch file that, when located in the Windows directory, automatically executes any commands within it as Windows is loaded. Any TSR programs executed are unloaded from memory when exiting Windows.

When Windows 95 is configured to use any of the Microsoft protected-mode clients, no network connectivity is established until after the processing of the AUTOEXEC.BAT file is completed. Any network-dependent TSRs in that file will, therefore, fail to load. The WINSTART.BAT file, however, is executed after a network connection is established. Migrating these TSR load lines there allows them to initialize properly.

As a result of these measures, a Windows 95 upgrade usually leaves a workstation with the same networking capabilities that it had before the process started.

Using NetWare Client Alternatives

Windows 95's backward compatibility and open architecture provides NetWare users with several alternatives to Microsoft's Client for NetWare Networks. Two of these alternative clients take the form of looking backward: Both of Novell's 16-bit real-mode DOS/Windows clients can be used with Windows 95; others look forward, providing even more features than are available with the Windows 95 client. The following sections consider all of these alternatives, outline their capabilities and their drawbacks, and cover their installation processes.

Gateway Services for NetWare

The first alternative method for gaining NetWare connectivity is actually not a client at all, it's a service. And what's more, it doesn't even run on a Windows 95 machine—it's for Windows NT Server.

Gateway Services for NetWare is an optional service available for versions 3.5 and later of Microsoft Windows NT. It allows a Windows NT machine to log into a NetWare server as a single user. As a result, a gateway is created so that all of the Windows network users that are logged into the NT server can access the volumes on the NetWare server, just as though they were normal Windows NT shares.

In this way, a workstation running Windows for Workgroups, Windows NT Workstation, or Windows 95 need not have a NetWare client installed at all. With only a Windows client, they can still gain access to NetWare-based file and print services.

Of course, Gateway Services for NetWare is not a practical alternative for prolonged use by a large number of workstations, as it pipes all of the NetWare requests through a single connection. But, for the user who needs only occasional access to NetWare files, or as a temporary measure to facilitate the transition between network operating systems, this can be a very useful tool.

File and Printer Sharing for NetWare Networks

Windows 95 has another unusual method for granting native NetWare users access to Windows 95 files, called File and Printer Sharing for NetWare Networks. Just as File and Printer Sharing for Microsoft Networks allows the Windows network client to share his workstation resources with other users, so File and Printer Sharing for NetWare Networks allows users of Microsoft's Client for NetWare Networks to do the same. To all NetWare users on the network, a Windows 95 machine running this setup appears to be a NetWare 3.12 file and print server.

Installation of the service creates a subdirectory called NWSYSVOL in the machine's Windows directory, which becomes the "server's" SYS: volume. When you share other Windows 95 drives or directories in the normal manner, they become additional volumes on the server.

Only user-level access to this server is allowed, and an actual NetWare server must be used as a "validator." You must select users that are to be allowed access to the shared drives from the actual NetWare server's user list, as shown in Figure 38.5. You then grant each user access rights to the shares, according to the standard NetWare model.

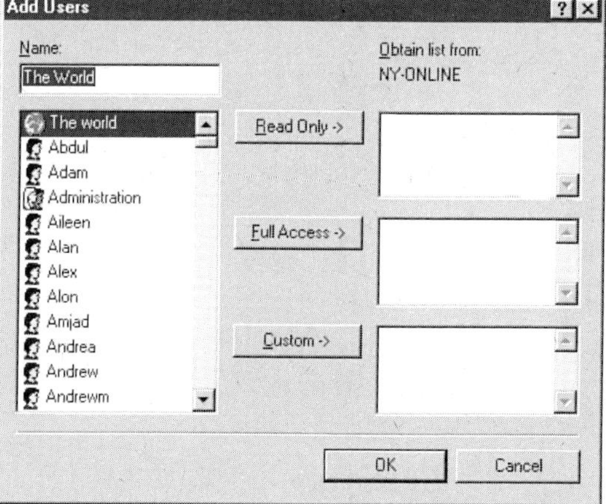

FIG. 38.5 Users for the new "server" are selected from a true NetWare server's user list.

Two options are available, in the service's Properties dialog box, for the way in which the new server is to be advertised on the network. *Workgroup advertising* means that the computer is seen as part of the regular Windows workgroup listing. *SAP Advertising* means that the machine appears to be a legitimate NetWare server to any other NetWare client workstation, through the SLIST command or any other utility that lists the NetWare servers on the network. You must use SAP (Service Advertising Protocol) advertising if you want users of the Novell NETX and VLM clients to be able to access the machine.

CAUTION

Use of the SAP Advertising feature in the File and Printer Sharing for NetWare service has been known to cause enormous increases in the overall SAP traffic on a network. Be sure to check with your network administrator before enabling this feature.

This service could be useful, for example, by granting Windows 3.1 NetWare users remote access to a CD-ROM drive without having to mount it as a volume on a real server, or access to a printer without having to attach it to a NetWare print server and a queue. However, use of a desktop computer as a file server is not recommended because these machines are not designed for the increased network traffic associated with the role of file server.

Using Novell Real-Mode Clients

Microsoft's NDS service for the Windows 95 Client for NetWare Networks and Novell's Client32 for Windows 95 both provide NDS access while retaining the advantages of a 32-bit protected-mode client. Both of these alternatives are considered later in this chapter.

Although there are other reasons to continue using the Novell real-mode clients, none of them have anything to do with performance. The real-mode clients are slower in every way than their protected-mode counterparts. They are also subject to the same conventional memory utilization problems as they were with Windows 3.1. It may be necessary, even with Windows 95, to implement a full memory management regimen, using the standard tools—EMM386.EXE, or a third-party package such as QEMM—to load some of the modules into upper memory.

However, situations such as those mentioned earlier in this chapter (when special TSRs are needed to gain access to critical network services) are still valid cases in which the real-mode clients might be needed—at least until the services in question can be upgraded. These cases are becoming less and less common, though, as many such TSRs are being rewritten as Windows 95 clients and services.

Using the NETX Client

When a workstation equipped with the NETX client is upgraded to Windows 95, it is automatically upgraded to the Client for NetWare Networks, unless TSRs are present that are incompatible with the 32-bit protected-mode client. If you want to continue using NETX with Windows 95 for any other reason, you need to remove the newly installed client first, in most cases, in order to restore NETX's functionality.

NOTE Even though Windows 95 may disable a workstation's existing networking configuration to install a new one, it will never delete the original files. Reinstalling the original client from the Control Panel locates and reactivates the original files.

Installing the NETX Client

When you install the NETX client in Windows 95, you should have a functional NETX client already installed on the machine, even if it isn't operating. Otherwise, you will be prompted to supply the necessary files during the installation.

CAUTION

The NETX and VLM client files do not ship as part of the Windows 95 package. You are responsible for supplying appropriate versions of all the necessary files. It's strongly recommended that the latest versions be installed on the system before the real-mode client is installed in Windows 95.

To install the NETX client in Windows 95, follow these steps:

1. Double-click the Network icon in the Windows 95 Control Panel.
2. If the Client for NetWare Networks, or any other NetWare client, is currently installed, select it and click the Remove button.

The NETX client can safely coexist with the protected-mode Client for Microsoft Networks on the same machine. Both can use the same IPX protocol, or two different ones can be installed. However, NETX cannot be used with the real-mode version of the Client for Microsoft Networks. Only one real-mode network client can run on a single machine.

3. In the component list of the Select Network Component Type dialog box, double-click Client.
4. In the Manufacturers list on the left side of the Select Network Client dialog box, select Novell. On the right side, choose Novell NetWare (Workstation Shell 3.X [NETX]). Click OK.
5. Notice that the NETX client, an adapter labeled Existing ODI Driver, and the Novell IPX ODI protocol have been added to the Network screen (see Figure 38.6). Click OK again to complete the installation. You will be prompted to restart your system.

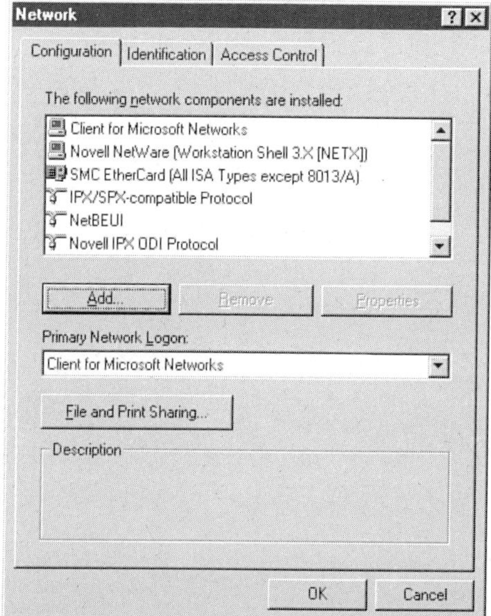

FIG. 38.6
Installing the NETX client automatically causes the Existing ODI Driver and the Novell IPX ODI Protocol to be installed.

NOTE Whereas the installation of the NETX client automatically includes the Novell IPX ODI Protocol and a 16-bit real-mode ODI adapter driver, either the Microsoft IPX/SPX-compatible protocol or its protected-mode NDIS 3.1 adapter drivers, or both, can be used instead.

Other NETX Client Issues

You need to consider several other issues when running the NETX client on a Windows 95 machine:

- Windows 95, by default, sets the LASTDRIVE= entry to the letter Z. To use NETX, you must include a line in the CONFIG.SYS file that indicates what the first NetWare drive letter will be. For example, adding LASTDRIVE=E will cause F: to be the first NetWare drive.
- If you will be running a login script that utilizes the %OS_VERSION variable, you must modify the Windows SETVER table by issuing the following command at a DOS prompt:

  SETVER NETX.EXE 7.00

SETVER, the MS-DOS version compatibility table, is no longer a separate TSR utility. It is now integrated into Windows 95 and automatically loaded with the operating system.

- Be sure that the NETX version of the NETWARE.DRV file is present in the Windows directory (see the "Windows 95 Clients and NETWARE.DRV" sidebar).
- You will not be able to store Windows 95 long file names on NetWare servers using NETX, or any real-mode client.

Windows 95 Clients and NETWARE.DRV

Whenever you elect to use a NetWare real-mode client with Windows 95, it's crucial that the correct version of the NETWARE.DRV file be installed in the Windows directory. There are different versions of this file for the NETX and VLM clients, and for Windows 95's own clients. Their approximate sizes are:

NETWARE.DRV	Windows 95	approx. 1.6K
NETWARE.DRV	VLM	approx. 160K
NETWARE.DRV	NETX	approx. 134K

Windows 95 replaces the current NETWARE.DRV with its own version when it updates a real-mode to the protected-mode NetWare client. The old version is renamed, however, as NETWARE.DR~ , so that it can be restored if necessary.

Using the VLM Client

The VLM client, if you are using it to log into a NetWare Directory Services tree, isn't replaced with the protected-mode client by the default Windows 95 installation routine. Like the NETX client, its settings are assimilated into the Windows 95 Registry and is loaded into conventional memory—unless you take steps to prevent this occurrence.

In addition, you must be aware of other concerns when using the VLM client with Windows 95, as well as issues that you must address when installing the client on an existing Windows 95 machine.

The VLM client offers considerably more functionality than NETX, but some of its features are not compatible with Windows 95. Its primary attribute is its ability to run NetWare NDS utilities like NWADMIN, NETADMIN, and CX, and to log into an NDS tree. To ensure this compatibility, you should use the DOS-based installation routine included with the VLM package to perform a complete client installation (with full Windows support). You should also make sure that you are installing the latest available version of the client software.

Obtaining the Latest Novell Client Software

The latest releases of the Novell NETX and VLM clients are required when you are running them with Windows 95. The most reliable source for Novell upgrade files is the Novell Support Connection Web site, located at **http://support.novell.com**.

All of the downloadable files can be found on the Novell Product Support page. This can be accessed by either clicking the Product Support icon or going directly to **http://support.novell.com/home**.

All of the Novell release files are self-extracting archives that you should execute in an empty directory. All contain extensive README files that you should read carefully before applying any updates.

Installing the VLM Client

When installing the VLM client onto a Windows 95 machine, use the Novell client installation program for the initial process rather than the Control Panel. When doing so, you must be sure to retain access to the VLM installation files throughout the process. You should therefore run the installation program either from floppy disks or a CD-ROM, or copy it to a local hard drive, rather than run it from a server drive.

To install the VLM client on a Windows 95 machine, use the following procedure:

1. Double-click the Network icon in the Windows 95 Control Panel and remove all existing network support components. Click OK to close the dialog box.
2. When asked whether to restart the computer, choose No. Open the Start menu, select Shut Down, choose Restart the Computer in MS-DOS Mode and click Yes.

The computer can also be started in MS-DOS mode by holding down the F8 key during the boot process and making the appropriate selection from the boot menu.

3. Run the VLM installation program from the DOS prompt in the normal manner. Be sure to include Windows support. If you are asked whether to overwrite the NETWARE.DRV file, select Yes.

4. Restart the computer and again open the Network dialog box. Windows 95 should detect that the VLM client has been installed and add the appropriate settings.
5. Click OK, and restart the computer once again.

Other VLM Client Issues

You must take note of the following issues when you use the VLM client with Windows 95:

- Due to a problem in the way that it makes calls to NETWARE.DRV, Windows 95, during its load sequence, attempts to restore any Windows-permanent network connections that you have specified before the NetWare login dialog box appears. This situation causes Windows 95 to generate error messages. One workaround is to ignore the errors and use the NWUSER program's Restore Now feature. Alternatively, you can log into the network before loading Windows to allow the permanent connections to be restored normally.

Placing a LOGIN command in the AUTOEXEC.BAT or STARTNET.BAT file causes the system's boot sequence to pause for user input and allows you to log into the network before the Windows 95 GUI loads.

- The VLM client's NWUSER program has an option to allow private drive mappings. These are drive mappings made in a DOS session that exist only in that session. This feature does not function under Windows 95. Be sure to leave the Global Drives and Paths box in the NWUSER program checked at all times. All drive mappings in Windows 95 are global. Changes made to drive mappings within a DOS session are always propagated throughout the whole system.
- As with Windows 3.1, all search drives must be mapped from a DOS prompt or a login script before starting Windows 95. Search drives cannot be mapped from a DOS session within Windows 95.
- As with NETX, Windows 95 long file names cannot be stored on NetWare servers with the VLM client. Instead, they are truncated to their DOS 8.3 equivalents. However, support is provided for the storage of user profiles on NetWare servers.

Using the Microsoft Service for NetWare Directory Services

Microsoft was well aware of the problems created by the lack of NetWare Directory Services (NDS) support in the Client for NetWare Networks at the time of the Windows 95 release. Within two months of that release, Microsoft resolved the problem by providing a Service for NetWare Directory Services (MSNDS).

This add-on service originally required the user to download the installation files from Microsoft's Web site, but the latest OEM Service Release (OSR2) includes the service in the base product. OSR2 is available in one form: preinstalled on new computers. If you have an older copy of Windows 95, or you have purchased Windows 95 as an upgrade, you must download MSNDS manually.

The addition of the service provides NDS users with full container, object, and user login script support, the ability to browse for NetWare resources through the NDS hierarchy, and access to all of the NDS-related NetWare utilities.

ON THE WEB

The Service for NetWare Directory Services is available for download from Microsoft's World Wide Web site at **http://www.microsoft.com/windows/software/msnds.htm**.

Installing the Service for NDS

NOTE Users of OSR2 do not need to download MSNDS. These users can simply install MSNDS from the Network Control Panel by clicking Add, Service, and Microsoft. The Service for NetWare Directory Services will be listed.

If you don't know if you are running the OSR2 version of Windows 95, open the System applet in the Control Panel. OSR2 is identified as version 4.00.950B.

To install NDS support into the Client for NetWare Networks, follow these steps:

1. Download MSNDS.EXE from one of the Microsoft online services.
2. Put the file in a directory by itself and execute MSNDS.EXE to extract the contents of the archive.

3. Double-click the Network icon in the Windows 95 Control Panel.
4. Click Add, double-click Service in the Select Network Component Type dialog box, and click the Have Disk button in the Select Network Service dialog box.
5. Enter the location of the directory containing the MSNDS files into the Install from Disk dialog box, and click OK twice.
6. Select the Service for NetWare Directory Services entry in the Network applet's Configuration page and click the Properties button.
7. Enter the name of your preferred NDS tree, and the full context of your workstation. Click OK twice to complete the installation.

CAUTION

When using the NDS Service to connect to a NetWare 4.01 NDS tree, only full-context names can be used. For example, a context of **.USER.ORGANIZATION** will not be acceptable. Enter instead: **.CN=USER.OU=ORGANIZATION**.

NOTE The installation of the Service for NetWare Directory Services adds a line to the system's AUTOEXEC.BAT file that runs a batch file called _NWNDS.BAT during the next system reboot. The batch file need only be run once, but this line will remain in the AUTOEXEC.BAT file. You can safely remove it after the installation is complete.

Other Service for NDS Issues

Although the Service for NDS provides users with the ability to access the NetWare Directory, you must address a number of compatibility issues before the service can be a suitable alternative to the VLM client. Some of these issues are easily addressed, some can be avoided by altering usage practices, and others are yet to be corrected. The following sections discuss these issues in detail.

NetWare Library Files Running the NWADMIN directory maintenance utility, as well as many other Windows network utilities, requires the support provided by the following NetWare library files:

- NWCALLS.DLL
- NWLOCALE.DLL
- NWIPXSPX.DLL
- NWNET.DLL
- NWGDI.DLL
- NWPSRV.DLL

These files are part of the NetWare VLM installation kit and are also available in the NWDLL2.EXE archive, both of which can be downloaded from Novell's NetWire service. If the VLM client has previously been installed on the workstation, these files should already be available. They must be located in the \Windows\System directory, or in another directory on the computer's PATH.

Windows 95 does not load these files into memory by default. It is possible that some networking applications may expect these libraries to be available in memory and will not function properly as a result. To work around this issue, Windows 95's System Policies feature can be used to preload these files. See "Advanced Installation Techniques" in Chapter 2 for more information on using the system policy editor.

NOTE The NW*.DLL files listed previously are not shipped with Windows 95. They are Novell release files and their use is subject to Novell's licensing restrictions.

Other applications may require access to the Unicode tables that are located in the \PUBLIC\NLS directory on a NetWare 4.x server. Adding this directory to the search path prevents any "Failed to Find Unicode Tables" errors from occurring.

Adding NDS Printers When using the Add New Printer Wizard with the Service for NDS to browse for printers, NDS printers are not visible. Bindery-based printers appear as they normally do. This discrepancy is due to a problem with the SHELL32.DLL file, which has been remedied by the release of Windows 95 Service Pack 1, available via Microsoft's Web site at **http://www.microsoft.com/windows95**.

See "Working with Network Printers," **p. 1049**

Service for NDS and NWUSER The Microsoft Service for NDS does not support the use of the NWUSER program that is included as part of the VLM client package. Most of the functions performed by NWUSER can be duplicated by other means in Windows 95.

Multiple Login Scripts When the Client for NetWare Networks and the Service for NDS are used alongside the Client for Microsoft Networks, Windows NT logon scripts always runs before NetWare login scripts, no matter which client is selected in the Primary Network Login dialog box.

Using the NetWare Client32 for Windows 95

Since the release of Windows 95, Novell has created its own protected-mode NetWare client, the NetWare Client32 for Windows 95. This client, as well as MSNDS, provides Windows 95 users with the basic NDS access that they requested. Novell's client, however, has proven to be a significantly more ambitious project than Microsoft's, and with good reason.

Client32 provides Windows 95 with NDS support, but it goes a great deal further by—for the first time—positioning NetWare Directory Services as a truly beneficial enterprise management platform. Client32's ability to deliver network applications to multiple users in the form of icons on the Windows 95 desktop is the first step toward making the Directory as useful for mid-sized and small networks as it is for giant enterprises.

Installing NetWare Client32 for Windows 95

Client32 provides a number of options with respect to its installation. Designed for the corporate environment, in which network administrators may be faced with the task of installing the client on hundreds of machines, it offers both automated and customized installation features.

For a network-based installation, Client32 can be added to the Windows 95 source files, and the installation script modified to make Client32 the default instead of Microsoft's NetWare client.

Client32 can also be configured to install itself automatically during a normal NDS login. A user's login script can be used to detect whether the client has already been installed on the workstation. If it hasn't, it performs the installation immediately.

Client32 can also be installed on demand by running a standard Windows 95 SETUP.EXE file from the source directory. All three of these processes can be customized to the administrator's exact preferences for multiple network installs. By default, they remove all existing NetWare client support from the Windows 95 machine and install the new client in its place.

For most single-user installations, running the SETUP program (see Figure 38.7) is the recommended installation procedure.

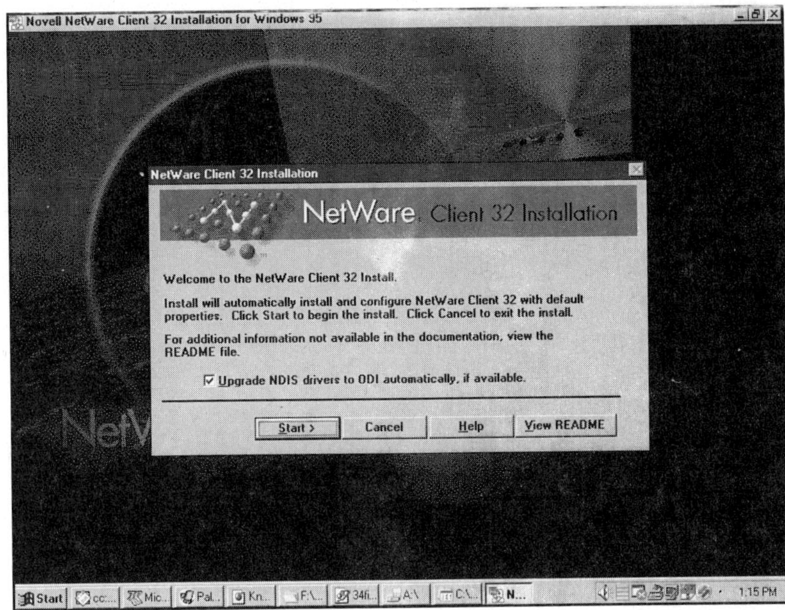

FIG. 38.7
The Novell NetWare Client32 for Windows 95 SETUP.EXE program completely automates the installation process.

The package also ships with its own 32-bit ODI drivers that, when compatible with the installed hardware, are recommended for use by Novell. Otherwise, you can use one of the NDIS 3.1 adapter drivers that ship with Windows 95.

Finally, Client32 can be installed using the normal Control Panel procedure, as follows:

1. Download NetWare Client32 for Windows 95 from Novell's World Wide Web site, place it in a directory by itself, and execute the file to expand it.

NOTE The Novell NetWare Client32 for Windows 95 can be downloaded from Novell's Web site at **http://support.novell.com** and then navigated to the appropriate page. To access the Client32 download page directly, point your browser at **http://support.novell.com/home/client/c3295/updates.htm**.

2. Double-click the Network icon in the Windows 95 Control Panel. Remove any existing NetWare support that has been installed.

NOTE Client32 is designed to automatically remove any existing NetWare client from Windows 95 before installing itself. However, in some instances, it can fail to do so, particularly when the Microsoft Service for NDS is present on the workstation. For large-scale client-upgrade projects, testing should be conducted on the existing environment to see if the installation method you choose behaves properly.

3. Click Add and double-click Client in the Select Network Component Type dialog box.
4. Click Have Disk and set the selector to the drive and directory containing the Client32 installation files.
5. When Client32 for NetWare Networks appears in the Select Network Type dialog box, select it and click OK.
6. After files are copied, the display returns to the Network's Configuration page, where the Novell NetWare Client32 is visible, as well as the IPX 32-bit Protocol for Novell NetWare Client32 (see Figure 38.8). If you want, and if your hardware is supported, you can manually install one of the 32-bit ODI adapter drivers included with Client32 at this time.

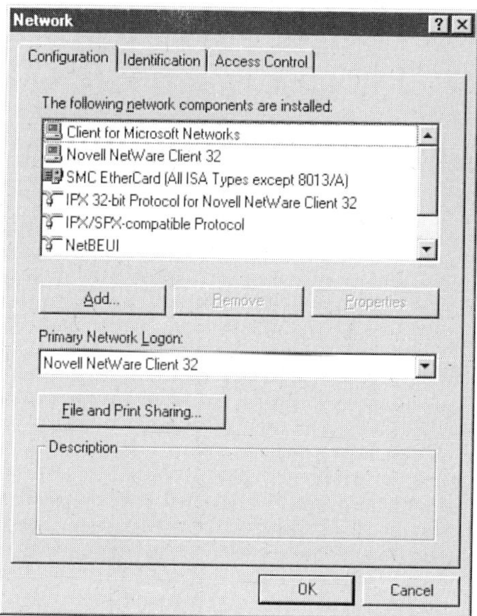

FIG. 38.8
Client32 is integrated into the Windows 95 networking environment, just as a Microsoft client would be.

7. Before closing the dialog box, if you will be logging into an NDS tree for the first time, select the client and click the Properties button. Then select the Client32 tab and fill in the names of your preferred server and NDS tree, the context of your user object, and select a letter to be your first NetWare drive letter.
8. Click OK twice to close the dialog box and complete the installation. Restart the computer when you are prompted to do so.

Other Client32 Issues

Once installed, Client32 makes itself your primary login client, and as soon as the machine restarts, you'll see how this client differs from Microsoft's. Additional features abound from the very first login screen.

Client32 provides support for browsing to a different preferred server or tree, executes a specific login script or user profile, specifies values for login script variables, or just performs a simple bindery login.

The client modifies the My Computer, Network Neighborhood, and Windows Explorer displays to include icons representing NDS trees, as well as other NetWare features not provided by any other client (see Figure 38.9). The network can also be browsed either through the NDS hierarchy or through a server list. Support is even provided for logging into multiple NDS trees simultaneously.

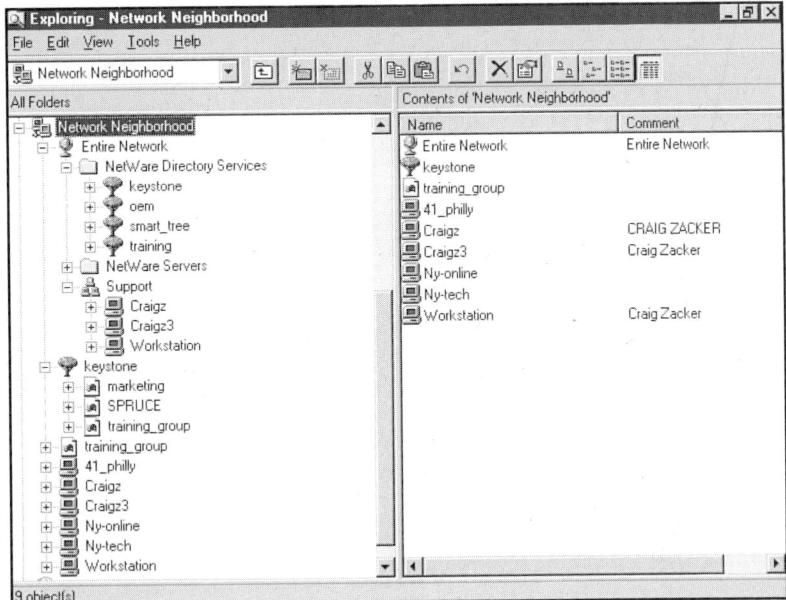

FIG. 38.9
Client32 integrates the NDS tree structure into the Windows Explorer.

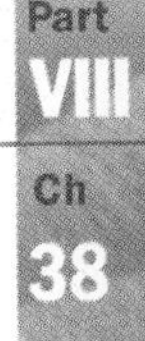

Of course, you can run NWADMIN and all of the other NDS-related NetWare utilities using Client32. All of the necessary library files are included in the package, so even if you have never run a NetWare client on the workstation before, no other downloads are needed.

NOTE Novell has recently released an updated version of the Netware Administrator for Windows 95, called NWADMN95. This release addresses some issues found when using the Windows 3.x version of NWADMIN under Windows 95, and can be downloaded from Novell's Web site.

Most impressively, the package includes a module called APPSNAP.DLL that adds additional schema to the NDS database, that can be used by the NWADMIN utility. Once the module is installed, you can create application objects in the NDS database, just as you would create user, group, or any other NDS objects.

When you assign a user rights to an object representing a network-based application, the icon for the application appears in a window on his desktop when he runs the NetWare Application Launcher, a utility that is also included with the client. By placing this launcher in the Windows Startup group on all users' computers, a network administrator can deliver an entire customized suite of applications to as many workstations as needed, simply by assigning rights to users, groups, or containers in NWADMIN.

Choosing an NDS Client

The possibilities suggested by the NetWare Application Launcher are numerous, and most enticing. Although it started slowly, NetWare 4 sales are increasing tremendously, and NDS finally seems to be garnering the attention that Novell has always hoped it would, from both users and developers.

For the majority of users, especially those who are better off shielded from the intricacies of NDS and networking in general, the Microsoft Service for NetWare Directory Services is the preferred alternative. It offers excellent performance, all of the features that the average user needs, and it merges seamlessly with the existing Windows 95 client installation.

At a price, Client32 offers power users a host of very attractive features, including advanced configuration options. Navigating through a network server or tree display is markedly slower than with the Microsoft client. Delays of several seconds are commonplace while scanning network directories.

Client32 ships with files that allow it to be managed by the Windows 95 system Policy Editor. Access to selected features can be restricted in order to customize the interface to suit the users' skill level.

It should be noted that network file transfer performance does not seem to be affected as much as simple directory scanning. Client32 provides its own client-side caching, while the Microsoft clients are able to share the unified Windows 95 system cache (VCACHE).

CHAPTER 39

Using Novell Network Resources in Windows 95

by Glenn Fincher with Sue Plumley

You can add a Windows 95 computer to an existing NetWare network by using Microsoft's enhanced NetWare connectivity tools. These tools are the first and best choices in almost every situation to ensure complete compatibility and integration with the very different architectures that Microsoft and NetWare represent. Additionally, Windows 95 has included many utilities and features you can use to communicate and connect to the NetWare network. This chapter discusses those Windows 95 utilities as well as several NetWare utilities and commands you can use from within Windows. ■

User Maintenance and Novell Utilities

Windows 95 includes a number of utilities useful for maintenance operations, and Novell utilities add additional functionality in a NetWare network.

Drive mapping and changing passwords

Two of the most important components of a network are maps and passwords, which add usability and security.

Connecting to other servers

It is extremely uncommon to find a site with only one server in the business world today.

Using network tape drives

Tape drives add backup security and insurance against the almost-inevitable system disaster.

Using Windows 95 and Novell Utilities

Windows support for Novell's NetWare makes performing general maintenance tasks, as well as requesting information from the server, quick and easy. You can perform many NetWare functions through Windows, such as mapping drives, listing your server connection, managing network print jobs, and so on, without ever using a command line.

Windows enables you to use many of NetWare's commands and utilities directly within Windows. You can check the status of network volumes, change your password, and use several administrative utilities from the MS-DOS prompt or the Run dialog box.

Mapping Drives

Windows provides an easy method of mapping drives from within the Network Neighborhood so you can avoid using Netware's MAP command. When you map a drive, you assign a drive letter to a network resource, such as a drive or folder. Mapping drives makes access to network resources faster and easier than opening several layers of windows to find the resource on the server or network.

TIP You can make mapping permanent so you don't have to set the mapping each time you log in to the server.

Additionally, if you're running a login script, mapping drives provides the search and drive maps created by the system administrator. If you choose not to run the login script, you can map the drives yourself within Windows.

You also can choose to connect the map as a root of the drive, which not only helps keep path statements from getting too long but makes your maps a bit more permanent. For example, you can map to a document directory using the path: F:\CARLOS\NOTEBOOK\WPDOCS.

Now suppose you go into the F:\CARLOS\NOTEBOOK directory and access the REPORTS directory. The next time you want to use the original mapping to the WPDOCS directory, the map has changed to the F:\CARLOS\NOTEBOOK\REPORTS directory.

Connect the map as a root of the drive to alleviate this problem. In this example, connect F:\CARLOS\NOTEBOOK\WPDOCS as "J." Whenever you want to access the WPDOCS folder, you simply type **J**. Not only is the path shorter and easier to enter, the path remains the same even if you access different folders within the NOTEBOOK directory.

NOTE If you have used Windows for Workgroups, mapping a drive in Network Neighborhood should seem familiar because it is similar to mapping a drive from File Manager.

The basic procedure for mapping a network drive is as follows:

1. Open the Network Neighborhood and select the shared folder you want to map to.

2. Choose File, Map Network Drive. The Map Network Drive dialog box appears, as shown in Figure 39.1. Alternatively, you can right-click the share and choose Map Network Drive.

FIG. 39.1
Windows displays the path you've mapped out by selecting each folder.

3. By default, Windows assigns the next available drive letter on your computer to the folder that you select to map. To assign a different letter, select it from the Drive drop-down list.
4. To reconnect to this drive or directory automatically, select the Reconnect at Logon check box. Choosing this option makes the mapping permanent.
5. If you want, choose Connect as Root of the Drive.
6. Choose OK to close the dialog box. View drive mappings in the My Computer window (see Figure 39.2).

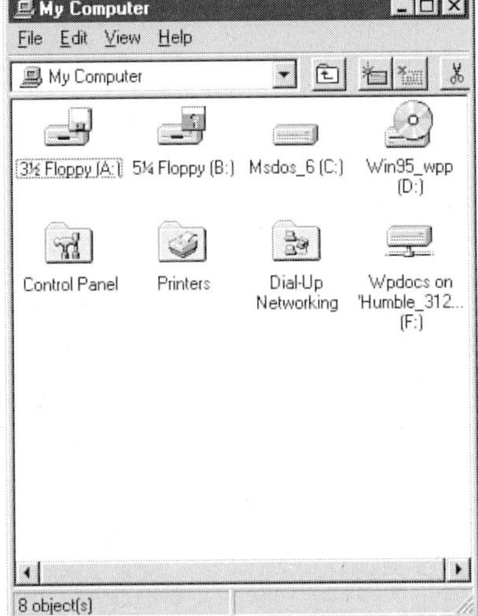

FIG. 39.2
Click the mapped drive icon to open the folder you want without wading through several other folders.

TIP If the toolbar is not showing in the Network Neighborhood window, choose View, Toolbar.

NOTE Windows supplies the Map Network Drive icon on the toolbar of the Network Neighborhood. However, mapping in this dialog box does not work with NetWare, but it does work with Microsoft peer-to-peer networking.

To disconnect a mapped drive, open My Computer and select the mapped drive. Right-click the mouse while pointing to the selected drive and choose Disconnect. The drive icon disappears from the window and the drive is disconnected.

If you want a list of the drives and mappings on your system, you might find the NetWare MAP command the best way to do so even though you can view mapped drives in the My Computer window. Enter **MAP** at the DOS prompt or in the Run dialog box, and you should see a screen similar to Figure 39.3.

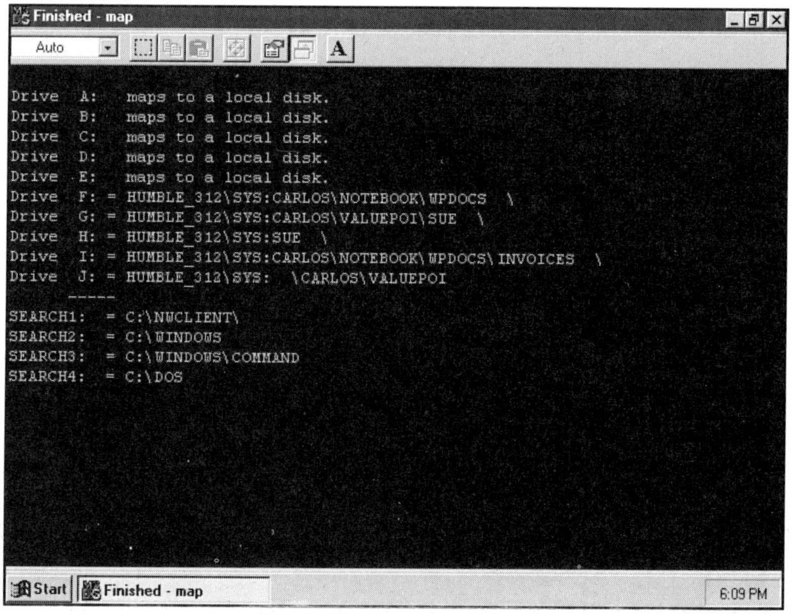

FIG. 39.3
The MAP command lists all the drive letters and the actual resources to which they are connected.

Finished - map

```
Drive  A:    maps to a local disk.
Drive  B:    maps to a local disk.
Drive  C:    maps to a local disk.
Drive  D:    maps to a local disk.
Drive  E:    maps to a local disk.
Drive  F: =  HUMBLE_312\SYS:CARLOS\NOTEBOOK\WPDOCS  \
Drive  G: =  HUMBLE_312\SYS:CARLOS\VALUEPOI\SUE  \
Drive  H: =  HUMBLE_312\SYS:SUE  \
Drive  I: =  HUMBLE_312\SYS:CARLOS\NOTEBOOK\WPDOCS\INVOICES  \
Drive  J: =  HUMBLE_312\SYS:  \CARLOS\VALUEPOI
          -----
SEARCH1:  =  C:\NWCLIENT\
SEARCH2:  =  C:\WINDOWS
SEARCH3:  =  C:\WINDOWS\COMMAND
SEARCH4:  =  C:\DOS
```

Start | Finished - map | 6:09 PM

The drive mapping displayed in Figure 39.3 shows drives F through J as mapped drives that you've created in Windows. These drives make it easier for you to access your work on the server. The search section of the drive mapping shows the search paths that the server follows when you try to access a file or folder. The search drives were added by the login script that ran when Windows first logged in to the server.

TROUBLESHOOTING

I connected a path as a root of the drive but now I cannot move up one level in the path. What am I doing wrong? You're not doing anything wrong; the problem is with connecting as a root of the drive. You cannot move up a level within the path. If, for example, you want to move up one level from

F:\CARLOS\NOTEBOOK\WPDOCS to F:\CARLOS\NOTEBOOK, you have to create a new mapping or enter the entire path. When connecting as a root of the drive, your only choice is the entire path.

I typed MAP in the Run dialog box, but I got a message that said "Cannot find the file 'run'." What do I do now? If you ran the login scripts and the search paths are established, then you can just type **MAP** in the Run dialog box; otherwise, type the path to the MAP command, beginning with the server, public folder, and then the command. A sample path might be \\HUMBLE_312\SYS\PUBLIC\MAP. HUMBLE_312 is the server, and SYS is usually the name given to the first drive volume on the server. PUBLIC is the directory normally used to store NetWare commands.

Changing Your NetWare Password

The only way you can change your NetWare password, short of asking the system administrator, is to use the SETPASS command. SETPASS enables you to create or change a password on one or more file servers. You must be attached to the server before you can set the password on it.

If you're attached to more than one server with the *same* password, SETPASS enables you to synchronize passwords (setting all passwords at one time to the same word).

To use SETPASS, follow these steps:

1. Open the Start menu and choose Run. The Run dialog box appears.

If you're unsure of the path, choose the Browse button and look for the PUBLIC folder (in SYS: volume). Then find the command.

2. In the Open text box, enter the path and the SETPASS command. An example of the path might be: \\HUMBLE_312\SYS\PUBLIC\SETPASS.
3. Choose OK. Windows opens the MS-DOS prompt with the prompt asking for a new password, as shown in Figure 39.4.
4. Enter the new password and press Enter.
5. Re-enter the new password to confirm and press Enter. SETPASS notifies you the password has been changed.
6. Click the Close button to close the MS-DOS prompt.

Checking the NetWare Version

You can check the version of the NetWare server from within Windows. You'll need to know the NetWare version if a specific application you use is version-specific or version-sensitive.

You can also find the NetWare server version information by running NVER.EXE in a DOS window.

FIG. 39.4
Set a new password using the SETPASS command.

To find the version of the NetWare used on the server, follow these steps:

1. Open Network Neighborhood and select the server.

TIP You also can display the properties sheet by right-clicking the server icon and choosing Properties.

2. Choose File, Properties. The properties sheet appears, as shown in Figure 39.5.
3. Once you have the version information, choose OK to close the properties sheet.

FIG. 39.5
The properties sheet lists NetWare server version information.

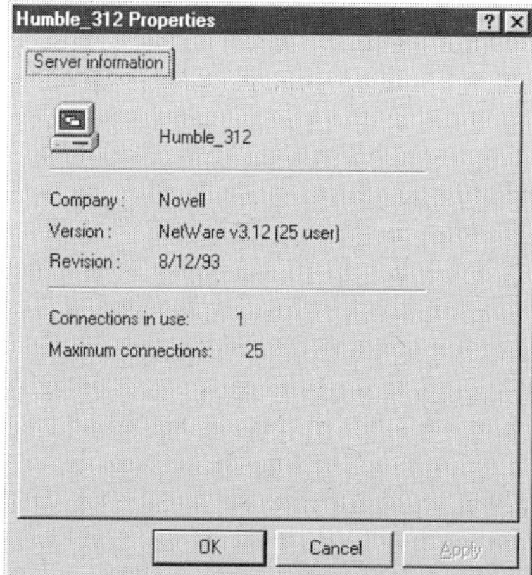

Checking the Status of Network Volumes

A *volume* is a physical portion of the hard disk that stores information on the file server. You can check the space on a volume as well as find out other information about different volumes on the server by using two NetWare utilities: CHKVOL and VOLINFO.

NOTE Usually the SYS is the first volume on a server and VOL1 is the second, VOL2 the third, and so on. Although these are the names Novell suggests, they are not always the names used.

To check on the status of the current volume, follow these steps:

1. Open the Start menu; then choose Programs, MS-DOS Prompt.
2. At the MS-DOS prompt, change the directory to the primary server drive (usually F:).
3. Type **CHKVOL**, and then press Enter. The results appear, as shown in Figure 39.6.

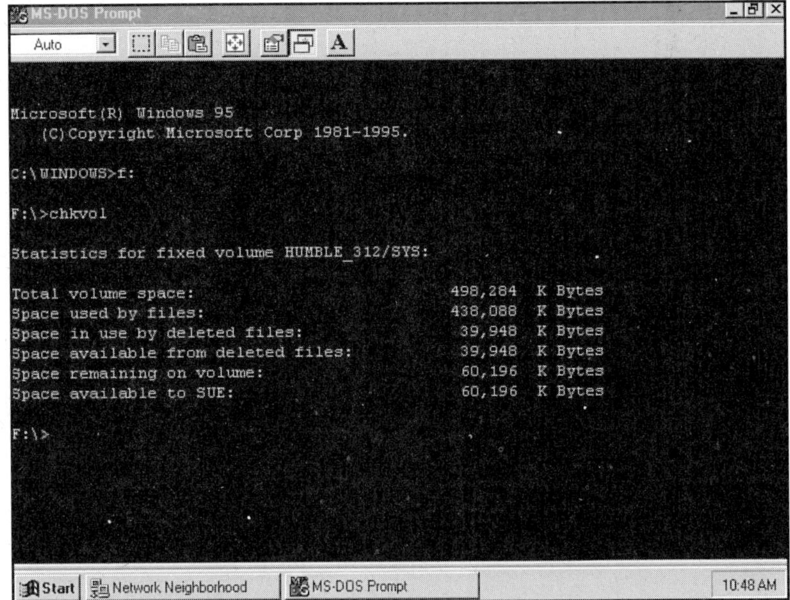

FIG. 39.6 Run CHKVOL at the MS-DOS Prompt or from the Run dialog box.

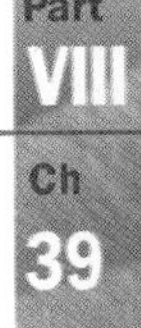

NOTE You may need to enter a path to the CHKVOL.EXE command; an example path might be \\HUMBLE_312\SYS\PUBLIC\CHKVOL.EXE.

4. Close the DOS window when you finish looking at the CHKVOL statistics.

The CHKVOL statistics list the total amount of space on the volume, the space used by files, the space in use by deleted files as well as the space available from deleted files, space remaining on the volume, and the space available to you.

Another NetWare information tool that you can use is VOLINFO.EXE, which quickly checks the status of drive usage. To use VOLINFO, follow these steps:

1. Open the MS-DOS Prompt and change to the primary server drive.
2. At the prompt, type **VOLINFO** and press Enter. The Volume Information utility appears (see Figure 39.7).

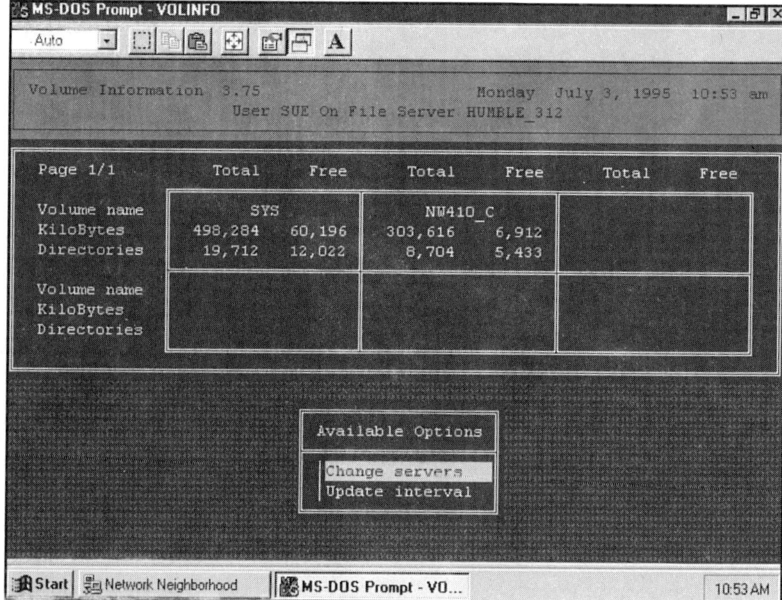

FIG. 39.7 Use Volume Information to view various volumes and their resources.

3. After viewing the volume information, press the Esc key. The Exit VolInfo dialog box appears.
4. Choose Yes, and then press Enter.
5. At the MS-DOS prompt, type **exit** and press Enter, or click the Close button in the title bar, to return to the Windows desktop.

VOLINFO reports the name of the volume you are viewing and refers to the storage capacity of that volume in kilobytes. It will report space in megabytes if the server has more than one gigabyte of storage space.

Listing Your Server Connections

Windows 95 provides a WhoAmI feature that is a graphical user interface (GUI) approach to NetWare's WHOAMI utility. This simplified version of the command shows only the most basic results: your user name and connection number. To see this information, right-click a server in the Network Neighborhood and choose Who Am I. The results are similar to Figure 39.8.

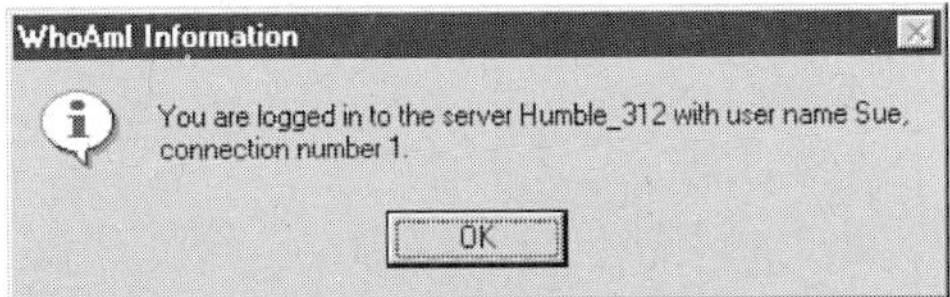

FIG. 39.8
The WhoAmI feature shows your user name, the server to which you're connected, and the connection number.

The NetWare command-line version is much more useful. For instance, if you enter **WHOAMI** at the DOS prompt, you get the same user, server, and connection information. Additionally, WHOAMI lists the NetWare version and allotted user number, date, and time of login, as shown in Figure 39.9.

If you're connected to more than one server, the WHOAMI command also lists those servers and your name on each, the software version on each, your login date and time for each server, and your rights and security equivalencies on each server.

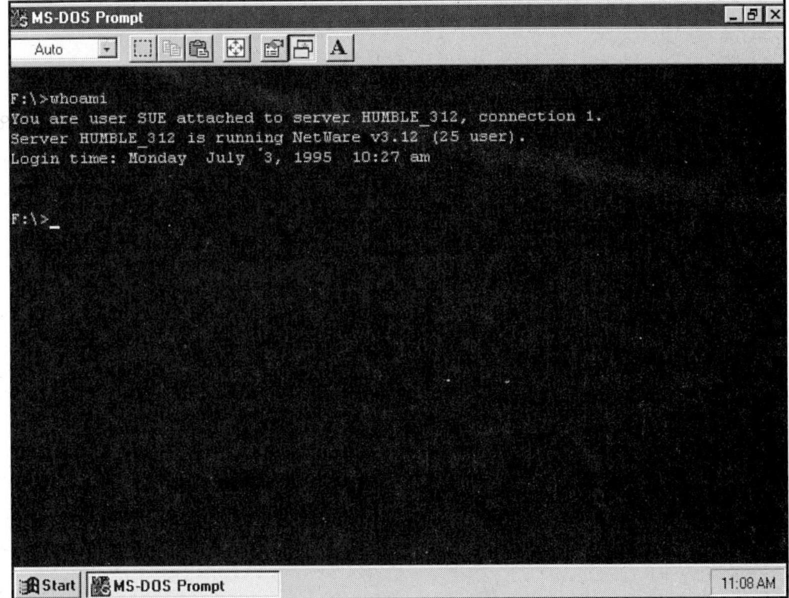

FIG. 39.9
Typical output from NetWare's WHOAMI utility.

You can enhance the command-line version's output with several parameters. Enter the command as **WHOAMI [servername] [option]**. The most useful parameters are those outlined here:

Parameter	Description
/s	*Security* lists the security equivalencies on each server you specify.
/g	*Groups* lists your membership in groups on each server specified.

continues

continued

Parameter	Description
/w	*Workgroup* lists workgroup manager information.
/r	*Rights* lists your rights on each server to which you're attached.
/a	*All* lists all the available information, including your group memberships, your security equivalencies, your rights, object supervisor, workgroup manager, and general system information.

Managing NetWare Printers

See "Understanding Network Printing," **p. 1050**

See "Solving Common Network Printing Problems," **p. 1062**

If you are comfortable with using NetWare and have done much work printing to a NetWare printer, you have probably seen or used NetWare's PCONSOLE utility for controlling print jobs. Windows 95 improves on PCONSOLE by adding to the printer's control applet in Windows 95 almost all these printer control functions for NetWare printers. Every common task for which you are likely to use PCONSOLE can be done from Windows. For example, checking the status of a print job and rearranging jobs in the queue (if you have sufficient user rights).

NOTE Even though Windows shows nine printer ports you can capture, Novell limits you to capturing on three: LPT1, LPT2, and LPT3. With Novell NetWare, Windows also tells you that LPT4 and higher are out of range.

PCONSOLE runs just as before, so if you are already familiar with it and want to continue using it, or if you want to access some advanced feature not available in Windows, you can still do so. However, if you only want to see how many print jobs are in front of you in the queue or to delete a print job that you sent accidentally, you can perform all these basic tasks in Windows, as described in Chapter 42, "Working with Network Printers."

Using Administrative Utilities

Most other NetWare utilities that you previously ran from a DOS prompt should now work in Windows 95 as well as from the DOS prompt. You might even find that some network utilities that were difficult to run in DOS 6.x, due to memory constraints, are easier to run in Windows 95 because more conventional memory is now available.

Table 39.1 lists some common Novell utilities that run in Windows 95. Many other unlisted utilities run as well.

Table 39.1 Some Novell DOS Utilities that You Can Run Under Windows 95 Command Prompts

Novell DOS Utility	Function
FCONSOLE	Monitors the file server and lets you perform such functions as broadcast console messages, down the file server, check file server status, and so on
RCONSOLE	Gives you access to the file server console from a workstation (NetWare versions 3.11, 3.12, 4.02, and 4.1)
FILER	Determines file creation date, last access date, size, owner, and so on
SALVAGE	Undeletes files from a NetWare volume
SESSION	Maps network drives with a menu
CAPTURE	Assigns network printers to local LPT ports
SLIST	Displays all NetWare servers on the network (through version 3.x)
SYSCON	Controls accounting, file servers, group, and user information (through version 3.x)

CAUTION

Deleted files and folders from a network drive are deleted permanently and do not go to the Windows Recycle Bin. There is no Undo, so be careful. If you do mistakenly delete an item you want, try the SALVAGE command as quickly after deleting the item as possible. When you delete files, the space it occupied remains on the server until the server needs space and is recoverable until that time.

Some utilities cannot run under Windows 95 when you use the Windows Client for NetWare Networks rather than the Novell VLM network drivers. You use these commands in NetWare 4.x networks that employ the NetWare Directory Services (NDS) to manage a multiserver domain. Table 39.2 lists these utilities, which operate under Windows 95, only when the Novell VLM network drivers are used.

Table 39.2 Novell Utilities that Work Only with Novell VLM Network Drivers

Novell Utility	Function
NWADMIN	Administers the NDS directory tree under Windows
CX	Changes contexts within the NDS directory tree
NETADMIN	Administers the NDS directory tree under DOS

NOTE NWADMIN, CX, and NETADMIN are all supported with NetWare's Client32 for Windows 95, which can be downloaded from the Novell Web site. In addition, if you are running OSR2 of Windows 95, you get MSNDS (Microsoft NetWare Directory Services), which allows a Windows 95 workstation access to NDS-based server resources. MSNDS also supports these Novell utilities.

See "Using Explorer with Shared Resources on a Network," **p. 354**

In addition to the utilities listed in Table 39.2 that do not work with the Windows Client for NetWare Networks, the NWUSER Windows 3.x utility is not supported under any configuration in Windows 95. This should not pose a problem because the Explorer application provides all the functionality of the NWUSER utility.

NWPOPUP, a utility administrators use to broadcast messages across the network, does not work in Windows 95; however, you can install WinPopup to work in its place. WinPopup is a Windows utility in which you can send and receive messages on the NetWare network. Find the WinPopup utility on the migration Planning Kit CD that ships with Windows 95 and look in the Admin95 folder, Apptools.

TIP In WinPopup, choose the Messages menu, Options button and select Pop Up Dialog on Message Receipt to be notified immediately of messages from the network.

You can add WinPopup to your Startup group (Start menu, Settings, Taskbar, Start Menu Programs tab) so WinPopup automatically starts when you start Windows, so you'll always know when a network message is broadcast.

TROUBLESHOOTING

I tried to enter a NetWare command in the Run dialog box but I got the message "Cannot find the file...." What did I do wrong? You may need to specify a path to the server and the folder in which the command or utility resides. If that still doesn't work, close the Run dialog box and use the MS-DOS prompt instead. In the DOS window, change the drives to the primary network drive (usually F:) and then enter the command and the path. Some NetWare commands just do not work from the Run dialog box.

I've forgotten where I placed a file on the server. Is there a NetWare command I can use to find the file? The easiest way to find a file or a folder in Windows is to use the Windows Find feature. You can use it for network drives as well as for your own drive. Choose Start, Find, and then Files or Folders. In the Find Files dialog box, choose the Browse button. In the Browse for Folder dialog box, double-click the Network Neighborhood. Double-click the server and then choose OK. Enter the file or folder name in the Named text box and choose Find Now. Windows searches the server drive for your file or folder.

Connecting to Other Servers

Connecting to and using the resources on servers within the local network is easy, but how do you connect to servers other than your usual "preferred server"? You accomplish this connection just as you would expect: by using all the standard tools previously discussed.

To connect to other servers, follow these steps:

1. Open the Network Neighborhood; all attached servers appear in the list.
2. Select the server name and then choose File, Attach As, or right-click the server name and choose Attach As. The Enter Network Password dialog box appears.
3. Enter your user name and password. Additionally, you can choose from the following options:
   - Save this password in your password list. Choose this option to save your password in a list so the next time you make this connection, you do not have to retype the password.
   - Connect as Guest. Log on as a guest if you do not have access to that server. Logging on as a guest gives you only limited access to the server.
4. Click OK to establish the connection. Note that your user name and password may vary from server to server.

If you have logins on multiple servers, this method is probably the easiest. Of course, if you frequently need to connect your computer to the same server, you might create a shortcut on the desktop for this connection.

Using Network Tape Drives

Windows includes a Backup program you can use to back up your files to a network tape drive. Windows 95 works only with 1992 or later versions of certain tape drives (find the list in Backup Help). You might also call the tape drive manufacturer for information about backup software you can use with Windows 95.

Several drives are not compatible with Windows 95, including Archive drives, Irwin AccuTrak tapes and Irwin drives, Mountain drives, QIC Wide tapes, QIC 3020 drives, SCSI tape drives, Summit drives, and Travan drives.

See "Backing Up Your Files," **p. 420**

In addition, Windows 95 includes an automatic backup feature, a backup agent that efficiently and regularly backs up your system, using industry-standard technology from Arcada (Backup Exec) and Cheyenne (ARCserve). These agents require network connections to a server.

NOTE These backup agents require the appropriate software running on the NetWare server. Windows 95 does not include the Arcada or Cheyenne backup software. Additionally, Arcada and Cheyenne are not Novell's native TSA backup agents.

Microsoft considers these agents a service. To install the service to Windows 95, follow these steps:

1. Open the Network dialog box from the Control Panel.
2. On the Configuration page, choose Add. The Select Network Component Type dialog box appears.
3. Select Service and choose Add. The Select Network Service dialog box appears (see Figure 39.10).

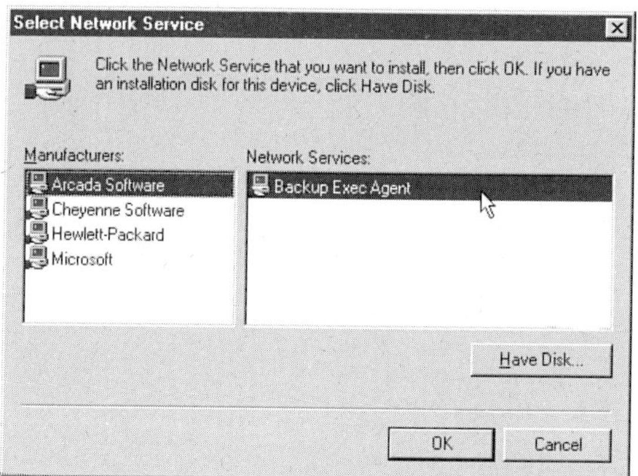

FIG. 39.10 Choose the service from the Select Network Service dialog box.

4. In Manufacturers, choose Arcada Software, and in Network Services, Backup Exec Agent becomes selected.

   Alternatively, choose Cheyenne Software in the Manufacturers list and choose ARCserve Agent.
5. Choose OK to select the service. Windows may prompt you to insert the Windows 95 CD. Follow directions on screen.
6. Windows returns to the Network dialog box. Choose OK to close the dialog box. Windows may copy more files from the Windows 95 CD.
7. Windows prompts you to restart your computer. Choose Yes.

The following sections take you step by step through a typical setup of both of these services. Remember, without one of these backup servers, you cannot use the backup agents.

NOTE If your NetWare server uses different backup software, you probably can still use it if you can run it from a DOS command line. Although Windows 95 might not support the software directly, you should still be able to run the software from DOS just as you could with previous releases of Windows.

Backing Up with Arcada

The Arcada Backup Exec agent as delivered with Windows 95 requires Arcada Backup Exec for NetWare, Enterprise Edition, or Single Server Edition, version 5.01. If your NetWare server is running either of these Arcada products, you can use the Arcada backup agent to archive important data regularly from your workstation.

Setting Properties After installing the Arcada service from the Select Network Service dialog box, follow these steps to set up the service:

1. In the Network dialog box, click the Configuration tab.
2. In the components list, double-click Backup Exec Agent. The Backup Exec Agent properties sheet appears, as shown in Figure 39.11.

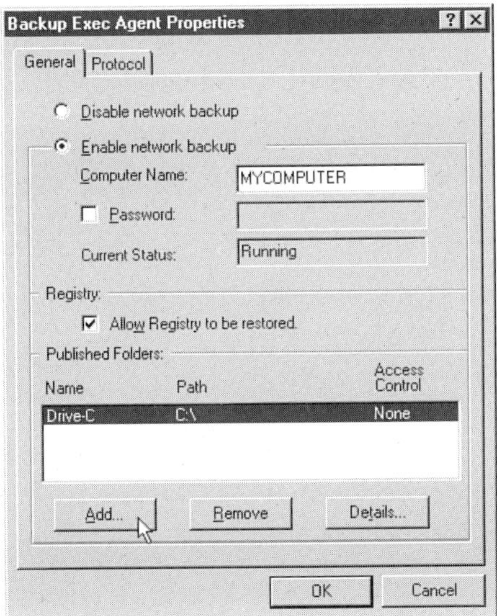

FIG. 39.11 Configure the Backup Exec Agent in the Backup Exec Agent properties sheet.

3. Click the General tab and choose to Enable Network Backup. The NetWare server software now considers the Windows 95 computer to be a backup source.
4. Enter the name of your computer (as the network knows it) and your password.

NOTE Select the Allow Registry to Be Restored check box if you want to enable the software to restore the Registry. If you select the Allow Registry to Be Restored check box, the software overwrites any changes that you made since your last backup.

TIP You can also choose to back up floppy and CD-ROM drives in the Select Folder to Publish dialog box.

5. In the Published Folders area, Drive C indicates your entire drive. If you do not want to back up the entire drive, choose Remove.

   To add specific folders, choose Add and the Select Folder to Publish dialog box appears (see Figure 39.12). Choose the folders you want to add to the backup and choose OK. The selected folders are added to the Published Folders list on the Backup Exec Agent properties sheet.

FIG. 39.12
Add drives and/or folders to the Published Folders list (backup list).

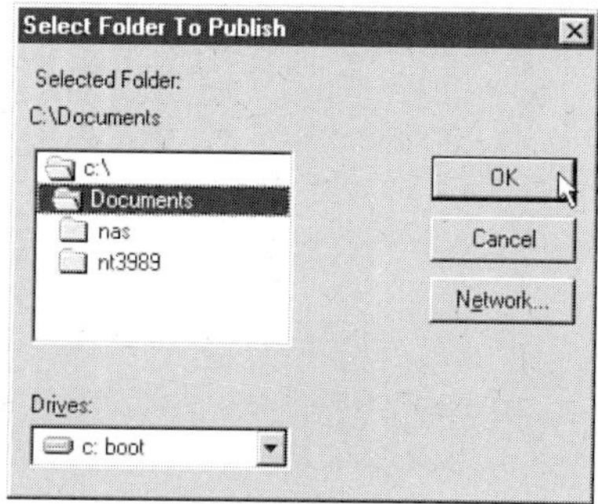

6. In the Published Folders area of the Backup Exec Agent properties sheet, select a folder or drive and choose Details. In the Folder Details dialog box, you can browse the folder's contents and set access limits (see Figure 39.13).

FIG. 39.13
In the Folder Details dialog box, you can assign the required access control.

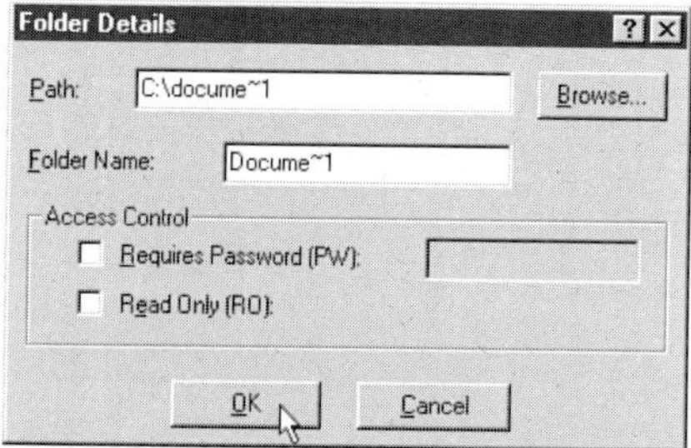

7. Choose OK to close the Folder Details dialog box. The dialog box closes and the access control limits appear in the Published Folders area of the Backup Exec Agent properties sheet (see Figure 39.14).
8. Click OK to close the Backup Exec Agent properties sheet.

NOTE When you first install your software, the properties sheet's Current Status indicates "Not Running." After you install and configure the agent, this status changes to "Running."

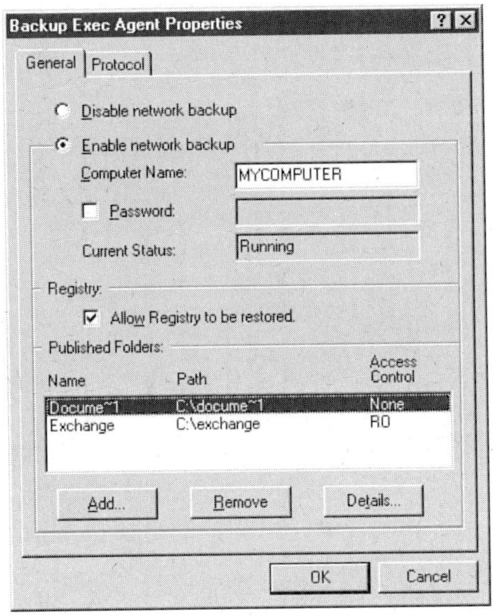

FIG. 39.14
The Published Folders area of the Backup Exec Agent properties sheet indicates the access control that you have set.

Setting Protocol You must set the protocol of the agent to match that of the server. To set the protocol for the Backup Exec Agent, follow these steps:

1. On the Backup Exec Agent properties sheet, click the Protocol tab (see Figure 39.15).

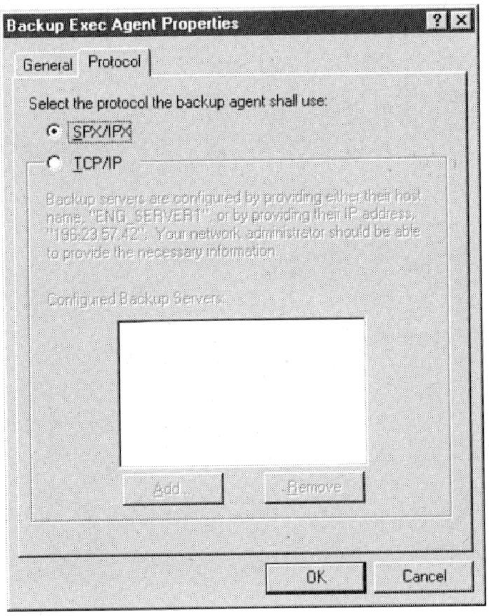

FIG. 39.15
The Protocol page of the Backup Exec Agent properties sheet.

2. Choose the SPX/IPX protocol for the backup agent.
3. Choose OK to close the dialog box.
4. Choose OK in the Network dialog box.
5. When Windows prompts you to restart the computer, choose Yes.

NOTE To use the Arcada Backup Agent, you might have to check whether the system administrator has the latest versions of the Arcada network loadable modules (NLMs) that have been updated for Windows 95. The necessary updated files are NRLTLI.NLM, TNRLAPT3.NLM, TNRLAPT4.NLM, TNRLTCP.NLM, and TNRLSPX.NLM. To get these files, you can contact Arcada directly or call Arcada's BBS at (407) 262-8139.

Backing Up with Cheyenne

If your server is running the Cheyenne backup software, and you've installed the ARCserve backup agent, you can set properties for the agent by following these steps:

1. In the Network dialog box, double-click ARCserve Agent. The ARCserve Agent properties sheet appears.
2. Click the General tab and choose Enable Network Backup. The Enable Network Backup area becomes available, as shown in Figure 39.16.

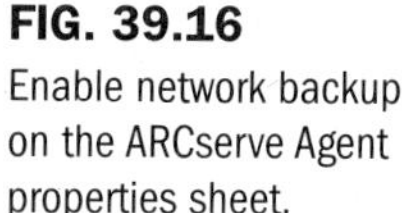

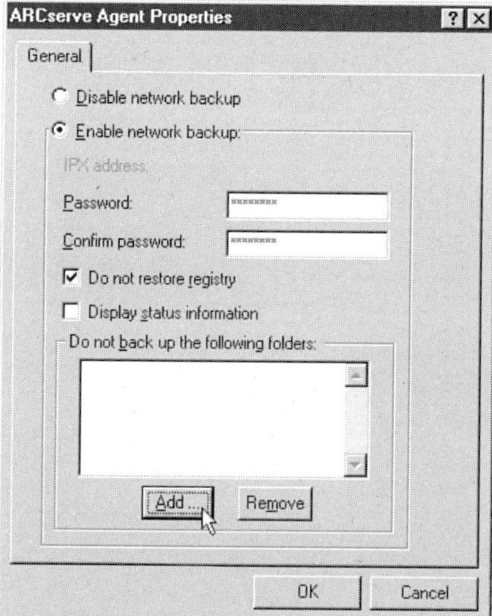

FIG. 39.16
Enable network backup on the ARCserve Agent properties sheet.

3. Specify the settings to configure the Cheyenne software:
   - **Password**. Enter your password.
   - **Confirm Password**. Enter your password again.

- **Do Not Restore Registry**. Select this option if you do not want your system's registry settings restored when your system is restored.
- **Display Status Information**. Displays information during the backup.

4. The Do Not Back Up the Following Folders list should contain only those folders you *do not* want to back up. By default, all folders will be backed up.

   To enter folders in the Do Not Back Up the Following Folders list, choose Add. The Add dialog box appears (see Figure 39.17).

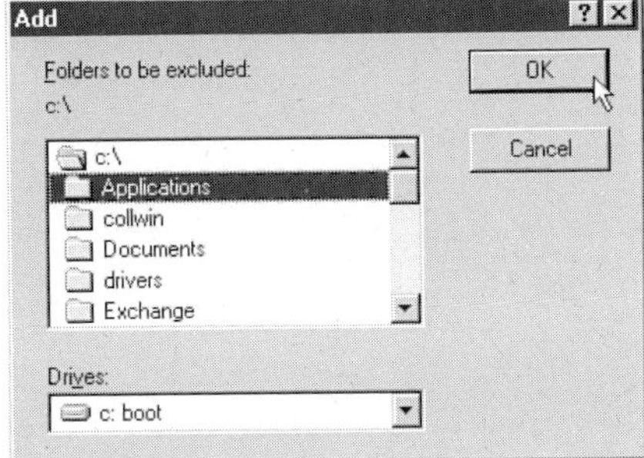

FIG. 39.17
Select the folder you *do not* want to back up in the Add dialog box for Cheyenne ARCserve agent.

NOTE If you mistakenly added a folder you do want to back up, select the folder and choose Remove.

5. Choose OK in the Add dialog box to return to the ARCserve Agent properties sheet. The folders you do not want to back up appear in the Do Not Back Up the Following Folders list box, as shown in Figure 39.18.

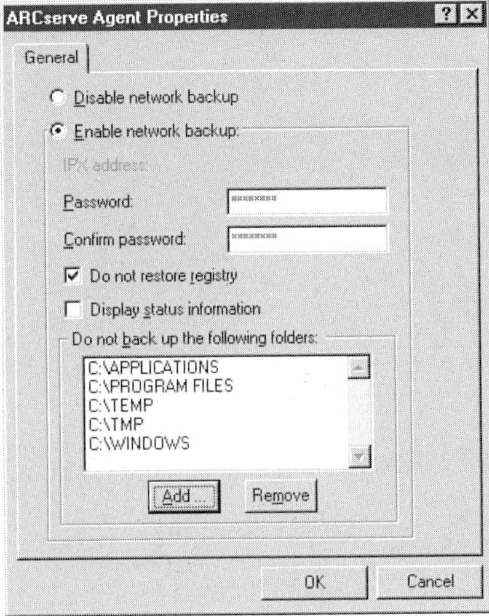

FIG. 39.18
The folders listed in the dialog box are those the agent will *not* back up.

6. Click OK to close the properties sheet.
7. Choose OK in the Network dialog box.
8. When Windows prompts you to restart the computer, choose Yes.

NOTE Cheyenne has updated the network loadable modules (NLMs) specifically for Windows 95. These updated files are APROCESS.NLM, ARCOPY.NLM, and WSTAPE.NLM. To obtain these files, contact Cheyenne directly at (800) 243-9832.

As you have seen in this chapter, Windows 95 and NetWare servers can coexist, and in fact, Windows 95 makes it easier to use NetWare server resources than previous releases of Windows. Microsoft has made Windows 95 truly a "well-connected client."

CHAPTER 40

Connecting Windows 95 to Windows NT Server 4.0

by Jerry Honeycutt and Craig Zacker

When Windows 95 is installed on a networked computer, the network client will, whenever possible, be upgraded to one of the new 32-bit protected-mode clients that ship with the operating system. However, if replacing the existing client will inhibit the workstation's network connectivity, Windows 95 will dynamically modify the client installation. Windows 95 may leave the entire existing client in place, or upgrade only the components that do not hinder network communications.

When networking support is not included as part of the Windows 95 operating system installation, it may be necessary for you to manually install the components needed to achieve network connectivity with Windows NT Server 4.0. This might require you to install and configure a network adapter; install and configure the networking client; and select the networking protocols; each of which you learn how to do in this chapter.

Install a network interface card in Windows 95

Before you can connect a Windows 95 workstation to a Microsoft Network, you must install a network interface card in your computer.

Install the Client for Microsoft Networks

The Client for Microsoft Networks helps your computer communicate with Windows NT Server 4.0. When you install it, you also install the other basic networking components, such as NetBEUI.

Install TCP/IP for use on a Microsoft Network

Most Microsoft Networks these days use TCP/IP instead of NetBEUI. Thus, you learn how to install and configure TCP/IP on a Windows 95 workstation in this chapter.

Installing a Network Adapter

A personal computer's network interface consists of two parts: the network adapter device itself, which usually takes the form of an expansion card or NIC (network interface card), and the adapter driver, which allows communication between the hardware and the network client software. Both the hardware and software components must be properly configured for network communication to occur.

When you install hardware conforming to the Windows 95 Plug and Play (PnP) standard, the operating system performs these configuration tasks for you automatically. However, many companies still purchase and use network interface cards that do not conform to the standard. When you install a non-PnP network adapter, you must configure the hardware and software yourself. Fortunately, even without Plug and Play, Windows 95 makes this configuration process easier than it has ever been before for a PC.

NOTE If you are using a PC Card network adapter, Windows 95 requires that you install a PC Card driver before the driver for the adapter. In many cases, the PC Card driver will provide Plug and Play recognition of the network adapter and its properties, even in computers without a Plug and Play BIOS.

Configuring Network Adapter Hardware

Every network interface card requires access to certain hardware and memory resources of your computer, such as an IRQ, a memory address, an I/O port, or any combination of these. The types of resources required differ for various adapters, but in nearly all cases, you must assign specific resource settings for the exclusive use of the card. The main obstacle to successfully installing a network adapter is locating settings acceptable to the card that are not already being used by the computer's other hardware.

You adjust your network adapter's hardware settings either by physically manipulating jumper blocks or DIP switches on the card itself, or by running a configuration program supplied the hardware. The program directly addresses the permanent memory on the card and stores your selected settings there.

Unless you are familiar with the IRQ, memory address and I/O port settings of all the components in your computer, the installation of a network card will be primarily a trial-and-error process. You insert the card into the computer, load the operating system, and see if there are any conflicts with the other hardware in the computer. If there are, you adjust the settings of the card and try again.

Windows 95 provides tools that can simplify this process, but before you can use them, you must first install driver support for the network adapter. You can do this from the Network properties in the Control Panel, but the easier method is to use the Add New Hardware Wizard.

Using the Add New Hardware Wizard

The Add New Hardware Wizard takes you through the process of identifying your network interface card to the operating system and installing the appropriate adapter drivers. You may elect to install the adapter hardware before running the wizard (although it is not essential), but it is recommended that you leave the task of resolving any hardware conflicts until afterward. Once you have installed the adapter driver, you can use the Windows 95 Device Manager to determine what devices are in conflict.

Before beginning the actual installation process of a new network adapter, it is a good idea to make a note of the adapter's default settings, either by examining the card itself, consulting the card's documentation, or by running the configuration software supplied with it. You may then physically insert the card into the computer (although this also may be done after the driver installation) and start the machine.

To install support for a network adapter, follow these steps:

1. Select the Add New Hardware icon in the Windows 95 Control Panel.
2. When asked if you want to let Windows 95 attempt to automatically detect your new hardware, select No.
3. From the list of Hardware Types, choose Network adapters and click the Next button. The Select Device dialog box, shown in Figure 40.1, appears.

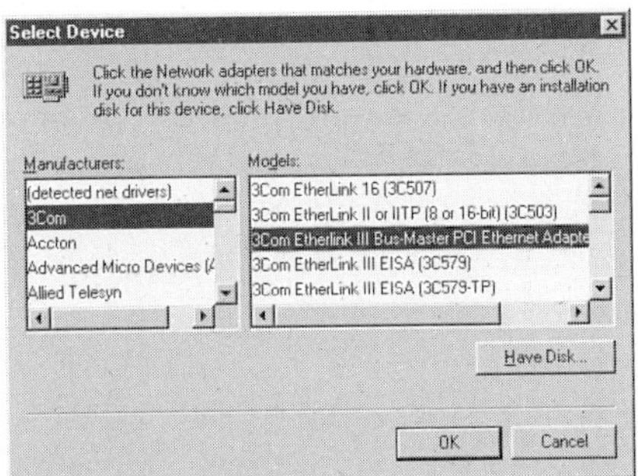

FIG. 40.1
The Select Device dialog box lists all of the network adapter drivers that ship with Windows 95.

4. Select the manufacturer of your network adapter from the scroll box on the left, and select the model on the right. If your adapter does not appear on the list, or if you have an updated driver that you want to install, click the Have Disk button and specify the location of the files.

NOTE The drivers supplied with the shipping version of the Windows 95 operating system support a large percentage of the network adapter cards in current use and available on the market today. However, new hardware is continually being released, as are updated drivers. Microsoft has posted a large number of updated hardware drivers on their online services. Updated drivers can also be obtained directly from the hardware manufacturer. While you may encounter cases in which newer

continues

continued

drivers are needed to enable certain networking features, you will rarely see the default Windows 95 installation package fail to achieve a network connection using the drivers provided.

Microsoft's updated adapter drivers can be found as part of the Windows 95 Driver Library, available on their World. Wide Web site at **http://www.microsoft.com/windows/software/drivers/network.html**.

5. Once you have made a hardware selection, click OK and Windows 95 displays a screen listing the hardware settings that must be specified for the operation of the adapter, as well as the default settings supplied by the driver software. These settings are not necessarily those to which the hardware has been configured. In a non-Plug and Play installation, the operating system is unable to detect the actual settings of the hardware. The values shown are proposed software settings for the driver to be installed.
6. Compare the driver settings displayed by the wizard with the adapter's hardware settings you have previously noted before the installation process began. If these values differ, then you must reconfigure either the hardware or software settings, or both. But first, the driver installation must be completed; click Next.
7. Windows 95 will now access its installation files and copy the appropriate driver files to the hard drive. You may be prompted to locate your Windows 95 installation source files. Click Yes when you are asked if you want to restart your computer.

TROUBLESHOOTING

After installing a new network interface card, my computer fails to boot properly. It either boots into Safe Mode or fails to boot at all. What's wrong? The network interface card is currently conflicting with the other hardware in your computer. Remove the card, boot the computer, and install support for the card using the Add New Hardware Wizard. (You can do this whether the card is physically installed or not.) Use the Windows 95 Device Manager to find new hardware settings that don't conflict with the rest of the system. Shut down the computer, reinstall the card with the new settings, and reboot.

Using the Windows 95 Device Manager

Unlike older operating systems, Windows 95 can monitor the hardware resources being used by every device in the computer (provided, of course, that you've also loaded the corresponding device driver). Windows 95 also includes a Device Manager that displays an inventory of the computer's contents. If you have determined during the adapter driver installation that adjustments to the hardware settings are necessary, you can use the Device Manager to see which hardware devices conflict and which settings must be altered.

You can access this inventory from the Windows 95 Control Panel by opening the System properties and selecting the Device Manager tab. This tab displays a tree, such as that shown in Figure 40.2. When you select a device on the tree, click the Properties button; then click the Resources tab. The hardware resource settings of the device's driver appear.

At the bottom of the Resources tab, there is a Conflicting Device List. If any of the current settings of your network adapter conflict with another device in the computer, then the setting and the device name appear in the Conflicting Device List.

If you attempt to modify a device's configuration to use a resource that has already been allocated, a message box warns you that you must make configuration changes.

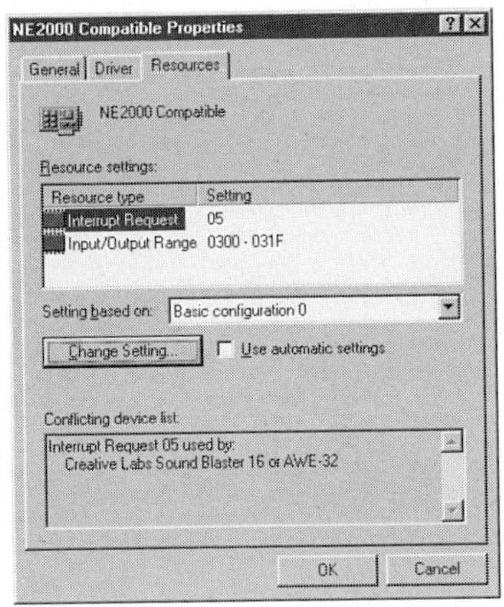

FIG. 40.2
The Device Manager screen displays an inventory of the computer's currently installed hardware.

Modifying the Network Adapter Configuration

At this point in the installation of the network adapter, you use the Device Manager to perform two distinct tasks:

- Determine whether the current hardware settings of the adapter are in conflict with other devices.
- Modify the resource settings of the network adapter's software device driver.

It is important that you distinguish between these two tasks. While you can use the Device Manager to examine the current hardware settings, it cannot modify them. You must do this by using the adapter's configuration program or by adjusting the hardware itself. Use the following procedure to locate proper hardware resource settings and configure the adapter driver to use them.

1. Double-click the System icon in the Control Panel, and click the Device Manager tab.
2. In the Device Manager tab, select your network adapter by name, and click the Properties button.
3. Click the Resources tab. A display of Resource Settings appears.
4. Click the first Resource Type in the Resource Settings selector; then click the Change Setting button. You'll see a dialog box similar to the one shown in Figure 40.3.
5. Modify the Value in the Edit dialog box to match your adapter's current hardware setting (which you noted before the installation process began). If another installed device appears in the Conflict Information window, that value cannot be used.

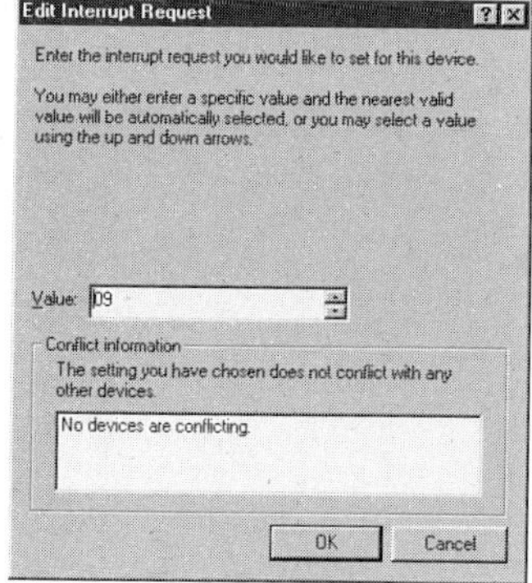

FIG. 40.3
You use essentially the same dialog box for editing IRQ's, DMA channels, and I/O addresses.

6. If necessary, modify the setting again to a Value that displays a No Devices Are Conflicting message in the Conflict Information window. Notice the new Value that you have selected for later use, and click OK.
7. Repeat steps 4–6 for each hardware setting displayed on the Resources tab. When you are finished, the Conflict Information window on the Resources tab should indicate that No Conflicts exist.
8. Click OK to close the dialog box.

Windows 95 displays a message stating that you should now shut down and power off your computer, and then modify your adapter's hardware settings. You need do this only if you encountered conflicts during the preceding steps. To change the settings, follow the instructions included with your network adapter. You may not have to power down the machine if a software-based setup program is available for the adapter. You do need to reboot the system, however, after any hardware settings are changed.

TROUBLESHOOTING

What do I do if I have tried all of the values for a particular resource setting, and they all result in a conflict? Today's network adapters usually provide a large selection of possible values for their resource settings. Other devices in your computer, however, may offer a different selection. If you cannot locate an nonconflicting value for a particular network adapter setting, you will have to modify the configuration of another device in your system to free up a resource for your network adapter.

The best way to handle this problem is to remove the network adapter from the computer and concentrate on reconfiguring another device, using either the Device Manager, a Control Panel application, or a dedicated configuration program to make the changes. Once you are certain that the other device is functioning properly, reinsert the network adapter and modify its resource setting to the newly available value.

I have modified the settings in the Device Manager so that there are no hardware conflicts, but my network adapter still does not function. What's wrong? If you made changes to the adapter driver settings, then you must also configure the hardware itself to use those settings. This can only be done by physically manipulating the hardware, using jumpers or DIP switches, or by using a software-based configuration program.

Installing the Client for Microsoft Networks for Windows NT 4.0

The adapter and its driver are the components that communicate directly with the network. For Windows 95 to access the resources on an NT server, you must next install the Client for Microsoft Networks, which communicates with the rest of the operating system, and a protocol, which links the client and the adapter.

The following procedure describes the installation of the Client for Microsoft Networks, and all of the other components necessary to gain access to a Microsoft network and attach to a Windows NT server.

1. Double-click the Network icon in the Control Panel and click Add.
2. In the Select Network Component Type dialog box (see Figure 40.4), double-click Client.

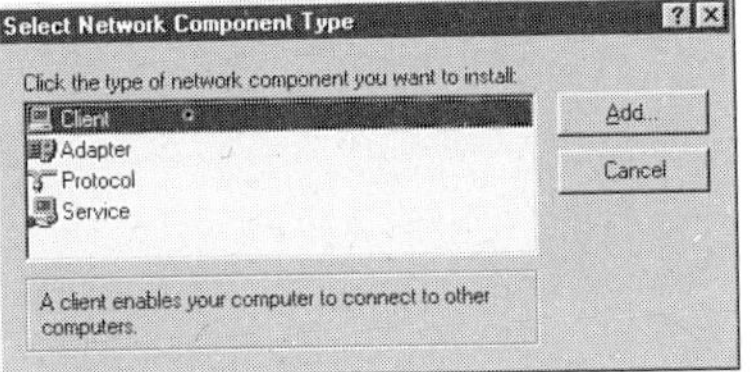

FIG. 40.4
Select the component to be installed from the list.

3. Choose Microsoft from the left side of the Select Network Client dialog box (see Figure 40.5) and choose Client for Microsoft Networks from the right side. Click OK. Back at the Network applet's Configuration tab, the client appears in the component list.

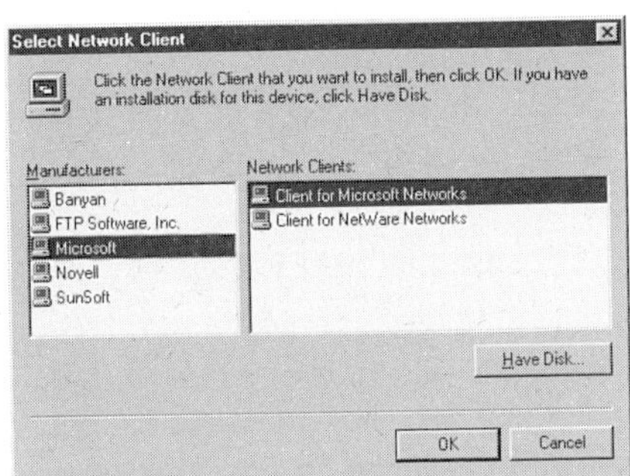

FIG. 40.5
Select the Client for Microsoft Networks to connect to a Windows NT server or a Windows peer-to-peer network.

NOTE If you had not already installed an adapter, you would be asked at this time to specify one, or allow Windows 95 to attempt to auto-detect one. You can install an adapter directly from the Network applet, or see "Using the Add New Hardware Wizard," earlier in this chapter.

4. Click the Add button again, and double-click Protocol in the Select Network Component Type dialog box.
5. Choose Microsoft from the left side of the Select Network Protocol dialog box and NetBEUI from the right. This is the default protocol for Windows NT and LAN Manager client/server networks, as well as for Windows peer-to-peer networks. Click OK. The Configuration screen of the Network applet should list the installed protocol, as shown in Figure 40.6.

NOTE With the introduction of Windows NT 4.0, Microsoft installs TCP/IP as the networking protocol of choice. Many networks still use NetBEUI, however. If your network is using TCP/IP, see "Installing TCP/IP for Windows NT 4.0 Networks," later in this chapter.

6. Review the following sections entitled "Primary Network Logon," "The Identification Tab," and "Domain Logons" and change any settings so that you can connect to the network after you restart your computer. After changing the settings described in those sections, click OK to complete the component installation process, and click Yes when you are asked if you want to restart the computer.

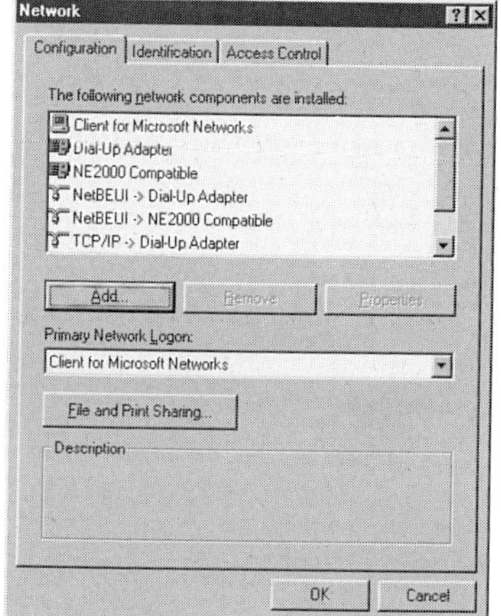

FIG. 40.6
A Windows 95 Network screen showing all of the basic components necessary to attach to a Microsoft Network running Windows NT Server 4.0.

Primary Network Logon

On the Configuration tab of the Network properties, select Client for Microsoft Networks in Primary Network Logon. This value determines which client is used to validate your logon. When multiple network clients are installed, you may select which one is to be the default login using this selector. If you choose Windows Logon, you'll see the Windows logon when you start your computer, and the passwords required to access the resources on Windows NT Server are retrieved from the password list.

The Identification Tab

On the Identification tab of the Network properties, enter a Computer Name and (optionally) a Computer Description. Windows 95 will use the names entered here to identify your computer to the network. Do not confuse the Computer Name with the user name that you use to log onto a network. A single Windows 95 computer can support many users, but it has only one single computer name. Also, for Workgroup, enter the name of the network workgroup or NT domain in which your workstation will belong.

Domains versus Workgroups

Microsoft Windows networking recognizes two types of logical machine groupings: domains and workgroups. A domain is a group of machines whose security is administered from a central location, that is, a Windows NT server. All users, groups, and passwords are stored on the server and administered by the server administrator. If you are logging onto an existing Windows NT network, there is probably a domain to which you will have to be granted access. Domain security information can only be stored on a Windows NT server; you cannot create a domain on a Windows 95 peer-to-peer network.

A *workgroup* is also a collection of Windows machines, any of which may be running Windows 95, Windows NT, or Windows for Workgroups. In a workgroup, each workstation is responsible for maintaining its own security information. The selection of which resources are to be shared and their access passwords are all controlled and stored on each individual workstation itself.

Every Windows computer running a Microsoft network client must declare itself to be a member of a domain or a workgroup, even if the workgroup consists of only one machine. Membership in a workgroup or a domain in no way prevents access to resources in other workgroups or domains.

Domain Logons

Since you'll be logging into an existing domain on the network, double-click the Client for Microsoft Networks in the Configuration tab of the network properties, and select the General tab in the Properties dialog box. Select Log on to Windows NT Domain, and enter the domain name in the Windows NT Domain field. You'll need to ask the network administrator for the domain name. Your username and password will be validated by the named domain controller.

Installing TCP/IP for Windows NT 4.0 Networks

TCP/IP (transmission control protocol/Internet protocol) is now the *de facto* standard protocol suite for all UNIX operating systems, as well as for the Internet. As well, most network installations of Windows NT Server 4.0 use TCP/IP instead of NetBEUI because NetBEUI packets can't be easily routed across subnets.

Windows 95 is the first popular desktop operating system to ship with fully integrated TCP/IP protocol support that is simple to use. It is also compatible with virtually every desktop Internet application available today. Microsoft's TCP/IP is installed like any other protocol and can be used as a general purpose LAN protocol. It can also be used to connect to the Internet, either through a LAN connection, or a dial-up connection. The Dial-Up adapter driver included with Windows 95 is explicitly made for this purpose.

Configuring TCP/IP for use on a Microsoft Network is more complicated than configuring NetBEUI. There are no default Plug and Play settings. You cannot expect to use the protocol without configuring certain options correctly, because they require unique values for every workstation on the network. In several cases, it will be necessary to ask your network administrator or Internet service provider for the correct settings. Before you read the following sections, which show you how to correctly configure TCP/IP, install the protocol on your computer:

1. Double-click the Network icon in the Control Panel, click Add, and double-click Protocol in the Select Network Component Type dialog box.
2. Choose Microsoft from the left side of the Select Network Protocol dialog box and TCP/IP from the right.
3. Click OK to add the protocol to your configuration. Review each of the remaining sections, and then change any settings described in them to make sure you've correctly configured TCP/IP. Then click OK to complete the component installation process. Click Yes when you are asked if you want to restart the computer. When your Windows 95 restarts, it'll prompt you for your NT user name and password.

The TCP/IP properties contains the standard Bindings, Advanced, and NetBIOS tabs that you can largely ignore. There are four other tabs that you must consider, however, which are described in the following sections.

DNS Configuration

A Domain Name Server is a server whose basic function is name resolution. That is, the DNS associates numeric IP addresses, such as 123.45.67.89, with named addresses, such as **www.microsoft.com**. The DNS does this by maintaining static tables of equivalent addresses, and by querying network entities for information to update the table.

The correct DNS address (or addresses) to use should be furnished by your network administrator or service provider Figure 40.7. You may enter multiple addresses in the DNS tab, so that if an entry is not found on one, the subsequent entries will be checked. You must also enter a host name for your machine, and the domain name for your organization (for example, **microsoft.com**). Use of a DNS is optional, because a DHCP server can be used for the same purpose.

Gateway

A gateway routes traffic from one network (subnet) to another. You'll usually have to configure a gateway when you participate in a network that's connected to another network and you need to access a resource on the remote network. For instance, if the network in accounting is attached to another network on which you participate via an IP router, you'd have to configure the IP router as a gateway if you wanted to access resources (such as the payroll) on the accounting network.

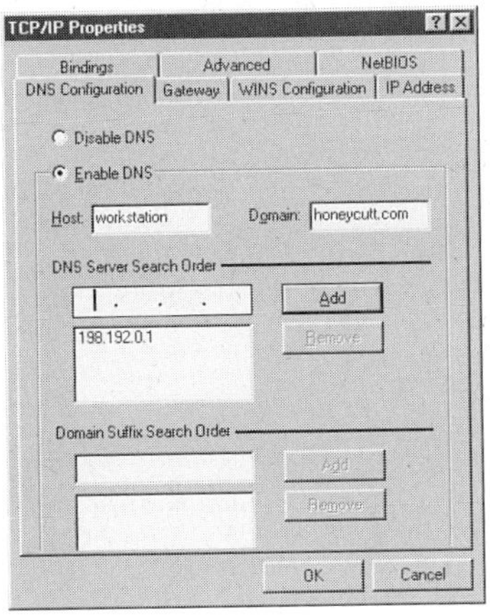

FIG. 40.7
In a corporate networking environment, you can probably ignore this tab as you're more likely to use DHCP in combination with WINS.

You use the Gateway tab to specify a gateway as shown in Figure 40.8. In fact, you can specify several gateway addresses. The protocol will proceed to the alternates when the first address is unreachable. This address should be supplied by your network administrator or service provider.

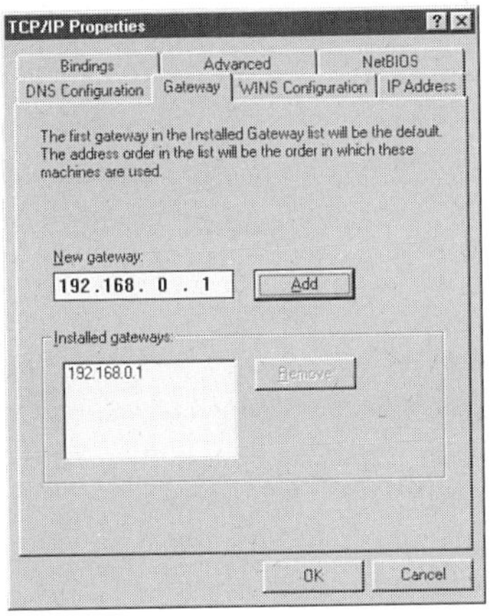

FIG. 40.8
If you've configured multiple gateways, TCP/IP will only use the second gateway in the list if, and only if, the first gateway is not working properly.

WINS Configuration

WINS, or *Windows Internet Naming Service*, is a realization of an existing published standard, implemented by Microsoft as a service for Windows NT Server. A WINS server performs essentially the same function as DNS, except that the WINS server does not require static addresses to maintain its data tables. They can be adjusted dynamically. When using a DHCP server to assign IP addresses, use of a WINS server is almost required, as a DNS server could not keep up with the continual IP address changes.

Configuring the TCP/IP protocol for the use of the WINS server in most cases simply involves entering the addresses of a Primary and Secondary WINS server in the spaces provided in the

WINS Configuration tab shown in Figure 40.9. Alternately, you can select the option that allows a DHCP server to provide the necessary addresses automatically.

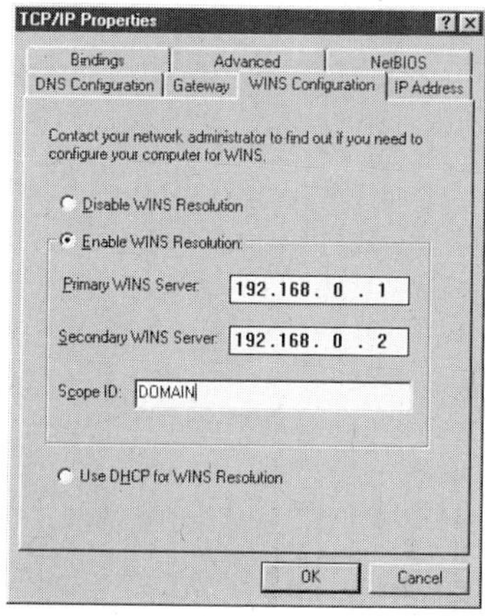

FIG. 40.9 If your network administrator configured DHCP to automatically provide WINS address, select Use DHCP for WINS Resolution.

IP Address

The IP address is the unique identifying address of your computer. It is composed of four octets of up to three digits each, separated by periods. In some cases, your computer may be assigned a specific IP address by your administrator or service provider. In that case, Select Specify an IP Address, and fill in the address and subnet mask supplied to you, as shown in Figure 40.10.

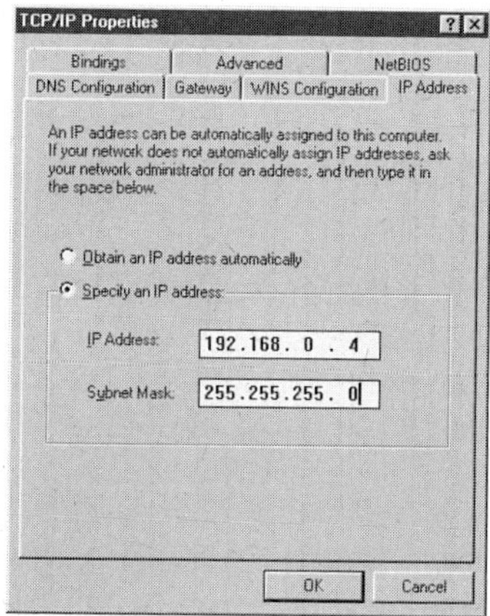

FIG. 40.10 It's more common to use DHCP than statically assigned IP addresses on a corporate network using Windows NT Server 4.0.

At other sites, a Windows NT server may be configured to act as a DHCP (*dynamic host configuration protocol*) server. This is a service that runs on Windows NT Server 4.0 that allocates IP addresses to network workstations requesting them, ensuring that no conflicts occur from two workstations using the same address. Such a server can also deliver a subnet mask, DNS and WINS information to the workstation. If your network uses DHCP, select Obtain an IP address automatically.

NOTE If you use dial-up connections to more than one Internet service provider, then individual IP address and DNS settings can be specified for each connection.

After completing the steps in this chapter, you should be able to connect to your Windows NT network. There's not much to look at yet, however, because you haven't learned how to use the resources on it. The next chapter, Chapter 41, "Using Windows NT Server Resources in Windows 95," shows you how to use such NT Server resources as shared drives and printers.

CHAPTER 41

Using Windows NT Server Resources in Windows 95

by Jerry Honeycutt and Craig Zacker

Windows 95 makes accessing shared network resources on an NT network as seamless as accessing resources on your own computer. In particular, you can access mapped and unmapped resources directly through the Network Neighborhood, which you see on your desktop once you configure your computer for network access.

This chapter tells you everything you need to know in order to get the most out of the resources on your NT network. It shows you how to configure which network logon prompt you see when you start Windows 95. It makes sure that you understand the Universal Naming Conventions for NT resources. It also shows you how to access shared drives, folders, printers, and more.

Demystify Windows 95 logon screens and passwords

This chapter shows you how to choose which logon screen you see when you start Windows 95. It also describes the Windows 95 password list.

Use the Universal Naming Convention

You can use the Universal Naming Convention to access shared network resources instead of mapping to specific network drives.

Access shared network drives

You can either map to a network drive or get access to it through Network Neighborhood. Either way, Windows 95 makes accessing network shares very easy.

Print to network printers

This chapter shows you how to install a shared network printer, print to it, and how to manage the print jobs on it.

Access shared network resources from DOS

You can use the NET.EXE program to get full access to shared network resources from the command line.

Logging onto an NT Network

When you configure Windows 95 to log onto an NT server, it displays a login screen each time you boot your computer. The choice of the primary client determines the type of network login screen. When Client for Microsoft Networks is installed, Primary Network Logon on the Configuration tab of the Control Panel's Network application offers two possible choices:

- **Client for Microsoft Networks.** Your username and password are validated by domain controller (Windows NT Server 4.0).
- **Windows Logon.** Your username and password aren't validated; but, Windows 95 uses both to open a password list (see "Working with the Password List," later in this chapter).

Additional entries will also appear in this list if you've installed additional network clients. When you select one of the network clients as the primary logon, that client's login screen appears first whenever the machine is booted, requiring the entry of a user name and password. The computer name that you have entered in the Identification tab of the Network properties is supplied as the username, by default, but you can change this to any valid network username, and the setting will be retained for future logins.

Logon onto an NT Server

When logging onto a Microsoft Network using the dialog box shown in Figure 41.1, Windows 95 uses the Logon Validation option specified in the General tab of the Client for Microsoft Networks' properties dialog box to determine whether a domain logon should be performed (see Chapter 40, "Connecting Windows 95 to Windows NT Server 4.0"). You must also specify a domain name on this tab. The General tab also contains an option to choose between a logon sequence that immediately verifies that each network drive is available for use, or one that waits until each individual drive is accessed before verification occurs. The tradeoff is between a brief delay when each drive is accessed, and a cumulative delay during the logon sequence, rarely more than a few seconds.

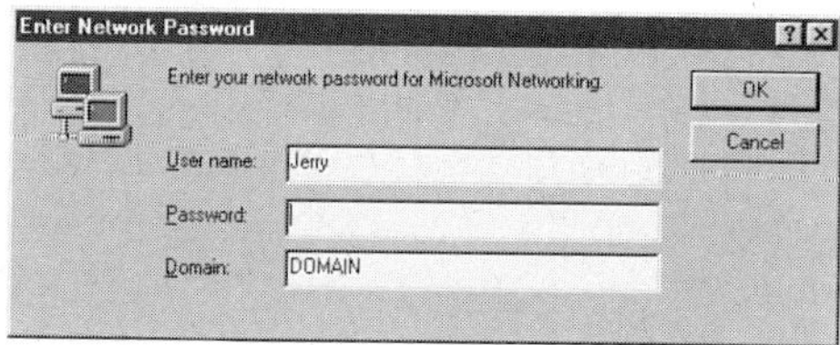

FIG. 41.1 The Microsoft Network logon screen allows access to Windows NT domains as well as peer workgroups.

After you log onto an NT server, the server executes a logon script. The logon script is a batch file that runs on the server. It does things like set environment variables or run programs. You can set an environment variable using the DOS command **set** as in **set PATH=C:\WINDOWS**. Then batch files or other programs can look up the variable called PATH and use the value you've assigned to it.

NOTE Windows 95 is incapable of setting environment variables that have been specified in Windows NT Server logon scripts in the normal manner. As a workaround, a utility called WINSET.EXE is provided in the \ADMIN\APPTOOLS\ENVVARS directory of the Windows 95 CD-ROM. You can use this program to set environment variables from a DOS session command line, a batch file, or a logon script. The syntax of WINSET.EXE is the same as that of the DOS SET command, except that entering the command without any parameters does not display the contents of the environment, as SET does.

TROUBLESHOOTING

Why doesn't a network login dialog box appear when I start Windows 95, no matter what the setting of the Primary Network Logon selector? If you select Shut Down from the Start Menu and then choose Close all Programs and log on as a different user, the correct login dialog box appears, after which everything functions normally. To eliminate this problem, open the Windows 95 Registry Editor (REGEDIT.EXE, located in the \WINDOWS directory), and proceed to the following key:

```
HKEY_LOCAL_MACHINE\SOFTWARE\Microsoft\Windows\CurrentVersion\Network\RealModeNet
```

Delete the value *AutoLogon=x*. A value of zero for the AutoLogon parameter causes the failure of the login dialog box to appear, and 1 is the default, but deleting the entire parameter is preferable to just changing the value. Save your changes and restart the computer. The primary login screen should now appear.

Working with the Password List

When logging into more than one network at the start of a Windows 95 session (Netware and NT Server, for example), you do not have to supply a duplicate password for each network, as long as both logins utilize identical usernames. Windows 95 automatically stores the secondary password in an encrypted password file called *username*.PWL, where *username* is your logon name, located in the workstation's \WINDOWS directory. You can use the Password application in the Windows 95 Control Panel to synchronize differing passwords used by the network logins.

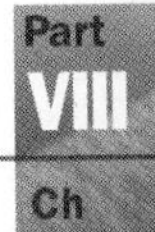

The primary network login password unlocks the password file for use during that Windows 95 session. As work progresses, the operating system automatically caches passwords for NT Server networks, and secures Internet resources and workgroup resources in this same file. Password-protected applications written to the Master Password API also can store passwords in this file. All passwords are stored in the file in encrypted form. No unencrypted password is ever sent over the network.

NOTE On December 13, 1995, Microsoft released a patch file that significantly enhances the security of Windows 95 .PWL files. This was in response to an algorithm posted on the Internet that could be used to crack the existing password files. The fix upgrades the encryption key to 128 bits (from 32), increasing the difficulty of cracking the file by 79228162514264337593543950336 (2^{96}) times. The patch file is called MSPWLUPD.EXE and is

continues

continued

now available as part of the Windows 95 Service Pack 1, on Microsoft's World Wide Web site at **http://www.microsoft.com/windows/software/servpak1/sphome.htm.** You don't need this patch if you're using OSR2.

Most logins to network devices include an option for password caching, such as a check box labeled "Save This Password in Your Password List." A network administrator also can use the System Policy Editor to globally disable password caching for specific users or user groups. This action forces users to log into network resources individually, each time they access them.

CAUTION

Password caching is a useful convenience, but it also can be a dangerous security hole if not used carefully. When system administrators work at a user's machine, for example, they must be careful not to insert their passwords into the user's cache and leave the user with a greater level of access to the system. If this does occur, one method of repairing the damage is to delete the user's .PWL file from the \WINDOWS directory, causing all of his cached passwords to be lost. The user now has to log into each network resource individually until Windows 95 assembles a new cache file.

There is an alternative to this solution, however. On the Windows 95 CD-ROM is a password file editing utility called PWLEDIT.EXE. You can install it by using the Add/Remove Programs applet in the Windows 95 Control Panel. Select the Windows Setup tab and use the Have Disk button to get to the \ADMIN\APPTOOLS\PWLEDIT directory on the CD-ROM.

Changing Your NT Server Password

You can change your NT server password at any time. Follow these steps:

1. Double-click the Password icon in the Control Panel, and the Password Properties dialog box appears.
2. Click Change Other Passwords, and you'll see the Select Password dialog box.
3. Select Microsoft Network from the list and click Change.
4. Fill in the Old Password, New Password, and Confirm New Password text boxes. Then, click OK. Windows 95 displays a dialog box telling you that it successfully changed your password.
5. Click OK to close the confirmation dialog box.

Understanding the UNC (Universal Naming Convention)

Windows 95 and most other network operating systems use a syntax called the *Universal Naming Convention*, or UNC, for addressing network resources. The syntax for the UNC is as follows:

```
\\SERVER\SHARE\DIRECTORY\FILE
```

Because most Microsoft operating systems offer both client/server and peer-to-peer networking capabilities, you must use naming conventions that are capable of addressing workstation as well as NT server resources. In actuality, the SERVER name listed in the syntax refers to any machine that is sharing its internal resources over the network, and not just Windows NT servers. A workstation that is configured to share its CD-ROM drive with a neighboring workstation is functioning as a server in that respect, and its machine name is used in place of the SERVER name shown in the preceding example.

SHARE refers to a logical name assigned by a user or administrator to a particular network resource that he is sharing with the rest of the network. All drives, printers, fax modems, and other devices that you can access over a Microsoft network are called *shares*, whether they're located on an NT server or a workstation. As a result, a share can be an entire drive on a particular machine, a single directory on a drive, a printer, or a fax modem attached to the NT server.

The name for a share is selected by the person electing to share it. It need not reflect the share's actual location on the NT server. In other words, in terms of file sharing, you need not give a user any way of knowing on which server drive a share resides, or whether or not that share represents the entire contents of the drive. Access rights flow downhill on a Microsoft network. When you assign a user rights to a share, you include all of the directories and subdirectories contained beneath it. The directory names are the same as they appear on the NT server itself, however. You cannot assign them share names unless you configure them separately as additional shares.

Finding Computers on an NT Network

You can search for a network computer using the UNC by typing ***SERVER***, where ***SERVER*** is the name of the computer you're looking for. This is particularly useful if the machine doesn't show up in the Network Neighborhood, but you're absolutely sure that it's on the network. Choose Find, Computer from the Start button; type the name of the computer for which you're looking in Named; and click Find Now. If Windows 95 finds the computer, you'll see it in the Find window as shown in Figure 41.2.

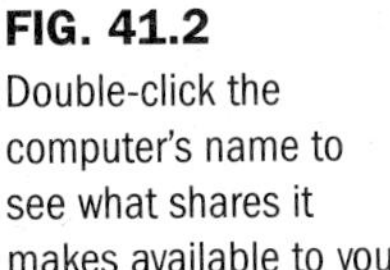

FIG. 41.2
Double-click the computer's name to see what shares it makes available to you.

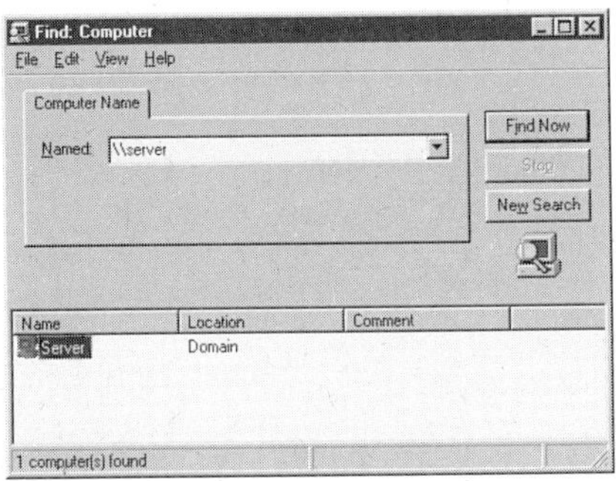

You can also open a folder that contains a computer's share by launching that computer's UNC name. Choose Run from the Start button, type the UNC name of the computer (**\\TheServer**, for example), click OK, and Windows 95 will open all of that computer's shared resources in a folder.

TROUBLESHOOTING

Why do I see some peer computers in Network Neighborhood, but not all of them? In order for you to see a peer computer in the Network Neighborhood, the peer has to be configured to participate in the same workgroup you do. See Chapter 40, "Connecting Windows 95 to Windows NT Server 4.0," to learn how to configure the workgroup in which you participate.

Sharing NT Network Drives

Unquestionably, the first and primary purpose of networking is to enable simultaneous multiple-user access to application and data files stored on hard disk drives. Although networking capabilities continue to expand, disk sharing is still the primary function of most local area networks.

Microsoft Networks provide two different ways you can access a shared network drive. You can use the traditional drive mapping method or you can use the Windows 95 Network Neighborhood. You learn about each in the following two sections.

Using the Map Network Drive Dialog Box

Drive mapping, the original network file sharing paradigm, which persists to this day, attempts to package network resources as though they are local devices by mapping NT server disk locations to workstation drive letters. The DOS conception of the drive letter is thus extended to include not only internal workstation devices, but network drives as well. In this case, the network client functions as a redirector, channeling requests generated by an operating system designed for stand-alone machines to devices at other locations on the network.

Within the Windows 95 graphical user interface, the Map Network Drive dialog box (see Fig. 41.3) provides a simplified means to map Windows NT Server or workgroup shares. The dialog box, which you can access from the Tools menu in the Windows Explorer or from the toolbar, contains two fields. The Drive field has a drop-down list with which you select the drive letter that you want to map. If a drive shown in the list is already mapped, you'll see the UNC path to which it is mapped just to the right of the drive letter. If you don't see a UNC path next to the driver letter, it hasn't been mapped and is available for you to use.

In the Path field, you specify the network share that you want to associate with the selected drive letter. The Path field also has a drop-down list, containing all of the network shares that you've recently accessed or have mapped. To map a drive to a new path, you must manually enter the name of the network resource into the Path field, using the UNC. If you are not currently attached to the resource you have specified, and if there is no password information in the cache for that resource, then you will be prompted to log in before the drive mapping is completed. Select Reconnect at logon to have Windows 95 to remap the drive letter each time the machine is started. In other words, make the drive mapping persistent.

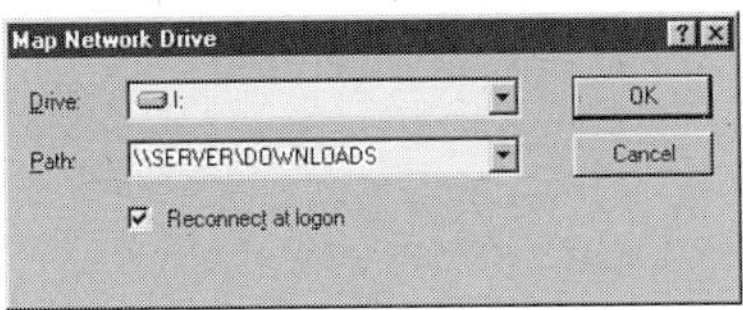

FIG. 41.3
The Map Network Drive dialog box allows network shares and volumes to be permanently associated with particular drive letters.

You also can access the Disconnect Network Drive dialog box from the Tools menu or toolbar of the Explorer or Network Neighborhood window. This dialog box displays a listing of the currently mapped drive letters and performs the opposite function of the Map Network Drive dialog box, allowing you to remove the selected mapping and free up its drive letter. Select a drive mapping and click OK to disconnect it. Click Cancel if you don't want to disconnect any drive mappings.

Using the Network Neighborhood

Besides supporting traditional drive-mapping methods, Windows 95 also provides another way of accessing network drives. The Network Neighborhood window displays all of the NT servers to which the user is currently attached as icons (see Figure 41.4). Double-clicking a server icon reveals the available Windows NT shares as folders.

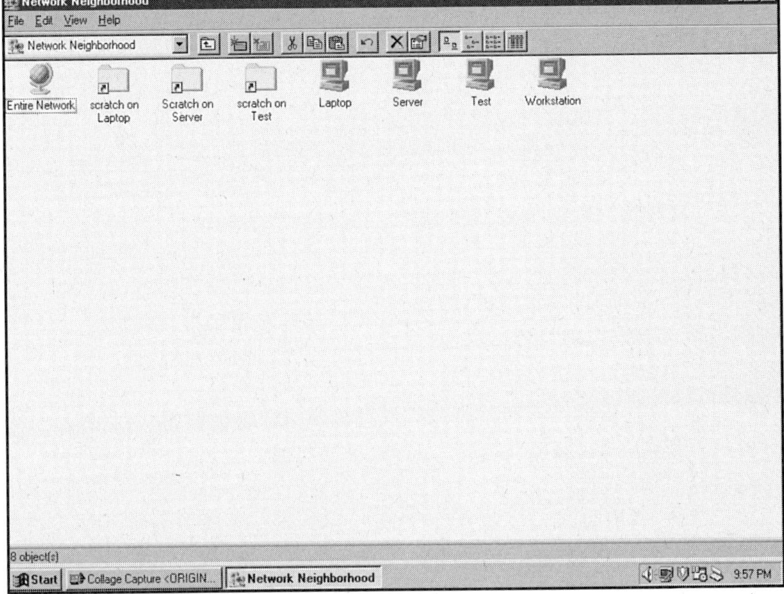

FIG. 41.4
The Network Neighborhood window displays all of the servers and workstations currently attached to the host machine.

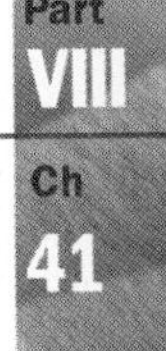

When a user double-clicks the Entire Network icon, all of the NT servers on the network are displayed, expanding his view even further. A user (with the appropriate permission) can access any shared drive or folder on the network from this interface, simply by double-clicking its icon. If the user is not currently attached to the NT server containing the share, he is automatically logged in, if a cached password is available, or presented with a login dialog box.

The Windows Explorer integrates My Computer with the Network Neighborhood to provide a single navigable interface for the more advanced user. Mapped drives coexist with NT server objects, even when both are referencing the same network machine, and users can manipulate files on both interchangeably by dragging and dropping, as well as with context menus. Many of the same tools are available in the Explorer and My Computer.

You can map network shares in Network Neighborhood, too. Right-click a share, and choose Map Network Drive. You see the dialog box shown in Figure 41.3.

For example, if the CD-ROM on an NT server is shared by the network administrator, you can access it through Network Neighborhood. Double-click the Network Neighborhood icon on the desktop, and then double-click the icon representing the NT server. You'll see a folder that represents the CD-ROM. Double-click that folder icon to view the contents of the disc that's currently loaded into the player.

Using NT Network Printers

Aside from drive-sharing and storage capabilities, the other fundamental reason for the widespread adoption of local area networking in the business world is the sharing of printers. As with hard drives, the original method for printer sharing was to redirect the local DOS output to the network, where it was stored in a queue on a print server, until it could be serviced by a printer. The introduction of Windows helped overcome this deception by adding the capability to address network printers directly.

Windows 95 takes this evolution several steps further. Installing support for a network printer is now a far easier process than it ever has been, and with some minor print server configurations, it can be made even easier for every Windows 95 user on the network. Windows 95 also allows workstations to exert a greater amount of control over network printing than they have been able to in the past, while maintaining the margin of safety important to network administrators. The following section discusses the process of printing to server-based devices located elsewhere on the network.

Using the Add New Printer Wizard

The procedure for installing a network printer is not much different from installing a local printer. After launching the Add New Printer Wizard, the first question that you are asked is whether you are installing a local or a network printer. When you select Network, you are then asked to furnish the location of the share or queue, as shown in Figure 41.5.

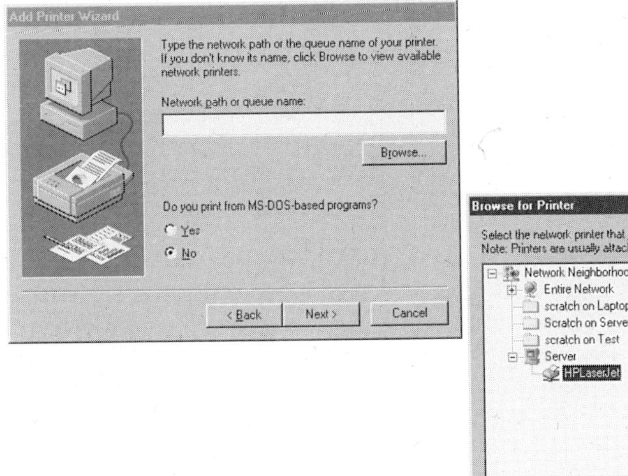

FIG. 41.5
The Add New Printer Wizard simplifies the installation of a network printer.

It is assumed that the printer you are installing has already been properly configured for network use. This involves the creation of a share on a Windows NT server. When you click the Browse button for the Network path or queue name field in the wizard, a Network Neighborhood display appears, in which you can expand servers until you have located the appropriate print queue. The correct path to the share or queue also can be entered directly into the dialog box, but it must be specified using a correct UNC path name; see the section "Understanding the UNC (Universal Naming Convention)," earlier in this chapter.

If the printer cannot be located at the path given, you receive a message to that effect, but you can still proceed with the installation. A network printer may be temporarily invisible to the network for any number of reasons.

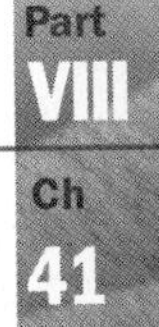

The Invisible Printer

One of the basic tenets of network printing is to keep the user working whenever possible. That is why network printing systems are usually designed to function normally, even when the actual printer is not working. Unlike printing to a locally attached device, all network print jobs are *spooled*. Spooling is the process by which an NT server accepts print jobs from applications and stores them on a disk until the printer can service them. Network users can continue to send jobs to print queues, even when the printer has run out of paper, jammed, or been stolen during the night.

The spooling process has two major effects:

- The actual time that the user's application spends printing is greatly reduced, because a hard drive can accept data at a much greater rate than any printer.
- The user cannot be sure that his job has been successfully printed until he actually walks over to the printer and checks.

continues

continued

The administrative capabilities of Windows 95 can help to make the latter point less of a problem. Printers become more interactive each year, and it is now possible to perform a number of maintenance tasks from a remote network workstation. This eliminates trips to the printer and avoids a backlog of jobs in the queue.

The second question asked in the Add Printer dialog box is whether you print from DOS-based programs. While most of the remaining major DOS applications, such as WordPerfect and Lotus 1-2-3, are capable of network printing, some Windows users may drop to the DOS prompt to use the small utilities that they have grown accustomed to over the years. These small programs are often not network-aware and print by default to the LPT1 port. What the wizard is asking with this question is whether it should configure the printer driver to capture local printer port output to the network queue.

The wizard then presents a standard Select Hardware dialog box to identify the printer model. Next, the wizard asks you to furnish a name for the printer. You may think it silly to name a locally attached device, but if you're printing on a network, printer naming can be essential.

Part of the advantage of network printing is the ability to access printers all over the network. This has obvious benefits when the printers are of different types. You may need access to a wide-bed dot-matrix printer for spreadsheets, a laser printer for correspondence, and a color printer for presentations. However, even in a company that has 50 identical laserjets on its network, the ability to send a document to someone in another department simply by printing it to his printer can be a real time-saver. For this reason, it is a good idea to name your various printers descriptively, identifying the printer type and its location.

After its interrogation is complete, the wizard then copies the appropriate printer drivers from the Windows 95 source files (possibly prompting you to insert a floppy or CD-ROM) and creates an additional icon in the Printers window. You may now use this printer just as if it were a local device, dragging and dropping files onto the icon or selecting it directly from your application.

Using Point and Print

One problem that is often faced by network users is how to know exactly which printer model to select during the installation process, when the printer itself may be some distance away from both their workstation and the file server.

A network printer may have to be associated logically with an NT server, but it does not have to be physically attached to it, except through the network medium itself. One of the most popular solutions for network printing today is to install a special network interface card, that also functions as a print server, into a laser printer. Print jobs can be spooled to a print queue on a server and then systematically fed to a printer located anywhere on the network.

NOTE The Hewlett-Packard JetDirect card is one of the most popular network interface cards, and Windows 95 includes a service with the operating system that provides an interface to the print server on the card.

So how do users know which printer to use and what printer driver to install? Point and Print is a Windows 95 mechanism that solves both these problems by associating the appropriate printer model with a print queue, and storing the correct printer drivers on the network, where all users can access them. If you remove from the Add New Printer Wizard the procedures by which the printer is identified and the drivers located, you are left with a ridiculously easy installation process that can be performed by anyone.

In fact, when you have set up a network printer for Point and Print, users need only browse the Network Neighborhood for the printer that they want to use and drag it into the Installed Printers window. Users are still asked if they print from DOS applications and whether the selected printer should be the Windows default. After those questions, however, the necessary drivers are automatically downloaded from the NT server and installed, and the printer is ready for use.

Monitoring NT Network Printers

Aside from simplifying the printer installation process, Windows 95 has also improved the administrative features devoted to network printing. When you double-click a network printer icon in the Printers window, a screen showing the current contents of the network print queue appears, as shown in Figure 41.6. The source application of each pending job is listed, as well as the network user who generated it, its size, and the time that it was submitted. A user can, therefore, tell when his job has been completed or estimate the delay until it is serviced.

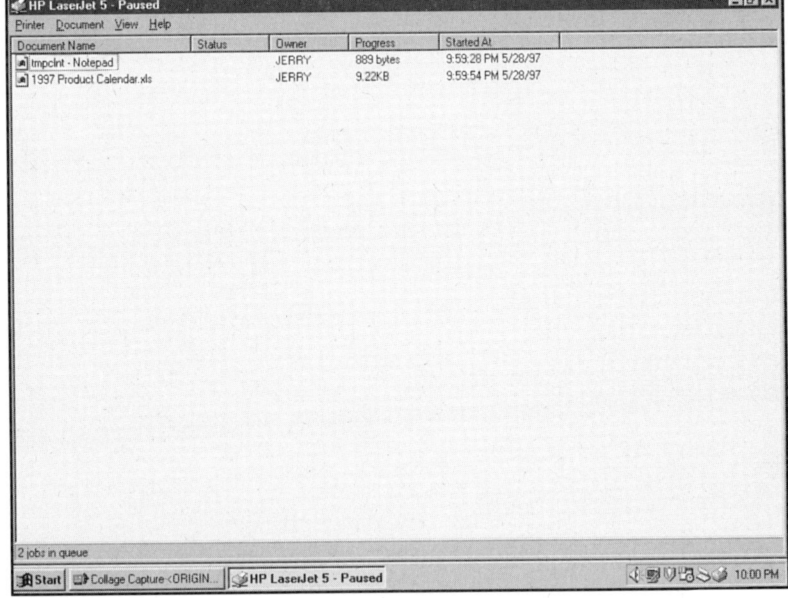

FIG. 41.6 The print queue window allows network print jobs to be manipulated directly from within Windows 95.

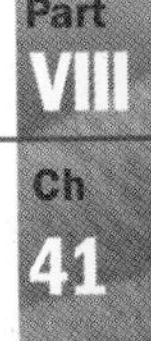

Accessing NT Network Resources from DOS

For users who first became acquainted with personal computing through DOS applications, perhaps you remember your first exposure to Windows and how long it took for you to gather up Windows versions of all of the DOS utilities you had collected. During those times when you just couldn't bring yourself to abandon your favorite DOS word processor or spreadsheet, it was a pleasure to exit from Windows and run that application in native DOS, rather than a DOS session.

Windows 95 is still capable of this, even when network support is required. Bring up the boot menu by pressing F8 as you start your computer, and you can easily boot to a DOS prompt. What you cannot do is boot directly to DOS mode with network support. You can, however, enable Windows 95's real-mode network clients with the NET START command, and map your drives with the NET USE command. Or you can create a batch file to perform all of these steps for you.

CAUTION

NET START can only be issued from the real-mode DOS prompt. It will not function in a Windows 95 virtual machine session. However, NET USE and many other commands can be used in a DOS window in place of their GUI counterparts.

Issue the NET START BASIC command from the DOS prompt to load the real-mode Client for Microsoft Networks. You then can map drives to any of the Windows shares available on the network, using the following syntax:

```
NET USE D: \\server\share
```

If you still use WordPerfect for DOS and need access to your network data files, using the real-mode client from the DOS prompt is the best way to run it under Windows 95. Also, in a troubleshooting situation in which video problems prevent you even from loading the standard VGA driver used by Safe Mode, this technique may help you out. And then, of course, there are those network multiplayer DOS games that you've been meaning to check out.

Mapping Drives with NET.EXE

Microsoft Networks provide utilities for mapping drive letters from a DOS prompt. You use the NET command. When using these utilities, you should be familiar with UNC.

You use the NET.EXE command line utility, with the USE parameter, for mapping drive letters on Microsoft networks. When you issue the NET USE command from any DOS prompt, all of the currently mapped devices on the system are displayed, including peer-to-peer mappings and captured print queues. When you issue the NET VIEW command, all of the shares on the network that are available for mapping are displayed.

Thc syntax for mapping a drive with NET is as follows:

```
NET USE X: \\SERVER\SHARE
```

NET USE also is capable of mapping LPT ports to shared network printers and contains many other options to control how drive mappings are created. This includes whether passwords are cached and whether the drive-mapping process should be interactive.

Performing Other Tasks with NET.EXE

NET is an extremely powerful command that you can use to perform nearly all of the network-related tasks that are possible from the Windows 95 GUI. It also has a number of real mode functions that can be used only when you boot Windows 95 to the command prompt; these functions will not operate from a DOS session within the Windows interface. Following is a summary of NET command functions. More detailed information about each one is available by typing the command followed by a **/?** at a Windows 95 DOS prompt (for example, **NET USE /?**).

NET CONFIG	Displays your current workgroup settings.
NET DIAG	Runs the Microsoft Network Diagnostics program to display diagnostic information about your network.
NET HELP	Provides information about commands and error messages.
NET INIT	Loads protocol and network-adapter drivers without binding them to Protocol Manager.
NET LOGOFF	Breaks the connection between your computer and the shared resources to which it is connected.
NET LOGON	Identifies you as a member of a workgroup.
NET PASSWORD	Changes your logon password.
NET PRINT	Displays information about print queues and controls print jobs.
NET START	Starts services.
NET STOP	Stops services.
NET TIME	Displays the time on or synchronizes your computer's clock with the clock on a Microsoft Windows for Workgroups, Windows NT, Windows 95, or NetWare time server.
NET USE	Connects to or disconnects from a shared resource or displays information about connections.
NET VER	Displays the type and version number of the workgroup redirector you are using.
NET VIEW	Displays a list of computers that share resources or a list of shared resources on a specific computer.

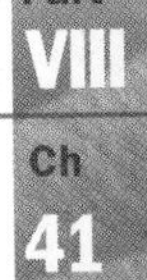

TROUBLESHOOTING

When using the NET USE command to map drives, why does the utility refuse to read passwords from the cache file and force me to enter them every time? The patch for the Windows 95 password cache file mentioned earlier in this chapter alters the NET.EXE utility. After the service pack containing the patch is applied, passwords are no longer extracted from the cache when you use NET commands. All passwords must be explicitly specified at all times.

CHAPTER 42

Working with Network Printers

by William S. Holderby

In Chapter 5, "Controlling Printers," you learned the basics of installing and working with printers—or at least those attached directly to your computer. Of course, not all printers are connected exclusively to your PC. In many workplaces, a local area network has multiple printer connections. Although Windows 95 makes network printers appear to operate as local printers, network printing may seem more complex. Local printers usually remain attached to the same port and are under your control. Network printers can change location and are controlled by other users or a network administrator. If problems arise when you are using a network printer, troubleshooting is much easier if you understand some of the differences between local and network printing.

This chapter takes printing a step further and discusses printing issues from a network perspective. ■

Print to network printers

One of the main reasons for establishing a network is to share print services.

Optimize print resources

Network printing can be a dream or a nightmare for users; the difference is often in how well the administrator has configured the resources.

Manage print files

You can prioritize, sort, manage, and even delete files after submission and before printing.

Solve common network printing problems

Printing problems are among the most common network-related problems that users face and administrators wrestle with.

Use custom printer drivers and utilities

In a perfect world, there would be no need for anything other than standard drivers. In the real world, custom drivers and utilities are often the norm more than the exception.

Examining Windows 95's New Network Printing Features

Windows 95 incorporates several new features and enhancements that markedly improve network printing. These new features include the following:

- *Network Point and Print* enables users to copy printer drivers automatically from network print servers to their local PC. This reduces the time it takes to set up a new printer and eliminates the need to find and copy vendor-driver software. This feature also eliminates the chance of configuring the wrong printer. You can access Network Point and Print from network servers running Windows 95, Windows NT Advanced Server, Windows NT Workstation, Windows for Workgroups 3.11, or Novell NetWare.
- *Windows 95's Network Neighborhood* provides tools to configure print resources quickly on Windows 95, Windows NT, and Novell servers. You can use this feature to find, use, and manage print jobs on printers interfacing any of these devices. Formerly, the user had to memorize locations and complex network commands. Network Neighborhood virtually eliminates this need through its new network user interface.
- *Compatibility with NetWare's PSERVER* enables you to access print jobs from NetWare's print spooler.
- *Deferred printing* provides you with the ability to save printouts until you reattach your printer. Deferred printing automatically stores print jobs after you detach your PC from the network, and automatically restarts them after you reestablish the connection.
- *Printer driver* provides command resources to remotely stop, hold, cancel, or restart print jobs located on shared printers.

Understanding Network Printing

Before delving too deeply into the nuts and bolts of network printing, you first must become familiar with the terminology you will see frequently in this discussion:

- *LAN Administrators* provide a management function to the local area network by assisting users and directing what resources are available on the network.
- *Systems policies* are software controls that are created by LAN Administrators to define what users can and cannot do on their desktops and the network. For example, you might use a system policy to restrict access to certain network programs.
- A *client* is a workstation that uses the services of any network server that can include server-based software systems, printers, and mass storage devices.
- *Print queues* contain print jobs that are not immediately printed. A queue holds the job until the printer is ready to print.
- *Windows Redirector* is the software module contained in the Windows network architecture that identifies software references to network devices and connects those devices to the workstation through the network.

- *Network resources* are software and hardware features that are available from servers and other workstations on the LAN. Resources such as shared drivers and server-based programs are available for network users.
- *Printing resources* are LAN resources that are dedicated to serving network users for the purpose of printing. These include shared printers, network printers, and print queues.
- *Print servers* service the printing needs of network clients.

Three network printer types are found on most networks:

- Printers attached to the network through a Microsoft Network-compatible server.
- Printers connected to a server running a compatible network operating system other than Windows, such as Novell NetWare and Banyan VINES.
- Printers directly attached to a network through a special printer network interface card (NIC).

Printing from Applications

Printing to network printers from within applications requires the same commands and menu items that you use to print locally. Windows handles the network communications and creates a printer driver for each attached network printer. As with local printers, you can access network printer configuration information in the Printer Properties sheet. In this sheet, you can change the network printer's properties for default or specific printing tasks.

CAUTION

Remember that other users can change a network printer configuration. Before printing, check all important parameters, including paper orientation and resolution. Don't assume that they are already set the way that you want them. Printing mistakes on network printers take extra time to recover.

When applications create a print file, they send a print stream to the network server through the Windows 95 Network Redirector. A print file contains spooled printer data and commands that are being temporarily stored prior to printing. The Network Redirector, which is part of Windows 95 network architecture, determines whether the print stream destination is a local printer. A print stream is the data that is being sent to a printer containing both printable and unprintable characters. Unprintable characters are used to control the printer. It also uses Windows network drivers to locate the designated printer.

Drag-and-Drop Printing

To perform drag-and-drop printing, you use the same procedure as you do for local printing. Remember, however, that drag-and-drop printing sends the print job to the system's default printer. If the selected printer is not the default printer, Windows asks you to make it the default printer prior to printing the file. When initially connecting your PC to a network, this printer might not be available. Be sure to log in to the network and verify the printer's network connection before setting it as the default printer.

See "Drag-and-Drop Printing from the Desktop," p. 150

Installing a Network Printer

Network printers are usually installed in one of two ways:

- The *Add Printer Wizard* from the Printers folder can be used for any printer connected to the network. The installation of a network printer doesn't change the printer, it simply loads an appropriate printer driver on your PC. Windows 95 uses that driver during printing.

NOTE If other users share a network printer, changes to the printer can affect every user. If you change a cartridge or make printer menu changes, you can affect everyone using your printer from the network.

- *Point and Print installation* from the desktop can be used for printers attached to servers that are Microsoft Client-compatible.

See "Setting Up a Windows 95 Peer-to-Peer Network," p. 939

See "Connecting Windows 95 to a Novell Network," p. 979

Using the Add Printer Wizard Installing a network printer involves the same Add Printer Wizard as the local printer installation described in Chapter 5, "Controlling Printers." However, there are some differences.

When you configure a local printer, the location of your cable to a specific printer port determines the port's selection. The network printer, on the other hand, requires an address. In the example shown in Figure 42.1, an HP 1200 CPS print queue is located on the AlphaNT server.

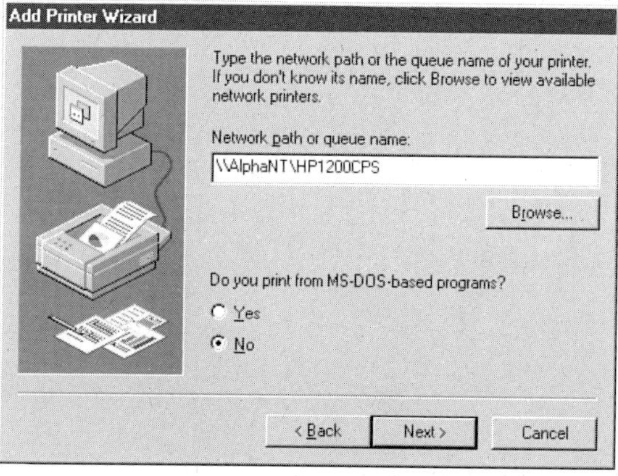

FIG. 42.1
The Add Printer Wizard requires a network address for printer installation.

If you're not sure of the correct address for the network printer, you can choose to browse the network. Browsing enables you to check which network printers are currently available. Some servers require passwords to view what network resources they have available. If you desire access to a server, but do not know the password, contact your LAN administrator.

To configure a network printer, you need to know its make and model. You can get this information from your network administrator. Microsoft network servers enable you to install printer drivers quickly.

To set up a network printer with the Add Printer Wizard, follow these steps:

1. Choose Start, Settings, Printers, and then double-click the Add Printer folder.
2. From the first Add Printer Wizard screen, click the Next button. Windows 95 displays the next Wizard screen which asks you to decide if you are adding a Network or a Local Printer.
3. Choose the Network Printer option to connect your PC to a network printer. Click the Next button located at the bottom of the window.
4. You must then identify the network path to the printer (refer to Figure 42.1). Click the Browse button to view the Network Neighborhood.
5. The Network Neighborhood displays a list of all servers and workstations connected to your network. Find the appropriate printer, select it, and click the Next button. The Wizard accesses the selected printer and determines whether its server can download an appropriate printer driver. If a driver is available, the Wizard automatically loads the driver and sets a default configuration for the printer. If a driver is not available, the Wizard asks you to specify the printer's make and model.

Use the Add Printer Wizard again if you have difficulty connecting to a printer using the Point and Print procedure.

6. Select the manufacturer and printer model by scrolling the Wizard screen lists; then click Next. The screen now offers a default name for your printer. The name should adequately describe the printer for later identification.
7. The Wizard asks whether you want this printer to be your default printer; select Yes or No. Follow this decision by clicking the Next button.
8. The final wizard screen provides the controls to print a test page on the printer you just installed. Choose Yes to print the test page, or choose No to not print the test page. As a general rule, you should always print a test page to verify the successful completion of the Add a Printer Wizard.
9. Click Finish.

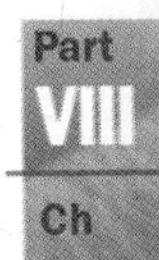

Using Point and Print Point and Print enables a workstation user to quickly connect to and use a printer shared on another Windows 95 workstation, a Windows NT Advanced Server, or a Novell NetWare server. When first connecting to the shared printer, Windows 95 automatically copies and installs the correct driver for the shared printer from the server.

1. Choose the Network Neighborhood icon on the Windows desktop.

2. Choose the Entire Network icon. Windows displays all the servers attached to your network.
3. Choose the Server that supports the printer you want to attach to your workstation. If you don't know which Server that is, ask the LAN administrator or select each server in sequence until you find the name of the appropriate printer or print queue. Windows displays the server's screen showing its shared resources.
4. Drag a network printer icon from a server's window and drop it on the desktop. You receive a diagnostic message that says "You cannot move or copy this item to this location. Do you want to create a shortcut to the item instead?" Answer Yes. Windows creates a shortcut icon and drops it on the desktop.
5. Drag a document from a local folder and drop it on the New Printer folder icon. Windows displays an information screen such as that shown in Figure 42.2. If you select Yes, Windows automatically connects to the printer and downloads the appropriate printer driver from the network printer's server. After loading and configuring the driver, Windows 95 begins printing to the network printer.

FIG. 42.2
If the printer driver is not loaded when you use Point and Print, Windows lets you install the driver on-the-fly.

Printing on a NetWare Network

To use a NetWare print queue, you must be logged onto a NetWare server. Windows 95 utilizes a PSERVER that can redirect print jobs from NetWare print queues to printers connected to Windows 95 workstations. In addition to the PSERVER capability, your PC must also use the Microsoft Client for NetWare Networks. Windows 95 automatically adapts to NetWare's security for printer and print queue access.

NOTE The network administrator can control how NetWare shares printers. If the administrator uses a *policy file* to disable print sharing, the network cannot access the printers. A policy file contains a set of commands that are used by your network administrator to set rules for the operation and configuration of Windows on a network. When entering a new network, check with your network administrator for a sharing policy before attempting to configure shared printing.

NetWare Print Servers Windows 95 provides printer services for NetWare networks, including a 32-bit PSERVER capability. PSERVER connects NetWare queues to printers shared by Windows 95 PCs. A NetWare print queue contains all the jobs waiting (queued) for a specific printer.

To connect your workstation to a Novell NetWare print server, follow these steps:

1. Choose the Network Neighborhood icon on the desktop. Notice that all servers (Microsoft and NetWare) appear in the Network Neighborhood screen. This screen displays an icon for each network drive currently attached to your system.
2. If you want to attach your workstation to a NetWare printer, choose the appropriate server by double-clicking its icon. The server dialog box opens and displays the shared directories, files, and print queues that are attached to the selected server.
3. Select the appropriate print queue. Choose File, Print and then select the Capture Printer Port control button.
4. The capture printer port dialog box contains the name of currently unattached LPT ports. Select the Reconnect at Logon check box if you want to maintain this connection and have it attached when you restart Windows. Then click OK to attach this print queue to your PC.

   Capturing the printer port attaches the NetWare print queue to the specified port. It does not, however, attach the associated printer to the desktop.
5. To attach the printer associated with that print queue, choose File, Create Shortcut. Windows displays a message warning that you cannot configure a shortcut printer icon in the Create Shortcut dialog box, but that you can create the icon on the desktop. Click Yes to create the icon.
6. Double-click the printer icon. Windows asks whether you want to set up a printer. Choose Yes.
7. Windows then displays the Add Printer Wizard. Follow the Wizard to finish installing an appropriate printer for the desktop.

NOTE You must know the type of printer attached to this print queue. This procedure is different than installing a printer attached to a Microsoft print server.

After configuring the printer, you can print by using the Point and Print procedure on the desktop.

Microsoft Client for NetWare Windows 95 Microsoft Client for NetWare Networks enables you to connect to new or existing NetWare servers to send files and interact with server-based software. With Microsoft Client for NetWare Networks, you can browse and queue your print jobs using either the Windows 95 network user interface or existing Novell NetWare utilities. The Microsoft Client for NetWare interfaces work equally well with both NetWare 3.x and 4.x servers running bindery emulation.

NOTE The Microsoft Client for NetWare does not support NDS-based NetWare 4.x networks. OSR2 comes with an option called MSNDS (Microsoft Netware Directory Services) that allows Windows 95 access to NDS-based server resources. Alternatively, you can use the 32-bit NetWare client available from the Novell site.

To use Microsoft Client for NetWare Networks, follow these steps:

1. Choose File, Print.
2. Your application might ask you to choose a destination printer. Most applications display a list of attached printers from which you can choose. If so, choose an appropriate network printer and choose OK.

   The Windows Redirector accepts the print stream and sends it to the selected printer over the network. Information concerning the status of the printing process automatically returns to you.
3. To monitor the status of your print job on a network printer, open the printer's folder and double-click the appropriate icon. The printer's local Printer Driver opens a status dialog box listing all print jobs in the printer's queue.

Point and Print for NetWare Print Queues

You can enable a Point and Print procedure to use a NetWare-compatible client as a destination. To do so, use the Point and Print procedure discussed earlier.

To print from the desktop to a network printer, follow these steps:

1. Open the folder that contains the document you want to print.
2. Select a document. Hold down the left mouse button and drag the selected document to the network printer's icon on your desktop. The document now appears as an outline.
3. Release the outlined document icon over the printer's icon. Windows 95 interprets the file type, starts the application associated with the file, commands the application to print the document, redirects the print job to the selected printer, and shuts down the application when the print job finishes.

NOTE Before Windows can perform the desktop printing operation, you must associate the document with an installed application. If the document is not associated with such an application, Windows displays a message box informing you that it cannot perform the printing task.

Printing on a Microsoft Network

To share files and printers on Microsoft networks, you also can set user rights remotely through the User Manager in a Windows NT Advanced Server.

To connect to a Microsoft print server, follow these steps:

1. Click the Network Neighborhood icon on the desktop. Notice that all servers (Microsoft and NetWare) appear on the Network Neighborhood window. This screen displays an icon for each network drive currently attached to your system.
2. To attach a printer through a Microsoft server, choose the appropriate Microsoft server by double-clicking that server's icon. The server dialog box, named after the appropriate

server, appears and displays the shared directories, files, and printers attached to the Microsoft server.

3. Select the appropriate printer queue. Choose File, Print and then select the capture printer port. The Capture Printer Port dialog box is displayed containing the name of a currently unattached LPT port.
4. In the Capture Printer Port dialog box, select the Reconnect at Logon check box if you want to maintain this connection and have it attached when you restart Windows. Click the OK button to attach this print queue to your PC.

NOTE Capturing the printer port attaches the printer to a specified port, but does not attach the associated printer to the desktop.

5. To attach the printer associated with the selected print queue, you must choose File, Create Shortcut. Windows displays a diagnostics message warning that you cannot configure a shortcut printer icon in the Create Shortcut dialog box, although Windows creates the shortcut on the desktop. Click Yes to create the icon.
6. Double-click the printer's shortcut icon. Windows asks whether you want to set up a printer. Choose Yes. Windows then displays the Add Printer Wizard.
7. Follow the Wizard to finish installing an appropriate printer for the desktop. The Add Printer Wizard identifies which printer make and model you are installing and completes the printer connection quickly.

After configuring the printer, you can print by using the Point and Print procedure on the desktop.

TROUBLESHOOTING

I can see a network printer using Network Neighborhood, but I can't print to it. Try the following:

- Check with your network administrator about your access rights to the printer.
- Verify that the printer is properly configured on your PC.
- Check with other users to determine whether they can access the printer.
- Try to print to another printer on the network to check your network connectivity.

I can't stop, cancel, or delete a print job in a network queue. Try the following:

- Check whether you have proper authorization from the network administrator to change the print settings. You might be authorized to change only your own print jobs, not others.
- If the print queue is on a shared printer, reload the printer driver or reset the printer properties. The system might not recognize that this printer is attached to your PC.

continues

continued

The network printer doesn't tell me that it is out of paper or toner. Have the network administrator configure WinPopup to broadcast printer-problem announcements. WinPopup is a utility that comes with Windows. This utility allows the network and network users to send "popup" messages that identify events and get the attention of other network users.

Optimizing Print Resources

Network printing involves many of the same facilities as local printing. Applications create print files that the Network Redirector streams to the destination network printer. When working with network resources, however, you must consider several other issues to ensure that you're getting the most from your system.

Network Printer Configuration and Management

The Printer Properties sheet contains information on each local and network printer attached to your PC. Each printer's properties are specific to its make, model, and hardware configuration.

See "Applications with Special Print Options," **p. 144**

You can make several changes to the properties to enhance your printing. The print quality can be enhanced by specific printers, setting device options, graphics, and the procedures for handling TrueType fonts. The following general procedure explores some of these changes:

1. After attaching a network printer, open its Printer Properties sheet by right-clicking the appropriate printer. From the drop-down menu that appears, choose Properties and then click the General tab. The pages in the Properties sheet are specific to your printer and display the options and selections that match the printer's current hardware and printer driver configuration.
2. Click the Device Options tab. Notice the options that the network printer offers.
3. Change the Device Options settings to match your printer's specifications. These options include such pertinent information as printer memory size and page protection. (If you don't see these options, check with your LAN administrator.)
4. Click the Details tab. Check the spool settings to determine whether the printer is set to print after the first or last page spools. Usually, waiting until after the last page spools yields better results. Experiment with this setting to gain a better understanding of your configuration.
5. Click the Graphics tab. Change the dithering settings to identify which setting yields the best results for both speed and printout quality.

TROUBLESHOOTING

When I print to a printer on the network, my printout quality and settings are not consistent. Try the following:

- Before printing, check the printer's Properties sheet. Change the settings, if required.
- Check with the system administrator for the printer settings, features, and hardware configuration. The printer might not be capable of handling your print job.
- Relate printout quality to changes in the property settings. Change your printer's properties and make test printouts to see how these changes affect the printouts.

Network Printer Drivers

Windows uses printer drivers to deliver your print files through the network to your printer. How well Windows performs this printing depends on how well the drivers perform. If you use drivers that are several revisions old, you might experience a slowdown. It is a good policy to check your printer drivers and update as revisions become available.

1. In the Control Panel, choose the System icon. Then click the Device Manager tab.
2. Verify that the network interface card driver is a virtual mode driver with a V×D extension. The driver will be listed including its extension. If a real-mode driver with a DRV extension is installed, contact your LAN administrator or printer manufacturer for an updated revision.
3. Verify that the configured printer driver is also a virtual mode driver. The driver should also have a V×D extension. If a real-mode driver with a DRV extension is installed, contact your LAN administrator or printer manufacturer for an updated revision.
4. Ask your LAN administrator whether your system is configured with the latest driver version for your network printers. If the drivers are not the most current revision, request the latest update from either your LAN manager or the printer's manufacturer.

Managing Print Files and Sharing

After creating print files and sending them to a network printer, you must verify that the print jobs are finished, on hold, or need to be purged. You can check the print job status on both local and remote printers by using the Windows Printer Driver. Print job control is a complex task that involves user security rights on remote printers.

Viewing a Network Print Queue

Although you can view queue information, you cannot change any print job characteristics unless the LAN administrator has authorized you to do so. For some systems, the network administrator is the only user who can control all print jobs, while another user can control only his or her local shared-printing resources. LAN administrator policies determine which users can delete, pause, or purge documents from the queue. Usually, users can change the status of their individual print jobs, but not those of other users.

To view the queue, simply double-click the printer's icon in the Printers folder or on the desktop. Windows displays the Printer Driver and print queue.

Shared Printing

Shared printing or *peer-to-peer sharing* provides other network workstations access to your local printer. Shared printing access is useful for transferring documents between workstations and for sharing expensive resources with other users. It is also an excellent way to maximize the use of often expensive printing hardware.

To share a printer, follow these steps:

1. Choose Start, Settings, Control Panel. In the Control Panel folder, double-click the Network icon. The Network tabs will appear. These tabs include Configuration, Identification, and Access Control.
2. On the Configuration page, select the Add button. The Select Network Component Type dialog box appears.
3. Choose Service and then click the Add button.
4. Choose Microsoft from the Manufacturers list box.
5. If your primary network logon client is Microsoft Networks, choose File and Printer Sharing for Microsoft Networks. If your primary network logon client is NetWare, choose File and Printer Sharing for NetWare Networks.
6. Choose OK to close the Select Network Service dialog box. For these changes to take effect, you must restart the computer.

TROUBLESHOOTING

My shared printer is unavailable to other workstations on my network. Try the following:

- In the Control Panel, double-click the Network icon. Choose the File and Print Sharing button. In the File and Print Sharing dialog box, verify that the I Want to Be Able to Allow Others to Print to My Printer(s) check box is selected.
- Verify that all users are running a compatible protocol.
- Verify that your PC shows up in the network browser on other connected PCs.
- Verify that you can print successfully to your attached printer.
- Use the Extended Printer Troubleshooting (EPTS) application available in your Help file.

Enabling Shared Printing After configuring the network setup by following the preceding steps, you must enable the sharing feature as follows:

1. From the taskbar, choose Start, Settings, Control Panel. In the Control Panel folder, double-click the Network icon.
2. In the Network dialog box choose the File and Print Sharing button.
3. In the File and Print Sharing dialog box, select the I Want to Be Able to Allow Others to Print to My Printer(s) check box (see Figure 42.3).

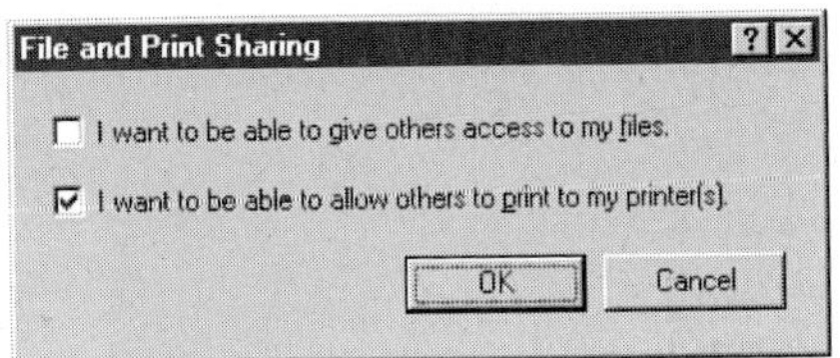

FIG. 42.3
The File and Print Sharing dialog box contains check boxes that enable you to share files and printers with other network users.

4. Choose OK to close the dialog box, and click it again to close the Network Control Panel. You must restart the computer for these changes to take effect.

NOTE If the I Want to Be Able to Allow Others to Print to My Printer(s) check box is grayed (disabled), your system does not support print sharing.

Disabling Shared Printing After your workstation printer is shared, you might find that too many users are creating an overload. To disable the share, follow this procedure.

1. From the taskbar, choose Start, Settings, Control Panel. In the Control Panel folder, double-click the Network icon.
2. In the Network dialog box, choose the File and Print Sharing button.
3. Deselect the I Want to Be Able to Allow Others to Print to My Printer(s) check box.
4. Choose OK to close the dialog box, and choose it again to close the Network Control Panel.

Creating Shared-Printer Security In Windows 95, creating shared-resource security is a multistep procedure. In order to effectively share a resource, you must be able to control who accesses that resource and, to some extent, what they do with it. If you share your printer, you can impose some level of security. Securing your printer requires several steps.

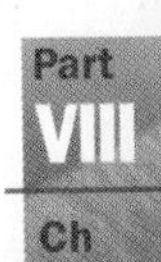

1. Choose the Passwords icon in the Control Panel folder. The Password Properties sheet appears. This Properties sheet has three tabs: Passwords, Remote Administration, and User Profiles.
2. Choose the Enable Remote Administration check box on the Remote Administration page.

3. Type a user-access password in the Passwords text box.
4. In the Confirm Passwords text box, retype the password. Record the password in your system workbook or manual.
5. Select OK.

Network users can now gain access to your system by using the password that you have just created. To access your shared printer, however, users must have the appropriate password information.

Deleting Connections to a Shared Printer When you delete a shared connection between your workstation and a workstation sharing its local printer, disabling sharing keeps your local printer from being shared by the network.

1. From the taskbar, choose Start, Settings, Printer's Folder. Windows displays a list of all printers, local or network, attached to your workstation.
2. Select the shared printer you want to delete.
3. Choose File, Delete.
4. Windows displays a dialog box warning that it will delete the selected printer. Click Yes.
5. Windows next displays a dialog box asking whether you want to delete this printer's drivers. Click Yes to delete the drivers.

CAUTION

Before you click Yes (and thus delete the printer's drivers), verify that you do not have any other printers attached of the same make and model. If you delete this printer's drivers, you might also disconnect other printers.

Solving Common Network Printing Problems

Windows 95 adds some basic Help tools to aid you in solving network printing problems. These basic tools include the following:

- Windows quickly displays descriptive information in diagnostic messages that appear when Windows encounters printing problems.
- The Help facility includes an interactive Printing Problem Help tool that takes you step by step through the most common solutions to problems.
- An enhanced Help tool incorporates even more detailed steps that can solve quite difficult network printing problems.
- The System Monitor is useful in diagnosing local PC problems caused by network connections.

Diagnostics

The facilities of the Windows Help system can help you diagnose printing problems as follows:

1. Choose Help, Troubleshooting, and Print Troubleshooting from your application or Windows. Windows displays a Windows Help screen with the Print Troubleshooter dialog box.
2. Answer each question by clicking the button next to the appropriate answer. The Help screens provide suggestions for many common troubleshooting problems.

If the troubleshooting Help information is inadequate for solving your problems, Windows provides the Enhanced Print Troubleshooter (EPTS):

1. Go to the Windows Explorer.
2. Choose the EPTS.EXE executable file. EPTS displays a Help screen that contains hypertext buttons. Next to each button is a brief statement describing a printer problem. Start by selecting the statement that best describes your problem.
3. Answer each EPTS question with the choice that best matches your problem. The EPTS helps you identify the most probable cause of your network printing problems.

Diagnosing network printing problems is more complex because the printers are not local and perhaps not readily accessible. After using EPTS, if you are still having difficulty printing to a network printer, call the local Help desk or your LAN network administrator.

Server Overload

A PC that shares a local printer with the network is a *print server*. If your PC is a print server, a percentage of your PC's resources are dedicated to the network. That percentage varies with the number of network connections to your PC. If your system slows down significantly, it might be suffering from *server overload*. This occurs when too many network users are either attached to or overusing your printer.

To test network loading, use the System Monitor to record your PC's server activities. Your Monitor charts might show large changes in network connection activity.

1. Choose Start, Programs, Accessories, System Tools, System Monitor.
2. Choose Edit, Remove to clear all Monitor chart variables.
3. Choose Edit, Add. Windows displays the Add dialog box.
4. Choose the Server Threads option from the Network Server category.
5. Choose the Bytes/sec option from the Network Server category.
6. Choose the NBs (network buffers) option from the Network Server category and then choose the OK button to complete the additions.
7. Choose Options, Chart. Set the update interval to one minute using the slide control in the Chart dialog box.
8. Choose View, Line Charts.

You have now configured the Monitor to show the level of resource loading associated with network clients. If the System Monitor displays large variations in the number of threads or bytes-per-second variables, discontinue printer sharing for a test period. This test period should help you determine whether you can eliminate overload as a cause for system sluggishness.

Using Custom Print Managers and Utilities

Windows 95 provides a standard platform that other vendors use to create software drivers and applications. These custom software packages integrate a specific product with Windows. As a result, many printer vendors work with Microsoft to create new drivers. Some vendors have created printing applications that can substitute for or replace the Windows Printer Driver. Many printer vendors provide custom property configuration utilities for accessing their printers' custom features. Two of these vendors are Hewlett-Packard (HP) and Digital Equipment Corporation (DEC).

- The HP JetAdmin Utility is a substitute for the Windows Printer Driver.
- The DEC utility provides additional property screens that the Windows Printer Driver can call.

Using the HP JetAdmin Utility

You can use the HP JetAdmin Utility to install and configure networked Hewlett-Packard printers that use the HP JetDirect network interface. The HP JetAdmin Utility substitutes for the Windows standard Printer Driver. You also can use JetAdmin to interface printers connected to a NetWare LAN.

Figure 42.4 shows the JetAdmin Utility's main screen. The dialog box is displaying a list of printers connected to a Novell NetWare network. The network printers are of diverse makes and models. The utility can identify most of these printers. However, if incapable of identifying a printer's make, model, or network adapter card, JetAdmin displays a large, yellow question mark to designate the unknown printer.

To obtain information about the printer, double-click one of the printers shown listed in the dialog box. The Printer screen shown in Figure 42.5 appears. The screen identifies the printer's make and model as well as its location, capabilities, and status.

Notice the traffic light indicator at the screen's lower-left corner. This indicator is useful for quickly isolating network printing problems. The following are traffic light patterns for diagnosing problem printers:

- A red light indicates that the printer has a critical error that you must correct before printing. Such critical errors include a lack of paper or an open door interlock.
- A yellow light signifies a noncritical error that will soon require service. For example, if the printer's toner is low, the yellow light comes on.
- A green light indicates that the printer is online and functioning normally.

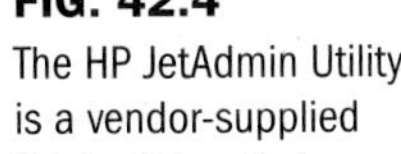

FIG. 42.4
The HP JetAdmin Utility is a vendor-supplied Printer Driver that monitors and controls HP network printers.

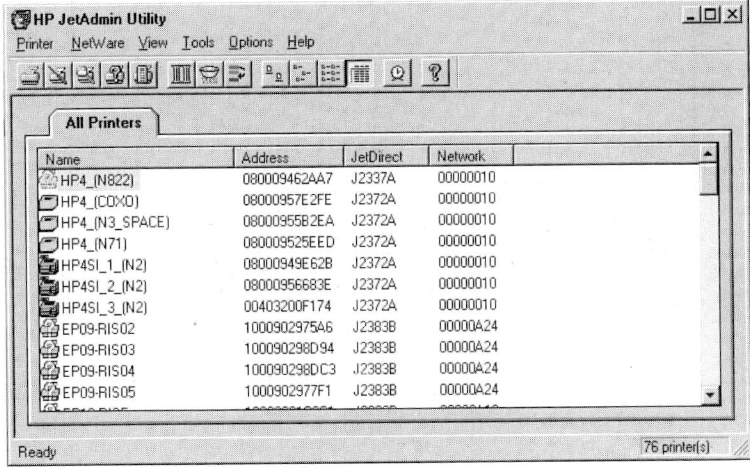

FIG. 42.5
The HP JetAdmin Utility's Printer screen displays current information about the selected printer.

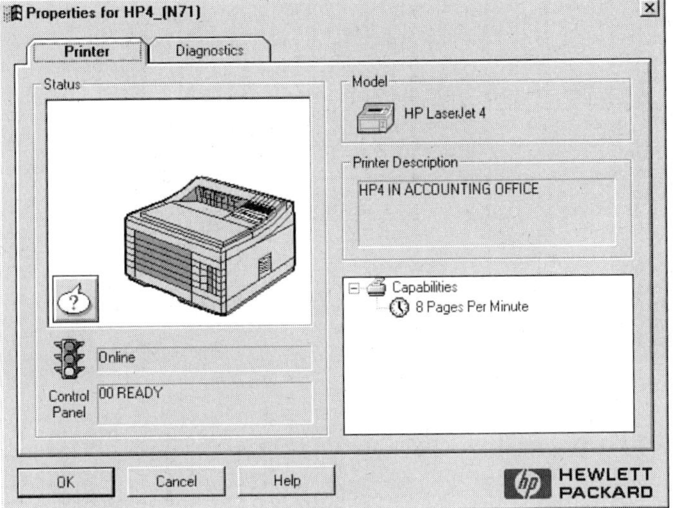

Figure 42.6 shows the Printer screen for a problem printer. JetAdmin has identified that the printer has a problem, as the question mark in the Status section denotes. Notice the traffic light patterns on this printer's display compared to that shown in Figure 42.5. The traffic light is now red, indicating a critical error has occurred.

Using the DEC Printer Utility

The DEC printer utility adds features to the standard Windows 95 Printer Driver and updates printer drivers. The utility includes a detailed Help file for configuring both local and network printers. In addition, the utility creates an enhanced set of property menus and screens for configuring DEC printers.

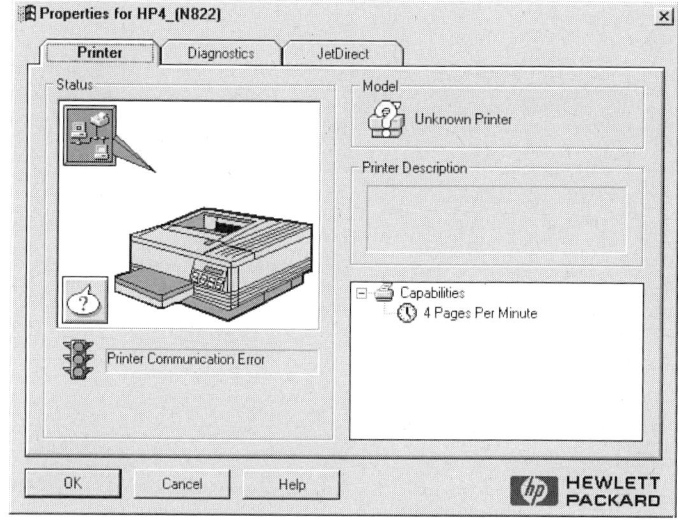

FIG. 42.6
The HP JetAdmin Utility's Printer screen shows the status of a printer whose current configuration is unknown.

Figure 42.7 shows the Device Options dialog box, which presents in detail the current conditions associated with the network printer. This dialog box also enables the user to install and quickly set special device options.

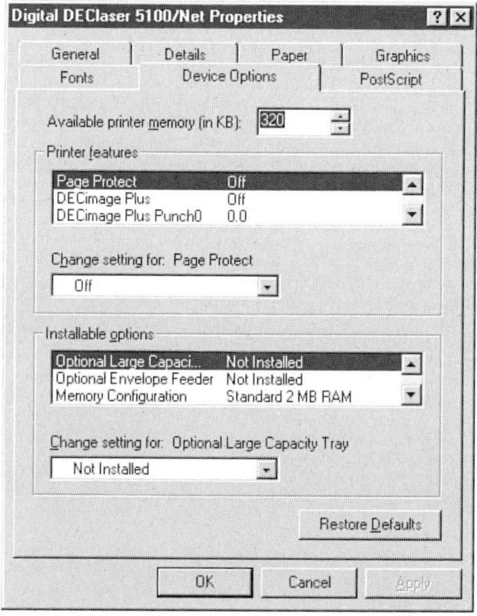

FIG. 42.7
The DEC printer utility's Device Options dialog box adds unique features to the standard Windows 95 Printer Driver.

As other printer vendors change their products and software drivers, other highly customized Printer Drivers will be available for use with Windows 95.

CHAPTER 43

Network Management and Security

by Gordon Meltzer

Creating network resources

The purpose of a network is to share resources, which must first be created and defined.

Monitoring network resources

You need to determine how well resources are being utilized and where potential problems lie.

Sharing network resources

Once created, resources must be shared for users to be able to reap their benefits.

Securing the network

No matter how small the network, never underestimate the damage that can be done if the network is not secure.

Managing the network

An administrator's job is never done, as there are always resources to be monitored, users to add, shares to create, and so on.

Using Dial-Up Networking

Windows 95 fully supports Dial-Up Networking to make it easier to compute with your network from any location.

Using Windows 95 with other networks

Windows 95 is an excellent client and workstation for every major network in widespread use today.

The motive for setting up a Windows 95 network is to share the resources associated with the computers on that network. *Resources* are disks (including CD-ROMs) and their files, printers, and fax modems.

A network, in which resources and information previously available only to people working on their private standalone personal computers now are available for sharing (and possible editing or deletion by the group), raises serious and complex issues. Network issues can best be understood by splitting them into two parts. This chapter examines these two parts: management and security.

In this chapter, you learn how to control the installation and configuration of your network. The chapter tries to expose weaknesses in the network design and tells you how to work around these weaknesses. The chapter provides tips for keeping your network up and running and for simplifying it without losing functionality. The chapter is a guide to help you understand the philosophy behind the Windows 95 network and make it work in your individual situation.

Creating Network Resources

The basic philosophy of peer-to-peer networks is that every file on every disk on the network is available for sharing by all members of the network. By extension, anyone can print to any printer on the network—and also delete any file, wipe out any directory, and erase any disk anywhere on the network.

That kind of peer-to-peer network, where everybody on the LAN is connected to everybody else's disks and printers, is an unmanageable network. If you draw a diagram of the connections in such a network, you'll see a crazy quilt of connections. With more than a few machines on the LAN, you'll be unable to follow all the connections. The worst parts of thoughtlessly connecting everybody to everybody are:

- **Confusion**. Time is always lost searching for data all over the LAN.
- **Data Loss**. Needed files get erased from one disk because somebody thought somebody else had a copy on another disk.

Don't be tempted to set up your Windows 95 peer network the crazy quilt way. The problem is that after you set up your network and declare your computer's hard drive to be shared, if you take no steps to manage the network, you've opened the door to network data-loss danger and file-finding confusion. You need to bring safety and sanity to your network environment, and you need to work with the other members of your workgroup to accomplish those tasks.

Data Storage Tips

Networks are designed to make office life easier. Peer-to-peer networks are supposed to eliminate something called the sneakernet, which is used when all computers in an office are standalone. Following are the steps involved in making a sneakernet connection:

1. You decide that you want to edit a document on which several people have been collaborating.
2. You visit each collaborator's computer, find the file in question, and record the date and time when the file was last modified. You're looking for the most recent version.
3. When you find the computer that has the most up-to-date version of the document, find a formatted floppy disk, copy the file to the disk, and take the disk back to your computer.
4. Copy the file from the floppy disk to your hard drive.

You think that you won't have to go through all that when you set up a network. All the computers will be connected, and you can copy the file to your hard disk over the wire. In fact, however, the default setup for peer-to-peer networks such as Windows 95 leaves each person's version of a collaborative file on his or her own hard disk, where other workgroup members cannot easily find it.

The solution to this problem is setting up your peer-to-peer Windows 95 network in a client/server model. The following sections show how this model enables all members of the network to get their work done but retains the flexibility that is the best feature of peer nets.

Choosing a Storage Area for Your Work

You really don't want to set up each computer on the peer network as a server; you want to make one computer on your network the server, the central storage area for data files. Data files are *work products*—the files created by the programs that you use. If you're not sure about which files are data files, remember that Microsoft Word creates files that have the DOC extension and that Excel creates worksheet files that have the XLS extension. The files with DOC and XLS extensions are the work product (data files) created by Word and Excel.

Files of this nature should be stored on only one computer in your workgroup so that everyone will know where to find them. If you don't do this, you have to search all the computers on your network for a file—and that makes the process very time-consuming and not superior to sneakernet at all.

Using a Dedicated Server

You don't have to have a dedicated server in your Windows 95 network, but if you can afford to dedicate one computer on your network to storing everybody's work product, do so. Following are the benefits of storing all the workgroup's data files on one machine:

- The individual workstations can use smaller, slower, less expensive hard drives.
- You don't have to search for the computer that holds the files that you want.
- Complex drive mappings are eliminated.
- In a LAN where all work product is stored on one central file server, File and Printer Sharing will not need to be turned on in Control Panel, Networks, on most of the computers in the LAN. Memory is used more efficiently on all the machines that do not use file and printer sharing.
- Backing up everyone's work is as simple as backing up one disk, because all the work is on that disk.

Setting Up a Data File Storage Server

Once you've decided that good network management involves setting up a central server, where you and your network neighbors will store their data files, follow these steps:

1. Choose the network machine that you want to use as the data server. This machine will always be turned on.
2. Enable File and Printer Sharing on the data server. Do this by going to the machine that will be your storage server. Use Control Panel and double-click the Network icon. Then choose File and Print Sharing and put a check in the box that says I Want to Be Able to Give Others Access to My Files.

NOTE If the server you're working on also has a printer attached, and if you and your workgroup members want to print on that printer, also put a check in the box that says I Want to Be Able to Allow Others to Print to My Printer(s).

3. Set up a directory structure that will make storing and finding documents easy.

NOTE You may create one folder for each user and then create subfolders for the users' projects. You may create a folder for each client and allow the workgroup members to store their work for that client in the client's folder. Setting up folders by project is okay, too, if the projects are long-term. Ideally, the directory structure on the data server should be long-lasting and timeless so that everyone in the workgroup can get used to it.

4. Map the server's network drive to each workstation using the same drive letter (for example, Z:).
5. Set up the applications on each workstation so that the default data directory for each application is the same.
6. Have workgroup members start saving their work to the appropriate subfolder on the network drive (not to their local C drives).

Getting the Best of Peer-to-Peer and Client/Server LAN Features

Although using a central server makes our workgroup look like a big client/server network, the flexibility of a peer-to-peer network still is available. You can call on this flexibility when you want to use a resource on the network that's attached to another computer—a color printer, for example. You can designate the printer as a shared resource, no matter whose computer the printer is attached to. You can't do that in a traditional client/server network.

Drive Mappings

Following a plan like the one shown in the section "Setting Up a Data File Storage Server" is important. If you don't, your workgroup ends up with a drive-mapping scheme that looks like a bowl of spaghetti. You don't want everybody in the network to be connected to everybody else's machines and drives. Point everybody in the workgroup to one machine for storage of working data files, and you'll always be able to find what you're looking for.

Suppose that you have a 10-user workgroup. If you set up the network in full peer-to-peer fashion, so that everyone is looking for files stored on other people's computers, your drive mappings look like Figure 43.1.

You can see why this kind of drive mapping is called spaghetti-code mapping. On each workstation, you have at least nine drive mappings to deal with. You'll have to look for files on all nine of the local hard drives if data files are stored on the local drive of each workstation.

Of course, you may be confused by having so many drive mappings and connections in place all the time. You may be dismayed by the drain on your system's performance caused by connecting to so many other workstations and having those workstations connect to yours. You are likely to disconnect from the other members' drives for normal work. Later, when you want to send a file to or retrieve a file from another computer, you must connect to the other computer, map that computer's drive to yours, and do your file transfer work.

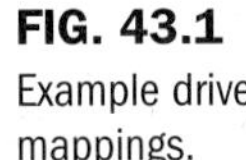

FIG. 43.1
Example drive mappings.

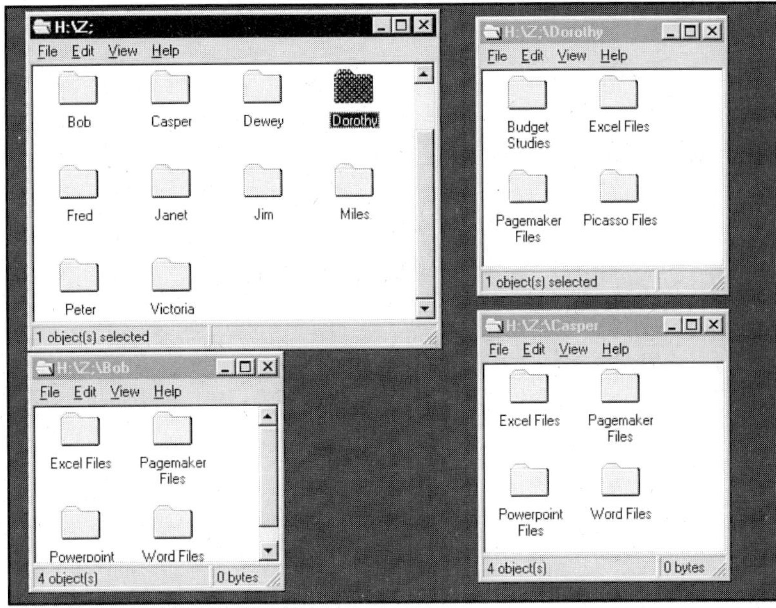

One more reason why all the computers in the workgroup should connect to one central data storage computer is that you can keep your computer connected to that computer at all times. This persistent connection can be configured to occur automatically when you start your computer or only when you actually try to access the drive. Because you don't have to worry about drive mappings or about connecting and disconnecting network drives, you can consider the network drive to be a permanent part of your computer—the place where you store your work.

Figure 43.2 shows three windows. The parent window shows a mapped network drive called Z. The first child window shows 10 folders on drive Z—one for each member of the workgroup. The smallest child window shows the folders in user Bob's main folder. The other users have similar folders. The number of folders that may appear in other users' main folders depends on the type of work each user does and the program he or she uses.

NOTE A parent window is the first window displayed by a program. Child windows appear as subsequent windows.

You don't have to structure the folder hierarchy on the data-server drive in any particular way. You should, however, have one data-server drive for your workgroup. All the members of the workgroup should connect to that drive permanently and store their work on that drive.

Keeping Applications and Data Separate

The preceding sections discussed only data files—the files that you generate by using your applications. But where should you store application files—your programs? The best method is to store applications locally on each user's C drive (if you have the space on your hard drive), because applications load and run noticeably faster if they run from the local hard drive.

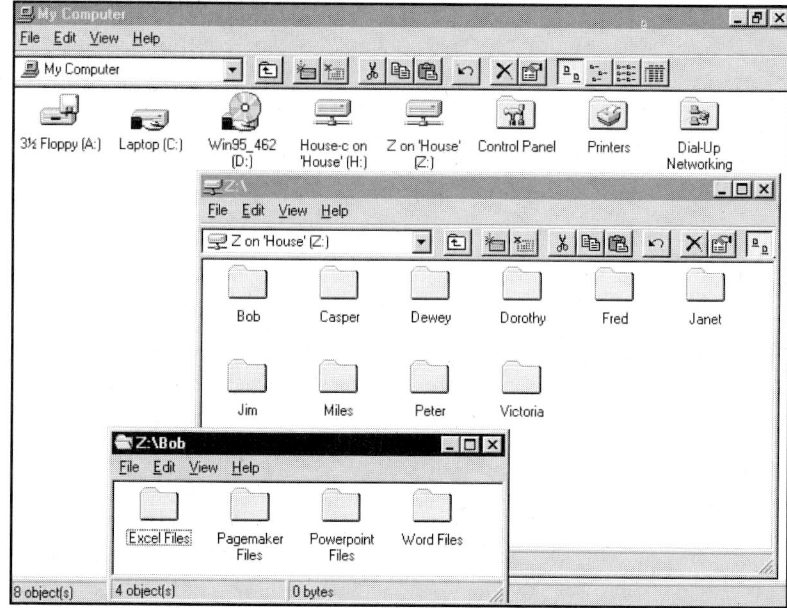

FIG. 43.2
This shows user Bob's folder structure on mapped network drive Z:.

Networks, and application-program vendors, certainly provide the capability for everyone in your workgroup to run programs from a single shared copy, located somewhere on a network file server. This method seems, at first, to be a very interesting way to operate, because that huge 15M installation of your favorite word processing program won't have to go on every computer—just on a file server. But the additional network traffic generated by the continual loading of program files over the network wastes bandwidth. Because Windows programs only load part of themselves from the disk into memory at one time, additional network traffic will be created as various parts of the program are called into memory as needed. If the application were stored on the local hard drive, all this unnecessary network traffic could be eliminated.

The users may complain that the program, coming to them from a server over the network, loads and runs too slowly. Finally, if the integrity of the network is interrupted, even momentarily, while a shared copy of an application is running, chances are good that every system running that application at that time will freeze while the application is being loaded. This could make some users think they need to reboot their machines. This procedure, of course, means that any unsaved data is lost in all applications.

The point here, of course, is that your workgroup will run much more smoothly if each user stores executable program files on his/her own computer's hard drive.

Being a Good Network Neighbor

If your workgroup is to function effectively, all the members of the workgroup must be good network neighbors. You can implement this simple concept by considering what resources are available on your computer and designating those resources as shared if other members of your workgroup need access to them.

▶ **See** "Sharing CD-ROMs and Other Removable Drives," **p. 963**

If yours is the only CD-ROM drive in the workgroup, for example, make it available for other members to use.

You also need to consider the continuity of shared resources. If you have the only CD-ROM drive or the only color printer and other users are connected to those resources, consider the effect on the rest of your workgroup if you turn off your computer without warning. In such a case, your resources disappear from the network and are no longer available to the other workgroup members. Don't discontinue sharing your resources without informing the rest of the workgroup. Use the WinPopup accessory program to send a message to your workgroup saying you are going to take your shared disk or printer offline. In your message, say how long it will be until you shut down. Communicating about a change in status of a shared resource you control is part of being a good network neighbor.

CAUTION

If a disk resource on your peer-to-peer network is disconnected from the network unexpectedly—if a computer that hosts a shared folder is turned off or if the folder-sharing properties are turned off—network users can lose data.

Network Management Tools

Windows 95 includes several useful tools that help you learn about and manage your peer-to-peer network. Although *network management* is a very broad term, management tools simply allow you to see how your network is functioning and to change almost everything about the entire network from your own computer. You can use these network management tools to enable or disable sharing of resources, add or delete passwords, disconnect users, and so on.

When you look at network management as being a series of toggle switches, with one switch for each possible setting on each possible resource, management tools become less mysterious. The trick is knowing how to set each parameter for optimum network efficiency.

NOTE Don't feel that you have to make every connection and map every drive just because you can. Simple is better.

Net Watcher

Net Watcher is installed in the Accessories, System Tools group, which you can find by opening the Start menu and choosing Programs. This utility is useful for examining which resources on which computer are shared. Net Watcher tells you about these resources, as well as who is using the shared resources and which files are open on the shared resources.

Net Watcher is a "per-server" utility. In order to display meaningful information, Net Watcher shows information about only one server computer at a time. Net Watcher shows information about computers that are sharing their disks or printers. These computers have File and Print Sharing for Microsoft Networks enabled.

Net Watcher provides three main views of the workgroup for each server:

- A view showing the users connected to the server called View by Connections. To see this view, start Net Watcher and choose View, Connections.
- A view showing the shared folders on the server called View by Shared Folders. To see this view from the main Net Watcher window, choose View, Shared Folders.
- A view showing the files that are open on the server called View by Open Files. To see this view, choose View, Open Files.

In the View by Connections, a list of users who are connected to the server appears on the left side of the screen. The right side of the screen displays the folders and printers to which the users are connected, as well as the files that the users have open. If multiple users are connected, you select one user at a time on the left side of the screen. You can then manage how that user interacts with the network, as you'll see next.

Figure 43.3 represents the View by Connections. In this example, you are looking at a server called HOUSE (as defined in the caption bar), to which one user, called LAPTOP, is connected.

View by Shared Folders shows detailed information about the disk folders and printers that have been declared sharable on the server. On the left side of the screen is a list of shared folders on the server, the names under which the folders are shared, the type of access available to the folder (full access or read-only), and any comment about the shared resource that was typed in the Comment box when the folder or printer was designated as sharable.

Figure 43.4 shows the Show Shared Folders view. In the figure, LAPTOP is connected to several shared folders and to one printer on the computer known as HOUSE.

View by Open Files is a full screen display. In Figure 43.5, Net Watcher shows the name of two open files on the server, the share name of the server on which the file is located, which computer is accessing the file, and whether the file is open for reading only or for reading and writing.

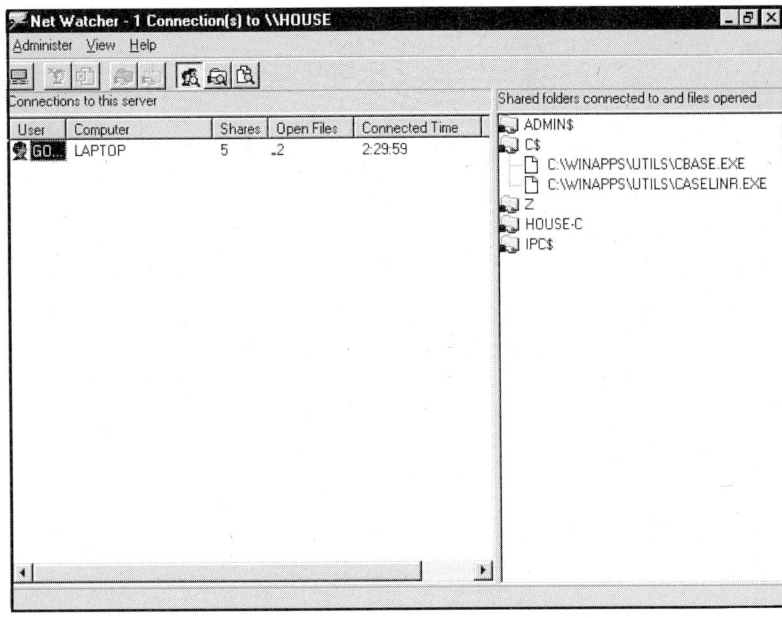

FIG. 43.3 The Net Watcher management program in View by Connections mode, showing user Laptop connected to server House.

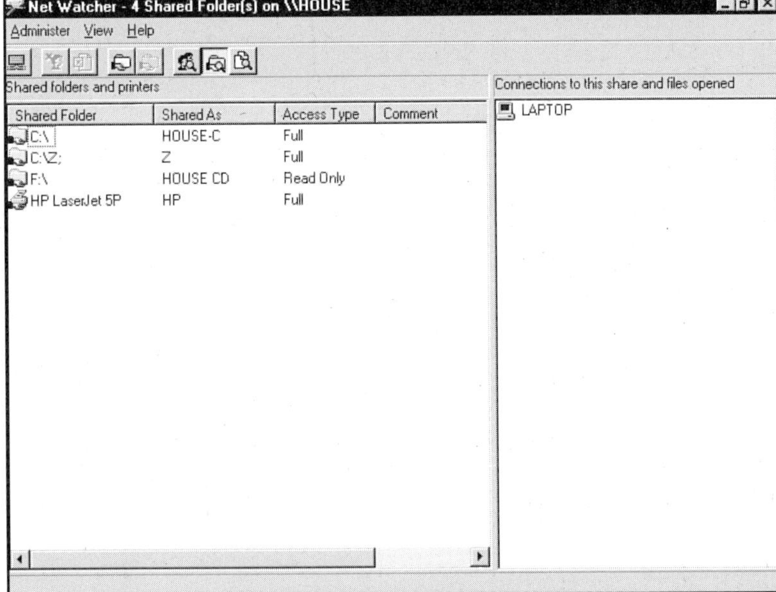

FIG. 43.4 The Net Watcher management program in View by Shared Folders mode, showing four shared folders on the server named House.

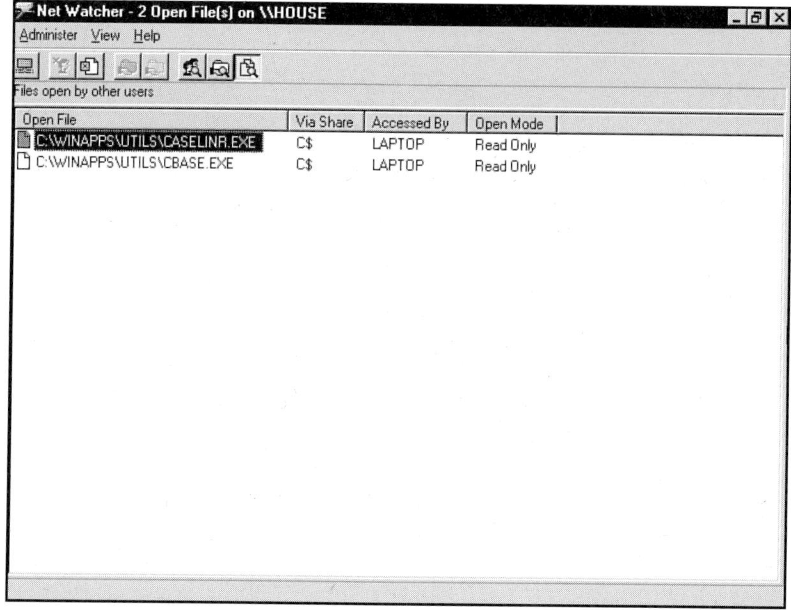

FIG. 43.5 The Net Watcher management program in View by Open Files mode, showing two open files on the server named House.

Net Watcher can do far more than simply report on network status, however; as a management tool, it can restructure the network. The following sections explain how you can use Net Watcher to accomplish these tasks:

- Disconnect a network user anywhere in the workgroup
- Close an open file anywhere in the workgroup
- Add a shared folder to any server in the workgroup
- Stop sharing folders on any server in the workgroup
- Change the properties of shared folders in the workgroup

Disconnecting a User from a Peer Server If you want to stop a user from connecting to your computer's shared folders and printers, use Net Watcher's Show Users view. Select the user whom you want to disconnect and then choose Administer, Disconnect User.

Disconnecting a user can have serious consequences for that user because data can be lost if there is any unsaved data at the time the disconnection occurs. In fact, Net Watcher issues a warning when you issue the Disconnect User command, as shown in Figure 43.6.

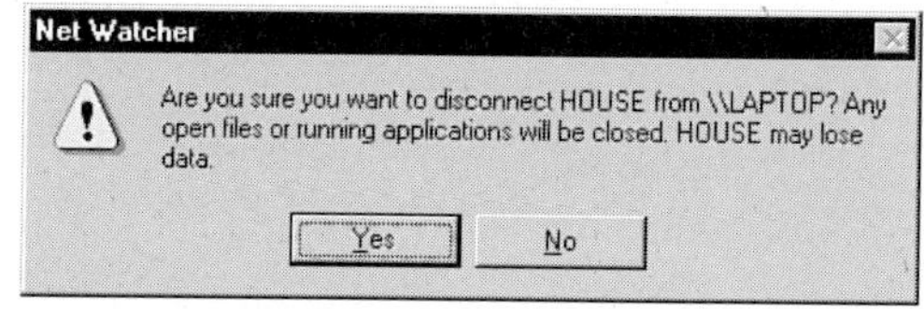

FIG. 43.6 The Net Watcher management program issues a warning when you use it to disconnect a server from a connected user.

Adding a Shared Resource on a Peer Server Adding a shared resource can be useful when you need access to a resource on another computer in your workgroup. Net Watcher can make the folder that you need sharable. Figure 43.7 shows the shared resources on the peer server called HOUSE—three shared folders and one shared printer. Anyone on a Windows 95 peer network can declare a share on any folder in which they have permission on the workgroup if the computer they are targeting is a server (has enabled File & Printer Sharing Services).

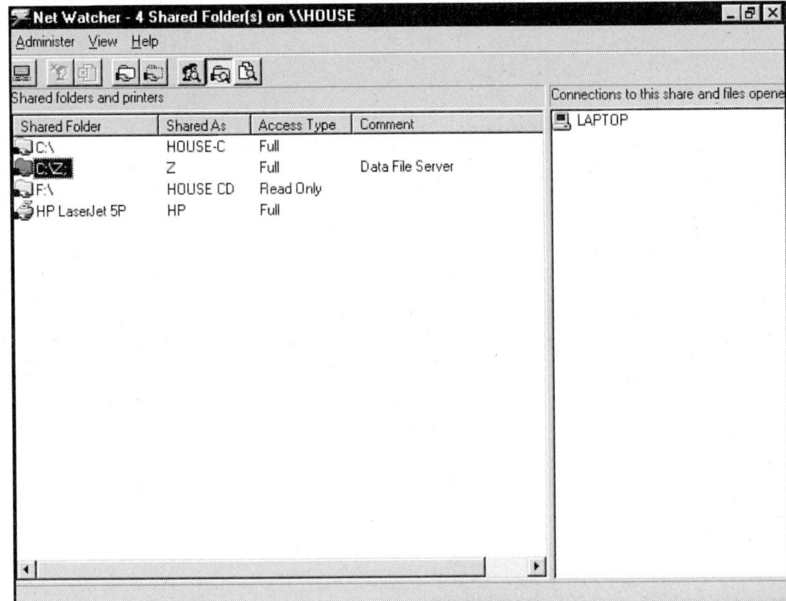

FIG. 43.7
Net Watcher in View by Shared Folders mode, showing three shared folders.

Suppose you want to access programs in the folder named SECURE on the computer named HOUSE. SECURE is not a shared folder, however, so you need to declare it to be sharable. You can do this, from any machine on the workgroup LAN, using Net Watcher. The three requirements are:

- Remote Administration is enabled on the server you are targeting (on which you want to set a resource shared).
- The folder, drive, or printer you want to share is on a server computer. A server computer has File and/or Printer Sharing enabled.
- No password has been established, controlling access to the folder or resource you want to share.

Starting from View by Shared Folders view on peer server HOUSE, choose Administer, Add Shared Folder, or use the Add Share button on the Net Watcher toolbar. Next, you'll see a dialog box asking for the path you wish to share. Then browse for the folder name, or type it in the Path box. Figure 43.8 shows the dialog box where you enter the path to the folder you want to share.

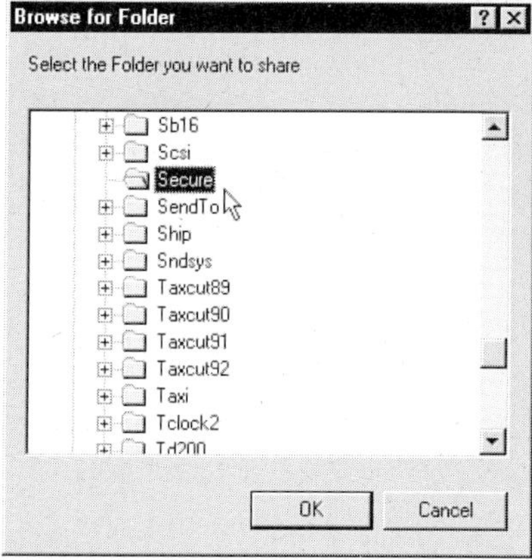

FIG. 43.8
To share a folder on your workgroup LAN using Net Watcher, browse for the folder you want to share and double-click to enter it in the Enter path dialog box.

When you select the folder you want to add, Net Watcher displays the Shared Folder properties sheet, shown in Figure 43.9. In this sheet, you declare the folder to be shared and set its shared properties: Shared As, Share Name, Comment, Access Type, and Passwords.

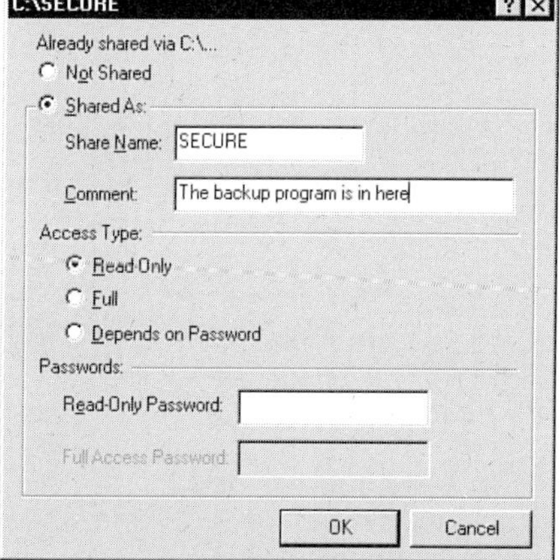

FIG. 43.9
In Net Watcher, you can edit the properties of your newly shared folder.

When you choose OK on the Shared Folder properties sheet, the folder becomes a shared resource on the workgroup and is added to Net Watcher's list of shared folders (see Figure 43.10).

CAUTION

The process of adding a shared folder just described has deep implications. Any member of the Peer-to-Peer workgroup LAN can add a shared drive or folder on any server computer in the network. The owner of the computer targeted to have a drive or folder shared doesn't need to agree. In fact, the owner of the targeted computer may not even know that a drive or folder has been set as shared, until she happens to examine the drive properties with My Computer or Windows Explorer, and notices the Shared Resource icon attached to one of her drives or folders.

Notice too, that any member of the workgroup, using Net Watcher to add shared drives or folders on server computers on the LAN, can also set passwords for access to the folders he declares as shared, effectively preventing anyone but himself from accessing those drives or folders over the LAN. Again, the owner of the computer containing these shared drives or folders will not know a password has been set without examining the properties for the shared drive or folder.

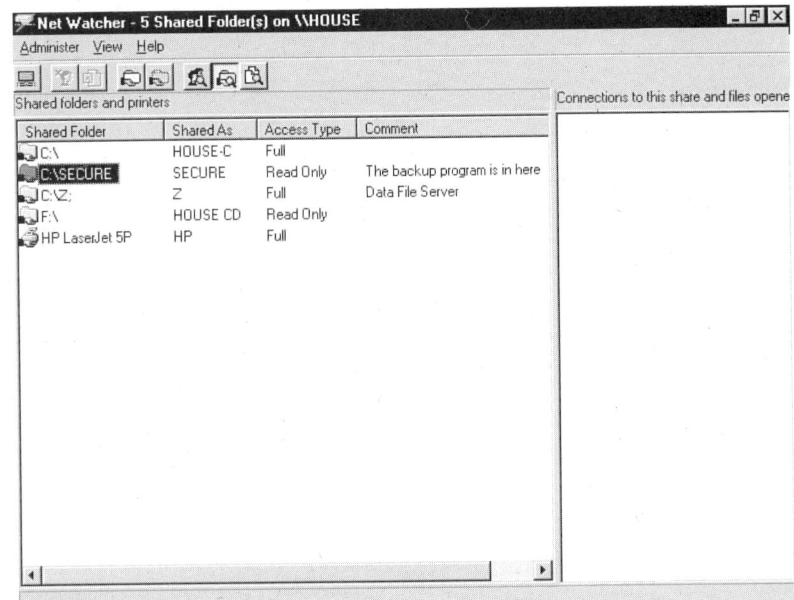

FIG. 43.10 The Net Watcher program has added your newly shared folder, C:\SECURE, to its list of shared folders on the peer server HOUSE.

TROUBLESHOOTING

Files on my hard disk drive are changing. Some are being deleted, some are just being modified. I haven't done anything to them. Why is this happening? The answer may be that another member of your workgroup LAN is causing these changes on your computer. If you have enabled File and Print Sharing in your network setup, another member of your LAN may have declared your hard drive and its folders to be shared. That person can then work with your files, modify them, delete them, or add new files to your disk.

Two ways to prevent having your drives and folders shared by others without your knowledge are:

- Turn off File Sharing in Control Panel, Network. Then, your computer is not a server and nobody can access your drives or folders over the LAN.

continues

continued

- Turn off Enable Remote Administration. You do this by using Control Panel, Passwords, and then clicking the page called Remote Administration. Only one setting is on this page. In the sole check box, deselect Enable Remote Administration of This Server.

Stop Sharing a Folder To stop sharing a folder, start in the View by Shared Folders view of Net Watcher. Select the Shared Folder that you want to stop sharing on the network and then choose Administer, Stop Sharing Folder. You also can choose the Stop Sharing icon on the Net Watcher toolbar. The warning message shown in Figure 43.11 appears. Click Yes to stop sharing the specified folder.

FIG. 43.11
When you use Net Watcher to stop sharing a folder, this confirmation dialog box appears.

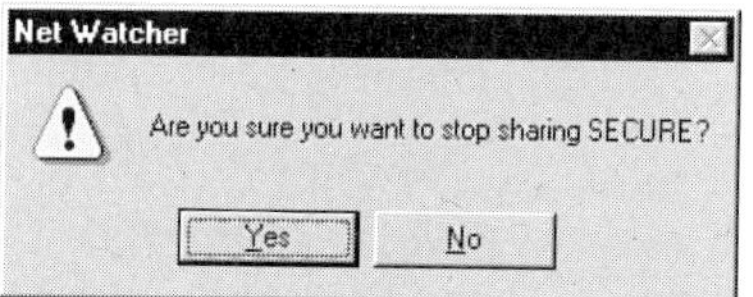

Change a Shared Folder's Properties This option allows you to stop sharing a shared folder, but it also allows you to change the name of the shared resource on the network, change the access type, and set a password for access. In Net Watcher's Show Shared Folders view, select the folder that you want to stop sharing on the network and then choose Administer, Shared Folder Properties.

Now you can perform these kinds of changes on the folder you selected:

- You can set the folder as Not Shared.
- You can set the folder as Shared. If you do this, you must also enter a Share Name. By default, Windows selects the folder name as the Share Name, but you also can change it.
- If you've set the folder to be Shared, you can set the access type to Read-Only, or Full, or Depends on Password. You also may enter a password for access to the folder.

Figure 43.9 shows the dialog box to change a shared folder's properties.

Stop Sharing a Printer If you need to stop sharing a printer on the workgroup, start in View by Shared Folder view of Net Watcher. Select the printer in the list of shared resources and choose Administer, Shared Folder Properties. The printer properties dialog box appears (see Figure 43.12) showing the name of the printer you're working with in its title bar. To stop sharing the printer, choose Not Shared in the dialog box.

Then, choose OK. No warning message appears before the printer is made unavailable to the workgroup.

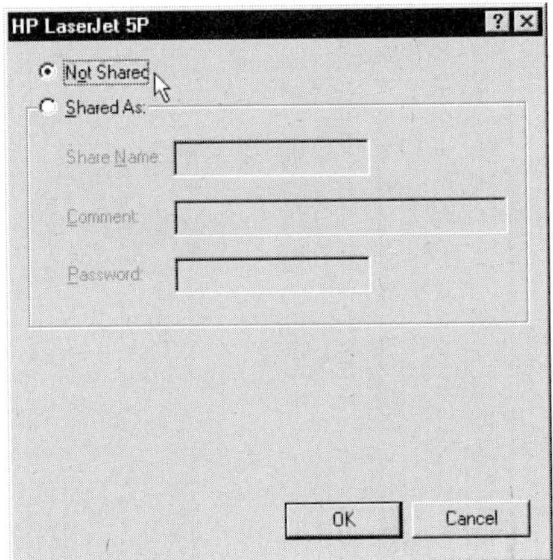

FIG. 43.12
Net Watcher uses this dialog box to allow you to stop sharing a network printer.

User Profiles as a System Management Tool

Many workgroups have users who may use more than one computer. Because Windows 95 is very customizable, a user who is sitting at what is not his or her main computer may be unable to work. Network connections may not be the same. Connections to the shared folders that the user needs may not be available. Printer connections may not be what the user expects. Menus may be different. In general, the workstation may be so customized for the primary user that another user may be lost.

See "Changing Custom Settings for Each User," **p. 889**

Some computers on your workgroup may have no primary user but a group of users, all of whom may have different needs or expectations. You also may have users who are true floaters who have no primary machine but need to be able to be productive on any computer.

To deal with all these cases, Microsoft introduced User Profiles to Windows 95. With User Profiles, the following settings on any computer can be customized for any user:

- Shortcut lists and their contents
- Items in the Start menu
- Items that can be configured by Control Panel
- Menu configurations (for Windows 95 programs and the applications bundled with Windows 95), toolbar configurations, status bar configurations, and font and display settings
- Appearance of the desktop, including shortcuts and icons
- Fonts in use
- Screen saver, screen background, screen colors, color depth, and screen resolution
- Network settings (such as persistent connections and printer connections)
- Network Neighborhood configuration

Enabling User Profiles on the Workgroup To use User Profiles, you must be sure the proper options are selected on the Passwords properties sheet. Follow these steps:

1. Open the Start menu and choose Settings, Control Panel, Passwords. The Passwords properties sheet appears.
2. Click the User Profiles tab.
3. Choose Users Can Customize Their Preferences, as shown in Figure 43.13.

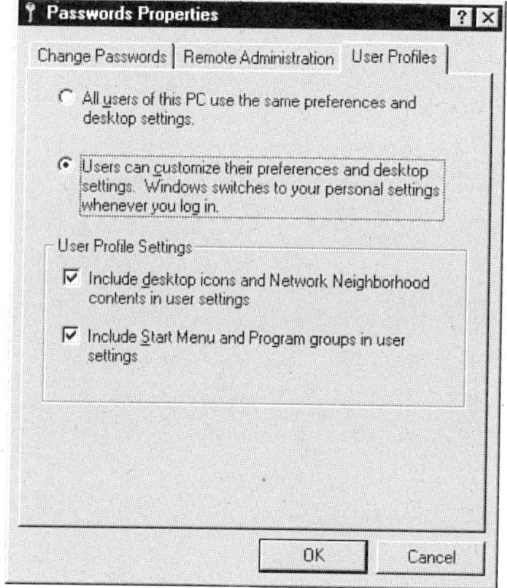

FIG. 43.13
Use the Passwords properties sheet to enable multiple User Profiles.

4. To make your User Profiles more powerful, choose Include Desktop Icons and Include Start Menu.
5. Click the Change Passwords tab.
6. Make sure that a logon password appears in this tab. You must have a password when you begin to work with User Profiles.

Working with User Profiles When a user logs on to a Windows 95 computer that has User Profiles enabled, the machine asks for a user name and password. The computer then creates a User Profile using default settings.

When you finish working at a profile-enabled computer, shut down with the Close All Programs and Log On as Different User option. This option prevents anyone from changing your profiled settings and preferences.

As the user sets up network connections, desktop preferences, and all the other customizable features of the workstation, Windows 95 waits for the user to log off and shut down the machine. Windows then saves all the settings that User Profiles can track (the settings listed in the preceding sections). Windows writes the User Profile information into the Registry, in the USER.DAT file, and saves the desktop and Start menu in the C:\WINDOWS\PROFILES folder, as shown in Figure 43.14. This figure shows profiles for five users on this computer; the hierarchy of subfolders is expanded for one of the users listed on the left side of the screen.

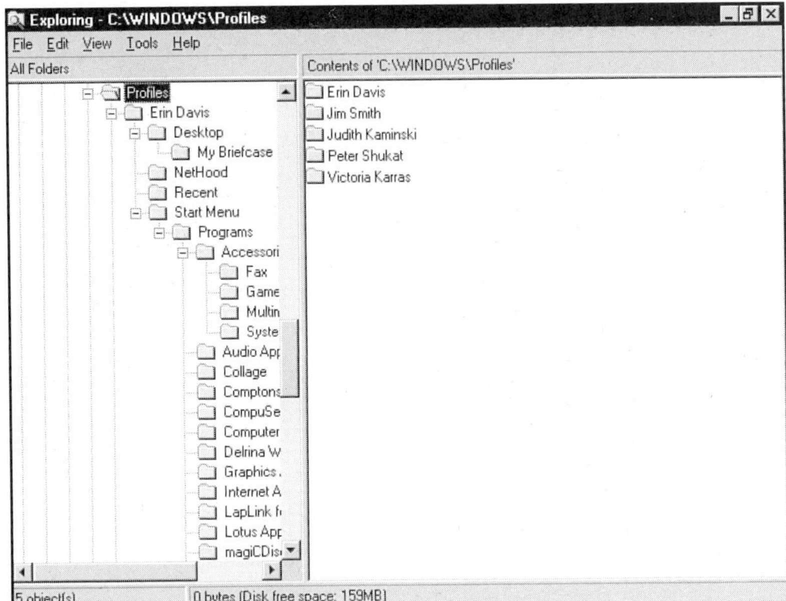

FIG. 43.14
Windows Explorer shows five User Profiles in the right half of the screen when five users have created Profiles.

User Profiles on the Network The preceding sections show how one machine can be customized for any number of users. This process is local use of User Profiles. An even more powerful type of User Profiles allows anyone to log in on any machine in the workgroup and have his or her settings restored, even if that user has never set up his or her profile at that machine before. This option requires the use of an NT or NetWare server. On an NT or NetWare network, you can log in from any computer on the LAN and use your customized User Profile. You can do this because your User Profile is stored on the NT or NetWare file server, not on the workstation.

Because the profile is stored on the NT or NetWare server, it can be accessed by any workstation on the LAN.

On an NT server, use the User Manager tool to create a home directory for each member of the workgroup. When a user logs off the Windows 95 workstation—if User Profiles are enabled— Windows copies the profile information to the NT server. When that user logs on to any other computer on the workgroup, the profile on the NT server is accessed and used to set up the current workstation. (This may not work in cases where you have a shortcut to an application such as Word, and the machine you log in from does not have Word installed.)

The same system works in a NetWare environment.

NOTE If the User Profile on the current workstation is newer than the copy on the server, the workstation copy is used, and the server is updated. The procedure also works in reverse, so that the user always has the most recent configuration available.

NOTE If you use Microsoft Exchange on a computer that has User Profiles enabled, set Exchange to query for an Exchange profile to use at startup, because User Profiles do not control Exchange profiles. (For more on Exchange, see Chapter 26, "Using Microsoft Exchange and Messaging.")

System Policies and Network Management

System Policies do many of the same things as User Profiles. System Policies are not used along with User Profiles but they are used instead of User Profiles. The members of a workgroup do not set System Policies, as they do for their own User Profiles. In this section, you'll see how the System Policy Editor can change the look and feel of your Windows 95 computer. Some features documented in this book may not be available to you if your network administrator has disabled some features using System Policy Editor. Let's see what can happen using System Policies which are created by the System Policy Editor program.

NOTE The System Policy Editor program, POLEDIT.EXE, is included on the CD-ROM version of Windows 95. It is not included on the floppy disk version of the operating system. If you do not have the CD-ROM version, you can download it from Microsoft's Web site (**http://www.microsoft.com**). The file is called POLICY.EXE and is included in the CD-ROM Extras.

The simplest way to understand System Policies is to know that these policies, which are created by a system administrator, are used to enforce predetermined User Profiles on a workgroup. The purpose of System Policies is to create a controlled workplace in which access to certain features of Windows can be restricted or eliminated. System Policies may restrict a user from accessing Control Panel or from getting to a DOS prompt, for example. These policies also may prevent a user from connecting to or disconnecting from shared resources on the network.

Used wisely, System Policies can increase the stability of a Windows workgroup by preventing users who like to experiment from disrupting needed network connections and thereby crashing the system. Used unwisely, System Policies can prevent the natural growth of understanding that is essential if members of a workgroup are to learn how to use their computers to maximum benefit.

System Policies are set through a tool called System Policy Editor, which is the most powerful of the network management tools included with Windows 95. This tool, which is designed to be used only by the network administrator, is inaccessible to users on the workgroup. The System Policy Editor should be kept in a nonshared folder on the administrator's computer.

With System Policy Editor, the administrator can set two types of policies. The first type of policies applies to individual-named computers on the network. The policies created for the named computer determine the default settings that are used when a user logs on to that computer.

The second type of policies applies to individual users, determined by user name at the time of logon. If policies exist for an individual user, they are combined with the System Policies that are in effect for the computer that is being used.

System Policies for Individual Computers The System Policy Editor can control the following settings on a per-computer basis:

Controlling the Network Group of Settings

- Access Control can be set to User Level. This requires the use of authentication on an NT or NetWare server to access the shared resources on the network.
- Logon features can display a warning at startup, saying that only authorized users should try to log on. Logon also can require validation by an NT server to access Windows 95.
- Settings for Microsoft Client for NetWare can be controlled.
- Settings for Microsoft Client for Windows Networks can be controlled.
- Password settings can be modified. Use of mixed alphabetical and numeric passwords, for example, can be required, and password caching can be forced off.
- Sharing can be disabled for the computer. In this case, no resources can be declared shared, and all shared information tabs disappear from properties sheets.
- Remote updating can be enabled.

Controlling the System Group of Settings

- The administrator can enable User Profiles.
- The network path to a shared copy of Windows Setup and Windows Tour can be specified.
- Items to be run at startup can be specified.

System Policies for Individual Users This area is where System Policy Editor can really show its power. Many options for individual users exist. For users, System Policy Editor works on five groups of settings.

Controlling the Control Panel Group of Settings

- The administrator can restrict the appearance of the Networks, Display, Password, Printer, and System icons in the Control Panel.

Controlling the Desktop Group of Settings

- The wallpaper and color scheme can be controlled.

Network Settings

- File and print sharing can be turned off for the user.

Controlling the Shell Group of Settings

- Custom Folder Functions can be disabled.
- Custom Programs Folders can be disallowed.
- Custom Desktop Icons can be disallowed.
- Start menu subfolders can be hidden.
- Custom Startup Folders can be disallowed.
- Custom Network Neighborhood can be disallowed.
- Custom Start Menu can be disallowed.
- The Run command can be removed from the Start menu.
- Folders and settings can be hidden so they won't show in the taskbar.
- The Find command can be disabled from the Start menu.
- The display of drives in My Computer can be hidden.
- Network Neighborhood can be hidden.
- Hide All items on the desktop can be hidden.
- The Shutdown command can be disallowed.
- Windows automatic saving of settings at shutdown can be disallowed.

Controlling the System Group of Settings

- Registry editing can be disallowed.
- The administrator can set up a list of allowed Windows applications and only the allowed applications can be run.
- The MS-DOS prompt can be disabled.
- MS-DOS mode can be disabled.

Figure 43.15 shows what the user would see if the administrator chose to restrict part of the System icon in Control Panel. The File System and Virtual Memory buttons in the System properties sheet are missing and the Device Manager and Hardware Profiles tabs are missing.

Figure 43.16 shows the System properties sheet before restrictions were applied by System Policy Editor.

CAUTION

System Policy Editor can be unpredictable. If the administrator selects a function and then deselects it, the function may not return to the state that it was in before editing. As a result, user settings can be destroyed without warning. The workaround is to tell your administrator to leave the setting neither selected nor deselected, but dimmed. Dimmed is an option when you edit a policy file.

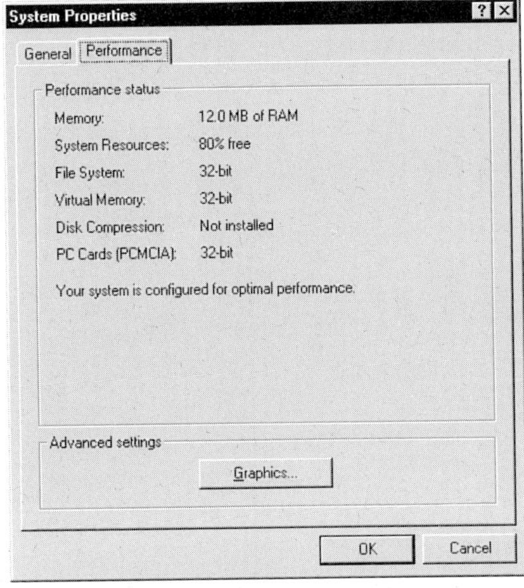

FIG. 43.15
System Policy Editor has removed features from System Properties in Control Panel.

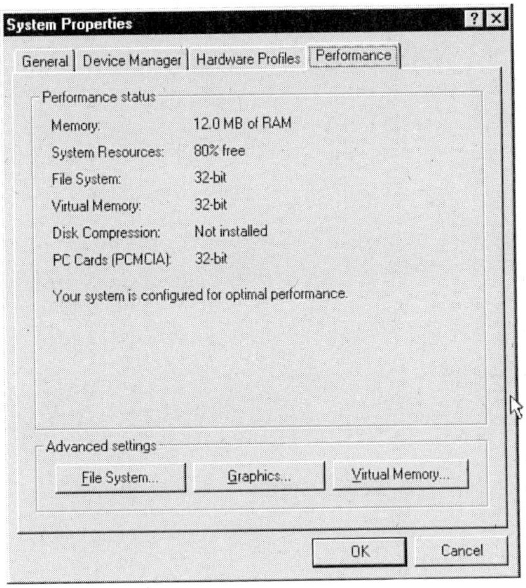

FIG. 43.16
System Properties in Control Panel looks like this before System Policy Editor removed features.

WinPopup

WinPopup is an applet that is included in the Accessories group when you install the network component of Windows 95. This tool normally is used to send short messages from one computer on the workgroup to another. WinPopup is designed so that when a message is received, the message pops up over anything else that is on-screen.

The real usefulness of the WinPopup program is that it automatically sends messages from a network printer when a print job finishes. WinPopup sends the message only to the computer that sent the print job for processing.

Figure 43.17 shows the simple network management function of a "print job is finished" notification.

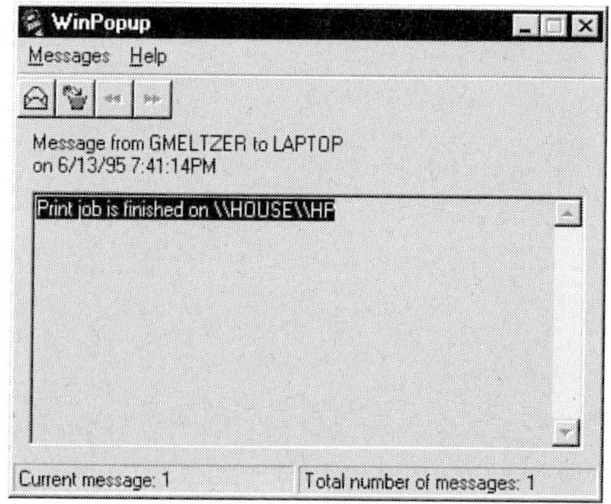

FIG. 43.17 WinPopup has sent a message to a user that the network print job is finished.

Network Security

Security on computer networks is designed to prevent unauthorized or accidental access to the information located on the disk drives on the network. Security can extend to preventing unauthorized users from using any network resource, such as a printer. Security systems also are intended to prevent unauthorized users from using computers on the network.

Windows 95 provides a wide range of network security options. Some of the most powerful security tools, however, are not available for a workgroup network that consists of computers that run only Windows 95. These functions require that a Windows NT or Novell NetWare server be connected to the network and programmed in a special way to enable Windows 95's advanced security functions.

The following sections examine the security tools that you can use in both environments.

All-Windows 95 Workgroup Network

In an all-Windows 95 workgroup, three types of security are available:

- Logon security
- Share-level password security
- System Policies security

Next, you will learn to use each of these security methods on your workgroup LAN. Whether you use one, two, or all of these techniques, the bottom line is that using security will prevent data loss.

Logon Security Although Windows 95 requires a logon password, you need to understand that the only things protected by this password are network resources, such as shared folders and shared printers. Windows 95 provides absolutely no password protection at the workstation level; anyone can sit down at your computer and access your local disks and attached resources.

If you need to control access to individual computers so that only a user with the right password can start the operating system, you should consider using Windows NT, not Windows 95, on individual workstation computers. NT requires a password before any user can work with the computer at all.

When Windows 95 starts, you see a screen that asks for your user ID and password. No matter what you do at this point, including clicking Cancel, Windows continues to load and to give you access to all the drives and printers on your computer.

Now that you understand that no logon security exists for the workstation in Windows 95, consider logon security for the network.

Windows Logon Password When Windows 95 starts for the first time, a logon dialog box asks for your user ID and password. Depending on your settings in Control Panel, Networks, you are prompted to log on to Windows 95 or the network. If your Network setting sets your Primary Network Logon as Client for Microsoft Networks, your logon screen looks like the one shown in Figure 43.18.

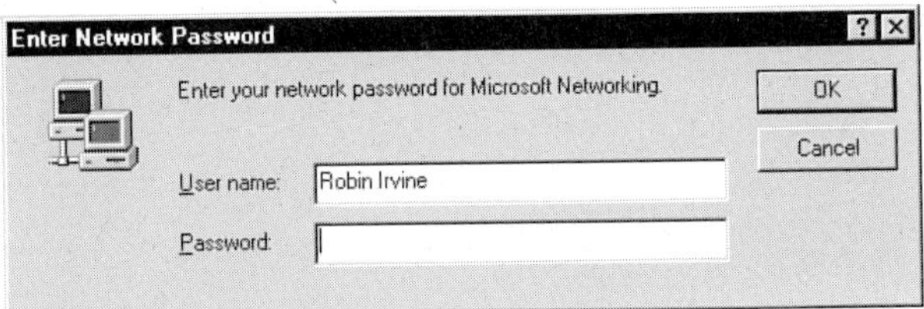

FIG. 43.18
This will be your logon screen if your Primary Network Logon is set to be Client for Microsoft Networks.

If you set your Primary Network Logon to be Windows Logon, you see a logon prompt like the one shown in Figure 43.19.

See "Removing Cached Passwords," **p. 1092**

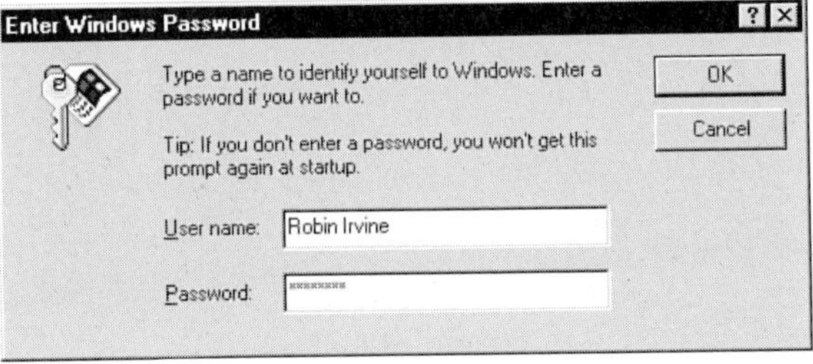

FIG. 43.19
The first time you run Windows 95 on your computer, you'll see this dialog box.

When you type the correct password for network access, you have access to all the shared resources on the network, as long as you know the password required to access them. In fact, you won't have to enter the passwords for network resources more than once; Windows stores the passwords that you enter in a cache so that they are entered for you automatically the next time you log on. Although the cache can be disabled by System Policies and by the Password List Editor program, in a normal installation, the password cache is active.

This chapter has mentioned passwords in connection with shared resources. The following sections examine the way that passwords work.

Access Control in Workgroups: Share-Level Access Control In Chapter 20, you learned how to enable peer-to-peer resource sharing on a Windows 95 workgroup. In this section, you set some passwords for those resources so that only authorized users can find them over the network.

Figure 43.20 shows two types of shared resources.

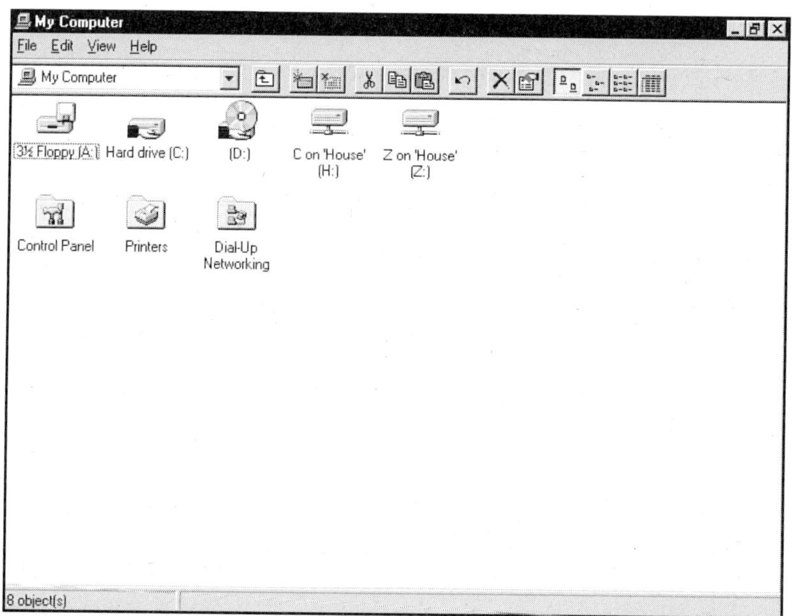

FIG. 43.20
There are two resources shared in this view of My Computer.

Notice that the icon for the local hard drive—Drive C—is shared. The icon includes the outstretched hand that signifies sharing. The hand does not mean that the disk is completely open to any user, however. To control how you will share your drive, right-click the icon and choose Sharing from the pop-up menu.

Figure 43.21 shows the sharing properties that are enabled for the local hard drive. Two passwords are set. You want to give full read-and-write access to users who know the full access password. Other users will be able only to read the disk, not to modify it in any way.

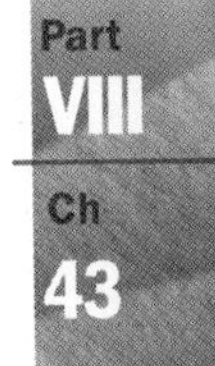

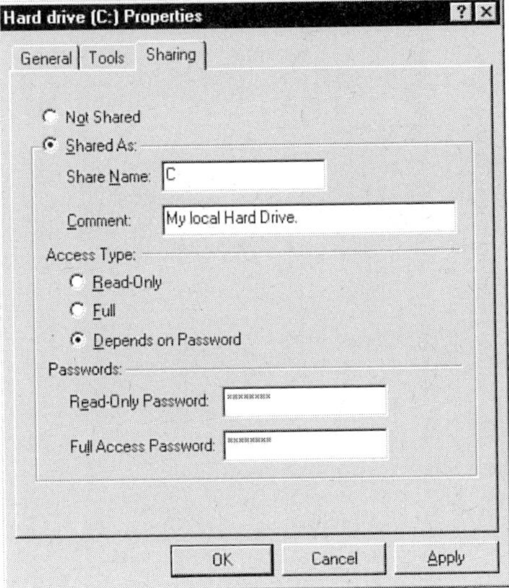

FIG. 43.21
The Hard Drive properties sheet controls password access to the drive.

This type of security is called *share-level access*, and it is the only kind of access protection available to workgroups in which Windows 95 (or Windows for Workgroups 3.1x) peer server is the only type of server on the network. To see how this access control is enabled, open the Start menu and choose Settings, Control Panel, Network; click the Access Control tab; and select the Share Level access-control option. The other option is not available for Peer-to-Peer networks.

Share-Level Access and Network Neighborhood If you enable sharing on a disk, folder, or printer on your computer, the shared resource appears in Network Neighborhood, from which users may try to connect to your resource or map a drive letter to it.

At times, you want to share a resource but not broadcast that fact to the workgroup. A mechanism for hiding shared resources exists. To do this, add a dollar sign character to the end of the share name. The resource still behaves in accordance with its password restrictions, but it does not appear in Network Neighborhood. Another member of the workgroup must know the exact name of the resource to connect to it.

Mapped Drives and Their Security Figure 43.20 earlier in this chapter, showed two types of shared resources in the My Computer window. This section examines the properties of the resources whose icons look like disks attached to cables. These resources are shared drives and folders on other computers. The owners of those resources may have enabled share-level security passwords for those resources. That security determines what you can do with the folders—whether you can write to them as well as read from them.

If the owner of a shared folder changes the password required to access that resource, your cached password no longer gives you access to the resource. You see a network drive icon with an *X* through the connection, like the one shown for the Z on House connection in Figure 43.22.

FIG. 43.22
An inaccessible network drive is shown with an X through its icon.

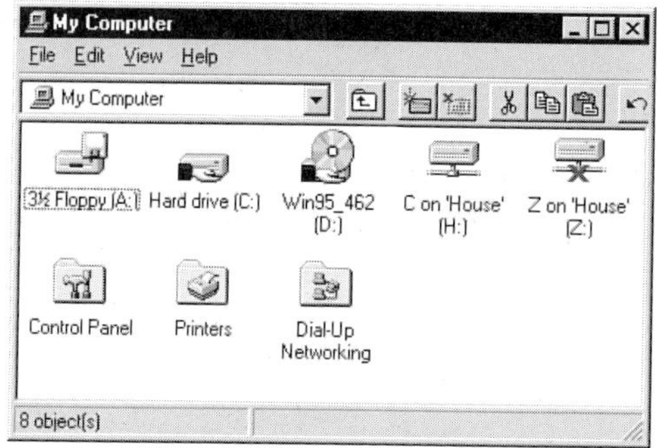

To access the resource again, learn the new access password. Then, when you want to access the shared drive again, you will have to restart Windows.

Removing Cached Passwords Because password caching is enabled in Windows 95 automatically, the system creates an encrypted file, in which it stores the password entries for all resources used by the computer. By default, the file name is SHARE.PWL. If User Profiles are enabled on the computer, the PWL files are not called SHARE but are created from the user names. When User Profiles are active, each user has a different PWL password list file, such as TOM.PWL.

If you are having trouble with a cached password, use the Password List Editor program, PWLEDIT.EXE. This program does not show you the actual passwords—it shows you that a password exists and gives you the opportunity to remove the password. This procedure forces you to log in with the correct password the next time you want to connect to the resource that you edited.

NOTE The Password List Editor program, PWLEDIT.EXE, is included on the CD-ROM version of Windows 95. It is not included on the floppy disk version of the operating system.

Figure 43.23 shows a Password List Editor screen. Password List Editor shows every password in effect on the computer on which it's running. In Figure 43.23, only one password is in effect. Although the display is not very informative, the text "Rna" shown in the Resource column is a hint that the password is for Dial-Up Networking. Rna, in Windows jargon, means Remote node access.

The only option is to remove the password.

Using Windows 95 with a Microsoft NT or Novell NetWare Server

If your network includes an NT or NetWare server, your options for workgroup security are greatly enhanced. You can use the features of those servers to provide and enforce user-level security on the workgroup. In this case, the NT or NetWare server is acting as a security provider and validator. This function works because those two network systems maintain lists of authorized users and those users' network rights and access privileges. This function does not exist in Windows 95 Peer-to-Peer networks.

FIG. 43.23 The Password List Editor program can remove passwords from any type of password protected resource on your computer.

Table 43.1 compares the features available in user- and share-level access control.

Table 43.1 Access-Control Comparison

Feature	User-Level	Share-Level
Read Files	X	X
Write to Files	X	X
Create Files and Folders	X	
List Files	X	
Delete Files	X	
Change File Attributes	X	
Change Access Control	X	

You can see that user-level security gives you much finer control of shared resources because you can enable any, all, or none of the preceding sets of rights. If you enable only List Files, for example, users who connect to the folder can execute programs from the folder, but they cannot delete or change anything.

User Lists in User-Level Security

In a Windows NT environment, the administrator uses the User Manager program to set up the security permissions for each user name. Windows 95 uses these permissions to set access rights for the listed resources. An NT administrator also can create groups and simplify workgroup administration by granting the same rights to several users or perhaps an entire workgroup.

The only thing to remember is that in the case of multiple NT domains, the Windows 95 computer must select one domain server to be the security and list provider.

In NetWare, the same list principles apply. Instead of using User Manager, however, NetWare relies on the Bindery feature. As a result, NetWare 4.x servers must be running Bindery emulation to act as security hosts for Windows 95 computers.

General Network Security Guidelines

As you've seen by now, network security in a Windows 95 workgroup LAN must be configured, cooperatively, by the network neighbors who are connected to the LAN. To avoid loss of your workgroup's valuable data, accidentally or otherwise, consider the following four guiding principles:

- Although setting up a completely open, password-free network is easy, resist the temptation. Even though you may not have to enter passwords with password caching enabled, require them because they will increase your options later.
- If you can make access to a shared resource read-only, do so. Use full read/write access only when it is necessary. This practice can prevent accidental deletion of important files and directories.
- Make sure that you and your network neighbors keep their passwords guarded and not written in plain sight on or near the computer.
- Don't use an obvious item, such as your name, as your Windows password.

Troubleshooting and Network Management Tools

If you're having problems accessing resources that you can see in Network Neighborhood, check to see whether you have the rights that you need to do your work. Windows provides an easy way to use Net Watcher for this purpose. In Network Neighborhood, right-click the computer that holds the resources that you need; choose Properties; and then click the Tools tab. Figure 43.24 shows the list of management tools that are available.

From this point, you can select Net Watcher and use it to see whether the folder that you want to use is shared. If not, you can designate the folder as shared. If the problem is that the folder is read-only and you need full access, use Net Watcher to adjust that situation, too.

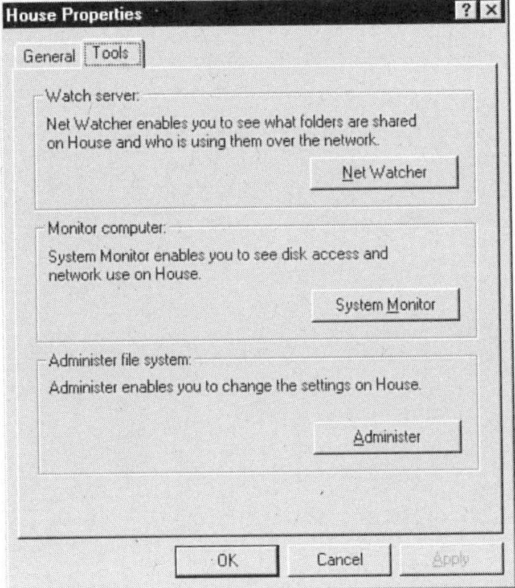

FIG. 43.24 Windows 95 provides Net Watcher, System Monitor, and Administer tools for network management.

Using Dial-Up Networking

Just as you can connect to shared resources on a network using a network interface card and network wiring, you can connect to the same kind of resources using a modem and telephone wires. This type of networking is called Dial-Up Networking. Dial-Up Networking is discussed in Chapter 8, "Special Features for Notebook Users," as this feature will be of most interest to laptop and notebook PC users. However, if you want to configure Dial-Up Networking to work on your desktop computer, all of the procedures are the same.

Appendixes

APPENDIX

What's on the CD?

What's on the Microsoft TechNet Sampler CD-ROM?

This section introduces the latest advancements in the User Interface for Que Shareware CDs and describes the CD installation.

The following information describes what you will find on the CD-ROM included with *Special Edition Using Windows 95, Second Edition*.

The Microsoft TechNet Sampler CD-ROM

The TechNet Sampler is an evaluation copy of the monthly TechNet, a vast database of Microsoft-related products and technologies. It includes more than 100,000 pages of articles, technical notes, service packs, and Knowledge Bases.

TechNet Contents Overview

The Microsoft TechNet table of contents contains 10 information categories (see Figure A.1). The following paragraphs describe those categories.

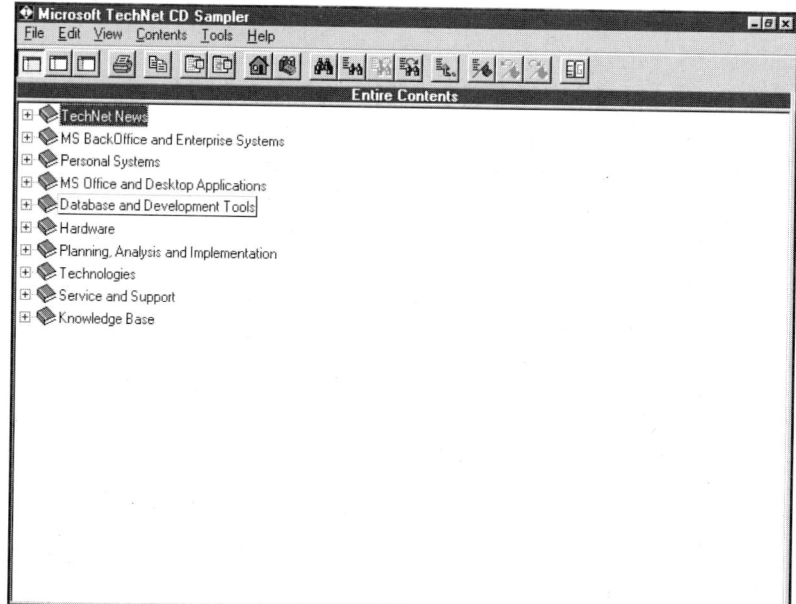

FIG. A.1 TechNet News is one of the available root categories in the TechNet table of contents.

TechNet News In the TechNet News category, you will find feature stories, announcements, columns, and editorials. You will also find out what's new and what has been deleted or moved to another location.

MS BackOffice and Enterprise Systems The MS BackOffice and Enterprise Systems category contains all the system information you need, including evaluation guides and migration strategies for the following Microsoft products: LAN Manager, Windows NT Server, SNA Server, SQL Server, Microsoft Mail, Microsoft Exchange, Windows NT Workstation, and DCA/MS Communications.

Personal Systems The Personal Systems category provides you with information covering MS-DOS and all the various Windows operating systems, such as Windows 95, Windows for Workgroups, and Windows 3.x.

MS Office and Desktop Applications The MS Office and Desktop Applications category contains up-to-date information about Microsoft Office software and desktop applications such as Microsoft Works, Microsoft Electronic Forms, and Microsoft Project.

Database and Development Tools In the Database and Development Tools category, you will find information on Microsoft Internet Studio, Microsoft Visual Basic, Microsoft Visual C++, Microsoft Visual SourceSafe, and Microsoft Visual FoxPro.

Hardware In the Hardware category, you will find information on ISDN, MS Natural Keyboard, printers, and hardware products architecture.

Planning Analysis and Implementation The Planning Analysis and Implementation category contains various items such as Saving Time, Money, and Expertise with the Self-Help Support System, UNIX Integration Project Report, and case studies.

Technologies The Technologies category is heavy with information in the following areas: DVD, MAPI, TAPI, Windows sockets, ODBC, OLE, Plug and Play, and WOSA.

Service and Support The Service and Support category contains access to such additional sources of information as the Microsoft Beta Tester Program, Product Support Services, Software Piracy, Microsoft Online Institute, U.S. Products Version List, Microsoft Solutions Provider Program Directory, Microsoft Certified Professional Assessment Exams, Microsoft Education and Certification, Microsoft Developer Network, and Microsoft Press book listings.

Knowledge Base The Knowledge Base contains thousands of Microsoft product support services, group notes, troubleshooting tips, and corrected problem documentation.

Getting Up and Running

To install the Microsoft TechNet Sampler program to your computer, run the SETUP.EXE file located in the TechNet folder. For further installation instructions, please read the MANSETUP text file located in the TechNet folder. This text file also contains the user license agreement for this product.

Searching TechNet

In order to search through the 100,000 pages of information on Microsoft products, Microsoft TechNet uses a powerful Full-Test Search Engine. Obviously, if you know what you are searching for, you will save a considerable amount of time when conducting searches. The Query dialog box (shown in Figure A.2) helps you to categorize your searches.

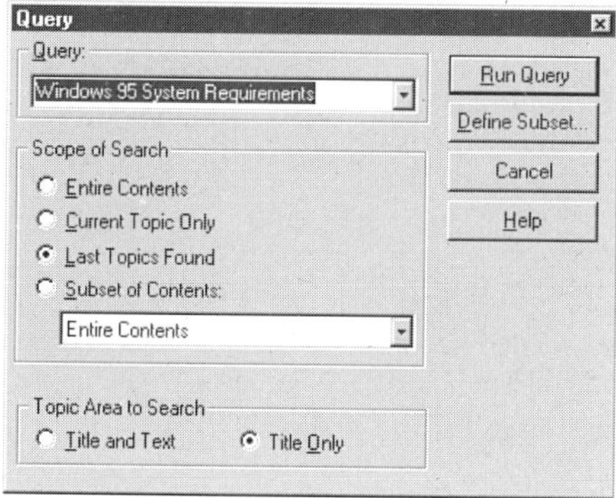

FIG. A.2
In the Query screen, you can limit the scope of your search to any of four options.

What's Your Objective? Spend a few minutes deciding what type of information you are looking for. Query results will obviously vary in size, depending on how general or specific the query might be. For example, a query for "Windows NT Workstation" will have thousands of results, but a query for "Windows NT Workstation Security" will produce a more specific area of query results.

Be Precise When conducting a search, the search engine looks for exact matches to the text you have entered. The search engine then returns a list of all strings in the TechNet CD that match the string you are looking for. Watch out for numbers, because they, too, can be difficult to use. A search for "Windows" will find topics containing "Windows" and "Windows 95," but a search for "Windows 95" will not find topics containing only "Windows."

Nail Down Your Objective After your initial search, there still might be too many results to look through (for example, there may still be 100 results); however, you can be reasonably sure that the information you want is in that list. You can use the New Query button along with the Last Topic Found option to initiate a search for a more specific topic using only the new list of 100 entries (see Figure A.3).

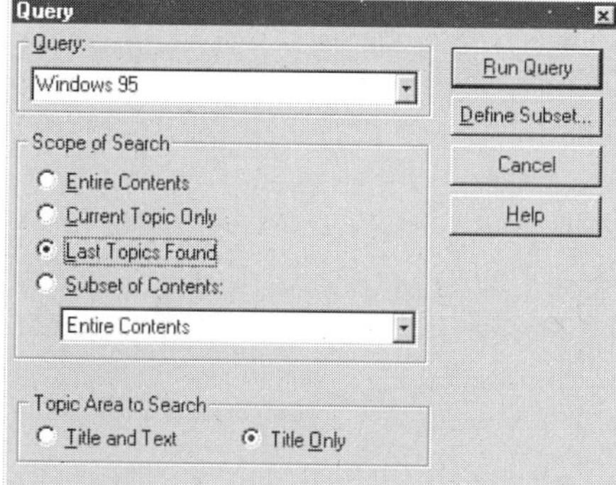

FIG. A.3
Clicking the New Query button directs you to the Last Topic Found option in the Query dialog box.

Basic Search Concepts The goal is not to make the query so broad that you have thousands of results. If you are looking for information on a certain feature of a product, use both the product name and the feature name in your query. If you already know the type of information you want—for example, system requirements for Windows 95—you can search that subset of the CD contents (see Figure A.4).

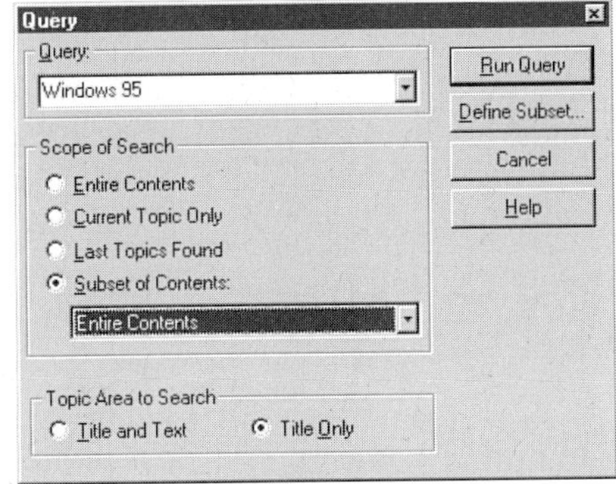

FIG. A.4
The Subset of Contents option can limit the scope of your search if you already have a general idea of what you are looking for.

Here are some basic concepts to remember when conducting searches:

- Type queries in either upper- or lowercase letters; queries are case-insensitive.
- Search for any combination of letters and numbers.
- Searches ignore punctuation marks such as the period (.), colon (:), semicolon (;), comma (,), and hyphen (-).
- You can use single or double quotation marks to delimit phrases.
- Use parentheses to nest expressions within your query.
- Use the four main operators (AND, OR, NOT, NEAR); use the OR function to search for synonyms.
- There are two wild card characters: question mark(?) and asterisk (*).
- Parentheses group expressions together.
- The search engine ignores words that occur too frequently to be useful in a search.

TIP If your initial query is too large or still has too many returned results, you can use a combination of both the Search Engine and the Browser. You do that by using the Display button shown in Figure A.5.

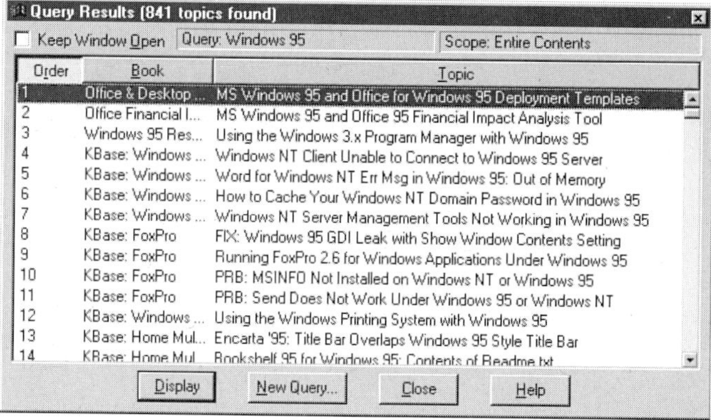

FIG. A.5
In the Query Results screen, you can further limit your search by clicking Display.

Obtaining Help and Information

The Microsoft TechNet online help describes in detail specific procedures for finding your way around the CD and using supporting files. It also includes general usage information and a usage guide to all buttons.

Customizing TechNet

You can customize TechNet using either bookmarks or topic annotations. While each of these is a unique customization tool, both expound on the power of TechNet and its adaptability to individual needs.

Bookmarks Bookmarks are one of the preferred customization tools with which Microsoft TechNet users mark their often used topics. Select Bookmarks from the Edit menu or click the Bookmark List button on the upper toolbar. Then double-click the bookmark's name in the list to return to that location. The Add Bookmark screen appears, as shown in Figure A.6.

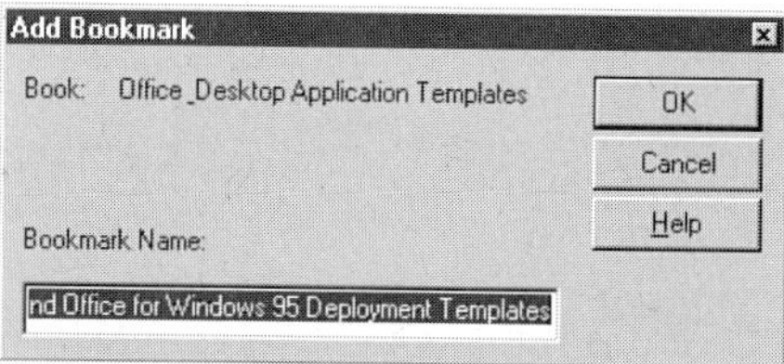

FIG. A.6
Confirm your selection by typing it in the Bookmark Name box and clicking OK.

Annotations If you need to add your own information (such as notes) to TechNet, annotations are a useful tool. Click the View Annotation button on the topic toolbar and type your notes in the Annotation pane. When the topic has been annotated, the View Annotation button is highlighted (see Figure A.7).

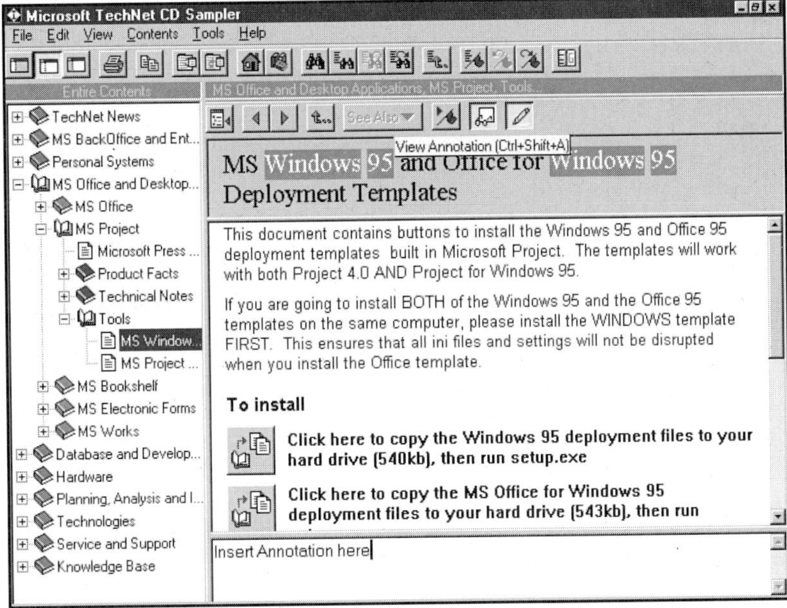

FIG. A.7
An alternative method to clicking the View Annotation button is to press Ctrl+Shift+A.

Additional Information About the TechNet Subscription

Microsoft TechNet is a monthly CD Software subscription giving you fast access to the most complete resource of Microsoft technical information available. If your job consists of evaluating, implementing, or supporting Microsoft business products, TechNet will keep you current with the latest patches and drivers.

With your first issue, you will receive a binder containing the following four color-coded sections (five for international subscriptions):

Monthly Issues

Utilities

Service Pack

Extras

International (if applicable)

Each CD is color-coded to match the tab color and is labeled to identify the contents of the CD. The following lists are typical examples of a Microsoft TechNet subscription.

Purple Tab Sheet titled Monthly Issues contains:

- Monthly issue CD
- Supplemental drivers and patches CD

Green Tab Sheet titled Utilities contains:

- Software Library Archive
- Client Utilities CD
- Server Utilities CD
- Windows NT 4.0 Resource Kit Utilities
- Back Office Resource Kit Utilities

Magenta Tab Sheet titled Service Packs contains:

- Exchange Service Packs CD
- Windows NT Service Packs CD
- Service Packs CD

Blue Tab Sheet titled Extras.

Subscribers to the international edition have another tab containing the International and Japanese supplemental CDs.

NOTE Each month, Microsoft sends out only the updated CD (not the complete binder).

A subset of Microsoft TechNet is available online at the TechNet Reference Desk. The TechNet Reference Desk is a central resource for operating and maintaining Microsoft business products.

These other items are also included on the Microsoft TechNet CD:

- Architecture white papers
- Case studies
- Reviewers' guides
- Product comparison articles
- Technical notes
- Resource Kits
- Service Packs
- Deployment Guides
- Training Materials
- Tools and Utilities

ON THE WEB

For more information on Microsoft TechNet subscription, log on at:

http://microsoft.com/TechNet

APPENDIX B

Additional Help and Resources

by Ron Person

Finding the right type of help

This appendix lists additional resources that offer help and support for Windows 95.

Using online help

This appendix includes a listing of Internet addresses that offer Windows 95 information.

Although this is one of the most comprehensive books written on Windows 95, there are many additional resources you can turn to for answers to user and technical questions. I have attempted to make this a comprehensive list of resources that includes all major sources. Over time, these sources will change: Books are revised and online services change their directories. To stay in contact with online services, use the Find feature found in most services to search for topics on Windows 95. To stay current with new books, call Macmillan Computer Publishing at the number listed later in this appendix.

Getting Telephone and FAX Support for Windows 95 and Microsoft Products

Microsoft has a wide array of telephone support systems for Windows 95. Numerous third-party companies are also dedicated to supporting individuals and corporations who use Windows 95.

If Windows 95 or other applications came preinstalled on your computer, your technical support for the preinstalled software will probably be through the hardware vendor who supplied your equipment.

Microsoft Telephone and FAX Support

For customer service and product upgrade information, call (800) 426-9400.

At the time this book was published, Microsoft used three methods of supporting Windows 95 with live support personnel. These numbers and support levels are outlined here:

Description	Type	Telephone
Support for 90 days from your first support call.	Free. Initial 90-day support.	(206) 635-7000
$35 charge to a credit card until the specific problem is resolved. Make sure you keep the charge code ID and incident ID assigned by Microsoft.	$35 per incident charged to a credit card.	(800) 936-5700
$35 charge to a telephone number until the specific problem is resolved. Incident ID is assigned by Microsoft.	$35 per incident charged to telephone.	(900) 555-2000

This support is available Monday through Friday, 6:00 A.M. to 6:00 P.M. Pacific Time, excluding holidays.

You also can receive help on Windows 95 via a fax that lists the most frequently asked questions and their answers. To get answers from FastTips, call (800) 936-4200.

Telephone Support from Non-Microsoft Vendors

Microsoft encourages the use of a stable of service providers who can give you or your company help on Windows 95. See the following list of service providers:

Name	Description	Support Options	Telephone
Sitel	Technical services	Wide range of services available	800-363-5448
Stream International	Backup for in-house support or staff	Windows 95 education and training	(800) 274-4707
Unisys Corporation	Support for home users and businesses	$35 per incident $2.95 per minute Prepaid callbacks	(800) 863-0436 (900) 555-5454 (800) 757-8324

Online Technical Support

You can also find support online through the Microsoft Download Service, the World Wide Web, and other computer bulletin board forums.

Microsoft Download Service

Microsoft maintains a software library containing sample programs, device drivers, patches, software updates, and programming aids. You have free access to the software in this library. Use HyperTerminal, which comes with Windows 95 and other PC communication software, to connect, search, and download files. You can connect to Microsoft Download Service at:

(206) 936-6735

World Wide Web

The World Wide Web is a huge, constantly changing collection of data. Because of this, you can waste considerable time searching for specific information on the Web. Your most productive searches for information will be through sites sponsored by Microsoft, PC Magazine, and vendors. Some valuable URLs are listed in Table B.1.

Table B.1 Helpful Web Sites

Name	Description	URL
Microsoft	Main Microsoft Web page	**http://www.microsoft.com/**
Microsoft	Table of contents for Windows	**http://www.microsoft.com/windows/**
Microsoft	Windows page and Windows 95 topics and software	**http://www.microsoft.com/windows/**

continues

Table B.1 Continued

Name	Description	URL
Microsoft Knowledge Base	Searchable database of white papers, technical notes, troubleshooting, tips, bugs, and workarounds.	**http://www.microsoft.com/kb/**
Microsoft	Home page for product support services	**http://www.microsoft.comsupport**
Microsoft	Free product upgrades, templates, and add-ons	**http://www.microsoft.com/ windows/support**, select a product, and then click **Go**
Microsoft TechNet	Troubleshooting database, drivers, upgrades; all the information from the TechNet CD-ROM	**http://www.microsoft.com/technet**

See "Getting Connected to the Internet," **p. 443**

Computer Bulletin Board Forums

Computer bulletin boards are computer services that enable you to retrieve information over the telephone line. Some bulletin boards contain a wealth of information about Windows and Windows applications. One of the largest public bulletin boards is CompuServe.

CompuServe contains *forums* in which Windows and Windows applications are discussed. You can submit questions electronically to Microsoft operators, who will answer questions usually within a day. CompuServe also contains libraries of sample files and new printer and device drivers. The Knowledge Base available in Microsoft's region of CompuServe has much of the same troubleshooting information that Microsoft's telephone support representatives use. You can search through the Knowledge Base by using key words. The Microsoft region of CompuServe is divided into many areas, such as Windows users, Windows software developers, Microsoft, Excel, and Microsoft languages, as well as sections for each of the major Microsoft and non-Microsoft applications that run under Windows.

After you become a CompuServe member, you can access the Microsoft user forums, library files, and Knowledge Base. (You must join CompuServe and get a passcode before you can use the bulletin board.) When you join CompuServe, make sure you get a copy of WinCIM, the Windows CompuServe Information Manager. It enables you to avoid typing many commands, and thus makes using CompuServe significantly easier.

Some of the Windows 95 services available on CompuServe are listed in Table B.2.

Table B.2 Windows 95 Services on CompuServe

Name	Description	Access With:
Windows Support	CompuServe's table of contents for Windows support, shareware, and so on	**GO WIN95**
Microsoft Connection	Entry service for Microsoft services	**GO MICROSOFT**
Microsoft Knowledge Base	Searchable database of troubleshooting tips, technical papers, and so on	**GO MSKB**
Microsoft Software Libraries	Free libraries of tools, software, patches, and drivers	**GO MSL**
Microsoft Windows Service Pack 1 upgrade	Free upgrades to Windows 95	**GO WINNEWS**
Windows 95 Setup	Specific setup questions for Windows 95 supported by WUGNET	**GO SETUP95**
Windows Users Group Network	Collections of useful software and information gathered by WUGNET	**GO WINUSER**

For information on joining CompuServe, contact a retail software store for a CompuServe starter kit or contact CompuServe at the following address:

CompuServe
5000 Arlington Centre Blvd.
P.O. Box 20212
Columbus, OH 43220
(800) 848-8990

Technical Support on Microsoft CD-ROM

One of the most valuable resources of technical knowledge on Windows and Windows applications is TechNet. TechNet is a compilation of troubleshooting procedures, technical papers, product descriptions, product announcements, drivers, and so on. It is available on a monthly CD-ROM for a fee or available over the World Wide Web for free. If you are a company with many Windows users or a consultant using Microsoft products, you must learn how to use TechNet.

If you support only a few people or do not have to frequently download files, the free Knowledge Base on the Web might work well for you. The Knowledge Base contains much of the same information as the TechNet CD-ROM, but it is free.

ON THE WEB

www.microsoft.com/kb

Although Knowledge Base is available for free on the Web, there are many times when you might want it on CD-ROM. If you frequently need files or need large files from TechNet, the CD-ROM is much more convenient than slogging through the Web. TechNet on CD-ROM has a much more flexible and faster search engine so you can quickly browse for related topics; for example, you can quickly find an answer while a client is on the phone. With the advent of CD-ROM drives built into portables, the TechNet CD is an indispensable tool for the traveling Windows consultant.

To subscribe to TechNet, contact them at this address:

Microsoft TechNet
One Microsoft Way
Redmond, WA 98052-6399
Fax: (206) 936-7329, Attn: TechNet
Voice: (800) 344-2121
Internet: **technet@microsoft.com**
Web: **www.microsoft.com/technet**

The Microsoft Windows 95 Resource Kit

Microsoft split the user documentation for Windows 95 in two parts. The first part contains the User's Guide, help files, tutorial, and so on. This part is aimed at the average Windows 95 user and covers the Windows 95 user interface and features.

The Windows 95 Resource Kit comprises the *rest* of the Windows 95 user documentation. This kit provides more depth and detail about topics that (in Microsoft's estimation) the average user isn't likely to need. You can find information about customized setup and installation, network configuration, and so on. The Windows 95 Resource Kit includes a manual, help files, and supplementary software utilities aimed at network administrators and others who must support other Windows 95 users.

It's important to understand that the Windows 95 Resource Kit is *not* a programmer's reference or software development kit—that's another area entirely. The Windows 95 Resource Kit is still part of the user-level documentation; it's just aimed at a higher-level user than the rest of the Windows 95 documentation.

The Microsoft Windows 95 Resource Kit is a book-software combination. The book and software come on the Windows 95 CD-ROM from which you might have installed Windows 95.

You can also download the book and software from online services or purchase it as a bound book from larger bookstores.

If you have the full CD-ROM version of Windows 95, you already have a copy of the Windows 95 Resource Kit. The Resource Kit chapters appear in the Windows 95 Resource Kit Help file, WIN95RK.HLP, which is located in the /ADMIN/RESKIT/HELPFILE directory. Double-click this file to open its help window. You can search and print in the file as you would any help file.

You can also find a number of useful user and network utilities on the Windows 95 CD-ROM. Look in the /ADMIN/APPTOOLS and /ADMIN/NETTOOLS directories to find these utilities. You also can find software tools on online bulletin boards. Many of these were listed earlier in this appendix, in the section "Online Technical Support."

NOTE Microsoft does not include the Windows 95 Resource Kit files when distributing Windows 95 on floppy disks. Also, other suppliers who are licensed to sell Windows 95 with their computer systems might not include the Windows 95 Resource Kit files.

Books from Macmillan Computer Publishing

Macmillan Computer Publishing (MCP) is the largest publisher of computer books in the world. Que Corporation is MCP's most successful book imprint. Que is the publisher of *Platinum Edition Using Windows 95* and the *Special Edition Using* series of books. Some of the best-selling books in this series are:

- *Special Edition Using Windows 95*
- *Special Edition Using Excel for Windows 95*
- *Special Edition Using Word for Windows 95*

For catalogs or individual or corporate purchases, contact Que and Macmillan Computer Publishing at:

201 West 103rd Street
Indianapolis, IN 46290
(317) 581-3500
(800) 428-5331

ON THE WEB

You can also search and browse book descriptions and download software at the Macmillan SuperLibrary site on the World Wide Web. To go there, use the URL:

http://www.mcp.com

Online WinNews Newsletter

Microsoft publishes WinNews, an online newsletter, that is available to anyone who can receive e-mail from the Internet (this includes CompuServe and America Online). WinNews includes information about new and free Windows 95 software, operating tips, releases of new hardware drivers, and references to additional information. It is published on the first and third Mondays of every month.

If you want to subscribe to WinNews, follow these steps:

1. Create an Internet e-mail message using the same account in which you want to receive WinNews.
2. Use a blank Subject line.
3. Type only the following as the message body:

   SUBSCRIBE WINNEWS
4. Send this Internet e-mail to:

   enews99@microsoft.nwnet.com

To stop receiving a copy of WinNews, follow the same instructions but use the following text as the only text in the message body:

UNSUBSCRIBE WINNEWS

Referrals to Consultants and Training

Microsoft Solution Providers develop and support applications written for the Windows environment with Microsoft products. They are independent consultants who have met the strict qualifying requirements imposed by Microsoft.

Microsoft also certifies training centers. A certified training center has instructors who have passed a competency exam and who use Microsoft-produced training material.

You can find the Microsoft Solution Providers and training centers in your area by calling (800) SOL-PROV.

Index

Symbols

A

B

C

D

E

F

G

H

J-K

L

M

N

O

P

Q

R

S

T

U

V

W

X-Z

Check out Que® Books on the World Wide Web http://www.quecorp.com

As the biggest software release in computer history, Windows 95 continues to redefine the computer industry. Click here for the latest info on our Windows 95 books

Make computing quick and easy with these products designed exclusively for new and casual users

Examine the latest releases in word processing, spreadsheets, operating systems, and suites

The Internet, The World Wide Web, CompuServe®, America Online®, Prodigy® —it's a world of ever-changing information. Don't get left behind!

Find out about new additions to our site, new bestsellers, and hot topics

In-depth information on high-end topics: find the best reference books for databases, programming, networking, and client/server technologies

A recent addition to Que, Ziff-Davis Press publishes the highly successful *How It Works* and *How to Use* series of books, as well as *PC Learning Labs Teaches* and *PC Magazine* series of book/disc packages

Stay on the cutting edge of Macintosh® technologies and visual communications

Find out which titles are making headlines

With six separate publishing groups, Que develops products for many specific market segments and areas of computer technology. Explore our Web Site and you'll find information on best-selling titles, newly published titles, upcoming products, authors, and much more.

- Stay informed on the latest industry trends and products available
- Visit our online bookstore for the latest information and editions
- Download software from Que's library of the best shareware and freeware

Copyright © 1997, Macmillan Computer Publishing-USA, A Viacom Company

Complete and Return This Card for a *FREE* Computer Book Catalo

Thank you for purchasing this book! You have purchased a superior computer book written expressly for your needs. To continue to provide the kind of up-to-date, pertinent coverage you've come to expect from us, we need to hear from you. Please take a minute to complet and return this self-addressed, postage-paid form. In return, we'll send you a free catalog o all our computer books on topics ranging from word processing to programming and the Internet.

Mr. ☐ Mrs. ☐ Ms. ☐ Dr. ☐

Name (first) ☐☐☐☐☐☐☐☐☐☐☐ (M.I.) ☐ (last) ☐☐☐☐☐☐☐☐☐☐☐☐☐☐☐

Address ☐☐☐☐☐☐☐☐☐☐☐☐☐☐☐☐☐☐☐☐☐☐☐☐☐☐☐☐☐☐☐☐☐☐☐

☐☐☐☐☐☐☐☐☐☐☐☐☐☐☐☐☐☐☐☐☐☐☐☐☐☐☐☐☐☐☐☐☐☐☐

City ☐☐☐☐☐☐☐☐☐☐☐☐☐☐☐ State ☐☐ Zip ☐☐☐☐☐ ☐☐☐☐

Phone ☐☐☐ ☐☐☐ ☐☐☐☐ Fax ☐☐☐ ☐☐☐ ☐☐☐☐

Company Name ☐☐☐☐☐☐☐☐☐☐☐☐☐☐☐☐☐☐☐☐☐☐☐☐☐☐☐☐☐☐☐☐

E-mail address ☐☐☐☐☐☐☐☐☐☐☐☐☐☐☐☐☐☐☐☐☐☐☐☐☐☐☐☐☐☐☐☐

1. Please check at least three (3) influencing factors for purchasing this book.

Front or back cover information on book .... ☐
Special approach to the content .... ☐
Completeness of content .... ☐
Author's reputation .... ☐
Publisher's reputation .... ☐
Book cover design or layout .... ☐
Index or table of contents of book .... ☐
Price of book .... ☐
Special effects, graphics, illustrations .... ☐
Other (Please specify): ______________________ ☐

2. How did you first learn about this book?

Saw in Macmillan Computer Publishing catalog .... ☐
Recommended by store personnel .... ☐
Saw the book on bookshelf at store .... ☐
Recommended by a friend .... ☐
Received advertisement in the mail .... ☐
Saw an advertisement in: ______________________ ☐
Read book review in: ______________________ ☐
Other (Please specify): ______________________ ☐

3. How many computer books have you purchased in the last six months?

This book only .... ☐ 3 to 5 books .... ☐
2 books .... ☐ More than 5 .... ☐

4. Where did you purchase this book?

Bookstore .... ☐
Computer Store .... ☐
Consumer Electronics Store .... ☐
Department Store .... ☐
Office Club .... ☐
Warehouse Club .... ☐
Mail Order .... ☐
Direct from Publisher .... ☐
Internet site .... ☐
Other (Please specify): ______________________ ☐

5. How long have you been using a computer?

☐ Less than 6 months ☐ 6 months to a year
☐ 1 to 3 years ☐ More than 3 years

6. What is your level of experience with personal computers and with the subject of this book?

	With PCs	With subject of book
New	☐	☐
Casual	☐	☐
Accomplished	☐	☐
Expert	☐	☐

Source Code ISBN: 0-7897-1381-0

7. Which of the following best describes your job title?

- Administrative Assistant ☐
- Coordinator ☐
- Manager/Supervisor ☐
- Director ☐
- Vice President ☐
- President/CEO/COO ☐
- Lawyer/Doctor/Medical Professional ☐
- Teacher/Educator/Trainer ☐
- Engineer/Technician ☐
- Consultant ☐
- Not employed/Student/Retired ☐
- Other (Please specify): ______________ ☐

8. Which of the following best describes the area of the company your job title falls under?

- Accounting ☐
- Engineering ☐
- Manufacturing ☐
- Operations ☐
- Marketing ☐
- Sales ☐
- Other (Please specify): ______________ ☐

9. What is your age?

- Under 20 ☐
- 21-29 ☐
- 30-39 ☐
- 40-49 ☐
- 50-59 ☐
- 60-over ☐

10. Are you:

- Male ☐
- Female ☐

11. Which computer publications do you read regularly? (Please list)

____

____

____

____

____

____

____

____

Comments: ______________________________

____

____

Fold here and scotch-tape to mail.

NO POSTAGE NECESSARY IF MAILED IN THE UNITED STATES

BUSINESS REPLY MAIL

FIRST-CLASS MAIL PERMIT NO. 9918 INDIANAPOLIS IN

POSTAGE WILL BE PAID BY THE ADDRESSEE

ATTN MARKETING
MACMILLAN COMPUTER PUBLISHING
MACMILLAN PUBLISHING USA
201 W 103RD ST
INDIANAPOLIS IN 46290-9042

Technical Support:

If you need assistance with the information in this book or with a CD/Disk accompanying the book, please access the Knowledge Base on our Web site at **http://www.superlibrary.com/general/support**. Our most Frequently Asked Questions are answered there. If you do not find the answer to your questions on our Web site, you may contact Macmillan Technical Support **(317) 581-3833** or e-mail us at **support@mcp.com**.